WILTSHIRE LIBRARY
& MUSEUM SERVICE

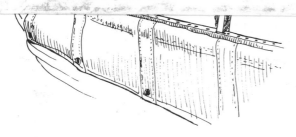

Plate I.

The steel keel LOXLEY belonged to Furley & Co.,
Gainsborough and was built at Thorne in 1925.

The Complete Book of
CANAL & RIVER NAVIGATIONS

Edward W. Paget-Tomlinson, M.A.

Wooden towpath bridge below Dutton locks,
Weaver Navigation.

Illustrated by A. J. Lewery and C. V. Waine
with maps by R. J. Dean

WAINE Research

Publications

This Book is Dedicated to:
Harry Bentley - Potteries Boatman,
Ken Keay - Walsall Boatbuilder and
Reginald Wood, Son of Albert Wood,
Canal Carrier - Sowerby Bridge.

2. Black Country day boat and horse. The harness is similar
to that for long distance boats; the towline attached to a
spreader to which the traces are secured.

© E. W. Paget-Tomlinson.

Published by:
Waine Research,
Mount Pleasant,
Beamish Lane,
Albrighton,
Nr. Wolverhampton WV7 3JJ.

First Published 1978.

ISBN 0 905184 01 7.

Reprinted 1980.

Printed & Bound in England.

Also in this Series:
Steam Coasters and Short Sea Traders
by Charles V. Waine, Ph.D.

Preface

This book could never be the work of one person. Without the help of very many it could not have been written. Much encouragement came from Dr. David Owen while Charles Hadfield was a most informative and understanding editor. Dr. Charles Waine has undertaken publication and has himself prepared the colour illustrations. Closely associated with the work has been Tony Lewery, the artist responsible for a fine series of line illustrations. Without his introduction to his many friends in the canal world, the book would have missed much. Richard Dean prepared the excellent series of maps. To Mrs. J. Stockdale of the Express Typewriting & Duplicating Service of Liverpool for typing the initial draft, to Mrs. Ann Smith for the final draft and to Mrs. F. J. Worrall for a large correspondence, to all these I extend my deepest thanks.

For help on the historical side, both with information and checking the text, my thanks are due to:- For the waterways of England; D. S. Akroyd, D. E. Bick, G. J. Biddle, J. H. Boyes, D. K. Cassels, Robin Chaplin, K. R. Clew, C. R. Clinker, H. Compton, A. J. S. Coombe-Tennant, C. B. Driscoll of the Port of Manchester, B. F. Duckham, A. H. Faulkner, A. Hayman manager of the Bridgewater Department of the Port of Manchester, Brian Lamb, Dr. I. Langford, C. M. Marsh, Frank Mullineux, P. A. Norton, J. H. Parker-Oxspring, Ronald Russell, Miss. Dorothy Summers, P. A. L. Vine, C. P. Weaver, and the late W. Howard Williams. For waterways of South Wales: P. G. Rattenbury. For Scotland: Dr. Jean Lindsay. For waterways of Northern Ireland: Dr. W. A. McCutcheon. For Southern Ireland; Mrs. D. R. Heard and Mrs. M. McCann. For places, thanks are due to; British Transport Docks Board Humber for Goole, Harold Darbyshire for Runcorn, the Forth Ports Authority for Grangemouth, the Lancaster Port Commissioners and K. H. Docton for Glasson Dock, the late F. Higgins and the late Mrs. E. Lightfoot for Preston Brook, S. H. Hobley for Weston Point and E. A. Wilson, for Ellesmere.

On engineering subjects I have received assistance from E. Baker, C. N. Hadlow, J. Overton, Geoffrey Wheat and Alan Richardson, the National Trust regarding both the Stratford Canal and the Wey Navigation, W. K. Masters and J. E. Mann of the Great Ouse River Authority, the Sussex River Authority. Particular thanks are due to the staff of the British Waterways Board who have given most helpful advice on a wide range of topics from tractor haulage to cruising guides, in particular; G. D. Bate, A. Blankharn, R. H. J. Cotton, J. E. Freeman, O. H. Grafton, B. P. Haskins, H. Holland, B. Houghton, R. J. Hutchings, A. J. Hunt, D. James, T. T. Luckuck, G. J. Pickbourn, H. C. Rutherford, Peter White, G. E. Willbond, also the Press and Publicity Office and the previous General Manager, D. J. Kinnersley. On cargoes, Messers Watts, Blake, Bearne & Co. gave advice on the ball and china clay traffic. On carrying, help has been received from; Norman Barraclough of Hull, Messrs John Harker of Knottingley, A. E. Hawksley of Swinton, G. D. Holmes of Immingham, R. H. Hunt of Leeds, G. Kitching of Gainsborough, the late F. Peate, of Oswestry, F. Scholes of Hull, L. P. Shirley of Stoke-on-Trent, Peter L. Smith of Wakefield, D. Tierney of Middlewich, D. S. Upton of Gainsborough, I. Broadhead and W. Walker of Messrs Hargreaves (West Riding) Ltd, Castleford and Keith Whitaker of Hull. Also on carrying matters, my thanks are due to R. K. Lang of the Hull River Craft and Lighter' Owners Association, and J. Wildblood of the National Association of Inland Waterway Carriers.

For information on narrow boats I have to thank: T. Appleton, C. Atkins, H. Bentley, Tom Chaplin, G. Crowshaw, H. R. Dunkley, the late Tom Foster, P. L. Froud, D. Jinks, G. Page, the late J. Roberts, M. Webb, A. Stevens, the late H. Theobalds, P. Wallace and R. J. Wilson. For Leeds & Liverpool craft; Messrs J. & W. Forshaw, J. L. Horton, J. Lawson, T. Taylor, J. Vickers, P. Watkinson, W. Wells. For Lancaster Canal boats; D. Ashcroft. For Bridgewater Canal craft; W. E. Leathwood. For Mersey and Weaver flats; the late J. Goodier, Dr. D. Chapman, H. Arnold, H. Copeland, Dr. G. F. Howard, Captain L. Mills, K. C. Rathbone, F. Rogers, L. Worth and for Weaver steam packets; Captain H. G. Alcock and J. Mills. For Yorkshire keels and other craft; Captain T. E. Claxton, T. E. Claxton, Captain J. Frank, T. Humphries, and R. Wood. For Trent craft;I. Argent, J. Hainsworth, L. G. Reid and Captain F. Schofield. For Severn craft; G. E. Farr, F. W. Rowbotham, R. Stiles, For South Wales craft; L. I. Heath and I. L. Wright. For Parrett barges; Commander J. E. G. McKee, RN. For Tamar barges; J. J. Adams. For East Anglian craft; E. Appleyard, Major J. A. Forsythe, J. E. Marriage, D. L. Sattin, and the River Stour Trust. For Scottish inland waterway craft; Dan McDonald and for Irish; J. B. Dalton, Dr. D. B. McNeill and Dr. E. M. Patterson. Advice on the history of the boat people has been received from H. Hanson and M. G. LeRoy over and above information supplied by boat people themselves already acknowledged. Boatbuilding techniques and boatyard history have been described by the late W. L. Cook, A. Deakin, A. Howard, K. P. Keay and his staff, H. Leyland, the late J. H. Taylor, J. Turner and L. Walton.

Thanks are also due to the following libraries, record offices and museums for their staff's unstinted help; British Transport Historical Records, Cheshire County Record Office, the libraries of Birmingham, Cambridge, Cheshire County, Gainsborough (J. S. English), Glasgow (the Mitchell Library), Kidderminster, Hull, Leeds, Lincoln, Liverpool, Manchester, Newbury, Nottingham, Runcorn, Stoke-on-Trent, York and the following museums; the British Museum, Cusworth Hall Museum, Doncaster and J. Goodchild, the Gloucester Folk Museum, Merseyside Museums and Messrs M. K. Stammers and A. E. Jarvis, the Manchester Museum, City Museum & Art Gallery, Stoke-on-Trent and A. R. Mountford, the Science Museum, South Kensington (Messrs R. J. Law and A. K. Corry), the Wisbech Museum. For general help on a miscellany of subjects, I have to thank the Inland Waterways Association, for details of pleasure craft history, the Canal Cruising Co. of Stone and David Wain of Christleton, Chester and for tramroads, Dr. M. J. T. Lewis. The entry on natural history has been prepared by R. P. Woods for which I am most grateful; while W. R. D. Hill helped regarding financial history.

E. W. Paget-Tomlinson, M. A. Cantab.,
Ulverston, January 1977.

3. Thames spritsail barges. Note the hard chine construction at the bow, in other words the angle between the side and bottom planking.

4. Mileposts: (left to right); Leeds & Liverpool, Trent & Mersey, Somersetshire Coal Canal, Grand Junction, Monmouthshire, River Severn.

Contents

5. Indexing and gauging craft at Etruria weigh dock on the Trent & Mersey. The three hand cranes load 1 cwt iron weights at the fore end, amidships and aft. Immersion is measured by a scale at points forward and aft each side of the hull.

1.

6. Canal surveying in progress, using level and staff to establish height. The assistant has a perambulator and surveyors chain to measure distance.

Some Events in Waterway History

LETTERS PATENT. When Parliament met infrequently, as in the first half of the seventeenth century, it was not always possible to secure an Act to undertake river improvement. But in the absence of Parliament, the Crown could give the required powers to purchase land and levy tolls, by the issue of Royal Letters Patent. Cromwell as Lord Protector had similar powers during the Commonwealth, powers which his predecessor, Charles I had, in the eyes of his opponents, abused by his grants of monopolies in trade and industry. In the case of waterways it was usual for the Letters Patent to grant a monopoly of carriage to the undertakers of the improvement. In return the grantee paid an annual fee or a percentage of the annual profits to the Crown. The rent asked was not large. Thus Arnold Spencer of the Great Ouse received Letters Patent which demanded £5 per year for every river he improved. After the Restoration, with Parliament more or less in regular session, Letters Patent ceased to be issued since Acts could be regularly passed.

ACTS of PARLIAMENT AUTHORIZING RIVER NAVIGATIONS and CANALS. Parliamentary authority was exercised over existing navigable rivers in the fifteenth century when fish weirs were ordered to be removed, while the first Act for navigational improvement was passed in 1424 for the Lee, long used commercially. Powers to improve rivers were vested in city corporations which could invade private property, and in Commissioners of Sewers, established by an Act of Henry VIII to watch over floods and drainage. Making rivers navigable was started in earnest in the seventeenth century by the granting of Royal Letters Patent. Similar powers could be granted by an Act of Parliament to trustees or to a joint stock company, trustees in the case of the Weaver after 1760, a joint stock company in the Douglas' Act of 1720. This was the year of the collapse of the South Sea Co., which led to a financial crisis. To stop further ones, caused by over investment in companies without sound prospects, an Act was passed in 1720 which forbade any public joint stock corporation to be set up without authorization by private Act. These included transport undertakings operating for the public and levying tolls; turnpike roads, river navigations and canals. The idea was that the establishment of corporations would be limited by the expense and trouble of getting an Act. Rivers had not needed to be joint stock corporations since they were cheap, but most canals had to be because of their cost. An Act was also needed for any canal, like any river improvement, which would have to purchase land, divert streams, cross highways and obtain water. Some canals were built at private expense on private land without an Act like the Torrington, but those seeking capital by the issue of shares to the public had, by the 1720 Act, to have this capital authorized by a private Act, together with stipulated maximum charges for tolls.

Because tolls were to be levied, a Bill had to be petitioned for, a very complete statement of the waterway's prospects had to be presented to Parliament, to show that it had a chance of success. An engineer was engaged to make a survey which was embodied into the deposited plan for Parliament showing property boundaries, proposed bridges, culverts, aqueducts, locks and tunnels. Before 1793 these plans were not required by Parliament, but then standing orders were revised and elegant maps appeared. The engineer had to estimate construction costs, likely traffic and revenue, and water supply and consumption. With the survey and estimates the promoters would prepare their petition for Parliament, to be embodied into a Bill. Meanwhile counter petitions were under way, organised by opposing interests, such as turnpike trusts, watermill owners, landowners, land carriers and other rivers and canals with whom the new waterway was likely to conflict. Early river and canal promotions escaped without much opposition because of their novelty. But in 1793 the new standing orders, drawn up because of the number of Bills at this time, demanded not only complete plans, but a book of reference detailing the owners and occupiers of land to be purchased, and listing those owners who agreed or disagreed with the scheme or who were neutral. Apart from the estimate of cost it was necessary to disclose the money already subscribed, which had to be a large proportion of the whole. These gave the opposition a more complete picture. If the standing orders were not complied with, the Bill was thrown out.

The Bill would include the following clauses:

1). Creation of a company of proprietors (the eighteenth century name for shareholders), so turning the unofficial promoters into a corporate body with a seal, a sign of corporate entity.

2). Authorization of the raising, by the issue of shares, of the capital, based on the engineer's estimate and supposed to be enough to complete the waterway. A further sum could be raised, generally a third more, by borrowing on interest or mortgaging the tolls, and often by additional calls on shares or the issue of new shares. This was generally needed and more besides, for which a further Act or Acts had to be passed, sanctioning the issue of shares or additional prior charges.

3). The value of shares, commonly in denominations of £100 or £50, although the Trent & Mersey were £200 each. Shares could also be purchased in fractions, half, quarter and eighth. Some Acts limited the number of shares to be held by one person.

4). Some early canal Acts limited dividends.

5). Election of a committee of management, by voters according to the number of shares held by each voter, one vote for one share, up to a maximum of fifteen or twenty votes.

6). General meetings to be called at intervals, plus an Annual General Meeting.

7). Provision for calls on shares, i.e. the instalments by which they were paid for.

8). Regulations for selling and transferring shares.

9). Proposed tolls, the maxima fixed by the Act. This would stipulate that certain goods must be toll free, like manure and road building materials, to compensate landowners whose land had been divided. These proved a handicap since the railways did not have such limitations.

10). Guarantees, if demanded, but rare, to competing rivers and canals of their dividends.

11). Powers to purchase land and assess its value.

12). Commissioners to be set up to settle land purchase and ownership disputes and to vary tolls in some early Acts. There was usually an appeal from the commissioners to a jury.

13). Powers to divert streams, cross highways and obtain water.

14). Powers to erect brickworks and sawpits on the canal line.

15). Stipulation of the confines of the canal line, usually 25 to 30 yards across or 100 yards in the case of wharves and passing places.

16). Powers of building public wharves.

17). Erection of mileposts to assess tolls.

18). Compensation for landowners.

19). Sanction for private branches, to make a canal or tramroad for a stated distance from the canal, up to 8 miles, but usually much less. The Neath was authorized with provision for tramroads within 8 miles of the canal and the Glamorganshire within 4 miles.

20). Powers to make collateral (parallel) cuts and branches.

21). Return of topsoil to land after cutting.

22). Directive on cattle watering places.

23). Rights of support to counter subsidence, important in salt and coal mining areas.

24). Rights of mills to water, for power, processing and steam condensation.

25). Provision of stop locks demanded by other canals to safeguard their water.

26). Demand for nearby steam engines to consume their own smoke (in the Barnsley Act).

27). Powers to establish bye-laws for regulation of traffic.

28). Powers to fix and exact penalties for bye-law offences.

29). Added as a schedule to the Bill; lists of people from whom land was to be purchased.

Drafted on some such lines the Bill would be presented to Parliament, supported by petitions and opposed by counter petitions already prepared and amended when the purport of the Bill was known. These would be presented after the second reading at the committee stage in the Commons and Lords, employing counsel and with witnesses, including eminent engineers, called to support or oppose. Much money was spent in obtaining an Act, sometimes too much, some canals almost exhausting their capital in obtaining an Act, and never doing much cutting, like the Exeter & Crediton Navigation. After three readings in the Commons and Lords the Act received the Royal Assent. Canals ended centuries of isolation, hence the bonfires, fireworks and bell ringing on the passage of the Act.

ACTS of PARLIAMENT, for SALE and ABANDONMENT. Acts had to be passed to sanction any change in the navigational authority, a sale or an abandonment, for only another Act could undo the work of the original Act. A sale to a railway was sanctioned by an Act unless the navigation was private, like the Yorkshire Derwent, and no waterway until 1888 could be abandoned as a navigation without an Act. Since the Railway & Canal Traffic Act of 1888 abandonment could be by warrant issued by the Board of Trade, later the Ministry of Transport. Land Drainage Acts also gave power to close, for example, part of the Market Weighton Canal under the Market Weighton Drainage Act of 1900. The Land Drainage Act of 1930 allowed drainage authorities to take over navigations and to vary navigation rights, powers which were reaffirmed by the River Boards Act of 1948. The 1947 and 1968 Transport Acts continued the procedure of abandonment by warrant. An abandonment Act does not necessarily mean total abandonment, but allows bridges to be lowered, culverts to be made and locks weired. For the waterway can still be a water supply channel.

1751. FORFEITED ESTATES FUND. Estates of men attainted or convicted of high treason for their part in the 1715 and 1745 Jacobite risings were confiscated and administered by the Crown. Revenue from them was consolidated into a fund created by an Act of 1751-2 for the improvement of the Highlands, placed under the care of commissioners. In 1784 the estates were returned to their owners, but the fund remained and in that year £50,000 from it was advanced to complete the Forth & Clyde Canal. Under an Act of 1799, the Forth & Clyde was authorized to repay the fund which then lent £25,000 to the Crinan, likewise stopped for a shortage of cash. The fund was wound up in 1806.

1792-3. CANAL MANIA. By the 1790s early canals were proving profitable and the inland waterway network impressive, with London joined to Birmingham via Oxford and Fazeley and the Thames & Severn providing a route to Bristol. Moreover, after the disastrous American War, the administration of the Younger Pitt had restored the economy and confidence and even events in France did not lessen optimism. Only one canal was authorized in 1790, but in 1791 seven received their Acts, in 1793 twenty, and in 1794 ten. In 1795 it was only four and by 1797 the canal boom was over, the country was now four years at war with France and costs were rising. Money appeared plentiful, although many subscribers may not have had it, as can be judged when £60,000 was subscribed in an hour in May 1791 for the Rochdale Canal. Even the rural Grantham received all its then expected capital of £40,000 at a single meeting in October 1791. People were further encouraged by the publication in July 1792 of John Phillips' GENERAL HISTORY OF INLAND NAVIGATION an enthusiastic book on the successes achieved by canals in Britain and the great future they had. Of the many canal projects authorized during this time of acute mania some were excellent schemes and proved profitable, like the Neath and the Swansea, and the Grand Junction and Dearne & Dove in Yorkshire. Others were useful canals, but not very profitable, like the Worcester & Birmingham, the Ellesmere and the Peak Forest. There were failures like the Herefordshire & Gloucestershire, authorized in 1791, but not reaching Hereford until 1845, and the Dorset & Somerset abandoned during construction, on hindsight the latter was unrealistic, but nothing compared with some ideas which never reached a Bill, let alone an Act. Bristol seems to have been the centre of projects, the Bristol & Western, from the Avon to Taunton, a canal from Bristol to Gloucester, and one from Bristol to Salisbury. Because of the considerable speculation, the date and place of promotion meetings were concealed until the last possible moment. Because of poor transport it was hoped to limit the attendance, so that only a chosen few could get at the subscription books which were believed to hold the key to wealth, not only because of the attractiveness of investment but because a speculator could quickly dispose of his shares at remarkable profits. Values could rise 100 per cent in a week and some people must have done well, but others were hit by a series of bank failures in 1793. These brought prices down, and with the War, contributed to the end of the frenzy.

A meeting of the Bristol & Western was kept secret, the promoters buying up all the newspapers which carried the advertisement. However the news leaked out but most speculators found the books full. The 'ride to Devizes' was the result of an elaborate trick to achieve the same end. The promoters of a Bristol-London canal (later the Kennet & Avon) arranged for a bogus meeting at Devizes on 12 December 1792. Speculators from Bristol rushed there, but found no meeting. To placate them one was hurriedly arranged and a Bristol - Salisbury canal considered, for which subscription books were produced and filled. People invested who could hardly have had any money, in 1792 the Ashby received share applications from a joiner, a serving man and a postilion. Many people doubtless borrowed from the bank to pay their deposits and first calls and would be badly hurt by bank failures. The mania was an English and Welsh peculiarity with less response in Scotland and not much in Ireland. The Crinan was authorized in 1793 and the Aberdeenshire was a mania proposal although it did not receive its Act until 1796. Many Scottish schemes were put forward later. On the other hand, the opening of the Forth & Clyde in 1790 was an encouragement to investment as the first coast to coast ship canal. Ireland had not the investment potential although the Royal, incorporated in 1789 was possibly encouraged by events in England. Few rivers were improved, an exception being the Leicester Navigation authorized in 1791.

1793. WAR WITH FRANCE. Further promotions were coloured by war fears and needs, thus the Caledonian, by which merchant ships could pass free from the attentions of privateers, and the Royal Military Canal, built as a defence line. During the Napoleonic period the waterways carried war supplies, the Carron Co., performing a particularly distinguished role via the Forth & Clyde. It was found possible to move troops by canal, from London to Liverpool and thence to Dublin, via the Oxford Canal in seven days in 1798. The Aire & Calder fitted out a small gunboat, the OUZE, in 1798, but the Government refused her and she had to be sold. In 1803 Pickfords' offered boats, waggons and horses, while the labour force building the Grand Junction formed a militia 'in support of our Laws and Property' in 1797 to resist revolutionary France.

1810. SECOND WAVE of INTEREST. Round about 1810 there was a second wave of canal interest, but not the same level of speculation. It was the time of John Rennie's encouragement of a string of grandiose schemes. In 1810 he was able to start the cutting of the long delayed Grand Western. This revived interest in a canal from Taunton to Bristol, part of a waterway route between London and Exeter surveyed by Rennie. He was at the same time planning a 'Grand Southern Canal' from the Medway to Portsmouth, but the only firm scheme which emerged was for a Thames or Medway to Channel waterway, the Wey & Arun Junction Canal sanctioned in 1813. In Scotland there were schemes for canals between the Forth and Loch Lomond with Stirling as the centre of a system, for a canal across Scotland from the Clyde at Dumbarton to Stonehaven and for a canal down Annandale to the Solway. But nothing came of any of these. Later the Manchester Ship Canal and European progress encouraged a host of ambitious schemes, including the Mid-Scotland Ship Canal first surveyed in 1889-90, and the Birmingham & Liverpool Ship Canal mooted in 1888. One partially came off, it was the Sheffield & South Yorkshire Navigation.

1817. EXCHEQUER BILL LOAN COMMISSIONERS. Unemployment and distress among ex-servicemen after the Napoleonic Wars led to the passage in 1817 of the Poor Employment Act. Under it Commissioners were appointed to control the lending of Government money to works which could employ the poor. Inland waterways came into this category and many of the later canals were saved by such timely help. Between 1817 and 1828 the Commissioners lent £623,000, notably to the Gloucester & Berkeley Ship Canal and to the Regent's Canal, neither of which would have otherwise been easily completed. They also advanced money to the Ulster Canal, the Birmingham & Liverpool Junction, the Montgomeryshire, the Thames & Medway, the North Wilts, the Edinburgh & Glasgow Union, the Glasgow, Paisley & Johnstone, the Portsmouth & Arundel, the Bude and the Norwich & Lowestoft Navigation, the last named being unable to repay the loan. To reclaim their money the Commissioners ordered its sale. In 1842 they were reformed as the Public Works Loan Commissioners, still in existence as the Public Works Loan Board.

1845. CANAL CARRIERS ACTS, 1845 and 1847. Railway expansion in Great Britain & Ireland led the Government to try and put the waterways on competitive terms. At the instigation of the Aire & Calder, two Bills were introduced. One was the Canal Tolls Act, the other the Canal Clauses Act, generally called the Canal Carriers Act. It specifically authorized canal companies to become carriers of goods upon their own and other canals. It allowed them to operate cargo boats, towage services, and road vehicles for delivery of goods, as well as warehousing. To further their carrying activities, canal companies were allowed to arrange with other canal or railway companies over the division of tolls. Such arrangements could extend to the leasing of tolls by one canal company to another for a period not exceeding 21 years. The idea was to strengthen the canal system by allowing more co-operation   and amalgamation. Historically the 1845 Act confirmed what had already been done by many canal companies, being a direct authorization to companies to run carrying fleets so that traffic would be kept on the water, should independent carriers desert water for rail. Further Governmental encouragement came in 1847 with the second Canal Carriers Act, which allowed companies to borrow money to set up a carrying department.

1845. CANAL TOLLS ACT. With the Canal Carriers Act, this one also inspired by the Aire & Calder, was designed to make the canals more competitive against the railways. The Act allowed navigation and canal companies to vary their tolls, rates and charges within the maxima granted to them by Parliament under their own Acts. This meant that they could depart from a flat ton/mileage rate applicable to the whole line of their waterway.   Now they could charge different mileage rates either to favour traders who were regular users over a certain length, or to encourage traffic over a little used section. They could also charge a higher rate for traffic passing through tunnels and other areas where maintenance was heavy, done, for example, by counting quarter miles as half miles. The Act was careful to say that varied tolls must be applied equally to all and a variation had to be agreed by the owners of the Navigation and Authorities.   Arrangements for through tolls variations had to be made with the consent of the navigations concerned, while any company subject to a limitation of profits, like the Glamorganshire, was not allowed to raise tolls above this limitation.

1854. RAILWAY AND CANAL TRAFFIC ACT.   By the 1850s railway owned canals were numerous and the Government were concerned to safegard their future. All waterways were to have as the Act said, 'reasonable facilities' for traffic and there were to be no favours shown to certain traders and no prejudices against others. There was to be no hindrance to the forwarding of traffic from one canal to another, whether railway owned or not, or from rail to canal or vice versa.

RAILWAYS and WATERWAYS. Horse tramroads had been built as feeders to the waterways and as competitive lines. The locomotive railway was different but was not immediately a threat. The Liverpool & Manchester Railway in its early years concentrated on passengers and light goods, leaving bulk haulage to water. This calm of the of the 1830s did   not last. The next decade saw the railway mania (1845) and the building of a great system , by which the waterways enjoyed a profitable few years with the carriage of construction materials. Great railway companies soon emerged, the Midland in 1844, the London & North Western in 1846, the Manchester, Sheffield & Lincolnshire in 1847. Railways   were   supported as they could break the old monopoly of the waterways and make them reduce their tolls. Of great importance was the increased speed of rail transport because it allowed manufacturers to store less raw materials. The effect here was better use of capital.   The people   could also move round more rapidly to sell goods, recruit labour and exchange ideas. Against the railways, the waterways were weak. There were few amalgamations, the Shropshire Union, the Birmingham and the Sheffield & South Yorkshire systems, all under railway control, and the independent Grand Junction. Nor had they arrangements for through tolls until the end of the nineteenth century. Unlike the railways they never had a clearing house. To meet the railways, they were forced to reduce their tolls or come to agreements with the railways over the apportionment of traffic. If one party carried more than their share, the other was compensated by monetary payment. Similar traffic agreements were made between waterway and waterway as a measure of co-operation. The Government tried to help the waterways by, from 1845, allowing them to vary tolls and act as carriers. Many sold out to railways, often at a good price. The newcomers might want the canal for several reasons, to silence opposition for their own Acts, to thwart future competition, or to build their own lines on the course of a canal. Thus the Midland had to acquire the Ashby Canal as the price of their Act for a railway into the Leicestershire coalfield. In the West Country the Bristol & Exeter Railway first leased and later bought the competitive Grand Western.   The Aberdeenshire was bought by the Great North of Scotland Railway in 1845 and used for part of its line. One or two railways were anxious to have a canal to increase their own operation; the North Staffordshire buying the Trent & Mersey and having eyes on the Bridgewater. Many of the waterways were impressed with railway possibilities and had ideas of wholesale conversion, for example, the Ellesmere & Chester and the Birmingham & Liverpool Junction around 1845. Sales of canals to railways was at first discouraged by the Government who tried to check the trend by an act of 1846, forming a Railway Commission under the Board of Trade to examine all amalgamation Bills to see if they were in the public interest. This was soon given up and railway take-overs became unrestricted although dependent on an Act. They were encouraged by the 1845 Canal Carriers Act which allowed canals to lease each other, including railway owned canals, the railways leasing through the canals they already owned. Actual passage of an Act for railway control was usually straightforward. Such Acts, called Transfer Acts, sanctioned the issue of railway shares in exchange for canal shares, or a pay-off in cash for those who did not want railway shares. The canal company was then dissolved. However there were exceptions. The Shrewsbury & Hereford Railway had agreed to buy the Leominster Canal as early as 1847 and the Act authorizing the sale was passed in that year. They had proposed to use the bed for the permanent way but later changed their route. Because of this they tried to evade their agreement and not until 1858 did the sale go through, after a case in Chancery. The Grantham and Nottingham Canals both sued a railway company because the agreed sale had not taken place. The Manchester, Bolton & Bury converted itself into a railway company in 1831, although the canal was not closed as intended, for the railway followed a separate route. By the end of the 1850s the waterway mileage under railway control was considerable, much of it leased, in addition to direct ownership. The Birmingham Canal Navigations were leased by the L.N.W.R. from 1846 and some ordinarily independent canals had spells of existence leased to railway interests, for example the Rochdale from 1855 to 1876. For a coherent waterway system this was to be deplored. The railways were not going to encourage traffic except in special circumstances of a waterway in rival railway territory. In GWR land the Shropshire Union was worked hard by the LNWR although they neglected their Huddersfield. Otherwise canals were closed, like the Oakham, immediately on railway purchase in 1846, or trade discouraged as it was on the Yorkshire Derwent by the North Eastern Railway. Acts were passed to safeguard the railway owned waterways such as the Act of 1873. It was difficult for the independent waterways to compete with the railways, their main weapons were toll reductions and their own carrying fleets. Flyboats were put on to give rapid delivery and steam tugs appeared on lock free stretches. Opening hours of locks were extended, making life harder for the keepers, but so much was out of date. Many independent carriers were small and made no effort to combine by rates agreements. Stoppages for repairs meant a complete cessation of traffic, tunnels were mostly one-way and few lock flights were duplicated. E. A. Pratt added many more shortcomings when he wrote at the time and after the 1906 Royal Commission. He described the problems of frost, subsidence, water supply for the high level Birmingham system, the remoteness of many canal wharves, and the lack of siding facilities where boats could be stored with their loads. He suggested modernization would be unwarrantably expensive and few canals tried to modernize. In the canal age they had given out too much in dividends, and railway competition hit their revenues hard, and so could not attract new capital. There were exceptions such as the compartment boat system of the Aire & Calder and the improvements on the Weaver. These are both rivers able to take larger craft and they came through the railway age successfully. Similarly the Manchester Ship Canal was successful, but the attempts of the Grand Junction to modernize their Leicester line around 1900 failed through lack of traffic. After the Act of 1888 stopped further acquisition of waterways by railways, the two settled down together until threatened by a common enemy, road transport, after the 1914-18 War. Perhaps it was in the period of decline between the wars that railway ownership of waterways was seen at its most unattractive. The LMSR were encumbered by much of the Shropshire Union and by the Huddersfield, their 1944 Act of abandonment was an effort to rid themselves of these liabilities, while the LNER succeeded in abandoning the Grantham in 1936 and most of the Nottingham in 1937. In Ireland railway dominance was less pronounced.

1855. CANAL ASSOCIATION. As British waterways yielded to the railways, so efforts were made to give the navigations a spirit of unified purpose. Associations to promote waterways had begun with the Inland Commercial Society in 1812, an assembly for the advancement of traffic by inland navigation. No national waterways body emerged until the founding of the Canal Association under the leadership of the Aire & Calder. The Navigation had previously invited other waterway owners to meet, for the purpose of pressing parliament to give greater freedom to carriage by canal and river, resulting in the Acts of 1845. The Association carried these meetings into a permanent organisation, to watch railway legislation and promote canal interests. At first it was called the United Body of Canal Proprietors, but from 18 June 1855 it was the Canal Association, with Col. J. G. Smyth of the Aire & Calder as chairman and Thomas Wilson, then the company's auditor as secretary. The Association was run from the Aire & Calder offices in Leeds. In 1858 there were 40 members including some of the railway owned waterways, the Shropshire Union, the canals of the Manchester, Sheffield & Lincolnshire Railway and a new member that year the St. Helens Canal & Railway Co. The annual reports of the committee are chiefly taken up with current Bills withdrawn and passed noting those with any canal interest. Sub-committees were appointed to consider various aspects of the industry, such as gauging boats, weighing and discharging cargoes, while a special one reported in 1864 on proposed standardized bye-laws. Of interest are the reports to the Association on technical advances on waterways, for example in 1859, on the introduction of steam scows on the Forth & Clyde and Monkland Canals. The Association lasted until nationalization, less the 1929 Grand Union who withdrew from membership in 1937 because the company wanted to escape from the Rail-Canal Conference set up in 1933 to end price cutting and apportion traffic.

1858. CHEAP TRAINS & CANAL CARRIERS ACT. This was about third class fares but the Aire & Calder managed to work in a clause to stop a loophole in the 1845 Canal Carriers Act. This had allowed canals to lease each other. Railway companies, through navigations they already owned,had successfully leased others, but the 1858 Act stopped this by forbidding a railway owned canal to lease another canal or railway unless specially authorized by an Act.

1873. REGULATION of RAILWAYS ACT. By the 1870s British manufacturers were subjected to the high charges of a near rail monopoly. Only the waterways, and coastal shipping could offer a competitive service. Already there had been legislation to encourage the waterways and check railways' take-over of waterways, but by this time something more positive was needed. The Act of 1854 had sought to safeguard the large mileage of railway owned navigation from neglect, but the 1873 Act, also called the Railway & Canal Traffic Act, 1873, was more far-reaching. It appointed Railway Commissioners, three in number, with an assistant under them. Their duties were to deal with complaints arising out of contravention of the 1854 Act, and they were also to arbitrate over disputes. The 1873 Act amended the through traffic facilities demanded by the 1854 Act to compel railway and canal companies to quote through tolls or rates by either or both means of transport. Most important was the forbidding of any further control of a navigation by railway company purchase, unless approved by the Commissioners, while the Act stopped agreement over working between canal companies allowed by the 1845 Act, unless sanctioned by the Commissioners. Railway owned waterways were to be properly maintained. This the railways did, often at no profit to themselves and thus saved some canals, for example the Macclesfield, which would have closed if independent.

1877. CANAL BOATS ACTS, 1877, 1884. George Smith of Coalville campaigned energetically for better conditions afloat, his particular concern being for the children of the boats. The first Act passed in 1877 was feeble with no penalties for non-observance, leaving all initiative to local authorities. They were to register and inspect boats used as dwellings and try to arrange education for the boat children. A registered boat, marked with the name of the local authority and a registration number, had to comply with the provisions of the Act; its certificate of registration sanctioned so many adults and so many children aboard, depending on the cabin size, with the provisions that the husband and wife's cabin should not be occupied by anyone else of the female sex above the age of 12, or any other male above the age of 14. Distinctions were drawn between fly-boats with crews working shifts and also between older boats, the date line being 30 June 1878. Older boats were allowed more cramped conditions. The local authorities were riparian, and their boats would pass by them, when they might be inspected. Unfortunately few local authorities bothered to register any boats, much to the disappointment of George Smith. However his perseverance triumphed and an Amendment Act passed in 1884. Now all craft which were lived in had to be registered, and a central inspector was appointed under the Local Government Board, who demanded reports from the local authorities on the inspections they had undertaken. The provisions regarding accommodation had to be enforced and a new registration certificate was required whenever the boat was altered. Local authorities were to make sure the children attended school, but this never proved workable. In other respects the Acts were a success and were untouched until the 1920s. A Ministry of Health departmental committee on the practice of living-in on canal boats, chaired by Neville Chamberlain, which reported in 1921, found little wrong with the boat people save their lack of education. In 1925 the two Canal Boats Acts were amended and in 1936 embodied in a new public health Act which tidied up all the old legislation. Local authorities responsible for inland waterway craft varied much in size. There were Birmingham, Manchester and Leeds, but also Daventry, Rickmansworth, Mirfield and Tamworth. Narrow boats had name and number (e.g.REGISTERED AT DAVENTRY No.374) lettered along the top of the cabin side, Runcorn adding a little ship and Chester a sheaf. Leeds & Liverpool boats had the number at the stern, with a "Liver bird" at the stern if Liverpool registered, while Manchester was signified by an "M" within a six pointed star,and Wigan by a "W" within a diamond.

1888. CANAL CONFERENCE. Up to the 1870s railway development had overshadowed the waterways. Then in the 1870s Britain's industrial lead was challenged by Europe and North America, while British agriculture was threatened by North American wheat. One reason for the success of foreign goods on the home market was the low cost of rail and water transport on the Continent compared with the high charges of British railways. A monopoly of British internal transport by the railways could be grave, hence the wish for an improved waterways system, modelled on the successful navigations of Europe and America. Interest was encouraged by developments on British rivers and canals, such as steam haulage and new locks on the Weaver as well as the Manchester Ship Canal project. Particular interest became focussed on a Bill which passed in 1888 as the Railway & Canal Traffic Act. This Bill reflected the national concern and on 10th and 11th of May 1888, while it was still before Parliament, the Royal Society of Arts drew attention to it and the waterways by summoning a conference on canals and inland waterways. The chairman was the scientist and administrator, Sir Douglas Galton. In his introduction he spoke of the impending Act and of the 1888 Local Government Act establishing county councils who would be responsible for highway upkeep as well as the severe foreign competition. Bigger waterways could provide the solution. He ended by considering state purchase of canals and navigations, and their management by the new county councils. The first papers were by canal engineers,Mr.L.F.Vernon-Harcourt, who described the great improvements then being carried out in France, and Mr.G.R.Jebb of the Shropshire Union and the Birmingham Canal Navigations, who outlined maintenance problems. Other contributors spoke of British canal history and of the mutual influence of railways and waterways in Great Britain; Mr.Forbes complaining that the legislature did not do enough for the canals. Mr.M.B.Cotsworth threw out suggestions of Government purchase or a big canal amalgamation. The second day opened with a paper on inland transport by land and water in the nineteenth century by F.R.Conder. He spoke of the European waterways and possible integration of rail and water transport, water taking the bulk cargoes. He spoke too of the way factories were migrating to the ports because of high railway charges in Britain. Mr. Lester in a following paper advocated public trusts to manage canals on the lines of that superintending the Weaver, but General Rundall made a plea for a national Water Commission which would be responsible for co-ordinating all aspects of water, supply and drainage as well as transport. The General suggested a Royal Commission, eventually set up in 1906. In the discussion public trusts were advocated as a matter of urgency to be incorporated, as they were, into the new Bill.

1888. RAILWAY & CANAL TRAFFIC ACT. It was in this mixture of concern and hope that further legislation, following the 1873 Act, was prepared to aid the canals. The canal conference secured an amendment authorizing local authorities to set up public trusts for administering waterways. Waterway tolls were too archaic for effective competition, and both these and railway charges had been the subject of an enquiry in 1887-8. The new Act demanded that each railway, canal and river navigation including those of Ireland and Scotland should submit a revised structure of commodities carried and their tolls to a new Railway & Canal Commission under the Board of Trade, superseding the Railway Commissioners set up in 1873. Its task was to approve the new tolls on behalf of the Board of Trade. The structure submitted was examined in an attempt to achieve uniformity between the companies. It also investigated the complaints, being endowed with powers of settling disputes between traders and companies, while any disagreement over charges between themselves and the companies could be settled by the Commission, although a company might appeal to a superior court. Once agreement had been reached the new scale of charges were the legal published ones, actually ratified by a long series of Railway & Canal Rates, Tolls & Charges Confirmation Order Acts passed between 1891 and 1894. This ended the old tolls maxima granted to waterways under their authorizing Acts. There were several extra canal provisions of special interest. Each canal company had to supply annual reports on their waterway and occasional traffic returns. They also had to notify stoppages to the Board of Trade. The Board of Trade demanded to inspect canal company bye-laws, and had powers to inspect canals themselves if the works were in a dangerous state or a hindrance to traffic. Railways and their officers were now expressly forbidden to acquire any canal interests. Canal companies were granted powers to set up a clearing house to deal with through traffic as on the railways, but it was never established. Abandonment of a waterway could be secured by a Board of Trade warrant if the canal was deemed 'unnecessary', alternatively the Board of Trade were able to issue a Provisional Order for future management of the canal by a specially constituted body under a local authority, or by a local authority itself, including the new county councils. This was in deference to the public trustees idea.

1906. ROYAL COMMISSION on the Canals and Inland Navigations of the United Kingdom, 1906-1911. The minutes of evidence, maps and reports are contained in 11 volumes, volume VII being the final report for England, Wales and Scotland, published in 1909. The Irish report came out last in 1911. Volume VI was the result of an enquiry into the waterways of France, Belgium, Germany and Holland, volume IX reported costs of the Commission's improvement proposals and volume X on water supplies. The Commission was the culmination of interest in British waterways. People were impressed with the successful completion of the new Manchester Ship Canal and creation of modern waterways in Cheshire and Yorkshire. Along with practical work came a series of books and papers on waterway subjects, holding up American and European rivers and canals as examples. There was a fear that Britain's industrial lead was slipping and one reason appeared to be high railway rates at home opposed to cheap water transport abroad. In this atmosphere the Associated Chambers of Commerce resolved in 1900 to ask for a Royal Commission to examine the problems, favouring the public trusts proposed earlier. Bills were introduced in 1901, 1904, 1905 and 1906 all on Chambers of Commerce initiative, but all failed. Finally the Associated Chambers did secure the Commission which first met in 1906, under Lord Shuttleworth as chairman, who had been Under Secretary of State for India and Parliamentary Secretary to the Admiralty. Under him were 18 Commissioners, including Sir John Brunner of Brunner, Mond & Co., Ltd, James C. Inglis, General Manager of the GWR and H. F. Killick, a director of the Leeds and Liverpool Canal. In making their recommendations the Commission drew on their knowledge of European waterways, remembering the special conditions in the British Isles of comparatively short hauls and a very dense railway network, as well as competition from coastal shipping. At the time of the Commission about 4670 miles of waterways were in use, nearly a third railway owned. England and Wales had 3639 miles while Scotland had 183 and Ireland 848. Some navigations had declined and closed while others had advanced. These were all wide waterways like the Weaver. In their final report for England, Wales and Scotland, they considered the reasons why private enterprise had failed to improve the waterways. They took evidence on the lack of standardization, the multiplicity of authorities and their lack of finance. Of particular concern was the 'rudimentary organization of carriage' and the difficulty there was in securing through rates. One witness, Mr. Hunt, the Leeds carrier, had said he had recently 'been about a month or five weeks trying to negotiate a through rate over five canals.' Four had been got 'into the humour of taking it', but one still 'stood out'.

Their evidence led them to recommend the improvement of the navigations forming the 'cross' in other words linking the Midlands with the four major estuaries; Mersey, Humber, Severn and Thames. Much was composed of narrow waterways which would have to be widened to at least 100 ton barge standard, although some favoured 300 ton standard, in order to compete with rail. On the larger rivers the Commission considered the use of craft of greater capacity, thus the Trent should take 750 ton vessels and the Severn 600 ton craft above Worcester and 750 tonners below, although some witnesses commented on the difficulty of finding consignments for the larger craft. The following system of enlarged existing routes was therefore proposed for which the consulting engineers, Sir John Wolfe Barry & Partners prepared plans and costs: -

A). Birmingham and Leicester to London(Brentford and Paddington), in other words the Grand Junction, to be improved to 100 ton standard. The Regent's could already take this size.

B). Leicester, Burton and Nottingham to the Humber. Here Fradley and Leicester were to be the terminal points for a 300 ton barge route. From Fradley there would be a much enlarged Trent & Mersey Canal to Burton and Derwent Mouth and a much enlarged Trent to Nottingham From Leicester the Soar would be enlarged to the Trent at Nottingham and below Nottingham the Trent was to be improved for 750 ton barges.

C). Wolverhampton and Birmingham to the Mersey. A 100 ton route to the Weaver already able to take 400 ton craft. Revived in 1943 when the Weaver reported on a 100 ton extension to Wolverhampton.

D). Wolverhampton and Birmingham to the Severn, the route joining A and C in Wolverhampton. The Staffs. & Worcs. to be enlarged to 100 ton standard to Stourport as well as the Droitwich and Worcester & Birmingham Canals, with the Severn taking 600 ton craft from Stourport to Worcester, 750 ton from Worcester to Gloucester, and 1200 tons on the Gloucester & Berkeley Canal. The Birmingham narrow network could not be enlarged because of waterside premises and was regarded as a feeder to the improved lines. There were no immediate plans to enlarge other canals, although trans-Pennine routes were to be considered after the 'cross' had been improved.

The cost of the 'cross' improvement would have been very high, some £17½ million plus the cost of acquiring the canals, according to the Barry Report. Some of the works would have been dramatic, for example 7 inclined planes between Worcester & Birmingham but the project was beyond the reach of private enterprise. The only solution was some form of public trust. Local trusts under local authorities were discounted as too parochial and the Commission recommended a central Waterway Board of three or five full time paid Commissioners. The Board would have powers to raise loans and issue stock to finance improvements. In Scotland they proposed that the Waterway Board should take over both the Caledonian and the Crinan. Ideas for enlarging the Caledonian were rejected although the Commission were impressed with schemes for an alternative canal to the Crinan from Loch Fyne. They were also interested in schemes for a mid-Scotland ship canal. The Royal Commission were far from unanimous. Some thought the improvements too ambitious and they would never pay. Mr. Inglis made a long report of his own which expressed the railway attitude, mentioning the many canals the railways had been required to save and maintain and suggesting there would not be enough water for enlarged canals. Nothing was done apart from works on the Trent. The scheme was seen as unfair to traders on unimproved waterways, and to the railways, for a state subsidized waterway system would be in competition with private enterprise railways. Railway interests had E. A. Pratt as their spokesman, with his two books, "British Canals" (1906) and "Canals and Traders" (1910). The former was subtitled "Is Their Resuscitation Practicable?" exactly describing his attitude. Public opinion considered the scheme too expensive and it was overshadowed by Irish Home Rule, the crisis over the House of Lords and eventually the 1914-18 War. After the War the cost had risen so much that implementation was out of the question. The Irish report of 1911 recommended a modest expansion, but nothing was done.

1912. WATERWAYS ASSOCIATION was dedicated to implementing the recommendations of the Royal Commission of 1906. It remained in being until 1922.

1914-18. WAR. The War deeply concerned the waterways. Railway owned navigations were immediately put under state control, being administered by the Railway Executive Committee while the independent waterways received no protection. Traffic fell because men left to join up and boats were commandeered for use in France. Eventually, in March 1917 the Canal Control Committee of the Board of Trade was formed to oversee, organize and subsidize the independent lines to relieve the railways. The Committee started a publicity drive for the waterways and soldiers from Transport Workers Battalions were drafted to work the canals and traffic increased, notably coal on the Birmingham system. The Caledonian successfully fulfilled its original strategic function in 1918 when mines were carried to Muirtown for laying across the North Sea. In 1920 the subsidy for the independent canals was ended and they returned to private control. Costs had risen and revenue prospects were dim. Waterways were allowed by the Ministry of Transport to raise tolls 150% and bypass their authorized maxima, the Ministry nominally taking over some, including the Trent, to allow this. Later when the maxima were abandoned and waterways fixed their own levels, they were returned to their owners.

1920. CHAMBERLAIN COMMITTEE. Increases in costs had made the improvements suggested by the 1906 Royal Commission out of the question, but the Government were concerned for the waterways . The future of some was gloomy, notably the Trent. The Ministry of Transport set up a departmental committee in 1920 under the chairmanship of Mr. Neville Chamberlain. It reported in 1921, an interim report in February and another in May but no final report. The February report concerned the Trent, taken over by the Ministry in 1920 to prevent closure. Under an Act of 1915 Nottingham Corporation were authorized to take-over the river from the city down to Newark, to improve it and, encouraged to proceed by the Committee, the corporation started work on new locks. The Committee had proposed a public trust, but Nottingham Corporation assumed control of their section of the river in 1927. While the Committee had considered that the Trent should be dealt with quickly, the remainder of their recommendations were for gradual implementation. The railways were being re-grouped and the Committee had similar ideas for the canals, proposing seven regional groups, each under a public trust composed of representatives of local users, public bodies, the Ministry of Transport and navigation company stockholders. It was felt that regional-ization would work because each group would centre on a commercially important waterway.

1922. NATIONAL COUNCIL for INLAND WATERWAYS. Based on Birmingham, it was founded in 1922 to further the proposals of the Chamberlain Committee. George Cadbury was one of its members.

NATIONAL INLAND NAVIGATION LEAGUE. It was founded sometime after the 1914-8 War, a precursor of the Inland Waterways Association. President of the league was George Westall, whose INLAND CRUISING was published in 1908.

1928. ROYAL COMMISSION on the Co-ordination and Development of Transport. Growth of road use lead to the formation of this Commission, to recommend plans for inland transport in Great Britain. Their chairman was Sir Arthur Griffith-Boscawen who led a team of eleven. The Commission reported in 1930, the section devoted to inland waterways being fairly short. After a brief historical survey, the report stated the proposals of the 1906 Commission, R. F. de Salis of the Canal Association and of George Cadbury for the National Council for Inland Waterways pleading for amalgamations to strengthen waterways. The Commission agreed to am-algamations, although how they were to be achieved was left open. Nothing was done due to the depression of the 1930s.

1933. NATIONAL ASSOCIATION of INLAND WATERWAY CARRIERS. The Association was formed for the benefit of the employers in the industry, separate from the Canal Association of 1855 representing owners of navigations. There had been in 1885, a Railway and Canal Traders' Association and there were additional regional groups, the Severn Waterway Traders Association, the Hull River Craft and Lighter Owners' Association and on the Thames the Association of Master Lightermen & Barge Owners. The new Association had its secretariat in the Bridgewater Department offices of the Manchester Ship Canal, but moved to Hull in 1974. Membership grew steadily and it worked closely with the original bodies. When the waterways were nationalized, the Association acted on behalf of the private enterprise carr-iers. Membership is either full or associate. Full members are companies whose main business is inland water carriage, the associates are those with an inland water fleet sub-sidiary to their other activities. In the 1950s there were 50 full members divided into regions, North Eastern, East Midlands, North Western, South Western and South East (London). The Association negotiates wages and liases between carriers and the British Waterways Board. There are regular meetings for the presentation of papers and discussion. The Hull River Craft and Lighter Owners' Association Ltd, founded in 1905, looked after carriers on the Humber, Trent and Yorkshire navigations. It merged with the National Association in 1976. There is also the Keel & Lighter Owners' Mutual Insurance & Protecting Society Ltd., founded in 1893, an insurance organization. The Severn Waterways Association was wound-up in 1971.

1939. WAR. During the 1939-45 War the waterways were given more careful consideration. The railway canals came, with the railways, under the Ministry of Transport. Again the independents were left, although from June 1940, carriers were subsidized. In 1941, Frank Pick of London Transport reported that waterways could contribute more to the War effort under Government control. Since the start of the War there had been six regional canal committees and a central commitee whose chairman was Parliamentary Secretary to the Minister of Transport. In 1942 the waterways and carriers most important for transport in wartime, were directly taken over by the Government. All revenue went to the Ministry, who in return paid out subsidies based on what the revenue had been just before the War, with more added to take account of the wear and tear of wartime traffic. Despite years of poor maintenance and the call-up, they carried considerable tonnages, particularly on the Severn. Bombs caused breaches, for example at Sheffield in 1940 and boats were lost.

1946. INLAND WATERWAYS ASSOCIATION. It was aimed at waterway preservation for commercial traffic. Much publicity came over the struggle to prevent abandonment of the Kennet & Avon, which ended in victory for the IWA by the later 1950s. It is a protest body campaigning in the press, speaking out at public meetings and organizing protest cruises as well as rallies and exhibitions. Their BULLETIN is now published quarterly. Now they have the ear of Parliament, a distinguished patronage, (A. P. Herbert was president from 1947 to his death in 1971), and an harmonious relationship with the British Waterways Board. There has been an Inland Waterways Association in Ireland since 1954 following the same policy.

1947. TRANSPORT ACT. This was the Labour Government Act which nationalized most of Britain's inland transport. Transfer to public ownership was to take place on 1st of January 1948, all nationalized undertakings to be vested in the British Transport Commission admin-istering the railways, railway owned ports and hotels, road haulage in a large measure and a large mileage of inland navigations. The Commission was to have a chairman and four to eight members, appointed by the Minister of Transport. The Commission had powers to carry, provide traffic facilities on inland navigations and at ports, to store and consign goods and build repair and maintain equipment for their own use. They could lend money to carry-ing enterprises, enter into business agreements and acquire other businesses such as carry-ing companies, warehousing and wharfage companies. The Commission was overall manager, but the running of the individual transport industries was entrusted to executives, the Rail-way Executive, Docks & Inland Waterways Executive and so forth. The Caledonian and Crinan Canals were transferred to the Commission from the Ministry of Transport. All carrying on nationalized waterways was to be subject to licences from the Commission, as they only took over fleets which were controlled by the waterways to be nationalized.

DOCKS & INLAND WATERWAYS EXECUTIVE (British Transport Commission). The passage of the Transport Act established this Executive to operate former railway owned ports and nationalized inland navigations. It had a full-time chairman, three full-time members and three part-time members, all appointed by the Ministry of Transport.   The chairman was Sir Reginald Hill, lately one of the deputy secretaries of the Ministry. At first the railway owned waterways were under the Railway Executive, until transferred gradually to the Docks & Inland Waterways Executive, whose navigation responsibilities   were divided into four regions, (but see officers and staff, canal companies to modern times for more details). Many waterways were left out of nationalization, which was founded on the Government's control of navigations during the 1939-45 War. Thus the east coast ones, contributing   little to the War effort, were excluded from control and nationalization. Also excluded were many rivers including the Thames and the Yorkshire Ouse, the Manchester Ship Canal   and   its satellite, the Bridgewater, because of its port status, some nearly disused canals   like   the Rochdale, some disused like the Neath and corporation owned waterways like the Exeter   and Beverley Beck. The Commission controlled 2064 miles of waterways. They acquired the Grand Union Canal Carrying Co., the Aire & Calder fleet, the Calder Carrying Co., (subsidiary   to the Calder & Hebble Navigation and soon sold) and Canal Transport Ltd,, on the Leeds   & Liverpool. The Commission had powers to acquire carrying companies not controlled   by canal companies, and bought Fellows, Morton & Clayton in 1949. In 1953 the Executive   was dissolved under the 1953 Transport Act and replaced from the 1 October 1953 by a Board of Management.

1953. ASSOCIATION of PLEASURE CRAFT OPERATORS. The original full title was the Association of Pleasure Craft Operators on Inland Waterways, APCO as it is   generally   known, looks after the interests of those who cater for the pleasure cruising industry.

1953. TRANSPORT ACT. This freed road haulage and abolished the Executives,   replacing them with a board of management, in each case under the British Transport Commission.

1953. RUSHOLME, BOARD of SURVEY. After the 1953 Act, the British Transport Commission decided on a private survey to make recommendations for the waterways. It was chaired by Lord Rusholme, a member of the Commission, and there were two independent participants. The results were reported in 1954 and published in 1955, listing many shortcomings in the system, particularly lack of traffic due to changes from water to rail and road. The survey decided that the nationalized system should be managed separately from the docks with a full-time general manager. The survey then suggested that the waterways should be considered in three groups: Group. 1. a small mileage (336), of already busy waterways which should be improved, Group. 2., a larger mileage, 994, of waterways to be retained because of their value for commercial transport in spite of a less certain future, and Group. 3., a mileage of 771, of waterways which seemed to have no commercial future and should be removed from the care of the British Transport Commission. The suggestion was also made that waterways in Group. 2. could be transferred to Group. 3. if their use dwindled. Scottish canals   were recommended for transfer to the Secretary of State for Scotland. The report was conditioned by the commercial value of canals, amenity being hardly considered. The groups were accepted by the British Transport Commission, although the BTC were not sure about the future of the Scottish canals. The public were unhappy about the future of the canals in Group. 3., many of which were valuable for pleasure cruising, so in 1956 an independent inquiry was appointed. The BTC sanctioned heavy expenditure on the Group. 1. waterways and work began in 1956 on a number of improvements, notably on the Trent.

1953. BRITISH TRANSPORT WATERWAYS was formed as a division under the BTC, after the Rusholme Report. The docks were put under separate management except for waterways ports (Ardrishaig, Weston Point, Sharpness, Gloucester, Regent's Canal Dock and Ellesmere Port, run jointly with the Manchester Ship Canal Co.). The new division was run by a general manager under a Sub-Commission. The General Manager, Sir Reginald Kerr continued the previous carrying policy and built new craft. The new division encouraged pleasure crusing, started a hire fleet at Chester in 1956, ran a hotel boat on the Witham and in 1962 opened the Waterways Museum at Stoke Bruerne on the Grand Junction. They introduced booklets on cruising and put up many hundreds of signs alongside roads and railways.

1956. BOWES COMMITTEE. Interest in waterways particularly for pleasure cruising was growing and the Government appointed this independent enquiry to be chaired by Mr. H. Leslie Bowes of the Pacific S. N. Co. Under him were seven members and their report came out in 1958. They recognized a small nationalized mileage (380) of what they called Class A. Waterways, useful for commercial traffic and worth developing. The second group Class B in the Bowes scale, a larger mileage (935) of nationalized waterways which were worth keeping navigable although commercially discouraging. A and B together formed what the Committee called 'the prescribed navigable system', other users being recognized, including pleasure and angling. It was suggested that A and B should be put in good working order and maintained up to standard for not less than 25 years. Profits on A were to be used for their maintenance and improvement, and the B system, with financial assistance was to be brought up to a standard which would allow passage of laden craft of the largest dimensions designed for these waterways. On B waterways, tolls were to be replaced by licences calculated on the capacity of the craft. Many nationalized waterways were left out of the prescribed navigable system. The Committee recognized their value although they could never pay. They were in many cases useful for water supply, drainage and recreation. Others could be eliminated as waterways although portions might be retained. Selection for redevelopment or for elimination should be made by an independent Waterways Redevelopment Board. This should have powers to tackle independent waterways as well. They reported specially on the Norfolk Broads for these also came within the scope of the Bowes enquiry, considering them essential to the economy of the area. They also recommended keeping the Caledonian and the Crinan open under the Secretary of State for Scotland. On future administration the Committee were divided. The chairman and three members felt that the nationalized waterways within the prescribed navigable system should remain under the British Transport Commission. Four

members of the Committee suggested an autonomus body which they called the Inland Water-
ways Corporation, to run all nationalized waterways, including Scotland. They said that the
IWC could also deal with waterways outside the prescribed navigable system. The IWC was
considered as a waterways authority in a wide sense, not just a transport authority. The
Government accepted most of the Bowes recommendations and set up an Inland Waterways
Redevelopment Advisory Committee, appointed in 1959, which made useful suggestions.

1962. TRANSPORT ACT . This abolished the British Transport Commission, establishing
independent Boards, including the British Waterways Board which took over on 1st January
1963. This now had powers to develop, lease or sell their land, make pipe-lines, make their
own equipment, acquire other undertakings and lend money. They were also given powers to
borrow money while the Minister of Transport was allowed to meet any deficit.

1963. BRITISH WATERWAYS BOARD. Its members (4 to 9), chairman and vice-chairman
were appointed by the Minister of Transport. They were all part-time but there was a full-
time general manager. The first chairman was F.D.Arney followed by Sir John Hawton and
Sir Frank Price. The Board continued the modernization policy, enlarged amenity facilities
and ended the Commission's policy of closure. Early in its life the Board made decisions
affecting the future of British canals. First, the smaller canals had so little future for
transport that they must be thought of as providing pleasure cruising, angling and amenity
facilities as well as water sales. Second, not to think of them as individual canals but as
a single network for pleasure cruising and maintained with Government financial help. These
decisions,   explained in 'The Future of the Waterways' (1964) and supported by 'The
Facts About the Waterways' (1965)   obtained   strongly expressed public approval,   and
were embodied almost exactly in the Act of 1968. The policy gave the smaller canals a secure
future and encouraged private investors to put money into hire cruiser firms, boat-building,
marinas and other amenities. The Board modernized their own hire cruiser fleet, provided
extra moorings and worked alongside voluntary restoration societies to reopen routes to cruisers. The Stourbridge restoration (1967) was an early success. On the other hand the Board
withdrew most of their narrow boat fleet and all their Leeds & Liverpool in 1963. But more
profitable were their ports, such as Weston Point and Sharpness, both much developed, and
their inland depots and warehouses. Administratively the Board in 1964 scrapped the four
divisions and replaced them by two regions, Northern and Southern, based on Leeds and
Gloucester, these were split into areas each headed by an engineer acting as a local manager.

1968. TRANSPORT ACT. An amplification of the 1962 Act, it gave wider powers to the Board
so that they could manage hotels, provide ordinary road transport apart from those linking
up with water transport, and provide amenity and recreational facilities including angling. Of
particular importance was the new three group classification of the Board's waterways into
commercial, pleasure cruising (cruiseways) and the remainder. The Minister of Transport
could transfer waterways from one group to another, and following the precedent of the
Railway & Canal Traffic Act of 1888, closure of a waterway could be secured by Government
order, again from the Minister of Transport. They were obliged to maintain their commercial
waterways to a suitable standard for freight carrying craft and the 'cruiseways' for pleasure
craft. Duties of maintenance were enforceable by the courts. The new Act abolished any
public or private right of navigation which might exist in any Act authorizing any particular
waterway, applicable to all waterways. This was to allow the Board and other owners to cut
out the dead wood. Remainder waterways, the third category were to be maintained   as
economically as possible and the Board was granted powers for their disposal, for example
to local authorities. Local authorities were also empowered to subscribe towards the cost of
improving waterways for amenity use, which they are doing. The Act also established   the
Inland Waterways Amenity Advisory Council of a chairman and not less than twelve members
who were to advise on cruiseways and recreation. It was disbanded in 1979.

Irish Waterways Legislation from 1715.

IRISH PARLIAMENT, before 1800. Navigations were projected by the Government to
open up the country. A general Act was passed in 1715 authorizing the improvement of certain rivers at the public expense both for drainage and navigation. They included the Shannon,
Barrow, Bann and Boyne and there were plans for a 'Grand Canal' to join the Liffey to the
Shannon. Each improvement was to be in the hands of a body of Commissioners.   However
little work was done and only the Maigue in Co. Limerick was tackled. An Act of 1721
revised the appointment of commissioners, henceforward to be members of parliament   and
justices of the peace in the counties where the works were undertaken. This was altered
in 1729 to a group of commissioners for each province. Complete centralization was achieved in 1751 by the establishment of 'The Corporation for Promoting and Carrying on an Inland
Navigation in Ireland', a group generally called the Commissioners of Inland Navigation.
They started considerable works, notably the Grand Canal and improvements on the Shannon,
but public financing of projects of this nature was scandalously corrupt and much less was
done than was paid for. After the Act of Union in 1800 and the end of the Irish Parliament,
the British taxpayer footed the bill for Irish waterway projects, undertaken with the object
of development and relief of distress. An Act passed in 1771-2 allowed the   Commissioners
to transfer works to private undertakers and another Act at the same time allowed partner-
ships to be formed to make navigations. Public expenditure had been much too high for the
small amount achieved, but more might be done by private enterprise. The Grand Canal was
transferred in this way. By an Act of 1787 the Commissioners were dissolved and a return
made to separate bodies of commissioners for each navigation.

1800. UNION PARLIAMENT after 1800. Money continued to be advanced from the state on a
generous scale, but in 1800, control was centralized in a new body of five Directors-General

of Inland Navigation appointed by the Lord Lieutenant. Under an Act of this year he was given power over all inland navigation works in Ireland and the Directors acted on his behalf. The local commissioners established by the Act of 1787 were abolished and the Directors took over all navigations not already under separate companies. They also made grants to enable private works to be completed, including both the Royal and Grand canals. In 1831 the power and properties of the Directors-General were transferred to the new Board of Public Works, established to oversee all government works, roads, bridges, public buildings, docks and navigations. Their biggest waterway responsibility was the Shannon, taken over after the improvements made by the commissioners were complete. The Board of Public Works built the Ballinamore & Ballyconnel Canal and the Lough Corrib Navigation, including the disastrous Cong Canal. Improvement of the Lower Bann was more successful.

_1919._ EIRE PARLIAMENT. By the Ministry of Transport Act of 1919 the navigational functions of the Board of Public Works passed to the new ministry, although the Board still carried them out. Founding of the Free State in 1922, placed the Board of Public Works under the Department of Finance, while the Ministry of Transport was replaced by the Department of Transport and Power. The Eire Government helped their waterways by their passage in 1927 of the Railway (Road Motor Services) Act which allowed railways and canals to operate their own road services. In 1932 a further Act, followed by another in 1933, was to limit road services to those run by railway, canal, shipping companies, and existing road transport concerns. Full nationalization came to Eire waterways with the formation of Coras Iompair Eireann in 1945, following the 1944 Transport Act, by this, CIE the Irish Transport Company, an independent body, but Government backed, acquired the railway owned Royal, and later in 1950 the Grand and the Barrow.

NORTHERN IRELAND PARLIAMENT. In Northern Ireland the Ulster Canal had been under Board of Public Works control from 1851, until transferred in 1888 to the Lagan Navigation Co., with the Coalisland Canal. In 1859 the Lower Bann had been handed over to a trust. In 1929 this was wound up and the navigation came under the Ministry of Finance of the Government of Northern Ireland. Under the 1954 Inland Navigation Act (Northern Ireland), the Ulster Government assumed responsibility for the Lagan, Coalisland Canal and Upper Bann.

In Ireland railway dominance was less pronounced, although competition had a crippling effect. Only the Royal was taken over by a railway, the Midland Great Western in 1845, who built their line alongside it to the detriment of traffic, but the railway tried a carrying fleet without much success. Coras Iompair Eireann ceased all carrying in 1960 to save money.

_1809._ IRISH WATERWAYS COMMISSIONS. In 1809 a commission met to examine the economic possibilities of the bogs and also considered how they could bring manure for their improvement. In 1880 a Royal Commission under Viscount Monck studied the future of inland navigation from north to south, from the Bann to Limerick. They felt prospects were poor but that navigation should not be hampered by drainage works which were of more concern than navigation. In 1885 the Viceregal Commission on Drainage was followed in 1887 by the report of the Allport Commission on Irish Public Works. This and the 1905 report of the Commission on Arterial Drainage recommended that drainage should be controlled by a government department to prevent conflict with other water interests. As already noted Ireland was included in the 1906 Royal Commission. Then soon after the founding of the Free State, the Dail established a commission to look at the waterways. It was chaired by Robert Tweedy and reported in 1923, following the recommendations of the Royal Commission, but nothing was done. Definite moves to greater government control came with the 1944 Transport Act. After the 1948 transport enquiry under Sir James Milne, CIE took over the Grand Canal in 1950. A further committee of inquiry chaired by J.P. Beddy in 1957 advised the CIE that they should cease their carrying on the Grand, Barrow and Shannon which they did in 1960.

Formation & Operation of the Waterway Companies.

PROMOTIONS of INLAND WATERWAYS. People who supported canals came from more varied backgrounds than the small groups of landed proprietors who undertook river improvements. However pressure did come from those with mineral wealth and promotions secured the patronage of local nobility. Thus the small Melton Mowbray Navigation had as shareholders two dukes, Rutland and Newcastle, and two earls, Ferrers and Harborough. Aristocratic patronage was similar in Scotland and Ireland. Colliery owners were particularly interested in canals to carry their coal, the Gresleys of Apedale near Newcastle-under-Lyme building a canal to that town. Elsewhere the landed classes wanted canals to improve their estates by bringing fertilizer, the Rolle family building a canal from the Torridge estuary to their estates at Torrington. In South Wales it was the ironmasters, the Hills, Crawshays and the Homfrays who lay behind much of the canal building. The Darbys and the other east Shropshire ironfounders developed the tub-boat system there to carry their goods. Josiah Wedgwood promoted the Trent & Mersey to carry clay to the potteries and distribute finished goods. The possibilities of controlling water fascinated the scientific minds of the day and canals were probably often discussed at scientific meetings such as those of the Lunar Society whose members included Wedgwood and Matthew Boulton, who invested in the Birmingham Canal. Clergy sat on many canal committees, notably the Oxford. In this case they were dons, for the University was a heavy subscriber, and the Oxford had a clergyman chairman until 1885. Local townspeople, manufacturers, merchants, millers, shop keepers and farmers promoted navigations for the benefit of the district. Merchants were important, a group in Manchester subscribing to the Mersey & Irwell, while a Leeds group were behind the Aire & Calder and a Halifax group the Calder & Hebble. Most were conceived as local projects to distribute coal to a district, to take farm produce to market, to send sea sand fertilizer to inland farms, to carry limestone for burning and iron ore for smelting; thus the haphazard extensions once the main routes were laid down. Locally initiated they were supported by local people, by those who would benefit directly and by local doctors and solicitors and during the "mania" by people who thought the canal would bring rapid wealth, small tradesmen and artisans with limited savings, small farmers and village craftsmen. Banks, in the canal age locally based, did not make a notable contribution to canal promotion, although they were a major source of finance. Bankers subscribed as individuals, notably William Praed, and clients would be persuaded to invest. Some corporations like Exeter built and owned a canal, Liverpool paid for surveys of the Sankey and Leeds & Liverpool, and others took shares in their local waterways, Chester in the Chester, and Swansea in the Swansea. Often the Mayor sat on the committee. A more positive part was played after the Municipal Reform Act of 1835. Manchester, Salford and Oldham supported the Ship Canal, Manchester saving the work by loans which enabled the canal to open. Nottingham by an Act of 1915 took over the Trent down to Newark. Engineers who prepared the surveys took up shares. Brindley was a major shareholder in the Trent & Mersey, the Dadfords invested in the Neath and the Aberdare while Leader Williams invested in the Manchester Ship Canal. They often felt called upon to help finance the canal so that their work could continue, apart from a stake in the results of their work. Finally there were the stock market speculators. Local interest lessened as the canal network spread; once canals were an old established transport system, say by 1810, they were considered as good stock for the ordinary investor wherever he might live.

In Ireland most of the system was financed by the state to open up the country. It proved costly with little reward, the more remunerative Irish waterways being completed and operated by joint stock companies, the Grand Canal and the Lagan Navigation. In Scotland construction of the Forth & Clyde was completed with Government help, but it was a joint stock company, while the state financed the completion and later took over the Crinan. The Caledonian was a state project because of its strategic value and it was intended to open up the Highlands.

The sequence of a typical canal promotion was:-

1). The group of promoters who had discussed the venture privately, advertised in the local paper and stuck up posters calling a public meeting, generally at an inn, for inns and town halls were the only available secular public meeting places in the eighteenth century.

2). At this first meeting a chairman and provisional management committee was elected and subscribers called for to finance the first survey and the cost of petitioning for an Act. These early subscribers were given the first opportunity to buy shares.

3). An engineer was appointed to make the first survey.

4). The engineer's report was presented to a succeeding meeting, with estimates of costs and probable receipts. The estimate of cost often proved inadequate due to rising expenses.

5). Meeting to resolve to apply to Parliament for a Bill.

6). Followed by a petition to Parliament in favour of the waterway, prepared by the provisional management committee. Also, after the revision of Parliamentary Standing Orders in 1793, a deposited plan was dispatched, accompanying a subscription list, books of reference and an estimate of cost signed by the engineer. A second copy of the plan went to the local office of the Clerk of the Peace.

7). Those who had objections to the waterway drew up counter petitions to Parliament.

8). Opening of the subscription book for shares and payments of deposits, those paying being enrolled as shareholders. Some of the deposit money was needed for legal and Parliamentary expenses.

9). The Bill went through the usual three stages, including after the second reading of the Bill, committees in both Commons and Lords. At the committee hearings the promoters had to appear, usually with their engineer for questioning. Objectors could also appear.

10). The promoters and shareholders became a corporate body on passing of the Bill, called the company of proprietors, with a seal. They elected a committee of management and a chairman. Officers were appointed including an engineer. If there were sufficient funds work began. After 1793 a large proportion had to be subscribed prior to applying for a Bill.

WATERMILLS and FISH. Though generally thought of as corn mills, there were fulling mills for shrinking and thickening cloth, mills for crushing dye woods, as well as driving furnace bellows and forge hammers. To ensure a good supply of water, millers found a reservoir necessary, fed by a stream. Reservoirs mean dams, and it was these which upset the navigators. They had to be pierced for the passage of boats, achieved by the moveable weir or flash lock. A miller would object to tampering with his supply, so there was perpetual antagonism between mills and navigational interests, although mill dams did ensure a good depth and sufficient water for a flash. Initially the millers would object to a navigation at all, often with success as on the Stroudwater. More usually objections were settled by the navigation's Act. Mills were compensated for loss of water. A miller could charge for passage of the dam, the charges being fixed by the Act, or be compensated if his wheels were stopped for lack of water, taken by the passage of craft. This latter would work out at so much per hour, on the Calder & Hebble 1s 3d, as laid down by their Act of 1758. Sometimes millers enjoyed free carriage for materials to be used in mill repairs. Navigations found that the best way to overcome mill problems was to buy or lease the mills. The Loughborough Navigation did this, first in 1780 renting a mill, then buying a half share in another. Thus the navigation could have a say in how the mills used their water. Canals drawing water from various sources might affect mills some distance away. Promoters therefore were opposed by milling interests. These might be strong enough as in the case of the Rochdale to defeat its first Bill in 1792 and nearly every act embodied compensation rights for millers. On the Lancaster, the mill at Capernwray was fed from the canal to compensate for the water the canal took from the River Keer. The Pennines became the biggest stronghold of water powered industry, hence the care with which Outram planned the water supplies for the Huddersfield so as not to interfere with mills. Eleven reservoirs were built and the Act said that the canal could only take water at times of flood.

It is well known how important fish were for food in mediaeval Britain. Apart from the demands of religion, fresh water fish were essential when meat was scarce and seasonal and sea fish limited to coastal consumption. Monasteries and great houses had their fish ponds, but good stocks could be maintained in mill reservoirs. Millers did well from fish sales, a further reason why they resented navigations. However, the reservoirs were often overfished and the dams were an obstruction to migratory fish. But additional dams were built to trap eels and the migratory fish. They were temporary affairs of stakes and nets or basketwork traps, obstacles rather than total obstructions to navigation. Generally they were removed to improve a river, like those in Tudor times on the Irish Barrow, where again in the 1760s weirs were removed by the Commissioners of Inland Navigation. They have survived on the Severn and some Irish estuaries.

CAPITAL for INLAND WATERWAYS. English inland waterways were built by private initiative to solve transport problems in an age of growing industry. River navigations were the first to be undertaken, often by individuals in the seventeenth century, like Sir Richard Weston on the Wey, or by groups of local landowners and merchants. These undertakers had the money to finance the works. River improvements were comparatively cheap, within the resources of a single undertaker or small group. The complete Warwickshire Avon cost Sir William Sandys £20,000 to improve before the Civil War. The Mersey & Irwell had cost about £18,000 when completed in 1736. Early canal schemes were not costly. The Sankey Brook Navigation needed £18,600 to complete, and the Duke of Bridgewater spent only about £7,500 on his first canal from Worsley to Manchester. Even a longer waterway like the Staffs. & Worcs., cost only £100,000 when opened in 1772. This canal kept within its estimate, but the Trent & Mersey proved far more expensive, it had an authorized capital of £130,000, but it cost £300,000 due to the expense of Harecastle tunnel and difficult work in the Weaver valley. The final cost included the Caldon branch; not allowed for originally. In most cases canals cost more than their original estimates. The engineers underestimated because of lack of information, hurried surveys and optimism, but early canals cost little by later standards, and after a few years made tremendous profits, encouraging a second wave of building in the 1790s. Costs then rose because of the War with France. The Grand Junction almost exactly the same mileage as the Trent & Mersey had cost £1,646,000 by 1811 when Wolverton aqueduct had been rebuilt. Admittedly the Grand Junction is broad but the costs are notably disparate. By 1815 most of the English canal system was complete, and those built thereafter were few and expensive, the Birmingham & Liverpool Junction cost by its opening in 1835 £800,000, although the authorized capital was half this, and even the short Wey & Arun Junction completed in 1816, cost £103,000. Capital was raised by the issue of shares to the amount stipulated in the canal's Act, with powers usually to raise up to a third more. If much more was needed, as it often was, then the company had to go to Parliament for further Acts. Most canal histories are stories of financial embarrassment. The authorized capital of the Huddersfield by its first act was £184,000, with powers to raise a further £90,000, but because of the cost of Stanedge tunnel a further Act was passed in 1800 to sanction wider borrowing powers, succeeded by another in 1806 authorizing an additional £100,000. When finally opened it had cost just over £400,000. The Somersetshire Coal Canal created a separate company to pay for its locks at Combe Hay. Some canals were financed and built privately without an Act, since there was no need for land purchase because the builder owned it. One was Lord Gower's Donnington Wood Canal in East Shropshire. It was however a toll taker. A purely private system without other carriers was the estate canal built by Sir Roger Newdigate. In the railway age, the attitude of the railway companies was by no means so negative as has been supposed. For example the Lancashire & Yorkshire, owners of the Manchester, Bolton & Bury Canal, paid for the subsidence repairs of the 1880s which included the retaining walls above the Irwell. The North Staffordshire Railway maintained the Trent & Mersey as an extension of their railway and in 1894 partially re-widened between Anderton and Middlewich. Municipal and county money was invested in waterways in the later nineteenth and early twentieth centuries, notably financing completion of the Manchester Ship Canal. When completed it had cost £14,347,891 the estimates had suggested £8,408,936. Nottingham Corporation offered help to the Trent, sanctioned under an Act of 1915, a condition being that they should take over the river from the city down to Averham weir. Money was also expected from the Development Commissioners, established to assist works that would find employment for those affected by war. They could not lend to profit making organizations, hence the transfer to the Corporation. Nothing was done until after the war, and in the end Nottingham spent £450,000 on its own section besides making a loan to the Navigation to rebuild one of Newark locks, assisted by a grant from the Unemployment Grants Committee. The Thames & Severn was taken over in 1900 by Gloucestershire County Council, who spent £20,000 on the leaking summit and reopened the canal in 1904. In 1948 nationalization placed a wider responsibility on the Government. State capital has been spent in efforts to keep or gain traffic on those waterways which appear to have a commercial future and much has been done on the Aire & Calder and Trent, also on the Caledonian and the Lee.

SHARES & DIVIDENDS. Shareholders in canals were protected under their Acts and were liable to lose their subscription only in the event of bankruptcy. This was in an age when limited liability was rare, hence the popularity of canal shares, usually issued in values of £100 or £50, with half, quarter and eighth shares for the smaller investor. They were bought by instalments or calls after an initial deposit had been paid as the holder's name was entered in the subscription book. Calls were made until the full nominal value had been paid, but not beyond unless the Act so provided or unless shareholders agreed. To encourage proprietors, that is the shareholders, to meet calls, interest was paid out of capital, or possibly out of revenue, if traffic had been able to start on some part of the canal. Proprietors were reluctant to meet calls, if the canal did not look like opening soon, but they were bound to meet calls up to the nominal value of the share. Forfeited shares which had been partly paid up were auctioned or even given away to people prepared to meet future calls. An additional inducement was the preference share, pioneered by the Thames & Severn in 1808. Here the need was to liquidate a large debt, achieved by converting it into £100 value new 'red' shares which the debt holders accepted since they received a preferential dividend of 1½ per cent, before the holders of the old or 'black' shares received their 1½ per cent dividend. By 1811 the £193,892 debt had been liquidated.

Early canal and river navigations paid well. The Sankey Brook Navigation was paying 20 per cent in 1772 and even with Bridgewater competition, the Mersey & Irwell were paying a steady 5 per cent in the 1780s. The Trent & Mersey after a shaky start were able to pay 5 per cent from 1781. Dividend rates increased as the canal and river network grew, the new lines bringing more traffic to the old. Really high dividends were paid in the early nineteenth century by the Oxford, 20 per cent between 1806-8, and a peak of 33⅓ per cent between 1824-6. These high figures are misleading because they represent the percentage on the original small share capital which all early canals thought would be sufficient. The Oxford's authorized capital was £150,000 although it cost £307,000 to build, the money raised to finance the completion not being added to the authorized capital. With such large dividends share prices climbed, in 1830 the Staffs. & Worcs., £100 share was worth £795. The Loughborough Navigation had an authorized capital of £7,000 in £100 shares, costing only £9,200 to complete. In 1830 each share was valued at £3,000, a year when the dividend was 151 per cent, for the Soar had become part of the line from the Derbyshire coalfields and the Trent to Leicester and London. Early investors who hung on to their shares did well, having taken the risk, and later buyers were sure of an increasing dividend plus capital appreciation. Some early canals had their dividends limited to 7 or 8 per cent, for example, the Derby Canal authorized in 1793, to check speculation and because it was felt that they should exist for the public benefit and that excess profits should go to the reduction of tolls. However it was found after 1800 that dividend limitation was an impediment to raising money and some of these limitation clauses were repealed. Sometimes a new canal, breaking into the preserve of older concerns, had to guarantee the latters' dividends as compensation, thus the Worcester & Birmingham had to make up the dividends of both the Stourbridge and the Droitwich. Later in railway days, railway controlled canals were subsidized, thus the LNWR guaranteed the dividends of the Birmingham Canal Navigations and of the Shropshire Union. This was offset by gains to the railways due to the absence of competition. High rewards had sparked off the canal 'mania' of 1792-3, but the canals promoted at that time did not do so well because of higher construction costs due to the War with France. The Worcester & Birmingham begun in 1791 was not fully open until 1815 and paid its first dividend in 1821, £1 for each £100 share. Canals started after 1800 did not do well either because of the continued high costs and because if further money had to be borrowed it was at a high rate of interest. Such canals were the Grand Union and the Regent's which had great difficulty completing its line. The Grand Union, opened in 1814 did not pay a dividend until 1826 and then only 1 per cent. Some canals never paid a dividend during their working life but only on winding up, such were the Portsmouth & Arundel and the Leominster.

Railway competition from the 1840s affected dividends but not too harshly at first, thus the Oxford was paying 26 per cent in 1846; in 1833 they had been paying 32 per cent. Canals who sold out to the railways did well from the sale, but those who remained independent usually did not maintain dividends. Exceptionally the railway controlled Shropshire Union was encouraged, and except for 1868 maintained a dividend free of railway support until 1874. The Birmingham Canal Navigations likewise did well, with a 4 per cent dividend guaranteed by the LNWR. The BCN only declined when the railways lost ground, but many independent canals lost ground as the railways advanced. Weakly financed canals collapsed completely, such as the Wey & Arun Junction and the Herefordshire & Gloucestershire, products of the later canal age, built at great cost with a rural trade assimilated by railways built on parallel routes. Older canals with a good dividend record survived and were able to keep profitable, the Oxford in 1860 paid 8¼ per cent and was able to maintain a dividend until the 1948 nationalization. It was a heavy coal carrier, a traffic able to co-exist alongside rail transport, but an increasing proportion of revenue in later years came from water sales and property. To some rivers like the Mersey & Irwell, the canals appeared as competitors, others became part of a new through route, for example the Kennet absorbed into the line of the Kennet & Avon Canal. Some were closed by the competing canals which bought them, such as the Derwent, acquired by the Derby Canal in 1795, others failed to pay their way, for example the Norwich & Lowestoft Navigation authorized as late as 1827. The Aire & Calder, largely canalized did supremely well, handling immense tonnages up to the present day. In 1825-6 it paid out £70,000 in dividends. Dividends were usually paid out twice a year and were declared at the twice yearly shareholders' meetings. They had to be applied for and because of this were advertised in the local press. The money had to be collected personally or by an agent, emphasizing the local nature of canal or river enterprises. With the spreading of the railways, these arrangements were replaced by mailed dividend warrants.

COMMISSIONERS. There were three main kinds of commissioners. Firstly people appointed under the Act for a river navigation or canal with judicial powers to settle valuation disputes over land purchase. These were a numerous body of local men, usually landowners above a certain property qualification. Acts allowed an appeal from the commissioners to a jury if the land values could not be agreed. In some cases under early canal Acts, such as that for the Staffs. & Worcs, commissioners could approve rises in the toll above the parliamentary maxima, although later Acts changed this. Secondly, on early river navigations there were commissioners who not only settled disputes, but regulated the undertakers, as the final administrative authority. They could appoint new undertakers if the old ones withdrew or died, but could not remove them. They were empowered, however, to take over if the undertakers failed to do their job. This happened on the Weaver in the early 1730s. A third type of commissioner, was given direct powers to build and maintain a waterway, as on the Thames, the Ure and the Driffield Navigation. The Thames Navigation Commissioners were at first, under the 1751 Act, simply granted powers to settle lock charges and correct abuses. Under the 1771 Act they were given administrative functions. The Ure Commissioners had powers to regulate carriers' freight charges. Elsewhere commissioners survived until recently, the Great Yarmouth Port and Haven Commissioners administering the Broadland rivers. The Irish Commissioners of Inland Navigation were a state body as were the commissioners appointed to administer the Caledonian Canal. The Exchequer Bill Loan Commissioners administered government funds for public works which would give employment.

COMMISSIONERS of SEWERS. Nothing to do with effluent, these sewers were watercourses for flood prevention and land drainage. To watch over both an Act of 1532 appointed commissions of principal local landowners to exercise these duties within their locality. They issued decrees or orders to keep channels clear but were not primarily concerned with navigation. They were generally appointed for a specific task, and money to clear obstructions and undertake flood works was levied from those whose land was threatened and would benefit by better drainage. However, their authority declined in the face of seventeenth century enthusiasm for navigation improvements. As landowners, they were not the people to undertake this kind of work although they tried and failed, for example on the Wye in 1622. Letters Patent from the Crown and Acts of Parliament gave powers to new commissioners and undertakers to make navigations, at the same time withdrawing the authority of the Commissioners of Sewers. However, in a few areas they survived until the creation of the Catchment Boards under the Land Drainage Act of 1930.

UNDERTAKERS. Those who were granted powers by Letters Patent or by an Act to improve a river, were called undertakers. They undertook to do the work and pay for it and were rewarded by the right to take tolls and generally in the case of Letters Patent by the right of exclusive carriage. Acts might also grant exclusive carriage, the Wey undertaker Sir Richard Weston was so favoured in 1651. Some like Daniel Wigmore on the Welland worked alone. They spent out of their own pocket and hoped to recoup themselves from the tolls and carriage rights. More often they were groups, sometimes disinterested like the Thames commissioners appointed from the University and City of Oxford in 1623-4. Landed proprietors were well to the fore, but interested because of the added value a navigation would bring to their estates, like the Sandys family. Then there were those with colliery interests like Lord Paget, the sole undertaker of the upper Trent, appointed in 1699. In the larger towns the mercantile element was interested in any navigation which would improve trade. They would form a company, possibly a joint stock company as on the Douglas. Beverley Beck, a corporation project, was financed by borrowing, while the Weaver was intended to be improved by the three original undertakers under a kind of trust. Once they had been reimbursed then the profits not needed for maintenance were to go to improve roads and bridges in Cheshire.

LEASES. When the undertakers of a river navigation did not want to administer it they leased it in return for rent. The amount depended on whether the tolls only were leased or whether the lessee was also responsible for maintenance when the rent would be lower. The lessee would hope to make a surplus for his own income. The Aire & Calder was run in this way from 1704 until 1774, when the sole lessee, Peter Birt was bought out. He had been lessee since at least 1758. The 1704 lease was for £800 per annum only, but by 1715 the undertakers wanted £1,800 per annum. They could not get it, settling for less, but in 1744 the lease was £3,600 per annum and by 1758 £6,000. Individual locks were also leased for rent, the lessee collecting the dues, for example Waltham lock on the Lee, once leased by a group of bargemen. Canal tolls or the complete canal were leased in a similar way but generally not until the railway age. Under the Canal Carriers Act of 1845, one canal could lease another for a period not exceeding 21 years. In 1854 the Aire & Calder leased the Barnsley Canal, including tolls, for 21 years, followed by purchase on expiry of the lease. Railways acquired canals by leasing them via canals they already owned, sanctioned by the Canal Carriers Act of 1845 but stopped by the Cheap Trains & Canal Carriers Act of 1858. Through a lease of tolls a canal company could be assured of revenue to finance maintenance and pay dividends. Leasing arrangements of one sort and another were widespread in the canal business. Boats were leased to traders, particularly passenger boats, for example on the Don in 1840, when two swift boats were leased to J. Ashforth as operator. Wharf and warehouse space was leased to traders and carriers, also cranes and hoists.

TOLLS. River navigations and canals were public highways and anyone could put a boat on them, but had to pay for the privilege unless the navigation was free, on an unimproved river. There were a few private waterways, but if the waterway was improved or artificial, then there would be some company charging tolls to pay for maintenance and make a living out of providing this service. Horse towing path companies also took tolls from their users. Bridges had been kept up in this way and during the seventeenth century in England tolls started to be charged for road use. On rivers the idea of charging tolls was certainly present in the Middle Ages, thus Richard II in 1378 granted the bailiffs of Droitwich the right to levy tolls on the Salwarpe. The right to charge had been granted to city corporations since the fifteenth century, while seventeenth century river improvers like Arnold Spencer on the Great Ouse and fellow undertakers elsewhere were granted toll taking powers by Royal Letters Patent. Similar powers could only be given by Act of Parliament after 1720. One of the main purposes of a navigation or canal Act was to fix the tolls. They could not be exceeded without further Parliamentary authority. In some early Acts, for example that for the Staffs & Worcs, local commissioners had been given powers to approve rises, and in the case of the Glamorganshire, the Quarter Sessions. But ordinarily the company could only levy tolls within the Parliamentary maxima. Tolls were calculated at a rate of so many pence per ton per mile, fractions of a mile being charged as a mile. Empty boats were sometimes chargeable, the Acts generally providing for this. Often they were free if they returned loaded down the same canal, or if the water was running over the weirs, or if they did not pass a lock. Where a canal company did its own carrying a rate including the tolls was quoted. Independent companies quoted the tolls plus their own carrying charges. Bulk commodities like coal, stone and lime were cheapest, iron ore was a higher rate because it was more valuable, while groceries, textiles and finished goods like iron castings paid a higher rate still. Fly boats carrying parcels and perishables of low tonnage could pay tolls in the form of an annual licence as did some of the colliery and ironworks boats on the South Wales canals, carrying their owners' products. To encourage long distance traffic, tolls were often refunded above a certain distance, encouraging carriers to find wider markets. These 'drawbacks' were used to develop the coal trade, and were expected to be passed on to the coal merchants and customers. Sometimes tolls were commuted in the interests of simplicity. Thus for craft owned on the Pocklington Canal, a single toll covered both the canal and the Derwent Navigation.

Early canals were given generous tolls maxima by Parliament to encourage people to invest in them, but this changed in the 1790s when they were shown to be profitable. Investors needed no encouragement now and Parliament reduced the maxima in the interests of promoting traffic. There were exceptions, where canals were rural and could not expect a large trade, or where they served a specific industry, terminating at a colliery or limestone quarry. In fact tolls were kept below the maxima by competition. With the advent of railways, tolls were drastically, often ruinously cut, to the extinction of the water route. Toll variations below the maxima were made by meetings of shareholders. Some bulk commodities were toll free, often to placate landowners whose land was being cut by the canal. Thus straw and manure were often exempt, and road building materials frequently were, to the advantage of the canal company, since they would be used to improve parish roads down to the canal wharves. Sometimes this freedom was conditional on no locks being passed, or a lock could only be passed if the water was running over the weir. Occasionally coal was carried toll free up to a certain tonnage, on the Derby Canal it was up to 5000 tons a year for the use of the poor, a way of making the canal company contribute to the poor rates of the town. Sometimes tolls were used for relief of county rates, the Weaver Navigation contributing hansomely to Cheshire, while tolls on the River Tone aided the poor of Taunton. A compensation toll was that which an old established canal company would charge a canal making a junction with it, in case the newcomer took away any of its traffic. The rate was often quite a high figure like 5d on all goods passing through. The maxima for coal tolls was usually about a penny per ton per mile. Extra tolls could be charged for the passage of locks. No company was allowed to grant special tolls for good customers or vary the rate over their line, so there was no way of encouraging a certain traffic, unless the canal company were also carriers and could vary their freight rates. This was remedied by the Canal Tolls Act of 1845 which gave the power to vary charges. The 1888 Act called for the complete reform of toll structures, carried out in the 1890s. Through tolls were the objective, but they remained difficult to secure.

Tolls were paid in cash by the boatman to the collector, unless the company had an account with the navigation. In any case the boatman was issued with a toll ticket as a receipt of payment. This gave details of the boat, her owner and steerer, cargo and where it was loaded, also the tonnage carried, toll payable and mileage to be travelled. Tonnage and tolls were arranged in column form since the cargo could well be mixed with a different toll for each commodity and destination, a reason why fly boats paid by annual licence. The cargo and tonnage entries would be copied by the collector from the waybill which the boatman received where the cargo was loaded. If the collector suspected the boat was carrying more than the waybill said, he would gauge it and enter the correct tonnage on to the toll ticket. If the boat passed on to another canal further tolls were payable at the junction and perhaps a new gauging. Credit to carriers with accounts was up to three or occasionally six months. The system lasted until nationalization and tolls, having been further rationalized in 1958, are still paid by carrying craft on commercial waterways, although pleasure boats and carrying craft on cruising waterways pay an annual licence; pleasure boat licences are calculated on length and commercial on capacity. Special tolls were charged for inclined planes, lifts and tunnel tugs. Inevitably there was fraud, excess loading discoverable by gauging and even weighing of boats. Hiding of high toll goods under low toll goods was much more difficult to detect. Then again there could be collusion between boatmen and collectors.

INDEXING and GAUGING of CRAFT. Tolls were charged on the weight of cargo, boatmen had a waybill, but more could have been put in than it stated, so canals and navigations evolved a means of measuring tonnage. It depended on displacement, and every new boat had to be indexed after a few trips to settle down. This was done at a special indexing dock, as at Etruria on the Trent & Mersey (5), at Tipton on on the Birmingham system, and at Northwich on the Weaver. Weights were loaded into the boat evenly, by crane. Weights were stone, but they became lighter due to abrasion and iron was substituted. Hydraulic cranes were used at Tipton, placing ton weights four at a time. The boat's empty freeboard, or height of the gunwale above the water was measured at four points, marked by metal plates placed on both sides of the ship at the fore and after end of the hull. Some canals used six indexing points for greater accuracy, such as the Swansea, Glamorganshire and the Oxford. The weights represented cargo and were loaded until the freeboard was reduced to the minimum consistent with safety. The maximum capacity was thus known, and as the freeboard was read and averaged with each ton of weights, so was the capacity in tons at different depths. Fittings and equipment aboard, such as coal for the cabin stove were noted. Items belonging to the boat, but not aboard were specially weighed, like cargo dunnage or bundles of sacks. All particulars were entered in a record book called the gauge tables, with a brief history of the boat, her dimensions and condition, for boats were indexed, say every ten years, because they became waterlogged and therefore slightly lower in the water. Gauge tables became general about 1810, previously the tonnage was marked on a scale on the boat's side, which many companies continued to demand. Opposite or below the particulars in the tables were columns for entering up the tonnage and freeboard called 'dry inches'. Thus in 1962 the wooden motor narrow boat DORSET was indexed at Tipton. At 2 tons she measured 35.22 dry inches, at 15, 20.13", at 25, 9.21" and at 33, the maximum, 0.65" only: almost awash. With tonnage in the first column and dry inches in the second; in the third the sinking rate was entered, or the difference between the freeboard every ton, lessening as the boat filled up. Copies of the gauge table were sent to every toll office on the canal and waterways where the boat traded, although they might also index her separately for their own records. About 1798 ten authorities in the Trent area achieved a common gauging arrangement, with gauge tables printed for them by the Trent Navigation, which have survived. The newly indexed boat was given a number at the indexing dock and this identified her in the tables. The number was prominently displayed. Long distance boats of the Fellows, Morton & Clayton fleet had several painted on the cabin side, including 1396 for the Thames, recorded at Waterman's Hall for FMC craft. The BCN issued cast iron number plates, displayed on the cabin bulkhead for example. On arrival at a toll office, the boatman would present his waybill. If the toll collector suspected it, he would gauge the boat at the same four points as in the indexing dock and by averaging, find the dry inches. He looked up his tables and against the dry inches would discover the tonnage. The collectors originally used a graduated staff with a bracket resting on the gunwale, but they had to bend down to read the dry inches. Later, a copper tube with a bracket for the gunwale well down the tube, contained a float carrying a staff. This protruded out of the tube at eye level, indicating the dry inches. Some BCN collectors gauged the freeboard by a staff with a bracket which was held up against the boat's bottom. Some companies insisted on boats carrying graduated scales, 'tonnage plates' down one side of their sternposts so that it could be quickly read off by the collector. Shropshire Union and Glamorganshire boats had them and many on the Leeds & Liverpool, where boats also had draft marks up one side of the stempost. Yorkshire keels carried scales of copper or lead to remain decipherable, on stem and stern posts as well as draught marks. Some companies had 'weighing engines' to weigh cargo, for example the Trent put one up at Newark in 1786 and the Calder & Hebble at Sowerby Bridge in 1805. Indexing means the initial measurement of the boat in the indexing dock, also called a weigh dock, gauging dock or gauging station. Gauging was what the collector did and still does if there is commercial traffic. Another phrase was taking the plates, reading the scales at stem and stern when fitted; the man who records the tonnage aboard laden compartment boats at Goole is called a plate taker.

BOAT WEIGHING MACHINES. There were so many ways of defrauding when a boat was gauged that some companies built weighing machines which weighed both boat and cargo in a great pan. Only suspect boats were weighed, false readings being given by listing the boat or having a higher gunwale at the gauging points. The first was built at Midford in 1831 on the Somersetshire Coal Canal. Housed under a roof supported by 8' stone Doric columns, the weighing machine in its dock remained in use until traffic collapsed in the 1890s. In 1914 it was dismantled. The Glamorganshire Canal in 1836 installed a machine at Tongwynlais, after several moves, it was sent down to North Road, Cardiff. It was used until the 1930s and is now at the Waterways Museum, Stoke Bruerne. The third and last of the boat weighing machines was installed in 1845 at Brimscombe Port on the Thames & Severn to deal with the variety of craft that appeared at the break of gauge there; trows from the Severn, western barges from the Thames, Stroud barges and Midlands narrow boats. So many were found suspect that the machine was able to recover £1154 of tolls in its first year, a greater sum than its capital cost. It remained in use until 1933 and was dismantled in 1937. There is a model in the Folk Museum at Gloucester. All three machines worked on the principle of the compound lever weighbridge, invented by John Wyatt of Birmingham in the 1740s as an elaboration of the old steelyard. They were inverted weighbridges with the levers at the top and the pan, bridge or cradle at the bottom of a dry dock into which the boat was floated. The water was drained off and the boat settled on the cradle which at Midford and Brimscombe Port was supported at each corner by five radial rods depending from the levers above, held up by a strong framework of pillars and beams, cast iron pillars at Brimscombe and Cardiff, stone at Midford. A final lever, at right angles to the machine, carried the weights in a small pan. At Brimscombe the leverage was on a ratio of $93\frac{1}{2}$ to 1 so that a 24 pound weight in the pan equalled a ton in the boat. This machine was the largest since it had to deal with barges and trows up to 90ft. long and 16 ft. beam.

Plate 2.

Motor Barge COURTDALE H.
DIMENSIONS: 138'0" x 17'6" x 8'6".
Tonnage 161 gross.

COMPLETED in 1958 by John Harker, Knottingley for their Humber fleet, she could carry 270 tons of black oil. She was scrapped in 1974 due to the increase in oil prices and falling bunker requirements, particularly of trawlers.

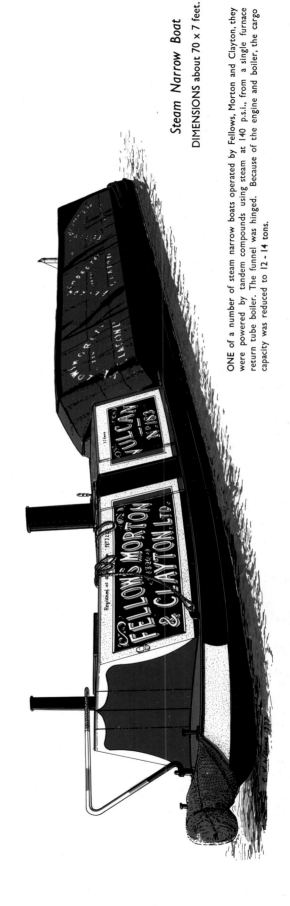

Steam Narrow Boat
DIMENSIONS about 70 x 7 feet.

ONE of a number of steam narrow boats operated by Fellows, Morton and Clayton, they were powered by tandem compounds using steam at 140 p.s.i., from a single furnace return tube boiler. The funnel was hinged. Because of the engine and boiler, the cargo capacity was reduced to 12 - 14 tons.

2.

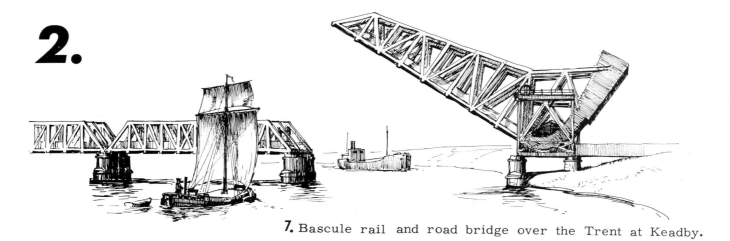

7. Bascule rail and road bridge over the Trent at Keadby.

Waterway Engineering, Facilities & Features

ENGINEERS. Those men generally called engineers, who planned canals and made rivers navigable were a varied assortment of talent. In the seventeenth century an engineer usually meant a military engineer, an expert on fortification; not until the second half of the eighteenth century did John Smeaton consider himself a professional engineering consultant. The men who made the waterway system were by training land surveyors, architects, estate agents, drainage experts and millwrights, or were landed proprietors without special knowledge. Landed proprietors were the first of Britain's waterway engineers, financing, planning and supervising much of the river improvement of the seventeenth century. William 'water work' Sandys was one of these 'engineer undertakers' of good family and an MP, wealthy enough to pay for his projects out of his own resources. Equally notable was Sir Richard Weston, who made the Wey navigable to Guildford, a landed proprietor and a farming expert. The amateur approach persisted into the canal age not only with inventive noblemen like the third Earl of Stanhope, but with the architect William Turner who worked on the Ellesmere. There were professionals in the late seventeenth and early eighteenth centuries. They were experts on waterworks not far removed from navigations. George Sorocold was a leader in the field. He built a dock on the Thames and a silk mill in Derby as well as surveying for navigations and erecting waterwheel driven pumps. Thomas Steers who worked under him had been an army officer, probably an engineer. Steers distinguished himself on dock and navigation works in the first half of the eighteenth century. Architects turned to navigation works, notably Robert Mylne, a competent bridge builder. He became a water supply expert, for he had long been engineer to the New River Co, although not a successful canal builder.

Land agents were drawn into waterway engineering since navigation works were often a part of estate development. William King, the Duke of Rutland's agent, worked on the Grantham Canal, but pre-eminent among them was the Duke of Bridgewater's agent John Gilbert who was also a mining expert. Mining engineers built canals to carry away coal especially in South Wales. George Overton was both a colliery engineer and proprietor, as well as a partner in the Hirwaun ironworks. These led him into tramroad and canal engineering, he built the Penydarren tramroad and finished the Aberdare Canal, while another mining engineer, William Kirkhouse, built both parts of George Tennant's canal. Estate work and mining demands skill in land surveying and a large number of canal engineers were surveyors. They were busy in the eighteenth century, an age not only of waterways and mines, but of land reclamation, drainage, enclosures, turnpikes and tramroads. John Eyes of Liverpool who worked on the Fidler's Ferry extension of the Sankey Brook Navigation was not only a surveyor, but made maps and charts. Many land surveyors took advantage of a local canal promotion to aid their practice. Thus John Priddey became the resident engineer of the Droitwich under Brindley and later moved to the Oxford. Some were employees of a landed proprietor, like James Green of Wollaton near Nottingham, who worked for Lord Middleton. William Jessop was actually a trained engineer, a pupil of Smeaton. The notable engineers of the age undertook a variety of commitments and like Jessop, established themselves in industry as mine owners, ironmasters or manufacturers. Brindley was a millwright by training and because of his skill with mills was called in to deal with mine drainage from which canals were a short step. As a man's commitments increased so he delegated more work to assistants. Brindley had an army of them, some good, a few indifferent. He himself became a consultant since his works were running concurrently. He checked the surveys after a cursory examination of the ground and looked in occasionally as construction proceeded. The elder Robert Whitworth was probably the most successful of Brindley's pupils, and John Varley the least. Engineers might be called upon to make a preliminary survey only, several of these possibly being made by different people or their assistants, as on the Grand Western, each estimating costs. If a man was asked to do the Parliamentary survey and estimates he would generally remain in charge as principal engineer if the Bill passed and work started, understudied by resident engineers on the site. Once opened the waterway would have an engineer on the staff for maintenance and other works. The picture is not quite as clear-cut as this however. Engineers were often replaced as construction went ahead and sometimes the engineer was also the contractor. Many who became engineers started as contractors, others gave up engineering posts for contracting. The elder Thomas Dadford had started as one of the Brindley team, but in the 1790s he and his son added canal cutting contracts to their engineering practice. They worked in association with the elder Thomas Sheasby who had started as a contractor on the Coventry. Payment was often generous, although some men in the early days had difficulty prising the fees out of the navigation, fees fairly charged considering their experience. The waterworks engineer John Hadley was well paid for his works on the Aire & Calder, receiving £420 for two year's work. On the Bridgewater Brindley was paid by the week, which suggests employment in a junior capacity. But as principal engineer or Surveyor General as he was titled, of the Trent & Mersey, he received £200 a year. His assistants were paid for by the company, Hugh Henshall, his brother-in-law receiving £150 a year as Clerk of Works out of which his own clerk had to be paid. Clerk of Works would mean resident engineer, the titles varying from navigation to navigation. Jessop reaped a rich reward in fees, for example he was paid £675 in instalments for his work on the Trent in the 1780s, then in 1787 engaged as the river's permanent engineer at £100 a year. In addition to engineers employed by the companies, there were those in government service, notably in Ireland. Thomas Omer was engineer for all the navigation works undertaken by the Commissioners of Inland Navigation, while John Brownrigg and John Killaly acted in similar capacities for the later Directors-General of Inland Navigation. These were salaried officials and Telford himself was very much of a government servant, as engineer of the Caledonian and the Highlands roads; after 1817 as engineer to the Exchequer Bill Loan Commissioners.

By the end of the canal age the profession of civil engineer was well established. The Smeatonian Society had been formed by Smeaton in the 1780s and was composed of his engineering friends and associates. In 1771 Thomas Yeoman, engineer of navigation works from Essex to Gloucestershire, became the first President of the Society of Civil Engineers. In the early nineteenth century this society became dominated by the Rennies, father and sons and in 1818 some of Telford's team founded a rival, the Institution of Civil Engineers, of which Telford became President in 1820. In 1828 the Institution was granted a Royal Charter. By now the waterways engineer was turning into a specialist. William Cubitt was perhaps the last of the versatile breed with his work on windmills, before he became committed to canals, rivers and docks. Under him on the Severn was the elder Leader Williams, a pure waterways man, whose son likewise concentrated on harbour and navigation works culminating in the Manchester Ship Canal. Other great names were W.H.Bartholomew on the Aire & Calder, Frank Rayner on the Trent and J.A.Saner on the Weaver. These engineers of existing navigations had the task of modernizing them to compete with rail. More can be learnt about the engineers from their biographies in Appendix.B.

AQUEDUCTS. As water channels they go back to the days of the Roman Republic, but for the passage of boats not earlier than the fifteenth century. There was one on the Martesana Canal from the River Adda to Milan built between 1462 and 1470, and by 1681 a major aqueduct had been built across the Repudre on the Canal du Midi in Provence, with a single arch of 30' span. In Great Britain, the New River Co. had by 1613 made a water supply channel from Ware into the Metropolis which involved the construction of several aqueducts over roads and streams, but the first British boat aqueduct was that at Barton over the Irwell to take the Duke of Bridgewater's canal from Worsley into Manchester. Completed in 1761, it carried the canal 38' above the Irwell, the centre arch having a span of 63' with sufficient clearance to allow sailing flats to pass beneath without lowering their masts. The two side arches were of lesser span, the Mersey & Irwell Navigation's towpath passing under one. The canal trough was lined with clay puddle and only about 18' wide, hence the later installation of semaphore signalling to control traffic. To resist the lateral water pressure a batter was given to each face wall of the aqueduct and each of the piers was buttressed as were the abutment walls. Lateral pressure was the problem in aqueduct design, not only of the water, but of the approach embankments, with a tendency to spread outwards. Then with the weight of the canal in its bed of puddle it was essential that arch construction be used, with the arches in equilibrium, balanced between their springings and keystones. Design depended on the level at which the canal would cross, from 100' above the river of Marple to syphon aqueducts. These syphons, also called crooked or broken backed weirs or culverts, overcame the problems of a near level crossing where the bed of the canal was lower than the water level of the stream crossed. The stream had to be dug out under the aqueduct and weired on the upstream side of the canal, so that the water would fall into the pool, pass under the aqueduct and come up the other side. John Rennie built two on the Lancaster Canal, over the Calder near Catterall and one further north. The Calder is nearly level with the canal but the weir drops it about 6' into a chamber which acts like a 'U' shaped syphon. Brindley carried his canals across rivers as low as possible, for a low aqueduct could be built on a massive and safe scale. On the Trent & Mersey he built two squat brick aqueducts, a twelve arch one over the Dove near Burton-on-Trent and a six arch one over the Trent at Brindley's Bank near Rugeley. On the Dove aqueduct the walls containing the aqueduct are 12' thick, each composed of two 18" wide brick walls with a filling of clay puddle between them, the canal crossing at a width of 28', an asset to traffic. The Dove arches have a span of 15' 4½" and a rise of 3' 6". After Brindley's death engineers continued to follow his aqueduct building precepts. By 1790 the elder Sheasby, with the advice of the elder Dadford had completed the three arch brick aqueduct over the Tame for the Coventry Canal. They were most enterprising in South Wales. On the Neath Canal the elder Sheasby carried on the work of the younger Dadford and built the five arch stone aqueduct over the Neath River at Ynysbwllog, while both Sheasbys built the three arched aqueduct over the Twrch at Ystalyfera on the Swansea Canal. That over the Usk at Brynich engineered by the younger Dadford is still navigable. It is a stone aqueduct of four low segmental arches with faces buttressed at each pier in addition to the batter of the face walls. The buttresses are shaped like cutwaters parting the river and checking scour. Further north, the younger Dadford with his brother John were engineers of the Montgomeryshire Canal. This crossed the Vyrnwy by a five arched stone aqueduct and the Rhiw by a four arched. Both proved problems, one arch of the Vyrnwy collapsed during construction, while later in 1823, all five were found to be fractured and had to be reinforced with tie rods to prevent outward collapse of the face walls and iron straps, linked by tie rods, to preserve the shape of two of the arches. By 1800 engineers were building more adventurously. In 1790 Robert Whitworth completed the four arched masonry aqueduct over the Kelvin in Glasgow for the Forth and Clyde, 400' long and 70' wide. The face walls above each arch have a concave curve, like an arch on its side, to resist lateral pressure. John Rennie on the Kennet & Avon had to cross the Avon twice between Bradford-on-Avon and Bath. He built masonry aqueducts on the grand scale, Avoncliff being finished in 1798, about 110 yards long. The centre arch over the river was elliptical and the two side ones segmental for the passage of flood water. The Dundas aqueduct at Limpley Stoke is more ornamental, with a 64' span segmental arch over the river, flanked by two narrow parabolic arches for flood water. Over the Lune above Lancaster he built a five arched stone aqueduct for the Lancaster Canal. Here the arches are semicircular and are reinforced by internal inverted arches between their crowns. He was very conscious of the need for lateral strength, and iron tie rods were concealed in the masonry of both Dundas and the Lune. The stone aqueduct over the Goyt at Marple, built for the Peak Forest by Outram was more daring. It was a delicate three arched structure carrying the canal 100' above the river, finished in 1800. The trough was only 7'6" wide and lined with bricks backed by puddle. To lessen the weight on the arches, their spandrels were pierced by 12' diameter holes.

William Jessop was unlucky with his masonry aqueducts. As engineer of the Cromford he built two, over the Amber at Bullbridge near Ambergate and an arch of 80' span over the Derwent below Cromford. In 1792 the Amber one partially failed and had to be extensively repaired. It was more of an embankment with a single culvert-like arch over the stream. The Derwent failed soon after, due to lateral pressure, one of the face walls cracking. His biggest disappointment was the collapse in 1808 of his three arched stone aqueduct over the Ouse at Wolverton for the Grand Junction Canal. But he was successful on the Rochdale with his Hebden Bridge aqueduct of four arches over the Calder. His largest masonry aqueduct, over the Dearne, had five arches and carried the Barnsley Canal. There were three major aqueducts on the Manchester, Bolton & Bury; two over the Irwell, at Clifton of three arches and at Prestolee of four. The Damside, 90' over the Tonge near Bolton, was demolished as unsafe in 1965. Britain's first cast iron aqueduct was completed in 1796, a very small 44'6" long trough at The Holmes on the Derby Canal. Outram was the engineer, since 1790 a partner with Jessop in the Butterley ironworks. Jessop took up the cause of cast iron with enthusiasm, since it combined lightness (for a puddle lining was not needed) as well as strength. The Holmes trough was built from wedge shaped plates flanged and bolted together and this became standard practice. While it was being built another was under way on the Shrewsbury Canal to replace Josiah Clowes' masonry aqueduct over the Tern at Longdon. It was designed by William Reynolds and Telford, the plates coming from the Ketley works. Longdon is an unattractive aqueduct, the trough resting on Clowes' old masonry abutments and supported by three piers of iron girders, built as inverted triangles, to spread the load.

It had already been decided to build the two great aqueducts of Chirk and Pontcysyllte of cast iron, though masonry had originally been intended. Iron would permit the Dee aqueduct to be high enough above the water (126'), to allow a level crossing. As built Pontcysyllte (8) was 1007' long with 19 arches, each of 45' span. It was completed in 1805, ten years after the laying of the foundation stone. The trough was built from wedge shaped plates, flanged and bolted together, and supported by segmental arches in equilibrium, built up in four arched rings or members, the inner two of open bar, the outer two plated over. Chirk forms a hybrid as if the engineers were playing safe. They produced a ten arched masonry structure enclosing an iron trough. The masonry gave lateral support to the ironwork, with the ironwork acting as a tie to the masonry, allowing it to be light, the upper parts of the piers being hollow with internal cross walls, as at Pontcysyllte, and the arch spandrels were left hollow too. In 1811 to replaced the collapsed aqueduct at Wolverton, Benjamin Bevan designed a cast iron trough with sides of wedge shaped plates supported by arched ribs fixed alongside. Between 1812 and 1816 the Stratford was extended from Lapworth to the Avon with three aqueducts at Yarningale, Wootton Wawen and Edstone near Bearley, the first of brick, the others of cast iron. In 1834 the brick Yarningale aqueduct was washed away by a burst and replaced by today's cast iron trough. Iron had one last triumph with the aqueduct completed in 1839 by George Leather which carries the Wakefield line of the Aire & Calder over the Calder at Stanley Ferry. This is a bowstring arched truss design, the cast iron arch supporting a cast iron tank by wrought iron rods. The aqueduct clears the river by a single 180' span and the tank is 24' wide, each side embellished with a frieze of Doric columns. In spite of the success of iron, masonry and brick continued to be used. Canals such as the Macclesfield have aqueducts of masonry and in the West Country there was the Beam aqueduct over the Torridge on the Torrington Canal, of five semi-circular arches and today used for the drive to Beam House. On the Barrow branch of the Grand Central Canal in Ireland a stone aqueduct with three shallow arches was opened in 1826 to replace a level crossing of the river which had needed locks. Hugh Baird, engineer of the Edinburgh and Glasgow Union copied Chirk for his three aqueducts on the advice of Telford. Telford re-

8. Donkeys or 'hanimals', here seen crossing the Pontcysyllte aqueduct, were used on the Ellesmere Canal. The trough over each arch is built up of wedge shaped plates, flanged and bolted together.

A.J.Lewery.

turned to wholly cast iron for the aqueduct named after himself on the Birmingham Canal Navigations. This carries the Engine branch over his new main line at Smethwick and the trough is carried on an arch of openwork design like the nearby Galton bridge. The trough sides are decorated with Gothic arcading. In the 1930s, the old stone Croxton aqueduct at Middlewich, built to barge standard, was narrowed when a steel trough was inserted, while in 1961 Rennie's stone Bulk Road aqueduct over the Kirkby Lonsdale road was replaced by a steel trough carried on pre-stressed concrete beams of 64' span. Aqueducts over roads are almost as frequent as those over water. Sometimes they are built like culverts, such as the two piercing the Shelmore embankment, others are bridges, as at Sedgwick on the Lancaster Canal. Generally of small span, road aqueducts are of pleasant variety, the tall stone one at Red Bull near Kidsgrove carrying the Macclesfield over the Sandbach road, and the cast iron ones of the Shropshire Union. There is a notable one in Glasgow taking the 10' deep Forth & Clyde over the Maryhill road. In common with the other Forth & Clyde aqueducts it has a lower arch in the middle to support the deep canal bed. Some, particularly over private drives were ornamental. The railway age brought further aqueducts. An early one was over the Grand Junction line at Preston Brook, completed in 1837. In 1971 it was rebuilt because of the Crewe-Glasgow electrification of the railway. Much larger is that taking the Basingstoke Canal over the lines from Waterloo to Southampton and Salisbury. Built in 1838 it had two arches, one for each track, increased to four when the line was quadrupled in 1900. It was built and extended without closing the canal, hence the excessive width as one half was built and then the other, the canal traffic being diverted as required. Smaller aqueducts over water are equally varied. Some are culverts like the Rye Water aqueduct of the Royal Canal near Leixlip under an embankment 100' above the water. The aqueduct on the Pitfour Canal over the Crooko Burn in Aberdeenshire, is rather crude, using two lintels instead of arches. There are two canal fly-overs in the Potteries area, the brick Pool Lock aqueduct built by the Trent & Mersey at Harding's Wood near Kidsgrove for their branch to the Macclesfield at Hall Green, opened in 1831 (163); and the Denford or Hazelhurst aqueduct built ten years later to take the Leek branch over the Caldon. This is of brick with a semi-circular arch. At Barton in 1893 the old aqueduct had to make way for the Manchester Ship Canal. As a replacement, Leader Williams designed the swing aqueduct in use today. This has a swinging span 235' long and weighs 1450 tons, for it is kept full of water to save taking it from the canal at each operation. The frictional loss through the roller bearings is reduced by a central hydraulic ram which takes 900 tons off the roller race. Rams are also used to drive home the rubber faced wedges which come into use at each end when the tank is united with the canal. These are tapered and designed to fit right around the sides and bottom of the trough. It was opened in 1893 and the old Barton aqueduct demolished.

BANK PROTECTION. River floodbanks were built up to a height of 8 feet or so above the water and not steeply sloped, while canal banks according to Rees' "Cyclopaedia" were to be a foot higher than the water with a slope of one in one and a half down to the canal bed. Protection against leaks and erosion was achieved in various ways. There was the puddle which made bank and bed watertight and to bind the sides rushes were planted. The engineers frequently left a ledge or berm just below water level, giving the rushes a foothold, and acting as a trap for earth which would otherwise roll in, the rushes breaking the eroding action of waves, aided by the berms. On the side away from the canal it was necessary to drain the banks if they were raised higher than the surrounding land to prevent them becoming waterlogged and liable to slip. If there was a slip, the water could be contained by two rows of hurdles with straw rammed between, a crude sort of cofferdam which could be amplified by piling. Where a bank was steep and so more liable to collapse into the canal the answer was camp sheeting, now called camp shedding, a row of piles holding behind them a wall of horizontal planks, the tops of the piles being tied back to the banks. On the Leeds & Liverpool this is called 'boarding and slabbing', the space behind the boarding being filled with rubble, and considered a good protection against erosion. To contain banks where the soil was loose, stakes were driven in at intervals to hold back a line of brushwood fencing. Infilling behind piling is vital because the water will pass through and by its sucking action when a boat passes, loosen the pile. Apart from their floodbanks, the natural banks of rivers needed protection from erosion, particularly on bends. In the nineteenth century on the Little Ouse to Thetford, alder poles were driven as piles, linked by horizontal lengths of alder and held back by wrought iron ties. Rivers with swift currents and tidal scour needed substantial piling and stone revetments to shore up weak places, the Severn being a costly river in this respect. Arrival of powered craft in the nineteenth century caused bank protection to be redoubled. More piling was done and many waterways lined the sides with stone pitching. Both allowed a vertical bank to be created, increasing the effective width of the waterway. The Bridgewater undertook stone pitching when they put steam tugs on in the 1870s and it had to be done on the Manchester Ship Canal because of the suction of the hulls and screws of laden ships. The pitching could either be rough stone or dressed stone laid without mortar. On the Weaver, three foot square and four inch thick blocks of 'bass' were used, the vitreous clinker from the salt pans, while the Leeds & Liverpool drove long slates vertically down to form a wall. A continuous wall of sheet piling could stop leaks and was also used to support lock walls and bridge abutments. In the eighteenth century it was made up of timber piles grooved on each side and driven close together, lengths of deal being slipped down the grooves to provide the seal. Modern sheet piling is of steel, interlocked and held firm by a horizontal waling of light railway line or road crash-barrier material. The wall is tied back every 10' to an anchorage in the bank called a pile block. Railway sleepers sawn into three were common, as on the Shropshire Union, while the Leeds & Liverpool used to cap their piles with a masonry coping. After the 1939-45 War, pieces of Anderson air raid shelters were used, followed by concrete in the 1950s and 1960s.

Piles have been driven by vertically falling weights since the eighteenth century, the pile driver usually being mounted on a boat. Mauls or beetles must have been used for earlier river improvement, a beetle being a hammer wielded by three men, having two shafts with a cross brace between them for the third man to lift by. Steam came to drive nineteenth century pile drivers (32) and modern ones have a motor winch with a hand clutch or are a compressed air unit suspended by a crane. It was essential that the weight or 'monkey' gave light blows to start the pile and heavier ones later on. There were also hand worked pile driving frames on the canals, six men tailing on to six ropes attached to the main rope for the monkey.

BRIDGES: Overbridges. Under a canal's Act bridges had to be provided for landowners and their tenants whose property the waterway would divide, and for highways. If the canal company failed to make a bridge, the Act allowed the landowner to make one at the expense of the company. If extra overbridges were required the landowners had to pay for them. To keep costs down some companies built their bridges as cheaply as possible and all tended to suit the canal rather than the road, although the Act might specify the width of carriageway and gradient of the approach roads. To save bridgeworks, fords were suggested for the Trent & Mersey and were built on the Tyrone (Coalisland) Canal. Usually the span had to be long enough to clear both canal and towpath, the canal being narrowed to a single boat width, a hindrance to traffic, hence the expression 'bridge hole'. On Fenland waterways the towpath passed behind the bridge requiring the hauling line to be unhitched. A canal bridge had to clear the boat and horse, yet the approach roads could not be too steeply ramped, but a hump-backed bridge was generally unavoidable. Unlike rivers, canals were often on a level with or higher than the roads which crossed them. Usually an arch construction was favoured, the Bridgewater and Trent & Mersey Canals setting the pattern. Brindley and his assistants employed a segmental arch, and to withstand the weight of the approach roads, gave to the bridge an arch shape in plan view with splayed abutments, in addition building each face with a curved batter. Many overbridges were deliberately built by locks to make use of the buttressing effect of the lock wing walls. Bridges spanning the canal in cuttings well above water level were not subject to so many limiting factors. Arches of strong curvature could be used, either semi-circular or segmental. Moreover the bridge could be designed to span the canal at full width. Brick is the usual material in the Midlands and South (33), sometimes laid in winding courses to form a strong arch. Winding courses are also found in skew bridges, a design first used by William Chapman on the Kildare Canal to Naas in 1787. Brindley had shunned any attempt at skew crossings, curving the approach roads to achieve the right angle. Stone bridges were used on most of the northern canals. Curiosities are the 'ball alley' bridges on the Ulster Canal (103), where the road is ramped up on each side of one approach, parallel with the canal, bounded by walls, hence the likeness to a ball or skittle alley. Metal was not widely employed for ordinary canal overbridges except in Yorkshire, steel for the Aire & Calder and Calder & Hebble bridges, although cast iron was used for towpath bridges on the BCN and northern Oxford when shortened in the 1830s. The railway age brought a greater use of iron and later steel. Railway style road overbridges were built on some of the later canals, notably the Cannock Extension of the BCN completed in 1863. Notable railway bridges are those of the London & Birmingham over the Grand Junction, made to a standard design with wrought and cast iron members, and the many on the BCN of brick, the engineering blue brick used on the BCN itself. Motorway construction has brought reinforced concrete into the canal scene. Timber overbridges have rarely been fixed, save in East Anglia, but timber was employed when canal companies sought to evade the cost of fixed bridges. A hand operated swinging or lifting span could be cheaply built to carry the road just above canal level and obviate the need to span the towpath. Swing bridges (sometimes called swivel or turnbridges) were built for the pioneer Sankey Brook Navigation to allow sailing flats up to St. Helens and according to Rees' "Cyclopaedia", were complete with a roller race, just as were those John Rennie built for the Kennet & Avon with races of 4" cast iron balls. To avoid obstructing the horses, swing bridges were made to pivot on the offside, although this made them difficult for boat people. Swing bridges are most numerous on the Leeds & Liverpool, many of the wooden ones being replaced by steel, and were also used on the Peak Forest, Cromford, Basingstoke, Grand Junction and Macclesfield and on the ship canals; Crinan, Caledonian (in Scotland they are called pivot bridges) and the Gloucester & Berkeley, the last named having until recently, bridges divided into two swinging spans, one operated by the resident bridge keeper, the other by a 'passman' who travelled with the ships, but since 1963 all have been replaced by single spans. Hand operated wood lifting bridges of more variety were used for cock-up bridges in the Fens, although some metal bridges were built in the nineteenth century, including the vertically rising Turnbridge on Ramsden's Canal in Huddersfield of 1865. On the Oxford Canal timber lift bridges are balanced by beams at an angle of about 140° from the platform, the whole pivoting about toothed segments of cast iron. The wooden lift bridges on the canal to Llangollen (9) have overhead beams with a balance box full of stones, the beams being braced together, unlike those on the Caldon where each beam is independent and separately counterweighted. Double leaved lift bridges were almost universal on the Forth & Clyde, operated by geared pinions and toothed quadrant, while there was an interesting example for a railway siding on the Monmouthshire Canal in Newport, where the two halves overlapped fully across the canal because the siding crossed at an angle to the canal and extra width was needed.

BRIDGES: Powered, Swing and Bascule. Railways, demanding stronger bridges, introduced the powered opening span. The power did not have to be excessive, since a swing bridge with a ball or roller race and a draw or bascule bridge could be designed to balance. Many heavy bridges could be hand worked by a capstan or windlass mounted on the span with a train of gears to the toothed ring on the swing bridge, or a toothed sector on a bascule, but the instant response of power reduced delays. Selby was the site of an early railway opening bridge (actually hand worked), a cast iron bascule with two leaves, built for the Hull & Selby Railway. It lasted until 1891 when it was replaced by the present electric swing bridge. These bridges were expensive and were limited to navigations used by vessels with fixed masts, such as the Gloucester & Berkeley Ship Canal. Hand worked bridges were satisfactory for road traffic, but the completion in 1879 of the Severn railway bridge above Sharpness demanded a steam swinging span. The two cylinder simple expansion engine and vertical coal-fired boiler, mounted on the span, were duplicated so that the bridge was always workable. However, clutches allowed the engines to work together. Operation of the bridge was interlocked with the railway signals. Like all opening bridges of any size, this bridge was locked in the 'closed to canal' position by wedges at each corner of the span. The biggest opening railway bridge over a British navigation must be the bascule bridge at Keadby over the Trent (7). Of rolling lift design, it rolled back and up. It was opened in 1916, to replace a swing bridge in use since 1864. The new span, the furthest downstream over the Trent, incorporates a road as well as the two railway tracks. With a total length of 440' the opening span, now fixed, measures 160' and gave an opening 150' wide. Sir William Arrol of Glasgow built the bridge to the designs of the American Scherzer Rolling Lift Bridge Co. Operation was by two 115 hp electric motors, the span being heavily counterweighted. Roads have demanded more elaborate bridges as traffic has built up, illustrated by two examples on the Leeds & Liverpool. At Plank Lane, near Leigh an electric swing bridge replaced a hand one in 1957, while at Litherland near Liverpool, a new electric lift bridge was opened in 1933, and the following year at Royston on the Barnsley Canal. The latter was built by the County Council, the hoisting gear and weights at each corner being housed in four brick towers. On the Manchester Ship Canal

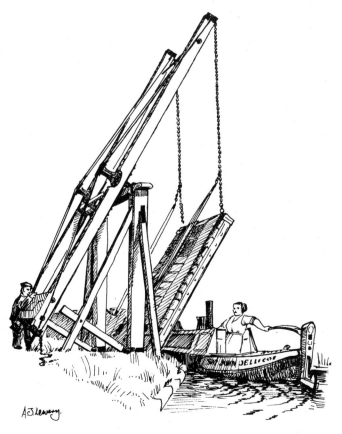

9. A lift bridge on the Ellesmere Canal. The boat is one of A. & A. Peate's, the Maesbury Hall, Oswestry, flour millers.

powered swing bridges are universal for road crossings except for the two motorway via-
ducts and the high level bridges at Latchford and Warburton. There are seven plus a dock
railway swing bridge at Trafford Park. All are hydraulically worked, with three cylinder
motors housed in the mounting. These drive by reduction gearing of 148 to 1, a toothed
rack on the bridge structure; this is 32' in diameter on three of the bridges. The truss is
of bowstring girder type but reinforced, since the bridge is supported at the centre only
when swung, but at the ends when open to the road. The Weaver swing bridges are electric
including the small one at Winnington. First to be built were two at Northwich, completed
in 1900. Because of the subsidence caused by brine pumping, the bridges are largely carried on floating pontoons. Tests were first carried out on an accommodation bridge at Marsh
lock. An old boiler formed the pontoon and it was a complete success, lasting 50 years. The
pontoons of the two Northwich bridges, Town and Hayhurst upstream (a new crossing point),
were made from four segmental tanks strapped together. They support about three fifths of
the weight and are integral with the bridge structure, turning with it. The remaining weight
is carried by eight steel piles round the outside of the pontoons and linked to each other by
a girder framework. On this is the roller path, the conical rollers being flanged on the inside to keep the bridge swinging true. Subsidence can be allowed for by screw adjustment of
the pile heads to keep the roller path at the correct level, while accumulated rain water
may be pumped out of the pontoons. The electric drive is by a 30 hp motor controlled from
the bank, which drives a winch which hauls on the steel cable passed round the roller race.
So successful were they that Sutton was replaced by a floating bridge in 1923 (107), and Acton
in 1932, although at both the ground was stable, because only a tenth of the power was needed to swing a floating bridge. At these larger bridges the piles were replaced by a concrete wall on which the roller path is laid. Within the chamber so formed, the pontoon, turning with the bridge, floats. The pontoon is open topped, but flood water is kept out by a
coaming, and water can be let in via a valve. Electrically applied band brakes are needed
because of the coasting action of the bridge once in motion. At Acton, the pontoon supports
560 of the total 650 tons. Here the bridge is centrally mounted, the other spans being offset and counterweighted with pig iron. Two men form the bridge crew, driver and gateman.

    BRIDGES: Lock Bridges. Although most lock gates act as bridges with platforms and
handrails, essential for their working, a special lock bridge speeded traffic, particularly on
broad canals where the gap between one closed gate and the other side of the lock was too
great to jump, so a bridge was frequently put across the lock tail where it would clear the
boat. On the Worcester & Birmingham there are or were bridges cantilevered out from one
side, the other being left unsupported, with a gap of a few inches so that a line could be
slipped through. More common are split bridges; on the Trent & Mersey these are wooden,
supported by elegant curved cast iron brackets, both halves of the bridge not quite meeting
in the middle. On the Staffs. & Worcs., they are cast iron with split handrails. Wooden
plank bridges with handrails are almost universal on the broad locks of the Leeds & Liverpool, and on the Lancaster. On the narrow canals there are some attractive cast iron examples (56), as at Bosley locks on the Macclesfield Canal, carried across by arched members, while on the Grand Union to Leicester, the Foxton flights are spanned by wood bridges.
Boatmen grew adept at passing towlines under the wooden lock bridges, swinging the rope
with one hand and catching it with the other. There are brick bridges on the Staffordshire &
Worcestershire and Trent & Mersey, serving a dual role as accommodation and access
bridges to lock cottages. They are buttressed by the wing walls of the lock tail, so span the
canal only, to the inconvenience of boat working.

    BRIDGES: Towpath Bridges. A continuous towpath meant bridging arms and basins, spec-
ial bridges at junctions, bridges over the weir stream on rivers, and bridges to take the
towpath from one side to the other, because of buildings or the farmer might have cattle
watering rights. They were designed to avoid unhitching the towline and go under several
names; on the Leeds & Liverpool they are called changeline bridges, elsewhere turnover or
just turnbridges (not to be confused with swing bridges also called turnbridges). They are
also called roving bridges, but this is not used by boatmen. The towpath must approach and
leave the bridge on the same face, which it does by gradual curves, a brick example is that
at High Onn on the Shropshire Union, or in stone, near Hyde on the Peak Forest. On the
Stratford-on-Avon Canal economy was achieved by the use of cast iron split bridges. There
was no need for the towpath to pass under the bridge, the horse merely walked across and
the line was dropped through the central gap. At junctions the towpath bridge had to carry
the main line path across the branch and the branch path round to the correct side without
the need to unhitch the line, resulting in some complex designs like the triangular junction at
Braunston where two cast iron spans cross from the Grand Junction to the Oxford via the
island in the middle. The Birmingham Canal Navigations have numerous junction bridges,
many of cast iron dating from Telford's improvements of the 1820s and after, made by the
Horseley Ironworks, Tipton. The same works cast side bridges over the arms and loops of
of the BCN. Side bridge is the boatman's term for a towpath bridge crossing an arm. Towpath bridges over the weir streams of rivers, over their tributaries and over the natural
river where it enters and leaves cuts often have large spans, like the pair of wooden arches
over the weir stream of the Weaver below Dutton locks, (title page). Towpaths are sometimes crossed by their own accommodation bridges; there is the 'towpath tunnel' on Marple
locks and another at Stone. Small bridges cross the tunnel top path over Hincaster tunnel on
the Lancaster Canal, linking fields, this path also passing under the main London to Glasgow
railway (72).

    BURSTS and LEAKS. When water leaks in great volume, the damage is described as a
burst, breach or blow. Either the canal is too full due to the result of heavy rain and
pressure of water too great for the banks, or the banks are too weak. They may have been

weakened by erosion on the water side or slips on the landward side, or a small hole may have been enlarged by water pressure. This could happen in a few hours, resulting in bank collapse. Holes made by rats, rabbits and moles weaken banks, hence the employment by many canal companies of a mole catcher. River floodbanks also have to be guarded particularly in the Fens. It is the duty of the lengthsmen to keep watch for leaks at all times, hence the regular inspections carried out at least weekly over the whole system. Subsidence was another danger, see page 61. Leaks which may lead to a burst are easily seen where they emerge from an embankment, but to find their source is a different matter, for water wanders before it shows. Water divining is useful and those on the engineering staff with the gift are in demand. If the leak cannot be traced it is a matter of trenching along the bank parallel with the canal until the seepage is found. Once the leak is marked, repuddling is carried out. Water rats make a hole just above the summer level, but the winter level of the canal will come up above the hole with every chance of a leak. Bursts were repaired with extreme urgency, as an alternative route might be very devious. Temporary repairs using a stank or cofferdam of sheet piling were used to seal the gap and allow the pound to be refilled. Work then proceeded without interruption to traffic.

CULVERTS. A culvert may be a passage for water to enter or leave a lock, a passage for a lock's bypass weir stream, or a miniature aqueduct set in an embankment to carry a stream or drain under the canal. To contain the stream, the culvert must be well built of brick or stone or made up from cast iron piping flanged together. This is to quote from Rees' "Cyclopaedia" (1819) while modern culverts use concrete pipes. Sometimes if the stream is near canal level it has to be syphoned under by a broken backed or moon culvert, so called because of its crescent shape. Canals abandoned for navigation but retained as water channels are themselves culverted under lowered bridges.

CANAL SURVEYING. First considerations were the gauge, broad or narrow, and the depth and width. In other words, the area of the canal's cross section on which depends the ability of craft to carry worthwhile payloads, to travel at a reasonable speed and to pass. The narrow canals were built 5' to 6' deep on average, with a width of 20' across the bed and 40' of water across the surface. The Aire & Calder's Knottingley-Goole canal was built with a bottom width of 40' and a surface width of 60' and a depth of 7' to take broad Yorkshire keels. The Gloucester & Berkeley Ship Canal opened with a depth of 18' and a surface width of 85'6". Sloped sides were the rule to stop slips, the angle depending on the soil, but one in one and a half was the usual gradient. If the bank could be walled with stone pitching the slope could be cut back to a near vertical, thereby increasing the cross sectional water area. Rules were worked out in the nineteenth century for the most satisfactory area. The least breadth of bottom should be twice the maximum beam of the usual type of trade boat, the least depth should be the greatest draught of a boat plus 18", and the least cross sectional area six times the area of the boat's midship section. Gauge was dictated by the traffic expected from other waterways, by cost and the attitude of adjacent canal proprietors. Thus the Leeds & Liverpool was built wide enough for Aire & Calder keels, while the narrow system of the Midlands was possibly the result of financial stringency. Apart from the extra expense of cutting, a broad canal needed more water. Choice of summit was most important for its water resources supplied the rest of the canal via the locks. It was soon observed that a long summit acted as a reservoir, and Brindley's canals achieved this, notably the Coventry and the Oxford, the former having a summit level 16½ miles long. The engineer and his assistants would decide on the summit level and its supply and work downwards towards each canal end, deciding the lock sites and noting the need for deep cutting, culverts and aqueducts. Careful consideration was given to tunnels because of their expense and slow construction. The acquiescence of landowners was necessary for the navigation's success through parliament and their wishes were respected by, for example, the Edinburgh & Glasgow Union who made a tunnel to avoid disfiguring the grounds of Callender House near Falkirk. The engineer tried to bring his canal as near the centres of commerce as possible, while striking a balance between sound engineering and cost. Brindley reduced his costs by following contours and avoiding earthworks arguing that more people would be within reach of the canal, when defending the twisting Birmingham canal, while in contrast the Birmingham & Liverpool Junction Canal ignored local traffic to drive a direct line to the Mersey. Choosing a line in the eighteenth century was made difficult by a lack of accurate maps and of geological knowledge. The first Ordinance Survey map appeared in 1801 and the country south of a line from Hull to Preston was not fully mapped until 1844. Trial excavations were made, but the effects of geological features were not understood until studied by William Smith, a canal engineer. The engineer was interested in the course of streams and the routes of intersecting roads, while the promoters needed to know the incidence of estate boundaries. Parliament required information on all these after 1793. By the eighteenth century, the principles of land surveying were known and practised. The course would be plotted by triangulation, which is the means of measuring horizontal distances on the ground by a series of triangles. The angles were measured by a theodolite, developed in the early eighteenth century from the surveying compass with its alidade or vane with sighting holes. The theodolite had a sighting telescope with cross wires. Jonathan Sisson, a London instrument maker made one in 1720, so they were available to canal engineers. The distances were measured using the Gunter chain of 100 links introduced by Gunter in the late sixteenth century. The chain was 22 yards long and metal arrows were planted in the ground as the chain advanced. Levels were taken with a spirit level coupled with a telescope with crosswire sights, an advance on the plum bob steadied in a tray of water. Heights were found by sighting adjustable markers on staffs. The levelling instrument was placed between two such staffs and the markers adjusted by the staffholders (6) until they coincided with the crosswires of the instrument. The surveyor would sight forward and back. Then the height of the markers above the ground would be measured and the difference between them would give the height of one staff position relative to the other. Successive heights would be found, the distance between each measured by chain. All levels as observed were apparent, true level depending on the subtraction of a figure to allow for the curve of the earth's surface. For future reference, some of the observed levels were marked on trees, posts or walls. These bench marks were noted and could be used in future levelling.

CANAL CUTTING METHODS. The depths to which a canal had to be excavated were marked by level pegs, arranged so that their crosspieces could be lined up horizontally and checked with a levelling instrument. The pegs were set every two or three chains, 44 - 66 yards, the frequency depending on undulations in the ground, and indicated the level of the top of the canal bank. Where embanking or deep cutting was required, as opposed to level cutting, special pegs were set up. Deep cuttings were marked out like tunnels, with pegs along the line of the work, the depth to be excavated known from surveys. With the level pegs in position along the proposed bank, always the upper bank if the canal was being terraced out, the engineers then marked the middle by stakes opposite each peg, called 'staking the middle range'. Trial excavations were made to see what the soil was like, to a depth three feet lower than the bed of the canal, to determine the work required. For the benefit of the cutters, the engineer's men would finally mark out the water surface of the canal by a series of small holes called slope holes, two or three chains apart on each side and joined by a shallow trench of a spade's depth called a lock spit. The slope holes and lock spit would indicate the course, with the bends marked by small pegs and the straight sections marked by a cord stretched between each slope hole. A good man was needed for the lock spit, actually two worked together from each side of the trench, the second man throwing out the wedge shaped turf which the first man cut from the outside, leaving the correct slope for the cutters to follow. The idea was to have banks of even slope. Another precaution the engineer's staff had to take was the marking out of puddling requirements. Puddle was the lightish loam or clay mixed with water which made the canal watertight. It had been used by tanners prior to the canal age, to line their pits and by Dutch drainage works in the Fens. The principle is to impregnate the earth or clay so that it will hold no more and so resist ingress of further water. It continues in use for lining canals and stopping leaks. Bentonite, the imported clay has also been applied in modern times successfully sealing cracks. It is poured in as a powder and swells when wet. If the canal was dug out of porous ground, both sides and bed would need to be fully lined with puddle, if the canal was in a watertight bed, then only the banks thrown up above ground level would need sealing with what was called a puddle ditch or puddle gutter. If the top strata was porous and the lower watertight, or if there was a middle porous layer, then a puddle ditch was made by trenching down to the watertight layer and filling with puddle. In the banks the puddle ditch was built up as the banks rose, the sides of the ditch being lined with sods or spits (spadefuls) of earth. The ditch was about three feet wide and went about a foot into the watertight layer to make a good seal. Another advantage of the ditch was that it formed a deterrent to rats and moles. The cutter and his mates, each of whom could probably shift 20 tons a day, dug inwards from the lock spit towards the centre of the canal, starting, if the canal was terraced, from the lock spit on the lower side. They would be especially careful to keep to the slope indicated by the lock spit, but would work back by vertical cuts which was known as 'reaching'. As they worked down to the bed, the cutters would consolidate the banks with the sods they dug out. The remaining spoil was used to form the banks, notably on the lower side, if the canal was being carried across the face of a slope. Spoil not required was carted away for embanking elsewhere.

Because of the need to line with puddle, most canals were excavated deeper and wider than indicated by the plan. It has to be very thick to be effective. Puddle was prepared by finely chopping loam, preferably mixed with coarse sand or gravel as a deterrent to rats, with a spade and mixing it with water to a semi-plastic state. It was then applied in layers, say 9" or 10" thick, each layer keyed by spadework to that below, and consolidated. Each was left to mature for several days, but not allowed to dry out, before the next was applied until the puddle ditch was complete. A similar method was used where the sides and the bottom were to be lined; and where the bottom was stones or chalk, an extra thick bottom course was applied. Following the bottom, the sides were done with stepped layers of puddle, the lowest 18" thick, the others 9" contained by a wall of sods or earth to prevent slips. With the puddle complete the water could be let in, the final task being the planting of rushes at the water's edge to consolidate the bank. The puddle had always to be fully immersed, otherwise it dried, cracked and leaked, so it was necessary to have water ready to let in before the puddle dried out. Where a canal was embanked on one side, this embankment was built on a terrace previously cut to ensure a stable foundation. Some deep cutting involved blasting through rock without the need for lining, as in the Clonsilla cutting, near Dublin, on the Royal Canal, while other canals were on such weak ground that a firm foundation for the bed had to be made of mortared stonework. The Shropshire Canal engineered over coal and ironstone workings was an example. During the canal age, excavation was by hand with pick, spade and shovel, wheelbarrow, horse and cart. When digging started back from the lock spit, removal of the spoil was easy, but problems increased with depth. Planks had to be laid for wheelbarrows to run up on to the bank and tip either on to the bank to strengthen it or into carts for removal. The wheeling planks were combined with horsing blocks to make barrow runs which could be laid obliquely up the sides of cuttings. Horsing blocks were open ended rectangular boxes stoutly strutted. Digging machines were tried to speed spoil removal rather than excavate. Carts or horse tramroads were used to move spoil along the line of the canal, while boats could be employed for longer distances. Spades with special narrow blades were used for placing puddle and keying it to the layer underneath. A wooden rammer or punner was used for consolidating the puddle and binding it to the layer below. The scoop, a wooden box with a long wooden handle, was used to ladle water over the puddle being worked in. Men engaged in puddling wore strong watertight boots whose weight would help puddle consolidation. Shot holes for blasting were prepared by hand turned augers. The charges were of black powder packed in loose and rammed home with an iron bar called a stemmer. This was most dangerous because the iron might strike a spark and ignite the powder. Copper stemmers were safer. The shot hole was sealed by clay and the charge ignited by a fuse of rope impregnated with saltpetre. The wheelbarrows came in two types; for earth removal, they had shallow sides and could hold about 2 cwt., for bricks and stones they had no sides, but a high board over the wheel, against which the bricks would be piled. For blocks of masonry, low two wheeled hand trolleys were used. Evidence for the appearance of this equipment comes from an illustrated record of the construction of the Warwick & Birmingham Canal in the 1790s. Many of the pictures are reproduced in "Canals and their Architecture" (1969). Barrows were used for distances up to 100 yards but for longer runs, two wheeled hand carts carrying about 4 cwt. Movement of spoil was measured by stages of 25 yards, taken into account when prices were fixed for contracting. For hauling spoil from tunnel shafts and deep cuttings, horse powered windlasses were used, the whims or gins of contemporary mines. The horse walked round and round yoked to a horizontal beam fixed to a revolving vertical shaft to which was fitted a large diameter (about 24 feet) winding drum from which the winding ropes were led over pulleys mounted on a framework above the shaft. By using two ropes the gin could haul up and down simultaneously, helped by the counterbalancing effect of the two skips. Two horses side by side could be used, blinkered to prevent giddiness. The skips were designed to be carried on three wheeled handcarts, off which they were lifted at the shaft bottom, one end of the skip being inclined for easy tipping. Hand windlasses, or jack rolls, were also used, simple barrels like those mounted over a well. Pumps were needed to clear workings unless a drainage sough was dug. This was recommended in tunnelling for it was efficient and cheaper. To clear cuttings of water, archimedean screws, either man or horse operated were used, the latter somewhat like a gin with a gear train between the vertical spindle and the inclined barrel of the screw. Water could also be hauled out in buckets, or a windmill pump might be erected to save the cost of a steam engine, for tunnel shafts.

CANAL CUTTING ORGANIZATION. For the resources of the eighteenth century, making a canal was an arduous task, because of the lack of mechanical equipment, poor transport and communications. Generally when the Act passed the man who had directed the surveys was retained as principal engineer. He would be too busy to oversee the work in detail. It was difficult to keep in touch by horseback and post chaise and the mail system was unreliable, so supervision fell to the resident engineers. A small canal might have one, a bigger two. Before handing over to the resident engineers, the principal engineer organized the distribution of cutting work to the contractors who supplied the labour for an agreed rate. Early canals and some later were built by men directly employed by the proprietors, as rivers had been improved by undertakers who took on men for the work. The Duke of Bridgewater achieved all his works by direct labour as did the Trent & Mersey. When canals multiplied and the demand for cutters, bricklayers, masons and carpenters grew, contractors appeared. They saved the canal companies trouble and the expense of a large supervisory staff, the only link between the company and the contractor being the former's engineering staff. Most of the contractors were men called hagmasters, employing or actually working at the head of a team of cutters (the skilled diggers) and labourers (the unskilled) who probably filled and wheeled barrows. They contracted for lengths of a few miles. There were also specialist contractors for tunnels and aqueducts, like Alexander Stevens & Son of Edinburgh who built the Lune aqueduct after the foundations had been prepared by the company. With iron aqueducts the contracting work became more complex, thus that on the Aire & Calder at Stanley Ferry had foundations built by Hugh MacIntosh and ironwork supplied and erected by William Graham & Co., of the Milton Iron Works, Elsecar.

Contractors tendered for work, the price being worked out per cubic yard of digging, also considering the distance the spoil had to be moved. Tools were usually found by the canal company. The engineers men made sure the work was not skimped. Money was paid on work done after a careful check by the canal's engineers. It could also be advanced, the 'subsist' money which kept the contractor solvent and his men paid. Some contractors failed or gave up and the company either carried on by direct labour or re-let the work. Often contractors had to find sureties before they started work, thus Jessop stood surety for £4,000 on behalf of John Pinkerton to enable him to get the Dudley tunnel contract. With contracts let, work proceeded, starting with locks and bridges, aqueducts and tunnels, all given priority because they were bigger undertakings. They needed sawpits, brick kilns, stone yards, horse gins, pumps and forges. Tunnels were the greatest problems for the engineers and contractors; they were started as soon as possible and were usually last to be finished. Specific lengths were the responsibility of sub or assistant engineers who might also be appointed with special responsibilities, such as William Cartwright, overseeing the foundations of the Lune aqueduct. The assistant engineer controlled a team of 'overlookers' closely watching the work of the hagmasters, and 'checkers' who counted the men under each contractor. The assistant engineer also superintended the work of the bricklayers, masons and carpenters via their own master craftsmen. These men were either directly employed or under contract. For the resident and his assistants the work must have been arduous, no telephones, few letters, but much riding in all weathers. Personal contact was vital to success, although the wrangling with the numerous contractors and suppliers must have been incessant. At the bottom of engineering hierarchy came the cutters and labourers, not called navigators until the 1790s, while the shortened 'navvy' was not recognized until 1832. In East Anglia they were called bankers. Most were paid fortnightly or monthly and a few weekly. Sometimes they were given notes which they had to cash at a discount. On the early canals they were probably local farm labourers. Local Highlanders were used on the Caledonian, not very successfully. Before the 1780s men were bound to their work and forbidden to leave. If they did, they were sought out and brought back at their own expense. During the earlier years of the French Revolutionary wars, men were let off canal work to help with the harvest in the national interest. In the nineteenth century, larger contractors like Joliffe & Banks, appeared. Men expert in tunnelling moved from canal to canal, becoming attached to specialist tunnelling contractors like Ralph Shepperd, one of several at Sapperton. Some of the canal companies appointed a doctor and the men formed sick clubs to cater for the frequent accidents. The canal companies supported them and gave donations to dependents of men killed on the works. Prisoners were used for work on the Oxford Canal in 1794-95, and on restoration of the lower Stratford in the 1960s. Soldiers built the Royal Military Canal.

DEEP CUTTING. These are the most difficult earthworks, liable to slips and rock falls. Brindley and his team avoided them by following contours and building more locks. Later engineers became bolder and undertook deep cutting to lower and extend the summit level, giving a greater water reservoir, tapping more feeder streams, and needing fewer locks. Expense was the main deterrent to deep cutting which demanded moving large quantities of spoil. Early canals left the spoil in banks. Cut and fill techniques were recognised by 1800, but difficult to achieve because of poor transport. For shallow work, planks laid on horsing blocks were sufficient, sited obliquely up the sides, but for deeper cuttings horse gins were used to hoist loaded wheelbarrows, an empty barrow helping to lift up the full one by its descent. The barrows were held by a rope with three tails, one with a hook to the wheel, the others with rings for the handles. A variant used in the railway age was the barrow run (10), where a rope linked ascending and descending barrows on inclined planes about 50 yds apart. A horse harnessed to the rope could pull either one way or the other. On the Trent & Mersey and Staffs. & Worcs., cuttings are short and shallow, but during the 1790s, they became longer and deeper as at Burbage on the Kennet & Avon summit, the cutting approaching the southern end of Wast Hill tunnel on the Worcester & Birmingham, Royston on the Barnsley Canal and Burrow Heights on the Lancaster. Telford is remembered for the deep cuttings at Tyrley and Grub Street on the Birmingham & Liverpool Junction, the former 90' deep and $1\frac{1}{2}$ miles long, cuttings in which slips are common today. At about 50º from the horizontal, the sides are too steep, and the water channel is narrow. Another of Telford's achievements is the Laggan summit cutting on the Caledonian Canal between Loch Lochy and Loch Oich. Rock cuttings are rare in Britain, there is a shallow one on the Leeds & Liverpool near Haskayne, a 50' deep one at Sowerby Bridge on the Rochdale, and some sandstone cuts on the Staffs. & Worcs., on one side only. More remarkable is the Clonsilla cutting on the Royal Canal in Ireland, 27' deep to water level and nearly two miles long, yet only a single boat's width.

CANAL DIGGING MACHINES. As canal cutting grew, several people proposed machines for speeding the work in the 1790s. As early as 1766 a machine was suggested for the Staffs. & Worcs., Canal. Among the first to be used was John Carne's for the Herefordshire & Gloucestershire's cut across Alney Island to reach the Gloucester channel of the Severn. It was tried in 1793 after digging out streams in Cornwall and operated until 1794 when it

10. Deep cutting: Removing spoil with barrow runs.

came to the deep cutting at Cofton Hackett on the Worcester & Birmingham summit level. It had a horse operated whim which wound out buckets of spoil from the cutting. They had to be filled by hand, but all barrowing was eliminated and the machine was portable, the staging, buckets and winding gear could be carried on two wagons. Eight men feeding it were able to shift 258 tons of spoil a day. Ralph Dodd designed the digging machine tried on the Grand Junction near Hayes in 1794, the same year Edward Haskew tried a barrow lifting machine on the Gloucester & Berkeley. Like Carne's it was intended to speed spoil removal. Joseph Sparrow's patent of 1793 is for what appears to be a bucket excavator. Steam excavators or shovels were introduced in the 1830s and 97 of them were used on the Manchester Ship Canal (78). Called American devils, (the invention was American), they were rail mounted, the jib slewing at the foot of a well braced pillar, the adjustable bucket arm allowing the bucket to feed into the work. Grab cranes were also employed for the softer spoil and two types of steam travelling cranes were adapted for excavating. Finally there were two types of ladder bucket excavators, land equivalents of the ladder bucket dredger, working from the top of the bank, four of these machines were French machines and three German. Floating bucket dredgers were used on the Caledonian and on the Manchester Ship Canal, allied with a spoil transporter on the latter, a floating conveyor which loaded railway wagons on the bank. Spoil carrying boats were also used, locomotive hauled from the bank, with the spoil in boxes for discharge by special steam cranes. For modern cutting and dredging, the shovel type excavator has been supplemented by the dragline, which dispenses with a rigid bucket arm, employing cables to move the scoop type bucket.

DREDGING, DREDGERS and MUD HOPPERS. The current on river navigations, particularly in flood, and the tide, bring silt which is deposited in bars and shoals, having been carried in suspension until the current or tide slackened. Tributary streams add their quota which forms a bar at their mouth, where their current loses its velocity on entering the wider channel. Banks become eroded by tide or current, while bridge piers and quay walls offer obstructions against which spoil is lodged. Still-water canals suffer from material brought in by feeder streams, bank erosion, particularly from powered craft and in urban areas, from rubbish thrown into the canal. A river's current can be made to help by its scouring action, although clearing the bed could speed up the current and not increase depth as happened on the Severn. In the early 1700s William Palmer narrowed the bed of the Yorkshire Ouse, probably by building out jetties, increasing the current and the scour. The work of the current could also be helped by loosening shoals with harrows or ploughs, the 'beake dragg' used on the Yorkshire Ouse in the 1730s being a device of this sort. John Grundy used 'hedgehogs' and 'porcupines' in the Fens and on the Cheshire Dee, wood cylinders studded with spikes. Palmer's jetties were the ancestors of the training walls which the Aire & Calder built on the Ouse below Goole from 1884 onwards. These also contained the banks and prevented encroachment. River dredging could be a herculean task, nowhere more so than on the Severn in the 1840s. Ledges of rock had to be cleared and the shoals of marl below Worcester removed by blasting as they had been found too hard to dredge. The latter work had to be stopped because the river began to flow faster rather than deeper with the removal of the obstructions. Silt is dredged up methodically, the dredger working along the channel and sweeping from side to side. Cross sections of the river are prepared using sounding rods, the dredger working to achieve a uniform depth. It had been found that if the dredger worked parallel with the current the bottom would resemble a ploughed field. On the canals the silt is mostly soft mud overlying the puddle. General siltation is tackled by what the engineers call straight line dredging, working as in river dredging. The cross section is measured every 50' using rods with a disc shaped foot so that they do not penetrate the mud. By comparing the measured cross section with the canal as built, the depth of silt can be determined. Apart from a full dredging programme such as this, there is concentrated dredging at known bad spots, at bridge holes, and at bends where boats have piled up silt on the inside. Removal of the spoil can be nine times as expensive as the dredging. A dredger working at a local bad spot may simply load a hopper or herself, but a full programme needs a tug and three hoppers, one loading, one in transit and the third unloading at the dumping ground. This has favoured the use of dragline excavators for the narrow canals, working from the towpath and tipping the spoil on the bank or in trenches in adjoining fields with the consent of local farmers. Very rarely has it been found possible to take a hopper with bottom doors to a deep part of a river navigation and drop the load. This was done on a length of the natural Weaver above Northwich, but it was soon filled up. The modern Weaver technique is to pump the spoil ashore as a slurry using floating pumping equipment which injects water into the spoil to liquify it, sucking out the slurry produced.

Dredgers were initially hand powered, using a scoop or bag on the end of a pole, (like the Norfolk dydle), which had a cutting edge like a hoe, 18" long and a ropework bag. A man pushed the scoop into the water until the scoop bit, while his mate winched the scoop out. The spoil in the scoop was then dumped into the boat. The man guiding the scoop stood on the gunwale while the winch was mounted outboard to exert a direct pull on the scoop holding about half a hundredweight. The work was called ballasting because the dredgings were once sold to ships as ballast. Sand was dredged with a leather bag, gravel in a net, the hoop extending the mouth being sharp edged to strike into the bottom. These early scoop dredgers were probably introduced from the Low Countries. They were limited to shallow water and could only handle soft stuff. The winch to draw up the scoop was the result of a Dutch patent of 1589 by Stevin. Further patents followed from Holland for spoon and ladle dredgers employing windlasses. In the canal age in Britain, the spoon or scoop dredger became established as the most used type and lasted into the mid-twentieth century. It had the advantage of being able to work in awkward corners, but was slow and cumbersome. Design

11. Scoop dredger working near Barnton Tunnel, Trent & Mersey Canal.

advanced from a simple punt to a canal boat with a crane which swung the scoop (11), like a shovel with drainage holes. Some became steam powered, the first about 1796 on the Wear. A Leeds & Liverpool dredger working on the Leigh branch in 1895 used a steam crane lifting a scoop, but still hand guided. The simple scoop developed into an excavator type bucket which in many designs had treadmill operated windlasses to move the bucket on its spar to the work and lift it when laden. Steam was used here too, a variant being the drag boat, an aquatic bulldozer which pushed spoil into a heap out of awkward corners, which an endless belt bucket dredger could not reach. Bristol and Bridgwater had one each, the latter dating from 1844 is at Exeter Maritime Museum. A single cylinder double acting engine was used for a winch to adjust blade depth and haul on warping chains made fast to the dockside. The Bristol one pushed up to 10 tons of spoil at one run. Modern variants are the diesel craft with hydraulic scoops for floating debris which can be exchanged for grabs for dredging. The endless belt bucket dredger was an old idea known to the Romans and was applied by the Dutch in the sixteenth century to what they called a mud mill, with boards set on edge working up a trough, buckets did not come until the eighteenth century. At first treadmill operated, horses were harnessed to the task in the early seventeenth century. Hull had such a dredger in the 1780s which John Rennie fitted with a steam engine in 1804, while in the following year William Jessop designed a steam bucket dredger for the Caledonian Canal. It was here that the bucket dredger proved itself, Bryan Donkin very likely following the lead of Jessop, when he designed two, built at the Butterley ironworks. They were delivered in parts, the first being assembled on Loch Oich in 1816. Donkin also supplied a dredger to the Calder & Hebble in 1817. For the cutting of the Manchester Ship Canal, self propelled and pontoon bucket dredgers were assembled from parts sent down from William Simons of Renfrew and Fleming & Ferguson of Paisley. For more restricted waterways the bucket type was not much used; there was one on the Ashton and Peak Forest Canals in the Great Central Railway days. Grab dredgers were more useful for canals since they could work close to a wall and excavate accurately. The Venetians used tongs in the sixteenth century, but the modern grab is the work of the Priestman brothers of Hull who took out their first patent in 1877. The company most associated with canal grab dredgers was Grafton & Co., of Bedford who in 1896 delivered one to the Grand Junction. This was a steam crane mounted on a pontoon, the boiler being in the hull separate from the slewing crane body. Many waterways used the Grafton (167), the Shropshire Union had them on 7' pontoons, but when working they had to be stabilized by extra pontoons on each side increasing the beam to 14' and one, the WHIXALL, lasted to nationalization days. The boat mounted diesel grab crane is satisfactory for wide waterways, but for narrow canals overhung by trees and with low bridges, several special grab units have been developed. They are hydraulic powered, using excavator buckets or grabs on arms which can reach about 15' and dig down 16'. The Grafton steam dredgers were not self propelled, depending on winch wires run out to the bank. Suction dredgers have been tried on river navigations, the Weaver's PORPOISE built in 1956 being a self-propelled example. With a rotary cutting head on the end of her suction pipe she did undertake direct dredging, but has been found more useful emptying spoil boats. There was one odd form of dredger used by the Yorkshire Ouse Navigation. This was their tug SIR JOSEPH RYMER built in 1909. Blades driven by the engine were lowered through a well and by their rotary action, cut up shoals.

Mud hoppers have had various names, spoil boats, mud boats, slutch boats in the north, and in Yorkshire, mallion boats. Often worn out trading boats were used, though various special craft have been designed for broad and narrow waterways. Mud hopper is a misleading term as few discharge through bottom doors, most being emptied by grab or suction pump with water injected to liquify the spoil. Modern hoppers are steel with a hold like an open topped tank. Those with hopper doors, opening longways, are kept shut by chains from a framework running along the line of the keel. A typical modern self-propelled hopper is the Weaver's DOLPHIN built in 1949, a diesel successor to the old round-bowed SHARK, WHALE and GRAMPUS, steamers built in the 1870s. The SHARK also worked as an icebreaker and the WHALE (29) once steamed to Belfast to work as a spoil boat. Most hoppers are dumb craft towed by a tug. Nowadays push towing of mud hoppers is standard practice on the Weaver and on the Trent.

EMBANKMENTS. To contain rivers and drain and reclaim land, embanking was practised from the earliest times. Earth for the task was won by digging alongside the river's course, called side cutting and the same technique was applied to canal earthworks. Whereas a river embankment kept the river to its course, a canal embankment was a daring advance, crossing valleys or holding the waterway to a level terraced out of a hillside, as on the Sankey Brook Navigation. A true embankment is pushed forward across open country. This was done in a minor way by the Newry Canal on flat stretches. Spoil was won either by side cutting or from excavations elsewhere. The Bridgewater was faced with a 'free standing' embankment on the approaches to the Irwell aqueduct and later to cross the Mersey near Stretford and the Bollin near Altrincham. The Bollin embankment was the work of Thomas Morris under the supervision of John Gilbert, and it seems much of the tipping was done from boats. The spoil was brought forward in a hopper carried between two boats each of which entered a wooden trough built out over the work, leaving a space between for the hopper to discharge. These caissons were apparently extended into locks to reach the lower part of the embankment. Brindley avoided earthworks if possible, although on the Trent & Mersey his brother-in-law, Hugh Henshall had to terrace out the canal between Anderton and Preston Brook, on the slopes of the Weaver valley, a method followed by the Dadfords and the Sheasbys in South Wales valleys. William Jessop carried the Grand Junction across the Ouse valley by an embankment at Wolverton, incorporating an aqueduct and similar embankments were built at Weedon and Bugbrooke. On the Ellesmere at the southern approaches to Pontcysyllte he built a 97' embankment. Rivalling this is the bank on the Royal Canal in Ireland near Leixlip which is 90' high. Other high embankments are Halberton on the Grand Western, Congleton on the Macclesfield and the straight mile at Burnley on the Leeds and Liverpool crossing the Calder valley. Over 40' high, it was completed in 1797, using spoil from the deep cutting and tunnel at Gannow to the south. Cut-and-fill was an improvement on wasteful side cutting. The extra land had to be bought and after the depredations of the workmen was of little value, degenerating into marshy hollows. Telford used cut and fill on the Birmingham & Liverpool Junction and on improvements to the main line of the Birmingham Canal Navigations, where an embankment was made at Tipton. Although planned as a direct canal demanding heavy earthworks, the Birmingham & Liverpool's greatest embankments were the result of deviations demanded by landowners at Nantwich and Norbury. The Nantwich was started in 1827 and ready by 1832 after much trouble caused by the clayey marl which slipped and spread when wet, limiting work to the summer, boats being used to bring spoil, probably from the cutting at Audlem. Last finished was Shelmore Bank, which subsided and spread because of the wet marl brought by waggon from the cuttings at Grub Street to the north and Cowley near Gnosall to the south. To gain more material, side cutting had to be undertaken and lighter sandy soil was mixed with the marl to bind it. The bank, over a mile long and 70' high was completed in 1835 (42). Where there is subsidence embanking is forced on the canal. Considerable embankments have thus grown up on the Bridgewater between Worsley and Leigh and on the Leeds & Liverpool's Leigh Branch. The canal bed is also raised to reduce the water pressure on the banks. Smeaton thought that the Grand could be cut shallow across the Irish bogs, but settling of the peat demanded embankments. Later when the canal was extended the peat was stabilised by draining and less embanking was needed. Subsidence did indeed take place, but was much reduced.

FLOOD CONTROL and DRAINAGE. Drainage involves control of flooding which could be difficult to achieve if a river was improved for navigation, as the locks and weirs raised the water level increasing the risk of flooding, hence navigations were often opposed by riparian owners. Canals with controlled water levels were not such a threat. Conflict did arise when a canal was dug for drainage and navigation, such as the Market Weighton Canal. Here the drainage interests were usually pre-eminent, the traffic suffering from the silt brought down drainage channels leading to the canal, while the Act stipulated that in the interests of drainage, locks had not to hold water back above a certain height. On the rivers, the watermills were obstacles to efficient drainage. It was in the miller's interest to have a good head for his wheel and even in flood conditions, he would demand this since the water in the tail race would be tending to rise. The great fear of riparian owners was summer flooding damaging crops. Winter floods were not so serious and might even be welcomed, the deposition of silt fertilizing the land. Generally the natural bed of a river is inadequate to contain floodwater and control means containing at least the summer floods. Several possibilities are open to the engineer, either embanking the river sides, enlarging the channel or making reservoirs to impound the floodwater, which is rarely practicable. Embanking and channel enlargement are the usual solutions, sometimes combined, as on the Trent in 1951, to protect Nottingham. Channel enlargement and improvement increases a river's capacity and improves the fall, leading to better dispersal of flood water. Shoals are removed by dredging, channels straightened and relief cuts made. The work involves bank protection and sluices for floodwater control. However, where the river has a small natural fall which cannot be increased, as in the Fens, embanking is the only practical protection. To pass water out to sea in the Fens, the ingress of the tide must be controlled so as not to back up the land water, deposit silt and cause flooding. Thus sluices have been built at the river outfalls, designed to control the tide so that its scouring action is not lost. To contain the floodwater not only are the rivers embanked, but banks are set well back from the natural channel. The lands between, the washlands, are inundated in flood conditions, and provide extra space for flood water. An additional Fens problem is subsidence due to the drainage of the peaty soil allowing it to dry and shrink, requiring pumping to keep it drained. The sluices some of which are automatic, have done much to lessen the flood risk, the idea being to manipulate the sluices so that a constant level is maintained. Today sluice keepers are in touch by telephone and keep records of the levels and operation of the sluices. In the event of a flood threat the police are informed. Administration of drainage and flood control has been under various authorities. In the old days there were local commissioners of sewers (page 24), but in 1930 the Land Drainage Act set up new Catchment Boards whose areas of control were equivalent to the catchment areas of a river or group of rivers for which each board was responsible. Each Board had powers to take over navigations and vary navigation rights. Within each Catchment Board were internal Drainage Boards financed by local land rating and government grants. The 1948 River Boards Act replaced the Catchment and Drainage Boards by River Boards with similar powers except in the case of the Thames and Lee; these Boards were also responsible for, fisheries, anti-pollution work and river gauging. The 1963 Water Resources Act replaced the Boards by River Authorities. An advisory Water Resources Board was placed over the River Authorities. On their own river navigations the British Waterways Board exercise flood control functions at sluices in co-operation with the River Authorities. Under the 1973 Water Resources Act, Regional Water Authorities were established covering England and Wales. Under these, water supply drainage and sewerage were unified, within the boundaries of the natural watersheds defining each Regional Water Authority. As they replaced bodies like the Thames Conservancy they have some navigational responsibilities.

FLOOD PADDLES. Also called ground paddles, waste gates, offlets, or let offs (79), these relieve a canal of excess water or drain a pound for repairs, usually turning the water into a stream. Early let offs were trap doors in the bed of the canal, pulled up by a chain. They were often difficult to work, becoming covered with mud and a horse was sometimes needed to shift them, while there was no discharge control. Lock type paddles which replaced them were controlled, working across a brick or stone lined culvert in the canal bed or at a waste weir. Some are sited on aqueducts, for example on the Edinburgh & Glasgow Union's Almond, while there is a plug in the middle of Pontcysyllte.

HEAD OFFICES. The early Calder & Hebble organization was so small that the part-time clerk worked from a room at the Talbot inn, Halifax. From 1761 he used his own house. Beech House at Ellesmere is a typical head office, a brick house near the canal company's maintenance yard. Overlooking the canal, the walls were rounded into a two storey turret, so that the agent could see what was going on. In those days the link between waterway and office was close. There were exceptions to this modesty. The offices of the Birmingham Canal Navigations were in a three storey octagonal building at the head of the old wharf in Paradise Street. Flanking the octagon were two wings pierced by archways for access to the quays. In such an office as this there would be a committee room, often absent in the smaller offices, the committee meeting in a local inn. Views of the Birmingham office show carved work round the jambs and lintel of the main entrance, a rococo mounted clock and a prominent cornice topping the walls. Built in 1773 it was demolished in 1913 when the company moved to Daimler House in Suffolk Street. In 1939 they moved to Sneyd near to Walsall, where they remained until nationalization. Offices of the Kennet & Avon survive in Bath (68), built over the canal in the Palladian style associated with the city. Also standing are the Shropshire Union Offices at Tower Wharf, Chester, built sometime after 1849 in a Regency style with dressed stonework. The Aire & Calder offices in Dock Street, Leeds date from 1906, now those of the Northern region of British Waterways Board. Other survivors are Canal House at Oxford and the Grand Canal offices at James Street Harbour, Dublin. Modern centralization, beginning with the railway owned canals has removed administration from the waterside, to London. The Grand Junction had its head office in the Strand and the Regent's was in the City. The nationalized authorities have had various London addresses. In 1823 the Ouse Navigation Trustees were more ambitious, building a banqueting house at Naburn lock below York in Regency style with elaborate decorative work on the main entrance.

HOTELS, PUBLIC HOUSES and STABLES. Today many have been redecorated or built to cater for the modern pleasure cruiser. However riverside hostelries date back to at least the Middle Ages, to refresh travellers waiting for ferries and crossing fords. When river horse towing paths were built, pubs were sited where they changed sides by ferry, as on the Severn at Ashleworth above Gloucester where the 'Boat' inn stands. At river wharves there were inns with stable accommodation for barge horses, important on trips that lasted many days. Before the introduction of permanent cabins on narrow boats in the 1790s, boatmen slept at canal side inns. Public houses were built for the canal, often by the company as on the Erewash, or on company land, sometimes in villages, sometimes isolated, while at town wharves several would compete. Some were beer houses licenced for beer only. All had stables, like the 'Broken Cross' near Lostock, Northwich on the Trent & Mersey, and the pubs on the long pounds of the Shropshire Union. For the long distance boatman the pubs were his relaxation. They were recognized tying up points where, once the horses had been led off to the stables, families could meet, the women sitting apart from the men. Some pubs had special functions, at Stoke Bruerne and Braunston they refreshed the professional tunnel legger, while some were built on the tunnel top paths to cater for the horsemen. Motor boats, making longer daily trips needed the pubs much less and as the canals declined and were abandoned, the pubs went too, some becoming farmhouses. The Llandoger Trow at Bristol recalls the craft trading down the Wye from Llandogo, while there are several 'Boats', an 'Old Boat and Horse' at Newcastle-under-Lyme.'Locks','Wharves' and 'Navigations' are frequent, but the 'Big Lock' at Middlewich is in honour of the special barge lock at the bottom of the Middlewich flight on the Trent & Mersey and the 'Old Packet Boat' at Broadheath near Altrincham recalls the Bridgewater passenger traffic. Canal pubs could be exchange points for the horses of fly boats and passenger packets. Hotels were built in both Scotland and Ireland to serve the more intense passenger services, a notable Scottish one being at Port Downie at Lock 16 on the Forth & Clyde near Falkirk. The Grand Canal provided a chain of hotels on its route across Ireland from Dublin to the Shannon, as at Roberts-town (66), but they failed because of the increased speed of fly boats introduced in the 1800s running without overnight stops, and to timetables which allowed direct connections with road coaches. There were others on the Barrow line and on the Royal Canal.

Stables: Horses were stabled each night and even for two or three hour waits. Every inn had stables so they were the usual stopping places. At public wharves, stables were provid-ed by the canal company, while the larger carrying companies had stables where their boats traded frequently. Fellows, Morton & Clayton used to have stables and ostlers at Preston Brook, while the Anderton and the Mersey, Weaver companies had stables sited at their main wharves at Middleport and Longport. As near monopolists of carrying on their own system, the Shropshire Union built stables from Ellesmere Port to Autherley. The Lancaster built stables for the passenger boat horses at eleven points between Preston and Kendal.   The hovels described by H.R. Robertson in his "Life on the Upper Thames" of 1875 were open shelters for the overnight stabling of the barge horses working on the river, with a flat roof of turf or straw on a wooden frame. Ordinarily stables were of weatherboard, brick or stone and with stalls rather than loose boxes closed by halved stable doors and ventilators on the roof (55). Often they might be part of a warehouse or wharf shed as at Burscough on the Leeds & Liverpool, or have a loft above for fodder. Some were large, particularly on the Birmingham system, like that of the Great Western Railway at Hockley with two floors. Canal company stables were under the care of an ostler or horsekeeper, the Shropshire Union hav-ing a day and a night man to handle the changes of horses for the fly-boats. Other carriers could put up their horses at company stables, paying say 6d a night or 2d for a short wait. Inns charged similar prices. The boatman could also buy feed at the stables. Stables were also built for contractors' horses when a canal was being built, such as those now demolish-ed at the Tunnel House by Sapperton tunnel on the Thames & Severn.

ICE - BREAKERS and ICE BREAKING. It is not just that a canal freezes over, but ice jams paddle gear and lock gates as well as between boats and the chamber sides. Aqueducts have to be emptied for fear of bursting. In the locks the ice was broken with a pounder, a stave with a wooden head shod with iron, or with an iron bound flail called a 'hockey stick'. On narrow canals, the ice breaking boat (12), was a slender 30' to 35' craft. Both ends were a similar shape and the cross section rounded, so that the boat would roll easily. If of wood, the hull was sheathed with overlapping iron plates. Pulled by as many horses as available, up to 24, the well raked stem rode up on the ice and cracked it. To create a wide channel, the ice-breaker was rocked by men standing each side of a platform and grip-ping a central rail, each side heaving in turn to rock the boat which was easily done, due to the rounded cross section. Several ice-breakers of this type survive, one is the old BCN ice-breaker NORTH STAR, built about 1910 and kept in the Black Country Museum. She has a rope to hang on to, tensioned by a screw, instead of a bar. There were other designs of horse or even man drawn ice-breakers. Iron was used very early, on the Ashby in 1808, on the Rochdale in 1811. Leeds & Liverpool ice-breakers were some 48'x 6' with a squared bow and stern, but rounded sides and two thicknesses of planking. Powered ice-breakers did not immediately replace horse drawn boats as thick ice could damage propellors. One of the iron steam tugs was used on the Bridgewater and the Leeds & Liverpool used the Foulridge tunnel tug for this work latterly, as well as fitting their own steam tugs with ice-breaking ploughs.   The motor AUTHERLEY kept at Norbury for the Shropshire Union was built like a horse ice-breaker except that she had a counter stern and was rocked like a horse drawn boat. Larger waterways used specially strengthened tugs. The steamer CONWAY (87) built in 1894 by Napier, Shanks & Bell was an example built for the Crinan. A spoon-bowed steel vessel measuring 63'x 18'x 8'7", she was kept at Ardrishaig solely for ice-breaking until scrapped in 1964. Still in service is the Caledonian's tug SCOT II, built for towing and ice breaking in 1931 and converted to diesel in 1961. There have been canal freeze-ups with ice a foot thick. Severe winters have been 1895, 1920, 1939-40, 1946-7, 1954, and 1962-3. The last stopped all traffic on the Grand Union for sixteen weeks. In these conditions even ice-breakers have been unable to move, for they could not break ice more than about 4" thick and because of packing of floes, ice could attain several feet in thickness.

12. Ice-breaker at work, men rock
   the boat to widen the channel.

Plate 3.

Steam Packet WEAVER BELLE

DIMENSIONS: 90'10" x 21'7" x 9'6".

Tonnage 156 gross.

THIS composite steamer (steel frames, wood planking) was built in 1900 by W. J. Yarwood & Sons Ltd., of Northwich for Henry Seddon & Sons Ltd., of Middlewich. She carried up to 200 tons of salt down the Weaver to Liverpool for export as well as towing a flat of 250 tons capacity.

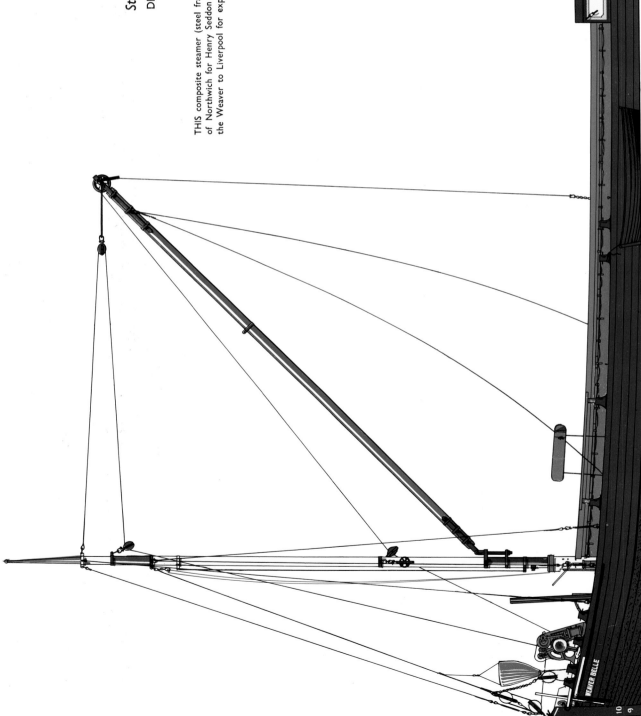

C. V. Waine 1977

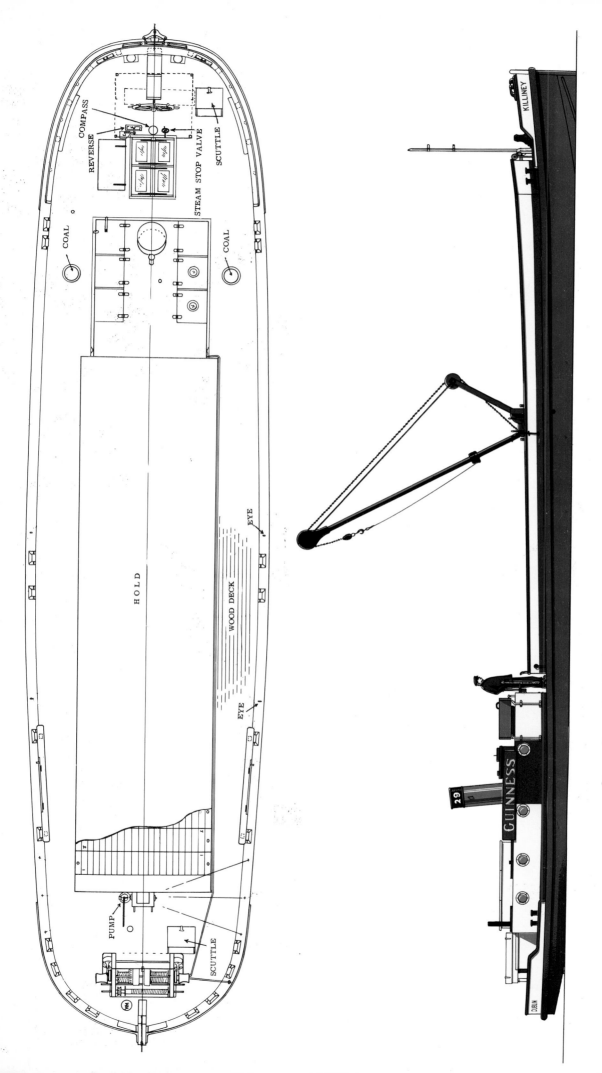

COMPASS

REVERSE

COAL

COAL

STEAM STOP VALVE

SCUTTLE

HOLD

WOOD DECK

EYE

EYE

PUMP

SCUTTLE

KILLINEY

GUINNESS

29

DUBLIN

Steam Barge KILLINEY
DIMENSIONS: 80'0" x 17'0" x 7'0".

Arthur Guinness, Son & Co., Ltd., had their own steam barges working on the River Liffey between their St. James's Gate Brewery and Dublin docks. Both funnel and crane were lowered to pass under bridges. Cargo capacity was about 90 tons. The last barge was sold in 1961.

INCLINED PLANES. Inclines have been employed to overcome severe changes in level, where water has been scarce, and locks too expensive or slow. The Greeks of the 6th century B.C. used rollers to move warships across the isthmus of Corinth and China had capstan worked inclined planes on her waterways, as early perhaps, as the first or second century A.D. In Flanders there was a waterwheel powered inclined plane at Watten which worked from the twelfth to the seventeenth centuries.

In the British Isles planes developed along differing lines as canals were built. Simplest of all were the chutes of John Edyvean on his St. Columb Canal of 1777, to send stone down to the beaches of St. Columb Porth and Mawgan Porth, containers of coal or sea sand being hauled up by a horse driven winding drum. John Edyvean also submitted proposals for a canal across the peninsula from Bude to Calstock using inclined planes with trucks, the cargo having to be transhipped at each plane. This sort became a tramroad connecting two water levels. The Coalbrookdale branch of the Shropshire Canal had a plane from 1794 from Brierly Hill down to Coalbrookdale, replacing two vertical shafts between canal and tramroad. About four years earlier the Donnington Wood Canal had replaced its twin vertical shaft link between its main line and branch at Hugh's Bridge by an inclined plane, with containers of coal and limestone carried up and down in trucks, later possibly using boats. Both planes were evidently double track with the trucks counterbalanced. A 237' plane was completed on the Tavistock Canal down to the Tamar at Morwellham Quay in 1817. Here copper ore was tipped from the tub-boats into trucks, the descending laden trucks helping to pull up the empties on the double track plane, although the main power came from a waterwheel.

First of the boat carrying planes in the British Isles were the three on the Tyrone Navigation in Ulster finally completed in 1777 by Davies Ducart for 10' x 4'6" boats. They were at first to run up and down on rollers laid across the timber ramps and Ducart proposed to use waterwheel power. He could not get sufficient energy and in 1773 Smeaton recommended a double line of ramps and rollers, allowing the laden coal boats descending to Coalisland to pull up the empties. Later the ramps were fitted with rails for the boats to be carried 'dry' on cradles. Locally called 'hurrys', a word also found in Cumberland meaning an incline or tip, these planes were tried intermittently until 1787. In 1788 came the first English boat plane on the Ketley Canal in Shropshire, designed and built by William Reynolds. It depended for operation on the laden boats pulling up the empties on a double tracked iron railway, the boats being carried 'dry' in cradles. Locks for each track were built at the top. The Ketley plane was only used until about 1816, but it inspired others on the mineral carrying Shropshire Canal. There were three, up from the junction with the Donnington Wood Canal at Wrockwardine Wood, down from the summit at Windmill Farm, and down again to the banks of the Severn at The Hay (now restored). All were double track with iron rails and the 5 ton tub-boats were carried dry, the cradles descending by reverse slopes into the top pound of the canal. At Windmill Farm and The Hay most of the laden traffic was descending, so horses and later the steam beam engines were normally required only to pull the cradles over the top sills and up the reverse slopes. At Wrockwardine Wood the laden traffic was uphill, so steam power was needed for the whole operation. These three planes were an improvement on Ketley because no lockage water was used, and as at Ketley the cradles were kept horizontal by means of carrying wheels of different diameters. Their level was ingeniously maintained over the sills and down the reverse slopes by use of an extra pair of wheels on the rear axle, which ran on specially sloped rails fastened to the walls of the chambers containing the reverse slopes. Very similar was the Trench plane built by the Shrewsbury Canal, completed in 1787 and working until 1921, the last in the country (36). These planes could handle a heavy traffic, six boats up and six down an hour was possible, while The Hay passed 100 boats a day at times. Latterly chain cables were used, replacing ropes, but both were prone to breakage with spectacular results. The underground inclined plane at Worsley in the Duke of Bridgewater's colliery was handling heavy traffic also for a time. This, ready for operation in 1797, joined the upper level with the main and worked entirely by counterbalancing, since the descending boats were always laden. As at Ketley there were locks at the top, to control the settling and floating of the boats on and off their cradles. Thirty laden boats could be passed in eight hours.

Heavy short distance traffic made successful the boat planes of Shropshire and the underground plane at Worsley, mainly in one direction. Moreover they could be repaired in an industrialised area. This was not so in hilly Devon and Cornwall where planes were the solution for the small agricultural canals. Here traffic was sparse and irregular, so counterbalancing of boats in dry cradles was not possible, and some form of direct haulage had to be employed. The chutes of John Edyvean were replaced by the considered proposals of Edmund Leach for the Bude Canal in 1785 where boats were to be carried on water filled counterbalanced caissons, and by the inventive work of Lord Stanhope, who strongly supported this canal. No work was done until 1819 when, under the engineer James Green, six double track railway planes were built all dependent on water power, five driven by water wheels, the sixth, and longest of any built in the British Isles, at Hobbacott Down, with a vertical rise of 225', operated by a bucket full of water heavier than the boat, descending a well. When the bucket reached the bottom an arm in the well tripped a valve which emptied the water. There were two buckets, the full descending one drawing up the empty one, ready to be filled for the next lift, with a steam engine in reserve. The water wheels drove an endless cable, passing round large diameter pulleys at top and bottom. Both ascending and descending boats could be attached to any part of the cable and the water wheel started. On the Bude the 4 ton capacity tub-boats were fitted with wheels which were guided on to the channel section rails at top and bottom by beams. Breakages of chains and gearing were frequent. The Bude planes were copied for Weare Giffard on the Torrington Canal opened in 1827, which was water wheel powered, the tub-boats probably being wheeled. In 1838 James Green completed the Taunton extension of the Grand Western as a tub-boat canal, with seven lifts and one inclined plane at Wellisford, working, like Hobbacott Down, although the boats were floating in a caisson. Again there was trouble with the buckets, this time they were too small, so a steam engine was built as a replacement. Green's influence was carried to the Chard Canal completed in 1842, where there were three counterbalanced double track inclined planes, probably water wheel assisted, employing caissons in which the tub-boats could be floated. The fourth Chard plane powered by a water turbine was only single track, the boats being carried dry.

James Green's influence extended to South Wales, where he designed three planes for the Kidwelly & Llanelly Canal for 6 ton tub-boats. Only two worked, at Pont Henry and Capel Ifan, between 1838 and 1867. These planes were counterbalancing, descending laden boats providing the power. Very different was that built in 1857 at Blackhill in Glasgow on the Monkland Canal, to relieve heavy coal traffic down two parallel lines of locks. This plane was 1040' long with a vertical rise of 96'. There were two caissons each 70' x 13' 4" x 2' 9" deep capable of floating a mineral scow (13), powered by a 25 hp steam engine.

CAISSON ON MONKLAND CANAL INCLINE.

ELEVATION.

END VIEW.
(Reduced.)

13. Blackhill inclined plane on the Monkland Canal from L.F. Vernon-Harcourt's 'Rivers and Canals', 1882 Edition. The caissons were carried on a 7' railway.

This plane was only used during the summer when water was scarce, for returning empty boats, hence the shallow caissons. It was discontinued in 1887 because the local mines were worked out. Passage took ten minutes.

On the same scale was the Foxton plane completed in 1900, to improve the Leicester line of the Grand Junction. The locks at Foxton and Watford were to be replaced by inclined planes to take wide boats, but only the Foxton plane with a vertical rise of 75'2" was built. As an experiment in 1896 the Grand Junction built a miniature incline at their Bulbourne works, the prelude to the large concrete ramp at Foxton laid with 16 rails, eight for each 80' x 15' wide caisson, capable of floating two narrow boats or a wide boat, which travelled laterally. Both caissons and the upper canal arms at Foxton were sealed by hydraulically operated guillotine gates. Movement was provided by a steam engine of low horse power. Each caisson had a pair of 7" steel wire hauling ropes passing round two large diameter drums in the engine house, while they were further connected by balance and tail ropes. Unfortunately the traffic did not materialise and in 1910 locks were reinstated for all traffic.

LIFTS or BALANCE LOCKS. Associated with inclined planes are lifts, designed to save water and the expense of locks, but less demanding in space. Lifts are faced with more constructional and mechanical problems and are descended from the vertical hoists used on the early canals. On the East Shropshire system hoists were installed at Hugh's Bridge on Lord Gower's Donnington Wood Canal in about 1770. Here a branch canal from limestone quarries ended below the main canal in a tunnel, communication being by two vertical shafts. In 1792 a similar arrangement was put to work at the end of the Coalbrookdale branch of the Shropshire Canal at Brierly Hill, communicating with a tramroad.

First in the British Isles were the experiments of Robert Weldon of Lichfield who made a model lift for demonstration purposes at Oakengates, Shropshire, in 1794. The model was the result of Weldon's approach to the Somersetshire Coal Canal Co., who asked him to proceed with the construction of the real thing, called a hydrostatic or caisson lock, at Combe Hay to lift narrow boats 46'. Work started in 1796. A single totally enclosed wooden caisson, big enough to take a narrow boat, was totally submerged in a water filled brick chamber, yet like a diving bell it retained sufficient buoyancy to be moved up and down in the chamber by hand operated rack and pinion gear. Water pressure held the caisson against the tunnel doors at the top and bottom levels of the canal. The lift worked experimentally, but was hampered by the walls of the chamber which bulged and presumably jammed the caisson. More realistic were the 1796 experiments, probably at Ruabon, on the proposed Ellesmere Canal from the Mersey via Chester to Shrewsbury, by Edward Rowland and Exuperius Pickering. Here the Weldon principle was followed by using a float immersed in a column of water. The float supported the caisson in which a boat could be carried in the normal manner, the float retaining enough buoyancy to be moved up and down by rack and pinion gear. Only a 12' lift was achieved, but because the canal was not completed, the work was stopped.

In 1794 Dr. James Anderson of Edinburgh had published a description of a lift or balance lock employing two counterbalanced water filled caissons, rising and falling in adjacent chambers and interconnected by cables passing over large diameter pulleys, spanning two chambers centre to centre. Complete balance was achieved by hanging chains underneath each caisson equal to the weight of the suspending cables. Movement could be effected by manual power at a windlass and the rate of descent controlled by a brake wheel. Experiments were undertaken by James Fussell at Barrow Hill on the Nettlebridge colliery line of the proposed Dorset & Somerset Canal between 1800 and 1802. Fussell carried 10 ton capacity tub-boats afloat in tanks under which were the balanced water filled caissons, guided in their chambers by rollers. The lift was 21' and a double purchase was employed for the suspension cables, with pulleys attached to the cradle and caisson framework. For narrow boats a lift was tried in 1808 at Tardebigge on the Worcester & Birmingham Canal on the site of the present top lock of the flight, hence its depth. Invented by John Woodhouse it had a 12' rise and was roofed over, the chamber containing only one water filled caisson balanced by counterweights of bricks, the balance being overcome by two men working a windlass. Entry to the caisson was by guillotine gates, both in the chamber and caisson. On trials the lift worked very well, passing 110 boats in twelve hours, but was regarded as not sufficiently robust for canal work over a long period. Embodying the counterbalancing principle, but assisted by hydro-pneumatic power, was the experimental 6' 8" lift built to the designs of Sir William Congreve of rocket fame by Maudslay's of Lambeth, at Camden Town on the Regent's Canal in 1815. First of British lifts to work regularly were those designed by James Green for the Grand Western's tub-boat extension to Taunton, completed in 1838. There were seven, of varying heights. Movement of the two counterbalanced water filled caissons was achieved by adding two inches of water to the descending one, with a controlling brake, and manual assistance if required. Until 1867 these lifts passed a steady traffic of 8 ton tub-boats, so they must have been fairly satisfactory. Successful and working is that at Anderton near Northwich, completed in 1875 to link the Weaver and Trent & Mersey Canal 50' above. By this time technology was equal to invention and an hydraulic lift was designed to float a pair of narrow boats or a single barge in each caisson. Edwin Clark proposed a counterbalancing lift with the two caissons supported by hydraulic rams (34), the descending one forcing up its fellow, since the hydraulic cylinders were interconnected at their ends. Movement was achieved by adding 6" of water to the descending caisson. The hydraulic cylinders were sunk in 50' deep shafts at the lift bottom called the camber which was open to the river, acting as an effective buffer. Additional hydraulic power was needed to complete the lift of the ascending caisson, because once the descending caisson had reached the water in the camber it lost its weight preponderance; this was provided by an accumulator fed by a 10 h.p. steam pump. At the top, the ascending caisson had to have its water level made up 6" via a sluice from the aqueduct leading on to the lift, while the descending caisson had to lose 6" through syphons so that the cycle of operations could begin again.

In 1882 one of the cylinders burst and the lift was out of action for nearly six months while both cylinders were renewed with thicker walls. Later, in about 1905 it was found that both rams and cylinders were going to need renewal because of corrosion and grooving, caused by the acids in the river water from the Northwich chemical works. Rather than have the lift out of action for another long spell, the Weaver Navigation decided on conversion to electricity. Already in 1903 electricity had replaced steam to power the accumulator and the guillotine gates were then fitted with electric winches (14). Conversion of the whole operation of the lift to electric power started in 1906 and was complete in 1908. The caissons were now to work independently, balanced by 250 ton counterweights, so that an electric motor of only 30 h.p. was required for each caisson. Over the existing structure they built a gantry for the 6' diameter pulleys, one end of each suspension cable being attached to the caisson via a pulley and the other to a weight. Drive from the motors to the pulleys is by 1800 to 1 reduction gearing.

FLASH LOCKS, WATERGATES and STAUNCHES. On the early river navigations passage of weirs was achieved by the flash lock and staunch, known to the Chinese and used on their waterways, in the last half century B.C. In Europe it was probably in use before the eleventh century, and was employed at both mill weirs, and at weirs built to improve water depth for navigation. The Chinese had used a series of horizontal planks one above the other like stop planks followed by the vertically rising gate, the stop planks, linked together, which in England became the vertically rising staunch used on some East Anglian rivers. It was known in Holland in 1056 and Flanders in 1116. Of a different origin is the horizontally swinging water gate known and used in England in the seventeenth century, an improvement on the old paddle and rimer flash lock, used on the Thames since the thirteenth century and only completely replaced in the twentieth. In the British Isles flash locks and staunches

14. A bottom gate of the electric lift at Anderton, showing the inclined face which makes a watertight seal with the tank.

were found on the Thames and its tributaries the Wey and the Lee (where the vertical staunches were called turnpikes), and the tributaries of the Severn, the Worcestershire Stour and the Warwickshire Avon, on the Wye and its tributary the Lugg. There were examples in Somerset on the Parrett and the Tone, on the navigable rivers of the South Coast from the Itchen round to the Kentish Stour, also the Medway and the Suffolk Stour, on the rivers of the Fens and on the Soar in Leicestershire and the Derbyshire Derwent. There were a few in Ireland, for example on the Nore. Navigation a 'rymer' lock was reported in 1759, and there were half locks on the Shannon noted by the engineer Richard Evans in 1783.

Paddle and Rimer Type: apart from the plank staunch, like the stop planks on a canal, used on the River Lark, the most primitive design of flash lock was the Thames flash weir, navigation weir or simple weir, also found on the Suffolk Stour fitted with paddles and rimers. Some were built at mill weirs, others for navigation only. Most of the structure was of timber but the shore abutments were often stone or brick. A wooden sill, generally elm, was laid across the river bed with a second beam above and parallel. This had to be above water level for it was used as a footbridge for working the lock and part or sometimes all could be swung for the passage of boats. The upper beam was pierced to take the rimers, or vertical guide timbers, which dropped against the sill. These rimers had rebated sides which allowed up to 21 paddles, acting as sluice doors, to be inserted between them. Attached to the paddles were handles for dropping them into position and lifting them clear. Water pressure held the paddles into their rebates, while the handles rested against a guide bar above the upper beam. To open the weir for a boat the rimers and paddles had to be removed from the movable part of the upper beam and this swung aside, unless the boat was small enough to pass underneath. On the fixed part paddles could be lifted to release water to increase the depth below the weir. There was no flexibility of control; the paddles were either in or out, the only variation being in the higher weirs say 4' or over where a second set of paddles, called the overfall, was inserted above the others. The flash would generally last for an hour or so, the downstream traffic descending first, helped over the shallows below by the flood of water, while the upstream, also lifted over the shallows, had to wait until the upper and lower reaches were approximately level before they were warped through the gap. Once craft were above the weir it was closed to enable the level to build up again for further progress upstream, the whole performance being repeated at the next weir.

Watergates and Staunches: It was a short step to make the movable beam into a single gate or pair of gates mitred together, with the paddles and rimers incorporated into the gate framework, the bottom of the gate bedding against the sill. They were employed on the Warwickshire Avon, the Tone and Parrett, the Itchen, the Lugg, the Great Ouse and its tributaries and on the Suffolk Stour. They were called watergates in the West Midlands and half locks in the West Country since they were half of a pound lock. They could also be called navigation gates or navigation weirs, the latter confusing them with the paddle and rimer type, while in East Anglia they were stanches or staunches, with either horizontal swinging or vertically rising gates or rather doors in the Fens. Their mode of operation differed from the flash lock proper and the reasons for the choice of a watergate, half lock or staunch when the pound lock was known were particular. Watergates did not upset the operation of mills, and it was because of this that two lasted so long on the Lower Warwickshire Avon, Pensham near Pershore until 1956 and Cropthorne until 1961. Moreover they were cheaper than pound locks, hence their construction on the Little Ouse and the Lark in the nineteenth century. They were not normally built by mill weirs because the gates were left open unless a boat was coming. A pound lock was chosen for a mill weir because of its economy of water when the paddle and rimer flash lock came to be replaced, but between mills watergates were installed at the weirs built for navigation. A pound lock would have the effect between mills of restricting the flow and backing up the water. An open watergate could do no harm. Operation of a watergate or staunch was slow, more tedious than a paddle and rimer flash lock. The river between staunches or between staunch and pound lock became in effect a very large pound lock chamber. Since horizontally swinging staunch gates could not be opened or 'drawn' against any head of water, boats had to wait until a level was made above and below the weir, and this was only possible if the staunch below the one being navigated was also closed or 'set', permitting the water to back up and the level rise, filled from upstream. Weir falls were small, between 2' and 4' only, but navigation took time because the reaches between staunches and locks were often long, particularly in East Anglia, up to 3 miles on the Nene. Design varied, on the Warwickshire Avon the gates were single but elsewhere they were mitred, meeting at an angle of about 90 degrees, more acute than the mitring of canal lock gates, making them easier to open. On the Tone balance beams alone were used, but elsewhere chains alone or chains and windlasses were employed. On the Lark, Ivel and Suffolk Stour the chains were secured from the mitre posts of the gates to the side walls, but generally a windlass was needed to overcome the pressure created by the current even if the levels were equal. Most gates were hung like lock gates in a hollow quoin, but on the Lark, Ivel and Suffolk Stour pintles were used like a field gate, facing upstream, so that the gates closed against their posts and kept watertight. Most gates had paddle gear.

Gates were set in chambers of varying length which had recesses as in pound lock chambers. The chambers could be either wood, brick or stone with their floors generally planked on a framework of timber. They were usually parallel sided, except on the narrow Lark where concave bays were made at each side for additional strength. Gates mounted on pintle hinges were prevented from falling inwards, being unbalanced, by a stride, a Thames word, or horizontal beam above the gates carried on extensions of the gateposts. These were found on the Lark, Ivel and Suffolk Stour and were in East Anglia called galley beams or lintels, being about 8' above the water so that boats were not impeded. Beyond the gates were the weirs, their length often broken by artificial islands. The weirs were made up of fixed sills and sluices, called cloughs (pronounced clows in East Anglia). These were vertically rising and held up by handles pierced for retaining pegs or wound up on a chain by a small barrel windlass. Some small narrow river navigations like the Dick Brook joining the Severn below Stourport and the Lark had no weirs. Here the gates acted as weirs, with their paddles as sluices. In East Anglia, Low Countries ideas influenced the pattern of some gates which were vertically rising like a guillotine. These were found on the Lee, Nene, Little Ouse, Nar and Bottisham Lode, a tributary of the Cam near Waterbeach. One on the last named survived in very rotten condition until demolition in 1969. Vertical gates had the advantage of easy drawing against the water pressure. They were raised and lowered by chains round a barrel geared down from a second spindle underneath, which carried a large spoked wheel of about 13' diameter. Plenty of leverage could be obtained by standing on the spokes and walking the wheel. It was reached from the ground by a ladder and platform which also served to cross the lock. The framework for the gearing cleared the top of the staunch chamber at Bottisham by some 8' allowing room for a boat to pass under the lifted gate. It would also act as a stride across the chamber to provide lateral strength. The big spoked wheel was held by a chain and hook round one of the spokes when the gate was up. The vertically rising staunches on the Nene were in many cases rebuilt in the early twentieth century with steel frames and steel gates, but all have now gone, although the Nene authorities use steel guillotine gates at many of their pound locks.

FLIGHTS of LOCKS. The earliest of any size was at Runcorn to bring the Duke's Canal down to the Mersey, the ten locks grouped in five staircase pairs with widened pounds between each staircase, both to allow boats to pass and to act as reservoirs, assisted by special reservoirs built adjacent to the flight. The later Runcorn flight of 10 was of single locks, with the intermediate pounds extended sideways into storage reservoirs. Towards the end of the canal age large lock flights were common. Two canals over the Pennines, the Rochdale and the Huddersfield were composed of flights from start to finish. Other Yorkshire concentrations were the 14 on the $1\frac{3}{4}$ miles of the Calder & Hebble's Halifax branch, 12 in a mile at Walton on the Barnsley Canal, and the 12 at Tinsley on the Sheffield and South Yorkshire Navigation, all within 1 mile $1\frac{1}{2}$ furlongs. The South Wales valleys were formidable barriers. On the Monmouthshire there were 42 locks on the 11 mile main line and 32 on the 11 mile Crumlin branch. For visual impressiveness there is nothing to beat the 29 locks straight up the side of Caen Hill, Devizes on the Kennet & Avon, while Tardebigge with 30 locks is reckoned to be the greatest narrow lock flight in the British Isles.

FLOOD LOCKS and FLOOD GATES. A flood lock or flood gate is put at the head of a river's navigable cut (37) to protect it from flood water. This cut would have an ordinary lock at its tail to overcome the change of level and in normal conditions the flood lock would be left open. At flood time however the flood lock or gates could be closed, so turning the swollen waters over the weir. Flood gates prevented the passage of boats when they were closed but a flood lock allowed navigation. Flood gates on a canal could be called confusingly stop gates (page 60) for example on the Grantham in 1841 when a pair were built at the junction with the Trent to protect the canal should the river rise above canal level. Flood gates and flood locks were most prevalent on the Calder & Hebble Navigation. The Calder is a river with a considerable fall, and liable to severe flooding. The cuts are protected by four flood locks and four pairs of flood gates, the locks with their top gate tops at a higher level than the lower. Flood locks and gates are usually designed like ordinary mitred locks. Exceptions are the locks on East Anglia waterways which serve a dual purpose, to overcome a change of level and to control flood water. A lock or sluice, which is what the fenmen call it, is normally closed and only opened to pass flood water, when it would cease to be used for navigation. Because of this function many nowadays have one set of their gates of guillotine pattern, which can be operated against a head of water and need no paddle gear. Generally these are the lower gates, the upper being horizontal mitred gates or pointing doors as they are locally named. Rules for the operation of such locks are strict because of their flood control functions. For example the paddles may be left open for regulating the flow of water, while if the pointing doors are chained open and the guillotine gate at the tail of the lock partially lifted, then flood conditions exist and the locks should not be used for navigation. (see entry for locks, regulating locks and locks, river locks, page 56).

LOCKS; OPERATION. Boatmen worked many locks themselves, and ingenuity achieved faster passages. Working uphill, a boat which fitted a lock closely could be checked and stopped by drawing a paddle at the head. A small boat had to be checked with a strap to the bank, for her water resistance was not so effective. Once in, the boat had to be kept well up to the bumping piece on the breast wall, because the drawing of top paddles creates a surge of water which curls back on itself and drives a boat forward out of control. Motor boats are put slow ahead, while horse boats were kept up either by a line secured to a post or to a cleat on the upper gate beam, or by the horse, also ensuring the helm was clear of the bottom gates. The latter was put hard over and the tiller removed. Keels used short cranked iron canal tillers which would not strike the lock walls. Once in the lock it was necessary to draw paddles carefully to avoid swamping a laden boat. Ground paddles allow the water to enter from below but gate paddles create a cascade over the top sill. They are generally drawn when their openings are covered otherwise the foredeck and cargo might suffer. Working downhill, it was vital to check the way of a boat entering a full lock otherwise it might damage the lower gates or burst them outwards. Powered craft put their engines astern but horse drawn must resort to strapping (15); special posts, pins or hooks were provided at the head of the lock and at the tail, for a boat entering an empty lock. In 1808 on the Chester Canal they were called snubbing posts. On many narrow canals they were on top of the breast post of the top gate. Posts were also provided along the lock side and by using them the horse towline could be used as a strap, taking several turns round as the horse stopped and the line fell slack. Laden boats might have to be persuaded to enter a full lock by drawing one or two of the bottom paddles so creating a current. This was regular practice on the Trent & Mersey's Cheshire locks for the Runcorn bound fly-boats laden with crated ware. Here it was combined with strapping to the top gate so that the water level was falling as the boat entered. So expert were the four men crews that the fly-boats would drop through the locks at a smart walking pace. Before descending the boat must be kept well up to the lower gates, otherwise there is danger of the stern sitting on the top sill which projects some two feet into the lock. Boats caught on the sill have broken their backs as the level fell. Moving a laden narrow boat out of a lock was heavy work for the horse because of water resistance, particularly in an empty lock where the cross sectional area of water was small. The horse could be helped downhill by a flush of water from above or by 'blocking' up or downhill, using the towline to create a two to one purchase (108). The line passed from the horse through a pulley block on the mast to a pin or projection at the lock head or tail. In this way the purchase was achieved but was converted to a direct pull when a toggle or block peg spliced into the line some 10' from the end, came up against the pulley block. The last 10' called the tack string now fell slack and slipped off the pin. On the Leeds & Liverpool this was called a block line and used for uphill work. Working pairs of narrow boats through narrow locks led to further ingenuity when aided by an engine. Ordinarily it was usual to let the motor go ahead and bow haul the butty up and down.

15. 'Strapping' downhill: Water resistance to the gate checks the boat's speed which in turn closes the gate.

On the Trent & Mersey's Cheshire locks some boatmen stabled ponies between Middlewich and Wheelock to work the butties; but the evenly spaced locks on the Shropshire Union flights at Audlem, Adderley and Tyrley leant themselves to 'lock lining' whereby motor and butty rose together in separate locks, the motor pulling the butty into and out of each successive one. A 150 yd. cotton line, five ordinary lines spliced together, was used but it was usual for uphill only (41).   Downhill working was speeded up by the motor steerer closing the bottom gates of the lock by a shaft as he left, so that it could be quickly re-filled for the butty. On the Grand Junction and new Grand Union a pair could enter each lock side by side. Empty boats travelled breasted up where the locks were frequent and up big flights like Hatton loaded boats might be breasted up. Otherwise loaded boats travelled with the motor towing the butty on a 20' snatcher; approaching a lock either up or down hill the motor slowed down, allowing the butty to close up. The motor steerer cast off the snatcher from his counter and laid it along the butty's cloths. Both entered the lock together and on leaving, the motor went ahead taking up the snatcher and making fast, pulling the butty into line behind him, so that the pair left by one gate. In an empty lock the motor, working downhill, could go astern and pull open one of the lower gates by a line from the mast passed round the handrail stanchion above the breast beams.   Only a round turn was used which freed as the boat moved ahead past the gate. A top gate could be pushed open by a motor's stem. On the Leeds & Liverpool where motor boats were often single manned and the locks deep it was common to attach a light line to the ahead and astern gear so that a boat could be moved out of an empty lock by a pull on the line from the lock side, the steerer stepping aboard at the tail. On larger waterways like the Weaver, the Trent, the Aire & Calder and the Caledonian Canal, initiative is in the hands of lock keepers. With the adoption of hydraulic power the work is done from a control cabinet, often in a building like a signal box. Traffic lights are mounted on gantries, as on the Aire & Calder (16), to warn craft of the state of the lock. Powered locks need fewer keepers and are speedier. Staff on the Caledonian have been reduced from eight men to two on shift work at Fort Augustus, moving from cabinet to cabinet up the staircase instead of sweating at cap-stan bars. Under hydraulic power, the paddles can be held at any position and used to draw in laden craft. On the Manchester Ship Canal the tugs handle ships while locks on the Lee below Enfield have powered capstans to warp lighters through.

PAIRED or PARALLEL LOCKS. To speed traffic and save water some canals duplicated their locks, occasionally they were called collateral locks (an Oxford Canal term of 1790) providing interconnecting or centre paddles between the two. Not only could boats pass rapidly, but about half the water from a full lock could be turned into its empty fellow for further use. Boatmen had other ideas for speeding their journey, particularly on the Cheshire locks of the Trent & Mersey, (102) which were duplicated between Kidsgrove and Wheelock during the early 1830s. They could empty a lock much faster if they used not only its bottom gate paddles, but the centre paddles, of which there were two, and the bottom gate paddles of the other lock. Duplicate locks were an advantage when boats were paired, and when repairs were made. The Monkland Canal duplicated their Blackhill flight of eight in four staircase pairs in 1841 for the heavy coal traffic, but they were not inter-connected, nor were the two flights of ten at Runcorn on the Bridgewater Canal. River locks are often paired for different sizes of craft, as on the Weaver and Aire & Calder. Vessels use the smallest necessary, the larger locks often having an intermediate set of gates to effect a similar economy.

POUND LOCKS. Historical: River navigations did not need locks as long as they re-mained unhindered by weirs, but once these were built for mills, and to provide depth for navigation, then a lock was wanted. Paddle and rimer flash locks, watergates and staunches were answers to this problem, but they were slow to operate, wasteful of water, and in the case of paddle and rimer flash locks dangerous to navigate. Pound locks solved all these problems; use of water was limited to the capacity of the lock chamber, and they were quick and safe to work, for only the chambers needed to be filled and emptied. The first known pound lock built in 983 A.D. in China had a chamber 250' long. In Europe the pound lock principle was probably arrived at independently. In 1376 a pound lock was built at Vreeswijk where a canal from Utrecht joined the Lek. It was more of a basin with vertically rising gates at each end, but a true lock was built some twenty years later at Damme near Bruges. In Britain the first pound locks were three with vertical gates on the Exeter Canal, built between 1564 and 1566. Leonardo da Vinci, engineer to the Duke of Milan built the first known mitred pair of horizontally swinging lock gates in 1497 for a canal at Milan. Mitred gates allowed wider lock chambers and more manageable gates. The mitring was against the head of water which by its pressure sealed the gates, forcing the mitres to close and the gates into their quoins. They were introduced into England on the River Lee at Waltham Abbey Lock in 1577 and the first three pound locks on the Thames, built in 1632 just below Oxford, had them. On an English canal mitred gates appeared before 1670, on the cut built for eight miles between Market Deeping and Stamford to bypass the River Welland. River pound locks sometimes had their chambers conforming to the shape of the banks for cheapness and ease of construction. Curious shapes were found, notably on the Bungay Navigation where some chambers are rounded, and on the Warwickshire Avon. Wyre lock on the Lower Avon is diamond shaped, as was Cleeve on the Upper Avon. The locks of Sir Richard Weston's Wey, improved by 1653, had turf sides, as did those on the Kennet Navigation built between 1718 and 1723, still extant in the 1970s. The banks sloped back at an angle of about 45 degrees, protected by timber piles to prevent boats grounding. Turf locks needed timber, brickwork or masonry abutments for the gates, but the rest of the

16. Mechanized lock on the Aire & Calder at Bulholme below Castleford. The gantry carries signal lights.

chamber could be dug out. Brindley built as few locks as he could to save water and expense. The more locks the greater would be the loss by leakage, but a few deep locks would draw heavily from the summit level and intermediate pounds. Theoretically a boat proceeding through the locks uphill would draw a single lockful off the summit and a further lockful for the descent, but she might find a lock full and have to empty it to get in, so using two lockfuls. This might demand the enforcement of waiting turns; in other words an ascending boat with the lock against it, had to wait until a descending boat came down to set the lock and vice versa. It was desirable in a flight that each lock should be well spaced and of uniform rise so that the intermediate pounds neither overflowed nor became too shallow. On the Thames & Severn Canal neither rule was followed, the locks sometimes as near as 30 yds. and of wildly unequal rise, from 11' at Wilmoreway to 6' at Cerney Wick. If the locks had to be near together, as at Devizes on the Kennet & Avon, then the intermediate pounds were extended sideways to act as reservoirs. William Jessop was careful to make the 92 Rochdale locks with a uniform rise of 10'. Gates could then be made to fit any lock. In the late eighteenth century, according to the canal writer John Phillips, narrow lock gates were not expected to stand a pressure greater than 12' to 13' head of water, so the rise of a lock was limited to an average of 6' to 10'. There are deeper narrow ones, for example Somerton on the Oxford Canal, 12' and the top lock of the Tardebigge flight on the Worcester and Birmingham, 14', exceptional because it replaced Woodhouse's experimental boat lift. Locks on the Glamorganshire Canal were deep, some as much as 14' 6", but in Eire, the two locks on the canal bypassing the Shannon hydro-electric power station at Ardnacrusha each have a 50' rise. They are sealed by guillotine gates. Early river improvements were generally seen in isolation. The Trent & Mersey Canal set the standards of the narrow system when Brindley designed locks for boats 70' x 7'. As engineer of the Staffordshire & Worcestershire, for a while of the Coventry and of the Birmingham and the Oxford, his gauge became general for the Midlands. The Leeds & Liverpool had to have locks for the broad keels of the existing river navigations of Yorkshire. Variations did not matter on the isolated canals in the South Wales valleys, but it was a mistake for John Killaly, engineer of the Ulster Canal, to design locks for craft only 62' x 11' when he knew that the adjacent Tyrone and Lagan Navigations had 14' 6" lighters.

Construction: Lock chambers demand strength to resist water and earth pressure. Early river locks, with their natural chambers, were extravagant with water, which the canal could not afford. An exception is the Stover in Devon where some of the chambers, over 100' long, are banked with earth, but this is a lateral canal by the Teign. To build a lock a rectangular pit was dug and the site for the upper sill selected. This determined the rise of the lock and so governed the rest of the measurements. Following the timber flooring used in early locks, like those on the Newry Navigation in Ulster and in the river staunches of East Anglia, it became usual to make an invert of brick or stone set in clay puddle if the ground was porous. This could be flat, but a shallow 'U' shape gave greater strength when combined with the side walls. The latter were sunk in good foundations and supported on piling along their length. Piles were driven under the top and bottom sills to support the gates which had to swing true, the upper sill being built on a strong breast wall across the end of the chamber. This had to be stout enough to contain the bed of the canal above. The lock side walls, to resist water pressure, were buttressed at intervals along their length on their outsides, the buttresses being hidden by spoil when the job was complete; while to resist earth pressure and expansion from frost the walls were given an outwards batter, while on the Louth Navigation in Lincolnshire, lock sides were divided into shallow concave bays. To check leakage the side walls were backed by puddle between the buttresses and because of this some canals such as the Nutbrook left the locks empty; at the same time reducing water pressure on the chamber sides. Bonded courses of stone or brick were the rule, brick in the Midlands, sometimes set in a timber framing, stone in the North, in Scotland and in Ireland. Choice of material depended on availability and the brick courses were capped with a stone coping. Telford had to rebuild one of the Beeston locks on the Chester Canal in 1827 as a cast iron tank because of running sand.

Gates (25): They are held by water pressure in a hollow quoin or curved recess in the chamber side, the quoin being built up of dressed masonry, moulded brick or an iron casting set in the masonry or brickwork. The timber heelpost of the gate is rounded to fit the quoin and from its foot projects a pin, the 'tan pin' which rotates in a 'pot' or socket in the lock invert. The top of the heelpost is held by a collar anchored to the chamber side, but this takes no real weight, water pressure keeping the gate in position.   On narrow canals single gates could be used, with their headposts closing against vertical clap quoins. Single gates were cheaper, and single top gates almost universal at narrow locks.   Single narrow bottom gates are known, on the Oxford Canal below Banbury, and on the Birmingham Canal Navigations, but a pair of mitred bottom gates was usual.   Some narrow locks have a pair of mitred top gates, at Ellesmere Port and on the Bosley flight of the Macclesfield. Heel and mitre posts or head or breast posts are connected by substantial cross timbers or bars, the bottom bars bedding against the sills which are of oak spiked to elm,   set in the brickwork or masonry of the invert. The oak taking the impact of the gates could be easily renewed, but the elm was almost permanent. The bars, heel and mitre posts are re-bated to receive the planking on the uphill side, the whole being of oak, reinforced by iron brackets at the morticed and tenoned joints and caulked like a boat. This is the frame gate but there was the solid gate, in which the whole was built up of solid timber, the same thickness as the heel and mitre posts. Iron gates were tried on the Oxford Canal in the 1830s at Napton and Claydon before being used on the duplicate locks at Hillmorton in 1840, and in the 1820s on the Montgomeryshire Canal and the Ellesmere. Care was taken to pro-tect locks from damage by boats, the gates were given wooden or iron bumping pieces, easily renewable, while the breast wall was protected by a stout iron faced timber pad in the way of a boat's fore end. Present British Waterways Board policy is to replace wooden gates by welded steel, cheaper to make and maintain. The gates on the Manchester Ship Canal, of up to 300 tons each, are of greenheart, working in hollow quoins.   Replacement gates are of steel, each lock has a set because sizes differ. There are rollers on the gate bottoms travelling on granite roller paths to take some of the weight. Horizontally swinging gates are generally opened by balances of squared timber beams or poles sufficiently   long and heavy to provide leverage and to counter the weight of the gates.   Old gates had rough beams, often crudely trimmed boles or boughs of trees. Some are built up from two short-er lengths, bolted together, standard on the Leeds & Liverpool and found latterly on the Rochdale Canal in Manchester. Near overbridges beams have to be shortened and specially adapted, thus the modern tubular steel cranked beams at Gailey on the Staffordshire and Worcestershire. The economical Basingstoke and the Wey have used telegraph poles, while the Pocklington had railway rails, a pair to each beam. Large gates are or were aided by a windlass on the bank, for instance the heavy lower gates of the big lock at Middlewich. The larger gates on the Weaver are worked by a Pelton wheel type of water turbine, but the smaller depend on a manually operated pinion and toothed sector mechanism.   On the Lee, Severn, Aire & Calder and the Trent hydraulic rams are used, pushing directly on the gates, but on the Manchester Ship Canal, chains pass through sheaves so multiplying the travel of the rams. Vertically rising gates did not find much favour once the horizontal gate had been tried. They were on some of the East Anglian staunches, on the Little Ouse and on the Nene but on canals they were rare, and used only in special circumstances. The stop lock at King's Norton on the Stratford Canal was so designed because the fall could have been either way. On the Shrewsbury Canal, whose very narrow locks were de-signed for tub-boats of 6' 4" beam, guillotine lower gates were fitted because the locks were designed to pass four tub-boats at once. Like the King's Norton gates they worked with the aid of counterweights, at first a box loaded with stones, later a weight ascending and de-cending in a well. One of the early type stands at Hadley Park (91), all the others being converted in about the 1850s. In frost, their guides froze and they were also liable to bounce up off the sill. On river navigations guillotine gates for pound locks have the ad-vantage of acting as sluices for flood control. They have been fitted on the Nene and the Great Ouse to replace staunches, vertically rising staunches in the case of the Nene but only the lower gates of the Nene locks are guillotine. They are worked by a bevel drive with considerable reduction, assisted by counterweights, so are slow as are the same navigation's three radial lower gates raised from the sill in an arc.   These have the same virtues as flood control sluices for they can be raised against a head of water. There is no paddle gear either. The radial gate is like part of the rim of a wheel pivoted about an axis, the gate edges running in guides and kept watertight by a rubber flap.

Paddles and Paddle gear: Horizontal gates cannot be opened against a head of water so must be provided with sluices either in the gate or chamber. Leonardo da Vinci designed a sluice or paddle (one of many names) like a swinging door, held closed by a catch, but because of water pressure a sluice moving in a vertical plane has become nearly universal. Elm doors slide in vertical guides; on the gates (gate paddles) they let the water straight through, but if they are sited at the bottom of the chamber side (ground paddles) then the water flow can be more rapid, by means of culverts, taking water via an opening in the wing wall or, as on the Ure Navigation in Yorkshire; directly in front.   It is usual on a canal to have ground paddles at the head of a lock assisted by gate paddles when the level has reached a certain height, to avoid swamping. The cheaper gate paddle is usually suffi-cient to empty a lock. Large locks on the Weaver and on the Manchester Ship Canal have ground sluices throughout because of their size and need for mechanical operation.   The Weaver lock sluices are almost all of a cylindrical pattern, a drum sliding in guide rods, in a cylindrical chamber. This is open to either the upper or lower pound depending on whether the sluice is at the head or tail of the lock. Operation is by worm and nut lifting the drum off the bottom of the chamber, either to fill or empty the lock, the lift uncover-ing the culvert communicating with the lock chamber. At first paddles were worked by a direct pull like the paddles of paddle and rimer flash locks and held by a catch of some sort, generally a peg and a series of holes in the paddle bar allowing variation. Paddles on the Wey were worked like this. The next step, was a chain on a wooden windlass barrel, the paddle gear on the Stover Canal in Devon was worked in this way, with a handspike. Detachable handspikes and later crank handles were needed to stop people tampering with locks. From the windlass, paddle mechanism progressed to the rack and pinion gear which was introduced in the 1750s. John Smeaton adopted it both on the Calder & Hebble Navigation for ground and gate paddles (17), and on the Forth & Clyde. His rack and pinion was hand spike operated with a pinion engaging the rack teeth and held by a pawl. Rack and pinion gear with a pawl or catch became almost universal on rivers and canals, undergoing many refinements to ease operation. In Ireland paddles are called racks, breast racks on the gates and land racks on the banks. Racks are generally doubled and staggered to give continuous engagement of the pinion teeth which are in two rings. While some mechanisms are direct, for example on the Grand Junction, many are geared, with one extra shaft as on the Birmingham Canal Navigations or two as on the Rochdale Canal, the latter enclosed in a dust tight casing with a friction wheel type of brake. A variant on the rack was the toothed sector found on the Leeds & Liverpool, operated by a pinion. Heavy paddles on the Aire & Calder are raised by worm gear meshing with a large pinion, in turn geared to the rack pinion, and a worm and nut mechanism raises the paddles on some waterways. This is smoother and safer (since the paddle cannot suddenly drop) though slower than the rack, and is used on the Leeds & Liverpool and on the new locks of the Grand Union's Braunston-Birmingham line completed in 1934. Glamorganshire top gates had paddles lifted and dropped by bell cranks linked by a yoke to a horizontal rod. Not all paddles are vertically lifting. The top ground paddles on the Trent & Mersey and Leeds & Liverpool are inclined so that the paddle slides on a face which takes some of the weight. On the Sankey Brook Navigation, opened in 1757, a swinging fan type was tried, and this radial arrangement, swinging in a vertical plane parallel with the gate or chamber side was widely adopted on the Leeds & Liverpool and on the Lancaster. Paddles are called cloughs (pronounced clows) on these canals, the top ground cloughs on the Leeds & Liverpool, termed jack or side cloughs, being simple, just swinging clear of the culvert by a handle fixed to their spindles. On many Leeds & Liverpool top gates and on some bottom gates, these radial cloughs are used, worked by a horizontal rack with pinion and crank handle, an arrangement also found on the Lancaster and formerly on the Stroudwater. Some paddles worked on the horizontal plane, sliding across a culvert in the canal bed. They were found on the Montgomeryshire Canal where they were made of cast iron, operated by a robust toothed sector worked by a two stage reduction gear (22). Some paddles are counterbalanced, the Leeds & Liverpool uses small weights on bottom gates hung by a chain from the paddle bar, while the Bridgwater & Taunton employed a ball hung by a chain passed over a roller on the paddle gear framework. Powered paddle gear has made use of a worm and nut mechanism on the Severn, driven by an electric motor, the worm climbing inside a housing with an indicator marking the position of the paddle and with lights for night work, to show whether the paddle is open or shut. On the Caledonian, hydraulic rams are employed with white discs to indicate the paddle position and rams are used on the Lee and Aire & Calder, and on the Manchester Ship Canal. Some hand worked paddles, recently installed, for example on the Brecknock & Abergavenny, depend on an hydraulic pump to lift the paddle bar. They are easier for pleasure boaters.

Lock Weirs: Every canal lock has to cope with excess water from the upper level. In river locks this is not so because they are built alongside the weir which takes the natural stream. Early canal locks were frequently designed to act as their own weirs. All lock gates can so perform, but it is usual to have a bypass stream, leaving the upper pound above the top gates and entering the lower below the bottom gates. Whereas most weirs are a simple brick or stone sill, the water passing down a spillway into a culvert or along an open leat, Brindley on the Staffordshire & Worcestershire Canal used circular weirs for increased capacity. These funnel shaped circular weirs are characteristic of this

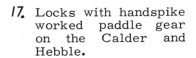

17. Locks with handspike worked paddle gear on the Calder and Hebble.

canal, some being ovoid. Also the big 'lobster pot' cages over the central hole kept out debris.

Lock Details and Decoration: Basingstoke Canal gates were painted all white, while the Lancaster had white for balance beams only. The idea was to show up at night and most balance beams are white tipped. The beams also carry the number of the lock and more rarely the name, either painted on or carved in, or cast in a plaque. The Crinan Canal locks have large metal numerals screwed to the beams. Leeds & Liverpool and Rochdale balance beams have legs or props at their outer ends to keep the open gates from swinging back, and it is usual to provide brick or stone treads on the ground below the balance beams for the boatmen's feet. At the lock tail there are often steps down to boat gunwale level and some locks have ladders or footholds within the chamber or on the gates; Leeds & Liverpool (18).

REGULATING LOCKS. A regulating lock protects an artificial waterway from the varied levels of a river or a lake, or tidal water. It is an all embracing term, sometimes even applied to stop locks at junctions. The stop lock at Marston where the Ashby joins the Coventry was called in 1798 a double regulating lock because it had gates opening both ways, in other words four sets, since the fall might be either way. A more typical regulating lock is Dochgarroch on the Caledonian Canal, where the canal leaves Loch Dochfour.

RIVER LOCKS. Akin to flood locks and tide locks, river locks are simply those which join a canal with varying levels of the river. Generally the canal is higher otherwise it would be inundated by floodwater. Examples are Thames lock at Brentford where the Grand Junction enters the river and the lock into the Douglas at Tarleton where the Rufford branch of the Leeds & Liverpool starts. Both are also tide locks, and the lock at Tarleton is protected by an extra pair of lower gates mitred the opposite way so that they close against the Douglas when a high tide brings the river higher than the canal. There are many river locks into non-tidal waters, such as Trent lock on the Erewash where it meets the river at Long Eaton, and River lock in Leeds where the Leeds & Liverpool joins the Aire.

SEA LOCKS and SEA GATES. Giving a waterway access to the sea or an estuary, they can be called tide locks. Sea locks range in size from the group at Eastham at the entrance to the Manchester Ship Canal, via the Victoria Lock at Lower Fathom at the entrance to the Newry Ship Canal, to that at Bude. They generally admit craft to a basin adjoining the canal, and are no different from the locks at the entrance to dock systems. If a full lock is not built, then a basin can be created by the simpler and cheaper sea or tide gates. They impound water in the basin at high tide and keep it in. An obvious disadvantage compared with a lock is that they can only be opened when the tide is level with the water in the basin as at Glasson Dock on the Lune.

LOCKS; SIDE PONDS. To save water, the side pond was patented in 1791 by James Playfair, a London architect. He designed a lock with ten, five on each side at different levels. The working would be impracticable and it seems likely as Rees' "Cyclopaedia" (1819) suggests, that another design of his with ponds shaped like sectors of a circle was tried in 1805 on the Grand Junction at Berkhampsted. Side ponds had to be large and shallow, otherwise the levels in the lock chamber and the ponds would equalize before the chamber was emptied of the required amount. More followed on the Grand Junction, dug, two to each lock, differing in depth and water level. The descending boatman turned water first into the upper pond until it levelled with the lock, then into the lower, each having its own paddle. When both were filled, he emptied the remainder of the lock into the lower pound. The ascending boatman drew first from the lower pond, next from the upper, finally from the upper pound. This took time and was not popular, use having to be enforced by lock keepers and warning notices posted threatening prosecution. About a third of a lock could be stored. On the Grand Junction there were double side ponds at Hanwell, Marsworth, Buckby and elsewhere single ponds; on the Coventry at Atherstone (166) on the Macclesfield at Bosley and on the Caldon at Hazelhurst. When several ponds were employed per lock, such a lock used to be called a compartment or combination lock. The Regent's tried some in 1816, copied from the combination locks with six side ponds which the Trent & Mersey had experimented with but found too time consuming. Paired locks also saved water, page 52.

LOCKS; STAIRCASES. A staircase (47) is two or more locks so close together that the chambers have common gates, the top gate of one acting as the bottom of the next above. They overcome steep slopes and save costs. A big pit for a two rise staircase would be cheaper than two pits, and one set of gates and quoins could be saved. A two rise staircase or staircase pair was no more extravagant of water than two separate locks. Staircases of more than two rises were the reverse, since an ascending boat finding all the chambers empty would keep drawing from the top pound to fill each in turn. The earliest two rise locks in the British Isles must be those on the Sankey Brook Navigation opened in 1757 called the Old Double Lock. Ireland was a great user of two rise staircases, called there double locks and confusingly to the English mind counted as single locks. On the Grand Canal there are five on the main line, and on the Royal there were ten. The only larger staircase in Ireland was the four rise one at Sprucefield near Moira on the canal section of the Lagan Navigation. Scotland has the greatest assembly of staircases, on the Caledonian Canal, headed by the eight rise 'Neptune's Staircase' at Banavie near Corpach. Water supplies are no problem here. No staircase approaches Banavie on any canal in England or Wales. Brindley is believed to have built a two rise at Salterhebble in 1765 on the Calder & Hebble, the next oldest after the Sankey staircase. On the Staffordshire & Worcestershire he built the unusual flight of three at the Bratch. These locks are so close

18. Leeds & Liverpool boatmen had to climb up the gates to get out and work the locks.

together that no boat can lie in the pounds between the locks, a similar arrangement being found on the Cefn flight on the Crumlin line of the Monmouthshire. Not far below the Bratch, Brindley combined two locks at Botterham into a two rise staircase of normal design. The only English canal with a large number of staircases is the Leeds & Liverpool, where between Leeds and Bingley there are three two rise, four three rise, and the Bingley five rise, impressive but extravagant on a canal which had a bad water supply record. Staircases were common in South Wales, headed by the treble locks at Nantgarw on the Glamorganshire, on which canal there were double rise locks as on the Monmouthshire.

STOP LOCKS. Although a new canal might bring fresh trade, fear of loss of water led to the demand for a stop lock at the junction. In 1785 the Birmingham Canal made the Dudley build a stop lock at the junction which would keep the Dudley Canal level 6" above the Birmingham's. Passage of a boat would give the Birmingham a shallow lockful of water, but no water could pass from the Birmingham to the Dudley. Stop locks were mostly designed like an ordinary pound lock with balance beams and paddles, but there were exceptions. The Stratford's guillotine gated stop lock at King's Norton survives. This is their level junction with the Worcester & Birmingham, so designed because the fall might be either way. Some stop locks had mitred gates facing in both directions to deal with this problem, a total of four sets. Where the Trent & Mersey's Hall Green branch met the Macclesfield, the former insisted on two stop locks, one controlled by themselves, the other a few yards away by the Macclesfield. Stop locks were also called regulating locks, for they rationed the water flow from one canal to another, page 56.

TIDE LOCKS and TIDE GATES. At a lock between tidal and non-tidal water the fall can be either way if the difference in level is small. This is so in the Fens, Salters Lode sluice between the Great Ouse and Well Creek has two pairs of navigation doors at the Well Creek end of the chamber and two pairs of sea doors at the Great Ouse and tidal end. There is another sluice at Salters Lode on the Old Bedford River just above its junction with the Ouse. This is not a lock but has a single pair of navigation doors and a single pair of sea doors, the navigation doors mitred towards the Old Bedford River and the sea doors to the Ouse, for again the fall might be either way. Both sets of doors are opened for navigation on the ebb tide whenever the levels coincide. Single sets of tide gates are in use at Sharpness at the present entrance to the dock and the Gloucester & Berkeley Canal. Here their purpose is to hold back the tide and create a harbour or tidal basin. A half tide lock, of which there is an example on the Thames at Richmond below the tidal limit of the river at Teddington, is designed to be used in the period between the half ebb and the following half flood. The weir at Richmond holds back the water at half flood tide level to give a greater depth. It is formed of sluices which are raised to allow the tide to flood but close when it has half ebbed. When the sluices are open, boats need not use the lock which comes into operation with their closure at half ebb. (see entry locks, river locks, sea locks).

LOCK WINDLASSES. Except on the mechanised locks, sluice or paddle operation has depended on manual power. Handspikes, levers, crank handles and wheels have all been used, sometimes detachable and carried only by lock keepers and boatmen, so that the paddles would not be tampered with and water wasted. Rack and pinion gear on the Forth & Clyde and Calder & Hebble and elsewhere in Yorkshire, was worked by handspikes, carried for the boat's anchor windlass. Adoption of rack and pinion gear for most paddle mechanisms favoured a detachable crank handle. In Yorkshire called a handling, on some canals in the past, a turn or just a handle, but more generally a windlass. This, with a square socket, fitted over the squared spindle end of the pinion shaft, or shaft of a worm and nut mechanism. Often both spindle end and socket were tapered to provide a tighter grip. The Grand Junction had a parallel sided spindle $1\frac{1}{4}$" square, the Shropshire Union used a socket tapering from $1\frac{1}{8}$" across the flats to 1", and the Trent & Mersey had $\frac{15}{16}$" tapering to three quarters. A boatman would prefer a small handle which he could stick in a pocket. Lengthsmen and lock keepers would carry a large windlass, because they needed to open stiff flood paddles. Most flood paddles or let offs have the same spindle as the company's locks, but the cautious Bridgewater has a triangular headed one, only issued to lengthsmen. The Trent & Mersey's Cheshire locks windlass from local Wheelock makers, C. H. Cooke, was stamped with that firm's pipe trade mark. In this design, often called a pipe windlass, the squared shank was chamfered at each corner, and each flat at the socket head nicked with a decorative scallop. Another modern modification is the double socket, $1\frac{1}{4}$" x $1\frac{1}{4}$" and $\frac{15}{16}$ " x $\frac{15}{16}$ " to cover the whole range of spindle sizes from Grand Union to Trent & Mersey.

GLOSSARY of LOCK TERMS.   See Appendix C.

LOCK HOUSES and HUTS.   Canal architecture is functional, evident in the design of the average lock cottage. They are generally two storied, built from local materials and after the style of the local farm cottages. They are strategically sited, at the top of flights with a second cottage at the bottom. From them the keepers could watch over the flight. Where the locks are spaced, on the Trent & Mersey (19) and Staffordshire & Worcestershire each has its cottage, often away from roads and without a piped water supply. Sited near the lockside some were designed with bay windows like a toll house for the better observation of traffic, as at Brighouse on the Calder & Hebble Navigation and it may have been visibility or just economy that prompted the circular cottages at Gailey and elsewhere on the Staffordshire & Worcestershire. Some lock houses have a particular style, as on the Shropshire Union and the Ulster Canal, also under Telford influence; they have shallow pitched roofs with wide eaves, possible because of the larger and lighter slates available by the 1820s. On the Stratford, six of the barrel roofed single storey houses survive, one floor also being usual on the Shropshire Union, although at Chester Northgate a house was built large enough for two families. Most attractive are the Regency bridgemen's houses on the Gloucester & Berkeley with their Doric porticoes. Many of the river lock houses are pleasant, for example at Torksey where the Fossdyke enters the Trent, and those on the Stort, each dated and bearing the initials of Sir George Duckett. At some locks simple huts were provided for the lock keeper as temporary shelters. Two round brick huts survive at Beeston and Tilston on the Shropshire Union (164) while on the Staffordshire & Worcestershire and Trent & Mersey there are beehive shaped brick huts.

MAINTENANCE CRAFT.   Many are dealt with separately, dredgers, ice-breakers and mud hoppers, but there are pump boats to empty lock chambers and de-water pounds, apart from salvaging sunken craft. Nowadays they carry motor centrifugal pumps, but in the past archimedean screws, a scoop wheel on the BCN and reciprocating hand pumps were used for de-watering, aided by syphons where these could be fitted. A crane boat has either a grab crane for dredging, or a crane for lifting lock gates. Modern diesel cranes do both. Other craft carry concrete mixers, generators for lighting in tunnels, air compressors and blacksmith's forges. Following these are the work boats, carrying piles, bricks, timber, clay puddle and tools, wheelbarrows, shovels, hand dredging equipment, kebs and the like. Maintenance craft follow the lines of their carrying sisters and are often old trade boats. The narrow canals use both motor and butty boats, stripped so that they are open holded. On the shallow Welsh canals, horse boats were used until the end of the 1950s. Historically interesting were the coal box narrow boats employed on maintaining the Worsley-Leigh length of the Bridgewater by the National Coal Board. A few narrow maintenance craft were specially constructed; the Shropshire Union had some with extra long foredecks giving good stowage space for tools below. In more recent times the LNER built a wooden motor maintenance boat the JOEL at their Ashton Canal's Gorton dock. Leeds & Liverpool maintenance boats are ex-carrying craft, some fitted with cranes, although the British Waterways Board are replacing them with shorter boats with shallower holds. Ex-carrying boats waste time going to wind or turn while their holds have to be built up to enable men to climb in and out easily. Specially built maintenance craft are more usual on the larger navigations. In Yorkshire they follow barge design, a typical example would be MCB 3 (motor crane boat No. 3) built in 1954 by Richard Dunston at Thorne and based at Stanley Ferry on the Wakefield line of the Aire & Calder. She has a diesel crane and grab. On the Weaver there is the SAMPSON a pontoon with twin jib cranes for lifting lock gates. The Manchester Ship Canal Co. have a 250 ton floating crane (28) for heavy lifts in the port and for handling lock gates. She was built in 1937 in Holland, with steam-electric drive, but not self-propelled, unlike the company's 60 ton crane, also Dutch built in 1921. At the other end of the scale are the punts bow-hauled by lengthsmen. They carry puddle to stop leaks, hedge trimmings and weeds. They have a little shelter for tea and meal breaks, with a stove. These would be called bank boats.

MAINTENANCE YARDS.   Every navigation, river or canal, had a yard and workshop. Here repair materials were stored, and tools and damaged equipment could be worked on and new made. Since most of the improvement work on rivers was minimal before the canal age, maintenance yards were doubtless small, but with the arrival of the artificial canal a new scale of repair facility was needed. The Duke of Bridgewater established docks and yards at Worsley where he built boats for his carrying fleet, both within the mines and without. He is believed to have employed 200 men. The Mersey & Irwell's premises at the Old Quay Runcorn were swallowed up by the Ship Canal Workshops. Each canal set up a maintenance yard, sometimes several if it was a long line, but there was generally a principal one. The Trent & Mersey made their company headquarters and chief yard at Stone, but there were other yards at Red Bull near Kidsgrove, Etruria and Fradley. These had similar facilities, an open yard where materials could be stored, a slip or a dry dock or both where maintenance boats could be repaired, frequently under cover, a saw pit, in later days a sawmill, and a series of workshops and stores for the several trades, carpenters, blacksmiths, painters and in modern times electricians and welders. Some isolated maintenance yards became the centre of a community; Norbury Junction on the Shropshire Union, Stanley Ferry on the Aire & Calder, successor to Lake Lock on the old Calder line

19. Lock house at Rump's lock
Middlewich. It was called
Joe Low's by the boatmen.

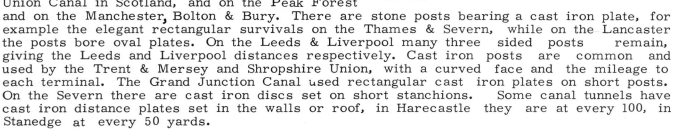

which had been established in 1802.   Banknewton
on the Leeds & Liverpool was a stone shed not unlike a farm building,   but Hartshill on the
Coventry Canal near Atherstone is like the stables
of a country house,   complete with the turret
clock in its cupola, and elegantly arched entrance
to the under cover dry dock.

MILEPOSTS and BOUNDARY POSTS.   Acts
stipulated that mileposts be erected to define the
distances which were the basis of toll charges.
They were placed at every mile,   and frequently
at half and quarter miles (4). Made to last,
many survive.   They bear the names of the
terminal points of their canal, either one, or
both. Wholly stone examples are common on the
Union Canal in Scotland, and on the Peak Forest
and on the Manchester, Bolton & Bury. There are stone posts bearing a cast iron plate, for
example the elegant rectangular survivals on the Thames & Severn, while on the Lancaster
the posts bore oval plates. On the Leeds & Liverpool many three sided posts remain,
giving the Leeds and Liverpool distances respectively. Cast iron posts are common and
used by the Trent & Mersey and Shropshire Union, with a curved face and the mileage to
each terminal. The Grand Junction Canal used rectangular cast iron plates on short posts.
On the Severn there are cast iron discs set on short stanchions.   Some canal tunnels have
cast iron distance plates set in the walls or roof, in Harecastle they are at every 100, in
Stanedge at every 50 yards.

Boundary Posts of river navigation (20) and canal companies were put up to mark the
limits of their property. On the Birmingham Canal Navigations they were foot high oval
section stone posts with a domed top, inscribed BCN. Very widespread are the boundary
posts the Great Western Railway erected on the Monmouthshire and Brecknock & Abergavenny Canals in the 1920s. They are short lengths of railway line, capped by a horizontal
disc, inscribed GREAT WESTERN RAILWAY with a date. They replaced stone posts, one
of which remains as a step at Llanfoist wharf on the Brecknock & Abergavenny.

RIVER IMPROVEMENT; ENGINEERING.   There were three main periods of activity,
dictated by the political and economic situation, 1662-65 after the Civil War, 1697-1700
before Marlborough's wars, and 1719-1721 in the boom before the South Sea crash.   The
river age then merged into the canal age and outlived it, for the Severn was not improved
until the 1840s, and the greatest works on the Weaver were done from the 1870s onwards.
The river age is far from dead in the 1970s with the improvement of the Aire & Calder.
Adequate depth was the first need and this could only be found by making dams. Fish weir
removal was the first stage in any river improvement, but it was impossible to shift mill
dams. To balance the needs of mills and navigations was difficult, and all river histories
are punctuated with mill disputes. Flooding was another problem if water levels were raised
by dams and fear of floods caused many objections to navigation schemes. When navigation
weirs were made, the usual practice was to separate the gate part from the fixed part by
some sort of pier. The main stream would pass over the weir and the gate would be in a
side cut. When pound locks were used the side cut was a more elaborate affair because of
the length of the lock chamber. A cut was the first step towards the canalization of a river
for it could be extended to eliminate a bend, could be provided with more than one lock,
and could join up with other side cuts above and below.   In the end, continuous side cuts
resulted in a lateral canal, parallel with the river and fed by its water. Historically however this was a late development, the improvers of the seventeenth century did not normally
achieve half so much. Thus William 'Water-work' Sandys improved the Warwickshire Avon,
building thirteen flash and pound locks. By the depth so created 30 ton barges could reach
Stratford, but he would not have done any other work. Because they did the minimum needed, with little excavation, these early improvers worked quickly. Thus on the Aire & Calder
a boat was able to reach Wakefield on the Calder in December 1699, while Leeds was
accessible at the end of 1700. Pound locks on short cuts were built on this navigation, the
natural stream being led over a weir. In calculating their depth requirements the improvers
had to know as much as possible about the river's conditions, how often and how deep the
floods, how frequent the dry spells and the least depth to be expected.   Much depended on
rainfall and the number and volume of the tributaries. Another need, when planning locks
and weirs, was to know the fall of the river, or how much the surface water level descended, expressed in feet and inches. A steep slope meant a swift current and a predeliction to
rapid rise and fall, resulting in sudden floods. The Yorkshire Swale fell into this category
and defeated its improvers in the late 1760s. Another steep Yorkshire river was the Calder
with a slope of 90" per mile, the total fall in the 24 miles of the navigation being 178'.
Locks were sited at the tail of each cut, because the scour from their paddles would help
to clear the inevitable bar of silt deposited across the lower mouth of the cut by the weir

stream. Ironically whereas both locks and training walls were designed to increase depth, locks also tended to check the current and so the scour. This happened on the Yorkshire Ouse when Naburn lock was opened in 1757. A big shoal started to form at Acaster Selby on a bend some $2\frac{3}{4}$ miles below the lock. Most effective of all was canalization, lengthening the artificial cuts. These could be extended to avoid bends and shallows, usually cutting across a loop. Sir Richard Weston had shown how on the Wey and by about 1665 the Welland had been bypassed by an $8\frac{1}{2}$ mile lateral canal from below Stamford to below Market Deeping. Almost complete canalization was achieved by the Aire & Calder in the late eighteenth and early nineteenth centuries. If bends were not avoided by a lateral canal, they could be eased by cutting back the banks, while always there were problems of bank protection to check erosion which would mean slips and the formation of shoals. If the river was liable to flooding it would have to be contained by artificial banks, the floodbanks so prominent on Fenland rivers.

STOP GATES, SAFETY GATES. Fitted to seal a length of canal rapidly, and stop the whole of a pound pouring through a breach, widening it and causing flooding. Early stop gates, credited to Brindley and sometimes called Brindley gates, were hinged to a sill on the canal bed and pulled up by means of a chain. Rees' "Cyclopaedia" (1819) describes some gates of similar design intended to be self closing, swinging upwards and butting into recesses in the side walls. They turned like a lock gate in a hollow quoin, were counter-balanced, and would work when a strong flow started, for the canal bed was shaped to direct the current under them. Because the current might flow either way there had to be two, swinging in opposite directions. The horizontal gates at Shebdon and on the Nantwich embankment are single and close like a lock gate. Aqueducts are also protected like the Basingstoke Canal's Frimley, over the railway lines from Waterloo to Southampton, Bournemouth and Exeter. Stop gates were used in Dudley tunnel to keep the water still when the locks at either end were drawn off so that boats would not be hindered by any current.

STOP PLANKS. By overbridges, locks, tunnel portals and aqueducts stop planks are kept to seal off a length of canal which can then be drained for repairs to lock chambers, tunnel inverts or bridge abutments. The planks slide down a pair of grooves cut in the brickwork or masonry of the bank. The bottom plank beds against a sill, either wood, brick or stone which has to be cleared by dredging with a scoop, aided by a scraper to shift rubbish in the grooves. Once the seven or eight planks, some as thick as 10" x 8", are in position they can be held down with wedges driven between each end of the top plank and the groove (21). To stiffen them against water pressure a stank bar may sometimes be driven into the canal bed on the side to be drained and held firm against the planks by a longitudinal piece of timber secured on the bank by stakes, the timber passing under a special lug at the top of the bar. Stop planks are stored in a frame or box on the bank generally roofed over. Designs vary from the brick boxes on the Shropshire Union, to the open framework at Claverton on the Kennet & Avon which is made up of lengths of railway line.

STOPPAGES. When a navigation is closed at any point a stoppage is said to be on. Natural conditions like frost, drought and flood can stop traffic, but a stoppage usually means an obstruction due to repairs or an accident. A waterway closure is likely to be absolute, unless the repair work can be stanked off to allow a passage for craft, or locks are duplicated. This proved a disadvantage against road or rail, and navigation history is full of examples of long stoppages, often due to bad construction, apart from necessary maintenance work and disasters like a breach or a boat sinking. Subsidence was a problem on many canals. Between 1843 and 1847 the Caledonian had to be closed for repairs, particularly at locks, due to faulty construction, while between 1801 and 1811 the Newry Canal in Ireland underwent a more or less complete reconstruction. Some canals did not have enough water and a dry spell would paralyse them, in 1819 the Huddersfield was closed for 39 days due to drought plus 10 days for ordinary repairs, while the Leeds & Liverpool had many drought closures. Accidents have been most felt by a port like Manchester, partially closed in March 1961 for nearly a month when the steam sand barge MARY P. COOPER sank fully laden at Stockton Heath. A canal dependent on lifts or inclined planes was peculiarly prone to trouble, notably the Bude. Stoppages are needed for maintenance, but they can be planned to interfere as little as possible with traffic. With pleasure traffic

20. A cast iron boundary post and a towpath gate, closing by its own weight, on the Weaver Navigation.

21. Stop planks at Barnton Tunnel on the Trent & Mersey. The man is 'racking off', shovelling in ashes as a seal. Behind him is a scraper and scoop to clear rubbish from the sill and plank grooves.

it is easier, stoppages being mostly confined to the winter.

SUBSIDENCE.   Coal Mining has been the greatest cause of subsidence, and the canals of South Wales, South Lancashire, Birmingham, the Black Country, the West Riding, the Potteries and Derbyshire have all had subsidence problems. Brine pumping in Cheshire, whereby the salt strata is dissolved, has had an unhappy effect on the Trent & Mersey Canal (35) and on the Weaver. The line of the Ellesmere Canal over Whixall Moss beyond Whitchurch has had to be embanked to counteract drying and shrinkage of the peat.   The Irish Grand,   crossing the Bog of Allen, had to be considerably embanked to overcome peat settling. Coal mining,   by removing strata, has led to some quite remarkable sinkings. In 1960 part of the Cannock Extension Canal due to open cast working sank 21' in a week, while in 1894 a section of the Dudley's Two Lock line collapsed overnight into a mineshaft. The St Helens Canal has had vertical movements of up to 20', while in the West Riding the Dearne & Dove Canal became so badly affected that it proved impracticable to maintain and mostly ceased to be navigated after 1934. Subsidence causes leaks or bursts through disintegration of the puddled clay and of the banks; while over shallow coal workings craters or 'crownings in' appear in the canal bed, possibly flooding the mine beneath. Locks are not only lowered,   but gates and chambers may become distorted and bridges and tunnels sink or collapse.   Both Butterley tunnel on the Cromford and Norwood on the Chesterfield became impassable because of subsidence. Aqueducts may be damaged and leak; in 1911 Jessop's at Barnsley suffered collapse of the wing walls and part of the approach embankment. Reservoirs and feeders are also affected, like Gad's Green near Netherton tunnel which became disused after 1915.   Subsidence, also called swagging, takes the form of either direct settlement or lateral pull, if the workings are a short distance from the canal; its amount depends on the thickness of the coal seam, the latter's depth beneath the canal, also on the direction and methods of mining.   Long walling, whereby a seam is attacked on a wide front is more conducive to subsidence than the old pillar and stall working. Brine pumping and rock salt mining have been equally damaging, often, in the case of the brine streams, miles away from the actual pumping. A side effect has been the widening of the Trent & Mersey at Billinge Green near Lostock Gralam into a lake. Damage causes expense, the apportionment of which has created difficulty. Some early river navigation Acts claimed the right to full support for the waterway, others defined the limits to which the waterway was entitled, varying from 10 to 100 yards in breadth, others again like the Nutbrook gave no thought to the matter, and the canal company had to choose between buying the support from the colliery company,   or coping with the subsidence. On the whole, if demanded by the canal company, reasonable compensation has been paid by coal owners and salt producers. On the Bridgewater from Worsley to Leigh, maintenance has been in the hands of the colliery companies, latterly the National Coal Board, ceasing in 1973 since no more mining takes place under the canal. Nevertheless the waterways have had to bear a heavy cost, because clear interpretation of the Acts was rarely possible. However, in November 1959 a new agreement was made between the British Transport Commission and the National Coal Board, following the passage in 1957 of the Coal Mining (Subsidence) Act. This has replaced all the old Acts and has apportioned the costs of subsidence repairs as follows: 70 per cent to be borne by the NCB and 30 per cent by the British Waterways Board, as successors to the British Transport Commission. The Board have their own mining engineer based at Leeds who has to inspect all mineral workings.

TOLL OFFICES.   These, also called check offices were for the toll-collector,   and sometimes incorporated into his house. As offices they were generally small one roomed buildings, as houses they could be large. Furniture would include desk, high stool, cupboard and shelves for the gauging books which could be numerous at busy centres, a brick fireplace and toilet facilities. Propped up against a wall would be the gauging staffs and in the canal age the collector might have a blunderbuss resting on wall brackets.   Like many lock houses the windows were arranged to watch the canal in each direction and the window

22. Carreghofa toll office with the monumental Montgomeryshire design of top ground paddle gear.

opposite the desk would have a small opening, as in a booking office. In the Birmingham area toll office design received particular attention because of the heavy traffic. On the busiest lengths they were built of octagonal shape on an island on the middle of the canal. The island allowed two boats at a time to be dealt with; the canal narrowing into two gauging stops of a boat's width each, one on each side, so that the toll-collector could gauge at the four prescribed points. Elsewhere similar gauging stops were used, or locks or a stop lock as on the Oxford Canal side of Hawkesbury junction, allowing access to both sides. The toll office at Carreghofa (22) where the Montgomeryshire Canal forms an end on junction with the Ellesmere, has a verandah for boatmen waiting at the toll window. When part of a house, the office was marked by a bay window as once at Aldersley, the junction of the Staffs. & Worcs. with the Birmingham system. Sometimes the houses were large like Wharf House, of three floors, standing at Marlbrook at the end of the Leominster Canal. This was a canal office, house for the toll-collector and warehouse for the Mamble tramroad which ran into two ground floor terminal wharves. Toll office furniture from Elland on the Calder & Hebble has been preserved at Cusworth Hall Museum, near Doncaster.

TOWING PATHS, GATES and STILES.   In horse traction days towing paths were as well looked after as the water channel. Early river navigations did not provide them, craft being hauled by men who stumbled along the banks. Landowners moreover maintained boundary fences, walls or hedges which had to be climbed; these multiplied in the eighteenth century with the enclosures movement. Even when horse paths were made they were not always satisfactory, and nowhere less so than in the Fens and East Anglia.   These 'haling ways' had to be on the flood bank some 8' above the river and separated from it by the wash lands. Before haling ways were built the horses or men struggled along the wash lands or waded. The haling ways changed sides without bridges, never passed under bridges and were bisected by 'jumps' or stiles. Elsewhere river paths became more organised as horse traction took over from men. The Don Navigation probably had one as part of the improvement below Doncaster under the Act of 1727. Lack of an overall river authority on the Severn led to the setting up of horse towing path companies to make paths, replacing the rough tracks which had been trodden into the banks through long usage.   A horse path involved gates at the boundary fences and bridges and culverts over minor streams.   Tolls were taken to pay for their construction and maintenance and because of these charges and the necessary purchase of land the paths were established by Acts of Parliament.   River paths were usually left unfenced since they crossed private land which had access to the water's edge, but they were kept gravelled, had gates which would shut by their own weight, behind the horse and driver (20). Canal towpaths were part of the land bought for the waterway, fenced off by hedge, wall or railings, as private property and were protected by bye laws against trespass. They were built 2' or 3' above the water, a little higher than the bank edge and it was considered good engineering to camber them down on the side away from the canal to allow horses a firmer foothold. They had to be wide enough for two horses to pass and were kept well gravelled with 'raffle' or chippings, cinders or ashes so that horses would find a good purchase. The path had to change sides to suit landowners, for example to allow cattle to come down to drink. The change was by a turnover or changeline bridge. Considerable care was taken to make the towpaths as safe as possible for horses.   Rails were sometimes provided on the water side where the path narrowed, under a bridge and in tunnels, and steep slopes up locks and over towpath bridges were paved with brick, with lines of bricks as treads. On the Birmingham system twin towpaths, one on each side of the canal, were built on the new main line between Birmingham and Wolverhampton, including Coseley tunnel. Later Netherton tunnel was built with a twin path, smoothing traffic flow. The shortened Oxford canal north of Braunston also had twin paths at some points, including the new Newbold tunnel, and they were provided on the Coalisland Canal in Co. Tyrone opened in 1787.

TOWPATH GATES   and STILES: Because of the rights of landowners, river navigations were often hampered by towing paths, crossed by hedges and fences. Men bow-hauling boats could clamber over, but when horses were used gates or stiles had to be provided.   Stiles became common in East Anglia, in the Fens called 'jumps' because the towing horses had to jump over them. The regulation height was 2'6" and lightermen pulled them down if they were higher. A more elaborate stile, on the Arun in Sussex was a section of fence composed of three pivoted rails each counterweighted at one end. If the rails were depressed the horse could step over. Most river navigations had gates made for the path. On the Weaver a special towpath gate was designed (20), of which examples remain.   It has a frame of tubular iron crossed by chains to form a barrier, but the frame is so shaped that the gate is out of balance with a tendency to close. Canal towpaths had gates and stiles

23. Rollers on two very sharp bends on the Leeds & Liverpool between Marton and Gargrave. The 6' high rollers at intervals round the bends outside the towpath kept towlines on canal property and held the lines out, otherwise the horse would be pulling the boat sideways.

at access points, generally from a public road near an overbridge. Stiles could be the ordinary sort with a single step, but the Montgomeryshire provided an attractive low two rail fence, with the two uprights splayed out and long enough to give a handgrip. Gates were generally of the wicket type, opening between two posts so that there was no need to latch them.

TOWLINE GUARDS and GUIDES. Horse towlines chafing on brickwork and masonry caused wear and canal companies protected them either by bands of iron or hardwood rollers. Most frequent are the guards or curbs to overbridge abutments on the towpath side found on almost all navigations. Towpath bridges received most wear, for horses not only passed underneath but crossed over, causing the lines to sweep over the coping of the parapet. The Lodge Hill towpath bridge, where the Glasson Dock branch leaves the main line of the Lancaster, has complex iron guard rails to keep lines off the squared coping (73) at the abutments. At narrow places on the towpath, and on all tunnel paths, railings were put up at the water's edge to stop horses falling in, and the top rail, generally of wood, was faced with a strip of iron with countersunk fastenings to avoid fouling the lines; moreover at each end of the railings the top rail was led down to the ground, so that the lines would not catch the uprights. Kinder on the lines were hardwood rollers; on the Leeds & Liverpool they were put on bridge abutments instead of iron curbs, while on the Marple flight of locks on the Peak Forest Canal there was a special horizontal roller at bridge 17 where the towpath leaves the canal to cross a public road, to protect the parapet. Rollers were put at two very sharp bends of the Leeds & Liverpool (23).

24.

TRAMROADS. Tramroads were in use in the British Isles since the early seventeenth century, with rectangular hardwood rails laid flat from colliery to river bank, notably the banks of the Tyne and Wear. Later the wooden rails were in two layers, so that the top could be renewed. From about the 1730s iron strips were laid on top of the rails to cut down wear, while from 1767 the Coalbrookdale Co. were casting rectangular iron rails to lie on top of the wood. Purely iron rails were unknown until the Dowlais ironworks at Merthyr Tydfil cast them in 1791. These were edge rails for flanged wheels as opposed to the flanged rail or plateway advocated and used by Benjamin Outram. Of edge rails, the strongest was the fish bellied used by William Jessop in 1792. By this time, tramroads were seen as useful adjuncts to, or replacements of canal lines, when reckless speculation was replaced by financial stringency. Canal promoted tramroads could extend the canal system particularly into hilly country, to reach mines and quarries, or could join up lengths of canal. A tramroad was cheaper to build, requiring simpler earthworks. Steep slopes could be overcome by inclined planes, simpler to operate with tramroad waggons. On the other hand a tramroad, even double track, could not manage the tonnage handled by a waterway, unless it was one product flowing in one direction, from mine or quarry down to canal basin. Here gravity would often aid the horses, (24). Early among the canal tramroads was that down from the Caldon limestone quarries to Froghall. The Act for this was secured in 1776 and it had a long and busy life. Another with traffic flowing in one direction was the Peak Forest, from Bugsworth seven miles up to the limestone quarries at Doveholes, opened in 1796 and not closed until 1925 (it had been relaid with steel plate rails in 1883). In South Wales tramroads were vital to shift the coal and iron from scattered collieries and ironworks down to the canals which could carry in greater volume to the sea. The Monmouthshire Canal had 14 miles made up of nine separate lines, some linking up with the tramroads of the Brecknock & Abergavenny Canal, which started as a tramroad operator in 1794 before it made a canal. A unique feeder was the Haytor Granite Tramway in Devon, with granite 'rails' laid as a plateway, and carrying granite from the Haytor quarries down to the Stover Canal at Ventiford, opened in 1820 and closed in about 1858. Tramroads built to join sections of canal were numerous. There were lines built to get traffic moving before the canal was finished, for example, the tramroad at Blisworth on the Grand Junction before completion of the tunnel in 1805. Then there were tramroads to link two levels as at Marple where a line was laid because the Peak Forest could not at first afford locks. A tramroad joined the northern and southern sections of the Lancaster Canal across the Ribble. Here a canal had been authorized but was never built due to lack of money. Joining two quite independent waterways was the Cromford & High Peak Railway, a 34 mile line from the Peak Forest Canal branch at Whaley Bridge to the Cromford Canal. From 1801, when the Surrey Iron Railway received its Act, came an increasing number of tramroads or railways promoted as public companies independent of both canal companies and of mine and quarry owners. In this category falls the Stockton & Darlington opened in 1825, planned originally as a canal.

TUNNELS.   Tunnelling for a waterway had to be both horizontal and straight.   The ancestor of the canal tunnel was the sough for draining mines, driven up from a stream into workings burrowed out of a hillside. One was made at Worsley and enlarged by John Gilbert into a level navigable by boats, and this became common practice. They were driven horizontally and some became a network of canals at different depths with branches to the working faces. For canal tunnelling, the line was laid out over the surface by a cord and the sites for shafts selected and marked. These were needed to enable as many headings as possible to be driven simultaneously, to remove spoil, empty the workings of water and ventilate them. The more shafts there were the faster the tunnel could be built and the more accurate it was likely to be. Lappal on the Dudley Canal's Selly Oak line, 3795 yards long had thirty shafts. The common spacing was 200 yards. The shafts had to be correctly aligned on the surface, by telescope. Shaft depths were worked out and plotted by use of a surveying level able to sight graduated staffs ahead and to the rear of the instrument, so establishing height differences. Shaft sinking was an old art allied to well sinking, some were square and lined with timber, others round and lined with brickwork, working downwards course by course as the shaft deepened, each course being held up by a wooden curb or ring which went down with the shafts, 'steining' this was called.   Once each had reached the right depth the future headings were aligned by dropping two plumb lines down each shaft on a still day, all lined up along the line of canal at the surface, again involving markers and a telescope. Once correctly aligned at the top they would be correctly aligned at the bottom and a cord held between them would indicate the line of the heading.   Then the men got to work, tunnelling in each direction from each shaft bottom and from the portals, so that at Lappal 62 headings could be driven at once. These were pushed through fast, to a small bore say 4' wide by 6' high, later enlarged to full tunnel size, for a small bore could more easily be corrected. Excavation was chancy because of lack of geological information, although shaft sinking provided a guide. Water and running sand were the main enemies, particularly the latter which William Jessop met at Braunston.   Water was lifted out of the shafts by horses or men winding out buckets or by pumps, either wind or steam, the latter used by Brindley at Harecastle. A drainage sough might be dug underneath and to one side of the tunnel line to carry water away to a natural stream at either entrance. Spoil, like water, was lifted up the shafts by horse gins, and left by the mouth of each shaft. At the portals tramroads were used and very likely from the headings to each shaft bottom. Work on the earlier tunnels proceeded slowly, the first Harecastle taking nine years, Stanedge 5456 yd, seventeen, and they were commenced as soon as the canal's Act was passed. Two to three hundred men were employed on the Sapperton (3817 yd) works, a gang of eight in each heading, three miners, two loaders, two waggon drivers and one emptying waggons at the shaft bottom. Later came carpenters and bricklayers or masons to erect centring and line the bore. Tools were simple; pick, shovel, crowbar, and auger for drilling shot holes. Illumination was by candle, in spite of the threat of fire damp in tunnels which passed through coal measures. Ventilation was achieved by lighting fires at the shaft bottom to create an upward current of air which would draw fresh air down an adjacent shaft, possible when the headings had linked two shafts. Most tunnels needed lining to prevent roof falls, although engineers hoped to avoid some of this. The 130 yd Armitage tunnel on the Trent & Mersey was left as a natural cavern and most of Stanedge likewise. Brick was the usual lining material, but sometimes it was masonry as at Ashford, 375 yd, on the Brecknock & Abergavenny. Lining included an invert to stiffen the side walls, sometimes laid on a bed of puddle if the strata was porous, while earth was rammed between the brickwork of the sides and roof and the natural strata to consolidate the lining. To lay the bricks, wooden centring was put up, taken down and rebuilt as the work progressed. Blisworth (59) was lined with 17" of brickwork round the sides and roof and 13" round the invert. With the tunnel completed the shafts were filled up although some might be left for ventilation. This was not considered worth the cost in the days of legging, no shafts being left at Harecastle, but steam tugs demanded them and more had to be added at Blisworth. Because the mouths of some shafts were within easy reach, their tops were protected by gratings to stop bricks and stones being tossed into the canal.   Early British main line canal tunnels were Preston Brook, 1239 yd, Norwood, originally 2850 yd on the Chesterfield Canal, near Staveley, and Harecastle, all the work of Brindley, although finished by Hugh Henshall, all opened in 1775. Because of economy on the privately financed British canal, they were built to small dimensions, the width of a single narrow boat and without towing paths. Broad canals had their tunnels built to the width of a single boat also without towpaths. Towpaths were only made through short tunnels like the 65 yd Cookley on the Staffs. & Worcs, until 1797 when a timber path was fitted to Berwick tunnel, 970 yd, on the

26. Carpenters at Bingley five rise (below) in 1904.

25. Repairs to the lower gate (above) of a pound lock on the Grand Junction.

27. Repairs to Blisworth tunnel lining in 1960 (below), following a slip.

66

28. THE 250 TON CRANE is the name of the Manchester Ship Canal's heavy lift craft, built 1937 and used for handling lock gates (as above), as well as cargo work.

29. No.3 bucket dredger, built in 1867 and the steam mud hopper WHALE at work (below) on the Weaver Navigation in February 1922.

tub-boat canal to Shrewsbury. This was built out over the water with bearers let into the side walls, but curiously it was removed in 1819. William Jessop and Telford provided tow-paths with guard rails for the horse in all three tunnels on the Ellesmere Canal. As an alternative, chains and wires were stapled to the tunnel walls for boatmen to haul themselves along, as in the Bruce Tunnel, 502 yd at Savernake on the Kennet & Avon, while in Shrewley, 433 yd on the Warwick & Birmingham, handles were fixed to the side walls and in Crimson Hill 1800 yd on the Chard Canal, there seem to have been rings in the roof by which men pulled themselves along with a hook attached to a harness as in the Worsley underground system. To speed traffic some tunnels were widened into passing places, Stanedge has four of these, with mooring rings. They were no solution for a heavily used route and it was on the Birmingham system that canal tunnelling reached its zenith. Following the lead of Newbold new tunnel on the straightened Oxford, completed by 1834, Telford planned Coseley tunnel, 360 yd on his new main line wide enough for two narrow boats to pass and with a towing path each side continuing the two paths of the canal. Netherton, 3027 yd, followed suit. Whereas Stanedge burrows 600 ft under the moors some tunnels have little cover, only 60 ft above Foulridge and about 20 ft above Hardham, on the Arun Navigation in Sussex. These shallow tunnels were made because they were safer than deep cutting, although most of Foulridge, all but 700 of the 1640 yd, had to be dug out as a cutting because the rock was too loose, and later covered. Owing to expense tunnel portals are almost all plain, unlike their flamboyant railway successors. The only really ornamental portals are those of Sapperton, Doric columns at one end with niches and a pediment, and castellations and finials at the other. Tunnels have many enemies, principally subsidence. One of the worst to suffer was the Dudley Canal, its three tunnels passing through an area of intensive mining, and was frequently stopped for repairs. Lappal closed for long stoppages in 1801 and 1805, and in 1917, closed completely because of subsidence. The 557 yd tunnel at Gosty Hill, Halesowen, was almost wholly rebuilt in 1881. Natural causes faced the engineers with problems; at Sapperton leakage through the fissures of the oolite eventually made the tunnel unnavigable, the bore also being distorted by water swelling the fuller's earth through which much of the tunnel passed. Some tunnels have been bypassed by later canal straightenings, the old one at Newbold and that at Wolfhamcote on the Oxford and Adwick on the Dearne & Dove. Ireland has no canal tunnels and Scotland only three, two very short ones on the Glasgow, Paisley & Johnstone Canal in Paisley and one in Falkirk on the Edinburgh & Glasgow Union. This takes the canal past the grounds of Callendar house and has a towpath, for the canal provided an efficient passenger boat service.

Tunnels over 1000 yards long are: Standedge or Stanedge (Huddersfield Canal) 5698 yds, Strood & Higham (Thames & Medway) 3946 yds, Sapperton (Thames & Severn) 3817 yds, Lappal (Dudley 3795 yds, Dudley (Dudley) 3172 yds, Blisworth (Grand Junction) 3056 yds, Netherton (BCN) 3027 yds, Butterley (Cromford) 2966 yds, Harecastle (Trent & Mersey) old, 2880 yds, new 2926 yds, Norwood (Chesterfield) 2850 yds, West Hill (Worcs. & Birmingham) 2726 yds, Morwelldown (Tavistock) 2540 yds, Oxenhall (Hereford & Gloucester) 2192 yds, Braunston (Grand Junction) 2042 yds, Crimson Hill (Chard) 1800 yds, Foulridge (Leeds & Liverpool) 1640 yds, Crick (Grand Union - old) 1528 yds, Southnet (Leominster) 1254 yds, suffered partial collapse and was never used. Preston Brook (Trent & Mersey) 1239 yds, Wren's Nest (Earl of Dudley's mine) 1227 yds, Greywell (Basingstoke) 1200 yds, Husband's Bosworth (Grand Union - old) 1166 yds.

TUNNEL MAINTENANCE. Apart from fighting subsidence and water pressure in rock fissures, canal engineers had to watch for signs of deterioration in the brick or masonry lining of tunnels. Replacing brickwork rotten from damp, either the whole depth of it, generally two layers, or the lining on the canal side, was the most frequent job. (27) Brickwork also suffered at water level from the passage of boats. Nowadays with seasonal pleasure traffic, repair work can be done in the winter and with the tunnel fully drained by means of stop planks. Though in commercial days every effort was made to keep the tunnel open, repairs being done in winter when the men could not work outside. On the Grand Junction with tunnels at Blisworth and Braunston and on the Leicester line at Crick and Husband's Bosworth, the engineers developed efficient damming arrangements. To work on the sides above and below water level they built longitudinal dams parallel with the axis of the tunnel at each side, but leaving a space for passage of craft in the centre. Each end of these dams was sealed by small cross dams so that the effect was of two boxes covering the sections for repair, or one box if for one side. If the whole width of the invert required attention then there was a stoppage and full cross dams would be put in to seal off the trouble spot. In the 1900s T. W. Millner the engineer of the Grand Junction's Northern District, designed special doors as cross dams. They were each shaped to half the lower cross section of the tunnel and held firm by a beam wedged across the tunnel above the doors and above water level. Through this beam there were four threaded holes, two above each door. Through the holes poked four screw jacks which pressed the doors down against the sides and bottom of the invert. There is a model of a cross dam at the Waterways Museum, Stoke Bruerne. Work on brickwork above water level was carried out from narrow maintenance boats fitted with staging or from flats, small punt shaped craft. Illumination in the old days was by candle, then petrol pressure lamps, acetylene and finally electricity with a boat mounted generator. To cure serious distortion of the invert the tunnel might have to be strutted with cast iron ribs, which would keep the way safe for traffic until a full stoppage allowed the engineers time to replace the damaged brickwork. This was done at Blisworth in 1849 when part of the invert was seriously affected by water pressure in fissures underneath. Hard wearing engineer's blue brick was much used for repairs particularly where boats rubbed against the sides. More recent practice has included removal of the first layer of brickwork, fitting metal reinforcement and cement spraying to consolidate the whole. Tunnel inspections were carried out by boat, with the water level let down so that as much as possible could be seen. The boat, often an ice-breaker, would be poled slowly through, while lights mounted on the hull and carried by the engineers would search out the faults.

WAREHOUSES and WHARVES: (48, 131). Storage at wharves was essential. There must have been warehouses on the Thames in Roman times and on the Dee at Chester. At Selby the mediaeval Abbot's Staith remains, a warehouse in the Norman style. Due to the difficulties and expense of construction they were built upwards rather than outwards, several together to house different commodities such as grain or salt. All the floors were of small area so that the goods could be quickly reached and by use of hoists and chutes it was easy to handle on and off the floors. The success of the Mersey & Irwell led to warehouse development by the Irwell in Manchester, starting with the Rock House, in use by 1734 when the navigation was open. Warehouses generally rose straight from the water, cranes handling goods for craft alongside via the loading doors at every floor. The Old Quay warehouse, in use on the Irwell by 1740, was five storeys high with brick walls and wooden flooring. The hoists were worked by a horse capstan and possibly at some stage a water wheel. Many were of wood with tiled or boarded roofs. At Newbury, one of the weatherboarded granaries at the head of the Kennet Navigation remains. The salt sheds on the Weaver were of timber, framed on the outside, originally without metal fastenings because of the corrosive salt. Trolley ways could be laid in the roof trusses to bring the salt in from the works and drop it on to the floor. On the quayside a canopy was built out over the water. Other specialized sheds were those for storing pottery ball clay which had to be kept moist. Warehouse construction on the stillwater canals reached a high level of ingenuity, pioneered on the Bridgewater at Castlefield, Manchester. Brindley's tunnelled out basin to the foot of a shaft which led up to street level is well known, but soon after 1765 the approach to the tunnel was straddled by a brick warehouse which boats could always enter and these 'shipping holes' became a feature of canal warehouse design. If boats could not enter a canal warehouse they could lie alongside under a canopy which became general, especially at public wharves. Some canal warehouses became elaborate. At Ellesmere Port, where Telford designed a harbour to handle the transhipment traffic between canal boats and sea going vessels, the grain warehouse was built of brick on two water levels. It was opened in 1843, the engineer being Telford's successor William Cubitt. On the upper level the warehouse ran alongside the quayside, two storeys high, but it was served from the dock below, achieved by building it like a letter E, the three arms of the E projecting as wings over the water. The wings were supported on piers and arches of sufficient height to allow flats under. With two arches to each wing, two flats at a time, could be accommodated under each arm of the E, cargo being handled through trap doors in the soffit of each arch. There were hundreds of little country warehouses by the local wharf. They may only have been single storey sheds, simple brick, stone or timber structures. The Shropshire Union had many, like the remote Tyddin at the end of the Guilsfield branch. Some lockhouses had cellars used for warehousing as on the Thames & Severn at South Cerney. On this canal the warehouse and wharfinger's house were combined, the house being central, flanked by the warehouse space. The Leeds & Liverpool established a chain of public warehouses at Wigan, Leigh, Blackburn, Church, Burnley, Nelson, Skipton, Keighley and Shipley. It was usual for the canal and navigation companies to build and own the warehouses which, if not public warehouses, were leased out in whole or in part to others. Thus the Rochdale carriers William Jackson & Son in 1845 rented space at Manchester, Rochdale and Sowerby Bridge from the Rochdale company. Warehouses if on a canal company's wharf, were under the overall authority of the wharfinger, but large ones would have their own managers assisted by warehousemen, porters and checkers. The small ones on the Shropshire Union line from Hurleston to Newtown were in charge of local farmers acting on behalf of the company and paid by commission, at say 6d per ton on all goods passing through their hands.

Wharves are the stations of navigations, officially so called on the Grand Canal in Ireland. Their frequency along the route was a measure of the waterway's importance and activity. Without them and warehouses there could be no efficient collection or distribution of goods. In waterway parlance a wharf does not mean just a quay, but quay, warehouse, shed, office, counting house, weighbridge and cranes. Most wharves were for handling cargo between water and land transport; those developed for transhipment between water and rail becoming very specialized, the largest being on the Birmingham system. Sea port wharves handled goods between ships and canal and river boats, while the wharves at inland ports dealt with transhipments between river and canal boats, or canal boats of different sizes. Wharves ranged from City Road basin in London with quays and warehouses on each side of the $2\frac{1}{2}$ furlong arm off the Regent's main line, down to country wharves like Aynho on the Oxford Canal. Ownership of wharves was divided. Those under the canal or navigation company were public and could be used by any carrier, but there were many private wharves, owned or leased by factories, collieries, gas and electricity undertakings. Local authorities had wharves for sending away refuse, while sand and gravel merchants, sawmills and brickyards had wharves dealing with these materials. The premises owned and rented by the larger carrying firms were often extensive. Fellows, Morton & Clayton rented wharves and warehouses from the Grand Junction at Brentford and Uxbridge.

WATER SUPPLY.   On a river the water is there although, exceptionally, reservoirs might have to be built, for example for the Foss Navigation in Yorkshire. But it must be controlled to make sure it neither floods nor dries up. Part of the art of river improvement is control of the feed of tributaries by weirs and sluices and the diversion of excess water over the weirs which bypass the locks and cuts. Enclosures in the eighteenth century involved the straightening and improving of watercourses which fed more rapidly into the rivers and so increased the flood risk. Canals take their water, some millions of gallons a day, from many sources. Basically it comes from rain which feeds the rivers, lakes, streams, and artificial reservoirs. The rain also gives rise to land drainage, and there are supplies from underground wells, springs and colliery drainage. The water is used up by boats passing through the locks and by evaporation, percolation and leakage through ill fitting lock gates or the banks. Water loss can take place at overflow weirs which are too low or through their brickwork. Weeds and rushes consume water by their transpiration. On the Leeds & Liverpool, leakage and water losses apart from boat consumption, work out at an average of $1\frac{1}{4}$" per day over the whole surface of the canal. Evaporation and other losses are severe in a dry spell and the summer rainfall can be discounted by them. Winter rain overcomes the loss rate and it is this which the reservoirs store via their feeders and their own catchment. Whereas gravity supply is desirable, pumping must be undertaken to make use of the underground supplies, or lower reservoirs.

Feeders are sometimes a natural stream turned into the canal, but usually such a supply was tapped by an artificial channel; the Peasey Beck (164) in Westmorland passes under the Lancaster Canal at Crooklands, the feeder being taken from the upstream side of the aqueduct. An artificial feeder could be an elaborate affair, sometimes navigable like that from the Dee at Llantisilio via Llangollen to the Ellesmere Canal at Trevor, a shallow and narrow canal flowing quite fast. Some were of commercial importance, like the Welford arm of the Grand Union up to Welford wharf, $1\frac{5}{8}$ miles long. This comes in from Welford and Sulby reservoirs, joined by another from the more distant Naseby reservoir. Feeders built like a canal, but too small to navigate, are open leats with a fall towards the canal, 6' or 8' wide and 2' deep or so. They may be culverted, but they also have embankments, cuttings and aqueducts. A notable masonry aqueduct of 10 arches carries the feeder from the Cusher river at Tandragee to the summit of the Newry Navigation at Scarva.

PUMPING ENGINES.   If the summit was higher than the water supply or if the consumption off the summit was heavy, then a company had the expense of pumping, from a reservoir, from wells fed by mine drainage, or returning water up a flight of locks. Some economically minded canals used windmills and waterwheels, but most had a steam engine to be sure of their supply. The Thames & Severn, with a leaky summit fed from underground springs, started with a six sailed windpump which they put up at Thameshead in 1790 but by 1792 a Boulton & Watt beam engine had replaced it. On the Oxford Canal windpumps had been installed about 1786 at Hardwick lock near Banbury and in 1789 at Hillmorton. The Kennet & Avon erected windpumps between Devizes and Wilcot to feed the long $16\frac{1}{2}$ mile pound between Wootton Rivers and the Devizes flight before the canal was completed and before the Crofton engines were in steam, and in 1833-4 the Wey & Arun Junction Canal installed two windmills, one at lock 17 near Cranleigh to replenish the summit pound, the other a larger one, by lock 18 to refill the Run Common pound. Neither was satisfactory; repairs were costly, and the wind would fail during the summer, when it was most needed and both mills were sold in 1853. The pumps were reciprocating, two 12" diameter cylinders on the smaller, lifting 550 gallons a minute. Waterwheels driving reciprocating pumps were more certain. A 24' diameter one was used on the Montgomeryshire at Newtown to lift water from the Severn, with a steam engine in reserve. On the canal section of the Arun Navigation between Pallingham and Newbridge a waterwheel driven pump lifted water from a stream at Orfold, while on the Glamorganshire, canal water was returned from the Melingriffith tinplate works by two waterwheel pumps (49) and are of a simpler design than those at Claverton on the Kennet & Avon. The hard worked but elevated Birmingham system was dependent on pumping since the few reservoirs could not meet the heavy lockage demand. There were eventually seventeen steam pumping stations on the BCN, twelve recirculating water, by pumping, back to the higher levels, leaving five providing a supply (mainly mine drainage) in concert with the reservoirs which were refreshed by pumping, for example Rotton Park, Chasewater, Lodge Farm and Sneyd. First to be installed was Spon Lane in 1778 pumping from the 473' Wolverhampton level up to Brindley's 491' summit, soon followed in 1779 by a more powerful engine at Smethwick at the other end of the short summit, to lift water from the 453' Birmingham level. Both were Boulton & Watt engines, the second being removed in 1898 to the BCN works at Ocker Hill for safe keeping. In 1960 the engine went to Birmingham Museum of Science and Industry. It is a typical Watt single acting condensing engine of the period, using low pressure steam with a wooden beam and arch heads at each end, from which chains hang to form the linkage for piston and pump rods. The beam engine remained common for canal pumps until the 1880s, when compound or triple expansion marine type engines were introduced. They drove either reciprocating ram pumps off their crankshafts with pump cylinders lined up beneath the steam cylinders or, at a higher speed, centrifugal pumps coupled to the crankshaft end (30). The centrifugal pump, available from the 1850s has the advantage of delivering a large volume of water at a low head, ideal for canal work where the lift is generally low. Thus the Smethwick beam engine of 1779 and her 1804 sister, scrapped in 1898, were replaced in 1892 by two vertical compound engines, each driving a 16" bore centrifugal pump. Meanwhile there was the Cornish cycle, which had shown great economies after exhaustive tests

Plate 4.

Single Masted Mersey Flat
LENGTH: 50 to 75 feet.

THESE craft were built to work on the Mersey and associated navigations. Four flats called 'powder hoys' and owned by the Liverpool Magazines Co., were used in carrying explosives for their powder hulk at Bromborough. The distinctive livery of these vessels is shown here on a typical single masted flat.

0   10 feet

C. V. Waine 1978.

Jigger Flat

DIMENSIONS: 71´6˝ x 15´6˝ x 9´
of example

THESE flats were designed for coasting voyages and derived their name from the jigger mast as their mizzen was called. Most were built at the end of the 19th century.

at the tin mines. The Cornish beam engine, widely used from the 1830s, was single acting with steam at 40 to 50 psi. The piston raised the heavy pump rods, being lifted to begin its downward stroke by the weight of the latter. Economy was effected because the engine worked on an early cut off of steam. Best known of canal Cornish pumps are the preserved pair at Crofton, which delivered into the short summit of the Kennet & Avon until 1959. Less well known is the single cylinder 50" bore Cornish engine at Lea Wood on the Cromford Canal, pumping up from the Derwent. This was built in 1849 by the Milton Ironworks at Elsecar near Barnsley and is preserved. The Carlisle had a waterwheel driven pump to lift water from the Eden, installed in 1824, but found ten years later that they had to augment the supply with a Cornish engine, built in 1838 by Harvey's of Hayle. The waterwheel, driven from the Eden, would not work when the river was low. The Portsea needed a steam pump for all its water. Ill starred canals generally had water supply as one of their problems, resolved by expensive pumping. But flourishing canals with a heavy traffic also had to pump. The Grand Junction pumped to the summit at Tring and traffic growth led to nine pumps being installed between 1834 and 1841 at the locks on the northern approach to Tring, from Fenny Stratford to Marsworth. The 'Northern Engines' they were called, each returning water up its lock or group of locks. Another canal entirely dependent on pumping was the Sheffield. Steam engines with their heavy coal consumption, (Crofton burnt about 30 tons a day), gave way to diesel, diesel electric or mains electric. At Tringford, the pumping station for the Tring summit, the steam engines were replaced, the first in 1911 by an 80 hp electric pump supplied by an 100 hp diesel generator, the second (the older steam engine) in 1926 by mains electric pumps. Modern electric pumps are centrifugal, needing no attendant and little maintenance.

Reservoirs: Early canals relied on natural streams, springs or drainage from mines, and the Newry Navigation on Lough Shark, a natural lake on the summit. The Chesterfield, opened in 1777, had to use an artificial summit reservoir at Pebley, above Staveley. This held the winter rainfall, via feeders and by its own catchment, supplying the canal in a dry spell when other sources failed. This is the principle of a reservoir, to help equalize the supply and demand. Pebley was anticipated in Britain by Smethwick Great Reservoir and Titford on the Birmingham, completed by about 1772. William Jessop was the most reservoir conscious of the canal engineers. His biggest problems were on the Grand Junction with two summits to supply. That at Braunston was taken care of by a reservoir at Daventry, but Tring was difficult to feed because the canal ran higher than any reservoir could be built. Here pumping had to be undertaken from, eventually, six reservoirs at lower levels. The shorter the summit the more vital the reservoirs, hence the Rochdale's need of eight with a summit of only $\frac{3}{4}$ mile. A long summit pound could act as a reservoir, like the Forth & Clyde's, some 15 miles long. It was sometimes necessary to amplify the feed down the locks by building reservoirs to supply lower pounds. On the Leeds & Liverpool, with summit reservoirs at Foulridge, Slipper Hill and Whitemoor, the Burnley pound, $23\frac{1}{2}$ miles long, was augmented by a reservoir at Rishton near Blackburn opened round about 1830. As traffic grew heavy canals found more reservoir building a necessity. The Trent & Mersey, dependent on mine water at the Harecastle summit, augmented by water off the Caldon branch and its reservoir at Stanley, became desperate by the 1790s. The situation was eased by the opening of Rudyard, authorized in 1797, but a second big reservoir had to be built at Knypersley near Biddulph, opened in 1829, and feeding into the Caldon. The hard pressed Birmingham system was helped by the opening in 1800 of Chasewater and Rotton Park in the centre of the town in 1826. Sometimes reservoirs were built to store excess water from the canal for re-use in dry spells. Tardebigge on the Worcester & Birmingham did this, built near the top of the locks with a pump to return water to the summit, while Barrowford on the Leeds & Liverpool, opened in 1885, takes surplus water from the Foulridge reservoirs which can be fed into the Burnley pound below Barrowford locks. Reservoirs have to leave unhindered any flow of water which existed before their construction. They do this by providing compensation water via a weir. Sometimes a canal had to build reservoirs to supply compensation water for mills. The Worcester & Birmingham, taking water from the rivers Rea and Arrow built five. Southfield reservoir, near Sykehouse junction on the Knottingley-Goole canal, makes good water losses from lock operation at Goole. The amount of water needed, measured in lockfuls, had to be determined and the supplies gauged for a year or more, to discover their volume. These would include streams, springs, land drainage and above all rainwater on which everything depended. In the Pennines there were well watered valleys to be damned and the valley sides provided a natural catchment. In the Midlands it was not so easy, contours are gentler and the same depth could not be achieved. Reservoirs had to be shallower with more artificial embanking. The Tring reservoirs are 10' to 15' deep, that at Daventry 32'. The bank foundations might need piling and to prevent percolation through the embankment a central puddle ditch was dug. Collection was by a strainer box in the reservoir bottom where a pipe led into an arched culvert running under the headbank. The pipe would have a valve to regulate flow and there would be a depth gauge. Records would show the capacity of the reservoir at different depths measured in lockfuls and because the pipe had a known rate of discharge, the varying needs of the canal could be met. Overflow would be normally by a fixed overfall weir on the crest of the head bank. In charge of the reservoir was a keeper who might have responsibility over several. There were cases of reservoirs bursting, as at Black-Brook in 1799 on the Charnwood Forest line of the Leicester navigation. The overflow weir was too small and flood water carried away the embankment. In 1925 a reservoir dam burst above Dolgarrog in the Conway valley, Caernarvonshire, causing much damage and loss of life. As a result the Reservoirs (Safety Provisions) Act was passed in 1930. This demands

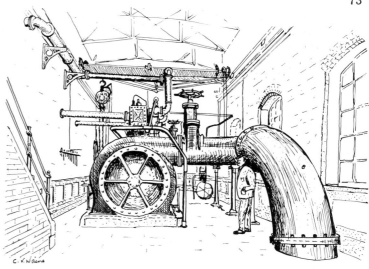

30. Centrifugal steam pump at Ellesmere Port for returning lockage water. The delivery pipe is in the foreground.

C. V. Waine

every ten years examination of each reservoir by an inspector appointed by the Home Office. He must check the repairs carried out, which are noted in a book assigned to every reservoir. Here are recorded weekly levels, signs of leakage and the repairs undertaken. The reservoir must have sufficient extra capacity to cope with the exceptional rainfall which can occur about once every 50 years. Reservoirs do more than feed canals. Some have been sold to local authorities, like the Rochdale ones, for local water supply. Others, while still supplying canals, are used by sailing clubs and for other water sports.

WEEDS and WEED CONTROL. Weeds are a natural hazard on any waterway although possibly less prevalent in the canal age for references are few. They are best kept down by frequent movement of craft, but on little used, shallow, canals and river navigations they impede traffic and consume water by their growth. Weed is either rooted in the bottom some species being totally submerged, or floating. Rooted weed is best eradicated, for cutting has a beneficial pruning effect. Cutting is easier but must be done annually by men wading in with scythes, or by making a chain of scythe blades sawed back and forth from the bank. Many canals have 1' draught paddle driven weed cutting boats (51). The cutter bar, making an 8' wide cut, works to and fro as on a hay mowing machine and can operate either ahead or astern. It can be raised and lowered by a wire to a maximum depth of 7'. With a 10 hp engine driving both the paddles and the cutters the craft can work as fast as 3 mph. When the weed is cut it is floated down to a boom laid across the canal, the current being created by drawing a lock paddle. Many companies used a hay type elevator to lift the weed out, otherwise it had to be forked. Often it was offered to local farmers as a manure. Total eradication has been achieved in modern times. Weed cutting is an all the year round job, different species demanding treatment at different seasons. They are best caught when young. Emergent weeds can be controlled by drowning them. Dependent on sunlight their growth is checked if they are submerged by the raising of the canal's water level. Few weeds grow under trees and none in tunnels.

WEIRS and SLUICES. A weir is a dam to hold back water. It may be pierced by openings whose apertures are controlled by sluice doors. A weir with no sluices is described as fixed, with sluices as a sluice; a fixed weir has a sill at its crest over which excess water flows, hence the description fixed overfall. Weirs create depth. Fish weirs were impermanent structures compared with mill dams, the latter pierced with locks for navigation. Land drainage and flood control demand weirs and sluices to regulate the flow of the tide inland and the discharge of fresh water into the tideway.

Canal Weirs: On the canal fixed overfall weirs are the regulators of water level in the pounds. Feeder streams and channels are brought in over weirs to regulate the flow into the canal, weirs are built at locks to send excess water down a bypass channel and there are waste weirs at salient points with their sills slightly above the top water level of the canal, turning excess water, which might otherwise burst the banks, into a stream. Flood paddles are additional precautions, but waste weirs are more used because they need no attention. Many extra have been built; it could need an 80' sill with 3" of water on it to equal the rate of discharge of one flood paddle. Weirs are used to gauge flow volume. A gauging weir is built with a sill like a notch, composed of a sharp edged plate along the crest and at each side, so that the length of sill is precise. Depth scales are set up three or four feet upstream of the weir edge to obtain a true reading, for the water level drops as it passes over the sill. With the depth of water and length of sill known, the volume passing over within a certain time can be calculated, either in locks per hour, later millions of gallons per day now metric. These 'sharp edged weirs' are sited at reservoir outlets, feeder inlets and pumping stations. Some have been replaced by continuously recording meters, such as the Venturi. Compensation water is required under a waterway's Act. The pre-canal flow of a feeder had not to be stopped, especially when supplies to mills were involved. So weirs of special design were built across feeder streams and below reservoirs. The compensation water is passed through a slot which delivers the amount demanded but no more. The slot, built of metal to precise measurements, takes water before any is fed to the canal, the canal feed passing over a sharp edged notch at a higher level, or as at Rudyard Lake over a long sill with a sharp edged weir lower down. A feature of compensation supplies, particularly noticeable at Rudyard, is the provision of a settling pond or lagoon above the compensation weir, to ensure that there is no head of water to force extra supplies through the compensation slot. At Rudyard the whole length of one side and one end of the 135' long narrow rectangular lagoon is a sill for the feed to the canal (168).

Fixed Weir Design: Mill dams on the rivers were made up of piled foundations capped by timber, of a piled framework filled by boulders resting on gravel, or of masonry resting on a piled foundation. Navigation weirs, as on the Severn, are a mound of rubble stone triangular in cross section with the two slopes protected by pitching, on the upstream side a layer of rubble, on the downstream an apron of fitted masonry. While the upstream side is sloped steeply, the downstream slope is gentle to break the force of the water. Pitching on the downstream side is continued beyond the foot of the slope to protect the river bed from scour. To prevent undermining, sheet piling is driven along the line of the sill and along the toe or foot of the downstream slope. The sill is stone or timber. Many weirs were built with the downstream slope stepped to break the force. Demand for a long sill to increase the rate of discharge, particularly on rivers with flood problems, led to some odd shapes. Many mill weirs were vee-shaped, the base of the vee pointing upstream so that the main flow was directed into a central channel. Navigation weirs were convex, on the upstream side, stronger than the vee. On the Severn, under the navigation improvements of the 1840s the overfall weirs were made oblique to the flow. At Castlefield, Manchester, Brindley built a six petalled foliated weir to achieve a total length of sill of 366 yd. Discharge was into a central hole. Here the Medlock was brought in to feed the canal, but led out via the weir to join the Irwell. The weir allowed for the fluctuations in the flow of the Medlock, but it became choked with mud and debris and was rebuilt on a smaller scale.

Sluices vary sill height by use of doors to deal with flood or drought conditions, (106) either impounding or freeing water. Fixed overfall weirs can be heightened on the sill by fitting boards or movable caps. Simplest of sluices are those with vertical draw doors, lifted to allow the water to flow over the sill beneath. In their most primitive form these were of the paddle and rimer type used at flash locks. Some East Anglian staunches were also vertically rising, the simplest way of overcoming water pressure. Modern draw door design has been helped by F.G.M.Stoney's patent rollers, first fitted to a sluice at Belleek on Lough Erne in 1883, and later to the Weaver outfall sluices built by the Manchester Ship Canal Co. Ten 30' span openings were made in the latter's river wall flanking the Mersey, the counterbalanced doors in each having a lift of 28'. Stoney rollers cut out friction in the vertical grooves, supplying rolling instead of sliding contact. They are mounted on frames linked to each door by chain cable, rising and falling in sympathy with the latter. Doors are made of timber, oak or greenheart, or of steel and timber. They are sealed by loose lengths of rubberfaced greenheart set along each vertical side, held in place in the grooves by water pressure. Along the top of many doors are timber boards, called ice caps, which guard the doors themselves from ice damage. Although many sluices remain hand operated, large doors are worked by electric or hydraulic power, the latter by rams. Counterbalances save power while some sluices are automatic, controlled by water height. Small sluices may be worked automatically by a vessel called a displacer, rising and falling in a well alongside. This is a float to which the gate is linked, water rising in the well causes the gate to open, falling to shut. Whereas draw doors create a limited aperture, some sluices are removed completely to allow uninterrupted passage for flood water. There was the American bear trap kind of shutter weir which collapsed into the bottom of the stream, so called because one door acted as a prop for the other like a bear trap. The tilting shutter pivots on a horizontal axis, possibly working automatically like that at

Throstle Nest on the Mersey & Irwell Navigation, installed in 1882. Here there were fourteen wooden shutters, each 12' long by 10' wide, with their axes above the centre of water pressure so that they would not open of their own accord. If the water rose they would tip and release more water, falling back as the level dropped. Tilting gates are common in modern drainage works, hinged at the bottom and worked manually or by electric motor. Radial gates date from the mid nineteenth century when in 1853 they were fitted to a Seine weir in Paris. Three are in use on the Nene serving as sluices and lock gates.

Syphon Weirs: Some weirs depend on syphonic action for discharge of surplus water. The weirs have fixed overfalls with tubes or barrels laid over the crest, their downstream ends discharging into a spillway and their upstream set at the required water level. If

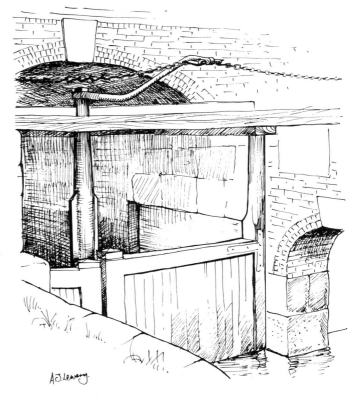

31. Scot's Float Sluice on the Eastern Rother above Rye. One of the four storm gates which can be quickly released for the discharge of flood water.

32. Overbridge arch repairs on the Grand Junction, note centring.

33. Bank protection; steam pile driving rig on the Grand Junction at Brentford (left) in the 1920s.

34. The Anderton hydraulic lift nearing completion prior to opening in 1875.

35. Subsidence; brine pumping caused this burst at Marbury, near Northwich (above) on the 21st of July 1907.
36. A tub-boat on its carriage at the Shrewsbury Canal's inclined plane at Trench, which worked until 1921.

this rises, air is driven out of the barrels and syphonic action starts, not ceasing until the upper level drops below the barrel's mouth, allowing air to enter and stopping the flow. Syphons take up little space, for a couple of barrels each 7' wide have a rate of discharge equal to an ordinary overfall weir sill 150' long. There are syphons at the Grand Union's Brent reservoirs.

Tidal Sluices. In the past these were mitred or 'pointing' doors which closed against the rising tide but opened as soon as the ebb dropped below the water level of the river behind the gates. Vermuyden used them in the Fens, but they have been modified to deal with the tide and land water. At Scot's Float Sluice (31) on the Eastern Rother above Rye, Sussex, there are four sets of storm gates and four sets of tide gates in the sluice, with a navigation pound lock alongside. The tide gates below are mitred against the flood tide which can only be admitted through paddles, but they swing open to the ebb. The sluice keeper can therefore shut out the tide or control its admission, depending on the amount of land water coming down. He can also hold back the ebb with the storm gates. Most historic of sluices is that at Denver, Norfolk.

WILD LIFE on WATERWAYS: (I) NATURAL HISTORY by R. P. Woods. Canals offer a fresh-water habitat to a variety of plant and animal species. All are inter-related with each other, and with the canal area. Canal water is of moderate depth and slow moving, and there is a pattern of life discernible in canals which is different from natural fresh water. Generally, slow running waters have a wider range of day and annual temperatures, and the bottom sand, clay or mud is stable, giving rise to a rich flora. This type of bottom receives the remains of dead plants and animals, providing food for scavengers. Green plants, ranging from single celled microscopic algae, to plants needing sunlight diminish as depth increases, or murky waters prevent the passage of light. Because green plants are able to manufacture food, they form the basis of life. Plant eating animals are themselves eaten by smaller numbers of meat eaters. Over a period of time, the water becomes crowded with plants, and silting occurs, until, instead of a fresh water habitat, a marsh will be established. Whilst there are numerous lower plants - algae, liverworts, mosses etc., these tend to be inconspicuous, although playing an important part in the food supply of herbivores. Higher plants - usually having some sort of flower, occupy several distinct areas - the bank and water's edge, the margin of canal water and the water itself. Marsh types, with their roots covered in water are found on the bankside, and include: Mares Tail, Meadow Sweet, Water Forget-me-not, Brooklime and Marsh Willow Herb, together with the beautiful flower of Yellow Flag, a relative of the garden iris. Sedges and rushes are plants with their 'feet' in water. Common trees on the waterside are Alder or Alder Buckthorn, if the ground is at all marshy. In undisturbed or disused waters, swamp plants such as reeds have creeping stems which penetrate the mud, and a single species such as Phragmites may take over and choke the water, but Bur-Reed (sparaganium) is often dominant in disused canals. True aquatic plants are either partially or wholly submerged, with leaves containing air-spaces, which allow them to float on or near the surface. In this way they obtain the energy of sunlight. Arrow-Head, named from the shape of its leaves, is familiar in many canals, even in the centre of cities. Yellow Water Lily has a smaller flower than that of the White Water Lily, but both flower between June and August. Frog-bit is locally common in canals in the south. It has either male or female flowers, and the flowers have three white petals. Various members of the indigenous Pondweed (potamogeton) family float in canals. Elodea, or Canadian Pondweed was introduced in the 19th century, and has spread throughout the waterways. A tiny plant, free floating on the surface, is Duckweed; this is the plant relished by ducks which makes still waters appear green. Amphibious Bistort is common with its clusters of small red flowers. It has two forms - one actually in the water, and the other, with shorter stemmed leaves, on the banks. One of the most striking of waterside flowers is a member of the Balsam family; this is Jewel-Weed which has orange flowers with blood red spots and is more likely to be found in the south. A noticeable plant, with upright stem, is water Figwort. It has small flowers, with dark red petals, arranged like another member of the same family, the Common Snapdragon. This garden escapee is sometimes found in the crevices of canal bridges, especially near buildings and cultivated ground.

Animals: The number of microscopic animals is vast. In still mud, on plant stems, on the slimy brickwork of the locks, are a variety of creatures which need considerable magnification to be seen. The majority are invertebrates, animals without backbones; Protozoas, Fresh Water Sponges, Hydra, Flatworms, True Worms, including Leeches; crustaceans such as Water Fleas and shrimp like creatures. Snails and Fresh Water Mussels are included in this range of animal types. Insects are obvious in their adult form but their dissimilar immature stages are aquatic, possessing gills which allow them to take oxygen from the water. Midges and Mosquitoes have caterpillar-like larvae, but Dragonflies are similar to the adult form, with definite jointed bodies and three pairs of legs. Of the many, the largest are the Emperor and the Golden Ringed Dragon-fly. Noticeable insects are those which move over the water surface. The Pond Skater has four long legs, and this dark brown insect propels itself upon its limb tips, making tiny indentations in the surface film. The more compact Whirligig Beetle gyrates in giddy fashion on the still surface. Other aquatic insects trap air bubbles which they carry under the surface when they dive, giving a silvery sheen to their bodies. Water Boatmen have their legs adapted in oar-like fashion, they 'row' through the water.

Birds: These are divided into those species which live on the water, or adjacent to it, and those which are visitors to stretches of water. In open country, Herons are seen, visiting waters which are stocked with fish, often some distance from a heronry. In flight the long neck is curled back in an 's' shape. Their prey is impaled by the sharp bill. The Mute Swan is common, using canals both for feeding and nesting. Their huge tangle of plant material is obvious, but in the season, well guarded. The male cob usually mates with the female pen for life and they are distinguished by the cob having a larger swollen black knob on top of the orange-red bill. They feed mainly on vegetable matter. Swans are good swimmers, but spectacular in flight, and when landing and taking off from water. Two birds which dodge amongst the stems of water plants are the Moorhen and the Dabchick or Little Grebe. The former is more common, with a conspicuous white flash at the rear, serving as a warning signal. It has a wide range of food, sometimes the chicks and eggs of other birds. Its own eggs are laid on a platform of dried water plants near the water. When danger threatens, Moorhens can sink under the surface, leaving only the bill protruding until the threat has passed. The males are fierce defenders of territory, and their fights can lead to damaged limbs. The smaller Dabchick has a dark brown back, chestnut breast and a pale face patch; and feeds on small fish, mainly the Stickleback. It is a weak flier but is a good swimmer, and diver. The young, which swim very soon after hatching, climb onto the parents' back and hide when the adult gives the 'twit twit' alarm. Besides the domestic ducks which swim on canals, the Mallard is likely to be seen. The duck is mottled brown; a useful shade when sitting on the nest, whereas the drake is a fine sight. He has a metallic green head, white collar and red brown chest, with lighter underparts, but this finery goes at the end of the summer when the drake is almost identical with the duck. Both have blue-purple wing patches. Mallards are mostly vegetarian, and build hidden nests on the ground, which are lined with down. The duck alone looks after the young until they fly, six or so weeks after hatching. The most brilliant of waterside birds is the swift flying Kingfisher, blue green above, orange chestnut below and with a forceful sharp beak. It fishes from a shallow perch and beats its catch before bolting it down in such a way that the fins and scales do not catch in the throat. Kingfishers tunnel into suitable banks, lining their nesting place with a thin layer of fish bones. The Reed Bunting is a sparrow sized bird. The cock has a white collar and black head, and together with the brown hen frequents the waterside. The flight is short and jerky, unlike that of those summer visitors which catch their insect prey low over the water. Swallows, Swifts and Martins are all members of the same family.

Mammals: The most common of waterside mammals is the Water Vole. It is often called the water rat, but, although about the same size as a common brown rat, it has a shorter tail, and a blunt face with short ears almost hidden in the fur, which is coarse and brown in colour. The Water Vole appears in the day, and several may congregate, as it is a sociable animal. It may be seen sitting up and grooming its fur on the mud under the bank overhang. When swimming, the Water Vole only uses the hind limbs, and the head and back are visible. If suspicious, the animal tends to sink down in the water, exposing only its nose. Diving is sudden, and the animal may remain under water for about a minute. A vegetarian, the Water Vole rarely takes small animals. Tunnelling is extensive, and nests are made of vegetation in the shelter of reed beds. Both the Common Brown Rat and Ship Rat are seen in canal areas, but the latter is smaller and more local; confined to waterside buildings. A shy and nocturnal animal rarely seen in the open, but a good swimmer, the Ship Rat is brownish or black, with lighter undersides. The usual colour of the Common Brown Rat is brown above, grading to off-white below. This shy animal appears in the day-time and follows regular pathways. Rats eat all types of food, and attack stored supplies. Nests are made under floors and in secret places, and are constructed from rag or paper scraps.

(II) ANGLING.   Fishing was an industry on the rivers before boats came, using weirs and traps, and a recreation. The artificial canals and their reservoirs were filled with fish from feeder streams, so the angler was presented in the later eighteenth century with a growing mileage of fishable water. Since the canals served towns, their banks were readily accessible to a growing urban and industrial population. The fishing of the waterways, rivers and canals has been parcelled out into leases to angling clubs who keep up fish stocks and control fishing. Nowadays club water is available to members and to those who buy day tickets. The numbers who fish are large, any Sunday might see 25,000 anglers on the banks. In the past, game fish, Salmon, Sea Trout, Brown Trout and Grayling were abundant in the rivers, but pollution caused their disappearance. A few game fish are found on canals like the Driffield which is clean, but the bulk of fish are coarse. Most often caught are Roach which move in shoals and average up to six ounces. Like them are Rudd, also shoal fish, common in Ireland. Bream are bottom feeders and average two pounds or so. Chub are larger still, moving in smaller groups. Chub and Dace are river fish which have been adapted to canals, the Dace being much smaller. Tench are bottom feeders reaching great weights, although two pounds would be good for a canal. Perch are shoal fish and feed on the fry of other fish. An average weight is half a pound. Pike are solitary and prey on other species, such as roach or bream. Average weights for Pike are up to seven pounds on a canal but much bigger fish have been caught, over fifty pounds. Eels are solitary scavengers, eating up dead fish, and migrate to sea to spawn. They average one or two pounds. Carp are occasionally found in canals. Among the very small species on the waterways are the Gudgeon, the Stone Loach, the very numerous Minnows and the tiny Sticklebacks with three, five or ten spines. The close season for fishing is from mid-March to mid-June.

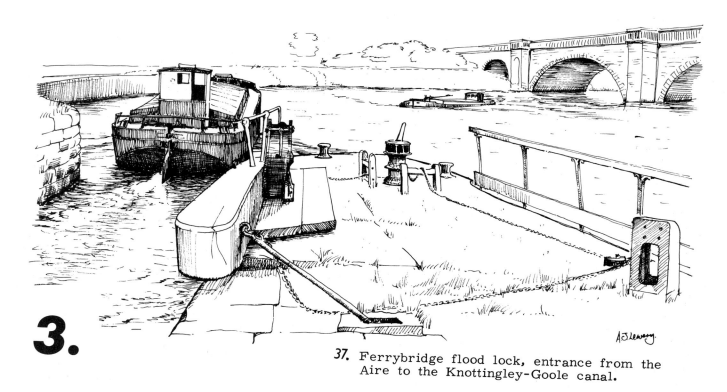

3.

37. Ferrybridge flood lock, entrance from the
Aire to the Knottingley-Goole canal.

Canal and River Navigations

OFFICERS and STAFF in the CANAL AGE.   Most canal companies were small. Their headquarters were in small places, the Trent & Mersey at Stone, the Wilts & Berks at Swindon (then a village) the Kennet Navigation at Newbury; some of the officers were part time, while the treasurer was honorary. The officers were appointed   by   the   canal's committee of management who ran the waterway as a board of directors with a chairman, responsible to the shareholders' meeting, the ultimate authority. The shareholders   were usually a small body (50 to 100) since the capital was not large, and they   met once   or twice a year to declare a dividend and possibly revise tolls within the maxima fixed by the canal's Act. They would also elect, normally annually, the committee of   management   and its chairman who was thus chairman of the company. The committee could   be from seven to fifteen, a few only attending meetings, monthly on a big canal, and three or four times a year on a small one. There were exceptions. On the Macclesfield a third of the committee retired each year, so each sat for three years, while on the Swansea and on the Mersey & Irwell from 1779 to 1794 all shareholders with five or more shares sat on the   committee. Some canals had sub-committees for works or finance, and big ones an executive committee which met frequently, for example on the Grand Junction. Committees took   decisions   on policy, wages and bye-laws, but daily administration was left to the officers.

The senior officers were the clerk, treasurer, engineer, accountant and the agent or in modern parlance, general manager. Some were part time, some combined several duties in the interests of economy.

Clerk: Usually a local solicitor paid an annual fee for canal work, he kept the minutes of both the shareholders' and the committee meetings and passed on   their   orders for execution. On a small navigation like the Loughborough he   could   also act as agent,   again part time.

Treasurer: A prominent committeeman and major shareholder   like   John   Hustler of the Leeds & Liverpool, he guided financial policy, particularly fund   raising during the con-struction stage. Having a large stake in the company he worked   hard for it and because of his position as a proprietor received no remuneration. After 1800 banks often took over the treasurership.

Accountant: More likely to be a full time employee, he kept the company's   books,   drew up the annual balance sheet and handed over the company's income to   the treasurer.   His daily duties were to collect the takings from the toll-keepers and check their   books,   also to take money from carriers with toll accounts on credit. Sometimes   he   was   called the clerk accountant and he was under the direction of the agent.

Agent or Superintendent: The canal's general manager, he was   full   time   and salaried, running the canal with the accountant as his immediate deputy. Under the agent's care were the toll-collectors, the clerical staff, the lock-keepers, the wharfingers   and   their   sub-sidiaries and the carrying staff if the company had a carrying fleet,   although   the   Grand Junction had a carrying manager.

Engineer: Not usually the engineer who built the canal but the man responsible for main-tenance and improvement, although William Jessop who had made the   Trent   Navigation remained all his life engineer. The engineer was often an ex-canal builder and contractor. His duties could be combined with those of agent, for the engineer ranked alongside rather than under the agent. Under the engineer were, on a large waterway like the Grand Junction, assistant and district engineers, and all maintenance staff.

Below the senior officers were the 'company' men, a name which has remained.

Toll-collectors: Stationed at each end of the company's system and at loading centres along the line, they took the tolls and handed the money to the accountant. They had to be honest and to ensure this, most companies picked them carefully and made them stand security for a certain sum in the event of dishonesty, when the sum would be forfeit. To take the correct tolls they had to check cargoes and gauge boats, both tasks liable to corruption. They were salaried and often given a house with an office. Their hours were dependent on the opening hours of the canal, the Nottingham being open from one hour before sunrise to one hour after sunset. If the canal was open all night the collector might have an assistant. They kept firearms, sometimes provided by the company, to defend themselves against thieves. Some were dismissed for dishonesty and embezzlement.

Lock-keepers: Under the agent were the lock-keepers, in the canal age at nearly every lock. They could do boat gauging and toll-collecting from boats loading near their lock, but their main function was to police the canal and see that traffic was running smoothly, to work the locks, aided by the boatmen, in order to speed traffic, stop quarrels over precedence and prevent damage to the lock machinery. They maintained the locks, prevented wastage of water and saw the bye-laws observed. On lock free canals similar men were employed as watchmen living in watch houses like that at Stretford on the Bridgewater. Lock-keepers were called 'lock tenters', (Macclesfield Canal and Leeds & Liverpool) 'water tenders' (Brecknock & Abergavenny Canal) or 'lock shutters' (Oxford Canal). They too were liable to temptation, boatmen might reward them for giving precedence or relaxing bye-laws, while they could have a business sideline, like those on the Bath & Bristol Avon who sold drinks to the passengers of the wherries. To deter these activities they were well paid and given the lock house, as well as a coal and candles allowance, the former to prevent theft from the boats. But hours were long and they had to be up at night if the canal was open and no night watchmen were available. For this they were paid extra, while night watchmen were employed to patrol the Cheshire locks of the Trent & Mersey into the twentieth century. Women were sometimes installed as lock-keepers apart from helping their husbands. The Weaver Navigation continued widows as lock-keepers, and some succeeded their late spouses as toll-collectors. Lock-keepers were specially appointed for junction stop locks. Tunnel keepers made sure traffic entered at the right times and later supervised tunnel tug operation. At lifts and inclined planes there were keepers who worked the mechanism and took the tolls. All were pensionable.

Constables: Under the Canal Constables Act of 1840 canal companies were empowered to appoint their own force. Only some of the larger companies like the Leeds & Liverpool did, although the small Aberdare had two policemen in 1846. The Derby Canal arranged for the town police to patrol the canal, and on the Neath and the Swansea the traders ran a police force to which the canal companies contributed. They were there to deal with pilferage and fighting, arresting and summonsing defaulters. They had their own superintendent and were uniformed. They supported the authority of the lock-keepers and remain as security men on the Lee. Special constables were enrolled from canal employees to deal with local disturbances; the bank rangers or lengthsmen of the Grand Surrey were formed into a force in 1811. On the Rochdale all the company's servants were sworn as specials.

Wharfingers: In charge of the public wharves and warehouses owned by the canal company, they acted as local agents or superintendents over local toll-collectors and lock-keepers. If the wharf were large then a warehouse manager was appointed. Under the wharfinger were warehousemen, porters, checkers and machine men to operate weighing machines and weighbridges. He could also be called wharf overseer and on the Yorkshire Ouse staith master. Because of temptation to theft, wharfingers were well paid and like most canal staff received pensions. They worked long hours particularly if there was much night traffic.

Dock and Harbourmasters: Canals and navigations which terminated at ports like Sharpness and Goole employed master mariners to supervise the movement of shipping. Here too would be stevedores, dockers and a pilotage service.

Clerical staff: The agent and the accountant would be backed by an under clerk or in modern parlance a chief clerk. He would supervise the book keeper, the cashier and the check clerks dealing with the issue and receipt of toll tickets, compilation of gauging books, invoices for warehousing charges and statements for carriers who had toll accounts with the company. Minor clerks copied correspondence into the letter books and were poorly paid.

Under the engineer were all the craftsmen and labourers concerned with canal maintenance. Most numerous were the Lengthsmen: They were called on the Leeds & Liverpool, bank rangers; on the Montgomeryshire, towpath men, and on the Bridgewater banksmen. They regularly inspected their length, say three miles, weekly, to watch for leaks or weak places in the banks. They repaired small leaks, but for major work sent in a report and after inspection by the engineering staff, these would be done by craftsmen, labourers and gangs of lengthsmen. Lengthsmen kept the towpath clear of growth and gravelled with 'raffle' or chippings. They trimmed hedges, cut weed and removed floating debris, but dredging was left to the spoon dredger and her crew of three.

Craftsmen: They were based at the maintenance yards and the company employed sufficient skills to deal with repairs to the canal and buildings. The carpenters who made lock gates, stop planks, arch centring for bridge repairs and stanks for tunnels were assisted by sawyers at the sawpit, labourers and apprentices. Masons and bricklayers inspected and repaired tunnel lining, aqueducts and lock chambers pushed out of true by frost. Blacksmiths shaped ironwork for lock gate collars, handrails and tie rods for weak bridges or aqueducts. There does not seem to have been much demarcation. The diary kept by the master carpenter at Banknewton maintenance yard on the Leeds & Liverpool during the 1860s records the wages and daily tasks of himself and his staff of three (later two) including an apprentice. They made and fitted lock gates, tarred them, painted swing bridges, fitted downspouts to lock cottages, pruned trees overhanging the towpath, and in winter went out with the ice-breaker, in particular freeing the locks. They never took holidays and worked a six day week, but it was a secure job with a pension. Over the ten years of the diary none of the men were sick. They probably worked twelve hours a day and were rewarded with ale for a heavy task like unloading oak at the yard. They put some work out to non-canal staff, slating and blacksmith work on their length from Skipton to Barnoldswick were done by outsiders and they bought paint, oil, nails, bolts and tar from local tradesmen. The master carpenter at Banknewton, who regularly inspected the locks and bridges on his length, got 4s a day, the journeyman or qualified carpenter 3/6 and the apprentice 1s rising to 1/8 until he was out of his time. This diary belongs to Merseyside Museums.

Labourers: Attached to each trade at the yard were the unskilled men. They had served no apprenticeship and worked at the direction of bricklayers, stone masons and carpenters, mixing mortar, stacking bricks, levering up coping stones, sweeping up sawdust, passing tools and brewing up. Like the craftsmen they were given a house, so that round each yard a community became established, at Norbury, at Fradley, at Banknewton and Stanley Ferry.

Reservoir Keepers: They lived on the job and watched the levels, regulating the feed to the canal. They would also be on the look out for weaknesses at the dam. Pumping stations would be manned by enginemen and firemen on shift.

Mole catcher: Because of the danger to embankments of mole runs and rabbit burrows, many companies had a full time catcher, others part time. The South Wales canals were particularly concerned about mole activity since they were embanked out of the valley sides. Carrying Department: If the company had one, it might be a subsidiary company or under a special superintendent of trade, as was the Thames & Severn's, with his clerks, boatmen, ostlers at the stables and boatbuilders at the company's dock. A large carrying department like that of the Shropshire Union employed hundreds of men.

OFFICERS and STAFF to MODERN TIMES. Railway owned navigations were absorbed into the parent organization and run as a department of the railway company under a canal manager and his staff. The committee was replaced by the railway's board of directors and the shareholders were railway shareholders. Sometimes the canal had its own engineer, but often it came under the railway's civil engineer. Traffic might be put under the railway's goods manager. Below the top men, the canal staff were retained under a railway authority. On the Shropshire Union, although under LNWR control, there was more autonomy, with an independent managerial staff and a canal engineer. From 1869 this officer was G.R.Jebb who in 1875 became engineer also of the Birmingham Canal Navigations, likewise under LNWR control but with its own administration. The Shropshire Union was under a joint committee composed of canal and railway men in equal numbers, to whom the canal manager was responsible. On independent navigations, committees were replaced by boards of directors, elected by the shareholders at their annual meetings. Clerks and treasurers were replaced by company secretaries, banks and chartered accountants. Under the general manager (the old agent) there would be local agents or superintendents, getting and keeping the business and overseeing local warehouse managers and toll-collectors. The word agent survived into the twentieth century, and people spoke of the Bradford agent, the Dewsbury agent and so on. Some agents were part-time, like the Shropshire Union's at Llangollen, and there were agents outside the company's system, acting as company representatives. Thus the Shropshire Union maintained goods agents in Liverpool and the Potteries, while the stationmaster at Manchester, Liverpool Road did the job part-time. Larger waterways were divided into districts with district engineers and inspectors. The Grand Junction had always been so divided, latterly into two, Northern and Southern, with the boundary at Fenny Stratford lock. The Shropshire Union was split into four districts, each with maintenance workshops, at Chester, Ellesmere, Welshpool and Norbury. A big organization like the Aire & Calder and the 1929 Grand Union had a managerial and technical staff commensurate with that of a railway. Both ran ports, operated large carrying fleets and had repair workshops and docks. During the 1939-45 War most of the waterways had been put under Government control and divided into six regions. Nationalization reduced them to four; the North Western based on Northwich (later Liverpool), the North Eastern on Leeds, the South Western on Gloucester and the South Eastern on Watford, the headquarters of the Docks & Inland Waterways Executive being London. The regions were called divisions, sub-divided into districts and the districts into sections. There was a Divisional Manager, with a Divisional Traffic Officer and a Divisional Commercial Officer under him, successors to the agents. The Traffic Officer, with his District Traffic Officers, was responsible for the carrying fleets of the Division and its toll offices, wharves and warehouses, while the Commercial Officer had the task of obtaining and keeping business and also handled pleasure craft. There was a Divisional Engineer with District Engineers under him, the Divisional Estate Officer and an Accountant. Local maintenance was under District and Section Inspectors responsible for stretches of waterway and supervising lengthsmen, craftsmen and lock-keepers. Toll-collecters remained under the Traffic Officer. Subsequent nationalization history has cut down staff and widened responsibilities. In 1964 under the British Waterways Board the four divisions were replaced by two regions, Northern and Southern, each with a manager and engineer. Headquarters of the Northern region became Leeds and the Southern Gloucester. The manager of each region is called the Marketing Officer and alongside him is the Principal Engineer for the region. In each region the freight services are administered by a group managers, in command of sales representatives, depot and dock managers, and superintendents of carrying fleets. The groups are based at Leeds, Nottingham, Weston Point, Birmingham, Gloucester and Brentford. There are also water sales and administration departments. Local administration is in the hands of Area Engineers with Area and Section Inspectors. Northern Region Areas are Wigan, Northwich, Castleford and Nottingham. Southern; Birmingham, Gloucester and Watford (the London area). The Gloucester Area Engineer has responsibilities in South Wales, the canals here in British Transport Commission days being under South Wales docks administration. Scottish canals are run from Glasgow, under the overall charge of the engineer and manager of the Caledonian who is based at Clachnaharry, Inverness, the canal being run because of its remoteness, separately from the other Scottish ones. British Waterways Board headquarters is at Melbury House in north-west London with the General Manager, Secretary, Chief Engineer and his assistants, Chief Estates Officer, Manager of the Freight Services Division and the Solicitor. The merchandise fleets in Yorkshire and on the Trent are managed from Hull and the Yorkshire coal compartment boat fleet by a superintendent at Goole. Pleasure boating and the amenity side come under the Amenity Services Manager at Melbury House, a post created in 1969, while an office in Watford handles pleasure craft inquiries and licensing. A mining engineer at Leeds deals with subsidence. Non-nationalized waterways, mainly in eastern England were under various bodies until the regional grouping of the Water Resources Act. Broadland was under the Great Yarmouth Port & Haven Commissioners, in the Fens there were the Great Ouse River Authority, the Welland and Nene River Authority and the Middle Level Commissioners, all with their administrative and engineering staffs. The Bridgewater Canal was a department of the Manchester Ship Canal Co., but run with its own offices in Chester Road, Manchester, while the Exeter Canal and the Beverley Beck are run by corporation departments. In Ireland the Grand was administered by a board of directors, a chairman and four members meeting weekly. Under them was the general Manager and Company Secretary, combined in the last days, who supervised the Chief Clerk, Goods Agent, Engineer, Chief Accountant, Cashier, Storekeeper and country agents at each of the 'stations'(wharves). The Goods Agent, who dealt with the traffic side, was in charge of the Dublin wharf, warehouse and motor lorry staff; the boatmen were under the supervision of the Cashier, while the General Manager was in charge of the country agents and of the head office staff. The latter also dealt with conditions of employment, salaries and wages. Under the Engineer was the Assistant Engineer, three district Inspectors and all the maintenance staff. When the Grand came under the control of Coras Iompair Eireann, the board of directors was dissolved and the General Manager, Chief Accountant, Engineer and Cashier were all retired, their staffs being put under existing CIE rail and road departments. The Assistant Engineer became the Assistant Engineer (Canals) and made directly responsible to the CIE Chief Civil Engineer.

COMPANY SEALS and EMBLEMS, Canal Heraldry. As corporate bodies, navigations had their seals, on which heraldic work might be included. Many were pictorial, canal scenes, portraits and allegorical figures. Father Thames was on the seal of the Thames Navigation Commissioners, a beatific figure paddling a boat, and later joined by the Severn nymph Sabrina, on the seal of the Thames & Severn Canal. The seal of the Wey & Arun Junction Canal carried the Arms of Guildford and Arundel, and the Shropshire Union had a seal with a multiple coat of arms characteristic of railway companies, embracing the towns the system served. The Shropshire Union stretched a point by the inclusion of Worcester and Stafford with Shrewsbury and Chester and the principality of Wales, but these had come within the company's railway ambitions. Many companies liked to portray the industries they served, particularly collieries whose main feature was a beam pumping engine. Engine houses with a nodding beam protruding occur on the Stourbridge seal, on the Somersetshire Coal Canal (98) and the Dudley. The Monmouthshire added a locomotive to their boat in 1849 when they became the Monmouthshire Railway & Canal Co. Mottoes are not so common, the Trent & Mersey had the well known 'In Patriam Populumque Fluat' (it flows for country and people), while the Chester Canal spoke of the domination of the waters. Tokens were issued as coinage during the national shortage of small change around the 1790s. They were struck on behalf of companies to pay their men and the contractor John Pinkerton had some showing a sailing barge as did a Thames & Severn token of 1795. More interesting is a token of 1789 showing the new Ketley inclined plane, the only surviving pictorial evidence. Some companies displayed a badge. The Weaver had a coat of arms identical with Chester's lions and sheaves. It was cast

38.

as a plaque on swing bridges, embellished staff buttons and was their seal (38). Many favoured a monogram like the Staffs. & Worcs., with S. & W. C. Co., etched on the windows of their committee boat the LADY HATHERTON. The new 1929 Grand Union adopted a map of their system enclosed by a circle, seen on their maintenance motor vans but not on their boats. Under nationalization the waterways have used badges following current railway and industrial trends. The life-buoy enclosing waves lasted from the days of the Docks & Inland Water-Ways Executive to the British Waterways Board. Its configuration allowed variations of the lettering without upsetting the design. In 1969 it was replaced by three stylized waves, a modern logogram. Badges are applied to notepaper, signboards, uniform caps and buttons. The Regent's Canal staff used to have the Prince of Wales' feathers on their buttons and Trent & Mersey men in later days, the knot of the North Staffordshire Railway on their coat lapels. The waves of the British Waterways Board do duty as a cap badge, while the Manchester Ship Canal use their coat of arms, which also appears on the gilt buttons of uniformed staff and the chromium plated buttons of the Ship Canal police. The arms are those of Warrington, Salford and Manchester. There are sleeve cuff badges of rank too, three stripes for a petroleum inspector, two for a senior lockmaster and one for an assistant lockmaster. Inland waterways fleets probably adopted easily recognized colour schemes from an early date, a simple use of shape and colour to act as a trademark. Pickfords' were bold, with a huge diamond on their cabin sides. Early river steam packet funnels had spirals of white and a colour, or white and red or black diamonds in a harlequin pattern from base to top. Later, funnels of inland navigation craft tended to follow the type used by deep sea ships. The Aire & Calder and the Rochdale had white with a black top, the Bridgewater Trustees and later the Manchester Ship Canal Co., black with two narrow white bands. The Severn & Canal Carrying Co's ATLANTA a coaster which came up to Worcester in the 1890s had a black funnel with a big white 'S' on each side, but badges on funnels became commoner by the 1950s. Imperial Chemical Industries affixed their ICI and two lines of waves on their Weaver packets. Motor narrow boats of the Grand Union Canal Carrying Co., went in for a diminutive motor ship style of funnel painted in bands of red, white and blue, their livery. Some were repainted in blue and yellow, the much discussed colours of 'British Waterways' until the early 1970s the yellow was replaced by white. Company or house flags were not so common on inland waterways; Brunner, Mond had a flag, blue with a gold crescent and the company's initials, while the Shropshire Union had a black flag with S U R & C C in white capitals, flown by their tugs on the Mersey. The Docks & Inland Waterways Executive had a flag which remained that of the British Waterways Board, blue with two thin gold lines paired horizontally across the flag at top and bottom. In the middle is a ship's wheel in gold.

ABERDARE CANAL, Glamorganshire. Promoted as a branch of the Glamorganshire Canal, it was intended to open up the Cynon valley and gain iron traffic from the Hirwaun works. It received its Act in 1793, for a canal from Abercynon on the Glamorganshire to near Aberdare with powers to build a tramroad extension and tramroad feeders within 8 miles of the canal. However money was scarce and the company found tramroad construction and the quarrying of limestone more remunerative, so the canal was neglected until 1810. The younger Thomas Sheasby became resident engineer, followed by George Overton and in 1812 the canal was opened, $6\frac{3}{4}$ miles long from the Glamorganshire at Abercynon to Ty-draw near Aberdare. There are three locks including the stop lock at Abercynon, large enough for Glamorganshire boats 60' x 8'9". Competition for ironworks traffic developed between the Aberdare and Neath Canals, although the Hirwaun works were quiet until 1819 when the Crawshays of Cyfarthfa took over. They virtually owned and managed the Aberdare Canal. From the 1840s iron was increasingly supplemented by steam coal from the Dyffryn and other pits, the heavy traffic causing a water shortage, so that a pump had to be used to raise water from the Cynon. However in 1846 a branch railway was opened to Aberdare from the Taff Vale followed in 1856 by a second railway in the Cynon valley. Increased coal production enabled the canal and railways to share the traffic, but more railway building in the 1860s led to a decline, the canal with the Glamorganshire being bought by Lord Bute in 1885. With subsidence affecting the waterway it was closed in 1900.

ABERDEENSHIRE CANAL. The Aberdeenshire was unique in being a seasonal waterway, restricted to summer operation from 1 April to 1 December because of ice and snow. It was proposed during the 1793 mania and an Act followed in 1796, with John Rennie as consulting engineer and George Fletcher as resident. Funds were insufficient and the company resorted to various shifts to have the line open, achieved by 1805. It was $18\frac{1}{4}$ miles long from Aberdeen to Inverurie with 17 locks 57' x 9', all near Aberdeen grouped in two flights at Stoneywood and Kitty-brewster. Goods traffic, mainly agricultural, started, followed by passenger boats offering a daily return service between Aberdeen and Inverurie. Speedier road coaches on the turnpike competed with the passenger boats and profits fell after 1816, the coaches running in winter. The terminal basin at Inverurie was called Port Elphinstone after the principal promoter of the canal, and the town flourished as a result of the traffic brought by the waterway. At Aberdeen, in 1834, the canal was connected to the harbour by a sea lock. This activity was threatened in the 1840s by the Great North of Scotland Railway, who saw the value of the canal as a rail bed as far as Inverurie and in 1845 made an offer which was accepted. Eventually in 1854 the canal was closed so that railway construction could proceed.

ABERDEENSHIRE PROJECTS, the PITFOUR CANAL. There were schemes for a canal on Deeside down to Aberdeen which came to nothing and for a canal started by James Fergusson in about 1790 along the north bank of the Ugie, north west of Peterhead, to bring shell sand from the sea by St. Fergus to his estate at Pitfour. A four mile lateral canal was built and apparently used, together with a branch cut in the early nineteenth century, just over $1\frac{1}{2}$ miles long, towards the village of Inverquinzie. The system was never fully complete and by 1868 was disused. Much of the canal works can still be traced.

ADELPHI CANAL, Derbyshire. A half mile private canal built about 1799 from the plant making cannon balls, known as the Adelphi works, established near Calow east of Chesterfield. The canal led from the works to a lane leading to Staveley and the Chesterfield Canal. $1\frac{1}{2}$ ton capacity boats were used. The plant, closed in 1850, drew condensing water for the works' steam engines from the canal.

River ADUR and BAYBRIDGE CANAL, Sussex. Although used commercially from the early 1700s the Adur was not improved until an Act of 1807 sanctioned work on the 14 miles from Shoreham to Bines bridge. Later, in 1825, came an act to canalize or at any rate widen the Adur for a further $3\frac{3}{8}$ miles to Baybridge. This was the so-called Baybridge Canal which had two locks 75' x 12'6". Railway competition from 1861 caused rapid decline, and closure in 1875, although the Ardur itself remained busy between Shoreham and the cement works and chalk pits at Upper Beeding until 1929, spritsail barges of 50-100 ton capacity handling the cargoes.

AIKE BECK (Lockington Navigation), Yorkshire. A tributary of the Hull, it was improved by the Hotham family about 1799, the works including a cut about a mile long to a wharf, used until the 1950s. There were two pound locks for craft 40' x 8'10" (not keels).

AIRE & CALDER NAVIGATION, Yorkshire, (38). There had been early attempts to extend the free navigation, which ceased at Knottingley, the tidal limit on the Aire. The Calder joining the Aire at Castleford, was un-navigable. Bills of 1621 and 1625 and efforts in the 1670s failed. The incentive was the West Riding cloth trade from Leeds and Wakefield. Surveys were made on the Aire by John Hadley, assisted by Samuel Sheldon on the Calder, for 15 ton boats to reach Leeds by the Aire and Wakefield by the Calder. The Act passed in May 1699. Undertakers from Leeds and Wakefield were to be responsible, commissioners were appointed to solve property disputes and four trustees, who could also be undertakers, were appointed to hold the navigation property. John Hadley was appointed engineer. He worked quickly upstream from Knottingley, for at the end of 1699 a boat reached Wakefield, and Leeds just under a year later. The Calder line was regarded as properly complete in 1702, the Leeds line being finished in 1701 except for the $1\frac{1}{2}$ mile long Crier Cut near Woodlesford opened in 1709. There were probably initially four locks on the Calder and twelve on the Aire, with masonry walls and timber flooring, each 58' to 60' long and up to 15' wide for 15 ton keels. The navigation commenced at Weeland some $8\frac{1}{2}$ miles below Knottingley, improvement of this lower section causing complaint, from landowners fearful of floods and traders who now had to pay a toll. Immediately on completion, the Navigation tolls were leased throughout most of the eighteenth century, the lessees also being responsible for repairs. A regular dividend was declared from 1718-19 and trade became buoyant. From 1744 Airmyn, only a mile from the confluence with the Ouse, became developed as a transhipment port. Like other river navigations the Aire & Calder came up against water mills, the undertakers pursuing a policy of controlling them so that the millers' tolls could be withdrawn to the benefit of traffic, and so that the undertakers would no longer have to compensate mills for lack of water. Since 1758 Peter Birt had been one of two lessees of the navigation, remaining when his partner dropped out. He stayed as sole lessee until 1774. He had a large carrying fleet and a big stake in the coal and cloth trades. From 1766 the Leeds & Liverpool Canal was being promoted and there were moves soon after to extend the navigation of the Ouse, and so it was not long before a Leeds to Selby canal was being considered. Such a canal would bypass the Aire, now thought out of date, as the undertakers, satisfied with their profits, had failed to make any improvements. The crisis came in 1771 when the tolls were again to be leased to Peter Birt for a 21 year period as from 1772.

Criticism of the Aire & Calder and their sole lessee led to their calling in John Smeaton who published his report in 1772. He recommended increasing the depth to suit 45 ton craft. But proposals came up for complete bypass canals from Leeds and Wakefield to the Don or the Ouse, encouraged by the completion of the Calder and Hebble to Sowerby Bridge in 1770, and schemes for what became the Rochdale Canal. One such was the Went Canal from Wakefield to Vermuyden's Dutch river; it would be 24 miles long and was surveyed by John Smith, but never reached Parliament. The other was the Leeds-Selby canal. Thomas Yeoman had estimated for this in 1769 and in 1772 John Longbotham did a survey for a canal direct from Leeds to the Ouse at Selby, which went forward as a bill at the same time as the Aire & Calder themselves were putting Smeaton's recommendations before Parliament. One of Smeaton's proposals was a bypass canal to avoid the Aire below Haddlesey. Jessop, his assistant, lengthened this and Parliament seemed to favour the Aire & Calder proposals, revised to make their canal enter the Ouse at Selby. The Bill for the Leeds-Selby was lost while the Act for the Aire & Calder proposals passed in 1774, including Jessop's Selby Canal. Jessop became engineer with John Grott as his resident and the Pinkerton brothers as contractors. In 1778 the Selby canal was open, but it was too shallow. It ran for $5\frac{1}{4}$ miles from the navigation at Haddlesey below Knottingley to the Ouse at Selby, with locks at Haddlesey and Selby. By 1785 most of the rest of the improvements had been completed as recommended by Smeaton and all old locks rebuilt. Selby became the main transhipment centre and in 1779 the Aire & Calder closed their Airmyn offices and started to develop Selby, although the old river was still busy. Because of the trade revival under the Younger Pitt, the Aire & Calder were thinking in the 1790s of more improvements, particularly at Selby. To increase their coal trade, the Aire & Calder started promotion of a canal to Barnsley in 1792. Pre-occupation with the Barnsley Canal and fund raising difficulties checked the Aire & Calder improvement programme, so the company became more interested in their carrying trade. This had been losing money but from 1796 was showing a profit, while the opening of the Rochdale Canal in 1804 was of enormous benefit to the Aire & Calder.

Partly because of the completion in 1816 of the Leeds & Liverpool Canal, a new basin was needed at Leeds for the increased trade, opened in 1818. Steam packets were established, in 1815 between Hull and Selby, in 1816 between York, Selby and Hull and by 1818 up the Trent to Gainsborough. These were passenger vessels but carried light goods too, including cloth. They encouraged fast road transport to serve them and undoubtedly worried the Aire & Calder, whose navigation was again becoming outdated. Fly-boats were an answer to compete with road transport and were soon introduced by the carriers. The time had come to make a better route to a lower point on the Ouse and entry to the Trent. Independent schemes appeared, the Aire & Dun Canal in 1817, followed by the Went & Wakefield, which spurred the Aire & Calder into action. The younger George Leather and John Rennie were called in to survey canals from Haddlesey to the Dun and to the Ouse respectively. Rennie's Ouse line was accepted, to run from below Knottingley to Goole, although altered in 1824 to start at Ferrybridge. A proposed branch to the Dutch River and therefore the Dun was deleted and the Act passed in 1820. George Leather was made engineer in charge, but Rennie was consulted on plans for Goole, proposing a basin there. Rennie however died in 1821 and the Goole plans were enlarged by Leather. Joliffe & Banks the contractors started at Goole in 1822. With a new canal line from Ferrybridge it was necessary to improve the navigation above, Rennie and Francis Giles had made recommendations but certain locks only were enlarged. Interest now centred on Goole which was expected to become a big transhipment port, eclipsing Selby and challenging Hull. Meanwhile Selby was flourishing because of the steam packets running to Hull. Many more appeared during the 1820s and to feed them fly-boat traffic on the Aire & Calder increased. The Company themselves entered the fly-boat trade in 1821. During this period the Aire & Calder was well served. In 1816 Joseph Priestley, son of the efficient manager of the Leeds & Liverpool, became head clerk, while Daniel Maude, one of the undertakers, was put in charge of finance. In 1825 Thomas Hammond Bartholomew became engineer. There were some minor private branches. Between 1815 and 1818 a 300 yard cut, the Haxby brothers' canal, was made off the Aire & Calder to limestone quarries, as was Staniland's Canal built at about the same time. Finally the Fairburn Canal, also to limestone quarries and about half a mile long was built in 1824 and was probably disused by 1850. In 1826 the Knottingley-Goole canal was opened, together with the basin, barge and ship docks at Goole. The Canal was 18¾ miles long with entrance locks at Ferrybridge (37) and Goole, and two intermediate ones. The Aire itself was left open as was the Selby canal, reached off the new canal by a branch which locked down to the Aire at Bank Dole below Knottingley. Passenger packets ran on the new waterway, offering a three hour service between Knottingley and Goole, connecting at the latter after 1827 with the Aire & Calder's own steam packet to Hull, the EAGLE. There was need for more improvement above Ferrybridge, the younger John Rennie having reported adversely on existing conditions. A 7' depth throughout was the aim, to be achieved by more canalization on both the Leeds and Wakefield lines. Telford looked over these and altered the Wakefield considerably, recommending an aqueduct over the Calder at Stanley Ferry. Work had also to be done on the Selby canal to placate Selby people and traders at York.

In 1835 the Leeds line improvements were finished under George Leather's superintendence, a canal now running alongside the Aire all the way from Hunslet to Allerton Bywater above Castleford. The canal was designed with masonry sides for steamers, 10 miles long, 7' deep and with seven 18' wide locks. A new dock was opened in 1843 at Leeds. The Calder canal line also under Leather was more difficult and took longer, mainly because of the aqueduct at Stanley Ferry. In 1839 the works were finished, the canal line adjacent to the winding Calder measuring 7½ miles from Wakefield to Castleford, and cutting five miles off the old river route. Later improvements were made nearer Castleford and completed in 1842. Meanwhile Goole was becoming known and was soon found too small to handle the nascent Continental trade. A new dock and entrance were built, the Ouse or Steamship dock. Railways threatened Yorkshire by the 1830s, the Leeds & Selby opening in 1834, connecting with a passenger and goods steam packet service to Hull. In 1840 a railway opened from Hull to Selby, a serious blow to the steam packets, which did however remain for about twenty years. Steam navigation on the Aire & Calder system itself was just beginning. A tug was put on in 1831 between Goole and Leeds, towing the fly-boats, soon followed by two more joining a steam passenger packet on the navigation, in competition with the swift twin hulled horse packets built in 1830 for the Knottingley-Goole canal, but the railways put an end to both. To face the railways the Aire & Calder increased their own carrying, while warehousing became very competitive, because the railways were building their own. In 1836 there was a scheme to join the Don with the Knottingley-Goole Canal, and in 1839 a project for an extension of the navigation in Leeds by a separate company up to Armley. This never came off although revived in 1865, but in 1845 the Leeds & Liverpool built their Arches lock branch on to the Aire. Railway competition became severe and the company made toll reductions, their main competitor being the Manchester, & Leeds Railway opened in 1841, but by 1845 a rates agreement was arranged. In 1845 the Wakefield, Pontefract & Goole railway was authorized which in 1847 was absorbed into the new Lancashire & Yorkshire company, along with the Manchester & Leeds. Traffic to Goole started in 1848 when the Railway Dock was opened at Goole. Inevitably a railway at Goole was damaging to Aire & Calder traffic, in spite of agreements over its apportionment. Corn and grain from Lincolnshire were main Aire & Calder cargoes, and some of this was transferred to rail, which gained much of the navigation's merchandise traffic. Joseph Priestley retired in 1851 and in 1853 the engineer Thomas Hammond Bartholomew died to be succeeded by his son. From 1855 the Aire & Calder abandoned agreements with the railways and to keep traffic, cut tolls. Inevitably in this period of intense competition there were railway offers to lease the Aire & Calder. In 1856 a joint lease was offered by the North Eastern and the Lancashire & Yorkshire. The Aire & Calder seemed willing, but the L. & Y., dropped out and A. & C., shareholders did not want a lease to a single railway, but a rates agreement was signed. For the navigation the 1850s were a critical decade, when railway competition hit hardest. On the Aire & Calder there were to be great carrying developments. Steam tugs were established, but in 1852 a fly-boat was given a steam engine and made into a cargo carrying tug able to pull other fly-boats. Hitherto the tugs were for the Aire & Calder's own carrying fleet but in 1857 two tugs were put on between Wakefield and Goole to tow bye traders' boats. Tugs marshalled boats into trains of six or seven and later up to thirteen when the locks were enlarged. Pollington on the Knottingley-Goole canal was the first to be extended, to 206', three times its original length, authorized in 1859. The others between Goole and Castleford followed, completed by 1867. In 1861 W. H. Bartholomew proposed the radical compartment boat system which saved the Aire & Calder's coal export trade from the railways. An experimental train was built and in 1865 commercial working started. Compartment boats did very well, carrying grain and merchandise on some of their return runs from Goole (39).

Meanwhile the Humber and Ouse approaches to Goole were being improved, including a dredging scheme in 1864. Lock lengthening was continued to Wakefield and Leeds, completed by about 1869 to the former and by 1873 to the latter, Woodstock lower lock on the Wakefield line being eliminated. In the 1880s the locks on the Selby line were rebuilt for craft 78'6" x 16'6". Further interest was being shown in the Humber and in the port of Hull where in 1871 the Aire & Calder bought a depot for their carrying fleets and in 1874 started on a wooden jetty at Blacktoft, replaced by concrete in 1956. This was for ships to moor to await the tide to Goole. Whereas the coal trade was doing so well because of the compartment boats and the construction of new colliery loading basins by the Aire & Calder, grain traffic was declining by the 1870s, mainly because of American imports. Merchandise was however increasing. Aside from the compartment boats the Aire & Calder had in the 1870s a carrying fleet of about 100 and also helped some of the independent carriers. They increased cranage and wharfage and in 1878 bought the Dewsbury old cut from Lord Savile's trustees, on which they created the Savile Town basin. Goole town became independent of the company in 1875 and eventually, in 1933, became a municipal borough. The Ouse (Lower) Improvement Act of 1884 transferred conservancy of the river, from York Corporation to the Aire & Calder, who on this $9\frac{1}{2}$ mile stretch from the railway bridge just above Goole down to Trent Falls, began a considerable improvement programme, building training walls to increase the scour and contain the channel. Much was done by 1894 but work went on into the 1930s, 1935 seeing the completion of the training walls at Trent Falls. More lock improvement followed in the 1880s between Goole and Castleford. Traffic was much improved when the New Junction Canal was built between the Don and the Knottingley-Goole Canal. Authorized in 1891, half the cost was to be borne by the Sheffield & South Yorkshire Navigation. It was to be $5\frac{1}{2}$ miles long from Sykehouse on the Knottingley-Goole canal to Kirk Bramwith on the Don. Work started in 1896 under Bartholomew, using direct labour, and the canal was opened in 1905. It is straight with one lock at Sykehouse 215' x 22'. Compartment boats could now work into South Yorkshire. In 1906 the Aire & Calder moved into new office premises at 1 Dock Street, Leeds. At the same time they were undertaking further lock enlargements from Castleford to Goole to a standard 215' x 22' x 9' on the sill which would allow by means of embayments, a train of 19 compartment boats to work through at one locking. On the eve of the 1914-18 War the Aire & Calder was doing excellently. War brought trouble, in 1915 there was air raid damage at Goole, while traffic declined due to the disruption of east coast trade. In the 1920s the navigation made a good recovery still with a considerable carrying fleet. The railway grouping helped them because Goole became an LMSR port, the only one in LNER territory. Goole therefore remained competitive and the LMSR used it well. During the 1939-45 War the Company's fly-boats were given up. In 1948 the Aire & Calder became part of the Docks & Inland Waterways Executive. Goole was separated from the navigation in 1953, the latter continuing under the waterways authorities. Traffic has altered. The smaller compartment boats have been withdrawn in large numbers because of the decline of the coal trade and the development of Immingham as a rail served port. Large 170 ton compartment boats were introduced in 1965 to supply the Ferrybridge C power station (39), but coal is not to be the navigation's mainstay. To replace coal, merchandise traffic has been encouraged. In 1958 the new depot at Knostrop below Leeds was opened and others closed, replaced by road services. The locks from Knostrop to Pollington and on the Wakefield line have been mechanized (16) and much bank protection and straightening done. Traffic was encouraging, well over three million tons in 1962. With a considerable oil contract signed in 1967, the British Waterways Board enlarged the Goole-Leeds line to take 500 ton barges. The 1971 tonnage was just over two million, some of it carried by 100 ton push tow barges operated by the British Waterways Board.

ALFORD CANAL, Lincolnshire. There was a scheme in 1805 for a canal from Alford south-east to Wainfleet, but it received little support. In 1825 an Alford canal was revived to run due east to the sea at Anderby creek. W. Tierney Clark looked over the line, proposing extravagant works on a canal $4\frac{1}{2}$ miles long for keels. Funds were raised and an Act passed in 1826, but there was insufficient money to do much if any work.

ANCHOLME NAVIGATION, Lincolnshire. Entering the Humber at South Ferriby, the Ancholme was used in the Middle Ages, and in 1287 a patent was granted for improvement up to Bishopbridge near Market Rasen. More important was the need to prevent flooding so the Ancholme remained under conflicting navigational and drainage interests. In 1635 a local landowner, Sir John Monsom, was given powers to make a new drainage channel and he built the New River Ancholme, a straight cut from Bishopbridge, by which the waters of the Ancholme, the Rase and numerous becks are taken out via Brigg to the Humber at South Ferriby. Navigation was not then considered of primary importance. One of the works was a sluice at South Ferriby to control the influence of the tide, which would otherwise deposit silt in the Ancholme channel. No more improvements were undertaken until the later eighteenth century, by which time the sluice at South Ferriby had become decayed and the drainage functions of the river much impaired. Riparian owners called in Thomas Yeoman to do a survey and he reported in 1766, explaining that the broken sluice was allowing silt to restrict the drainage channel. An Act for navigation and drainage improvement was passed in 1767, under commissioners, with emphasis on navigation. A new sluice and lock, were completed at South Ferriby in 1769, the lock being 70' x 14'9" on a separate channel from the sluice drain. Bishopbridge was difficult for craft to reach and in the late 1770s there was talk of a lock at Harlam Hill, $2\frac{1}{2}$ miles from Bishopbridge. Between 1781 and 1792 tolls were leased, the lessees also being responsible for some maintenance, but after 1792 the commissioners took the management back. Their drainage problems were by no means solved and in 1800, Isaac Leatham presented a report followed in 1801 by John Rennie, both recommending expensive works. Later Rennie reduced his estimate and the commissioners decided to proceed on his proposals. Under an Act of 1802 work began slowly because of lack of funds. Another lock was now proposed in addition to that at Harlam Hill, and mooring posts were to be provided at one mile intervals, also acting as mile posts. The elder Rennie died in 1821 and in 1824 his son was called in to consider how the works should continue. He planned a new sluice at South Ferriby and suggested a larger lock for 60 ton Yorkshire keels. A further Act was obtained in 1825 and work began again, although hampered by financial difficulties. However more was achieved, including the graceful iron bridge at Horkstow, a mile and a quarter above Ferriby Sluice. By mid-1828 the navigation was regarded as improved to Bishopbridge. All that remained to be done was the present sluice and lock at Ferriby Sluice, not opened until 1844. The work included a swing bridge which was replaced by one of similar design in 1935. The navigation was now 19 miles long. A passenger packet was started in 1856 from Brigg to Ferriby Sluice, connecting there with a steamer to Hull. The Ferriby Sluice service lasted until about 1905 (40), while there was a market boat from Bishopbridge to Brigg up to 1915. Coal and cattle food were principal cargoes to Brigg, with corn, bricks and manure downstream. The railway reached Brigg in 1848 and navigation takings declined although they were improving again by the end of the nineteenth century. Brigg is still accessible for commercial craft, but only pleasure boats can reach Bishopbridge. Drainage improvements were undertaken in the 1930s, Harlam Hill lock now having an upper guillotine gate for flood control but mitred lower gates.

39. A train of compartment boats passes the chutes at Castleford on the Aire & Calder (below, left). Note the recesses in the 'stern' to take the 'stempost' or knee of the succeeding boat. The compartment boat tipples at Ferrybridge C power station (below, right) one of the large compartment boats is shown in this view from the cab of the 'Jumbo' or boat manipulator. These large modern craft carry 170 tons.

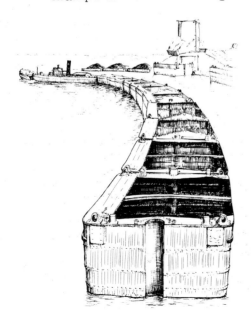

40. Horse drawn pass-
enger packet GEM
at Ferriby Sluice.

ANDOVER CANAL, Hamp-
shire. Robert Whitworth made
a survey in 1770 for a canal to
run from Andover down the
Test valley to Redbridge on
Southampton Water. The scheme
lay dormant until 1788 when he
made another survey, used in 1789 by an Act. As completed in 1794 the canal, via Stockbridge and Romsey was 22 miles long with 24 locks for craft 65' x 8'6". Trade was
mainly in coal and agricultural produce. No dividends were ever paid to the shareholders,
and railways in the area from 1851 sealed the fate of this rural waterway. In 1859 it was
bought by the Andover & Redbridge Railway who closed it, using about $14\frac{1}{4}$ miles of the
canal as a railbed (see also page 94).

ANGUS SCHEMES. William Keir in 1767 surveyed a line from Perth to bring coal to
Angus. The Commissioners of Forfeited Estates were keen, Smeaton, Mackell and Brindley
being asked for help. Then in 1770 James Watt suggested a 36 mile level canal from Perth
via Coupar Angus to Forfar. Later in 1788 Robert Whitworth surveyed a canal from near
Arbroath to Forfar. Most remarkable was a canal proposed in 1810 to run from the Clyde
at Dumbarton via Stirling and Perth to Stonehaven. There were plans for a canal between
Brechin and Montrose and in 1817 Robert Stevenson surveyed a further canal between
Arbroath and Forfar.

ANNANDALE and NITHDALE CANALS SCHEMES, Dumfriesshire. In about 1810 a canal
was proposed from Lochmaben down to Annan parallel with the Annan River, but nothing
was done, nor did a similar scheme materialise to cut a canal by the Nith from Dalswinton above Dumfries to the Solway at Caerlaverock Castle.

River ARUN & ARUN NAVIGATION, Sussex. Partially navigable since the Conquest,
the Arun was much improved in the sixteenth century, particularly the port of Arundel,
and boats could reach Pallingham in Elizabeth's reign. Arundel became a busy port in the
seventeenth century and a shipbuilding centre in the eighteenth. However the river above
the tidal limit at Houghton needed more improvement and an Act was passed in 1785 to extend the navigation as far as Newbridge near Billingshurst. The works were completed by
1787 and involved a canal from Pallingham running alongside the river to Newbridge,
crossing it by an aqueduct at Orfold. To avoid the Arun's bend round by Pulborough a cut-
off canal was next dug from Coldwaltham to Stopham piercing the low Hardham Hill by a
375 yard tunnel, opened in 1790. There were six locks, the distance from Newbridge to
Houghton, via the Coldwaltham cut, being $12\frac{1}{4}$ miles, and from Houghton to the sea at
Littlehampton $15\frac{1}{2}$ miles. Not until 1816 with the opening of the Wey & Arun Canal did the
Arun become more than just a farmers' waterway. Although in the 1830s the navigation did
quite well, railway construction sealed its fate. By the 1880s the Pallingham to Newbridge
canal section was in a poor state and the last barge passed in 1888. Hardham tunnel was
closed the following year, although the two artificial cuts were not officially abandoned
until 1896. The river lasted longer, during the 1900s there was a steady brick traffic from
Harwoods Green below Pallingham and chalk from Houghton Bridge, finally stopped in 1938
by the substitution of a fixed structure for the old rolling bridge at Ford, on the newly
electrified Havant-Brighton line. Now, however, restoration is in progress to link up with
the Wey.

Earl of ASHBURNHAM'S CANAL, Carmarthenshire. About 1796 a canal $1\frac{1}{4}$ miles long
was built for the Earl of Ashburnham from Frwd near Pembrey to the estuary of the
Gwendraeth, with a $\frac{1}{4}$ mile branch to Coed, the latter probably built in 1805. Another local
canal was the very short Bowser's Level from a coal level near Ffrwd to a nearby road.
It was mostly disused by 1816 when joined by the Kidwelly & Llanelly near Ffrwd, offering
an alternative route to the coast, and completely so by about 1867 when the Kidwelly &
Llanelly Canal became disused.

ASHBURTON CANAL PROJECT, Devon. Proposed from above Totnes to Ashburton, a
survey was made in 1793 and a Bill sought, but because of the war against the French the
project was dropped.

ASHBY-DE-LA-ZOUCH CANAL, Warwickshire, Derbyshire, Leicestershire. Called the
Moira cut by boatmen because it was built only to Moira and not to Ashby-de-la-Zouch as
intended. It was started for two reasons, the upper Trent navigation to Burton were keen
to gain a coal supply, independent of the Trent & Mersey, while the landowners wanted
to develop the local coalfield at Ashby-de-la-Zouch. A through canal from the Trent at
Burton to the Coventry Canal was suggested in 1781 and surveyed by Robert Whitworth. In
1787 the scheme was revived, William Jessop making a report. The Ashby mania promotion was intended to pass coal off the Coventry down to the Trent and feed it to the many
limeworks in the Ashby-de-la-Zouch area. Robert Whitworth put forward a plan checked by
Jessop for a canal between the Coventry and Ashby-de-la-Zouch only, but the 1792 Bill
was lost. The Bill, introduced again, passed in 1794. It was to be a broad canal to suit
river boats because of a possible junction with the Trent. Cutting began and the junction
with the Coventry was made at Marston outside Bedworth but tramroads were built instead

to the limeworks on the high land north of Ashby-de-la-Zouch. The engineer was Robert Whitworth jointly with his son Robert. Both were dismissed in 1797 and replaced by Thomas Newbold. Meanwhile the Ashby had become involved with the 1796 project for the Commercial Canal which was defeated and the Ashby was left to consider a line on to the Trent as originally proposed. There were unsuccessful moves to amalgamate with the Burton Boat Co. who leased the upper Trent. Work pressed on and in 1798 the canal was open from Ashby Woulds (Moira) about three miles west of Ashby-de-la-Zouch to Market Bosworth. The tramroads from the canal to Ticknall and Cloud Hill north of Ashby-de-la-Zouch were started in 1799 and opened in 1802, Benjamin Outram having advised on construction. In 1804 the canal was open from Marston to Ashby Woulds. But the collieries around Ashby-de-la-Zouch were not developing well, and so no local coal was carried until the Moira colliery, sunk in 1804 by Lord Moira, introduced their popular domestic coal to London and the Midlands in 1815, so that by the 1820s and 1830s the Ashby was carrying a heavy traffic. The canal was 30 miles long with only a 14' wide stop lock at Marston, following the 300' contour on the western side of the Charnwood Forest uplands. A short 250 yd tunnel was driven at Snarestone near Measham, built broad. In 1816 a passenger boat had been started privately, while another useful traffic was cheese from Measham. In 1819 the Marston stop lock was narrowed, for the Coventry and Oxford had never been widened and only narrow boats were using the Ashby. The passenger service took a more remunerative turn when in about 1826 medicinal salt water was found in the Moira pits. In 1833 came the Coleorton Railway from the canal's Coleorton tramroad to join the Leicester & Swannington, but in 1846 the Midland bought the Ashby, traffic being safeguarded by the enforcement of low tolls. Moira coal continued to go by canal, the colliery having their own fleet of narrow boats. The colliery also in 1856 started a tug, the PIONEER, ideal on the lock free Ashby. The Midland objected to her use because of possible damage to the banks but a court case in Chancery found in favour of the tug and the PIONEER was joined by the VOLUNTEER, both working trains of boats down to Braunston. Eventually the canal succumbed to railway developments. Subsidence was another enemy, the canal being closed in 1918 by a burst embankment near Moira. A new length had to be built, opened in 1919. By 1944 the subsidence was serious around Moira, the colliery still sending coal by boat but now wanting to mine beneath the canal. The LMS, successors to the Midland, had tried to give the canal to the Coventry who refused it, but now they emptied the upper $2\frac{1}{2}$ miles between Moira and Donisthorpe. The British Transport Commission abandoned a further $4\frac{7}{8}$ miles down to Measham in 1957 but between Measham and Marston the canal remained open. The Ashby Canal Association in 1969 took over the organisation of the coal trade from their own canal and from the Coventry to John Dickinson's paper mills at Croxley near Watford on the Grand Junction. This ceased in 1970 but the Association's Ashby Canal Transport continue their support of working narrow boat operators.

ASHTON CANAL, Lancashire, Cheshire. The Ashton was encouraged by the moves in 1791 for the Rochdale Canal. It was promoted in isolation, to run from Manchester to Ashton-under-Lyne with a branch towards Oldham, the Act passing in 1792. Thomas Brown had done the surveys but construction proceeded under no official engineer. In 1793 the branch towards Oldham was authorized to extend to Hollinwood nearer the town and another branch to Stockport was sanctioned, with a branch to Denton. Most of the main line was ready by about 1796 together with the Hollinwood branch, and the line to Stockport and the short Fairbottom branch off the Hollinwood opened in 1797. Earlier, this same Hollinwood branch had been extended by a private canal 1 mile long owned by the Werneth Colliery Co. The branch to Denton was abandoned in 1798 because of difficult cutting. Finally in 1799 the Ashton was extended from Ancoats into Manchester, Piccadilly, where in 1800 it made the Ducie Street junction with the Rochdale. By 1800, the Peak Forest was open from its junction with the Ashton at the latter's 40 yd Dukinfield branch across the Tame, and the Huddersfield was nearly finished. As completed the Ashton main line was $6\frac{3}{4}$ miles long with 18 narrow locks, the Stockport branch $4\frac{7}{8}$ miles on the level, the Hollinwood branch (excluding the Werneth Canal) was $4\frac{5}{8}$ miles with 7 locks including a staircase pair at Waterhouses where the level Fairbottom branch, $1\frac{1}{8}$ mile went off. Finally there was a $\frac{1}{4}$ mile branch and associated arms in Islington, Manchester. It was a canal of aqueducts, over the Medlock at Waterhouses where there was also a 110 yd tunnel, opened out in 1914, over the Tame at Dukinfield, over Store Street in Ancoats and again over the Medlock at Beswick Street. Water came from the Medlock, from reservoirs at Hollinwood and Audenshaw, from mine pumping via the Werneth Canal and from the Huddersfield and the Peak Forest. A beam engine pumped back up the Waterhouses flight. The Ashton worked in close harmony with the Peak Forest and the Huddersfield, the closest ties existing with the Peak Forest passenger packet services introduced in 1797 between Stockport, Ashton and Manchester for a short time. Opening of the Macclesfield and the Cromford & High Peak Railway, both in 1831, brought more traffic to the Ashton, as did the Sheffield, Ashton-under-Lyne & Manchester Railway coming in 1841 right by the canal at Guide Bridge near Dukinfield. Canal passenger services were quickly started between Guide Bridge station and Ashton, but a rail branch killed this enterprise in 1845. The future was dim and the shareholders welcomed an offer by the railway which took effect in 1848. The railway ran a small carrying fleet in connection with goods trains at Guide Bridge, however this was given up in 1892. Road services after the 1914-18 war hastened the canal's end, and it was now seriously affected by colliery subsidence. The Hollinwood branch was closed in 1932, the Stockport ceased to be used about 1933 and the main line carried little after the 1939-45 war, traffic ceasing in 1950, and by 1960 it was quite impassable. In 1968 a large scale programme to clean up the Ashton by voluntary labour was started by the Peak Forest Canal Society and the Inland Waterways Association with the ready help of the British Waterways Board. In 1971 the British Waterways Board promised full restoration, and in 1974 it was reopened as part of the 'Cheshire Ring' along with the lower Peak Forest, the Rochdale section following in 1976.

River AVON, Hampshire, Wiltshire. Never properly improved, the Hampshire Avon from Christchurch up to Salisbury received an Act in 1664-5. Work started in 1675 under Samuel Fortrey for Salisbury Corporation but stopped in 1677. A private group took over and improvements were completed after a fashion by 1684, although additional work was done at the very end of the century, resulting in the building of flash locks and perhaps three pound locks on the 36 mile navigation. There does not seem to have been any commercial traffic after 1705.

River AVON , Somerset. See Kennet & Avon Canal.

River AVON, Warwickshire, Worcestershire, Gloucestershire. William 'Water-works' Sandys of Fladbury, Evesham financed and engineered improvements to the Avon from 1636 and by about 1639 the river was passable from its junction with the Severn at Tewkesbury up to Stratford for 30 ton craft, with 13 watergates and pound locks to placate millers, a distance of $45\frac{3}{4}$ miles, a most impressive and costly achievement. Further work was done by William Say during the Commonwealth, while from 1664 a syndicate, which included Andrew Yarranton, built six more locks above Evesham. By the 1750s control of the river had passed into many hands, and to remedy confusion the borough of Evesham in 1751 together with others, obtained an Act to open the Avon to all and fix tolls. After this, the lower river, below Evesham, passed into ownership of the Perrott family who made improvements, while the upper river remained under the control of Lord Windsor's family, granted the ownership in 1664. By the end of the eighteenth century the Upper Avon was in poor condition with no horse path which neither navigation was ever to possess. It was rescued by William James who in 1813 gained ownership between Evesham and Stratford. With James' bankruptcy the Upper Avon was sold in 1824 to a syndicate closely connected with the Stratford Canal who built more locks and undertook dredging to restore traffic which did improve, coming off the Stratford Canal which itself leased the upper river in 1842. The Upper Avon, $17\frac{1}{2}$ miles long, now had eleven pound locks and one watergate at Bidford, able to take craft about 58' x 11'6". The Lower Avon was now under the control of the Worcester & Birmingham Canal who had leased the navigation from the Perrott family in 1830. Arrival of the Oxford, Worcester & Wolverhampton Railway at Evesham in 1852 took upper river traffic and after 1857 it became disused, although acquired in 1859 on behalf of the railway company. Complete decay followed, but under the Upper Avon Navigation Trust the river was reopened to Stratford in 1974, and there are ideas of continuing to Warwick. The Lower Avon also suffered railway competition from 1864 onwards. In 1872 the second lease of the Worcester & Birmingham Canal expired and was not renewed. Nevertheless the navigation, $28\frac{1}{4}$ miles long with seven pound locks taking craft 70' x 14'6" and two watergates, struggled on, but during the 1939-45 War became unnavigable above Pershore, although grain traffic to Pershore remained until 1972. However in 1950 because of pleasure boating, the Lower Avon Navigation Trust was formed by local parties and the Inland Waterways Association to restore the river, the first of such projects. In 1962 boats could reach Evesham and in 1964 Offenham, two miles above.

Loch AWE CANAL PROJECT, Argyllshire. In 1793 a company was formed to make a branch from the Crinan to the south-west end of Loch Awe.

Rivers AXE and BRUE and PILLROW CUT, Somerset. The Axe rising near Wells reaches the sea near Weston-super-Mare, the Brue flows into the Parrett estuary at Highbridge, while the Pillrow Cut used to join the two. This last was developed in mediaeval times from a natural waterway into a canal for navigation and drainage and used by Glastonbury Abbey, but after the Dissolution decayed. The Brue and the Axe were navigable until the drainage Acts of 1801 and 1802.

AYLSHAM or UPPER BURE NAVIGATION, Norfolk. The lower Bure down to Yarmouth was commercially used for centuries, but wherries could not go above Coltishall and Aylsham relied on land transport. In 1773 there were moves to extend the navigation and an Act passed. Work started in 1774, the surveys having been done by a Mr. Biederman, and estimates prepared by John Adey. By 1777 money was short, but the navigation far from finished, the engineer John Smith submitting estimates for completion. Loans were raised locally and work continued under Smith who was in 1779 joined by John Green of Wroxham. The navigation opened in October of that year. The course of the Bure was largely unaltered save for a mile of cut at Aylsham to the basin, with a further cut to the mill pool, so that wherries could load and discharge alongside the flour mills. With a length of $9\frac{1}{2}$ miles the navigation had five locks for small 10 to 13 ton wherries (54' x 12'8") drawing up to 2'6". For a hundred years the navigation was busy with 26 or so wherries trading to Aylsham. They carried coal, corn and timber to Aylsham and flour from the town's mills. Bricks were another cargo from a yard near Oxnead and marl from Horstead Hall estate. The pits on the estate were served by a system of navigable dikes. Decline came with the opening in the 1880s of the Wroxham-Aylsham and the North Walsham-Melton Constable railway lines. Water traffic survived until the great floods of 1912 badly damaged the locks. Repairs were beyond the resources of the navigation and the waterway was formally abandoned in 1928.

BALLINAMORE & BALLYCONNELL CANAL, Co Leitrim, Cavan, Fermanagh. It seemed worthwhile to join the Shannon with Lough Erne, linked with Lough Neagh and Belfast by the Ulster Canal. The project began in the 1780s, when the River Woodford improvements started from Lough Erne up to Ballyconnell, but the work languished until 1839 when William Mulvany surveyed for a canal to join Lough Erne and the Shannon. Because land drainage was involved, the Board of Works took an interest, encouraged by the completion in 1842 of the Ulster Canal and works on the Shannon. So public money was allocated and work began in 1846 on the canal which was completed in 1859. It had a total length of 38 miles, partly canal, partly river navigation with artificial cuts, and partly lough. The 16 locks were made for boats 82' x 16'6". The loughs precluded horse haulage and from the point of view of traffic the canal was a disaster, with few trade boats and only occasional pleasure craft and by 1873 the canal sections had become too shallow for navigation. It may possibly be reopened for pleasure craft.

Lower BANN NAVIGATION, Co Antrim, Londonderry. Lough Neagh's outlet to the sea, the Lower Bann was shallow and liable to floods. Improvement of the Lower Bann was discussed during the 1700s. The need to alleviate distress in the 1840s by providing work led to an Act in 1842. Elaborate plans were made to deepen the Lower Bann and remove the ridge of rock at Portna which was obstructing the channel, at the same time building locks for an efficient navigation, so that screw steamers could reach Lough Neagh from the sea. Works started in 1847 under the Board of Public Works with Charles Ottley as engineer. In 1859 the works were completed and the navigation put under a trust from Antrim and Londonderry. As completed it was $32\frac{3}{8}$ miles long from Coleraine to Toomebridge, with 6 locks (2 a staircase pair) large enough for craft 120' x 19'. There was no towpath, so presumably powered vessels were expected, including tugs towing lighters in trains, but by 1859 there were plenty of railways in the Lough Neagh area. The works were a fair success from the drainage and land reclamation angle. Two passenger and goods steamers were tried on the Lower Bann from 1863 until 1871, but by the 1880s the Lower Bann Navigation was near abandonment but seemed likely to be saved by improvement of the port of Coleraine, undertaken between 1879 and 1884. Unfortunately the development of Belfast overshadowed both Coleraine and the Bann and traffic dwindled still further and by 1905 had almost ceased. In 1929 the trust was abolished and the river put under the Ministry of Finance of the Government of Northern Ireland, who became responsible both for drainage and navigation. Today the Lower Bann is still open, although the government are more concerned with its drainage efficiency. Sand and gravel are the main cargoes, handled by motor barges and there are a few pleasure craft.

Upper BANN NAVIGATION, including the BLACKWATER, Co Tyrone, Armagh, Down. Almost all the inland waterways of Ulster depended on access to Lough Neagh and three of them made use of rivers feeding the Lough. The Newry Navigation entered the Upper Bann just south of Portadown, the Coalisland Canal entered the Blackwater about 3 miles from Lough Neagh, while the Ulster Canal entered the Blackwater some 9 miles south west of Lough Neagh. The Upper Bann and the Blackwater were unimproved until work was done contemporary with that on the Lower Bann. The Board of Public Works completed work on the Upper Bann and Blackwater by 1858. The limits of improvement were Whitecoat Point where the Newry Navigation entered the Bann, and Blackwatertown on the Blackwater, 3 miles above Charlemont, the latter the junction of the Ulster Canal, a total combined length of $21\frac{1}{4}$ miles. No lock work was involved and on completion control was vested in trustees drawn from Tyrone, Armagh and Down. With the decline in canal traffic the navigation suffered. There was no traffic on it after the early 1950s and it was officially closed in 1954.

BARNSLEY CANAL, Yorkshire. By the 1790s the demand for coal led to a shortage. The solution was to develop more coalfields, and build waterways to them. In 1790 the Aire & Calder had a project for a canal and colliery north-west of Wakefield, but it was dropped in favour of a waterway between Wakefield and Barnsley. Surveys were made, but William Jessop was too busy to do more than check the work, but led in putting forward an estimate. A controlling interest was to be taken by Aire & Calder shareholders. The line was to go from Heath, on the Aire & Calder just below Wakefield, past Barnsley to Barnby Bridge, in the centre of the coalfield. Water supply looked like being a problem, but Jessop also planned a summit reservoir. The Dearne had not to be tapped and so it was resolved to pump up from the Calder. A rival scheme of 1793 appeared from Horbury on the Calder & Hebble to Haigh Bridge and on to Barugh, with a branch to Barnby Bridge, and was surveyed by John Hodgkinson. It got as far as a Bill and the Barnsley promoters compromised, abandoning their proposed Haigh Bridge branch from Barugh and agreeing not to object should the Horbury canal scheme be pushed forward. The Barnsley Act passed in 1793. Jessop was the engineer and his associate John Pinkerton did the cutting. In 1799 the canal was opened to Barnsley, but not until 1802 to Barnby Bridge, the coalfield section. The Dearne & Dove, opened in 1804, joined the Barnsley at Barnsley. 11 miles long to the Dearne & Dove junction and 15 to Barnby Bridge, the Barnsley was an engineering achievement. There were 20 broad locks, 15 within the first $2\frac{3}{4}$ miles including the entrance lock at Heath and 5 at Barugh beyond the Dearne & Dove junction, all large enough for keels 78'6" x 14'6". At Cold Hiendley there was a notable deep cutting and a five arched masonry aqueduct carried the canal over the Dearne near Barnsley. No water was taken from the Calder, although pumped from the summit reservoir at Cold Hiendley, and an engine was installed in 1801 at Barugh to pump back up the locks. There was a serious lack of traffic, since the Barnsley coalfield was in its infancy. A tramroad was needed to Silkstone, but an Act had to be obtained in 1808 to raise more capital. With some of the money the tramroad was laid and opened in 1810. Coal traffic now improved, other cargoes being lime upwards for land improvement, linen yarn for the mills and corn for Barnsley. Water remained a problem, the canal company covertly tapping the Dearne although checked by the Don Navigation. A second reservoir was planned but not built; the

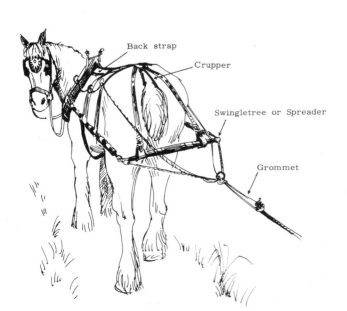

Back strap

Crupper

Swingletree or Spreader

Grommet

Plate 5.

Boat Horse and Harness

pumping power at Cold Hiendley was however increased. The North Midland Railway was opened from Derby to Leeds in 1840, and the following year the Great North of England from Darlington to York. The latter upset the Barnsley's coal trade to the North Riding. Up to 1840 the canal had been doing well, with a peak toll revenue in 1837, but railways meant rate cutting. In 1845 there were talks and agreement with the Don over a lease and then a purchase, the Don being anxious to prevent the Barnsley and the Silkstone coal trade falling into railway hands. The Don then offered the Barnsley to the Aire & Calder. The Don failed to take it over and the Barnsley refused offers of a lease from the Aire & Calder leaving them isolated within a growing railway network. By 1846 the railway was near Silkstone, coal being sent by rail from that year. Leases were now offered by the Barnsley first to the Manchester & Leeds Railway, then to the Aire & Calder. Eventually in 1854 the Aire & Calder agreed to a lease for 21 years. On 1 December 1854 this took effect, the Barnsley company remaining to receive the rent, all operations being taken over by the Aire & Calder. Under Aire & Calder management the Barnsley at first did well, traffic to Hull and Goole rose and improvements were made. There were two problems, mining subsidence and water supply. Subsidence cost money in repairs and in buying rights of support under the canal from the colliery companies. Water from the Dearne's catchment area was the Barnsley's main supply but in 1870 it was stopped because of increased water needs by Barnsley Corporation. The Aire & Calder decided on direct purchase of the Barnsley when the lease ran out on 30 November 1875. This was authorized by an Act of 1871 which also solved the water problem by legalizing abstraction from the Dearne at Barugh mill, which the Aire & Calder had bought in 1862 to try and safeguard the Dearne supply. Aire & Calder ownership brought more improvements. The Cold Hiendley reservoir was to be extended and another pump was installed in 1874. Between 1879 and 1881 the locks below Barnsley were enlarged to 84' x 15' x 6'6" on the sills for craft of 6' draught. In 1893 the short length above Barugh wharf which included five locks was abandoned owing to disuse. Subsidence became the ever increasing menace and in 1911 the wing walls of the Barnsley aqueduct gave way and the canal was closed for over seven months. Traffic remained good up to the 1940s and only declined when canalside collieries closed. One modern feature was the West Riding County Council's electric vertical lift bridge at Royston, built in 1934. Subsidence eventually closed the canal. The aqueduct was in danger and in 1945 there was a serious burst at Littleworth near Barnsley, entailing heavy compensation. The Aire & Calder were determined on abandonment, agreed to before nationalization, but not enforced until 1953, and Barnsley aqueduct was demolished as unsafe.

BARROW NAVIGATION, Co. Wexford, Kilkenny, Carlow, Leix, Kildare.   Navigable today from its junction with the Grand Canal at Athy to St. Mullins where a lock leads on to the tidal section of the river down to the sea, the Barrow Navigation is $41\frac{7}{8}$ miles in length from Athy to St. Mullins. In 1715 the Barrow was to be improved under the authority of local commissioners. No work was done until about 1760 when weirs and obstructions were removed and a lock and lateral canal built for a short distance, Thomas Omer being in charge. The work proceeded by grants of public money, but by 1790 the river had still not been fully improved as far as Athy, although seven locks were built. Impetus was given to the Barrow by the completion in 1791 of the Grand Canal's Barrow branch to Athy, and the previous year the Barrow Navigation Co. had been incorporated. William Chapman surveyed the project, recommending a total of 27 locks. Works went ahead under Chapman: he built 10 new locks and reconstructed 4 of Omer's. The locks in 1973 numbering 24, are of varied size, the narrowest 13'8", although Chapman was working to a standard of 80' x 16'. In 1790 the towing path between Athy and St. Mullins was completed. Traffic developed during the nineteenth century, but the extreme shallowness of the river in summer limited boats to 10 tons on only 18". Passage boats were tried but ceased between Athy and Carlow as early as 1809. Grain and flour were the main cargoes to and from the watermills. Flooding was caused by the navigation works, but nothing was done to remedy this. In 1894 the Barrow Navigation was merged with the Grand Canal, the canal company putting a tug on to assist barges in winter and erecting no less than 70 winches with wire ropes at points along the banks to help craft upstream. Latterly the river was much used by the firm of Minch, Norton who had maltings at nine places on the Barrow. In 1950 the Barrow was transferred with the Grand Canal to Coras Iompair Eireann (CIE) and there was no commercial traffic after 1959.

BASINGSTOKE CANAL, Surrey, Hampshire.   The Basingstoke was suggested as early as 1770 as part of a scheme to bypass the Thames and to open up northern Hampshire, with the canal bringing chalk to fertilize the barren lands of Bagshot Heath and to take away farm produce. The project was shelved until 1776, when a survey was made by Joseph Parker, followed by an Act two years later. The American War intervened and no work was done until 1788, since no capital had been forthcoming. William Jessop was appointed surveyor and consultant engineer with John Pinkerton as the contractor. Money ran out but a new Act empowered fresh capital and the canal was opened in September 1794. From Basingstoke to the Wey at Byfleet it was $37\frac{1}{2}$ miles long with 29 locks, 14 in the Frimley flight, built for boats 72'6" x 13'6" wide. From the lock at Aldershot a 21 mile pound ran to Basingstoke, with a 1230 yard tunnel at Greywell near Odiham. Financially the Basingstoke was almost bankrupt from the start. Salvation came in 1797 with a new and energetic chairman Dr. Robert Bland, a London gynaecologist. The war with France promoted an upsurge in traffic, but the canal was too heavily in debt to pay a dividend. Between 1792 and 1808 there were many schemes to continue westwards to either

Andover or Winchester. More persistent was the proposed Berks & Hants Junction Canal from Basingstoke to the Kennet encouraged by the opening of the Kennet & Avon Canal in 1810. Traffic on the Basingstoke had for long been threatened by improved roads. The London & Southampton Railway was opened as far as Basingstoke in 1839 and in 1849 came the Guildford-Farnham Railway. A move was made to sell the canal in 1850, but fortunes revived with the construction between 1854 and 1859 of Aldershot Camp. Nevertheless in 1866 the canal was in Chancery. It became the plaything of speculators, between 1866 and 1910 changing hands no less than nine times, towards the end of that period coming within Horatio Bottomley's fraudulent empire. A modest traffic did revive during the 1914-18 war due to the enterprise of the Harmsworth family, who were carriers, and owners of the canal from 1923 to 1949. However, trade to Basingstoke ceased in 1910, and to Aldershot in 1921, but the Woking timber traffic continued until 1949, when the New Basingstoke Canal Co. took over, the canal remaining navigable as far as Woking until about 1968. Its restoration is being led by the Surrey and Hants Canal Society, the parts of the canal lying within Hampshire and Surrey having been purchased by the Hampshire and Surrey County Councils in 1973 and 1976 respectively.

Proposed Links Between the BASINGSTOKE CANAL and the ITCHEN or ANDOVER CANAL. At the time of its construction a westward extension from the Basingstoke Canal seemed worthwhile and in 1789 John Rennie made a survey for a line towards Salisbury which would have proved difficult to build, although the Andover Canal could have been utilized. Earlier in 1788 there had been ideas to extend the Basingstoke down to the Itchen and these were revived in 1792, by two surveys for the London & Southampton Ports Junction Canal and in 1807 when money was subscribed, although it was abandoned in 1809. In 1810 came another idea to join the Basingstoke and Andover Canals, and finally as late as 1902 when, after experiments with electric traction on the Wey, a proposal was put for a 64 mile canal from the Itchen by way of Alton and Guildford to the Thames at Ditton, electric locomotives towing 250 ton barges.

BATH & BRISTOL CANAL PROJECT. Closely linked with the Kennet & Avon Canal proposals in 1795, was the proposal for the canal to continue to Bristol. John Rennie surveyed a line but due to local opposition no Act resulted. In 1809 the scheme was revived by South Wales ironmasters and Rennie made a second survey, an Act following in 1811 for a broad canal. No work was ever done, because the Kennet & Avon proposed to improve the Avon.

BEDALE BECK, Yorkshire. See River Ouse, (above York).

BEVERLEY BECK, Yorkshire. A tidal creek off the River Hull running for $\frac{3}{4}$ mile up to Beverley. By 1344 the Beck was navigable, previously the town wharf had been at Grovehill where it joins the Hull. Beverley Corporation looked after the Beck, an Act of 1727 allowing the corporation to borrow money for repairs. These were completed by 1731 but proved insufficient. Tolls were let from 1748 and revenue improved in the 1770s, probably as a result of the opening of the Driffield Navigation and the Selby Canal so that access to the Aire & Calder was improved. In 1802 a lock was put in at Grovehill, designed by William Chapman. The lease continued, the lessees usually being traders. In 1846 the Hull & Bridlington Railway reached Beverley, but traffic remained on the Beck, whose water supply was improved at the end of the century by pumping up from the Hull at Grovehill lock. Most keels were bow-hauled up the Beck until motor barges came. However at the turn of the century a steam launch was used as a tug for a short while. Grovehill lock was rebuilt in 1958 and takes craft 65' x 17'6", the Beck allowing a 6'6" draught. Traffic continues, and the Beck remains under the Corporation of Beverley.

BILLERICAY CANAL PROJECT, Essex. It was proposed to link the Crouch with the Thames by a canal from Battlesbridge on the Crouch, following the Mardyke (page 189) to Purfleet on the Thames, with a branch to Billericay which would be heavily locked. Surveys were made in 1825, but the expense of such a canal was far beyond any likely revenue.

BIRMINGHAM CANAL, BIRMINGHAM & FAZELEY CANAL, BIRMINGHAM CANAL NAVIGATIONS, Staffordshire, Warwickshire, Worcestershire. What became known as the BCN started simply enough. The Trent & Mersey failed to make a branch to Birmingham and the Staffs. & Worcs. bypassed the town too, so local interests in 1767 sought to make a canal from Birmingham to the Staffs. & Worcs, outside Wolverhampton. James Brindley did the survey via Smethwick, Oldbury, Tipton, Bilston and Wolverhampton to the Staffs. & Worcs. at Aldersley and with support from Matthew Boulton and other members of the Lunar Society the Act was passed in 1768, with branches at Ocker Hill and Wednesbury. Brindley was appointed engineer, the actual work being done by his assistants Robert Whitworth and Samuel Simcock. Cutting was rapid between Wednesbury and Birmingham because the supporters were anxious to tap Wednesbury coal and this section, about 10 miles long, was completed in 1769, with a one mile summit level at Smethwick. Coal traffic into Birmingham started at once and the canal company had a near monopoly of the trade. Not until 1770, after pressure from the Staffs. & Worcs, was construction pushed on to Wolverhampton. In 1772 the junction at Aldersley was made via the 20 (later 21) locks at Wolverhampton (41). It was a devious canal of $22\frac{5}{8}$ miles, following contours and intended to serve as wide an area as possible. The original Wednesbury line, leaving the main at Spon Lane, was $4\frac{3}{4}$ miles long, and the Ocker Hill branch $\frac{5}{8}$ mile. The locks at first totalled 32, the 20 at Wolverhampton plus 6 at Spon Lane and 6 at Smethwick on to and off the summit. The Birmingham Canal did well, and was wealthy enough to finance improvements out of profits. Monopolies are resented and it was not long before a rival canal was being considered. The Birmingham & Fazeley story started in 1770 with ideas

41. Lock lining, a pair of Thomas Clayton oil boats on the Wolverhampton flight of 21. Motor and butty rise simultaneously in their respective locks.

for a canal from Walsall via Lichfield to Fradley on the Trent & Mersey. This was revived in the 1780s as a canal from the Birmingham at Wednesbury to Fazeley and on to the Coventry Canal. The promoters in 1782 concluded an agreement with the Trent & Mersey, Coventry and Oxford companies. This was an effort to complete the Coventry's authorized line between the Trent & Mersey and the Oxford. It arranged that the Birmingham & Fazeley would build half of the Coventry's line from Fazeley to Fradley, the Trent & Mersey building the other half while the Coventry itself would push on to Fazeley from Atherstone. All depended on the Fazeley getting their Act, but meanwhile the Birmingham were disturbed and lost no time in promoting a rival canal linking their own system to Fazeley. The Act which was passed in 1783 sanctioned not only the Birmingham's project for a canal to Fazeley, now from Farmer's Bridge, but also another scheme, the Broadwaters Canal from Rider's Green on the Wednesbury branch towards Walsall. The promoters of the original Birmingham & Fazeley Canal now agreed to join the Birmingham's project and in 1784 an amalgamation was achieved, from 1794 called the Birmingham Canal Navigations. John Smeaton was appointed engineer both of the Fazeley and Rider's Green lines, completing the latter some way to Walsall in 1786 with eight descending locks at Rider's Green. The Birmingham & Fazeley was completed in 1789 with 38 locks descending from Farmer's Bridge, 13 on the Farmer's Bridge flight, 11 at Aston, 3 at Minworth and 11 at Curdworth. The total distance was $20\frac{3}{4}$ miles, including the $5\frac{1}{2}$ miles from Fazeley to Whittington Brook, half way to Fradley, built under the Coleshill agreement for the Coventry. Meanwhile Smeaton endeavoured to improve the water supply to Brindley's Smethwick summit, fed from reservoirs at Smethwick and Titford, and by water pumped back at Spon Lane and Smethwick locks. But this was insufficient to cope with the increased traffic from the Rider's Green and Fazeley Canals so it was decided to lower the summit by 18 ft to the level of the long Wolverhampton pound. To disrupt traffic as little as possible this was carried out in two stages and the work was completed in 1790, eliminating three of the six locks at Spon Lane and at Smethwick. The Smethwick three were duplicated. The Birmingham were worried about rivals bypassing their system, in particular the 1792 schemes of the Dudley to join the Worcester & Birmingham at Selly Oak. In 1798 this was completed, the Worcester & Birmingham themselves having no physical connection with the Birmingham at the Worcester Bar junction point, until in 1815 the Bar was removed. On the other hand the Birmingham Company welcomed canals which joined their system, in 1792 the Wyrley & Essington was authorized and in 1793 the Warwick & Birmingham. They also supported and built on behalf of a separate company a canal to Walsall, opened in 1799 as the Walsall Canal. It was an extension of their own branch from Rider's Green to Broadwaters and totalled $7\frac{1}{4}$ miles. Later in 1805 the Ocker Hill tunnel branch (for water supply only, to feed the recirculating pumps at Ocker Hill) was opened, and later still in 1849 the Bradley locks branch (9 locks) linking the Walsall with Brindley's old main line at Bradley. The old line became known as the Wednesbury Oak loop. Traffic had become so heavy by the 1790s that there were proposals to straighten Brindley's line, but because of the war with France and financial difficulties nothing was done. However by the 1820s the congestion was serious and in 1824 Telford was called in. His proposals were accepted because the BCN was probably concerned about railway building between Birmingham and Liverpool, and because there might be a new canal from Wolverhampton to the Mersey, eventually completed in 1835 as the Birmingham & Liverpool Junction. Work started, water supplies being eased by the completion in 1826 of a new reservoir at Rotton Park. In 1827 came the straightening of the line between Birmingham and Smethwick, with a towing path on each bank. The 1790 summit level was bypassed by a new 71' deep cutting, and extended on the same level all the way from Birmingham to Tipton to three new locks at Tipton Factory, which took the canal up to the 473' Wolverhampton level. The cutting at Smethwick was completed in 1829. Finally work was started on the length from Bloomfield near Tipton to Deepfields, completed in 1837. It involved a 360 yd tunnel at Coseley authorized in 1835 and opened with a double towpath. In 1838 the new main line was ready. Brindley's route had been shortened from $22\frac{5}{8}$ miles to $15\frac{5}{8}$. The new canal, called the Island line, because it cut through the high ground at Smethwick known as the Island, crossed the line of the Tipton Green-Toll End communication which was a useful route on to the Walsall level; this from the old main line to the Walsall had been completed in 1809. Finally the BCN deepened and improved the canal between Deepfields and Aldersley on the Staffs. &

Worcs., and branches were built. The BCN system had been evolved on a series of levels. Brindley's old line was on the 453' level from Birmingham rising to a 491' summit at Smethwick and returning to the 453' on the branch to Wednesbury. His Wolverhampton line struck a new level of 473' from half way down the six Spon Lane locks where it parted with the branch to Wednesbury. Smeaton's summit was cut down to 473', the Wolverhampton level, while Telford's new main line maintained the 453', the Birmingham level, to Tipton Factory, Brindley's 473' line continuing as a loop from Spon Lane to Tipton Factory. This was joined in 1847 by the Titford branch rising by 6 locks to a new 511' level at Oldbury, called because of its height the 'Crow's Nest' or the 'Crow'. The 408' Walsall level ran from the bottom lock at Rider's Green to the bottom lock at Walsall, including the Tame Valley Canal as far as the top lock at Perry Bar and the Rushall Canal up to the bottom lock of the Rushall flight. The lowest level was at 209' on the Birmingham & Fazeley, whilst the highest was reached on the Essington locks branch at 527'. Telford's straightening added to the congestion at Farmer's Bridge, the only exit for the Fazeley and Warwick lines. There was no room for parallel locks because of the number of canalside works, so a direct canal following the River Tame was decided on. Acts were secured in 1839 and 1840 for the Tame Valley Canal, open in 1844, from the Walsall Canal near Ocker Hill to the Birmingham & Fazeley at Salford Junction. It was $8\frac{1}{2}$ miles long with 13 locks at Perry Barr and avoided the Farmer's Bridge and Aston locks. At Salford also a junction was made with the Birmingham & Warwick Junction Canal. In 1847 the Rushall Canal, $2\frac{7}{8}$ miles and 9 locks was opened between the Tame Valley and Wyrley & Essington's Daw End branch. This was built as a result of the 1840 merger of the Wyrley & Essington with the BCN, two other links also being completed, in 1841 the 8 locks at Walsall to join the BCN's Walsall Canal to the Wyrley's branch from Birchills, and in 1843 the $3\frac{3}{8}$ miles Bentley Canal with 10 locks from the Wyrley at Wednesfield to the Anson branch of the Walsall Canal. Water was a problem, much came from Cannock Chase reservoir which had been constructed by the Wyrley & Essington as early as 1800, but the BCN had to rely heavily on expensive pumping back up flights of locks, with engines at Ashted, Titford, Perry Barr, Walsall and Park Head on the Dudley. There was also recirculation between levels, at Ocker Hill between the 408' and 473', and at Smethwick between the 453' and 473'. Further pumping took place back into reservoirs at Rotton Park, Cannock Chase, Lodge Farm and Sneyd. Most important of all, water was pumped from coal mines in agreement with their owners and the South Staffordshire Mines Drainage Commissioners. Railways appeared in 1838, with the completion both of the Grand Junction between Birmingham and the Liverpool & Manchester, and of the London & Birmingham, while in 1840 a railway was opened from Birmingham to Derby. The BCN had ideas of railway building on its own account, but instead, allied with the new London & North Western Railway. An Act of 1846 confirmed that the canal could be leased to the LNWR, the BCN continuing to manage it, the rent being in the form of a guaranteed 4 per cent dividend which the railway would if necessary make up from their own resources. The BCN was therefore given security in the railway age and developed to serve railway needs. Because Birmingham and Black Country industries had grown up alongside the canal, it was easiest and cheapest for the railway companies to gain traffic and achieve distribution via the waterway network. Boatage services to canal-rail transhipment basins began in the 1850s. Large depots were built at Wolverhampton, Great Bridge, Tipton, Bloomfield and later Hawne, to deal with the tube traffic from Stewart's & Lloyd's Halesowen, plant. There were 26 railway basins, 12 LNWR, 11 GWR, 3 Midland. To tap new colliery workings more canals were built. In 1854 the Cannock Extension Canal was authorized to run from the Wyrley & Essington at Pelsall to Hednesford basin; $5\frac{5}{8}$ miles long on the level it was opened in 1863 and via the 13 descending Churchbridge locks joined up with the Hatherton branch of the Staffs. & Worcs. This canal, wide straight and deep, had railway style overbridges as did the Anglesey branch, so called when the feeder from the Cannock reservoir was made navigable in 1850. The 3027 yd Netherton tunnel, built to provide a more rapid route between the Birmingham system and the Dudley and Stourbridge lines, was completed in 1858. To cope with the increased traffic the tunnel would bring, the Dudley was straightened and a cut off, the Two Lock line, built in 1858 to avoid the congestion of Dudley tunnel traffic at Park Head. Finally the nine Delph locks at Brierley Hill on the Dudley's old line up from Stourbridge were replaced by eight in 1858. But canals were becoming less profitable: as tonnages and receipts rose, operating costs rose too. From 1874 the LNWR had to be called upon regularly to guarantee the 4 per cent dividend from its own resources. In 1906 at the time of the Royal Commission the BCN totalled some 159 miles with 216 locks. It was still viable, but maintenance was becoming a problem because of subsidence. The Two Lock line had to be closed in 1909 and Lappal tunnel near Selly Oak in 1917. But it was road competition after the 1914-18 War which brought tonnage down, affecting the railways and so the canals. The BCN remained busy even after the 1939-45 War, particularly on the Cannock Extension Canal. In the 1960s however traffic fell away, due mainly to the contraction of coal mining. The Cannock Extension north of the A5 road was closed in 1963 because of subsidence caused by opencast mining at Churchbridge. There had been other closures before this; in 1954 Ogley locks on the Wyrley down to Huddlesford, in 1962 the locks at Park Head on the Brierley Hill side of Dudley tunnel, the tunnel itself remaining navigable, but not used commercially since 1951. Other branches too were abandoned, including in 1961 part of the Bentley. By 1973 some 52 miles of the system had been abandoned but all the main routes are there and likely to remain, as 'cruiseways', with the locks at Park Head reopened in 1973 so that the Dudley tunnel again forms part of a through route.

42. Shelmore Embankment completed in 1835 on the Birmingham & Liverpool Junction Canal. One of two road tunnels.

BIRMINGHAM & BRISTOL IMPROVED NAVIGATION PROJECT. The Manchester Ship Canal Act of 1885 encouraged large schemes elsewhere, including this of 1886 to make an improved waterway between Bristol and Gloucester and enlarge the Worcester & Birmingham for vessels of up to 250 tons capacity.

BIRMINGHAM & LIVERPOOL JUNCTION CANAL, Cheshire, Shropshire, Staffordshire. Traffic on the BCN had by the 1830s reached such proportions that improvements were imperative, undertaken between 1824 and 1838 to the recommendations of Telford, whose report in 1824 also suggested a new canal northwards to the Mersey, to run from Autherley on the Staffs. & Worcs., to Nantwich, the terminus of the Ellesmere & Chester. By this time railways were in the forefront of the public mind, but Telford's support won the Act for the canal in 1826, of which he was appointed engineer, later to be assisted by William Cubitt. The canal was direct and straight, possible between Autherley and Nantwich, for speed against future railway competition; hence the earthworks, Tyrley and Grub Street cuttings, Nantwich, Shebdon and Shelmore embankments (42). Completed in 1835 after trouble with Shelmore, the canal was 39½ miles long with 26 narrow locks plus the stop lock at Autherley, and with one short 81 yd tunnel at Cowley near Gnosall. There was one important branch, authorized by an Act of 1827, from Norbury on the main line, to Newport and on to Wappenshall near Wellington to join the Shrewsbury Canal, linking the East Shropshire network with the Midlands system. Opened in 1835, the Newport branch was 10¼ miles long with 23 locks and had the short Humber Arm of ¾ mile to Lubstree wharf, owned by the Lilleshall Co. This arm had been intended to go to the Lilleshall ironworks but a road, and from 1870, a railway, connected the works and the Donnington Wood Canal at Muxton bridge to the wharf, a distance of some 3½ miles. Soon after the canal was ready railway competition began to be felt, and it was forced to cut its tolls. In addition the early days were hampered by water shortage, Knighton reservoir near Market Drayton was finished in good time, not so Belvide near Brewood, which was dependent for its completion in 1842 on the Exchequer Bill Loan Commissioners, who had already come to the aid of the canal during construction. The Newport branch gave the iron traffic from Coalbrookdale a more direct outlet to the country's canal system, the iron coming by road from the Dale and Horsehay to Wappenshall for loading into narrow boats. In 1843 the company, who had become carriers the previous year, put on steam tugs between Autherley and Ellesmere Port to haul their own and other carriers' boats in trains. However steam was found to be uneconomic and after a few years horses returned. Early in 1844 moves were made towards amalgamation with the Ellesmere & Chester achieved the following year, but in 1846 overtaken by the Shropshire Union.

BIRMINGHAM & LIVERPOOL SHIP CANAL PROJECT. Passage of the Manchester Ship Canal Act of 1885 encouraged similar schemes, one in 1888 was for a canal for 300 ton craft between Birmingham and the Mersey, to run from the Weaver at Winsford to Stafford, Wolverhampton and Birmingham by way of the Potteries. The North Staffordshire Railway therefore decided to widen the Trent & Mersey between the Potteries and Preston Brook, hoping that the new canal would choose their route and in 1892 an Act for this widening was passed. Meanwhile the Shropshire Union were interested in enlarging to Autherley. Nothing came of the ship canal scheme, so the NSR did little widening and the Shropshire Union none.

BIRMINGHAM, WALSALL & LIVERPOOL JUNCTION CANAL PROJECT. In 1825 a new canal was announced to make a more direct link with the Mersey. This was to run from Birmingham via Perry Bar and Walsall to the Wyrley & Essington at Wyrley Bank, then to the Staffs & Worcs at Otherton near Penkridge.

BIRMINGHAM & WARWICK JUNCTION CANAL, Warwickshire. Traffic increased on the improved BCN with the opening in 1835 of the Birmingham & Liverpool Junction Canal, and to help the flow the Tame Valley Canal was completed in 1844. This avoided the congested Farmer's Bridge locks but directed traffic on to the Fazeley line rather than the Warwick & Birmingham. To avoid such a trend the Warwick & Birmingham proposed a canal from Salford Junction, where the Tame Valley met the Fazeley, direct to its own. An Act of 1840 authorized a canal from Salford up to Bordesley to join the Warwick & Birmingham line coming from Digbeth. The new canal, engineered by James Potter, was 2⅝ miles long with six narrow locks rising to Bordesley and opened in 1844, on the same day as the Tame Valley. The Birmingham &

Warwick Junction was financed and staffed by the two Warwick canals who held all the shares. Management was undertaken by the Warwick & Birmingham and the junction canal followed the fortunes of the other two Warwicks, in 1917 coming under their joint committee of management and in 1927 being bought by the Regent's, becoming in 1929 a part of the Grand Union, although the locks were not widened under the improvement scheme.

River BLACKWATER, BRIDE and LISMORE CANAL, Co Waterford, Cork.   Entering the sea at Youghal the Blackwater is tidal 18 miles up to Cappoquin and navigable, but there were plans in the 1750s to extend the navigation to coal pits west of Mallow, 45 miles above Cappoquin. William Ockenden started the works about 1759 and by 1761 had completed nearly 5 miles of canal between Mallow and Lombardstown to the west, probably with two locks. Later in 1800 there were moves to make a new navigation from Cappoquin up to the collieries, but nothing was done, except for the Duke of Devonshire's private Lismore Canal completed by about 1814 from Cappoquin 3½ miles westwards to Lismore. This had a lock for vessels 71'6" x 19'6", but is now derelict. A tributary of the Blackwater, the Bride is today navigable from its junction for 7½ miles up to near Tallow; there were also ideas of improving it.

BLYTH NAVIGATION, Suffolk.   In the eighteenth century Halesworth was the centre of a prosperous farming district. Local interests wanted a link with the sea via the River Blyth and Southwold harbour, the main promoter being Thomas Knight, a Halesworth brewer. John Reynolds made a survey and estimate in 1753 but no Act came until 1757, followed by a re-survey by Langley Edwards and a report by John Grundy both in 1759. By 1761 the river was open to Halesworth basin, 9 miles long with four locks. Thomas Manning had been the engineer. Successful at first, the Blyth's future depended on the preservation of Southwold harbour, subject to the feeble scour of the tide, made feebler by the local landowners who enclosed the saltings by Blythburgh upstream from Southwold. Gradually the harbour was ruined, in spite of a short lived prosperity for the navigation in the 1830s due to the energy of a Halesworth maltster, Patrick Stead. By the 1850s there was little trade on the Blyth and the last wherry came in about 1906. In 1911 abandonment was proposed and the locks were closed in 1934. But the river is still navigable up to Blythburgh.

BO'NESS CANAL, West Lothian, Stirlingshire.   The Act for the Forth & Clyde of 1768 had provided for a branch to Bo'ness, to be made by an independent company. Following a survey by James Watt in 1772 money was raised after a delay of ten years, work starting in 1783. The canal was to run from Bo'ness to the Forth & Clyde at Grangemouth, with aqueducts over the Avon and the Grange Burn, the former being almost completed. But money was exhausted and the canal abandoned.

BOURNE EAU, Lincolnshire.   The Bourne Eau runs from Bourne to the River Glen which it joins some 3½ miles below Bourne. It had become a much decayed navigation, but in 1781 an Act was passed to revive it. Trustees were appointed to do the work and the eau was cleared of silt and wharves built at Bourne. Traffic was in farm produce down to Boston and back with groceries and merchandise. This lasted into the 1920s. There were two locks.   See also River Welland Navigation.

BOYNE NAVIGATION, Co Meath, Louth.   The river used to be open for 19 miles from Drogheda via Slane to Navan, the first work towards this starting in 1759 with public funds under Thomas Omer. By 1789 13 miles had been improved but most unsatisfactorily, for in the following year the River Boyne Co was incorporated to improve the river as far as Trim. But by 1800 Navan only was reached, there being 20 locks on the 19 mile navigation for craft 78' x 14'6". Because the Boyne Co had failed to reach Trim, it forfeited under its Act the Lower Boyne from Slane to Drogheda which came under government control. In 1894 the latter took over the Upper Boyne, above Slane, from the old River Boyne Co. In 1896 a new Boyne Navigation Co was formed to take over the whole navigation from Drogheda to Navan and put it into good repair. But traffic was sparse and in 1913 the company went into liquidation selling the navigation in 1915 to the Navan corn millers John Spicer & Co., Ltd. After the 1914-18 war they were the only traders using the river and they stopped their two horse boats by about 1925.

BRADFORD CANAL, Yorkshire.   A canal to Bradford from the Leeds & Liverpool at Shipley was considered profitable and an Act was obtained in 1771. John Longbotham acted as engineer, the canal opening in 1774, 3⅜ miles long with 10 locks rising to Bradford for Leeds & Liverpool size boats. By this time the Leeds & Liverpool was ready between Skipton and Shipley so limestone traffic could begin from the Craven quarries to the canalside kilns outside Bradford. Because of the rapid growth of Bradford's industry and housing, the canal became excessively polluted, the 1849 cholera epidemic causing a public outcry. By this time the Leeds & Bradford Railway was competing. By the 1860s the canal had become so noisome that there were moves afoot to force the company to clean it up, impossible because it was fed by the heavily polluted Bradford Beck. A court order of 1866 forbade the canal to take water from this, so the company had no feedwater and decided to close the last ¼ mile, hoping to lease the remainder to the Leeds & Liverpool. However there was a further court order in 1867 so the Bradford Canal closed and was drained. Without a canal the quarry owners and stone merchants were at a loss so a new company was created which in 1873 reopened the canal for 3 miles. Traffic was difficult to revive but the canal was rescued by its joint sale in 1878 to the Leeds & Liverpool and Aire & Calder. They were able to build up traffic and very fine warehouse facilities were provided, but the canal was costly to maintain because all the water had to be pumped. Losses increased after 1910 and road transport became cheaper. So in 1922 the

Bradford Canal finally closed.

River BRANDON.   See Little Ouse.

BRAUNTON CANAL and River TAW SCHEMES, Devon.   There were ideas between 1810 and 1813 to develop drainage channels around Braunton into navigable canals.   Much later in 1850 a cut was made on the united Caen river and Knowle Water below Braunton up which there is still a trade in gravel.   In 1845 there was a plan for a canal up the Taw from Barnstaple to Umberleigh bridge.

BRECKNOCK & ABERGAVENNY CANAL, Breconshire, Monmouthshire.   This canal was proposed at about the same time as the Monmouthshire but was at first to have no connection and to run as the Abergavenny Canal from Newbridge-on-Usk via Abergavenny to Brecon.   The Monmouthshire, authorized in 1792, changed this attitude and the younger Thomas Dadford, engineer of the Monmouthshire, made a survey to join the Abergavenny to that canal at Pontymoile below Pontypool.   The Act for the Brecknock & Abergavenny passed in early 1793 at the height of the canal mania and by it the canal company were allowed to build tramroads within 8 miles of the waterway, which they did before starting on the canal, probably because of the needs of local ironmasters; but the Monmouthshire became insistent that the canal works should start.   Their own engineer, Thomas Dadford junior, was in 1795 appointed part-time engineer, because he was still working for the Monmouthshire, becoming full-time from the end of 1798.   Cutting started in 1797 from Gilwern upwards towards Brecon.   Twelve miles were open by 1799 and Brecon was reached in 1800 via the four arched masonry aqueduct over the Usk at Brynich and the 375 yd Ashford tunnel near Talybont-on-Usk.   There are six locks on this section plus the junction stop lock at Pontymoile, for boats 64'9" x 9'2", the same size as on the Monmouthshire. Money was now all spent and work stopped, but was restarted in about 1802, to continue the canal down to Llanfoist where the wharf for Abergavenny was to be built.   Thomas Cartwright was now engineer and carried the canal through to just short of Llanfoist by 1805.   Coal and lime were the principal traffic on this isolated canal, undertaken by the Brecon Boat Co, a mine and quarry owning concern who carried their own products, largely owned by canal shareholders.   Under the younger William Crosley, work restarted in about 1809, cutting upwards from the Monmouthshire at Pontymoile.   Eventually in 1812 the canal was fully open, a total of 33¼ miles, 23 of which were a level pound just below the 400 ft contour.   Neither the canal nor its tramroads were as profitable as hoped, the end of the Napoleonic wars and the end of the demand for munitions having a depressing effect. In 1845 the Monmouthshire's Act to make a railway from Newport to Pontypool passed and the Brecknock & Abergavenny tried to sell their canal.   There were more attempts to sell the canal, for by the later 1850s the iron trade had moved from water to rail.   The Brecon Boat Co gave up in 1865 and the canal outlook was gloomy.   Salvation came however by amalgamation with the Monmouthshire in that same year.   The Brecknock & Abergavenny was of little value as an artery of trade but important as a source of water drawn from the Usk at Brecon, to supply the docks at Newport and works along the Monmouthshire's line.   In 1880 both canals passed to the Great Western Railway and traffic declined heavily. There were few boats by 1914 and the market boat service from Newport ceased at about this time.   No tolls were taken on the canal after 1933 but it remained open as a water channel.   Because of its great beauty the canal in the 1950s became increasingly popular with pleasure craft.   The Brecon Beacons National Park was created and from 1968 restoration was put in hand as a joint effort of the British Waterways Board and Monmouthshire and Brecknockshire County Councils.   This has been a success and was capped in 1970 by the opening of a lift bridge at Talybont to replace a fixed bridge, so allowing boats to reach Brecon.   A breach in 1975 isolated the upper pounds but reopening is expected.

BRIDGEWATER CANAL, Lancashire, Cheshire.   The Bridgewater was the largest waterway project in the British Isles to be financed by one man.   Its success encouraged the great period of canal construction which followed in the 1760s and 70s.   It started modestly with the authorization in 1759 of a canal to run from the Duke of Bridgewater's mines at Worsley to Salford.   In 1737 the Mersey & Irwell Navigation had secured an Act to make the Worsley Brook navigable down to their own waterway.   No work was done, but the idea was revived in the 1750s when a group planned a canal from Salford via Eccles, Worsley and Leigh to Wigan, to carry coal from the Wigan field direct to Manchester. Francis Egerton, third Duke of Bridgewater was brought up in an atmosphere of eighteenth century big business, for one of his guardians was Lord Gower who had mining and smelting interests in Staffordshire and Shropshire.   Gower had been considering a canal from the Trent at Wilden Ferry, Shardlow, to Stoke, and it is likely that he encouraged the Duke to revive a canal project between Worsley and the Irwell.   John Gilbert, the Duke's agent, probably drew up plans for the canal to Salford which the 1759 Act sanctioned, together with another canal from Worsley to the Mersey & Irwell at Hollins Ferry six miles below Barton.   Work started by direct labour under Gilbert with James Brindley brought in to assist.   The canal was driven from Worsley both towards Salford and south-westwards towards Hollins Ferry, while the Worsley underground system was also begun.   In October 1759 the Duke decided to push the canal through to Manchester itself.   By crossing the Irwell, he would bring his coal within reach of Cheshire as well as Manchester, moreover he was possibly now planning to carry his canal through north Cheshire towards the lower Mersey and Liverpool, bypassing the Mersey & Irwell.   It looks as if the Hollins Ferry canal was merely a ruse to gain the acquiescence of the Mersey & Irwell who were now unable to prevent passage of a new Act in 1760 authorizing the line to Manchester, crossing their navigation at Barton and including a ½ mile branch from Stretford to Longford bridge on the Chester road, for the distribution of coal into Cheshire.   Crossing the Irwell at Barton faced Gilbert and Brindley with the need to build an aqueduct. In 1761 it was opened in the presence of the Duke and the canal reached Stretford at the end of that year. In 1763 the canal was in Manchester but the first wharf at the Castlefield terminus was not in use until 1765. By 1765 the Worsley underground system was well advanced. Completely separate from the Worsley system was a $1\frac{1}{2}$ mile underground canal from Boothstown on the Leigh branch to Mosley Common, opened in 1822. Meanwhile the Longford bridge branch had been completed in 1761 and Brindley surveyed onwards from there to the Hempstones on the Mersey about $2\frac{1}{2}$ miles above Runcorn. He also surveyed for a branch from Sale to Stockport but this was not included in the Act for the Hempstones extension which passed in 1762. The Mersey & Irwell opposed strongly and to stifle them the Duke tried but failed to buy them out. This Mersey extension did not, considering the competition from the Mersey & Irwell, look a very rewarding canal until 1765, when Josiah Wedgwood's Trent & Mersey project was being seriously considered. John Gilbert was successful in persuading Wedgwood and his associates to join the Duke's canal, giving them a route to Manchester as well as the Mersey. The problem was where the Duke's canal would join the Mersey. He had ideas of making an aqueduct over the Mersey to take it into Liverpool itself, but this was abandoned in favour of a compromise with the Trent & Mersey by which his canal would join theirs at Preston Brook and he build, at his own expense, their line to Runcorn all authorized by their Act of 1766. In this way the Duke succeeded in controlling the Mersey exit of the whole Midlands waterway network. On the Runcorn line work proceeded steadily with the embankment and single arched aqueduct over the Mersey at Stretford. Altrincham was reached in 1766 and Lymm via the Bollin embankment at Dunham in 1769. All the canal from Worsley was on one level but at Runcorn the descent to the Mersey had to be made by 10 locks, grouped in staircase pairs. They were opened in 1773 to barge standard for craft 72' x 14'2". By this time the canal was complete save for a short length at Norton Priory where the owner Sir Richard Brooke refused to sell land. He did not give way until 1776, when the whole canal was open with a short branch at Preston Brook to meet the Trent & Mersey. The Bridgewater was 33 miles long between Worsley and Runcorn plus $\frac{3}{4}$ mile for the Preston Brook branch and 2 miles of the canal from Worsley towards Hollins Ferry which was never completed, although the length cut was used until the 1800s, together with a short branch of 1614 yd cut between 1799 and 1803. There was another short branch of about $\frac{5}{8}$ mile built before 1785 into Chat Moss to carry moss. Water for the system came from the Worsley mines, from Worsley Brook, from the Trent & Mersey and from the Medlock in Manchester. Water also came later via the Bank Top tunnel, a navigable sough which fed into the Medlock, completed in 1789 and used by boats until about 1800. When the Ashton and the Rochdale Canals were completed in 1799 and 1804 respectively, they too contributed. Traffic had been heavy since the opening of the length into Manchester in 1765, the Duke doing his own carrying from the start, but the line to Runcorn on the completion of the Trent & Mersey started to bring colossal receipts. By 1791 further basins were ready at Runcorn and in 1783 the Duke opened his own dock in Liverpool. Preston Brook too was developed as a transhipment port. Passenger traffic had started as early as 1767 between Broadheath near Altrincham and Manchester and was extended as the canal progressed. From 1775 services were also run between Worsley and Manchester, and as soon as the canal was open to Runcorn passenger services operated between there and Manchester. The Duke kept the passenger packets in his own hands. On his own account the Duke in 1795 gained an Act to extend from Worsley to near Leigh, all on the level, and using part of the Hollins Ferry line completed the $6\frac{1}{4}$ mile extension in about 1799. Later in 1820 it was joined by a branch of the Leeds & Liverpool from Wigan. (44). Passenger services were started to Leigh in 1800. On March 3 1803 the Duke died, a bachelor, the title becoming extinct. His nephew the second Marquess of Stafford inherited a life rent in the canal, the mines and the estates. This passed on his death in 1833 to his second son Lord Francis Egerton who, in 1846 was created Earl of Ellesmere. The Duke placed all these properties under the control of three trustees headed by his legal agent and canal manager Robert Haldane Bradshaw, as superintendent of the trust who exercised a very complete authority. Competition in passenger carrying to Runcorn came in 1807 from the Mersey & Irwell, causing the Bridgewater Trustees to arrange for connecting sailing packets between Runcorn and Liverpool. In 1815 a steamer, the ELIZABETH was tried on this run. Other steamers appeared in 1817. In 1827 the new flight of 10 locks at Runcorn was completed with 5 intermediate reservoirs, to enter a tidal basin about 350 yd downstream from the old line. Opening of the Liverpool & Manchester Railway in 1830 distressed neither the Mersey & Irwell nor the Bridgewater, although some rate cutting followed, Bradshaw thinking that the canal could remain competitive. He refused any rates agreement with the Liverpool & Manchester, but in 1834 he resigned, to be followed by James Sothern as superintendent of the trust, who in 1835 came to terms with the railway over rates. Surprisingly Bridgewater passenger services held up well against the railway. Since 1821 there had been daily services between Manchester and Liverpool via Worsley and the newly opened Leigh branch of the Leeds & Liverpool. Iron swift boats were introduced in 1843 which offered a sensational improvement in the Runcorn service now reduced to $3\frac{1}{2}$ hours with two boats a day each way. Sothern, who tried to be independent of influence by Lord Francis, did not last long, being bought out of his post for £45,000 by Lord Francis in 1837. James Loch now became superintendent of the trust. An important move in this period was the completion in 1838 of the three locks at Hulme, Manchester, which joined the Bridgewater with the Irwell. By 1840 the Bridgewater was feeling competition from other railways for in 1837 the Grand Junction had been completed to Birmingham. This resulted in rate cutting and more energetic carrying by the Bridgewater. The 1840s were indeed a difficult time because the Mersey & Irwell were trying to force an alliance with the Manchester & Leeds Railway in opposition to the Liverpool & Manchester and the Bridgewater. This broke down, the Manchester & Leeds joining with the Liverpool & Manchester against the waterways in 1842. Price cutting was the result, the Bridgewater being unwillingly involved, and to preserve peace with the railways, Loch determined on control of the errant Mersey & Irwell. Lord Francis in 1844 bought the navigation which two years later was handed over to the Bridgewater trustees, a new rates agreement being secured in 1845 between both waterways and the Liverpool & Manchester Railway. The Bridgewater trustees entered deeply into Midlands carrying, entrenching themselves at Wolverhampton by an agreement with local carriers and offering services down to Stourport, Gloucester and Bristol. A difficulty was railway control of many of the canals which fed Manchester, and since 1846 the Trent & Mersey had been owned by the North Staffordshire Railway, so the Bridgewater felt encircled and itself tried to find a railway ally. The Great Western was chosen because the Bridgewater could offer deep penetration into rivals' territory, but nothing tangible resulted. In 1855 came a positive offer from the North Staffordshire Railway to lease the canal but its Bill failed and the offer was turned down by Lord Ellesmere, convinced by his canal manager George Fereday Smith that the canal had a good future under the trustees. Now started a period of improvement. First came the Runcorn & Weston Canal, authorized in 1853 and built at Lord Ellesmere's expense. It was completed in 1859, $1\frac{1}{4}$ miles long with 2 locks, for craft 72'3" x 18'5" between the Francis dock at Runcorn and the basin at Weston Point. It was intended for the salt trade. Fereday Smith made further improvements at Runcorn; in 1860 a new tidal basin was made, followed by the Alfred dock. The swift boats were withdrawn in 1855 and passenger packets operated only between Preston Brook station and Runcorn. In spite of Smith's activity, the trustees sold out to railway interests, Sir Edward Watkin of the Manchester, Sheffield & Lincolnshire and W. P. Price of the Midland. This was in 1872 and a new company was formed, the Bridgewater Navigation Co, with Edward Leader Williams, late of the Weaver, as general manager and engineer. He made many improvements notably the introduction in 1875 of steam screw canal tugs (45). More improvements were made at Runcorn, another dock had been started by the trustees and this was completed in 1875 as the Fenton dock; part of the Runcorn & Weston Canal was enlarged by the following year into the Arnold dock and a big programme of canal bank walling was carried through, completed in the late 1880s, to preserve the banks from the tugs' wash. The Bridgewater was still efficiently run but was overshadowed by the moves towards the Manchester Ship Canal. The Act for this passed in 1885 and provided for the purchase of the Bridgewater Navigation Co, including the Mersey & Irwell which the Ship Canal had to have to build its own waterway. Construction of the Ship Canal entailed the demolition of the old aqueduct over the Irwell at Barton, so Leader Williams designed the swing aqueduct opened in 1893. Now known as the Bridgewater Department of the Manchester Ship Canal Co, the canal continued to be busy. Although the Ship Canal robbed it of much Liverpool-Manchester traffic, it retained important feeder services, including road cartage. But as on other waterways, there was a decline between the wars. Nevertheless improvements continued, in 1947 the length between Hulme and Stretford was deepened and in 1962 Hulme locks were rebuilt as a single deep lock to facilitate the grain traffic from Manchester docks to mills on the canal, notably Kelloggs at Trafford Park but this ceased in 1974. The Bridgewater is now under a joint trust of local authorities and the Manchester Ship Canal Co.

BRIDGWATER & TAUNTON CANAL, Somerset. Although projected as the Bristol & Taunton and obtaining an Act in 1811, there was so much objection from north Somerset landowners that the scheme was dropped until revived in 1822 as a canal from Taunton to the Parrett at Huntworth, bypassing the Tone. An Act was obtained in 1824, and with James Hollinsworth as engineer the $13\frac{1}{2}$ mile line, with six locks, supplied by water from the Tone was opened in 1827. Immediately hostility began between the canal and the Tone Conservators, resolved in 1832 when the canal bought the river. The waterways

44. Two 'box boats', used for carrying coal in containers, at Astley Green colliery near Leigh on the Bridgewater.

45. 'Duker' flat and tug, locally known as a little packet, on the Bridgewater.

were threatened by the Bristol & Exeter Railway, completed 1844. To withstand railway enterprise the canal had in 1841 extended one mile to Bridgwater and built a dock there, closing the Huntworth basin and lock. Now the canal was 15¼ miles long including the dock with seven locks, including Firepool into the Tone at Taunton, the entrance lock from the canal into Bridgwater dock and the barge lock from the dock into the Parrett. The canal locks took 18 ton craft 54' x 13', the same size as those on the Tone. The Bristol & Exeter finally bought the Bridgwater & Taunton in 1866. For ten years the railway used the canal fully, modernizing Bridgwater dock and the Parrett wharves at Bridgwater and Dunball. However the GWR, which controlled the Bristol & Exeter from 1876, neglected the canal. Shortage of water after 1896 turned more traffic on to the GWR and in the year 1907 the canal carried no tonnage. It has remained disused ever since, now owned by the British Waterways Board.

BRISTOL to SALISBURY CANAL SCHEMES.   See Page 11.

BRISTOL & TAUNTON CANAL, Somerset.   During the canal mania of 1792/3 schemes were revived for a canal from the Bristol to the English Channel. One was the Bristol & Western from the Avon at Bristol to Taunton, possibly making a junction with the Grand Western. Re-named the Bristol & Taunton it promoted a Bill in 1796 which was defeated. A Taunton to Bristol canal again looked attractive in 1810 as part of a scheme for an inland water route from London to Exeter, and a line was surveyed by John Rennie. The revived Bristol & Taunton obtained an Act in 1811 against formidable landowner opposition which effectively killed the scheme although a little cutting may have been done. In 1822 it was revived and built as the Bridgwater & Taunton.

BROHARRIS CANAL, Co Londonderry.   The Broharris was an isolated two mile level cut on the south eastern shore of Lough Foyle running inland towards Limavady. It was made in the 1820s as both a drainage and commercial cut, the main traffic being kelp and shellfish for use as fertilizer.

BUDE CANAL, Devon, Cornwall.   This was built to carry shell sand for agricultural fertilizer. As early as 1774 there was a 95 mile canal project by John Edyvean to carry the sand by tub-boat from Bude to the River Tamar at Calstock. An Act for this was passed in 1774 but no work was done. In 1778 John Smeaton recommended locks on the Bude river, a short canal, and more locks on the Tamar, while in 1785 Edmund Leach proposed a route involving two inclined planes and a long tunnel. Lord Stanhope, an advocate of tub-boat canals and planes who owned land at Holsworthy, keenly supported a canal which was surveyed by John and George Nuttall in 1793. No Act was passed, and the project lay fallow mainly because of the war, until 1818, when a line was surveyed by James Green and Thomas Shearn, from Bude to near Okehampton with a branch down towards Launceston. An Act was secured in 1819 and construction started, involving a breakwater, entrance lock and basin at Bude, and a barge canal with two locks, 63' x 14'7", as far as Marhamchurch. In 1823 the canal was opened; from Marhamchurch the tub-boat line went to Red Post where it divided, one branch eastwards to Blagdonmoor just beyond Holsworthy, with a navigable feeder from the Alfardisworthy reservoir, supplied from the Tamar, and another branch southwards to Druxton about three miles short of Launceston, completed in 1825, the whole system measuring 35½ miles. There were six inclined planes, at Marhamchurch, Hobbacott Down and Venn (on the Holsworthy branch) and Merrifield, Tamerton and Werrington (all on the Druxton branch). The tub-boats carried 4 tons each, horse hauled in gangs of six or eight. Their small wheels ran in channel rails up the planes. It was usual for barges to bring the sand from Bude to Marhamchurch where it was transhipped. Traffic was encouraging at first, but maintenance costs were high. Railway encroachment and the spread of artificial fertilizers removed much traffic after 1880, yet the canal staggered on until the tub-boat sections were closed in 1891; while in 1901 the whole undertaking was sold to the Stratton & Bude Urban District Council, who used part of the Holsworthy branch as a water channel from the Alfardisworthy reservoir, and kept the barge portion navigable to Marhamchurch until 1924. Today with the broad locks closed, only the basin and entrance lock remain. In 1967 the reservoir and water channel were transferred to the North Devon Water Board.

BURNTURK CANAL, Fife.   Two small canals were made in 1800, to bring limestone to kilns at Burnturk colliery in the centre of Fife, and send coal and lime down to Kings-kettle village. The first, 2 miles long ran between the quarry and the colliery, the second ½ mile, from the colliery down to Kingskettle. Inclined planes were used to load at the quarry and discharge at Kingskettle but they did not carry boats. These were very likely tub-boats, 4 to 10 tons capacity on the longer canal, only 2 tons on the shorter. They were bow hauled.

BURRY & LOUGHOR RIVERS, Carmarthenshire, Glamorganshire. The Burry is the estuarial successor of the Loughor which flows down from the Black Mountain, Carmar-thenshire. Both were improved for navigation under an Act of 1815, the Loughor being used for the shipment of coal from a colliery at Llangennech on the Carmarthenshire side until a railway was built in 1833.

BURY & SLADEN CANAL PROJECT. The Manchester, Bolton & Bury were anxious to defeat moves towards a trans Pennine canal via Rochdale by promoting their own line into Yorkshire. When the Rochdale failed to obtain an Act in 1792, the Sladen scheme was pushed on towards Sowerby Bridge. Longbotham did the extension survey and proposed a long tunnel of 8428 yd to reach the Calder near Halifax. A Bill was put forward in 1793, it failed but was reintroduced in 1794. Again it failed but in the same session the Act for the Rochdale passed, ending the Bury & Sladen project.

CAISTOR CANAL, Lincolnshire. Because of improvements to the Ancholme after the middle of the eighteenth century, ideas of extending were put forward. One was to link Caistor to the Ancholme by a canal. William Jessop made a survey in 1792, and although the Ancholme Navigation Commissioners were worried about upsetting the drainage of the area, they agreed to the proposals, the Act passing in 1793. The resident engineer was Robert Dickenson and work started on a canal which left the Ancholme four miles south of Brigg and ran easterly towards Caistor for about four miles, but never reached the town. The terminal basin was at Moortown on the Market Rasen - Brigg road. Traffic began in about 1800 on this five lock waterway. There were never many cargoes to and from Caistor and by 1877 the canal was disused. It was abandoned in 1936 on the application of the River Ancholme and Winterton Beck Catchment Board.

CALDER & HEBBLE NAVIGATION, Yorkshire. In the early eighteenth century, with the Aire & Calder established, there were ideas of extending up the Calder from Wakefield. In 1740-1 John Eyes and Thomas Steers made a survey to improve the Calder and its tributary the Hebble. A Bill was defeated by landowners fearful of floods and by owners of cloth fulling mills. John Smeaton was asked to do a survey in 1756, but was too busy on the Eddystone lighthouse to come until the following year. He proposed a scheme to use the Calder and then go up the Hebble or Halifax brook to Salterhebble below the town. This time both land and millowners approved, and the scheme was extended to Sowerby Bridge on the Halifax-Rochdale turnpike. John Eyes did a survey to Sowerby

46.

Bridge and in 1758 the Act passed for a complete Calder navigation to Sowerby Bridge and a Hebble navigation to Salterhebble. Commissioners and not undertakers were responsible for the work, daily affairs being run by a committee, with Smeaton as engineer. Just before work started in 1759 a Tewkesbury man, John Kemmett, offered to make a navigation which would not upset the mills, by having cranes at each mill weir to tranship cargo in containers, but the Calder refused it. Smeaton was assisted by Joseph Nickalls, also from the Eddystone, while the treasurer was Richard Townley of Belfield near Rochdale. By 1762 some of the lower Calder was navigable and in 1764 the river was open to Brighouse. Then came a crisis, because one group of commissioners wanted to end at Brooksmouth, where the Hebble joined the Calder, while the others wanted to push on to Sowerby Bridge. The latter won and a new committee was formed to press on with the work, Brindley being called in 1765 to advise. Smeaton was dismissed and the same year the navigation reached Brooks-mouth, Brindley acting as engineer. He is believed to have left in 1766 after revising the line upwards from Brooksmouth to Sowerby Bridge. In about 1767 Salterhebble was reached with its staircase pair of locks, probably designed by Brindley. As soon as the navigation was open to Salterhebble it was damaged by floods, in late 1767 and early 1768. Smeaton returned to do repairs but more floods closed the navigation. To reopen, more money was needed. With the assistance of Sir George Savile, the Whig MP, an Act was obtained in 1769. This incorporated the existing subscribers as the Company of Proprietors of the Calder & Hebble Navigation. Previously it had been the Calder or the Upper Calder Navigation. Richard Townley was chairman of the new company. Work went ahead quickly with Luke Holt and Robert Carr as resident engineers, and the navigation was re-opened to Salter-hebble in 1769 and to Sowerby Bridge in 1770. The locks were built for 14' beam keels but only 57'6" long. There were soon proposals for branches. In about 1768 John Longbotham had surveyed from the navigation above Brighouse to just short of Halifax. In 1770 he sur-veyed a canal from the Calder & Hebble at Dewsbury up to Birstall and another via Cleck-heaton to Bradford. Apart from the wool and corn for which the navigation had been built, coal soon became important. From the start the Calder & Hebble did well, they had always had a horse towing path and it was not long before they planned more improvements. Jessop surveyed a new cut between Mirfield and Shepley Bridge, excavated by John Pink-erton. Smeaton recommended alterations in the locks in 1779, and the Salterhebble staircase and single lock at Brooksmouth were replaced by three single locks. Then in 1785 Battye Ford cut was extended above Mirfield under Jessop. Carrying was not undertaken by the Calder & Hebble but they found carriers and received payment for the freight, which they accepted at their wharves. Because of this they could advertise what was in effect a carrying service. Passage of both the Huddersfield and Rochdale Acts in 1794 encouraged more improvements. In 1796 a bigger warehouse was opened at Salterhebble, a year later a new one at Sowerby Bridge. In about 1798 the Thornhill cut was opened at Dewsbury, and more stables and wharfage were made at Sowerby Bridge to cope with the expected Rochdale traffic which began in 1804.

Benefits to the Calder & Hebble were enormous - the company now worrying about fraud. A weighing machine was set up at Sowerby Bridge in 1805 to check cargoes. So many cargoes were found to be overweight that the company in 1808 compelled boats to carry gauging marks. There were toll reductions and navigational improvements, by 1808 a new cut at Brookfoot above Brighouse and in 1815 an extension of the Elland cut to join the final one to Sowerby Bridge. About 1812 the Calder & Hebble had built an extended cut at Fall Ing, Wakefield, replacing the old single lock with two new ones. The Calder & Hebble pursued a mill buying policy so that they could control the water. With the Rochdale open, corn traffic to Manchester from Lincolnshire became heavy, and encouragement was given by drawbacks both to this and the malt trade off the Trent. Warehousing space at Wakefield was extended. Fly-boats started in 1825 between Manchester and Wakefield, but the company never countenanced Sunday working. In 1828 the Calder & Hebble's branch canal opened to Halifax off the navigation at Salterhebble. In the steep sided upper Calder valley, it was a heavily locked waterway, 14 locks of the same size as those on the main line, in a total mileage of $1\frac{3}{4}$. Water had to be pumped up to the summit from Salterhebble basin via a tunnel and shaft. The engineer was their own Thomas Bradley. More improvements were undertaken in the 1830s, matching those on the Aire & Calder's Calder line. The idea was to canalize most of the navigation, but plans had to be modified because of mill needs. The authorizing Act of 1834 was ambitious, to improve to Mirfield with a view to continuing to Brighouse. Locks were to be larger, 70' x 18'6" and two were to be made at each place, parallel with each other so that they could act as side ponds. What was done was not so extensive. A new cut was made at Horbury replacing the old and two new locks built to the larger dimensions (Broad Cut Upper and Lower). To communicate with the river and the old cut on the other (north side) of the Calder a side cut and lock were made just above Horbury Bridge. Finally a new lock was built at Thornes, above Fall Ing, again a large one alongside the original small one. All this work was finished by 1838, but no more locks were lengthened. On the Calder & Hebble the position now was that the locks up to and including Figure of Three above Horbury were 67'6" long or more and 18' wide. The remainder stayed at a craft limit of 57'6". There were 28 locks, four flood locks and four sets of flood gates. In 1841 the Manchester & Leeds Railway was opened, parallel with the Rochdale and the Calder & Hebble. Rate cutting followed and Calder & Hebble share prices fell sharply. To save themselves the Calder & Hebble decided in 1843 to lease their navigation to the Manchester & Leeds and terms were agreed. Under railway control from 1844 the old waterway's management was made more efficient. But in 1847 the lease was given up because it had never been legally authorized. The Calder & Hebble however wanted an alliance with somebody, the Aire & Calder refusing to lease them, although otherwise co-operative. With the railways the Calder & Hebble were keen to make traffic agreements, but they failed and cut tolls instead. Eventually in 1855 the Calder & Hebble succeeded in making a traffic agreement with the Aire & Calder. This was not however sufficient protection for the former, they wanted amalgamation. Compromise was reached in 1865 when the Aire & Calder leased the Calder & Hebble for 21 years, with an option on purchase. The Aire & Calder hoped to make a useful through navigation of the Calder & Hebble to take their own and Rochdale craft. Work was started on the locks, altering them to Rochdale standards. However by the end of the 1860s the lock work had stopped. One crafty move of the Aire & Calder during this period was their 99 year lease in 1878 of the Dewsbury old cut. The Calder & Hebble had sold this in 1861 to Lord Savile's trustees. It was derelict, but the trustees covered its banks with houses and business premises. Under Aire & Calder control the cut was reopened to traffic and a new basin built at Savile Town, as the new development was called; this is the site of a Museum dedicated to Yorkshire waterways. Purchase of the whole navigation was in the Aire & Calder's mind, but the Calder & Hebble favoured amalgamation. The Aire & Calder were keen to continue the lease, but refusing amalgamation, since their shareholders would not benefit. They were still interested in enlarging the locks, which restarted in 1882 under the supervision of W.H. Bartholomew. Their lease, 21 years from 1865, still had a few years to go. Funds were put up by the Calder & Hebble to undertake the work and much was done, the idea being to improve initially to Mirfield. The two locks at Fall Ing were converted to a single one, 130' long and one of the Thornes locks just above was lengthened to the same size. But again the work was stopped because the Calder & Hebble wondered if it was worthwhile. However 90 ton craft 120' x 17'6" could now reach the tail of Broad Cut Top lock. There were now 26 locks, plus 4 flood locks and 4 flood gates. Above Broad Cut Top the old 57'6" x 14'2" remained. The navigation measured $21\frac{1}{2}$ miles. At the end of 1885 the Aire & Calder's lease expired but the Aire & Calder had lost money towards the end of their tenure and did not want a further lease. The Calder & Hebble now had thoughts of continuing the lock enlargement programme, but instead rebuilt their overbridges in steel. The Calder & Hebble also became interested in creating a carrying department, actually a subsidiary, the Calder Carrying Co. founded in the early 1900s. Twentieth century Calder & Hebble history was one of traffic decline. The company kept their dividend up, but this meant nothing was ploughed back and capital could be found only by issuing debentures or selling property. Modernization was limited to new cranes and coal storage facilities. The 1929 proposals to enlarge Broad Cut Top lock came to nothing, and another blow was the end of through

Plate 6.

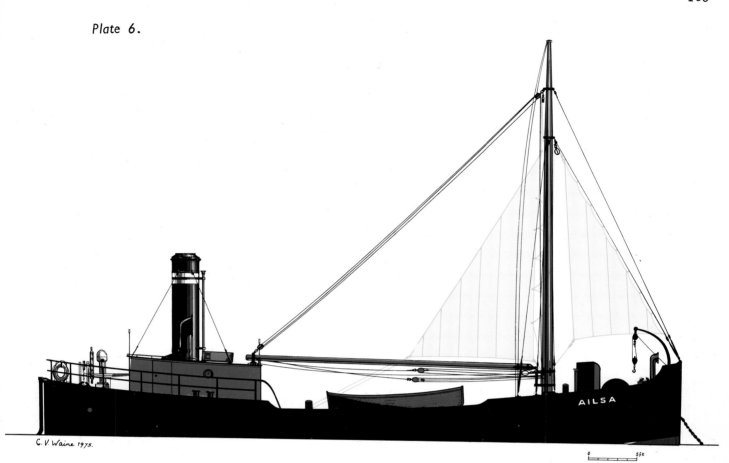

C.V. Waine 1975.

Steam Coaster AILSA
DIMENSIONS: 66′6″ x 18′4″ x 8′10″

THE 'puffers' AILSA and GARMOYLE had the distinction of being built by Wm. Denny & Bros., Dumbarton, who usually constructed passenger steamers. They were completed in 1904 for A. McG. Leslie of Glasgow who sold them both to A. F. Henry & Macgregor, Leith, for their local trade as shown here. AILSA was sold to the Light Shipping Co., Ltd., managed by Ross & Marshall Ltd., of Greenock, in 1920 and became HEADLIGHT. She was broken up at Bowling in 1939.

Tug WORCESTER
LENGTH 45′1″ BREADTH 6′10″

This tug was completed in 1908 by Isaac J. Abdela and Mitchell Ltd., Brimscombe for service on the Worcester and Birmingham Canal. She was fitted with a single cylinder Bolinders engine of 30 horse power in 1929 and this still powers the boat to-day. She now forms part of the collection of the Boat Museum at Ellesmere Port.

traffic on the Rochdale in 1937. In 1942 the Halifax branch was abandoned because it had become unprofitable. In 1944 the Calder & Hebble bought the whole of Sir John Ramsden's Canal and part of the Huddersfield from the LMSR. Nationalization came in 1948, the Calder & Hebble paying a dividend to the last. Their carrying subsidiary, the Calder Carrying Co. was bought by the Hargreaves group. In the 1950s traffic declined sharply, the Rochdale being abandoned in 1952. There were no cargoes up to Sowerby Bridge after 1955 and by 1958 little above Thornhill power station, below Dewsbury. The power station traffic continues into the 1970s from a local colliery staithe (162) but above Dewsbury the navigation is scheduled as a cruiseway.

CALEDONIAN CANAL, Inverness-shire.   Dividing the Highlands, the Great Glen lends itself to a waterway from coast to coast. As early as 1726 one was considered, but it was after the '45 Rebellion that the project took shape, as part of government policy. Under the direction of the Forfeited Estates Commission, James Watt made a survey in 1773-4. The waterway was considered as an aid to the fishing industry, allowing boats to follow the seasonal migrations of the herring, but no work followed. Further surveys were made by John Rennie in 1793 and Thomas Telford in 1801-2 during the war with France, when a canal took on an added significance as a means of evading privateers. This spurred the government who appointed commissioners of eminence to administer the canal including Lords Castlereagh and Dundas, and Telford as principal engineer with William Jessop as consultant. To raise money, Acts were passed in 1803 and 1804. Work was concentrated at the two sea entrances and basins at Corpach near Fort William and at Clachnaharry near Inverness, and on the cuts towards Loch Lochy and Loch Ness. Telford grouped his locks in staircases to save expense, for there was no water shortage. At Banavie he built Neptune's staircase of 8 locks, at Muirtown of four, at Fort Augustus of five, with double locks at Corpach and Laggan. The remainder were single and the total came to 29 including the sea locks at Corpach and Clachnaharry and a second lock at Gairlochy added in 1844. They were to pass vessels 160' x 36' wide, whose height was unrestricted because swing bridges were provided. The depth was designed to be 20' but on completion only 12' was achieved on the summit, deepened to 17' in 1847. The final cost totalled £905,258, although Telford estimated £350,000 in 1802. In 1822 it was complete, totalling 60 miles. The war was long over, and steamers were beginning to trade, for which the north of Scotland spelt less danger, so traffic did not develop as hoped, also sailing ships had great difficulty navigating the lochs. In 1847 tugs were introduced to help them, although horses remained on the canal sections. From the start passenger steamers worked throughout the system, a service which lasted until 1914, although until 1929 there was a truncated service from Inverness to Fort Augustus. Much of the construction was found to be faulty, notably at locks, so there were stoppages, including a very long one from 1843 to 1847. But traffic never prospered, poor harvests meant less grain and potatoes moving westwards, the use by the Moray Firth fishermen diminished, while at the same time during the 1850s and 60s, navigation of the Pentland Firth was improved by new charts and sea marks. Railway competition came from the coast to coast lines to the south. Nevertheless the canal proved its worth during the 1914-18 war, enabling the American naval bases at Muirtown and on the Cromarty Firth to be supplied, and in 1918, vast numbers of mines needed for the field between the Orkneys and Norway were delivered via the canal to east coast ports. During the 1939-45 war it was likewise busy but afterwards road transport robbed it of practically all traffic except fishing boats. In 1919 the old commissioners had been replaced by the Ministry of Transport who in 1948 handed over to the British Transport Commission. From 1966 traffic has been encouraged into the enlarged sea lock and basin at Corpach by the opening of the Wiggins Teape mill nearby, while all the locks are now mechanised. The British Waterways Board run their tug cum icebreaker SCOT II on excursion sailings from Muirtown locks to Castle Urquhart on Loch Ness. Yachts and fishing boats form the bulk of the through traffic, with a small amount of coastal cargo, and local hire pleasure cruises.

River CAM, Cambridgeshire and associated LODES, SOHAM LODE. The Cam enters the Great Ouse 3 miles above Ely at Pope's Corner. Although navigable for the 14½ miles up to Cambridge and used during the Middle Ages to send stone up to the university and corn down to King's Lynn, the Cam was found in poor shape by a survey of 1618. With the expanding university dependent on the Cam and Great Ouse for food supplies and building materials, an Act for improvement above Clayhithe was passed in 1703, the work to be in the hands of conservators, still the authority above Bottisham lock, with powers amended by an Act of 1857. There are three Cam locks, able to pass craft 98' x 15'. Bottisham lock is now electrified, the other lock being Baitsbite and the third Jesus Green, on the outskirts of Cambridge, moved upstream to the present site in about 1837. The river carried traffic to the wharves above the colleges at Silver Street and to Quayside below Magdalene bridge, replacing the old wharves which had become the college Backs. There was also traffic to the annual Stourbridge Fair below Cambridge, which supported passenger services. During the early nineteenth century the Cam was prosperous, so much so that in 1826 the conservators commissioned a 'state barge' and at about the same time built a Flemish style banqueting hall at Clayhithe. Off the main river were drains or lodes, some navigable since Roman times. Bottisham Lode, probably Roman, with one staunch was used until about 1900 for 2½ miles up to Lode village; Swaffham Lode, also probably Roman with an entrance staunch went up for 3⅜ miles to a wharf at Swaffham Bulbeck. Further downstream Upware was the junction for lodes to Reach, Burwell and Wicken. Reach Lode with an entrance lock at Upware, replacing a Roman waterway, was about three miles long, Burwell Lode about the same, a branch off Reach Lode. Both were used commercially until the 1940s, clunch, a chalk for building, being quarried at Reach, while there was a fertilizer factory at Burwell. Wicken Lode was a 1½ mile branch, off Reach Lode, and was used into the 1939-45 War for the carriage of peat and sedge. Soham used to be reached by the Lark and Snail, the latter navigable in the eighteenth century to Fordham, but in about 1790 the Snail was diverted to enter the Great Ouse at Barway below Stretham and made into the navigable Soham Lode, entered by two sets of gates mitred in opposite directions, so not a lock but rather a staunch. Malt, corn, flour, coal and timber were the main traffic, but most cargoes ceased in the 1890s. The London-Cambridge Railway line was opened in 1845 and the following year the Cam Conservators cut their rates. Some traffics however survived into the twentieth century. Coal, bricks and timber came up to Cambridge, many cargoes being handled by a 70 ton steam barge, the NANCY which worked between King's Lynn and Cambridge up to 1914. Gas water from Cambridge gas works went by tug hauled tank barges to the West Norfolk Manure Co's fertilizer works at King's Lynn up to 1938, but a post 1945 trading venture with a motor barge failed, as did the motor NANCY II in 1927-9.

CAMPBELTOWN CANAL, Argyllshire. James Watt in 1773 surveyed a canal across Kintyre from the Argyll colliery by Machrihanish Bay to Campbeltown. Three miles long it was completed in 1794, lasting until 1856 when replaced by the Campbeltown & Machrihanish Light Railway.

CAMPSIE CANAL PROJECT, Stirlingshire, Dunbartonshire. An Act of 1837 sanctioned a canal from Campsie where there was an alum works to the Forth & Clyde near Kirkintilloch.

CANN QUARRY CANAL, Devon. Proposed in 1778 by John Smeaton, nothing was done until the Earl of Morley, the slate quarries' owner, opened a 2 mile mill leat navigable by small tub-boats in 1829. This was connected to the Plymouth & Dartmoor Railway, a horse operated line, by a half mile branch tramroad, ten years later extended to supplant the canal.

CAR DYKE, Cambridgeshire, Isle of Ely, Huntingdonshire, Northamptonshire, Lincolnshire. A channel from the Cam near Waterbeach, via Peterborough to the Fossdyke near Lincoln. It is believed to be a Roman work for drainage and navigation, supplying Lincoln with wheat, hides and wool. Much is traceable, see Witham and Fossdyke Navigations.

CARLINGWARK CANALS, Kirkcudbrightshire. Two short canals for carrying marl were built to improve the Dee near Castle Douglas between 1765 and 1789. One was 1½ miles long from the Dee to Carlingwark Loch, the source of the marl, the other, built nearer 1780 was a ½ mile cut with a lock to avoid a stretch of the river, boats taking marl to New Galloway at the head of Loch Ken. They became disused by 1840.

CARLISLE CANAL, Cumberland. West Cumberland coal came to Carlisle by the Eden and there were moves to improve the river, an Act passing in 1721, but nothing was done. In 1807 William Chapman reported on the possibility of either a ship canal down to Bowness-on-Solway or an ordinary canal to Maryport. Telford was called in to advise, proposing a ship canal (he called it the Cumberland canal) to Bowness, but nothing was done until 1817 when Chapman again surveyed between Carlisle and the Solway. This time the promoters obtained their Act in 1819 and started work, Chapman acting as consulting engineer although he was later dismissed for negligence. The canal ran from just east of Bowness, where the entrance to the Solway was named Port Carlisle, 11¼ miles into Carlisle, with an entrance lock from the firth and 7 other locks for vessels 74' x 17'6", the provision of lifting bridges allowing sailing vessels up. Water came from a reservoir fed by the Eden. It opened in 1823. Traffic was slow in starting, the canal company having to hunt for cargoes. Things improved when a Carlisle-Liverpool steam packet service began about 1825, the company building a jetty at Port Carlisle and starting a canal packet in connection with the steamer services. Meanwhile a Carlisle-Newcastle Canal had been revived, (see Tyne schemes), Chapman being called in to estimate the cost of this or a railway. A railway was selected after the successful completion of the Stockton & Darlington and in 1829 the Newcastle & Carlisle was authorized, completed in 1839. It proved of benefit to the canal, bringing coal from the pits at Greenhead near the Roman Wall, goods from Europe for north-west England and Ireland, and German emigrants, for Liverpool and the United States. Both canal receipts and dividends responded favourably. Meanwhile another steamer service had started between Port Carlisle, Annan and Liverpool. The Carlisle Canal was not to enjoy prosperity for long. In the 1840s competition developed, coal from Greenhead was threatened by West Cumberland coal loaded at Maryport, and in 1845 the Maryport & Carlisle Railway was open, joining up with the Newcastle & Carlisle. More serious was the arrival in 1847 of the Lancaster & Carlisle Railway over Shap Fell, followed in 1848 by the Caledonian. Although tolls were cut the canal could not go on, closing in 1853. Plans were made to convert it into a railway, opened in 1855.

River CART, Renfrewshire. To improve water transport to Paisley there were moves to modify the White Cart. An Act was passed in 1753, but nothing was done until a second Act of 1787 authorized a cut, which was made.

CASSINGTON CUT, Oxfordshire. Because of the increased Thames traffic from the Oxford Canal the Duke of Marlborough sought to benefit by building a private cut off the river below Eynsham to the Eynsham-Cassington road. It was started about 1800 and extended in stages for the ¾ mile to the road, being complete about 1814. There was one lock similar in size to those on the Thames, large enough for vessels 100' x 14'. The cut ceased to be used in about 1870.

CHARD CANAL, Somerset. It was encouraged by the completion in 1827 of the Bridgwater & Taunton, local people wanting a canal from the latter to Chard. James Green made a survey for a tub-boat line from the Bridgwater & Taunton at Creech St. Michael, with two lifts, two inclined planes and two tunnels. An Act was passed in 1834. Possibly because of his difficulties with the Grand Western lifts, Green was replaced as the Chard engineer by Sydney Hall who replaced the proposed lifts by inclined planes. A third tunnel was driven at Ilminster, a lock built at Dowlish Ford, and the Chard Common plane heightened. By 1841 the canal was open to Ilminster and by 1842 to Chard, an extension to Chaffcombe was never built, so the total mileage remained at 13½. Water came from the specially built Chard reservoir. Apart from the 300 yard Ilminster tunnel in which tub-boats could pass, there were the 1800 yard Crimson Hill and 314 yard Lillesdon single line tunnels, none having towing paths. The Chard Common plane was single line with one caisson, the other three planes at Thornfalcon, Wrantage and Ilminster being double track. Quite a brisk trade started with 26' x 6'6" tub-boats. Unfortunately the year the Chard was opened the Bristol & Exeter Railway reached Taunton, from where land carriage was easy. To boost trade the Chard manager started a carrying company, the Bridgwater & Chard Coal Co., for by 1844 only two years after completion, six of the original twelve carriers had left the canal. The canal succumbed in 1867 when it was bought by the Bristol & Exeter and closed the following year, for in 1866 this company had completed their railway from Taunton to Chard.

CHELMER & BLACKWATER NAVIGATION, Essex. Ideas to make the Chelmer navigable down to Maldon on the Blackwater were first put forward by Andrew Yarranton, who described his survey in his "England's Improvement by Sea and Land" - published between 1677 and 1686. Maldon was against the scheme because improvement of the Chelmer would allow traffic to bypass Maldon and go direct to Chelmsford. After Yarranton's scheme nothing was done until 1733 when John Hore of Newbury made a survey. He proposed either a river improvement or a canal on a new line. Again Maldon objected and overrode the proposals. John Smeaton and Thomas Yeoman made surveys in 1762, and Yeoman a further survey in 1765, used for an Act passed in 1766 to make the Chelmer navigable from Maldon to Chelmsford. The money raised was insufficient so no work started. The scheme was revived in 1772 as a possible canal without locks, but nothing was done. The Chelmer navigation languished until the 1790s by which time Chelmsford found itself out of date, and pressure to make a waterway increased. In 1792 a scheme was put forward which would avoid Maldon and end the navigation near Heybridge, some way below Maldon on the Blackwater estuary at Colliers' Reach. John Rennie was in charge of the surveys and sent two assistants, first Charles Wedge, and secondly Matthew Hall. Maldon opposition was unavailing and the Act passed in 1793. Work was nominally under John Rennie, but his assistant Richard Coates was actually in charge. Watermills had to be passed by cuts and locks, the other works being a half mile cut at Chelmsford and a 2½ mile cut from Beeleigh down to what became known as Heybridge Basin. Here there was a sea lock for coastal vessels 107' x 26' and there were twelve locks on the 13⅞ mile navigation for barges 60' x 16'. The cut below Beeleigh crosses the Blackwater on the level and there are two locks, one on each side of the Blackwater, which protect the cut from Blackwater floods and ensure sufficient depth in drought conditions. Even so the Chelmer & Blackwater is very shallow, 2' being the ruling draught. With work on the Chelmer & Blackwater under way Maldon now tried to join up. They called in Latrobe who had worked under Smeaton. In 1793 he recommended deepening the Blackwater and the following year suggested a junction with the Chelmer. This latter was put to Parliament to the concern of the Chelmer & Blackwater who saw their Beeleigh-Heybridge Basin cut as possibly valueless. Fortunately nothing came of Maldon's proposals. By the spring of 1796 the lower part of the Chelmer & Blackwater was open to traffic, but the whole navigation was not open until 1797. As on so many river navigations, floods quickly became a problem because of the deposition of silt which formed almost impassable shoals. Rennie's work was criticized and he was called upon to suggest remedies. Nor were the millers satisfied, because of water losses at the locks. But traffic increased in spite of a severe frost in early 1799, and the facility with which coal could be shipped to Chelmsford encouraged a gas works to start there in 1819, the second in Essex. Dividends fell after 1843 when the Eastern Counties Railway reached Chelmsford, but the Chelmer & Blackwater were fortunate in that no direct railway was made between Chelmsford and Maldon. Later history of the Chelmer & Blackwater has been uneventful, coal, timber, bricks and stone were the main upward cargoes, with grain and flour downwards (53). After the 1939-45 War the sea lock at Heybridge Basin was enlarged for bigger timber ships from the Continent. There was one branch canal built privately, a line of about half a mile leaving the navigation just below the locks at Beeleigh. Originally called Mr. Westcomb's Navigation because it crossed his land, it later became known as Langford cut because it served Langford mill. It was opened at the same time as the main navigation. The last barge came up the branch in 1881. On the main line, traffic in timber continued from Heybridge Basin to Chelmsford up to 1972. Now pleasure craft use the navigation and fishing is popular. Below the lower of the Beeleigh locks, the pound down to Heybridge Basin is a yacht centre and the still independent navigation derives revenue from mooring fees.

CHESTER CANAL, Cheshire. In the eighteenth century the Dee was still a busy commercial river although silting, but better inland communications were needed, thus the promotion in 1771 of a canal from the river at Chester to join the Trent & Mersey near Runcorn, later changed to Middlewich, with a branch to Nantwich, and so provide a second western outlet. But the Duke of Bridgewater, arbiter of the Trent & Mersey's fortunes, desired no rival connection at Middlewich, indeed the proposed canal was not to come nearer than 100 yd, to which the Chester people were forced to agree. On this basis an

Act was obtained in 1772 for a barge canal and Samuel Weston was appointed engineer, although later replaced. A tidal basin led off the Dee from which the canal was carried up to the city at Northgate by a five rise staircase (47). In 1775 it was opened to Beeston and by 1779 to Nantwich, but lack of money prevented a line to Middlewich. With a total length of $19\frac{1}{4}$ miles this broad canal today has 16 locks for craft 74'11" x 14'3", plus the river lock into the Dee, the two at Bunbury and three at Northgate being staircases. Because it had no developing hinterland the canal had little traffic. The company tried prospecting for salt at Nantwich and carrying on the Trent & Mersey, both unsuccessfully; equally unremunerative was the Chester-Beeston passenger packet service. In 1787 one of the Beeston locks collapsed and traffic above stopped until there was money to repair it. Salvation came with the promotion of the Ellesmere Canal which received its Act in 1793, for a waterway from the Mersey to the Severn with which the Chester hoped to join; a hope realised when the Wirral line was built from Netherpool (later Ellesmere Port) to the Dee making in 1797 a junction with the Chester Canal. Later the Chester Canal received a second connection with the Ellesmere when that canal's Whitchurch branch was completed to Hurleston near Nantwich in 1805. The Ellesmere was dependent on the Chester Canal for access to the Mersey, resolved in 1813 when the two amalgamated. As the Ellesmere & Chester Canal the new company pursued a forceful policy, to gain traffic and effect repairs. On the

47. Northgate locks, Chester originally a five rise, but a three since 1797 when the Wirral line was made.

Chester Canal this meant the 1827 rebuilding of both Beeston locks, the lower with an iron chamber. The previous year the Chester had been put firmly on the canal map with the passage of the Act for the Birmingham & Liverpool Junction Canal, followed in 1827 by the Act for the canal to Middlewich, agreed to by the Trent & Mersey when they learnt of the passage of the Birmingham & Liverpool Act. In 1845 came amalgamation of the Ellesmere & Chester with the Birmingham & Liverpool, under the title of the former, a short lived independence, because in 1846 the Shropshire Union was formed.

CHESTERFIELD CANAL, Nottinghamshire Yorkshire, Derbyshire. Because the River Idle was unimproved, local mineral interests favoured a canal from the Trent westwards to Chesterfield to cut out the road transport to Bawtry at the limit of navigation of the Idle. In 1769 James Brindley surveyed a narrow canal from Chesterfield and Staveley, via a tunnel at Norwood, to Worksop, East Retford and Stockwith below Gainsborough on the Trent. With the Act passed in 1771, Brindley was made engineer and work started, including the 2850 yd tunnel, later when the nearby railway was built, lengthened to 3102 yd. In 1774 it was agreed to broaden the length from Retford down to the Trent including Drakeholes tunnel (154 yd) built like Norwood without a towing path. By this time Brindley was dead and the supervision devolved on his brother-in-law Hugh Henshall, with John Varley as resident engineer. Norwood tunnel was opened in 1775. The whole line was open in 1777, 46 miles long with 65 locks, 6 of them broad, one of these being a tide lock at the junction with the Trent. There were two summit levels and three branches, one of a mile to Norbriggs near Staveley to connect with the Chesterfield road, a $\frac{3}{4}$ mile private one, to a quarry near Worksop and a third to a colliery tramroad near Staveley. Finally there was an isolated underground level, on the Worsley pattern, at Hollingwood pit owned by the Duke of Devonshire, navigated by 20' tub-boats. Water came from four, later six, reservoirs, Pebley being the largest, also from the Idle at Retford, the Ryton at Thorpe and Worksop and the Rother at Chesterfield. With coal as the staple traffic the canal did well and there were ideas in the 1820s to extend westwards to collieries and limestone quarries, in 1824 a prospectus being issued for, the Grand Commercial (or Scarsdale & High Peak) Canal to run from the Peak Forest Canal at Bugsworth to the Sheffield Canal with another line running down to the Chesterfield and Cromford Canals. From 1793 onwards there were schemes to connect the Chesterfield Canal with Sheffield and the Don culminating in a proposal of 1852 for a Sheffield & Chesterfield Junction Canal. In 1847 an Act was passed for a railway from Staveley to Worksop to join the Chesterfield Canal. With this line the canal company amalgamated, but in the same year (1847) the new company joined with the Manchester, Sheffield & Lincolnshire. To accommodate the new railway the canal was partially realigned reducing its length by $\frac{1}{2}$ mile and Norwood tunnel lengthened. Under railway control the canal continued to carry a fair traffic, the MS & LR putting on a small carrying fleet which lasted until 1892. By the early twentieth century the canal was declining, mining subsidence causing serious damage to Norwood tunnel, which in 1908 had to be closed.

During the 1920s and 30s in LNER days, parts of the canal were narrowed between Retford and West Stockwith, the last traffic, between West Stockwith and Walkeringham three miles up, ceasing in 1955. Today owing to the enthusiasm and hard work of the Retford and Worksop Boat Club the canal has been restored to navigation up to Worksop.

CINDERFORD CANAL, Gloucestershire. This was a private canal, about $1\frac{1}{4}$ miles long completed by 1795 from the dam pool at Broad Moor to the Cinderford ironworks. It probably served a double purpose, small boats carrying coke and the water feeding a wheel providing the furnace blast.

Vale of CLWYD CANAL PROJECT, Denbighshire. A canal was proposed in the 1770s from collieries near Whitford inland from Mostyn, down to the coast at Foryd on the other side of the Clwyd from Rhyl, with a branch up the Vale of Clwyd to Rhuddlan, St. Asaph, Denbigh and Ruthin. Although revived in 1807 no bill was ever sought.

COALISLAND CANAL   -   See Tyrone Navigation.

COD BECK - See River Ouse above York.

COLNE NAVIGATION, Essex. Colchester was a Roman town and port at the head of navigation of the tidal Colne. In the reign of Richard I, the river was put under the new corporation of Colchester. An Act of 1623 gave Colchester better control of the river, but it needed improving to remain navigable. A further Act of 1698 authorized this as far down as Wivenhoe, four miles from Colchester. Commissioners were appointed to oversee the works. They included a lock about half a mile below Hythe bridge, Colchester, allowing vessels to lie at the Hythe quays at a constant level. Unfortunately Colchester suffered a severe slump in the 1700s and the navigation was allowed to decay. The lock collapsed and by 1749 the Colne was derelict, the corporation having given up control and any attempt to collect dues. However an Act of 1719, which had extended the time limit for completion of improvement works authorized by the Act of 1698, also allowed others, who were not members of Colchester Corporation to supervise the Colne. These others secured a further Act in 1750 which vested control in the justices of the East Division of Essex and reformed the toll structure. The lock was rebuilt to the benefit of Hythe quays and the channel below, because it provided a head of water to scour out the tideway. But no further improvements were undertaken, although in 1842 two schemes were put forward, one for a ship canal from Wivenhoe to the Hythe and another for a barge canal along the Colne valley, for $2\frac{1}{4}$ miles to link up with the Eastern Counties Railway which skirted the town. By this time the Colne was deteriorating and the condition of the lock poor; it was nearly a hundred years old. More ideas were put forward in 1847, one of which, by Peter Bruff, who had proposed the barge and ship canals, suggested removal of the lock and the building of a new one about a quarter of a mile downstream. In the end it was the railway which decided things, when later in 1847 a line was opened round from the Eastern Counties Railway to the Hythe. The river was widened and deepened and the old lock removed, so that today Colchester is a busy port. Since 1892 the Colne has again been under the corporation, who have jurisdiction from East Mill Colchester to Colne Point below Mersea, a distance of 11 miles.

COMMERCIAL CANAL PROJECT. Not to be confused with the Grand Commercial Canal (see Peak District canal projects). It was promoted in 1795-6 as a broad canal from the Chester Canal at Nantwich to join Sir Nigel Gresley's Canal near Newcastle-under-Lyme, involving a tunnel near Harecastle. From Newcastle the Commercial was to cross the Trent & Mersey at Burslem, continuing to Uttoxeter and via the Dove valley join the wide part of the Trent & Mersey at Burton. Below Burton the Commercial would cross the Trent, join the then broad Ashby Canal, and provide, as long as the Coventry to Hawkesbury and the Oxford to Braunston were widened, a broad water route between the Thames and the Mersey, for the Ellesmere's Wirral line was open. The Commercial was supported by the Ashby and by Sir Nigel Gresley and the Burton Boat Co, lessees of the Trent from Wilden Ferry to Burton. The Grand Junction were not in favour, because they were hoping to make the Oxford, Coventry and Trent & Mersey widen their own lines, nor were the Trent & Mersey because the Commercial would bypass them. Robert Whitworth and William Jessop had made surveys, but the strong opposition prevented any Bill being introduced and in 1797 the canal was dropped.

COMPSTALL NAVIGATION, Cheshire. Cotton mills on the Etherow at Compstall near Marple, built in the 1820s were water powered, the channel from the river weir to the storage reservoirs being used in the mid-nineteenth century to bring coal to Compstall village from pits near the weir in boats 22' x 6'5" x 3'6" two of which have been found.

CONG CANAL, Co Galway, Mayo. To join Lough Corrib and Lough Mask in Connaught the Board of Public Works during the 1850s built a 3 mile canal with four locks. It took five years labour but would not hold water, the limestone having swallow holes. So the canal was abandoned and never used.

COOMBE HILL CANAL, Gloucestershire. This broad waterway was authorized by an Act of 1792 to run from the Severn towards Cheltenham to bring coal to the growing spa town. It was probably opened by early 1796, $2\frac{3}{4}$ miles long, entering the Severn down two locks six miles above Gloucester and running inland to the village of Coombe Hill, from whence the coal went by road five miles into Cheltenham. By 1808 there were plans to extend the waterway to the town, although this was successfully opposed by the Gloucester & Cheltenham tramroad, later built to bring Forest of Dean coal. From 1822 the canal came under the control of the Worcester & Birmingham who leased it in 1825. Their lease was renewed in 1829 and in 1844 they proposed to buy the canal and extend it to Cheltenham to fight railway competition. However they did not and in 1849 it was leased to the Staffs. & Worcs, to extend their traffic, the lease ending in 1867. The canal rapidly declined and was sold in 1871 to private interests who secured an Act of abandonment in 1876.

COTTINGHAM & HULL CANAL PROJECT, Yorkshire. There were ideas in 1802 of making a canal from Cottingham to Hull four miles or so away. Estimates were made by Thomas Dyson. A suburban passenger service was expected, and milk traffic on the passage boats. The war with France had just been resumed and the prospects for such a canal did not look good.

COVENTRY CANAL, Warwickshire, Staffordshire. Promoted by local interests to improve the supply of coal to Coventry, Brindley selected a route from the Trent & Mersey at Fradley near Lichfield via Fazeley, Atherstone, Nuneaton and Bedworth. The Act was passed in 1768 and work started, the length from Coventry to Bedworth being opened the following year, absorbing the $\frac{5}{8}$ mile private canal from Richard Parrott's colliery at Bedworth to Hawkesbury. By this time the idea of making the Coventry part of a canal to Oxford and the Thames had taken shape, for the Act for the Oxford Canal was passed in 1769. That same year the Coventry had to dismiss Brindley because of lack of attention. In his stead the elderly Thomas Yeoman was called in, but was soon replaced by Edmund Lingard with Samuel Bull as his assistant. By the end of 1771 the canal reached Atherstone still 21 miles from Fradley where it stayed for a long time, an isolated local line, conveying coal to Coventry. Reasons for this halt were primarily lack of money. Not until 1781 was any positive move made to persuade the Coventry to push northwards, later in 1782 impetus coming from the Birmingham & Fazeley project. By an agreement made to rescue the Coventry Canal, the Birmingham & Fazeley would build half the Coventry's line from Fazeley to Fradley, as far as Whittington Brook, the Trent & Mersey being responsible for the canal from thence to Fradley. Meanwhile the Coventry itself had to complete the line to Fazeley. This joint work was authorized by an Act of 1785, but even now the Coventry were loath to go on. The Trent & Mersey completed to Whittington Brook in 1787 and the Birmingham & Fazeley reached the same place in 1789, the following year the Coventry arrived at Fazeley, via the Tame aqueduct near the town, so the route was open from Fradley, to Coventry and through to Oxford. With traffic from Liverpool, Manchester and the Potteries, from Birmingham and the Black Country able to reach the Thames, the Coventry began to do better. It bought the section from Whittington Brook to Fradley, but the Fazeley - Whittington Brook length remained under the control of the Birmingham & Fazeley until 1948, as a part of the BCN. The Coventry owned a total length of $32\frac{1}{2}$ miles, $5\frac{1}{2}$ being the detached Whittington Brook - Fradley length; there were 13 narrow locks, 11 on the Atherstone flight and two at Glascote near Tamworth plus the stop lock (only a gauging stop), at Hawkesbury. Water came from Oldbury reservoir near Atherstone, later by pumping at Hawkesbury from mine drainage. There was a $\frac{3}{4}$ mile private branch to Griff colliery near Nuneaton opened in 1787 by Sir Roger Newdigate and used until 1961, latterly owned by the National Coal Board. Sir Roger also developed his own private canal system at Arbury which joined the Coventry main line nearby. Railway competition in the 1840s meant reduced tolls and agreements with other canals to keep traffic on the waterways while maintaining the Coventry's share. They had enough money to finance improvements, notably the purchase of two steam tugs in 1860-61. Like the Oxford, the Coventry never succumbed to railway control or other control. On the other hand it failed in 1880 to either buy or lease the Fazeley-Whittington Brook section from the BCN, so remained until nationalization a curiously divided waterway. Dividends were however paid until 1947 and traffic remained constant until the early 1960s, most of the canal borne coal for London coming from pits on the Coventry.

CRINAN CANAL, Argyllshire. The Crinan was a result of governmental policy to open up the Highlands after the '45 Rebellion. In 1771 Glasgow interests approached the Forfeited Estates Commission who requested James Watt to make surveys for a canal across the Kintyre peninsula to save fishing vessels and coasters the passage round. More surveys were undertaken in 1792 by John Rennie, for the Duke of Argyll and the Marquess of Breadalbane, for the canal was now to be promoted by public subscription with governmental encouragement. In 1793 the Act was passed, with much of the finance coming from England. Shortage of labour caused the work to proceed slowly, the route via Daill involving deep cutting on the summit and much rock excavation near Crinan. To complete the line the government had to step in with a £25,000 loan. In 1801 the Crinan was opened although not finished, a total of 9 miles from Ardrishaig on Loch Fyne to Crinan, with 15 locks able to take vessels 88' x 20'. Not until 1809 was the canal pronounced satisfactory, although there were more long stoppages for repairs. Water supply was dependent on a chain of little lochs, their capacity amplified by dams, feeding into a summit level less than $\frac{3}{4}$ mile long between the locks at Dunardry and Cairnbaan. In 1816 because the canal company had incurred heavy debts from the government, the Crinan was put under the latter's control, authority being exercised by the Commissioners of the Caledonian Canal. Their engineer Thomas Telford was made responsible for putting the works into good order. Passenger services started in 1818 with Bell's COMET, followed by other steam vessels as part of a service from Glasgow to Fort William and after the opening of the Caledonian Canal in 1822, Inverness, passing through the Crinan under their own power. Horses were provided by the canal for sailing vessels and for canal passenger boats. Steam navigation reduced the Crinan's value, for the Mull of Kintyre was not now such an obstacle. In 1848 the Crinan was placed completely under the Commissioners of the Caledonian Canal, although the original promoters had tried to get it back. With the advent of larger steamers (too large for the canal) passenger traffic increased from the Clyde to the

West Highlands, mostly carried on the canal section by the horse drawn track boats until in 1866 Hutcheson's introduced their twin screw LINNET solely for canal use. By the 1880s cargo through the canal was mainly in the hands of steam 'puffers' suitable for the Crinan locks. Traffic declined in the 1914-18 War because many of the 'puffers' were requisitioned by the Admiralty, and in 1919 the canal was taken over by the Ministry of Transport. In 1948 the Crinan came under the British Transport Commission and its future is assured because of its value to the economy of the Hebrides, although yachts form the bulk of present traffic.

CROMFORD CANAL, Nottinghamshire, Derbyshire.   To tap more of the coal deposits in the Erewash valley, an extension of the Erewash Canal towards Pinxton was proposed in 1787. The following year Sir Richard Arkwright, owner of the mills at Cromford backed promotion of a canal to Cromford and a survey by William Jessop recommended a line from the Erewash at Langley Mill to Cromford with a branch to Pinxton. The Act followed in 1789 and with Jessop as engineer and Benjamin Outram as his assistant, work commenced. The $14\frac{5}{8}$ miles long canal involved considerable engineering works, the 2966 yd Butterley tunnel (extended to 3063 yd when the railway was built above it), three shorter tunnels between Butterley and Cromford, Buckland Hollow (33 yd) Hag (93 yd) and Gregory (76 yd), and two aqueducts, over the Amber at Bullbridge and a larger one over the Derwent at Lea Wood near Cromford. The 14 locks, all between Butterley and Langley Mill were built broad, but the tunnels were narrow. The level $2\frac{3}{8}$ miles branch to Pinxton left the main line at Ironville. Water for the new canal came from reservoirs at Butterley and Codnor Park, also from Bonsall Brook feeding into the head of the canal at Cromford and from the Derwent by pumping at Lea Wood. In 1794 the canal was open, Butterley tunnel proving a bottleneck to traffic, taking about three hours to leg. The $2\frac{1}{2}$ furlong Lea Wood branch, privately built to serve works and quarries was completed in 1802. Traffic in limestone, lime and coal, iron, gritstone and lead became heavy, the canal being fed by horse tramroads including the line down from Crich quarries to Bullbridge and the Mansfield & Pinxton, projected in 1803 as a canal, then as a tramroad and opened in 1819. In 1831 the Cromford & High Peak line was opened over to Whaley Bridge and the Peak Forest Canal, so that Manchester traffic came on to the Cromford. During the 1840s railway competition caused toll reductions and lower dividends and in 1852 the canal passed to the Manchester, Buxton, Matlock & Midlands Junction Railway whose line down to Ambergate followed the canal. In 1870 the Midland bought both. Mining subsidence closed Butterley tunnel in 1889 which was reopened in 1893, but permanently closed by further subsidence in 1900. In 1936 the private Lea Wood branch became disused and the following year the LMS proposed to abandon the isolated upper section for navigation, this was refused although the last traffic passed in 1938. But in 1944 the railway secured abandonment of the whole canal for navigation save for the final $\frac{1}{2}$ mile to Langley Mill. The last traffic had passed in 1943, the branch to Pinxton becoming disused before that date. Traffic in coal on the last $\frac{1}{2}$ mile to Langley Mill finished in 1952 and in 1962 it too was abandoned, much of this lower length being now filled in, although the lock at Langley Mill has been reopened, together with the Nottingham's basin there, to serve pleasure craft while work is in progress to restore more of the lower section and at the Cromford end.

CROYDON CANAL, Surrey.   The Croydon Canal received its Act in 1801. Ralph Dodd planned it on the lines of the canals of East Shropshire with inclined planes for 10 to 20 ton boats. John Rennie, called in to advise, also favoured planes because of a likely water shortage on the summit, but in the event reservoirs were built, so locks could be used for 30-35 ton craft 60' x 9'. As opened in 1809 with Dudley Clark as engineer, the Croydon ran $9\frac{1}{4}$ miles from Croydon to join the Grand Surrey Canal at New Cross instead of continuing to Rotherhithe as originally planned. 26 of the 28 locks came in the first $2\frac{1}{2}$ miles from New Cross to Forest Hill. Both the canal and the Surrey Iron Railway competed for traffic so that neither paid very well. In spite of the reservoirs at Sydenham and Norwood and a pumping station at Croydon the canal was often short of water to the end of its career in 1836, when it was bought by the London & Croydon Railway and closed.

CRYMLYN BOG CANAL, Glamorganshire.   In early times, possibly the Middle Ages, there was, it is believed, an artificial cut in the Crymlyn bog, between the estuaries of the Tawe and the Neath.

River CUCKMERE, Sussex.   In 1791-2 there was a proposal to make a canal from the Ouse eastwards to the Cuckmere and in 1813 a further suggestion to make the Cuckmere itself navigable.

CYFARTHFA CANAL, Glamorganshire.   In 1765 at Cyfarthfa near Merthyr Tydfil, Anthony Bacon from Whitehaven built iron furnaces, later leased to the Homfrays and Crawshays. Bacon probably built a small tub-boat canal in the late 1770s for two miles on the level between coal pits and the ironworks. The canal was given up in about 1836, and is now untraceable.

DANE NAVIGATION PROJECT.   When the Weaver's Act passed in 1721 there was also a move to make its tributary, the Dane, a navigation. It would have been useful to the Middlewich salters and a separate Act was passed for its improvement in 1721. There were further moves a few years later to improve the Dane, but a new Bill was defeated.

DARTFORD & CRAYFORD NAVIGATION, Kent.   Although the River Darenth or Dartford Creek was in the early nineteenth century navigable $3\frac{1}{2}$ miles up from the Thames for 50 ton barges on spring tides, at other times cargo had to be transferred to small 10 to 12 ton punts or lighters. Improvements came under an Act of 1840 which sanctioned shortening and dredging both Dartford and Crayford Creeks to take 150 ton barges. These works were completed in 1844 with a lock below Dartford, the total length of the navigation being $2\frac{3}{8}$ miles excluding Crayford Creek. It is still busy with Thames lighter traffic under the control of the Dartford & Crayford Navigation Commissioners.

DEARNE & DOVE CANAL, Yorkshire. The Dearne enters the Don below Mexborough while the Dove enters the Dearne below Barnsley. With the Don navigable up to Rotherham by 1740, Swinton near Mexborough became the road transhipment point for Barnsley. The road was bad, so plans were formed to make the Dearne navigable. The Marquess of Rockingham had the river surveyed in about 1773 but nothing was done until 1792. Now a canal was in view, the object being the Barnsley coalfield. The Don company saw a Dearne valley canal as a subsidiary and asked William Jessop to do the survey but he was too busy. Apparently the work was undertaken by the Don's own engineer John Thompson assisted by William Fairbank. Robert Mylne reported on the surveys. The Dearne & Dove Act passed in 1793. John Thompson was in charge of construction, but he died in 1795 and was replaced by Robert Whitworth. He died in 1799 and the canal was probably finished by one of his sons, Robert or William. Most was open by 1799, including the branch to Earl Fitzwilliam's Elsecar colliery. He had considered making this himself but the canal company eventually did it with his money. Finally in 1804 the Dearne & Dove was fully open, a total of $9\frac{5}{8}$ miles from Swinton on the Don to the junction stop lock with the Barnsley Canal in Barnsley. There were two branches each of $2\frac{1}{8}$ miles, to Elsecar and Worsbrough which also acted as feeders from the two reservoirs at their respective heads. The main line had 19 locks including the junction lock, grouped into flights, 6 at Swinton, 4 below the junction with the Elsecar branch, then the 8 Aldam locks below the junction with the Worsbrough branch. On the Elsecar branch there were six locks. They were built to take keels 58' x 14'10". There was a short 472 yd cut and cover tunnel at Adwick above Manvers Main. Because the Rochdale Canal also opened in 1804, the Dearne & Dove became part of the new through route from the Don to Manchester and Liverpool, for the Barnsley Canal had reached Barnsley in 1799. Apart from a hesitant coal trade the Canal also suffered initially from water shortage. They were obliged in 1804 to give water to the hard pressed Barnsley but were themselves closed in the summers of 1805 and 1806 through drought. Dearne & Dove coal was vital to the Don who wanted the navigation improved in the 1830s. There was always the fear that the coal would go the other way via the Barnsley Canal if depth was not increased. Eventually to safeguard the coal trade the Don bought the Dearne & Dove. Moves towards this started in 1845, and from 1 January 1846 the Don leased the Dearne & Dove, in 1857 purchasing it. From 1850 the Don and the Dearne & Dove were part of the railway and waterway combine called the South Yorkshire & River Dun Co. The Dearne & Dove in the late 1830s had contact with the North Midland Railway who were building alongside the canal. The earthworks allowed the canal to bypass its own Adwick tunnel and come close to the railway so that an interchange wharf could be built. Later Dearne & Dove history is part of the Don's and from 1895 of the story of the Sheffield & South Yorkshire Navigation. The canal had a bad record of subsidence and was mostly abandoned in 1961. See also Don Navigation, Yorkshire.

DERBY CANAL, Derbyshire. Brindley had proposed plans for a canal via Derby in the early 1770s, and in 1791 one was promoted from the Trent & Mersey at Swarkestone to Derby, with another proposal from Shardlow to Derby. Benjamin Outram did surveys for a broad canal from the Trent to the Trent & Mersey at Swarkestone then on to Derby, with a line up the Derwent to Denby near Belper and a branch to Sandiacre on the Erewash. Promotion was confused by Trent & Mersey proposals for a Trent Canal to Nottingham which would have a branch to Derby, but William Jessop resurveyed Outram's route, altering the Denby line to stop at Little Eaton and Bills for both the Derby Canal and the Trent Canal, called with its Derby branch the Derby & Nottingham, went before Parliament in 1793. The latter was thrown out but the Derby Act passed in May 1793. Benjamin Outram became engineer. The line from Derby to Little Eaton was complete in 1795, and in the same year the line to Sandiacre on the Erewash. Outram had considered an aqueduct over the Derwent but he changed this to a level-crossing in Derby. It meant the construction of a 300' long weir below, to give sufficient depth, but in 1796 this was completed, together with the country's first iron aqueduct over a small tributary of the Derwent at The Holmes in Derby. The canal was open in 1796, $\frac{3}{8}$ of a mile from the Trent to the Trent & Mersey at Swarkestone, $5\frac{3}{8}$ miles from the Trent & Mersey to the Derwent in Derby, then on to Sandiacre, a total of $14\frac{1}{2}$ miles. On this line, Swarkestone to Sandiacre, there were 8 broad locks plus a flood lock, and four locks on the section from the Trent to the Trent & Mersey. The one furlong Phoenix branch off the Derwent - Sandiacre section returned to the river at Phoenix lock, boats using the Derwent to go $1\frac{1}{2}$ miles upstream to Darley Mills. Then came the line to Little Eaton, $3\frac{1}{8}$ miles with four locks and a 4 mile tramroad continuation to Smithy Houses, locally called the Little Eaton gangway. This was owned by the Derby Canal and connected at Smithy Houses near Denby with private colliery and works tramroads. All the locks suited 72' x 14' craft. Water came from the Derwent by a special feeder for the Derby-Trent section, and also for the Little Eaton and Sandiacre lines. The short line from the Trent to the Trent & Mersey at Swarkestone was a failure mainly because it had to pay a compensation toll to the Trent & Mersey. Traffic on it is believed to have ended in 1817 and it was dry in 1837. The rest of the system became very busy, particularly coal traffic on the gangway. Later in 1820 the Denby pottery traffic came on to the tramroad. Passengers travelled on the canal by the weekly market boat from Swarkestone into Derby. To fight the railways, the canal cut tolls, but was driven into further decline when in 1855 the Midland Railway opened a branch to Ripley parallel with the canal, to Little Eaton and its gangway. In 1872 the Derby offered their canal to the Midland and to the LNWR, but neither wanted it. The Little Eaton gangway was closed in 1908 which meant no more traffic on the branch canal, and indeed there was hardly any traffic on the whole system by 1927. The Little Eaton branch was abandoned in 1935, but further abandonment was delayed by Imperial Chemical Industries who wanted water. The Derby Canal was never nationalized but in 1964 they succeeded in complete abandonment and the company was wound up in 1974.

River DERWENT, Derbyshire.   Although navigable before the thirteenth century the river became blocked by mills and weirs. It was probably reopened towards the end of that century but must have deteriorated by the early 1600s because Charles I ordered Vermuyden to restore navigation, a work prevented by the Civil War. After the Restoration there were Bills for improvement but no Act passed until 1720. This authorized a navigation from Derby down to the Trent, but no major works were undertaken in spite of earlier plans by George Sorocold. Ten miles long the navigation may have been aided by a couple of flash locks, but in 1759 its traffic was reduced by the completion of Cavendish bridge taking the Derby road over the Trent at Wilden Ferry. The cutting of the Trent & Mersey Canal meant greater losses and in 1794 the navigation was sold to the Derby Canal, who retained 1½ miles in Derby as a navigation.

DERWENT NAVIGATION, Yorkshire.   The Derwent enters the Ouse at Barmby-on-the-Marsh, and runs up to Malton, its source being on the moors behind Scarborough. The lower Derwent was always navigable up to Stamford Bridge. At the end of the seventeenth century George Sorocold did surveys, but Bills of 1695 and 1698 for its improvement were unsuccessful. One of 1701 passed after more surveys by Sorocold, and gave powers to five undertakers to make a navigation up as far as 'Scarborough mills'. No work was done, but the undertakers kept changing, finally settling on Thomas Wentworth. With him as owner, improvement began in 1720, the engineers being Joshua Mitchel and Mark Andrew of Knottingley. By 1724 the river was probably navigable as far as Malton, 38 miles from the confluence with the Ouse. Five locks were made for small keels 55' x 14', the tide at springs now reaching the lowest lock at Sutton, 15½ miles from the Ouse. A towpath was made for bow-hauling but converted to a horse path in 1756. There were ideas in the 1770s of extending to Scarborough as the 1701 Act had sanctioned, and in the 1790s further ideas of reaching Scarborough and Whitby. Smaller craft were getting up to Yedingham some 13½ miles above Malton, and delivered lime up two tributaries, the Rye and the Costa Beck. Another plan followed in 1799, which revived the previous drainage cum navigation scheme, and included improvements to the Rye, the Costa Beck and the Holbeck, to serve the Helmsley and Pickering areas. William Chapman was called to advise and reported in 1800. Those behind the scheme were scared of the Derwent Navigation's owner, now Earl Fitzwilliam and the Muston Drainage Act of 1800 sought to placate him. Earl Fitzwilliam preserved the right to extend his navigation above Malton, while the drainage channels built were to be suitable for navigation. Earl Fitzwilliam went ahead with plans to extend above Malton, George Leather being asked in 1809 to do the surveys, actually undertaken by his son. The Rye was also looked over. Work began at Malton in 1810 but little was done to the navigation, most of the expense being a new drain round Malton. Nevertheless in 1813 the Derwent was regarded as improved to Yedingham, and boats may have reached Foulbridge, about 1¼ miles above. There was some traffic above Malton into the 1840s. Meanwhile below Malton the Derwent was doing quite well. Leases of tolls continued up to 1808, thereafter Earl Fitzwilliam managed the navigation himself, owning boats to serve his own estates. Malton was his pocket borough and in the election of 1807 he raised tolls against those who had failed to support one of his nominees. Fortunately the nominee was later declared elected, his rival's victory being found invalid, and tolls were reduced. Earl Fitzwilliam kept the Derwent in good order to face railway competition. A steam dredger was at work in the 1830s, while Thomas Rhodes did a survey in 1837 after which more improvements were made. The navigable depth was now 5'4" in winter and 4'10" in summer. The York & North Midland Railway passed through Malton and opened in 1845. It was very damaging to the Derwent, but in 1853-54 an agreement over traffic allocation was reached between the Aire & Calder, the York & North Midland and the Derwent. Agreement with the railway was soon followed by sale, concluded in 1855 by Earl Fitzwilliam to what had since 1854 become the North Eastern Railway. The sale was arranged in a roundabout way to avoid illegality, the river being bought personally by the NER's manager, engineer and solicitor and then leased to the NER. Under the North Eastern traffic declined, discouraged by the railway, for the sale had been private without an Act, so the railway raised tolls while maintaining attractive railway rates. The lease arrangement continued, for the NER failed to purchase. The 1873 Regulation of Railways Act would have made this difficult, but the NER, not being owners, were cleared of their obligations under the Railway & Canal Traffic Act of 1888. There were strong local objections, the river now being so badly silted that trade was only possible below Sutton. Finally in 1913 came the opening of the Derwent Valley Light Railway and the virtual end of river commerce. The LNER had the river after the 1923 grouping, but in 1935 responsibility moved to the Yorkshire Ouse Catchment Board who ended public navigation. They did however rebuild the lowest lock at Sutton and in 1937 the river was reopened to navigation for a short while. Traffic lasted to 1960 and restoration for pleasure traffic up to Malton has been proposed, Sutton Lock opening in 1972 allowing boats to Stamford Bridge.

DICK BROOK, Worcestershire.   Andrew Yarranton built a blast furnace in 1653 at Astley on the west bank of the Severn three miles below Stourport, and made the Dick Brook, a tributary of the Severn, navigable for ¾ mile in order to bring ore up to the works. Yarranton built two locks on the brook measuring 70' x 10'9". The remains suggest a flash locks.

The DOCTOR'S CANAL, Glamorganshire. Mining speculators on Dr. Richard Griffiths' land introduced Rhondda coal to the world from a pit at Hafod near Pontypridd in the late eighteenth century. The doctor suggested a branch canal from the Glamorganshire at Denia to Treforest with a tramroad thence to the mine. In 1813 the canal, one mile long on the level, was joined to the Glamorganshire after some delay, since the latter were uncertain about the water supply for the newcomer. Traffic declined with the opening of the Taff Vale Railway's branch to the Rhondda in 1841, but some of the tramroad and the canal remained in use, although disused by 1914 and derelict by 1918. It passed in 1826 to a nephew of Dr. Griffiths, the Rev. George Thomas and his brother, hence the title The Rev G. Thomas's canal sometimes used.

DON NAVIGATION, Yorkshire, SHEFFIELD & SOUTH YORKSHIRE NAVIGATION. The river is now spelled Don, but the navigation Dun, after the old spelling of the river. It was a river with two exits, one to the Aire, the other to the Trent. It was always navigable to Doncaster. A change of flow came in the early seventeenth century when Cornelius Vermuyden turned the Don into a single channel to the Aire as part of his drainage work on Hatfield Chase. Flooding resulted so Vermuyden had to cut a new channel from Newbridge to the Ouse at Goole. This was the Dutch River and because of its greater fall, the Aire and Trent exits silted up. Tides were kept out by sluices at Goole but in 1688 these were destroyed and not replaced. Tides now made up the Dutch River and allowed larger craft up the Don. At the end of the seventeenth century came the first moves towards improvement, but a Bill of 1698 was defeated as was a second of 1701. However Sheffield and Rotherham were interested but their Bill of 1721 failed. Surveys followed by William Palmer of York, Joseph Atkinson and Joshua Mitchell. At last in 1726 an Act passed to make a navigation from just below Doncaster up to Tinsley, above Rotherham, but three miles short of Sheffield. The 1726 Act related only to the Don as far as Holmstile just below Doncaster, now it was the turn of the lower river. Joseph Atkinson did a survey and the Act passed in 1727, the undertakers being Doncaster Corporation who also took over the ¾ mile of the Sheffield portion of the river just below the town. Doncaster's responsibility went down to Wilsick House which is near Thorpe in Balne, but they could do works below. The two improvement authorities did not remain separate for long, amalgamating in 1731. A new Act was passed in 1733 to make the whole concern a joint stock company. By this time the Sheffield people had done much work, John Smith being the engineer. Eleven locks had been built on the two sections and a number of cuts and in 1740 the Don was navigable to Rotherham. Tinsley was reached in 1751, three more locks being built between Rotherham and Tinsley. Meanwhile an Act of 1740 sanctioned improvement from Wilsick House down to Fishlake Old Ferry, bedevilled by shallows and dependent on the tide. Two locks and a long cut were made below Wilsick House, the lowest lock being at Stainforth, and this was now the limit of the tide. Thorne became the effective end of the navigation and a transhipment port for Hull between river and coastal vessels. The Don was a navigation of 33 miles, with twelve locks above Doncaster and five below. In 1738 the navigation tolls were leased, the lessees having to maintain the works, but in 1759 the company took over management themselves, considering improvements by the 1800s. One was the Sheffield canal opened in 1819, and much helped when the Don made a horsepath from Rotherham to Tinsley in 1822. By this time passenger services were well established on the navigation. There was a sailing packet in 1809 between Hull and Thorne and a steamer from 1816. The idea of a junction with the Aire & Calder was proposed in 1817 as the Aire & Dun whose engineer was William Smith. The Don supported it, but its Bill was lost in 1819 because of Aire & Calder opposition. Another project followed also in 1819, the Went & Wakefield Canal, which was planned to run from the Barnsley Canal at Cold Hiendley to the Dutch River. William Smith was the engineer. But the Aire & Calder opposed. Under an Act of 1821 the Don improved their main line. George Leather undertook the surveys and became engineer of three new cuts. The longest, from Long Sandall to the start of the Stainforth cut, now made the navigation from near Doncaster to Stainforth a continuous canal. They were open by about the end of 1823. By a further Act of 1826 more cuts and a new lock went ahead, albeit slowly. They had been delayed by more ideas to join the Don with the Aire & Calder, consequent on the opening in 1826 of the latter's Knottingley-Goole canal. Steam towage was present in the 1830s to handle fly-boat traffic, and passenger services continued. Most interesting were the two Scottish built swift boats which the Don themselves operated from 1840 between Swinton and Doncaster, called aquabuses. Railways had been overshadowing Don affairs since the mid 1830s, and to counter them yet more improvements were planned. By 1845 all the bridges below Doncaster were made opening so that fixed mast vessels could reach the town. Railways arrived in earnest with the opening in 1838 of the Sheffield & Rotherham, with which the Don were keen to co-operate. The navigation's policy was to work in with railways, so that traffic could be shared. In 1845 an agreement was made to amalgamate with the proposed South Yorkshire Coal Railway which would run up from the Don to the Barnsley coalfield. On the railway's behalf as well as their own the Don were concerned to safeguard their coal supplies from the Barnsley field by control of the canals which served it. They had in 1845 tried to buy the Barnsley Canal to save it from possible opposing railway clutches. They failed but were more successful with the Dearne & Dove taken over in 1846. In 1848 the Don were able to buy the Sheffield Canal from the Manchester, Sheffield & Lincolnshire Railway. Finally in 1849 the Don leased the Stainforth & Keadby. The following year the now enlarged Don merged with the South Yorkshire, Doncaster & Goole Railway as the South Yorkshire Coal Railway was now called. The Don controlled a considerable waterway empire totalling 63 miles. The united rail and water company was called the South Yorkshire Railway and River Dun Company. The idea was to use the navigation to export coal via Keadby as successfully as the Aire & Calder used Goole. Soon however the railway side of the company were determined to extend their track, done in 1855 by building a line on the banks of the navigation down to Thorne, extended to Keadby in 1859. But the railway side of the company had wider horizons, culminating in the leasing in 1864 of the South Yorkshire Railway and River Dun Co. to the expanding Manchester, Sheffield & Lincolnshire Railway, to whom the Don was of minor importance. In 1874 the South Yorkshire Railway & River Dun Co. was dissolved and everything was transferred to the MSLR. The Don and its associated waterways continued in the 70s and 80s to do quite well but they were out of date. On the Dearne & Dove Canal there was subsidence trouble, when in 1884 a section of the Worsbrough branch collapsed, while the Sheffield Canal depended on costly pumping. Its Greenland arm was sold about this time. Local opinion in the late 1880s hardened against the railway's conduct of its navigation. Parallel with the criticism went the feeling that South Yorkshire could have a big modern waterway, encouraged by the promotion and construction of the Manchester Ship Canal. In 1888 the Sheffield Chamber of Commerce started an enquiry into a new waterway to the sea, to be independent of the existing navigations, but serving Sheffield, Rotherham, Doncaster and the south Yorkshire coalfield. Much enthusiasm was shown and an influential committee was formed. They commissioned a report from the engineers Charles Hawksley and James Abernethy who considered that the best solution was use of the existing waterways down to Keadby with bigger locks for 300-500 ton craft, rather than for 'Sheffield size' keels. The engineers recommended a new canal from Tinsley up to Sheffield. The committee acted quickly, forming a promotion company in 1888, the Sheffield & South Yorkshire Canal Co. Ltd, to get an Act for a new waterway. Financial backing came from the Duke of Norfolk and Earl Fitzwilliam, and Sheffield Corporation supported the venture. The Bill passed in 1889 and after opposition from the railway and from the Hull shipowners who forced the company to give up their plans for a steamship line. The promotion company was now augmented by an operating company, the Sheffield & South Yorkshire Navigation Co. Ltd, who were to have a capital of £1½m. Their problem was to raise the money in order to make an improved waterway, and buy the Don, the Sheffield Canal, the Dearne & Dove and the Stainforth & Keadby from the MSLR. Support for the navigation was impressive and the board was a strong one, including steel and colliery magnates. However they had to deal with the powerful MSLR who were naturally unwilling to sell their waterways and fought a delaying action which lasted several years. Meanwhile the Sheffield & South Yorkshire were altering their own plans with a view to using Goole instead of Keadby. This meant a connecting canal with the Aire & Calder large enough for compartment boats and in 1890 the Sheffield & South Yorkshire made an agreement with the Aire & Calder to jointly build the New Junction Canal from Bramwith on the former to Sykehouse on the latter. 5½ miles long, it was to have one lock at Sykehouse. The canal was authorized in 1891, although the Sheffield & South Yorkshire then had no funds to finance their half share of construction. A sale figure was finally agreed in 1894 but to find the £1,140,000 needed proved beyond the powers of the Sheffield & South Yorkshire. They raised £625,000 in preference shares, of which the MSLR took up £125,000. The MSLR also took up the remainder of the required capital, gaining the right to nominate five of the ten directors. So the Sheffield & South Yorkshire started as a waterway dependent on the railway it sought to oppose. In 1895 with their capital found, the Sheffield & South Yorkshire took over the navigations except for the Don below Fishlake Old Ferry, and the Dutch River. Unfortunately they could not raise the extra capital needed for improvement and never managed the enlargements. Sheffield basin was modernized with new warehouses and cranage and much dredging and bank work was done. They also contributed their share to the New Junction Canal on which construction started in 1896, with completion in 1905. But the Dearne & Dove cost them heavily because of mining subsidence. Traffic was declining and in 1906 they closed the Worsbrough branch except as a feeder. They did not try and check subsidence but sold and leased the coal under the canal.

The important compartment boat traffic to Goole had to wait not only for the New Junction Canal but for some straightening at Doncaster and Sprotbrough completed in 1907. Compartment boats started, but the locks could only take three at a time. Nevertheless with them traffic increased, although never on the scale of the Aire & Calder. The New Junction and Stainforth & Keadby Canals were the main Sheffield & South Yorkshire outlets, indeed Stainforth lock, below the junction with the Stainforth & Keadby, was closed in 1939, ending the use of the Dutch River. Improvements continued up to 1914, including the lengthened lock at Doncaster. Inevitably the war was a bad time, coal traffic falling because of requisitioning of Hull trawlers by the Admiralty. But even during the war there was talk of improvement, led by Sheffield City Council. An engineering report was prepared and in 1920 a scheme presented to the Government to deepen, widen and straighten between Tinsley and Keadby. The locks were to be replaced by 18 new ones, 270' x 22', able to take a 300 ton craft. There were now 18 locks on the Don, 12 on the Sheffield Canal, two on the Stainforth & Keadby Canal and 25 on the Dearne & Dove. The Government turned it down, and Sheffield was not prepared to go ahead by itself. However the company did do some improvements. In 1932 they completed the lengthening of Bramwith lock above Stainforth and built a lay-by for compartment boats at Hatfield Main colliery on the Stainforth & Keadby. By 1934 they had also completed some straightening at Doncaster for which the corporation largely paid, and built a new wharf and warehouse there. The Dearne & Dove was continuing its history of subsidence. In 1928 the Elsecar branch was closed and in 1934 the last boat went through to Barnsley. The Dearne & Dove remained open until the British Transport Commission abandonment Act of 1961. The traffic from Manvers Main Colliery had ceased in 1952 and after 1961 the only open portion was the half mile at Swinton serving a glassworks and Waddington's boatyard. The post-1945 outlook was more cheerful. Oil traffic was growing and from 1946 the company ran an efficient goods collection service in Sheffield. Under nationalization more improvements were undertaken, coal staiths at Mexborough, and a new 215' lock at Long Sandall below Doncaster. This was completed in 1959 and with Sykehouse, Bramwith and Doncaster locks already 215', 17 boat compartment trains could reach Doncaster and Hexthorpe. The lock was later fully mechanised. During the 1960s and 70s there have been schemes to enlarge the Sheffield & South Yorkshire. A plan of 1961 proposed a waterway for 250 ton barges with a new terminal depot at Rotherham. This depot was built and has expanded. Another improvement of 1963 was a new deep lock at Tinsley. A further but rejected plan of 1966 proposed rebuilding the line between Bramwith and Rotherham with ten 225' mechanized locks to replace the existing twelve. Finally in 1972 came a plan for a waterway which could carry 750 ton barges to Mexborough and 400 tonners to Rotherham. This was approved by the Government in 1973, but since shelved.

DONNINGTON WOOD CANAL, Shropshire.   Inspired by the success of the Duke of Bridgewater's Canal from Worsley to Manchester, his brother-in-law Lord Gower planned a smaller canal, using 3 ton capacity tub-boats, to move the coal and ironstone mined on his land to local furnaces. As estate agent Gower had Thomas Gilbert, brother of the Duke's agent, so the experience was there to make the private Donnington Wood Canal 5½ miles eastward to Pave Lane on the Newport-Wolverhampton turnpike. This was probably completed in 1768, but a branch with several arms (total 2 miles) was added later from Hugh's Bridge near Lilleshall to limekilns and stone quarries; there were seven locks on the branch, but the main line was level. Water for the former came from local ponds, for the latter from the Donnington Wood colliery, where there were, it is believed, underground canals, possibly linked by an inclined plane. The lower branch met the main line 42'8" down in a tunnel, communication being by two vertical shafts. In about 1790 an inclined plane with trucks replaced the shafts, while the tub-boats themselves may also have been carried. From 1802 the canal was leased to the Lilleshall Partnership, later the Lilleshall Company. Gower, who had been created Marquess of Stafford in 1786 was a principal partner, but he died in 1803, being succeeded by his son who in 1833 was created Duke of Sutherland. Hence the waterway is variously called the Donnington Wood, the Marquess of Stafford's or the Duke of Sutherland's canal. The branch was abandoned in about 1873 when the Lilleshall limeworks closed, while the main line was cut and much of the eastern end obliterated in 1890 by the Duke of Sutherland's new carriage drive from Lilleshall. Final abandonment came in 1904 because the Lilleshall Company were using their mineral railway from Muxton bridge on the canal to Lubstree wharf on the Humber Arm of the Newport branch of the Shropshire Union.

DORSET & SOMERSET CANAL, Somerset.   The Dorset & Somerset was projected to run from coast to coast, from Poole to the Avon at Bath. Surveys were made by Robert Whitworth and William Bennet, and there were hopes of a big coal trade southwards and of clay being sent northwards from Wareham. But so much landowner opposition arose to the southern section that an Act was secured in 1796 for a line from Limpley Stoke via Frome and Wincanton only to Gains Cross near Blandford, with a branch from Frome to Nettlebridge collieries. Work started on this branch and nearly eight miles were dug, but the canal was never opened. Of particular interest was the scheme to replace locks by lifts. James Fussell, the ironmaster from Mells near Frome, had experimented with these and had one tested on the branch at Barrow Hill.

DOUGLAS NAVIGATION, Lancashire.   In the 1700s there were moves to make the Douglas navigable, a river which flows from coal producing Wigan to the Ribble at Hesketh Bank. Thomas Steers made a survey in 1712 but an improvement Bill of 1713 was rejected and the scheme was not revived until 1719, the Act being obtained in 1720. Steers however did little for the Douglas which was also called the Asland. He and his fellow promoters were accused of raising money by false pretences and the whole matter was dropped until 1733 when it was revived by local landowners. By 1742 the river appears to have been made navigable up to Wigan, 17½ miles from the Ribble with 8 locks apparently large enough for the coastal sailing flats of the day. Moves in the early 1750s to make the Sankey Brook navigable to St. Helens were an obvious threat to the Douglas and from about 1753 the proprietors of the navigation, headed by Alexander Leigh started on the making of a bypass cut below Gathurst. In 1771 Leigh, the majority shareholder of the Douglas, sold all his shares to the Leeds & Liverpool, who made use of his cut for their canal to Wigan so by-passing the river. By 1781 the Leeds & Liverpool completed their branch parallel with the river down to Rufford and into the Douglas at Sollom, extended to Tarleton in 1805. By 1801, the river had lost all traffic to the canal.

DRIFFIELD NAVIGATION, Yorkshire.   John Smeaton was consulted about 1765 on making the upper Hull navigable, for keels to reach Great Driffield. His ideas were enlarged by John Grundy, who recommended a longer artificial section, from Frodingham Beck to Driffield. The local merchants accepted Grundy's plans and the Act passed in 1767. The whole navigation was complete in 1770, the canal being 5 miles long from Fisholme on Frodingham Beck to Driffield and the river section ¾ mile from Emmotland, the junction with the Hull, to Fisholme already navigable. There were then four timber

48. Sailing keels came up to Driffield basin, but because of locks and bridges, left their masts and leeboards behind.

floored locks all on the canal section, large enough for craft 61' x 14'6". In the early years the navigation was not very successful, the Hull River needing improvement and a certain amount of dredging was done in the 1780s. On the canal length the lowest lock at Snakeholme was rebuilt as a staircase pair in 1776. Trade was increasing so there were ideas for further improvement. In 1796 William Chapman was called in to make plans and estimates and in 1801 an Act was passed. This also set up a fresh administrative body of commissioners for the new navigation, working alongside the old navigation commissioners. Chapman was made engineer and the works were completed by 1805. Hull Bridge was raised, and a new lock was built at Struncheonhill on the Hull below Fisholme, at the tail of a new cut avoiding a big bend on the river. Struncheonhill, probably first a single lock, was soon made a staircase pair. The last work was the navigation to Corps Landing on the Hull, not finished until 1811. The new navigation started at Aike Beck 3¼ miles above the Hull bridge. In 1817 a steam passenger packet started to run between Driffield and Hull but was not too successful. Steady prosperity was the keynote of Driffield history in the 1800s, wheat traffic being important. In 1846 the railway came to Driffield and to keep traffic the navigation cut tolls and in the 1850s began to consider improvements. Edward Welsh made a report in 1855 but fear of flooding caused the scheme to be withdrawn. A steam keel was put on, probably in the 1860s and lasted into the 1900s, and coal traffic kept up while grain fell. In the twentieth century traffic fell away, the last keel came to Driffield in 1944 (48) and to Brigham in 1948. Above Struncheonhill the navigation has become unnavigable but the Driffield Navigation Amenities Association, formed in 1970, is determined on restoration and a survey has been undertaken.

DROITWICH CANAL and DROITWICH JUNCTION CANAL, Worcestershire. Local interests in the 1750s subscribed to this short waterway, since earlier efforts to make the River Salwarpe navigable had failed. Although Brindley surveyed the route the resident engineer was John Priddey. The canal, 6¾ miles, follows the Salwarpe, has 8 locks, and was opened on 12 March 1771. The locks were for vessels 64' x 14'6", so that suitable trows could trade to Droitwich, becoming known as 'Wich barges'. Between 1810 and 1821 the Droitwich was managed by the Worcester & Birmingham company. During the 1820s there was a considerable revival in the salt trade, although in the early days the canal had suffered from road competition and lack of a horse towing path until 1806. Railway plans matured in the 1840s and 50s. and were countered in 1854 by the Worcester & Birmingham, who opened the 1¾ mile Droitwich Junction Canal from their own Hanbury wharf to the Droitwich Canal in Droitwich, with 6 narrow locks. At the same time the locks on the Droitwich Canal were lengthened for narrow boats. Rescue of the Worcester & Birmingham and Droitwich Canals from growing insolvency came in 1874, when they were taken over by the Sharpness New Docks Co. who improved both by dredging; from 1889 the Droitwich could accommodate vessels of 6' draught. Nevertheless the salt trade deserted the canal and the Droitwich and Droitwich Junction were abandoned in 1939 having been disused for many years. Now however the Droitwich is being restored.

SIR GEORGE DUCKETT'S CANAL. See Hertford Union Canal.

DUDLEY CANAL, Worcestershire, Staffordshire, Warwickshire. Linked with the Stourbridge Canal, the Dudley was promoted to take coal from the mines round Dudley to Stourbridge and on to the Staffs. & Worcs. Canal. Lord Dudley backed both, indeed in 1775 the first Bill introduced them as one scheme, after a survey by Robert Whitworth, but it was withdrawn due to opposition by the Birmingham Canal. So fresh Bills were introduced for two separate canals and both received their Acts on 2 April 1776. Thomas Dadford senior was made engineer and work began on the 2¼ mile line from the open fields between Dudley and Brierley Hill to join the Stourbridge at Black Delph down the nine Delph locks, later reduced to eight (55), finished in 1779. Plans were prepared during the 1780s to join the Birmingham Canal. They were encouraged by the limestone and coal mining activities of Lord Dudley at Castle Mill and Wren's Nest. In 1775 he had begun to make a private canal from the Birmingham main line at Tipton through a short tunnel which led first into Tipton colliery and then on to a basin at Castle Mill, deep in the limestone, but open to the sky. To join this the Dudley proposed a tunnel from their canal to Castle Mill, involving an extension via five (later four) locks at Park Head to the projected southern portal. This tunnel was to be a major work, 2942 yd plus 34 yd across Castle Mill basin and 196 yd of Lord Dudley's tunnel, making a complete length of 3172 yd. The Act for this extension totalling 2⅜ miles passed in 1785. Thomas Dadford senior remained as consulting engineer for the tunnel, with Abraham Lees as resident. The contractor was John Pinkerton but he proved unsatisfactory and the company took over the work themselves under the charge of Isaac Pratt, a member of both the Dudley and Stourbridge committees. Little progress was made and errors were discovered in the line, so in 1790 Josiah Clowes was

49.

A model in the National Museum of Wales of waterwheel powered pumps, built in 1807, to return water to the Glamorganshire Canal taken by the Melingriffith tinplate works outside Cardiff (top). One of the last boats on the Glamorganshire (middle), seen here at Gabalfa lock, Cardiff in 1943. Note bell crank linkage for the upper gate paddle gear. Motor weed cutting boat (bottom), on the Oxford Canal in 1956. They could work ahead or astern.

50.

51.

52. Packard's steam barge TRENT RIVER (top) on the Gipping (Ipswich & Stowmarket Navigation) at Bramford in the 1920s.   Chelmer and Blackwater, a timber laden motor craft approaching Little Baddow lock (middle), in the 1950s.   The Coalbrookdale Co's castellated warehouse (bottom), for tramroad to river traffic interchange on the Severn about 1880, with an upriver trow alongside.

53.

54.

55. Stables at Brierley Hill down the 'nine locks' (actually eight) on the Dudley Canal.

called in, and in 1792 the work was finished with a new junction with the Birmingham at Tipton to replace Lord Dudley's private cut, generally called Lord Ward's, because Lord Dudley bore the dual title of Viscount Dudley and Ward. Clowes also built a small reservoir at Gad's Green, Netherton. The Dudley then determined to extend south eastwards to tap the collieries about Netherton and join up with the newly promoted Worcester & Birmingham Canal. John Snape, who had done preliminary work for the Dudley tunnel line, made the survey and an Act was obtained in 1793. From the Dudley at Blower's Green by Park Head the new line was to run level via Netherton, Rowley Regis and Halesowen to Lappal and Selly Oak where it would join the Worcester & Birmingham, a distance of $10\frac{7}{8}$ miles including two tunnels, one of 557 yd at Gosty Hill and another of 3795 yd at Lappal. Josiah Clowes was made engineer and work began in 1794. But he died a year later and was succeeded by William Underhill. In 1798 the new line was complete, fed by Gad's Green reservoir extended in 1802, but the Worcester & Birmingham were very far from Worcester, although a useful traffic could start from 1802 with the Grand Junction via the Stratford at King's Norton and the two Warwick Canals. But the Dudley Canal were much hampered by their two huge tunnels, both single line and dependent on legging or shafting. In 1840 mechanical haulage, probably a cable, was suggested for Dudley but found too expensive. At Lappal however in 1841 a steam pumping engine combined with stop locks created a current which could flow either way to help boats through, an ingenious practice which continued until 1914. Subsidence was the other menace to Dudley traffic, particularly at Lappal. Throughout their independent existence the Dudley were trying to win traffic from the Birmingham, but on the whole trade preferred the latter's route to London. The company had a capable superintendent in Thomas Brewin appointed in 1812, and under him the Dudley improved their line by building cut-offs to shorten their route to Selly Oak. One of these included a 75 yd tunnel named after himself, opened in 1838. Two branches on the Selly Oak line had been authorized but only a short length of one, at Windmill End, Netherton, was ever started, back in 1803, although in 1842 a $\frac{1}{4}$ mile branch was built to Withymoor near Primrose Hill. Water supply to the Dudley's Selly Oak line was improved by building Lodge Farm reservoir near Netherton in 1836. In 1846 the Dudley Canal amalgamated with the Birmingham Canal Navigations, who made considerable improvements.

EARDINGTON FORGES and CANAL TUNNEL, Shropshire. This almost entirely subterranean canal is by the Severn, 3 miles south of Bridgnorth and was cut by 1782 to join Eardington Upper forge with Eardington Lower forge. The canal fed by the Mor brook is about $\frac{1}{2}$ mile long, almost wholly in a tunnel 9' x 6' high which ends abruptly on the banks of the Severn, 30' above the river with no physical connection. There was evidently a river wharf and presumably a crane for the transfer of pig iron and completed forgings. The forges closed in 1889 and the canal with them.

EAST LOTHIAN & BERWICKSHIRE SCHEMES. Two canals were suggested for East Lothian in about 1805, one up the East Lothian Tyne from the sea to East Linton and another across the peninsula from the mouth of the Tyne to Aberlady on the Forth. In Berwickshire there were moves in the 1740s to divert traffic from Berwick to Eyemouth by diverting the Whiteadder into the Eye, allied to a scheme to make a canal from Eyemouth via Duns to Kelso. The Kelso project was revived in 1789, by a scheme for a canal down to Berwick reported on by Robert Whitworth.

EASTERN ROTHER and BREDE, Sussex, Kent. Entering the sea at Rye the Rother had been navigable from very early times, stone for Bodiam Castle came by boat. Also an early navigation was the Brede joining the Rother at Rye. Trade continued on the Rother up to Newenden, $12\frac{1}{4}$ miles from Rye, the limit of regular navigation, until 1909 and to Maytham into the 1920s. The Brede remained navigable to Brede throughout the nineteenth century, and the Rother is still navigable. In 1806 the Royal Military Canal was completed which joined the Rother at Iden lock, barges passing through Scots Float sluice and lock on the Rother to Iden and the Canal. Scots Float sluice, for craft 45' x 12' was rebuilt in 1844 (31).

EDINBURGH & GLASGOW UNION CANAL, Stirlingshire, West Lothian, Midlothian. Coal was needed for Edinburgh and a canal was proposed in 1791-2 to bring it from Lanarkshire, to cross Scotland from Leith to the Clyde at the Broomielaw in Glasgow. John Ainslie and Robert Whitworth made surveys of four possible routes and John Rennie recommended a fifth further to the north. However with the French wars the whole project was shelved until 1813. In that year Hugh Baird, engineer of the Forth & Clyde drew up a plan for a canal from the Forth & Clyde at Falkirk into Edinburgh. Telford supported Baird's line and the waterway, not a ship canal like the Forth & Clyde, closely followed Telford's recommendations, with arched masonry bridges on the English style, the three aqueducts being close copies of Chirk. In 1817 the Act passed, the Chairman being Robert Downie, an Indian nabob, who gave his name to Port Downie, the basin by Lock 16 on the Forth & Clyde where the Union joined the older waterway. With Baird as engineer, work started in 1818. Three rivers were crossed, the Water of Leith at Slateford by an eight-arched aqueduct, the Almond near Ratho by a five-arched and the Avon near Linlithgow by a twelve-arched 80' above the river. There was one tunnel of 696 yd just south of Falkirk to avoid the grounds of Callendar House, with a towpath for the passenger boats, and water came from the Almond fed by the reservoir at Cobbinshaw in the Pentland Hills. All was complete by 1822 and the canal, 31½ miles long, opened for traffic, the eleven locks taking boats 69' x 12'6" wide. The company became carriers and had some wooden scows built and also passage boats with sleeping accommodation. Some boats ran only to the top of the eleven locks at Falkirk, the passengers having to walk down to Port Downie; this walk was shortened for them in 1823 by the building of a ¼ mile branch above the locks to a new basin called Port Maxwell, after a prominent supporter of the canal. Coal became the main traffic into Edinburgh and the passage boats were a success. Competition from road coaches had been a healthy stimulus but in 1840 a new factor appeared, the Slamannan Railway from near Airdrie to the canal at Causewayend near the western end of the Avon aqueduct. This started a joint rail canal service into Edinburgh, road coaches also meeting the trains. But two years after the Edinburgh & Glasgow Railway was completed and the passenger trade quickly lost, being abandoned by the canal company in 1848. The Union fought the railway by improving cargo services, steam tugs were put on in 1844 and new scows ordered the following year. In 1849 the canal was taken over by the Edinburgh & Glasgow Railway which in 1865 became part of the North British. The NBR tried to encourage canal traffic but without success, the basins at Port Hopetoun being sold in 1921 and commercial traffic finally ceasing in 1933 by which time the canal was owned by the LNER. Port Downie and the locks were filled in and the canal remained solely as a water channel, used by a few pleasure boats on the summit. Recently pleasure traffic has revived and restoration works are proposed.

EGLINTON CANAL, Co Galway. Lough Corrib could not be reached from the sea because of the unnavigable Corrib River. Nothing positive was done until the nineteenth century, as part of a plan to open up Mayo to navigation via Lough Corrib and Lough Mask. In 1838 the Lough Corrib Improvement Co. was formed but did little work, being rescued in 1847 by the Board of Public Works. Using government money a ⅝ of a mile canal was built with two locks for vessels 130' x 20'6" wide, and opened in 1852, by the Earl of Eglinton, Lord Lieutenant of Ireland. In 1860 a steamer service was started from Galway via the canal to Maam at the head of Lough Corrib. The service did well until the opening in 1895 of the railway from Galway to Clifden, goods and passenger traffic declining sharply thereafter, ceasing about 1930. Replacement of the swing bridges over the canal in the mid-1950s by fixed concrete spans closed the waterway which up to that time was still used by pleasure craft.

ELLESMERE CANAL, Shropshire, Cheshire, Flintshire, Denbighshire, Montgomeryshire. The Ellesmere was a product of the 1792-3 canal boom, although there had been proposals in 1789 and a scheme launched in 1791 at a meeting in Ellesmere, for a canal from Netherpool on the Mersey to the Dee, and from the other side of the Dee via Overton to Shrewsbury. Such a canal would appeal to the ironmasters and colliery owners of the Wrexham-Ruabon area. At the same time there were counter proposals for a more easterly Dee-Severn line making use of part of the Chester Canal and passing nearer Whitchurch. After surveys by local engineers, William Jessop came to advise; he favoured the Overton-Ruabon line with differences, proposing a 4607 yd tunnel at Ruabon, an aqueduct over the Dee at Pontcysyllte, another tunnel at Chirk of 1236 yd, then via Frankton with a 476 yd tunnel at Weston to Shrewsbury. Between the Dee and Ruabon the canal had to climb 303 ft, needing many locks. Jessop planned branches to Holt on the Dee and Llanymynech. Money was easily raised, but the promoters of the more easterly line backed by the Chester Canal also sought subscriptions, although their plans were neutralized by the Ellesmere, who surveyed a branch to join the Chester Canal near Nantwich. In the end the two groups amalgamated and the Ellesmere's Act was passed in 1793 for a narrow canal, although a broad was really wanted. Jessop was the engineer assisted by John Duncombe, Thomas Denson, William Turner and Thomas Telford as general agent. First completed was the Dee-Mersey section, called the Wirral line, finished to broad standard in 1795 with basins adjoining the Dee, and in 1797 joining the Chester Canal. A successful goods and passenger traffic between Chester and Netherpool (after 1796 called Ellesmere Port) began on the Wirral line, 8¾ miles long with two broad locks down from the canal to the dock at Ellesmere Port and a third from the dock into the tidal basin leading into the Mersey. In 1796 the Llanymynech branch was opened from the bottom of the locks on the main line at Frankton to Carreghofa just outside Llanymynech, 11 miles with three locks, where it met the Montgomeryshire Canal completed in 1797. The middle section of the main line was started in 1793-4 from Trevor near Ruabon to Frankton, a three arch masonry aqueduct being proposed over the Dee at Pontcysyllte with locks leading down to it, but in July 1795 Jessop recommended a cast iron aqueduct carrying the canal across on the level and a similar iron aqueduct over the Ceiriog at Chirk. Chirk was open in 1801 and the canal open from Vron with its limestone quarries to the bottom of Frankton locks in 1802. Pontcysyllte was completed in 1805. 1797 saw the opening of a further section of main line from the Frankton locks (55) to Weston, about 15 miles north west of Shrewsbury, but no more was cut because the Shrewsbury Canal had already reached the town and the state of the upper Severn was then so poor that through traffic was unlikely. Also abandoned by 1800 was the whole main line from the Dee to Trevor because of tramroad competition from the collieries at Hawarden and Flint to the Dee. Part of it, the Ffrwd branch, about 2 miles, was cut and filled with water in 1796 but probably never used, being dismantled after 1809. Another abortive project was the experimental lift built and tried near Ruabon by Edward Rowland and Exuperius Pickering in about 1796. Opening of the Pontcysyllte aqueduct (8), brought the main line to terminal basins at Trevor from where tramroads led to works and quarries, followed in 1830 by a $\frac{5}{8}$ mile private canal to the collieries at Plas Kynaston. Water supply to a canal which never reached its summit level was solved by the completion in 1808 of a navigable feeder up from Trevor to the Dee at Llantisilio where the weir called the Horseshoe Falls was constructed, while Bala Lake, the source of the Dee, was raised. A branch from Frankton to Whitchurch and on to the Chester Canal was started in 1787 to run via Ellesmere and the difficult peat bogs of Whixall Moss. Many embankments, cuttings and an 87 yd tunnel at Ellesmere had to be built to reach Tilstock Park near Whitchurch in 1804. From here it was carried forward to Hurleston on the Chester Canal at the end of the following year, with a $3\frac{3}{4}$ mile branch completed in about 1806 from Whixall Moss to Quina Brook on the Whitchurch-Wem road, although intended to reach Prees. There was also a $\frac{1}{4}$ mile branch to Ellesmere completed 1804, and a mile branch completed in 1811 to Whitchurch itself from the top of Grindley Brook locks. Although now connected via the Chester Canal with the Mersey and Dee, the Ellesmere built up only local traffic in coal, lime and limestone. Their main line from Trevor to Weston was $17\frac{3}{4}$ miles long with six narrow locks and two tunnels, Whitehouses (191 yd) and Chirk (459 yd), while the branch to Hurleston was 29 miles with 19 narrow locks, there being no locks on the shorter branches.

ELLESMERE & CHESTER CANAL.   Because the Chester Canal formed a part of the Ellesmere's line to the Mersey, amalgamation of the two was proposed in 1804 and finally agreed in 1813. The new company encouraged long distance traffic off their system to the Mersey. They put a steam ferry on the river in 1816, the COUNTESS OF BRIDGEWATER to run between Ellesmere Port and Liverpool but she was uneconomic, being withdrawn in 1819. More successful were the Chester-Ellesmere canal packets, only ousted by the Birkenhead Railway in 1840. The new company succeeded in joining up with the rest of the country's inland waterways by opening the branch to Middlewich in 1833, $9\frac{3}{4}$ miles long from Barbridge with three narrow locks to join the Trent & Mersey's Wardle branch and lock at Middlewich. Opening of the Birmingham & Liverpool Junction Canal in 1835 brought so much traffic on to the Ellesmere & Chester that Ellesmere Port had to be extended. A second flight of narrow locks from the canal to the dock was made and the works were ready in 1843. Because the Ellesmere & Chester was now so dependent on the traffic of the Birmingham & Liverpool Junction it was not surprising that in 1845 a further amalgamation between these two companies was achieved, the Ellesmere & Chester title remaining. However in 1846 the new group was taken over by the Shropshire Union scheme.

EMMET'S CANAL, Yorkshire.   A mile long level canal built in about 1782 to bring coal and ironstone to a furnace near Birkenshaw, four miles south-east of Bradford, set up by John Emmet and three partners. In 1815 the works closed, but much of the canal can be traced.

ENGLISH and BRISTOL CHANNEL SCHEMES, Devon, Somerset.   Earliest was the 1769 project, surveyed by Robert Whitworth under Brindley's supervision for a canal from the Exe to Uphill near Weston-super-Mare. He also examined a line from the Parrett to Seaton via Chard which was revived by Whitworth in 1793. A further proposal surveyed by Josiah Easton involved a more extensive route, but both were dropped in favour of the Grand Western (page 135). In 1809 the Chard plan had also been revived under a new title the English & Bristol Channels Canal and John Rennie was asked to make a survey. He recommended a small ship canal from Seaton to Combwich at the mouth of the Parrett, but again nothing was done. In 1821 James Green suggested a tub-boat canal from the Tone to Beer, but this English & Bristol Channels Junction Canal was dropped because it was not considered ambitious enough. Instead Telford and Captain Nicholls were asked in 1824 to make a survey for a ship canal, which they recommended should run from

56. Iron lock bridge at
Frankton locks,
Ellesmere Canal.

Stolford on the Parrett estuary to Beer. There was opposition to the scheme, although an Act was secured in 1825, but no work was ever done. As late as 1870 someone proposed a Great Western Maritime Ship Canal.

57.

EREWASH CANAL, Derbyshire, Nottinghamshire. The valley of the Erewash was a rich coal producing area. A canal was suggested by some of those who had supported the Loughborough Navigation. John Smith, their engineer, did a survey in 1776, from the Trent just above Soar mouth, the start of the Loughborough Navigation, to Ilkeston and Langley Mill, and the Act passed in 1777. John Varley was made engineer and cutting proceeded quickly, some of the line being open in 1778 and all in 1779. The total length was $11\frac{3}{4}$ miles with 14 broad locks for boats 78' x 14'6". A heavy coal traffic built up, not only to the Soar, but also the Trent. From 1787 there were moves to extend the Erewash to Pinxton and later Cromford, promoted as the Cromford Canal. Later in 1792 the Nottingham Canal was authorized, competitive with the Erewash. The Erewash fought back by trying to gain direct access to Nottingham. First they tried to make the Beeston Cut themselves, eventually built by the Trent Navigation, then in 1793 they became involved with the Trent Canal scheme to continue the Trent & Mersey to Beeston and Nottingham. With the arrival of the Nutbrook Canal in 1795, joining the Erewash at Stanton, and of the Derby Canal in 1796, joining lower down at Sandiacre, more traffic came on to the Erewash together with more water. Most water came from the Erewash River feeding in at Langley Mill, helped by lockage water off the Cromford and the summit level of the Nottingham. The opening in 1834 of the Leicester & Swannington Railway made Leicestershire coal competitive with Derbyshire so that Erewash revenue declined, but much more serious was the authorization in 1844 of an Erewash Valley Railway, opened in 1847 parallel to the waterway. Competition was severe and the Erewash had to make toll reductions. But the coal trade still fell away, the only relieving feature being the founding in 1846 of what became the Stanton ironworks. The Erewash kept in business and there were ideas in 1863 of a general amalgamation of all the canals between the Midlands and London. After 1894 through toll agreements were made by the Grand Junction with the Leicester, the Loughborough and the Erewash. This was part of a plan to develop the Derbyshire coal trade to London by creating a wide waterway throughout. In 1932 the new Grand Union bought the Erewash, together with the Leicester and the Loughborough Navigations in a second attempt to secure a wide route to the Trent and Derbyshire coalfield. The Erewash continued to carry traffic and in 1932 the new owners founded a carrying subsidiary, the Erewash Canal Carrying Co. Traffic lasted on the Erewash until 1952 and in 1962 the section between Langley Mill and Ilkeston was abandoned, but the whole canal is still used by pleasure craft.

EXETER CANAL, Devon. Mediaeval navigation of the Exe was hindered by weirs so that ships for Exeter had to unload at Topsham. In 1563 John Trew of Glamorganshire was authorized by the Corporation to build a canal to bypass it, from outside the city walls to just below Countess Wear a distance of $1\frac{3}{4}$ miles. This was complete in about 1566 and possessed three pound locks with guillotine gates, the first in the country, with a single gate where the canal entered the Exe. Unfortunately the waterway could only take 16 ton vessels, entering at high water. The Civil War encouraged decay, so in the 1670s the corporation decided on dredging and an extension half a mile nearer Topsham with a larger entrance, completed by 1676. This was a time of great prosperity for Exeter, and very soon the canal had to be further improved, now straightened and enlarged with one new lock, the so called long chambered Double Locks which acted as a passing place, to replace John Trew's three. By the 1800s further improvement was needed. James Green undertook dredging and further straightening, he also rebuilt the Double Locks, completed in 1821, and recommended a new pound lock entrance at Turf 2 miles lower down the estuary; in addition the banks were raised throughout to permit 14' draught ships to proceed and a new basin was built in Exeter, by 1830, while in 1832 came the sidelock into the Exe opposite Topsham. Until the coming of the railway in 1844 canal traffic was immense, for ships of 350 tons could use it. The Bristol & Exeter Railway caused a severe decline. Trade continued to fall during the nineteenth century partly because ships had become larger. Today with a total length of 5 miles the canal remains under corporation ownership. Double Locks are 317' x 27' wide. Exeter Maritime Museum now occupies part of the basin.

EXETER & CREDITON NAVIGATION, Devon. Proposed in 1792 to run from Crediton to Exe bridge. An Act passed in 1801, the expected traffic being lime for land improvement. A little work was done, about half a mile, abandoned in 1818.

FIFE SCHEMES. A canal was suggested up to Cupar from the coast via the valley of the Eden but the possible trade hardly justified it.

Water of FLEET CANAL, Kirkcudbrightshire. From Gatehouse to the sea the river was always navigable but in 1824 was improved by a 1400 yd canal cut privately by the owner of Cally Park on the eastern side of the estuary.

FLEET CANAL, London. From the Thames up to Holborn, the Fleet River was navigable from the twelfth century and used during the Middle Ages and later, although an open sewer as well as a navigation. Sir Christopher Wren improved the lower part of the river after the Great Fire, making it into a 50' wide canal from the Thames for 700 yd up to Holborn bridge. The work was finished in 1674 and the canal kept busy until about

1733 when it was partially arched over, becoming a covered market.

FLETCHER'S CANAL, Lancashire. Brindley was working in the 1750s at Wet Earth colliery at Clifton near Salford, using water power to drain the mine, the water coming via a ½ mile channel from the Irwell. Later the channel was extended to serve another nearby pit at Botany Bay, to drive a waterwheel winding coal. Matthew Fletcher had developed this colliery and in about 1790-1 he widened the channels into a canal, although not then joined up with the adjacent Manchester, Bolton & Bury. Some years later a lock was built, to the MB & B, to large dimensions, 90' x 21' able to take three narrow boats. The Canal was 1½ miles long. Fletcher is also believed to have driven underground canals on the Worsley pattern. Inevitably subsidence affected this canal, but it continued carrying coal until in 1928 when Wet Earth Colliery was closed. Felspar and clay went to a tile works near the entrance until 1935, but it was completely closed in 1952.

FLINT COAL CANAL, Flintshire. Promoted by a group of copper, iron and lead mining magnates including Thomas Williams of the Parys copper mine Anglesey, the Flint Coal Canal was surveyed by William Jessop in 1785 to run from the Dee to Greenfield and take 100 ton ships, Greenfield and district being a centre of copper and brass smelting and coal and lead mining. An Act was obtained in 1788 but no canal work was done.

FORTH & CART CANAL, Dunbartonshire. Designed to make through navigation possible from Paisley via the Cart to the Forth & Clyde Canal, the Forth & Cart was authorized in 1836 and completed in 1840, ½ mile long from the Forth & Clyde at Whitecrook near Clydebank down to the Clyde, directly opposite the Cart, an improved navigation. There were three locks, two combined as a staircase, each 67' x 15'. It was never a success, in spite of offering the Forth & Clyde another entry to the Clyde, possibly because its locks were a bit narrower. In 1855 the Forth & Cart was transferred to the Forth & Clyde, passing in 1867 to the Caledonian Railway and closing in 1893.

FORTH & CLYDE CANAL, Dunbartonshire, Lanarkshire, Stirlingshire. Considered as early as the reign of Charles II this took a more positive form after a survey of 1726 by Alexander Gordon. Later the elder Pitt favoured a canal built at public expense and this, revived by the Board of Trustees for the Encouragement of Fisheries, Manufacturers and Improvements in Scotland, led to a survey completed in 1764 by John Smeaton. Two routes were suggested, one by Loch Lomond, but neither would pass very near Glasgow whose tobacco lords wanted to re-export American tobacco to the Continent. They commissioned a survey by Robert Mackell. Both proposals found support and both were moving towards a Bill, when Smeaton altered his ideas and put forward a scheme for a canal of greater depth, 7', for sea-going vessels, and in 1768 the Act for Smeaton's canal was passed, to be financed as a joint stock enterprise, to run from Grangeburnfoot on the Carron, to the Clyde at Dalmuir. Much support came from Sir Lawrence Dundas of Kerse, a landowner at the eastern end. The Act also gave powers to cut a branch into Glasgow, Smeaton being appointed engineer with Mackell under him. There was trouble over the eastern entry into the Carron, opposed by the Carron Company, who commissioned James Brindley and others to survey a fresh canal with an entry into the Carron further upstream, to the advantage of their iron works. Meanwhile Smeaton's canal was proceeding westwards following the line of the Antonine wall. By the end of 1770 all the eastern locks were completed and the following year work started on the main reservoir, Townhead near Kilsyth. In 1773 the canal reached Kirkintilloch, but money was running short, although cutting continued as far as Stockingfield, the junction for the Glasgow branch, and work started on this. But no more was done to the main line after July 1775, the branch continuing to the terminal basin at Hamiltonhill, opened to traffic in 1778. Smeaton had resigned in 1773 and Mackell died in 1779. Funds permitted no more work westwards. However improvements were made to the eastern entry and a cut started to the Forth parallel with the Carron River, the beginnings of the port of Grangemouth. In the end it was the Forfeited Estates Fund which saved the Forth & Clyde, the government agreeing in 1784 to lend £50,000. Bowling was now to be the western entry into the Clyde, where the river was deeper. Robert Whitworth was appointed engineer in 1785, finding water to be a serious problem, solved by using the Monkland as a feeder. The greatest work on the cut to Bowling was an aqueduct over the Kelvin with four masonry arches. At last in 1790 the Forth & Clyde was complete and fully open to Bowling, 35 miles long on the main line, with 39 locks large enough for craft 66' x 19'8", plus the 2¼ miles of the lock free Glasgow branch to Hamiltonhill, soon to be extended for ½ mile to new basins at Port Dundas and a further mile to join the Monkland by the 'cut of junction'. These works were completed in 1791. Although other branches were expected only two were ever made; the Carron Co. completing one in 1782 between the canal and the river, a mile long, but it closed in about 1810; and a ¼ mile branch to a lime works at Netherwood near the eastern summit lock. The canal had a summit level of some 15 miles. Traffic developed well, the canal being used by fishing boats following the herring, and for the carriage of minerals to feed the industries of central Scotland. Water continued a problem, partially solved in 1798 by the completion of a large reservoir at Hillend above Airdrie to feed the Monkland, more reservoirs following in the nineteenth century, the Lily Loch in 1837 and Roughrigg in 1852, both also feeding into the Monkland. The war with France made the canal a safe route for coasters between east and west. Passenger services commenced in 1809 between Port Dundas in Glasgow and Lock 16 near Falkirk whence passengers proceeded by coach to Edinburgh. Completion of the Edinburgh & Glasgow Union Canal in 1822 allowed boats to go direct to Port Hopetoun in Edinburgh and in 1824 a night service was started. Grangemouth by this time was developing into a major port, the Carron River being straightened so that land

could be reclaimed and basins dug. Railway proposals spurred the Forth & Clyde to greater improvements; the Monkland & Kirkintilloch had arrived by the canalside at Kirkintilloch in 1826 bringing Lanarkshire coal to the canal, but the schemes of the early 1830s
for a line between Glasgow and Edinburgh were a danger. Passenger services were speeded
up and cargo services too, a boat carrying carts coming into use in 1833 and several
tramroad waggon boats two years later, operating from the railhead of the Monkland &
Kirkintilloch. The canal itself tried locomotive haulage of boats over $\frac{1}{2}$ mile in 1839.
Opening of the Edinburgh & Glasgow Railway in 1842 caused competition with the canal,
whose passenger traffic had already been damaged by the completion in 1840 of the Slamannan Railway from near Airdrie to the Union Canal at Causewayend, leading to a joint
rail and canal service to Edinburgh. However passenger traffic continued and in 1846 the
Forth & Clyde strengthened their position by merging with the very profitable Monkland
Canal, the chief supplier of coal to Glasgow. During the 1850s and 60s horse traction was
being replaced by steam. Grangemouth by now was a major port on which the Caledonian
Railway cast envious eyes, and in order to gain control of this they were obliged in 1867
to take over the Forth & Clyde. Inter city passenger traffic had ceased by 1848, but shorter services were still operated, a screw steamer the ROCKVILLA CASTLE appearing in
about 1860. Later the canal was much used by pleasure steamers, running between Port
Dundas, Kirkintilloch and Craigmarloch near Kilsyth. These were the 'Queen' steamers
owned by James Aitken & Co. of Kirkintilloch, the first being the FAIRY QUEEN of 1893
and the last and largest the GIPSY QUEEN which ran until 1939. Goods traffic continued
on the Forth & Clyde until the 1914-18 war but was much reduced by the wartime closure
of Grangemouth and post war depression. It remained open until 1963, by which time
commercial traffic had vanished, oil being one of the last. Yachts and fishing boats used
the canal to the end, to the latter the canal was of real benefit, and there are restoration
proposals for pleasure traffic.

River FORTH SCHEMES, Clackmannanshire, Stirlingshire.   Robert Mackell and James
Watt surveyed a canal from Tillicoultry to Alloa, to improve transport of coal to the
Forth, navigable up to Stirling. Then Smeaton had ideas in the 1760s of improving the
Forth to Cambus below Stirling, including a canal. James Watt proposed in 1767 to make
the Forth navigable as far up as Aberfoyle from Stirling. In 1810 Alexander McGibbon
suggested a whole network of canals between Loch Lomond and the Forth centred on
Stirling, including a main line from the Forth to Loch Lomond. A proposal to join Stirling
to the Forth & Clyde in 1835 also fell through.

FOSS NAVIGATION, Yorkshire.   The Foss, joining the Ouse in York, was considered
as a navigation as early as 1725. William Jessop did a survey in 1791 as far as Sheriff
Hutton, but the promoters were also interested in drainage and land improvement, for the
Foss was prone to flooding in York. Money was put up and the Act passed in 1793, the
navigation to be extended to Stillington. It was to be large enough for keels 58' x 14'6",
with the water supply amplified by two reservoirs. Jessop was now too busy elsewhere and
an inferior man, John Moon, was employed. He altered Jessop's plans for the worse and
work began. It went on slowly and expensively, so much so that John Rennie was called in
1795 to advise, and Moon was dismissed. However sufficient money was raised to complete
the navigation to Strensall, some 5 miles short of Sheriff Hutton. It was opened in about
1796 and a modest traffic started but revenue was low. In 1800 a further Act was passed
to raise more capital to push on to Sheriff Hutton. A cut was made away from the river
to the river bridge near Sheriff Hutton, and a basin was built there, and completed by 1804.
The navigation now totalled 11$\frac{1}{2}$ miles with eight locks, including that at Castle Mills in
York. Agitation commenced to continue to Stillington and in 1810 a survey was prepared.
Revenue reached its peak in 1809 and then declined because of Ouse and Derwent competition. Traffic became very small above York, yet in the city there was plenty of short
haul movement. With the arrival of railways the Foss were keen to sell, since the York -
Scarborough line, opened in 1845, ran close alongside as far as Strensall. Railway competition killed Foss traffic above York and in 1852 the proprietors sold out to York Corporation.
The latter were mainly concerned with pollution, which the old company had tried to
tackle in the late 1840s. In 1859 York Corporation gained an Act to abandon the Foss save
for just over a mile in York. They were left with one lock, Castle Mills, a quarter of a
mile above the junction with the Ouse. Traffic within the city remained considerable. Most
important was that of Henry Leetham & Sons, the flour millers for whom the city, from
1887, granted specially favourable tolls on the Ouse and Foss, and for whom they rebuilt
Castle Mills lock in 1889 to take steam keels 97' x 18'6" carrying 230 tons. Traffic increased but in 1930 Leetham's (from 1928 part of Spillers) moved to Hull. They had had a
court action with the Corporation over the 1887 tolls agreement, found to be invalid.
Leetham's refused a new agreement and their departure meant that very little came up the
Foss. However commercial traffic uses the navigation in the 1970s.

FOSSDYKE NAVIGATION.   See Witham and Fossdyke Navigations.

GALTON'S and BROWN'S CANALS, Somerset.   Both were short cuts from the Brue,
the first built by Mr E. Galton in about 1801 for 1$\frac{3}{8}$ miles between the Brue and the North
Drain, with a small lock and used to carry silt for fertilizer. Nearby another canal,
Brown's, a mile long from the Brue to the North Drain was cut for the same purpose.

GIANT'S GRAVE & BRITON FERRY (JERSEY) CANAL, Glamorganshire.   An extension
of the Neath Canal made in about 1815, firstly round the end of Giant's Grave pill to a new
wharf, then extended for just over half a mile to another wharf, completed by about 1832,

and finally in 1842 a further extension was made to the site of the original Briton Ferry. All this was done privately, first by Lord Vernon's agent, later by the Earl of Jersey, who succeeded to the Vernon estate. The canal, able to take boats 60' x 8'10", seems to have become somewhat decayed during the 1860s, although it is still used as a water supply.

GLAMORGANSHIRE CANAL. The Glamorganshire was promoted to improve transport to the coast from the ironworks and coalmines in the Merthyr Tydfil area. The Merthyr ironmasters, led by Richard Crawshay and Francis Homfray, proposed a canal for which money was readily found and an Act obtained in 1790, to run from Merthyr via Pontypridd and Melingriffith to the Taff below Cardiff. The Glamorganshire was built by the Thomas Dadfords, father and son, and the elder Thomas Sheasby working as engineers-cum-contractors. It was navigable throughout in 1792 although not fully completed until 1794. By this time it had been extended half a mile to a point near the Crawshay ironworks at Cyfarthfa. The canal rose 543', clinging to the hillside above the Taff. At the top several locks were paired in two rise staircases and at Nantgarw nine miles up from Cardiff the company built a staircase of three, the treble locks. There was a short 115 yd tunnel under Queen Street, Cardiff. The boats were something like narrow day boats but were 60' x 9'. It was not long before the seaward end of the canal was extended a mile to a new basin and sea lock for ships up to 90' x 24'. This was called the Sea Lock Pound, the originally planned entrance never having been built. The canal now measured 25½ miles, and finished up with 51 locks plus the sea lock but including New lock. From 1798 a lasting quarrel blew up between the Crawshays and the other ironmasters who complained that the Crawshays as the biggest shareholders ran the canal for their own benefit. More remarkable was the quarrel in 1794 between the two Dadfords and Thomas Sheasby with the canal company. This was over money which was owing to the engineer-contractors, the company refused to pay, so the former withdrew their men and in reply the company had them arrested. Robert Whitworth, the engineer, was called in to arbitrate and found in favour of the Dadfords and Sheasby.

Like all the South Wales canals the Glamorganshire was dependent on tramroads for much of its traffic. But because of the ironmasters' quarrel tramroad building took the form of the rival Penydarren tramroad from Merthyr down to Abercynon parallel with the canal. By the early nineteenth century the Glamorganshire was busy. Water supply was a problem because of the heavy lockage and disputes with ironworks over the supply from the Taff. As a result, a reservoir was built soon after 1806 at Glyn-dyrys near Merthyr and a pumping engine erected at nearby Pontyrun to pump back Taff water. Nearer Cardiff at about the same time, waterwheel driven beam pumps were set up at Melingriffith to return water taken out by the works there. A reservoir was added in 1821 below the Nantgarw treble locks to try and improve supplies to the lower pounds. This considerable traffic from the Merthyr ironworks and collieries brought revenue which could not be passed on as dividends because the Glamorganshire's Act had limited them to 8 per cent, so tolls and rates were reduced successively over these golden years. Increased traffic brought congestion at Cardiff. In 1814 the sea lock was lengthened and George Overton recommending what was in effect a dock. Here the canal company came up against the Marquess of Bute who had his own dock plans. He was advised in 1828 by James Green who recommended a ship canal separate from the Glamorganshire. So in 1830 the Act passed for the Bute Ship Canal to be 1½ miles long with a dock and two lateral connections with the Glamorganshire. No ship canal was built but in 1839 the West Bute dock was opened. There was a connecting cut from the dock to the Glamorganshire who built an extra lock, New lock, just below the junction. Meanwhile the Glamorganshire was doing well, the first cargoes of steam coal being sent down in 1830, and tolls again reduced. Much of this came off the Aberdare Canal which joined the Glamorganshire at Abercynon and the short Doctor's Canal which joined the Glamorganshire at Denia. The continual passage through locks caused a downhill current which limited up going boats to cargoes of 15 to 18 tons. Water was always short and the loading limitations of Merthyr bound boats caused foreign iron ore to pile up at Cardiff. To some of the ironmasters therefore a railway seemed attractive, for the Penydarren tramroad was likewise unable to handle the uphill traffic. The Hills of the Plymouth works and the Guests of Dowlais were keenest and went ahead with railway plans which emerged as the Taff Vale Railway authorized in 1836. It reached Merthyr in 1841, and for a while there was sufficient traffic, notably steam coal from the Rhondda, to keep both the railway and canals going, but from the 1860s, Glamorganshire tonnages fell sharply. By this time there were more railways and the railway served East Bute dock opened fully in 1859. The canal tried to fight back by proposing docks of their own in the mid-1860s which were countered by an offer from the Bute trustees to buy the canal. After 1876 the 8 per cent canal dividend could not be maintained, indeed in 1882 it was as low as 1½ per cent, the year the company built the railway to serve their Sea Lock Pound. A second offer from the Bute trustees to buy the canal in 1883 was accepted and became effective in 1885 and included the Aberdare Canal. By this time the Glamorganshire had fallen into a poor state, but the Marquess of Bute did some improvements to the Sea Lock Pound. A steam boat was introduced in 1893 but by this time the section from Cyfarthfa to Merthyr had been disused since 1865, and after 1898 there was no traffic above Abercynon. After a burst in 1915 there was no traffic above Pontypridd while a burst at Nantgarw in 1942 closed the whole canal except for part of the Sea Lock Pound. In 1943 the canal was bought by Cardiff Corporation who secured abandonment, the Sea Lock Pound becoming disused in 1950.

GLAN-Y-WERN CANAL, Glamorganshire.   Edward Elton owned a colliery at Glan-y-wern to the north of the Crymlyn bog. He built a $3\frac{1}{2}$ mile canal across the bog and eastwards to Red Jacket pill on the Neath River although the canal stopped short of the river, the coal being transhipped from small canal boats to river vessels.   The canal was completed in 1790 at Elton's expense, but after his death in about 1810 it became disused.   It was revived after 1816 by George Tennant who made it part of his scheme to link the Tawe and the Neath. A lock was built at Red Jacket to connect with the pill.   The Glan-y-wern could then take 60 ton capacity craft. It remained in use until about 1910 but was derelict by 1918. This canal went under several names, the New Chapel Canal,   Crymlyn & Red Jacket Canal, Briton or Britton Canal, and Llanywern or Lanywern Canal.

GLASGOW, PAISLEY & JOHNSTONE CANAL, Renfrewshire.   At the end of the eighteenth century the Clyde was shallow up to Glasgow and there were possibilities of developing Ardrossan as a port connected by canal with Glasgow. This was the hope of the twelfth Earl of Eglinton the principal landowner in the Ardrossan district and in 1791 he formed a committee to promote the idea. John Rennie made a survey in 1800 and the project was reported on by Telford. The Act for the canal, called the Glasgow, Paisley & Ardrossan passed in 1806 and the Earl of Eglinton became chairman, work starting between Johnstone and Glasgow. Telford seems to have guided the engineering, designing the aqueduct over the White Cart at Blackhall in Paisley, the canal being opened to Paisley in 1810 and through to Tradeston on the south bank of the Clyde in Glasgow the following year. The canal was 11 miles long, without locks, but with two short tunnels in Paisley with towpaths. The terminal basin at Tradeston was named Port Eglinton. But the company were without money to continue and the Government refused to help, because Clyde improvements had made the canal to Ardrossan unnecessary. The open section earned a good and increasing revenue. After 1820 no more plans were advanced for extending to Ardrossan, although there were ideas of replacing the canal by a railway and an Act passed for this in 1827. Part was built between Kilwinning and Ardrossan. Meanwhile the canal was developing a passenger boat service which reached its heyday in the 1830s, the time from Glasgow to Paisley was reduced from $1\frac{1}{2}$ hours to 1 hour 11 minutes, and only 45 minutes back to Port Eglinton. Cargo traffic competed fiercely with road carriers, cotton from the Johnstone mills being a principal item, carried in light fast boats no more than 7'4" beam, Scottish equivalents of narrow boats. Screw steamer propulsion was tried in 1840 but the canal was too shallow to achieve success. With the completion in 1840 and 1841 of two railways between Glasgow and Paisley the canal was doomed; for a while it tried to compete at ruinous rates but in 1843 the parcels and passenger services were given up and the horses and passage boats sold. In 1869 the canal itself was sold to the Glasgow & South Western Railway, but traffic declined and in 1881 it closed, a railway being laid in its bed (95).

GLASTONBURY CANAL, Somerset.   About 1825 there were proposals for a canal from Highbridge to Glastonbury, the Act being passed in 1827. Original plans for the route were revised in 1828 by the younger John Rennie who recommended a waterway suitable for local coasters, with a sea lock at Highbridge and one intermediate lock at Shapwick, each 64' x 18'6". It was completed in 1833, the total length being $14\frac{1}{8}$ miles. The Glastonbury started well, since the town was open to coasters, but prosperity was short-lived because in 1842 the Bristol & Exeter Railway reached Highbridge, and bought the canal in 1848 to prevent its use by a rival railway as a railbed. In 1852 the Bristol & Exeter were happy to dispose of it to the new broad gauge Somerset Central Railway who built their line along the canal bank. With the railway open in 1854 the canal was abandoned, save for a short length at Highbridge turned over to the local commissioners of sewers and abandoned in 1936.

River GLEN.   See River Welland Navigation and River Glen.

GLENKENS CANAL PROJECT, Kirkcudbrightshire.   John Rennie surveyed a canal to run from Dalry parallel with the Rivers Ken and Dee down to Kirkcudbright, an Act passing for this in 1802. Trade was too limited to justify construction.

GLOUCESTER & BERKELEY SHIP CANAL, Gloucestershire. Moves were made in 1783 for a canal from Gloucester to join the Stroudwater, and a further proposal came in 1792 for a ship canal to take 300 ton vessels from Gloucester to Berkeley Pill bypassing the shallows of the lower Severn.   After preliminary work by Richard Hall and Josiah Clowes, a further survey was undertaken by Robert Mylne who underestimated the cost, leading to trouble after passage of the Act in January 1793. Work started in 1794 from Gloucester with the trial of various patterns of cutting machines. In 1797 Mylne was dismissed and James Dadford carried on, although he left in 1800, with only $5\frac{1}{2}$ miles built, and no more money. Ideas were put forward for continuing the canal, for example to raise money by lottery and to end only at Hock Crib near Frampton-on-Severn, about two thirds of the distance to the finally selected ending at Sharpness, proposed in 1813. In the end the long abandoned

58.

waterway was rescued by the Exchequer Bill Loan Commissioners. They made sizeable advances so that in 1819 cutting could be resumed, although money ran out again in 1820. With more public money work recommenced in 1823 and in 1827 the canal was at last finished, $16\frac{3}{8}$ miles long on one level, with a short 1 mile navigable feeder to Cambridge. As completed it could take 600 ton ships, being 86'6" wide and 18' deep and spanned only by swing bridges. Trade built up slowly and the canal was hampered by water problems, supplies coming from the Cam, the Stroudwater and the Severn at Gloucester. Unlike most canals the Gloucester & Berkeley welcomed railways as feeders to Gloucester, while on the other hand they resisted improvements to the Severn, fearing that Gloucester might yield to Worcester. They wanted a railway to Sharpness and across the Severn to the Forest of Dean and South Wales. This was secured by an Act of 1872, while, starting in 1869, Sharpness was enlarged for the increased size of vessels. Modernization was achieved under the direction of W.B. Clegram the Company's engineer, involving a new entrance lock $\frac{3}{4}$ mile downstream and a 2000' long wet dock. In 1873 the company had bought the Worcester & Birmingham Canal so on completion of the Sharpness works in 1874 a new title was created, the Sharpness New Docks & Gloucester & Birmingham Navigation Co. In 1879 the Severn Railway bridge was completed with a swinging span over the canal, and extensive sidings laid alongside the Sharpness quays. Revenue did not increase as hoped, because of depression and competition from Avonmouth, until the 1900s. Today the canal called the Gloucester & Sharpness is busy, mainly with oil traffic.

Sir John GLYNNE'S (SALTNEY or HAWARDEN) CANAL, Flintshire. A very short local coal canal, only about a mile, built privately about 1768 from Sir John Glynne's Sandycroft colliery near Bretton to Saltney just outside Chester. It remained in use until about 1779.

GRAND CANAL, Co Dublin, Kildare, Offaly, Leix, Galway. Ireland's largest canal system is aptly named, for it carried the heaviest traffic of any Irish river or canal, reaching a peak of 379,047 tons in 1875. An Act of 1715 sanctioned the improvement and the project was revived in the 1750s, Thomas Omer making surveys for the Commissioners of Inland Navigation. He was working under the authority of resolutions of 1756 which authorized a canal from Dublin to the Shannon, to be built with public money. Omer started work in 1756 on a route crossing the Bog of Allen and cutting proceeded quickly although expensively on independent lengths. An interest in water supply was shown from 1763 by Dublin Corporation and they obtained more government funds towards this, the canal becoming a joint venture between the Commissioners of Inland Navigation and Dublin Corporation. But by 1770 it appeared that the whole scheme might be beyond the capabilities of the Commissioners. Rescue came from private enterprise assisted a little by Dublin Corporation and in 1772 the Act forming the Grand Canal Co. passed the Irish parliament, authorizing the raising of funds by subscription. The year before, John Smeaton had been invited over to survey the new Grand but he was too busy to come until 1773, when he brought his assistant William Jessop. Smeaton and Jessop found much wrong with Omer's survey and the workmanship of the contractors, Omer having planned a canal for very large vessels of 175 tons, completing locks 137' x 20' wide. Smeaton advocated a canal for boats only 56' x 13' to 14' beam and the locks were eventually built to something like these dimensions. Work re-started before Smeaton arrived, the resident engineer John Trail (succeeded in 1777 by General Tarrant) busy replacing the lock work of Omer and his successors. Jessop was now given the post of consulting engineer, paying occasional visits, and by 1779 15 miles had been opened. Money was perpetually short and the government had both to give and lend. By 1780 the canal had reached Sallins, Richard Evans, from about 1785 the resident engineer in place of Tarrant, crossing the Liffey by a seven arched masonry aqueduct. When Lowtown was reached, 8 miles west of Sallins, construction turned from the Shannon line to the branch to the Barrow, completed to the river at Athy in 1791, $28\frac{1}{2}$ miles from Lowtown with 9 locks, two of them doubles, so 11 by English reckoning. On the main line, Tullamore was reached in 1788 but more Government money had to be procured to continue, John Killaly now being resident engineer. He selected the route to the Shannon down the Valley of the Brosna, suggested by Jessop. In 1803 the junction was made with the Shannon at Shannon Harbour, although because of leakage the canal was not declared open until 1805, 79 miles 3 furlongs between James Street Harbour, the Dublin terminal, and Shannon Harbour, with 36 locks (41 English), some two rise to take craft 70' x 13'7". The locks on the Barrow line and on the other branches had similar dimensions, varying from a length of 69'8" on the Ringsend circular line to 73'6" on the Naas branch. Most important of the branches was the Ringsend link with the Liffey and the sea at Dublin. This was planned in the early 1780s at first to be a direct line from James Street Harbour to the Liffey, but altered by William Chapman to a circular line south of the city to enter the Liffey at Ringsend below the bridges, where docks were built by the canal company. With Government assistance the branch and docks were completed in 1796. There were several other branches, that to Naas with five locks was built by the separate Kildare Canal Co. whose resident engineer was Chapman, reaching Naas from the main line at Soldier's Island near Sallins in 1789. In 1808 the Kildare was bought by the Grand who pushed the branch further south to Corbally, $7\frac{7}{8}$ miles from the main line. More ambitious were the schemes in 1800 for the Queen's County Canal to go from Monasterevan on the Barrow line to Kilkenny and the collieries at Castlecomer, enlarged in 1811 to a canal down to the Suir at Carrick. But all that was built was a branch from Monasterevan to Mountmellick $11\frac{1}{2}$ miles away, with 3 locks, completed as late as 1830 by the Grand. Mountmellick had been reached with money from the Exchequer Bill Loan Commissioners who also financed the 8 mile level Kilbeggan branch from Ballycommon, opened in 1835. Much earlier in 1802 a one mile level branch had been opened to Edenderry from the main line in the Bog of Allen, and in 1828 came the completion of the line to Ballinasloe from opposite Shannon Harbour, $14\frac{1}{2}$ miles long with 2 locks. Money again came from the Exchequer Bill Loan Commissioners. Water for the Grand came from 19 feeders as well as two reservoirs, Blackwood and Milltown, on the summit level via navigable feeders. Traffic increased steadily on the Grand; turf, farm produce and building materials going to Dublin, with coal, manure and merchandise coming westwards. In

1780, well before completion, passenger traffic started between Sallins and Dublin, becoming quite profitable, although the lavish hotels which the company built did not prove so successful. The Napoleonic Wars benefited canal trade but a depression followed Waterloo, Ireland becoming particularly unsettled, marked by malicious breaching of the canal bank. Railway competition appeared in 1847 with a line to Kildare, the Grand having earlier considered an atmospheric railway between Portobello and Sallins. As elsewhere railway construction also brought a traffic boom, so that the Grand did well in the mid-1840s, but the post famine period from 1848 brought a recession. To avert a financial crisis the company was in that year reconstituted and the following year themselves became carriers, and tugs on the Shannon were started in 1849 and in 1865 extended to the canal. Because of railway competition passenger services ceased in 1852. The Midland Great Western Railway, already owning the Royal Canal, tried to buy the Grand too and pending settlement leased it for seven years from 1853, but on expiry of the lease in 1860 however, the offer was withdrawn because the canal had operated at a loss. In 1878 the Grand acquired the trade of the Barrow Navigation Co. north of Athy, and in 1894 the navigation itself from Athy down to the tidewater at St. Mullins. By this time Grand fortunes were being restored by the energetic James McCann who had become chairman in 1891 and revolutionized by the first motor boat in 1911. Between 1917 and 1920 the canal gained Government help over finance and policy because of the war but traffic was seriously affected by the national crisis, followed during the 1920s by increasing road competition to which the Grand replied in 1932 by starting its own fleet of lorries. The fuel shortage of the 1939-45 War was beneficial to the canal, wooden 'emergency' horse boats being built. In 1950 the canal was taken over by Coras Iompair Eireann, who allowed traffic to decline. The bye traders were driven off by 1957 and in 1959-60 CIE withdrew their own boats, the last cargoes being for Guinness, so that all commercial traffic ceased. Today the main line, the Ringsend line, the Barrow line and the Edenderry branch are open and used by pleasure craft, but the other branches were closed to navigation in 1960-61. In 1973 the Grand was transferred to the Eire Government Board of Works.

GRAND CONTOUR CANAL SCHEME. As recently as 1942 J.F. Pownall proposed a remarkable scheme for a wide waterway serving the principal industrial areas of England. The whole canal would be on one level, following the 310' contour. This would take it from near Southampton up to Tyneside, from Hartlepool to Chester, with a branch to Birmingham, and from Bristol to near Nottingham. Manchester, Leeds and the Potteries would lie close to the line, which was to be large enough for coastal craft drawing some 15' of water, the depth being 17' and the surface width 100'. Although there were no locks, communication with the ports would be by lifts of considerable height at Newcastle, Hartlepool, Preston, Chester and Bristol.

GRAND JUNCTION CANAL, London, Middlesex, Hertfordshire, Bedfordshire, Buckinghamshire, Northamptonshire. With the Midlands canal network taking shape a direct canal route to the metropolis was needed and in 1791-92 surveys were made by James Barnes and William Jessop from Brentford, crossing the two summits of Tring and Daventry, to the Oxford at Braunston. Designed as a broad canal for 70 ton barges the Grand Junction was well supported under the chairmanship of William Praed, the banker. On passage of the Act in 1793 Jessop was appointed principal engineer with Barnes as resident. Work started quickly, particularly on the two tunnels at Braunston and Blisworth. Braunston (2042 yd) was opened in 1796 but Blisworth proved a problem due to flooding and a new line had to be set out. By 1800 the canal was complete save for this tunnel and traffic could flow, via a road over Blisworth Hill replaced in the same year by a double track horse tramroad. Not until 1802 did work start on the new line of Blisworth (3056 yd) which was completed in 1805 (59). The canal was $93\frac{1}{2}$ miles with 101 broad locks, later 102, with an extra at King's Langley, excluding those 9 leading to a level crossing of the Ouse at Wolverton. These were just a temporary arrangement, for Jessop replaced them by an embankment and masonry aqueduct. A wooden trough was built until a new iron aqueduct was completed in 1811. In 1795 the $13\frac{1}{2}$ mile long level branch to Paddington was authorized (completed in 1801) from the main line at Bull's Bridge near Hayes, with a basin in Paddington and many private arms to brickfields along its route, much extended during the nineteenth century. A proposed branch to Daventry was never built, but there was one of $\frac{5}{8}$ mile to the new barracks at Weedon, opened in 1804. The branch to Northampton was delayed by non-arrival of the Union Canal from Leicester. A tramroad was built from the Grand Junction main line to the town, followed in 1815 by the 5 mile branch canal from Gayton with 17 narrow locks falling to Northampton. In 1801 the $10\frac{1}{2}$ mile Buckingham branch was complete with two narrow locks, running via Stony Stratford. Branches proposed to St. Albans and Watford were never built, but in 1799 the $6\frac{3}{4}$ mile navigable feeder was completed from wells at Wendover to Tring summit, with one stop lock. There was also a side lock into the Colne at Rickmansworth to serve wharves on the river. In 1811-12 there were ideas to join the Ouse at Bedford, but all that resulted was the independent Newport Pagnell Canal opened in 1817. In the other direction there were proposals to extend towards the Kennet & Avon and the Wilts & Berks, for example to Abingdon to meet the latter, the Grand Junction to make the line as far as Aylesbury. This they did, from Marsworth on the main canal $6\frac{3}{8}$ miles with 16 narrow locks down to Aylesbury, reached in 1815 but never extended. Last of all the branches was the level 5 miles to Slough opened as late as 1882. Water requirements were very large for the heavy lockage over the Chilterns and for the second summit by Daventry. The long Paddington branch was a useful supply fed by the River Brent, by reservoirs at Ruislip and Aldenham and after 1835 by the Welsh Harp at Hendon. The summit at Tring was fed from the nearby reservoirs by pumping up into the canal and by the feeder from the wells at Wendover, while the Daventry summit took water from local reservoirs. With the opening of the Grand Union Canal in 1814 more water came down from the reservoirs on the wolds about Naseby. Traffic built up quickly. For the first time the Midlands and Manchester were able to exchange goods direct with London. Traffic on the canal became so heavy that water was commonly short. Curiously passenger traffic did not develop, although from 1801 a service operated between Paddington and Uxbridge, but lapsed after 1820. Although built as a broad canal most of the Grand Junction was little used by barges or wide boats. They were common enough below Berkhampstead and on the Paddington branch, but elsewhere narrow boats were the carriers. From 1805 the company discouraged, although they did not prohibit wide boats in Braunston and the newly opened Blisworth tunnel because of the delays they caused. Railway threats for a London-Birmingham line came as early as 1824. In reply the Grand Junction contemplated locomotive haulage of boats and steam tunnel tugs, while at the same time there were plans to improve the canal line between London, Birmingham, the Severn and Mersey. In 1827 came the scheme for the London & Birmingham Junction Canal from the Stratford Canal to Braunston later altered to Ansty or Brinklow, but it never obtained an Act. It was followed by William Cubitt's Central Union scheme of 1832 from the Worcester & Birmingham near Worcester Bar across via Solihull to the Oxford at Ansty, while in 1833 came James Green's London & Birmingham Canal, from Stratford direct to the Regent's, bypassing the Grand Junction Canal entirely. It was dropped, but did stir the Grand Junction into making improvements. To speed up traffic the Stoke Bruerne locks were duplicated in 1835 and new larger reservoirs built at Tring summit to ease a serious water shortage. In 1838 the London & Birmingham Railway was opened, against which the Grand Junction fought gamely, agreeing with other companies on toll reductions and in 1848 entering the carrying trade. From 1864 steam narrow boats were acquired, working with a butty, and these penetrated right up the Erewash. Depots were set up in places well away from the canal in an effort to capture traffic, but carrying was given up in 1876 because it did not pay. Steam tugs were however put on for Blisworth and Braunston tunnels from 1871, replacing a short lived experiment with an endless wire rope at Braunston. As early as 1863 there were plans for a general amalgamation of canals on the London to Birmingham, Coventry and Leicester lines, but this never took shape. There were then moves towards the acquisition of the Leicester line by the Grand Junction, spurred on by Fellows, Morton, & Clayton. In 1894 the Grand Junction bought both the Grand Union and the Leics. & Northants. Union and improvements began, listening to the pleas of Fellows, Morton who offered to put wide boats on the line if the locks of the Grand Union were enlarged. It was hoped to recapture the coal trade from Derbyshire. In 1896 the Grand Junction decided to build an inclined plane alongside the narrow locks at Foxton with caissons large enough for a pair of narrow boats or a barge. This was completed in 1900 and at the same time the widening of the Watford locks was authorized, to complete a wide waterway from London to Derbyshire. But the traffic did not develop and the widening at Watford was countermanded, in 1902 the locks being rebuilt to narrow standard. From 1910 the locks were passing the bulk of the traffic at Foxton. In 1925 the Grand Junction made a move to acquire the three Warwick canals, which was followed by discussions with the Regent's on a merger. This was agreed to in 1926 as long as the Grand Junction bought the three Warwick canals, which were in fact purchased by the Regent's. From 1 January 1929 the new amalgamation came into force as the Grand Union Canal Co. Ltd., an old name resurrected. All that was left under Grand Junction control was its property in Paddington. The last regular coal traffic on the main line ceased in 1970, although local traffic in the London area remains.

GRAND SURREY CANAL, Surrey. Promoted to run from the Thames at Rotherhithe to Mitcham on the Wandle, with branches to Deptford, Peckham, the Borough and the Thames at Vauxhall. By its Act of 1801 the canal, with Ralph Dodd as engineer was called the Surrey & Kent, but it developed more as a dock business, and never got nearer Mitcham than Camberwell, 3⅜ miles from Rotherhithe, reached in 1810. Much later in 1826 a ⅝ mile branch was opened to Peckham. Traffic on the canal was considerable, and the two 109' x 18' locks leading into the dock system and river were large enough for Thames lighters and spritsail barges. Although the company had plans to extend their canal, all their efforts went into dock building, in 1855 changing their name to the Grand

59. Blisworth Tunnel with an empty Grand Union pair emerging, the butty cross strapped to the motor.

Surrey Docks & Canal Co. In 1864 some of the canal was absorbed by the extension of the Greenland Dock. In the same year the company amalgamated with the rival Commercial Docks Company to form the Surrey Commercial Docks system absorbed by the Port of London Authority in 1908, together with the canal which was used until 1971.

GRAND UNION CANAL (Old)., Leicestershire, Northamptonshire. For the Grand Junction the failure of the Leicestershire
& Northamptonshire Union to join up with their line was a disappointment. To gain Trent traffic and that from the Notts-Derby
coalfield a connecting canal was essential and in 1808 Thomas
Telford and James Barnes made preliminary surveys at the instigation of the Grand Junction. Although the old Union was broad,
together with the rest of the line to the Trent and up the Erewash
valley, the new canal was built with narrow locks. For the Grand
Junction wanted only narrow boats on its line, it found barges and
wide boats caused delays, since they could not pass in Braunston
or Blisworth tunnels. However bridges and tunnels on the Grand
Union, as the new waterway was called, were built broad. Benjamin Bevan was made engineer and selected Barnes' rather than

60.
Telford's line because it was cheaper and shorter. The Act passed in 1810 and work
started on the $23\frac{1}{4}$ mile line. The summit level was over 20 miles, piercing the hills by
tunnels at Crick (1528 yd) in the south and Husband's Bosworth (1166 yd) in the north.
Crick tunnel had to be realigned because of quicksands, but both were ready when the
canal was opened in 1814. The locks were grouped at Watford, descending from the summit
to the junction with the Grand Junction at Norton and at Foxton where the canal dropped
down to join the old Union. There was a staircase of four and three single locks at
Watford and two staircases of five at Foxton with a passing place between them. Water
came from reservoirs on the wolds at Welford, Naseby and Sulby, which via the Welford
arm, a navigable feeder $1\frac{5}{8}$ miles long, supplied water not only to the Grand Union, but
also to the old Union and the Grand Junction. The new canal was dependent on what the
other companies sent on the long line between the Grand Junction and the Derbyshire coalfields, there being five separate authorities between Foxton and Cromford. Thus the Grand
Union did not do well and had to be financially supported by the Grand Junction who by
about 1840 gained a majority shareholding. Railway competition forced tolls down and in
the 1860s the canal sought refuge by close working arrangements, just short of amalgamation, with the old Union, itself equally hard pressed. By the 1880s both were in a bad way
but rescue came to both by outright purchase by the Grand Junction in 1894.

GRAND UNION CANAL (1929), London, Middlesex, Hertfordshire, Buckinghamshire,
Northamptonshire, Warwickshire, Leicestershire, Nottinghamshire, Derbyshire. A final
bid to make a canal network pay in the face of rail and road competition, the Regent's
Canal, under its chairman W.H. Curtis, appears as the mainspring of this amalgamation.
In 1925 he suggested purchase of the Grand Junction, itself proposing to buy the three
Warwick canals. For convenience the Regent's agreed to buy them in 1927 and take over
the Grand Junction, since 1894 owner of the canals to Leicester. Acts were obtained in
1928 and from 1 January 1929 a new company was born, the Grand Union. Plans were made
to widen the line from Braunston to Birmingham for craft of 12'6" beam with the aid of a
government grant. This was sanctioned by an Act of 1931 and work began, the company also
proposing to widen the locks at Watford and Foxton on the Leicester line for which another
Act was passed in 1931. But here the government refused help, although the Grand Union
had committed themselves to extending their line to the Trent by the purchase of the
Leicester Navigation, the Loughborough Navigation and the Erewash Canal, completed in
1932. So all efforts were concentrated on the Birmingham line. To gain complete control
of this it was hoped to buy the Oxford Canal, still owning the five miles between Napton
and Braunston, and also the Coventry. But neither were acquired, the Grand Union being
allowed to improve the Napton Braunston length at their own expense. Widening as far as
the top of Camp Hill locks meant the abandonment of 52 narrow locks, converted into
weirs, and the construction alongside of 51 broad locks, for on the Knowle flight six were
replaced by five, and at Bascote a staircase pair replaced two single locks. In addition 26
miles of bank protection work was carried out and throughout a uniform depth of 5'6" over
the lock sills was achieved. Between Braunston and Birmingham the canal was dredged to
this depth and the bottom widened to 26' so that 12'6" beam boats could pass, but bottom
widening south of Braunston was never achieved. In 1934 the Duke of Kent opened the
Hatton flight of 21. Although this marked completion of the wide locks, other improvement
works were not finished until 1937. By this time the Grand Union had nearly ended an ambitious narrow boat building programme. In 1937, because of the disappointing interchange
rate of goods from ship to canal boat at Regent's Canal Dock, the company started its
own shipping subsidiary, the Regent's Line running between the Thames, Antwerp and later
Rotterdam which provided valuable additional traffic for the narrow boats. To complete the
provision of cargo services the company set up Grand Union (Stevedoring & Wharfage) Co.
Ltd, and their own agency in Antwerp. With new warehouses at Birmingham and improved
ones at Brentford, Northampton and Leicester, this extension of business looked promising
although the war interrupted development. Nevertheless in 1943 the Grand Union expanded
further, acquiring road hauliers Cartwright & Paddock, and forming Transport, Estate,
and Warehousing subsidiaries and Grandion to run their Ruislip lido, opened in 1936. In
1948 came nationalization and the acquisition of all the Grand Union interests by the British
Transport Commission, who quickly sold off the ships and in 1951 the lido. By the 1970s

61. Two river Parrett barges at Bridgwater, a pre-1883 view. Note the stern of the trow lying beyond the Bridge.

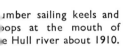

...umber sailing keels and ...oops at the mouth of ...e Hull river about 1910.

63. A view of the Trent near Keadby, taken in the early 1930s. In the foreground are the two sailing keels, SAMARITAN and BRASSO built in 1883 and 1924 respectively, the latter owned by Reckitt's of Hull, makers of the polish. The tug RIVERMAN was built in 1915 for United Towing of Hull who did the towing for the Trent Navigation Co., between Hull and Nottingham. In the background are three Trent pans under tow, and a steam keel towing two keels which have set sails to help.

64. A ferry (top) over the Trent at Stockwith, below Gainsborough about 1900.

65. Suffolk Stour lighters worked in gangs of two (middle). A scene at Nayland in 1905, the Cardy family.

66. Grand Canal hotel at Robertstown, with the summer horse-drawn trip boat, 1971.

the main line of the Grand Union carried no regular commercial traffic save for a little in the London area.

GRAND WESTERN CANAL, Devon and Somerset.   To link the Bristol and English Channels was the dream of many. Surveys were made or revised by Robert Whitworth, John Longbotham and Robert Mylne, followed by recommendations of William Jessop and his assistant Hugh Henshall, and an Act was passed in 1796, although the canal committee also called in John Rennie, who altered Jessop's plans. Because of war and a shortage of labour and materials, construction did not begin until 1810, when work began in the middle to gain stone traffic from the Burlescombe quarries. Rennie had lowered the summit level, and more expensive earthworks were required. By 1814 the 11 mile section, part main line and part branch, from Lowdwells to Tiverton was complete without a lock, but there was little money to continue, yet a modest barge traffic in coal and limestone started.   There were proposals for continuing the canal, as least to Taunton, but not until 1830 did James Green submit an extension to Taunton for tub-boats using an inclined plane and seven vertical lifts. By 1838 this was complete, although trouble had been experienced with the plane and the lifts. Their caissons could only accommodate single 8 ton boats measuring 26' x 6'6", with a loaded draught of 2'3". The Grand Western was moderately prosperous, carrying coal and limestone, until the arrival of the Bristol & Exeter Railway in 1844.   Then fortunes declined, the canal was leased to the railway in 1854 and sold ten years later. In 1867 the tub-boat portion was closed, but the barge canal remained open until about 1924, latterly carrying roadstone in two small boats. In 1971 the British Waterways Board gave the canal to Devon County Council for restoration for pleasure craft, which now use it.

GRANTHAM CANAL, Nottinghamshire, Leicestershire, Lincolnshire.   Promoted in 1791 it followed the inception of the Nottingham Canal, designed to bring coal to the city and the Trent. A canal from the Trent eastwards to Grantham would bring more markets for this coal. William Jessop did a survey, but the first Bill was lost and introducing a second the promoters altered the junction with the Trent to West Bridgford, directly opposite both the city and the Nottingham Canal. The Act passed in 1793. Jessop was put in overall charge but the resident engineers were James Green who was working under Jessop on the Nottingham Canal, and William King, the Duke of Rutland's agent.   The canal was soon built, opening in 1797, a total length of 33 miles with 18 broad locks rising to Grantham, able to take craft 75' x 14', the same size as the Nottingham so that boats could work right through from the Nottinghamshire collieries. The canal took water from reservoirs at Knipton fed by the River Devon and at Denton, both on the wolds above Grantham, as well as from feeder streams. The $3\frac{5}{8}$ miles branch authorized to Bingham was never built. In spite of the small population it served, the Grantham did fairly well, and a passenger service ran from 1798. All the time the Grantham worked closely with the Nottingham. There was in 1833 a proposal to make a canal on from Grantham to Sleaford, where cargoes would be unloaded and sent on by road to the South Forty Foot Drain for Boston. In 1845 the Grantham had agreed to sell out to the Ambergate, Nottingham, Boston & Eastern Junction Railway when they completed their line from Ambergate to Grantham.   In 1850 the railway opened but no sale took place, the Nottingham Canal having also agreed to be bought out. Eventually, after a series of court cases, the unwilling railway was forced to buy both canals. The Grantham was taken over in 1854 and in 1861 came under Great Northern control. Traffic declined under the GNR and the LNER closed the Grantham in 1936. There had been no traffic for over ten years. There are moves to reopen it for pleasure traffic, and some restoration work has been done.

GREASBROUGH (PARK GATE) CANAL, Yorkshire.   To serve collieries near Rotherham the Marquess of Rockingham planned a private canal in 1769 from the Don at Park Gate to near Greasbrough. John Varley did a survey, and another was prepared in 1775 by Smeaton. At last in 1778 William Fairbank surveyed and William Jessop built the canal. It was probably completed in 1780, with four broad locks and a reservoir. It was only $1\frac{1}{2}$ miles long with one short branch to Sough Bridge. Another branch canal soon followed for about $\frac{1}{2}$ mile to Newbiggin. Coal from Earl Fitzwilliam's Park Gate colliery was boated in containers. Railways from the 1830s captured much of this and the colliery tramroads and upper part of the canal were disused by the 1840s. The Newbiggin branch closed before 1900 and the lower $\frac{5}{8}$ mile probably ceased to be used at the end of the 1914-18 War.

River GREAT OUSE, Bedfordshire, Huntingdonshire, Cambridgeshire, Isle of Ely, Norfolk.   The Great Ouse rises near Brackley in Northamptonshire but has never been navigable above Bedford. Its length is about 160 miles from source to its outfall below King's Lynn. In the Middle Ages it ran via Upware and Wisbech but changed course before the end of the thirteenth century to come out at King's Lynn. This more direct channel helped navigation to Ely, to Thetford on the tributary Little Ouse, and to Cambridge on the Cam. It became of value for trade in the more settled years after the Conquest. The tides then penetrated some 48 miles inland and the tideway was considered an open navigation under Crown protection. During the fourteenth century the Ouse was probably not navigable above St. Ives except between each mill dam, and there was little attempt to improve the river in any way, responsibility below Huntingdon being under successive Commissions of Sewers since the mid-thirteenth century. With them drainage was paramount but land conditions in the Fens deteriorated so badly that by the seventeenth century the government took action, surveys being made in 1605 and 1618. Under Letters Patent granted by the Crown in 1617 to John Gason, the navigation was to be improved above St Ives. Gason assigned his rights to Arnold Spencer and Thomas Girton and work began on six pound locks between St. Ives and St. Neots. Girton withdrew in 1625 but Spencer carried on and by 1635 reached Great Barford, some $7\frac{1}{2}$ miles short of Bedford.   The Civil War ruined him and his works decayed, to be revived after the Restoration. An Act passed in 1665 to make the Ouse navigable to Bedford, but nothing was done until a lease of the site was secured in 1674 by Henry Ashley of Huntingdon. By 1687 he had restored the navigation to Great Barford and in that year became sole undertaker of the proposed navigation to Bedford, which was reached in 1689. Control between St. Ives and Great Barford was secured in 1680 by his son, also Henry, who rebuilt the staunch at St. Ives in 1720. There were now probably ten pound locks in the 31 miles between St. Ives and Bedford, plus five staunches and artificial cuts, and haling ways (towpaths) were made. Traffic benefited; coal, salt and merchandise came up while corn was probably the principal export. Drainage of the Middle and South Levels of the Fens between the Great Ouse and the Nene was undertaken by Vermuyden, the first stage being completed in 1637, including the old Bedford River, the straight cut between Earith and Salters Lode below Denver. The second stage included the completion of the 21 mile New Bedford River, or Hundred Foot because it was 100' wide, although now much wider, parallel with the Old, and the building of the sluice at Denver above the junction of the Hundred Foot with the Ouse, plus the Hermitage sluice below Earith to turn upper Ouse water into the Old and New Bedford Rivers. Both sluices and the Hundred Foot were finished in 1651. Whereas the Hundred Foot formed a valuable short cut to the upper Ouse, Denver sluice was harmful to navigation both above and below. Above, the Ouse was deprived of its current and silted up, below the great volume of land water coming down the Hundred Foot, combined with the tide, made the sluice impassable, for it had no lock and could only be navigated if water levels agreed. Opposition to Denver was formidable, from King's Lynn to Cambridge, but nothing was done until in 1713 the sluice collapsed due to water pressure. The effect was disastrous, floods and debris with more siltation, but between 1748 and 1750 the sluice was rebuilt by the Swiss engineer Charles Labelye, this time with a pound lock. Navigation remained difficult because of the lack of tidal scour below the sluice. In spite of the problems, boat traffic had been on the increase since the 1660s, notably to Cambridge, on the Cam. No tolls were charged by the drainage authority, the Bedford Level Corporation, while the towing horses damaged their banks. Navigation interests tried to secure an Act in 1749 to legalize their use of horses as long as they made good damage to the haling ways, but this was lost and not until 1789 did an Act pass, which regulated the haling, laid down a scale of tolls and put the administration of navigation up to Denver under commissioners representing both drainage and navigation. The upper river (above St. Ives) was in the hands of Ashley and Jemmatt descendants.

By this time concern was felt for the Ouse outfall and King's Lynn. Denver sluice, 14 miles above Lynn was blamed for siltation, and mooring was hazardous because of the tidal bore or aegre. In 1766 Smeaton recommended that the outfall waters should be concentrated to increase the scour. Above Lynn the river took a great bend which in 1751 Nathaniel Kinderley had seen as a hindrance to velocity. By the end of the eighteenth century plans were formed for a cut off channel from Eau Brink to Lynn harbour. Although strongly opposed by navigation interests, since its passage would demand tolls on what they considered a drainage work, the Act passed in 1795. No work was done until 1817, the $2\frac{1}{2}$ mile cut being completed in 1821 under John Rennie the elder and Thomas Telford. It proved a success, increasing the scour and deepening the river below Denver, although silt was deposited in the harbour. More repair work was needed on the upper Ouse by the early nineteenth century. The then joint owners, Sir Thomas Cullum and John Francklin (the former an Ashley, the latter a Jemmatt descendant) undertook staunch (three replacing four) and lock rebuilding from 1832 onwards, at great expense with little revenue prospects. Although the upper Ouse had done well in the first years of the nineteenth century, from 1805 it faced competition from the Grand Junction Canal which carried off the coal trade. Plans followed to join the upper Ouse to the canal system with the river acting as a feeder. Between 1811 and 1824 ideas recurred for a canal from Bedford to Fenny Stratford on the Grand Junction, and there was a plan to extend from Bedford to the proposed London & Cambridge Junction Canal authorized in 1812. The Newport Pagnell Canal was thought of as a possible link in 1817, but none of these expensive proposals came to anything. By the early nineteenth century the old drainage authority, the Bedford Level Corporation were in financial difficulties, but under the Act of 1827 some of their responsibilities were tranferred to two new bodies, the South Level Drainage and South Level Navigation Commissioners who united the divergent aims of drainage and navigation. They worked in harmony with the Eau Brink Act of 1795. The Navigation and Drainage Commissioners combined to build the staunch at Brownshill above Earith, completed in 1837. This checks the flow of the tide coming up the Hundred Foot, but tidal effect remains between Brownshill staunch and Hermitage sluice below Earith. In 1830 the South Level Drainage and Navigation Commissioners opened a 6 mile cut from below Ely to Littleport. Both Eau Brink and South Level united to dredge the Old West River, that is the Ouse between Earith and the junction with the Cam, completed in 1838. The section between Ely and Littleport is the Ely Ouse, and between Littleport and Denver the Ten Mile River. There were two navigable lodes off the Old West, the two mile Cottenham Lode from Twentypence Ferry and the Willingham Lode from below Hermitage sluice. They served the villages of those names. Railways soon upset Ouse traffic, providing severe competition from the 1850s. Freight rates were cut but river tonnages fell. Sir Thomas Cullum, part owner of the upper Ouse, died in 1855, and both his widow and Francklin were glad to get rid of the navigation in 1869 to John Kirkham. During 1870s the works decayed so much that boats could not get above Eaton Socon after 1878. Amazingly at this late stage plans were put forward for a canal from the Ouse at Bedford to Soulbury on the

Grand Junction. A Bill of 1892 was dropped but in 1893 the old upper navigation was bought by Leonard Taylor Simpson, a stockbroker. Between 1893 and 1899 he repaired the 15 locks and 3 staunches from St. Ives upwards and founded the Ouse Transport Co. with steam tugs and lighters. A good traffic developed up to Bedford from King's Lynn, although Simpson found himself legally unable to charge realistic tolls. He was opposed by the county councils and by Bedford and Godmanchester Corporations who combined to force closure of the navigation in 1904. Simpson retained ownership and derived some rent by leasing locks for the passage of pleasure traffic. In 1908 there were moves to reopen to traffic, headed by Bedford Corporation, to combat high rail charges, but Simpson was uncooperative, wishing only to sell. Insufficient funds could be raised to buy him out and he and his executors retained navigation rights until 1935 when they were acquired by the Great Ouse Catchment Board. The Catchment Board, established in 1932 under the Land Drainage Act of 1930, united drainage and navigation. There had been no navigation above St. Ives since 1909, but the Catchment Board reopened the river as far as Godmanchester in 1935 and Eaton Socon in 1939. In 1951 the Great Ouse Restoration Society was formed to reopen to Bedford. The locks at Bedford and Cardington have been repaired, in 1972 Roxton lock above Tempsford was opened, all by the efforts of the society and the Great Ouse River Authority, and now the navigation nears Bedford. Between St. Ives and King's Lynn traffic held up better, rail interchange docks and wharves being established at Ely and Littleport. Coal went by water to Fenland pumping stations, osiers for baskets were a useful local traffic and in the 1920s sugar beet cultivation expanded. Waterside beet factories were established at Ely (136) and Wissington on the Wissey, but traffic declined in the 1950s with road improvements; blue clay or gault is still carried by water for bank repairs and diesel by barge to the pumping stations until 1975. The navigation of the Ouse measured $74\frac{3}{4}$ miles from Bedford to the Wash via the Hundred Foot, the old course of the river from Earith, via Ely to Denver measuring $31\frac{1}{4}$ miles. The maximum size of craft up to Bedford was 101' x 10'8" via the Hundred Foot, but the old course to Earith, via Denver and Ely, limited craft to 90' x 12'6".

Sir Nigel GRESLEY'S CANAL, NEWCASTLE-UNDER-LYME CANAL, NEWCASTLE-UNDER-LYME JUNCTION CANAL, Staffordshire. Owning collieries at Apedale north-west of Newcastle-under-Lyme, Sir Nigel Gresley Bt. and his son Nigel Bowyer Gresley obtained an Act in 1775 for a private canal three miles long on one level from the mines into Newcastle. This waterway, probably completed in about 1776, gave the Gresleys a monopoly of coal sold in Newcastle, the Act controlling the price for a period of 42 years. Rivalry to Gresley's Canal came with the completion in about 1800 of the Newcastle-under-Lyme Canal (authorized by an Act of 1795) from the Trent & Mersey at Stoke, 4 miles on the level into Newcastle, but the new canal was not allowed to carry coal save for pottery manufacture, in order to preserve the Gresley monopoly. With two canals into Newcastle but unconnected, a move was made to join them by means of the Newcastle-under-Lyme Junction Canal authorized in 1798, one of the promoters being Sir Nigel Bowyer Gresley. Only $1\frac{1}{8}$ miles long with no locks, it had a sorry history. Like the Newcastle Canal it could carry coal only for the potteries, but it never linked the two other waterways, running only from Sir Nigel Gresley's Canal to Stubbs Walks in Newcastle. The Junction Canal carried little traffic throughout its career which lasted until its sale to the North Staffordshire Railway in 1851, the waterway ceasing to exist by 1864. In 1856 the NSR built a rail branch to the Apedale collieries, so the Gresley Canal closed, probably the following year. The Newcastle Canal proper was leased to the NSR in 1863 and worked as a section of their Trent & Mersey. Part was closed in 1921 and the remainder abandoned in 1935.

GROSVENOR CANAL, London. This creek of the Thames between the present Chelsea bridge and the bridge into Victoria Station was used from 1724 by the Chelsea waterworks as their supply, on lease from the Grosvenor family, but in 1823 the lease expired and the Earl of Grosvenor made the creek into a $\frac{3}{4}$ mile private navigable canal with a tide lock and basin; opened in 1824 and used for coal traffic to south-west London. Railway development shortened the canal, first in 1860 when Victoria was opened, and again in 1902 when the Victoria network was expanded. In 1904 the remainder was sold to Westminster City Council. For some years its basin has been used as a loading depot for refuse boats.

GWAUNCAEGURWEN CANAL, Glamorganshire. There were in 1757 navigable levels in a mine at Gwauncaegurwen at the head of the Upper Clydach River, the boats carrying both men and coal.

HACKNEY CANAL, Devon. The Hackney was promoted by Lord Clifford of Chudleigh in 1843 to transport pottery clay to the Teign estuary and sea-going vessels, from quarries around Kingsteignton. The $\frac{5}{8}$ mile canal has one lock at Hackney into the river, to take two River Teign barges. Pottery clay traffic was brisk in the nineteenth century but declined with increased rail and road facilities, finishing in 1928.

HASLINGDEN CANAL PROJECT, Lancashire. This arose about 1793 from the ideas of the Manchester, Bolton & Bury and the Leeds & Liverpool to join up. The Haslingden Canal was to run from Bury via Haslingden to the Leeds & Liverpool at Church near Accrington, obtaining an Act in 1794 for a tub-boat canal using twelve inclined planes. No work was ever done.

HAYLE-CAMBORNE CANAL SCHEME, Cornwall. An 1801 proposal for a canal from Hayle to Camborne to export tin ore, which did not materialize.

HEDON HAVEN, Yorkshire. Hedon is built on a natural creek near Hull. In the Middle Ages the creek was extended by two cuts disused by the 1500s. Hedon decayed until an Act of 1774 authorized improvement of the tidal creek called Hedon Haven. The works were completed about a year later. The town corporation in 1803 sought powers to make a new cut to bypass the creek but nothing was done. Hedon Haven was used into the twentieth century.

HELSTON CANAL PROJECT, Cornwall. Robert Fulton was the main planner of this tub-boat canal to cross Cornwall from the Helford to the Hayle rivers and a survey was made in 1796.

HEREFORDSHIRE & GLOUCESTERSHIRE CANAL.   Proposed as early as 1774, this canal was reported on by Robert Whitworth, the idea being to connect Hereford with the Severn directly, not making use of the Wye. It was revived in 1789 and a Bill sought the following year after a survey by Richard Hall. The Act passed in 1791 after a further survey by Clowes.   The new narrow canal was to be 35½ miles long from the Severn at Gloucester to Hereford with two tunnels and an aqueduct.   In 1791 a further survey was made by Henshall who took the main line by way of Newent with a third tunnel at Oxenhall, and work began;   Whitworth replacing Clowes as engineer after the latter's death in 1795. The aqueduct idea was dropped and the canal entered the western

67.

branch of the river at Over so that boats would work round to Gloucester by the Upper or Lower Partings, although in 1794 a cut had been made across Alney island using John Carne's cutting machine, but it is doubtful if boats ever used it.   Some of the canal had been opened in 1794 and a ¼ mile branch to collieries at Oxenhall near Newent was completed by 1796 but disused by 1800. In 1795 the canal was open from Over to Newent and in 1798 to Ledbury with the 2192 yd tunnel at Oxenhall. There were 13 locks on the 16 mile canal, built of unusually great depth, some up to 12'6" and most averaging 10'10", for craft 70' x 7'6" wide. The company had now exhausted its funds but the canal was still 18 miles or so from Hereford. Traffic was very light and water became desperately short, because the canal had failed to reach the River Frome on which the summit was to depend.   From 1800 the committee seems to have given the Herefordshire & Gloucestershire up as hopeless. However from 1827 matters improved when Stephen Ballard was appointed clerk. He increased its water supply and in 1830 started work on the line to Hereford with the main object of getting water from the Frome. No real progress was made until 1839 when a new Act empowered the raising of more funds. Walsopthorne tunnel, shortened from 1192 yd to 400 yd, was completed in 1842 and in 1845 the canal at last reached Hereford via an aqueduct over the Lugg and the 440 yd Aylestone Hill tunnel, 34 miles from the Severn to Hereford, with 22 locks and an 8½ mile summit level. Pursuing an independent career the canal company did succeed in increasing its traffic, but in 1862 was leased to the West Midland Railway and the GWR. Under railway control part was used for the new railway between Over, Newent and Ledbury, being closed from Ledbury to the Severn in 1881. It is assumed that the Ledbury- Hereford section closed soon afterwards.

HERTFORD UNION CANAL, London, or LEE UNION, or SIR GEORGE DUCKETT'S CANAL.   As owner of the Stort navigation Sir George Duckett was impressed by a possible connecting canal between the newly opened Regent's Canal and the nearby Lee Navigation into which the Stort flowed near Hoddesdon. He obtained an Act in 1824 for a 1¼ mile canal from Old Ford on the Regent's to the Lee, and in 1830 it was opened, with three locks wide enough for barges. Francis Giles was the engineer. Unfortunately traffic was disappointing because of the tolls demanded by himself and the Regent's.   By 1848 the Hertford Union was disused. Sir George sold the canal in 1857 to the Regent's who reopened it.

HOPKIN'S CANAL, Carmarthenshire.   A tiny ½ mile canal from the Burry estuary existing in 1825, but about which little is known.

HORNCASTLE CANAL, Lincolnshire.   Through the market town of Horncastle flows the Bain, a tributary of the Witham, being joined by the Waring at Horncastle.   In the canal age there were ideas of making the Bain navigable to join the Witham Navigation. They were encouraged by the existing Tattersall Canal a couple of miles long,   also called Gibson's Canal. It had been built privately some time in the 1780s with one lock. Horncastle extension schemes were considered in 1791, including two from William Jessop, one avoiding the Bain. However it seemed that the Bain would afford sufficient water for canalization and the Act passed in 1792. It sanctioned the purchase of the Tattershall Canal for incorporation in the new project, and limited dividends to 8 per cent. Work began under William Cawley of Mickle Trafford, Chester although other engineers followed him. By 1797 the canal had reached Dalderby about two miles below Horncastle, but it stopped there for lack of funds. John Rennie was called in to advise and reported in 1799. He made recommendations for continuance, which led to a petition to Parliament for more money, particularly necessary because of flood damage to completed works. A second Act passed in 1800 allowing more capital and also lifting the dividend limitation. Thereafter the work proceeded under Walker one of the shareholders and it was opened in 1802.   It measured 11 miles and there were 11 locks for craft 54' x 14'4" and 3'6" draught.   Two basins were made at Horncastle and a small one at Tumby later extended. Above Kirkby on Bain the waterway was largely a lateral canal, below, it was the canalized Bain, leading down to the Tattershall Canal which joined the Witham. Traffic built up,   although no dividend appeared until 1813, the main cargoes being coal, lime and timber to Horncastle and farm produce from the district.   Railways soon arrived, the Horncastle enjoying a brief spell of activity carrying railway construction materials. In 1848 the Boston to Lincoln railway was opened along the banks of the Witham, some goods being transhipped for a while between boat and rail at Dogdyke on the Witham below the Horncastle Canal junction. More serious for the canal was the opening of the line to Horncastle from Woodhall Junction in 1855. Traffic by water fell away and by the 1870s there was very little. The last boats came and went from Horncastle in 1878, but the canal still kept open. There were no company meetings after 1884 and in 1889 the canal was reported as defunct.

HOWDEN CANAL PROJECT, Yorkshire. A canal from Howden to the Ouse, considered in 1796 and a Bill petitioned for but not introduced, although in 1825 the idea was briefly revived.

HUDDERSFIELD (Narrow) CANAL, Lancashire, Cheshire, Yorkshire. This would probably not have been built but for the keenness of the Ashton Canal promoters for a trans-Pennine route of their own. A survey for a narrow canal was undertaken by Nicholas Brown and a report prepared by Benjamin Outram who proposed the summit tunnel at Stanedge 656' above sea level between Diggle and Marsden, the highest canal summit in the British Isles. The Act passed in 1794 for a canal to run from the Ashton terminus at Ashton over to Huddersfield to join Sir John Ramsden's. Water was the big problem with the stipulation that none should come from rivers save at flood time, so that millowners' supplies would not be jeopardized. Ten reservoirs were built, on the moors above Stanedge. Outram became the engineer and work started immediately on the summit tunnel, the rest of the canal being by comparison easy, for in 1797 it had reached Uppermill near Saddleworth on the Ashton side and Slaithwaite on the Huddersfield. The canal was complete except for the tunnel in 1799 and traffic started using the road over the top. By now however money was short. The enterprise was really saved by John Rooth, who in 1801 took over superintendence of the canal and tunnel works, trade being more actively encouraged and the company's financial structure rearranged. In 1809 the two headings met and in 1811 the tunnel was complete, today 3 miles 418 yd, for it was extended in 1893-4 to accommodate the railway at Diggle. At last the Huddersfield was fully open, $19\frac{7}{8}$ miles with 74 standard narrow locks for 70' x 7' boats, and apart from Stanedge, a 198 yd tunnel later opened out at Stalybridge and a 220 yd tunnel at Scout near Mossley, with a towing path and handrail, plus five aqueducts, one partially of iron at Stalybridge. Working the great tunnel proved immensely difficult and slow, there being no towing path and only single line traffic. A steam tug hauling itself along by a chain laid along the tunnel bottom was tried from 1824 but in 1833 was replaced by professional leggers who were used until the end of the nineteenth century. Standard narrow boats were too long for the short barge locks of Sir John Ramsden's Canal and the Calder & Hebble. Huddersfield became a transhipment centre until, from 1822 short narrow boats were built to pass on to the Calder & Hebble. Because of competition in the early 1830s from other canals, tolls were cut, but the Huddersfield was soon faced with railway threats from the Manchester & Leeds. It opened in 1841 through to Leeds but the Huddersfield became more directly menaced by a proposed railway from Stalybridge to Cooper Bridge near Huddersfield. This line, the Huddersfield & Manchester, quickly arranged to buy the canal, which in 1845 became railway property, this particular railway with the canal coming under LNWR control in 1847. It was opened with its own tunnel at Stanedge in 1849. Traffic was well maintained during most of the nineteenth century but less and less came to use the summit, ceasing over the top by 1905. After the 1914-18 War there was little traffic at all and the LMS in 1944 abandoned all but a $\frac{1}{2}$ mile at Huddersfield which was transferred to the Calder & Hebble, this too being abandoned by the British Waterways in 1963. However the canal is a water channel and for this reason the tunnel is kept open and there are restoration proposals.

River HULL, Yorkshire. The Hull is still navigable and, since the fourteenth century, a free navigation. Previously the Archbishops of York had charged tolls. In the seventeenth century the Hull was navigated to Wansford below Driffield. There were other navigable tributaries, the Arram Beck just above Beverley near Leconfield, and the Old Howe and Earl's Dyke above Frodingham, the last two in 1800 incorporated into the Beverley & Barmston Drain. By the early nineteenth century traffic on the Hull within the port of Hull became congested with deep sea vessels as well as river craft. It was relieved by dock construction. The tide remains the chief motive power for navigation.

HURLET CANAL SCHEME, Renfrewshire. James Watt in 1773 surveyed a canal from collieries at Hurlet to Paisley, to be 3 miles long but no more was done.

River IDLE, Nottinghamshire. In the sixteenth century navigable from Bawtry, 10 miles to the Trent, the Idle had to wait until 1720 before it received an Act for improvement to extend to East Retford; but no work was done and the river lost traffic to the improved Don and later the Chesterfield Canal so the river was disused by 1828. The only real improvement was by Vermuyden in the early seventeenth century, who re-aligned it as part of his drainage schemes, while about 1760 a sluice was built at Misterton about 1 mile from Stockwith, incorporating a lock which limited river craft to 48' x 13' to 14' beam, carrying between 12 and 24 tons. As late as 1928 a little traffic was reported on the Idle, then open from Misson near Bawtry 8 miles down to Stockwith. Later a road bridge across the river's entrance into the Trent prevented boats going up and in 1937 the Trent Catchment Board made a sluice just inside the entrance.

INVERARNAN CANAL, Dumbartonshire. A $\frac{1}{4}$ mile canal off the River Falloch at the head of Loch Lomond to the inn at Inverarnan, this is still in existence and was used by the Loch Lomond steamers.

IPSWICH & STOWMARKET NAVIGATION (RIVER GIPPING), Suffolk. The Gipping joins the Orwell above Ipswich. It was navigable to Stowmarket in the Middle Ages; Caen stone came up for the abbey at Bury St. Edmunds. The river was still used in the seventeenth century but no serious improvements were undertaken until the Act of 1790 appointed six trustees to administer the newly created Ipswich & Stowmarket Navigation Co. There had been moves towards improvement up to Stowmarket since the early eighteenth century, always blocked by Ipswich Corporation, fearful of their own trade. 15 locks were now made and numerous cuts across bends in the $15\frac{7}{8}$ miles between Ipswich and Stowmarket. Three of the locks were of timber, the remainder brick or stone, all for craft 55' x 14'. William Jessop was consulted about the junction with the Orwell and John Rennie reported on the works in 1792. A further Act had to be passed in 1793 to raise more money and the navigation was not completely finished until 1798, having suffered flood damage in 1796. A plan of 1790 for a canal from Stowmarket to Bury St. Edmunds came to nothing. Traffic grew from modest beginnings, and in a few years 30 to 40 barges were at work. In 1846 the Navigation leased their river to the Ipswich & Bury St. Edmunds Railway which followed the valley of the Gipping. Barge traffic fell away and in 1888 the railway lease, by then to the Great Eastern, ran out. The old company resumed control but by 1900 there were few traders. Manure to Stowmarket was one latter day cargo, another gun cotton from the explosives works below the town. Of greater importance was the traffic in fertilizer, raw materials from Ipswich docks up to works at Bramford handled by Fison's and Packard's (52). They had steam barges capable of towing two dumb craft. Both firms undertook lock maintenance and weed clearance up to Bramford four miles above Ipswich. Fison's gave up in the 1920s and Packard's in 1930. In 1929 the navigation company had wound up their affairs and in 1932 the river was transferred to the East Suffolk Rivers Catchment Board, later the East Suffolk & Norfolk River Board, whose main concern was drainage and pollution. There has been no traffic since the 1930s.

ISLE OF DOGS CANAL, London. Between Limehouse and Blackwall the Thames makes a loop to the south by Greenwich, almost surrounding the so called Isle of Dogs. A canal across the top of the Isle would save sailing ships and was mooted in 1771. In 1799 the Government authorized a ship canal under the West India Docks Act to be 900 yd long and 6' deep, protected by flood locks at each end. This was to be built by the City of London with public money. Cutting took a long time, the canal not being opened until the end of 1805. Financially it was a failure, no tolls were charged at first to encourage use but when they were, few ships used the cut. The advent of steam made it unnecessary. In 1829 the City sold the canal to the West India Dock Co and it became part of the South West India Dock.

River ITCHEN, Hampshire. Although navigable in the Middle Ages from Alresford to Southampton, the Itchen decayed and was not revived until an Act of 1664-5. As completed about 1710 the navigation was $10\frac{3}{8}$ miles long from Winchester to Woodmill on the estuary, with 15 pound locks, 12 of them turf sided, for craft 72' x 13' and two half locks. At Woodmill there was a tide lock while the proprietors built wharves down the estuary at Northam. The Itchen was involved in several schemes, first an Act in 1795 to canalize the river from Woodmill to Northam, then ideas to join the Itchen to the Basingstoke Canal in 1796. The Basingstoke Canal took much of the traffic and by 1840, when the London & Southampton Railway was opened, trade was very low, although the last tolls were not taken until 1869.

River IVEL, Bedfordshire. The Ivel joins the Great Ouse at Tempsford and in 1756 there was local pressure to make it navigable to Biggleswade, authorized by an Act of 1757. Commissioners were appointed to manage the navigation and work began on the 7 miles from Tempsford to Biggleswade. Five pound locks were built with 110' x 12' chambers plus one horizontal swinging gate type staunch like those on the Great Ouse. The improvements were completed in 1758 and gangs of lighters brought modest returns. Coal, iron, timber and farm produce were the main cargoes and funds were put aside for the authorized extensions to Shefford, Baldock and up the Hiz to Hitchin. The canal age brought ideas to join with the Grand Junction at Fenny Stratford or the Lee at Hertford, but Shefford pressed for a navigation from Biggleswade, and Benjamin Bevan made a survey and estimate in 1807, but the commissioners thought the expense unjustified. Later it was revived, with Francis Giles making a survey. Work started in 1819, the Ivel being improved up to Langford whence a canal was cut to Shefford, some 3 miles from the river. Five more locks were made, the same size as the others, and in 1823 the extension was opened, the navigation now extending 6 miles from Biggleswade, and 13 from Tempsford. At the same time there were ideas of extending to Hitchin with a canal on to Hertford, but both were too expensive. For the Ivel modest prosperity continued, dependent on the needs and produce of a rural community, but succumbed to the railways which served the district, the navigation closing in 1876.

River KENNET, River AVON, KENNET & AVON CANAL.

River Avon, Somerset. Tidal up to Hanham Mills $14\frac{1}{2}$ miles above Avonmouth, the Avon has been used by ships since the Middle Ages. Powers were granted to Bath Corporation in 1619 to improve the river to that town, but laid aside until 1712 when a Bill was passed for river improvement. Work was delayed by local opposition until 1724 when control passed to a group of proprietors. The work, completed in 1727, with John Hore as engineer, had six locks in the $11\frac{1}{2}$ miles from Hanham to Bath. Passenger wherries were immediately put on between Bath and Bristol. From 1796 control passed to the Kennet & Avon Canal.

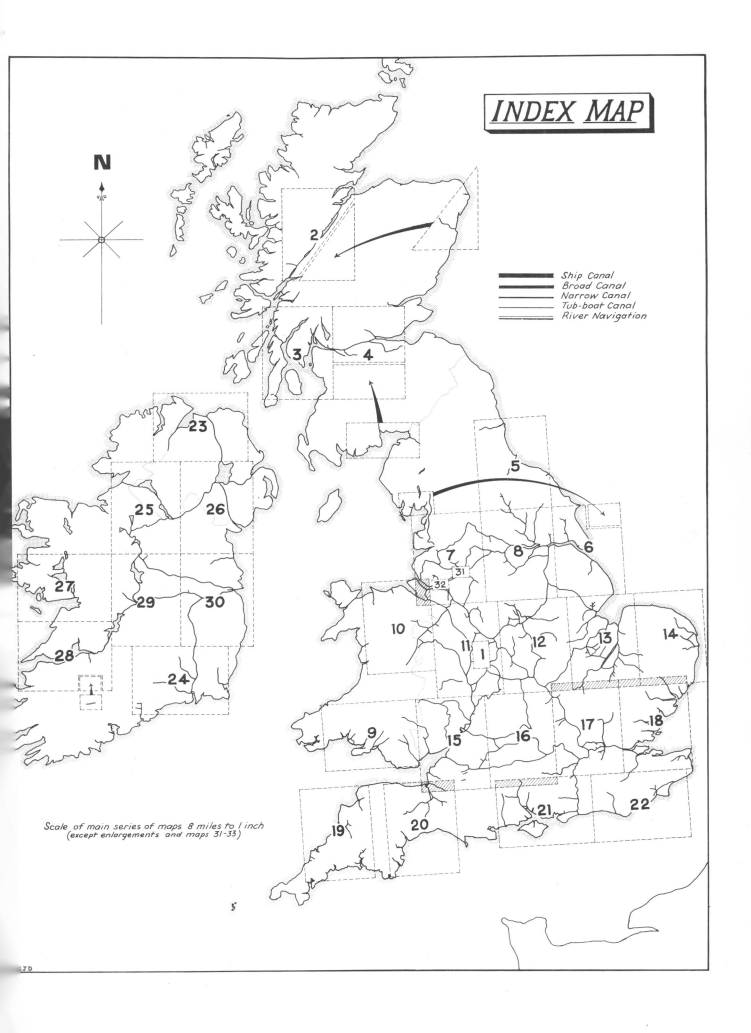

INDEX MAP

N

Ship Canal
Broad Canal
Narrow Canal
Tub-boat Canal
River Navigation

2

3   4

5

23

25   26

27   7   31   8   6

29   30   32

10

28   11   1   12   13   14

24

9   17   18

15   16

19   20   21   22

Scale of main series of maps 8 miles to 1 inch
(except enlargements and maps 31-33)

JD

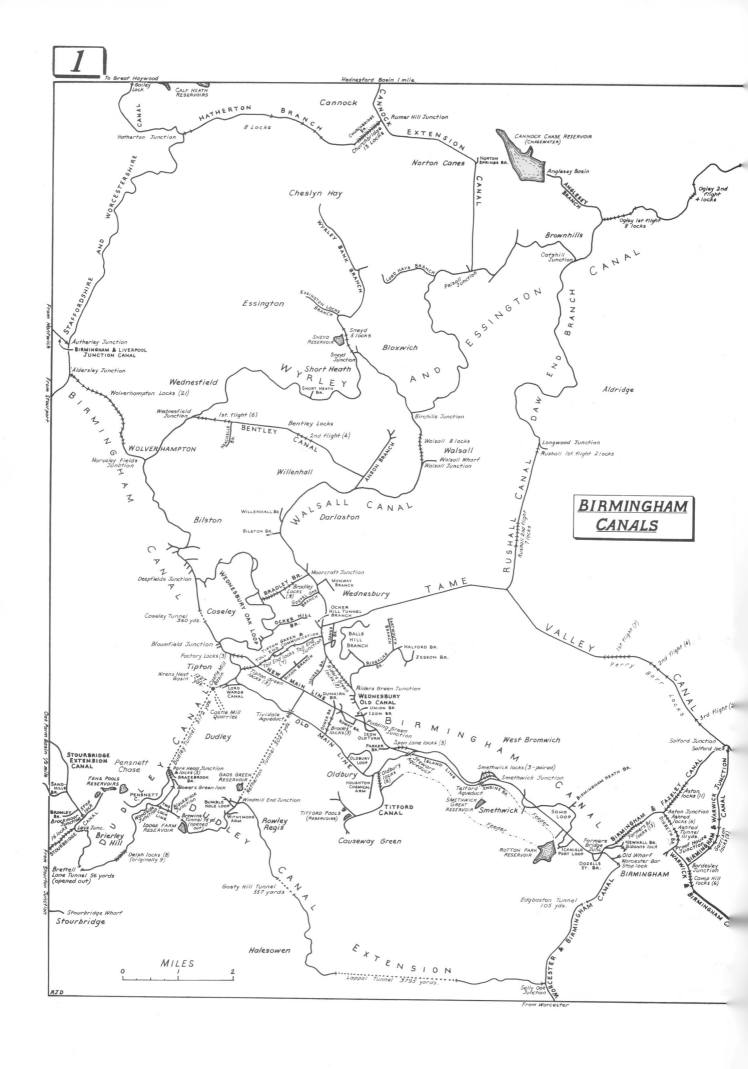

1

To Great Haywood

Gailey Lock

Calf Heath Reservoirs

Hednesford Basin 1 mile

Cannock

HATHERTON BRANCH

Hatherton Junction

8 Locks

CANNOCK EXTENSION

Churchbridge Br.
Churchbridge 13 locks

Rumer Hill Junction

Norton Springs Br.

CANAL

Norton Canes

Cannock Chase Reservoir (Chasewater)

Anglesey Basin

Cheslyn Hay

ANGLESEY BRANCH

Ogley 2nd flight 4 locks

Ogley 1st flight 8 locks

Brownhills

Catshill Junction

STAFFORDSHIRE AND WORCESTERSHIRE

Essington

WYRLEY BANK BRANCH

Lord Hays Branch

Pelsall Junction

DAW END BRANCH CANAL

Aldridge

From Nantwich

Autherley Junction
BIRMINGHAM & LIVERPOOL JUNCTION CANAL

Aldersley Junction

Wednesfield

Essington Locks Branch

Sneyd Reservoir

Sneyd 5 locks

Sneyd Junction

Short Heath

Short Heath Br.

Bloxwich

AND ESSINGTON

From Stourport

BIRMINGHAM

Wolverhampton Locks (21)

Wednesfield Junction

1st flight (6)

WYRLEY

Bentley Locks

2nd flight (4)

Mitchells Br.

BENTLEY CANAL

Birchills Junction

Walsall 8 locks

Walsall Wharf
Walsall Junction

Longwood Junction

Rushall 1st flight 2 locks

WOLVERHAMPTON

Horseley Fields Junction

Willenhall

ANSON BRANCH

Walsall

RUSHALL CANAL

Rushall 2nd flight 7 locks

CANAL

Bilston

Willenhall Br.

Bilston Br.

WALSALL CANAL

Darlaston

Wednesbury

TAME

BIRMINGHAM CANALS

Deepfields Junction

WEDNESBURY OAK LOOP

BRADLEY BR.

Bradley Locks (9)

Gospel Oak Branch

Moorcroft Junction

MONWAY BRANCH

VALLEY

Coseley Tunnel 360 yds.

Coseley

OCKER HILL BR.

Ocker Hill Tunnel Branch

DARTMOUTH BRANCH

1st flight (7)

CANAL

Bloomfield Junction

Factory Locks (3)

Tipton

Wrens Nest Basin

Dudley Tunnel 3172 yds.

TOLL END
TOLL END COMMUNICATION
Toll End locks (8)
Toll End Junction

DIXON BRANCH

HAINES BR.

DUNKIRK BR.

RIDGACRE BR.

BALLS HILL BRANCH

Halford Br.

Jesson Br.

2nd flight (4)

Perry

Barr locks

3rd flight (2)

Castle Mill Basin

LORD WARDS CANAL

Tipton Green locks (3)

BOWEN BR.
Brades locks (3)

ROWAY BR.

Riders Green Junction

WEDNESBURY OLD CANAL

Union Br.

IZON BR.

Salford Junction

Salford Lock

Castle Mill Quarries

Tividale Aqueduct

Netherton Tunnel 3027 yds.

Dudley

OLD MAIN LINE

NEW MAIN LINE

DUDLEY CANAL

Park Head Junction & locks (3)
GRAZEBROOK BR.

GADS GREEN RESERVOIR

Blowers Green lock

Tipton Green locks

PARKER BR.

Pudding Green Junction

IZON OLD TURN

Spon Lane locks (3)

West Bromwich

Island Line

Steward Aqueduct

Smethwick locks (3-paired)

BIRMINGHAM CANAL

Birmingham Heath Br.

Aston locks (11)

WARWICK CANAL

STOURBRIDGE EXTENSION CANAL

Pensnett Chase

FENS POOLS RESERVOIRS

SAND-HILLS BR.

BROMLEY BR.

Brockmoor Junction

16 locks

STOURBRIDGE CANAL

Leys Junc.

PENSNETT C.

Woodside Lock Line

Blackbrook Br.

LODGE FARM RESERVOIR

Brierley Hill

Delph locks (8)
(originally 9)

DUDLEY CANAL

Brewins Tunnel 78 yds. (opened out)

WITHYMOOR ARM

Bumble Hole Loop

Windmill End Junction

Rowley Regis

TITFORD POOLS (RESERVOIRS)

Oldbury Loop

HOUGHTON CHEMICAL ARM

Oldbury

Oldbury locks (6)

TITFORD CANAL

Causeway Green

Telford Aqueduct

SMETHWICK GREAT RESERVOIR

Smethwick Junction

Smethwick

Feeder

Soho Loop

Feeder

ROTTON PARK RESERVOIR

Farmers Bridge Junc.

NEWHALL BR.
Gibsons lock

Old Wharf
Worcester Bar Stop lock

Icknield St. Br.

Oozells St. Br.

BIRMINGHAM

ENGINE BR.

Farmers Br. locks (13)

Digbeth Br.

BIRMINGHAM & FAZELEY CANAL

Aston Junction

Ashted locks (6)

Ashted Tunnel 111 yds.

Proof House Junction

Garrison locks (5)

Bordesley Junction

Camp Hill locks (6)

WARWICK & BIRMINGHAM C.

From Stour Junction

Oak Farm Basin 1/2 mile

Stop lock

STOURBRIDGE CANAL

Brettell Lane Tunnel 56 yards (opened out)

Stourbridge Wharf

Stourbridge

Halesowen

GOSTY HILL Tunnel 557 yards

DUDLEY EXTENSION CANAL

Edgbaston Tunnel 105 yds.

Lappal Tunnel 3795 yards

WORCESTER & BIRMINGHAM CANAL

Selly Oak Junction

From Worcester

MILES

0   1   2

RJD

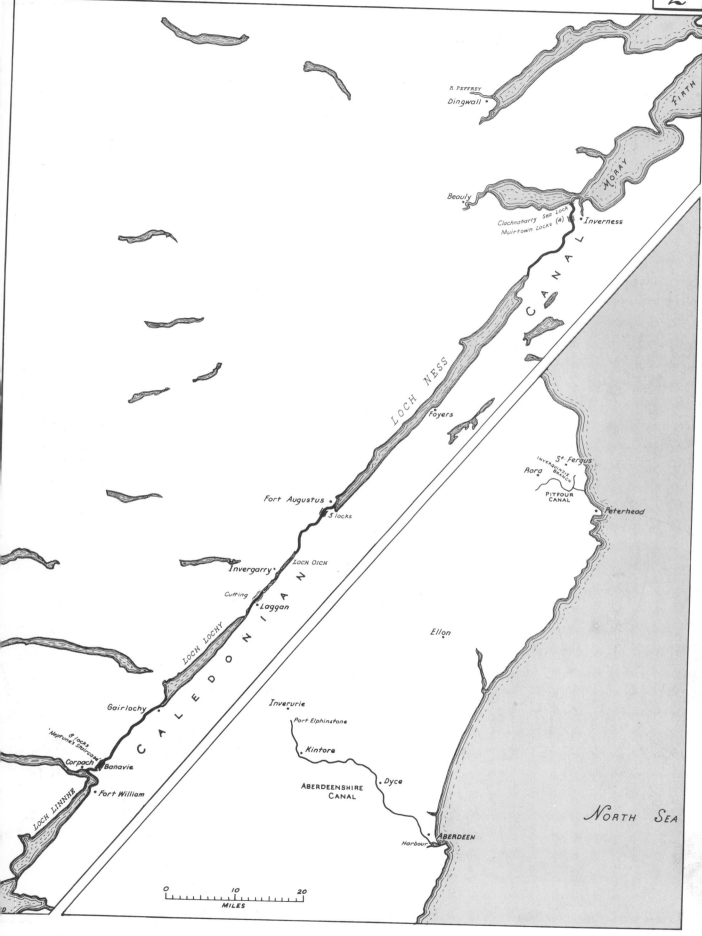

2

R. PEFFREY
Dingwall

FIRTH

Beauly

MORAY

Clachnaharry Sea Lock (★)   Inverness
Muirtown Locks (★)

CALEDONIAN CANAL

LOCH NESS

Foyers

St. Fergus
Aora
INVERQUINZIE BRANCH
PITFOUR CANAL
Peterhead

Fort Augustus
5 locks

LOCH OICH
Invergarry

Ellon

Cutting
Laggan

LOCH LOCHY

Inverurie

Gairlochy
Port Elphinstone

8 locks
'Neptune's Staircase'
Kintore

Corpach   Banavie
Dyce
ABERDEENSHIRE
CANAL

LOCH LINNHE   Fort William

NORTH SEA

Harbour   ABERDEEN

0   10   20
MILES

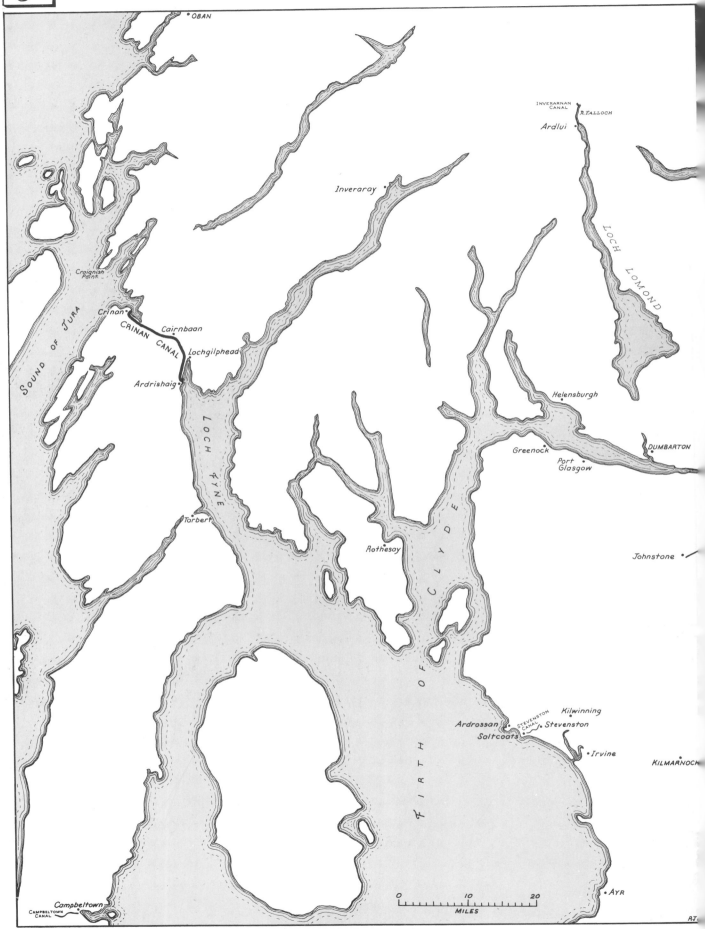

3

• OBAN

INVERARNAN
CANAL
Ardlui • • R. FALLOCH

LOCH LOMOND

Inveraray •

Craignish
Point •

Crinan • CRINAN CANAL Cairnbaan •
Lochgilphead

Ardrishaig •

SOUND OF JURA

LOCH FYNE

Helensburgh •

Greenock •
Port
Glasgow •
DUMBARTON •

Torbert •

Rothesay •

Johnstone • —

FIRTH OF CLYDE

Kilwinning •
STEVENSTON
CANAL
Ardrossan • • Stevenston
Saltcoats •

Irvine •

KILMARNOCH •

Campbeltown •
CAMPBELTOWN
CANAL •

0   10   20

MILES

• AYR

AJ

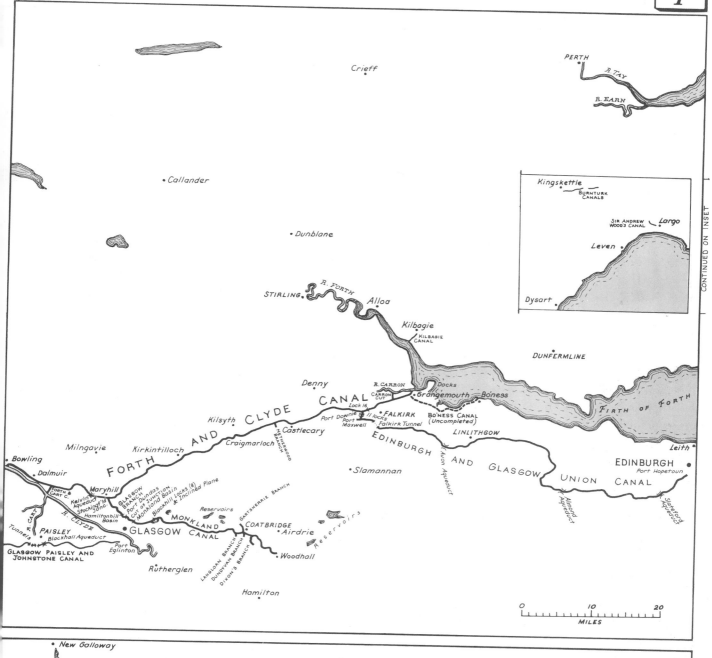

PERTH

R. TAY

R. EARN

• Crieff

• Callander

CONTINUED ON INSET

Kingskettle •
BURNTURK CANALS

SIR ANDREW WOOD'S CANAL   Largo

Leven •

Dysart •

• Dunblane

STIRLING •   R. FORTH   Alloa •

Kilbagie •
KILBAGIE CANAL

DUNFERMLINE

FIRTH OF FORTH

Denny •   R. CARRON   Docks
CARRON CUT   Grangemouth   Boness

Lock 16   CARRON CUT
FORTH   AND   CLYDE   CANAL

Kilsyth •   Port Downie 11 locks
Port Maxwell   FALKIRK   Falkirk Tunnel

Bo'NESS CANAL
(Uncompleted)

Milngavie •   Kirkintilloch •   Craigmarloch •   Castlecary •
NETHERWOOD BRANCH

LINLITHGOW

EDINBURGH   AND   GLASGOW   UNION   CANAL

LEITH

Bowling •
• Dalmuir

FORTH & CART C.
Kelvin Aqueduct
Stockingfield   Maryhill •
GLASGOW BRANCH
Port Dundas
Cut of Junction
Monkland Basin
Blackhill Locks (8)
Blackhill Inclined Plane

• Slamannan

Avon Aqueduct

Almond Aqueduct

EDINBURGH
Port Hopetoun

Slateford Aqueduct

R. CART
Hamiltonhill Basin

Reservoirs

MONKLAND   CANAL

GARTSHERRIE BRANCH

Tunnels   PAISLEY •
Blackhall Aqueduct

GLASGOW   CANAL

COATBRIDGE •   Airdrie •

Reservoirs

R. CLYDE

Port Eglinton

GLASGOW PAISLEY AND
JOHNSTONE CANAL

Rutherglen •
LANGLOAN BRANCH
DUNDYVAN BRANCH
DIXON'S BRANCH   • Woodhall

• Hamilton

0   10   20
MILES

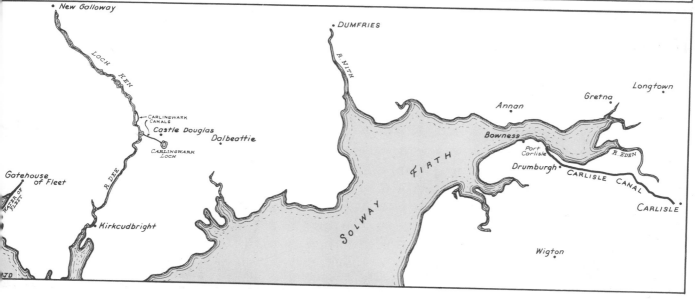

• New Galloway

• DUMFRIES

R. NITH

LOCH KEN

Longtown •

Annan •   Gretna •

CARLINGWARK CANALS

Castle Douglas •   Dalbeattie •

CARLINGWARK LOCH

Bowness •
Port Carlisle
R. EDEN

R. DEE

Gatehouse of Fleet •

Drumburgh   CARLISLE CANAL

CARLISLE

• Kirkcudbright

SOLWAY   FIRTH

• Wigton

JD

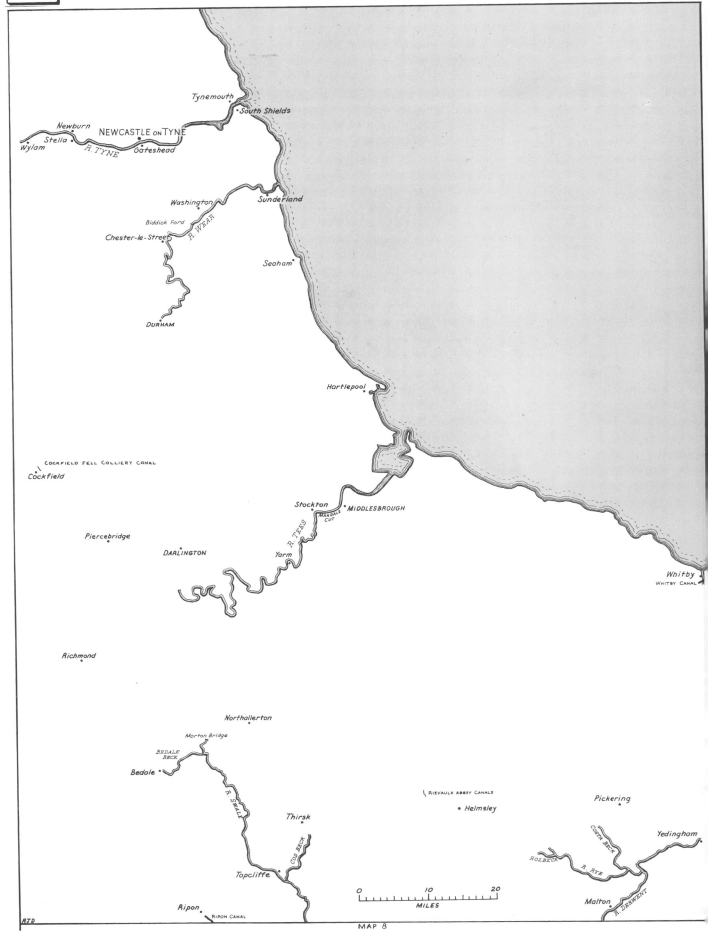

5

Tynemouth
•South Shields
Newburn
NEWCASTLE ON TYNE
Stella•
Wylam•   Gateshead
R. TYNE

Washington•   Sunderland
Biddick Ford•
Chester-le-Street•   R. WEAR
Seaham•
DURHAM

Hartlepool

COCKFIELD FELL COLLIERY CANAL
Cockfield•

Stockton   •MIDDLESBROUGH
MANDALE CUT
Piercebridge•   R. TEES
DARLINGTON   Yarm
Whitby•
WHITBY CANAL

Richmond

Northallerton
Morton Bridge
BEDALE BECK
Bedale•
RIEVAULX ABBEY CANALS   Pickering
R. SWALE   •Helmsley
Thirsk•   COSTA BECK   Yedingham
COD BECK
HOLBECK   R. RYE
Topcliffe
0   10   20
MILES
Ripon•   Malton   R. DERWENT
RIPON CANAL

RJD   MAP 8

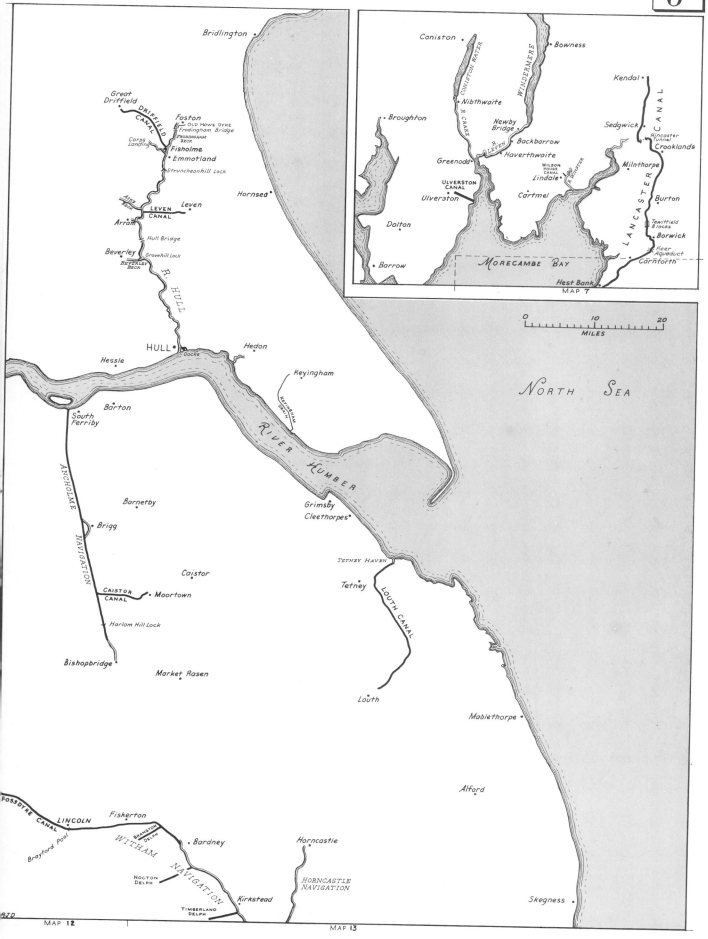

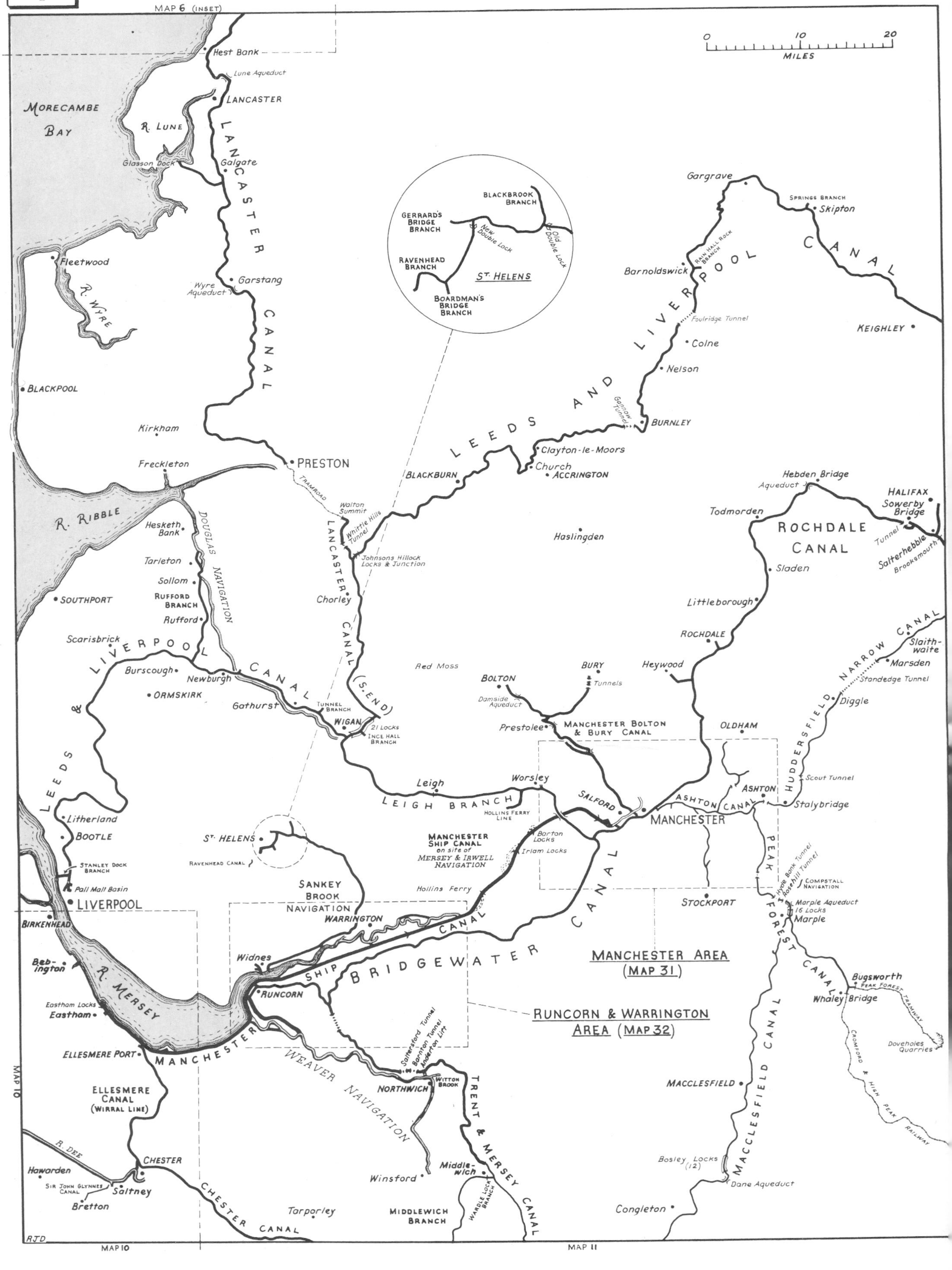

MAP 6 (INSET)

0   10   20
MILES

MORECAMBE BAY

R. LUNE

Hest Bank
Lune Aqueduct
LANCASTER
Galgate
Glasson Dock

LANCASTER CANAL

Fleetwood

R. WYRE

Wyre Aqueduct
Garstang

BLACKPOOL

Kirkham

Freckleton

PRESTON

Tramroad
Walton Summit
Whittle Hills Tunnel
Johnsons Hillock Locks & Junction

BLACKBURN

Clayton-le-Moors
Church
ACCRINGTON

Haslingden

Red Moss

BOLTON

BURY
Tunnels

Heywood

LEEDS AND LIVERPOOL CANAL

Gargrave
SPRINGS BRANCH
Skipton

Barnoldswick
RAIN HALL ROCK BRANCH

Foulridge Tunnel
Colne
Nelson

Gannow Tunnel
BURNLEY

KEIGHLEY

Hebden Bridge
Aqueduct Jc.
HALIFAX
Sowerby Bridge

Todmorden

ROCHDALE CANAL

Tunnel
Salterhebble
Brooksmouth

Sladen

Littleborough

ROCHDALE

INSET:
GERRARD'S BRIDGE BRANCH
BLACKBROOK BRANCH
New Double Lock
Old Double Lock
RAVENHEAD BRANCH
ST. HELENS
BOARDMAN'S BRIDGE BRANCH

Slaithwaite
Marsden
Standedge Tunnel
Diggle

HUDDERSFIELD NARROW CANAL

Scout Tunnel

Prestolee
Damside Aqueduct
MANCHESTER BOLTON & BURY CANAL

OLDHAM

Leigh
Worsley

LEIGH BRANCH

SALFORD
ASHTON CANAL
MANCHESTER
ASHTON
Stalybridge

St. HELENS

Hollins Ferry Line

Barton Locks
Irlam Locks

MANCHESTER SHIP CANAL on site of MERSEY & IRWELL NAVIGATION

STOCKPORT

Ince Bank Tunnel
Woodhill Tunnel
COMPSTALL NAVIGATION
Marple Aqueduct
16 Locks
Marple

PEAK FOREST CANAL

LEEDS & LIVERPOOL CANAL

Scarisbrick
Burscough
Newburgh
ORMSKIRK
Gathurst
WIGAN
TUNNEL BRANCH
21 Locks
INCE HALL BRANCH

Litherland
BOOTLE

Ravenhead Canal

SANKEY BROOK NAVIGATION

WARRINGTON

Widnes

Hollins Ferry

MANCHESTER AREA (MAP 31)

RUNCORN & WARRINGTON AREA (MAP 32)

Bugsworth
PEAK FOREST TRAMWAY
Whaley Bridge

STANLEY DOCK BRANCH
Pall Mall Basin
LIVERPOOL

BIRKENHEAD
Bebington

R. MERSEY

MANCHESTER SHIP CANAL

BRIDGEWATER CANAL

RUNCORN

Eastham Locks
Eastham

ELLESMERE PORT

WEAVER NAVIGATION

Saltersford Tunnel
Barnton Tunnel
Anderton Lift

NORTHWICH
Witton Brook

TRENT & MERSEY CANAL

MACCLESFIELD CANAL

MACCLESFIELD

Doveholes Quarries

CROMFORD & HIGH PEAK RAILWAY

ELLESMERE CANAL (WIRRAL LINE)

R. DEE

Hawarden
SIR JOHN GLYNNE'S CANAL
Saltney
Bretton

CHESTER

CHESTER CANAL

Tarporley

Winsford
Middlewich
WARDLE LOCK BRANCH

MIDDLEWICH BRANCH

Congleton

Bosley Locks (12)
Dane Aqueduct

MAP 10

MAP 10

MAP 11

MAP 11

RJD

R. RIBBLE

Hesketh Bank
Tarleton
Sollom
RUFFORD BRANCH
Rufford

SOUTHPORT

DOUGLAS NAVIGATION

LANCASTER CANAL (S. END)

Chorley

LIVERPOOL CANAL

SOUTHPORT

MAP 5

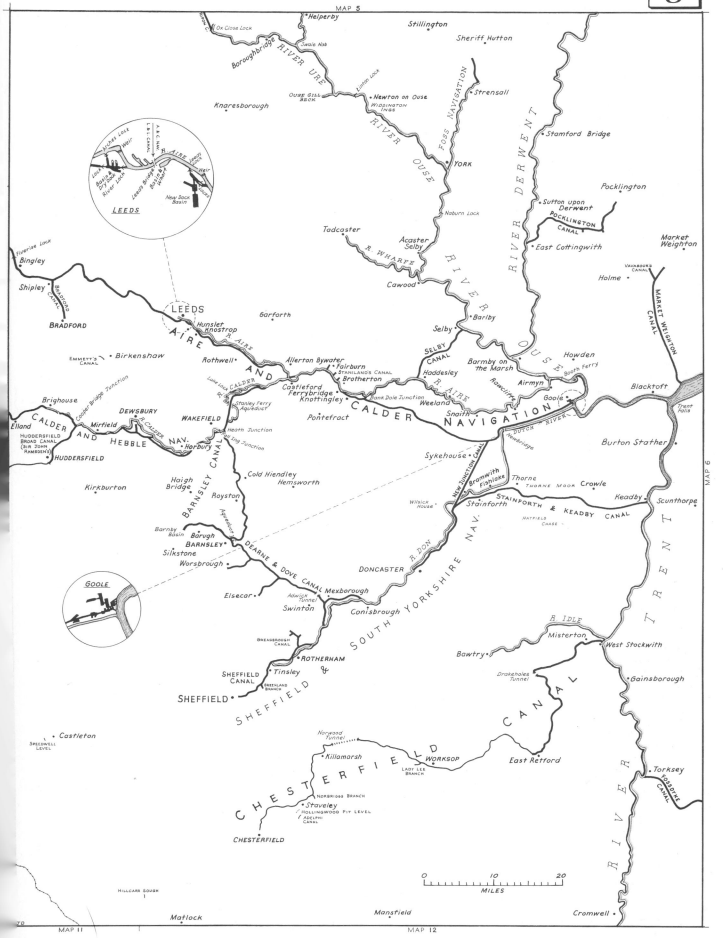

Helperby

Stillington

Sheriff Hutton

Ox Close Lock

Boroughbridge

RIVER URE

Swale Nab

Strensall

Newton on Ouse

Knaresborough

Ouse Gill Beck

Linton Lock

Widdington Ings

Stamford Bridge

Pocklington

Sutton upon Derwent

POCKLINGTON CANAL

East Cottingwith

Market Weighton

RIVER DERWENT

York

RIVER OUSE

FOSS NAVIGATION

Naburn Lock

Tadcaster

Acaster Selby

R. WHARFE

Cawood

Holme

VAVASOUR'S CANAL

MARKET WEIGHTON CANAL

LEEDS

Arches Lock

Weir

Lock

Basin & Dry Dock

River Lock

A.&C. NAV.

L.&L. CANAL

R. AIRE

Leeds Lock

Leeds Bridge

Basin & Wharf

Weir

Leeds Dock

New Dock Basin

Fiverise Lock

Bingley

Shipley

BRADFORD CANAL

BRADFORD

LEEDS

Hunslet

Knostrop

R. AIRE

AIRE AND

Garforth

Rothwell

Allerton Bywater

Fairburn

Staniland's Canal

Brotherton

Selby

Barlby

SELBY CANAL

Haddesley

Barmby on the Marsh

Howden

Booth Ferry

Airmyn

Rawcliffe

Goole

Blacktoft

Trent Falls

EMMETT'S CANAL

Birkenshaw

Lake Lock

CALDER

Castleford

Ferrybridge

Knottingley

Bank Dole Junction

Weeland

R. AIRE

Snaith

CALDER NAVIGATION

DUTCH RIVER

Brighouse

Cooper Bridge Junction

Mirfield

DEWSBURY

R. CALDER

WAKEFIELD

Stanley Ferry Aqueduct

Pontefract

Elland

CALDER AND HEBBLE NAV.

HUDDERSFIELD BROAD CANAL (SIR JOHN RAMSDEN'S)

HUDDERSFIELD

Horbury

Heath Junction

Fall Ing Junction

Newbridge

Burton Stather

MAP 6

Sykehouse

NEW JUNCTION CANAL

Bramwith

Fishlake

Thorne

THORNE MOOR

Crowle

Keadby

Scunthorpe

Kirkburton

Haigh Bridge

Cold Hiendley

Hemsworth

BARNSLEY CANAL

Royston

Wilsick House

Stainforth

STAINFORTH & KEADBY CANAL

HATFIELD CHASE

Aqueduct

Barnby Basin

Barugh

BARNSLEY

Silkstone

Worsbrough

DEARNE & DOVE CANAL

Mexborough

R. DON

DONCASTER

SOUTH YORKSHIRE NAV.

GOOLE

Elsecar

Adwick Tunnel

Swinton

Conisbrough

R. IDLE

Misterton

West Stockwith

GREASBROUGH CANAL

ROTHERHAM

Bawtry

SHEFFIELD CANAL

Tinsley

GREENLAND BRANCH

SHEFFIELD

SHEFFIELD

Drakeholes Tunnel

Gainsborough

Castleton

SPEEDWELL LEVEL

Norwood Tunnel

Killamarsh

Lady Lee Branch

WORKSOP

East Retford

CHESTERFIELD CANAL

Torksey

FOSSDYKE CANAL

Norbriggs Branch

Staveley

HOLLINGWOOD PIT LEVEL

ADELPHI CANAL

RIVER TRENT

CHESTERFIELD

0   10   20

MILES

HILLCARR SOUGH

Matlock

Mansfield

Cromwell

MAP 11   MAP 12

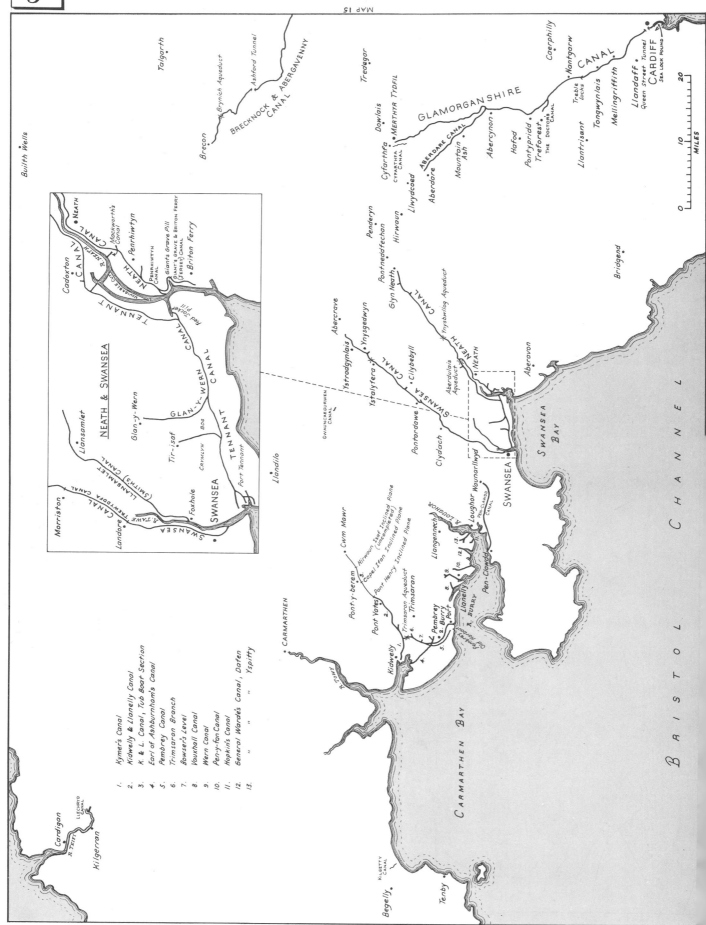

MAP 15

CARDIFF
Sea Lock Pound
Queen Street Tunnel
Llandaff
Mellingriffith
Tongwynlais
Nantgarw
Coerphilly
Treble Locks
Llantrisant
THE DOCTOR'S CANAL
Pontypridd
Treforest
ABERDARE CANAL
Abercynon
Hofod
Mountain Ash
Aberdare
CYFARTHFA CANAL
Cyfarthfa
Dowlais
MERTHYR TYDFIL
Tredegar
GLAMORGANSHIRE
CANAL

BRECKNOCK & ABERGAVENNY CANAL
Brynich Aqueduct
Ashford Tunnel
Brecon
Talgarth
Builth Wells

Penderyn
Hirwaun
Pontneddfechan
Llwydcoed
Glyn Neath
Ynysbwllog Aqueduct
NEATH
Abercrave
Ynysgedwyn
NEATH CANAL
Abergulais Aqueduct
NEATH
Aberavon
Ystradgynlais
Ystalyfera
Clydach
SWANSEA BAY
GWAUN-CAE-GURWEN CANAL
Cilybebyll
Pontardawe
Clydach
SWANSEA

Llandilo

NEATH & SWANSEA

Neath
Mackworth's Canal
Penrhiwtyn
Cadoxton
PENRHIWTYN CANAL
Giant's Grave Pill
GIANT'S GRAVE & BRITON FERRY (JERSEY) CANAL
Briton Ferry
Red Jacket Pill
Liansamlet
GLAN-Y-WERN CANAL
Glan-y-Wern
Tir-isaf
CRYMLYN BOG
Foxhole
Port Tennant
SWANSEA
Morriston
Landore
R. TAWE TREWYDDFA CANAL
CANAL
LLANSAMLET (SMITHS) CANAL

CARMARTHEN

Cwm Mawr
Pont-y-berem
Hirwaun Isaf Inclined Plane
Capel Ifan Inclined Plane (Uncompleted)
Pont Henry Inclined Plane
Pont Yates
Trimsaran Aqueduct
Trimsaran
R. TOWY
Kidwelly
Pembrey
Burry Port
Pen-Clawdd
R. BURRY
Llanelly
R. LOUGHOR
Llangennech
Loughor
Gorseinon
Wounarllwyd
PENCLAWDD CANAL
8. 9. 10. 11. 12. 13.

CARMARTHEN BAY

BRISTOL CHANNEL

Begelly
Tenby
KILGETTY CANAL

Cardigan
R. TEIFI
LLECHRYD CANAL
Kilgerran

Bridgend

1. Kymer's Canal
2. Kidwelly & Llanelly Canal
3. K & L. Canal, Tub Boat Section
4. Earl of Ashburnham's Canal
5. Pembrey Canal
6. Trimsaran Branch
7. Bowser's Level
8. Vauxhall Canal
9. Wern Canal
10. Pen-y-Fan Canal
11. Hopkin's Canal
12. General Warde's Canal, Dafen
13. " " " Yspitty

0   10   20
MILES

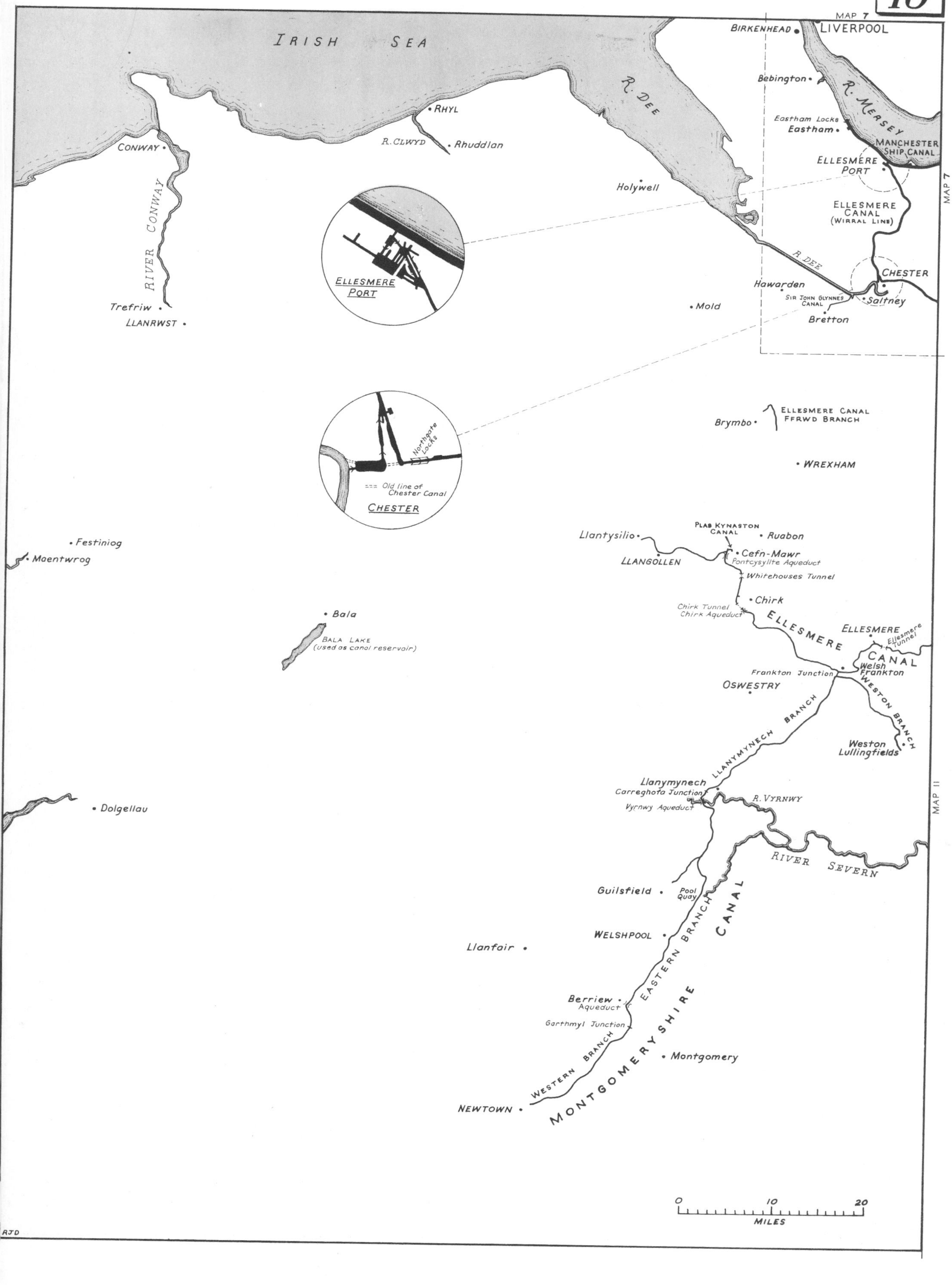

MAP 7

10

IRISH SEA

R. DEE

R. MERSEY

BIRKENHEAD •
LIVERPOOL

Bebington •

Eastham Locks
Eastham •
MANCHESTER SHIP CANAL

• RHYL

Rhuddlan •

R. CLWYD

ELLESMERE PORT

ELLESMERE CANAL (WIRRAL LINE)

CONWAY •

Holywell •

R. DEE

Hawarden •
Sir John Glynnes Canal
CHESTER

Saltney •

Trefriw •

• Mold

LLANRWST •

Bretton •

RIVER CONWAY

ELLESMERE PORT

Northgate Locks

=== Old line of Chester Canal

CHESTER

Brymbo •
Ellesmere Canal Ffrwd Branch

• WREXHAM

• Festiniog

Moentwrog •

Llantysilio •
Plas Kynaston Canal
• Ruabon

LLANGOLLEN
• Cefn-Mawr
Pontcysyllte Aqueduct
Whitehouses Tunnel

• Chirk
Chirk Tunnel
Chirk Aqueduct

ELLESMERE

ELLESMERE
Ellesmere Tunnel

CANAL

• Bala

BALA LAKE (used as canal reservoir)

Frankton Junction
Welsh Frankton

OSWESTRY

WESTON BRANCH

Weston Lullingfields •

LLANYMYNECH BRANCH

Llanymynech •
Carreghofa Junction
Vyrnwy Aqueduct

R. VYRNWY

• Dolgellau

RIVER SEVERN

Guilsfield •
Pool Quay

WELSHPOOL •

Llanfair •

EASTERN BRANCH

MONTGOMERYSHIRE CANAL

Berriew •
Aqueduct

Garthmyl Junction

WESTERN BRANCH

• Montgomery

NEWTOWN •

0   10   20
MILES

RJD

11

MAP 7   MAP 8

MACCLESFIELD CANAL
MEERBROOK SOUGH
CROMFORD & HIGH PEAK RAILWAY

CHESTER CANAL   MIDDLEWICH BRANCH
Barbridge Junction
Hurleston Junction   • CREWE
Hall Green Junction   • Leek
Pool Lock Aqueduct   Leek Tunnel
Hardings Wood Junct.   Kidsgrove   Leek Br.
Nantwich Basin   Harecastle New Tunnel
Harecastle Old Tunnel   Old line 5 locks (1766-1800)
New Junction   Bedford Aqueduct (1841)   Leek Br.
• Nantwich   THE POTTERIES   Old line & Staircase Lk.
Burslem   Main line & Staircase Lk. 1800-1841
ELLESMERE CANAL   Foxley Branch   1800-1841
Sir Nigel Gresley's Canal   R. CHURNET   HAZELHURST
• Audlem   Etruria   Hanley   Tunnel   WOODEAVES CANAL
BIRMINGHAM &   Newcastle Junction Canal   Froghall   Fenny Bentley
NEWCASTLE   • STOKE ON TRENT
• Whitchurch   NEWCASTLE UNDER LYME CANAL   • Ashbourne
• Longton   Alton Tunnel   Crumpwood Weir
R. CHURNET   UTTOXETER BRANCH
• Market Drayton   LIVERPOOL   • Meaford   Uttoxeter
• Stone
PREES BRANCH   • Prees   • Uttoxeter
Quina Brook Wharf
JUNCTION   Great Haywood Junction   Horninglow
BURTON on TRENT
• Norbury   STAFFORD   R. Sow   Shobnall
NEWPORT BRANCH   Norbury Junction   Baswich Bridge   Bond End Canal
Cowley Tunnel   • Rugeley   Tunnel   • Alrewas
• Newport   Armitage   Fradley Junc.   • Fradley
Hugh's Bridge Inclined Plane   Huddlesford Junction
Londgon   Pave Lane   Penkridge   COVENTRY CANAL
• HUMBER ARM   DONNINGTON WOOD CANAL   • Gailey   Hednesford Basin
Aqueduct   Lilleshall   Cannock •   • Lichfield   Whittington Brook Junction
Berwick Tunnel   Wappenshall Junction   SHROPSHIRE CANAL   • Tamworth
SHREWSBURY   • Wellington   STAFFORDSHIRE   WYRLEY & ESSINGTON CANAL   • Glascote
R. Severn   • Oakengates   Sutton Coldfield   • Fazeley
• Atcham   SHROPSHIRE CANAL   Autherley Junction   Aldersley Junction
Horsehay   • Shifnal   • WALSALL   Curdworth Tunnel
COALBROOKDALE BRANCH   Stirchley Tunnel   WOLVER-   BIRMINGHAM & FAZELEY CANAL
• Coalbrookdale   Windmill Inclined Plane   HAMPTON   BIRMINGHAM
Ironbridge   Hay Inclined Plane   CANALS MAP
• Coalport   Oak Farm Basin   Salford Junction
WORCESTERSHIRE   DUDLEY   MAIN LINE   BIRMINGHAM
WOMBRIDGE CANAL   Worcester Bar   • BIRMINGHAM
Trench Inclined Plane   Wrockwardine Wood Inclined Plane   STOUR-   WARWICK AND
SHROPSHIRE CANAL   BRIDGE   • STOURBRIDGE
Snedshill Tunnel   CANAL   Kings Norton Tunnel
KETLEY CANAL   • Oakengates   AND   • Bridgnorth   Dunsley Tunnel   SOLIHULL
Ketley Inclined Plane   Tunnel   EARDINGTON FORGE CANAL   STRATFORD
Stop Lock   Tunnel   Cookley Tunnel   • Kings Norton
RIVER SEVERN   West Hill Tunnel   BIRMINGHAM
• Ludlow   Arley   BITTALL ARM   • Kingswood
• KIDDERMINSTER   Kingswood Junction
• Bewdley   R. STOUR   • BROMSGROVE   Shortwood Tunnel   Lapworth   Shrewley Tunnel
• Mamble   Pratt's Wharf   Tardebigge   Tardebigge Tunnel   AVON
LEOMINSTER CANAL   Southnet Tunnel   STOURPORT   56 Locks   • REDDITCH
Rea Aqueduct   Newnham Tunnel   Pensax   Shorwood Tunnel   Yarningdale Aqueduct
• Tenbury   • Astley   DROITWICH   CANAL   Wootton Wawen   • Aqueduct
Teme Aqueduct   Dick Brook   JUNCTION CANAL
Putnal Field Tunnel   R. SALWARPE   Hanbury Wharf   Edstone Aqueduct   • Bearley
• Kingsland   Droitwich   WORCESTER AND   • Alcester
• LEOMINSTER   • Hawford   BIRMINGHAM CANAL   Dunhampstead Tunnel
R. Lugg   Bromyard   • WORCESTER   STRATFORD upon AVON
Diglis Basin   R. AVON
R. Teme   Powick Bridge
0   10   20
MILES

RJD

MAP 15   MAP 16

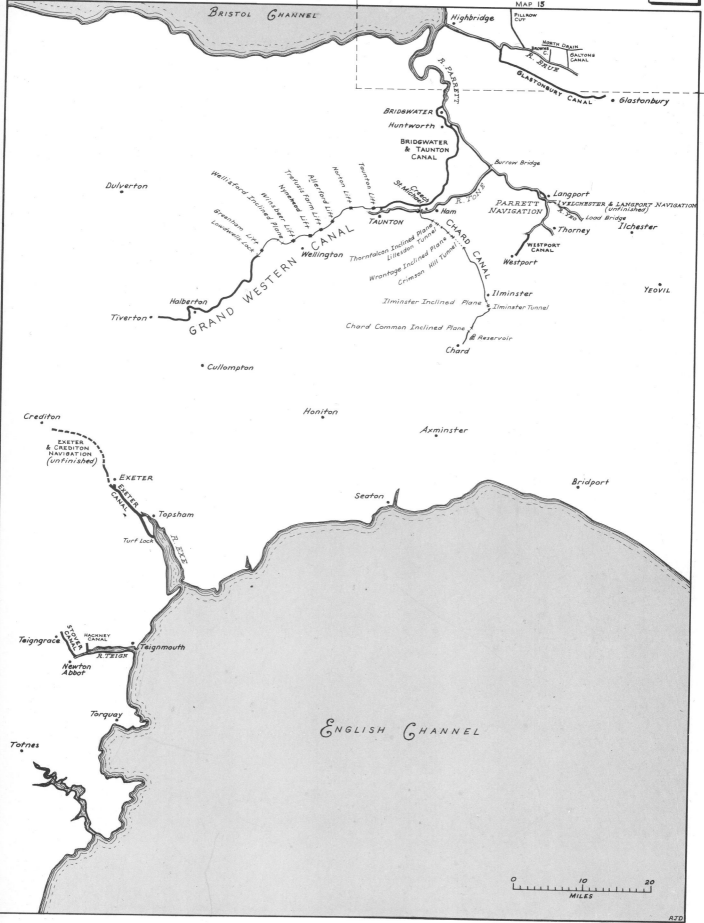

MAP 15

BRISTOL CHANNEL

Highbridge

PILLROW CUT

NORTH DRAIN

BROWNS C.

SALTONS CANAL

R. BRUE

GLASTONBURY CANAL

· Glastonbury

R. PARRETT

BRIDGWATER ·

Huntworth ·

BRIDGWATER & TAUNTON CANAL

Burrow Bridge

Dulverton ·

Wellisford Inclined Plane
Greenham Lift
Lowdwells Lock
Nynehead Lift
Winsbeer Lift
Trefusis Farm Lift
Allerford Lift
Norton Lift
Taunton Lift

GRAND WESTERN CANAL

Creech St. Michael

R. TONE

· Langport

IVELCHESTER & LANGPORT NAVIGATION (unfinished)

PARRETT NAVIGATION

R. Yeo

Load Bridge

· Ilchester

· Wellington

TAUNTON

· Ham

Thornfalcon Inclined Plane
Lillesdon Tunnel
Wrantage Inclined Plane
Crimson Hill Tunnel

CHARD CANAL

· Thorney

WESTPORT CANAL

· Westport

· YEOVIL

Halberton ·

Ilminster Inclined Plane

· Ilminster

Ilminster Tunnel

Tiverton ·

Chard Common Inclined Plane

Reservoir

· Chard

· Cullompton

· Honiton

· Axminster

Crediton ·

EXETER & CREDITON NAVIGATION (unfinished)

· EXETER

EXETER CANAL

· Bridport

· Topsham

Seaton ·

Turf Lock

R. EXE

Teigngrace ·

STOVER CANAL

HACKNEY CANAL

· Teignmouth

R. TEIGN

Newton Abbot

· Torquay

ENGLISH CHANNEL

Totnes ·

0   10   20
MILES

RJD

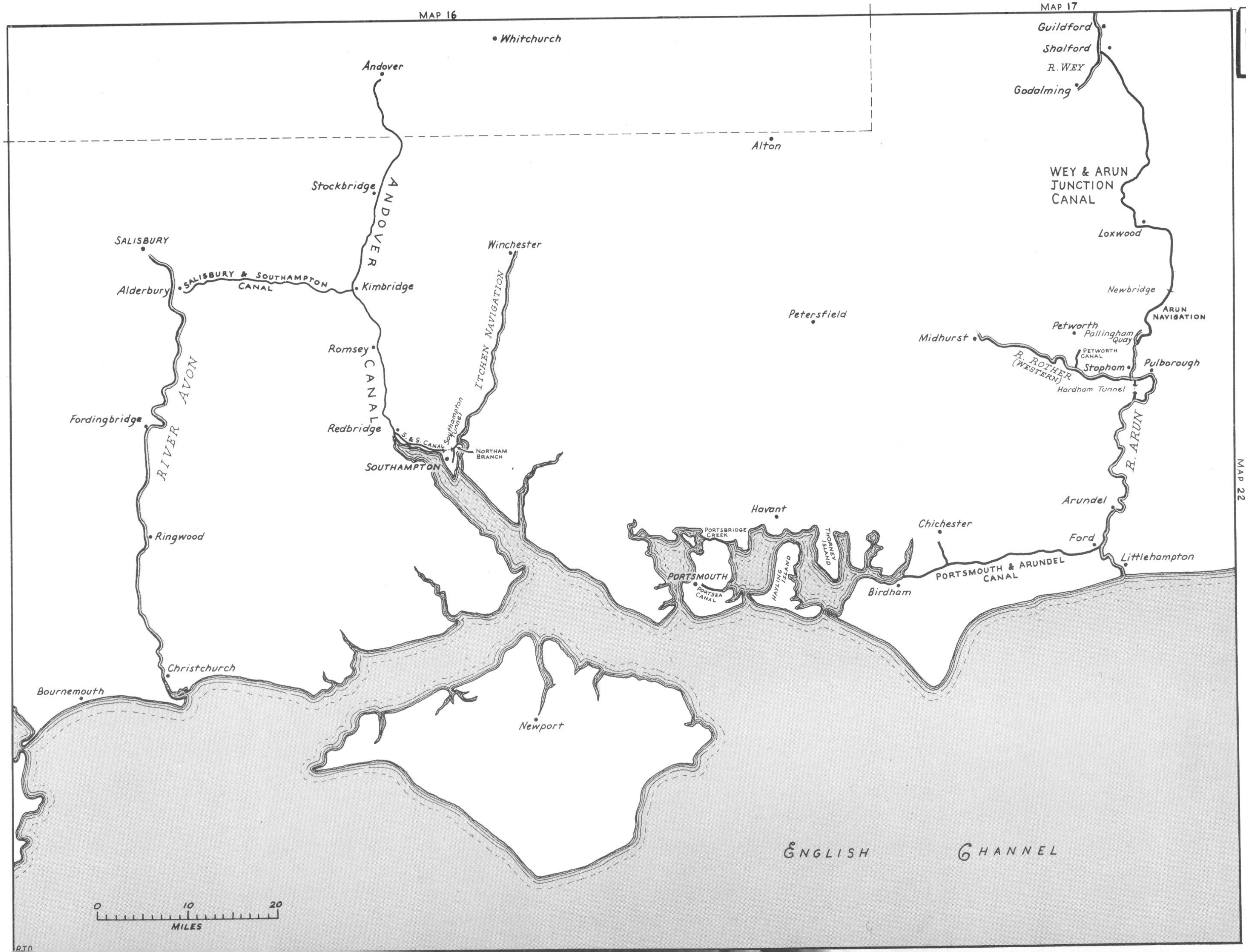

MAP 22

MAP 17

MAP 16

Guildford

Shalford

R. WEY

Godalming

WEY & ARUN JUNCTION CANAL

Loxwood

Newbridge

ARUN NAVIGATION

Pulborough

Petworth

Pallingham

PETWORTH CANAL

Stopham

Hardham Tunnel

R. ROTHER (WESTERN)

Midhurst

R. ARUN

Littlehampton

Arundel

Ford

PORTSMOUTH & ARUNDEL CANAL

Chichester

Birdham

THORNEY ISLAND

HAYLING ISLAND

Havant

PORTSBRIDGE CREEK

PORTSEA CANAL

PORTSMOUTH

Petersfield

Alton

ENGLISH CHANNEL

Whitchurch

Winchester

ITCHEN NAVIGATION

NORTHAM BRANCH

Southampton Tunnel

S. & S. CANAL

SOUTHAMPTON

Newport

Andover

ANDOVER CANAL

Stockbridge

Kimbridge

Romsey

Redbridge

SALISBURY & SOUTHAMPTON CANAL

SALISBURY

Alderbury

RIVER AVON

Fordingbridge

Ringwood

Christchurch

Bournemouth

MILES

0   10   20

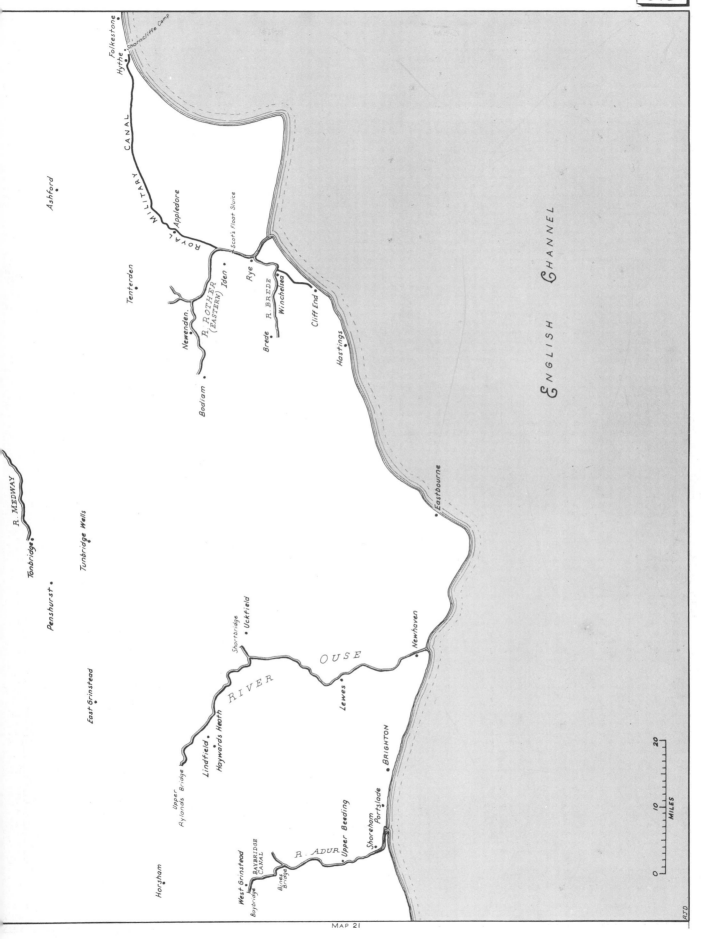

22

ENGLISH CHANNEL

Ashford

Folkestone
Hythe
Shorncliffe Camp

ROYAL MILITARY CANAL

Appledore

Scot's Float Sluice

Tenterden

R. ROTHER (EASTERN) Iden

Newenden

Rye

R. BREDE
Brede
Winchelsea

Bodiam

Cliff End

Hastings

R. MEDWAY

Tonbridge

Penshurst

Tunbridge Wells

Eastbourne

East Grinstead

Shortbridge
Uckfield

RIVER OUSE

Lindfield
Haywards Heath

Newhaven

Upper
Rylands Bridge

Lewes

Horsham

West Grinstead
Baybridge
BAYBRIDGE CANAL

Bines Bridge

R. ADUR

Upper Beeding

Shoreham
Portslade

BRIGHTON

0   10   20
MILES

RTD

MAP 21

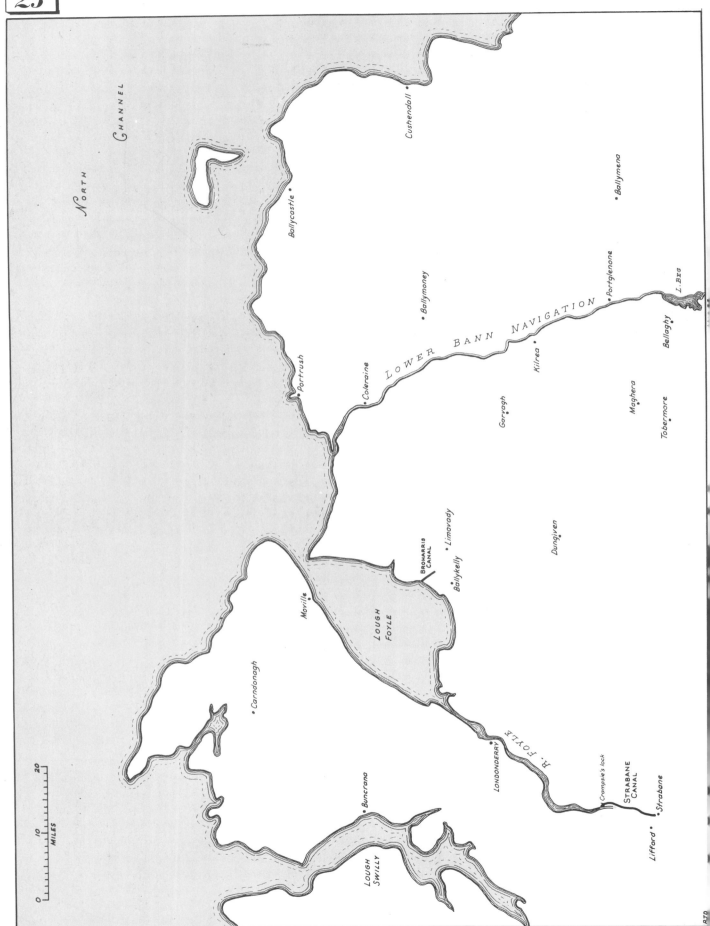

North Channel

North

Ballycastle

Cushendall

Ballymoney

Ballymena

Portrush

Coleraine

LOWER BANN NAVIGATION

Portglenone

L.Beg

Garvagh

Kilrea

Bellaghy

Maghera

Tobermore

Moville

BROHARRIS CANAL

Limovady

Ballykelly

Dungiven

LOUGH FOYLE

Carndonagh

R. FOYLE

LONDONDERRY

Crampsie's lock

STRABANE CANAL

Buncrana

Lifford

Strabane

LOUGH SWILLY

20

10

MILES

0

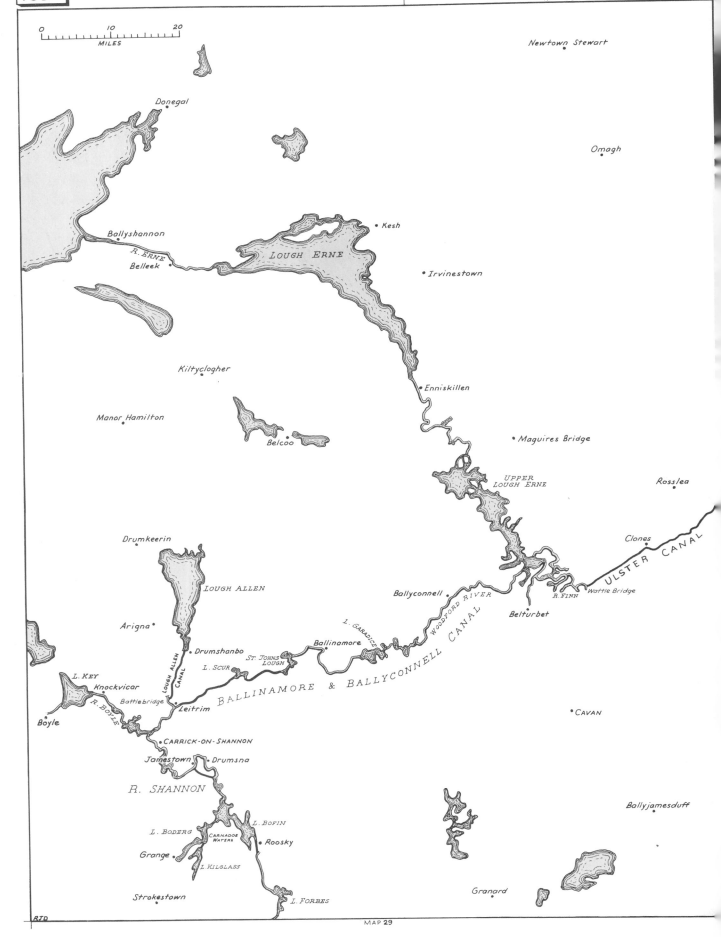

25

MAP 23

0   10   20
MILES

Newtown Stewart

Donegal

Omagh

Ballyshannon
R. ERNE
Belleek

• Kesh

LOUGH ERNE

• Irvinestown

Kiltyclogher

• Enniskillen

Manor Hamilton

• Maguires Bridge

Belcoo

UPPER
LOUGH ERNE

Rosslea

Drumkeerin

Clones

ULSTER CANAL

LOUGH ALLEN

Ballyconnell
WOODFORD RIVER

R. FINN   Wattle Bridge

Arigna •

L. GARADICE

Belturbet

Drumshanbo
ST. JOHNS
LOUGH
L. SCUR

Ballinamore

BALLINAMORE & BALLYCONNELL CANAL

L. KEY
Knockvicar
R. BOYLE
Battlebridge
Leitrim

LOUGH ALLEN CANAL

Boyle

• CAVAN

• CARRICK-ON-SHANNON

Jamestown • • Drumsna

R. SHANNON

Ballyjamesduff

L. BOFIN
L. BODERG
CARNADOE
WATERS
Grange •
L. KILGLASS
• Roosky

Strokestown
L. FORBES

Granard

MAP 29

RJD

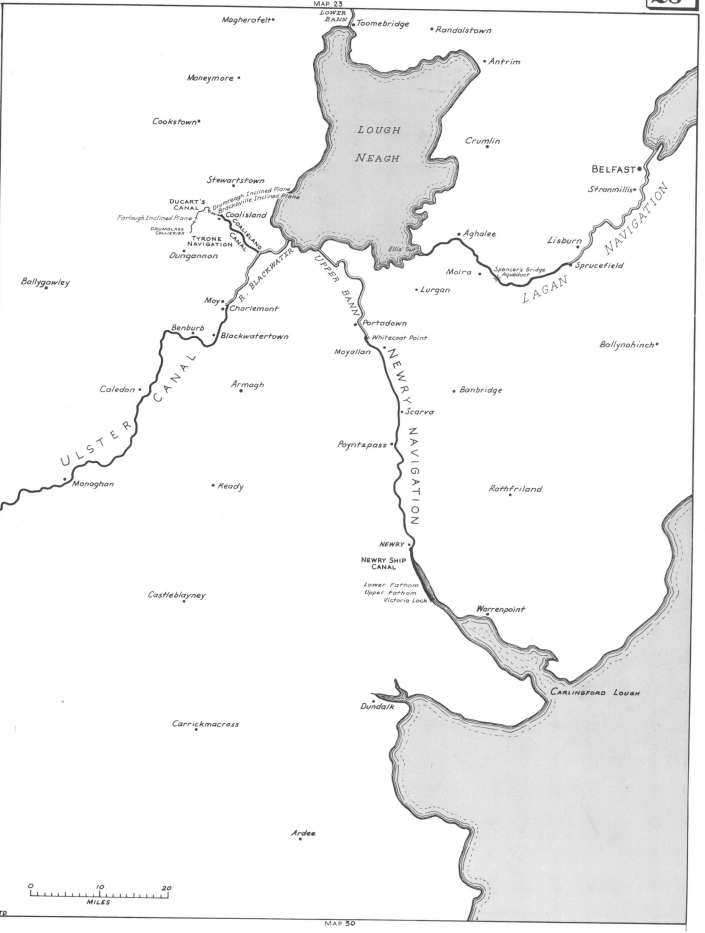

MAP 23

Magherafelt•

LOWER
BANN

•Toombridge

•Randalstown

Moneymore •

•Antrim

Cookstown•

LOUGH

NEAGH

•Crumlin

BELFAST•

•Stranmillis

Stewartstown•

DUCART'S
CANAL

Drumreagh Inclined Plane
Brackaville Inclined Plane

•Coalisland

Farlough Inclined Plane

DRUMGLASS
COLLIERIES

TYRONE
NAVIGATION

•Aghalee

Ellis' Gut

•Lisburn

•Sprucefield

Dungannon•

Ballygawley

R. BLACKWATER

UPPER BANN

•Moira

Spencer's Bridge
Aqueduct

LAGAN

•Lurgan

Moy•
•Charlemont

•Portadown

Whitecoat Point

Ballynahinch•

Benburb•

•Blackwatertown

Moyallan

NEWRY NAVIGATION

Caledon •

ULSTER CANAL

•Armagh

•Banbridge

•Scarva

• Monaghan

•Keady

Poyntzpass•

Rathfriland
•

Castleblayney•

NEWRY•

NEWRY SHIP
CANAL

Lower Fathom
Upper Fathom
Victoria Lock

•Warrenpoint

CARLINGFORD LOUGH

Carrickmacross•

Dundalk•

Ardee
•

0   10   20
MILES

MAP 30

MAP 29

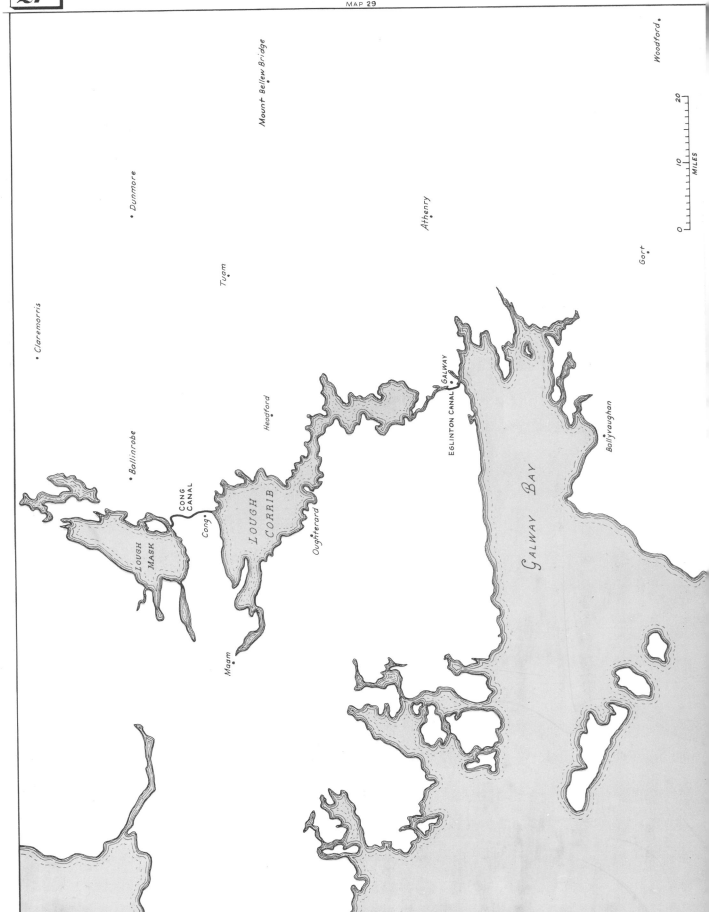

Woodford.

Claremorris

Dunmore

Mount Bellew Bridge

Ballinrobe

Tuam

Athenry

Gort

Headford

LOUGH MASK

CONG CANAL

Cong.

LOUGH CORRIB

Oughterard

Maam

GALWAY

EGLINTON CANAL

Ballyvaughan

GALWAY BAY

0   10   20
MILES

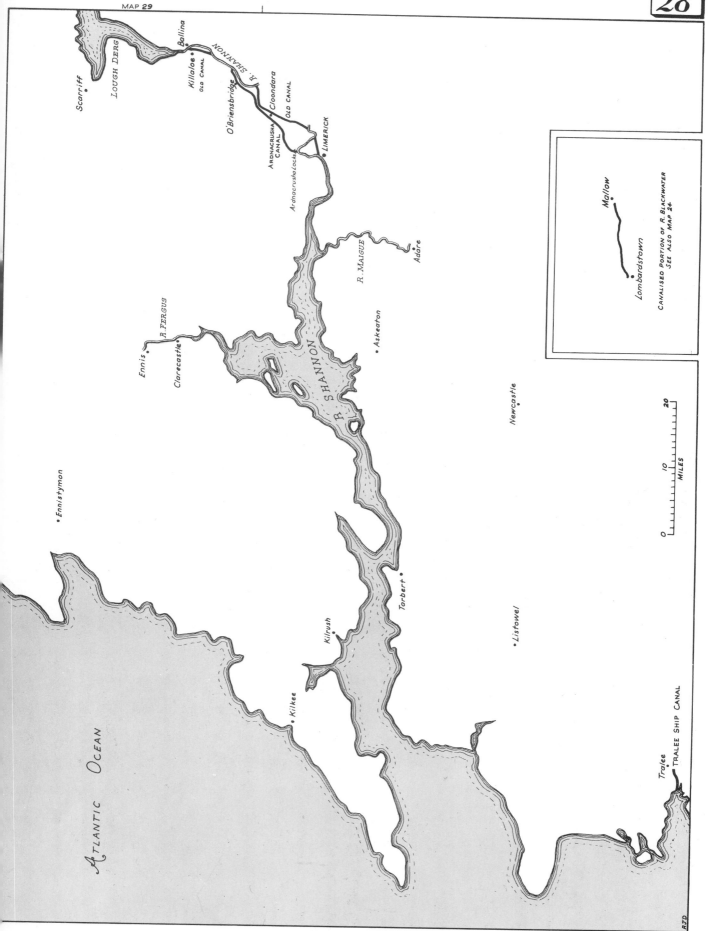

MAP 29

Scarriff

LOUGH DERG

Ballina

Killaloe OLD CANAL

R. SHANNON

O'Briensbridge

ARDNACRUSHA CANAL

Cloondara OLD CANAL

Ardnacrusha Locks

LIMERICK

R. MAIGUE

Adare

R.FERGUS

Ennis

Clarecastle

R SHANNON

Askeaton

Newcastle

Ennistymon

Mallow
•
Lombardstown
•

CANALISED PORTION OF R. BLACKWATER
SEE ALSO MAP 24

Tarbert

ATLANTIC OCEAN

Kilrush

Listowel

Kilkee

Tralee TRALEE SHIP CANAL

0   10   20
MILES

R.J.D.

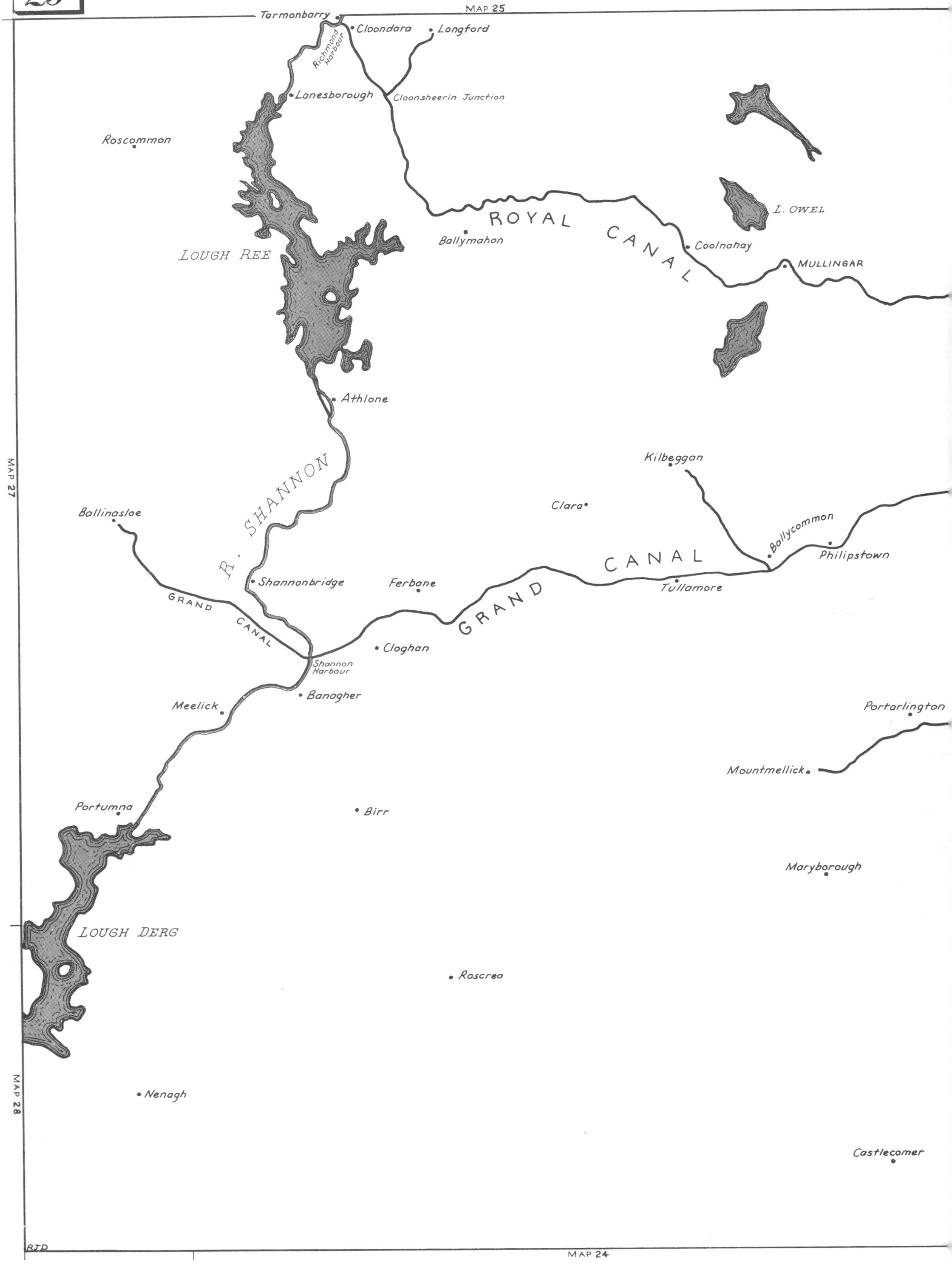

MAP 25

Tarmonbarry

•Cloondara •Longford

Richmond Harbour

•Lanesborough Cloonsheerin Junction

Roscommon

MAP 27

ROYAL CANAL

•Ballymahon

L. OWEL

•Coolnahay

•MULLINGAR

LOUGH REE

•Athlone

Kilbeggan

Clara•

Ballinasloe

R. SHANNON

GRAND CANAL

•Shannonbridge •Ferbane

GRAND CANAL

•Bollycommon

Philipstown•

•Tullamore

•Cloghan

Shannon Harbour

Meelick•

•Banogher

•Portarlington

Mountmellick•

•Portumna

•Birr

Maryborough•

LOUGH DERG

•Roscrea

MAP 28

•Nenagh

Castlecomer•

MAP 24

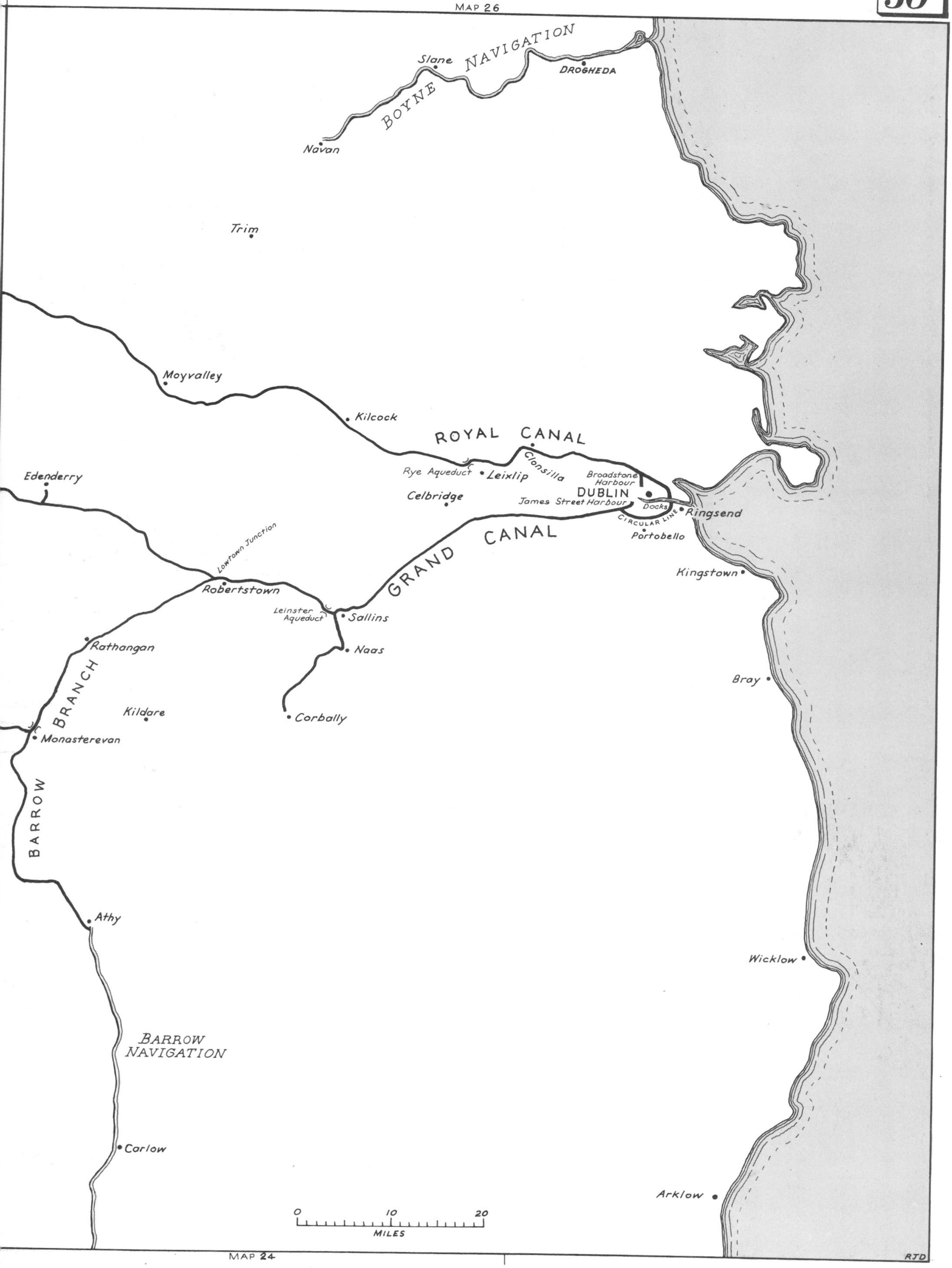

MAP 26

BOYNE NAVIGATION

Slane

DROGHEDA

Navan

Trim

Moyvalley

Kilcock

ROYAL CANAL

Clonsilla

Rye Aqueduct *Leixlip*

Broadstone Harbour

Celbridge

DUBLIN

James Street Harbour *Docks* *Ringsend*

Edenderry

CIRCULAR LINE

Portobello

Lowtown Junction

GRAND CANAL

Robertstown

Kingstown

Leinster Aqueduct *Sallins*

Rathangan

Naas

BRANCH

Kildare

Bray

Corbally

Monasterevan

BARROW

Athy

Wicklow

BARROW NAVIGATION

Carlow

Arklow

0   10   20
MILES

MAP 24

RJD

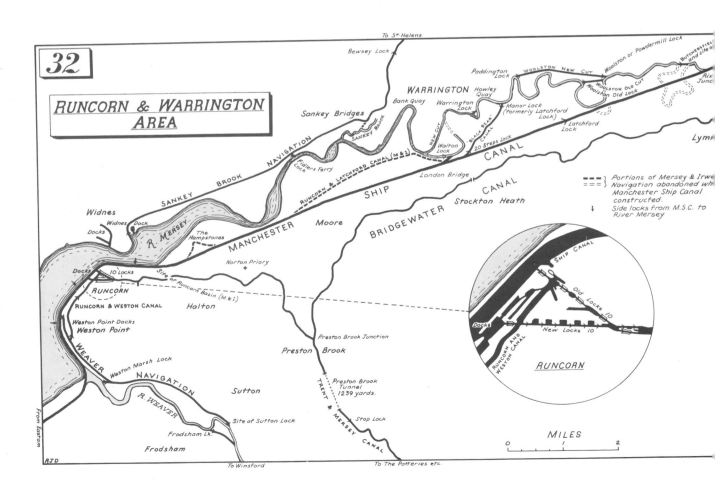

River Kennet, Berkshire. Joining the Thames at Reading the Kennet was made a navigation under an Act of 1715 from Reading to Newbury, with John Hore as engineer. $11\frac{1}{2}$ miles of cuts were made to straighten the river and 20 turf sided locks built. By 1724 the works were complete, including a horse path, and the total distance of $18\frac{1}{2}$ miles became navigable for 80 ton Thames barges. The Kennet, short of money and badly run, was opposed by millers and Reading bargemen, since the centre of distribution had moved upstream to Newbury. From 1767 Francis Page, a coal trader owning barges, became a proprietor later gaining control. He did much to improve the river, enlarging the locks for craft 122' x 19', to take the large 110 ton 'Newbury' barges. Page was keen to proceed with a canal to join the Avon, an enthusiasm continued by his son, also called Francis. The Kennet was bought by the Kennet & Avon Canal in 1812.

Kennet & Avon Canal, Berkshire, Wiltshire, Somerset. A canal joining the Kennet and the Avon had been an idea in the reign of Elizabeth I and various Bills for it were introduced under Charles II, the last in 1668, but none passed. In 1788 came a meeting at Hungerford chaired by Charles Dundas of Kintbury near Hungerford, both M.P. and a J.P. for Berkshire. Although called to consider merely an extension of the Kennet to Hungerford the meeting resolved to join the Rivers Kennet and Avon. Initial surveys were made by Samuel Weston, Samuel Simcock and James Barnes, followed by John Rennie. No money was subscribed until 1792. It was found by a Bristol group who joined with the old Hungerford group and a new committee was formed in 1793. Rennie made a further survey altering the line to pass through Devizes, and the Act passed in 1794. Work started on a broad line for 60 ton boats from Newbury to the Avon at Bath. The canal, eventually 57 miles long with 79 locks for craft 73' x 13'10", was opened piecemeal to get trade moving and raise revenue, so in 1798 Hungerford was reached and in 1799 Great Bedwyn. The last section between Pewsey and Great Bedwyn over the summit and the great flight of 29 locks up Caen hill, Devizes was completed in 1810. Feed water for the short summit was taken by steam pumps at Crofton from Wilton Water, a small reservoir fed by springs at a lower level on the other side of the valley. Other water came from the Seend feeder, from the Wilts. & Berks. and Somersetshire Coal Canal where they joined the Kennet & Avon at Semington and Limpley Stoke respectively and from the Avon at Claverton, raised by waterwheel driven pumps built in 1813. Later steam pumps were built at Bath to return water up the Widcombe flight of locks, for a time. Traffic built up well, coal coming off the Somersetshire Coal Canal. Fly-boats ran between Bristol and Reading from 1818, a steam barge had been tried in 1813, but doubtless was discouraged because of bank damage. A further traffic feeder from 1827 was the Avon & Gloucestershire Railway from the collieries near Mangotsfield to the Avon above Keynsham. Completion of the Great Western Railway in 1841 took the Bristol to London through traffic. In 1847 the Berks & Hants railway reached Hungerford. Canal tolls were cut and staff reduced, while in 1845 the Kennet & Avon had tried but failed to promote its own railway along the line of the canal. From 1848 the company entered the carrying trade with a mixed fleet of trows and locally built Kennet barges. With further toll reductions the whole waterway from Hanham to Reading was taken over by the GWR in 1852. The carrying business ceased after 1873 and there was no profit from the canal after 1877. As traffic declined so did the state of the canal, aggravated by a water shortage. Nevertheless the GWR did try to keep the canal going by repairing the pumps at Crofton and Claverton and dredging out Wilton Water. By 1909 traffic was local, the last through cargoes from Bristol having passed in about 1900, Welsh slates for Reading. After the 1914-18 War came road competition, although the GWR undertook a big dredging, repuddling and lock repair programme in the early 1930s, in accordance with an agreement given to a local trader that the canal would not be allowed to deteriorate. The last traffic on the Bath-Newbury section ended in 1937, although pleasure boats struggled through up to the late 1940s. Abandonment, proposed in 1955 was withdrawn after public pressure and portions of the waterway are regularly navigated by pleasure traffic, after attempts to keep commercial traffic going to Newbury in 1949 and 1950. The Kennet & Avon Canal Trust, successor to the Kennet & Avon Canal Association, are committed to full reopening. They have done much repair work with the full co-operation of the British Waterways Board. The locks at Bath have been restored so that boats can enter from the navigable Avon, where commercial traffic, tar from Bath gasworks, ceased in 1967.

KENSINGTON CANAL, London. In 1824 an Act authorized a short canal from what is now Olympia to the Thames at Chelsea, making use of $1\frac{3}{4}$ miles of a natural stream. A lock was built at the entrance to the terminal basin, the rest of the cut being tidal. The Kensington Canal was opened in 1828 but

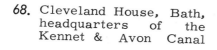
68. Cleveland House, Bath, headquarters of the Kennet & Avon Canal

it did not do well and in 1839 took the opportunity of selling to a newly promoted railway, the West London, who were to build a line from the canal basin to join the GWR and the London & Birmingham. This was a failure but in 1859 the West London Extension Railway was promoted, and the Kensington Canal was transferred to it, part of the canal bed being used for the railway and more filled in. Today only 3 furlongs inland from the Thames remains open, owned by the British Waterways Board. It is wholly tidal and the top end dries at low water.

KETLEY CANAL, Shropshire. Here was built the first inclined plane for boats in England. Richard Reynolds and his son William built the $1\frac{1}{2}$ mile canal privately to bring coal from Oakengates to their Ketley furnaces. It was completed in 1788 for tub boats of 8 tons capacity, which were carried up and down the 73' fall of the inclined plane on carriages. Choice of the plane rather than locks had been dictated by the severe slope down to Ketley and water shortage. Very soon after completion, the Ketley was able to join the newly promoted Shropshire Canal, by means of an extension with a lock to overcome the 1' difference in level. This of course brought more traffic to the Ketley, but with the dismantling of the Ketley ironworks in 1816 the canal closed.

KEYINGHAM NAVIGABLE DRAINS PROJECT, Yorkshire. Keyingham Drain ran down to the Humber south-east of the Hull from Holderness. There were proposals in the 1790s to make it navigable to Keyingham Bridge and in 1797 William Chapman made a survey. The Act passed in 1802 authorizing navigation, together with improvement of the drains for boats. But use was subject to a majority approval by landowners, which does not seem to have been forthcoming.

KIDWELLY & LLANELLY CANAL, Carmarthenshire. A canal had been suggested in 1793, to run up the Gwendraeth Fawr valley from Kidwelly, later revived as an extension to Kymer's Canal, with a branch to Llanelly. In 1812 the Act passed and there were ideas of pushing further up the Gwendraeth valley. Work was first started on the line to Llanelly from Kymer's Canal near Spudder's Bridge to join the Earl of Ashburnham's Canal near Ffrwd, Pinkerton (probably James) being the engineer. The line as far as the junction with the Earl's Canal was completed about 1816 with one lock and a $\frac{3}{8}$ mile branch to Moat Farm continued to Trimsaran colliery by a tramroad, the main line crossing the Gwendraeth Fawr near Trimsaran by an aqueduct. Work also started up the Gwendraeth Fawr valley, about 2 miles with two locks being completed, but lack of funds checked progress for many years, although by means of the Pembrey Canal, completed in about 1824, the Kidwelly & Llanelly was able to reach the Burry estuary. In 1833 however James Green was called in to advise. The year before the new harbour at Burry Port had been completed and Green proposed that the canal should be extended there, ignoring the Pembrey. Work restarted and Burry Port was reached in 1835. For the Gwendraeth Fawr valley Green proposed a tub-boat extension with three inclined planes and work began, two more locks being built and two inclined planes at Pont Henry and Capel Ifan. The third inclined plane at Hirwaun-isaf does not seem to have been completed and the canal above Pontyberem seems only to have been a water channel from the proposed reservoir at Cwm-y-glo. In 1835 the Kidwelly & Llanelly leased the old Kymer's Canal and about three year's later the canal up the Gwendraeth Fawr was working, using 6 ton tub-boats over the planes and probably 20 ton boats elsewhere. The total mileage opened was 9 with five locks and two planes. During the 1860s there were ideas of railways up the Gwendraeth Fawr valley. The K. & L. Canal in 1865 turned itself into a railway company, in 1866 amalgamating with the Burry Port Co. to become the Burry Port & Gwendraeth Valley Railway who used the canal bed for their lines to Kidwelly, Pontyberem and Cwm Mawr, the canal being closed in about 1867.

KILBAGIE CANAL, Clackmannanshire. A mile long cut made in about 1780 to take grain from Kennetpans near Alloa on the Forth up to a distillery at Kilbagie. It was disused by 1861.

KILGETTY CANAL, Pembrokeshire. For the shipment of coal from Lord Milford's colliery at Kilgetty near Saundersfoot, his miners are believed to have started to cut a mile long canal, probably for tub-boats, to the coast during the 1790s. It was never finished and probably not used.

KILMARNOCK CANAL SCHEME, Ayrshire. To serve Kilmarnock elaborate canal schemes were drawn up in 1797 to connect the town with a new harbour at Troon, with a branch up towards the River Irvine, but a cheaper tramroad was subsituted.

KNARESBOROUGH CANAL SCHEME, Yorkshire. Knaresborough was a flax spinning centre at the end of the eighteenth century, the mills depending on water power, which was inadequate, so a change to steam was made. Coal had to come by road, for the Nidd was never navigable. A canal was advocated in 1800 and William Chapman did the survey for a canal to either the Ouse or Ure, the latter being favoured. It was to leave the Ure just below Swale Nab and come within $1\frac{1}{2}$ miles of Knaresborough. The canal could not actually reach the town without heavy lockage. It did not look attractive unless coal could be brought down from Durham by water. Waterway schemes in the North Riding were vague but in 1818 Telford made a survey for a canal either to the Ouse just below Linton Lock or to the Wharfe above Tadcaster. This was revised in favour of a canal cum railway, since a railway could enter Knaresborough, but failed to attract investment.

KYLE NAVIGATION PROJECT, Yorkshire. A navigation from the Ouse at Newton to Easingwold was discussed in 1769 and revived in a different form in 1772. Part of the river Kyle would have been used, together with a tributary.

KYMER'S CANAL, Carmarthenshire.   Authorized in 1766 to bring coal and limestone down from the Gwendraeth Fawr valley to the port of Kidwelly. It was opened in 1769, having been financed by Thomas Kymer, owner of the collieries and quarries. There were no locks on the three mile line nor did the canal enter the River Gwendraeth, but ended at Kidwelly quay. Kymer's later became part of the Kidwelly & Llanelly's line, being leased to the latter in 1835. With the Kidwelly & Llanelly it became disused in about 1867.

LAGAN NAVIGATION, Co Antrim, Down.   Use of the Lagan was put forward as early as 1637 but coal in east Tyrone provided the incentive. Arthur Dobbs, the H.M. Surveyor General, surveyed the river in 1741 by which time the Newry Navigation was nearly complete, a further reason why Belfast should have a waterway to Lough Neagh, so that Newry did not get all the traffic. The Act did not pass for the Lagan Navigation until 1753. It was to be partly Government financed through the Commissioners of Inland Navigation and partly local, work starting in 1756. The river was to be improved to Spencer's Bridge with a canal thence to Lough Neagh, and Thomas Omer was put in charge. Work on the Lagan proceeded rapidly from Stranmillis in Belfast where a tide lock was made on the north side of the river, and in 1763 Lisburn was reached. Two years later the Lagan had been improved as far as Sprucefield but there work stopped for lack of money. In 1768 Robert Whitworth was called over and advised either a canal the whole way separate from the river, or to continue as a canal from Sprucefield. The second was adopted and more funds were raised by local subscription. Most of the money was provided by the Marquess of Donegall, under whom in 1779 a company was formed to take over the navigation from the Commissioners as a joint stock enterprise. Richard Owen became engineer onwards from Sprucefield. In 1792 his canal reached Aghalee whence a road led to Ellis' Gut, a bay on Lough Neagh, so that traffic could start, the canal itself reaching Ellis' Gut in 1794. The Lagan Navigation was $25\frac{3}{4}$ miles long with 27 locks, large enough for craft 62' x 14'6". Tyrone mining was meeting increased competition from England and Scotland in the early nineteenth century and the Lagan became busier with cross-channel coal upstream to Lough Neagh, while building materials, earthenware, sand and road metalling went to Belfast. In 1810 control of the navigation passed from the Donegall family to a group of Belfast merchants who undertook deepening, lock repairs and started on a proper horse towing path. As a result traffic speeded up and a lighter (69) could reach Lough Neagh in 28 hours from Belfast. Traffic increased still further, with coal, foreign timber and chemicals moving upstream, and grain, flour, potatoes and sand down from Lough Neagh. The growth of industry in the lower Lagan Valley and canal improvements enabling 60 to 80 ton lighters to be used, so stimulated traffic on the eve of the railway era that Lisburn in particular became an important inland port. Competition came from road haulage because the hauls were often very short, and the Ulster Railway which reached Portadown from Belfast in 1842. Mills and factories had been built on the Lagan to make use of water power and transport, and in the early days the railways tended to feed the navigation. By this time the company had been reconstituted, in 1843 the old 'Company of Undertakers' was dissolved and a new Lagan Navigation Co. incorporated. This reflected the relative prosperity of the Lagan because most Irish waterways had since 1831 been transferred to the government Board of Public Works. Traffic continued to expand, steel lighters were introduced in 1880 and tugs employed from the Belfast quays to Stranmillis, and on Lough Neagh. Traffic remained heavy until the 1930s, coal and grain being the main upstream cargoes, with sand and gravel downwards, but just before the 1939-45 War there was a sudden decline, for road competition had increased. The Lagan became so short of funds that from 1937 they were subsidized by the Government of Northern Ireland, who were fearful of taking over a decayed navigation, for the 1843 Act put the waterway under Government control if it fell into disrepair and commercial traffic ceased. Because of the considerable subsidies the Government decided to take over the navigation and close it, this was done by an Act of 1954 when the canal section between Sprucefield and Lough Neagh was abandoned. In 1958 the rest of the navigation was abandoned from Stranmillis to Sprucefield. There had been no traffic above Lisburn since about 1947, and none at all after 1956.

LAKE DISTRICT WATERWAYS, Cumberland, Westmorland, Lancashire (Furness). Lakes Coniston and Windermere were busy during the eighteenth century, taking locally made charcoal down to iron furnaces. This finished in the 1780s but both lakes carried other traffic in the nineteenth century, copper and slate coming from Coniston to Nibthwaite for overland carriage, while the gunpowder works at Low Wood near Haverthwaite sent blasting powder up both lakes to the mines and quarries of Tilberthwaite and Langdale. The Crake appears to have been navigable up to Penny Bridge $\frac{1}{2}$ mile from the shores of Morecambe Bay and was used for the slate traffic at the end of the eighteenth century. The Leven was navigable up to Haverthwaite and used for iron shipments. Another Lakeland navigation was the Cumberland Derwent from the coast at Workington up to Cockermouth but this had decayed by the 1740s. Apart from the Ulverston Canal there was one other artificial waterway, the Wilson House Canal near Lindale-in-Cartmel, dug in the 1750s by Isaac Wilkinson, the father of the ironmaster, possibly using iron boats, to bring peat to his iron furnace at Lindale.

LANCASTER CANAL, Lancashire, Westmorland.   Ideas for such a canal arose because of the difficulty and expense of supplying coal to north Lancashire and south Westmorland. The Lune had been improved in the mid-eighteenth century and Glasson Dock completed in 1787, but local people thought a canal from the Wigan coalfield would serve them better. In 1772 Robert Whitworth had surveyed from the Leeds & Liverpool's intended line near Chorley across the Ribble and up to Lancaster and Kendal. In 1791 John Rennie was invited to do a survey for a line to broad standard from Westhoughton near Bolton to Kendal. It was to carry on from Westhoughton to Worsley, yet they lost their Act for this, but the Act for the Kendal-Westhoughton canal passed in 1792. Work started on the Lancaster with John Rennie as engineer and William Crosley the elder as his assistant. An Act of 1793 authorized the branch which Rennie had suggested to Glasson Dock to give the canal a sea outlet, while in 1794 work started on the Lune aqueduct. In 1797 this was complete and boats could navigate the long level pound, $42\frac{3}{8}$ miles, between Preston and Tewitfield north of Carnforth. 1798 saw much of the work complete south of Preston, and in 1799 the canal was ready between Bark Hill above Wigan and Johnson's Hillock near Chorley; but the company were still faced with the Ribble crossing. Jessop and Rennie favoured a stone aqueduct. William Cartwright suggested a tramroad between the two halves of the system, with which Jessop and Rennie concurred, but only as a temporary measure. A double tracked tramroad was built with three steam worked inclined planes, between Preston basin and Walton Summit to which the canal was extended from Johnson's Hillock via the 259 yd Whittle Hills tunnel. The Ribble was crossed by a trestle bridge, the third inclined plane taking the tramroad up to the level of the canal in Preston. Opened in 1803 the tramroad became permanent, for there was never enough money to build the aqueduct. Traffic had been using parts of the canal since 1796 but the tramroad helped receipts considerably, the southern section between the Ribble and Wigan being the busiest. A passenger boat service had been put on in 1798 between Preston and Lancaster. Tewitfield remained the terminus and Kendal was still without a canal. No further work was done until 1813 and the line to Kendal was not finished until 1819. It included the eight locks at Tewitfield and the 378 yd tunnel at Hincaster, built without a towing path (72).

69. Lagan Navigation lighter at Belvoir Park, Belfast

Thomas Fletcher was the engineer and the younger William Crosley resident, and their achievements included the reservoir at Killington on the moors between Kendal and Sedbergh, to feed what now became the canal's $13\frac{3}{4}$ mile summit level. Water also came from becks at Stainton, Crooklands and Farleton and south of Lancaster, from Catterall Beck. At Preston a tunnel was cut down from the canal to the Ribble up which water was pumped by a steam engine. The final task was the long delayed $2\frac{1}{2}$ mile branch to Glasson Dock started in 1819 and completed in 1825, by the younger William Crosley with six locks from the junction with the main line at Lodge Hill near Galgate (73). A large basin was made at Glasson inland from the existing one of the Lancaster Port Commissioners. By 1825 the Lancaster Canal was 57 miles long from Preston to Kendal with 8 locks, plus the $2\frac{1}{2}$ miles branch, the locks admitting boats 72' x 14'6". South of Preston, the Leeds & Liverpool used the already built section of the Lancaster from Walton summit to Bark Hill, to reach Wigan, the Lancaster having made no progress from here to Westhoughton. The Leeds & Liverpool met the Lancaster 'South End' at Johnson's Hillock, the Lancaster building $\frac{1}{2}$ mile on from Bark Hill to what became Wigan Top Lock, and $\frac{1}{2}$ mile of canal and seven locks at Johnson's Hillock as a branch from their canal to meet the Leeds & Liverpool coming down from Blackburn. From Walton Summit to Wigan Top Lock at Kirklees the Lancaster ran on the level for $13\frac{1}{4}$ miles, the tramroad between Walton and Preston measuring 5 miles. The great feature of the 'North End' of the Lancaster, between Preston and Kendal, were the passenger services run in the face of railway competition. In 1833 a swift boat was ordered to run a new fast daily service between Preston and Lancaster, 30 miles in 3 hours. A parallel railway between Preston and Lancaster was ready by 1840 but the swift boats offered a far more comfortable journey, so that no passengers were lost to the trains. Indeed in 1842 the Lancaster Canal took the bold and unusual step of leasing the railway, called the Lancaster & Preston Junction. They were soon faced with further railway promotion northwards, the Lancaster & Carlisle being authorized in 1844 and two years later reached Kendal in 1846. This brought about the surrender by the canal of their railway, by an Act of 1849 becoming a part of the Lancaster & Carlisle. Meanwhile the Lancaster Canal were considering the future of their South End, in 1845 they offered to sell it to either the Leeds & Liverpool or the Lancaster & Carlisle Railway, and in 1851 succeeded in leasing the tolls on this section to the Leeds & Liverpool in return for an annual payment as rent, a lease in perpetuity followed in 1864. Railway growth by the 1850s was upsetting canal traffic, and the coastal traffic distributed by the canal from Glasson Dock. To counteract this the canal company entered the coastal trade with their own ships and in 1855 put a steam boat on the canal. Traffic declined to such an extent that from 1860 railways were approached. The leasing arrangements of 1864 to the LNWR were followed in 1885 by the outright purchase of the whole canal. This meant that the North End came under direct railway control, but the South was still leased to the Leeds & Liverpool, their rent now going to the railway company. The old tramroad from

Walton Summit to Preston was finally closed in 1879, (it had been closed from Bamber Bridge across the Ribble to Preston in 1864) traffic having dwindled away, the last being coal to mills at Bamber Bridge. The coal traffic to Kendal gasworks ceased in 1944 when it went over to road, and the final commercial traffic, coal to a mill in Lancaster ceased in 1947 when the mill changed to oil firing. By this time the LMS had taken steps to try and close the canal, in 1941-2 the ½ mile north of Kendal gasworks was closed because of leakage, but because of the gasworks traffic they failed to gain abandonment of the whole canal in 1944. After nationalization the British Transport Commission were authorized by an Act of 1955 to close the canal, in fact it was drained from the Stainton feeder up to Kendal, again because of leakage through fissures in the limestone. The last 2 miles into Kendal were filled in, as was the last ¾ mile or so into Preston. More of the canal was drained and piped at Burton and the M6 roadworks effectively closed Tewitfield locks. To-day the canal south of Tewitfield and the Glasson Dock branch is full of pleasure craft, water also being supplied to ICI at Fleetwood from the Killington reservoir, for part of the summit remains as a water channel. The South End between Johnson's Hillock and Wigan Top Lock is an integral part of the Leeds & Liverpool and open, but the line to Walton Summit, last used in 1932, is absorbed by motorway construction.

LANCASTER-MORECAMBE SHIP CANAL PROJECT. Because of the difficulty of navigating the Lune, particularly in the 1840s, there were ideas for a 3½ miles long ship canal from the coast at what is now Morecambe to the Lune at Lancaster. In 1845 a Morecambe Bay Harbour Co. was floated to make the ship canal, but a railway was preferred and built.

LANGSTONE DOCKS and SHIP CANAL PROJECT. To provide Portsmouth with new docks, promoters suggested a ship canal from Spithead to Eastney leading into two new docks which would also be open to Langstone Harbour in 1846.

River LARK, Cambridgeshire, Suffolk. Joining the Great Ouse about four miles below Ely, the Lark was navigable for 12 miles to Mildenhall but impassable from there to Bury St Edmunds. The Romans are believed to have improved the river between Prickwillow and Isleham, but under an Act of 1700 the younger Henry Ashley improved the 13 miles from Mildenhall to Bury by building pound locks and staunches. The Lark remained under the ownership of the Ashleys and their descendants into the 1850s. Traffic was coal to Bury, with wheat, rye and malt coming downstream. During the canal age there were plans to join the Lark and the Suffolk Stour by a canal from Bury to the Stour estuary at Mistley. John Rennie did a survey in 1790. Another proposal of 1790 was a canal from Bury to Stowmarket on the Gipping. Traffic declined during the French wars but in the 1830s and 40s the Lark's owner Sir Thomas Cullum of Bury St. Edmunds, also joint proprietor of the Upper Ouse, undertook improvements. There were now eleven pound locks and fifteen staunches on the Lark for craft up to 48' x 10', all except Isleham staunch were above West Row near Mildenhall, Isleham being under the control of the South Level Drainage and Navigation Commissioners. Cullum, the last Ashley family proprietor, died in 1855 by which time traffic on the Lark had nearly ceased because of rail competition, principally from the Bury-Ipswich line opened in 1846. There were plans in 1863 to re-establish the Lark for coal traffic and to exploit local clunch (a chalk for building) and flint deposits. Nothing was done until, in 1889, the navigation was acquired by the Eastern Counties Navigation & Transport Co. Ltd. They worked to re-open the Mildenhall-Bury section to steam towage, repairing the staunches, three of which were eliminated and one converted into a pound lock. They also made the tributary Tuddenham mill stream above Mildenhall navigable with a single staunch. They were able to improve up to Fornham, a mile short of Bury, by 1894, but a receiver was appointed at the end of the year. The river above Icklingham was then abandoned. Later the Lark was bought by Parker Bros. of Mildenhall, but commercial traffic ceased in the 1920s. However Isleham lock is open and pleasure craft can go about two miles above this.

LEE NAVIGATION, Hertfordshire, Essex, Middlesex. Navigation on the Lee (old spelling Lea) goes back to prehistoric times and it was an important Saxon waterway. Nothing written has survived earlier than a licence issued probably in 1190, from the King granting the Abbot of Waltham powers to improve the navigation by making a cut. The Lee was the subject of the first Act for the navigational improvement of any river in the British Isles, passed in 1424, followed by a second in 1430. It was put under commissioners, local landowners who could levy tolls to pay for improvements. An Act of 1571 granted improvement powers to the Lord Mayor and City Council of London who were concerned about grain supplies via the navigation. They were allowed to make new cuts to link the Lee with London, but they confined themselves to improving the Lee at Bow. This section, called the Bow River, was granted freedom from toll, a privilege which still exists. In 1577 came the opening of the pound lock at Waltham Abbey. There were already staunches on the Lee, or turnpikes as they were called, like the East Anglian staunch with vertically lifting gates. The Waltham Abbey lock was made with a timber planked chamber 70' x 24' and probably had the first mitred gates in the British Isles. By 1590 this lock seems to have fallen into disrepair and turnpikes continued to be built at the mills, the millowners charging for their passage. Apart from the consumption of water by mills, the Lee became of increasing importance as a supplier of water to London. The New River Company had opened their channel in 1613, a forty mile artificial watercourse from near Ware to London,

70.

the supply coming from springs at Amwell and Chadwell. But the springs proved insufficient and from the 1750s Lee water was being abstracted to the detriment of both the mills and the navigation. Parliament had to step in to resolve a petition presented in 1736-7 and in 1739 an Act was passed to remedy the situation. Trustees were established to control the navigation through their own staff. A survey was made of the river by William Whittenbury a Hertford carpenter, who became more or less surveyor to the Lee, although not formally appointed. He continued to recommend the turnpike type of staunch and one was erected at Broxbourne Mill in 1741. Millowners remained dissatisfied with the supply of water and more drastic remedies were needed. John Smeaton made a survey in 1765 and another in 1766 assisted by Thomas Yeoman, the latter becoming surveyor to the Lee Navigation in 1767. Smeaton suggested that pound locks should replace flash locks, and that new cuts should be made, including a new entrance cut from the Thames at Limehouse up to Bromley. All this was embodied in an Act of 1767. Yeoman's greatest achievement was the completion of the Limehouse cut opened in 1770. This brought the navigation into the Thames above the Isle of Dogs, upstream from the natural entrance via Bow creek. The new cut soon had to be widened so that barges could pass anywhere and this was completed towards the end of 1777. The trustees were able to raise sufficient money to pay for their works and other cuts proceeded at Waltham, Edmonton and Hackney with their pound locks, opened in 1769. In 1803 the elder John Rennie surveyed the Lee valley to see if it could be flooded as an anti-invasion measure. He found it would take three months to fill, the water being impounded by a series of dams, which were completed, after the invasion threat had gone. Meanwhile an Act had passed in 1805 to improve the Lee's function as a water supply and because of this the Act limited craft to 40 tons. In 1850 an Act sanctioned improvement up to Tottenham locks, allowing 70 ton barges, although 100 ton powder barges were coming down from the Royal Powder Mills at Waltham. These dated from the 1650s and were served by branch canals with two locks. Further upstream was the small arms factory established at Enfield lock in 1804 and expanded in 1816, using the Lee both for power and transport, also with branch canals entering above and below Enfield lock. A major reconstruction of Lee administration came in 1868 when the trustees were replaced by the Lee Conservancy Board, responsible for navigation and flood control. Water abstraction for London grew apace during the nineteenth century, the East London Waterworks starting to take water in 1808. Foundation of the Metropolitan Water Board in 1902 united eight water undertakings, including the New River Co, and more reservoirs were built, following those built at Walthamstow in the nineteenth century. The King George V at Enfield was opened in 1915 and the William Girling below it in 1951. There had been a pollution crisis in the 1880s, due to the increased discharge of sewage into the Lee from the growing towns of the valley and due to the use of old leaky boats for the upstream manure traffic. A Royal Commission of 1886 reported and slow improvement resulted. In 1911 the Lee bought the Stort and improved both it and their own river. By the 1930s, 130 ton barges were able to reach Enfield and 100 tons Ware and Hertford. In 1930 the Lee Flood Relief Act started canalization in the West Ham area and work was done in the Bow Back Rivers, that complex system improved to serve mills, possibly as early as the sixteenth century. A new lock at Bow was opened in 1935, and a new lock at City Mills, while Carpenter's Road lock was given radial gates to act as flood relief sluices. Under nationalization the Lee has been further improved. During the 1950s the locks up to and including Ponders End were duplicated and mechanized, now taking craft 85' x 18'6". The manual ones above take craft 85' x 16'. In 1968 the British Waterways Board opened a new cut between the Limehouse cut and Regent's Canal Dock, closing the Lee's Limehouse cut entrance and entrance lock to the Thames. An earlier link between the Lee and Regent's Canal Dock, opened in the 1850s, had been closed because of the new Regent's Canal Dock entrance lock opened in 1869, but the Limehouse cut entrance lock was then widened from 16' to 20'. In 1969 the British Waterways Board opened a new depot at Brimsdown, Enfield which attracts heavy towed lighter traffic, although commerce goes up to Ware, and Hertford is reached by pleasure craft. The main line of the Lee, Limehouse to Hertford, measures $27\frac{3}{4}$ miles, on which there are 19 locks (excluding the Limehouse cut entrance lock). There are three locks on the Bow Back Rivers system, plus sluices.

LEEDS & LIVERPOOL CANAL, Lancashire, Yorkshire. First considered in the 1760s, the Leeds & Liverpool was seen as a broad canal for Yorkshire keels to join Liverpool to Hull via the Aire & Calder. In 1766 there was a public meeting at the Sun Inn, Bradford called by an engineer John Longbotham of Halifax and a Bradford wool merchant, the Quaker John Hustler. The Leeds & Liverpool surveys were prepared by Longbotham and submitted in 1768. To gain wider support the new canal was promoted by two committees based on Liverpool and Bradford, the latter controlling finance. They disagreed over the canal line in Lancashire, because as planned it avoided the towns. A revised Lancashire route, surveyed by John Eyes and Richard Melling, was found too long and expensive by the Bradford committee. Eventually Brindley arbitrated in favour of Longbotham's original line favoured by Hustler. In this uneasy atmosphere the Act passed in 1770 and money was soon raised so that work could begin. Brindley was appointed chief engineer but he asked to withdraw, so that Longbotham became both chief engineer and clerk of works. Two treasurers were appointed at first but from 1771 John Hustler of Bradford held this office alone, so the Yorkshire side controlled affairs. By April 1773 the canal was open between Bingley and Skipton and traffic started,

71.

while the following year it was ready between Liverpool and Newburgh and up a cut parallel with the Douglas which had been started by the Douglas proprietors as early as about 1753. This the Leeds & Liverpool extended to rejoin the Douglas at Gathurst, while by 1780 it was pushed on to Wigan. At Newburgh a start was made with the intended main line. In 1774 the five rise staircase at Bingley was completed and in June of that year the canal reached Gargrave (23), but now the money was spent. Longbotham resigned in 1775 being replaced in 1777 by Richard Owen. Borrowed funds enabled work to go on and in 1777 the canal joined the Aire by the river lock in Leeds, while in 1781 the branch from Burscough via Rufford was completed to enter the Douglas at Sollom. Fortunately the canal by now was sufficiently open for traffic to start, coal from Wigan and limestone from Skipton. However Owen was dismissed as engineer in 1782 and work came to a stop. Nothing further was done until 1789 when Robert Whitworth reported on the cost of completion. He varied Longbotham's line to include a summit tunnel at Foulridge and a revised route on the Lancashire side, all authorized by an Act of 1790, which also sanctioned more capital. Whitworth left the Forth & Clyde to be engineer of the Leeds & Liverpool. Foulridge tunnel soon proved to be a major obstacle because of the rotten rock and the expert Josiah Clowes was called in, recommending continuance. In 1794 an Act passed authorizing a considerable deviation via Blackburn to run parallel with the South End of the Lancaster near Chorley to meet the Manchester, Bolton & Bury at Red Moss and cross the Lancaster above Wigan, where the existing length of the Leeds & Liverpool would be joined. This same Act allowed yet more capital, for Foulridge tunnel was proving expensive; it opened in 1796 after six years work, 1640 yd, all but 700 yd being built on the cut and cover principle, for the water level was only 60' or so beneath the surface. About two years later the first of the Foulridge reservoirs, to be called Foulridge Lower, was made but it was soon found necessary to extend it. Work was now in progress towards Blackburn, Whitworth crossing the Calder valley at Burnley by the $\frac{3}{4}$ mile embankment, 46' high, which was followed to the south by the 559 yd Gannow tunnel. In 1799 he died, to be replaced by Samuel Fletcher who in 1801 completed the canal as far as Enfield wharf at Clayton-le-Moors near Accrington.

Blackburn was reached in 1810 and it now seemed best to complete the canal by using the South End of the Lancaster. The Lancaster themselves made short connecting extensions, from Bark Hill to Kirklees to join the flight of 23 locks which the Leeds & Liverpool had to build up from Wigan, and from Johnson's Hillock to Copthurst near Heapey with seven locks. In 1816 the route between Liverpool and Leeds was complete, a total of $127\frac{1}{4}$ miles including $10\frac{3}{4}$ miles of the South End of the Lancaster with 91 locks, although lock history became complicated because of removals and replacements in the Wigan area, due to subsidence and there were later 92. The locks were designed for boats 62' x 14', the keels of the Aire & Calder and the canal's own short boats although between Wigan and Liverpool they had been built 72' long for the flats which used the Douglas. The Rufford branch, $7\frac{1}{4}$ miles to Tarleton, completed in 1805 with 8 locks, could only take 62' boats. There were other branches too, in 1796 one was authorized to Rain Hall Rock, a limestone quarry worked by the company near Barnoldswick and gradually extended partially in a tunnel, finally in about 1862 measuring $\frac{3}{8}$ mile. The Springs Branch from the main line at Skipton to quarry staiths was a private canal $\frac{1}{2}$ mile long completed in 1797. In about 1800 a $\frac{1}{4}$ mile private branch was made at Crooke near Wigan wholly tunnelled to serve a colliery. Later in the nineteenth century came a $\frac{1}{2}$ mile branch to the Ince Hall Coal & Cannel Co. off the lower end of the Wigan flight, but it was closed in 1900 following a burst. Coast to coast trade would depend on the water situation on the summit which was to prove a problem to the canal company for the whole of its history. In fact trade grew in volume on the Lancashire and Yorkshire sides in much greater proportion to that carried over the summit, Lancashire traffic benefiting much from the somewhat delayed completion in 1820 of the branch from Wigan to Leigh to join the Bridgewater $7\frac{1}{4}$ miles long with at one time four locks, although because of subsidence they have been reduced to two. Originally these were only large enough for 62' boats but in 1822 were lengthened, together with the bottom two locks of the Wigan flight below the junction with the Leigh branch, so that 70' narrow boats could reach Liverpool. Railways came with the authorization in 1825 of the Bolton & Leigh Railway and the following

72. Towpath bridge over Hincaster tunnel, Lancaster canal. The tunnel path has its own accommodation bridges and tunnel under the Carlisle railway.

73. Lodge Hill where the Lancaster's Glasson Dock Branch leaves their main line. Note the iron guard rail on the left hand side of the towpath bridge to protect the parapet from towlines.

year of the Liverpool & Manchester with which the Bolton & Leigh connected in 1831. The canal was not upset by these early lines which could not manage the traffic as adequately as boats, but the competition led the canal to make improvements. There was no Mersey connection until the completion in 1846 of the Stanley Dock branch, $\frac{1}{4}$ mile long and descending from the main line at Lightbody Street by 4 locks, built for 72' boats. At Leeds, navigation of the Aire to Armley was proposed in about 1839, involving a cut and lock to bypass a weir. Nothing came of this although in 1845 a cut and lock were made into the Aire above Leeds weir from the Leeds & Liverpool basin. This was the 90 yd Arches lock or Monk Pits branch, so called because the lock was underneath the arches of the Leeds & Bradford Railway Station. For 62' boats, it was in use until about 1960 and by it traffic went up the Aire for just over half a mile. Passenger services had started in 1774 between Gathurst and Liverpool. In 1806 the canal company took over the Liverpool-Wigan packets which had been extended from Gathurst as soon as the canal reached Wigan in 1780, and in 1808 a daily Liverpool-Wigan service was started. From 1814 there were suburban services between Liverpool and Old Roan at Aintree and the opening of the Leigh branch allowed a Manchester-Scarisbrick service (for Southport) to start in 1821.

From the 1840s the canal was faced with three recurring problems, railways, shortage of water and the poor state of Foulridge tunnel. This had collapsed as early as 1824 leading to closure for repairs and a road over the top to keep traffic moving. There was a further collapse in 1843. Water shortage had closed the summit in 1824 and 1826, so further reservoirs were needed. Foulridge Lower was deepened in 1832, and a new reservoir nearby, Whitemoor completed in 1840. The long Burnley pound was fed from another new reservoir, Rishton near Blackburn, opened about 1830. A carrying department was started by the company in 1848 to try and maintain prosperity but in 1850 the canal company decided to come to terms with the principal local railway companies by leasing certain traffic tolls to them in return for an annual rental. On the South End of the Lancaster, the Leeds & Liverpool undertook from 1851 to take the lease of Lancaster tolls in return for an annual rental to the Lancaster. These arrangements, because the railways increased the tolls, helped the Leeds & Liverpool, but the railway lease lasted only for 21 years and in 1874 was not renewed after a two year extension. In 1864 the Lancaster leased their South End to the Leeds & Liverpool in perpetuity. Between 1855 and 1859 several miles of the Liverpool end were widened and in 1871 steam tugs were introduced on the long pound between Appley Bridge and Liverpool. With traffic back in their own hands the company energetically strove to keep it by means of improvement work and were successful. In 1880 a steam tug was put into service at Foulridge. Another tug was introduced for Gannow tunnel in 1887. Also in 1880 four steam fly boats were ordered and steam remained a feature of the Leeds & Liverpool until the 1950s. During the 1880s there were serious water shortages on the summit. The remedy was more reservoir building, a new one being opened in 1885 at Barrowford to hold surplus water from those at Foulridge and from the canal, while in 1893 the large Winterburn reservoir in the moors north of Gargrave was opened which fed water by pipeline to the summit pool at the head of

Canal and River Navigations

Greenberfield locks. Even in the twentieth century the company were faced with more drought stoppages and in 1902 Foulridge tunnel collapsed again, while subsidence repairs were reaching major proportions, causing lock rebuilding below Wigan; Pagefield lock was added in 1904 and later Crooke lock removed. The company's carrying subsidiary continued until 1921 but was then given up because of the end of the wartime Government subsidy, higher wages and the eight hour day. However in 1930 carrying was resurrected in another guise when the company invested in Canal Transport Ltd. Today the canal is kept in good order and pleasure traffic has increased. All is open except for a short length to the Liverpool terminus at Pall Mall, closed in 1960. The last regular main line traffic was coal (78) to Blackburn's Whitebirk power station and to Athol Street gasworks in Liverpool which ceased in 1963, and 1964 respectively, but coal traffic to Westwood power station at Wigan from pits on the Leigh branch lasted until 1972.

LEICESTER NAVIGATION, Leicestershire. In 1778 the Loughborough Navigation was open and there were ideas of extending the Soar navigation to Leicester. The first proposals came in 1780 and included a branch canal to the coalfield in Charnwood Forest, revived in 1785 because road charges were high, and Bills were introduced and lost in 1786 and 1789. Also involved was the Wreak to Melton Mowbray. William Jessop surveyed for the Leicester navigation, the Charnwood Forest canal and the river navigation to Melton. The latter was taken over by a separate company, but the Act for the other two passed in 1791. Jessop was made engineer with Christopher Staveley as assistant and work started on the Soar and on the canal into Charnwood Forest which Jessop considered should be partly canal and partly tramroad because of the gradients. The Forest line started from the basin in Loughborough of the Loughborough Navigation as a tramroad to Nanpantan 2½ miles away. Then came a 7½ mile level canal fed by the reservoir to be made at Blackbrook. This split at a junction with short branches going north and south, both extended by tramroad systems, to limeworks at Cloud Hill in the north, and to collieries at Coleorton and Swannington in the south. There were 8¾ miles of canal open by 1794. It was a failure. The colliery owners would not support it, favouring the proposed Ashby Canal on the other side of the Forest, so at first only demonstration loads were carried by the canal company. A little revenue came in later but water proved a problem. The Blackbrook reservoir was not ready until 1797, then in 1799 it burst, badly damaging the canal works, but it reopened in 1801, although there was no traffic. Again the reservoir failed and the Forest line closed. The Soar up to Leicester was more successful, opening in 1794. There were 10 broad locks for craft 83' x 14'6" and an eleventh lock, Limekiln in Leicester, was added in the late nineteenth century by the Corporation to control flooding. The navigation was 15¾ miles long, joined above Cossington by the Wreak Navigation to Melton Mowbray. Mountsorrel granite was important apart from coal and wool for the Leicester mills. Leicester prosperity ended in 1832 with the opening of the Leicester & Swannington Railway which spoilt the waterborne coal trade from Derbyshire by bringing in coal from the Charnwood Forest field. The Leicester considered competing with this by re-opening their old Forest line as a horse tramroad but it was never done. Tolls dropped and dropped again when the Midland Counties Railway opened in 1840 from Derby and Nottingham to Leicester and then later on to Rugby. However the Leicester kept going on granite traffic. It did not support a Grand Junction scheme of 1863 to amalgamate all the waterways on the London, Leicester, Birmingham and Coventry lines but later in 1894 the Grand Junction negotiated low through tolls. It was bought in 1932 by the new Grand Union in an effort to build up traffic between London, the Trent and Derbyshire. Commercial traffic was maintained on the Leicester until the 1960s and has recently revived.

LEICESTERSHIRE & NORTHAMPTONSHIRE UNION CANAL. This was planned in 1792 as a broad extension of the Leicester Navigation to Market Harborough, to go on to Northampton and join up with the proposed Grand Junction line to London. Surveys were done first by Staveley, then by Varley, while William Jessop was appointed overall engineer. The Act passed in 1793 and money had been readily subscribed but the canal as authorized would have been very costly. There were to be four tunnels piercing the wolds. Work started from Leicester, with the Soar made navigable from the Leicester Navigation at West Bridge for two miles to Aylestone, whence the canal ran parallel with the river for just over two miles before turning east to Blaby and Wigston. Costs outran funds and by 1795 the company, with the canal open as far as Kilby Bridge, were considering ending at Market Harborough.

74.

Saddington tunnel (880 yd) was finished in 1797 by which time the canal had reached Debdale wharf about six miles from Market Harborough. There work stopped, 17 miles from Leicester with 25 broad locks (reduced to 24 in 1890, one at Leicester being removed) water coming from a reservoir on the summit at Saddington. In 1799 and 1802 James Barnes surveyed lines to join the Grand Junction at Braunston. All the Union did was to secure an Act in 1805 to continue to Market Harborough, which they reached in 1809, a further 6¾ miles on the level. Initiative for continuing passed to the Grand Junction who from 1808 promoted the Grand Union to connect at Foxton with the Union, to be called the old Union, from their own line. Completion of the Grand Union in 1814 boosted traffic considerably, Derbyshire coal now coming down for London. Later railways competed with the canal and by the 1840s the old Union was suffering, in spite of drawbacks on coal. From the 1850s their revenue dropped sharply, and by the 1880s their fortunes were at a very low ebb. Salvation came in 1894 by outright purchase by the Grand Junction.

LEOMINSTER CANAL, Herefordshire, Shropshire, Worcestershire. Also called the Kington & Leominster it was promoted to link Herefordshire with the Severn, originally as a canal from Bridgnorth to Leintwardine on the upper Lugg, to be made navigable down to Leominster. The opening of the Staffs. & Worcs. Canal to Stourport suggested a Severn connection here and in 1777 Robert Whitworth proposed a line from opposite Stourport to Leominster, Hereford, Ledbury and Gloucester. Nothing happened until 1789 when the younger Thomas Dadford surveyed between Stourport and Leominster, proposing four tunnels, while at the same time the people of Kington asked for a canal thence to Leominster, so the two schemes were combined for a 46 mile canal from Stourport via Leominster to Kington. In 1791 the Act was passed and work began on this very rural canal. In 1794 part was open from Marlbrook near the Mamble mines via Tenbury to Woofferton the nearest point to Ludlow, and Mamble coal was brought to Ludlow and Tenbury. By 1796 the canal had nearly reached Leominster and the 1254 yd tunnel at Southnet had been finished, but fell in and the canal proprietors could not afford repairs. Work stopped towards Stourport, but 1796 saw the canal open from Marlbrook to Leominster, $18\frac{1}{2}$ miles with 16 narrow locks, a 330 yd tunnel at Putnal Field between Leominster and Tenbury, a 94 yd at Newnham. Aqueducts were built over the Teme at Woofferton and the Rea at Marlbrook. No further progress was made and the canal remained isolated. Efforts were made to build tramroads and after 1803 a short length was built to Mamble from Marlbrook wharf. The Shrewsbury & Hereford Railway proposed to buy it in 1847 but the sale did not go through until 1858 after a case in Chancery, due to the railway's abandonment of its ideas of using the canal bed for the permanent way. Once under railway ownership the canal was drained in 1859, part being later used by the Tenbury Railway.

Vale of LEVEN CANAL SCHEMES, Dunbartonshire, Perthshire. In 1841 the second Marquess of Breadalbane proposed a canal from Bowling up the Leven to Loch Lomond, and also one from the head of Loch Lomond over to Loch Tay some 20 miles away.

LEVEN CANAL, Yorkshire. Leven, about four miles to the east of the River Hull, is in the centre of a drainage scheme made in the 1760s by John Smeaton and John Grundy. William Jessop reported on the works in 1786, advising that a navigation could be incorporated. The idea was revived in 1791, but nothing happened, until in 1801 two schemes were put forward, one by Mrs Bethell, a local landowner who asked Jessop to survey a canal from the Hull below Aike to Leven, and the Act passed in 1801, with completion probably in 1804. Most of the $3\frac{1}{4}$ miles were dead straight and there was one entrance lock off the Hull, able to take keels 64' x 14'10". A basin was built at Leven. During the 1820s there was at least one regular carrier from Leven. The York & North Midland Railway had powers to buy the canal in 1847 but did not exercise them. However the canal continued busy until the Hull & Hornsea Railway opened in 1864. Thereafter traffic, after a brief revival in the early twentieth century, declined. The Bethell family closed the canal in 1935 and sold it in 1963 to Mr Frank Hopkinson of Conisbrough who died in 1969.

LINTON LOCK, SWALE, BEDALE BECK, Yorkshire. See River Ouse (above York).

LISKEARD & LOOE UNION CANAL, Cornwall. The Liskeard & Looe was projected to carry lime and sea-sand inland as a manure. First considered in 1777 nothing was done until 1823 when James Green made a survey for a tub-boat canal with inclined planes from Sandplace, which would be linked to the sea by a barge cut. Another survey was made by John Edgcumbe and others for a locked canal, which was adopted, the Act passing in 1825 with the line fully open in 1828. In a length of $5\frac{7}{8}$ miles from Terras Pill, Looe, to Moorswater about a mile from Liskeard, there were 25 locks, one large one at Terras Pill, the others above Sandplace 57' x 13'6". From the start the canal did well, costing little more than the estimate. By 1836 traffic in fertilizer was declining but the canal was saved by the new Caradon copper  mines opened in 1837 and 1840. From the mid-1840s the mines and the Cheesewring granite quarries were joined to the canal head by a tramroad and traffic became such that it could not cope. So a railway was built by the canal company between Liskeard and Looe and opened in 1860. The canal quickly became disused, although the lower section from Terras Pill to Sandplace, which could take bigger boats, lasted until about 1910.

75.

LITTLE OUSE or BRANDON RIVER, Norfolk, Suffolk, LAKENHEATH LODE. The Little Ouse enters the Great Ouse at Brandon Creek. It was probably used from the early Middle Ages, an Act of 1670 sanctioned improvements from Wilton Bridge, $9\frac{1}{2}$ miles from Brandon Creek, to Thetford (13 miles). The work was executed by the Earl of Arlington and the navigation from Wilton Bridge remained in his family until 1696, when the rights passed to Thetford Corporation. Under Thetford the navigation works decayed, although from 1742 the Corporation built staunches, for the collapse of Denver sluice in 1713 caused unhampered movement of waters. Tolls and maintenance had been leased, but the lessees failed to do their work properly and by 1820 Thetford Corporation were in direct supervision. They rebuilt all the staunches between 1827 and 1835. Thetford were responsible for seven staunches, all of the vertical guillotine gate type, affording an opening for craft of 12'6" beam, but there was an eighth, Crosswater staunch, outside their jurisdiction at Botany Bay, the junction with the 3 miles Lakenheath Lode on which there was one staunch, Highbridge. Crosswater, under the South Level Drainage and Navigation Commissioners, had a pair of mitred gates, replaced before 1908 by a guillotine. There were no pound locks on the Little Ouse because there were no mills below Thetford and so no mill-navigation conflict. Trade was heavier and more profitable after the rebuilding of the

76. A typical Leeds & Liverpool motor short boat.

staunches, with coal and timber coming up from King's Lynn and flints, chalk and marl were useful local traffics. As many as forty lighters were at work, but in 1845 the Norwich-Ely Railway was opened via Thetford and Brandon. Thetford Corporation cut tolls and the navigation continued to pay its way because of the local traffic, to which was added fertilizer. James Fison had works at Thetford and Two Mile Bottom. At the end of the nineteenth century Fison's were using a steam tug towing trains of lighters between Thetford and Lynn. By the turn of the century there was little traffic save for Fison's who lent the Corporation money to keep the river open. No tolls were taken after 1901, but Fison's continued to use the river and bear expenses until 1914. By the 1930 Land Drainage Act the Little Ouse came under the authority of the Great Ouse Catchment Board, navigation rights remaining with Thetford Corporation. During the 1950s the Great Ouse River Board, successor to the Catchment Board, replaced the delapidated staunches with steel sluices. Concrete ramps were built to haul pleasure rowing boats round, but ordinary craft can only go as far as the tail of Brandon staunch. Lakenheath Lode was probably last used in the 1920s.

LITTLE PUNCHARD GILL BOAT LEVEL, Yorkshire. An underground canal to boat away lead ore in a mine in Arkengarthdale above Richmond in Swaledale. It was closed in 1860.

LIVERPOOL CANAL PROJECT. In 1765 the Duke of Bridgewater had considered taking his own canal over the Mersey at Runcorn Gap into Liverpool. It was revived in 1768 by a Liverpool group when Brindley did a survey and a combined road and canal aqueduct over the Mersey was considered. This became a part of the 1770 Liverpool Canal scheme for a waterway from the Trent & Mersey via Cronton, Halewood and Toxteth to join the new Leeds & Liverpool. Later the line was varied to include Wigan and a junction with the Lancaster. When in 1772 a Liverpool Canal Bill was introduced, both the Sankey and the Leeds & Liverpool combined to defeat it, the latter worried at a rival in Wigan.

LLANDEILO & LLANDOVERY CANAL PROJECTS, Carmarthenshire. There were proposals for canals up the Loughor and Towy valleys from the coast to Llandovery, the first in 1770, and again in 1793 when Thomas Sheasby made a survey from Pen-coed on the estuary of the Loughor up to Llandovery via Llandeilo. By 1798 the proposal had been wound up, although discussed later in various forms between 1810 and 1824.

LLANSAMLET (SMITH'S) CANAL, Glamorganshire. Built by John Smith, son-in-law of Chauncey Townsend and owner of a colliery at Llansamlet to take coal 3 miles to the River Tawe at Foxhole above Swansea, and completed about 1784. It was initially busy but it probably ceased to be used after 1852.

LLECHRYD CANAL, Cardiganshire. In about 1772 a cut was made from the Teifi near Llechryd about six miles above Cardigan, to a tinplate works at Castle Malgwyn. This may have been a water channel but there is evidence of barges carrying iron ore and timber. The tinplate works was closed in 1806, but the Teifi was used into the 1900s to carry quarried stone.

LONDON & CAMBRIDGE JUNCTION CANAL PROJECT. Such a waterway would have made through communciation possible between London and King's Lynn, as the link between the Stort and the Ouse. Robert Whitworth did a survey in 1779-80 from Bishop's Stortford to the Cam at Cambridge. In 1789 John Rennie suggested cuts to join the Fen lodes and much later Francis and Netlam Giles, working for Rennie, surveyed for a canal from Bishop's Stortford to the Cam at Clayhithe below Cambridge, with a branch from Sawston to Whaddon. An Act passed in 1812 for this London & Cambridge Junction Canal but the required funds had not been subscribed. A further Act passed in 1814, which allowed work to proceed as far as the capital allowed, but little was done. Completion of the Eau Brink Cut at King's Lynn in 1821, giving an improved navigation at the mouth of the Ouse, revived the Cambridge proposals, the younger Sir George Duckett, owner of the Stort, being particularly interested.

LONDON - PORTSMOUTH SCHEMES. In 1803 John Rennie planned a 100 mile canal with 41 locks and a 4400 yd tunnel and expected naval stores, chalk and coal to be carried on this waterway, which would run from the Croydon Canal to near Portsmouth dockyard. Rennie revived the idea in 1810 as a 'Grand Southern Canal' from the Medway to Portsmouth but again the Bill was defeated.

LOUGHBOROUGH NAVIGATION, Leicestershire, Nottinghamshire. There had been plans as early as 1634 to make the Soar navigable to Leicester, Thomas Skipwith being granted letters patent by Charles I. His funds ran out after a few miles of improvement and nothing further was attempted until 1734 when a Bill was considered. In 1765-6 the project was revived and an Act for the Soar to be made navigable to Loughborough passed in 1766. Brindley made a survey for the commissioners. He recommended a canal for part of the route but since the commissioners had no power to make this, the scheme had to lapse. It was not revived until 1775 when a local group sought and obtained in 1776 an Act which allowed cuts and canal work. The Loughborough Navigation, now a company of proprietors, was to be for local traffic and the authorized capital was low, £7000. John Smith was made engineer and work started. Staunches on the East Anglian pattern were made at Redhill and near Loughborough, but found unsuitable, being replaced by locks on the recommendation of young William Jessop. He was called in to report in 1777 because the promoters saw that this was going to be more than a mere local waterway, for the Erewash Canal had been authorized. By 1778 the navigation was fully open and by 1780 Jessop's improvements had been made, so that in the $9\frac{1}{4}$ miles between the Trent and Loughborough six locks had been built, for craft 72'3" x 14'3". A seventh, Kegworth flood lock, was later added. The navigation had cost only £9,200. Traffic was much helped by the opening of the Erewash. A first dividend of 5 per cent was paid in 1780, but in 1790 this had reached 20 per cent. There were now plans to extend the navigation to Leicester, make the Wreak navigable to Melton Mowbray, and build a canal to the collieries in Charnwood Forest. Apart from the Leicester and Melton traffic, the Loughborough benefited from the opening of the Oakham Canal and of the Leicestershire & Northamptonshire Union, and when in 1814 the Grand Union was opened from the Grand Junction. The dividends became remarkable, 80 per cent average in 1803-5, and in 1827-9 a maximum of 154 per cent. In 1830 Loughborough shares were at £3000 each. The opening in 1832 of the Leicester & Swannington provided competition, much increased in 1840 by the Midland Counties Railway from Derby and Nottingham to Leicester, running parallel with the Soar. Share prices fell but the navigation carried coal in competition with rail, and the Mountsorrel granite traffic remained important. In 1863 the Grand Junction put forward a scheme of amalgamation of all the waterways to Birmingham, Coventry and Leicester, but it lapsed. It was revived when in 1894 the Grand Junction bought the Leicestershire & Northamptonshire Union, the Grand Union and arranged low through tolls with the Leicester, the Loughborough and the Erewash, with options to purchase. Not until 1932 was the Loughborough, with the Leicester and the Erewash bought by the new Grand Union. Commercial traffic remained on the Loughborough until the 1960s and has recently revived.

LOUTH NAVIGATION, Lincolnshire. This navigation was partly a canalization of the River Lud, built to open the town and district of Louth to the Humber. A survey was made in 1756 by the drainage engineer John Grundy at the request of Louth Corporation. He recommended a line to the Humber at Tetney Haven below Grimsby. John Smeaton was called in later as consultant, and reported in 1760, favouring Grundy's route. The Act passed in 1763, establishing commissioners to administer the navigation. Money could only be raised under the Act by borrowing on the credit of the tolls and the commissioners had the task of finding possible lenders which took time, but work started in 1765. Some of the navigation was ready by 1767, but it was not complete to Louth until 1770, a distance of $11\frac{3}{8}$ miles, with eight locks of varied size, including the sea lock at Tetney Haven. The minimum size was 85'11" x 15'3", six of the locks being built with chamber sides composed of four segmental arches in the vertical plane, to resist lateral earth pressure. Traffic upwards, merchandise, coal, groceries and timber, was in the hands of keels and billyboys to wharves at Louth. Wool and corn were the principal exports. Tolls were leased and from 1770 were taken by one of the commissioners, Charles Chaplin. He also took over maintenance. Later in 1777 he secured a 99 year lease, but neglected the navigation, which fell into a bad state. A grandson, George Chaplin, looked after the works better and the family seem to have done well. Inevitably in the 1840s the navigation was threatened by railways, in particular the Grimsby-Louth line. It came under railway control in 1847 when the Great Northern bought the remainder of the Chaplin lease. Eventually in 1876 the 99 year lease ran out, but the GNR did not apply for renewal, since they were not bothered about any competition the Louth Navigation might offer. Further leases were arranged but traffic was on the decline and ceased during the 1914-18 War. In 1920 the commissioners applied to be relieved of maintenance, the bridges being taken over by the local authorities. In 1924 all the navigation property was sold and the waterway allowed to become derelict.

LYDNEY CANAL, Gloucestershire. To market Forest of Dean coal there were two water routes, via the Severn and the Wye. The problem was transport between the mines and the rivers. In 1801 a scheme was proposed for a tramroad between Lydney on the Severn and Lydbrook on the Wye although this was not authorized until 1809, spurred by the construction of a rival tramroad from the Forest to a proposed new dock at the harbour of Bullo Pill, 12 miles up the Severn from Lydney. John Rennie suggested a canal link between the tramroad at Lydney and the river, because Lydney pill was so shallow. In 1810 a small ship canal was authorized to join the much earlier Pidcock's Canal. Under this 1810 Act the tramroad and canal became the Severn & Wye Railway & Canal Co. and work proceeded on both projects; the tramroad was completed to Lydbrook on the Wye in

1811, while the canal was finished in 1813. There had been several changes of engineer, first Astley Bowdler, soon replaced by a Jessop probably Josias, in 1811 replaced in his turn by the younger Thomas Sheasby. The proposed outer harbour was built in 1821, 400 ton vessels could use this but only 300 tonners could enter the canal, one mile in length with a tide lock able to take ships 100' x 24'. During the 1830s Lydney Canal trade improved although railway proposals were in the air. The rival Bullo Pill line became a broad gauge railway in 1854 but the Severn & Wye carried on as a horse line until steam locomotives were introduced in 1864. Lydney kept busy as a railway port although in 1927 the coal tips at the top end of the canal were removed. Today under British Transport Docks Board control the port is still open although only the seaward end of the canal is used and no coal has been shipped since 1960, rail access to the harbour ceasing by 1965, but West African logs, for a local plywood mill, came up from Avonmouth by barge until 1976.

MACCLESFIELD CANAL, Cheshire. The Macclesfield received its Act in 1826, although there had been several earlier schemes. The canal was to provide a more direct line from Manchester to the Potteries and the South, joining the Peak Forest above the top lock at Marple and the Trent & Mersey by a junction at Hall Green near Kidsgrove, built by the latter. Although the Macclesfield was planned by Thomas Telford, the engineer was William Crosley the younger. There are eight aqueducts on the $26\frac{1}{8}$ miles main line, and twelve locks with masonry chambers grouped in a flight at Bosley. Water is supplied from surface streams and from two reservoirs, Sutton near Macclesfield and Bosley. The canal was opened for traffic in November 1831. There is one branch at High Lane near Stockport $\frac{1}{4}$ mile long. After a short independent career during which tolls were reduced because of railway competition, the Macclesfield sold out to the Sheffield, Ashton-under-Lyne & Manchester Railway, (later the Manchester, Sheffield & Lincolnshire) in 1846. Traffic on the Macclesfield was never heavy compared with the Trent & Mersey, although steam tugs were encouraged and a passenger packet put on in the 1840s; and the railway owners started a carrying fleet which lasted until 1892. In the early twentieth century Macclesfield traffic was mainly coal, raw cotton, grain and stone. Coal lingered until 1953 when the Goyt mills near Marple changed over to oil fuel. The canal is much in demand as a pleasure route.

77.

MACKWORTH'S CANAL, Glamorganshire. In about 1696 a 300 yard tidal cut was possibly built from a pill on the River Neath to Sir Humphrey Mackworth's lead and copper works about a mile below Neath, later sealed by gates, so that craft of up to 100 tons could reach the works. It seems to have been disused by 1720.

MANCHESTER, BOLTON & BURY CANAL, Lancashire. This was promoted with the support of the Mersey & Irwell who wanted to extend their trade. The initiative seems to have come from Bolton, some of whose citizens commissioned the 1790 surveys and estimates from Matthew Fletcher. More surveys were prepared by Hugh Henshall for the canal to join the Irwell. After the parliamentary survey by Charles McNiven the Act passed in 1791 for a narrow canal to divide at Prestolee near Kearsley, one line going to Bolton, the other to Bury. Fletcher was put in general charge of the works and Henshall retained as consultant. The Manchester, Bolton & Bury put forward two projects to rival Rochdale proposals; in 1791 a canal from Bury over to Hebden Bridge, followed in 1792 by the Bury & Sladen Canal to join the Rochdale at Sladen above Littleborough. In the other direction the Manchester, Bolton & Bury were interested in joining up with the Leeds & Liverpool's proposed line to Wigan at Red Moss. Bills for both were introduced in 1793 and failed, although the Red Moss line continued to be advocated. The Leeds & Liverpool were amenable, and an agreement was made in 1794 between them and the Manchester, Bolton & Bury, the latter deciding to build broad locks, converting the narrow ones already constructed. Bolton was reached in October 1796 and Bury three weeks before, traffic having begun over part of the canal the previous year; while in 1796 a passenger packet was put on between Bolton and Salford. The canal was not joined to the Irwell. In 1800 the Manchester, Bolton & Bury were considering an aqueduct over the Irwell to join the Rochdale. Eventually they cut through to the river in 1808 and this completed the canal. It was 11 miles long from the Irwell to Bolton running up the Irwell valley, the route to Bury continuing above the Irwell, $4\frac{3}{4}$ miles from the top of Prestolee locks, while the Bolton line ran above the Croal to extensive basins in the town. There were seventeen locks able to take barges or flats 68' x 14'2" and either a pair of short narrow boats or a single standard one on the skew. Many of the locks were in staircases, the Prestolee flight of six being made up of two three rises. Above Prestolee the lines to Bolton and Bury were level, with two tunnels at Bury of 66 yd and 141 yd, the latter on a wharf extension only wide enough for narrow boats, there were also two short tunnels in Salford, really bridges of 34 yd and 50 yd. It was a canal of aqueducts, a three arched stone one over the Irwell at Clifton, a four arched stone one also over the Irwell at Prestolee below the locks, and a three arched brick aqueduct over the Tonge on the line to Bolton. Water came from the Elton reservoir near Bury fed by Irwell floodwater. The company did not give up ideas of joining the Leeds & Liverpool at Red Moss until in 1809 they heard of the latter's Bill to build a branch from Wigan to the Bridgewater at Leigh. The Manchester, Bolton & Bury became a prosperous local coal carrying canal from the collieries at Clifton and Kearsley down to Salford and Manchester and up to mills at Bolton and Bury. Passenger services were run, at first between Bolton and Salford, from 1810, between Bolton and Bury.

Plate 7.

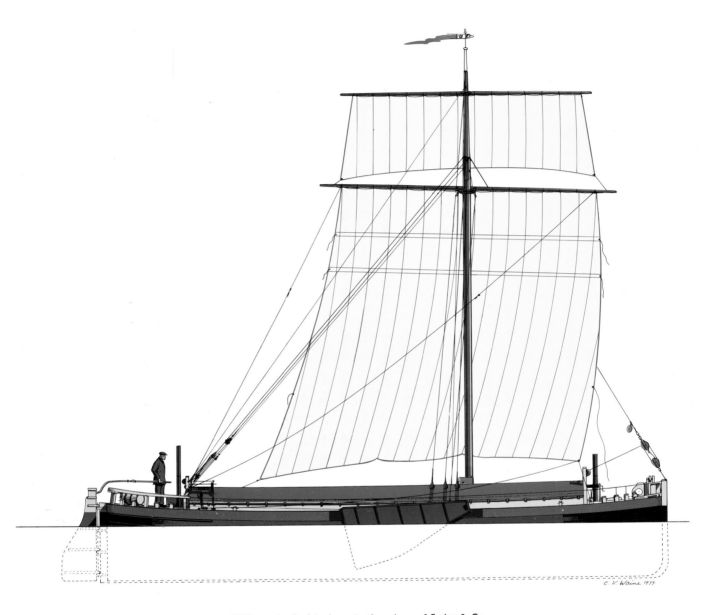

C. V. Waine 1977.

Sheffield Size Keel
DIMENSIONS: 61'6" x 15'6".

THIS wooden keel is shown in the colours of Furley & Co.,
of Gainsborough. The normal crew was two, the mate living
in the forecastle where most of the cooking was done. The
captain lived aft, sometimes with his wife.

Suffolk Stour Lighte
LENGTH of example 46'

Norfolk Wherry
LENGTH: about 50 to 80 feet.

HULLS of wooden wherries (a few were built of iron) were well rounded with plenty of flare at bow and stern and a 'V'- bottom, much attention being paid to the design as they were so shallow draughted. Oak was used for the hull planking, with garboard strakes of elm.

THESE lighters were worked in pairs carrying a total of 26 tons on a draught of 2 feet 5 inches. Accommodation was under deck forward in the second lighter for the two man crew or a family. They were double ended and clinker built.

Railways entered the Manchester, Bolton & Bury scene at an early date with the Act of 1825 for the Bolton & Leigh. By 1830 the canal company were promoting a railway between Bolton and Manchester to use the canal line and by an Act of 1831 turned themselves into a railway company, a second Act the following year authorizing the railway, not exactly following the canal, which had to be kept and maintained. Jesse Hartley built this line which was opened in 1838, but did not do too well, in 1847 becoming part of the Lancashire & Yorkshire. Large tonnages of coal were handled by canal until the 1930s when some of the principal mines had closed, notably in 1928 Wet Earth on the private 1½ mile Fletcher's Canal which joined the Manchester, Bolton & Bury at Clifton and had been navigable since about 1791. With coal went subsidence, from which the canal suffered seriously in the late 1870s, coupled with a burst at Agecroft in 1881 which led to reinforcement work where the canal ran close above the Irwell. LMS policy was not favourable to the canal. In 1936 there were more bad bursts including one at Prestolee above the locks, which cut the Bury line. It was not repaired although traffic had been brisk. In 1939 the Ministry of Transport ordered the piping of a ½ mile section at Agecroft to protect the nearby works of the Magnesium Electric Co, should bombing cause a breach in the canal. In 1941 the LMS closed the canal above the Clifton aqueduct through to Bolton, leaving the Bury line as an isolated waterway on which coal moved from Ladyshore colliery near the 1936 burst to Bury until in 1951 this colliery closed. For a few years until 1956 coal was ferried across the canal, still using the old containers, from a road served wharf to Crompton's paper mills, and below Agecroft traffic lasted until the early 1950s. There had been no traffic to Bolton since 1924 and from 1961 the canal was completely abandoned.

MANCHESTER & DEE SHIP CANAL PROJECTS.   A Mersey-Dee canal was suggested at the time of the Chester Canal Act of 1772. Then in 1823-4 Robert Stevenson surveyed a line for 400 ton craft from Dawpool near Heswall via Frodsham and Lymm to Manchester, but the Bill was lost in 1825. William Chapman revived this for smaller 250 ton ships. Reverting to a Mersey-Dee line, in 1828 Telford, Stevenson and Alexander Nimmo advised on a ship canal from Wallasey pool across the Wirral to the mouth of the Dee at Hilbre Island. A Manchester ship canal was revived by Sir John Rennie's survey of 1837 which proposed a canal from Liverpool to Warrington which could be extended to Manchester. This was seen in the 1840s as an enlargement of the Mersey & Irwell Navigation for 400 ton vessels. In the 1870s the project was revived as the Manchester Ship Canal.

MANCHESTER & SALFORD JUNCTION CANAL, Lancashire.   The Manchester, Bolton & Bury were keen to join the Bridgewater across the Irwell, but the Duke feared loss of traffic to the Mersey & Irwell. The Manchester, Bolton & Bury nevertheless pressed their junction, in 1800 planning an aqueduct over the Irwell, but were strongly opposed by the Mersey & Irwell. In 1805 the Mersey & Irwell themselves proposed a canal between the Irwell and the Rochdale Canal and other ideas followed. On their side the Bridgewater trustees suggested in 1835 a link at Hulme between their canal and the Irwell, opened with three locks in 1838. In spite of this the Mersey & Irwell pressed for a Rochdale connection and secured their Act in 1836. John Gilbert was the engineer and the canal, an independent company, the Manchester & Salford Junction, was opened in 1839. It was only ⅝ of a mile long with a 499 yd tunnel and 4 locks rising to the Rochdale for craft 71' x 14'. Because the Rochdale refused any water, it all had to be pumped up the locks from the Irwell by two steam engines, one by the river the other by a small summit reservoir. No heavy traffic came because of the Hulme link and the canal seemed unlikely to pay. To stop closure the Mersey & Irwell took it over in 1842. Revenue was never large and in 1875 part of the canal was closed to enable the Cheshire Lines Committee to carry their railway over into Manchester Central. In 1899 the new Great Northern Deansgate goods station was joined to the canal by two hoist shafts for railway interchange traffic between Manchester docks via the Irwell. The canal was now under Ship Canal control who abandoned it in 1936, for it had not been used since 1922.

MANCHESTER SHIP CANAL, Lancashire, Cheshire.   Mancunians were fearful of a rail monopoly between Liverpool and their town and Liverpool's port charges. This was given added point when in 1872 the Bridgewater Canal was bought by railway interests, and ship canal ideas were seriously revived. They started in a modest way by a letter to the "Manchester Guardian" in 1876 from Mr. George Hicks, later auditor of the Manchester Ship Canal Co. He observed the shortcomings and possibilities of the Mersey & Irwell as a navigation. An engineer, Hamilton Fulton, made a report to the Manchester Chamber of Commerce but because of depression the idea was dropped. However in the early 1880s interest revived. At the head of the scheme was Daniel Adamson, a Durham man who owned an engineering works at Hyde in north-east Cheshire. James Abernethy, the engineer, said a ship canal was feasible; so from 1882 meetings were called, pamphlets written and money raised. Hamilton Fulton returned with plans for a tidal canal up to Manchester on one level. This appeared cheap and was strongly supported but wisely not adopted. Abernethy favoured a canal with locks and another consultant, Leader Williams, concurred, and became engineer. Support now came from Manchester and Salford city councils, but the parliamentary struggle was bitter because of the opposition of Liverpool, of the railways and the railway controlled Bridgewater Navigation Co. Two Bills were thrown out but the third passed on 6 August 1885 after many alterations to satisfy Liverpool. The latter feared their port would be silted up if the canal made use of the reservoir of tidal water upstream. So the ship canal entrance was moved from Runcorn to Eastham. Such an extension added to the cost, now estimated at £6,311,137 for the works, plus the cost of the Bridgewater Navigation Co. This the Ship Canal Co. had to buy to give them control of the Mersey & Irwell, whose navigation and water they needed.

Money was the Ship Canal Co's problem, for an issue of shares failed, since two thirds of the £8m capital had to be raised within two years. They set up a consultative committee to examine the soundness of the scheme and its estimates. This found in favour of the canal but recommended a stronger Board of Directors. Daniel Adamson then resigned as chairman in favour of Lord Egerton, a descendant of the Duke of Bridgewater. Money came in better, aided by the creation of preference shares, but the Bridgewater was bought only a month before the closing date. The contractor was Thomas Andrew Walker and cutting then proceeded employing 11,000 men. The canal was built with a minimum depth of 26' and a general minimum bottom width of 120' save at the Latchford narrows where it is only 90'. At times up to 17,000 men were engaged on the works and 80 steam shovels (78) and dredgers. Some 1,228 miles of railway track were laid and 173 locomotives and 6300 wagons employed. The Weaver mouth had to be sealed and water led into the Mersey via sluices. More sluices (Randles) were built above Runcorn to carry off ebb tidal water, for the tide was allowed to flood up the canal from Eastham if it exceeded 14' 2". Below Frodsham the River Gowy was syphoned under the canal. Many bridges had to be built, either swinging spans or sufficiently high to clear masts and funnels. Most of the road bridges were hydraulic swing bridges to a standard design, but all the railway bridges were high level except that in Manchester for the dock railway. Apart from the entrance locks at Eastham where three were built side by side, locks were built at Latchford above Warrington, Irlam, Barton and Mode Wheel. At Eastham the three locks measured 600' x 80', 350' x 50' and 150' x 30', the other locks were duplicated, all to a standard size, the larger 600' x 65', the smaller 350' x 45'. Both were fitted with intermediate gates so that the chambers could be divided. Side locks were built into the Mersey; Weston Mersey lock opposite Weston Point for the port and Weaver traffic 600' x 45', Bridgewater lock opposite Runcorn docks and the Bridgewater Canal 400' x 45', and Old Quay lock just above Runcorn where the old Mersey & Irwell's Runcorn & Latchford Canal had entered the Mersey. This measured 250' x 45'. The final piece of hydraulic mechanism was the swing aqueduct at Barton, not opened until the very end of construction, on 21 August 1893, after which the old aqueduct was demolished.

Walker the contractor died in 1890 which was a year of floods, notably at Latchford where the Mersey overflowed into the works, first in January, then again in November. Later mishaps were bank slips at Ince in 1891 and the collapse of the Bridgewater lock in 1892. There was trouble with Walker's executors and at the end of 1890 the company decided to carry on with direct labour, which immediately led to unrest. It was now clear that the company's capital could not complete the canal. Manchester Corporation came to the rescue and an Act of 1891 allowed them to lend the canal company £3m on debentures, and to nominate five directors. As well as cutting a canal the company were creating a port. Their first was the little Saltport opened in 1892 at the mouth of the Weaver on the Eastham side, to tap the navigation's traffic from Winsford and Northwich. At Manchester and Salford they planned a considerable dock system, three docks at Salford for ocean-going ships, and four smaller ones up the canal in Manchester for coasters. The smaller docks were built on the site of Pomona Gardens in Manchester and have kept the old name, the larger are called Manchester docks. Individually they are numbered not named, a later addition being No. 9 opened in 1905. A No. 10 was planned but not built. There is no No. 5 although it was started opposite the Pomona group. In 1892 Manchester Corporation advanced another £2m also on debentures. With it came the right of the Corporation to appoint a majority of the directors until half the £5m they had lent was paid off. The 36 mile canal was opened to traffic on 1 January 1894. First boat up the waterway that day was Mr. Samuel Platt's steam yacht NORSEMAN with his fellow directors aboard, but the official opening took place on 21 May 1894, by the Queen. The canal had cost a total of £14,347,891 due to increased labour, material and flood damage costs.

The railways were unco-operative and at first it proved difficult to attract the liner companies. Manchester was cheaper than Liverpool and tonnages slowly climbed. The port's own shipping company, Manchester Liners, started its services to Canada and the United States in 1898, and the canal was fed by traffic from the established ports along its length, Ellesmere Port, Weston Point and Runcorn. These found the ship canal a better way out than the upper Mersey estuary. Because sea-going ships could use it, the canal became a centre of industry, attracted by the ease with which raw materials could be brought and products exported. This has led to the idea of the Manchester Ship Canal as a 36 mile long dock served by rail and road, with the Trafford Park industrial estate, the Shell Chemicals plant at Carrington and the oil refineries at Stanlow. Here in 1922 and 1933 the Ship Canal Co. built two oil docks and in 1954 opened the Queen Elizabeth II Dock at Eastham for oil tankers. This has a separate entrance lock down the Mersey, so sited because of siltation problems in the Eastham approaches. The lock is 807' x 100' and is not connected to the canal. Manchester has participated in the container revolution with a special berth and cranage, cars are exported from the Vauxhall works at Ellesmere Port, and heavy electrical equipment is handled by roll-on roll-off ferries. Vessels of 15,000 tons deadweight can reach the oil berth at Ince above the Stanlow refineries and 12,500 tons deadweight ships can reach Manchester. The port handles nearly 17m tons of goods a year and about 5000 vessels use the canal annually. The 'masting crane' at Eastham will remove masts, funnels and radar scanners which would otherwise foul the fixed high level bridges. Ships can pass except at Latchford where the narrows demand single line working.

MARDYKE CANAL PROJECT, Essex. The Mardyke helps to drain the marshland north of Grays and enters the Thames at Purfleet where part of it was used by craft

78. A steam navvy working on the Manchester Ship Canal. Most were made by Ruston & Proctor, each of theirs could shift 2,500 tons of spoil in 12 hours.

C.V WAINE.

coming to the powder magazines there. In the later eighteenth century there were ideas of extending the navigation. A canal was proposed in 1776 but received little support. Not until 1833 was a Mardyke Canal again considered, a survey being made by Edward Lapidge. During the 1870s the Mardyke was used to take manure to local farms, the boats returning with produce.

MARKET WEIGHTON CANAL, Yorkshire. A navigation with a three fold purpose, land drainage in the plain of York, better transport and agricultural improvement. It was discussed in 1765 to run from the Humber to Market Weighton and Pocklington on the edge of the Yorkshire wolds, but Pocklington was dropped and the project became a drain cum navigation from Market Weighton to the Humber, using the Foulness River. The Act passed in 1772 and land drainage was the first consideration, to the extent that locks had not to hold back water above a certain height. Commissioners were to make the works and the completed scheme was to be handed over to trustees. John Smith the younger made the survey and was appointed consultant. Samuel Allam was resident and James and John Pinkerton the contractors. Smith's work was checked by the more competent Grundy who became consultant in his place. Cutting went ahead slowly, some of the canal being open by 1776 and a portion of the Foulness River the following year, but work stopped and did not start again until 1780, most of the money having been spent. There had been a new estimate for finishing the canal to smaller dimensions in 1778 and Grundy proposed to stop on Weighton Common because of the rise of land for the last mile and a half into Weighton. This was done, the canal ending down a by-road at River Head some two miles from the town. As completed in 1782 the canal, including the canalized river, was $9\frac{5}{8}$ miles long with an entrance lock and three others. The change in dimensions allowed keels of 66' x 14'10" into the lower pound via the entrance lock, called Weighton lock, but craft of only 57' x 14'2" up the other locks to the canal head. In 1834 there were ideas to extend to Market Weighton but nothing was done, except probably at this time, the building of the $\frac{3}{4}$ mile Holme canal from a little below the terminal basin at River Head to the Holme road at Canal Head. This was a private branch called after its owner, Sir Edward Vavasour. Railway threats came with the York-Beverley line which reached Market Weighton in 1847 and in 1850 the shareholders sold out to the railway, the York & North Midland later the North Eastern. The trustees however remained in control while Sir Edward Vavasour's Canal remained private. From the mid-1860s the upper $3\frac{1}{2}$ miles or so were allowed to silt up and by 1894 were considered unnavigable. The main traffic was now to Henry Williamson & Co, brick and tile makers of Newport. From 1897 they agreed to make up revenue for 20 years as long as the lowermost 4 miles were kept open for them. Under the Market Weighton Drainage Act of 1900, the NER abandoned their interest and powers were given to abandon the canal above Sod House lock, the lowest apart from the entrance lock. Williamson's found they had to make up the revenue every year and by 1917, the last of their twenty year guarantee, traffic had almost ceased. Williamson's were allowed to continue use at their own risk and in the 1920s, after some dredging, traffic revived a little. There was none at all after 1958 and in 1971 the entrance lock was abandoned, but since there have been moves towards restoration.

River MEDWAY, Kent. The Medway has always been navigable to Maidstone and attempts were made in the sixteenth and seventeenth century to improve it to Yalding 6 miles above Maidstone. Under an Act of 1740 the river was improved to Tonbridge, a distance of 16 miles with 14 locks, the works being completed about 1750, although authorized to be further improved to Forest Row near East Grinstead. The navigation undertakers had a carrying monopoly. In 1792 came an Act to improve the lower Medway from Aylesford to Maidstone followed by another in 1802 which resulted in the building of Allington tidal lock so that barges could reach Maidstone on all tides. Following an Act of 1824 improvements from downstream at Halling up to Maidstone, a distance of 9 miles were made, the obstructive Aylesford bridge rebuilt and a horse towing path made. Meanwhile the upper Medway had been doing very well. From 1828 the owner of Tonbridge Mill, Mr. Christie proposed to extend the upper navigation to Penshurst under the powers of the 1740 Act, although little work was done. Arrival of the railway at Maidstone in 1844 forced the upper navigation to cut its tolls and a decline set in. The company was reformed in 1892, 1899 and 1903 to try and rescue the navigation by modernisation, with no success. By an Act of 1911 a new conservancy authority was established backed by Kent County Council, which made improvements, replacing 13 old locks by 10 new ones. Re-opened in 1915, losses were great at first but later diminished; no tolls were taken after 1927-8. In 1934 the Conservancy was replaced by a catchment board later under the Kent River Authority. Pleasure craft can still reach Tonbridge but barges do not go above Tovil paper mills just above Maidstone. In 1881 the lower Medway authority was divided, the old Company being now confined to the 6 miles between Maidstone and Hawkwood, below to Sheerness the Medway Conservancy took over. In 1969 the Conservancy was replaced by a new Medway Ports Authority which also absorbed the Lower Medway Navigation Company. The lower river is still commercially active.

MELTON MOWBRAY NAVIGATION, Leicestershire. A tributary of the Soar, the Wreak was considered in the late eighteenth century suitable for improvement so that boats could reach Melton Mowbray. The passage of the Act in 1796 for the Leicester Navigation encouraged the promoters and in the same year the Act for the Melton Mowbray Navigation was secured, it was opened in 1797, $14\frac{3}{4}$ miles from the Soar at Turnwater meadow near Syston where the Wreak was used as a part of the Leicester Navigation, to Melton Mowbray. There were 12 broad locks 91' x 15'. The Leicester Navigation had been open in 1794 and once complete the Melton Mowbray did well, although there was competition from land carriage and the Grantham Canal. The arrival in 1846 of a railway between Syston and Melton doomed the navigation, who sharply reduced their tolls. In 1862 the Melton was offered to the Loughborough Navigation and to the Midland Railway, but neither were interested and the navigation kept going until 1877 when it closed under an Act of abandonment.

MERSEY & IRWELL NAVIGATION, Lancashire. Manchester, on the Irwell, depended on road communication with Liverpool and the sea until the eighteenth century, for the Mersey, which the Irwell joins below Irlam, was unnavigable above Warrington, and obstructed by fish weirs below. Attempts were made to secure an Act to make the Mersey and the Irwell navigable in the 1660s but without success, although the fish weirs were cleared in the 1690s, so that there was traffic between Liverpool and Bank Quay, Warrington. Thomas Steers surveyed the Mersey and the Irwell in 1712, with the object of reaching Manchester and providing a navigation to within 28 miles of the navigable rivers of Yorkshire. The Act for the Douglas was passed in 1720 and for the Weaver in March 1721, the Act for the Mersey & Irwell passed June 1721. The three navigations were interdependent, the salters of the Weaver needing the coal which would be brought down the Douglas and the Mersey & Irwell. Work started on the Mersey & Irwell in 1724 and the navigation was open in 1736, with 8 locks for craft 68' x 17'6". The navigation was $20\frac{1}{4}$ miles long between Bank Quay, Warrington and Quay Street, Manchester. More improvements followed over the next two decades, for by 1761 two long cuts had been made, the Howley in Warrington and the Woolston old cut above the town, with a third at Butchersfield near Rixton planned. There was a towpath for man haulage. The Mersey & Irwell had around 1736 proposed to enlarge its system by making the Worsley Brook navigable from the Irwell to Worsley with a canal to Booth's Bank, providing water transport for Worsley coal into Manchester but although Steers surveyed the brook and an Act was passed in 1737 no work was done. In the 1750s the Mersey & Irwell supported a canal from the Irwell at Salford to Wigan via Eccles, Worsley and Leigh but the Bill for this was thrown out in 1753-4. From 1759 when the Duke of Bridgewater obtained the Act for his canal, the navigation operated under competition. The 'Old Quay Co.' so named after their Manchester quay, were seriously damaged by the opening in 1776 of the Duke's canal to Runcorn, and in 1779 the whole navigation, including the company's carrying fleet, was offered for auction. Under new management the Mersey & Irwell prospered despite the rival Bridgewater Canal. More cuts were made between Warrington and Manchester, but the company were concerned about the river below Warrington. So the Mersey & Irwell went ahead with a canal from Latchford above Warrington down to Runcorn. It was opened in 1804, $7\frac{3}{4}$ miles long with a lock up from the navigation at Latchford and a river lock from the canal's basin in Runcorn, probably supervised by C. McNiven. The Mersey & Irwell now had a total of 11 locks. In 1807 the Old Quay Co. started a passenger service between Manchester and Runcorn, competing with that on the Bridgewater Canal.

Steam navigation was considered on the Mersey & Irwell in 1815. Improvements started with the extension of the Woolston cut now to be $1\frac{3}{4}$ miles long, completed in 1821, while at Runcorn they built a second larger lock parallel with their existing entrance lock and a new larger basin so that traffic would be speeded in and out of the canal. These were completed during the later 1820s. At this time the Mersey & Irwell were successfully holding their own against the Bridgewater, both profiting by a sharp increase in trade. The threat of the Liverpool & Manchester Railway did not upset the Mersey & Irwell, but they opposed the Bill which passed in 1826 and from 1828 carried out certain improvements, two new cuts and two parallel locks at Butchersfield, and in 1830 started with steam tugs. Continuing their initiative in the face of the railway competition, they decided on a new canal between the Irwell and the Rochdale in 1835, a revival of an 1805 scheme. This, the

Manchester & Salford Junction, was authorized in 1836 and completed in 1839. In the 1830s they added swift boats to the regular passenger packets and in 1838 put their own steamer the stern wheeler JACK SHARP on the Mersey between Runcorn and Liverpool, with the pleasure steamer the COUNTESS OF ELLESMERE running on the Irwell to Pomona Gardens. In 1840 the navigation was extended $\frac{3}{4}$ mile to Hunt's Bank, Manchester near the later Exchange Station, the total mileage to Runcorn now being $28\frac{3}{4}$. During the early 1840s the Mersey & Irwell was profitable and confident enough to consider a close working association with the Manchester & Leeds Railway but found the railway interests against them. This led to a rate war, much to the annoyance of the Bridgewater who were unwillingly involved, and led to the latter's determination to gain control of the Mersey & Irwell in order to preserve peace with the railways. So in 1844 Lord Francis Egerton, the heir to the canal by the Duke of Bridgewater's will, bought the navigation for a total of £550,800. In 1846 the Mersey & Irwell was transferred to the Bridgewater trustees. Passenger services lasted on the Mersey & Irwell until a little after 1865. Much of the short haul traffic remained on the navigation, particularly on the Runcorn & Latchford Canal and in Manchester itself. By the 1880s the Manchester Ship Canal was under discussion, although the Bridgewater hoped to make this unnecessary by enlarging the Mersey & Irwell. Improvements were made; new sluices were built to increase the scour, a cut made at Mode Wheel and one of the locks, Calamanco, removed in 1883. There were plans for much more but the Ship Canal was now moving towards a Bill which passed in 1885. The new waterway, almost entirely swallowed up the Mersey & Irwell. The Runcorn & Latchford Canal was partly absorbed and the rest mostly disused. Bank Quay was now reached off the Ship Canal via the Walton lock branch. The Woolston new cut remained used together with the navigation up to the Butchersfield cut, where the Ship Canal was rejoined at Rixton junction. Traffic remained on parts of these truncated sections of the old navigation, although much reduced by the 1939-45 War. However Barges still use Walton lock to reach the works and mills at Bank Quay, although the Woolston new cut was last used in the 1930s and Howley Quay in 1970. Howley remains as a road haulage depot and warehouse for the Manchester Ship Canal Co.

MIDDLE LEVEL NAVIGATION, Huntingdonshire, Isle of Ely, Cambridgeshire, Norfolk. The Fens as a whole, were subdivided for drainage into three levels, the North, from the Nene to the Witham, the Middle, between the Nene and the Great Ouse, and the South between the Great Ouse and the Eastern Highlands of Norfolk and Suffolk. The Middle Level includes the old course of the Nene, flowing through March, Well Creek and Whittlesey Dyke. Well Creek is descended in a complex way from the Wellstream, which was the course of the Great Ouse to the Wash, joining the Nene and both entering the sea below Wisbech. Towards the end of the thirteenth century the Great Ouse changed direction to King's Lynn and the Nene formed a delta which covered much of the Middle Level. These delta channels were probably used for navigation during the Middle Ages but there was no improvement until the early seventeenth century, apart from the Nene's Morton's Leam of the late fifteenth century. In 1605 Lord Chief Justice Sir John Popham and other undertakers completed Popham's Eau as a drainage channel between the old Nene and the Ouse at Salters Lode above Downham Market. This took land water into the Ouse and was resuscitated by Vermuyden who was responsible for most of the Middle Level system, using gravity to carry water to his two Bedford Rivers, the hub of his drainage plan. Thus he cut the Forty Foot River from the old Nene to the Old Bedford, the Twenty Foot River from Whittlesey Dyke into the old Nene, whence water would flow by Popham's Eau and Well Creek to the Ouse, and the Sixteen Foot from the Forty Foot to Popham's Eau. These works were finished by 1651 which marked the second stage of Vermuyden's task and the completion of the drainage of the Great Level. The Twenty Foot was an extension of an earlier work of Vermuyden, Bevill's Leam, completed in 1631 from the Black Ham Drain to Whittlesey Dyke. The names Sixteen Foot, etc. refer to the original widths of the drains, nowadays much wider. Vermuyden left water levels sufficient for navigation, but there do not seem to have been any Acts authorizing navigational improvements until the nineteenth century. There was a general one in 1810, and two in 1844 and 1848 respectively for Well Creek. In 1862 the Middle Level was separated from the Bedford Level Corporation, the drainage authority established by the General Draining Act of 1663, and put under its own commissioners with offices at March. The South Level had been separated in 1827 and the North Level in 1858, although the Bedford Level Corporation remained in existence until 1914. A finance Act followed for the Middle Level in 1867 and a navigation rights Act of 1874 authorized bye laws. Meanwhile gravity drainage had been improved by the cutting of the 150' wide Middle Level Main Drain in 1844. This was a continuation of the Sixteen Foot down to the tidal Ouse at St. Germans and passed under Well Creek, which was supported by a single span aqueduct. The new channel achieved drainage of Whittlesey Mere in 1851-52 but in 1862 the outfall sluice at St. Germans was destroyed by a storm. A new sluice was ready in 1880, and in 1934 the works were enlarged when it was decided to pump all Middle Level waters into the Ouse, necessary because of peat shrinkage and land settlement. In 1966 the St. Germans pumping station was given greater capacity. Most commercial navigation finished on the Middle Level in the 1940s. Sugar beet traffic was the last, with fertilizers, coal, corn and hay among the later cargoes. Well Creek, the old Nene and Whittlesey Dyke were busiest, the route between Peterborough and the Ouse at Salters Lode. Well Creek became impassable as a through navigation but the Middle Level Commissioners reopened it in 1975. There are a few locks of modest rise on the Middle Level, as follows:- Stanground from Whittlesey Dyke into the Nene, Horsey off Whittlesey Dyke on to the Farcet River, Whittlesey or

Ashline on Whittlesey Dyke, Marmont Priory on the old Nene, giving access to Well Creek, Salters Lode between Well Creek and the Ouse, the Old Bedford sluice at Salters Lode which is not a lock, but a pair of navigation doors and a pair of sea doors, so craft can pass when the ebb tide makes a level between the Ouse and the Old Bedford River, and finally two on the Forty Foot, Horseway and Welches Dam. Stanground sluice is the smallest of all, taking craft 46' x 11'. There were about 108 miles of navigable waterway on the Middle Level according to De Salis.

MIDDLESBROUGH-REDCAR SHIP CANAL PROJECT, Yorkshire. To help Middlesbrough, suffering from competition with Sunderland and Hartlepool, a ship canal was proposed in 1832 from the Tees to a new port at Redcar.

MID-SCOTLAND SHIP CANAL PROJECT. To provide a route for warships from the Clyde to the Forth, this was a result of the successful promotion of the Manchester Ship Canal, and received further impetus from the completion in 1895 of the Kiel Canal and Germany's naval preparations. Surveys were made in 1889 and 1890, one proposing a canal from the head of Loch Long via Loch Lomond to the Forth at Alloa the other following the line of the Forth & Clyde. During the 1914-18 War further reports were prepared, to be revived during the 1939-45 War.

MILLWALL CANAL, London. A revived version of the Isle of Dogs canal, the Millwall was authorized by an Act of 1864 to run across the Isle of Dogs more to the southward as a dock, with a branch northwards to the West India Docks. After alterations of plan because of railway developments, the western part was opened as a dock, the Millwall Canal Co. becoming in 1870 the Millwall Dock Co.

MONKLAND CANAL, Lanarkshire. Promoted to bring coal from the Lanarkshire field to Glasgow as early as 1769, when James Watt made a survey from the Monkland district of north Lanarkshire. The project was well supported and the Act passed in 1770, Watt becoming engineer. By 1773 the canal had reached Barlinnie prison north west of Glasgow but stopped (Watt having left for Birmingham in 1774) for 9 years while more capital was raised. In 1782 cutting recommenced westwards to Blackhill and thence at a lower level into the centre of Glasgow, the locks being built later. These needed more water and an Act of 1790 authorized an extension eastwards to the River Calder at Woodhall, the canal also now being considered as a feeder to the Forth & Clyde, which it was to join at Port Dundas via the 'cut of junction'. By 1793 all was complete, the Monkland now $12\frac{1}{4}$ miles long from Woodhall to its Glasgow basin, with two locks at Sheepford and four staircase pairs at Blackhill, taking scows 66' x 13'6". Traffic developed as the north Lanarkshire collieries became more intensively worked. Railway competition arrived in 1826 with the completion of a horse line from the Monkland collieries to the Forth & Clyde at Kirkintilloch, while in 1831 came the locomotive worked Glasgow & Garnkirk, from Port Dundas to near Gartsherrie, nearly parallel to the canal. Both lines left the Monkland unmoved, for colliery traffic was heavy. The earliest canal branch was built by the Calder Coal Co. in 1799-1800, a mile long and called Dixon's cut. The Gartsherrie branch, less than $\frac{1}{2}$ mile long, was made in 1827 to serve two pits there, the Gartsherrie ironworks being built in 1828. The $\frac{1}{4}$ mile Langloan branch served a colliery and after 1841 an ironworks, while the Dundyvan branch ($\frac{1}{4}$ mile) served the coaling basins at Palacecraig of the Monkland & Kirkintilloch Railway. Passenger boats were introduced and people changed craft at the Blackhill locks which incidentally had to be doubled in 1841 for the heavy traffic. By this time the Monkland had a steam tug which was sold in 1846, the year the Monkland merged with the Forth & Clyde. Traffic was a strain on the water supply, solved in 1850 by an inclined plane at Blackhill (13) for empty boats to the pits and a reservoir built in 1852. During the 1860s steam scows were replacing the horse drawn ones, although limited in size by the fixed bridges eastwards from Blackhill. Prosperity was ending as coal seams were worked out. In 1867 with the Forth & Clyde, the Monkland was taken over by the Caledonian Railway, competition by this time coming from the new rail served coalfield round Wishaw. In 1870 most of the traffic was captured by the new North British line between Glasgow and Coatbridge, the Blackhill plane being closed in 1887. The last traffic was coal to a few works and the power station at Port Dundas, but there was none after 1935. Yet the Monkland was still needed as a feeder to the Forth & Clyde and could not be abandoned until 1950. It still supplies water, in particular to the modern Ravenscraig strip mill at Coatbridge.

MONMOUTHSHIRE CANAL. Promoted in 1791 to run up from Newport to Pontnewynydd above Pontypool with a long branch from outside Newport to Crumlin, the Act was secured in 1792. The younger Thomas Dadford was engineer. The line from Newport to Pontnewynydd was open in 1796 and Crumlin in 1799. Both were 11 miles long and heavily locked, 42 on the main line and 32 on the Crumlin, including a flight of ten at Cwmbran and 14 at Cefn near Rogerstone on the Crumlin line. There were three short tunnels, two at Newport, one of 140 yd under Barracks Hill, a second under Mill Street and an 87 yd one at Cwmbran. Boats became standardized at 64'9" x 9'2" with a capacity of 25 to 28 tons of coal. While the canals were building, the company was also laying feeder tramroads which their Act sanctioned within eight miles of the waterway. In Newport the canal ended in a basin by the Usk but was extended to a better site in 1798 alongside river wharves. The whole canal was regarded as complete in 1799. Meanwhile the canal company were extending their tramroad empire. An Act of 1802 authorized the Sirhowy, outside the 8 mile limit since it ran 24 miles from Newport up to the Sirhowy ironworks via the Sirhowy valley, running parallel with the Crumlin branch of the canal at Risca. Because of increased traffic the basin at Newport was by 1804 becoming full and John Hodgkinson proposed plans to extend it. These were carried out about 1808 and later augmented. In 1818 a lock was built from the basin at Potter Street into a private cut leading to the Usk. This was Potter Street lock from which the elegant Monmouthshire Canal cast iron mileposts measure distance. More tramroad construction followed in the 1820s. The Crumlin line of canal was often short of water as was the topmost section of the Pontnewynydd. Water came from the Afon Llwyd and the Glyn ponds for the Pontnewynydd section and from a pond at Hafodyrynys for the Crumlin line, while the much of the main had a good supply from the Usk via the Brecknock & Abergavenny which joined at Pontymoile. Because of water shortage an extension of the Blaenavon tramroad was opened in 1829 to Pontypool. Eventually when the Monmouthshire came to build railways this top length of canal was abandoned, down to Pontypool in 1849 and to Pontymoile in 1853. They became a railway company by an Act of 1845, which authorized a railway from Newport to Pontymoile with a branch to Pontnewynydd and to the dock in Newport. From 1849 the concern was officially called the Monmouthshire Railway & Canal Co, the railway from Newport to Pontypool was opened to passengers in 1852 and goods in 1854. By the 1860s the canals were little used. In 1865 the Brecknock & Abergavenny Canal was bought, but canal closure was now the concern of the Monmouthshire. In 1854 they had filled in half a mile of canal in Newport and more was closed in the town in 1879. In 1880 the Monmouthshire Railway & Canal Co. amalgamated with the Great Western, and canal traffic speedily declined. Market boats carrying miscellaneous goods had been a feature, running between Newport and Crumlin and Newport and Brecon. The latter ceased in 1915. There were no cargoes on the Crumlin line after 1930 and none to Pontymoile after 1938. By that time the canal was being abandoned in sections, first more in Newport, while the Crumlin line was closed by the British Transport Commission in 1949. The line to Pontypool via Pontymoile was closed under Acts of 1954 and 1962; but the canal remains as a supplier of water, some of it can be navigated, and a restoration scheme is under way.

MONTGOMERYSHIRE CANAL.   Wholly within the county of Montgomery, promotion started in October 1792 as a move to extend the Llanymynech branch of the Ellesmere down to Welshpool, but it was decided to extend to Newtown, and an Act was passed in 1794 for a narrow canal from about three miles north of Llanymynech, down to Newtown with a branch to Llanymynech to join the Ellesmere's branch and another to Guilsfield north of Welshpool. John Dadford was engineer with his brother Thomas (junior) to help him. The Montgomeryshire was planned as a canal to support agriculture, to supply limestone to be burnt into lime for the new enclosures, from the quarries around Llanymynech. In fact the section to the Porthywaen quarries in the Act was never built, being replaced by a tramroad to Crickheath on the Ellesmere's line to Llanymynech, so the Montgomeryshire's branch to the Ellesmere at Llanymynech became part of its main line, joining the latter at Carreghofa (79) just outside the village. Construction of the Montgomeryshire proceeded well and included aqueducts over the Vyrnwy near Llanymynech and over the Rhiw at Berriew. By the end of 1797 the canal had reached Garthmyl, $16\frac{1}{4}$ miles from Carreghofa with 13 locks, and the $2\frac{1}{4}$ mile level branch from Burgedden near Pool Quay to Guilsfield had also probably been finished. By this time Thomas Dadford senior had replaced his son John as engineer. But the Montgomeryshire had no more money to continue and Garthmyl remained its terminus for many years. Traffic developed well, for it was wartime, with high grain prices. Peace brought a recession, although moves were already afoot to extend to Newtown. In 1813-14 Josias Jessop was called in to estimate, but dissension arose. The solution was a separate company which received its Act in 1815 for a narrow canal from Garthmyl to Newtown, built to Jessop's plans with John Williams as resident engineer. This became the Western Branch and reached Newtown in 1819, $7\frac{3}{8}$ miles with 6 locks being completed in 1821 with help from the Exchequer Bill Loan Commissioners. Water for the Western came from the Severn via a feeder at Penarth near Newtown, aided by a pumping waterwheel with a steam pump in reserve in Newtown. Water for the Eastern Branch, as the original length was now called, came also from the Severn at Garthmyl and from the Tanat at Carreghofa. The two companies never combined. Both earned good revenue in spite of improved local roads and from 1836 fly-boats ran from Newtown to London. During the early 1840s there was a trade depression but traffic picked up after 1844, although in 1845 the Eastern Branch considered becoming a railway. Later that year the Eastern agreed to be taken over by the Ellesmere & Chester and in 1847 joined the Shropshire Union, from which the Western held aloof until 1850.

MORAYSHIRE SCHEMES.   The flat lands bordering the Moray Firth seemed ideal for canal work and several proposals were put forward, from Findhorn to Forres, also one by the Spey from Garmouth to Rothes, about 1811. Two canal routes were suggested between Elgin and the sea, either to Burghead or Lossiemouth, but no waterway was ever cut.

Loch MORLICH CANAL SYSTEM, Inverness-shire.   Four miles east of Aviemore in the Forest of Rothiemurchus a waterway system is believed to have been made at a height of over 1000' to extract timber and float it down to the Spey. It was based on streams but in the mid nineteenth century was replaced by a light railway.

MORRIS'S CANAL, Glamorganshire.   Built in about 1790 to bring coal to copper works in each of which trades John Morris had an interest. It was just over a mile long and in 1794 became a part of the new Trewyddfa Canal, in its turn part of the line of the Swansea Canal.

MUIRKIRK CANAL, Ayrshire.   A canal was built in 1789 to serve an ironworks at Muirkirk, one mile long, to bring ore, coal and power waterwheels.

MUNDON or WHITE HOUSE FARM CANAL, Essex.   A canal, about two miles south-east of Maldon, from Southey Creek on the Blackwater to White House Farm, Mundon, it was built privately in 1832 on his land by the local landowner J. Marriage. It ran for about 1¼ miles and its entrance was protected either by a lock or by tidal doors. It was operated as part of the Mundon Hall Estate, a flourishing agricultural enterprise. By the 1880s the canal had ceased to be navigable and is now just a rush filled cut.

River NAR, Norfolk. Entering the Great Ouse above King's Lynn, the Nar was improved under an Act of 1751, which sanctioned work to West Acre 15 miles from King's Lynn. Narborough, 12 miles from the Ouse, became the limit of navigation, with 10 staunches in the uppermost five miles. One staunch, at the bonemill below Narborough originally had, like the others, a guillotine gate, but was converted into a kind of pound lock by the addition of a pair of mitred gates 185' upstream. This would benefit the mill, for the staunch by itself would have lowered the level for the whole 1,100 yds up to the next staunch. Latterly the navigation was owned by the Marriot brothers, maltsters of Narborough, malt and coal being the main cargoes. There was no traffic after 1884.

NEATH CANAL, Glamorganshire. In 1790 a canal up the Neath valley was proposed by local people led by Lord Vernon. A survey was made by the younger Thomas Dadford who intended to make use of the Neath River, although this was given up. Coal and iron ore would be carried for the Neath Abbey works. In 1791 the Act was passed for a canal from Neath to Glynneath, with access to the river at Neath, which had been improved sufficiently for 200 ton ships to reach Neath. Thomas Dadford junior remained as engineer with Jonathan Gee under him as engineer cum contractor, but Gee was followed in 1792 by Thomas Sheasby senior, who took over from Dadford as well, because the latter was busy on the Monmouthshire. The Neath Canal took some time to complete because Sheasby was arrested at the instance of the Glamorganshire Canal in 1794 and the Neath owners had to finish off themselves. It was cheaply built in spite of the six arch masonry aqueduct over the Neath River at Ynysbwllog and was fully open in 1795, 10½ miles with 19 locks. These could take boats 60' x 9' carrying 25 tons. Water came from streams in the valley. At Neath the river connection was never built but by 1799 the canal had been extended 2½ miles down to Giant's Grave on the estuary below Neath, ending in a basin by Giant's Grave pill where vessels could lie. They could not enter the canal. There were three private canal branches built, one near the head of the canal towards Maesmarchog in 1800 with a tramroad to collieries, a second, the Cnel Bach (1817) ran from near Aber-clwyd about two miles below the head of the canal to a limekiln near the river, and a third at Court Sart (about 1812) near Giant's Grave was also to a colliery tramroad. All three were about ¼ mile long. The Neath did well, the principal traffic being downwards, coal, culm or small anthracite, iron, ironstone and fire-clay, culm heading the list for quantity. Giant's Grave was developed as a port, although the canal company were keen to improve the facilities at Neath from 1818. Railway competition came in 1851 when the Vale of Neath line was opened up the valley but the canal kept its business and paid good dividends up to the late 1860s. By 1900 canal traffic was very light, while Giant's Grave had seriously declined by the 1880s. Traffic had almost ceased by 1921 although the last toll was taken in 1934, and today the canal is a water channel owned by the Neath Canal Co, although restoration is underway, mainly on the upper pounds with a view to re-opening.

River NEATH, Glamorganshire. Navigable before 1790 to Neath, the river was used higher up to reach works near Aberdulais, via a cut parallel to the river and sealed at each end by a lock. These locks were built before the canal age, the lower possibly by 1700, the upper about fifty years later, and used until the opening of the Neath Canal. The lower lock could apparently pass 100 ton vessels.

River NENE, Northamptonshire, Huntingdonshire, Isle of Ely, Norfolk, Lincolnshire. The Nene enters the Wash below Wisbech. Up to the end of the thirteenth century it did this via the Great Ouse, but the latter changed course to King's Lynn, and the Nene was left to form a delta. Navigation was hampered by the silted outfalls. The delta had two main arms, through Spalding and through March (still called the old Nene), Wisbech being on a subsidiary with insufficient scour to maintain a deep channel. Drainage of the once good farmland was essential and the first works were undertaken by Bishop Morton of Ely between 1479 and 1490. Morton's Leam was cut from Peterborough to Guyhirne to carry flood water seawards. It also carried traffic but became neglected until restored in the seventeenth century. Now it supplements the main Nene channel. There were no further navigation proposals until 1713, when the first Act for the Nene was passed, to make it navigable to Northampton. By then boats were reaching Alwalton above Peterborough but no undertakers came forward. An Act of 1724 was followed by a scheme to improve in sections. Two undertakers were found to finance work between Peterborough and Oundle and this length was considered complete by 1730. Work continued to Thrapston under one of the two, being completed after 1736. This

79. Flood paddles on the Montgomeryshire, the canal's safety valves.

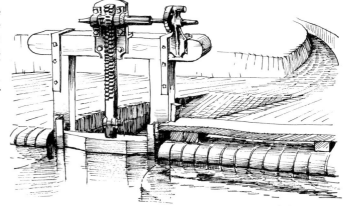

length, Peterborough to Thrapston, was called the Eastern Division. Meanwhile there had been proposals for the outfall into the Wash. The elder Kinderley had a scheme for training walls below Wisbech to increase the scour. These were to have been built by the North Level drainage undertakers helped by Wisbech, but the latter withdrew support. Not until 1773 was an outfall cut built, named Kinderley's Cut, in honour of both father and son Kinderley. By this time the Peterborough-Wisbech channel was improved as Smith's Leam, Peterborough to Guyhirn, completed in 1728, part of the modern main Nene channel parallel with Morton's Leam. An Act of 1756 sanctioned work above Thrapston up to Northampton, reached in 1761. This was called the Western Division under separate commissioners who were responsible for settling disputes over land purchases, and were the final authority over the undertakers. There were now 34 pound locks and 12 staunches (probably rebuilt in the 1830s and later improved when two became locks) from Woodstone above Peterborough to Northampton. The locks would pass craft 84' x 10' and the mileage from the Wash to Northampton was $91\frac{3}{4}$. There were branches in Northampton, one of $5\frac{1}{2}$ furlongs to West Bridge, the main line at Northampton later joining up with the Northampton branch of the Grand Junction Canal opened in 1815; at Peterborough one of $\frac{5}{8}$ of a mile to join the Middle Level Navigations at Stanground sluice, actually a lock. The 1827 Act for the Nene outfall extended Kinderley's Cut and the works were completed in 1830 under Telford and the younger John Rennie, following his father's plans. Sir John Rennie put forward proposals for more outfall and navigation improvements in 1836, notably a lock at Dog-in-a-Doublet below Peterborough. In 1848 came a report on the drainage of the upper Nene, while in 1852 the Nene Valley Drainage and Navigation Improvement Act passed, dividing the valley into districts, with commissioners to administer each. Former Nene Acts were repealed but the new authorities were hampered by lack of funds, and lack of support from Wisbech, which was only interested in the seaward end. Navigation was hard hit by the railways and the Northey Gravels, shoals below Peterborough. The latter protected a fresh water intake for the village of Thorney, owned by the Duke of Bedford, who gained a perpetual court injunction against their removal, which would have allowed tide borne salt water into the intake. By the twentieth century the Nene was decayed as a navigation although most of the staunches were modified in the 1900s. The Nene Catchment Board, established in 1931, undertook a major reconstruction, under their chairman George Dallas and engineer Harold Clark. Between 1937 and 1944 the old vertical gate staunches and locks were replaced, seven staunches being eliminated and three made into locks. So all staunches now became locks with lower guillotine and radial gates, acting also as flood control sluices. There are three radial gates, and 34 guillotine, all above Peterborough. Below the city, the Board completed a new electrically worked sluice in 1937, with a lock, at Dog-in-a-Doublet, removing the Northey Gravel shoals and by excluding the tide, ensuring a permanent water level at Peterborough. Dog-in-a-Doublet, named after a pub, will take craft 140' x 20', the upstream locks 78' x 13'. From the drainage angle the new works were excellent, but river commercial traffic has never been heavy due to low bridges. Pleasure cruising is on the increase. The Catchment Board's successors were the Welland and Nene River Authority, later merged into one of the Regional Water Authorities. The river is pronounced Nen in Northamptonshire, but Neen below Peterborough.

NENT FORCE LEVEL, Cumberland. John Smeaton was involved with a plan to drive an underground level or sough to drain a lead mine at Alston. Work started in 1776 with the idea of also using the level for boating out ore. It was too small and in 1777 John Gilbert, who had mining interests at Alston, recommended widening, at no great expense in his estimation. Progress was slow because of the hard basalt rock, but by 1810 the tunnel had gone in 2 miles 921 yd where the navigable part stopped. The level became a tourist attraction and was still used into the twentieth century.

NEWCASTLE-UNDER-LYME CANAL, NEWCASTLE-UNDER-LYME JUNCTION CANAL. See (Sir Nigel) Gresley's Canal.

NEWDIGATE CANALS, Warwickshire. Arbury near Nuneaton was the seat of the Newdigate family, who were colliery owners and in the 1700s developed a system of small 'boatways' to carry coal. These were extended by Sir Roger Newdigate from the 1770s onwards. Eight connected canals were built at different dates, serving a worsted factory and Arbury Hall, as well as the pits, carrying estate materials, coal and pleasure parties. Some started as mill leats but were expanded to carry boats and in the end the system had 13 locks. Separate from the Arbury network was the Griff Hollows Canal, built by Sir Roger from the Coventry Canal $2\frac{1}{2}$ miles south of Nuneaton to his Griff colliery, a distance of about 1320 yds. This, opened in 1787 remained in use until 1961 and is now closed, whereas the Arbury network did not long survive Sir Roger's death in 1806.

NEWPORT PAGNELL CANAL, Buckinghamshire. With the promotion of the Grand Junction went a scheme for a branch to Newport Pagnell, surveyed in 1793 by James Barnes, although the Grand Junction decided against making it. In 1813 the project was revived by local interests. After another survey by Benjamin Bevan, the Act passed in 1814 and the canal opened in 1817, $1\frac{1}{4}$ miles long from Linford on the Grand Junction with 7 narrow locks down to the town, plus a stop lock at Linford. The canal did fairly well, but in 1863 was sold to the proposed Newport Pagnell Railway and closed the following year, the Railway being partially built on it.

NEWRY NAVIGATION and NEWRY SHIP CANAL, Co Armagh, Down. The inland section of the Newry has the distinction of being the first summit level canal in the British Isles. As early as the 1640s there were ideas of connecting Newry by a canal to Portadown on the Upper Bann which flows into Lough Neagh. In 1703 the project was revived and a Bill drafted. Coal had been discovered in east Tyrone, which would find a ready market in Dublin via Newry. It was evident that any schemes would have to be financed by the Government, since private capital was sparse. Tyrone coal was expected to make Ireland independent of outside supplies and in 1731 work on the Newry Navigation began under Richard Castle. He is believed to have built the first stone chambered lock in Ireland but was dismissed in 1736 with the canal far from complete. Thomas Steers was invited to carry on, and in 1742 the canal was open. It ran 18 mile from Newry where it entered the tidal Newry River over the 78' summit at Poyntzpass down to the Bann just above Portadown. There were 14 locks for craft 44' x 15'6". Water came from Lough Shark and feeder streams but it barely sufficed in a dry season. Construction had been poor possibly because of inexperience. More serious however was the condition of the tidal channel of the river below Newry. Without Newry as an outlet, the value of the inland canal was nil so in 1759 improvement work began under John Golborne. He made a very small and useless cut parallel with the river, but Thomas Omer replaced this with a ship canal of more generous dimensions with a sea lock at Lower Fathom 130' x 22' for coasters; it was finished in 1769, $1\frac{3}{4}$ miles long. The ship canal did much for Newry, which by 1777 was the fourth trading town of Ireland. The Commissioners of Inland Navigation were disbanded in 1787 and the canals came under local control. By this time the inland canal had fallen into a poor state but nothing was done for it, in spite of the completion in 1787 of the canal from Lough Neagh to Coalisland in the Tyrone colliery district, and in 1794 of the Lagan Navigation from Lough Neagh to Belfast. Both brought more trade to the Newry which was eventually rescued by the appointment in 1800 of the Directors-General of Inland Navigation. They took over and between 1801 and 1811 both canals were extensively repaired. On the inland canal, locks were rebuilt and enlarged for craft 62' x 14'6" the same size as those on the Tyrone Navigation. By this time (1811) there was very little coal from Tyrone and the canal soon became busier carrying cross-channel coal inland from Newry. In about 1833 a passenger service was started between Newry and Knock Bridge near Moyallan on the Upper Bann.

Even after the repair programme the ship canal section remained unsatisfactory because of silting. Steamships now had to be considered and Sir John Rennie recommended in 1830 an improved natural channel from the sea lock down to Warrenpoint. In fact the ship canal was extended further downstream to Upper Fathom where the new Victoria lock was made, 220' x 50'. The ship canal, now 3 miles long, was completed in 1850 with a new basin, the Albert, at Newry, while below the lock the natural channel was improved down to Warrenpoint. The work had been done by a local company created in 1829, the Newry Navigation Co. After 1858 the inland canal did less well and its condition deteriorated. Railways were the main reason. By this time too Belfast had replaced Newry as Ulster's chief port, although Newry tried hard to compete, in the 1880s deepening and widening the natural channel to take 5000 ton ships. Public control returned to the Newry Navigation in 1901 when the company was replaced by the Newry Port & Harbour Trust, which represented town as well as navigational interests. Improvements were made to the harbour and ship canal, and efforts made to keep the inland canal in working order. There was no traffic on it after 1938 and the canal was abandoned in 1949 as far as Newry, the town section to the Albert basin being abandoned in 1956. In 1958 the Dublin road swing bridge was fixed so craft could not enter the inland canal, but the channel was kept as a feeder to the harbour and ship canal and for land drainage. The ship canal remained open under the control of the Newry Port & Harbour Trust until 1976 when the large harbour planned for Warrenpoint to handle traffic for the new city of Craigavon was opened.

NEWTON ABBOT CANAL PROJECT. James Green of the Exeter Canal submitted a plan in 1827 for a half mile canal from the Teign into Newton Abbot, to improve the berthing of ships.

NORE NAVIGATION, Co Kilkenny. Joining the Barrow below St. Mullins where both rivers are tidal, the river was one of those mentioned in the Act of 1715 as ripe for improvement, but nothing was done until 1755 when work started under Thomas Omer. Boats were able to reach Kilkenny by 1761, Omer's assistant William Ockenden having built as part of the improvement a 4 mile canal with 12 very large locks, 200' x 21'. But the work was never completed due apparently to Ockenden's death in 1761. During the 1780s many proposals were made to extend the navigation. Nothing was done and during the nineteenth century the Nore became derelict including the existing works below Kilkenny. Today the river is navigable only on the tidal section from the junction with the Barrow for 7 miles up to Inistioge the tidal limit.

NORTHERN IRELAND PROJECTS. In 1808 John Rennie surveyed a canal from the coast at Larne to Lough Neagh. He put forward another line involving a waggon inclined plane down to Larne, but sufficient money could not be raised. Coleraine on the Bann had a difficult seaward approach and around 1814 there were ideas for bypassing it with a ship canal to Portrush. Between 1827 and 1836 however Sir John Rennie built a harbour at Portrush which became as important as Coleraine so the need disappeared. Between Lough Foyle and Lough Swilly, the flat country attracted several schemes in the eighteenth century, followed by specific surveys in 1807 and 1831. Later in the nineteenth the canal idea became involved with tide control and land reclamation proposals on Lough Swilly. With the Strabane Canal open in 1796 there were ideas of extending to Lough Erne in the early nineteenth century. In 1800 there were plans for an inland navigation between Lough Neagh and Dublin, which included consideration of a canal from Armagh to the Blackwater. Although the Broharris Canal was in existence in the 1820s more ambitious ideas were afoot to make a canal from Lough Foyle to Limavady.

NORTH WALSHAM & DILHAM CANAL, Norfolk.   The Ant was already navigable to Dilham, but round about 1810 there were ideas of extending to North Walsham. Surveys were made by John Millington of Hammersmith and an Act for a canal passed in 1812. Nothing was done for many years, probably because of a claim for damages by one of the Dilham traders, Dilham fearing that with a canal open, North Walsham would become the distribution centre of the district instead. The damages were settled and work started in 1825 under Millington as engineer. The navigation was quite independent of the course of the Ant and therefore a true canal. Cutting was in charge of contractor Thomas Hughes. He found Norfolk peat difficult but achieved completion in August 1826. Leaving the Ant just above Wayford bridge near Dilham, the canal ran to North Walsham and on to Swafield and Antingham Ponds, a total distance of $8\frac{7}{8}$ miles. There were six locks 50' x 12'4" x 3' draught, for small wherries carrying about 20 tons. Coal traffic did not develop as expected because it was cheaper to land it on the nearby coastal beaches and bring it overland to North Walsham. However corn, flour, timber, cattle cake and animal feeding stuffs were important cargoes and there was the 'cabbage' wherry taking vegetables from Antingham to Yarmouth market. The canal never made money and in 1866 powers were acquired to sell it. It was finally sold in 1886 to a local miller, Edward Press of Bacton Wood mill near North Walsham who ran his own wherries, and so had an interest in the maintenance of the canal and its water supply to his mill. However after 1893 the canal above Swafield locks to Antingham Ponds was abandoned. In 1906 Edward Press died and the canal was auctioned, being bought by the General Estates Co, who were involved with many enterprises, the tolls of Selby bridge, the Gorleston ferry and the Yarmouth & Gorleston Steamboat Co. They kept the canal until 1921 when it was bought by the local Ebridge millers E. G. Cubitt and G. Walker, who formed the North Walsham Canal Co. Meanwhile its condition was deteriorating, the severe floods of 1912 which closed the Aylsham Navigation, breached the North Walsham. Attempts at improvement were made, for the canal was still of importance as a water supply to the mills. Cubitt and Walker in 1927 dredged from Wayford Bridge to Bacton Wood, although at the same time they dewatered the Swafield locks - Antingham Ponds length, which has been converted back to farmland. The last wherry passed in 1934 and today the locks are derelict. Pleasure craft may however navigate up from Wayford bridge to the first lock at Honing.

NORWICH & LOWESTOFT NAVIGATION, Norfolk, Suffolk. The Yare has carried traffic since Roman times, but no improvements were made to the river until the nineteenth century, apart from dredging. Under an Act of 1698, duties on coal had been charged at Yarmouth for the maintenance of the haven there, but because of the shallowness of Breydon Water, cargo for Norwich had to be transhipped. Norwich wanted to be a port for sea-going vessels and the Norfolk engineer William Cubitt proposed an outlet at Lowestoft, via a canal from Reedham on the Yare to Haddiscoe on the Waveney, and from the Waveney a navigation via Oulton Dyke, Oulton Broad and Lake Lothing to Lowestoft. Objections were made by the Aylsham Navigation and by the North Walsham & Dilham Canal, fearful that traffic would leave the Bure if Lowestoft was developed, and naturally there was opposition from Yarmouth. However in 1827 the Act for the navigation passed and work commenced, all the money coming from the Exchequer Bill Loan Commissioners. Harbour works at Lowestoft were completed in 1832 and the Reedham-Haddiscoe canal, the New Cut, was opened in 1833. Norwich was now open to sea-going vessels but no docks were ever built. The navigation was a failure because the entrance dock at Lowestoft was constantly blocked by sand and the harbour works undermined. The Exchequer Bill loan could not be repaid so the Government forced the sale of Lowestoft harbour in 1842. In 1844 this came into the hands of Samuel Morton Peto, the railway contractor. The following year the Eastern Counties Railway bought both the harbour and the navigation and developed Lowestoft as a railway fed port. Although Lowestoft flourished the navigation did not, because in the 1840s the Yarmouth authorities dredged the Breydon channel so that sea-going ships could use the Yare up to Norwich. The New Cut has remained open, $2\frac{3}{8}$ miles from Reedham to Haddiscoe, as has the rest of the navigation to Lowestoft, 9 miles from Haddiscoe via the Waveney to the port, with one lock at Mutford Bridge between Oulton Broad and Lake Lothing. This limits craft to a length of 85' x 20'. At present the owners are the British Railways Board, successors to the Eastern Counties Railway, the Great Eastern Railway and the LNER. The Yare itself has no locks in its $18\frac{7}{8}$ miles from Yarmouth to Norwich, where navigation ends on the Wensum, about $2\frac{3}{4}$ miles above the confluence of the Wensum and the Yare. The authority over the Yare and indeed the other Broadland navigations, with some exceptions, was the port of Great Yarmouth, administered by the Great Yarmouth Port and Haven Commissioners.

NOTTINGHAM CANAL, Nottinghamshire.   Promoted in 1790 to bring coal into Nottingham direct, William Jessop was asked to do the survey but was unable to complete it because he fell ill, the work being finished by a local surveyor James Green. This broad canal was to run from the Cromford at Langley Mill to the Trent at Nottingham with a branch from Lenton to the Trent upstream of the city at Beeston. The branch was to bypass the dangerous Trent bridge section of the river but was dropped from the Bill, because the Trent Navigation wanted to make it themselves. The Nottingham's Act passed in 1792. Jessop, with Green under him, was appointed engineer and work began, the first length being opened in 1793 between the lock on the Trent and the Nottingham wharves. In 1796 the canal was open, $14\frac{3}{4}$ miles long from Trent lock, below Trent bridge, where it joined the river, up to Langley Mill where it met the Cromford. Jessop had built 20 broad locks for craft 75' x 14', one of these being a stop lock at Langley Mill. The summit was reached at Wollaton, west of Nottingham, by a flight of 14 locks. Water came from a reservoir at Moorgreen above Langley and by many feeder streams. Branches were cut to premises in Nottingham and to collieries outside the town. Most important in Nottingham was the junction with the Trent Navigation's Beeston Cut at Lenton, also opened in 1796. This made the Nottingham part of the through river navigation. There were branches near Nottingham Castle and at Sneinton, the latter called the Poplar arm, $\frac{1}{8}$ mile long. Completed in about 1794 it was, in the mid-1830s, extended a furlong by the Earl of Manvers. Off this Poplar arm ran the $\frac{1}{8}$ mile Brewery branch, and there may have been a link between the canal and the river at Trent bridge. Above Wollaton locks was the Bilborough cut, completed privately by about 1799, $1\frac{5}{8}$ miles long, with tramroads to collieries, also the $\frac{1}{8}$ mile Greasley cut built in about 1800 and the $\frac{3}{8}$ mile Robinett's cut in the Erewash valley opened in about 1796, both serving collieries. In 1846 a further branch was opened in Nottingham, the private Westcroft, actually a loop of about $\frac{1}{2}$ a mile, serving coal wharves. It had a short life, being disused by 1860. In 1840 the Midland Counties Railway opened their line between Nottingham and Leicester, soon followed by others. Their appearance quickly caused the Nottingham's receipts to fall. To survive, the Nottingham determined to amalgamate either with other canal companies or with a railway, and in 1855 succeeded in selling out to the Ambergate, Nottingham, Boston & Eastern Junction after a struggle. The agreement to purchase had been made as early as 1845, to be completed when part of their line was opened. This took place in 1850 but no purchase followed. Only a series of court cases, ending in the House of Lords, settled the matter in 1855. The Ambergate line was leased in 1861 to the Great Northern Railway who maintained the Nottingham Canal on which traffic steadily fell. It was busiest in Nottingham from the Trent to the city wharves and with traffic to the Beeston cut. In 1923 the canal passed to the LNER and commercial traffic ceased above Lenton in 1928. In 1937 the whole canal was abandoned save for the Trent lock - Lenton section, and in that year leased to the Trent Navigation, who bought it in 1946.

NUTBROOK CANAL, Derbyshire. Proposed in 1791 as a branch of the Erewash, the main promoters were the colliery owners Edward Miller Mundy and Sir Henry Hunloke. A survey was made by John Nuttall but no Act was obtained. Tenants of Lord Stanhope started to cut a private canal from the site of a proposed ironworks near Dale to join the Erewash Canal. The project was supported by local colliery owners including Mundy and Sir Henry Hunloke, and in 1793 an Act was obtained to extend up to Shipley beyond Ilkeston and down to the Erewash. William Jessop did the survey and Outram was appointed engineer. Most of the canal was built by direct labour and completed by about 1796, a broad waterway $4\frac{1}{2}$ miles long with 13 broad locks from Shipley Wharf to its junction with the Erewash at White House, Stanton. Water supplies came from a reservoir at Shipley and local brooks, including the Nutbrook itself. In 1821 a second reservoir was made at Mapperley. Dividends ceased after 1885 by which time the railways had captured most of the traffic. During the 1870s mining subsidence caused considerable expense to the company, whose claims to support were not defined by their Act, and low rainfall and seepage combined to produce a chronic shortage of water. By 1895 the canal was insolvent with no traffic save from Stanton ironworks. By 1907 the Nutbrook was derelict save for $1\frac{1}{4}$ miles at Stanton retained to serve the ironworks, slag and pipes being carried from their wharves. In 1924 the Mundy's, still principal shareholders in the canal, sold out to Shipley Collieries Ltd, from whom in 1946 the Stanton ironworks acquired the bulk of the canal to preserve their water supplies. Between 1941 and 1947 Stanton operated their own boats to the Nutbrook, but after 1949 there was no traffic and since that date much has been filled in and the water piped. A curiosity of Nutbrook bye laws was the regulation requiring boatmen to leave all locks empty when proceeding uphill, this was in order to preserve the lock chambers by relieving them of unnecessary water pressure.

OAKHAM CANAL, Leicestershire, Rutland. First considered in 1785 when the improvement of the Wreak to Melton was under discussion, it was thought that a canal line could be taken from the river at Melton to Oakham. William Jessop was commissioned to make a survey but the work was done by Robert Whitworth and there were ideas of extending to Stamford. With the Acts for the Leicester Navigation and that to Melton Mowbray passed in 1791 the Act for the Oakham Canal followed in 1793, supported by the local nobility and landowners. Christopher Staveley was made engineer but in 1797 he was replaced by a Sheffield man William Dunn who completed the canal in 1802, after more money had been raised. It was $15\frac{1}{4}$ miles long from its junction with the Wreak at Melton Mowbray to Oakham with 19 broad locks rising to the summit at Oakham. Water was always a problem and boats probably did not reach Oakham until 1803. In 1809 the extension to Stamford was revived, this time via the Welland and the South Forty Foot to Boston with another line to the Nene at Peterborough, but nothing materialized. The canal did much for Oakham until the arrival of the railway in 1848. It was abandoned two years before; the proprietors had anticipated the rapid demise of the canal and sold out to the Midland Railway.

River OUSE, Bedfordshire etc. See River GREAT OUSE.

River OUSE, Sussex. Below Lewes the Ouse had always been open tidal navigation. After a survey by William Jessop in 1788 an Act of 1790 authorized improvement to beyond Hammer bridge, Cuckfield, and a further Act of 1791, improvement both for navigation and drainage on the tidal portion between Lewes and Newhaven. Work above Lewes proceeded very slowly due to lack of funds and poor workmanship. Eventually between 1808 and 1812 with William Smith as engineer, the navigation was completed to Upper Ryelands bridge near Haywards Heath, short of Hammer bridge, $22\frac{1}{2}$ miles from Lewes, with a

$\frac{3}{4}$ mile branch to Shortbridge near Uckfield, and 18 locks for boats 48' x 13'3". On the upper river traffic lasted into the railway age, indeed there was a brief period of activity carrying material for the great Ouse viaduct at Haywards Heath. Competing railways pressed more and more heavily on the navigation which in 1861 became disused above Lindfield and in 1868 above Lewes. Below Lewes the river is still navigable but carries no commercial traffic above Newhaven.

River OUSE, Yorkshire (below York). Always navigable to York the Ouse was a difficult river, and the city became less used as a port as the size of vessels increased. Edward IV made the Corporation conservators of the Ouse, Humber, Wharfe, Derwent, Aire and Don. They saw that the Ouse was dredged and in the early seventeenth century had plans for locks and cuts, even a bypass canal, putting forward a Bill for improvement in 1621. It failed, but an Act passed in 1657, although nothing was done. In 1699 Thomas Surbey did a survey and recommended a big lock at Naburn below the city. John Hadley was called to build it, but the Bill for the work failed in 1700. In the early eighteenth century the lower Ouse became much busier with Aire & Calder and Don traffic, both of whose Acts removed York's claim to conserve the Aire and the Don. William Palmer of York did a survey in 1727 and the improvement Act passed in that year. The river was to be administered by trustees from both members and officials of the Corporation, and Palmer was then taken on as engineer. He built jetties to try and increase the scour and dredged, but not very successfully. The lock 90' x 21'6" at Naburn was the answer and this was opened in 1757. While the lock increased depth above, the flow was reduced below and a large shoal formed. Completion of the Foss Navigation in 1804 brought more traffic, although the lower river was bypassed by the completion of the Stainforth & Keadby Canal in about 1802. A steamer service started between Hull and York in 1816 and four years later there was a service between York and Gainsborough. Goole was now the leading lower Ouse port and York wishing to share the prosperity, decided on more river improvement. Thomas Rhodes was called in and reported in 1834. He recommended and undertook dredging, bank protection and suggested a larger lock at Naburn. With the removal of the two mile shoal below Naburn, 60 ton craft could reach York at all times. Railways did irreparable damage to the Ouse from 1839 and Naburn lock was still the great obstacle. W.H. Bartholomew was called to advise in 1866 and again in 1871. He recommended lengthening of the chamber and dredging below the lock. Traffic improved, largely because of Henry Leetham's flour mills at York, opened in 1850. Not until 1886 was a new lock built at Naburn, 150' x 26', alongside the old one. Traffic increased in the 1900s, handled by the trustees' own tugs and by Leetham's steam keels. By 1918 the Ouse was in a poor way, and, like other waterways, unable to increase their tolls sufficiently to cover greatly increased costs. The trustees approached the Ministry of Transport asking to be taken over, but were refused. Most serious to the Ouse was the loss in 1930 of Leetham's traffic. Recently Selby traffic has increased, with sea going ships coming to the cattle food mills there, but tonnages to York have fallen away. Prospects for Selby appear good, while Howden Dike is now another Lower Ouse port.

River OUSE, Yorkshire (above York). Above York it was usually navigable to near Linton, but boats could also sometimes reach Boroughbridge on the Ure which is the continuation of the Ouse above Ouse Gill Beck, and occasionally reach Topcliffe on the Swale. William Palmer in 1726 surveyed the river above York, and ten years later, came schemes to improve the Swale even to Richmond, allied with lower Don improvements, to build up traffic between north and south Yorkshire. The Don works went ahead but Swale plans were not revived until the 1760s when John Smeaton did a survey of the Ouse and Ure. Three Acts were passed in 1767, for the Ouse and Swale to Morton Bridge, with a branch navigation up Bedale Beck, for the Cod Beck and for the Ure and Ripon Canal. Commissioners to build and maintain were appointed in three groups, for the Ouse, for the Swale and the Bedale Beck, and for the Ure and Ripon Canal.

Linton Lock, the Swale and Bedale Beck - Smeaton had estimated for the Ouse and the Ure and Ripon Canal, while John Grundy had done the same for the Swale and Bedale Beck. The 1767 Act for the Swale included improvement of the Ouse up to Swale Nab, the junction for that river, and improvement of the Swale for 18 miles up to Morton Bridge. The Bedale Beck was to be improved from the Swale up to Bedale with artificial cuts. There was to be one lock on the Ouse at Linton, four on the Swale and two on the Bedale Beck. John Smith the younger was consulting engineer for the whole project. The Ouse work centred on Linton lock went ahead well, the lock being opened in 1769. It took craft 60' x 15'4". All the Ouse works were completed in 1771 and traffic began, since the Ure and Ripon Canal were soon ready. On the Swale there were money difficulties and labour troubles. Only one of the locks was opened (at Topcliffe) and keels were able to reach there although it was announced that the Swale was navigable to Morton Bridge in 1769. Work was started on other locks and a towpath was made. The very variable levels of this river were a difficulty, but it was lack of money which stopped the work. To raise fresh capital an Act was passed in 1770 to establish a company but it was unsuccessful, and the whole scheme including the Bedale Beck where one of the locks had been completed, was wound up. The Swale remained navigable to Helperby, three miles up from the Ouse confluence. Coal traffic lasted on it into the nineteenth century. Although the Linton lock Navigation, $9\frac{3}{4}$ miles from Widdington Ings above York to Swale Nab, was part of a through route it had a difficult start. Tolls could only be collected at the lock so the rest was toll free. Shallows were a problem, dealt with in the 1830s by the steam dredger from the Ouse. Traffic depended on the Ure and declined with it when the railways came. Sand and gravel were principal cargoes, carried by the local firm Blundy, Clark & Co. Ltd, of Boroughbridge, but trade fell during the 1914-18 War. It was revived in the 1920s and the revenues of the commissioners were helped from 1920 by York's lease of land at Linton lock for a hydro-electric station. Lock repairs were done and dredging undertaken from 1937 by Blundy's, who received payment from the commissioners. During the 1939-45 War traffic was low and the navigation has only been saved by pleasure craft interests. Money for repairs was lent by the Linton Lock Supporters Club, the Ripon Motor Boat Club and others, and these came forward to save the lock which was reopened in 1967 after repairs by the British Waterways Board. Commercial traffic still passes on to the Ure and the commissioners (Linton Lock not being nationalized) gain revenue from pleasure traffic and anglers.

Cod Beck. In 1767 an Act was passed to improve the Cod Beck which leaves the Swale below Topcliffe and runs up to Thirsk. Four or five locks were intended, but only one built. Some work was done on a basin and wharf at Thirsk and the beck was deepened up to the one lock. A second lock was probably started, but funds ran out and work stopped. In 1770 two craft went from Thirsk to York, the first and probably the last to use this ephemeral navigation.

Ure Navigation and Ripon Canal. In 1767 came the Act for the Ure to be made navigable to Ox Close above Boroughbridge with a canal from there to Ripon. Commissioners were appointed to administrate who had unique powers of varying freight charges on this navigation. William Jessop did the survey work as Smeaton's pupil and built the waterway under his supervision. The whole was probably open in 1773 with two locks on the river, the canal entrance lock at Ox Close and two more locks on the canal, all able to take keels 58' x 14'6". The complete navigation was $10\frac{1}{4}$ miles long from the Swale's confluence at Swale Nab, $2\frac{1}{4}$ miles of this being canal. A half mile private cut was made to Bishop Monkton. Opened in about 1810 it was used up to the 1840s, but by 1906 it was reported as silted up. The commissioners ceased to exercise control after 1820. The works degenerated, but a company of proprietors was incorporated under an Act of 1820, fresh capital raised and repairs undertaken. The navigation was deepened and 70 ton cargoes could reach Ripon. Fly-boats were also put on to Hull. In 1847 the Ure Navigation was sold to the Leeds & Thirsk Railway, together with the Ripon Canal, in 1854 passing into North Eastern hands. In the 1860s there was a steady coal trade to Boroughbridge but by the 1890s revenue was low and there was no traffic on the Ripon Canal. The NER tried to abandon the whole navigation in 1894 but local opposition was too strong. By 1906 Ripon could not be reached, and there was only one coal boat trading to Boroughbridge apart from sand and gravel handled by Blundy, Clark & Co. Ltd. Under the British Waterways Board the Ure still carries some sand and gravel traffic and a growing number of pleasure boats. Part of the Ripon Canal has been reopened from Ox Close lock and cabin cruisers can reach the tail of the next lock, Littlethorpe.

OXFORD CANAL, Oxfordshire, Warwickshire, Northamptonshire. Ideas for a canal from the Thames at Oxford go back to Andrew Yarranton who planned to make the Cherwell navigable from Banbury to Oxford. The idea was revived as an extension of the Coventry Canal authorized in 1768, to carry Warwickshire coal southwards and give Midlands boats access to the Thames and London. Brindley laid out the line for the Oxford and in 1769 the latter received its Act. Appointed engineer, Brindley was assisted by Samuel Simcock with James King as clerk of works. There was trouble over the junction with the Coventry, due to the apportionment of tolls. By changing the junction from Bedworth to Longford the Coventry Canal would have the benefit of tolls on Oxford bound coal from Bedworth colliery. By 1771 10 miles of

80.

the Oxford had been made, Simcock succeeding Brindley on his death. Napton was reached in 1774 and Banbury in 1778 after more money had been raised. Not until 1790 did the canal reach Oxford, with the Duke of Marlborough building the $\frac{1}{4}$ mile private Duke's cut from the canal to the Thames in 1789. This had one lock, and in 1798 was leased to the canal company, who in 1796 had made their own junction with the Thames via Isis lock. In 1785 a more sensible junction with the Coventry was made at Hawkesbury nearer Bedworth. Robert Whitworth surveyed the final Banbury-Oxford line after a survey in 1785 by Samuel Weston to see if the Cherwell could be made navigable. A canal was chosen, making use of the river for a mile near Shipton, the Cherwell also crossing the canal on the level at Aynho, 91 miles long with 43 locks including a shallow lock at Hawkesbury all narrow except originally Isis lock, made for Thames barges, but narrowed in the later nineteenth century. The Oxford was the supreme example of the contour canal, not only north of Rugby but on the 11 mile summit level between Claydon and Marston Doles, encircling the spur of Wormleighton hill. Water for the Oxford came from four reservoirs between Marston Doles and Cropredy, one of which, Boddington, completed in 1815, was paid for by the Warwick & Napton, both Warwick canals paying for its enlargement in 1833. The Oxford also took water from the Warwick & Napton's Napton reservoirs via a navigable feeder, one third of a mile long, and from the Cherwell, while a windmill pump was built in 1786 near Banbury, followed by another at Hillmorton, in 1789 replaced by a steam engine. To economise, side ponds were made at Hillmorton locks, which in 1840 were duplicated to speed traffic. The canal had one 12 arch aqueduct, Brinklow Arches. There were four tunnels, Newbold, 125 yd, Wolfhampcote 33 yd and the two at Fenny Compton, 336 yd and 452 yd respectively. Trade on the new canal developed well, taking cargoes away from the Thames & Severn, but the Oxford's southern section was hurt by the Grand

Junction route to London, although the northern part benefited from the junction at Braunston. On the Thames the canal fostered a local trade which suffered after 1810 from the Wilts. & Berks. and Kennet & Avon competition. In 1829 through fear of a new canal promoted two years before from the Stratford-upon-Avon to Braunston, altered to Ansty or Brinklow, the Oxford determined to improve their waterway, having resisted Grand Junction appeals to widen. After surveys by Sir Marc Brunel and Charles Vignoles an Act was secured in 1831 to shorten from 91 to $77\frac{3}{8}$ miles, concentrating on the busy route north of Braunston. The old tunnels at Newbold and Wolfhampcote were abandoned and a new 250 yd Newbold tunnel driven with two towing paths, the Brinklow aqueduct was embanked and a new iron aqueduct built over the Rugby-Lutterworth road. William Cubitt was consultant for the scheme, completed in 1834, some of the old route becoming branches, for example to Stretton and Brinklow and at Braunston part of the old course became a basin. In 1836 improvements were made to Hawkesbury junction and in 1840 came the final branch, a $\frac{1}{4}$ mile private canal to Wyken New Colliery. Another branch was the $\frac{3}{8}$ mile Alexandra arm, also off the Wyken loop, to Alexandra colliery. Railway competition upset the excellent dividends, the worst threats being the lines from Banbury to Birmingham and from Bletchley to Banbury and Oxford. But the canal still showed a profit, a final improvement being the opening up of the two Fenny Compton tunnels completed in 1870. Dividends were maintained until nationalization, the canal never coming under railway or even Grand Union control in the 1930s.

PADSTOW - LOSTWITHIEL SCHEME, and the POLBROCK CANAL, Cornwall.   A survey was made in 1794 for a barge canal across Cornwall to join the Camel and Fowey rivers, which John Rennie considered of little value so near Land's End, although a waterway could carry sea-sand inland from Padstow. Under his direction a further survey was made for a canal from Polbrock on the Camel to near Bodmin. An Act was secured for this in 1797 but no work was done. In 1825 M. Brunel proposed a Padstow-Fowey ship canal.

PAR CANAL, Cornwall.   In 1847 a canal of $1\frac{7}{8}$ miles with three locks, was opened from Par harbour to Pontsmill to a tramroad. The canal carried tin, lead ore and china clay in containers transhipped from the tramroad trucks to the boats. With the extension of the tramroad to Par harbour in 1855 the canal declined though it remained open until 1873.

PARNALL'S CANAL, Cornwall.   Only half a mile long, this canal, cut about 1720 by a Mr. Parnall, was almost wholly in a tin mine. Very small boats in trains were moved to the tunnel mouth and upended, the ore sliding down a chute into carts.

River PARRETT, Somerset. IVELCHESTER (ILCHESTER) & LANGPORT NAVIGATION, WESTPORT CANAL.   Tidal almost to Langport, vessels for centuries used the Parrett to Bridgwater and well upstream to Thorney, also going up the Yeo or Ivel tributary to Ilchester if there was sufficient water. Through navigation was impossible because of Langport bridge, cargoes being transhipped. A scheme emerged in 1794 for a navigation, the Ivelchester & Langport, bypassing the bridge and improving the Yeo to Ilchester. An Act was obtained in 1795 and work started with William Bennet as surveyor and Josiah Easton as engineer. Due to lack of money the project was abandoned about 1797, but the Yeo continued to be used in its unimproved state regularly to Load Bridge, $3\frac{3}{4}$ miles. More promising were later plans to improve the Parrett from above the junction with the Tone at Burrow Bridge to Thorney adding a canal to Westport via a section of the River Isle at Muchelney. An Act was passed in 1836 and the scheme completed in 1840 with William Gravatt as engineer. Langport bridge was also re-built so that cargoes of up to 24 tons could pass throughout. Between Burrow Bridge and Thorney, $10\frac{1}{2}$ miles, there were four locks and one half-lock, measuring 73'6" x 16'. Traffic was good at first, although the Chard Canal took some. However from 1845 railway schemes threatened and a line from Durston Junction on the Bristol & Exeter to Yeovil was opened in 1853. The Parrett lost traffic and became a threat to local drainage. In 1878 it was vested in the Somerset Drainage Commissioners who abandoned it, although boats could and did reach Langport and even Ilchester after 1900.

PARROTT'S CANAL, Warwickshire.   Richard Parrott was a coalowner at Bedworth and around 1765 built a private canal which ran for about $\frac{5}{8}$ mile from his pit to near Hawkesbury. The canal was absorbed into the line of the Coventry Canal authorized in 1768, Parrott himself being a principal shareholder.

PEAK DISTRICT CANAL PROJECTS.   By 1800 there were four waterways to the edge of the Peak, the Peak Forest, the Don, the Chesterfield and the Cromford. To join them across the top was attractive. First came a proposal in 1802 for a canal from Bakewell to the Cromford, revived in 1810 as the High Peak Junction Canal fostered by the Grand Junction when they were backing the Grand Union to complete a line to Leicester. The Grand Junction considered it as an extension of the Cromford to join the Peak Forest. In another form the High Peak Junction was revived in the 1820s as the Grand Commercial Canal to run from the Peak Forest Canal to Sheffield with a branch to Chesterfield and then on to the Cromford Canal. Also called the Scarsdale & High Peak this was in 1824 submitted to Telford who proposed to go by Woodhead and Penistone from the Peak Forest at Hyde to Sheffield. Eventually the idea of joining the Peak Forest and the Cromford went ahead as a railway.

Severn Trow

LENGTH: **64** to **75** feet.

THE open hold was protected by canvas side cloths. The last trow under sail was the ALMA built in 1854, which traded as a ketch until 1943, while the PALACE of 1837 carried stone from Tintern until about 1939.

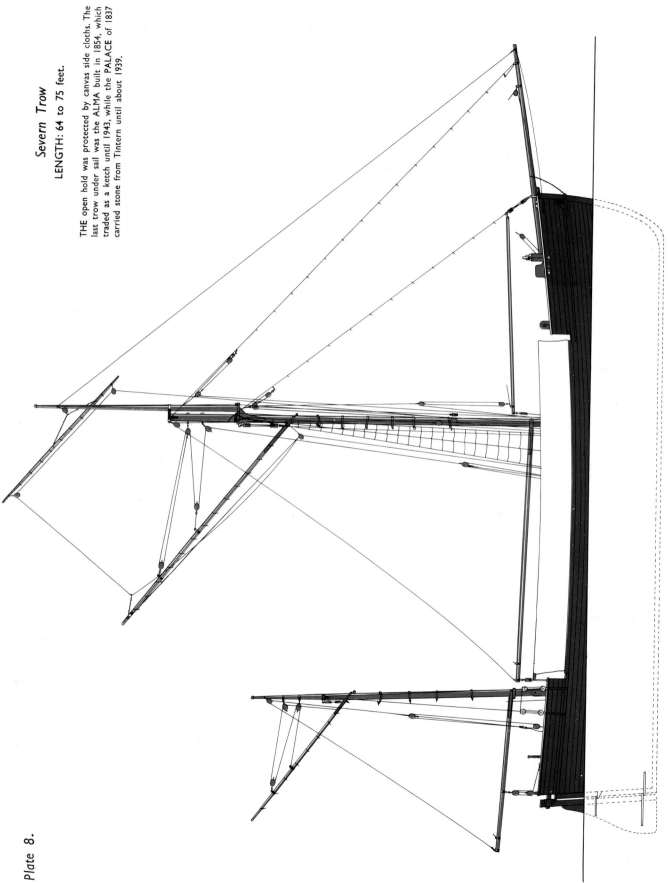

Plate 8.

81

PEAK FOREST CANAL, Cheshire, Derbyshire.   The canal was promoted to serve the limestone quarries. The driving force and a heavy investor was Samuel Oldknow, associated with the Arkwrights of Cromford and himself the owner of a cotton mill at Mellor near Marple. The Act passed in 1794 and authorized a canal from the Ashton at Dukinfield to Chapel Milton below Chapel-en-le-Frith with a tramroad onwards to limestone quarries at Doveholes. In fact it was decided to end the canal at Bugsworth (now Buxworth) about $2\frac{1}{2}$ miles short of Chapel Milton. Outram became engineer and work proceeded including the masonry aqueduct at Marple, 100' above the Goyt, completed in 1800. By this time money had become short and instead of building the 16 locks at Marple to take the canal to its summit, a single track tramroad had been laid by 1798 to connect the two levels, with a $\frac{1}{2}$ mile canal branch to Whaley Bridge. So in 1800 limestone traffic began, the $6\frac{1}{2}$ mile tramroad onwards from Bugsworth also being ready. Traffic developed so quickly that the Marple tramroad was doubled in 1801, but it was decided to build the 16 locks, completed in 1804. The Peak Forest Canal was $14\frac{3}{4}$ miles long with three short tunnels at Woodley 167 yd, Hyde Bank 308 yd, and Rosehill 100 yd, later opened out, near the Goyt aqueduct. Water came from two reservoirs, Toddbrook and Coombs above Whaley Bridge.   Traffic assumed prodigious proportions as the demand for lime increased. The appearance in 1831 of the Macclesfield Canal at the top of Marple locks and of the Cromford & High Peak Railway the same year at Whaley Bridge brought more traffic to the Peak Forest which now became part of a through line to the Potteries and London.   Still a busy canal the Peak Forest covered themselves against decline in 1846 by selling out to the Sheffield Ashton-under-Lyne & Manchester Railway who also bought the Macclesfield and the Ashton under their new (1847) title of the Manchester, Sheffield & Lincolnshire Railway.   The MSLR worked all three canals as a single unit, the Peak Forest limestone remaining exceptionally busy and profitable. The railway company themselves ran a fleet of narrow boats until 1892. As on the Ashton a passenger packet boat service ran in the 1840s at first from Macclesfield to Dukinfield, later from Marple only.   The Bugsworth tramroad line was abandoned in 1925 by the LNER so that the upper level of the canal soon became disused. Traffic however came off the Macclesfield and the Ashton until 1959, the last being coal for the Hollins cotton spinning mill at Marple.   The locks remained usable until the early 1960s but then deteriorated, the aqueduct suffering a breach during frost in January 1962. It has been repaired and now with Marple locks re-opened in 1974, the Peak Forest forms part of the 'Cheshire Ring', with the Ashton and Rochdale.   Above the locks the Peak Forest with the Whaley Bridge branch has always been open, and great efforts are being made by the Inland Waterways Protection Society to restore the Bugsworth system of basins.

River PEFFREY, Ross & Cromarty.   Dingwall burgh improved the Peffrey for navigation to the town, between 1815 and 1817, making an artificial cut for part of the river.

PEMBREY CANAL, Carmarthenshire.   Built to bring iron ore from the Kidwelly & Llanelly Canal to furnaces at Pembrey, it was probably completed in 1824. 2 miles long with a lock near Pen-y-bedd, it ran from near Ty-gwyn to Glo Caled from which it was connected to Pembrey Old Harbour by a short tramroad. With the extension of the Kidwelly & Llanelly to Burry Port in 1835 the Pembrey lost its value, although it remained in existence until the 1840s.

PEN-CLAWDD CANAL, Glamorganshire.   In 1811 an Act authorized a canal to run from the Burry estuary at Pen-clawdd on the Gower peninsula $3\frac{5}{8}$ miles inland to collieries at Waunarllwyd and Pont Lewitha. There were at least two locks on the canal completed in 1814, but the collieries had closed by 1818. It was still usable in 1825.

PENRHIWTYN CANAL, Glamorganshire.   Between 1790 and 1795 Lord Vernon built a canal from the pill at Giant's Grave on the River Neath to iron furnaces at Penrhiwtyn, about $1\frac{3}{8}$ miles long. The Neath Canal took it over in 1797 as part of their own extended line to Giant's Grave.

PENSNETT CANAL or LORD WARD'S BRANCH, Worcestershire.   This short line was built in 1839-40 by Lord Dudley's trustees, from the Dudley Canal's Park Head basin for $1\frac{1}{4}$ miles on the level to Lord Dudley's Round Oak ironworks. It was mostly disused by the 1940s although a short section remained until 1950. It was called Lord Ward's branch because of the dual titles of the Dudley family. This canal must not be confused with the Lord Ward's branch from the north end of Dudley tunnel at Tipton to join the Birmingham Canal's main line.

PEN-Y-FAN CANAL, WERN CANAL, Carmarthenshire.   Possibly in 1750 there was a canal from collieries at Pen-y-fan near Llanelly to the west. There was certainly a canal later, from Wern colliery to the sea, built in about 1795. The canal, 1 mile long, probably with a branch, was disused by about 1811.

PERTHSHIRE SCHEMES.   West of Perth Strathearn was a centre for canal projects, encouraged by the Commissioners of Forfeited Estates, who, in 1773, asked James Watt to look over a line up to Crieff which it was later considered could be extended to Loch Earn. The second Marquess of Breadalbane resurrected the idea in 1806.

PIDCOCK'S CANAL, Gloucestershire.   Made in about 1779 it ran from Lydney pill $1\frac{1}{2}$ miles up to Middle Forge, Lydney, later owned by John Pidcock and George Homfray. The Lydney Canal, completed in 1813, joined Pidcock's which appears to have been open until the mid-1840s. There were three locks just below Middle Forge.

PLAS KYNASTON CANAL, Denbighshire. Built by about 1830, this was a $\frac{5}{8}$ mile private canal from the basins at Trevor of the Ellesmere Canal to works at Plas Kynaston near Cefn-mawr. It had been authorized in 1820 but was cut in stages, the work being undertaken by the younger Exuperius Pickering. Later the canal passed to the Wynn estate but was closed by 1914.

POCKLINGTON CANAL, Yorkshire. There were ideas for a canal from the Derwent to Pocklington around 1777, but nothing was done until 1801. Henry Eastburn was then asked to do a survey from the Derwent to Pocklington, an alternative scheme to the Ouse at Howden having been dropped. The report was presented by William Chapman in 1802, who revived the Howden idea, in opposition to Earl Fitzwilliam, the owner of the Derwent Navigation, who would have been deprived of Pocklington tolls and possibly of Derwent water. Eventually it was Fitzwilliam who ordered a survey from the Derwent to Pocklington. It was done in 1813-14 by the younger George Leather. The canal was planned to end on the turnpike short of Pocklington, an extension into the town being dropped. The Act passed in 1815 and work commenced with Leather as engineer and it was opened in 1818, $9\frac{1}{2}$ miles long with nine locks. They were deeper than usual, averaging 11'3" and took keels 58' x 14'3". The junction with the tidal Derwent was at East Cottingwith, where the entrance lock was built. Water came from Pocklington Beck at the canal head and again from the beck at the tail of Thornton lock. There were two very short branches, to Melbourne and to Bielby. The canal was so rural that traffic was small. It was bought in 1848 by the York & North Midland Railway which had reached the Pocklington area the year before. Traffic declined and there were ideas in the early 1850s of conversion to a drainage channel with a tramroad on the towpath for local traffic. The canal became badly silted, the last keel passing in 1932. However recent history has been more cheerful. In 1969 the Pocklington Canal Amenity Society was formed and is restoring the waterway for pleasure. Much is already open.

PORTSMOUTH & ARUNDEL CANAL, Sussex, Hampshire. The Portsmouth & Arundel was the last link in the London to Portsmouth barge route. During the Napoleonic Wars it would have been a useful canal, but its Act was not passed until 1817. With John Rennie as overall engineer the line ran from the Arun at Ford to Birdham on Chichester Harbour, with a branch to Chichester from Hunston. Dredged channels between the mainland, Thorney and Hayling Islands allowed barges to reach Portsea Island, where a short canal from Milton led up to the terminal basins at Portsea, the whole system being 28 miles long. Under an Act of 1818 the Portsea Canal and the Birdham, Hunston, Chichester section were enlarged to ship canal size, the whole opened in stages, Birdham to Chichester in 1822, then the Portsea Canal, finally in 1823 Hunston to Ford. The company had to dredge the tidal channel between Birdham and Milton and provide a steam tug to tow barges between these places. Water supply was a problem, at Ford a steam pump was required to raise water from the Arun, while another supplied the Portsea Canal from a well. The locks were at the sea and river entrances, a flight of two at each, making a total of six, to raise the waterway 12' above High Water Spring Tides. Trade never developed because shippers preferred the coastal route. Carriage of bullion brought welcome receipts for a while, and an enterprising move was the commissioning of the steamer SIR FRANCIS DRAKE in 1824 to carry goods and passengers from Portsmouth to Plymouth and Falmouth. A sensible economy was achieved in 1830 with the closure of the Portsea Canal, an alternative barge quay being opened in Portsbridge Creek near Cosham. Trade declined. In 1840 the tug was broken up and the last barge sailed from Chichester to London. The ship canal to Chichester remained useful until the 1900s, although no traffic was carried after 1906, but restoration is under way.

PRESTON SHIP CANAL SCHEMES. Founded in 1803, the Ribble Navigation Co. had the task of improving the river up to Preston, but they achieved little, though a group in 1834 considered a ship canal on the north bank from Lytham into Preston, for 200 ton vessels. Soon Preston was developing her quays for vessels of increasing size and in 1842 a dock was opened at Lytham. Later Preston Corporation started to build Preston Dock which was opened in 1892.

PUBLIC DEVONSHIRE CANAL PROJECT. This was a product of the canal mania, arising out of the limited aims of the Exeter & Crediton Navigation. Several proposals were advanced, from Coleford past Crediton to join the proposed Grand Western at Topsham, or from Barnstaple to Topsham to take narrow boats.

Sir John RAMSDEN'S CANAL, Yorkshire. Robert Whitworth made a survey in 1766 up from Cooper Bridge on the Calder & Hebble and in 1773 another was made by Luke Holt, an ex-engineer of the Calder & Hebble, on behalf of the Ramsden family, owners of much of the land needed for the canal. The Act passed in 1774 having been promoted by Sir John Ramsden's trustees, since he was a minor. The short $3\frac{3}{4}$ mile canal with its 9 broad locks was opened in 1774, the locks admitting craft 58' x 14'2". Traffic became quite substantial and tramroads were later built down to staiths from nearby collieries. Sir John Ramsden's Canal never benefited much from the Huddersfield Canal, and was regarded more as a branch of the Calder & Hebble, whose prosperity it shared. When in 1845 the Huddersfield Canal was bought by the Huddersfield & Manchester Railway, the Ramsden Canal followed suit. Both came under the LNWR. Local carrying held up into the twentieth century, a disadvantage of Ramsden's Canal being its shallowness compared with the Calder & Hebble, so that boats had to lighten to 50 tons. In 1945 the Calder & Hebble bought the canal, together with a short length of the Huddersfield from the LMSR, but nationalization soon followed. Coal had been the last traffic, ending in 1953, but it is open as a cruiseway with a marina at Aspley basin, Huddersfield.

RED MOSS EXTENSION CANAL PROJECT. Red Moss is a flat wasteland just south of Horwich. In the canal age it was on a possible line between Bolton and Wigan and also from Blackburn to Wigan. Red Moss was of interest to the Manchester, Bolton & Bury Canal as a means of joining up with the Leeds & Liverpool. In the end the Manchester, Bolton & Bury were disappointed, for the Leeds & Liverpool became more interested in a branch from Wigan to Leigh and the Bridgewater.

REGENT'S CANAL, London. Although Robert Whitworth planned a canal from the Lee at Waltham Abbey to Marylebone nothing further was done until the arrival of the Paddington branch of the Grand Junction in 1801. The following year a line was surveyed from Paddington to the London docks and money subscribed, but no water was forthcoming from the Grand Junction. It was resurrected in 1810 by Thomas Homer, a carrier and wharf owner on the Grand Junction who gained the support of the architect John Nash, while the Grand Junction agreed to supply water. After surveys had been made by Nash and his assistant James Morgan, the Act for the canal was secured in 1812, the route to be from Paddington to the Thames at Limehouse, entering the river just above the Limehouse Cut of the River Lee. Although at first to be called the London Canal, the Prince Regent blessed the new undertaking with his name. James Morgan became the engineer and Thomas Homer superintendent. To save water it was proposed to pair the locks so that they would act like side ponds, while Sir William Congreve proposed hydro-pneumatic lifts. One was built as a trial in 1815 at Camden Town. Money was short, aided by Homer's embezzlement. Nevertheless by August 1816 the length from the junction with the Grand Junction at Paddington to Camden Town was ready with a $\frac{5}{8}$ mile branch to Cumberland Basin. This included Maida Hill tunnel (272 yd) and the length through Regent's Park which Nash incorporated into his schemes there. An Act of 1816 sanctioned the raising of more money, but few subscribed. The project was saved by the Poor Employment Act of 1817, which seems to have sprung from the suggestion by the canal committee to the Society for relieving the Manufacturing Poor, that the Government should lend money for public works to relieve unemployment. The Act set up the Exchequer Bill Loan Commissioners who advanced money. Telford made a new survey on behalf of the Commissioners and work restarted in 1817, the canal being complete in 1820, $8\frac{5}{8}$ miles long with 12 locks to broad standard and two tunnels Maida Hill and Islington (960 yd) neither with towing paths. There was one more important branch, $\frac{1}{4}$ mile to the City Road basin in Islington, which supplanted Paddington as the main London canal depot. At Limehouse a ship basin was excavated, ancestor of Regent's Canal Dock, with an entrance lock from the Thames.

The water situation eased, the Regent's taking more from the Grand Junction. Later the Regent's shared water from the Grand Junction's reservoirs at Ruislip and Aldenham, although the latter ceased to be used after 1861. It was the Regent's who in 1835 completed the Welsh Harp reservoir fed by the River Brent. This had been authorized for the Grand Junction and it supplied both canals. Once open the Regent's did well, traffic increasing and building development proceeding along the banks. More basins were added and a chain tug was put on for Islington tunnel in the 1820s to speed up the traffic. In 1830 the Hertford Union Canal linked the Regent's directly with the Lee. The Regent's acted as an artery of the Thames, handling a large volume of sea borne coal destined for local use. Railway plans left the Regent's unharmed for it was well placed to act as a feeder. With the completion in 1838 of the London & Birmingham Railway, transhipment began between rail and canal at Camden Town, later transferred to the special dock completed in 1848 at Hampstead Road. Because it linked so many approaches to rail termini, the Regent's thought of becoming a railway itself. No lines were built, instead the company increased its interchange facilities with the railway companies; with the Great Northern at Maiden Lane near King's Cross in 1850, subsequently with the GWR, Great Eastern, Midland and Great Central. An aqueduct had to be built to carry the canal over the King's Cross line. As the nineteenth century advanced so did the size of the basin at Limehouse. The Welsh Harp had to be enlarged in 1853, and in 1865 pumps were installed to return water to the summit from the dock. Railway building ideas recurred in the 1880s when the Regent's sold out to a new company, the Regent's Canal City & Docks Railway Co. In 1900 the company became the Regent's Canal & Dock Co, still doing well, distributing sea borne coal and timber, mostly local traffic. Like other canals the Regent's considered electric traction using overhead cables. The Regent's were the prime movers in the formation of the Grand Union. In 1925 they discussed with the Grand Junction purchase of the latter together with the three Warwick canals; agreement was reached in 1927, and in 1929 the new Grand Union was born. The Regent's continued to carry a heavy traffic under the new management although during the 1930s they suffered from closure of smaller power stations resulting from the opening of the giant at Battersea supplied direct by flatiron colliers. Shipping into Regent's Canal Dock was encouraged to feed the canal and from 1937 the Regent's Line was started.

Regent's Canal Dock, London. With the Regent's Canal completed in 1820, a four acre basin was built for ships at the Limehouse end, entered from the Thames by a lock 125' x 31'. Originally only a barge dock was planned, but collier brigs were using the basin from August 1820, transhipping into canal boats. The dock, initially the 'New Basin',

was called the Regent's Canal Dock from June 1822. By 1842 the basin or dock was enlarged to the northward and included a barge basin built under the London & Blackwall
Railway. In 1849 a new barge entrance was opened alongside the ship entrance, with a
lock 79' x 14'6" and by 1852 further extensions had been made eastwards and southwards.
At the same time a connection was made with the Limehouse cut of the Lee which entered
the Thames only a few yards downstream. New quay sheds and hydraulic cranes appeared
during the 1850s at Regent's Canal Dock, but there was need for a new entrance lock to
take steam screw colliers. It was opened in 1869, 350' x 60', cutting across the connection to the Lee which was closed. As a compensation their Limehouse cut entrance was
widened from 16' to 20'. Between 1877 and 1879 there were more dock enlargements eastwards and to the south, flanking the new entrance. In 1897 the first ship entrance was
partially filled in and wholly by 1922, while the parallel barge lock was closed in 1924.
In 1968 the wheel came full circle when the British Waterways Board closed the Limehouse
cut entrance to the Thames and once more made a connection with the Regent's Canal
Dock, Lee craft using the dock's entrance lock. In 1969 the dock itself was closed because
of its small size.

The RETYN and EAST WHEAL ROSE SCHEME, Cornwall. A mine waterway was
proposed in 1821 from the River Gannel above Newquay inland to Retyn, with the object of
carrying sea-sand inland and lead ore to the coast.

RIEVAULX ABBEY CANALS, Yorkshire. The Cistercians used two short canals to
transport building stone for the abbey. They were made in the twelfth or thirteenth centuries, and one seems to have had a means of changing level, perhaps a half-lock.

RIPON CANAL, Yorkshire. See River Ouse, (above York).

ROCHDALE CANAL, Lancashire, Yorkshire. Richard Townley of Belfield near Rochdale called the first promotion meeting in 1766. They wanted a direct line between Manchester and the West Riding, to the Calder & Hebble Navigation. Brindley did two surveys
for the promoters, but nothing more happened for nearly thirty years. In 1791 the Rochdale
scheme was revived and John Rennie was commissioned to do a survey. The Duke of
Bridgewater had to be consulted about a Manchester junction with his own canal to which
at first he objected, but later relented because he feared a rival waterway from the
Mersey & Irwell Navigation into Yorkshire as an extension of the newly authorized Manchester, Bolton & Bury. A Bill for the Rochdale was put forward in 1792 but lost because
of millowner opposition, however a second Bill for a narrow canal went forward in 1793,
Rennie assisted as before by the elder William Crosley. This Bill too was lost in spite
of the Duke's influence, and the promoters tried again, now with Jessop doing some of the
survey work, Rennie only directing Crosley who prepared the deposited plans. At last in
April 1794 the Act passed for a broad canal from Manchester to Sowerby Bridge which the
Calder & Hebble had reached in 1770. There had been much argument whether the Rochdale
should be broad or narrow, the Duke for example had wanted a narrow canal so that he
could keep the Bridgewater trade in his broad boats, and the Act sanctioned sufficient
capital for a narrow canal, although work started on a broad canal. Rennie now took no
part although Crosley remained as the resident engineer and Jessop as principal. In 1798
the canal reached Todmorden from Sowerby Bridge and later the same year Rochdale,
while in 1799 it was ready in Manchester between its junction with the Bridgewater at
Castlefield and its junction, actually made in 1800, with the Ashton Canal at Ducie Street,
Piccadilly.

Long distance carrying between Hull and Manchester started in 1799 on the incomplete
canal, the road being used between Manchester and Rochdale. More money had to be
raised, and the Rochdale was completed in 1804, the resident engineer from 1802 being
the younger William Crosley. The Rochdale was a fine achievement, the first of the trans-
Pennine canals to be opened, 33 miles long with a total of 92 broad locks, standardized
with a 10' rise so that water would not be wasted and gates interchangeable. The locks
could take boats 74' x 14'2", and were therefore open to Mersey flats. There was a four
arched masonry aqueduct over the Calder at Hebden Bridge and a short tunnel under Deansgate in Manchester, originally 336 yd, now opened out to 78 yd, and at Sowerby Bridge
(40 yd). A $\frac{1}{2}$ mile branch into Rochdale had been opened in 1798, but the $1\frac{1}{2}$ mile Heywood
branch was not made until 1834. Water was a serious problem for such a heavily locked
route. At first there were three reservoirs, finally the canal had eight, on the Pennines
between Littleborough and Todmorden. From the start the canal was a success. Coal,
grain, stone and merchandise were principal Rochdale cargoes, the corn coming from
Lincolnshire by this new direct route. Fly-boats locally called 'fly-outs' are first mentioned in 1825, these were keels or flats running to a timetable, together with bale vessels
carrying cotton and wool, Sowerby Bridge becoming an increasingly busy transhipment
centre. Prosperity was the keynote of the Rochdale story in the 1830s, the new Liverpool
& Manchester Railway feeding the canal. In 1839 a railway was opened from Manchester
to Littleborough and through to Leeds and Hull in 1841, many carriers changing to rail,
although by cutting rates the Rochdale hoped to remain competitive. In 1843 the Rochdale,
Calder & Hebble and other waterways except the Aire & Calder came to a rates agreement
with this Manchester & Leeds Railway. Soon after there were ideas of converting the
Rochdale into a railway. Conversion schemes were followed by proposals for a Manchester
& Leeds Railway take over of the Rochdale, a Bill was introduced in 1847 but defeated by
the Aire & Calder. Nevertheless the Rochdale was able, in 1849, to take part in an agreement over rates between themselves, the Bridgewater and the Calder & Hebble (now free
of railway control) and the Lancashire & Yorkshire Railway as the Manchester & Leeds
had become; this was succeeded in 1855 by a 21 year lease of the Rochdale by four

83. Canal flats of the Rochdale Canal Co. locking up in Manchester.

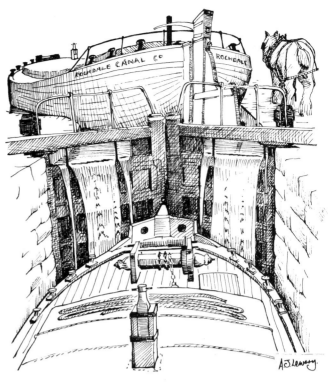

railway companies which lasted until 1876. Traffic was falling by then and to revive it the again independent canal company ran a carrying department. Until the 1914-18 war the Rochdale was still busy, the Manchester Ship Canal swelling the traffic exchanged at Manchester, but in 1921 the carrying business had to be given up. There was now little through traffic, the last being in 1937, commercial traffic ceasing altogether in 1958. The Rochdale Canal Co. were not nationalized and an Act of 1952 allowed them to close all the canal to navigation except for the length in Manchester to just beyond the Ashton's junction from Castlefield. A further Act of 1965 allowed this to be closed if the Ashton were closed, but because of the Cheshire Ring proposals for pleasure cruising, realised in 1976, the company kept this $1\frac{1}{2}$ miles open, and there are plans to restore more of the Rochdale, with much achieved.

RODING NAVIGATION, Essex. Navigation of the tidal part of the Roding from the Thames up the creek as far as Barking was possible in the Middle Ages and was under the control of Barking Abbey until the Dissolution of the Monasteries. It was, apparently quite busy, but Barking remained the head of navigation until the eighteenth century. However Ilford was interested in improvement and in 1736 one Joseph Goodman made an agreement with local landowners that he would undertake the works. These failed and had to be followed by an Act which passed in 1737. Goodman resumed work under the Act, but died before completion and his navigation and wharf were acquired by John Webb in 1764. Webb finished the works and traded from his wharf at Ilford bridge. Other proprietors followed Webb, vessels now trading regularly between St. Katherine's, where the dock had been opened in 1828, and Ilford. Nowadays the $1\frac{3}{4}$ mile navigation is open under the Barking & Ilford Navigation Co. (1961) Ltd. There is no lock, the only control being by a single pair of gates below Barking bridge which are wide enough for 17' beam vessels. The depth is limited to 7'6", craft only being able to enter when the tide makes a level with the river, the tide then flooding up the river as far as Ilford bridge. There is little traffic, 100 ton capacity vessels being the maximum practicable, one obstacle being the low headroom of the bridge by the 'lock' at Barking.

ROMFORD CANAL, Essex. Proposed in the early nineteenth century to bring farm produce to the London markets, the first scheme appeared in 1809, for a canal from Rainham creek on the Thames towards the River Beam on which Romford lies, using the river valley. Ralph Walker was behind this project and a subsequent one of 1812. Although laid before Parliament, the 1812 scheme was dropped and nothing further was done until 1818, when a canal which could be used to carry timber from Hainault forest (Crown property) to the royal dockyards was suggested. The Crown Estates were unimpressed and refused any help, nor was any local encouragement forthcoming. A further plan followed in 1824 which would have breached the Dagenham embankment, but it was not pursued because of opposition. However an Act was applied for in 1874 to make a canal from the Thames near the outfall of the River Beam to Romford, and passed in 1875. Money was raised and work started, one lock being built for craft 135' x 16'6". A tunnel was driven under the London, Tilbury & Southend Railway, but when this was widened to accommodate the District line extension to Upminster, the new railway embankment was made solid. The lock and the tunnel can still be traced. Work ceased in 1877 and in 1910 the company was liquidated.

River ROTHER, Sussex, Kent. See Eastern Rother.

River ROTHER, Sussex. See Western Rother.

ROYAL CANAL, Co Dublin, Kildare, Meath, Westmeath, Longford. Built nearly parallel to the Grand, the route of the Royal was considered in 1756 for the former and revived by the energetic John Binns in the late 1780s as a rival canal to the Shannon. He led the project with the backing of the Duke of Leinster, Lord Longford and others, petitioning for a Bill plus Government financial assistance. The Royal was incorporated by charter in 1789 and work began under Richard Evans as engineer and John Brownrigg as surveyor. As the canal progressed the Government was approached for more money which was granted to provide work rather than complete an economically unjustified canal. On Richard Evans' death in 1802 John Rennie came to advise on the project, and pointed out that Evans' estimates were too low. By 1811 the company's financial difficulties made it unlikely that the canal, which by 1809 had reached the western end of its summit beyond Mullingar, 58 miles from Dublin, would ever be complete. Traffic had started in 1806 with passenger services between Dublin and Mullingar, reached that year. The Government however decided to dissolve the canal company, whose charter was surrendered in 1813 and the canal put under the Directors-General of Inland Navigation who were authorized to complete it, achieved by 1817. The main line of the Royal was $90\frac{3}{8}$ miles from the Liffey to Cloondara where the Shannon was joined at Richmond Harbour. There were two level branches, a $\frac{3}{4}$ mile one in Dublin to terminal basins at Broadstone Harbour completed early on in 1796 and a 5 mile one to Longford. There were 56 locks by English reckoning on the Royal's main line, many staircases of two, in Ireland classed as one for statistical purposes, taking craft 75' x 13'3" wide. Water came via a main feeder from Lough Owel into the 15 mile summit near Mullingar, aided by others elsewhere. On completion the canal was handed over, free of debt to the New Royal Canal Co. subject to a Government Board of Control, who were able to show an immediate profit from traffic. The passenger traffic was quite a success too and the company built hotels at Broadstone and Moyvalley near Enfield. The Midland Great Western Railway, planning to build westwards from Dublin to Galway and Sligo, in 1844 offered to buy the canal to use the land alongside as a railbed, between Dublin and Habsborough. The offer was accepted because it was clear that the Royal would never rival the Grand. Under MGWR control from 1845, Royal traffic naturally declined, and the passenger services were withdrawn. The railway company experimented with carrying, in 1875 putting four steamers into use, but both the steamers and their horse boats were withdrawn in 1886. In the twentieth century the main cargoes were porter, both full barrels and empties, and bog iron ore, used for removing sulphur from town gas. In 1945 the canal passed to Coras Iompair Eireann. During the 1939-45 war the turf traffic had revived but in 1951 the last trader gave up, and the canal, with the Longford branch, was closed to navigation in 1961, the last boat a pleasure cruiser having passed through to the Shannon in 1955, however restoration is under way.

ROYAL CLARENCE SHIP CANAL PROJECT. Planned in 1812 to ease navigation of the Thames, the scheme envisaged a cut from below Woolwich Arsenal to Erith and later a cut from below Greenwich to above the Arsenal. Nothing matured.

ROYAL MILITARY CANAL, Kent, Sussex. Built as a defensive work, to resist the expected landing and deployment of Napoleon's troops on Romney Marsh, which the Government had considered flooding, although they more readily favoured the canal which was the idea of Lt. Col. Brown, the Assistant Quartermaster-General. He made a survey and work commenced in 1804 at the height of the invasion scare, with John Rennie as consulting engineer. Although construction was hastily pushed on with the approval of Pitt, completion was not achieved until October 1806, when the threat of invasion had gone. The canal ran a total of 30 miles from Shorncliffe Camp via Hythe, inland to Appledore to join the Eastern Rother at Iden lock (72' x 16') from where it became part of first the Rother and then the Brede, turning into a canal again from Winchelsea to Cliff End on the coast. This was not connected to the Brede by a lock and probably never navigated. From Shorncliffe to the Rother the canal was accompanied by a military road and a parapet, with bends every so often on which guns could be mounted to enfilade each length. The canal was used by traders from the Rother as far as Bonnington, while the army had a few barges pulled by horses of the Royal Waggon Train. Sand, bricks, stone and timber were the principal cargoes, the last barge passing in 1909. Today Iden lock is a sluice, so the main part of the canal is isolated. Pleasure boats use the eastern section owned by Hythe Corporation, while $3\frac{1}{2}$ miles of the canal eastwards from Appledore belongs to the National Trust.

ST. COLUMB CANAL, Cornwall. The St. Columb was the brainchild of John Edyvean, who wanted a waterway to carry sea-sand inland for use as a fertilizer. In 1773 an Act was passed for his canal to leave the sea at Mawgan Porth and go inland by way of St. Columb Major to return to the sea again at Lower St. Columb Porth, some thirteen miles. Two lengths were built to tub-boat standards, one about $4\frac{1}{2}$ miles inland from near Mawgan Porth, the other about 2 miles inland from near St. Columb Porth. Inclined planes were apparently built, to link the canal with the beaches. A horse operated winding drum hauled containers of coal or sand up, while in the other direction stone slid down by gravity. The whole system closed in about 1781, having opened in about 1777-9.

ST. HELENS CANAL. See Sankey Brook Navigation.

SALISBURY & SOUTHAMPTON CANAL, Wiltshire, Hampshire. Brindley in 1768 made a survey for a canal from Salisbury to Redbridge on Southampton Water. When the Andover Canal was revived in 1788 the Salisbury idea likewise reappeared. Various routes were put forward using the Andover Canal which the Salisbury would join at Kimbridge, and leave again at Redbridge, to cut across to Northam and the Itchen. After a survey by Joseph Hill of Romsey an Act was secured in 1795 and cutting began, including an 880 yd tunnel under Southampton. If completed the canal would have been $9\frac{1}{2}$ miles from Salisbury to Kimbridge and $3\frac{1}{2}$ miles from Redbridge to Northam with 15 locks, probably about 65' x 8'6", but money ran out. The canal never reached Salisbury and it is doubtful if the Southampton tunnel, was ever navigated. A little trade was done on the Kimbridge length and between Redbridge and the tunnel between 1802 and 1806-7, but in 1808 the company was defunct.

River SALWARPE, Worcestershire. Running up from the Severn to Droitwich, the Salwarpe may have been used for the salt trade in mediaeval times but later became impassable. Andrew Yarranton proposed a navigation scheme in 1655 but nothing was done until the Restoration, when Lord Windsor built five locks out of the six intended, yet left the scheme unfinished. Further work was done by others later, and a Bill to improve the river was introduced in 1693 and another in 1747. However the Droitwich salt proprietors had to wait until the completion of the Droitwich Canal in 1771.

SANKEY BROOK NAVIGATION, (St. Helens Canal) Lancashire, and the Ravenhead Canal, Lancashire. Coal was mined around St. Helens but land carriage to Liverpool was expensive because of the turnpike tolls, the prices in the winter of 1753 leading to riots. Liverpool Council determined to ease the situation by seeing if the Sankey Brook could be made navigable beyond Sankey Bridges towards the St. Helens pits. The survey was done by Liverpool's dock engineer Henry Berry assisted by William Taylor, the two leading promoters on the council being John Ashton and the younger John Blackburne. The Act was passed in 1755, for a navigation because of likely opposition to a canal. Berry however knew that the Sankey was too small to be improved and with the private agreement of Ashton determined on a full canal, for a clause in the Act allowed him to make navigable cuts. Work proceeded quickly on a lateral canal following the course of the brook. In 1757 it was open from Sankey Bridges via Winwick and Earlestown to collieries round Haydock and Parr, two years later reaching Gerard's Bridge between Parr and St. Helens. The line of the Sankey became very complex because of the collieries, the main was considered to end at a staircase pair of locks called the old Double lock, 8 miles from Sankey Bridges. Here the branch, 1½ miles went on to Gerard's Bridge, but off it was first the Blackbrook branch, ⅝ mile, completed in 1762 and then the Boardman's Bridge branch, itself with a branch to Ravenhead to serve copper and glass works, another 1⅛ miles, and finished in about 1772. There was a short branch off the Ravenhead to Sutton Colliery. There were 10 locks for craft 68' x 16'9" on the main line, including the Old Double lock, and a staircase pair called the New Double lock on the Boardman's Bridge branch, the system being spanned only by swing bridges, so that sailing flats did not have to be unrigged. Water came from the streams which fed the Sankey brook itself and later from a reservoir at Carr Mill not owned by the canal. There were also two private canals in St. Helens, the Ravenhead approximately ½ mile opened in about 1773 from collieries at Thatto Heath to the new glass works at Ravenhead but unconnected with the Sankey, and about a ½ mile extension of the Blackbrook branch to mills at Carr, known to be in use in 1784.

Navigation up the brook to the canal became unsatisfactory because of the tides. John Eyes did a survey and the Act for extension downstream to Fidler's Ferry passed in 1762, the extra 1⅝ miles of canal with a river lock being soon completed. Coal for the Cheshire salters and for Liverpool brought great profits. The Liverpool & Manchester Railway would cross the Sankey but it was not seen as a useful mineral line by the colliery proprietors, who decided to build their own railway to take coal down to the Mersey. As the St. Helens & Runcorn Gap Railway this was authorized by an Act of 1830 to which the canal replied by an extension to Runcorn Gap, to be called Widnes, also authorized in 1830. The canal would now avoid the tides and sandbanks of the Mersey above Runcorn Gap and work proceeded under Francis Giles as engineer. An extra 3⅜ miles from Fidler's Ferry, the canal entered the river by a pair of locks side by side, larger than those of the original canal, measuring 79' x 20'. Completed in 1833, the works included a dock beside the dock built by the railway company. It was a most unsuccessful railway and the canal did much better, Liverpool steamships needing Sankey coal for their bunkers. There was talk of union between canal and railway, agreed in principle in 1838 and in practice by 1844, the authorizing Act passing in 1845 for the St. Helens Canal & Railway Co, hence the change in the canal title from Sankey Brook Navigation to St. Helens Canal. By 1845 the Weaver salt industry had ceased to be the largest market for Sankey coal, and the new company sought to develop their railways, to a new dock at Garston opened in 1852, and by a new line to Warrington in 1853. Canal tonnages increased, although waterway maintenance was neglected, until in 1864 the LNWR took over both railway and canal and had to spend large sums on the latter because of chemical pollution and subsidence effects. By the twentieth century the pattern of St. Helens Canal traffic had changed, coal giving place to raw materials for local works and their products, notably chemicals, sugar, copper and silica sand for the glassworks. In 1898 ½ mile of the Ravenhead arm was closed. No craft worked up to St. Helens after 1919 and because of road widening schemes in St. Helens, all the canal north of Earlestown was closed by the LMS in 1931. Traffic remained to the wharves of the Sankey Sugar Co. at Earlestown until 1959, handled by power barges, but the whole canal was abandoned in 1963, yet remains a water channel.

SCARBOROUGH and WHITBY CANAL SCHEMES, Yorkshire. The Derwent had under its Act been authorized to be improved as far as Scarborough mills, but by 1793 the works had only reached Malton, hence the idea of a canal from Malton to Scarborough. An engineer called Cockshutt surveyed the line from the sea at Scarborough to Pickering with a branch to the Derwent for Malton and another branch to Kirbymoorside. The canal was expected to hinder drainage, and it was considered just as satisfactory to extend the Derwent Navigation so a branch off the Derwent to Pickering was suggested. Meanwhile Whitby wanted a canal inland to Pickering. William Crosley, probably the elder, did a survey in 1793-4 for a 25 mile narrow canal but it was not taken further.

River SEVERN, Montgomeryshire, Shropshire, Worcestershire, Gloucestershire. Longest of the rivers of the United Kingdom, the Severn rises on Plynlimmon and flows for 220 miles to the Bristol Channel. It is tidal up to Gloucester, but before the improvements of the 1840s the tides regularly reached Worcester. The Severn is subject to violent changes of level as the flood waters come down from Wales, a rise of 18' in five hours being known and heights of 25' above the average low water level not uncommon, render-

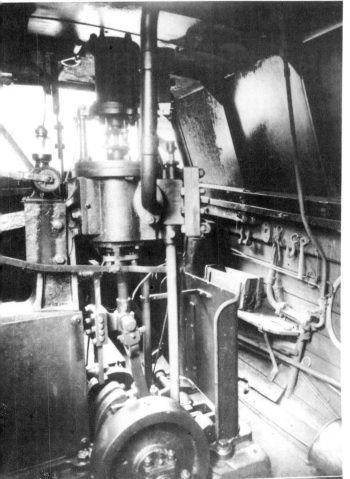

84. ICI's Weaver packet CALEDONIA of 1904 (top left), locking down Hunt's Locks at Northwich in 1957.

85. Tank barges (top left) locking out of the Royal Edward Dock, Avonmouth in 1956.

86. The tandem compound engine (left), of the Leeds & Liverpool tug No.57.

87. Crinan Canal icebreaking was done by the steamer CONWAY, built 1894 and broken up in 1964.

88. Severn trow WILLIAM (above), built in 1809 at the Bowyer yard, near Broseley, Salop, in Cumberland basin, Bristol.

89. Fitting out steel barges for the Wolverhampton Corrugated Iron Co's Ellesmere Port steelworks fleet at W. J. Yarwood's yard, Northwich.

90.

ing the river unnavigable. The tidal portion also has high water springs reaching 28' at Sharpness and 10' at Framilode 16 miles upstream, which cause the tides to flow at up to 7 knots past Sharpness Point. Finally there is the bore, created by the funnel shape of the estuary, which forces the incoming tidal wave to increase in height, forming the bore, which can reach nine feet, although a height of four feet is usual. The larger bores occur with the equinoctial tides, though most spring tides have a bore. Until the nineteenth century improvements, upstream navigation was dependent on flood water, for the Severn is shallow with shoals of gravel and rock ledges. Traffic followed the seasons, held up in summer by the low water but able to proceed in winter. The flood water or 'freshes' from Wales were amplified by water drained from the bog lands north west of Shrewsbury. Traditionally the limit of navigation was Pool Quay, $4\frac{1}{2}$ miles below Welshpool, reached in times of flood. However in the eighteenth century there was a steady coal traffic from East Shropshire down to the Droitwich salt works and for domestic use. Upstream came pig iron from the Forest of Dean and from the 1750s, foreign iron ore. Other important trades were salt from Droitwich and corn from the Vale of Evesham, while the Severn brought the merchandise and manufactures of Cheshire, the Potteries and the Black Country down to Bristol, Bristol sending up her imports. The Severn was left unimproved, the trows and barges waiting for the freshes to proceed upstream, in charge of gangs of bow hauliers or 'towing men'. Canal construction put the Severn in a new position. First came the Droitwich in 1771, then in 1772 the Staffs. & Worcs. Canal reached the river at Stourport. Later came the Stroudwater Navigation, joined in 1789 by the Thames & Severn Canal, so providing a through water route to London. Canals put traffic on the Severn which led to demands for improvement and a horse towing path. In 1784 the Staffs. & Worcs. Canal commissioned William Jessop to make a survey and he proposed to make the river navigable at all seasons between Diglis below Worcester and Coalbrookdale by providing locks. Below Diglis Jessop proposed dredging and he also proposed collecting floodwater into reservoirs. A Bill was introduced in 1786 but failed to pass. After another survey in 1790 by Robert Mylne, a fresh Bill was introduced and passed, although the work done was quickly destroyed by hostile boatmen, and no more was attempted. But more canals as well as tramroads were completed to feed the river, in 1798 came the Herefordshire & Gloucestershire Canal to Over on the western channel of the river opposite Gloucester, in 1813 the Lydney Canal and Severn & Wye tramroad, also bringing Dean coal down to the river. In 1815 came the Worcester & Birmingham Canal. Well upstream was the tub-boat canal system of East Shropshire, completed by 1796 and bringing traffic to the river at Coalport. But still there were no river improvements, transhipment being necessary at Gloucester and Tewkesbury for upriver cargoes from the trows into the lighter draughted barges (54) which plied up to Coalbrookdale and Shrewsbury. There was an exception to this, the authorization in 1793 of a canal down from Gloucester to bypass the treacherous estuary below the city, the Gloucester & Berkeley Ship Canal.

As early as 1761 there had been a petition for a horse path between Bewdley and Worcester while in 1772 an Act was passed for a path between Bewdley and Coalbrookdale, although because of opposition from the traders no work was done. In 1797 Richard Reynolds the ironmaster built at his own expense a path for two miles between Ironbridge and Coalport, to demonstrate its practicability and by 1800 the Severn Towing Path Co. under the old 1772 Act completed a horse path from Coalbrookdale down to Bewdley, 24 miles. In 1803 an Act was passed for an extension from Bewdley to Diglis under the Severn Horse Towing Path Extension Co; completed in 1804. In 1809 came an Act for a path upstream to Shrewsbury, completed that year. Finally in 1811 came the Act for a path from Diglis down to the Lower Parting below Gloucester under the Gloucester & Worcester Horse Towing Path Co, completed in 1812 and crossing several times from side to side. Completion of the Gloucester & Berkeley Ship Canal in 1827 brought yet more traffic to the Severn because vessels were no longer dependent on the tide except below Sharpness. By this time too, steam navigation had appeared on the river. For these reasons during the 1830s demands for improvement increased, particularly from the Worcester & Birmingham Canal. They were concerned for their coal trade from the Midlands, down the Severn. In 1831 they dredged some shallows and a few years later used what must be one of the earliest hydrographic models of a part of the river to study its behaviour. Then came a proposed Severn Navigation Co. which under its engineer Thomas Rhodes planned to build locks and weirs up to Stourport. Their Bill was defeated in 1837, but in the same year the Worcester & Birmingham Canal promoted their own Severn Improvement Co. and the following year the Severn Navigation Co. came to an agreement with the Worcester & Birmingham to form a new Improvement Co. and introduce a fresh Bill. This too was defeated by the opposition of the Staffs. & Worcs. Canal who objected to improvements only as far as Worcester. In 1840 the Improvement Co. was wound up and a new Severn Improvement Association was formed to press for a Bill to set up a Severn Commission, the Act passing in 1842. The new Commission was authorized to take tolls in return for improvements between the entrance lock of the Gloucester & Berkeley Canal in Gloucester and the Gladder Brook just above Stourport, $42\frac{5}{8}$ miles, plus the western or Maisemore channel from the Upper Parting down to the entrance lock of the Herefordshire & Gloucestershire Canal at Over ($1\frac{7}{8}$ miles). The Staffs. & Worcs. Canal guaranteed the money needed for the enterprise and work began in 1843, with William Cubitt as engineer assisted by Leader Williams senior, who became engineer in 1847. Locks and weirs were built at Lincomb, Holt and Bevere between Stourport and Worcester, able to take craft 87' x 15'6" while at Diglis just below Worcester and below the entrance to the Worcester & Birmingham Canal, two locks side by side were built, one 94'7" x 20', the other 142'5" x 30', allowing 135' x 22' vessels up to Worcester. Between Worcester and Gloucester the marl shoals had to be blasted away but still the intended 6' depth below Diglis could not be maintained, and although these works were completed by the later 1840s another lock was recommended at Tewkesbury. This was authorized in 1853 at Upper Lode and opened in 1858. The entrance lock into the Gloucester & Berkeley Canal was too shallow and the river channel poor. An Act of 1869 authorized improvements and also extended the jurisdiction of the Commission to the Lower Parting a further $\frac{3}{4}$ mile. To increase the depth into the Gloucester & Berkeley a lock and weir were built on the eastern channel at Llanthony on the outskirts of Gloucester while a weir and lock were also built at Maisemore on the western channel to divert more water into the eastern. Maisemore lock was only for narrow boats entering the Herefordshire & Gloucestershire Canal, but Llanthony was built for craft 87' x 15'6" because of the coal traffic from Bullo Pill. All these works were completed in 1871, financed by the Staffs. & Worcs. and Gloucester & Berkeley Canals. By this time railway competition was felt, particularly above Stourport, where the river remained an open navigation. The last barge had come to Shrewsbury in 1862 and by this time too there was no traffic up to Pool Quay. In 1885 the Coalbrookdale-Shrewsbury horse path had been given up, and barges must have ceased to come up to Coalbrookdale during the 1880s for the Coalbrookdale-Bewdley path ceased to take tolls in 1884. By the 1920s there was little traffic at all above Stourport, and that only to Bewdley and Arley. Steam navigation ended the life of the lower horse paths in the 1900s. By 1894 a depth of 10' had been achieved up to Worcester and 7' to Stourport, all the locks being deepened except Upper Lode which did not need it. Although steamers of up to 200 tons capacity were put on to Worcester, the improvements did not increase the traffic and revenue fell. The 1906 Royal Commission recommended that the Severn should be improved sufficiently to take 750 ton vessels to Worcester and 600 tonners to Stourport. Maisemore lock was disused by the early 1920s, (since the closure of the Herefordshire & Gloucestershire Canal in 1881, narrow boats had come only to a coal wharf at Maisemore) and Llanthony lock after 1924, for the Bullo Pill coal traffic had practically ceased by 1902, being much affected by the opening in 1879 of the Severn railway bridge. Indeed the Severn was decaying until rescued by the growing oil and petrol traffic of the late 1920s. New oil wharves were built at Diglis which the Commission extended in 1944. Motor barges of 280 tons capacity were trading to Worcester and dumb barges of 330 tons, but since the 1960s the oil traffic has fallen away due to pipelines, bulk trains and road transport. There has been very little oil traffic on the Severn to Diglis since 1969, instead the British Waterways Board have improved the Gloucester & Berkeley Canal to take 1000 ton tankers up to the oil wharves at Quedgeley below Gloucester. There is still timber traffic to Worcester and grain to Tewkesbury but nothing to Stourport since the aluminium traffic finished. The Diglis and Upper Lode locks were mechanised in the 1960s and the rest followed in 1972-3.

River SHANNON, Co Cavan, Leitrim, Roscommon, Longford, Galway, Offaly, Clare, Tipperary, Limerick, Kerry. Longest river in the British Isles, the Shannon was always navigable in certain lengths. It has a course of 224 miles from its traditional source Shannon Pot, in the Cuilcagh mountains. On its way to the sea it traverses Lough Ree and Lough Derg, the former 18, the latter 24 miles long. The Shannon was being considered for improvement as part of a general policy of settlement after the Williamite wars, but nothing was done until the Irish Parliament's Act of 1715 authorized a programme for several rivers and the construction of connecting canals. The Shannon scheme was for a navigation from Limerick to Carrick-on-Shannon and certain individuals undertook to do the work. They did very little, and the river had to wait for Thomas Omer in the mid eighteenth century, engineer to the Commissioners of Inland Navigation. He started in 1755 on the upper river and between Limerick and Killaloe at the foot of Lough Derg. A certain amount was done, including a lock at Meelick below Banagher, and in 1767 undertakers were appointed to continue work on the Limerick-Killaloe section. Progress was very slow both here and on the upper river between Jamestown and Lough Allen, where sections of lateral canal were started in the 1780s. This is a confused period of Shannon history, but it seems that by 1769 some sort of navigation existed for 80 miles of the river between Killaloe and Roosky, complete with locks and cuts. Some of the locks appear to have been flash locks. Concern for the Shannon was shown by the Grand Canal who depended on its condition for the success of their own waterway. In 1806 they were given a Government grant to improve, maintain and control the middle section. They built new locks and deepened the channel. The Directors-General of Inland Navigation were particularly worried about the Limerick-Killaloe section, which The Limerick Navigation Co. had been struggling to improve since the 1760s. Eventually in 1803 the Directors-General took over this section. Floods in 1809 held up the job, but it was finished in 1812. Improvements were continued piecemeal, including the $4\frac{1}{2}$ mile lateral canal from Battlebridge into Lough Allen, built to the plans of John Killaly by 1822. Traffic was poor, partly because of lack of wharves, warehouses and bad roads. Sea transport round from Dublin to Galway and Sligo was preferred. Nevertheless, the Grand and the Royal were dependent on the Shannon. John Rennie was ordered to make a survey in 1821, carried out in 1822 by John Grantham. Grantham had been working more on flood relief and drainage but traders on the river pressed for improvement. They were headed by Charles Wye Williams of what became the Inland Steam Navigation Co. A commission was set up in 1831 with the engineer Thomas Rhodes as a member. Rhodes did two comprehensive surveys, in 1832-33.

Authority over the river was now to be united and in 1835 the first Shannon Navigation Act was passed. Commissioners for its improvement were appointed, including William Cubitt and Rhodes. Work was sanctioned to start in 1839 with Government funds. New bridges were built and new locks and a new cut made at Meelick, while the old Jamestown canal was enlarged and the lock re-sited. Policy was to deepen the river, achieved with three steam dredgers. Commercially the Shannon was not very satisfactory because the locks were not to a standard gauge. The result was as follows:- on the Shannon between Killaloe and Battlebridge, the start of the Lough Allen canal, there were five locks 120' x 30', on the Lough Allen canal the two locks were 67'4" x 12', while the Limerick-Killaloe section with fourteen locks by the English reckoning took 74'9" x 15'2" vessels. The 14 locks were reckoned as 11 by the Irish, for three of them were staircase pairs, counted as one lock in Ireland. The navigation from Limerick to Lough Allen now totalled 128 miles. Tributary improvements were also carried out; the Boyle joining the Shannon just above Carrick was improved with a lock below Lough Key. A navigable passage was made into the Carnadoe waters, that is the Grange Lough, with the intention of making a further cut into Kilglass Lough to serve nearby Strokestown; and on Lough Derg the Scarriff river was improved up to Scarriff. The works came too late, since their completion coincided with railway development. Passenger steamer traffic ended in 1862, although services were revived in 1897. Floods were a recurring problem and there followed the suggestion that north of Athlone the navigation should be closed to aid drainage. Traffic on the upper river was certainly low but the government were not keen to abandon their expensive waterway. From 1852, on completion of the works, the Board of Works assumed charge of the river in succession to the Commissioners.

In 1930 the hydro-electric power station at Ardnacrusha above Limerick was opened. This demanded several alterations in the navigation. Lough Allen became a storage reservoir and the Lough Allen canal was closed, so that the present head of the navigation is Battlebridge, however the canal was reopened in 1977. The Boyle remains open and so do the Carnadoe waters, with a cut through to Kilglass Lough reopened in 1965. This last had never been completed in the improvements of the 1840s. Below Killaloe a length of river was expanded into a reservoir and from this the headrace led off on a course away from the old canal and river to Limerick. The headrace became the new navigation with a staircase pair of locks at Ardnacrusha to overcome the fall. These are for craft 105' x 19'6", still not conforming to the 120' x 30' of the middle section locks. With guillotine gates they have a total fall of 100' and take boats down into the tidal tailrace. Traffic on the Shannon reached its lowest in 1960 when the Grand Canal boats were withdrawn, but since then the revival has been due to pleasure craft.

SHEFFIELD CANAL, Yorkshire. Tinsley below Sheffield was the limit of navigation of the Don. The road to Sheffield became very busy, so that by 1792 there were moves to extend the Don navigation. The Don suggested a canal from Tinsley or Rotherham with a branch southwards to Eckington, a colliery area. The Chesterfield Canal objected to this incursion into their territory, but Robert Mylne did a rapid survey in December 1792. The project was carried forward by a semi-independent group led by Dr. John Browne of Sheffield. Outram did a survey in 1793 which included the Eckington branch, now apparently thought of as the main line from Sheffield, with a branch to the Don at Tinsley, and a junction with the Chesterfield Canal. The Sheffield Canal was not revived until William Jessop did a survey in 1801. The Eckington branch had been forgotten but the Cutlers' Company were keen on a canal to Sheffield. William Dunn, then engineer of the Oakham Canal did a survey in 1802. A Bill was introduced in 1803 but failed owing to Don opposition, the navigation fearing loss of revenue since Tinsley would cease to be the terminal basin. So again nothing was done until 1813 when William Chapman surveyed a possible canal from Sheffield to Rotherham, on the initiative of the Cutlers' Company, a branch to Eckington and to the Peak Forest being considered. At last the Act passed in 1815, the Duke of Norfolk being the leading subscriber, followed by Earl Fitzwilliam. Henry Buck was resident engineer and work proceeded quickly. It was opened in 1819, $3\frac{7}{8}$ miles long from the Don at Tinsley. There were twelve locks grouped into two flights at Tinsley, large enough for keels 61'6" x 15'3". There were three reservoirs but much of the water came from mine pumping. The $\frac{5}{8}$ mile Greenland branch was built down to Darnall for Handsworth colliery. Dividends were paid to Sheffield shareholders from 1826, modest at first but improving in the 1830s. Water supply was a problem because of the dependence on mine pumping which became deficient in 1834. An agreement for ten years had to be made from 1836 with the Sheffield Water Works Co. to provide supplies. By this time the Sheffield Canal were worried about railways. When in 1838 the Sheffield & Rotherham Railway was opened the Sheffield Canal began to do less well, although there were extensive services, even direct to London. Fly-boats, steam towed on the Don but behind a horse on the Sheffield Canal, worked to Hull, while there were regular services to Manchester, York, Leeds and Gainsborough. The Sheffield Canal were amenable to proposals of amalgamation and in 1845 the Don were interested. At this stage the Sheffield Canal takeover was not pursued because of the Don's railway preoccupation, but the Sheffield & Lincolnshire Junction Railway heard in 1846 that the Sheffield & Rotherham were trying to take over the Sheffield Canal, so they also tried and succeeded in reaching an agreement. They went ahead with a Bill in 1847 to secure the canal, which passed, much to the concern of the Don. The latter now tried to acquire the Sheffield Canal from the railway. This was agreed to in 1848, an Act of 1849 transferred the canal to the Don. The rest of Sheffield Canal history is that of the Don and the Sheffield & South Yorkshire Navigation.

SHREWSBURY CANAL, Shropshire.   Longest of the East Shropshire tub-boat canals, it was promoted in 1792 to supply Shrewsbury with coal from Donnington Wood.   After a survey by George Young, the Act was obtained in 1793, with Clowes as engineer. He died in 1795 and was replaced by Thomas Telford. At Shrewsbury there was no connection with the river and the canal went for 11 miles without a lock,   passing through the 970 yd Berwick tunnel and crossing the Tern by the famous cast iron aqueduct at Longdon-on-Tern. Between Long Lane and Trench there were eleven locks,   all 81' x 6'7", with guillotine bottom gates, designed to take 4 of the 20' long 5 ton tub-boats at a time, mitred lower gates not allowing sufficient clearance (91).   At Trench the canal made a junction with the Wombridge, 1 mile 88 yd of which the Shrewsbury   bought   to   reach Donnington Wood and join the tub-boat canal there. To reach the   Wombridge level the Shrewsbury built an inclined plane (36). In 1797 the canal was complete, 17 miles long to the junction with the Wombridge, and a steady coal trade began. Completion of the Newport branch in 1835 allowed standard narrow boats down the Shrewsbury and the two locks at Eyton were widened to receive them, but not the nine up from Wappenshall to Trench, so special 6'2" beam narrow boats had to be built for trade to the bottom of the plane, where goods were transhipped.   In 1846 the Shrewsbury became part of the   Shropshire   Union. Trade continued until 1921 when the Shropshire Union ceased carrying. This meant the end of the Trench traffic and closure of the plane in that year, the last traffic being grain to Bullock's Donnington Wood Mills.   No traffic went to Shrewsbury   after 1936 and none to Longdon after 1939, so the whole canal was abandoned by the LMSR Act of 1944, including the Newport Branch.

SHROPSHIRE CANAL, Shropshire.   The Shropshire was a tub-boat canal from industrial East Shropshire to the banks of the Severn where cargoes were transhipped. It was a public undertaking of local industrialists, led by William Reynolds, who made the survey, taking advice from William Jessop and the Act followed in 1788. From a junction with the Donnington Wood Canal at Wrockwardine Wood the new canal went by way of Oakengates, with tunnels at Snedshill (279 yds) and Stirchley (281 yds), through Madeley to the Severn at Coalport, although not linked with the river, a distance of $7\frac{5}{4}$ miles, with a $2\frac{3}{4}$ mile branch from Stirchley to Horsehay and Coalbrookdale. In such hilly country with little surface water the canal was only possible by use of inclined planes, at Wrockwardine Wood, at Windmill Farm Stirchley and The Hay above Coalport. At the last place there had been an earlier attempt in 1787 to cut an underground canal and sough from the Severn to serve local collieries, but 300 yds inside a deposit of tar and pitch was struck and the yield from the 'Tar Tunnel' was then used commercially. Further in they discovered brine so the work was abandoned. All three inclined planes were double track for the 5 ton capacity tub-boats. By the end of 1792 the canal was complete, having been opened in stages and joined by the Ketley Canal near Oakengates. In 1794 another plane was built on the Coalbrookdale branch at its Brierly Hill terminus for the waggons of the Coalbrookdale horse tramroad which ran down to the Severn. It was superfluous after 1800 when the tramroad was continued to Horsehay, and the canal from Horsehay to Brierly Hill became disused. Before the inclined plane there had been two vertical shafts at the 'Wind' as Brierly Hill was called. Until the 1850s the Shropshire Canal, in 1849 leased by the Shropshire Union, was busy, the coal and iron traffic paying regular dividends in spite of the low tolls imposed by owners who were also intensive users. In 1857 however the Act for the LNWR branch to Coalport was passed, which provided for purchase of the canal by the railway.

Under the LNWR the canal, already in a poor state because of mining subsidence, was gradually closed,   in 1858 from   Wrockwardine Wood to the bottom of the Windmill plane, as well as the branch to Horsehay, in about 1894 from Blist's Hill furnaces to Coalport, including The Hay plane,   and in 1912 the final coal traffic passed from local collieries to Blist's Hill ironworks,   closed in that year. Official abandonment   came   with   the LMSR Canals Act of 1944, although part of the canal together with the Hay Plane has been restored by the Ironbridge Gorge Museum Trust.

SHROPSHIRE UNION RAILWAYS & CANAL CO, Cheshire,   Staffordshire,   Shropshire, Flintshire, Denbighshire, Montgomeryshire. In 1845 the Ellesmere & Chester Canal took over the Birmingham & Liverpool Junction Canal. The new company was threatened by

91. Hadley Park Lock, Shrewsbury
     Canal, with a lower guillotine
     gate of the original pattern.

92. The barge dock Goole about 1900. Note the Aire & Calder fly-boats.

93.

Leeds & Liverpool steamer WILLIAM ROBINSON (below), later No.30, on the summit pool prior to 1914.

94.

Potteries narrow boats (J. & G. Meakin and the Anderton Co.), (left), with the Alfred Dock crate warehouse beyond.

95.

96.

Committee boat; inspection in May 1882 of the Glasgow, Paisley and Johnstone Canal in the iron fly-boat SUNBEAM after the canal had closed.

Sunday School outing about 1905 at Gilwern, Brecknock & Abergavenny Canal.

97. Leeds & Liverpool; boatmen outside a Liverpool dock road pub about 1910.

railway proposals for their area and could only counter these by promoting railways laid in the beds of their canals. So in 1845 James Loch, superintendent of the Bridgewater trust, and on the board of the Ellesmere & Chester, proposed to create a union of railway and canal companies in the area, converting most of the waterways to railways and building more railways. The following year the scheme took shape with the passage of three Acts for railways; under the name Shropshire Union Railways & Canal Co. which it acquired in that year the Shrewsbury Canal and powers to buy the Montgomeryshire (both branches). The Eastern Branch was bought in 1847 and the Western in 1850 while in 1849 the Shropshire Union had leased the little Shropshire, ending up with a 200 mile system. In 1846 they commenced to build one of their proposed railways, from Stafford to Shrewsbury. The new railway and canal combine was swiftly overtaken by railway developments, because of the ambitions of the new LNWR of 1846, which saw the Shropshire Union railway schemes as a threat. Hence the LNWR offer in 1846 to lease the Shropshire Union in perpetuity, which was accepted. In 1849 the Stafford to Shrewsbury railway of the Shropshire Union was opened, running via Newport and Wellington, and operated by the LNWR, who refused to allow further Shropshire Union railway building. The Shropshire Union canals suffered from rival railway building and because of this the waterways were encouraged. With the canal head office moved in 1849 from Wolverhampton to Chester, the Shropshire Union carrying business, started in 1842 by the Birmingham & Liverpool Junction, was extended to cover the whole system and penetrate rival waterways. An inevitable step was the gradual closure of the Shropshire Canal bought outright by the LNWR in 1857. On the other hand the Shropshire Union in 1870 leased the Lubstree Wharf on the Humber Arm of the Newport branch from which a railway was built to the Lilleshall Co. works. Carrying on its own system, with little competition so that most of its revenue came from freight rates rather than tolls, became the keystone of Shropshire Union policy from the 1870s onwards, and was extended to provide boatage services from rail to canal on the BCN, the Staffs. & Worcs. and the Stourbridge Canal. The company also managed railway depots, and provided railway cartage services at Chester and in the Potteries. On the Mersey the Ellesmere & Chester had since 1838 operated a fleet of barges and the Shropshire Union expanded this considerably during the 1870s and 1880s, acquiring many more flats and the steam tugs to handle them, and establishing, about 1872, a Liverpool headquarters at Manchester basin near Canning Dock.

Completion of the Manchester Ship Canal brought a new importance to Ellesmere Port, the Shropshire Union building a new quay for 4000 ton ships alongside the Ship Canal. Greater raw materials imports caused the Shropshire Union to enlarge the facilities between 1892 and 1912. Although the carrying business was so extensive the company only earned enough to provide a small surplus over expenses, dividends and interest on loans having to be found by the LNWR as lessor of the company. This reached serious proportions with the 1914-18 War, although the Government subsidised the canals from 1917. This was withdrawn in 1920 and the following year the company gave up carrying, added difficulties being the new 8 hour day and higher wages. The LNWR refused financial aid, although at the end of 1922, just before the railway grouping came into force, the LNWR took over the Shropshire Union completely. All the boats were sold, but the canals were still kept open and tolls hoped for, from bye traders. The LNWR itself in 1922 took over the still necessary boatage services, while from 1922 the Manchester Ship Canal took a lease on Ellesmere Port and the GWR acquired the Shropshire Union premises at Manchester basin, Liverpool. The lease, later ratified under an agreement of 1931 between the MSC and LMSR (successors to the Shropshire Union) is for 999 years and is maintained by the Ship Canal Co. and the British Waterways Board. As successors, the LMSR without a carrying fleet could do nothing. Traffic declined, aided by two bursts, the first in 1917 on the old Ellesmere line from Frankton to Shrewsbury, latterly called the Weston branch, which limited traffic to Hordley ¾ mile from Frankton, the second more serious in 1936 on the Llanymynech branch near Frankton which isolated the whole Montgomeryshire system, abandonment being secured by the LMSR Act of 1944. By 1939 there was no traffic on the line from Hurleston to Ellesmere and Llangollen, and that same year saw the last traffic on the Shrewsbury as far as Longdon; on the Newport branch there was a little trade until 1943, but the Humber Arm had not been used since 1922 and the last remaining open portion of the Shropshire Canal ceased to be used in 1913. The private Plas Kynaston Canal was disused by 1914. All were abandoned under the 1944 Act, leaving only the main line from Ellesmere Port to Autherley and the branch to Middlewich. One of the abandoned lines, from Hurleston up to Llantisilio was saved as a navigable feeder to the main line, its preservation secured in 1955 by an agreement between British Transport Waterways and the Mid & South East Cheshire Water Board, the former gaining revenue from the supply of water pumped up from the Dee at Vron to the reservoirs and treatment plant at Hurleston. By this time it was becoming popular with pleasure craft to such an extent that improved maintenance was essential, achieved over the next decade. The short branch to Ellesmere is open, although the Whitchurch branch and the Prees branch are not. The Montgomeryshire is under restoration, and the main line is busy from Chester southwards with pleasure boats, although commercial traffic finished during the 1960s.

River SLANEY, Co Wexford, Wicklow. Under the all embracing Act of 1715 for the improvement of Irish rivers the Slaney was mentioned as a possible navigation from Wexford to Baltinglass in Co Wicklow. Nothing was ever done although schemes were revived in 1795 and 1832, to improve the tidal section between Enniscorthy and Wexford, 19 miles long, always navigable, and still so today.

SLEAFORD NAVIGATION, Lincolnshire. From the navigational point of view Sleaford in the 1750s was isolated, although an important place on the Peterborough-Lincoln road. In about 1774 there had been a survey for a canal from Sleaford to Grantham, but in the early 1780s there was more interest in the River Slea and its continuance, the already navigable Kyme Eau, if it could be opened to the Witham. The Kyme Eau had been a mediaeval waterway, but before extending it the promoters were concerned to secure a satisfactory toll agreement with the Witham commissioners, which were too high on the Witham to encourage traders to use any proposed navigation. By the end of 1783 the Witham commissioners were more accommodating, but the Sleaford project was not pursued until Jessop and J. Hudson made a survey of the Slea and Kyme Eau in 1791. An Act for the Sleaford Navigation passed in 1792, having Boston Corporation as a subscriber, hoping to gain trade for the port of Boston. Seven locks were made, measuring 60' x 15', on this $12\frac{1}{4}$ mile navigation from the Witham, via the Kyme Eau to Sleaford. For Sleaford traffic on the Witham, Witham tolls were to be halved, so there was some incentive to traders. Sleaford tolls were leased from the opening of the navigation in 1794. In the first half of the nineteenth century the Sleaford did quite well and there were ideas in 1833 of extending it westwards to join the Grantham Canal and so the Midlands. By the 1870s, owing to poor traffic receipts proprietors secured an Act for abandonment in 1878 and closed in 1881. Actually over half of it remained navigable until the 1940s when Kyme Lower lock was converted into a sluice. Below this the Kyme Eau is used by pleasure craft and the whole navigation remains a drainage channel.

SOMERSETSHIRE COAL CANAL, Somerset.   This was first proposed in 1792 by local colliery owners. Surveys were prepared by William Smith, under John Rennie's direction, while Jessop also made a report for a line from Limpley Stoke, on the projected Kennet & Avon Canal up through Dunkerton to Paulton with a branch or a second main line through Wellow to Radstock, both to serve local collieries. Although at one point the idea was to use tramroads for the two summit levels, waterways along the top met with more favour and the canal committee hoped for a solution to the gradient problem in Robert Weldon's hydrostatick or caisson lock, built at Combe Hay. The single lift built did not prove satisfactory and in 1800 a tramroad was laid instead, with three locks leading down from its lower terminal. This involved a double transhipment from boat to truck to boat, although there had been a scheme to

98.

carry the trucks on rafts. From the summer of 1801 the canal from Paulton to Limpley Stoke was open, with a short tunnel at Combe Hay and two aqueducts at Dunkerton, so that coal could reach Bath via the Kennet & Avon. However the incline was not a success, because of transhipment and broken coal, so locks were decided upon, 19 at Combe Hay in addition to the three already built, and 19 on the still unconnected Radstock line. A special 'lock fund' was opened for these as a separate company. The Combe Hay flight was built but money proved insufficient for locks, except the bottom one, on the Radstock line. A tramroad was therefore laid from the junction of the two lines at Midford to Twinhoe at the end of the Radstock canal summit level. The boat-tramroad transhipment on the Radstock line was unsatisfactory and in 1815 this whole length was converted into a tramroad, leaving $10\frac{1}{2}$ miles of waterway. From 1810, with the Kennet & Avon and Wilts. & Berks. fully open, the Somersetshire Coal Canal had a busy and profitable time. But in 1874 the Somerset & Dorset Railway reached Bath, having in 1871 bought the canal's Radstock tramroad as a railbed, while in 1873 the Bristol & North Somerset Railway also reached Radstock. Canal traffic slumped and there were also colliery closures. In 1893 a Receiver was put in and the canal closed in 1898, being abandoned in 1904. The GWR bought the bed to Paulton for their branch from Limpley Stoke to Camerton, using Combe Hay tunnel.

SPEEDWELL LEVEL, Derbyshire.   Following on the experience gained at the Worsley mines, John Gilbert tunnelled a half mile navigable level into the Speedwell lead mine near Castleton. Work began in 1774 and was completed in about four years. The level has remained navigable and visitors are taken on it by boat to this day. Similar levels were driven into Hillcarr near Darley Dale and Meerbrook near Leek, Staffordshire.

SPRINGS BRANCH or LORD THANET'S CANAL, Yorkshire.   Lord Thanet owned limestone quarries behind Skipton Castle but the Leeds & Liverpool Canal declined to take their line to them so he obtained an Act in 1773 for a branch. In 1785 the Leeds & Liverpool took over the lease of both canal and quarries, and developed them, starting to extract limestone from Haw Bank $\frac{3}{4}$ mile further on and 200' higher up. This new quarry was served by an extension of the canal in a deep cutting, now measuring $\frac{1}{2}$ mile, completed in 1797 and a tramroad which ended at staiths or drops. After 1888 railway sidings were put in from the Midland Railway's Skipton-Ilkley line but the canal continued to be used until 1947 when the plane was dismantled. The branch is still open.

STAFFORDSHIRE & WORCESTERSHIRE CANAL.   Also called the Wolverhampton Canal and colloquially the Stour Cut this has retained its eighteenth century atmosphere, perhaps because it was never under railway dominance and indeed from 1772 to 1948 it was run from the same offices at 87 Darlington Street, Wolverhampton. The canal sprang from the movement for the Trent & Mersey, but was independently promoted by James Perry and a group from Wolverhampton who pushed forward a Bill which passed on the same day, 14 May 1766. Initial surveys had been done by Henshall and Simcock for a narrow canal from the Trent & Mersey at Great Haywood near Stafford to the Severn near Bewdley. Brindley was made surveyor but he left the engineering work to Simcock and Thomas Dadford senior. The canal was $46\frac{1}{8}$ miles long with 43 locks including the two barge locks at Stourport as the junction with the Severn was named. Water came from the reservoirs at Gailey and Calf Heath and later from the Wyrley brook via the Hatherton branch. In 1772 the canal was complete and open, with the Trent & Mersey open from Derwent Mouth to Great Haywood so that cross country traffic could begin. More important was the completion in 1772 of the Birmingham Canal which joined at Aldersley just outside Wolverhampton, later in 1779 came the Dudley and Stourbridge Canals, joining the Staffs. & Worcs. at Stourton Bridge. Stourport itself became a transhipment centre between Severn craft and narrow boats, with a new road bridge across the Severn. From the start the Staffs. & Worcs. did well with a strong interest in the development of the Severn for the traffic to Bristol and in the waterways which were to join the river lower down, the Stroudwater in 1779 and in 1789 the Thames & Severn. In the following year however the Oxford Canal was opened. More serious was the completion in 1815 of the Worcester & Birmingham Canal with a more direct route to the Severn upsetting Staffs. & Worcs. dividends. Stafford had been bypassed but from 1805 was joined by a tramroad, and later in 1816 the Sow was made navigable to the town from an artificial junction with the canal at Baswich, with one lock. Serious for the Staffs. & Worcs. was the completion in 1835 of the Birmingham & Liverpool Junction Canal, joining at Autherley and traffic declined sharply on the Staffs. & Worcs. between Great Haywood and Autherley. The new canal however made the $\frac{1}{2}$ mile Autherley-Aldersley section exceptionally busy for which the Staffs. & Worcs. charged lucrative compensation tolls, to such an extent that a new line to pass over the canal was considered in 1835 and a Bill promoted. However they reduced their charges and the Bill was withdrawn. Later the canal was able to finance from their own income the Hatherton Branch named after their chairman Lord Hatherton and opened in 1841. This gave them a direct route to the Cannock coalfields and in 1863 they made a junction with the Churchbridge branch of the Birmingham Canal Navigations, the 13 Churchbridge locks being paid for by the Staffs. & Worcs. leading to the Cannock Extension Canal and the Wyrley & Essington. The Hatherton branch was $3\frac{1}{2}$ miles long with 8 locks. To counter railway competition the Staffs. & Worcs. suggested a canal combine and gave heavy financial support to the work of the Severn Commission, guaranteeing all the money authorized for the project and lending more for further improvement in 1856. In spite of railways the canal continued to do well until 1860, because of the heavy traffic on the BCN, the Stourbridge and the Shropshire Union. In 1851 they had entered the carrying trade and also took over a Severn tug business around 1860. Between 1860 and 1864 they ran two small steam coasters fitted with drop keels between Worcester and the Continent. After 1860 the Staffs. & Worcs. were less successful, becoming more dependent on the BCN for traffic and water down the Wolverhampton locks. In 1895 the old canal joined the Thames & Severn trust because it wanted the latter to continue distribution of Staffordshire coal, and in 1897 there were proposals to enlarge the canal from Stourport to Aldersley for Severn vessels around 200 tons. In 1923 the canal was the scene of experiments with electric haulage at Kidderminster, not pursued. The Stafford branch ceased to be used in the 1920s; as did Pratt's lock, the side lock into the Stour just outside Stourport, giving access to Wilden ironworks $1\frac{1}{4}$ miles up the river, about 1948, while in 1949 the last coal came off the Hatherton branch. The Staffs. & Worcs. paid a dividend until nationalization.

STAINFORTH & KEADBY CANAL, Yorkshire, Lincolnshire. Brindley advised on a Don-Trent canal in 1763 but the matter rested until 1772. It was probably revived because of the Marquess of Rockingham's plans to build a navigation from the Don to the Barnsley coalfield. The Don's engineer John Thompson did a survey from Stainforth on the Don to Althorpe above Keadby on the Trent; the attraction being another Humber entrance to replace the Dutch River. Surveys were again done in 1792 by Thompson with Robert Mylne. The Act passed in 1793 authorizing a canal from Stainforth to Keadby with a branch from Thorne to the Don again at Hangsman Hill, but this was never built. John Thompson was in charge of construction until his death in 1795. He was succeeded by Daniel Servant. About 1802 the canal was opened, $12\frac{3}{4}$ miles long with entrance locks at Thorne and Keadby. Mylne had advised a large Keadby lock and it was built 81' x $22\frac{1}{2}$' for ships of up to 200 tons capacity. All the bridges were swinging spans to take rigged craft. The canal gave Keadby a new importance. The Hull-Gainsborough sailing packets called there, and steam arrived in 1815. To connect at Keadby, a horse passenger packet started on the canal from 1815, running between Thorne and Keadby, lasting until at least 1839. Stainforth & Keadby history in the early nineteenth century seems to have been uneventful except when threatened by other canals. One such was the Trent & Balby of 1828 which was to run from Stockwith on the Trent to Doncaster on the Don. The canal was disturbed in 1836 when the Don decided on a new Ouse exit at Swinefleet above Keadby. This would mean a new canal from Stainforth, and to make it the Don wanted two miles of the Stainforth & Keadby. Naturally the latter were opposed and the Don decided to compromise with them and offered to buy the Stainforth & Keadby on generous terms. This would have given the Don control of the Keadby exit to the Humber, but the sale, although agreed in 1837 fell through. The Don were determined on control and finally, in 1849, a lease was arranged to be followed by a purchase, but the terms were not as good as the first offer. In 1850 with the Dearne & Dove, the canal became part of the South Yorkshire & River Dun Co. Later Stainforth & Keadby history is integral with that of the Don and with the Don it became part of the Sheffield & South Yorkshire Navigation in 1895.

STEVENSTON CANAL, Ayrshire. To speed the export of Ayrshire coal to Ireland Cunningham, the local colliery proprietor, built a $2\frac{1}{4}$ mile level canal from his pits at Stevenston to Saltcoats harbour, completed in 1772. Branches were added some six years later from newer pits and the system closed about 1830.

River STORT NAVIGATION, Essex, Hertfordshire.   The Stort joins the Lee above Feilde's Weir near Hoddesdon and in 1759 an Act was passed to make it navigable to Bishop's Stortford. Insufficient money was raised, but a further Bill was introduced and the Act passed in 1766. Three undertakers had come forward with funds, provided they could take the tolls, Charles Dingley, William Masterman and George Jackson. Work was pushed ahead under Thomas Yeoman as engineer and in 1769 barges could reach Bishop's Stortford, 13¾ miles from the junction with the Lee. Largely canalized, 15 locks were made on the Stort for craft 88' x 13'3" and drawing 5'. Grain from riverside maltings to East London breweries was a principal downstream traffic, with timber coming up from the Thames. George Jackson continued as the sole undertaker until his death in 1822. In 1797 he changed his

99.

name to Duckett to gain an inheritance, being already a baronet. His son, also Sir George, continued as owner of the Stort and in 1824 secured an Act to make the Hertford Union Canal from the Lee to the Regent's. His idea was to divert traffic off the lower Lee and benefit the Stort by this link with the canal system. In 1859 Sir George sold the Stort to Gurney & Co, the Norwich bankers. By this time traffic was seriously undermined by the railway, open to Bishop's Stortford from London since 1842. Later the Stort passed to the Gilbey family and in the 1900s they commenced negotiations with the Lee Conservancy Board. Bishop's Stortford were also interested, but nothing positive was done until 1909 when Roydon lock collapsed. Sir Walter Gilbey now offered the Stort to the Lee free of charge, but in 1911 he made it a nominal sale for five shillings. The Lee authorities started on much needed improvement works to all the locks, completed after the 1914-18 War, but the chambers were not widened to Lee dimensions, so special steel lighters were built for Stort traffic. This continued to decline until 1945, after which little passed. Malt cargoes had gone some years before, but timber had continued in the War years. There has been some traffic since, and the Stort is busy with pleasure boats.

River STOUR, Kent.   Navigable from Sandwich to Fordwich, 2½ miles downstream from Canterbury, the Stour began to be improved during the sixteenth century by harrowing of weeds and scouring, following an Act of 1515 to make the stretch between Fordwich and Canterbury navigable, which resulted in the building of two flash locks so that some craft were able to reach Canterbury. Neglect was succeeded by improvement during the seventeenth century, while during the eighteenth further schemes followed, notably a canal between Fordwich and Canterbury proposed in 1792. An Act was passed in 1811 for a canal from St. Nicholas Bay near Margate down to Canterbury, partially parallel with the Stour. In 1824, a new scheme proposed improving the Stour from Sandwich to Canterbury for 100 ton vessels. This was commended by Telford and in 1825 an Act was passed for the Canterbury Navigation & Sandwich Harbour, which included a new cut from Sandwich to the sea. In the same year came the Act for the Canterbury & Whitstable Railway which effectively killed the waterway project. Nevertheless more schemes followed, the last in 1864 when the Downs Dock Act authorized a canal from the sea near Sandown Castle across to Sandwich. The Stour itself was carrying commercial traffic until the 1870s.

River STOUR, Suffolk, Essex.   Probably used before the seventeenth century in its unimproved state, the Stour was in 1638 the subject of a grant of Letters Patent by Charles I to Arnold Spencer, but nothing was done because of the Civil War, although considered again in 1658. The Stour remained unimproved until an Act of 1705, promoted by the Mayor and Corporation of Sudbury, appointed undertakers to do the work between Manningtree and Sudbury, 25 miles upstream. The improvements were probably complete by 1709 when coal was coming up to Sudbury. They included 13 staunches of paddle and rimer type (later gate type staunches) and 13 pound locks, each 95' x 10'9", capable of taking two of the local lighters, Brantham, the lowest lock, excluding the tide. After a poor start due to lack of capital for maintenance, traffic developed; coal upstream, bricks from Ballingdon, chalk and corn being principal downstream cargoes, transhipped to sea-going craft at Mistley quay. A proposal of 1787 for a canal from Bury St. Edmunds to Mistley was surveyed by Rennie in 1790 but no more was done. Stour life remained uneventful, the tolls were leased in 1821, the lessees also being responsible for repairs. A survey ordered by the undertakers and completed in 1836 by William Cubitt recommended improvement of the towpath to avoid ferrying the boat horses over, there being 26 of these 'boatings' at that time. Other hazards were the stiles or jumps portrayed by Constable in the 'Leaping Horse', 123 of them, replaced by gates after 1850. Cubitt wanted the staunches removed, but this was not done, although two more pound locks were built on the new Wormingford cut near Nayland, increasing the number to 15, with uprights and lintels spanning the lower gates. Railway competition came in the 1850s with a line from Marks Tey to Sudbury, the navigation offering to sell out to the railway. This was refused and the Stour proprietors had to reduce their tolls. They had considered extending to Clare, about 13 miles above Sudbury, but instead in 1862 they put a steam barge on the river. She was soon withdrawn, although a steam dredger was more successful. But by 1890 the Stour was in debt and becoming silted. To keep solvent, land was sold, the proprietors being replaced in 1892 by the River Stour Navigation Co. Ltd. This went into voluntary liquidation in 1913, but the shareholders formed themselves into a trust to keep the navigation open. They succeeded for a few years, but the last lighter went through Boxted lock below Nayland in 1916. One of the trustees was Percy Clover who operated the last traffic, grain to his mills at Dedham in 1930. The trust was wound up in 1937, but the South Essex Waterworks Co, under their Act of 1928, built four new locks at Brantham, Flatford, Stratford and Dedham. They were never used. A new River Stour Trust, founded in 1968, aims to restore the navigation and has made progress, with Flatford Lock reopened.

River STOUR, Worcestershire.   The Stour navigation was authorized by an Act of 1662, from the Severn to the Stourbridge collieries, with eleven locks for 6 ton boats and two branch tramroads. Andrew Yarranton undertook the work, mainly financed by Lord Windsor, and built 12 locks and four half locks for 16 ton craft between Kidderminster and Stourbridge, completing the task in 1667. Boats used this section but lack of money prevented further improvement downstream, although the river was navigable down to the Severn. Robert Yarranton tried to continue the work below Kidderminster but again there was a shortage of money and soon afterwards floods destroyed the works.

STOURBRIDGE CANAL, Worcestershire, Staffordshire, Warwickshire.   Considered as a local narrow line to bring coal from the Dudley mines to the iron and glass works of Stourbridge, the Stourbridge hoped to join up with the Staffs. & Worcs. The Dudley Canal was at first a part of the Stourbridge promotion but later became a separate scheme although Lord Dudley as the local mining magnate was the chief promoter of both. Robert Whitworth made the surveys and in 1775 the Bill for the Stourbridge and Dudley was introduced, but opposed by the Birmingham Canal and thrown out. In 1776 the two were put forward as separate Bills and passed. The Stourbridge was to run from Stourton on the Staffs. & Worcs. to Stourbridge with branches, one from Wordsley junction to the canal's reservoir at The Fens on Pensnett Chase, while the other off this first branch went on to Delph below Brierley Hill to meet the Dudley. Thomas Dadford the younger was engineer with Green, probably the father of the West Country engineer, as his assistant. Work commenced on the intended main line from Stourton to Stourbridge and on the two branches to Pensnett Chase from Wordsley junction, with its flight of 16 rising locks, while the second ran to Delph on the level from Lays Junction. Although built as branches, the two came to be accepted as the main line, with Stourbridge on a branch. The whole canal was completed by 1779, the line from Stourton to Delph measuring $5\frac{1}{8}$ miles, while from Wordsley junction to Stourbridge it was $1\frac{1}{4}$ miles, and from Lays junction to Pensnett Chase $\frac{3}{4}$ mile, where two more reservoirs were built in 1779. Apart from the flight of 16, four locks were built at Stourton and there was a 56 yd tunnel under Brettell Lane near Delph, later replaced by a bridge. The new canal started their own coal merchant's business at Stourport and assisted the Dudley with their plans to join the Birmingham Canal. In 1785, the year the Dudley extension was authorized, they planned a canal, from Stourbridge to the Severn at Diglis below Worcester. Its Bill failed but the scheme was revived in 1789 as the Worcester & Birmingham. A first Stourbridge dividend was paid for 1785 and thereafter the canal became quite prosperous in a district of increasing industrialisation. With the opening of Dudley tunnel, the Stourbridge became part of a through route to the Midlands, continuing to work closely with the Dudley. It was to benefit from their Selly Oak line and from the opening of the Worcester & Birmingham in 1815, because of a new through iron trade. Colliery tramroads were built down to the Pensnett Chase branch in the early nineteenth century and traffic was further helped by the completion in 1840 of the Stourbridge Extension Canal. Appearance of the Oxford, Worcester & Wolverhampton Railway, opened from Droitwich via Stourbridge and Dudley to Tipton in 1853, did not upset the Canal; they worked together, and canal to rail transhipment wharves were built. Later in 1855 the LNWR backed BCN offered amalgamation with the Stourbridge probably because it was under GWR influence, the OWWR having been absorbed by the Great Western. BCN overtures were refused for the Stourbridge was still prosperous. Later in the 1880s revenue declined but revived in 1904 when the company began an improvement programme. Between the wars however road competition brought a severe decline and commercial traffic ceased in the 1950s. The canal fell into some disrepair but was rescued by the joint efforts of the British Waterways Board and the Staffordshire & Worcestershire Canal Society. Work started in 1964 and in 1967 the Stourbridge was reopened.

STOURBRIDGE EXTENSION CANAL, Staffordshire.   In 1829 the Shut End Railway (then called Shutt End) was opened from the coal and ironstone deposits around this village near Kingswinford to the Staffs. & Worcs. Canal at Hinksford. Meanwhile the Stourbridge Canal Co. were planning an extension also to tap the Shut End deposits but were opposed by Lord Dudley as principal promoter of the railway. Nothing further was done until 1836-37 when a canal was planned from the Stourbridge via Shut End to the BCN at Bloomfield. This never matured and the promoters had to be content with a small extension from Brockmoor on the Stourbridge to near Oak Farm beyond Shut End. Although the Stourbridge Co. offered to build, the promoters formed their own company, with Stourbridge support, and in 1837 the Act for the Stourbridge Extension Canal was passed. William Fowler was made engineer, followed by Benjamin Townsend and then William Richardson of Dudley. Opened in 1840 the main line to narrow standard was 2 miles long with a $\frac{5}{8}$ mile branch to Sandhills, another branch to Bromley, only $2\frac{1}{2}$ furlongs, was added in 1841. There was one stop lock near the Bromley branch, $1\frac{1}{2}$ furlongs from the junction with the Stourbridge. Traffic from the Extension in coal and ironstone was of benefit to the Stourbridge and the former paid immediate dividends. However it was not independent for long, being bought in 1847 by the Oxford, Worcester & Wolverhampton Railway, who worked it hard. The GWR acquired the canal in the 1860s (the boatmen called it the Great Western Extension), but although tonnage fell, the canal was still profitable in the 1880s and was used until after the 1939-45 War. Some had been abandoned in 1935, and the remainder in 1960.

STOVER CANAL, Devon.   Promoted by James Templer of Bovey Tracey, this was built to bring pottery clay from the pits around Chudleigh for transhipment at Teignmouth.

Construction was completed in 1792 but not as far as Bovey Tracey, nor was a branch to Chudleigh ever dug. Ventiford became the terminus, from where the canal ran for $1\frac{7}{8}$ miles down to the Teign at Jetty Marsh, with five locks, able to pass barges 54' x 14' x 3'6" draught. Other outward traffic was lignite (low grade coal) from Bovey Tracey and granite from Haytor, the latter much increased with the opening of the Haytor Granite Tramway in 1820. In 1829 the canal was sold to the Duke of Somerset, who in 1862 sold it to the Moretonhampstead & S. Devon Railway, later a part of the Great Western. From the 1850s it declined and was leased by the GWR to the clay companies, in particular to Watts, Blake, Bearne & Co, although the canal was disused by 1939.

STRABANE CANAL, Co Tyrone.   Privately built by the first Marquess of Abercorn this extended the navigation of the Foyle up to Strabane. Richard Owen was in charge and the canal was built between 1791 and 1796. It left the Foyle some 10 miles above London-derry and ran parallel with the river 4 miles to a basin in Strabane.   There were two locks, an entrance lock into the Foyle 117' x 24' and another about half way to Strabane, 108' x 23', which were intended to take coasting schooners and ketches, the canal being crossed by swing bridges. Water came mainly from a feeder rising on Moorlough on the slopes of Knockavoe. Initially the Marquess ran the canal himself but from 1820 it was leased to a Strabane group. Lighters were towed in trains by a tug up the Foyle to the canal entrance. On the canal, horses towed both lighters and coasters.   As early as 1847 a railway was built from Londonderry to Strabane, more lines coming in the 1850s so that canal traffic began to suffer seriously. In 1860 the group of lessees were replaced by the Strabane Steam Navigation Co. who carried on until 1890 when they were replaced in their turn by new lessees, the Strabane Canal Co. By about 1900 only two or three lighters a week were coming up to Strabane. The canal was sold to the Strabane & Foyle Navigation Co. Ltd. in 1912 who attempted to improve the draught and brought a steam tug for use on the Foyle. The attempts failed and traffic declined still more, vanishing in the early 1930s.

STRATFORD-UPON-AVON CANAL, Warwickshire, Worcester-shire.   In 1792 there were moves to build a canal to Stratford and Warwick from either the Digbeth branch of the Birmingham or from the Worcester & Birmingham. The Warwick part went a-head as the Warwick & Birmingham, leaving the Stratford as a separate project from the Worcester & Birmingham at King's Norton to Stratford but without a connection with the Avon. John Snape surveyed the line, the Act passing in 1793. Before work started the company were considering an extension, either to join the Oxford Canal at Fenny Compton or the Warwick & Birmingham via Lapworth and Kingswood, the latter only requiring a short branch. The idea was to pass on through traffic, bypassing the excessive charges of the Birmingham Canal.   After negotiation a

100.

supplementary Act was passed in 1795 for the Lapworth branch, to the Warwick & Birmingham at Kingswood. Work on the Stratford began in 1793, with Josiah Clowes as engineer, the summit level running from King's Norton to Hockley Heath, $9\frac{3}{4}$ miles. The latter was reached in 1796, the work having cost as much as the estimate for the whole canal, including the 352 yd King's Norton tunnel. No more money was available and Clowes had died in 1795. The Stratford was discouraged by the unfinished state of all its connecting canals, but as they progressed, so the Stratford's will to continue revived. A new Act to raise more money was passed in 1799 and the line altered to bring the canal within $\frac{1}{8}$ mile of the Warwick & Birmingham at Kingswood. Work recommenced under Samuel Porter, lately Clowes' assistant, and the 18 locks down from the summit and the junction at Kingswood were completed in 1802. Now able to pass trade on to the Grand Junction, the Stratford had no interest to continue to Stratford. However William James pressed for continuation and took charge. Money was raised and in 1812 work began under William Whitmore as engineer, reaching Stratford in 1816 where it was joined to the Avon, the portion above Evesham being under James' ownership.   The complete waterway was $15\frac{5}{8}$ miles long with 56 locks, 25 of them down from the summit at Lapworth, one a stop lock at King's Norton and one a barge lock into the Avon at Stratford, the remainder being narrow. There was also a lock on the Kingswood branch.   A single arched aqueduct of brick crossed over the Cole near Shirley, while south of Kingswood came three cast iron aqueducts, Yarningale, Wooton Wawen over the Stratford-Birmingham road and the Edstone over Edstone Brook. Water for the canal came from the feeder streams until the building in 1821 of the reservoirs at Earlswood on the summit.   Most of the Earlswood supply had to be pumped into the canal, the beam engine working from 1823 to 1936, in that year being replaced by electric pumps.

Traffic developed on the northern section as a through route, but was not so heavy to Stratford. Completion of the Stratford & Moreton tramroad in 1826 helped to advance trade, the Stratford leasing the Upper Avon from 1842. Meanwhile tolls had been reduced on the canal and connecting waterways to counter railways. Railways entered the Stratford scene directly in 1845 when the Oxford, Worcester & Wolverhampton Railway approached the canal with a view to buy and were accepted, the sale being completed in 1856. Once under railway control the Stratford declined, traffic being diverted to rail. In 1863 the GWR ab-sorbed the OWWR and canal traffic fell still further, particularly between Kingswood and Stratford. The northern part has remained open continuously, the southern ceased to be navigable about 1945 and would have been abandoned in 1958 had not the National Trust leased it in 1960. In 1964 after the efforts of teams of volunteers, the canal was re-opened to the Avon, being transferred to the National Trust in 1965.

STROUDWATER NAVIGATION, Gloucestershire. In the late seventeenth century ideas were put forward to make the Stroudwater navigable to Stroud. These were revived about 1728 by John Hore who proposed a canal, although an Act passed in 1730 envisaged a river improvement. Because of millowner opposition nothing was done except a survey in 1754. In 1758 an idea was put forward to cut out locks and install cranes at each change of level so that cargo in 1 ton boxes would be transferred at least 14 times. Under an Act of 1759 improvements were started with this in view, 5 miles being completed and installed, but probably never much used. More surveys were made in 1774 by the younger Thomas Dadford and John Priddey, followed by Thomas Yeoman who had prepared the 1754 survey. At that time Yeoman had proposed a navigation, but now, like Dadford, he recommended a canal. Work was started under the 1730 Act, although opposed since the Act had not sanctioned a canal. So a new Act was obtained in 1776 and the canal opened in 1779 from Framilode on the Severn to Walbridge, Stroud, a distance of 8 miles, with 12 locks, 72' x 15'6", able to take trows and Severn barges. Bow hauling was done until 1827 when a horse path was completed. With the opening of the Thames & Severn in 1789 the Stroudwater became part of a through route, while at the same time it was involved in the Gloucester & Berkeley which later crossed the Stroudwater on the level at Saul. Coal for the Stroud mills was the main traffic, much of it from South Wales. The opening of the North Wilts. Canal in 1819 provided a second and better route to the Thames, while in 1820 the Gloucester & Berkeley reached Saul. The Stroudwater enjoyed considerable prosperity until the arrival of the GWR at Stroud and Gloucester in 1845. Even so locks were widened in 1859 to allow a steam barge up to Ryeford mill, but later tolls had to be reduced, particularly when the Stonehouse & Nailsworth Railway (later the Midland) gained its Act in 1863. By the 1930s the Stroudwater was in a poor state, the last traffic passing in 1941. The navigation was abandoned by an Act of 1954, but restoration is under way.

SUIR NAVIGATION, Co Waterford, Kilkenny, Tipperary. Tidal to above Clonmel $29\frac{1}{4}$ miles above Waterford and navigable to Carrick-on-Suir, about 15 miles above Waterford, the first moves towards improvement came in 1759, with ideas of extending the navigation to Clonmel. About 1800 came proposals to join up with the Shannon, the proposed Kilkenny navigations and the Grand Canal. Improvements were restricted to the section below Carrick, an Act of 1836 setting up the River Suir Navigation Co, who proceeded to make a short ship canal at Carrick, completed about 1840. Traffic was never heavy on the river, hindered particularly by the rapid current.

River SWALE, Yorkshire. See River Ouse (above York).

SWANSEA and TREWYDDFA CANALS, Glamorganshire, Brecknockshire. In 1790 there was a survey for a canal up the Tawe and another in 1793 by the elder Thomas Sheasby for a line into Brecknockshire. The Act passed in 1794, although one of the main opponents, the Duke of Beaufort, was allowed to build under the same Act a part of the Swansea canal from Landore to Fforest copper works. This was the $1\frac{3}{8}$ mile Trewyddfa Canal completed about two years later, on which the Duke took tolls. The Swansea was to be built by direct labour and costs did not prove high, first under Charles Roberts as engineer, later under the elder Thomas Sheasby with his son Thomas assisting him. In 1796 the canal was partially open, in 1798 completely so, $15\frac{1}{8}$ miles long from Swansea up to Henneuadd but broken into two by the $1\frac{3}{8}$ miles of the Trewyddfa Canal, so the whole line up the valley into Brecknockshire measured $16\frac{1}{2}$ miles. There were 36 locks for boats 69' x 7'7" carrying 25 tons, and several aqueducts including a three arched stone one over the Twrch at Ystalyfera. Traffic on the Swansea built up well as the Tawe valley was developed, in spite of the arrival in 1824 of the Tennant Canal at Port Tennant. The Swansea was served by many tramroads from collieries as well as the Brecon Forest tramroad from near Devynock to the canal near Ynysgedwyn, completed about 1834. The main canal line was also fed by private branch canals, a $\frac{1}{2}$ mile one from Ynysgedwyn ironworks, a short one from Ystalyfera ironworks, a $\frac{1}{4}$ mile one at Cilybebyll to join colliery tramroads, a short one to the river at Pontardawe and finally soon after 1852, the canal company built a branch alongside the new North dock in Swansea. Railway competition arrived in the early 1850s from the Swansea Vale line, in 1861 reaching Ystradgynlais near the head of the canal, with a route parallel to the canal on the opposite side of the Tawe. Then in 1864 came the Neath & Brecon Railway who attempted to lease the canal. Tolls were reduced to win back traffic from the railways, but the canal was also hit by the growth of rail served steelworks, and the decline of iron. By this time the Swansea Canal was owned by the GWR who bought it in 1873 together with the Duke of Beaufort's Trewyddfa Canal. The GWR worked the canal hard because they were competing with the Midland who in 1876 absorbed the Swansea Vale Railway. Until the mid-1890s the canal was profitable but carrying finally ceased in 1931. Since 1904 only the lower six miles had been in use; there had not been traffic to the head since about 1880. Today under British Waterways Board control the Swansea Canal is a water channel, although abandoned as a navigation by a series of Acts from 1928 to 1962.

TAMAR MANURE NAVIGATION, Devon. This navigation was designed to carry fertilizers, in this case lime, inland. The Tamar itself had been navigable since the twelfth century as far as Morwellham, but the canal mania produced a scheme, to join the proposed Public Devonshire Canal, and more realistically the projected Bude Canal. An Act was obtained in 1796 to improve the river from Morwellham to Blanchdown, and make a tub-boat canal on to Tamerton bridge to the Bude. The canal section was never started, and the river was only improved as far as Newbridge near Gunnislake, a distance of $2\frac{3}{4}$ miles, with one 70' x 20' lock at Weir Head, Nutstakes a mile below Newbridge. Traffic continued to Newbridge until about 1929, when the river ceased to be navigable.

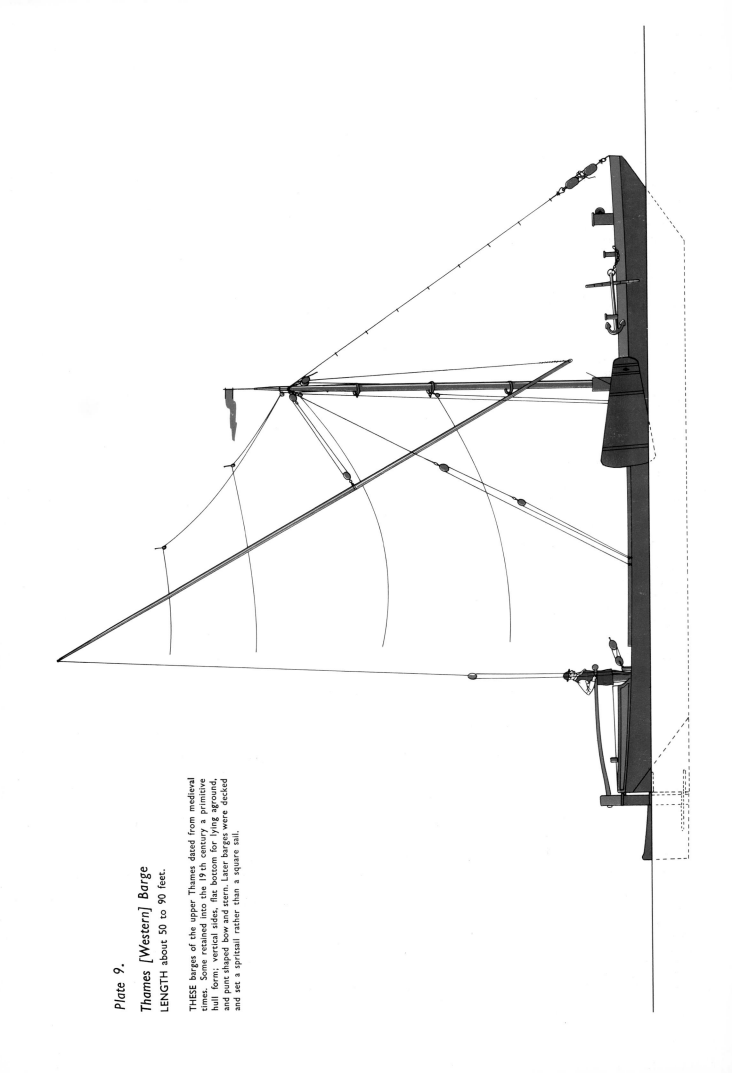

Plate 9.

Thames [Western] Barge
LENGTH about 50 to 90 feet.

THESE barges of the upper Thames dated from medieval
times. Some retained into the 19 th century a primitive
hull form; vertical sides, flat bottom for lying aground,
and punt shaped bow and stern. Later barges were decked
and set a spritsail rather than a square sail.

TAVISTOCK CANAL, Devon. Built to export copper ore from the local mines via Morwellham quay on the Tamar. A survey for a four mile tub-boat canal from the quay to the River Tavy at Tavistock with a branch to the Mill Hill slate quarries was made in 1802 and an Act passed the following year. John Taylor, manager of the Wheal Friendship mine was engineer for a waterway which included the aqueduct over the River Lumburn, a 2540 yd tunnel through Morwelldown and an inclined plane 237' down to the quay. There were no locks, but the canal was sloped down from Tavistock so that a current was generated to drive mining and mill machinery and help the ore laden boats. In 1817 the tunnel was finished and the canal open, save for the Mill Hill branch, with another inclined plane, opened in 1819. The canal made a steady profit, carrying limestone, slate, and a little granite. Whereas the short double track inclined plane on the Mill Hill branch carried tub-boats, that down to Morwellham quay carried trucks into which the cargoes were transhipped. After 1831 the Mill Hill branch was closed, re-opening as a tramroad in 1844. Because of threatened railway competition the main canal experimented with water wheel driven cable haulage through Morwelldown tunnel in 1859, but arrival of the railway at Tavistock in the same year ended the canal's usefulness, and it was sold to the Duke of Bedford in 1873 who closed it. In 1933-4 the canal was resurrected to provide a water channel for a hydro-electric plant at Morwellham.

TEES SCHEMES, the STOCKTON & DARLINGTON CANAL, Co Durham. The Tees was navigable to Yarm above Stockton, but coalfield expansion led to ideas of a greater navigation, though only a short length of canal at Cockfield Fell colliery was actually built in the 1760s and an experimental flume used to move coal in boxes by an artificial current. Both were the work of the colliery lessee George Dixon. A canal was proposed in 1767 from the collieries north-west of Darlington via that town to Stockton on the navigable Tees. Brindley was asked to do the survey but his assistant Robert Whitworth was sent. At the same time at Cockfield Fell, George Dixon was planning a 10 ton tub-boat canal which would be linked with the main canal by an inclined plane. A Stockton to Darlington canal to extend to the collieries was again projected, Ralph Dodd doing the survey in 1796. He more or less followed the Whitworth line. A survey was done in 1800 by George Atkinson for the North Riding Canal, from the Ure to Piercebridge west of Darlington, with branches to Bedale and Richmond, and towards the Tees. In 1808 the Tees Navigation Co. was formed, dedicated to river improvement, and for them in 1810 Chapman built the short Mandale cut to save 2¼ miles of river. Rennie in 1812 gave advice on a Stockton to Darlington Canal along the old Whitworth line, revised in 1816 as a canal-rail project. Other canals were considered at about the same time, for example the Stockton & Auckland, but railways were preferred and built. Finally, on the Tees there was an 1825 plan for a ship canal to extend Chapman's 1810 cut downstream.

River TEME, Worcestershire. William Sandys in the 1630s was granted powers to make the Teme navigable from the Severn towards Ludlow, but he never did anything, although the river was used by boats in its unimproved state serving mills and forges. During the nineteenth century the 1½ miles of river from its junction with the Severn near Worcester up to Powick Bridge was used by coal boats.

TENNANT CANALS, Glamorganshire. Red Jacket (Neath & Swansea Junction) canal. In 1816 George Tennant bought properties near Neath and proposed a canal system to link the River Tawe at Swansea with the Neath River, because the former offered better shipping facilities. He first leased the Glan-y-wern Canal from about 1816 and enlarged it, building a lock from it into Red Jacket pill on the Neath River, able to take 60 ton capacity craft. Tennant then built, without an Act, the Red Jacket Canal from the Glan-y-wern to the Tawe with a lock into the river. His engineer was William Kirkhouse and the whole was completed in 1818 at Tennant's expense, the main line between Red Jacket and the Tawe measuring 4 miles with the remainder of the Glan-y-wern as a 1⅜ miles branch. Traffic was not on a large enough scale, and the enthusiastic Tennant found he needed a direct link with the Neath Canal. At first he proposed simply to make a lock from the Neath Canal at Giant's Grave into the River Neath, so that boats could cross over to the Red Jacket pill on the opposite side, this was superseded by the Neath & Swansea Junction Canal. The Red Jacket Canal became disused by about 1922.

Tennant (Neath & Swansea Junction) Canal. In 1810 George Tennant proposed a line to join the Red Jacket and Neath Canals. The canal would run alongside the Neath River to join the Neath Canal at Aberdulais, giving a line throughout from Neath to Swansea. Work commenced in 1821 under William Kirkhouse at the expense of George Tennant, no Act being passed to authorize compulsory land purchase. It is thought that Tennant may already have had a short canal built over a part of the new line near his Rhyddings estate to bring coal down to the Neath River, with an inclined plane near Cadoxton to load boats on the river. The new canal crossed the Neath at Aberdulais by a low ten arched masonry aqueduct. In 1824 the 4⅞ mile line was complete, level except for a lock at Aberdulais, large enough for boats 60' x 8'10" carrying 25 tons; the whole Tennant system now measured 8½ miles, including Port Tennant where the canal entered the Tawe. Officially it was the Neath & Swansea Junction, although after 1845 was generally known as the Tennant. Traffic was steady in minerals, timber and sand and from 1827 there was a passenger service between Neath and Port Tennant. By the early 1840s the Tennant had acquired many short branches, the ½ furlong Dulais built in 1840 with one lock to a quarry, the ½ furlong private Neath Brewery branch built in 1839, and earlier in 1828 a lock into the River Neath below the town, also in the same year a private ½ furlong branch to the Neath Abbey works. Two more branches were built during the second half of the nineteenth century, the private 1 mile Tir-isaf Canal to a colliery near Port Tennant opened in about 1863, and another branch between the canal and the Neath River in about 1879 with a lock above the Crown copperworks at Neath, the older (1828) River Neath branch now being closed. Earnings were maintained by the canal to the end of the nineteenth century. There was no commercial traffic after 1945, the canal suffering bomb damage. The Tir-isaf and Glan-y-wern Canals, disused after 1910, were derelict by 1918. The system is owned by the Tennant family and remains as a water channel, and is being restored and reopened.

River TERN, Shropshire.   Entering the Severn at Atcham half way between Shrewsbury and Wellington, the Tern was used in the early eighteenth century by craft to carry pig iron from the Forest of Dean and Coalbrookdale to a forge at Tern Hall, about $\frac{3}{4}$ mile from the Tern's junction with the Severn. Boats also went up a further $1\frac{1}{2}$ miles to Upton Forge and possibly higher, likewise carrying pig iron. The Tern Hall forge closed in 1757, but the river may still have been used until 1797 when part of the entrance lock into the Severn was removed. This was 24' x 7'8".

River THAMES, Gloucestershire, Wiltshire, Berkshire, Oxfordshire, Buckinghamshire, Middlesex, Surrey, Kent, Essex.   By a charter of 1197 the conservancy of the river was vested in the Mayor and Corporation of London whose jurisdiction really only extended to Staines. Above Staines the river was maintained by local communities. In the Middle Ages there were plenty of water mills and fish weirs on the river. From the twelfth century boats could reach Oxford and flash locks were a feature since the thirteenth century. Although navigable to Oxford the river above Abingdon needed improvement and schemes were put forward in the early seventeenth century to extend to Cricklade. This was authorized by an Act of 1605 which appointed commissioners. The work was partially done, but a further Act of 1624 replaced them by the Oxford-Burcot Commission for the river below Oxford. This group built the first pound locks on the Thames. They were at Swift Ditch (Abingdon), Sandford and Iffley further upstream, and were open by 1635. Overall control was provided at first by a commission of the justices of the riverside counties established in 1695 and more permanently by the establishment in 1751 of the Thames Navigation Commissioners, to oversee the considerable traffic. There was room for improvement and in 1770 the City of London took the initiative and called in Brindley. He recommended a canal for 200 ton barges to bypass the river between Monkey Island below Maidenhead and Isleworth below Richmond on the tideway. Soon the Monkey Island canal idea was being extended to Reading, and there were ideas of a canal from Monkey Island to Basingstoke. The city supported Brindley's Monkey Island-Isleworth scheme now called the London Canal. It never reached Parliament, although three Bills were put forward in 1771; for two canals, that from Reading to Monkey Island, and from Monkey Island to Basingstoke, while the third Bill was for Thames improvement. Only the third passed in 1771. It was an important Act, the number of commissioners was increased, the river was divided into five districts above Staines, the limit of London's control and the commissioners were given wide powers of improvement. They were financed by toll revenue and by the borrowing powers granted under their Act. They built eight new pound locks, between Maidenhead and Reading, including the famous Boulter's at Maidenhead. These were completed by 1773 with turf sides. Horse paths were also extended. The new locks gave a canalized river from Maidenhead to the mouth of the Kennet which had been improved since 1723, but new locks were soon added on the Thames above Reading, at Caversham in 1778, at Mapledurham in 1777. Above Oxford the river was in poor state. The Thames & Severn was authorized in 1783 to join the river at Inglesham and expected improvement. Another likely arrival was the Oxford Canal direct from the Midlands. The commissioners were ready for them with 10 new locks built between 1787 and 1795, three of them replacing the 1635 locks of the Oxford-Burcot Commission. However there was still the river between Oxford and Lechlade for which William Jessop prepared a survey in 1787. New locks were needed and a horse path, and the commissioners showed a willingness to co-operate with the Thames & Severn. The latter's resident engineer, Josiah Clowes, designed new pound locks and by 1791 they were built, at St John's (Lechlade), Buscot, Rushey and Pinkhill.

Improvement was needed on the river below Maidenhead, Boulter's being the lowest pound lock. The old London Canal idea was revived in 1790 and Robert Mylne did a survey for the commissioners and reported in 1793, favouring a canal. Rival canal and river improvement proposals were prepared for Parliament but the river supporters won. John Rennie now did a river survey and an Act passed in 1795 sanctioning new lock construction below Maidenhead. One, Romney near Windsor was soon built and opened in 1797. The old idea of bypassing the lower river was revived in 1792 by an Oxford Canal promotion, the London & Western or Hampton Gay Canal to run from Hampton Gay on the Oxford to Isleworth. Then came the Grand Junction, authorized in 1793. In 1794 came the Act for the Kennet & Avon Canal and in 1796 that for the Wilts. & Berks. In 1802 the Basingstoke had ideas of a cut from Kingston to the Wey, to bypass the lower river, and a few years later the Kennet & Avon were full of schemes, once they had successfully opened their own line. First they wanted a canal from the mouth of the Kennet to Windsor, and a second canal from Datchet below Windsor to Isleworth. More attractive was a canal from near Maidenhead to Cowley on the Grand Junction, suggested in 1795 and revised in 1810, 1815 and 1819. It was called the Western Union and surveys were made by John Rennie with Francis Giles. The Wilts. & Berks. who entered the Thames at Abingdon inspired extension projects. First was the Western Junction Canal from Abingdon to Aylesbury and Marsworth on the Grand Junction proposed in 1803 and again in 1809. Part of it was actually built as the Grand Junction's Aylesbury branch opened in 1815. Extension proposals to Abingdon continued into the 1820s. One reason for the failure of the canal schemes was that the lower

Thames was improved in the early nineteenth century. John Rennie and William Jessop did a survey in 1805 and made suggestions for part canalization. This was not undertaken but more pound locks were built, the lowest, Teddington, in 1811 followed by eight more, the last being Cookham in 1830. There were still however plenty of flash locks. Passage of the river was slow, an additional complication being the varied sizes of the pound locks, 110' x 14' from Lechlade down to Godstow, and 120' x 18' lower down. From Inglesham where the Thames & Severn Canal entered, down to Teddington where the tideway commenced, the navigation was 125½ miles long. With the opening of the Great Western Railway to Reading in 1840 and Bristol the following year Thames traffic began to suffer. The line from Didcot to Oxford followed in 1844. River tolls were cut, and funds fell very low. Rescue came by the formation of the Thames Conservancy in 1857 to take over the City's responsibility up to Staines, extended in 1866 to control the commissioners' lengths up to Cricklade. Weirs and paddle and rimer flash locks remained for some years yet. By 1880 most had been removed but four stayed into the twentieth century, the last not being dismantled until 1937. This was Hart's weir near Buscot on the upper river. The Thames Conservancy did much more to improve the river in the later nineteenth century, because of hopes of revived traffic off the Thames & Severn. A new lock was built in 1884 at Osney, Oxford, and four more followed on the upper river between 1892 and 1898. Then in 1894 a half tide lock was built at Richmond below Teddington to improve depth in the upper tidal reaches. There were 38 locks in 1888 and 43 by 1954, still of the same two sizes and now mechanized. While commercial traffic has fallen pleasure traffic has increased and the Thames Authority revenue relies much on the sale of water to the London water undertakings. Nowadays commercial traffic is mainly below Shepperton; the Thames below Teddington has been under the jurisdiction of the Port of London Authority since its formation in 1908.

THAMES & MEDWAY CANAL, Kent. It was advocated in 1799 by Ralph Dodd, a great promoter of canals in the London area. A canal between Gravesend and Strood on the Medway would, he argued, be of exceptional value to the Government in time of war. In 1800 Dodd's canal received its Act and work started, but there was not enough money to finish. A further Act of 1804 authorized more money, and Dodd having left, Ralph Walker proposed a deviation and a larger cutting. Later Walker proposed a second deviation and a tunnel which was accepted by an Act of 1810, followed by one of 1818 which sanctioned more money. Work on the Higham-Strood tunnel started in 1819 with William Tierney Clark as engineer. Finished in 1824 the tunnel was only for single line traffic, and in 1830 the centre was opened up to provide a very necessary passing place, and there was a towpath. The canal was 7 miles long with basins and entrance locks from river to basin and basin to canal at Gravesend and Frindsbury on the Medway. Water came from the spring tides and a steam pump at Gravesend. Although there was no war when the canal opened trade built up, particularly during the hop and fruit seasons. Passenger services were limited because the steamer damaged the banks, but the tunnel was a tourist attraction. Later a steam tug was put on for it. However the canal became a railway, work starting in 1844 and a single track line was laid alongside the canal from Gravesend to Strood. Opened in 1845 and at first carrying only passengers, trains and barges shared the tunnels until 1847, the South Eastern Railway having bought the canal company in 1846. The canal remained open from Gravesend to Higham until abandoned in 1934. The basin at Gravesend remains, used today by pleasure craft. A late revival of the Thames & Medway Canal was the scheme which in 1902 actually received an Act, to provide a 5⅛ mile waterway for boats operated by electric traction, to bypass the Isle of Grain.

THAMES to CHANNEL SHIP CANAL PROJECTS 1823-8. 1823-4 were years of financial optimism when some amazing canals were promoted for deep sea ships between London and the Channel. Their value in time of war and their safety to sailing ships were emphasised. In 1824 two rival schemes emerged from James Elmes and N. W. Cundy, money being subscribed to the latter's Grand Ship Canal from London to Arundel Bay. In 1825 came a plan from George and the younger John Rennie for a London to Portsmouth Ship Canal. In 1827 Cundy made another proposal for a Grand Imperial Ship Canal which died the following year. By this time the financial boom was over.

THAMES & SEVERN CANAL, Gloucestershire. As early as 1610 there were ideas for a Thames-Severn waterway to join London and Bristol. Between 1662 and 1668 various bills for a canal were proposed, the project being revived in the eighteenth century under the impetus of the Stroudwater Navigation. The Thames & Severn was promoted largely to carry south Staffordshire coal to the Thames, and in 1781 a survey was made by Robert Whitworth, the Act following in 1783. The canal was opened to Chalford in 1785 and throughout from Walbridge, Stroud, the junction with the Stroudwater, to the Thames at Inglesham in November 1789, Josiah Clowes being the resident engineer. In its 28¾ miles the Thames & Severn had 44 locks and the 3817 yds Sapperton tunnel. The locks were in two sizes, since somewhere on the line there would have to be a transhipment point between the Severn trows from the west and the Thames barges from the east. Brimscombe became the site for this inland port, the locks to Walbridge measuring 68 - 69' x 16'1" - 16'2" and those to Inglesham 90' - 93' x 12'9" or 13', one at The Bourn just above Brimscombe being 90' x 16'1" suitable for either type of vessel. The canal was built too late to benefit from the great days of the London-Bristol trade. The bulk of the trade remained local, to and from the woollen mills of the Golden Valley. The summit level from the start was beset by leakage and an inadequate water supply, although helped by the building of a windpump at the Thames Head springs in 1790 replaced in 1792 by a Boulton & Watt atmospheric engine. Nevertheless the canal began a modestly successful career, the company from the start building and operating their own boats. The North Wilts Canal completed in 1819 from Latton to Swindon gave them a new and much better access to the Thames at Abingdon via the Wilts & Berks Canal. Railway competition from 1845 when the Swindon-Gloucester line opened, caused canal traffic to decline, accelerated by the completion of the Gloucester to Chepstow line in 1854 which captured the Forest of Dean coal traffic. No dividends were paid after 1864 and plans were made to turn the canal into a railway in 1865 and again in 1882 when the GWR acquired a majority shareholding in the canal. In 1895 they transferred their holdings to a trust, which mismanaged the canal until 1900, when it was taken over by the Gloucestershire County Council. Both the trust and the County Council had tried to put the canal into good working order. Traffic by this time was negligible, the last cargo boats crossing the summit in 1911. To avoid further expense the County Council closed the line east of Chalford in 1927 and the whole in 1933, but now restoration work has been undertaken, notably at Sapperton tunnel.

THORNE and HATFIELD MOORS PEAT CANALS, Yorkshire, Lincolnshire. Peat from Hatfield Chase east of Doncaster was sent down to the Don's old line to the Trent. Later when the Dutch River was made in the 1630s the Don's Trent mouth closed and the peat cutters appear to have built a canal from Hatfield Chase to the Trent. Other canals were cut westwards from Thorne Moors to the Don in the mid eighteenth century. There was at least one lock on the system near Thorne; it was busy by the 1790s. However peat was overtaken by coal and enclosures and drainage reclaimed the cuttings for agriculture. A new drain, as part of the enclosures was cut in 1815, and was probably navigable, but there is unlikely to have been much traffic after the 1830s. The turf boats were 28' x 6', and clinker built. Peat traffic revived in the 1880s, for use as horse litter. A new waterway system was built, or adapted from old drains and peat cuttings, by a Dutch company. It ran to the rail served litter works and was used until the 1920s.

River TONE, Somerset. Joining the Parrett at Burrow Bridge six miles above Bridgwater, the Tone as early as 1638 was made navigable by John Mallet, to Ham Mills about 3 miles below Taunton, so that boats could bring coal from Bristol. Under Acts of 1699 and 1707 conservators made it navigable as far as Taunton, with one lock and at least two half locks, able to pass boats of just over 15 tons capacity. From 1792, the river became involved in various Bristol to Taunton canal projects and others to link the Bristol and English Channels. One became the Bridgwater & Taunton, with a lock into the Tone at Firepool, Taunton, strongly opposed by the Tone Conservators whose river was now bypassed. By this time the Tone is known to have had four full locks taking craft 54' x 13' and four half locks on the upper three miles between Ham Mills and Firepool. After some years of hostility the canal company bought the river in 1832, maintaining it as a navigation. In 1834 a cut with two locks was made between the Tone and the Grand Western Canal which was extending to Taunton as a tub-boat line. Until 1907 there was traffic in Taunton from Firepool lock for $\frac{3}{4}$ mile upstream to Taunton gasworks and until 1929 between Burrow Bridge and Ham Mills. Distances were $11\frac{5}{8}$ miles from Firepool to Burrow Bridge and $17\frac{5}{8}$ miles from Firepool to Bridgwater, plus the $\frac{3}{4}$ mile stretch upstream from Firepool to French weir and the gasworks.

TORRINGTON or ROLLE CANAL, Devon. The Torridge was navigable to Weare Giffard four miles above Bideford, to which coal and limestone were brought for road distribution inland. Denys Rolle, a local landowner, was a strong advocate of tub-boat canals. Nothing was done for a canal to Torrington until 1823 when Lord Rolle, the son of Denys, started at his own expense to cut one, without parliamentary sanction. James Green was his engineer, who made a tide lock and basin at Weare Giffard, followed by an inclined plane, from the top of which the canal followed the course of the Torridge for 6 miles to New Mills just beyond Torrington, crossing the river by the Beam aqueduct. Opened in 1827 the Torrington carried a steady upward traffic of limestone and coal, with return cargoes of agricultural produce. In 1852 the canal was leased to a local merchant and banker George Baginton, who went bankrupt in 1865, so that it reverted to the Hon. Mark Rolle. That same year an Act was passed for a railway from Bideford to Torrington, although the company, the LSWR were not keen and wanted to abandon the project. Mark Rolle however insisted on the railway going ahead and so the canal closed in about 1871.

TRALEE SHIP CANAL, Co Kerry. Authorized by an Act of 1828, but not built until about 1847 it runs for $1\frac{1}{2}$ miles from Tralee Bay up to Tralee for 400 ton ships though siltation had reduced it to 250 ton craft by 1923. Its role was altered by the arrival of the railway at Fenit on the north side of Tralee Bay in 1880. A pier and harbour were built and henceforward the canal was used mainly by lighter traffic to Fenit. The canal and its basin in Tralee are still open under the Tralee and Fenit Pier and Harbour Commissioners.

River TRENT, Derbyshire, Nottinghamshire, Leicestershire, Lincolnshire. Below Wilden Ferry in Derbyshire, just south of Shardlow, the Trent was naturally navigable for the 94 miles (7) down to Trent Falls below Keadby where it enters the Humber. It was under no authority and had for centuries carried cargoes transhipped at Gainsborough. Here the river is tidal, a feature being the bore which on spring tides attains 5' above Keadby. Navigation was difficult, boats relying on man haulage. Above Wilden Ferry there was no navigation until an Act of 1699 sanctioned improvements to be made under the authority of commissioners; the undertakers were headed by Lord Paget who put up most of the money. His two locks and cuts allowed boats to reach Burton. On completion early in the eighteenth century, this length, extending  *101.*

$18\frac{3}{4}$ miles above Wilden Ferry, was leased to various local people, in 1762 being renewed in favour of the Burton Boat Co, carriers. However it was eclipsed by the arrival of the Trent & Mersey Canal in 1770. The Trent below Wilden Ferry benefited from this canal and in 1772 came the first Act for improvement. It was a local project to bring traffic nearer Newark by the channel that passed close to the town, for the river divides at Averham two miles above Newark. The works, under the Newark Navigation Commissioners, included two locks, completed in 1773. There was a move to have the river dredged, cuts and locks made, and above all a horse path. The Thomas Dadfords, father and son, did a survey, and a Bill was prepared but opposed by the bow haulers or 'higging' men, and by merchants who did not want to pay tolls. It was withdrawn, but William Jessop was asked to make a further survey. In 1783 an improvement Act was passed and Jessop was made engineer of a company who proposed to undertake works between Wilden Ferry and Gainsborough. They operated downstream, improving the river section by section, tolls being taken when each was completed. By 1787 the works were considered complete, and included a horse path. Nothing was done below Gainsborough where jurisdiction ceased and the navigation became free. Jessop remained the Trent Navigation's permanent engineer and was able to build his first lock in about 1793 at Sawley above Nottingham, with the agreement of the local landowner. It was later joined by a flood lock. The Trent & Mersey and Erewash had ideas of a canal parallel with the river but the Navigation were able to defeat this by promising further improvements, which had to include a canal to bypass the dangerous Trent bridge in Nottingham. William Jessop and Robert Whitworth made surveys and a further improvement Act was passed in 1794. More effective work was now done to canalize the navigation through Nottingham. In 1796 the $2\frac{1}{2}$ miles Beeston cut, leaving the river above Nottingham by a lock, was completed. This joined the new Nottingham Canal's line to the Trent at Lenton Chain which had one lock, plus the Nottingham's Trent lock back into the river. The following year the Cranfleet cut with one lock was opened opposite the mouth of the Soar where it was shallow and in 1800 the Holme cut below Nottingham with a lock and flood lock. These locks varied in size but all could pass barges 81' x 14' wide. The improvements were completed by 1801 and the river became busy, with a steam passenger service from Nottingham to Gainsborough from 1817. The Burton Boat Co. were still lessees of the Trent above Wilden Ferry and about 1787 cut a canal from the river at Burton to Bond End to try and join the Trent & Mersey. But the latter refused a connection until scared by the efforts of the Burton Boat Co. to make a canal either to the Coventry or the Ashby, so in 1793 they agreed to the junction at Shobnall which was probably made in 1795. The cut was only $1\frac{1}{8}$ miles long with a stop lock to protect the Trent & Mersey and a shallow lock at Bond End. The river, often short of water, caused boats to lighten their cargoes. In 1805 the leading proprietor of the Burton Boat Co. died and the carrying fleet closed down. This was the virtual end of river traffic above Wilden Ferry, while the Bond End branch canal was disused by about 1870. Arrival of the railways upset the fortunes of the Trent, tolls had to be reduced and the Navigation even wanted to amalgamate. They were particularly badly placed because almost all their connecting waterways became railway controlled. By the 1870s the river was in a bad way and various ideas followed for improvement, notably wire rope haulage, the rope being laid on the river bed. It was not installed, but in 1882 the Navigation started a carrying fleet of tugs and barges. The river itself needed improvement but the old Navigation were financially powerless. A new limited liability company was formed in 1883 but superseded in 1884 by a company which was intended to be taken over by Nottingham Corporation who in the event did not. A third company was formed in 1887 the Trent (Burton-upon-Trent and Humber) Navigation Co, which went ahead on improvements, having secured increased capital powers in 1892 and a change of name, back to Trent Navigation Co.

At first improvements were limited, but in the early 1900s prospects for river traffic looked sufficient for large schemes to be considered. To maintain depth dredging was insufficient, locks were needed and recommended by Sir Edward Leader Williams. An Act was passed in 1906 to authorize these. The engineer in charge of the river since 1896 had been Frank Rayner and under him work began in 1909 on Cromwell lock at the tidal limit below Newark; Newark Town lock, one of the two built in the 1770s by the Newark Navigation Commissioners, being deepened. Cromwell lock was opened in 1911, 188' x 30'. Petroleum traffic began to help the river just before the 1914-18 War and the Trent Navigation Co's carrying fleet was providing an efficient service between the Humber and Newark, Nottingham, Loughborough and Leicester with cartage and warehousing in each town. Unfortunately the Trent Navigation could not finance any further improvements but Nottingham Corporation came to the rescue. They were authorized by an Act of 1915 to take over the Nottingham-Newark section, but the War stopped any work on locks. Nottingham Corporation saved the Trent from closure, for like other waterways, it was receiving a Government subsidy during the war. This ended abruptly in 1920, leaving the Trent Navigation with increased costs, but no powers to immediately raise tolls. The Ministry of Transport took over the river until Nottingham could proceed with the proposed improvements in 1921. By 1926 they had built locks at Holme, Stoke Bardolph, Gunthorpe and Hazelford and in 1927 took over their section which was managed for them by the Trent Navigation. The Navigation themselves in 1926 rebuilt Newark Nether lock but could not obtain the money to rebuild Newark Town lock. These new locks were 180' x 29', but in and above Nottingham the locks were the old Jessop size, for craft 81' x 14', as was Newark Town lock and the flood lock at Holme. In 1936 the Trent Navigation leased and in 1946 bought the Nottingham Canal section which formed part of their route through the city. They had also in 1935 extended Cromwell lock by building a second pair of gates below, so that it became a staircase. Nationalization did not neglect the Trent. Newark Town lock was rebuilt to the size

of the others below Nottingham, in 1952, and two years later Holme flood lock was eliminated, the last of the small ones below the city. In 1957 a further improvement programme was started which included bank protection, new plant and workshops and some
locks mechanized. In 1960 the lower Cromwell lock was incorporated in the main chamber
so that eight barges could be passed through at once. Traffic was on the increase, topping
a million tons in 1964. But there was then no commercial traffic above Nottingham. The
Nottingham trade uses 250 ton capacity motor craft up to 142' x 17'6" and drawing 6' and
push towed trains of three 100 ton 55' long dumb barges. The authority of the British
Waterways Board ends at Gainsborough, below, the navigation comes under the jurisdiction
of the British Transport Docks Board Humber, replacing in 1968 the Humber Conservancy.
The Newark Navigation Commissioners remain as a link with the eighteenth century, leasing their section to the British Waterways Board.

TRENT & MERSEY CANAL, Cheshire, Staffordshire, Derbyshire.   This canal brought
both Hull and Liverpool into water communication with Staffordshire. Commonly called the
Grand Trunk, from it grew the limbs which brought both the Severn and the Thames into
the inland waterway network. Another name was the Staffordshire Canal, and in railway
ownership days the North Staffordshire Canal. As early as 1758 there had been a proposal
for a canal from Stoke down to the Trent at Wilden Ferry, where the river became a free
navigation, Lord Gower commissioning Brindley to make a survey, while in 1761 Smeaton
recommended a westward extension to the Irish Sea. Stoke was the principal source of promotion for the new canal, as the north Staffordshire potters were at the mercy of bad
roads; a secondary one was Liverpool. Josiah Wedgwood became the leader, with his friend
and later business partner Thomas Bentley in command of the Liverpool faction. Brindley
now proposed a canal route to narrow dimensions from the Trent to the Mersey, entering
the Trent at Wilden Ferry and the Weaver at Frodsham bridge just below the jurisdiction
of the Weaver trustees, with a branch to Birmingham via Tamworth and another to Newcastle-under-Lyme. With Lord Gower as patron the canal became involved with the
schemes of his brother-in-law the Duke of Bridgewater. John Gilbert, the Duke's agent,
suggested a junction of the new canal with the Duke's waterway to the Mersey, because it
would give the Trent & Mersey a route into Manchester as well as an outlet to the Mersey
and Liverpool. Possession of the western end of the Trent & Mersey became a struggle
between the Weaver trustees and the Duke, although Wedgwood and his friends could not
discover where on the Mersey the Duke meant to bring his own line. An aqueduct across
the river was even proposed to take the canal to Liverpool itself. In the end the Duke's influence won. Another controversy centred round the administration of the new canal,
whether it should be run by a company or a trust. Wedgwood favoured the latter, which
would have acted like a turnpike trust. If such a trust had been set up, other canals might
have followed suit, so that the waterways would have eventually become toll free like the
roads, on the abolition of the trusts. The Act was passed on 14 May 1766. Officially
called the Navigation from the Trent to the Mersey, the canal was to run from Wilden
Ferry actually extended to Derwent Mouth $1\frac{3}{8}$ miles downstream, to Runcorn, joining the
Duke's canal at Preston Brook. For he had now moved his Mersey outlet from the Hempstones, about two miles upstream of Runcorn Gap, and agreed to bring his line on to
Preston Brook and build the last section of the Trent & Mersey to Runcorn as part of his
own canal at his own expense. Brindley was appointed Surveyor General with Hugh Henshall
as clerk of works. The flatter eastern end from Derwent Mouth via Shardlow to Shug-
borough near Lichfield was open via a 130 yd tunnel at Armitage by 1770, and extended in
1771 to Stone. The canal was built broad from Horninglow near Burton to Derwent Mouth,
but narrow westwards to Middlewich, becoming broad again from Middlewich to Preston
Brook. Greatest of all the engineering works was the 2880 yd summit tunnel at Harecastle. This was completed for single line working and without a towpath in 1775 and by
the autumn of that year the canal had reached Middlewich down the great flight of the
34 Cheshire locks (102) from the $5\frac{7}{8}$ mile summit level (Red Bull to Etruria). Preston
Brook tunnel (1239 yd) had been completed and the only remaining section was along the
side of the Weaver from Acton to Middlewich, with two short tunnels at Barnton (572 yds)
and very close by at Saltersford (424 yds) where a terrace would be difficult to contain.
The whole canal was complete in 1777. It was an impressive achievement, $93\frac{3}{8}$ miles from
Preston Brook to Derwent Mouth with 74 locks (seven being wide, six at the eastern end
and the barge lock at Middlewich) plus the wide stop lock at Dutton. Some of the Cheshire
locks were doubled, between Wheelock and Red Bull, during the 1830s, while a little
earlier a staircase of three on the Lawton flight had been replaced by four single locks on
a new alignment making the present total 75 plus the stop lock.

The Trent & Mersey promoted branches. In 1773 two were proposed, to Leek and to
the Breedon limestone works near Ashby-de-la-Zouch, although neither then matured; in
1776 a $17\frac{1}{2}$ mile branch was authorized from the summit at Etruria eastwards to Froghall
using the bed of the Churnet for $1\frac{1}{2}$ miles at Consall with a tramroad thence to the Caldon
limestone quarries. Opened in 1779 with 17 narrow locks and a 76 yd tunnel at Froghall
the Caldon carried a heavy traffic, also acting as a feeder from the reservoir at Stanley.
By an Act of 1797 the Caldon was extended to Uttoxeter, $13\frac{1}{4}$ miles, crossing the Churnet
on the level but with 17 narrow locks, an iron aqueduct over the Tean and a 40 yd tunnel
at Alton, all completed in 1811. Also in 1797 a branch was authorized to Leek from the
Caldon, together with a great and much needed reservoir at Rudyard from which a feeder
led to the Leek branch. $2\frac{3}{4}$ miles long with no locks but a 130 yd tunnel at Leek, this was
completed in 1802 joining the Caldon on its extended summit level at Hazelhurst, a junction
which in 1841, involved the construction of the Denford aqueduct, taking the Leek branch

102. Paired or parallel locks down from the Potteries, the Trent & Mersey's Cheshire locks have centre paddles between the chambers, allowing faster emptying.

over the Caldon to join it on the opposite side. Finally in 1797 a short branch was authorized to Burslem $\frac{3}{8}$ mile on the level, completed in 1805, while before 1809 a private branch had been cut from the Caldon near Burslem to ironworks at Foxley, $\frac{5}{8}$ mile with one lock. About 1795 a very short branch was opened from Shobnall to Bond End to join a branch from the Trent. In its earlier days the Trent & Mersey did not do so well, although it captured the pottery traffic hitherto handled by the Weaver, but not much of the latter's salt trade. To encourage more interchange with the Weaver a transhipment centre was built at Anderton near Northwich; this was operating by 1793 and grew into a complex of salt chutes and tramroads. From the start the Trent & Mersey had their own carrying subsidiary, Hugh Henshall & Co. which brought welcome revenue, and as more branches were added so Trent & Mersey prosperity increased; in 1806 a 40 per cent dividend was declared as other connecting canals opened. Improvements came, a second tramroad was built to the Caldon quarries followed in 1849 by a cable worked line, tramroads were built in the Potteries, and a second tunnel at Harecastle (2926 yd), again single line; but with a towpath, in 1827, so that two way traffic could operate. Another new reservoir was completed in 1829 at Knypersley near Biddulph to feed into the Caldon. At the same time the Trent & Mersey was subject to increasing competition, in 1831 the Macclesfield was opened. It joined the Trent & Mersey by a fly-over junction near Kidsgrove actually built by the latter as their Hall Green branch, 1½ miles long from Hardings Wood to join the Macclesfield at Hall Green, both companies building stop locks and the Trent & Mersey demanding a special toll on coal from the Macclesfield. In 1835 the Birmingham & Liverpool Junction Canal was opened, a serious rival since it was allied to the Middlewich branch of the Ellesmere & Chester Canal. This the Trent & Mersey allowed to join at Wardle outside Middlewich by building a 1/16 mile branch opened in 1833 with a single deep lock. Again the Trent & Mersey charged special tolls for this branch. Trent & Mersey security was assured by the promotion of the North Staffordshire Railway incorporated in 1846, to which the Trent & Mersey had offered itself in 1845. In 1847 the railway took over the canal and began to work it hard as an extension to their system, using a carrying subsidiary, the North Staffs Railway & Canal Carrying Co. using rail-water interchange facilities to advantage, for example at Willington junction between Burton and Derby. In 1847 the railway closed the Uttoxeter branch. Although more traffic was transferred to rail, the Trent & Mersey continued busy throughout the nineteenth century. In 1863 the Trent & Mersey took over the Newcastle-under-Lyme Canal. Building of the Manchester Ship Canal led to an interest in a possible Birmingham & Liverpool Ship Canal of which the Trent & Mersey might form a part, prompting a Bill in 1891 to widen and straighten the canal between Preston Brook and Stoke and in 1894 some work was done between Anderton and Middlewich. The Preston Brook-Middlewich section had been designed for flats, found too big for the tunnels, so only narrow boats had used the line, consequently narrow structures had since been added. It was again reduced to narrow gauge by the rebuilding of the Croxton aqueduct in the 1930s. By the early twentieth century however the canal was in decline, in 1895 the North Staffs Railway & Canal Carrying Co. was taken over by the Anderton Co, while in 1905 a new rail link with the Caldon quarries made the Caldon branch more or less redundant and after 1920 it was little used beyond Stoke. After 1952 there was no commercial traffic on the Caldon save for a recent revival, the specialised catamaran craft which since 1967 have carried pottery from Hanley to a packing station four miles up the Caldon. The LMSR, owners of the Trent & Mersey since the 1923 grouping, closed the Leek branch in 1944, except as a feeder from Rudyard. On the credit side in the twentieth century was the inauguration in 1914 of the electric tug through Harecastle new tunnel, the Brindley tunnel having become disused by this time. Steam tugs were used for the towpathless Preston Brook, Saltersford and Barnton tunnels from 1864. In 1958 because of brine pumping, a new steel chambered lock with guillotine gates was built at Thurlwood, and a 580 yd deviation was built at Marston near Northwich. Up to 1971 there was the occasional load of salt from the warehouses at Preston Brook and until about 1966 felspar was taken up to the Potteries from Weston Point, after which commercial traffic ceased. However the Leek branch as far as the tunnel and the Caldon to Froghall were reopened in 1974.

TYNE SCHEMES, Durham, Northumberland.   In 1710 there was a scheme to extend navigation of the Tyne to Hexham, and in 1778 Smeaton had surveyed for a canal to bypass the river upwards from Stella. During the early 1790s the attraction was for a canal, from Tyne to Solway. Ralph Dodd surveyed in 1794 but those interested had a second opinion from Chapman and Jessop. Dodd's canal was too narrow for the easy passage of the Tyne keels which he expected to use it. Chapman reported in 1795 on a barge canal of 93½ miles from Newcastle via Carlisle to Maryport for small seagoing vessels as part of a through route from Ireland to the Continent, and Jessop agreed. Money was found for the section from Newcastle to Haydon Bridge beyond Hexham, but a Bill introduced in 1796 failed. Also in 1796 John Sutcliffe followed Dodd by proposing a canal from Stella to Hexham which could be extended to the west coast. The war had caused costs to rise and money was tight, so it was dropped. Chapman put forward the commercial and now military advantages. The final breath of a Tyne-Solway canal came in 1810 after a survey by Barrodall Robert Dodd, possibly Ralph's son. All that was built was the Carlisle Canal itself, by Chapman.

TYRONE NAVIGATION, COALISLAND CANAL, DUCART'S CANAL, Co Tyrone.   Overland carriage of coal was too expensive and as early as 1709 a canal was suggested from the collieries to Lough Neagh. Dublin was the best market and plans for the Tyrone went with those for the Newry Navigation, which would take the coal to Newry, for shipment to Dublin. Establishment of provincial commissioners of inland navigation in 1729 brought proposals to a head and the waterway, to be built from public money, was authorized in 1732 to run from the River Blackwater to Coalisland on the edge of the mining district. It was to be a lateral canal parallel with and fed by the River Torrent, and work started in 1733 under Acheson Johnston. As cutting proceeded it was realized that Coalisland was not near enough to the pits and concern was now felt about the progress and expense of the canal. To solve transport from the collieries down to Coalisland, Thomas Omer in 1760 proposed a canal extension from Coalisland and about ½ mile was cut before the project was found too expensive. It was superseded by a proposal for a smaller canal to which the Government agreed in 1767, but this was replaced by ideas for a tub-boat canal, put forward by Daviso de Arcort, generally anglicized to Davis Ducart. He proposed a canal entering a tunnel at one colliery to reach the bottom of a shaft, with another canal at a higher level from the top of the shaft via tunnels to a second coal working. These were accepted and work went ahead on Ducart's Canal from about 1767, the shaft and tunnels being replaced by inclined planes to take the tub-boats. The canal was probably completed in 1773, but not the three inclined planes, for Ducart could not find sufficient water to drive the wheels to haul up the boats. Advice was sought from Smeaton, then working on the Irish Grand Canal. Smeaton suggested making the planes counterbalanced, for loaded boats would always be descending and could pull up the empties, and Ducart agreed. In 1777 they were finished and the coal could move to Coalisland. Ducart's Canal was 3½ miles long, the planes overcoming all changes in level. The tub-boats were 10' x 4'6" carrying about 2 tons. In 1787 the main canal was finished, 4⅜ miles with 8 locks (two combined into a staircase) for craft 62' x 14'6". Towing paths were provided at both sides, presumably because traffic was expected to be heavy. By the time the Coalisland canal was ready, Ducart's had been found a failure, the planes would not work properly, and because of seepage the levels were short of water; it was soon disused. In 1787 the Commissioners of Inland Navigation were dissolved and both the main canal and Ducart's were put under local trustees. The main canal proved useful, carrying coal to the linen bleachers of east Tyrone and north Armagh, although the output of the Tyrone pits was declining. Its condition deteriorated until it was rescued by the Directors-General of Inland Navigation, appointed in 1800, who had it fully repaired. Ducart's Canal was abandoned and filled in. Coal now came to Coalisland by road, but more was coming over from England and Scotland, so that local production suffered. The canal however carried merchandise, and 70 ton capacity lighters could reach Coalisland from Lough Neagh. Railway competition by the 1870s caused a decline in Coalisland traffic. The canal had since 1831 been under the Board of Public Works who in 1888 sold it to the Lagan Navigation. The latter deepened it for 80 ton capacity lighters, increasing traffic and profits. Belfast took increasing quantities of bricks, tiles and building sand from the Coalisland area, while maize imported into Belfast went up in large quantities to be milled at Coalisland for pig feed until 1914. Final decline started in the early 1930s because of road competition and by 1939 there was very little traffic. It ceased altogether in 1946 and the canal, coming under Government control in 1954, was immediately abandoned. It is still a drainage channel and the locks are weired.

ULSTER CANAL, Co Armagh, Tyrone, Monaghan, Fermanagh.   In 1778 there were ideas for a canal parallel with the River Erne from Ballyshannon to Lower Lough Erne, with a possible extension to the Shannon. Some work was done in the 1780s under Richard Evans but money ran out and it was abandoned in 1794. The canal was to have linked Limerick with north-west Ireland, but by 1814 Lough Neagh and north-east Ireland offered greater attractions and a canal from Lough Neagh to Lough Erne was proposed by the Directors-General of Inland Navigation and John Killaly made a survey. As a link with the Shannon was considered, it is extraordinary that Killaly should recommend locks narrower than those of the Lagan, Newry and Coalisland, so precluding through traffic. Nothing further was done, but the demands from both canal companies and landed gentry were too strong to be denied and in 1825 with Government blessing, the Ulster Canal was authorized by Act. Killaly became the engineer, but because money had to be borrowed from the Exchequer Bill Loan Commissioners, their engineer, Telford looked over the line. He later ordered a new survey which was done by Killaly in 1831. From this the canal

WARWICK & BIRMINGHAM CANAL, Warwickshire.   Although supported by the Birmingham Canal because it would give them a direct line to the proposed Grand Junction, the Warwick & Birmingham, with the Warwick & Napton, was mainly promoted by Warwick interests. After a survey by Samuel Bull, the Act was passed in 1793 for a canal from the Birmingham's Digbeth branch $22\frac{5}{8}$ miles to Saltisford Wharf in Warwick. For its length it was heavily locked, from Digbeth there were 6 at Camp Hill rising to Bordesley, a 10 mile summit level, then 6 locks at Knowle and 21 at Hatton descending to the Avon valley. One tunnel, Shrewley (433 yd), was made between the Knowle and Hatton flights. There was a stop lock at Digbeth, for water was a problem on this hilly route, fed by a reservoir at Olton near Solihull. From 1796 an engine was pumping back up the Camp Hill locks. In spite of shortage of money and a change of engineer, William Felkin being replaced in 1797 by Philip Henry Witton, the whole line was ready at the end of 1799. The Warwick & Napton was open the same year and the Grand Junction, on which both relied for much of their traffic. Competition was fierce with other canals, at first with the Birmingham & Fazeley and Coventry for Birmingham traffic off the Grand Junction until in 1810 a rates agreement was reached with the Coventry. Roads improved and in 1838 the London & Birmingham Railway opened and caused a severe loss of trade to the Warwick canals. No dividend was declared on the Warwick & Birmingham after 1853, when a receiver was appointed. There were ideas for converting the canal into a railway, but instead the company was reorganized and dividends reappeared from 1859. In 1895 both Warwick canals agreed to amalgamate with the Grand Junction, although nothing was done, nor did the offer by Fellows, Morton & Clayton in 1903 to lease the canals and convert them to electric traction come to anything. In 1917 the Birmingham & Warwick Junction, the Warwick & Napton and the Warwick & Birmingham put themselves under a joint committee of management which remained until their purchase by the Regent's Canal in 1927, in 1929 being incorporated into the new Grand Union.

WARWICK & NAPTON CANAL, Warwickshire.   Conceived with the Warwick & Birmingham as part of a new through route from Birmingham to the Grand Junction, the Warwick & Braunston as it was first called was promoted by the same interests at the same time. After a survey by William Felkin, engineer of the Warwick & Birmingham, Samuel Bull and others, the Act was passed in 1794. This authorized a canal from Warwick to Braunston. From the start the new canal was administered by the same clerk and treasurer as the Warwick & Birmingham. In 1795 work began under William Felkin, but in the same year it was agreed to shorten to Napton. From the second Act of 1796 sanctioning the Napton line, the company was called the Warwick & Napton and work continued, Felkin being replaced by a local man Charles Handley. The canal was complete in 1800, $14\frac{1}{2}$ miles from the junction with the Warwick

104.

& Birmingham at Budbrooke $\frac{1}{2}$ mile west of the latter's terminus at Saltisford, to the Oxford at the foot of their Napton flight, with the two Cape locks down and 23 rising to Napton. The Warwick & Napton decided to build its own reservoir at Napton, duplicated in 1814, and it also paid for the Oxford's reservoir at Boddington completed in 1815, for the Warwick & Napton inevitably took much of its water from the Oxford. Boddington was enlarged in 1833 at the expense of both Warwick canals. In 1815 a branch was proposed to Southam but never built, the only arm being a $\frac{3}{4}$ mile private one (Kaye's) to a limeworks and quarry from near the bottom of Stockton locks. This crossed the canal, although the northern portion to the quarry was closed in the early 1930s. Later history of the Warwick & Napton followed the pattern of the Warwick & Birmingham.

River WAVENEY NAVIGATION, Norfolk, Suffolk.   Before the 1650s the Waveney was navigable up to Bungay, but by 1670 vessels could only reach Beccles. An Act of 1670 restored the navigation to Bungay. Later there were ideas of extending up the Waveney and down the Little Ouse to Brandon. During the late eighteenth century the navigation prospered, particularly under Matthias Kerrison, a Bungay merchant, who died a near millionaire in 1827, having owned the navigation for over forty years. Up to Beccles there were no locks, but to Bungay $7\frac{1}{2}$ miles upstream, there were three, able to pass vessels 70' x 16' with a 3' to 4' draught. The improved section started about a furlong below the lowest lock and $4\frac{3}{8}$ miles below Bungay. In 1847 the Waveney below Beccles was the subject of an Admiralty enquiry, aimed at improving the navigation to that town from Yarmouth. By this time there were two steam tugs working between Yarmouth and Beccles. In 1889 the improved navigation above Beccles was bought by the local maltsters W.D. & A.E. Walker, who were succeeded in 1919 by the brewers Watney, Combe, Reid & Co. Ltd. By the 1920s the navigation was declining and in 1934 it closed.

WEALD of KENT CANAL PROJECTS.   Proposed in 1800 the Kent & Sussex Junction Canal was to run from the Eastern Rother's Newmill Channel near Tenterden to the Medway near Yalding between Maidstone and Tonbridge, to provide a Thames-Channel waterway avoiding the Foreland. In 1809 a similar scheme was promoted from Brandbridges near East Peckham on the Medway to Iden on the Rother, but withdrawn and promoted again in 1812 as the Weald of Kent Canal between Brandbridges and Appledore on the Royal Military Canal.

WEAR SCHEMES, Co Durham.   The Wear was navigable to Biddick Ford near Washington, but there were plans for improvement, and an Act of 1726 expected navigation to be extended to Chester-le-Street, and one of 1747 made further demands. Eventually in 1758 an estimate was prepared. Durham Corporation wanted the Wear navigable to Durham and obtained an Act in 1759. Smeaton produced a plan for locks and cuts. Ralph Dodd did a survey in 1796 for a Durham Canal. This involved making the Wear navigable upwards to just above Durham, and a heavily locked canal between the Wear and the Tyne, running via the Team valley. It would have a branch to Beamish and an inclined plane there, to a tub-boat system serving the collieries.

River WEAVER NAVIGATION, Cheshire. The Weaver was always navigable to the tidal limit at Pickerings, about 7 miles upstream, but no moves towards improvement were made until 1663 and 1670. By this time salters of Northwich and Winsford were using coal to evaporate brine. This came by cart or packhorse from Staffordshire and Lancashire, crossing the Mersey by boat, an expensive business. Four Bills were introduced between 1711 and 1720 but none were successful because of the opposition of the land carriers. However in 1721 an Act was at last secured to improve the Weaver as a navigation to Winsford, an improvement later aided by the lakes or flashes caused by subsidence, which act as traps for the silt brought down by the upper river. Also to be improved was the Witton Brook up to Witton bridge. Work began on Weaver improvement about 1730, Thomas Robinson acting as surveyor general. By 1732 vessels were reaching Winsford $10\frac{3}{8}$ miles from Frodsham bridge, passing through eleven timber sided locks between 15'6" and 16' wide with their attendant weirs and towed by men along a rough path, or sailed when possible. Opening of the Sankey Brook Navigation in 1757 brought coal nearer the Weaver. Under the 1721 Act it had been put under the control of undertakers, eminent men of Cheshire, few of whom took an active interest in the river, which remained in a poor state. Administering them were commissioners, entitled to appoint undertakers and to take over the works should the undertakers fail. They did take over in 1757, sanctioning expenditure and appointing staff. Responding to improvement demands, Henry Berry in 1758 surveyed the river and started new cuts and lock construction. Under the 1721 Act the commissioners were not supposed to be directly responsible, but an Act of 1760 regularized the situation, 105 public trustees replacing the old undertakers, with a small management committee, surplus revenue, as ordained by the 1721 Act, going to the county of Cheshire for use principally in road and bridge improvement. Under the trustees the new Weaver works, with locks taking craft 68' x 16'9", continued under Robert Pownall as engineer, the $\frac{3}{4}$ mile Witton Brook section being made navigable with one lock by 1765. While the Trent & Mersey canal was building, the Weaver went ahead with improvements so that trade would be kept. Even so when it opened Weaver revenue fell, pottery raw materials and finished ware in crates being particularly affected. Payments to the county from surplus revenue had started in 1771 but soon stopped because of the money needed for improvements and falling revenue. In the 1780s traffic recovered because of salt trade developments, notably from Winsford, and the trustees undertook improvement between Northwich and Winsford, replacing the timber sided locks with chambers of brick and stone. A horse towing path was made as far as Anderton by 1793 and was later extended to Winsford. From the start the Weaver had been hindered by the tides. The solution was a new deep water entrance and Weston Point on the upstream side of the Weaver estuary was judged the best place for this. The Act for the four mile Weston Canal and basin at Weston Point passed in 1807 and the trustees' own engineer John Johnson was put in charge of the works. He found the burden too heavy and Telford assumed control as consultant. In 1810 the canal and basin were ready and both did well from the start. The 1830s became a busy decade with more shortening cuts; now there were 12 locks including the river lock into the Mersey at Weston Point and a lock at Frodsham on what was now the old line of the navigation to the Weaver estuary. By this time the trustees were thinking of a navigation for coastal vessels but William Cubitt dissuaded them, recommending more improvements to take 100 ton capacity flats (133), including new locks which could be duplicated. Work on these locks, with chambers 88 ' x 14' proceeded during the 1840s, when three churches were built by the trustees at Weston Point (105), Northwich and Winsford. The trustees were employers with a strong sense of welfare, including spiritual, of both their employees and the flatmen, paying pensions, employing widows of employees and founding schools at Northwich, Winsford and Weston Point. It was a long time before railways were built down to the river, because the companies were loath to offend the trustees who had considerable parliamentary influence. All their improvements were financed from revenue and by 1845 they had handed over half a million pounds to the county. Cubitt's advice on duplicate locks was followed when in the later 1840s larger 100' x 22' locks were built alongside the 88' x 18'. In 1856 a new basin was opened at Weston Point and that same year Edward Leader Williams junior became engineer of the navigation. During his tenure of office the Weaver rose to new heights of efficiency, utilising steam craft, though the first packet did not appear until 1864. Now the trustees returned to their earlier proposals of the 1830s to make the Weaver suitable for coasters. Leader Williams prepared reports on both the river and Weston Point which led to an Act of 1866 for the construction of a new Mersey entrance 50' wide, and the Delamere dock, opened by 1870. On the river he proposed locks large enough to pass a steam packet and three towed flats at once, but at this stage only Sutton was enlarged, hitherto the smallest on the river, and in 1870 a steam coaster loaded salt and coal at Anderton for Dublin. He also had in mind a boat lift at Anderton, because of the likelihood of increased transhipment traffic with Staffordshire. The lift was opened in 1875 and worked well. But it brought no great additional traffic off the Trent & Mersey and Bridgewater routes and the salt chutes continued to be used. Between 1871 and 1897 the navigation was in effect rebuilt (106). By this time there

105. A jigger (ketch) rigged Mersey flat at Weston Point with the Weaver Navigation Church beyond.

were nine pairs of locks. Leader Williams' report was implemented and larger locks 229' x 42'6" with gates operated by water powered Pelton wheels were built alongside the 100' x 22' at Hunts and Vale Royal. 220' x 24' locks were built at Saltersford and Dutton by the larger locks, also 229' x 42'6". All others were eliminated save for those at Frodsham and Sutton where a new 42' wide lock was built, although only used at times of flood or high spring tides. In 1885 a new dock, the Tollemache, was opened at Weston Point, and during this period the river was dredged to a uniform 12', in the eighteenth century it had been 4'6", improved to 7'6" in the 1830s and 40s. Construction of the Manchester Ship Canal helped the Weaver because ships no longer needed to lock out into the Mersey at Weston Point, but could use the ship canal down to the deep water channel at Eastham at reduced rates. The ship canal provided a side lock into the river, Weston Mersey, allowing Weston Point traffic to pass into the river free of toll. In 1891 they built Weston Marsh lock from the Weston Canal direct into the ship canal. The pattern of Weaver traffic was changing, salt and coal tonnages had dropped sharply by the 1890s, because of brine pipes and rail transport, but were replaced by chemicals carried to and from the works of Brunner, Mond & Co. established at Weston and Winnington alongside the navigation. The 1888 County Councils Act led to a necessary reorganization of the Weaver trustees, who from 1895 were to number 38, composed of 6 existing trustees, later reduced to 4, 22 from the new Cheshire County Council, 14 from the traders on the river, 1 from Northwich, 1 from Winsford. In 1903 the gates and hydraulic pumps on the Anderton lift were converted to electricity, followed by the whole lift, because of wear on the hydraulic rams. The work, taking over two years, was completed in 1908, the lift now being both quicker in operation and cheaper to maintain (14). By 1900 two swing bridges had been installed at Northwich, three fifths of their weight supported on buoyancy tanks because of subsidence. The larger swing bridges at Sutton Weaver built in 1923 (107) and Acton built in 1932 followed the same principle. The stone bridge at Hartford, replaced by the present steel structure in 1938 now allowed coasters with fixed masts to reach Winsford. After 1918 the prospects were not so good, tonnages dropping to just over half the pre-war figures, but the trustees were able by 1935 to extinguish the debt incurred by their modernization. The river was becoming more used by coasters, of increasing tonnage up to the present 600, which are the bulk of today's traffic to Winnington, Winsford traffic ceasing at the end of the 1950s. There were plans during the 1939-45 war of extending the Weaver Navigation to Audlem as part of a 100 ton waterway to Wolverhampton, and an Act secured in 1945 gave powers to develop as far as Nantwich. Weston Point traffic which had fallen badly by 1948 has risen dramatically, particularly since the start of container services. Frodsham lock on the old river parallel with the Weston Canal was closed in 1955 and Sutton lock eliminated at about the same time. The dredged depth today is 13' to Winnington, although 15' is intended, the locks at Dutton and Saltersford have 15' over the sills. From Weston Point to Winsford bridge the navigation is 20 miles.

River WELLAND NAVIGATION and River GLEN, Lincolnshire, Northamptonshire. Navigation of the Welland had much declined by the sixteenth century because of the number of mills. An Act of 1571 granted Stamford Corporation powers to improve from their town to Spalding and the sea. From 1663 Stamford leased the river to Daniel Wigmore who carried out more improvements, including an 8½ mile lateral canal from below Stamford to below Market Deeping. The outfall into the Wash had been improved in the 1630s, previous siltation being so bad that boats were being carried down to the sea on carts. From Stamford to the Wash at Fosdyke Bridge the navigation measured about 34 miles, all the twelve locks were above Spalding and for craft of 7' beam, the locks on the lateral canal being the first mitred gates on an English canal. Other lessees followed Wigmore, but by the early nineteenth century the Welland to Stamford was little used, although Acts of 1774 and 1794 gave powers to improve the outfall. A cut was made, but no sluices, while in 1800 Jessop and the elder Rennie were making drainage proposals. There had been ideas for canals westwards from Stamford to the Leicester line, the Melton Mowbray Navigation and the Oakham Canal. They were revived as the Stamford Junction in 1809, 1815 and 1828, one idea being to make the Welland itself navigable up to a junction with the Leicestershire & Northamptonshire Union Canal. In 1824 trustees were appointed for the Welland and under the 1794 Act the New Cut was made, from the junction with the Glen, called the

Reservoir, for $2\frac{3}{4}$ miles down to Fosdyke Bridge. Under the 1837 Welland Outfall Act training walls were built to maintain the tidal scour. River GLEN: The Earl of Lindsey was draining the area in the 1630s and traffic was probably then passing up into the Bourne Eau. The new Welland trustees placed tide gates at the confluence of the lock free Glen and Welland in 1824. Commercial traffic lasted on the $11\frac{1}{2}$ miles up to the junction with the Bourne Eau into the 1920s. The Welland itself was improved for navigation by the construction in 1955-56 of the lock at Fulney, Spalding, the limit of the tide, able to take craft 110' x 35'. Pleasure craft can reach Deeping St. James, $22\frac{1}{4}$ miles from Fosdyke Bridge and the site of the first of the locks on the old navigation to Stamford.

WESTERN ROTHER NAVIGATION and PETWORTH CANAL, Sussex.   A survey was made by William Jessop and an Act passed in 1791, the 3rd Earl of Egremont being sole proprietor, much of the work being done by his estate men. As completed in 1794 the Rother was navigable from the Arun at Stopham up to Midhurst, a distance of $11\frac{1}{4}$ miles. Two miles were artificial, and there were eight locks. A $1\frac{1}{4}$ mile canal with two locks was cut from the river to Haslingbourne Bridge near Petworth. Traffic on the Rother was steady, continuing well into the nineteenth century, until the railway arrived at Midhurst in 1861. Decline quickly set in, although traffic remained until 1888.

WEY & ARUN JUNCTION CANAL, Surrey, Sussex.   Although the navigable Wey and the navigable Arun were only 15 miles apart it was not until 1810 that the Earl of Egremont started to promote his Wey & Arun Junction Canal. The preliminary survey was made by Josias Jessop, the Act passing in 1813, time being required to raise capital. As completed in 1816 the canal had a length of $18\frac{1}{2}$ miles from Newbridge on the Arun Navigation to Shalford on the Wey, with 23 locks and 2 aqueducts. Trade at the start was unpropitious, because the Napoleonic war had ended, and through traffic preferred the sea. However during the 1830s the canal enjoyed a brief prosperity. Railway promotion between the 1840s and 60s ended this, aided by an old problem of water supply. The canal was fed from the inadequate Vachery Pond near Cranleigh, but the summit level had a bed of porous sand, and there were many locks. Recourse was had to two windmills, built in 1833-4 pumping back to the summit. Then as soon as the Mid-Sussex line of the LB & SCR was opened in 1865 traffic fell off. An Act for abandonment was passed in 1868, yet the canal was offered for sale as a going concern in 1870, but found no buyer. In 1871 it was officially closed, although William Stanton's barges traded from the Wey up to Bramley until June 1872. Now restoration is in progress.

WEY NAVIGATION, GODALMING NAVIGATION, Surrey.   Navigable to above Weybridge since the sixteenth century, the Wey was improved by Sir Richard Weston under an Act of 1651 as far as Guildford, $15\frac{1}{2}$ miles from the Thames, with lengthy cuts and twelve pound locks. Work was completed in 1653 but more improvements followed under an Act of 1671. By an Act of 1760 the navigation was extended $4\frac{1}{2}$ miles to Godalming, with four locks, under a separate authority. Both prospered in the late eighteenth century with the carriage of Government stores to Portsmouth. In 1796 the Basingstoke Canal brought additional traffic and the Wey & Arun Canal was completed in 1816. With the war over, trade on the new route was not brisk and during the 1820s the Wey became neglected, although rejuvenated after 1825 under the new superintendent Charles Hodgson. During the 1830s the Wey prospered in spite of the water demands of local millers, but suffered severely when the railway reached Guildford in 1845 and Godalming in 1849. Nevertheless it enjoyed a welcome revival at the turn of the century, with pleasure traffic added and experiments in electric traction undertaken. From about 1900 to 1963 the Wey was owned by the Stevens family of Guildford, who had long been carriers. In 1963 Mr Harry W. Stevens gave the navigation to the National Trust to maintain as a pleasure waterway. Commercial traffic ended to Guildford in 1958 and in 1969 grain and linseed ceased to be carried from London Docks to Coxes Mill at Weybridge. Trade stopped between the wars on the Godalming Navigation, the gunpowder traffic from Chilworth having ended in 1921, but here again pleasure cruising is increasing, and the navigation was given to the National Trust in 1968. Two of the Wey locks were

106. Weaver sluice at Northwich. The gate is lifted by hand worked reduction gearing.

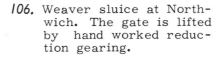

107. Sutton swing bridge on the Weaver, one of the 'floating' bridges.

still turf sided until 1966, but all have now been rebuilt in brick and concrete for boats 73'6" x 13'10½".

River WHARFE, Yorkshire.   Joining the Ouse above Cawood, the Wharfe in the seventeenth century was navigated to Tadcaster, goods coming by road from Leeds. For this reason Tadcaster was opposed to the Aire & Calder Bill of 1698. Aire & Calder improvements reduced the Wharfe to merely local traffic and later Wharfe history is sparse. Railway proposals might have helped Tadcaster, there were ideas in 1846 for a transhipment port from rail to water. Traffic continued until 1914 when the last boat came to Tadcaster. Earlier, in 1890, an Act was passed to incorporate the Wharfe as a navigation to serve a Tadcaster brewery. The proposed improvements would have allowed 50 ton craft to reach the town. Some work was done, but in 1898 the Wharfe River Navigation Co. was wound up.

WHITBY CANAL, Yorkshire.   This was to bring corn to a mill on the Esk estuary. Ordinarily boats could only reach the mill on spring tides, but the cut allowed them to come up in neaps. The mill was built in 1752 and the canal was probably disused before the end of the eighteenth century.

WILTS. & BERKS. CANAL, Wiltshire, Berkshire. NORTH WILTS. CANAL, Wiltshire, Gloucestershire.   Because of the likely success of the Thames & Severn Canal, but remembering the poor condition of the upper Thames, a canal was proposed in 1784 from the Thames & Severn at Lechlade to the Thames at Abingdon. Ten years later this was revised to link the newly proposed Kennet & Avon with the Thames at Abingdon, and an Act was passed in 1796 for a narrow canal from Semington on the Kennet & Avon to Abingdon. As built the main line was 51 miles long with 42 narrow locks and many lift bridges and branches as follows: Calne 3⅛ miles, 3 locks; Chippenham 2 miles; Wantage ¾ mile; and the later authorized Longcot ½ mile. William Whitworth was the engineer, but owing to money difficulties work proceeded slowly, the canal reaching Abingdon in 1810, opening at the same time as the Kennet & Avon. However the Wilts. & Berks. wanted to go further and put forward various schemes; to link up with the Grand Junction, to make a canal from Wootton Bassett to Bristol, to join up with the Stratford-upon-Avon Canal. What did emerge was a useful link with the Thames & Severn, the separately subscribed North Wilts. Canal receiving its Act in 1813. It was opened in 1819 from Swindon to Latton near Cricklade, 9 miles long with 12 narrow locks. Coal from Somerset was the main traffic with corn and farm produce the other way. Fly-boats were run from Melksham to Bristol and Abingdon, but through traffic did not develop as hoped. In 1841 the GWR was open to Bristol, the line running parallel with the canal. Nevertheless the coal trade from Somerset remained important to the end of the 1860s. In 1874 a Bill was promoted to close it, but instead the canal was bought in 1875 by a group of interested traders. In 1882 it was leased to some Bristol merchants who experimented with sectioned boats. In 1891 came a new owner, the United Commercial Syndicate, but the canal could not be revived and with traffic ending in 1906 the whole system, including the North Wilts, was closed by an Act of 1914.

WIMBLEDON & WANDSWORTH CANAL PROJECT, Surrey.   In 1865 there were plans for a canal from Wandsworth parallel with the Wandle, to Wimbledon to serve factories on the Wandle and Wimbledon gasworks. A Bill was introduced in 1866 but defeated.

WISBECH CANAL, Isle of Ely.   The Wisbech Canal was made to join the tidal Nene and the Middle Level Navigations, so that craft could go from Peterborough and Wisbech to King's Lynn without crossing the Wash, for the Middle Level is linked to the Ouse. A survey was made in 1792 under John Watté and the project was backed locally, as well as by people in the Midlands. There had already been a linking navigation, the Elm Leam, but this was no longer open. The Act passed in 1794 for a canal from Wisbech to Outwell on Well Creek which the promoters were allowed to improve. The new canal was $5\frac{1}{4}$ miles long with locks at Wisbech and at Outwell of varied size, that at Wisbech being 50' x 13'6" that at Outwell 97' x 11'6", so that boats which could pass right through had to be comparatively narrow. The 50' limitation of length could be discounted when the canal made a level with the tide at Wisbech, but this waterway was never able to take craft of more than 3'6" laden draught. Water supply was the difficulty with the Wisbech Canal, for it was dependent on spring tides on the Nene at Wisbech when the river rose higher than the canal and water could be let in. This happened only once a fortnight, 'putting the tide in' it was called. The Wisbech Canal was opened in 1797, although traffic did not become at all heavy until the 1840s when coal cargoes increased, due to a toll reduction. By the end of the nineteenth century coal had ceased to be a regular cargo and traffic was lessening. Passengers had been carried for a few years preceding 1883. There were some steam craft on the canal and possibly some pioneer motor boats. However decline had been inevitable ever since the opening in 1884 of the Wisbech & Upwell Tramway, a steam worked line which ran parallel to the canal via Outwell. By the 1914-18 War canal traffic was dropping, ceasing in 1922, the company already having tried to secure abandonment. This was achieved in 1926 at the hand of the Isle of Ely County Council, the ownership of the waterway being transferred in 1944 to Wisbech Corporation.

River WISSEY, Norfolk. Improvements were planned for the Wissey, a tributary of the Great Ouse, as early as 1438, but whether anything was done is unknown. The river was certainly navigable without locks at a later date for 10 miles from its confluence with the Ouse, up to Stoke Ferry, and this remains the limit of navigation for pleasure craft. The sugar beet factory at Wissington received beet by barge until the late 1950s.

WITHAM and FOSSDYKE NAVIGATIONS, Lincolnshire. WITHAM NAVIGABLE DRAINS. The Fossdyke is the $11\frac{1}{8}$ mile cut from the Witham at Brayford Pool or Mere in Lincoln to the Trent at Torksey where there is an entrance lock, while the navigable Witham continues from Lincoln to the Wash below Boston, $36\frac{1}{8}$ miles. Both owe their waterway status to the Roman military station and colony at Lincoln. Their engineers improved the drainage of the Witham and made it navigable down from Lincoln, extending the drainage cut to the Trent. This was the Fossdyke joined by the Car Dyke, the former possibly navigated in Roman times, certainly by the Danes and in the Norman period. Henry I ordered local landowners to maintain the Witham and the Fossdyke, and by 1121 had the latter improved by scouring. Landowner and monastic administration was not very successful and both waterways decayed. In 1670 the Fossdyke was put under the care of Lincoln Corporation, and under Acts of 1671 the Corporation were to become undertakers for the improvement of both the Fossdyke and the Witham. They did not undertake the Witham, although they were interested in its future. Between 1672 and 1675 some work was done on the Fossdyke by Samuel Fortrey, but a Witham survey of 1733 by James Scribo reported adversely. In 1740 Richard Ellison of Thorne, a Don shareholder, became sole undertaker of the Fossdyke under a 999 year lease from Lincoln Corporation. He started improvements and by 1744 the Fossdyke was in better shape. In the 1760s Lincoln Corporation were showing more interest in the Witham and an Act passed in 1762 for drainage and navigation works, after reports by Nathaniel Kinderley, Langley Edwards and John Grundy. There was the usual conflict between navigation and drainage interests, landowners being worried about the level of the Fossdyke if the Witham were improved. Work started under commissioners with Langley Edwards as engineer. In 1763 the Grand Sluice at Boston was completed, excluding the tide, the lock here following in 1766. By 1770 locks were completed at Kirkstead near Woodhall, Barlings above Bardney, and at Stamp End, below the High Bridge in Lincoln. Witham traffic now improved, and more wharves were built at Lincoln. The High Bridge under Lincoln's High Street, at the eastern end of Brayford Pool, the junction point of the Witham and the Fossdyke, was a serious bottleneck to traffic. William Jessop reported in 1791, finding only a foot of draught under the bridge, while the other link between the Witham and Fossdyke, the Sincil Dyke, had become disused. The High Bridge route was improved by 1795, paid for by the Witham commissioners, and the Horncastle Canal and Sleaford Navigation, who would both benefit. From 1801 and the Witham drainage Act of that year, John Rennie was being consulted. To drain fenland north of Boston he improved the channels by a new Maud Foster drain, completed in 1807 and replacing the 1598 cut. The longer Hobhole drain entering the Witham at its Wash outfall was completed in 1806. From 1804 Rennie was also draining land on both sides of the Fossdyke. The Ellison family continued improvements to this and Brayford Pool, which by 1820 could take 50 ton vessels, of the keel type. Horse drawn passenger packets had been introduced on the Fossdyke in 1805 and on the Witham in 1809, steam soon followed on the latter, certainly by 1816, with regular Lincoln-Boston services. Rennie planned further improvements to Witham drainage. In 1807 he recommended dispensing with the locks at Kirkstead and Barlings, and his views were incorporated in an Act of 1812, passed after severe floods. Work was not begun until after his death in 1821, under his son John. New straightening cuts were made and the Witham assumed its present character, notably the straight six miles between Dogdyke and Langrick. Stamp End lock was rebuilt in 1826. Associated with the Witham were side drainage cuts or 'delphs', some being navigable. The Kyme Eau had been a mediaeval waterway, and much had been done north of Boston in the earlier seventeenth century, Sir Anthony Thomas was at work in this area in 1631, and gave his name to Anton's Gowt, a cut with a lock added in 1821, where a large drainage system converged on the Witham. The South Forty Foot Drain, made in the 1630s by the Earl of Lindsey, gave a navigation from Boston to Bourne, 24 miles, a sluice later being erected

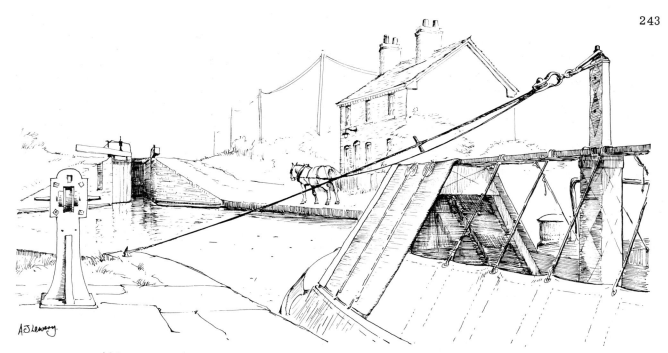

108. Lock operation; 'blocking', moving a laden narrow boat up the Tardebigge flight, Worcester & Birmingham Canal. A two to one purchase became a direct pull when the toggle came up against the pulley block.

at the drain's entry to the Witham. This was the Black Sluice, made under an Act of 1765, which gave its name to the drain to Bourne. By 1816 the elder Rennie reported three navigable delphs completed further upstream, Timberland Dyke, Nocton Delph and Branston Delph. In 1828 one of the younger Rennie's assistants surveyed for a canal from the Witham at Bardney to the Ancholme, this Witham & Ancholme Junction Canal being revived by Rennie in 1844, but never built. Whereas the Witham was 6' deep after the 1820s improvements, the Fossdyke, still under Ellison control, was only 3'6", the depth required by their lease of 1740. Traffic now demanded 5' and there were complaints. A legal dispute over the lease started in the 1820s, and continued until 1839, when settled by the Court of Chancery in favour of the Ellisons. The family now proposed to sell out, but both navigations were overtaken by the railways. A line was promoted in 1844 and proposed amalgamation with the Witham and Fossdyke. The incorporation of the Great Northern Railway by an Act of 1846 overtook the proposals, and the new company leased the Witham and Fossdyke in 1848, the year the Lincoln-Boston railway was completed along the Witham bank. Remarkably the steam passenger packets survived to 1863, the GNR putting on 4th class coaches at $\frac{1}{2}$d a mile to compete. Under railway control a new cut and lock were made on the Witham at Bardney, completed in 1865. While Witham traffic declined, the Fossdyke continued and indeed Furley's of Gainsborough were sending grain up to Lincoln until 1972. Regular Witham traffic ended in 1952 although there were some timber cargoes to Boston in the 1960s. Boston Dock is a busy coaster port, making use of the $4\frac{3}{8}$ miles tidal Witham below the Grand Sluice. Pleasure traffic continues on both navigations and the Witham is renowned for its fishing. The Witham locks, now Grand Sluice, Bardney also called Horsley Deeps, and Stamp End, the last given a top guillotine gate in 1950 for flood control, can pass craft up to 78' x 15'2". The Fossdyke's Torksey lock is of the same size.

WOMBRIDGE CANAL, Shropshire. William Reynolds the Ketley ironmaster built a private $1\frac{3}{4}$ mile level canal to bring coal and ironstone in tub boats from deposits at Wombridge to the furnaces at Donnington Wood, joining the existing canal there. The new line was probably complete in 1788, but in 1792 most of it was sold to the newly formed Shrewsbury Canal, from the top of the Trench inclined plane to Donnington Wood. The unsold portion must have been abandoned during the early nineteenth century. The Shrewsbury part lasted until 1921, being actually abandoned in 1931.

Sir Andrew WOOD'S CANAL, Fife. Purely ornamental and of no commercial value this $\frac{1}{4}$ mile canal, was made it is believed, for Sir Andrew Wood of Largo, the fifteenth century Scottish sea officer. The canal ran from his residence, Largo House, to Largo Church, which he attended by barge.

WOODEAVES CANAL, Derbyshire. Near Ashbourne and unconnected with any other, this waterway $1\frac{1}{4}$ miles long was built in about 1802 to carry limestone to cotton mills near Fenny Bentley in Dovedale, serving also as a reservoir for the mill waterwheels.

WORCESTER & BIRMINGHAM CANAL, Warwickshire, Worcestershire. A more direct line from Birmingham to the Severn than the Staffs. & Worcs. Canal was proposed in the 1780s by the Stourbridge Canal Co, to run from near Stourbridge via Bromsgrove to Worcester. A Bill was introduced in 1786 but opposed by the Staffs. & Worcs. and defeated; it was revived to run direct from Birmingham via Tardebigge to Worcester and a Bill introduced in 1790 but again defeated, opposed now by the Birmingham as well. However in

1791 the Birmingham acquiesced and the Bill passed, although there was to be no connection in Birmingham, the result of this being the notorious Worcester Bar. Surveys were undertaken by John Snape and Josiah Clowes who laid out a broad waterway but because of cost and junctions with the narrow Dudley and Stratford, a narrow canal was built although bridges and tunnels are broad. Thomas Cartwright became the engineer and construction proceeded. Selly Oak, to be the junction with the Dudley Canal was reached in 1795, and King's Norton the junction with the Stratford Canal in 1796, with West Hill tunnel (2726 yd) completed in 1797. Subsequently lack of money caused cutting to be slowed. However in 1807 Tardebigge old wharf was reached via Shortwood tunnel (613 yd) and both a cargo and passenger service started, with road carriage to Worcester. Lifts as well as locks were suggested for Tardebigge, one being erected in 1808 on the site of the present top lock at Tardebigge, the invention of John Woodhouse, who in 1809 succeeded Cartwright as engineer on the Worcester & Birmingham; but the canal found sufficient water for locks and construction proceeded in 1812 with renewed energy under William Crosley, who had become engineer in 1811. In 1815 the canal was at last finished, with a reservoir at Tardebigge, that at Upper Bittall being built in 1832 to cope with the increased traffic. Lower Bittall had been built to provide compensation water to mills on the Rea and Arrow from which the canal drew water, four other compensatory reservoirs being provided. The Worcester & Birmingham is 30 miles long; in addition to tunnels already noted there are Edgbaston (105 yd) Tardebigge (580 yd) and Dunhampstead (230 yd) nearer Worcester, and 58 locks (108) including the two barge locks down from Diglis basin Worcester to the Severn, with a total fall of 428'. On completion, Pickfords commenced a fly-boat service, the Worcester Bar being pierced by a stop lock in 1815. Traffic thereafter built up and the company's finances slowly improved. The W. & B. benefited from the Gloucester & Berkeley completed in 1827 and they also extended their traffic in 1825 by leasing the Coombe Hill Canal, followed in 1830 by their lease of the Lower Avon. Rock salt from the newly discovered deposits at Stoke Prior provided a lucrative traffic during the 1830s but the completion of the Birmingham & Gloucester Railway in 1841 was a bad blow, the railway running parallel with the canal and taking much of the salt traffic. To counter railways the canal had promoted Severn improvements, while in 1848 they began a carrying business associated in Birmingham with the North Staffordshire Railway & Canal Carrying Co. of the Trent & Mersey. Another move to gain traffic was the completion in 1854 of their Droitwich Junction Canal, but a receiver was appointed in 1868. Salvation came in 1874 when the Sharpness New Docks Co. bought both the Worcester & Birmingham and the Droitwich Canals, sinking much capital into the improvement of both, but receipts steadily declined. Commercial traffic lasted on the canal until 1961, chocolate crumb to Bournville from Cadbury's factory at Frampton-on-Severn, although today the canal has plenty of pleasure boats, Diglis basin being a yacht marina.

WORCESTER & GLOUCESTER UNION CANAL PROJECT. With the long awaited Gloucester & Berkeley nearly open, in 1825 there was a move to extend this to the Worcester & Birmingham Canal at Worcester. For the Severn was then unimproved and it was expected that a bypass canal would speed up the Birmingham-Bristol traffic. Telford did a survey and the scheme was welcomed by the Worcester & Birmingham but finance became a problem and nothing was done.

WORSLEY, Lancashire. Worsley Old Hall near Manchester was the Lancashire seat of the Egerton family from the early seventeenth century, who owned coal mines in the district. Drainage of these was a problem. The remedy at Worsley was to cut a sough or culvert running from a sump within the workings out to the Worsley brook, completed during the 1730s by John Massey, agent to the 1st Duke of Bridgewater. John Gilbert, agent to the third Duke developed the drainage system to take boats into the mines, his own idea. By 1759 this navigation level was completed. By 1840 46 miles of underground canal had been built. The main level was 4 miles long and the upper $1\frac{3}{4}$ miles, there were also two lower levels, the bulk of the total of 46 miles being the combined lengths of the numerous branches. The main level was 10' to 12' wide and 8' high above water, which averaged 4' depth. The main level forked 500 yds inside to reach the delph or basin at Worsley by two entrances, one 6'6" high for loaded boats, the

109. Entrance to Worsley underground system. The sluice was opened to create a current and float out laden boats.

other 8' high for empties (109). Much of the system was brick lined with some complex work at the junctions with the branches. Just before his death Gilbert designed an inclined boat plane to link the main and higher levels, replacing the lowering of coal in boxes down vertical shafts. Completed in 1797 it worked until 1822. The underground system was last used for coal extraction in 1887 but was maintained and inspected until 1969, for these canals were a source of water for the Bridgewater Canal.

Rivers WYE and LUGG, Monmouthshire, Gloucestershire, Herefordshire.   Navigable up from Chepstow before the seventeenth century, boats on the Wye were obstructed by mill weirs. During the Commonwealth there were proposals to improve the river and at the Restoration Sir William 'Water Work' Sandys was appointed with his cousin and grandnephew under an Act of 1662, to make both the Wye and the Lugg navigable. Sandys probably built flash locks on the Wye but did nothing for the Lugg, but by 1695 the Wye was back to its unimproved state. An Act of that year appointed trustees for the rivers. A further Act of 1727 sanctioned more work on both rivers so that boats could now reach Hereford 69½ miles from the Severn and even Leominster on the Lugg, the latter improved by half locks or water gates. The Lugg probably remained navigable on its lowest five miles up to Lugg Bridge until about 1860. During the eighteenth century the trustees sought further improvement. But no work was done on the Wye until 1809 when an Act was obtained for a horse path from Hereford downstream to Lydbrook, 37 miles. The path was open in 1811, traffic improved, and the Wye Steam Boat Co. experimented with a tug as early as 1825. In the early nineteenth century trade continued steadily up to Hereford and there were passengers and pleasure boat services; some boats could even go up to Hay on flood water. Wye traffic benefited from the opening of the Severn & Wye tramroad from Lydney to Lydbrook in 1811, but the Hereford tramroad, opened in 1829 must have damaged the trade. The Newport, Abergavenny & Hereford Railway opened in 1854, followed in 1855 by the Hereford, Ross & Gloucester Railway, ended Wye traffic to Hereford and the towing path company was dissolved. In 1876 the Wye Valley Railway was opened and river traffic ceased above Brockweir, just above Tintern, and later because of silting stopped at Tintern itself, stone being shipped down from the Lancaut quarry 5 miles below Tintern.

WYRLEY & ESSINGTON CANAL, Staffordshire.   This was promoted to bring coal from pits round Wyrley and Essington on the southern edge of Cannock Chase to Wolverhampton and Walsall. The original Act of 1792 provided for a main line from Horseley Fields on the Birmingham Canal near Wolverhampton to Sneyd near Walsall. Here there were to be branches, one up to Wyrley Bank with a branch off this to Essington, and another branch to Birchills nearer Walsall. Two years later a second Act extended the canal a long way, to Brownhills and past Lichfield to Huddlesford on the Birmingham & Fazeley's portion of the Coventry line. There were also to be more branches, the Daw End from Catshill Junction to limestone quarries and limeworks at Hay Head, and Lord Hay's branch from the main line near Bloxwich. The line to Huddlesford was built with its own capital, but William Pitt was the engineer to both, and later the finances were amalgamated. Part of the original line to Sneyd was opened in 1794, after which work proceeded on the extension, and in 1797 the main line was open throughout. It was built to narrow gauge with a summit level from Horseley Fields junction to Ogley top lock (Brownhills) some 16½ miles. From Ogley 30 widely spread locks descended to Huddlesford, making a total of 23½ miles. Water came from Sneyd reservoir and from Norton bog, drained to feed the canal, and from the Birmingham Canal, but supplies were short until the building in 1800 of Cannock Chase reservoir (Chasewater). The branches followed the main line, that from Sneyd to Wyrley Bank was completed in 1798, 2¼ miles with 5 locks, as was the branch off that to Essington, ¾ mile with 4 locks. In 1800 the Daw End branch was finished, 5⅜ miles on the level, and Lord Hay's branch, 1¼ miles on the level was also completed. The 2⅛ mile Birchills branch to Walsall had been finished in about 1798 but the following year the Birmingham Canal came to Walsall so the branch was little used.

The Wyrley & Essington carried much heavy traffic, coal to Lichfield, coal to the brickworks near Sneyd, and general merchandise for the growing industries of Walsall and Bloxwich. Unfortunately the limestone quarries on the Daw End branch were worked out by 1809, but the Wyrley Bank branch was extended to serve more pits, now terminating 3½ miles from Sneyd. Extra revenue was gained after 1835 by the sale of surplus water to the Birmingham & Liverpool Junction and occasionally to the Staffs & Worcs and Dudley Canals. Moves to join the Birmingham Canal at Walsall during the 1830s led to amalgamation in 1840 with the BCN. The Walsall junction was then made (1841) by a ⅝ mile link with 8 locks, and in 1843 two others, at Wednesfield with the BCN's Bentley Canal, and via the Daw End branch with the new Rushall Canal.

4.

Boatbuilding

110. A plank, once rendered pliable in the steaming box, could be secured to the hull by cramps. The illustration shows the planking up of a Birmingham tug, the counter block lies in the foreground.

BOATBUILDERS.   The terms yard and dock are synonymous, both meaning a place where boats were built and repaired. Docking means repairing in inland waterways parlance. Long before the canals, there were building yards on the rivers, increasing as the rivers were improved. With the arrival of the canals, yards of similar type became established on them. In the days of wooden boatbuilding it was not expensive to establish a yard. All that was required was flat land by the bank, a slipway with timber baulks, a sawpit, a steaming box and a shed for stores and workshop containing a bench for smaller   tasks. The stores contained oakum for caulking, kept in what was sometimes called an oakum hovel, pitch and tar, paint and nails. Timber was stored out of doors in stacks for season-ing, after conversion from the round into planks and frames by the sawyers. The overall space needed was small, with a water frontage not much more than the length of the boats to be built, or less if launched end on. Ironwork was put out to a local blacksmith,   the like of guard irons, towing studs and rudder pintles. In such a yard the work force could be two or three, with six as a good average. Youths would serve an apprenticeship and become qualified shipwrights, then moving on to another yard to gain experience.   Many were family businesses. On the rivers boatbuilding centres grew up, villages and towns became the homes of competing yards, with the bulk of the population employed as ship-wrights, sailmakers and rope makers. For the establishment of a boatyard   meant   the founding of ancillary industries, ropewalks, sail lofts, blockmakers, blacksmiths and in larger centres foundries for the manufacture of windlasses, anchors and   chain   cable. Reedham on the Yare and Coltishall on the Bure were the great Norfolk wherry building places, and on the Don, Thorne had two yards by the 1790s. More obscure were the yards on the Vyrnwy at Carreghofa near Llanymynech and at Pallingham on the Arun in Sussex. On some canals building and repair work became concentrated from an early date at the larger yards. The Duke of Bridgewater established a barge and boatbuilding yard at Wors-ley for his own fleet where he employed about 200 men building a variety of craft.   The great economy of a large yard was that all the trades could be concentrated under one au-thority and little work need be put out. Fellows, Morton & Clayton found it worthwhile to have two boatyards, at Uxbridge as well as at Saltley, Birmingham. They even built some of the tandem compound engines for their steamers. Usually engines were supplied from outside, certainly all diesels were. If a carrying company did not build they often had their own repair dock. Thomas Clayton, the bulk liquid carriers, had a dock at Oldbury and John Toole of Bradley near Bilston docked or repaired not only his own fleet but that of Stewarts & Lloyds. For the smaller carriers, owning their own boatyard was usually out of the question, although ownership might come with the carrier's growth, as it did for the Samuel Barlow Coal Co. when in 1941 they bought the Nurser yard at Braunston.   Most of the bye traders and many company fleets went to independent boatbuilders for new craft and for repairs. The independent yards were numerous, like garages today, particularly on the Birmingham system. Well known builders were Worsey's successors to   Luffkins, Worsey's in 1922 having yards at Toll End, Tipton, Plume Street, Aston and Icknield Port Road, Birmingham.   Then there was Braithwaite's with docks at Rider's Green and West Bromwich, Spencer Abbott's at Gravelly Hill, Aston and Peter Keay at Birmingham and Walsall. These yards turned out day boats by the hundred, also tugs and some long dis-tance boats, for example Braithwaite's built for Fellows, Morton & Clayton between 1912

III. Wood boat-building; bostocks (in the middle), jacks and packing tilt a Black Country day boat for easier caulking.

and 1914. Building of long distance wooden narrow boats tended by the twentieth century to be concentrated at a limited number of yards who had established reputations. Among the leaders was William Nurser of Braunston who started business in about 1870. Nurser's built and repaired the Samuel Barlow fleet and built for Thomas Clayton, Henry Seddon the Middlewich salters, John Green the Macclesfield carrier, and for Fellows, Morton & Clayton. Nursers' rivals were Lees & Atkins of Polesworth who started in the late nineteenth century and remained in business as builders until just before the 1939-45 War, although they undertook repairs in the post war period. Both yards built pairs of horse boats for number ones on the Grand Junction who paid by instalments, a narrow boat costing some £225 in the 1920s. In earlier days there were boat clubs, rather like building societies, the boats paid for by subscription and sometimes apportioned by lottery. New construction was generally concentrated on the winter months because repairs were then difficult, since rotten wood could not be detected if the water it held was frozen. A narrow horse boat would take about 6 weeks to build with eight men working on it, the whole Lees & Atkins labour force. Some repairs could take as little as a week, simply making good caulking, re-blacking the hull and repainting and decorating the cabin inside and out. Nearer London famous yards were L.B. Faulkner of Leighton Buzzard, Walker's of Rickmansworth who built for Ovaltine and for the new Grand Union, Bushell Brothers of Tring who built the wide boat PROGRESS, and James Pollock of Faversham on the north Kent coast who were the British agents for the Bolinder engine. In the North West narrow boats were built by Simpson Davies at Runcorn who were also carriers, by Samuel Fox of Longport, Burslem and by Rathbone's of Stretford. The latter were better known as barge builders and builders of craft for the Leeds & Liverpool. On this canal builders were likewise plentiful; Mayor's of Tarleton and Wigan later concentrating at Tarleton, Jacob Sheldon at Parbold, J. & J. Crooke of Riley Green near Blackburn who were building wooden short boats until the late 1940s and on the Yorkshire side G.E. Ramsey of Windhill, Shipley. The Rathbone yard was founded in 1878 by Henry Rathbone at Stretford, moving to the Longford Bridge site in 1892. Henry was succeeded by two sons, John and Herbert who in 1932 sold the business to the Wigan coal carriers T. & W. Wells. The yard not only built carrying craft but specialized in rowing boats for park lakes, a side which continued in the 1970s. Reflecting Clydeside activity, small specialist yards were established on the Forth & Clyde at Bowling, Maryhill, Hamiltonhill, Blackhill, and Kirkintilloch building iron and steel craft. Fellows, Morton & Clayton made composite hulls at their Saltley dock, but much metal construction centred on Northwich, and on yards in Yorkshire. Richard Dunston's was founded in 1858 at Thorne, although Dunston himself originally had a small yard at Torksey. Their Hessle shipyard was acquired in 1932 from Henry Scarr Ltd. Dunston's build deep sea vessels, tugs and trawlers as well as river and canal barges. They are interested in push towing and built the tugs for the Cawoods Hargreaves large capacity compartment boat fleet. Yorkshire's rivers are large enough for deep sea shipyards and Goole and Selby have long been centres. Beverley too had shipyards and one survived, the old yard of Cook, Welton & Gemmell, into the 1970s under a new management. Waterways encouraged the foundation of boatyards who built craft for a wider market. Two examples are outstanding, Hayes of Stony Stratford on the Grand Junction founded in 1840 and in business until 1925, and Isaac J. Abdela & Mitchell at Brimscombe Port on the Thames & Severn, who closed in 1933. This firm also had a yard on the Chester Dee at Queensferry. Edward Hayes was an agricultural engineer who turned from portable steam engines to marine engines and then boats. In 1896 W.J. Yarwood took over a yard with a vessel on the stocks at Northwich. Building at first for the Weaver trade, and continuing wood construction up to the 1914-18 War, Yarwood's expanded to fulfil orders for owners overseas and elsewhere in the British Isles. They became specialists in tugs, river steamers and dumb barges, (89) building their own engines and boilers which demanded a heavy capital investment. In the

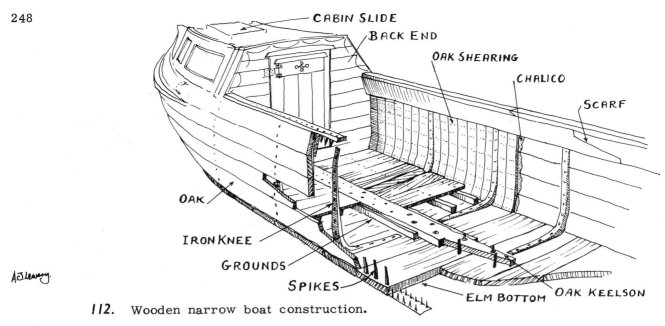

CABIN SLIDE
BACK END
OAK SHEARING
CHALICO
SCARF
OAK
IRON KNEE
GROUNDS
SPIKES
ELM BOTTOM
OAK KEELSON

112.   Wooden narrow boat construction.

1920s and 30s they expanded further, embarking on steel narrow boat building for the Grand Union Canal Carrying Co. and others. Paralleling their history was that of Isaac Pimblott, established in 1867. They built for the Leeds & Liverpool's Canal Transport, for the Bridgewater Department of the Manchester Ship Canal Co, and some of the last narrow boats to be ordered, by British Transport Waterways. Nowadays the accent is all on pleasure craft and several old yards have had a new lease of life catering for the boom. New yards have started, to manufacture steel and fibreglass hulls. They are often very small, in the old tradition, the welding set making steel fabrication remarkably easy.

BOATBUILDING.   Construction of inland waterway craft followed the techniques of deep sea shipbuilding with the same changes from wood to iron and steel, with the half way house of composite construction, and the more recent abandonment of rivetting in favour of welding. Wood survived on inland waterways longer than at sea. Iron and steel were indeed, save for some notable exceptions, latecomers to the inland waterways largely because much of the construction was in the hands of small yards and docks, capable of working with wood, but without the capital to invest in the equipment needed for iron and steel fabrication. Wood is also easier to repair. Many inland craft were built on sea-going ship lines, that is with a keel, timbers or frames to shape the planking and a keelson to hold the frames in position. The planking ran longitudinally from the keel round the bilge to the gunwale. But there were variations. The early western barges on the Thames were simply and cheaply built with flat bottoms, an angular bilge, no projecting keel and swim heads, that is with bow and stern shaped like those of a punt. Choice of hull form depended on the method of propulsion and on the types of waterways on which the craft were to trade. To work to windward sailing craft had to have some form of fin to grip the water. Thus Mersey flats had a keel, although it did not project very far, and Humber keels and sloops and Thames spritsail barges, leeboards. Most inland waterway craft were flat bottomed

113.   Composite narrow boat construction.

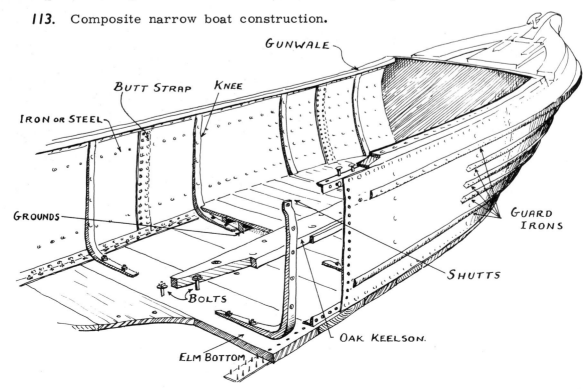

GUNWALE
BUTT STRAP
KNEE
IRON OR STEEL
GROUNDS
BOLTS
GUARD IRONS
SHUTTS
OAK KEELSON.
ELM BOTTOM

Decorative Canal Boat Painting

THREE flower styles are illustrated: Anderton Co., or knobstick (top).
Lees & Atkins, Polesworth (middle) and Nurser, Braunston (bottom).

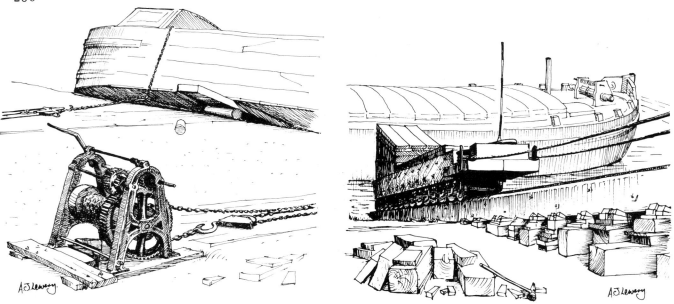

114. 'Pulling out' a narrow boat at a Walsall dock with a windlass and roller (left).

'Pulling out' at the Liverpool Lighterage Co's slip on the Weaver at Northwich, (right). The wedges were used to lift both the slip and carriage to take the weight of the hull off the bilge blocks when the repairs were complete and the vessel ready to return to the water. The depth stick showed how deep the carriage went.

because they were so often aground; in tidal waters they lay on the mud to work cargo, in rivers they might be grounded for lack of water. Cargo was more economically carried in a flat bottom; the capacity was the maximum possible, and the flatness made shovelling and stowage of packages easier. Powered craft needed new hull designs. Whereas horses would pull boats of the bluffest shape, propellers demanded a good flow of water. Propeller driven craft had to have a more gradual run in towards the stern, so that there was plenty of water reaching the blades and rudder, since manoeuvrability was dependent on the stream of water created by the propeller. So in the nineteenth century there was a revolution in stern design which continued into the twentieth. Many horse drawn and sailing craft had a square stern; it was fairly easy to make, and allowed a fuller hull for more cargo than a pointed stern craft. Examples were the Severn trows and the Weaver flats. On the Leeds & Liverpool Canal most of the horse boats had the square stern, but the appearance of steamers in the 1880s forced the adoption of a rounded one to suit the propeller. On the Weaver the steam packets were built with a round stern from which the rudder was hung outboard, while the powered river craft of Yorkshire kept the lines of their horse hauled and sailing parents, for these had sufficient deadwood aft to accommodate the propeller and provide a good flow to it. The deadwood is the final thin wedge shaped taper of a vessel's stern into the stern post. Associated with the propeller was the development of the counter to overcome cavitation. This is the creation of a 'hole' in the water by the rotation of the propeller, so that it loses grip, common when the propeller is working near the surface. To overcome it, water has to be made to flow over the blades and this a counter could be designed to achieve. Counters were therefore fitted to tugs which needed a powerful thrust. The powered craft of the Trent, the Yorkshire waterways and the Bridgewater Canal have rounded or elliptical counters. The counter came to the rescue of the steam and motor narrow boat, working in shallow water. The problem was solved by fining the underwater part of the stern into a wedge, while keeping the upper part at near full beam until it was rounded off as a counter, aft of the propeller. The bottom of the counter acted as a cavitation plate, preventing air entering over the blades. When horse narrow boats were converted into motors it was found necessary to build a counter round or replace the old pointed stern. Narrow boats evolved a form of wooden construction different from other inland craft (112). They were hard chine, their sides making an angle with the flat bottom. This construction is found in the small mine boats used in the Worsley underground system which are believed to have been the ancestors of the narrow boat. They had cross bottom boards to which the bottom side planks were spiked from underneath, and cross bottoms have remained characteristic of narrow boats, having the advantage of easy replacement. Unlike keels and flats, narrow boats rely on their planking for strength. The knees, originally wood, later iron except at the fore end and stern where they remained wood because of the shaping required, tie the planking together and form brackets between the bottoms and sides. The first iron hull in the British Isles was tried on a river, John Wilkinson's Severn barge TRIAL launched at Coalport in 1787 and quickly followed by others. Thereafter iron entered the inland waterway scene spasmodically. In 1810 a 50 ton capacity iron lighter was built at Broseley for the Severn and another for the Thames, sent to London in parts. Later in the 1830s iron sailing flats were introduced by the Mersey & Irwell Navigation, who also had iron canal flats, without sails, built for their trade up the Rochdale Canal, while iron narrow boats were ordered by the Oxford Canal in 1865. In Yorkshire an iron sloop was built in 1818 and the Aire & Calder had iron fly-boats in the early 1840s, while iron compartment boats were introduced commercially from 1865. Iron had the advantage of strength combined with lightness. This meant a bigger payload. For larger craft the keel, frames and keelson were made up of iron bars and angle, likewise the stem and stern posts, while the planking was replaced by rivetted plating, overlapped or butted with butt straps and laid in strakes. Narrow boats were built with an iron keelson, iron bottom plates and side plates, secured to the bottom plating by lengths of angle iron, which was also the method in composite craft. This mixture of wood and iron found more favour for narrow boat hulls than wholly iron construction. Composite narrow boats introduced in the 1890s were given iron sides but elm bottoms which were easily replaced, and an oak or pitch pine keelson (113). Iron composite boats were built as late as the 1930s by Yarwood's for Fellows, Morton & Clayton, following some steel composite hulls. Between the wars, the Grand Union Canal Carrying Co. ordered large numbers of all steel boats, some wholly iron ones, and a good many steel and iron composite. The all steel craft followed the principles of wooden construction with a keelson and knees. The keelson was of steel channel with a deal filling and the knees of specially rolled 'T' section with a bulbous stem. Composite construction also found favour in its better known form of iron or steel frames and wooden planking. W.J. Yarwood of Northwich built some of the larger Weaver dumb barges like the GOWANBURN of 1902 in this way and also a series of 18 canal flats for the Rochdale Canal Co. Iron hulls were more quickly adopted in Scotland than in England, for all types of inland craft. On the Forth & Clyde iron scows were in use in 1824. Later scows were built of steel, the last in 1948. The steam scows were all iron as were the canal puffers which followed them, parents of the well known Clyde and West Highland puffers, built of iron at first, later of steel. On the Grand Canal in Ireland horse drawn iron boats were introduced probably in the second half of the nineteenth century. Steel succeeded wrought iron for frames and plates towards the end of the nineteenth century, when Siemens mild steel became widely available. Thus the composite hulled Weaver packet WEAVER BELLE built by Yarwood's of Northwich in 1900 was steel framed, while Brunner Mond's packet CALEDONIA built in 1894 was wholly steel. In Ireland the Grand Canal Co took delivery between 1925 and 1939 of 49 diesel powered steel canal boats. These pre 1939-45 War craft were rivetted, except eight narrow boats built by Charles Hill of Bristol in 1934-5 for the Severn & Canal Carrying Co. They had sides of welded steel but elm bottoms. Welding was developed during the war and the last narrow boats built for British Transport Waterways in the late 1950s and early 1960s were welded steel, as were three short boats built by Harland & Wolff of North Woolwich for the Leeds & Liverpool in the mid 1950s. An all welded hull was more rapidly built and lighter than a rivetted one. Nowadays the inland waterway power barges built by Richard Dunston at Thorne and John Harker at Knottingley are all welded.

    BOATBUILDING; LAUNCHING. On many inland navigations space was the problem so craft had to be put in sideways. On the Weaver, vessels were built parallel with the bank and fixed ways constructed which ran at right angles to the keel down to the river's edge. For a harbour tug seven fixed ways were usual, the hull having been built up on wedged and packed keel blocks. When the time came for launching the wedges would be removed and the weight transferred from the blocks to the sliding ways, forming a cradle for the hull, laid atop the fixed ways, both being greased with soft soap and tallow. The vessel was held back by triggers or daggers at each end of the hull which locked the sliding ways to the fixed. Heavier vessels were allowed a longer run, 67' being the maximum and 40' the minimum at Yarwood's at Northwich, the expected speed down the ways being 12' per second. Simultaneous movement of both ends of the ship was essential and could only be achieved by simultaneous release of the two daggers. Two long hollow boxes were arranged vertically at bow and stern over each dagger with a weight in each box, held up by a common line, passing over pulleys at the top of each and coming down to the launching platform. At the naming ceremony the line was cut by a guillotine and the weights dropped to release each dagger. The fixed ways ended at the bank edge, some 5' above the river, but the sliding ways overran them and tipped so that the vessel entered the water well heeled over. Nobody was aboard in case of accidents. A Black Country narrow boat is launched sideways in a simpler fashion. Having been set up on bostocks, launching ways are built up fore and aft under the hull. They are temporary, formed of loose timber cross wedged to prevent disintegration under the weight of the boat, and are topped by rails made from old guard irons. The bostocks are so angled that the inland side of the boat's bottom rests against the ways. In this position the water side of the bottom is propped up by a single stout timber. When this is knocked away the bostocks tip and shoot the boat on to the ways so that she slides into the water.

    BOATBUILDING; GLOSSARY OF TERMS, but see glossaries of narrow boats, keels, flats etc.
1. Boatbuilding in wood.
BADGING; wooden filling put behind the shearing where the curve of the planking is acute, to save bending of the shearing and give it backing. BOSTOCKS; stout bearers for supporting narrow boats on the slip. They are 9' or so long with a rounded foot resting on a block. Placed across the bottoms at the fore end and the stern they allow the boat to be tilted either way for repair and caulking of the bottoms. The boat is kept stable by packing amidships, easily adjusted by jacks (111). BOTTOMS; whereas the barges, keels and Leeds & Liverpool short boats had longitudinal bottom planking carried round the bilge and up the sides, narrow boats are absolutely flat bottomed with an angle between bottom and side. The cross bottom planks were 3" thick when fitted and 12" to 18" wide, and projected slightly beyond the side planking often with an iron guard because of wear. Elm untreat-

115. Boatyard worker rolling oakum
into a loose rope before threading into a seam.

ed with tar was always used for long distance
narrow boats since it remains sound as long as
it is allowed to absorb water. In composite
boats, the wooden bottoms were bolted to an
angle iron to which the plating was rivetted.
CATCHING UP; pulling a boat far enough out
of the water to get at the bottom but not right
up the slip, see also Pulling Out. CAULKING;
to make the seams of a wooden boat watertight
they have to be caulked with oakum. This used
to be untreated rope teased into loose hemp and
impregnated with linseed oil, more recently it
has been made of hessian, likewise treated with
linseed. The oakum comes as a sliver which before use is rolled into a rough rope (115). This
forms the thread which is forced between the
planks by the caulking irons (116). First the
seam may have to be opened out to receive the
oakum, although it was possible to caulk a seam
as narrow as $\frac{1}{8}$". Generally the seam has to be
$\frac{1}{4}$" or even $\frac{3}{8}$" wide, made so by the sharp stubby
'opening iron' hit by a mall. Oakum is intro-
duced to the seam by the sharp edged 'threading
in' iron. This pushes the material into a loose
bunched thread outside the seam and is followed
by the 'knocking back' iron which rams the oakum into the seam. A narrow boat with 2" thick
planks will take up to 6 threads of modern oakum
in each seam, or three of rope oakum. The threads are packed tight together by the 'making up' or 'hardening' iron which completes the caulking. Both this and the 'knocking back'
iron are of varied thickness, depending on the width of the seam, the thicker irons having
two or three grooves. The irons are hit by a special caulking mallet made of lignum vitae
or beech, which has a head of up to 15" in length and a square section haft or style of
about 18". The striking faces are reinforced by malleable iron hoops which can be moved
inwards as the faces wear. The hand which holds the iron also feeds the thread up to the
face of the iron, presenting a fresh bunched up length to the seam between each blow of
the mallet. Oakum is threaded initially into several seams, then knocked back before a
second thread is introduced. There are other irons, a narrow spike iron for caulking round
spikes and a curved bladed 'following' or 'travelling' iron for seams on the curve. Immediately a seam is caulked it has to be treated with pitch 'paid up' or applied hot. Otherwise
the oakum will work its way out. Decks are treated in the same way, their seams caulked
and then pitched. CHALICO; an historic Midlands preparation for treating the inside of
the side planking. It was a mixture of gas tar, with a little tallow, horse dung and horse
or cow hair, applied hot and backed by brown paper smoothed over it, all held in place by
the oak shearing or a similar thin wooden backing. When dried out it had the effect of
roofing felt, the hair binding the mixture into a tough waterproof fabric. The preparation
is still made up at some boat docks, backing the mixture with roofing felt. The tar is
heated and lumps of pitch melted in with it,
in a proportion of $\frac{3}{4}$ of tar to $\frac{1}{4}$ of pitch. The dried
dung is added at a rate of two bucketfuls per 5
gallons of the tar/pitch mixture. But before this
the dung has to be prepared by 'rubbing up', in
other words reduced to a powder with the hard
bits like beans picked out, the whole lot stirred
up or 'boxed up' into a paste and applied hot to
the planking with a wooden spreader. As soon
as it is on, it is backed with the paper or felt,
the shearing being added later. OAKUM; see
caulking. PULLING OUT; self explanatory
but as opposed to 'catching up' this means pulling the boat right out of the water well up the
slip. Both 'catching up' and 'pulling out' were
usually done sideways because of space problems. At boat docks without a dry dock there
was a slip with three ways, for the fore end,
midships and stern. At the head of each would

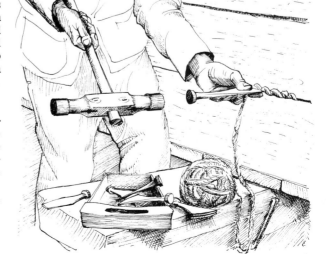

116. Caulking; threading oakum
into a seam.

be a windlass with a wire rope shackled to a length of chain. The chain was passed either right round the hull, going underneath first and the hook at the end attached to a link, or the hook was hung over the offside gunwale. In both cases the effect was to make the pull come on the boat at the bottom. Skids were passed under the hull, lined up with each slip-way and the boat rode up on these, both skid and way being greased with tallow. In the Black Country oak rollers were used. Some slips had railed carriages, for example those of the Mersey, Weaver Co. at Burslem while the nearby Anderton Co. had electric tackle to lift a narrow boat on to the slip with other tackles to pull her up it. On the Weaver the Liverpool Lighterage Co. had four double tracked railed ways or baulks with a 10 rollered carriage on each. The slip could handle 100' barges (114). Once in the right position a narrow boat could be jacked up on the water side, attached to the windlass ropes, with one side resting on the skids. It was packed on the water side then jacked up on the land side clear of the skids and packed. Once packed high enough the bostocks could be put under and the hull lowered on to them (see above). On the Weaver the boat or barge once pulled out was transferred from the carriages to blocks under the bilges, the shift of weight being accomplished by wedges. To put the boat on these blocks the wedges were driven under the packing on the blocks. To return her to the carriage the slips themselves were raised by wedges. They had to be driven in unison, 'rallying', by a gang of men working along each baulk in turn.   RAMPERS; spikes driven laterally between adjacent planks to hold them together, in narrow boats both the bottoms and the side planks. A pocket is cut to enter them at the right angle and a hole drilled.   ROVE; domed washer for holding a clenched bolt, with a square section hole to fit the squared bolt. Roves (pronounced roughs) were driven on by a rove bunter, a kind of punch. The bolt was clenched or 'roved off' by nicking it at each corner with a cold chisel just above the rove. The unwanted length of bolt with its point was then snapped off and the four projections left by the cold chisel rivetted down over the rove.   SCARF; the means of joining two lengths of timber in one plane and retaining as much strength as possible. It is essential to canal boat building, particularly narrow boat building where the strength of the hull lies in the planking. For the side planking ordinary scarfs were used but they were staggered to avoid any single point of weakness. The plank lengths were usually up to 30' with not more than two scarfs per strake. Each scarf would be held by two through bolts, their heads countersunk and their ends clenched in another countersunk hole which would be filled with cement and tarred over. The longer the scarf the stronger it was, 2' being considered a minimum in narrow boat building. Keels and keelsons had also to be made up out of scarfed timber, a narrow boat keelson being made up out of two 35' pieces of 12" x 4" oak or pitch pine scarfed with a hook and butt scarf, that is a scarf cut so that it was hooked at each end, a complex piece of sawing. Such scarfs would measure 4' long and be held by at least two clenched bolts, and by spikes. These would lie horizontally in the boat, because the scarf was across the 12" width of the keelson.   SHEARING; $\frac{1}{2}$" oak boarding applied to the inside of a narrow boat's side planking. It served to back the seams to prevent the oakum being driven right through and to hold the chalico sealing. The shearing had to be pliant so was warmed over a fire, not steamed, and very quickly applied, all hands gathering to complete the work.   SPIKE; not a nail because it has a blunt point and so cannot be directly driven. It is of square section and grips because it is driven down an undersize round hole.   SPOIL (or Spile); the curve and bevel of a boat's planking. Boats were planked from the bottom upwards so that the correct bevels could be made for each successive strake. To maintain the shape of the fore end and stern certain planks had to be cut to a curve or 'spoiled' and then bevelled to fit. The curve was measured by use of a spoiling board laid along the line of the top edge of the proposed plank, the vertical distances being read at intervals to the plank below.   STEAMING; planking to be bent had to be steamed to loosen the wood fibres and make them pliable. This was done in a long wooden box in which the section of plank to be steamed was laid (118). The steam at some docks came from a crude boiler, with pipes to the 12' long box. More modern yards used high pressure steam in a sealed iron box, long enough to contain a complete plank. Ordinarily the steam was passed in at very low pressure, the ends of the box being roughly plugged with sacks to contain it. The softening process varied with the thickness of the timber, a 2" plank would be sufficiently steamed after two hours. The use of pressure did not apparently alter the softening rate, under pressure a 3" plank took four hours. On withdrawal from the box the plank had to be quickly put in position and held by cramps. (110). If allowed to cool it would stiffen and either refuse to pull round or split. If the plank was particularly awkward to put in position quickly, for example a bottom strake, it could be crippled on a former, in other words bent to the correct curve and then left, to be actually fitted cold. Some yards assembled stacks of crippled planks for later use.   TRENAIL; an oak peg used as a fastening in wooden shipbuilding up to the present day, universal in barge building and probably in narrow boat construction before iron fastenings were adopted. The trenail would be about 1" diameter and slightly tapered. At its head a hole would be made and a square plug inserted to hold the trenail tight.

2. Boatbuilding, iron and steel.

BUTT STRAP; when plates in a rivetted vessel are jointed, they may be butted flush and held by a strap rivetted on the inside. Iron and steel narrow boats were constructed in this way, butt straps linking the side plating of the hull, double rivetted, that is with two rows of rivets each side of the join.   CAULKING; iron and steel ships have to be caulked by burring over the plate edges with a pneumatic hammer to form a tight seal at the overlap or butt joint.   FRAMING; iron and steel barge and boat construction followed wooden practice, with frames set up to take the plates. Metal allowed lighter and more slender frames to be used at wider centres. Various shapes were rolled for inland waterway

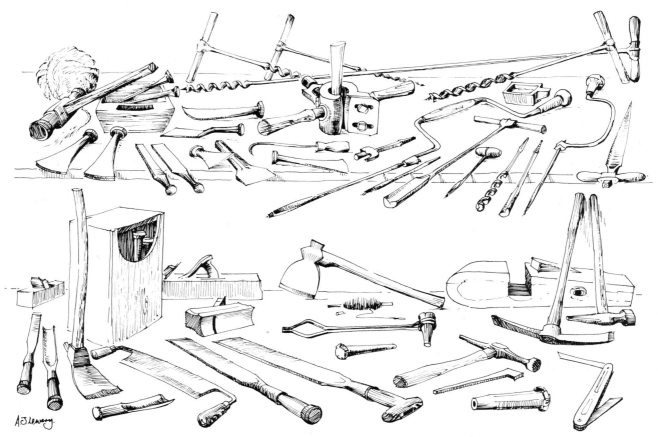

117. Wooden boatbuilding tools;   Along the back; caulking
mallet and irons, augers,   pole plane and braces.
Along the front;   gouges, chisels, adze, draw knife,
planes, shearing hammer, broad axe, mattock, mall,
rove bunter, punches, bevel and game block in which
planks were wedged for boring.

craft construction, most following shipbuilding practice and employing an angled girder.
Fellows, Morton & Clayton boats used a knee of rounded back section, those Yarwood's
built for the Grand Union had a ribbed knee of T section, $5\frac{1}{2}''$ across the top of the T.
KNUCKLE;   a bend or angle, making a break in the line of framing or plating. PLATING;
plates are laid like planks in strakes much wider than any plank, yet individually not so
long. To work out plating (called   shell plating) re-
quirements the lines of the   plates are drawn out on
a half model and then traced. Spread out flat the tracing paper gives the required shape of the plate, the
necessary full scale measurements being taken from
the drawing. Plates are supplied cut   approximately
to the sizes required but have to be trimmed by a
cropper which shears off the rough and leaves a true
edge. Bending is done by a set of rollers, but if a
compound or two way curve is needed, the plate has
to be heated in a plate furnace and shaped over a
cast iron former or die. Offered up to the hull the
plates are bolted into position, all the holes needed for
the rivets having been drilled or punched. When lined
up with a fellow plate, the two sets of holes are
reamed through to ensure perfect alignment. Plates
are either butted flush and held by butt straps or
overlapped with edges scarfed, the scarfing being
done by a milling machine or planer. Plates can be
overlapped by a joggle or kink along the edge of one,
put on by a joggling machine, while any gap between
frame and plate has to be filled with liner pieces,
slender tapered lengths of metal. Plating is started
from the top downwards and outwards from the keel,
the bilge being the last area to be completed, formed
by wrapper plates. These are laid over both bottom

118. Boatbuilding; using an adze
to shape a plank with the
steaming box in action behind.

119. A drydocked Leeds & Liverpool short boat being caulked.

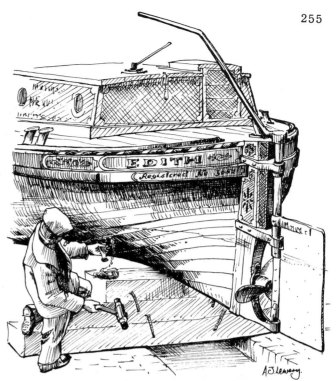

and side plates with overlap on both sides.
Welded plates can be butted together without
butt straps and need no holes except a few
for holding bolts. RE-FOOTING or RE-
HITCHING;   a term used, certainly by Midlands boatbuilders, to describe repair work
on iron and steel narrow boats. Hull side
plates deteriorate from the inside outward,
behind knees, in cabins and at the fore end,
generally along the bilge, hence the term re-
footing. Repairs are effected by cutting out
the bad plates and, nowadays, welding in new
plates often referred to as hitching plates.
RIVETTING;   until the advent of welding in
the 1930s and 40s all iron and steel vessels
were fastened by rivets. The rivets were
heated in a small portable furnace, entered
and held up on one side and rivetted over by
a hammer on the other. Hand hammers were
used for shell plating until replaced by pneumatic hammers. Since the 1860s there were
various patterns of hydraulic rivetting machine, a welcome tool to boilermakers since
it closed up seams much better. But these
were rarely used for shell plating.   There
were three men in a hand rivetting gang, the holder upper, the rivetter, with his hammer,
and the heater tending the furnace and passing the rivets to the holder upper. A gang was
expected to average 350 rivets in an 8½ hour day, they could manage 700 if the work was
straightforward, perhaps only 100 if the location was difficult. Rivets were spaced on the
basis of their diameters, 7 diameters were sufficient for attachment, 4 for a watertight
and 3½ for an oiltight joint.   WELDING;   one of the earliest applications for inland waterways would appear to have been the building in 1934-5 by Charles Hill of Bristol of a class
of eight motor narrow boats for the Severn & Canal Carrying Co. They were given welded
steel sides and elm bottoms. W.J. Yarwood of Northwich built some welded bomb scows
during the 1939-45 War but did not take up welded construction fully until after the war.
A welded vessel could be assembled faster, using less metal, by electric arc welding.
Large sections were put together on the building berth, methods which John Harker of
Knottingley and Richard Dunston of Thorne have applied to barge construction. To speed
assembly, parts can be put in a manipulator, a frame which can be tilted and moved for
ready access by the welder. The British Waterways Board workshops at Bradley near
Wolverhampton on the Birmingham system have one large enough to take a complete narrow
hull. It is fitted into a dry dock, the boats being floated into the manipulator.
  BOATBUILDING TOOLS AND THEIR USES.
1. Glossary of Tools for Wooden Boatbuilding (117).
ADZE;   like an axe but with the blade set at right angles to the plane of the long handle
so that the chopping is done with a downwards swing (118). The adze, of prehistoric origin
is the pre-eminent shaping tool in a wooden boatyard. Stem and sternposts are shaped by
the adze from the sawn block, and the top plank would be trued up by the adze before the
gunwale was spiked down. AUGER;   for long holes, such as required by the stern tube
of a propeller shaft, hand turned augers, which date back to the early Middle Ages have
to be used. It is a rod with a drilling head and at the other end a handle passing through
an eye. The drilling heads vary. Most common are twist augers, with a spiral head, dating from about 1800. Also used are the earlier shell or spoon augers known to Viking
shipwrights, with a gouge shaped head which will not clog with shavings, so that the auger
does not have to be withdrawn. Some augers can be used to ream or enlarge holes. They
are blunt headed with a cutting bar for the sides. BRACES; for boring holes for bolts
and spikes boatbuilders used a brace to which a boring down bit was permanently attached.
The brace, which dates from the fifteenth century, was of the usual cranked shape, iron,
with a brass ferrule on the crank and a wooden handle. The boring down bit could be as
long as 16", drilling a 5/16" hole; it had a gouge shaped head like a shell auger. Attachment to the brace was by the square tapered end of the bit fitting into a block on the brace.
The pointed end of the taper was heated and bent over to hold the tool. The great length
was necessary for boring from edge to edge of a plank. CAULKING IRONS and CAULKING
MALLET;   see page 252. CHISEL;   unlike the ordinary chisels used by joiners, the
boatbuilder's variety is usually wholly steel like a cold chisel, forged in one piece and
therefore without shoulders to the upper part of the blade. It has to stand up to frequent
hammering, including sideways blows to loosen it. Chisels are used to cut ½" shearing and
for rebating. Some do have wooden handles and are notable for the width of blade, not unlike a plane iron. DRAWKNIFE;   a heavy duty spokeshave with two handles and a curved
blade between them for shaping work, notably for shafts, mast and spar work. GAME
BLOCK;   a slotted block used to hold a plank while boring it from edge to edge. They
were often made from an old ram's head, the slot being cut by sawing into the hole for
the tiller. The plank would be held in by a wedge and the whole block could be chocked up

at an angle to suit the operator. The plank would be moved through the slot as the work progressed. GOUGE; a hefty wooden handled tool for making pockets for rampers and for cutting the holes to receive bolt heads. MALL; the heavy hammer used by shipwrights for driving spikes and bolts. It has a long handle like a sledge hammer and a head of some 5 lbs. The non-striking end of the head is pointed and simply acts as a counterbalance. MATTOCK; like a pickaxe, but with one blade broad and flat as on an adze, set at right angles to the handle. The mattock is used for pulling out rotten planks. PIT SAW; the cross cut saw used in the sawpits to convert round timber into planks. An average one measured about 7' long, tapering from top to bottom. The upper handle, called the tiller was bolted on, it had a wrought iron stem and a wooden T shaped handle. The lower handle called the box was simply wedged on to the blade, and consisted of a short wrought iron stem and again of a wooden T shaped handle. When the wedge was released the box could be taken off and the saw withdrawn from the cut. This was necessary to move the log along on its supports as the sawing advanced. PLANES; ordinary wooden stock planes, which date back to classical times, were used by shipwrights. They came in three sizes, the short smoothing plane 7-9" long, the jack plane 16" and the long tryplane 18-28". There were also special rebating and moulding planes with shaped soles for beading and decorative work. These had several irons set for each configuration of the moulding. The 'pole plane' was for cylindrical objects like shafts. It was made in the form of a clamp with a hollowed out portion to receive the work. The iron was straight edged and planed across the circumference of the work. PUNCH; a short round bar for driving down rampers, the punch taking the hammer blows. ROVE BUNTER; a punch for driving roves (pronounced roughs) or domed washers. SHEARING HAMMER; about the size of an ordinary joiner's hammer, the head has a chequered striking face for hitting rose

head nails, for a plain face would be liable to slip. The opposite side where one would expect a claw or a flat pein is lengthened into a round tapered spike, although blunt ended. This is simply a counterbalance. Mostly used to nail shearing. TUP; more of a blacksmith's tool, the tup, a sort of punch or sett held by a wire handle, is held against a bolt head for the final drives of the mall. In narrow boat work, it performed its greatest task fastening the bottoms to the bottom strake. The bolts were driven so far, then the seam between the bottom strake and the bottoms was caulked. 'Tupping up' drove the bolts home, the hollow at the head of the tup enclosing the bolt head, and ensuring a countersunk finish with a tightly caulked seam.

2. Tools for Iron and Steel Boatbuilding. ANGLE FURNACE; a special furnace used to heat frames before they are shaped on the bending block. BENDING BLOCK; a large iron casting punctured with square holes like a honeycomb. On it vessels' frames are bent to shape, following the curve of the set iron, itself formed from the scrieve board. The frames are held by 'dogs', steel clips which stand in the holes with a bent over portion gripping the frame. The holes allow any shape to be manipulated. The frame bending is done by sledge or pneumatic hammers working on the red hot metal. BEVEL BOARD; associated with the scrieve board the bevel board has the angle of bevel of each frame marked out upon it. The frames' outer sides have to follow the curvature of the hull so that the plating lies fairly upon them. The angles are put on the frames by a bending machine, templates being taken off the bevel board to ensure accuracy. JOGGLE; a kink in a plate edge so that it laps over its fellow and fits flush against the frames. The machine could be an hydraulic press or a rotative stamp driven by an eccentric.

120. Narrow boat cabin side and stern lettering styles, Fellows, Morton & Clayton, Thomas Clayton (Oldbury), Samuel Barlow, Joseph Skinner (a number one) and Noah Webb of Brierley Hill.

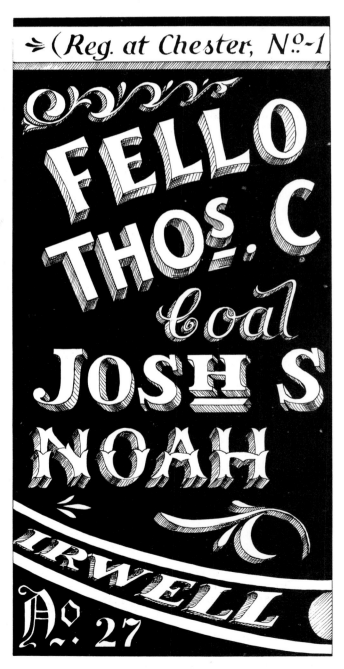

A.J.Lewery.

121. Castle styles; left - Lees & Atkins, Polesworth
right - Anderton Co (knobstick) painting.

PLATE FURNACE;   used to heat plates before shaping on a former or die, or in the
case of iron, not so ductile as steel, before rolling. Furnaces are made with hearths of
various widths depending on the size of plates in use. W.J. Yarwood of Northwich had a
5' wide furnace.   PLATING ROLLS;   for putting a curve on a flat sheet of plate, rolls
are made for various widths, the larger power operated, the smaller hand. Two of the
rolls run in fixed bearings, but the third, above them, is adjustable for different plate
thicknesses. Curvature is produced by the pressure exerted by the top roll.   SCRIEVE
BOARD;   the means by which frame shapes are transferred from the measured drawings
to the shipyard bending blocks. The board can be a vast blackboard made to the depth and
half the beam of the vessel, so that the frames can be marked on full size. All the frames
can be accommodated, only one side needing to be shown.

     BOAT REPAIRS: DRY DOCKS and SLIPS.   Since inland waterways are mainly non-
tidal, vessels can rarely be beached to be worked on between tides. Special facilities must
be provided. Cheapest is the slipway which can be laid down any river or canal bank with
baulks of timber running into the water. For reasons of space most inland waterways slips
haul the boat out sideways. Narrow boat slips in the Black Country were and are timber
baulks leading down to the water up which the boats are dragged on skids and rollers by
hand windlasses (114). But barge building and repair yards dealing with larger, heavier
craft have wheeled carriages, their baulks being faced with iron or steel plates or laid
with rails. Windlasses here have to be powerful to handle craft 100' long and are low geared. In early days it was all hand working but steam and later electricity came to the rescue. Dry docks are expensive but large centres generally have them (119). It is quicker
and simpler to put a boat on a dry dock. Care must be taken to line her up properly with
ropes to the sides so that she comes to rest evenly on the blocks as the water level falls.
There are marks at one or both ends of the dock to show the centreline of the blocks,
with which the bow and stern must be lined up and extra marks along the sides corresponding to the blocks so that the boat can be placed evenly without excessive overhang. Dry
dock entrances are closed either by stop planks, or if the entrance is wide, by mitred lock
gates as at the Shropshire Union dry dock in Chester, or by a guillotine type gate. As for
emptying and filling this is often contrived without pumps. The Weaver dry dock at Northwich is cunningly sited. Boats enter it via the weir stream which leaves the navigation
above Hunts locks, the dock being dug out of the high bank just below the locks, with the
bottom above the level of the lower reach of the navigation. It is emptied straight into the
reach via a sluice. So that work can proceed in all weathers most dry docks are covered,
as at Wigan.

     DECORATIVE CANAL BOAT PAINTING.   Most boats are decorated in some way as a
matter of pride or recognition. Earliest and simplest is the use of bright and contrasting
colours applied to shapes like triangles and lozenges, much used to embellish river and
canal craft, the blue and white of the 'standing and shifting right ups' (hatch coamings) of
a Norfolk wherry, the geometric work along the gunwale of a Leeds and Liverpool short
boat, and the lozenges on the towing mast of a narrow boat. Many never progressed beyond this, apart from the addition of some scroll or decorative work round the name, on
the transom of a Thames spritsail barge; but on the narrow boats of the Midlands this was
not so. Early narrow boats were simply decorated. An oil painting in the collection of
the British Transport Historical Relics shows the Pickfords' boat HOPE with crimson and
dark blue on top strake, cabin sides and cabin doors. E.W. Cooke's 1829 engraving of a
pair of Pickfords' narrow boats on the Thames shows a lozenge on the inside of each
cabin door and a crescent on the top strake, features which remained with narrow boats,

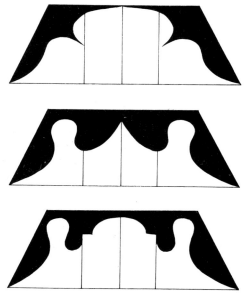

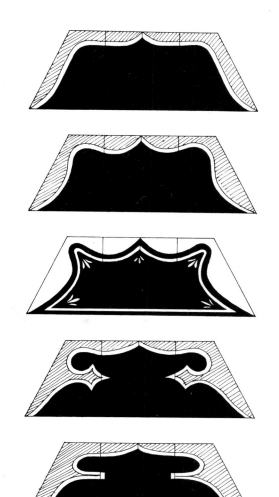

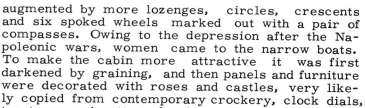

122. Narrow boat cabin rear end design. The five (right) are long distance 'cabin' boats, the three (above), Birmingham day boats whose designs were meant for easy recognition.

augmented by more lozenges, circles, crescents and six spoked wheels marked out with a pair of compasses. Owing to the depression after the Napoleonic wars, women came to the narrow boats. To make the cabin more attractive it was first darkened by graining, and then panels and furniture were decorated with roses and castles, very likely copied from contemporary crockery, clock dials, tea trays and cottage furniture. Rarely was the outside of the cabin so treated, although the serif lettering was well proportioned (120), often elaborately shaded, and surrounded by scroll work, Plates 2 and 10. Narrow boat painting styles varied greatly. Carriers had their own liveries as described under each of them, but the roses and castles varied from district to district and painter to painter. Decorative painting was possibly first done professionally at the docks, the boatmen then took a hand and cabin stools, door panels, hand bowls and cabin blocks were painted by them. Some clear floral styles emerged with variations, the slick abstract roses and daisies of Braunston, Banbury, Bedworth and Leighton Buzzard, secondly the more naturalistic roses of Polesworth, and thirdly (probably in the twentieth century) the real looking 'knobstick' roses of the Potteries yards, Plate 11. Castle designs varied much more, from painter to painter, some preferring cottages and farms, while many castles looked more like churches (121). North western painters sometimes used other motifs, a stag on a cabin block, and a horse's head on the underside of a handbowl or the sailor from a Player's cigarette packet complete with a HERO hatband. Dates are difficult, Robertson's "Life on the Upper Thames" of 1875 illustrates a narrow boat cabin side with a painted panel of a cottage, bridge and stream, these panels he says were called 'cuts' by the boatmen, while "Household Words" describes a castle panel on the cabin side of a Grand Junction fly-boat in 1858. Southern boats reached a higher pitch of decoration than northern, while the 'Number Ones' outshone the carrying companies with a wealth of floral and geometric work and castle panels both inside and out. Little old painting has survived, because everything, including cans and handbowls, was repainted and redecorated when the boat was docked, hence the difficulty of tracing the history of the art. One or two curiosities remain, firstly the use of hearts and clubs but never spades which bring bad luck, on narrow boat cabin slides and deck lids, secondly the exterior curvilinear painting on the rear bulkhead of the cabin (122). This may not be a very old idea, perhaps not earlier than the 1890s, but it became wide-spread, varying in shape. In its simplest form it looked like curtains drawn back to reveal the doors. Leeds & Liverpool short boats never adopted the castles decoration although floral painting was seen. More favoured was geometric and scroll work in contrasting colours of red, yellow, blue and white along the gunwale at bow and stern; the square sterns of horse boats allowed space for elegant shaded lettering, stars, scrollwork and lining, scrollwork also surrounding the name at the fore-end. Steamers and motor boats continued the decorative tradition, although their rounded sterns did not allow so much scope.

CABINS and FITTINGS.   Inland waterway craft cabins evolved from the canvas tilt, spread over a framework, generally hooped. The western barges of the upper Thames, originally undecked, had a canvas cover over a hooped frame at the stern for the protection of their crew. This lasted on many into the nineteenth century. Once a craft was decked, then a cabin could be contrived below. This could be no more than a cuddy, a

123. Narrow boat cabin (right) looking forward to the bed-hole, replaced during the day by a seat board. The view looking aft (left) shows the table cupboard, bottle stove, coal box and food cupboard outside in the hatches.

small pokey space under the deck reached by a hatch, which developed into a well appointed cabin in keels and flats. Some craft remained undecked, or partially decked. The Norfolk wherry had a cabin with sides and roof built up above deck level and entered from a cockpit by a pair of doors. Most numerous of the undecked craft were the narrow boats and their wider sisters. In his "Tour of the Grand Junction" of 1819, John Hassell shows some undecked boats with cabins and these have a rounded roof like the tilt of a western barge. It is possible that some early narrow boats made do with a canvas tilt until more permanent cabins were adopted by the 1790s. That they were adopted and standardized early in the nineteenth century is clear from E.W. Cooke's engraving in his "Shipping and Craft" published in 1829. The pair here on the Thames have cabins almost identical with those of the present day, while some had cabins entirely below deck on the Chesterfield canal and Trent. Dickens' magazine "Household Words" in vol. 18, 1858 describes a journey from London to Birmingham by a Grand Junction narrow fly-boat the STOURPORT. This craft had a cabin interior layout almost the same as that found a hundred years later. The range was on the left, forward of it the table cupboard, across the back the main bed or crossbed and down the right hand side a seat with a locker under it. The table, hinged out from the table cupboard, had a looking glass on its back, there were hooks round the walls for rope lines, the smacking whip and a scrubbing brush, and straps in the roof. These were above the main bed for an umbrella and a saw, and by the doors for documents. Decoration in the cabin is not described. The social tale "Rob Rat" published in 1878 had some cabin interior illustrations, bereft of decoration apart from brass knobs on the back of the table, and a few pictures. These were the first steps in a long process of cluttering up the cabins with ornaments to make them more interesting and bearable. The women needed decoration, hence the lace pelmet over the bed curtains, the lace fringes fronting the table cupboard shelves, the lace edged plates hanging down the side of the table cupboard, the brass drying rails over the range, the miniature brass lock windlasses hanging in front of the plates. The effect was to pile ornament on ornament, so that none were seen to advantage. Layout of a narrow boat cabin became and remained stereotyped. The main bed had a hinged centre which folded up to one side, allowing access via the bulkhead door into the hold or in motor boats the engine room. During the day this was replaced by a seat board (123). Powered narrow boats made little difference to the tradition. Motor boats and butties were permanently paired, the motor cabin being regarded as an annexe, the butty as home. Motors did not usually have ranges, just a stove, either the old fashioned bottle stove which, with a hob, did duty as a cooker in nineteenth century narrow boats, or more recently slow combustion solid fuel stoves. Ranges were neatly designed, measuring about 24" x 16" x 18" high, with a hot plate and oven. There was one cabin disliked by the health authorities and indeed by the boatmen themselves. This was the forecabin, probably introduced into nineteenth century narrow boats after the Canal Boats Acts of 1877 and 1884 laid down minimum space requirements. Children were packed into these hutches forward of the cargo, measuring just over 6' long, at the back the full width of the boat but narrowing forward. They too had a cross bed and a side bed with lockers and a bottle stove. They were entered by a slide. The Leeds & Liverpool horse boats, many of them family boats, had under deck cabin space fore and aft, the after cabin being the captain's, with his family (124). Here the open stove was on the centreline, flanked by berths. One of these was a wide double bed built into a box recess, the other an open berth called the 'spare side' for children. There would be seat lockers in front of the 'bedhole', and right aft the whole width of the craft would be taken up with locker space with a table cupboard in the middle. Some Leeds & Liverpool stern cabins were roomy enough to have closed in bunks on both sides and a small open berth across the back. The fore cabin was smaller and used by the mate, with the same arrangement of box bed, spare side and table cupboard. But much of the space was taken up with lines and fenders. The cabins were entered from a hatch or scuttle on deck down a companion ladder. Decked craft like keels, flats and trows had underdeck accommodation fore and aft, the main cabin being aft. In keel and flat after cabins there was a double bed on the bed side, and a single smaller bed on the spare side. This could be for a mate in a non family boat or for young children. Both might be box beds, the bed side certainly. Fo'c'sles were cluttered by one or two chain lockers, each with a removable front so that the anchor chain could be properly stowed in layers. Space was also taken up by the pump barrel and there might be one of these in the after cabin too. Old keels' fo'c'sles were entered by a pole studded with wedge like steps, later came an iron ladder. In narrow boats the mattress for the main bed had to be folded or rolled up into one corner to allow access to the hold. Probably before the women came aboard the mattresses were simply chaff filled palliasses, but the women would bring feather or flock mattresses and these remained until the age of Dunlopillo. To store their bedding narrow boat wives used to pack it in a deep drawer under the main bed or in a tin trunk, or both, along with the best clothes. Preventing clothes becoming crumpled was a serious problem. In a narrow boat the only movable furniture was the low stool, strongly made and decorated with floral painting, very often by the boatmen. Coal was kept in a box pulled out from under the single step which formed the threshold of a narrow boat cabin, the front of the box frequently painted with scalloped edges and a roundel in the centre. Keelmen kept their coal in the lockers which were built round the cabin sides as seats. Usually water was kept by the narrow boat people in cans (125) carried on the cabin top, although "Household Words" of 1858 talks about a water can hung up in the cabin. These cans, of galvanized iron, were given spouts, a carrying handle and a hinged lid. Two are normally carried, each holding three or four gallons. Because of their shape and prominence they have had more decoration

124. The fore end cabin of a Leeds & Liverpool boat.
Note box 'bedhole'.

lavished on them than any other single article aboard. Groups of roses on a dark green blue or black ground form the major part of this, with a broad band round the waist bearing the name of the owner or boat or a simple motto like 'Good luck' or 'Live and Let Live'. Some have been called Buckby cans because boatmen bought them at the shop at the top of Buckby locks on the Grand Junction. Cans were placed close up to the chimney, and resting partly on the cabin top handrail. Allied to the cans were the hand bowls or dippers which were used as basins or dipped in the canal to draw water for washing and peeling potatoes. They too were decorated with flowers, the older ones having curved sides, the more recent straight. Round the base there might be a motto like 'Use me well and keep me clean.' All boats carried a mop, generally made from rags, old stockings or jerseys. Narrow boats had theirs with a handle decorated in spirals of contrasting colour like a barber's pole, Plate 10. It was stowed on the cabin top, the handle resting on the cans and against the chimney. Narrow boat chimneys are easily detachable because of low bridges and are held by a chain, often brass and decorated with brasses or, just after the 1939-45 War, made of brass clips from army haversacks.

Apart from the decorative lace edged Staffordshire plates, crockery and cutlery were undistinguished. In 1858 "Household Words" spoke of rudimentary spoons and forks with two prongs, while the sugar it said was mostly ladled out of a drawer. In the 1880s the curious brown Measham teapots were bought by the boat people, probably more for decoration than use, for they are an impractical knobbly shape. Keelmen had their beef kettle, a round three legged cooking pot for boiling stews, and some kept an earthenware pickle pot for preserving pork or beef.

Cabin illumination was by oil lamp, larger craft like keels had sufficient headroom for a lamp, hung on a long rail so that it could be slid from end to end of the cabin. Also there were wall lamps with a reflector behind the glass. These were found on narrow boats, a variant being a lamp on a swinging bracket by the table cupboard. Before oil lamps there were candles, and tallow dips for the poorer boats, but motor boats with their generators changed all this.

Lavatories were rarely a feature of small inland craft due to lack of space. Crews could get ashore and this seemed to be the practice at tying up places. Some of these became very foul, notably the path under Broad Street in Birmingham. The canal company purified it with chloride of lime. Aboard narrow boats the only sanitary equipment was a bucket, used in a corner of the engine room or in the deck at the fore end. Water closets were fitted to larger powered craft. If one considers family life in a boat cabin as cramped, squalid and insanitary, remember that the boatman, his wife and children were rarely in it except to sleep for a few hours and when waiting to load or unload. Their home was the towpath driving the horse or in the hatches steering, and for the evening a pub bar. The open air acted as an antidote to the ills which a frowsty, verminous, over crowded cabin could bring.

125. Chimney and water can (below, left), and the 'cratch' of a narrow boat (below, right), note the decorative strings securing the top cloth, deck cloth and stem fender.

5.

126. Arun Navigation spritsail barge.

Canal and River Craft

BARGES:

ARUN NAVIGATION, RIVER ARUN.   Heavy goods were carried by lighters and sailing barges of up to 100 ton capacity and by spritsail barges of 30 to 40 tons, and light goods by 20 ton boats, both sailed and horse hauled, often travelling fly between London and Portsmouth. Lower Arun lighters and sailing barges, the former unrigged and working with the tide and shafts, could pass no higher than Arundel, usually with South Wales coal, while the smaller spritsail barges generally went up the Arun Navigation, the Western Rother and the Wey & Arun Canal as far as Cranleigh, occasionally beyond, with stone, chalk and timber. Groceries and farm produce, like carrots, cider and hops tended to go by the 20 ton boats, sailed up to Pallingham, but horse hauled on the Wey & Arun Canal and Wey Navigation. Arun navigation spritsail barges could be square or pointed sterned; the average beam was 12' but length varied from 40' to 70' and all had flat bottoms, rounded bilges and an open hold. Pallingham was the main building centre.   Occasionally the accommodation for the two or three man crew was under deck aft, but more frequently they had to make do with a tent on deck or sleep in the hold.   No   deck   erections   were possible because of low bridges on the Wey & Arun Canal. Some appear to have been two masted, but a single mast a little forward of amidships in a tabernacle, so that it could be lowered, was more usual. The spritsail was similar to a Thames barge and a foresail was always set. Decoration was limited to a painted transom and rudder head, while the hull was tarred. Owners were numerous, the majority having one barge only. The Arundel Barge Co. had a fleet of seven in 1830, well known carriers were James and later William Stanton of Bramley near Godalming, the last trader on the Wey & Arun Canal. Lower Arun sailing barges had a capacity of from 50 to 100 tons, rigged with a spritsail, squaresail or lugsail, akin to the barges of the Adur and Sussex Ouse. They traded between Littlehampton and Arundel and on the Portsmouth & Arundel Canal. These larger decked craft had hatch boards and coamings. The smaller spritsail barges perished some seven years before the closure of the Arun Navigation in 1896. The lower Arun barges lasted until the mid-1930s.

BASINGSTOKE CANAL.   The average capacity of a nineteenth century Basingstoke barge was 50 to 54 tons and up to 72'6" x 13'6". They seem to have been square or tran- som sterned like Wey barges. In the early days of the canal there were some sizeable fleets. In 1826 John Birnie took over the 12 barge fleet of Wallis & Foyle, in addition to his work as clerk to the canal company. Best known of the Basingstoke carriers was A.J. Harmsworth who commenced trading in 1902. He acquired a number of barges and narrow boats either second hand or from other builders before he started to build his own barges at Ash Vale in 1918. Harmsworth's barges loaded 75 to 80 tons on the Thames, but were limited to 50 up the canal to Woking. They were transom sterned and round bilged, with an almost straight upright stem and washboards fore and aft for the tideway.   Many had living accommodation aft complying with the Canal Boats Acts for the crew of two.   These were the residential boats or 'reso's' as opposed to the 'odd'ns' or odd boats used for day work, lightening other barges so that they could get up the Wey and the canal. All had a single long hatch with coamings to which the cloths were secured by battens and wedges in addition to lashings. The last Basingstoke barge to be built at Ash Vale, the ARIEL I in 1935, was the last to trade, ceasing work in 1967.

BRISTOL AVON. Akin to the Severn barges were those on the Avon stone trade, retaining a single squaresail into the twentieth century. Many were old trows, but some were built for shallow water, retaining the trow hull characteristics with less depth.

MOTOR BARGES. Most numerous are the river and tidal motor barges of Yorkshire generally called river craft, and motor keels and sloops when they were motorized, leading a commercially active existence in the 1970s. There was one on the Sheffield & South Yorkshire as early as 1906, but they were not common until the 1930s. Early ones had Gardner hot bulb semi-diesel engines, and Gardners have remained popular for Yorkshire craft. New construction was mostly in steel and building was concentrated into the hands of specialists, John Harker, Knottingley, Richard Dunston, Thorne and Hessle and the one time yards of Joseph Scarr & Son, Beverley and T.H. Scarr of Howden Dike. The vertical sternpost of the keel was kept until the 1939-45 War, when use of hard chine construction to save bending and speed completion led to angular sterns of swim headed form. Welding replaced rivetting, but the bow has retained the bluffness of a keel, complete with the prominent hawse ports. Wheelhouses were often small and made with a collapsible roof and windows because of the low bridges. Engine controls were grouped here and it was possible for one man to run a motor although two were more common. Some motor craft possess the wooden stern rail of a keel while others have a steel bulwark formed like a turtle back. Regulations demand steaming lights, so they step a short mast forward for a white light and have side screens by the wheelhouse for port and starboard navigation lights. Craft also carry life-buoys and inflatable rafts to replace the cog boat or dinghy. Sizes and capacities vary. Calder & Hebble boats had to be no more than 57'6" long to get up above Broad Cut below Dewsbury, although down from there they could be 120'. On the Don section of the Sheffield & South Yorkshire Navigation and on the Sheffield Canal craft are limited to 61'6" or 'Sheffield size' but on the main line of the Aire & Calder they can go up to 180'. Sheffield & South Yorkshire craft carry 90 tons, but those on the Aire & Calder some 300 tons of dry cargo (127). Demands for oil led to the first Yorkshire motor tanker craft built for and by John Harker from 1925. Tanks in these are subdivided and come up to the height of what would in dry cargo craft be called the hatch coamings. The largest Yorkshire tankers by 1973 measured 180' x 18'9" x 8'3" laden draught, carrying up to 520 tons. Motor barges on the Trent are similar to the Yorkshire ones, with capacities of up to 250 tons, the navigation accommodating a length of 142' up to Nottingham, Plate 2. Above Nottingham cargo could be handled by 50 to 60 ton capacity barges about 72' x 14'. See Barges, River Trent. On the Severn petroleum traffic saved the navigation from decay in the 1930s. The Severn & Canal Carrying Co. built five tanker barges between 1933 and 1937 suitable for work in the river and the Bristol Channel. They also assembled a fleet of dry cargo barges in the 1930s, the first being the SEVERN TRADER, built in 1932. She was followed by two more, all three and the five tankers being built by Charles Hill of Bristol and intended for Bristol Channel service as far west as Swansea (85). They had a gross tonnage of 122 and were handsome craft, with bulwarks, cruiser sterns, enclosed wheelhouses and a derrick over the single long hatch. In 1952 they were joined by the SEVERN SIDE built at John Harker's Sharpness shipyard. With a capacity of 360 tons, she measures 134'6" long overall by 21'3" x 8' laden draught. Her engine is a five cylinder Ruston diesel and she is capable of 7 knots laden. Her routes under British Waterways were from Worcester to Avonmouth, Cardiff, Penarth and Bridgwater, crewed by captain, mate, engineer between Worcester and Avonmouth but four in the Bristol Channel. All the fleet have been sold, the SEVERN SIDE to Healing's mills Tewkesbury. Largest of Severn craft are the coastal tankers operated by Bowker & King Ltd. carrying refined petroleum products from Swansea to the terminal at Quedgeley on the Gloucester & Sharpness Canal. They can carry 1000 tons and measure 211' x 30' with a loaded draught of 11'6". In the north-west, motor vessels were introduced on the Weaver in 1911 with the EGBERT of Brunner, Mond & Co. While the EGBERT could carry only 130 tons, the JAMES JACKSON GRUNDY of 1947 could carry 285. She was followed by six more for ICI, later able to carry 300 tons because of increased river depth. The Bridgewater Department of the Manchester Ship Canal Co. ordered some counter sterned power barges after the 1939-45 War to handle their fleet of dumb craft and carry a useful 80 ton payload themselves. Isaac Pimblott of Northwich built four and W.J. Yarwood two in 1951-2. All names began 'Par' something, the first, the PARADINE had an overall length of 71', a maximum breadth of 14'9½" and a moulded depth of 6'3". She had a 68 bhp Gardner. In Ireland there were motor barges on the Shannon, an early one being the CAMBRIA built in 1921 by W.J. Yarwood at Northwich for James Bannatyne & Sons Ltd, the Limerick flour millers. On a 4'6" draught she carried 60 tons. Her engine was a 40 bhp Robey. The same firm's ECLIPSE FLOWER remained on the Shannon service until the 1960s latterly under the ownership of Rank's (Ireland) Ltd. The Grand Canal Co. had motor barges-cum-tugs on the Shannon, transhipping from canal boats at Shannon Harbour and running down to Limerick, towing motor canal boats which could not always cope with the Shannon currents and lake storms. The steel ST. JAMES was built for them in 1938 by the Ringsend Dockyard Co in Dublin. 73' x 14'8" beam she had an 80 hp twin cylinder Bolinder. Two other barge-cum-tugs were acquired in 1945, the ST. BRIGID and the ST. PATRICK ex AVON QUEEN and AVON KING respectively. They were larger than the ST. JAMES and had Bolinders. All were sold in 1960 when traffic ceased on the Grand and Shannon. In Ulster there are motor barges on the Lower

127. A 250 ton powered Yorkshire
craft taking a dumb craft in
tow.

Bann and Lough Neagh carrying sand. Two, owned
by H. & W. Scott, sand merchants of Toomebridge
are ex Guiness steam barges from the Liffey. See
also Irish inland waterway craft.

River PARRETT and Associated Waterways; Craft used on the Parrett, the Tone, the
Bridgwater & Taunton Canal and associated
waterways seem to have been interrelated. Three
main sizes are known, the 15 ton capacity barges
(61) which worked down the Parrett for the estuary silt used to make bath brick, similar to the
18 ton canal barges; and 5 ton boats called 'shoes'
used on the Bridgwater & Taunton Canal and probably on the Chard and the Grand Western. Additionally there were boats used by farms to carry
produce, turf, peat and withies for Somerset
basket making. Clinker planking gave them strength
for lying on the mud when loading silt and also sufficient for the open hold unstiffened by
beams. They were some 53' long by 13' beam, Plate 12. Fore and aft there were short
decks and aft also a bridge deck with a portable steering platform just forward of it like
the thwart of a rowing boat, for the steering sweeps were handled by two men, the barge
depending on the tide. They had a little cabin under the foredeck with sitting headroom
only and a stove. The two 25' sweeps worked in grooves, one cut in the head of the sternpost, the other in a grooved block called the monkey which fitted at the fore end. A rudder
was stowed on the after deck but only shipped for canal work or if under tow. Drag chains
were used to stop or slow the vessel, hove overside to 'ride the bottom'. The chains were
secured aft by substantial cleats called clinks and forward by three forked posts called
livers, held by iron brackets to the forward bulkhead of the hold. The livers were of natural timber, the forks being used to hold bights of chain. Planks were carried for wheelbarrows, loading silt in the estuary and unloading at the Bridgwater kilns. Four shafts,
locally called geds, were carried, both for manoeuvring and as mooring stakes. A hand net
was carried for salmon and the crew baled with a wooden scoop like that of narrow boats.
Decoration was limited to a white line round the black hull below the gunwale and the name
of the owner was painted on the after bulkhead. The Somerset Trading Co. had a lozenge
painted on the inside hull aft, while Pocock's went in for painted animal figures on the
after bulkhead. Parrett barges also carried bath bricks, building bricks, tiles, and coal for
the kilns. Decline in the silt traffic began during the 1914-18 War because of the introduction of cleaning powders. The last barge was broken up just after the 1939-45 War but
they had done well for their owners, notably Symons & Co, H.J. & C. Major Ltd, Pocock's
and the Somerset Trading Co. The barges were mostly built at Bridgwater, Pocock's being
builders and owners. Barges seem to have been numbered rather than named. The five
ton shoes measured 20' x 8' x 3' usually with square sterns of up to 6' in width. Shoes
would be horse hauled on the canals possibly in trains, but the small turf and withy boats
were more likely to have been drawn by manpower or poled.

RYE River. Described by Leopold A. Vidler in the "Mariner's Mirror" vol 21.(1935),
these worked on the Eastern Rother, the Brede and the Royal Military Canal. They were
strongly constructed lugsail rigged craft drawing 3' laden, with flat bottoms to lie aground
when loading shingle, and had rounded bilges. Capacity was 20 to 25 tons but one of the
later barges could carry 40. Those which worked on to the Royal Military Canal and up the
Rother had to be small enough for Scots Float sluice lock, for craft 45' x 12', but many
were limited to Rye and the lock free Brede. Most were built of wood, locally at Rye, although a few iron ones were launched in the nineteenth century, all having a pointed stern
and a flat sheer because of the low river and canal bridges. The hold was open, the barge
having short decks fore and aft, each with a cabin forward for the crew of two and a
locker aft. The sixteenth century sprit rig was replaced by a standing lug, the mast stepped in a tabernacle because of bridges and unstayed. The sail was only used in a fair wind,
the men quanted if the wind was foul or non-existent, or bow hauled on the upper reaches.
By the later nineteenth century cargoes were reduced to coal, timber, bricks, manure and
above all shingle for road metalling and ship's ballast. In summer, barges might go outside
Rye Harbour for this, but usually kept within the Rother, the crew loading at low water
with planks and wheelbarrows. These craft did not survive the 1939-45 War.

River SEVERN; Barges, Frigates, Flats, Wherries: In the mid-eighteenth century
smaller Severn traders were called frigates or barges, the difference in size from the
trows continuing into the nineteenth. Frigates handled the trade to Coalbrookdale (54) and
Shrewsbury, transhipping into trows at Gloucester and not working below that city. In the
1750s frigates could carry 20 to 40 tons and trows 40 to 80, but by the 1840s both types
had grown, the frigates or barges (the latter the more usual term by then) handling up to
80 tons. Originally there would be little difference in hull form between the frigate or
barge and the trow, since both met with the same river conditions, a keel-less flat bottom
being essential. But the barge kept her old shape into the nineteenth century, bluff bowed,
large open hold and dish shaped cross section because of the shallow river. A 30 ton

capacity frigate would measure about 50' x 15' x 3' loaded draught. Eighteenth century frigates were square rigged, some possibly adopting the fore and aft spritsail during the 1790s, while during the nineteenth some were probably rigged like trows. Barges lasted in the stone trade until about 1910, still with a single square sail. The mast could lower by a forestay tackle. John Wilkinson had pioneered iron hulls with the 30 ton capacity Severn barge TRIAL built at Willey near Broseley in 1787. She was followed by several more, designed for shallow water, 8" laden draught in one case. A 100 ton capacity Severn barge was developed in the early nineteenth century; measuring 120' x 16' to 20' wide by about 5' draught. No evidence of their rig exists, but their dimensions suggest an unhandy vessel, able to sail with a following wind, but relying on man and horse power. Flats, introduced towards the end of the eighteenth century for shallow water work, were able to carry 20 tons on an 18" draught, and wherries were two man boats for general river work with oars and a sail, probably a sprit. They carried passengers and small consignments. See also trows, and 'wich barges.

STROUD: The Stroudwater was a broad waterway used by Severn trows and salt barges but during the 1820s a special craft was built for the Forest of Dean coal trade from Bullo Pill to Framilode and up the canal to Brimscombe and Chalford. This was the double ended, flat bottomed, hard chine Stroud sailing barge with a massive keelson, many of which were built at The Bourn, Brimscombe by the Gardiner family. They measured about 68' x 12'6", about 50 tons capacity, short enough for the locks below Brimscombe, and narrow enough for those above. Accommodation was below short decks fore and aft, and the large open hold was stiffened by moveable beams. A stout tabernacle supported by a fixed beam received the mast, rigged with a single square sail. For canal work all were lowered and haulage was done by men and horses. Some lasted until the 1930s, owned by James Smart of Chalford, but by this time they were unrigged and towed on the Severn by tugs.

River TAMAR: Working between Calstock and Plymouth these sailing barges also came up to Morwellham and on to the Tamar Manure Navigation to Newbridge near Gunnislake. They carried coal, coke, grain, limestone and timber upriver, returning with bricks and granite from Calstock and copper ore and arsenic from the mines above Morwellham. They had a capacity of 50 to 80 tons measuring about 50' overall by 16', small enough to pass through the one lock on the navigation at Weir Head, Nutstakes. They were flat bottomed, with well rounded bilges and a keel about 12" deep and so sailed well to windward. The stem was straight and slightly raked; the stern could be rounded or square, usually the latter. One or two had wheel steering. There was a long hatch and the accommodation for the crew of two was below deck aft. These craft were cutter rigged, with a large gaff mainsail, foresail and jib set on a long bowsprit. Some of the larger ones had topmasts and jackyard topsails. The mast could be lowered in its tabernacle or saddle. Most were built on the Tamar, many at Calstock, but their traffic was killed by the completion of the railway viaduct at Calstock in 1908 for the Bere Alston & Callington line. During the 1914-18 War these barges had been commandeered to carry stores and some survived on these duties until after 1945 although with engines. The sailing barges were frequently given tows on the Tamar, otherwise they depended on the tide, and could use sweeps if the wind fell. There was a towing path from below Calstock up to Newbridge, from which the barges could be bowhauled by up to six men with a hauling line from the masthead. In shallow water they could be shafted. **One is now preserved in the museum at Cotchele.**

River TEIGN, STOVER and HACKNEY CANAL: Barges carrying pottery clay down the Stover and Hackney Canals and River Teign to Teignmouth were probably unchanged in appearance from 1792 when the Stover Canal opened to the end of trade before the 1939-45 War. Carrying 25 tons, they were either bow hauled or sailed on the canals and used wind and tide on the river. The wooden hulls usually measured some 50' x 14' x 5' depth, with a flat bottom, bluff bow and wide transom stern. The hold was served by a long wide hatch and a large square sail was hoisted whose mast, unsupported by shrouds, was set in a tabernacle at the forward end of the hold, so that it could be lowered. Two formed the crew, usually from Kingsteignton, the profession passing from father to son. Barge owners were the Templer family, the first proprietors of the Stover Canal, and the Clifford family proprietors of the Hackney. Later the GWR operated barges on the Stover Canal, as did the clay companies, particularly Watts, Blake, Bearne & Co, who towards the end of their lease of the Stover Canal employed the motor tug KESTREL, built locally in the 1920s, to tow the barges, now bereft of sails.

THAMES, SPRITSAIL: They carried a rig which could be operated by two men and were sufficiently shallow draughted to be at home among the sandbanks of the Thames estuary (3). Some could load as much as 300 tons but 150 to 175 tons was average, and they handled much of the local coasting trade to and from London up to 1939. They stemmed from the same root as the western barges which worked up the Thames to Oxford and above. Hull form was similar but with the spritsail and lee boards, making the Thames sailing barge distinctive. Chapman in his "Architectura Navalis Mercatoria" of 1768 shows a spritsail rigged chalk barge with the punt shaped bow and stern, the rudder hanging from a fin or skeg which the bargemen called a budget. She has lee boards, which would enable her to go to windward, but has an open hold. From about 1840 the punt shape, called swim headed, began to be replaced by the rounded bow and transom stern, although the flat bottom and the hard chine or square bilge remained. Empty barges needed no ballast, for the wide flat bottom provided sufficient stability. Swim headed barges were common until the 1900s. Rig varied. The early spritsail ones, like Chapman's chalk barge, had a mainsail and foresail, but no topsail and came to be called stumpies. A mizen was introduced round about 1800 and adopted on all barges. It too was a spritsail but mulies or mule rigged barges had a gaff mizen. Then there were the coasting boomies, built with barge hulls and lee boards but rigged like coasting ketches with a boom mainsail and mizen. To work up rivers and canals sailing barges could lower their masts, both main and mizen, sometimes with sail set. This was necessary on the Medway, the shooting of Rochester bridge being a dramatic accomplishment. Barges worked up as far as Tonbridge and the Thames & Medway Canal was built to save them passage of the lower Thames and Medway. On the Thames, sailing barges went well upriver and one class was built for the locks on the Regent's Canal. Much of the trade was to East Anglian ports, for example Heybridge basin at the entrance to the Chelmer & Blackwater Navigation. They could not go up the river, but the entrance lock could take barges of up to 107' x 26', which was large enough for any spritsail barge. Grain to mills on the Orwell and the Stour was another important trade. See also under Lighters, Thames and Lee.

THAMES; WESTERN BARGES: Not to be confused with the spritsail barges of the lower Thames and Medway, the barges of the upper Thames, trading from Oxford and the west, dated back to mediaeval times. They retained until the eighteenth century a primitive hull form with vertical sides and a punt shaped bow and stern, undecked, rectangular and flat bottomed, because they had to lie aground in shallows. During that century their lines were improved to a more rounded cross section and a more refined bow and stern, retaining the punt or swim headed shape. Some barges became decked. The Thames & Severn Canal may have stimulated further improvements when in 1790 they completed the EXPERIMENT at The Bourn above Brimscombe with a pointed bow, rounded sides, and a transom stern, like a Severn trow. Western barges stepped a single pole mast in a tabernacle, since it had to be lowered for bridges, and they could set a squaresail or later in the eighteenth century a spritsail. Towing was from the masthead either by men or horses, two barges generally working together, eleven horses sometimes being needed on the Thames to drag one barge against the current. On the undecked barges the three man crew lived under a temporary canvas tilt aft, stretched over hoops, but below deck accommodation was provided in the improved barges, Plate 9. Dimensions of barges varied widely, an Act of 1768 limited them to 3' draught, while a 1775 barge trading to Lechlade measured 87'6" x 11'7" and drew 4' fully laden with 65 tons. Downstream barges were larger, up to 146 tons in the Weybridge area. 80' x 12' was the average size of those passing on to the Thames & Severn Canal. They could use this as far west as Brimscombe, because below there the locks were too short. The smaller 60' x 12' salt barges worked through from Droitwich to London. From 1841 however the Thames & Severn Canal was closed to most western barges because the locks were shortened by 20' to save water, and they were killed off soon after by railway competition and the poor state of the upper Thames.

River TRENT: Trent craft were divided into those that went above Nottingham to Wilden Ferry and before about 1805 as far as Burton, and those of the river below Nottingham which went down to the Humber. Upper Trent craft would not go below Keadby, but those on the lower river were of the Humber keel type suited to estuary conditions. Keels would come up from Humber ports and from the Don via the Stainforth & Keadby Canal but because of the shallowness of the Trent, they could not carry their full tonnage. With Jessop's improvements, a minimum depth of only 2'6" was achieved by the early 1800s. So Trent river vessels were designed to carry a load of 40-50 tons on a draught of 2'6" with 3' as a maximum, while the locks below Nottingham imposed a length not exceeding 81' and a breadth not above 14'. Trent catches (a corruption of ketch), on the Trent, Fossdyke and Witham were like keels, double ended and rigged with a squaresail on the main mast and fore and aft on the mizen. They measured about 74'9" x 14' and could load to 5'6" draught. However the Trent became shallower, as little as 20" in the 1880s and was not sufficient for 100 ton craft until the 1920s. Some of these were lighters towed in trains of three by a steam tug, others were sailing keels. The new locks were 180' x 29', but no individual craft could exceed 82'6" x 14'6" (Trent standard size) until the older locks were eliminated. The Trent steel dumb lighter or pan was of this size carrying 100 tons on 5' draught. The ANCHOLME built to this size in 1921 at the Trent Navigation Co's Newark dockyard could carry 120 tons. She was a wooden boat, the Navigation naming their carrying fleet after rivers. In 1954 the last of the older locks were eliminated and so vessels measuring 142' x 17'6" carrying 250 tons came up to Nottingham. Above Nottingham the size of 72' x 14' was dictated by Jessop's locks. Following his improvements vessels averaged 60' x 11' to 14' beam and carried 50 tons, either horse hauled or sailed. They had open holds with keel rig (128). Lee boards and mast were put ashore if going up the River Soar or the Grantham and the Nottingham canals, similar craft lasting into the twentieth century. The iron open holded Nottingham pan 72' x 14' was a dumb craft working to Burton-on-Trent, Leicester and Grantham. The usual capacity for powered craft was 50 to 60 tons working to Shardlow or Leicester until the end of commercial traffic in the early 1960s.

River WEY: Horse haulage remained on the Wey until 1960, hulls of the wooden barges were similar to the Lower Arun and Thames spritsail barges. Wey barges were fully decked and transom sterned with a round bilge and flat bottom. Forward, some Wey barges carried washboards for the tideway. Immediately aft of the hold the deck was bounded by low coamings like a shallow well. Here the steerer stood, the great tiller coming right up over the after deck proper, which was built higher. The barge's name was painted on the low bulkhead between the two decks, pierced by cabin windows. All these barges had a colossal rudder which needed the big flat tiller to work it. This was fitted with a vertical wooden handle for the steerer. For Thames work Wey barges had an anchor and windlass on the fore deck. A small hatch here gave access to the fo'c'sle where spare lines and

128. An Upper Trent craft.

C.V.Waine.

gear were kept plus a berth for the third hand, the accommodation for the captain and mate being aft, reached by a sliding companion hatch. The barges varied a little, the maximum being 73' x 13'10". They could carry 80 tons on the Thames and up to Coxes lock, the second after the Thames lock below Weybridge, but less upstream, and less still on the Godalming Navigation, which was limited to 3'6" draught. Horse towing was from a timber head forward. Tugs were used after 1960 until the last grain barges, manned by the captain only, came to Coxes Lock mill in 1969. Many were built at Dapdune Wharf Guildford by the Stevens family, who not only owned the Wey and Godalming Navigation, but most of the barges too. Transoms were painted white and lettered in black 'William Stevens and Sons Guildford'. Top strakes were light green, as were the wash strakes forward. Also green were the rudder head and the tiller, the remainder of the hull being tarred black. The covering boards, coamings and windlass were red. See also barges, Arun Navigation.

'WICH BARGES.   See Trows.

BILLYBOYS, YORKSHIRE: The Billyboy was a coaster but many were built and owned at Knottingley on the Aire. They worked up the Aire & Calder and even the Barnsley Canal. During the nineteenth century, fore and aft ketch and cutter rigged billyboys were common and there were some schooner examples with square topsails, with capacities of 80 to 100 tons. Like the keel, to which she was related, the billyboy had leeboards, and was flat bottomed, with very bluff bow and stern. Unlike the keel she had bulwarks, more sheer and was clinker built. The crew of three berthed forward, while the captain lived aft, often accompanied by his wife. Until the end of the 1914-18 War billyboys were still trading on the East Coast. See also Keels and sloops, Humber (sailing).

BOATS:

CHELMER & BLACKWATER, IPSWICH & STOWMARKET NAVIGATIONS.   The Chelmer & Blackwater Navigation was opened in 1797, the locks accommodating craft 60' x 16', but the ruling draught was only 2'. Because of their beam however, they were able to manage 25-27 ton cargoes; they were double ended or square sterned, decked aft, the open hold extending to the stempost. Horse drawn wooden boats, of hard chine, flat bottomed construction continued on the Chelmer until the late 1950s when they were replaced by similar steel craft (53), powered by Harbourmaster drive inboard-outboard diesels, mounted on deck. The horses hauled on a timber head at the side, towards the fore end. Timber was the latter day cargo, piled well above the gunwale, the boats being run by Brown & Sons Ltd. to their Chelmsford sawmills. Traffic ceased in 1972. Similar shallow draught boats worked on the Gipping or Ipswich & Stowmarket Navigation where they could draw 3' laden, the maximum dimensions being 55' x 14'. Gipping barges carried 30 tons. In the 1900s wooden steam barges were used on this navigation towing two dumb barges (52). Fison's used them until the 1920s and Packard's until the 1930s. They carried to the fertilizer works at Bramford, four miles upstream from Ipswich.

COMMITTEE Boats: A committee inspected their waterway, generally once a year, usually in the summer (95). Smaller companies would probably just fit a cargo boat or a maintenance boat with seats and an awning, as was done on the Bridgwater & Taunton, using a horse drawn Parrett barge. Or they could hire a pleasure boat for the day as the Linton Lock Commissioners did from York, first a steam launch, later petrol. But many had special craft. The Duke of Bridgewater had a yacht or private boat on his canal in the 1790s, but river committee boats have an ancestry back to the Lord Mayor of London's river procession to Westminster which started in 1454, he and the livery companies travelling upstream in state barges. A Lord Mayor of London's barge of 1816 had a grand saloon 56' long and could seat 140 at dinner. Eight horses were needed to tow it upstream. An early river committee boat was the SAVILE (rebuilt in 1801) on the Calder & Hebble, named after the navigation's supporter Sir George Savile. A new SAVILE followed in 1825. These were horse drawn but steam was ideal because neither space nor fuel consumption was important. Thus the Weaver trustees had their steam launch the DELAMERE. At the opening of the Rochdale Canal in 1804, the committee borrowed the Calder & Hebble's SAVILE which was accompanied by the TRAVIS, a private craft which had belonged to the late chairman Archdeacon George Travis who died in 1797. Not until 1832 did the Rochdale order their own craft THE ROCHDALE from Liverpool builders. On the Bridgewater the yacht tradition persisted. The Earl of Ellesmere built a special state barge for Queen Victoria's visit to Worsley in 1851. About 45' long she was quite fine lined, with carved work at the stemhead and at the stern. She was hauled by two grey horses ridden by postilions in dark grey jackets. Still (1977) in commission as a pleasure boat is the LADY HATHERTON of the Staffs. & Worcs. She is built on narrow boat lines but finer, with a cabin running for most of her length. Named after the chairman's wife she was in service with the company from 1896 to 1948. Whereas the LADY HATHERTON was horse drawn most committee boats were steamers. Thus there was the SWALLOW of the Worcester & Birmingham, and the DOLLY VARDEN of the Trent & Mersey built by the North Staffordshire Railway Co. in 1904 for their directors' use. These boats were built as steam launches of late Victorian opulence. On the Leeds & Liverpool was the WATER WITCH built in 1915 at James Mayor's yard at Tarleton replacing an earlier boat of 1878. This second committee launch, 61' long, lasted until 1951. In 1928 the Grand Junction had a directors' boat, the KINGFISHER, driven by a petrol engine. She retained the elegance of her steam predecessors and was used by Sir Reginald Kerr, general manager of British Transport Waterways, for his inspections in the 1950s. Inspection boats used by the engineers were no less stylish than the former but would not have the facilities for meals such as the KINGFISHER could provide. The Lancaster used the old swift passenger boat WATER WITCH II, which is why she lasted until the Second World War. She was horse drawn, as was the INSPECTOR based at Ellesmere, used until 1934 on the Shropshire Union's Welsh section. The Grand Junction had smart steam launches, for example the clinker built GAD-FLY used by T. W. Millner, engineer of the Northern District from 1896 to 1930. Some carriers had inspection boats. There was the steam launch PACIFIC of the Salt Union, used for tours of the Winsford salt works, while H. R. de Salis of Fellows, Morton, & Clayton had his DRAGONFLY, built for his personal use in 1895. Then there were the tug/tenders of the Manchester Ship Canal Co. First they had the CHARLES GALLOWAY delivered new in 1895 with limited passenger accommodation. She was broken up in 1929 and replaced by the RALPH BROCKLEBANK bought from the Shropshire Union in 1922. In 1936 this vessel was refitted and renamed DANIEL ADAMSON.

COMPARTMENT Boats: By the 1830s, 36 cwt colliery tubs were being loaded into boats on the Don and the Aire & Calder. W. H. Bartholomew, the latter's engineer went a stage further when in 1861 he proposed his compartment boat system, large floating colliery tubs, coupled up in trains. Placed in service in 1865 after a period of experiment, they were rectangular iron boxes, each 21' x 15' x 8' and drawing 6'6" when loaded with 35 tons of coal. Their true ancestors were the tub-boats of East Shropshire and the West Country. But Bartholomew broke new ground with his patent of 1862 because he arranged for his trains to be push towed in groups of six, hence the particular importance of his bow section to give a boat shape to the train, which was held tight by chains passing through fairleads down each side from the 'dummy bows' and secured to a winch on the tug's foredeck. The chains were for steering, to be slackened and tightened to give curvature to the train. Up to twelve boats were pushed but the longer trains which the trade needed were impossible. Push towing lasted into the 1900s but then it was abandoned in favour of trains behind the tug, the bow section being retained at the head of the train to improve propeller flow and steerage and to prevent the wash of the tug swamping the leading boats when loaded. Steerage was further improved by loading the first three boats of the train to a lighter draught roughly equal to that of the 'dummy bows' so that they curved down to the deeper boats behind. These first three, to aid steerage, were bound rigidly to the bows by chains or wires passing through fairleads on either side, and taken up by a windlass on the deck of the 'dummy bows'. The remainder were close coupled by chains passed round timberheads and through fairleads and for rapid handling at locks by chains made fast on one boat and held by quick release stoppers on the other. To give articulation the bow of each boat was fitted with a rounded 'stempost' fitting into a recess in the 'stern' of the craft next ahead, and to straighten the train up after a bend, spring loaded buffers were mounted on each fore end acting on wooden pads on the stern of the boat ahead (39). Empty compartment boats rode high drawing only a few inches; they were towed in the same way except that because of their light draught their 'dummy bows' also known as the cutwater, headpiece or Jabez Head had to be pushed ahead of the tug. It was secured by chains from its windlass to timber heads on the tug's foredeck. Trains of up to 40 boats were known, although 30 was a more average figure, two men being in charge of the train plus two on the tug. Between the wars trains became shorter, limited to 19, for the locks had been enlarged in the 1900s between Castleford and Goole sufficiently to take a tug and train at one penning. Above Castleford the trains were limited to 17, penned in two portions, 10 and then 7 and the tug. Flexibility has been the virtue of the compartment boat system. Trains could be adjusted to suit the traffic, moreover the boats, like colliery tubs, could be handled to load and discharge their coal. They were marshalled under the drops at waterside collieries, although in 1891 one colliery near Stanley Ferry built a special railway and slipway into a basin, for the boats to be loaded on to a 12 wheeled bogie wagon which a locomotive hauled to the colliery drops. Goole was the unloading point for all the compartment boats and here Bartholomew designed hydraulic hoists, one being on a pontoon, to lift one boat at a time and tip it so that the coal fell into the hold of a sea-going collier. The boat ascended in a cage containing a cradle, shaped to receive the hull, which was floated in and clamped to the cradle. Hydraulic rams lifted the cage, tipped the cradle and altered the angle of the coal chute. In 1913 Aire & Calder compartment boats carried a million and a half tons of coal down to Goole where they could be unloaded at the rate of 200 tons per hour per hoist. At one time there were as many as 1100 in service. Every boat tug and 'dummy bows' bore a number, each tug being paired with a 'dummy bows' of the same number; later diesel tugs were named. Tugs and 'dummy bows' were painted in the green and white livery of the Aire & Calder, succeeded by the blue and yellow of British Waterways, the compartment boats being black. Gangways were fitted down the side of each boat and some were built with coamings and sockets for spars over which cloths could be spread and secured by lashings, because return cargoes were occasionally obtained from Goole, such as wire rope and grain. Like the boats the 'dummy bows' were iron-built, on the lines of the fore end of a keel. In the 1970s the 35 ton compartment boats are being rapidly scrapped because coal for export is increasingly handled by rail to Immingham, while a new design of compartment of 170 tons capacity has been created for internal traffic, push towed in trains of three or more (39). These work to

Ferrybridge C power station near Castleford where they are lifted 40' and tipped by a hoist of special design. They have been in service since 1965. Each is 56' x 17'3" x 9'6" deep, linked as a rigid three section unit by wires and chains kept tight by means of a screw tensioning apparatus on each boat and on the tug. Each boat has two stemposts or knees fitting into recesses in the stern of the boat ahead. Peter Brotherhood Ltd of Peterborough built some welded steel narrow compartment boats for the Grand Union in 1932, each measuring 18' x 7' x 4'6" deep with a 10 ton capacity. Four could fit in a narrow lock. They remained experimental as did a British Transport Waterways design of 1957 for the Birmingham system, with a capacity of 2 to 4 tons. The British Waterways Board have returned to the idea with their 100 ton push tow barges introduced in 1970 for traffic on the Aire & Calder, Sheffield & South Yorkshire and Trent. They are formed into trains of three, each boat being 55' long. They have hatches and are suitable for use by a barge carrying ship.

CONTAINER Boats: Boxes of materials transferred from mine or quarry to boat and from boat to terminal wharf, saved time and labour at the awkwardly sited early wharves. Worsley coal on arrival at Castlefield, Manchester had to be brought up to street level, and Brindley designed a waterwheel powered crane to do this. The coal was packed in boxes, filled within the mine. These were iron, each with a capacity of 8 cwt, the mine boats taking an average of twelve apiece. Similar boxes were used on the tub-boat canals of East Shropshire, first on the Donnington Wood, later on the Shropshire Canal to serve the Coalbrookdale tramroad. Here again the main reason must have been awkward handling; the Coalbrookdale branch of the Shropshire ending at Brierly Hill 120' above the Dale Co's tramroad, where vertical shafts were sunk. The Shropshire boxes were of iron with a capacity of up to 2 tons, coal, ironstone and limestone being the main loads. The tub-boats took four at a time. Use of boxes for the coal traffic on the Duke's and neighbouring waterways stayed until the mid twentieth century (44). The boxes were loaded by crane into narrow boats which could take up to a dozen. The boxes themselves varied in capacity, the maximum being 35 cwt. Design seems to have advanced to a hopper with iron bottom doors. Four lugs were fitted for the four lifting hooks and the doors were closed by chains round a spindle turned by a detachable crank handle. A ratchet and pawl held the doors closed and they were opened by releasing the pawl. The most common boxes measured 6' x 4'6" x 4' deep, dimensions which allowed the majority of them to lie across the boat except at the ends. The narrow boats used were called 'box boats'. Many were 68' long so that two together could enter the locks of the Manchester, Bolton & Bury Canal. This and the colliery-owned Fletcher's canal, became busy box boat waterways and the boxes remained in use as late as 1956 when traffic had dwindled to a crossing of the canal at Bury from a wharf to a works. Capacities of the M.B. & B. boxes varied from 10 to 35 cwt. On the Derby Canal's Little Eaton 'gangway' the use of tramroad waggons with demountable bodies became standard practice. They brought coal down from the pits above Belper to the canal wharf at Little Eaton where a substantial crane transferred the bodies to boats. A narrow boat could take up to five of these 33 to 37½ cwt capacity boxes. The tramroad remained open until 1908. With the modern interest in containers, their possible use on inland waterways has not been neglected. The British Transport Commission tried some small ones for the Continental trade in 1959. More promising was the British Waterways Board's development of their 100 ton push tow barges on the Trent, Aire & Calder and Sheffield & South Yorkshire which could carry containers. On the narrow canals, containers, or at least open topped boxes, have been used in recent years to carry Hardy Spicer motor car transmission components on the Birmingham system. Akin to the box is the pallet, designed for handling by a fork lift truck, and the flat, of a floor area similar to a container, lifted by a crane. The Rochdale Canal had the latter in the later nineteenth century for use with their fly-boats. Called flats or flatbottoms they were trays with four lifting eyes and carried bales of textiles and packets of perishables. They were transferred by crane from the boats to the company's horse lorries.

FLY-BOATS: ran a fast or express service to a timetable, with precedence over other craft and such privileges as permission to pass locks at night. They carried miscellaneous goods, discharging and loading at intermediate points as well as the termini. Because of the speed, demanding changes of horses, they were expensive to run, so they carried freight which paid a high toll. Also called express boats they became widespread during the early nineteenth century, their road equivalent being the light van which offered competition or co-operation, like the 60 hour Leeds to Manchester service of the 1820s, by van from Leeds to Dewsbury and fly-boat on the Calder & Hebble and Huddersfield Canals. Fly-boats, first appearing in the 1790s, were the waterways' reply to road services, but they were not ideal, carrying a small tonnage and disruptive to other traffic. In Yorkshire, road transport was allied with scheduled steam packet services on the Ouse in the years after Waterloo. The steamers carried high toll goods, including textiles, which were brought down by road. In reply, Aire & Calder carriers put on fly-boats, and the Aire & Calder improved its navigation, from 1821 themselves running fly-boats between Leeds and Selby and Wakefield and Selby to connect with the Ouse steamers. Like keels but probably narrower, the fly-boats would run with relays of horses but there was no indication that they carried double crews to work shifts, since the trips were comparatively short. Leaving Leeds every evening they travelled overnight and took 12 hours to reach Selby, catching the morning steamer to Hull which was reached in the afternoon. From 1831 fly-boats were towed by tugs on the Aire & Calder, although horses remained on the Calder & Hebble for the Aire & Calder's services. Latterly the Aire & Calder had a monopoly of fly-boat traffic on their navigation, the horse boats and tugs amplified by steam keels. The Leeds & Liverpool Canal Co. started their own carrying department in 1848 of which

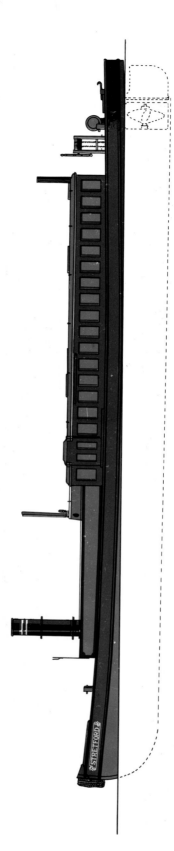

Canal Tug STRETFORD
DIMENSIONS: 61'0" x 7'7".

River Parrett Barge
LENGTH of example 53 feet.

Swift Boat CREWDSON
DIMENSIONS: 72'0" x 6'0" x 2'6".

Plate 12.

THESE screw tugs (top) were built of Low Moor Iron for the Bridgewater Canal Co., from 1875 onwards and were fitted with horizontal single **cyl.** engine exhausting to the atmosphere. The large screw was driven by bevel gears. The boiler was of locomotive type. The 25 ton capacity river barges (middle) were flat bottomed and clinker built, pointed at both ends with little parallel mid-body, the design dating from the 16th century or earlier.

Scottish swift passenger boats were introduced on the Lancaster Canal in 1833 and eventually there were four, one of which was the CREWDSON. Seats were arranged along the cabin sides and 90 passengers were carried, first class forward and second class aft, with the stewards pantry amidships. There were also seats in the open wells fore and aft. The CREWDSON (bottom) later became the inspection boat WATERWITCH II.

Glamorganshire Canal Boat
DIMENSIONS: 60'0" x 8'6".

Short Boat
LENGTH: 62 feet.

Canal Flat BRIAR
DIMENSIONS about 72 x 13.5 feet.

0   10 feet

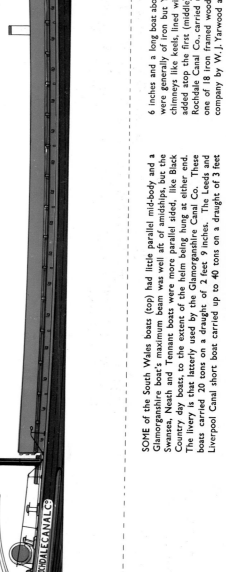

SOME of the South Wales boats (top) had little parallel mid-body and a Glamorganshire boat's maximum beam was well aft of amidships, but the Swansea, Neath and Tennant boats were more parallel sided, like Black Country day boats, to the extent of the helm being hung at either end. The livery is that latterly used by the Glamorganshire Canal Co. These boats carried 20 tons on a draught of 2 feet 9 inches. The Leeds and Liverpool Canal short boat carried up to 40 tons on a draught of 3 feet 6 inches and a long boat about 70 tons on a draught of 5 feet. Chimneys were generally of iron but Yorkshire boats had square sectioned wooden chimneys like keels, lined with metal. For extra draught a second was added atop the first (middle). BRIAR (bottom), built in 1908 for the Rochdale Canal Co., carried up to 90 tons on a 5 foot draught. She was one of 18 iron framed wooden flats built between 1906 and 1914 for the company by W. J. Yarwood and Sons Ltd., of Northwich.

fly-boats formed an important element. Competition was now with the railways and the fly-
boats were an attempt to run like railways, to timetables so that deliveries could be assured. On these longer distance craft, double manning was practised, with a crew of four
working two shifts. Horse fly-boating meant organization to deal with the changes of animal,
a chain of stables, a large reserve of horses, and horse-keepers on duty night and day.
These were beyond the average carrying company, so that the fly-boats were the preserve
of the larger carriers like Pickfords', of canal companies such as the Rochdale with their
'fly-outs' or of private carriers supported by canal companies as on the Thames & Severn.
Fly-boats remained into the days of steam and motor craft. Canal Transport had motor
fly-boats on the Leeds & Liverpool in the 1930s. Fly-boat services were not common on
the mineral carrying canals of South Wales and Scotland. There was one on the Swansea
Canal from 1835 running in connection with the Brecon Forest tramroad called the BRECON
FOREST. Her schedules coincided with steamer sailings to Liverpool. Boats carried distinguishing marks so that their precedence would not be in doubt, on the Aire & Calder the
company's boats were lettered ACN LICENSED FLY BOAT in bold white capitals on the top
strake, Leeds & Liverpool craft also bearing the legend FLY BOAT, (92). Narrow boats
carried roundels at the fore end (see narrow boats, fly-boats).

LANCASTER CANAL: Similar to the boats on the Leeds & Liverpool the broad beamed boats working on the Lancaster from Preston to Kendal measured 72' x 14'6" x 5' depth
of hold (73). They carried up to 50 tons of coal on a loaded draught of 3'4". They were
always horse drawn, occasionally with two horses, the tall towing mast being stepped at
the side of the vessel in the angle between the edge of the hold and the forward bulkhead,
and moved as required to the side nearest the tow path. All Lancaster boats had square
sterns with a wide deck for the steerer. Latterly they were all iron or steel, built on the
Ribble by W. Allsup & Sons, Preston, and towed round to the canal at Glasson Dock.
Wooden boats seem to have died out on the Lancaster Canal during the nineteenth century
probably because repair facilities were few. The hold was stiffened by two beams and
could be covered by tarpaulins to protect perishable cargoes, although latterly the boats
carried coal, bricks, tiles, roadstone, timber and limestone. The space under the fore
deck was entered by a door from the hold, and used for horse fodder and spare lines. To
gain extra headroom in the cabin aft, the deckhead was raised to form a coach roof pierced by narrow windows which the boatmen called a 'booby hatch'. Entrance was via steps
down an open companionway on the port side just abaft the hold bulkhead and in by a door
and a scuttle, the latter a removable lid fitting over the deck opening. Inside, the cabin
had the main double bed across the stern, the latter pierced by a couple of square or circular 'air holes', one each side of the stern post, and closed by slides. There was a side
bed on the starboard side with drawers under for clothes, and opposite, side lockers and
cupboards for food and crockery. A table could be set up in the middle, while the stove
was central against the hold bulkhead. Water was carried in a rectangular iron tank,
mounted on deck, generally near the tall iron chimney which was made up in two sections.
Boats were either crewed by man and wife or by two men, family boats being common on
this canal until the end of carrying in the 1940s. Boats were more decorative in the old
days with scroll work on the square stern. Lancaster boatmen favoured stars and roundels
and the name in large letters across the stern. One of the principal carriers, the Wigan
Coal & Iron Co, had red sterned boats with rows of white five pointed stars along the gunwale and across the stern, while Baines Bros, with their buff coloured sterns, had a dot
dash decoration in black and yellow along the gunwale at the fore end. There were many
small carriers on the Lancaster, some of whom were taken over by Baines. W. & J.
Turner of Preston ran a couple of Leeds & Liverpool steamers for three years in the
1930s, later returning to their own canal. Used as tugs and cargo carriers they were the
only power boats on the Lancaster apart from an experimental screw steamer in 1855 and
the ice-breaker cum steam dredger PET. The last carriers were the Ashcrofts, who took
over some of Baines' boats in 1941, and continued until 1947 with coal to Storey's mill in
Lancaster. Changeover to oil firing meant the end of all traffic.

LIGHTENING Boats: Any boat receiving goods from a carrying craft which was forced
to partly unload to make progress up a shallow river or canal. Lightening boats could be
barges or narrow boats and were regularly used on the Thames in the eighteenth century,
accompanying the larger barges. Latterly on the Basingstoke Canal, they followed the
carrying boat to her destination. On the Market Weighton Canal the trustees provided a free
lightening boat when the water was down.

LONG BOATS: See Short Boats.

MARKET and LUGGAGE Boats: Local passenger boats brought people to market, and
carried produce and parcels. One was on the Derby Canal in 1816, running between Swarkestone and Derby every Friday. Market boats were an early feature of the Gloucester &
Berkeley and stayed until about 1930. Into the 1920s there were market boats on the south
Yorkshire navigations pulled by two horses and locally called fly-boats. In South Wales,
where a proper passenger service operated only on the Tennant Canal, there ran in 1848 a
thrice weekly market boat between Cardiff and Aberdare. Scotland linked the swift boats
with secondary craft. The Forth & Clyde started them in 1783 and a nineteenth century illustration shows a beamy bluff bowed craft like the cargo scow, with cabin accommodation
fore and aft and space for goods amidships. They were also called luggage boats. In Ireland market boats travelled on the Grand and Royal for the farming population and their
produce. On the Royal they went at night no faster than 4 mph, to leave the day clear for
the packets. On the Shannon steamers towed cargo boats of 60 to 70 tons capacity called
'luggage boats', although there were boats carrying passengers' luggage towed behind the

passenger steamers. Many market boats did not carry passengers or only unofficially, but produce and parcels like the carrier's cart on the roads. There were market boats of this type on the Beverley Beck in the early eighteenth century and in the nineteenth on the Wey & Arun Canal which may have carried a few passengers to Guildford on market day. The Bridgewater ran a parcels, perishables and farm produce boat between Runcorn and Manchester until the 1939-45 War, she was an ordinary narrow boat loaded to about 15 tons.

MINE Boats, Bridgewater Canal: Designed to work in the 46 mile Worsley underground system and built with oak side planking and elm bottoms, they are probably unchanged since the 1760s. Existing examples, used as maintenance boats before the system was sealed off in 1969, measure 36' x 4'6" x 4' deep, able to carry 8 tons on a 2'6" draught, although there were larger 55' boats able to carry 10 tons and narrower shallower tub-boats only 19" deep limited to 2 tons. They are double ended craft of square cross section with substantial knee timbers unprotected by inner shearing and without a keelson. They were built at Worsley, those for the lower level being sent vertically down a shaft which opened out sufficiently at the bottom to allow the boat to be launched horizontal. Those for the upper level entered by an adit from a boatyard just outside and those for the main level, between upper and lower, from the delph or basin.   Propulsion was by legging against the roof in the smaller side arm tunnels, but in the main line, empty boats were drawn along by means of a hook secured by a line to a canvas harness worn by the boatman (129).   The hook could be attached to a series of ring bolts in the roof at 8'6" intervals, and the boatman walked down his craft, to pull it towards and past the ring, unhooking at the right moment.   These boats had no rudders and for manoeuvring into the side arms, wooden hand grips were provided.   Loaded boats were marshalled into trains in the main line of the main level and flushed out by a slow current created by sluices at the entrances.   Although Phillips the historian says coal was loaded from 10 cwt tubs which tipped into the boats from a stage over the canal, it seems that 8 cwt iron containers were widely used.   These were stowed in the tunnel boats which worked through to Manchester in short trains of 5 or 6 pulled by a single horse and steered by a sweep.   No doubt also the containers were transhipped in the delph.

Canal PASSENGER (GIG or SWIFT) Boats: On the Bridgewater, passenger boats were started by the Duke in 1767 and extended as the canal pushed towards Runcorn.   At first they ran between Manchester and Altrincham, later in 1769 to Lymm.   Initially they were converted barges, but in 1774 two packet boats were built with three cabins for three classes and refreshment bar.   They were slow, taking 8 hours for the Manchester-Runcorn trip.   The neighbouring Manchester, Bolton & Bury started a passenger service in 1796, operating their own craft which had a 'state' cabin amidships and second class aft.   Meals could be prepared and eaten on the move, an impossibility in a road coach, and were available on the Duke's packets, although stops were made at inns, for example at Lymm. The Leeds & Liverpool had passenger services between Liverpool and Wigan as soon as the canal was opened in 1774 and these continued until the late 1840s.   The Leeds & Liverpool Canal Co, who ran the packets, remained conservative in the 1830s, sticking to an old design of boat when other operators were using the Scottish light swift boats.   Canals of the English Midlands and the South never developed passenger services to the extent of the North-West, except for short distances, and even then often late in the canal age when in 1843 swift boats were available between Birmingham and Wolverhampton.   There were services from the later 1790s on the Derby Canal and from 1797 on the Cromford Canal between Cromford and Nottingham.   Passenger boats seemed more successful when linked to river services.   At Runcorn the Bridgewater packets met the sail and later steam packets to Liverpool.   An operational snag were locks, at Runcorn for instance the boats stopped at the top of the locks and people had to walk down with their luggage.   Later English canal passenger boat design was based on developments in Scotland.   Wales was never a great centre for passenger services, they were only run regularly on the Tennant Canal from 1827 to 1857 between Port Tennant near Swansea and Neath, apart from the much later excursion services between Newmarton and Llangollen on the Welsh line of the Shropshire Union started in the 1880s.   The Forth & Clyde started a passenger service in 1809 between Port Dundas in Glasgow and Lock 16 near Falkirk whence a coach ran to Edinburgh.   In 1819 they put a large iron boat VULCAN into service, 63' long, for 200 passengers.   The services were improved in 1822 when the Edinburgh & Glasgow Union Canal opened. Through passenger working was possible between Glasgow and Edinburgh, although some services involved a change of boats at Falkirk, people having to walk down the Union's locks to the Forth & Clyde.   Night boats with sleeping accommodation were started in 1824, named 'hoolits' because their warning trumpets sounded like the hoot of an owl.   There were passenger boats too on the Monkland, from 1807 on the Aberdeenshire and on the Crinan and Caledonian.   These last two had steam passenger boats from the start of the services, not limited to the canal, although the Crinan also had horse drawn track boats.   On the Glasgow, Paisley & Johnstone Canal passenger boats reached their zenith.   In 1830 William Houston of Johnstone Castle a member of the canal's committee, arranged trials of a gig as used in rowing matches.   This, carrying 10 or 12 passengers and pulled by one horse achieved 12 mph.   She was followed by a gig shaped boat designed by himself, 60' x 4'6" beam only, with a draught of 10".   Intended for 36 passengers, she carried up to 50 in service and on trial this pencil like craft attained an average 10.8 mph when planing.   By 1835 other boats of gig shape followed, built of iron, 70' x 6' x 1'10" depth.   Pulled by two horses they cut the time from Glasgow to Paisley from 1½ hours to 1 hour 11 minutes, with only 45 minutes back to Glasgow.   90 passengers were carried in two classes, the best forward, the second best aft, with luggage compartments at each end.   Lightness was the key to success, the overall roof being of cotton spread over thin ribs.   The Forth

& Clyde followed the Paisley experiments with some trials of their own in July 1830. They had the idea of twin hulls which would even out the surge and contain much of the turbulence between the hulls. First, two rowing gigs were lashed together and then a lightly timbered twin hulled passage boat was built called the SWIFT. She was 60' x 8'6" wide over the two hulls, with room for 50 to 60 passengers. Empty she weighed 27 cwt. The trials were extensive and it was found that whereas at 6 to 7 mph a wave was created, sometimes flooding the towpath, above this the surge greatly diminished even at the maximum 14 mph, with two horses at full gallop. Three horses were generally used for the trials and the boat averaged 8 to 9 mph between Glasgow and Edinburgh. Horses were exchanged for a man worked paddle wheel set between the hulls, a successful modification which led the Forth & Clyde to order a passenger steamer from the Manchester engineer William Fairbairn. This was the LORD DUNDAS completed in 1831, twin hulled of iron, 68' x 11'6" and 4'6" deep, with a 9' diameter paddle wheel between the hulls and room for 100 to 150 passengers. A central paddle wheel, although creating turbulence in the middle of the canal, left the banks scarcely disturbed. English canal companies were impressed with the Houston designed craft called swift or gig boats. One was brought down from Scotland in 1833 for trials on the Oxford Canal where it achieved 11.8 mph. Four English firms paid for the trials, the Oxford, the Wilts. & Berks, Grand Junction and Kennet & Avon, the last named buying the boat, called the SWALLOW and running her between Bath and Bradford-on-Avon. She was of wrought iron with two classes in the long cabin, an open foredeck and an open cockpit for the steerer. The Bridgewater introduced iron boats of Scottish design in 1843 which cut the Manchester-Runcorn times to $3\frac{1}{2}$ hours from the previous seven or eight. The first swift boat on the Lancaster was the WATER WITCH. She was put into service in 1833, and reduced the Preston-Kendal times from ten to eight hours. By 1839 three more had joined the fleet, the SWIFTSURE, SWALLOW and CREWDSON, Plate 12, and competed successfully with the parallel railway. The 50 passengers sat along the sides looking inwards, the first and second class cabins separated by a steward's pantry. There were seats too in the open at the fore end and in the open cockpit aft. The boats were 72' overall with a well raked stem but only 6' wide. Two fast passenger boats were put on the Knottingley-Goole canal. They were built in 1830 at Wells, Norfolk and named in that accession year WILLIAM IV and QUEEN ADELAIDE. They lasted until 1834, succumbing to steam packet and then railway competition. They were twin hulled. A northern waterway which concentrated on passenger traffic was the Carlisle Canal who in 1825 secured the BAILLIE NICOL JARVIE second-hand from the Edinburgh & Glasgow Union. She ran until replaced by a Houston boat, the ARROW, in 1834 followed by another the SWALLOW in 1838. Second-hand boats from Scotland appeared on other English canals when Scottish railway competition bit hard. The Paisley Canal gave up the packets in 1843 and some were sold to John Boulton who started a service on the Ashton Canal between the railway station at Guide Bridge into Ashton. Boulton also ran ex-Paisley boats from Macclesfield, later from the bottom of Marple locks to Dukinfield station. This was the final phase of regular canal passenger operations, to feed the trains, except for the steam packet service on the Gloucester & Berkeley which lasted until 1932, because roads are few. But canal excursions were already popular from Sunday School outings in swept out narrow boats, 'scholar boating', to the steamers on the Forth & Clyde and Crinan Canals. The Forth & Clyde 'Queen' steamers ran between Port Dundas and Craigmarloch from 1893 to 1939, while MacBrayne's (formerly Hutcheson's) LINNET operated on the Crinan between 1866 and 1929. Ireland used canal passenger boats to provide transport in an underdeveloped country. The Grand's chain of hotels was intended for overnight stops but in the 1800s 'fly-boats' were introduced which ran day and night. The schedules were improved when swift boats were introduced after 1834, able to reach 10 mph. On the Royal Canal similar boats were running in the 1840s but travellers complained that cabins were scarcely wide enough to turn in. Two or three horses in tandem were the usual, the last being ridden by a postilion, jockey, or in Scotland a 'riding boy'. The line was secured to a timber head at the boat's fore end. The horses were trotted or galloped on the swift boat services, the rider ducking under bridges, and there were frequent changes of animals, those on the Lancaster were replaced every five miles or so, or eleven times between Preston and Kendal. Passenger embarkation points were often roofed, with waiting rooms and a ticket office, for example on the Bridgewater at Castlefield. Once aboard the passengers were sometimes well entertained, not only with food and drink, but with a string band on the Kennet & Avon's 'Scotch' boat, while on the Scottish boats they could hire backgammon tables and buy newspapers. Crews on the Grand Canal boats were lavish; a captain, a steerer, a stop man, a boy, a cook (usually the captain's wife) a barmaid and several stewardesses. The captains of these Irish boats wore a blue frock coat and scarlet waistcoat and it was usual for the postillions to be uniformed, a black cape and scarlet jacket on the Paisley, a red jacket on the Bridgewater and a yellow cape and blue jacket on the Grand Junction. These boys carried horns to warn other boats which dropped their lines allowing the packet the towpath side. Bridgewater packets carried a symbolic curved knife on the stempost.

River PASSENGER Boats: Passengers were probably carried on the Yorkshire Ouse and the Great Ouse in the Middle Ages. The vessels would be sailing craft and they probably carried cargo too. There were sailing passenger craft on the Trent, possibly the Shannon and possibly on the Mersey & Irwell, although the Mersey & Irwell's own services which started in 1807 were by horse drawn boats. These followed the style of canal packets if the river was sufficiently canalized for their safety (40). Thus the Don in the 1840s had two iron swift boats called aquabuses and built in Scotland. The Mersey & Irwell ones were pulled by two or three horses, two of the three being ridden by red jacketed jockeys. The leading jockey had a horn and on May Day his horse was decorated with ribbons and bells. The team was kept going at a fast trot or even a gallop with right of way at locks. Slower services were run by boats of more barge like dimensions, 66' x 15' with two or more horses, ridden by jockey boys. They worked between Salford and Warrington, trotting downstream and walking up. They also took light goods, and would stop at any landing stage to suit passengers. The most unusual horse drawn swift boat was introduced by C.W. Williams on the Limerick canal, the canalized section of the Shannon between Killaloe and Limerick. Called the NONSUCH she appeared sometime after 1830 with hinged bow and stern sections. These were necessary because of the locks, Williams appreciating that a long slender craft was essential for speed, but the 74'9" locks of the Limerick canal did not allow much scope, hence his unusual idea. Following the pioneers, steam was quickly taken up. In 1813 there were trials on the Aire at Leeds of a steam packet, the EXPERIMENT, intended for the Norwich & Lowestoft Navigation where she commenced a Yarmouth-Norwich service in 1814, while that same year there was a passenger and luggage boat on the Severn. These early steamers were only practicable as tugs or passenger boats; the space demanded by their engines, boilers and bunkers ruled out any worthwhile cargo capacity, except for small, valuable, consignments. Steam paddle packets appeared on the Trent in 1817 between Gainsborough and Nottingham, on the Yorkshire Ouse in 1816 with the WATERLOO between Hull, Selby and York, and on the Great Ouse between King's Lynn and Cambridge by about 1824. There was the iron paddler MARQUIS WELLESLEY on the Shannon in 1826, operated by the engineer John Grantham. In Ulster the first passenger steamer seems to have started in 1842 on the Upper Bann and Lough Neagh. She was the GRAND JUNCTION which ran a service connecting with the trains at Portadown. The iron LADY LANSDOWNE built in 1833 by William Laird at Birkenhead, measuring 133' x 17' x 9'6" was possibly the largest steamer ever on the Shannon and too big to leave Lough Derg. More typical was the 80' LADY BURGOYNE which ran on the river up to Athlone. With the arrival of the railways, steam packet services tended to decline from the 1840s, though the 150 passenger stern wheeler JACK SHARP was put on by the Mersey & Irwell in 1838. On the Yorkshire Ouse passenger services lasted until the 1870s, while the Trent retained passenger craft on the lower reaches until the period between the wars, to serve the more isolated villages. On the other hand paddle and screw excursion steamers continued to be built for the Shannon, Thames and Yare among others, Salter's of Oxford starting their Oxford-Kingston steamer service in 1888. They remained on the Shannon until 1914, and excursion sailings on Lough Ree have been revived by Coras Iompair Eireann since 1954 with two motor vessels the ST. BRENDAN and ST. CIARAN. Salter's maintain their Thames craft although their last steam propelled vessel ceased to run in 1966. On the Yare the double ended screw steamer RESOLUTE built in 1903 was withdrawn in 1969.

PLEASURE Boats: Growth of pleasure cruising is a post mid-1950s phenomenon. Lack of commercial traffic is one reason, others are more money, and leisure. The economic depression of the 1930s was not conducive to holidays of this sort, although there was a boat hire firm on the Shropshire Union, founded in 1935 by Mr G.F. Wain at Rowton Bridge near Chester. In the 1930s moreover, information about the inland waterways was very limited. Certain rivers had a long record of pleasure boating, but the canals were a different world, although their Acts had often granted riparian owners toll free use of the canal bounding their property for their pleasure craft. The attraction of rivers and canals was their isolation and the great distances one could go. Because so much mileage is through remote districts, early pleasure cruisers of the 1950s found a new world of quiet. The past tense is used advisedly here, because this peace is going. The canal and river mileage has proved insufficient and moves are being made to re-open derelict and abandoned waterways. Pleasure boating is favoured by the ease with which a canal may be navigated. It is different on the rivers. Boats are hired or owned and special hulls have been evolved for canal work. They are subject to the limitations imposed by locks, bridges and depth. Strength is a prime need because of the inevitable bumping, while the hull sides should not be too flared otherwise they will always be marked by the lock sides. Early pleasure voyagers in the 1900s like George Westall used an open launch in which he camped, but during the 1960s there was a revolution in cruiser design. Planked hulls had already given way to plywood, now fibreglass came to triumph over both, as it needs little maintenance. On the other hand it is easily holed, as is plywood. Many are attracted by the protection afforded by a welded steel hull. British Transport Water-

129. Mine boats; working an empty train in the Worsley underground system.

ways shortened a steel narrow boat for their first hire craft in 1956 and followed it up with other shortened steel hulls. They were successful and in 1966 a new steel hull was made specially for a private pleasure craft. The idea caught on and soon boatbuilders were in competition for a growing market. Hulls of varied shapes and sizes are offered to the public. Narrow boats have been converted, following on Mr Rolt's CRESSY. They are spacious, but maintenance is a problem, particularly of the wooden ones. Some have been shortened. Leeds & Liverpool short boats have also been converted and even a few steel motor craft in Yorkshire. Motive power is equally varied. One couple have been happy to bowhaul their house boat, outboards proliferate, there are a few steamers, the rare horse boat, and many petrol and diesel units. There have been canoes on the canals since a pioneer trip from Manchester to London in 1869. They can be carried round locks and with camping equipment large mileages can be covered, remembering that for safety, canoes are prohibited in tunnels. Canoes can navigate waterways not normally accessible, like the Montgomeryshire, since weired locks and culverts are no obstacles. Apart from boats one can hire, some craft operate as mobile hotels. The first, a narrow boat, appeared in the late 1940s, and in the 1950s British Transport Waterways had a wide boat on the Trent, Fossdyke and Witham. Hotel boats have proved a success, recent examples being built on narrow boat lines. Some operate as a pair, motor and butty, others as single motors. They carry a maximum of twelve passengers. Camping boats have enjoyed a growing vogue, for youth clubs, and others. Finally come the day trip motor boats. Most of these too are narrow boats, although a Bridgewater operator uses an ex-Amsterdam water bus. The 1968 Transport Act recast most of the open mileage as 'cruiseways' to be maintained to 'cruiseway' standard. The history of the authorities interest in the pleasure boater dates back to the mid 1950s with the publication of cruising booklets and the first British Waterways hire boat began operating at Chester in 1956. British Transport Waterways had a stand at the National Boat Show from 1955. In 1957 tolls were replaced by annual licences, an increasing item in the revenue of the British Waterways Board, amplified by mooring fees and rent from marinas and dry docks.

SHORT and LONG BOATS, LEEDS & LIVERPOOL CANAL.   Horse Drawn Boats: The Leeds & Liverpool was intended for Yorkshire keels since it joined the Aire & Calder, but traders on the canal created a type with keel affinities which became the 'short boat', Plate 12, short enough to fit the 62' locks between Wigan and Leeds, on the Rufford branch and at first on the Leigh branch. The locks between Wigan and Liverpool could hold 72' boats, having been built to take the flats of the Douglas Navigation, so that another canal craft appeared, the 'long boat'. After 1822, when the Leigh branch locks were extended for 72' craft, these could reach Manchester and the Bridgewater Canal to Runcorn. Both long and short boats were of the same beam, not exceeding 14'3", built on barge or keel like lines, round bilged with all the planking running longitudinally, held in shape by frames and floors (130). Although open, the decks fore and aft were linked by narrow side decks, with the accommodation below deck. A short boat could carry up to 40 tons of coal on a draught of 3'6", a long boat 70 tons on a draught of 5' or so. Probably the square stern was universal in the earlier Leeds & Liverpool boats of both types, lasting until recent years (18). The round stern was used for the Leeds & Liverpool Canal Co's fly-boats. The bow was bluff, with a stem bar flanked by guards, including a top one or rubbing iron which passed the full length of the hull. Very many Leeds & Liverpool boats were run by families when horse hauled, the family in the larger after cabin, and a mate living forward. On deck aft was a little wooden kennel shaped ventilator which could be moved and replaced by a metal cover to exclude air. The dog kennel which boatmen kept on the stern deck was often a store. A 5 gallon water barrel laid on its side in chocks was also on the stern deck. emptied by a dipper, together with a 'proven' tub. Chimneys fore and aft were up to 6' high, clearing the bridges but detachable. Generally they were iron, in two sections pushed together, but Yorkshire boats copied keels and had square sectioned wooden chimneys tapering in to the top. They were metal lined and fitted over a cast iron base. For extra draught one wooden chimney would be sat atop the other. Three sheeting rails made up in sections were laid parallel along the length of the hold, supported on forked iron stanchions which held the ends of each section. The stanchions or stands were socketed into the beams across the hold. The centre sheeting rail or middle plank was higher than the other two. Joining the headledges or end coamings were side coamings to which the side cloths or covers were nailed, or in iron or steel boats made fast by battens and wedges. Fore and aft were the end covers, generally nailed to the headledges. The sequence of sheeting up was to spread the end covers over the sheeting rails, then lay the side covers, three a side, kept taut by lashings across the rails from one cover to its opposite and finally the three top covers held down by strings to cleats along the coamings. Leeds & Liverpool coal boats had an open hold with the two fixed beams. All craft were provided with timber heads fore and aft and some had rails on each quarter across which the spare tiller would be laid. For the steerer to see over a high load, a steering plank was laid across the rails. Centrally against the bow beam in the hold was stepped the lutchet or post into which the towing mast fitted, the bottom of the lutchet being socketed into the keelson and the top held by a through bolt from the beam. Leeds & Liverpool fly-boats had square section lutchets like the Yorkshire keels, but other boats an iron tube. The mast had an iron pin or 'nib' for the eye of the hauling lines and was pierced with holes for a second pin, so that the height could be adjusted. The fly-boats always hauled from the mast in the lutchet, but other craft only used it when working up locks with a block line to get a double purchase with the horse, a pulley block being attached to the masthead. Three other masts were carried, simple tapered poles, a long one of 9' or 10' and two short of 6'6". They fitted in sockets in the shutts or floor boards and through

130. Short and long boats on the Leeds & Liverpool Canal.
A square sterned long horse boat passes a short motor
boat and her tow.

brackets at deck level, either side of the forward headledge or at each end of the bow beam nearest the towpath. The taller mast was useful for clearing the line over another boat, although officially it had to be dropped underneath, and the short masts were for an empty boat. Boats were built with oak frames, keel and keelson, and pitch pine planking. Construction differed between the Lancashire and Yorkshire ends of the canal, the Yorkshire builders making a bluffer bow because they gave less shape to their floor timbers. Yorkshire boats often had hawse timbers either side of the stempost, like keels, but no hawse holes since there was no anchor. Iron boats were introduced in the later nineteenth century and steel between the wars for motor boats. The last horse boat, H. & R. Ainscough's PARBOLD, built in 1936, was steel; she was a 'long boat' like that company's fleet of steel motor boats and dumb barges which had coamings and hatch boards.

GLOSSARY OF LEEDS & LIVERPOOL SHORT and LONG BOAT TERMS: BEAMS: there were two fixed beams in the hold, the bow beam and the stern beam. A loose beam could be fitted between them. Some boatmen towed off the stern beam if the wind was tending to push the boat into the towpath side, thus keeping the bow out. FAN SHAFT; with an 'S' shaped double hook it was used for clearing the propeller. Otherwise one short and two long shafts were carried, called stowers in Yorkshire. LOCK TILLER; shorter than the normal wooden horse boat tiller which could be up to 9' long, also of wood, but was short enough not to need unshipping in locks. PROVEN TUB; the box shaped provender tub for the horse feed on the stern deck, measuring some 3' x 4' x 3' high. It had a lid although the top was partly boarded over, because the box was tipped on its side to mix the feed. RUDDER LINE; a painted chain or decorative cotton line from the rudder head to the end of the blade, the cotton rope sometimes being braided. SCUTTLE; the hatch to the cabin space fore and aft, which fitted like a lid over the opening, neither slid nor hinged. It was held down by hasps and staples and inside by bolts. SPARE SIDE; the open bed on top of a locker on the other side of the cabin from the bed hole. WIGANER; Lancashire and Cheshire description of a long Leeds & Liverpool boat which could work between Liverpool, Wigan, Leigh, Manchester and on the Bridgewater to Runcorn, but not up the Wigan locks and beyond.

Steamers: Because of the success of steam tugs introduced in 1871, the Leeds & Liverpool decided on the building of new steam fly-boats, and in 1880 four were ordered for the company's carrying fleet. They were round sterned and narrower than the horse boats, with a 13' beam. The engines and boilers were designed to be as compact as possible. Most of the engines were vee-type but there were also horizontal and inverted ones. Compounds were almost universal, the vee-engines of the fly-boats and most of the long distance craft being four cylinder tandems. The boilers were vertical with Field water tubes protruding into the firebox, and a single flue up to the chimney, but there were horizontal examples. Cylinders were of 6" or 8" stroke, and propellers 3'3" diameter, for low revolutions. The power plants took up 10 tons of cargo space, leaving a payload of about 30 tons so steamers generally towed two or three dumb barges. Engines were non condensing and exhausted up the funnel, the steam passing through a feed water heater on the way. Coke was usually burnt and working pressure was 150 lbs. psi. Controls passed to the deck, the engineman attending to the fire, water level, ash disposal, lubrication and cylinder drains. Because of bridges and tunnels the funnel was hinged and could be quickly pulled down by a rod. The four crew lived forward (93). Many steamers were wooden short boats for the fly traffic, and the canal company themselves had the largest number, but they and others had long ones also. Steamers remained on the Leeds & Liverpool until the early 1950s, one of the last operators being James Gore & Sons Ltd, of Bingley, by then worked singly.

Motor Boats: The Leeds & Liverpool Company experimented with a motor in an ex-steamer before the 1914-18 War. One of the early post war motors was the INA, a wooden square sterned short horse boat, owned by the Clayton Carrying Co, of Morley near Leeds. She was given a rounded stern to improve propeller flow and equipped with a

13 hp Kelvin engine. To keep the propeller immersed a water ballast tank was fitted aft. G.E. Ramsey of Shipley began to specialize in motor boat work in 1921, fitting a 30 hp Widdop oil engine into a short boat owned by the Burnley Brick & Lime Co. The following year they built four motor boats for Leeds & Liverpool carriers. The early Widdops were semi-diesels, but later came the 24 hp single cylinder full diesel, which became standard for many of the craft. Motor boats had a bigger cargo capacity, than steamers, up to 45 tons, so it was usual for them to work singly, although they could tow. This was common in the coal trade where hauls were often short and limited to one level. Because accommodation was now moved forward, family boating died out on the Leeds & Liverpool and the motors ran with two men or even one. If a family was carried in a motor, the mate had to sleep in the engine room. During the 1930s the newly formed Canal Transport embarked on a boatbuilding programme, ordering steel boats from W.J. Yarwood, Isaac Pimblott and John Harker, with 24 hp single cylinder Widdop diesels, They were named after rivers. More craft followed, wooden and steel (76). Finally in 1952-3 came three high tensile steel boats built by Harland & Wolff of North Woolwich, designed to carry 10 per cent more cargo since they were of lighter construction and had a beam of 14'6" with a 4' laden draught. Other steel short boats were built between the wars, for Ranks to carry grain from Merseyside to mills at Blackburn. Later in the 1950s these went over to coal for power stations at Blackburn and Wigan. Between Liverpool, Wigan and Manchester a larger class of motor boat operated, 72' x 14'5" with a 60 ton capacity. Again during the 1930s and 40s W.J. Yarwood built a number for H. & R. Ainscough Ltd, the Burscough and Parbold millers. These were all steel and unlike the short boats, had high hatch coamings and hatch boards held down by cloths, battens and wedges. Ainscough's boats carried grain from the Liverpool and Birkenhead docks, up to their mills, so were allowed across the Mersey, with a tug in attendance.

SOUTH WALES: They were mostly day boats, for hauls were short and the family boat rare, although boatmen would stay away from home several days at a time. So much of the traffic was mineral that most of the boats were open, but cloths could be spread over cargo likely to be spoiled. The South Wales boat came to a point at both ends, with a slight tumblehome to her top strakes (50). Construction followed narrow boat lines, flat bottoms of elm, oak side planking and oak knees. Glamorganshire boats had five planks a side, Monmouthshire and Brecknock & Abergavenny boats four. An iron boat was built experimentally in 1810 for the Glamorganshire by the Dowlais Iron Co, but the majority were wood. Glamorganshire boats were provided with two rubbing strakes called fenders on each side, running the whole length of the hull. Cabins were usual on the longer haul boats, on the Glamorganshire, Monmouthshire and Brecknock & Abergavenny, but uncommon on the Neath, Swansea and Tennant. The stove was forward on the centre line against the bulkhead, flanked by cupboards, while the two berths were along each side tapering aft as the cabin narrowed. Chimneys of cast iron were square and latterly very short because of bridges lowered by mining subsidence. Haulage was by horse except when the Glamorganshire in 1893 put a 20 ton capacity steam barge into service. Named the BUTE, for the canal was then owned by the Marquess of Bute, she was iron, built by W. Allsup & Sons of Preston and was used as a tug and ice-breaker. Horses pulled from a mast stepped in the keelson and lashed to the forward movable beam in the hold, the middle beam only being fixed, with another portable one aft. The mast was some 6' long, with an iron ferrule at the top for the towline. Horse fodder was kept forward under the deck, with an access door from the hold, the cargo being held back by a temporary planked bulkhead. The crew stowed their provisions in a similar space right aft which they called the larder. Decoration was limited. Latterly the carrying fleet operated by the Glamorganshire Canal Co had a light blue colour scheme for the cabin ends and tops and a blue strip on the gunwale round the steering well. The remainder was black. On the cabin sides were gable-end shaped wooden boards on which the iron plate bearing the boat's gauging number surmounted by the initials G. C. Co, was secured, Plate 13. Another iron plate bore the registration number under the Canal Boats Acts, both were protected from the rain by the roof of the gable. According to a boatman's model in the National Museum of Wales, some boats had a lozenge painted on the top strakes each side fore and aft, quartered in contrasting colours, in addition there might be a pair of four petalled flowers on the cabin side looking like ship's propellers, while the rudder post could be red with a band of blue. One company, the Star Fuel Co. of Blackweir near Cardiff had a star painted on or cut into the gunwale. Two was the usual crew. They lived in the canalside villages, on the Glamorganshire at Tongwynlais, Nantgarw and Treforest. Building and repair docks were likewise scattered up and down the canals, there were at one time ten on the Glamorganshire and the Aberdare. The last docks in use on the Glamorganshire were in the Cardiff area, including the canal company's at Gabalfa. Called the Cambrian yard, it built the company boats and did the last repairs in the early 1940s. While Glamorganshire Canal Co. boats were known by their gauging numbers, others owned by the hobblers or owner boatmen had a name on the forward bulkhead of the cabin. On other canals named boats were common, the name being cut in the top plank. Glamorganshire, Monmouthshire and Brecknock & Abergavenny boats measured some 60' x 8'6" carrying 20 tons, on 2'9" draught. Neath and Tennant boats were 60'x 9', loading a maximum of 24 tons, on 2'9". Swansea boats were 65' x 7'6", carrying 20 tons, on 2'9". Some Swansea boats were sent by the GWR, as owners of both, to the Monmouthshire, and the GWR sent South Wales boats as maintenance craft to the Kennet & Avon.

TUB-BOATS: They may have been used as early as 1720 on Parnall's Canal in a Cornish tin mine, only 6' x 4' x 1' deep, suited to small canals and inclined planes, and they remained a favourite of the West Country. Their advantage was cheapness and flexibility, each boat need only be quite small and shallow, but coupled in a train they could carry a substantial tonnage, behind one horse. Moreover a tub-boat need never be winded. In the West Country these merits added up to projects for rural waterways to carry sea sand inland for use as fertilizer. Robert Fulton seems to have been the first to propose wheeled boats to save carriages on inclined planes and when James Green completed the Bude Canal in 1825 wheeled boats were used, 20' x 5'6" x 2'9" deep carrying 4 to 5 tons of sand or coal. In 1970 one of these craft was recovered from the canal at Bude. It had cast iron 14" diameter wheels fitted within the beam of the boat, to reduce damage to canal puddling. In industrial East Shropshire tub-boat traffic was heavy and continuous. The Shropshire Canal and Shrewsbury boats measured about 20' x 6'4" x 2'9" deep carrying 5 tons on 2' draught. In the pounds between the planes tub-boats were made into trains of 20 behind a single horse, manoeuvred by a shaft from the bank. Construction was simple, with cross boarded bottoms reinforced by a keelson and on an average three plank sides and ends held by wooden knees, later iron, with stout posts at the four corners, protected on their outside by angled plates. Some tub-boats had the sides partially built up with an extra board, and some were iron. They were coupled by chains passing round timber heads at each end. On the two mile Cyfarthfa Canal near Merthyr Tydfil, the boats were iron, bow hauled by one man in trains of up to six and steered by a shaft wielded by a second man or even a girl in the leading boat. They measured about 14'8" x 8'2" across. Tub-boats were also used on the Kidwelly & Llanelly Canal's extension engineered in the late 1830s. In 1836 the Grand Western Canal was extended from Lowdwells to Taunton as a tub-boat line, designs of lift and plane allowing for 8 ton boats, 26' x 6'6", as did the Chard. In Ulster Ducart's Canal made use of small tub-boats to bring coal down to Coalisland via three inclined planes. At the basin the boats were tipped to discharge into sea going vessels. See also Compartment Boats.

FERRIES: There are rowing boats called 'cock boats' sculled over the stern as public ferries on the Manchester Ship Canal, successors to those in Mersey & Irwell days. Some were large enough for a waggon and horses (64). The Thames had 'flats' to take horses and carts; for example at Hampton Ferry. On the Severn at Arley above Bewdley the last of the current worked ferries plied until 1972. There were others, at Ironbridge and Coalport taking carts and horses as well as people. The swift stream of Severn allowed these boats to swing across the current pendulum wise from a rope upstream of the landing points. This was led to a pulley at the masthead and down to the deck, so that the ferryman could adjust it to suit the water level. His main job was to handle the large rudder to work the boat across the current. The Arley craft was finely shaped forward but with a wide square stern, to stem the current, the bow pointing upstream. Aft there was a shelter cabin with a stove. Slow Fenland rivers relied on chain and rope worked ferries, with a windlass on the bank or on the boat. A more primitive type, whereby a rope was stretched across the river, the ferryman pulling himself across hand over hand, is described by H.R. Robertson in his "Life on the Upper Thames" of 1875, used for people and boat horses. It was a punt, the rope passing through vertical guide rollers and kept tensioned by a handspike windlass on the bank. The chain ferry developed from the simple 'grinds' on the Cam to the powered vehicular ferries of Lake Windermere and the Clyde. Ferries replaced fords when rivers were improved for navigation. The horse towing paths were forced to cross from side to side by the dictates of landowners. They could make use of existing bridges, but sometimes had to have their own ferry. There were boat horse ferries on the Mersey & Irwell, at Calamanco lock near Irlam and at Holmes Bridge lock, used when the plank footbridge was submerged. The Aire & Calder had boat horse ferries at Castleford and Wakefield and there was one at Broad Cut on the Calder & Hebble crossing the Calder. It could take one horse at a time, tethered to an upright stake in the boat. In Ireland the canal ferry is common because accommodation bridges are scarce. Thus on the Grand, isolated farms in the Bog of Allen have their punts for shifting stock, and there are private punts and rowing boats at many English canalside dwellings.

FLATS:

BRIDGEWATER CANAL: Flats and Lighters: Much traffic was handled since the Duke's day by barges, either flats, which being decked could go out into the Mersey to Liverpool, or canal lighters. At his death in 1803 the Duke owned 60 flats and 46 lighters, all called 'dukers', the name applied to craft, from a tug to a narrow boat, owned and operated by the Bridgewater Canal authorities, the Duke's trustees, the Bridgewater Navigation Co, or the Bridgewater Department of the Manchester Ship Canal Co. Modern steel grain barges both dumb and powered were still known as dukers. Before 1914 the flats operated by the Bridgewater numbered up to 490, plus lighters, the latter just numbered. The duker flats came in three sizes, the large Birkenhead, River Mersey craft, too big to go up Runcorn locks, the Preston Brook or Preston, and the smaller Manchester flats. None were really small, the minimum length being about 71' x 14'3" beam, and the capacity on the canal 80 tons on a 4' draught (131). The most a flat could take was 90 tons on a draught of 5'. The open holded lighters were about the same length and breadth but drew less water, carrying 50 tons at 3'6". Because of their estuary work flats carried an anchor windlass and anchor navigation lights and life-buoys. Many of the dukers, flats and lighters had the old square stern which was usual before about 1850, later vessels had rounded sterns. They were built at the Duke's dock at Worsley carried on by the trustees, and later by Rathbone Bros. of Stretford. None of the dukers were family boats but were run by a crew of two who kept with the same vessel all the time, taking pride in her upkeep, the NEVA being one of the smartest between the wars. Horse towing seems to have

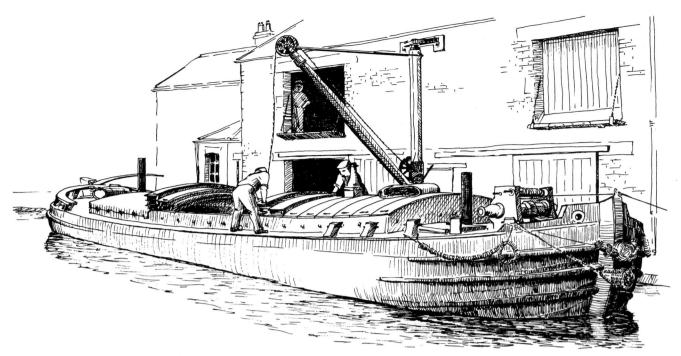

131. Unloading a duker (Bridgewater) flat at the
warehouse by the top of Runcorn locks.

been done from the timber heads forward. Two horses were needed between Runcorn and Preston Brook for the larger Preston flats, but one was sufficient on to Manchester. The tugs called 'little packets' or 'Jack Sharps' handled four flats on the canal, both tugs and horses meeting the flats at the top of Runcorn locks. Coamings and hawse timbers were painted a dull red, replaced after 1939 by the later green and yellow although the power barges had red top strakes. The name was carved in the stem and stern rails. Apart from flats and lighters, there were floats, barges decked for their full length to carry deck cargoes only, like logs and lengths of steel. Wooden hulls were universal in the duker fleet until after the 1939-45 War when steel barges, both powered and dumb, were ordered from W.J. Yarwood's and Isaac Pimblott's at Northwich. The dumb had a much increased cargo capacity of 114 tons on a draught of 5'6".

MERSEY: Canal Flats: The flats of Lancashire and Cheshire were a large family, some sailing, some dumb, some coastal, some river, some canal. Flats designed for canal work were unrigged, being towed by a horse or a tug. They measured 68' to 72' long by 13'6" to 14'9" wide, loading up to 90 tons on a 5' draught. Because they worked on to the Mersey they had an anchor and windlass, and were also fitted with hatch coamings, hatch boards and cloths. Their routes were widespread, on the Leeds & Liverpool from the Mersey to Wigan and down to Leigh and Manchester, on the St. Helens Canal, the Mersey & Irwell Navigation, the Manchester Ship Canal, and the Bridgewater. They were numerous on the Weaver and Mersey, and traded over the Rochdale Canal (83) as far as Sowerby Bridge. Many were square sterned, particularly the early ones of the late eighteenth and early nineteenth centuries. Canal or 'cut' flats had a single long hatch spanned by a middle beam and forward of this the main beam, to which in the Rochdale traders the tabernacle or 'lutchet' stepped in the keelson was secured; in this the long or short towing mast, the 'neddy' was fixed: other flats towed from a timber head forward. On the after deck was a 30 gallon water cask, while the long wooden tiller passed over the stern rail, although a rail right across the stern was not universal. Most flats followed keel practice with a manrope rigged from a stanchion on the tack timber forward to the first stern rail stanchion aft. Accommodation for the two man crew was forward and aft, the mate living forward and the captain aft, sometimes both being accompanied by wives and families. Flats were built at many yards, those for Weaver service at Northwich and Winsford, those for the Rochdale Canal by Rathbone's of Stretford and Muggs' of Stretford, while others were built at Chester and on the Leeds & Liverpool and St. Helens Canals. Pioneers of iron flats in the 1830s were the Mersey & Irwell Navigation, while between 1906 and 1914 the Rochdale Canal Co. had 18 flats built by Yarwood's of Northwich with steel frames and wooden planking. Rochdale flats were designed with side decks wide enough to take a bale of cotton. Some worked fly with small tonnages, for example those of the Rochdale Canal Co. to Sowerby Bridge. Distinctive colours were applied to top strake, rudder head, hawse timbers, covering board and timber heads, for example Albert Wood, the Sowerby Bridge carrier, favoured yellow, green and red, the Rochdale Canal Co, Plate 12, white, red and blue, the Shropshire Union white and black; the first named colours in each case being predominant, applied to the top strakes at bow and stern.

MERSEY: Sailing Flats: 'Mast' flats, as opposed to the canal or 'cut' flats went up the St. Helens Canal, the Weaver, the Mersey & Irwell Navigation and the Runcorn & Latchford Canal. Some were coasters trading to Preston and Fleetwood, to Beaumaris and Penmaenmawr for stone and further afield, while others kept within the Mersey. During the eighteenth century the change was made from square to fore and aft rig, coupled with a square stern, to enable vessels of larger capacity to pass locks on the Weaver and Mersey & Irwell Navigation. From the mid-nineteenth century the rounded stern came back and two classes of sailing flat or sailing barge emerged, the coaster with finer lines, and the river vessel (132). Both types varied in size from 50' to 75' in length, with a capacity from 80 to 150 tons. At the same time there was an advance from the high peaked gaff mainsail and foresail of the single masted flat to the ketch rigged jigger (105) and Plate 4. Most of the jiggers were coasters but one or two stayed in the river. With the late nineteenth century came some big coastal flats, like the E.K. MUSPRATT of 1894 built for the United Alkali Co. Ltd., measuring 82.2' x 21.2' beam, with bulwarks, unusual for flats; which had either a rail the full length of the hull or just at the stern, which gave them the name 'bare or naked flats'. Coal, stone, chemicals and sugar were common cargoes and some carried explosives, Plate 4, the largest being able to carry 200 tons in the river laden to her scuppers, and 175 tons outside on a draught of 7'6" to 9'. Others went up the St. Helens Canal to Earlestown with raw sugar from Liverpool docks, returning with coal. All sailing flats were carvel built, flat bottomed and round bilged with little external keel, but had a massive internal keelson or hog as deep as 3'. There were two hatches, a small one forward of the mast and a long main hatch. Latterly most flats had fixed masts stepped in the keelson, but earlier vessels must have had lowering masts to pass under Frodsham bridge on the Weaver and the fixed bridges over the Mersey & Irwell Navigation. Accommodation was aft for the crew of two in the river flats, although the coasters carried a third hand who berthed forward. Flats were built of oak at Northwich, Winsford and Sankey Bridges near Warrington, on the St. Helens Canal, although in the 1830s the Mersey & Irwell had some of iron. Most sailing flats disappeared between the wars due to the competition of powered craft and road motors, although some like the E.K. MUSPRATT and the WINIFRED were fitted with auxiliary engines, while others were unrigged, like the JOHN & WILLIAM and the EDWARD both of United Alkali, to trade as dumb barges on the Weaver. Sailing flats were simply decorated, the timber heads and rail stanchions being picked out in red, blue or green, also the water barrel on the after deck, the little wooden skylight aft, the main windlass and the small halliard windlass at the foot of the mast. Most distinctive were the bands of recognition colours at the masthead above the hounds. The small

132. Mersey Flat under sail

crews, two in the river and three outside, needed running rigging easy to handle, with large sheaved blocks and latterly wire rope made in Warrington. Flats, in spite of little keel and their bluff bows and sterns, would go about quite well light, although sluggish when laden. On the navigations and canals hired horses would be employed, or the crew would bow haul for short distances on canals, sometimes aided by the foresail. Because of this, posts were set up by the side of the St. Helens Canal between Widnes and Sankey Bridges to protect the adjacent railway from swinging spars. When steam tugs were generally available, flats were towed on the Mersey, and of course they made use of the tide.

GLOSSARY OF FLAT TERMS (see also keels glossary):
BULK LASHINGS; longer than snug lashings, securing cloths to coamings when bulk loads were carried (canal flats). BULK TILLER; a special cranked tiller of iron although some were wood, for use with a steering plank when bulk loads were carried (canal flats). CANAL FLATS; or 'cut flats' non-sailing flats working on canals and under tow in the Mersey. CHECK LINE; attached to rudder blade, used to pull rudder over in a lock (canal flats). COCK BOAT; a sailing flat's punt or row boat. DRAGGING OR DRIVING; working a flat stern first down the Weaver in flood, the anchor just touching bottom to control the speed. FLATTIE; a member of a flat's crew, a flatman. HOBBLERS; owners of spritsail gigs on the Mersey who carried messages and people from ship to shore, or ran

lines to dock walls.   INSIDE FLATS;   sailing flats working within the Mersey.   JIGGER FLAT;   a sailing flat rigged like a ketch with main and mizen (jigger) masts.   JIGGER SLOOP;   a coasting ketch with counter stern, bowsprit and bulwarks.   KEDGE DRUDGING; kedging off (sailing flats).   MAIN OR MAST BEAM;   across the hold of a canal flat in way of the lutchet which was secured to it.   MIDDLE BEAM;   across the hold of a canal flat or keel aft of the main beam, detachable, but with a tensioning chain alongside, necessary because of the tendency of some hulls to spread.   NO MAN'S LAND;   the space between two sets of hatch boards of the main hatch.   OUTSIDE FLATS;   coastal sailing flats.   RONGE;   rough water in the Mersey.   ROPE BOARD;   platform between the hawse timbers and the anchor windlass of a canal flat, also used on Yorkshire keels, for the stowage of rope.   SANDHOOKERS;   flats carrying Mersey sand.   SILL FENDER;   lowest of the three fenders at the stem of a canal flat or keel to protect it from impact with the upper gate sill.   SNUG LASHINGS;   shorter than bulk lashings for securing hatch cloths to coamings (canal flats).   When complete the flat was said to be 'laying snug'. STEERING PLANK;   when a canal flat was bulk loaded a plank with battens was laid across the stern rail for the steerer, so that he could see over the load.   STERN STRAP; line from a timber head at the stern, secured to a strapping post or check pin on the lock side to check a boat's way entering a lock.   STOWER CLOGS;   a Yorkshire term to describe the rests on the hatch covers of canal flats for the boathooks and stowers (see keels glossary).   TELL TALE HOLE;   a special hole on each quarter of a sailing flat which became immersed if the vessel was deep laden, warning of possible leaks from the dry seams by the hissing of water running into the bilge.   It could be plugged and was marked by a circle of red or yellow paint.   TIDY BETTY;   a wooden pad with a handle like a ping-pong bat, for a kettle or pan to stand on when taken off the cabin stove, also used in Yorkshire and sometimes made of iron.   TRANSOM;   sailing flat term for the foresheet horse, some flats had a short one for the mainsheet.   WHISKERS;   the guards at the bow, so called because a flat's or keel's bow with the hawse ports or eyes represented a face.   This seems to be a Yorkshire term applied also to the keels.   Boat builders called them false bins or false bends.

WEAVER;   Dumb Flats: The Weaver was much used by sailing flats until the 1850s but the advent of steam packets and tugs in the 1860s robbed them of trade and they were replaced by dumb barges, towed by a horse, a steam packet or a tug.   These flats grew into considerable vessels 90' x 21' beam carrying 230 to 250 tons.   Such was the steel framed but wooden planked GOWANBURN built in 1902 and later owned by Henry Seddon & Sons Ltd, of Middlewich, working as a pair with the steam packet WEAVER BELLE. More typical were the smaller flats owned by the Salt Union, loading 80 to 90 tons, with a length of about 70'.   These were christened Black Flats because they were tarred black, or 'Salties', and came down from Winsford with bagged salt for export from Liverpool and Birkenhead.   None were rigged, although they had to step a short mast in a tabernacle to hoist a steaming light when under tow.

WEAVER;   Sailing Flats: Too narrow for regular navigation under sail, although sails were used whenever possible, the Weaver was the home of a sailing flat which in the eighteenth century was bow hauled by men, in the nineteenth, horse towed on the river, yet sailed on the Mersey and made coastal voyages.   They may in the earlier eighteenth century have been square rigged, but the gaff fore and aft sail was probably introduced by the 1770s.   Their masts must have lowered in a tabernacle to pass under Frodsham bridge,

and these eighteenth century flats would have averaged 50' x 14' carrying 30 tons, on 4' of water (133). As the Weaver was improved during the nineteenth century, so the sailing flats increased in size and capacity up to 50 tons. When the locks were enlarged from the 1870s, steam packets towing dumb barges put the sailing flat out of business. A few survived, probably into the first decade of the twentieth century, owned by their captains, or relatives, hence the expression 'Number One Flat' to describe a sailing Weaver flat. Like the more numerous Mersey single masted sailing flats, the Weaver type were rigged with a foresail and high peaked gaff mainsail, some with two hatches, the smaller forward of the mast, or with a single hatch. For steamers see under Packets.

FRIGATES etc. See Barges, River Severn.

133. Characteristic square sterned Weaver Flat hoisting sail.

GABBARTS, Scotland: 'Gabart - a long narrow, flat vessel or lighter, with a hatchway extending almost the length of the decks, sometimes fitted with masts, which are made so that they may be lowered in passing under bridges.' The definition given by the 1863 edition of Young's 'Nautical Dictionary' of the craft listed as gabbarts in the Mercantile Navy lists. It describes the river lighters, dumb craft, used on the Clyde and after the appearance of steam tugs in the 1820s, towed by them between Greenock and Glasgow. The steam lighter or 'puffer' superseded them and some were converted to steam propulsion. In 1790 the Forth & Clyde was fully open to the Clyde at Bowling and was used by river and estuary traders, sloop rigged sailing craft, also called gabbarts on the West Coast of Scotland. They were rigged with a gaff mainsail and forestaysail, and measured about 60' x 13'6", drawing 5'6" laden. They were round bilged and double ended, with the rudder outboard. Their long hatch gave access to a hold with a capacity of 70 to 80 tons, accommodation for the crew of two or three being aft. Some had low bulwarks but most an open stern rail, with timber heads to support the wooden baulks which acted as fenders. They did not have bowsprits or set topsails. The sloop rigged gabbarts went to Oban and possibly Mull, and down the Forth from Grangemouth, while because of their lowering masts they could get above the Glasgow bridges. On the Forth & Clyde and Monkland Canals they were horse hauled carrying minerals and timber. All were wood, built mostly at Bowling and Dumbarton, although no new ones appeared after the middle of the nineteenth century because of puffer competition which killed them by 1900. Coastal smacks and ketches also called gabbarts survived longer, ketches working through the Crinan Canal and carrying coal to Rothesay until the 1920s, until replaced by puffers, also sometimes referred to as steam gabbarts. Gabbarts had distinctively painted mastheads and prominent weather vanes. Hull decoration on the gabbart was limited to a painted strake. In Ulster the variant 'gabbard' was used in the early eighteenth century to describe trading sailing craft on Lough Neagh.

ICE BREAKERS. See Icebreaking, Section 2.

IRISH WATERWAY CRAFT: On the Shannon in early times there were hide covered wicker boats carrying turf (peat), later handled by 50 ton capacity sailing sloops, two of which lasted until the 1920s. Generally Irish craft were broad beamed, decked barges. In Ulster they were called lighters, some square sterned, but most round. Lagan lighters (69) had wide side decks and the hatch was covered by boards and cloths. Dimensions varied, Lagan, Coalisland, and Newry lighters were up to 62' x 14'6" carrying up to 80 tons, too wide for the Ulster for which special narrow lighters were used. Steel lighters were built in 1880 by MacIlwaine & Lewis of Belfast for William Barbour & Son of Hilden. Motor lighters were introduced on the Lagan about the 1914-18 War with capacities of up to 80 tons but horses remained in use until the end of traffic in the 1950s. Decoration seems to have been largely absent from these grey craft, apart from a painted bulwark and strake, generally white, below gunwale level. Many were family boats. Steam lighters were introduced on the Newry Navigation in the late nineteenth century and one craft, the ULSTER was fitted experimentally with two enormous propellers which worked semi-immersed, in 1893. There were also steam barges (134) on the Liffey, notably the Guinness fleet working between the brewery and the docks, Plate 3. The last was sold in 1961. Southern Irish canal craft were open holded without the hatch covers of the Lagan and other lighters. Some had round sterns and some square, the latter being commoner. Most numerous were the horse boats on the Grand Canal measuring some 60' x 13'. Photographs of the 1900s show Grand Canal Co. boats as round sterned with wide side decks like Lagan lighters and accommodation aft and forward. The cargo was covered by tarpaulins if perishable. The Royal Canal had four steam boats from 1875 to 1886, put into service by the Midland Great Western Railway, but the Grand went over to motor boats from 1911 onwards, (see below motor boats, Grand Canal, Ireland). The Grand also introduced their own motor barges on the Shannon (see barges, motor) from 1938. Later nineteenth century Grand Canal Co. horse boats were built of iron by yards in Ireland and Scotland, the Dublin Dockyard Co, Ross & Walpole of Dublin, the Passage Dock Co. near Cork, Bewley, Webb & Co, Dublin and Cumming & Ellis of Inverkeithing on the Forth. They were numbered rather than named. A final series of wooden horse boats was built by the Irish Government during the 1939-45 War to carry turf. They were built of native timber with a short life expectancy.

Motor Boats, Grand Canal, Ireland: In 1911 the Grand fitted a Bolinder semi-diesel into a horse boat. More horse boats were converted until 30 had been done. It had never been the practice to name Grand Canal Co. boats and the motors were numbered with an M suffix, signifying motor (135). From 1925 the first of a new series of all steel M boats was built, the last being completed in 1939. There were 49 with 15 bhp Bolinders. Construction was shared between the Ringsend Dockyard Co. and Vickers (Ireland) Ltd, two sizes being turned out 60' x 13' and later 61' x 13'3". The Ringsend boats were swim headed fore and aft, the Vickers with a swim bow and a more normal faired-in stern with a round bilge. Both carried 45 tons on 3'9" draught and could navigate the Shannon down to Limerick. The hold could be covered by tarpaulins. Accommodation was forward for the crew of four, after 1946 three, with a turf burning stove. Fresh water was carried in a barrel on deck. Bye traders on the Grand bore a number and a B suffix, some being converted wooden and iron horse boats, others built as motors. They were the same size as the Grand Canal Co. boats, and were often chartered to the company when they were short of tonnage. On the other hand some ex-Grand Canal boatmen hired Grand Canal boats and plied as bye traders. See also Barges; Motor.

KEELS:

NORFOLK: Keels possibly also called keel wherries, these dated back to the Middle Ages and were the carriers of Norfolk until superseded by the fore and aft rigged wherry during the eighteenth century. The keels were square rigged and unhandy, their clinker built, usually transom sterned, hulls decked but free of bulwarks, with a single long hatch. A model in the Science Museum, South Kensington, of an early nineteenth century keel shows a round bilged V-bottomed craft 54.5' x 14.5' wide with a capacity of 30 tons. Because of wherry competition during the latter part of the eighteenth century, keels grew larger, varying from a group of eight of 70 tons, burthen, built in 1770 to the 97 ton SUCCESS of 1795. These needed a crew of four, which made them uneconomic against the wherry handled by two men. Few keels were built after 1800. They operated on all the Norfolk rivers, those on the Yare being the largest, those on the Bure the smallest.

HUMBER: Sailing Keels and Sloops: Because of their single square mainsail, keels (169) appear as descendants of the mediaeval cargo ships. Probably rig and hull form did not change significantly for centuries, modification coming in the eighteenth with the increasing introduction of a fore and aft sloop rig (62, 63) and some sloops were built larger and so more suitable for coastal trading. Both varieties survived to the 1939-45 War but then succumbed to road competition. They were carvel or clinker built with oak sides, (but there were many built in iron and steel also), a rounded bilge and a flat bottom built of oak, so that they could take the ground safely, with a shallow external keel. Dimensions varied depending on the canals used by keels and sloops, there being many sizes, for example Barnsley 78'6" x 14'6", Sheffield 61'6" x 15'6", Driffield 61' x 14'6", Manvers (Manvers Main colliery on the Dearne & Dove Canal) 58' x 14'10" and Lincoln 78' x 15'2". The depth of the hold averaged 7'6" and the laden draught 5' to 6', giving 60 to 80 tons capacity. Keels and sloops went up the Ouse, the Trent, the Aire & Calder, the Derwent, the Don, the Ure, the Market Weighton Canal, the Fossdyke and the Louth Navigation from Tetney Haven. Sloops went on coastal passages to the Thames, but keels rarely. Cargoes were varied, coal being pre-eminent, followed by grain, flour, cement, bricks, stone, sugar beet, slag, ironstone, sand, particularly moulding sand and fertilizer. Two were specially built with tanks for carrying oil and tar. Builders were numerous, at Thorne, Hull, Selby, Rotherham, Stainforth, Goole, Wakefield, and Boston on the Wash. Most were family and captain owned in small fleets of one, two or three. Keels and sloops had leeboards for tacking, handled by special windlasses, and apart from the large anchor windlass, there

134. Guinness steam barge KILLINEY.

was a winch at the forward headledge for heaving up the mast and at right angles to this, the tack rollers, port and starboard, for pulling down on the tack of the square mainsail in keels. Sheet winches were fitted on the coamings of the square sail keels which carried a mainsail, above it a topsail, but rarely a topgallant, all untanned. Latterly all the standing and much of the running rigging was of wire, the shrouds being set up by deadeyes and lanyards. For canal work, keels and sloops generally put ashore their cog-boat, anchors and leeboards, and either lowered or put ashore their masts. In place of the mast they stepped a 'neddy' as a towing mast for the horse, using a 120' line. Bow hauling or 'bow yanking' was also practised, while the crew could quant with the stowers. If the wind served, horse haulage could be avoided by a light square sail from the derrick pole which all carried for cargo working. Because of low canal bridges, an empty Humber keel had to be ballasted down with water, let in by a tap under the floor of the after cabin. Working keels and sloops on the Humber, Ouse and Trent under sail was dependent on the the tide. Speed and steerage in a fast current could be controlled by a weight dropped over the stern from which lines were led to each quarter, the lines being worked in combination with the leeboards which prevented sideways drift. Again running stern first with a tidal stream the anchor crown was allowed to trail on the bottom. This slowed the keel and gave steerage way relative to the tide. Keel and sloop decoration was straightforward. At the masthead was a 6' vane of turkey red bunting atop a gilded truck. Mast, rails, winch posts, covering boards and bitt heads were linseeded and varnished, save for the mast of a sloop where the hoops slid, this was linseeded only. Graining was applied to the coamings and headledges, and paintwork to the timber heads, horse, top strake, winches and tiller. The hull was either tarred or occasionally painted, red or grey being the usual. Favourite colours for top strake and deck fittings were green or blue, sometimes marked off in panels with dark green or dark blue. Keels on the Sheffield & South Yorkshire Navigation favoured blue. Two was the normal crew, the mate living in the forecastle where most of the cooking was done. The captain lived aft, sometimes with his wife. On the canals a keel could be managed by a man and his wife, but not on the Humber. Water was kept in a 30 gallon cask on the after deck and had to be baled out with a dipper. Wages were paid from the keel's earnings in thirds or fourths, in thirds it would be two thirds to the captain who found his own mate and a third to the keel's owner, or in fourths, a quarter to the owner and three quarters to the captain, if the earnings were low. In both cases the captain paid the mate, horse and tug hire and casual labour. Sloop mainsails and foresails were usually tanned. **(see page 320).**

GLOSSARY of Humber and Yorkshire keel and Humber sloop terms: (see also Flats Glossary). BEAMED UP; swelled up, referring to the planks of the hull, swollen and tight. BINS, RUBBING BINS or BINDS; the 3" thick rubbing strake round the hull just below deck level. Also along each side were three wedge shaped skids, below the bins to stop them catching on the lock sides. BLOPPING BOARD; a board placed between the coamings and the side for sliding stones overboard to make a training wall. BOAT ABOUT; to move the keel by manpower. BOATIE; a boatman. BOW YANKING; pulling the keel by manpower, bow hauling. BRIDGE RUNNING; passing under river and canal bridges with lowered masts, and raising the mast under way the other side. BRIGGAGE, or TO GIVE BRIGGAGE; to allow clearance under canal bridges. Yorkshire keels had enough but Humber keels had sometimes to be ballasted down. BRIGHOUSE FENDER; an intricately made rope stem fender for Yorkshire keels, Mersey flats had a turk's head fender. BUFFET; the rear end of a keels cabin, which had lockers and space for a clock. CANAL TILLER; of iron and cranked to avoid fouling the stern rail when the rudder was put hard over in a lock. CLIFF CLAMS; jaws for loading stone, Cliff being the chalk quarry near Barton-upon-Humber. CLOG or **STEM CLOG**; a detachable wedge of wood, frequently decorated with a star or scrollwork, above the stemhead, **behind which stood the stay** chock. This stopped the forestay's lower stayfall block from dropping down on the anchor gear windlass. COAL CADGERS; men who unloaded canal boats. COG BOAT; a keel's punt or skiff towed astern, about 12' x 4'6" beam. CROP; the camber of a keel's deck, designed to clear canal bridges or 'give briggage'. CUTWATER; extra area of wood at the leading edge of a leeboard. DENNINGS; the flooring in the forecastle and after cabin. DERRICK POLE; spar for cargo work, secured to the foot of the mast when not in use. DOG LEG; a hook shaped anchor for mooring to banks like the rond anchor of the Norfolk Broads. DRIVE; to go with the tide, trailing the anchor on the bottom to give steerage way. FEATHERINGS; coamings which join together the hawse and long timbers, usually decorated.

135. The fore end of the Grand Canal motor boat No. 52M built in 1928. Note depth scales for calculating the tonnage.

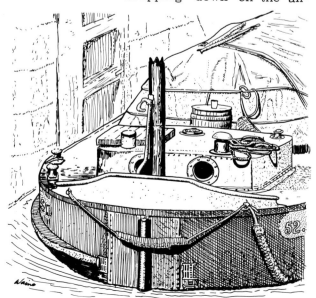

FETTLING; to treat canvas with preservative.   FUTTOCKS; these are the doubling timbers where the floors and the frames meet, the shape of the futtocks describing the shape of the bilge.   HANDLING; a lock windlass, or any crank handle for a windlass aboard the keel.   HANDY BILLY; a short shaft some 10' long.   HAULING; horse hauling as opposed to towing by a tug, a keel carrying two sizes of hauling line a river line (long) and a useful line (short) for canals.   HAWSE PORTS; at the bow through which the anchor cables pass, they were also called pipes or eyes, keels could be recognised by the position and colour of their eyes.   HAWSE TIMBERS; the stout timbers either side of the stempost which contained the hawse ports, they were distinctively painted and a stem clog, usually decorated with a star, slipped between them on short stemmed keels.   HEADLEDGES; the hatch coamings which ran athwartships at bow and stern. HORSE; the rail across the stern bearing the name and port of registry of the keel on the outside and the name and address of the owner on the inside, also on Mersey canal flats, the side rails being scarfed to it.   HORSE MARINE or MARINE; the man in charge of a boat horse, which the keels hired.   KELSEY; Yorkshire word for keelson.   LEGS of SAIL; the clews or bottom corners of a keel's square mainsail.   LIVER; to liver means to discharge, livered to have discharged.   LOCK PENNY; a coin thrown to a lock or bridge keeper, a custom carried on to the present day.   LONG TIMBER; the timberheads either side of the hawse timbers.   LUTCHET; the tabernacle for the mast.   MANGLING; warping up to a mooring by working the windlass. Keels had a 90 fathom line for warping in dock systems.   MANROPE; a light line secured fore and aft along the gunwale between the fore deck timber heads and the stern rails as a life line. It was kept taut by a lanyard and deadeyes, but could be lowered when working cargo. Found on all keels and some flats.   NEDDY; the short mast for canal towing stepped in the lutchet.   PULLING OUT; using a horse to operate a crane or derrick to work cargo.   PURCHASE MAN; an extra man hired to do the shafting.   RIDGE CHAINS; found on Yorkshire keels, between the long and tack timbers as handrails.   SEAL; a canvas harness, worn round the shoulders, for the 'bow yanker'.   SEALING; or ceiling; the planking inside the frames.   SHOOTS; the floor of a keel's hold, with loose limber boards alongside the keelson to allow the waterways below to be cleaned out.   SHORT STEMMED; a keel or sloop whose stempost did not rise above deck level. Sloops with bowsprits were necessarily short stemmed, but many were so built, as opposed to the 'long stemmed' where the stempost came level with the top of the hawse timbers. They had no stem clog,   SKATING; describes a leeboard veering away from a keel's side.   SOUNDING ROD; a graduated depth gauging shaft 16' long for gauging the depth.   SPRING TIMBER; or lazy timber (because little used) timber head a few feet aft of the forward deck, to which mooring springs were secured. STOWERS; 22' wooden shafts, with 'grains' or a bifurcated ferrule at the bottom and a pommel at the top to put one's shoulder against. They and the 16' boathooks were laid on 'stower clogs' on the hatches, the boathooks having an 'S' shaped grain.   SUCK IN; description of a keel stuck by suction in mud as the tide rose. Chains were worked round the hull to break the vacuum.   TACK TIMBER; the aftermost of the timber heads on the foredeck.   TAFFEL TIMBER; the timbers which supported the stern horse with projecting heads above the rail, handy for securing the cog boat.   THIEF BARS; irons bars securing the companion hatches to the forecastle and after cabin. Each hatch had two bars forming a cross with a hole for a bolt in the middle.   TOWING; by a tug as opposed to horse hauling, the keel carrying a hemp towrope for the tug.   WINDHOLE; wide place for turning a keel.

NON-TIDAL KEELS, Yorkshire: These keels did not work out on to the Humber. They never stepped a mast and sail or rigged leeboards. The Aire & Calder Navigation had a large fleet of them, many built of iron or steel, and simply numbered. Coal boats or barges had a wide hatch with the coamings coming to the edge of the covering board on the gunwale, but no hatch boards or cloths. There were others fitted with hatch boards and cloths, while some were termed 'umbrella' or 'hen peeked' boats. These had forked iron stanchions on which three parallel lines of rails were laid like hen perches (peeks in Yorkshire), over which the cloths were spread. Although the round stern was usual, many non-tidal craft had a square stern, like the iron 'spouts' on the Aire & Calder. Non-tidal keels were also called boats, for example coal boats, or broad boats as opposed to narrow boats, or short boats as opposed to long boats (Mersey flats). These terms were important at Sowerby Bridge where two waterways of different gauges met, but they became confusing. Those on the Calder & Hebble were called 'West Country' boats, to distinguish them from the bigger keels on the Aire & Calder.

TIDAL KEELS: On the canals and rivers of Yorkshire the keel was the principal carrier, varying in size. Yorkshire keels were a foot less in hold depth at 6'6" than Humber keels, many Yorkshire keels loading to 4'11", with a length of 57', so that they could go up the Calder & Hebble Navigation to Sowerby Bridge and by the Rochdale Canal to Manchester and Liverpool on a draught of 3'11". Tidal Yorkshire keels with hatch boards and cloths worked on the Humber and the Mersey and some were rigged like the Humber keel with a square sail and leeboards. In hull form they were similar to the Humber keel, and in the canals they stepped a 'neddy' for horse hauling in the 'lutchet'. Of the two man crew, the mate lived forward and the captain aft. These were frequently family boats. Each cabin had a stove, often with a square or round wooden chimney metal lined on the inside. Water was kept in a 30 gallon cask on the after deck. Decoration was limited to painted or varnished top strake, stern rail, timber heads and hawse timbers, with the hawse ports or 'eyes' picked out in a contrasting colour, each carrier having his colours, red and blue, red and green, white green and red, yellow green and red, with the addition of scroll work on the feather boards between the hawse and long timbers. Some owners varnished the decks. An iron sloop was built as early as 1818 at Hunslet, below Leeds, and in later days a good many were built of iron or steel, or with iron or steel.

STEAM KEELS: were introduced by the Aire & Calder Navigation in 1852 to their own fleet as tugs cum cargo carriers, for merchandise and later mineral traffic. Some steam fly-boats were still in service in the early 1950s on the Barnsley Canal, which would limit their length to 78'6", other steam keels were 80' long or more and 17' beam working on the Aire & Calder main line. The hull was similar to the sailing keel but finer aft because of the propeller. Accommodation for the crew of three, captain, mate and engineer, was forward, followed by the long hatch. One steamer at least had a midships steering position, generally it was aft. Hatch boards with battened down covers were fitted. All underdeck space aft was used for engine and 'Scotch' boiler with a single furnace and generating steam to 120 psi for the usually compound engine with surface condenser. The funnel was hinged for bridges. Propellers were up to 4' in diameter because of the comparatively slow speeds of the engines. All were iron or steel, mainly built by the two Scarr's of Hessle and Beverley. Capacities were 120 tons or more, the main cargoes being flour from the Hull mills to bakeries in Leeds or grain from the docks to mills at York. Steam keels would tow three or four barges, either sailing keels or sloops, unrigged for inland navigation, or dumb barges. Five steam keels were owned by Rishworth, Ingleby & Lofthouse Ltd, and Henry Leetham of York had four. These firms were flour millers and Leetham's operated 230 tons capacity steam lighters up the Ouse and its tributary the Foss to their mills. On the Trent the gravel traffic was handled by steam 'gravel packets'. Mostly 120' x 15'6" x 7' depth of hold, carrying about 100 tons.

KEELS; MOTOR: See Barges, motor.

LIGHTERS:

FEN Lighters: Fenland rivers have carried commercial traffic for most of recorded history. In the seventeenth century lighters were horse and man hauled and set a single square sail, the mast being lowered for bridges. Some Great Ouse 130 ton lighters were decked, but 30 tons seems to have been common in the eighteenth century, plus some 15 tonners. By the early twentieth the average wooden lighter measured 42' x 10' across the gunwales, with a capacity of 25 tons on a draught of 3'6", but drawing only 12" empty. There were bigger lighters on the Great Ouse, 70' x 14' carrying 70 tons on 3'6" draught, and small ones of 8 tons. All were double ended and flat bottomed with an identical rounded bow and stern. Dutch influence seems evident in the wide 15" clinker planking and the sheer at bow and stern, the topstrake being given a pronounced tumble home fore and aft. While some lighters had short decks fore and aft, and a cramped cuddy under the fore deck reached by a hatch, many were open. The hold was stiffened by three beams and could be sheeted over with tarpaulins, although decked lighters had coamings and hatch boards. Lighters had no rudder because it had become the practice by the eighteenth century to work them in trains or gangs. Five was as much as one horse could manage. When steam tugs were introduced the gangs were up to fourteen (136). Each was linked to the other by 'jesses ropes' secured to the stem/stern posts, control being achieved by a long steering pole made fast to the forward beam of the second lighter in the gang. This projected well over the stern of the leading lighter and was used as a giant tiller. The steerer was helped by a stout rope which secured the leading end of the pole to either gunwale of the first lighter. Similar but shorter 'jorming poles' were secured to each successive lighter, their leading ends being held by ropes called 'quarterlies' to each gunwale of the lighter next ahead. The poles gave some rigidity to the gang, otherwise it would bunch up if the horse slowed. A sail might be set if the wind was fair, as was done by lighters working alone. Because many had no accommodation, one lighter of a gang was fitted with a cabin built as a rough superstructure, for the two men, one driving the horse the other steering. This was the 'house lighter' the cabin being called the boathouse. In addition a special lighter might be attached to ferry the horse over when the towpath changed sides, and there was always the 'cock boat', a dinghy. The horse hauled from one of the timber heads of the leading lighter or if the lighter had a mast, from this. Masthead hauling had the advantage of enabling the line to clear bushes and posts on the bank. Horse's harness followed canal boat practice, with traces and chains from a spreader which were married some 5' behind the spreader and ended some 2' further back in a hook for the hauling line. This could be long on a twisty stretch, up to 480', but 80' or so was more normal if the river or lode was straight. Sometimes gangs of lighters were bow hauled or were quanted like the Norfolk wherries, having walkways along each side. One man walked back pushing the quant, called a 'spread' or 'sprit' in the Fens, while the other walked up to commence his turn. Steam tugs were introduced towards the end of the nineteenth century. Prentice's of Burwell near Cambridge and Jackson's of Peterborough were noted tug and lighter owners. Prentice's had their boatyard at Burwell where the last wooden lighter was built, the READY MONEY in 1914 for Jackson's. The last gang of wooden lighters traded up to 1945. With the tugs came steel lighters. They too worked in gangs but had rudders and so were towed spaced out, a man aboard each. A tug could manage up to eighteen. Some were fitted with tanks to carry gas water from Cambridge gasworks. The old cargoes stayed until lost to road haulage. By the nineteenth century with rail competition, coal, bricks, grain and timber predominated, plus local cargoes; clunch like chalk and used as a fertilizer, osiers for basket making and coprolites. These were the fossilized droppings of animals used as a fertilizer. Small wooden lighters of 12" laden draught carried turf or peat and sedge for thatching. They would be bow hauled and were shaped like punts. Later steel

136. Fen lighters loaded
with sugar beet at
the Ely sugar beet
factory in 1926.

lighters were swim headed, without rudders and towed in trains,
secured stem to stern. They handled, with some of the remaining
wooden lighters, the sugar beet
traffic, the last cargo of importance in the Fens, finishing in 1959.
Nowadays steel lighters carry
'gault' (clay) for building up banks
and stopping leaks. Fen lighters
were named and carried the name
of their owner at bow and stern.
Some had white quadrants at the
bow, like Norfolk wherries.

SUFFOLK STOUR: The lighters
worked in pairs, the locks on the
Stour being sufficiently long to
pass a gang of two, coupled together with seizing chains, the
second craft, acting as a rudder,
controlled by a hefty 30' long steering pole secured to the fore end and passing right over
the stern of the leading lighter to where the steerer stood between the two hatches, Plate 7.
John Constable's paintings have made the Stour lighter familiar and there seems to have
been no alteration in design, to judge from the craft lifted in 1972 from Ballingdon cut near
Sudbury by the River Stour Trust. She measures 46'9" overall and 10'6" across, with a
depth of 3'2" amidships. She is double ended with wide clinker planks, and excessive rake
to the stem and stern posts. The holds were covered by hatch boards and each lighter
could load 13 tons on a draft of 2'5". The gang therefore carried 26 tons behind a single
horse (65), or upstream two horses, the cargoes being mostly coal, grain, fertilizer and
flour. Accommodation was under the deck forward in the second lighter for the two man
crew or for a family. The mate or horse leader rode and jumped the stiles, the horses
towing from a post in the steerer's well. With the path changing sides without a bridge, the
horses were ferried or 'boated' across on the foredeck of the leading lighter. They were
trained to jump on and off from little piers. Lighters were sailed, and poled (or 'stemmed')
below Cattawade bridge on the tideway, the sail probably a crude square one. They used
the tide up to Brantham where horses were picked up, and because of it carried anchors.
There was no traffic above Boxtead after 1916 and none at all after 1928. The River Stour
Navigation Co were themselves carriers.

THAMES & LEE; Lighters: Early Thames craft of many types were swim headed, the
bow and stern squared off and sloped down like those of a punt, in fact the smaller Thames
lighters are called punts by the watermen. For the dumb lighters of the Thames and Port
of London the swim headed design has been retained to modern times. When steel replaced
wood, the shape was kept, simple to make. Size would vary, those using the Lee Navigation not exceeding 85' long, their width varying from 18'6" below Enfield to 16'0" up to
Hertford. Many of the Lee lighters have a normal shaped bow and rounded stern with a
rudder and tiller and low wash boards to protect the decks. Some have hatch boards and
cloths, others are open. Small steel barges not exceeding 13'3" were built for the Stort
after the Lee had rebuilt their locks by the 1920s. Lighters are dependent on a tug, or the
tide, where movement is guided by the lighterman's long oars or paddles. On the Lee and
Regent's Canal they could be horse, tractor or tug drawn. The British Waterways depots
at Brentford and Enfield handle considerable transhipment traffic between road and lighter.

Barges: On the Lee there used to be open holded sailing barges with a stumpy spritsail rig, with a hull like a Thames spritsail barge's also with a transom stern. They were
later built unrigged, some 72' long by 13' - 15' beam. Barges of similar shape, but unrigged worked up the Regent's Canal and the Grand Junction from Brentford. Emmanuel Smith
of Brentford was a well known owner. Accommodation for the two man crew was aft. High
hatch coamings were fitted and the hatch was covered by boards and cloths. Some of these
barges were elegant, with the name on the transom enclosed in a scroll, turks head ropework at the head of the rudder post and elaborately worked rope fenders. Wood gave place
to iron and steel for the hull, but horse traction lasted on the canal above Brentford until
the later 1950s. The horse towed from one of the timber heads forward, as did succeeding
tractors.

NARROW BOATS:

NARROW BOATS: Historical: The Trent & Mersey was designed with locks about 75' by
7' wide. Brindley proposed cargo boats which according to the canal historian John Phillips,
were to be 70' x 6' with a loaded draft of 2'6", able to carry 20 tons of coal and also able
to transfer the rudder from one end to the other, crewed by a man and a boy and pulled
by a single horse. It was hoped that the horse could manage a train of these boats, but it is
doubtful if this was done. A fairly convincing picture emerges of a double ended flat bottomed

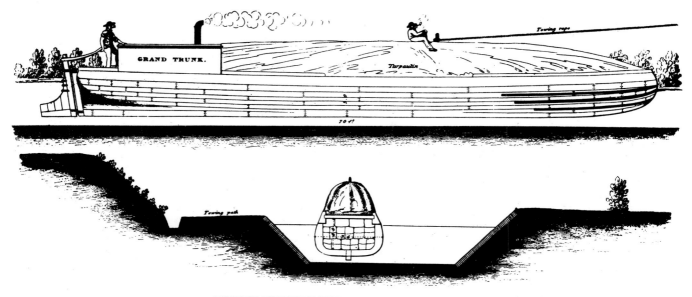

SECTION THROUGH THE CENTRE OF THE BOAT.

137. A Trent & Mersey or 'Grand Trunk' boat of the 1820s, with a hold depth of as much as 5'. It was drawn for William Strickland's report on canals, railways and roads of Britain, to the Pennsylvania Society for the Promotion of Internal Improvement, 1826.

craft, with a cabin and a towing mast like the day boats of the Birmingham Canal Navigations. Hull form may have followed the tunnel boats used at Worsley. Although small by twentieth century standards, the 15 to 20 tons carried by narrow boats was a considerable advance when introduced, compared with a road waggon, or packhorse. But while good coal carriers, narrow boats were not so suited to handle timber and lighter bulky goods and were limited to small tonnages. During the 1820s illustrations appeared of Pickfords' boats, in E. W. Cooke's engraving for his portfolio 'Shipping and Craft' published in 1829. They are superior craft with well shaped sterns and flared bows designed for long distance work. They have high cabins and a bulky cargo clothed up and secured by ropes This and also other contemporary pictures of Pickfords' boats on the Regent's Canal show how little the present day butty differs from its early nineteenth century ancestor. By the mid-nineteenth century the narrow boat emerged with gang plank and side cloths according to an illustration of 1859 of a Thames & Severn boat and a description in Vol. 18 of 'Household Words' (1858), with details of a Grand Junction fly boat, the STOURPORT. She had stands, planks, and cloths but apparently no cratch, the planks curving down to the fore deck. The different builders created their individual styles and regional characteristics became apparent. Then there were boats for special trades such as the Thomas Clayton tar boats.

Wood has been used for narrow boat construction throughout their history (112). With the ready availability of iron from the early nineteenth century, iron knees were introduced followed by iron sides, the transverse elm bottoms being kept in this form of composite construction. In the twentieth century, steel replaced iron and between the wars and since, many boats have been built wholly of steel. Wooden boats were being built at Braunston until 1960, while as early as 1865, two iron boats were delivered to the Oxford Canal Co. Horse traction lasted until the 1970s for shorthaul traffic and until the 1950s there were some long distance horse boats. Many boatmen preferred mules to horses as they worked harder, while a few boats were hauled by donkeys, two side by side. Many horse boats became butties, while others were converted to motors. By the 1930s motor and butty had pretty well triumphed over the single horse boat. Standard narrow boats ventured far from their home in the Midlands. In the north they could reach Manchester, Wigan and Liverpool and Sowerby Bridge via the Rochdale Canal. A shortened type could pass from the last named on to the Calder & Hebble, while short boats were normally used on the Huddersfield Canal, for transfer on to Sir John Ramsden's and the Calder & Hebble, although the locks of the Huddersfield could take 70 footers. There were shortened narrow boats also on the Manchester, Bolton & Bury. Extra narrow narrow boats worked on the Shrewsbury Canal to the bottom of the Trench inclined plane, while standard narrow boats were used for the broad Grantham, the broad Kennet & Avon, Thames & Severn, also the Weaver and even the the Aire & Calder. Boats of a similar design but different dimensions were used on the isolated canals of South Wales, but were never introduced to Ireland where the canals were broader and in Scotland the only narrow canal with similar boats was the Glasgow, Paisley & Johnstone.

'AMPTON BOATS: See Wharf Boats.

DAY BOATS; these undertook short haul work carrying bulk goods which needed no weather protection and were not lived in. They operated on the Black Country system, in South-East Lancashire, the Potteries and South Wales, the latter not exactly narrow boats and therefore dealt with separately. They were a basic type with an ancestry back to the open coal boats of the Worsley underground system. The cabinless open narrow boats in this area were of simple construction 'narrow gutted', with perpendicular sides narrowing to each end without flare. Locally called 'starvers', some carried coal in boxes (44), others loose. The Black Country canal network was the home of the greatest number of day boats. Coal was the basic traffic, but other traffic included bricks, pig iron, foundry sand, slates, cinders, timber, gravel, rubbish, dung, limestone, forgings, castings and more recently pipes and car components. These day boats, like their sisters of the Manchester area, were vertical sided, with near vertical stem and sternpost, little sheer or lift and no flare. Without cabins they were called 'open' boats, with cabins 'box cabin' boats, and here the word 'Joey' was more specifically used to describe a day boat with a cabin (2). Many were 'double ended' open boats meaning that the helm could be hung at either end to save winding, others were round stemmed boats where the helm could be hung at the stern only. These latter could have a more shapely rounded stempost and might have descended to day boating from long distance work. Some were specially built for certain traffic; 'hotholers' were of iron or steel throughout and carried the cropped ends of tubes from the works at Coombeswood, Halesowen to the Bilston steelworks, returning to Halesowen with steel billets. The name arose because the boats unloaded alongside the Bilston furnaces. The 'Rowley raggers' carried granite or rag from the quarries near Dudley. The 'station' or 'railway' boats were a superior class of non-cabin wood or iron boat working between factories and canal-to-rail interchange basins. Day tar boats were called black boats because of their contents and because of their black cabin sides. Black country day boats were the maximum size possible for the locks, 71'6" x 7'2" and about 3'10" deep. They could load 40 tons if the water allowed it, the hull being stiffened by five beams, the fore beam, the fore mast beam, middle beam, stern middle beam and bulkhead beam. The mast was a pole about 9' long stepped in a socket in the keelson and bearing between chocks against the fore mast beam (138). If this was a double ended boat going the other way, then the stern middle beam was used. Wooden knees were used to secure the planking until the arrival of iron grabs in the 1880s caused damage. Likewise the keelson had to be protected from grab jaws by laying timbers to raise the bottom level up to it. On the outside a day boat was well protected, timbers 5" x 1" were laid, 3 a side at each end, faced with iron, to act as guards, iron boats having wholly iron guards. Fairly cheap materials were used, deal or spruce for the bottoms. Between the wars a wooden boat cost only £120 to £150 and £80 before 1914. Some boats were composite, with iron sides and wooden bottoms, or occasionally with a wooden bottom strake of planking as well. Some were wholly iron, but wood remained popular because it was cheap. There were no decks, the steerer stood on a platform below the gunwale at either end and for tug work there were towing posts at each end, offset to clear the helm. Cabins if fitted were about 5' long with a bench across the back called the cross bed while another ran down the side, the side bed, with room for a stove. The cabins were locked up by a bar swung across the doors and secured by a padlock on the inside reached by an arm hole. Black Country day boats were quite lavishly decorated. Some were named, others just numbered, but the decoration made the boats readily recognisable, for crews changed from boat to boat. Carriers had their own distinctive patterns of crescents, circles and diamonds along the top bend and much ingenuity was displayed to vary the design on the rear cabin bulkhead, from a simple scallop pattern in contrasting colours of say black and white or red and white to some bulbus creations (122). The painting was done by the very many docks in the Black Country and they dictated the decorative styles. Peter Keay & Son of Walsall had a way of dating their dockings, making use of a string of diamonds down the waterway of the cabin side. The top diamond contained the initial K, the second the day of completion, the third the month, the fourth the year, thus K 27 8 32.

The carriers did not always find their own crews, but might contract the working to firms called steerers who found the men on a casual day to day basis as the traffic demanded. The men, there were two to a boat, one steering, the other horse driving, changed with their horse to another boat when they reached their destination. They carried from boat to boat their helm, mast, tiller, stove and water can, the latter a former chemical carboy or a stone jar. The horses would drag the mast and helm a fair distance sometimes (139). The stoves were bottle stoves in the box cabin boats, fire buckets in the open, which could be transferred alight, the fire buckets being tins with holes punched in the bottom and sides. For tunnels duck lamps were carried, like a teapot with a paraffin soaked wick in the spout.

138. Black Country day boats towed from a mast chained to the foremast beam, but stepped in different positions depending on the wind's tendency to blow the boat in or out.

139. 'Going Overland'. Black Country horses pulled the helm, tiller and mast along when the men changed to another day boat at their destination. One man is carrying the horse's nose tin, the other the fire bucket and shaft. The corn sack lies across the horse's back.

A single horse could pull two loaded boats or four empties, while the tugs averaged four loaded boats. Sometimes in strong winds the boats had to be guided by lines from men on the bank, while in an empty horse boat, the towing mast, lowered to pass under bridges, could be positioned at angles to vary the direction of pull. In tug trains a system of hand and mouth whistle signals was used between boat steerers and tug drivers, one whistle and a hand up meant stop, two whistles and a wave go on. Potteries day boats brought coal from pits south of Stoke into the Five Towns, and pottery materials from railway yards to the wharves of manufacturers. These were former long distance boats.

FLY-BOATS. Best known were those run by the Shropshire Union. They had little parallel side and a well rounded cross section although flat bottomed. Tumble home was pronounced, with well raked stem and stern, hollow bow lines and long foredeck without much lift to the stempost. They never loaded to the tonnage of a general carrying boat and 15 to 18 tons was about average. The Shropshire Union fly-boats were distinguished by a black spot or roundel on the white top bend forward. The No. 1. fly was the Birmingham to Ellesmere Port, two trips a week, leaving Birmingham at 5.00 p.m. on Saturdays and Tuesdays. Arrival at Ellesmere Port was at 10.00 p.m. on Sundays and Wednesdays, a 29 hour journey, the turn-round time being four hours, for the departure was at 2.00 a.m. Arrival back at Birmingham was at 10.00 a.m. and the only night off was Friday. There were other fly services from Ellesmere Port to the Potteries, Shrewsbury, Trench, Newtown and Llangollen with intermediate calls. Whereas the Birmingham fly changed horses five times, at Ellesmere Port, Bunbury, Tyrley, Norbury and Autherley and with a sixth change at Birmingham, that to Shrewsbury only had one intermediate change at Barbridge. Schedules had to be maintained to catch the Ellesmere Port sailings which depended on the tide. Extra horses were allowed if the boat had been delayed say by fog. (140). Fly-boat services were established elsewhere competing with road and to win traffic from other canals. Pickfords' schedules were extensive, from London to Manchester and Liverpool, Birmingham to Leicester, Birmingham to Stourport for transhipment to Bristol. Running to a timetable the boats had regular stops at wharves on the way, for example Warwick and Market Harborough on the Birmingham to Leicester run. There were also stage boats for slower schedules, carrying heavier cargoes. Pickfords' fly-boats worked in pairs as did those worked by the Grand Junction. These were narrow boats, each pulled by its own horse, one buttying the other, in other words setting the locks for it. These narrow fly-boats did not follow a special design but could be distinctively marked, for example the diamond on Pickfords' boats, while those of the Anderton Co, had two red roundels on the top bend forward. The Grand Union Canal Carrying Co. during and just after the 1939-45 war operated a service taking Guinness from their Park Royal brewery to Birmingham and bringing back empty barrels. The round trip had to be completed in a week, for loading at Park Royal the same day the following week. The crews were four handed and specially selected. Fly-boats were registered to comply with the Canal Boats Acts of 1877 and 1884. Boats worked by shifts had to have the crew all above twelve years old. The Rochdale 'fly-outs' were Mersey flats loaded to 20 tons, only drawing 3 feet so they could go faster. They provided an overnight service from Manchester to Sowerby Bridge, leaving Manchester at 7.00 or 7.30 p.m. and arriving at Littleborough or Todmorden at 4.00 or 5.00 a.m. and Sowerby Bridge about noon. For more details see under Flats, canal.

HUDDERSFIELD CANAL. Although this canal was built with narrow locks long enough to take a standard 70' boat, at Huddersfield it met the barge locks of Sir John Ramsden's Canal for 57'6" craft. A couple of narrow boats were shortened as early as 1811 and afterwards this became the standard length for boats on the Huddersfield. In appearance they followed northern narrow boat practice with timber heads at each side fore and aft and a stand in place of the cratch. Similar shortened narrow boats were used on the Manchester, Bolton & Bury Canal whose locks were built for 68' craft. Most of these were day boats carrying coal in container boxes. There were also some 62' narrow boats for working up to Blackburn on the Leeds & Liverpool Canal. See also under Northern Narrow boats.

NORTHERN BOATS; Manchester Area: Of eighteenth century descent were the day boats on the Bridgewater Canal coal trade. Some of their features were transferred to the cabin boats of the area, the timber heads and sometimes the wedge shaped fore end, this lacking much flare, made construction easier. Other northern narrow boats were given a full fore end and deep hull, up to six planks a side. The gang planks were supported by a stand at the fore end, and the cloths came together in front of it. Latter day narrow boats operated by Jonathan Horsefield of Runcorn and J.E. Southern & Co. of Manchester in the coal trade between the Lancashire pits and Runcorn gasworks were large, carrying about 30 tons of coal. Many were built by Simpson Davies of Runcorn, who converted some to motors, altering the pointed stern into a counter. The horse boat style of cabin was kept, the roof appearing low, but because of the depth of hull it was quite roomy. Decoration was not lavish on these northern boats with no roses and castles on the exterior and rather plainly styled lettering on the cabin sides.

Potteries Boats: For traffic in pottery raw materials and finished ware in crates the Anderton Co. developed at its own Middleport boatyard, a fine lined type for its fleet and other Potteries carriers. Both fore ends and sterns were narrow while the sides were barrel shaped with considerable tumblehome. Because of the bulkiness of crated ware, most of the load was above the water line and the boat rolled when people moved about, but the barrel sides ensured that the hull returned to the upright. All Anderton Co. boats were wooden, both horse and motor. They and other potteries boats had cratches, side and top cloths, for carrying crates, bagged flour, salt and pottery materials. Anderton Co. boats were always called 'knobsticks' and their crews 'knobstick men'. Similar to those of the Anderton Co. were those of the Mersey, Weaver Co. built by their own dock at Longport.

PASSENGER BOATS: See BOATS: Canal passenger (Gig or Swift) Boats.

ROYALTY CLASS, GRAND UNION and BRITISH WATERWAYS Boats: The 'Royalty' Class prototype all steel motor and butty were launched in 1929 by the Steel Barrel Co. Ltd, of Uxbridge, to the order of the Regent's Canal Co. who proposed starting a carrying fleet. Named GEORGE and MARY they had greater depth and fuller lines than the standard narrow boat, with a capacity of 70 tons between them, being intended to work on to the Thames. In 1931-2 a similar six pairs were delivered to the carrying subsidiary of the new Grand Union Canal Co, Associated Canal Carriers Ltd, which in 1934 became the Grand Union Canal Carrying Co. Ltd. The new motor 'Royalties' were all steel, four built by W.J. Yarwood of Northwich and two by James Pollock of Faversham, but the butties were wood. The motors were 4'11" deep in the hold and to maintain stability on the Thames, had water ballast tanks, one forward and one either side of the propeller shaft.

In 1934 the new Grand Union Canal Carrying Co. embarked on a narrow boat building programme, the wide boat experiment having failed. Design was modelled on the 'Royalty' class, although the company cautiously built six wooden pairs in 1934. In 1935 came a big order for 82 pairs from Harland & Wolff, Yarwood's, Walker's and Woods', most were composite craft, although Yarwoods built eight all steel pairs with vee bottoms to reduce wear on the chine and Walker's and Woods' delivered wooden boats. All were named after constellations, stars and planets. The 'Town' class were ordered in 1936 and designed to carry cased goods, when the 'Stars' designed for bulk cargoes, were still being delivered. Whereas the 'Stars' had 4'2" (a few 4'6") deep holds the 'Towns' were deeper (4'9½"), suitable for the Thames, and 86 pairs were ordered, all steel, motors and butties, from Harland & Wolff, all steel motors from Yarwood's and wooden butties from Walker's (141). Deliveries continued into 1938, but this fleet, totalling 186 pairs, was never fully employed in spite of the improved line to Birmingham and the gaining of new traffic from the Continent. These Grand Union boats are very distinctive with their bluff fore ends, low sheer and squat cratches necessary since they had a greater freeboard when empty than other narrow boats. All had electric headlights, and looked smart in their red, white and blue 1937 Coronation Year livery, replacing the earlier light and dark blue and white, and in 1943 being supplanted by blue and maroon.

The Docks & Inland Waterways Executive took over narrow boats from the Grand Union Canal Carrying Co. and Fellows, Morton & Clayton, but in the later 1950s new construction was commenced in an effort to make these craft pay. Having had a few conventional boats built in the early 1950s, new designs were prepared for boats of greater capacity. They emerged as the 'Admiral' class of six pairs, four from Isaac Pimblott, and the remaining two pairs from Yarwood's. Both motors and butties were of welded steel with very bluff fore ends, and in the Pimblott series, swim headed below the waterline. In the new boats the planks were carried on shallow hoops spanning the hold and socketed into brackets on the coamings. The cloths were spread over the hoops and secured to cleats on the coamings by

140. Lines of the horse boat SATURN built at Chester in 1906 by the Shropshire Union Railways & Canal Co., for their own fleet. She follows narrow fly-boat lines with a hollow stem although engaged on Cheshire cheese traffic from Barbridge to Manchester. About 1925 she passed to the Birmingham fleet of the LMS and much later became, and still is a hotel boat.

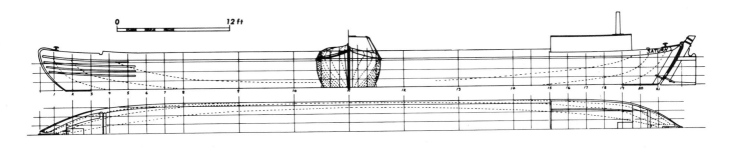

141. Narrow boats of the Grand Union Canal Carrying Co. The butty has running blocks for the adjustment of the towline and trails her downhill strap in the water, for locks are frequent.

wedges. With a capacity up to 30 tons the 'Admirals' were placed in traffic on the Trent & Mersey and Shropshire Union. In the later 1950s British Transport Waterways tried a new design for the Grand Union, the 'River' Class, again of welded steel. They were built by Harland & Wolff of North Woolwich, 23 of them butties, the holds being covered by blue fibreglass covers which interlocked. They were quickly christened 'blue tops'. Two motors were also built with the 'Harbourmaster' type of inboard-outboard diesel drive, but they proved difficult to steer.

RIVER SEVERN: In the Severn area called long boats, these were employed on the river between Gloucester and Worcester, up the Worcester & Birmingham Canal, up the Stroudwater from Framilode, and up the Staffs. & Worcs. from Stourport. Under horse haulage they worked singly on the river, but when steam tugs were introduced, the narrow boats were formed into fleets of two parallel lines behind the tug. There were stout timberheads at each side fore and aft for the tug's towrope and in hull form they developed into a very capacious cargo carrier, with six plank sides, a draught of up to 3'9" loaded, and a bluff fore end. At an overall length of 72' and a maximum beam of 7'2" they were the largest narrow boats, carrying 45 tons. Motor canal boats arrived on the Severn after the 1914-18 War. These could work independently of the tugs, and could, if powerful enough, tow a butty (called a trailer on the Severn) against the stream. In 1934-35 the Severn & Canal Carrying Co. built eight 9 h.p. Petter engined boats with welded steel-sided hulls but elm bottoms and cabins forward of the engine room, but they were too weak to tow a loaded butty upstream. Severn & Canal Carrying Co. boats were nicknamed 'toe rags'.

SHREWSBURY CANAL: Completion of the Newport branch of the Birmingham & Liverpool Junction to Wappenshall in 1835 brought narrow boats on to the Shrewsbury Canal for the first time. To accommodate them, the Shrewsbury widened the two Eyton Locks and the bridges so that they could reach Shrewsbury, but the locks and bridges up to the foot of the Trench plane from Wappenshall were left to the old tub boat standard, so a specially low and narrow boat was built for this traffic. A fleet of 'Trench boats' was maintained until 1921 when the Shropshire Union ceased carrying. Some were fly-boats, while others were called reserve boats for local traffic. They were 70' long but with a beam of 6'2" and low cabins, the low clearances demanding removal of all planks, stands, cratches and chimneys if the boats were empty. They carried 16 tons, but could manage as much as 18.

STEAMERS: With their wide locks, steamer and butty operation appealed to the Grand Junction. In 1864 they put the DART into commission between London and Braunston. A small fleet was assembled, but sold in 1876, the Grand Junction leaving carrying, mostly to Fellows, Morton & Clayton. Over the next 50 years FMC operated an efficient service, building boats at their Saltley, Birmingham dock, Plate. 2, fitted with their own engines, although later engines were bought from outside makers, notably A. H. Beasley & Sons, Uxbridge and Haynes of Smethwick. Some were wooden, others composite with iron sides and elm bottoms, all with rounded counters. Because the engines revolved slowly, 280 rpm was the maximum on a canal, 300 rpm on the Trent and Soar, the propellers, at first steel, later phosphor bronze, were large, 2'10½" in diameter. In order to clear the blades, the counter had to be given a noticeable lift. Because of the propeller shaft, the cabin of a steamer was built higher than that of a horse boat, the forward part being extended some 10' to contain the engine and boiler. The funnel was hinged to clear river bridges at flood time. With 10 tons for engine and boiler, the cargo capacity was reduced to 14 tons. The engines were inverted tandem-compounds. All were given surface condensers, while the steam at 140 psi came from a single furnace horizontal return tube boiler. Coke was the Fellows, Morton fuel, consumption averaging 10 cwt between Bull's Bridge and Braunston, the bunker holding one ton. A round trip to Nottingham, or Birmingham consumed up to 2 tons, the boats bunkering at depots there. The bunker was under the roof and down each side of the boiler, loaded via the roof hatch. Some steamers were coal burners, for example those owned by the lime and cement manufacturers Charles Nelson & Co. Ltd of Stockton on the Warwick & Napton Canal. With their low cargo capacity, steamers, called 'engines' by their crews, were worked fly, the crew of four working shifts, the captain taking watch with the driver's (engineer's) mate

142. Wharf boat traffic on the BCN; an 86' long wharf boat, tugs and tows.

and the captain's mate paired with the driver. There were no wives carried except during the latter part of the 1914-18 War when wives acted as drivers on steamers which managed to work fly with husband and wife only. On the shorter Brentford-Braunston run a crew of three was needed, but most services were longer, from City Road Basin, London to Birmingham and Coventry, and from either Brentford or City Road to Leicester, Nottingham and Derby, also occasionally Market Harborough. The longer round trips took a week, but the Brentford-Braunston boats could manage three in a fortnight. Butties were not permanently paired with steamers, but exchanged, notably at Braunston, where some were taken on to Birmingham by horse. Steamers also worked down the Thames from Brentford into Bow Creek, and on to the Lee from the Regent's via Sir George Duckett's Canal. For the Thames tideway an anchor, life buoys, navigation lights and sweeps had to be carried, while on the Trent they had to take on a local waterman as pilot. Many steamers were converted to motors and others sold to Number Ones, the ex Fellows, Morton EARL being the last in service as a steamer, finally sunk at Hillmorton in 1931. An odd craft was the SENTINEL built in 1927 by J. H. Taylor & Sons of Chester for C. Payne Crofts of Northampton. A wooden boat, she had a Sentinel steam road waggon engine and vertical boiler, soon replaced by a motor because of the difficulties of ash disposal.

TANK BOATS. Akin to tar boats were narrow boats fitted with portable tanks for carrying chemicals, mainly acids. Best known were those owned by W. H. Cowburn & Cowpar of Manchester. In 1933 W. J. Yarwood & Sons of Northwich built them two composite motor boats for single operation, the SWAN and the SWIFT, followed by eight all steel motors, with rounded bilges. All could be fitted with two portable cylindrical tanks arranged in tandem for the carriage of highly inflammable carbon disulphide. Between the engine room and the after tank was a cofferdam, while in the event of fire the hold could be flooded by a special cock.

TAR BOATS or GAS BOATS. For the bulk carriage of tar, creosote and ammonia water from gas works, hence 'gas boats' and petroleum, narrow canal tankers replaced transport in barrels. An iron tank boat was registered in 1873, but few were built of iron or steel. The cargo space stiffened by beams, was decked over, the deck pierced by hatches or lids for cargo handling, the tar being pumped in or out (41, 47). Steam was used to liquefy it before discharge and for washing out. The tank was sub-divided, transverse partitions sliding in grooves and resting on the keelson, to act as swill boards, to prevent the liquid surging. Motor boats were given bulkheads with an aperture closed by a paddle so that the trim could be controlled. Against each bulkhead was a safe loading mark. Horse boats were loaded 2" down by the head, so that the pull of the horse would bring them level. Best known of the tar boat operators were Thomas Clayton of Oldbury, Plate. 11. Most of their fleet were wood but some were iron, including their first motor the LINDOLA acquired second hand from Fellows, Morton & Clayton about 1936. Other operators were Chance & Hunt of Oldbury who ran local and long distance boats; they were chemical manufacturers, like the Brownhills Chemical Co. who had local boats on the Black Country system. There were also short haul boats in the Potteries run by the Staffordshire Chemical Co. of Tunstall. Because the hold was useless for anything save tar, horse boats were given a generous space under the fore deck for the stowage of hay, corn and lines. Many had a fore cabin and in these the foredeck space was reduced so that hay and corn had to go in a tent-like cover which the boatman called a cratch, on deck behind the towing mast, together with a barrel for oats and bran feed. Motor boats had no towing mast but had a short mast at the fore end for a headlamp which acted as a guide for the steerer, of particular value when the boat was empty. The hold was sealed fore and aft by narrow cofferdams, used as lade holes for pumping out and to protect the cabins from cargo seepage and fumes.

WHARF BOATS; also called 'Ampton' boats or 'Ampton flats' (Wolverhampton), these were coal boats built on narrow boat lines like Birmingham day boats but wider and longer, since they worked the lock free level from the Cannock Extension Canal and Anglesey basin along the Wyrley & Essington via Horseley Fields junction to Wolverhampton, Bilston, Tipton and Brindley's old main line. They could measure up to 86' x 7'9" beam, the turn at Horseley Fields being the limiting factor to their size. They had a hold depth of 3'9" carrying 45 to 50 tons (142). They were made up into trains of five behind a tug, or drawn by a single horse and were managed by two men. See also narrow boats; day boats.

GLOSSARY of NARROW BOAT TERMS: (Boat types, Boat parts, Boat Operation).

1. Boat Types, not already covered:

BACK O'THE MAP; refers to canals and boats on the other side of the ridge from Oldbury Smethwick, Tipton and Wolverhampton; the Dudley Canal, the Stourbridge Canal and the Stourbridge Extension.   BUTTY; a Staffordshire word for foreman and when a pair of horse boats travelled together, the butty led ('Household Words' vol. 18, 1858). Butty also, according to the Oxford English Dictionary, meant mate, so when steamers and motors were introduced the boat or boats they towed were called butties. Pairs of boats could butty each other, working through the locks in succession, the leading pair setting them.   CABIN BOATS; the day boatmen's description of a long distance narrow boat with a living cabin.   CHANGE BOAT; the spare boat kept by carriers for use when one of the fleet went on dock.   Number ones, or owner boatmen often had a change boat and some docks hired them out.   HIGH DECK BOAT; found in advertisements of the early nineteenth century to describe a cabin boat.   LOW COUNTRY BOAT; Black Country description of a long distance narrow boat, operating further than the plateau on which the Black Country system lies.   MONKEY BOAT; London area term for narrow boat.   MOTOR; a motor narrow boat.   RAILWAY BOAT; these and STATION boats operated as day boats between factory wharves on the Birmingham and Black Country system and the canal-to-rail interchange basins owned, as were the boats, by the three railway companies of the area, the GWR, LNWR and Midland. They also went down to Stourport, the 'Stour lifters', via Kidderminster. Many were wood but some were iron and later steel, with elm bottoms or wholly metal. For speed a number were built fine lined and were christened fly-boats. Most had no cabins and all were horse drawn, the horses trotting in the fly-boat services. Thirty eight steel boats were built by Yarwood's for the LMS between 1928 and 1931 with a final six in 1937-39. During the 1950s a few were converted to long distance cabin boats.   WATERCRESS BED; a badly leaking boat.   WOOSER; also 'worser' or 'wusser', a South Midlands name for a narrow boat, used for example on the Thames and on the Kennet & Avon Canal. It is a contraction of Worcester and was applied first to boats on the Worcs. & Birmingham Canal.

2. Boat Parts (See also Cabins and Fittings, page 258):

ANSER PIN; an iron or steel lug bolted to the top bend or top strake of a narrow horse boat or butty, one on each quarter, at the stern. On motor boats they are on the gunwale by the aft bulkhead of the cabin. A shackle or hook can be secured to them for mooring and breasting up, and for tunnel work (tunnel hooks) when boats were towed in trains by a tug.   BACK END; the back of the hold up against the forward bulkhead of the cabin. A space was made here for horse feed or coal.   BEAMS; portable, but placed across the cargo space with their ends socketed into brackets secured to the gunwales. Long distance boats have three beams, the mast beam, middle beam and stern beam. The mast beam is shaped; cut out to receive the mast, held in place by a chain while the other two are slotted to receive the stands. Some Runcorn canal boats simply had iron ties permanently fixed.   BLADES; propeller blades, and so the name for the propeller.   BOXMAST; the box shaped towing mast (143) of a long distance narrow boat, socketed into the keelson and held upright by the mast beam. Inside the wooden box is the actual mast, also of wood, of 4" x 4" timber, adjustable for height by a pin, because of the varied height of banks and the need to keep the line out of the water.   BOX PUMP; square section pump made of wood with a square wooden piston sealed by leather. It could be worked from two places in a loaded boat, by the mast and at the back end. A variant was a piece of iron piping with an iron piston which could be worked from anywhere, see below, lade hole.   BULK; some narrow boats had cratches with built out wing-like extensions forward. These were entirely decorative, the deck cloth being stretched over them, forming a curved 'bulk'. Hay or straw could be used for extra padding, see cloths, deck cloth.

CABIN BLOCK; acting as a chock for the rear of the stern plank, the last of the series of planks over the cargo, where it curved down to the cabin roof.   CABIN SLIDE; the sliding door in the cabin roof above the stern entrance doors.   CABIN SIDE STRINGS; ornamental ropes with fancy knots at their ends, each about 2' 6" long, passed through a brass ring on the cabin top, used to secure the coiled towline for fear of theft.   CHAINS; passed across the hull under the portable beams, they act as the deck beams would in a decked craft. They can be removed during loading but in a laden craft are hooked on and tightened by bottle screws to hold the shape of the hull.   CLOTHS; narrow boats depended on tarpaulins to protect their cargoes. Side cloths (see endpaper) were permanently fastened to the gunwale and extended by lines called strings, passed over the planks from one side, rove through eyelets in the opposite side cloth, passed back and made fast. These ran the full length of the hold from cratch to cabin. Their main purpose was to prevent water slopping inboard and to stop small coal rolling overside. Overhanging them on each side were the top cloths, either three or four, overlapping each other. They were made fast by strings passed through rings along the gunwale

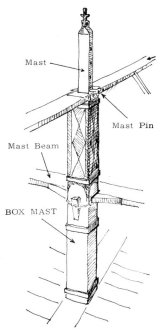

Mast

Mast Pin

Mast Beam

BOX MAST

A.J.Lewery.

143.

and kept the weather out. The fore cloth was often a semi-permanent fixture for the first three feet, between the cratch and the false cratch, under which the lines, fenders, and the cloths themselves were stored. Under the fore cloth some boats, notably those of Fellows, Morton & Clayton, had a shaped deck cloth covering the cratch and the forward few feet of the side cloths. The tippet was a long narrow cloth running along the top planks over the top cloths to protect them from the boatman's feet. Cloths were generally black tarpaulin canvas, although the Shropshire Union used undressed white canvas for their cheese boats. CRATCH; (see endpaper), the triangular boarding at the fore end of the hold to support the top planks. Many narrow boats never adopted it. They had instead a simple stand, the cloths being folded round the front. Early cratches were lashed to this same stand, the lashings being tightened by a wedge driven down between the stand and the cratch. In some boats the cratch was built up like a tent, with a 'false cratch' set 3' aft, linked to it by 'cratch boards' generally three a side. DECK; follows the accepted maritime sense, but 'in the deck' means the space under the fore deck used for storing lines and coal. DECK LID; the hatch to the 'deck' under the fore deck, hinged like a lid. DOOR HOLE; the aperture closed by the cabin doors. Hole is the narrow boatman's term for any space, such as 'engine hole' for engine room. FAN; propeller, hence 'fan hold' when the propeller bites. FENDERS and FEND-OFFS; because of the locks these were generously provided (148). The round stem fender took the shocks of hitting the breast wall of a lock and there might be a sill fender below it also. Horse boats and butties also had a small fender on the trailing edge of the rudder. Motor boats had banana shaped 'tip cat' fenders round the back of the counter, usually two, plus a buffer shaped stern fender long enough to protect the rudder. All were made from rope, either coiled up into a tight ball or cylinder sometimes surrounded by a rope basket, or in the case of tip cats, the ropes were lashed into a banana shaped core with a rope net worked round it. A chain was laid in the middle with its ends left hanging out for securing to the boat. FORE END; the bow of a narrow boat, universally used, bow never being heard. GIRDER ROPES and CHAINS; stout ropes lashed round the top planks where they overlapped and made fast to the gunwales by girder chains. Shafts were carried attached to the girder ropes. HATCHES; the cockpit of a butty or horse boat, a shallow well about 1'8" in depth, measuring back from the cabin doors about the same. In the hatches was a food locker, taking up a triangular space between the well and the stern post. HELLUM; helm, particularly the large wooden rudder of a horse boat or a butty, motor boats having an iron or steel balanced rudder with a lug on top to stop it swinging under the counter. HOOD ENDS; rebates in the stem and stern posts which receive the planking. ICE PLATES; thin sheets of galvanized iron. At the fore end they are tacked in overlapping vertical strips, each about 8" wide and they continue aft at full depth for about 10' and then as two strips, one along the loaded, the other along the empty waterline as far as the run in for the stern. KEB; a long handled rake with 9 or 10 tines carried by narrow boats to dredge coal out of the canal. The tines could be formed into a kind of sieve to hold small coal by weaving a rope between them. LADE HOLE; a sump or well in the shutts for pumping out. There were two in long distance boats, by the mast and at the back end (see Box Pump). LUBY; possibly spelt looby. The pin at the towing mast head to which the horse line was attached. It was mounted on a spring loaded pivot which allowed the pin to tip back if the boat overran the horse, so allowing the line to slip off and prevent the horse being dragged into the water. PIGEON BOX; the engine room skylight, each side hinged for ventilation and often pierced by round portholes. RAM'S HEAD; the top part of a wooden rudder post above the rudder itself, socketed for the curved tiller. It is decorated by painting and turk's head ropework above the tiller socket with a little 'wheel' of white cord or another turk's head below (147). Some boats used to sport a white horse's tail from the top of the ram's head. RUNNING BLOCKS; sited on the top planks but lashed to the gunwales, there were usually three, their purpose being to pass a towline from a pulley block on the mast aft to the cabin top, where it could be made fast to a stud bolted ahead of the cabin slide. By this means the steerer could ease the towline when the horse rounded a bend or cast off in an emergency. The practice was carried through to motor boat operation. SCOOP; pronounced scope, a wooden 5' handled shovel or scoop for bailing water out of the hold. SHAFTS; narrow boats generally carried three, two

144. The arrangement of the deck cloth at the fore end, the top cloth being
      spread and the tippet laid along the planks.

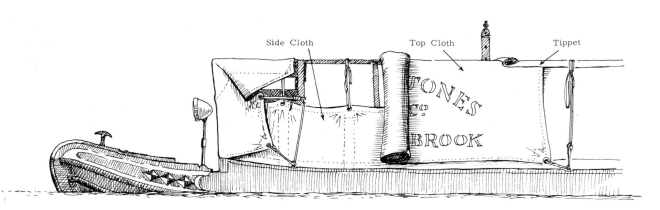

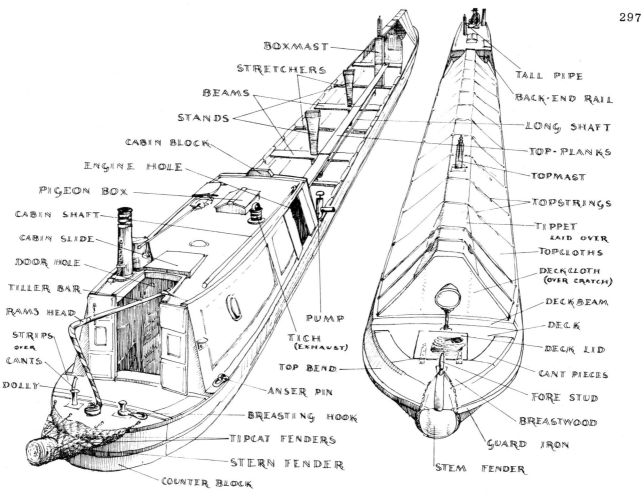

BOXMAST
STRETCHERS
BEAMS
STANDS
CABIN BLOCK
ENGINE HOLE
PIGEON BOX
CABIN SHAFT
CABIN SLIDE
DOOR HOLE
TILLER BAR
RAMS HEAD
STRIPS OVER CANTS
DOLLY

PUMP
TICH (EXHAUST)
TOP BEND
ANSER PIN
BREASTING HOOK
TIPCAT FENDERS
STERN FENDER
COUNTER BLOCK

TALL PIPE
BACK-END RAIL
LONG SHAFT
TOP-PLANKS
TOPMAST
TOPSTRINGS
TIPPET LAID OVER
TOPCLOTHS
DECKCLOTH (OVER CRATCH)
DECK BEAM
DECK
DECK LID
CANT PIECES
FORE STUD
BREASTWOOD
GUARD IRON
STEM FENDER

145. Motor Narrow Boat details.

146. Horse drawn Narrow Boat details.

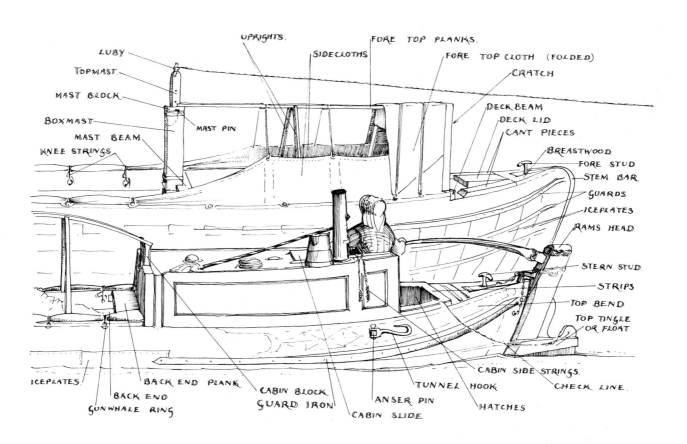

UPRIGHTS.
FORE TOP PLANKS.
SIDECLOTHS
FORE TOP CLOTH (FOLDED)
CRATCH
LUBY
TOPMAST.
MAST BLOCK
BOXMAST
MAST BEAM
MAST PIN
KNEE STRINGS

DECK BEAM
DECK LID
CANT PIECES
BREASTWOOD
FORE STUD
STEM BAR
GUARDS
ICEPLATES
RAMS HEAD
STERN STUD.
STRIPS
TOP BEND
TOP TINGLE OR FLOAT

ICEPLATES
BACK END PLANK
BACK END
GUNWHALE RING
CABIN BLOCK
GUARD IRON
CABIN SLIDE
ANSER PIN
TUNNEL HOOK
HATCHES
CABIN SIDE STRINGS.
CHECK LINE.

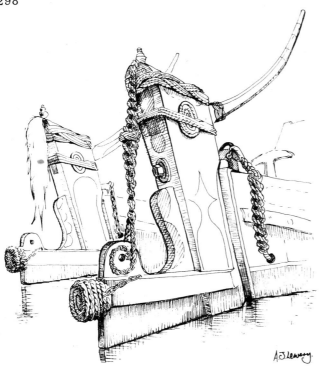

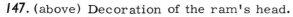
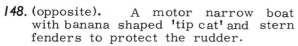

147. (above) Decoration of the ram's head.

148. (opposite).   A motor narrow boat
with banana shaped 'tip cat' and stern
fenders to protect the rudder.

long ones of about 20' and 15' respectively and a short cabin shaft of about 6' made of ash.
All had the boathook type spike and reverse hook, but some canal companies forbade spiked shafts because of damage to the puddle lining of the canal bed, for example the Stroudwater Navigation in 1778 issued special spikeless shafts at Framilode to incoming boats in
exchange for their own. Their use for shafting through tunnels was not encouraged either,
because of damage to the brickwork or masonry, but it was done.   SHUTTS; or shoots, the
floors in the hold which are secured to battens or grounds and are removable in sections.
The word is also found in Yorkshire keel terminology. STANDS; detachable wooden uprights
(149) socketed into the keelson and passing up through slots in the middle and stern beams.
They had rectangular heads to support the top planks which either overlapped or butted together with strengthening pieces in way of the stands. STEM POST; Black Country boatmen
talk about the fore stem post and the stern stem post because they are dealing with double
ended craft. STERN STUD; a 'T'-stud of iron like the fore stud but with the 'T' across the
boat. A safety chain from the top rudder pintle was secured to it by a collar, another chain
from the top pintle passing through a hole in the stern post to hold the helm down and prevent it being knocked up out of the thimble and top hole by any obstruction under the water.
STIFFENERS; thinner stands socketed into the keelson and used as an extra support for the
top planks, for example where they curved down to the cabin top. STRETCHERS; additional
to the beams, there could be three or four, held in brackets. They and the beams were of
particular importance if the boat was heavily laden in the bottom, the water tending to force
the sides inwards. SWAN'S NECK; decorative well scrubbed ropework from the top of the
ram's head to the lug at the end of the rudder. It was generally formed by continuous wall
or crown knotting with five or six strands of cotton rope over a shaped core and finished off
with two or three turk's heads. TILLER; of wood in a horse boat and butty, generally ash,
it is socketed into the ram's head and easily detached in locks. When not in use it is put in
upside down to clear people's heads. Motor boat tillers are of round iron bar, swan's neck
shaped; the handle, a wooden extension, held by a decorated brass 'tiller pin'. TOP BEND;
the top strake of planking of a narrow boat, particularly at the fore end and stern.   TOP
PLANKS; to pass quickly along the boat, there were generally 4, the fore plank from the cratch
to the top of the box mast, the back o'the mast plank from the mast to the first stand, the
middle plank between the stands and finally the stern plank from the last stand to the cabin
block. UPRIGHTS; not upright but diagonal struts between the gunwales and the top planks to
give extra support. They were in pairs and there could be as many as four pairs.

3. Boat Operation:

BACKERING; a well trained boat horse 'would go of 'isself' without leading. This was called
'backering'. BLOCKING; or 'blocking a boat out', see Locks, operation. BREASTED UP; a pair
of narrow boats secured side by side are breasted up. They are generally moored in this
way, but it was common for empty pairs on wide waterways to travel breasted up. Secured
in this way only one boat need be steered. CROSS STRAPS; for close up towing between a
motor and butty with the butty behaving like a trailer and so without the need for a steerer,

it was the practice to cross two short straps between the pin or
dolly hook on the motor's counter and the fore stud of the butty.
(see endpaper). CROSS WINDED; pronounced with a short 'i' it is
when a boat approaches a lock or bridge hole and fails to make
a clean entry, entering crooked and hitting one side wall, binding
against the other and maybe jamming. HOBBLER, HOBBLING; going
ahead to set the locks, also called lock wheeling. A hobbler was
also a casual chap who would help boats up locks. In South Wales
he was an owner captain or number one. HOLD IN, HOLD OUT;
steering directions, in to the towpath, out away from it. HORNS;
to give a warning at blind turns and bridge holes, horse boats
either sounded a brass mouth horn or cracked their 'smacking
whip'. Steamers had whistles and motor boats either a handle
operated klaxon making an ugly burping sound or an electric car
horn. LOCK LINING; this is a particular method of working
a motor and butty up flights of locks, see under locks, operation.
A variant of the practice was called 'missing a lock', the motor
being two locks ahead of the butty using 10 ordinary lines. LOCK
WHEELER; member of the crew sent ahead to set locks, generally
on a bicycle. Also called a 'hobbler'. RINGHOLE DEEP; a Black
Country and Birmingham term for a laden day boat, so low that
the water came level with the top guard. Another phrase described the boat as so low that the sparrows could drink off the side.
SAILS; not designed to be sailed, narrow boats used them on the

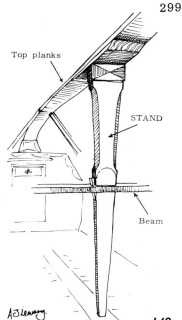

Top planks

STAND

Beam

149.

Thames, the Trent and on the Mersey & Irwell Navigation. To maintain stability under sail a
pair would travel breasted up with the mast stepped between them, according to the evidence
from E. W. Cooke's engraving of a pair under a single square sail on the Thames, published
in 1829. The shrouds go to each side outside the gunwale and the braces and sheets are led
back to one of the boats. Narrow boats passing on to the Trent from the Chesterfield Canal
set a square sail like a keel. The water sail used on the Severn by narrow boats was to aid
them when running down river independent of both tug and horse. A top cloth was suspended
in the water secured to the timber heads at the fore end and to the towing mast. The current
pressed upon it and the boat was given added steerage by lashing a shovel to the end of a
shaft. SNATCHER; a short rope also called a short strap, used for pair working through the
wide locks of the Grand Junction and its successor in 1929 the Grand Union. It was generally
of 3" manilla and about 15-20' long towing from the butty's fore stud, see locks, operation.
SNUBBER; was of 2" manilla and 60' long or over. It was employed for motor and butty
working on the Grand Junction between groups of locks. The idea was to keep the butty clear
of the motor's wash. STEMMED UP; run aground or into the bank. STEMMING; a method of
linking up Birmingham and Black Country day boats in trains behind a tug, see under tugs.
STRAP; any sort of rope of say 3" circumference for towing or boat handling, thus the cross
straps (see above) for close towing. A stern strap is most often employed to check a boat's
way, particularly when entering a full lock, see locks, operation. A strap is also used to help
a boat round a sharp bend. Then it is led from the fore end to a specially sited post right
on the corner. With the fore end held, the stern swings out, pivoting on the former, the strap
keeping the fore end in as the boat makes the turn. TACK STRING; an extra line 'tacked' on
to the towline of a horse boat, used in certain situations on the Birmingham Canal Navigations, also the line with the block peg used to block the boat out of a lock, see locks, operation.

PACKETS, RIVER WEAVER. Packet was the name for a Weaver steam barge and is still
applied to all motor barges on the navigation. The first steamer was introduced by A. T. Falk
in 1864, for his Winsford salt traffic and they soon supplanted the Weaver sailing flats and
towed the latter, many of which became dumb barges. After the locks were enlarged from
the 1870s, a packet and her tow of three barges could pass through each big lock at one
operation. Early packets were wooden steamers built until the 1900s. A few were composite
with steel or iron frames and wood planking; some early ones were built of iron salvaged
from salt pans, with stem posts of railway line, but after 1910 they were all-steel. Builders
were local, some Winsford salters building their own vessels. In 1888 many of these merged
into the new Salt Union combine (150). Their rivals were the larger Brunner, Mond packets,
this Company having started carrying in 1874. Steam packets were from 70' to over 120'
long by up to 21' beam (107), the largest vessels having a capacity of 300 tons on a draft of
10'. All had a single long hatch, and a mast and steam operated derrick, which was mounted in a tabernacle because of the low road bridge at Hartford and in the early days, the
fixed Town bridge at Northwich. Funnels were hinged and had counterweights. By the steam
winch on the foredeck was the companion to the fo'c'sle accommodation for the crew of three
comprising captain, mate and engineer, or in the larger packets four, the fourth being an apprentice deckhand or engineer. The engineer called colloquially the 'engine driver' was also
fireman, the engines being controlled from the helm. In nearly all the Salt Union boats and
one of the Brunner, Mond, the boiler was mounted athwartships to gain more hold space, so
that the funnel was offset (84). Boilers were of the return tube type. The engines of the powerful
HERALD OF PEACE, built in 1877 had two cylinders arranged in a vee, with the connecting
rods working on to a common crankpin. Most Salt Union packets had vertical two cylinder
simple or high pressure engines which used steam at 120 psi exhausting to the atmosphere via

150.

The Salt Union steam packet VALE ROYAL loading a salt cargo by chute; Anderton circa 1914.

the feed water heater, while others used compounds with jet condensers. Brunner, Mond boats on the other hand had compound engines with surface condensers. Wheel steering was universal, the Salt Union steering from right aft and the later Brunner, Mond boats having a small bridge just forward of the funnel. Salt, usually bagged, and chemicals were the main cargoes of the packets, some making two or three trips a week down to Liverpool and Birkenhead, so the crew lived aboard. Other owners were Henry Seddon of Middlewich, salt manufacturers, who had the WEAVER BELLE, Plate 3, which towed the large composite built, 90' barge GOWANBURN; the Northwich Carrying Co. with their ALICE CAPPER, built in 1875, carried foodstuffs and the United Alkali Co. Ltd., who had coasters and river steamers named after elements like RODIUM and SODIUM. The last steamers were built as late as 1946, the ANDERTON and the DAVENHAM, for Imperial Chemical Industries, but in 1947/49 seven similar motor vessels followed and the steamers were withdrawn over the next 15 years. Decoration was limited to painted strakes at bow and stern and painted hawse ports, timber heads, rails and windlass drums, in red, green or yellow. Some of the Salt Union packets sported a light blue trailing edge to the rudder, flanked by varnished bulwarks against the rudder head. The sailing flat practice of painting distinguishing bands of colour at the masthead was continued for the packets, the Salt Union having red with a white band while Henry Seddon had red, cream and blue from top to bottom, with a gold truck.

PUFFERS, SCOTLAND. The puffer of the West Highlands had her roots in the cargo scows of the Forth & Clyde Canal. In 1856 the iron horse scow THOMAS was converted into a steam lighter by James Milne, the Forth & Clyde Canal's engineer. A small vertical boiler and two-cylinder simple engine were fitted, with no condenser, hence the name puffer, although the exhaust simmered rather than puffed. In 1858 there were seven steam scows on the Forth & Clyde Canal and two years later 25. They carried mainly minerals such as coke, ironstone, foundry sand and limestone. With a single long hatch and hatchboards they could also carry perishables, but were unable to venture into the river because they had no anchor gear. Improvements were made and the range increased. Derricks were fitted, not always with a steam winch, for cargo work and for putting a man ashore to work locks and drawbridges on the canal. These iron hulled craft were called canal puffers and with their three man crew, skipper, mate and engineer, ventured down the Clyde as far as Greenock and to Leith on the Forth. They were allowed no further for they had no bulwarks abreast the hatch, being flush decked with little sheer (151). To go under Glasgow bridges their masts lowered in a tabernacle, while they retained tiller steering suited to canal work. The canal puffer measured 66' by 14' to 16' beam, carrying 80 tons on a draught of 6' or 7'. Engines and boilers were more powerful than those in the scows and Currie's of Leith (the Leith, Hull & Hamburg S.P. Co. Ltd.) had some with single furnace return tube boilers needing tall thin funnels to obtain sufficient draught. Some of the Currie boats had vee type diagonal engines. Other prominent owners were the Carron Co., whose sea-going vessels and puffers carried a cannon ball at the masthead, H. Salvesen, Jacks & Co., and John Hay. It was common for a puffer to tow a scow on the Forth & Clyde although they were cargo carriers rather than tugs, transhipment taking place at Grangemouth, Leith and Bowling. By 1870 puffers were being built for coastal service, an early one built in 1868 being the KELPIE. They were given bulwarks and later a quarterdeck, a punt for getting ashore from an anchorage, and a foresail and gaff mainsail to save coal, the mainsail degenerating into a trysail. Their hull was modelled on the sailing gabbarts and had more sheer than canal puffers. Two types appeared, the smaller 'shorehead' boats within the Firth of Clyde, and the coasters or 'outside' boats which penetrated the West Highlands to the Outer Isles via the Crinan Canal and across to the coasts of Antrim and Donegal. On the east coast they went up to the Moray Firth and down to Tyneside and Middlesbrough. The shorehead boats with a crew of three measured up to 66' by 15' to 16' with a loaded draught of up to 7', carrying 80 tons. The coasters, Plate 6, with a crew of four including a deckhand were 66' by up to 18'6" beam with a loaded draught of 9'6", the limit for the Crinan Canal, carrying up to 120 tons. At a reduced draught they could still use the Forth & Clyde Canal, where indeed many were built of iron and later steel, at Hamiltonhill, Maryhill and Kirkintilloch. Others were built at Larne, Greenock and notably at Scott & Sons, Bowling. Wooden puffers were rare, one was built on an Arran beach in about 1895 by the Hamiltons of Brodick, their first GLENCLOY. Some puffers were 'rose on' or heightened by the addition of solid bulwarks to make them shorehead or outside boats, while later some of the 66' boats were lengthened 19' up to 85', the maximum for the Crinan Canal. Wheel steering appeared by the 1870s, placed aft with the engine controls alongside. By about 1910 open bridges were being fitted on the engine casing abaft the funnel, not enclosed to form a wheelhouse until the 1920s. Accommodation had been in the forecastle for all the crew, but by the 90s the captain was given a tiny semi-circular cabin aft over the propeller. Sea-going puffers had compound condensing engines. Most of the compounds were two-crank, although the Burrell yard at Hamiltonhill favoured the single-crank, tandem arrangement. Vertical boilers stayed almost to the end of puffer building, some being Cochrane type. Motor puffers were introduced as early as 1913 by the Coasting Motor Shipping Co., of Glasgow, 65' long with counter sterns and oil engines of Scandinavian make, some of them Bolinders. Unfortunately they were not a success, due to lack of experienced engineers, and were sold during the 1914-18 War. Not until 1953 did a motor re-appear with Hamilton's GLENSHIRA and from then the demise of steam was rapid.

RAFTS: These were an easy method of moving timber lashed together and towed, for example on the Norwich river behind wherries, one of which is recorded as towing a raft 100 yards long by 20 feet wide up to Norwich. It had to be broken up into sections to get round some of the corners. Wherries also towed timber lashed on either side, still managing to sail. There were rafts on the Regent's Canal in the early nineteenth century but the Severn was the great rafting river. From the thirteenth to the eighteenth centuries timber felled along its banks was sent down in this way, although damaging to bridges. In addition on the Severn, rafts, called floats or drags, were used to handle heavy and bulky cargoes, including the beam engine cylinders cast and bored by John Wilkinson at Broseley.

SCOWS, SCOTLAND. Canal boats in Central Scotland are called scows. They measured about 60' x 13'6" carrying 70 to 80 tons on a draught of 5' or 6', narrow enough for the Monkland locks, although those going up the locks of the Union Canal were a foot narrower. They were round bilged double ended craft, earlier examples being wood although iron was used early in the nineteenth century, certainly from 1824. Fore and aft were short decks with a small day cabin below deck aft, for the three crew. One man was in charge of the towing horse, usually a Clydesdale towing from a stud on the foredeck, the others steered and worked locks and drawbridges. Some scows were open but those carrying perishables had a hatch and hatch boards, the open ones being used for minerals, pig iron, coal, coke, limestone and foundry sand. In 1833 the Forth & Clyde Canal experimented with an iron scow carrying carts, it was able to take up to 18 on deck, while two years later tramroad waggon scows were successfully tried, carrying 14 waggons loaded with a total of 40 tons of coal. The waggons were run on to the deck at the canalside terminus of the Monkland & Kirkintilloch Railway at Kirkintilloch. The Forth & Clyde had a large fleet of scows and another important owner was the Carron Co, users of the canal from the start, and the Leith, Hull and Hamburg S. P. Co., shipowners. In 1856 one of the Forth & Clyde's iron horse drawn scows, THOMAS was converted to steam to operate between Port Dundas and Falkirk and the puffer was born. The steam scows lasted on the Monkland until about 1900 and on the Forth & Clyde until the 1920s, they never went on the Union Canal because the fixed bridges were too low for them. A few became steam suppliers to grain elevators in the Glasgow docks and three were at work as late as 1954 (152). Dumb steel scows were built for canal use as late as 1948 and they remained until the late 1950s on the Forth & Clyde, towed by puffers. See also Puffers above.

SLOOPS; see keels.

TROWS:

TROWS and 'WICH BARGES, SEVERN. Cargo sailing vessels on the Severn, Wye and associated waterways have from the fifteenth century, been called trows (to rhyme with crows). Sketchy pictorial evidence of the late sixteenth century shows open double ended boats sailed or bow hauled. The square sail later joined by a square topsail, persisted through the seventeenth to the eighteenth century, and the trow became a flat bottomed,

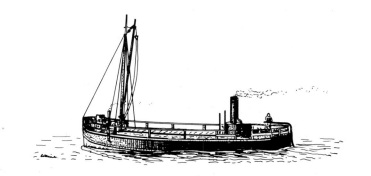

151. Carron Co., puffer, probably No. 12, built 1878.

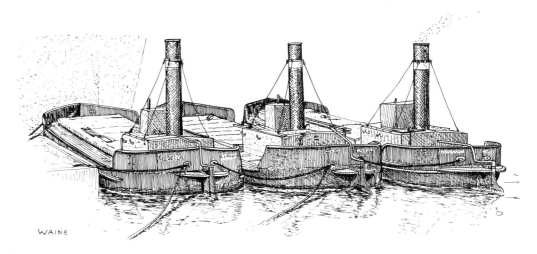

152.

Steam Scows.   WAINE

beamy, transom or square sterned craft with an open hold designed to carry as much cargo as possible on a shallow draught, characteristics probably dating from the seventeenth century. The flat bottom was necessary in case of grounding on the changing sandbanks of the Severn. A heavy keelson gave the craft strength to lie aground. Mid-eighteenth century trows averaged 40 to 80 tons capacity, in the nineteenth some could carry over 100 tons. The main feature was the deep D shaped transom, the D lying on its curved back, sometimes pierced with a square window or windows, one each side of the rudder post, the rudder being hung outboard. Some trows, notably those built at Brimscombe, were double ended with a round stern. The hold was open, protected by vertical canvas side-cloths (88) between the bulwarks at bow and stern, and across the ends of the hold. The cloths were held up by rails laid on stanchions with forked ends, higher than the fixed bulwarks fore and aft. They were said to be floating on their side cloths when deeply laden. The bilge was rounded as was the bow, sometimes with a fiddle shaped cutwater attached to the upright stem. The square rig remained well into the nineteenth century, particularly on the 'Wich barges so called because they traded up the Droitwich Canal, although fore and aft sails were introduced as early as 1799. This innovation may have been due to the enterprise of the Thames & Severn Canal Co., who ordered a fleet of new trows, ketch rigged, for the Welsh coal trade. Some appear to have had fixed keels and must have resembled coasting trows of the later nineteenth century, others had a movable keel or 'keelboard' which became a regular trow feature, used when the vessel was light and held by brackets fore and aft with a securing chain round the stern.

From the 1830s much traffic on the Severn was handled by tugs and lighters so the sailing trows went further afield, into the Bristol Channel, Plate 8. Open trows were modified into 'half box' or 'box' trows, the former protected by permanently building up the ends and sides of the hold level with the bulwarks, the latter having side decks and hatch coamings in the normal manner. The hatch was covered with a tarpaulin stretched over a central rail, but some 'box' trows had hatch boards. Box trows had continuous bulwarks and were decked with waterways at each side of the hatch coamings, the waterways being at the level of the fore and after decks in the coasting trows, but in the canal and river trows often built up level with the bulwarks to increase the capacity of the hold, which was covered either by boards

Valuable cargoes were carried: A 'lock up' trow had a special enclosed part of the hold reserved for cargoes liable to be pilfered such as wines and spirits, which could be secured by padlocks. A tabernacle winch on the forecastle abaft the windlass was used for raising and lowering the mast and sails. A trow's boat or punt was used for towing a trow when becalmed. They were up to 23' x 7'4" x 2'8" with four or six oars. Large coasting trows were built, notably at Bridgwater. Some had counter sterns and some were schooner rigged, with wheel steering, fixed masts and keels. During the nineteenth century the ketch rig became common for coastal and river trows although the smaller 'Wich barges favoured the smack or sloop rig. Many trows ended as lighters on the Severn and Gloucester & Berkeley Canal. Some had unusually long lives, the WILLIAM (88) built on the Severn at the Bowyer yard at Bentall near Broseley in 1809 lasted under sail until 1939, by then the oldest British merchant vessel trading. Until the railways, trows and smaller barges went up to Shrewsbury and beyond, and up the Wye to Hereford. This trade depended on the depth of water, the Severn never being improved above Stourport. Trows traded up the Droitwich Canal for salt (which ensured some well preserved hulls), and the Stroudwater Navigation and the Thames & Severn Canal as far as Brimscombe, for the locks above were too narrow. Early in the nineteenth century small trows were built for through Severn-Thames work, via both the Thames & Severn and Kennet & Avon Canals. Mast, bowsprit, rigging, anchors and cables were removed for canal work. During the nineteenth century trows were active in the Forest of Dean coal trade from Bullo Pill to Bristol Channel ports, and from the 1850s, took coal from South Wales to Highbridge for use on the Somerset & Dorset Railway. Other later cargoes were gravel, stone from Tintern and sand. Trows were built at Framilode, Brimscombe, Lydney, Saul, Hereford, Bristol and Cardiff the latter two building ten iron trows with counter sterns, for Benjamin Danks & Sons of Stourport between 1843 and 1876. Small trows were built on the Kennet & Avon Canal at Honeystreet near Pewsey and at Aldermaston in Berkshire. Trow decoration was sparse, some had a line of painted ports copying deep-sea tradition, but more normally a white or yellow strake relieved the tarred black of the hull. Frequently two life buoys were hung over the transom. Trow sizes varied from the 64' x 14' of a 'Wich barge to the 75' overall by 19' 6" of the coastal trow NORAH. The coastal trows in the nineteenth century had a crew of three, two sleeping forward and the captain aft. The 'Wich barges had a crew of two living aft. Before the 1850s trows had bigger crews, three in the non-tidal part of the Severn and five in the tidal. See also Barges; Bristol and River Severn.

TUGS, Introduction: The first steam canal tug was built on the Bridgewater at Worsley about 1797. She was apparently designed by Robert Fulton, the Newcomen engine with two cylinders being supplied by Bateman & Sherratt of Salford. She worked well enough, towing eight boats with 25 tons of coal in each from Worsley to Manchester. Then Symington's CHARLOTTE DUNDAS was tried on the Forth & Clyde in 1802. With her single stern mounted paddle wheel she was able to tow two 70 ton laden scows for nearly 20 miles, but the paddle wash was unacceptable. The Duke of Bridgewater was sufficiently impressed to order from Symington similar tugs to the CHARLOTTE DUNDAS for his canal, but on his death in 1803 the trustees cancelled them.

River Tugs: Currents and obstructions made horse towing and sailing a risky business. Tug's could handle several craft at once and were more economical in the long run, with an added value in tidal water. As early as 1818 there was a tug on the tidal Trent between Hull and Gainsborough and on the Humber between Hull and Goole from 1826, services soon being extended further up the Ouse. The Aire & Calder began steam towage of fly-boats between Goole and Leeds in 1831 via the Knottingley-Goole canal. From 1830 a tug was operating between Bristol, Gloucester and Worcester. Appropriately called SABRINA, she cut towage times and could handle a 60 to 70 ton laden trow at 8 m.p.h. The Mersey & Irwell were cautious, they considered steam towage as early as 1815 but found fuel consumption too heavy. From the early 1830s they had steam tugs working between Runcorn and Liverpool as did the Bridgewater trustees, but not on their own navigation until much later. Early nineteenth century tugs were all paddlers. Paddle tugs were a great advantage in shallow water where a screw would fail to grip, but a screw allowed a more compact engine layout. The Bridgewater trustees, and their successors had a fleet of paddle tugs on the Mersey towing flats between Runcorn and Liverpool. The Manchester Ship Canal took them over but in 1926-7 replaced the four survivors by four screw tugs built for army use on the French canals during the 1914-18 War. The last two paddle barge tugs were the DAGMAR and the ST. WINIFRED. The screw river tug has evolved as a smaller edition of the harbour tug with the same full bow but fine run aft to give a good propeller flow, with the stern shaped into an overhanging elliptical counter which presses down on the water as the screw takes hold, stopping cavitation. Steam has been gradually replaced by diesel power. There have been conversions from steam to diesel, for example the Severn & Canal Carrying Co's SEVERN VICTOR, built in 1904 was converted to diesel in the early 1950s. Other Severn & Canal tugs, for example the SEVERN ENTERPRISE, built in 1930 and the SEVERN PROGRESS were built with diesels, the former with a twin cylinder Widdop. Some craft were built for special towing purposes such as the Aire & Calder Navigation's compartment boat tugs, first steam with 120 h.p. engines and from 1957 diesel, squat beamy craft with bluff bows and sterns and a curious reverse sheer at the fore end. Towing is done from timber heads. For push towing on the Yorkshire navigations more specialist tugs have been introduced. Those operated by the Cawoods Hargreaves consortium pushing the 170 ton capacity compartment boats have rectangular hulls, and a diesel powered Harbourmaster inboard-outboard drive, using the propeller as a rudder. Tugs revolutionized Fenland water transport. On the Lark a narrow canal type steam tug was used to tow coal lighters up to Bury St. Edmunds in the 1890s, but on the Great Ouse a larger class of vessel could be employed like the OLGA and ANNIE of the West Norfolk Manure Co., each with a tall thin funnel. Steam tugs were also employed on the Lee until replaced by diesels in the 1950s. These handle the dumb lighters which do all the carrying on this navigation. On the Severn, craft were towed in two parallel lines with up to a dozen in each, narrow boats, trows and barges all mixed together. With this arrangement, the tug's wash passed down between the two columns and did not hinder steerage. On the Mersey, the Bridgewater tugs could handle up to 16 flats, again in two parallel lines, while the compartment boat tugs (39) on the Aire & Calder could handle up to 40 units.

Canal Tugs: Still-water canals were slower in adopting tugs because of damage to the banks, moreover they were of little use if locks were frequent. Only on long pounds could their cost be justified. Here boats could be coupled up in long trains as on rivers, a tug perhaps being stationed in each long pound to take over the tows as they passed through the intervening locks. Among the first canal tugs were those put on for tunnels. For canal towage proper the earliest, apart from experimental vessels, seem to have been on the Macclesfield and the Ellesmere & Chester, incorporating the Birmingham & Liverpool Junction, both with long pounds between lock flights. Each started tug haulage in the 1840s, but the Shropshire Union found the system uneconomic and reverted to horses except on the lock free Wirral line. The Shropshire Union also had river tugs for barge work on the Mersey, some of which carried passengers between Ellesmere Port and Liverpool. After they gave up carrying, the Midlands & Coast Canal Carrying Co., tried to revive tug towage between Wolverhampton and Ellesmere Port using the motor tug ENERGY. She had a large windlass for working boats through locks but her career was not very successful. Another lock free canal was the Ashby where in 1856 the Moira Colliery Co., introduced the steam tug PIONEER. She had twin contra rotating screws to minimise wash, and was joined by the VOLUNTEER and both worked trains of coal boats down to Braunston. A third tug on this service was the HARRISON acquired in 1861. Tugs found more favour on broad canals with their larger barges. The Grand in Ireland had tugs from 1865, towing up to six barges on the two long levels between Robertstown and

Ballycommon. The Forth & Clyde having condemned the CHARLOTTE DUNDAS in 1803, did not try another steam tug until the CUPID was put on in 1828 and later developed the steam lighter towing scows. In England the Leeds & Liverpool introduced company tugs in 1871. They worked between the principal lock flights; between Liverpool and Wigan, Wigan and Johnson's Hillock, Johnson's Hillock and Blackburn, and Blackburn and Barrowford, with horses at each flight. With a beam of 8' they were shortened short boats, with a raised cabin for most of their length covering crew accommodation, engine and boiler. In winter some were used for ice breaking. Leeds & Liverpool traders had tugs too, for example the Wigan Coal & Iron Co., with four steamers, the ENGLAND, IRELAND, SCOTLAND and WALES. In 1875-6 Leader Williams ordered six tugs for the Bridgewater and the fleet eventually amounted to 26 (45). They were built of Low Moor iron with horizontal engines which exhausted to the atmosphere, the drive to the large diameter and low revving screw being by bevel gears. They had counter sterns and wheel steering and were named after local places like STRETFORD (Plate 12), THELWALL and ROCHDALE. Built by Richard Smith of Preston and by Edward Hayes of Stony Stratford on the Grand Junction, they measured 59'3"-61' overall, by 7'7"-8'9" by 3'9" draught. Called packets, they could tow three flats on the Bridgewater and six on the Manchester Ship Canal in two lines of 3 and even more on the Mersey. They saved money but the company spent it walling the canal sides. From about 1926 they were converted to diesel, some with 70 h.p. Gardner engines, the first conversion being the STOCKTON.

There were tugs on the Grand Junction mainly handling the gravel boats in the London area; on the Regent's operated by the Thames lighterage companies, while the Thames and Severn put some into service in the 1870s to try and revive their fortunes. The Portsmouth & Arundel had to have one to tow barges between Birdham on Chichester Harbour and Milton on the Portsea Canal. On the Birmingham and Black Country system with intensive short haul traffic, tugs hauling several boats would achieve considerable economies. Steam screw tugs were introduced in the later nineteenth century, built on narrow boat lines with a shortened hull. Chance & Hunt, the Oldbury chemicals manufacturers, had them, DISPATCH being one of them, and this firm introduced the first motor tugs to the BCN, the STENTOR and HECTOR, each fitted with a 25 h.p. Bolinder. The STENTOR was built in 1919 under subcontract from James Pollock of Faversham by Walkers' of Rickmansworth. She was more elaborate than the usual BCN motor tug, able to sleep seven people in two cabins, front and rear. The average tug was 40' or so feet long and drew 3' of water. The engine was amidships and could be as powerful as 36 h.p. Most had a day cabin with a stove and benches astern of the engine room. If they had a sleeping cabin it was forward. It was common for up to nine empty boats to be marshalled behind a tug, or about four loaded ones. To save steerers of the towed boats, 'stemming' was practiced, that is they were paired, each having their stem and stern posts overlapping and lashed. The second boat had to be steered with reverse helm pushing the leading boat round. Push towing is now favoured for all purposes including mud boats. No one need be aboard the tow which is fully under the control of the pusher, the pushed barges needing no rudders. The Brentford firm of E.C. Jones have since 1948 developed the 'Bantam' tug for this, although some Bantams tow in the traditional way. The British Waterways Board use many Bantam pusher tugs for maintenance work. Larger tugs have been converted to push work, for example the FRANCE HAYHURST on the Weaver while the more recent NORTHWICH on the same river was built as a pusher in 1961.

Ship Canal Tugs: Britain's few ship canals need or have needed tugs to handle seagoing ships, vital in sailing ship days. At first the Gloucester & Berkeley had only horse haulage but tugs were introduced in the 1850s. One Gloucester & Berkeley iron screw tug, the MAYFLOWER built in 1861, remained in service until 1966. Today they are all diesel, handling only barge traffic, an example being the RESOLUTE built in 1897 as a steamer for the Sharpness New Docks Co., She was converted to diesel in 1956 reducing her crew from five to three. The Manchester Ship Canal Tugs work one ahead and one astern, and guide as well as propel the ships under tow. The first ones were paddlers, the last of these, the MSC RIXON, being withdrawn in 1955. Since 1966 when the MSC BISON and MSC BADGER were withdrawn they have all been diesel, the modern ones with hydroconic hull form and excellent wheelhouse visibility, for the funnel has given way to twin uptakes forming two legs of a tripod mast. They are twin screw and highly manoeuvrable.

Tunnel Tugs: Steam power was seen as a solution for canal tunnels with no towpath and a steam tug was considered for Standege on the Huddersfield Canal as early as 1816. This was to haul itself along by winching in and paying out a chain cable laid along the tunnel invert. In 1824 a cable tug was put into service, followed in 1826 by one in Islington tunnel on the Regent's Canal. Other canal authorities followed suit after the successful development of the screw propeller, which gave more flexibility, but there was always the problem of ventilation. The Grand Junction would have preferred to keep steam tugs away from their two long tunnels, but they were forced to start a service in 1871 after cable haulage experiments failed. The Grand Junction tugs were each 49' x 7' x 4'5" and coal fired. They had condensing engines. Two were stationed at each tunnel, one in steam, one in reserve, the Braunston tug providing an hourly service backwards and forwards, the Blisworth an hour and a half. Each had a driver and steerer who worked shifts because the timetable ran from 5 a.m. to 9 p.m. About 20 narrow boats could be handled at once, totalling 500 tons. Because of the large numbers of motor boats by the 1930s, the steam tugs were withdrawn in 1936. Steam tugs were introduced in 1876 for the three summit level tunnels of the Worcester & Birmingham Canal. The Sharpness New Docks Co., put two into service, BIRMINGHAM and GLOUCESTER, one to work in the long West Hill tunnel, the other in the Shortwood and Tardebigge tunnels. Later three more tugs arrived, WORCESTER, STOKE and DROITWICH. With the coming of the motor tugs from 1908, the steamers were withdrawn, the SHARPNESS and her sisters

153. Tunnel tugs; one of the wheeled tugs taking up her tow at Preston Brook.

WORCESTER (Plate 6) and BIRMINGHAM undertaking not only tunnel work but also towing on the Severn, the Gloucester & Berkeley and from Tardebigge to Birmingham, together with ice-breaking. At the northern end of the Trent & Mersey the three tunnels at Preston Brook, Saltersford and Barnton were given tugs by 1864. They provided a 50 minute service through the tunnels from 6.00 a.m. to 8.30 p.m, with two shifts of tugmen. To save steering, two of the tugs were fitted with guide wheels on a vertical axis (153), two each side. The engines were single cylinder horizontals without condensers which drove the screws by right angled bevel gears. Locomotive type boilers were used to raise steam to 90 p.s.i, fired on coal. The guide wheel tugs, numbered 1 and 2 were joined about 1910 by No. 3, a larger vessel which could only work through Preston Brook. She had a two cylinder simple vertical engine. Services lasted until about 1943. Also on the Trent & Mersey was the electric tug for the Harecastle tunnel. The North Staffordshire Railway planned to use a non-steam tug in the new tunnel as early as 1904, but there were objections to the toll. However a tug was placed in service in 1914 by which time the old Brindley tunnel had become impassable, so that a tug was vital. Since there were no ventilating shafts only an electric tug was possible, haul-ing itself along by cable. Two 15 h.p. motors provided the traction, taking current from batteries loaded in a narrow boat behind, while a second boat was charged by a plant at the Chatterley end and another was on stand-by. After the 1914-18 War overhead wires replaced the battery boats, the current being picked up by a trolley pole. One of the narrow boats was retained to issue tunnel toll tickets. Working an hourly service, the tug had a long day from 6 a.m. to 10 p.m. She was withdrawn in 1954 when ventilating fans were installed at Chatterley and motor boats allowed to proceed through under their own power.

To save winding, a double ended design of tug was used at Foulridge and Gannow on the Leeds & Liverpool. The Foulridge tug was ordered in 1880 and the Gannow started work in 1887. Both these steamers had propellers at each end with clutches, the compound engine of the Foulridge also driving an air pump to charge bottles to be used in case of asphyxiation. The Foulridge tug, which had provided an hourly service, was withdrawn about 1935 but con-tinued as an ice-breaker, while the Gannow tunnel tug came off in 1937. Rather similar to the Leeds & Liverpool design was the blunt ended tug put on in 1914 to work a half hourly service through Gosty Hill tunnel on the Dudley Canal. She had a propeller at each end which could be engaged by a clutch. Named GEORGE II she was sold about 1935. Her engine was a 20 h.p. Bolinder burning paraffin, the original plan being to have a 15 h.p. Bolinder at each end. A motor tug of similar design worked through the long Dudley tunnel. She was the GEORGE I, but fumes caused her early withdrawal. Working steam tunnel tugs was an ardu-ous business. Each night at Preston Brook the fire was banked up and the boiler tubes swept every morning. Only on Monday mornings was steam raised from cold, (for there was no Sunday service), taking two hours. Before each tow the fire was made up so that by the time the tug was under way it was burning clear with no smoke. The leading narrow boat of the train, which could number up to 20 boats, put on the 20' tug's towrope, the rest of the train, coupling up with their own lines. Because the special winding hole was so close to the portal at each end of the tunnel, the tug could never draw its train clear. The first three boats to emerge were attached to their horses, the tug cast off, and the train pulled further out by three horse power. These three would then leave and the next three or four horses come down and pick up their boats. Towing was from the fore end T-stud of the leading boat so that it could be easily slipped. Because of the strain on this and on the stempost, the trains at Harecastle were limited to 21 loaded boats although the tug could manage 30.

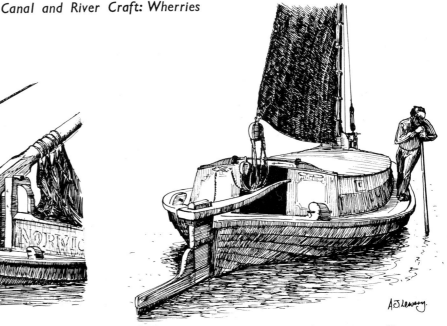

154. Lowering the mast of a Wherry,
the windlass swings to one side
to allow the heel to rise.

155. Quanting a Wherry, the man walks
along the plankway.

Tunnel Sweeping Boat; with the establishment of steam tugs in Blisworth and Braunston tunnels from 1871, some method had to be devised for regular sweeping of the tunnel walls. After using a large hawthorn bush on a narrow boat, in 1908 a mud hopper was fitted with 3 specially shaped wire brushes. The brushes were fitted forward of the well so that the soot dropped into it. The hopper was towed by a tug and on the first sweeping operation 10 tons of soot were collected from both tunnels.

WHERRIES, NORFOLK. Sixteenth century wherries were passenger and light cargo carriers; they did not rival the Norfolk keels as cargo vessels until the eighteenth century. The nineteenth century was the heyday of the wherry despite railway competition, but road transport took their trade after the 1914-18 War. Larger wherries traded on the Yare, Waveney and Lowestoft Navigation, smaller on the Bure and Ant, including the Aylsham Navigation and the North Walsham & Dilham Canal. Wherries also traded to Bungay, on the Chet to Loddon, and on the Blyth Navigation, with occasional local coasting trips. Cargoes were varied, coal, sand, marl, manure, bricks, ice for fishing smacks, wheat, barley for the maltings, timber, reeds for thatching and latterly sugar beet. Before the railways everything came by keel and wherry. One Norwich wherry the ENCHANTRESS, had tanks for carrying tar in bulk. Hulls of wooden wherries, a few were built of iron, were well rounded with plenty of flare to bow and stern, and vee bottomed, much attention being paid to the design, since they were so shallow-draughted. Most were clinker built, some with pointed sterns, some with square transoms (favoured on the Bure). A typical wherry, the GLEANER (ex ORION) of 1894, was 52' overall, 14' beam and 4' depth; loaded to the gunwale she could carry 25 tons; largest of all was the WONDER of Norwich carrying 90 tons and built in 1878. One of the smallest was DOROTHY, trading up the Dilham Canal, carrying 14 tons. Oak was used for all the hull planking with garboard strakes of elm. The hatches were long and wide with the top half of the coamings or 'right ups' removable for easier cargo handling, abaft the hatches came the 7' long cabin for the crew of two. Either side of the hatches were the 'plankways' edged by a white painted covering board or 'plancea', on which the men walked aft when quanting (shafting), the white being useful at night as were the white painted quadrants on either bow called 'nosings'. Wherry decoration was simple, black hull, blue 'standing right ups' and white 'shifting right ups', vermilion hatch boards and cabin top, the cabin doors in red, white, yellow and blue, the rudder post and tiller white, picked out with red and blue, Plate 7. Wherry builders were scattered about the Broads, but the greatest concentration was on the Yare at Reedham, and at Coltishall on the Bure where Allen's launched the last sailing wherry in 1912. Most wherries in the eighteenth and nineteenth centuries had a single large gaff main sail with a loose foot. The sails were black, dressed with tar and seal oil and hoisted by a windlass on the foredeck, with only one halliard, frequently tapered to allow space on the windlass barrel, the peak of the gaff being raised by a complex system of 'spend block' chain 'spens' and a wire 'martingale'. Some wherries had peak and throat halliards. The mast, in a tabernacle at the forward end of the hold and counterweighted with lead could be lowered for bridges (154). There were no shrouds, for these would have made quanting difficult. The mastheads were painted in bands of colour signifying the owners, and at the truck was a vane pronounced 'wane', comprising a tin framework and a length of scarlet bunting, either this could be a 'gate' or 'low' vane with a decorated plate to leeward, or a 'high' vane with a figure in tin on the windward side, often linked with the name or owner of the wherry. A Welsh girl holding a bunch of leeks became popular, because of a nineteenth century song about Jenny Morgan, the 'Jenny Morgan' figure being adopted by Morgan's Brewery in Norwich.

Because of the high peak of her gaff sail and because her mast was stepped so far forward a wherry could sail well into the wind, and because there were no shrouds, the gaff could swing well out for running before the wind. Quanting was done by both men, each walking down either plankway. For working under the Yarmouth Haven bridge a 30 fathom dropping chain was used, the wherry shooting the bridge stern first, the weight of chain paid out from the bow controlling her speed. Larger wherries had fixed keels of the 'rocking horse' pattern, but the smaller craft had slipping keels which could be detached and left ashore when proceeding up the Ant or the Bungay Navigation. An innovation since 1880, they were secured by bolts through the keelson and were guided into position by chains from the stem head.

GLOSSARY of further WHERRY TERMS: BIN IRON; Half round guard iron, extending round the wherry's side, called a 'hairpin iron' where it goes round the stem. 'Down to her bins' means a heavily laden wherry (see also Keels and Sloops). BOKE; a cargo loaded higher than the shifting right ups, a wherry is then said to be 'boked'. BOWSING; hauling a wherry against the stream by means of a tackle to a post ashore, the windlass and mainsheet blocks could be used. CABIN SLIP; sliding hatch in the cabin top, found in the high sternsheet wherries. CARLING BOARD or 'curling way' the hatch covering the aperture in the foredeck in which the foot of the mast swings. COBURG; wood faring around the stove pipe on the cabin top. DEAD HATCH; hatch board in way of mast tabernacle. HARPENS; overhangs of the covering board fore and aft. HERRING HOLE; hole at the masthead for the halliard sheave. HIGH STERNSHEET WHERRIES; large type of wherry, with no cockpit, steered from the deck. HOOD; the hatch covers. HORSA; the horse for the mainsheet block. KILLER; wooden wash bowl. KINDLE; the wind kindles up when it starts to freshen. QUANT; wooden 24' pole for pushing a wherry, with a 'bott' or knob on the shoulder end, a 'foot' to prevent it sinking in too far, and a pointed iron 'shoe' at the bottom. ROND ANCHOR; an anchor with one arm which is driven into the 'rond' or bank to secure a mooring line. ROOT; when a heavily laden wherry tends to sail her nose under. RUNGS; the mast hoops. SINGLE LOADED; all cargo below hatches. SOLE; cabin floor. SWIPE; the pump, 'to have a swipe', to try the pump. TAKING OFF HATCH; one of the hatch boards in the middle not interlocked with the rest, so that half the hatch could be opened independently. TROLLEYS; parrel balls secured by a parrel lashing to keep the gaff jaws to the mast. WALING; loading timber over the plankways to form a deck cargo.

Wide Boats

Horse Drawn; these were open holded boats, built on narrow boat lines but wider. They were introduced on the Grand Junction, but not encouraged through Blisworth and Braunston tunnels because of congestion, so were mainly found on the southern part. To reduce water resistance their sides were rounded in from 9' to 11' beam on the gunwale to 7' across the bottom. With a length of 70' to 72', they had stands and planks, and a cabin like a narrow boat, although some were decked over for bulk liquid carriage. Many were employed in the chalk, brick and gravel trade, one owner being George Garside, the Leighton Buzzard sand merchant. Fellows, Morton & Clayton wide boats carried general goods in clothed up holds. Wide boats were used on the Kennet & Avon and on the Bridgewater, Leeds & Liverpool and Rochdale. Because they were wide but looked like narrow boats they were called bastard boats in the north and mules on the Kennet & Avon.

Powered; Grand Union Canal: Completion of the wide locked London to Birmingham waterway by 1934 encouraged the building of 65 ton diesel wide boats of 12'6" beam. Two were built of wood, the PROGRESS by Bushell Bros., of Tring for the Grand Union and PIONEER by Fellows, Morton & Clayton at their Uxbridge yard in 1935 for their paper mill traffic. They were not a success as the bottom width of the canal was not extended, so there were few places where they could pass; moreover they were unable to pass any other craft in tunnels. The PROGRESS spent much of her life as a maintenance boat, becoming a house boat in 1963. In 1910 Fellows, Morton built an oil fired steam 10'6" wide boat, the SWAN which they operated to Braunston.

HAULAGE & PROPULSION of VESSELS

CABLE HAULAGE. Powered craft on rivers faced currents and shoals and on canals their wash was damaging to the banks. A solution which was much tried and fairly widely adopted in Europe was to lay a cable in the river or canal and have a tug haul herself along it, taking in and paying out. British engineers were impressed by this. As early as 1852 cable haulage had been suggested for the Severn because of the swift current, using several flexible iron bands which a tug could grip between rollers. They were to be laid all the way from Gloucester to Welshpool. On the Trent, rope haulage was proposed in 1878 and in 1902 cable haulage was suggested for the Suir in Ireland, because of the current. It was tried experimentally by John Fowler on the Bridgewater Canal about 1873. Leader Williams however preferred tugs, the disadvantages of the cable being its inflexibility on a canal where traffic was heavy, stops frequent and the distance short. Two cables for passing traffic would have undoubtedly been needed. Cable towing was advantageous in canal tunnels. A tug had only to go backwards and forwards to a timetable and could be attached permanently to the cable. A chain tug was put on at Stanedge in 1824, although taken off in 1833 and replaced by company leggers. The chain system put on in 1826 at Islington tunnel on the Regent's Canal, lasted until the 1930s. Finally there was the Harecastle electric tug from 1914 to 1954. A moving wire rope driven by two waterwheels was tried about 1859 through Morwelldown tunnel on the Tavistock Canal. It scored the sides and invert and did not last long. Then the Grand Junction considered moving wire ropes for Blisworth and Braunston. One was tried in the latter in 1870 but was unsuccessful because the curves of this tunnel strained the rope and maintenance looked like being heavy. The rope passed down each wall with guide pulleys at intervals. There was an enormous horizontal pulley at the north end, the engine being at the south end.

Finally there was direct cable haulage from a capstan on the bank to warp a vessel into a navigation entrance as at Framilode where the Stroudwater met the Severn.

ELECTRIC HAULAGE: In the late 1890s electric traction was being introduced to street tramways and transferring the trolley pole of a tramcar to aquatic use on a still water canal was an attractive possibility. This was first tried on the river Wey at Guildford, and in 1900 a barge canal from the Thames to Southampton was proposed, although here electric loco-motives were to be used. Another electric traction canal was promoted in 1902 and author-ized, a 5⅛ mile line between the Thames and the Medway passing inside the Isle of Grain. In 1901 the Calder & Hebble had shown interest in the possibilities. In 1903 Fellows, Morton & Clayton, suggested their taking a lease on the Warwick & Birmingham and Warwick & Napton Canals and electrifying them, while about 1905 the Regent's put forward a modern idea, to build a motor road over their canal and use the underside of the road for suspending the wires. The only other electric experiments were those of 1923 on the Staffs. & Worcs. Canal. Here a short length of canal near Kidderminster power station was equipped with poles and over-head wires. The boat picked up the current via a trolley pole which drove an 18 hp electric motor. This was mounted over a hole in the bottom of the boat encased by a cylinder, the motor driving a centrifugal pump which drove the boat by water jet. The pump was the work of the Gill Propeller Co., of King's Lynn and could not only reverse its flow to drive the boat astern, but could also steer by rotation of the whole power unit. The motor and pump were designed to be detachable and transferred from boat to boat. Trials seem to have been successful, a speed of 6 m.p.h. being achieved. Also there was no turbulent wash and the pump was protected against large floating debris. The only long term application of electric power was the Harecastle tunnel tug. (see page 305).

HORSE HAULAGE and BOAT HORSES: There was never a boat horse strain, the scows on the Forth & Clyde and the Monkland were pulled by Clydesdales, but in England, on the narrow canals, a smaller animal of about 15 hands was favoured because of the low bridges. Welsh heavy vanners were the usual for narrow boats, cobs with short legs, although some boat-men had hardly more than ponies. Number ones on the Grand Junction used Shires to pull a pair of narrow boats, but almost every type of horse was represented in the inland water-ways. Cart horses, much used by the Bridgewater, bread van horses, old carriage horses, anything between 14 and 17 hands. Most were mares or geldings, stallions being rare, and all had to be broken to boat haulage. To move a loaded narrow boat, a horse had to hang forward into its collar, until it broke the boat's inertia, straining until it could take another step. As the boat gathered way, it could step out more often, and when the boat was moving properly, the work was easier. The Duke of Bridgewater had mules to work his carrying fleet as they had staying power and were hard working. Some were in use until the end of horse haulage. The well known Oxford Canal number one boatman, Mr. Joseph Skinner had the last of several for his FRIENDSHIP in the 1950s. Then again there were donkeys or 'hanimals' as the boatmen always called them. They worked in pairs, side by side, particularly on the Staffs. & Worcs., Worcester & Birmingham, Droitwich, Stroudwater and Thames & Severn Canals. They also worked on the Welsh section of the Shropshire Union from Trevor basin (8).

Number one boatmen owned their own horses as did some boatmen employed by the carrying companies, they could be hired, for example on the Severn, from towing path companies who also provided drivers. On the Yorkshire waterways horses and horse marines or drivers were available for hire by the sailing keels, while from 1847 the Regent's Canal provided horses and drivers for lighterage traffic, continued under nationalization but operated by tow-age contractors with British Waterways men as drivers. Many of the larger carrying firms supplied horses, notably the Shropshire Union who in 1905 had 328. The boatmen were issued with an identity card for their horses, so that they could claim it at the stables, each animal being numbered by branding into one fore hoof, with SUC branded into the other. The company had their own farriers and paid for outside stabling and veterinary care. Such organisation was economic because the Shropshire Union had a near monopoly of carrying over their own system, but other companies provided horses, Fellows, Morton & Clayton, Thomas Clayton of Oldbury and Henry Seddon of Middlewich. On the Birmingham system, steerers or companies who contracted to work fleets of day boats provided both men and horses. Some carrying companies provided horses which the boatmen could buy in instalments. The Anderton and the Mersey, Weaver companies both did this, the boatmen eventually owning a horse which if paid for quickly enough could be sold at a profit. When the company provided the horse it was often kept by the same man for quite a while, and it was usual to have a number of spare horses in case of illness or injury. Horses worked from 5 or 6 a.m. to 7 or 8 p.m., so they had to feed and drink on the way, out of a nose tin (156), slowing down but not stopping. The tin was held on by a strap passing round the neck just behind the ears, and a horse might be muzzled with a wicker basket when not feeding to prevent grazing so that it would go without being led. In 1809 according to a company order, muzzles were to be regulation wear on the Worcester & Birmingham. The horse was often fed at regular places, which they would recognize, stopping until the nose tin was filled. Thus on the Shropshire Union there were four feeds between Autherley and Market Drayton a matter of 26 miles, a day's run. The feed varied little, Fellows, Morton & Clayton had an official horse corn mixture fed dry, a ton of feed being composed of 8½ cwt of hay, 1½ cwt of straw, 1½ cwt of bran, 1½ cwt of peas, 2½ cwt of oats and about 4 cwt of dredge which is chaff or husks of grain, the hay and straw also being cut up into chaff. Oil cake would be added and some boatmen gave their horses conditioning powders or tealeaves and boiled linseed as a tonic, also vegetable scraps like potato peelings and boiled carrots. It was usual for the carrying companies to provide the feed and most, like the Anderton Co., made it up at their main stables. Some boatmen, who cared for their horses, might buy extra, and number ones bought their own. Although the vet

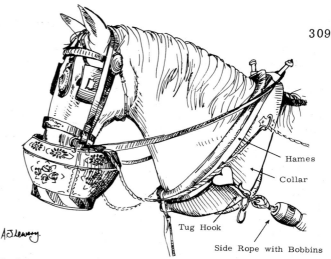

Hames

Collar

Tug Hook

Side Rope with Bobbins

A.J.Lewery.

156.

The nose tin for feeding a
boat horse.

could be called in, boatmen often used canal
side plants as herbal remedies. Sores from
the collar were common, a remedy for them
being a salve prepared from boiled up oak
bark and alum. Boat horses were specially
shod because of their need to grip the path
to start the boat, and needed re-shoeing
every two weeks or so. Some carriers,
notably Thomas Clayton, used a collar cloth with leather lined holes for the harness, to keep
the collar dry, if it got wet it chafed. Because they worked hard, horses were generally
stabled at night to avoid chills and were covered with a canvas horse cloth, particularly when
standing after work. To protect them against flies, some boatwomen used to crochet ear caps.
Apart from occupational complaints, a common accident was falling in the water. This could
be serious if it was a river with a strong current. The boatman had to go in, keep it standing and take the gears off. Although canals are shallow, banks are steep, often with vertical
walling. If the boatman could not find a shallow spot to lead it out, he might remove a coping stone from the towpath edge. The Bridgewater provided steps at some places and the
Regent's and Grand Junction in the London area, sloping concrete ramps parallel to the towpath. Otherwise it could be a matter of ropes and planks to make a ramp. If a telegraph pole
was handy it was used as a purchase for a line. As long as one foreleg could be eased on to
the bank there was a chance the horse would heave itself out. They fell in from many causes,
either slipping, being jostled when another boat passed, or they bolted, trains being a frequent
cause of this. Horses harness or 'gears' were simple and practical and the towline so arranged to the boat's mast that it could be quickly cast off, Plate 5. Tug hooks for the side
ropes were fastened to the hames which passed round the collar. Their ends stuck up like
horns, but in narrow boat gears certainly, were kept short because of the danger of fouling
bridges. The side ropes to the swingletree or spreader, were supported by the pad across
the back, the hip strap further to the rear and the girth underneath. From the top of the
collar ran the back strap ending in the crupper round the tail, and from the bottom of the
collar, the martingale, back to the girth. Horses wore blinkers, decorated with brasswork,
and a brass too would hang from the brow band of the bridle, and sometimes several from
the martingale. Most side ropes were threaded through hardwood bobbins to prevent chafe to
the flanks, although Thomas Clayton and many Leeds & Liverpool carriers used lengths of
leather tubing and some used leather traces. The bobbins or spools were painted red,blue,
white, green or yellow, or more decoratively, with bands of contrasting colour, or even in
a lozenge pattern. The gears were shown off at shows held specially for boat horses, for
example at Broken Cross near Northwich.

Towlines were attached to the 3' long swingletree and this could either be painted in a
single colour or decorated with bands of contrasting shades. Some narrow boat towlines were
attached to the swingletree hook by an eye spliced into the line; this was the method of the
potteries carriers. Fellows, Morton & Clayton and Thomas Clayton used a bridle from the
swingletree, to which the towline was secured by a short rope grommet passed through the bridle
and through itself like the tag on a luggage label, Plate 5. The grommet was also threaded
through a brass ring for holding the rope reins, and the free loop of the grommet held the
towline, kept from slipping through by a knot or toggle. Cargo fly-boat horses did not feed
much on the way, a Shropshire Union fly-boat stage varying between 10 and 20 miles, while
swift passage boat stages were very short, on the Bridgewater, five miles or so. These
horses were provided by the canal company or by the carrying firm and those used for the
faster passage boats must have been comparable to carriage horses. Passage boat horses
worked in tandem pairs on the faster services, the second one being ridden. They were not
strictly in tandem according to a print of a Forth & Clyde swift boat, for each had its own
swingletree, the towline being parted into two tails.

Horses could be taught to go by themselves without leading; stopping or starting to a word
of command or the crack of the smacking whip, used not for chastisement but as a signal to
the horse and approaching boats. A clever horse could pull off a grounded boat. Hauling and
towlines had to be light to save the horse a sagging weight, and for the same reason as short
as possible. On twisting rivers a long line was unavoidable, towing from as high up as
possible, to stop the line sagging into the water. Hauling and towlines had to stretch so that
the load came gradually on to the horse, they were made of cotton which sinks, so that
passing boats could go over a dropped line. Lines were bought in 94' lengths weighing 5 to
6 lbs.; a river line might be several spliced together, with the horse 100 yards from the boat,
but for canal work the horse might be less than a boat's length ahead. Towlines wore out
quickly, lasting only 5 or 6 weeks on long distance narrow boats. They were jealously guarded for the boatmen generally had to buy them. On the Weaver, loaded narrow boats towed
from a stud on the cabin top just forward of the slide. This gave the steerer control of the
line in case of emergencies, he could cast off if the boat hit an obstruction and there was

a danger of pulling the horse into the water. Running blocks allowed the steerer to control the length of line, paying out more for bends and hauling in when the channel straightened. The line passed through a pulley at the head of the mast and the three blocks, to a stud temporarily fixed through the cabin roof ahead of the slide. When working through many locks the horse line was attached to the fore end stud of a narrow boat, and on twisting canals the point of the tow could be carried forward from the mast by a bridle passed from the fore stud round the towline and back to the stud. This would make the horse pull the fore end round. Alternatively the boatman would take a turn of the towline round the fore stud. Horse haulage suffered from difficulties of passing and overtaking. Bye laws to regulate the traffic formed a large part of a canal company's regulations. One boat had to give way, fly-boats having precedence. Empty boats might give way to loaded boats, but when two laden boats were to pass, the usual rule was for the drivers to keep their horses to the left and steerers to steer their boats to the right. This had the effect of sending one boat and horse outside the other, the driver of the outside horse having to stop and lower his line, possibly even unhooking it, so that the inner boat and horse could pass over it. On the Shropshire Union it was the rule to drop the line, but boatmen preferred to clear it over because there was a danger if dropped of it catching the iron shoe or skeg under the other boat's stern and pulling the horse into the canal. On the Birmingham system it was usual to clear the line over both the inside boat and horse, the steerer shouting to the horse driver: 'Heave it up'. Telford's main line had a towpath on each bank, to end the chaos of heavy traffic on a narrow path. Horses were ordered by most company bye laws to be led, or 'driven' (the correct word). On the narrow canals children would do this, sometimes even riding, but in Yorkshire and elsewhere, where horses and drivers were hired, men were in charge. Horses in East Anglia had a lively time. The banks were often divided by bounds, fences crossed by stiles or 'jumps', some, says De Salis, as high as 2'7". The horse had to jump them, frequently getting bruised or cut.

Donkeys worked in pairs, generally side by side with the towline forked, one tail to each swingletree. On a wide canal like the Bridgewater, one horse could manage a pair of narrow boats. Simpson Davies of Runcorn worked regularly in this way as did the number ones on the Grand Junction, but two were needed to pull the big duker flats between Runcorn and Preston Brook. On the Birmingham system, wharf boats in pairs were pulled by two horses while one horse could manage two loaded day boats or four empties. On difficult river navigations large numbers of horses were often demanded to move craft upstream against the current. The Thames was notorious, the larger western barges, carrying up to 140 tons, needed as many as 14 horses to negotiate the shallows below the flash locks.

LEGGING and SHAFTING: Few canal tunnels went to the expense of towpaths. The horse had to be replaced by manpower. Indeed few horses cared for tunnel towpaths and boats had to be bow hauled through Telford's Harecastle tunnel. Others had chains or rails along the side walls for boatmen to pull themselves through, but most had nothing so legging was used. If the tunnel was low one man could lie on the cabin top or on the gang planks of an empty boat and push with his toes. Otherwise it had to be pushing against the side walls, best done by two men on the foredeck. Each walked the tunnel, rhythmically bringing one leg past the other (157). If the tunnel was wide like Blisworth and Braunston, but used by narrow boats, then the men or women, used to lie on a plank lashed to the fore stud, a dangerous position since one person's incautious movement could derange the plank and imperil his fellow. Some were drowned this way, but the situation was saved by the use of individual boards or 'wings' with a hook which passed through a ringbolt on the deck. Probably these were introduced in the 1850s, varying in length to suit the width of the tunnel. Those on the broad Grand Junction were about 6' long with their far ends rounded into a seat shape for the boatman's bottom. He held his position by gripping the sides of the wing. Legging was slow and exhausting and passage through single line tunnels like Dudley took four hours. For this reason in Stanedge passing places were provided. In two way tunnels such as Braunston and Blisworth, boats could pass, the leggers swinging both themselves and their boards clear at the last moment. In 1827 the Grand Junction had instituted professional leggers for these tunnels to speed traffic and because casual leggers had been terrorizing the boatmen. They wore brass armbands with their registered number. George Smith of Coalville met one of them, William Benjamin, 'Ben the legger' at Braunston who had legged 50 to 60,000 miles in his working life. At Blisworth a gang of 12 in pairs was stationed at each end, four out of each gang specializing in night work. They waited in a hut at each portal, the Stoke Bruerne men being responsible for northbound traffic and the Blisworth for southbound. They ceased work when the tugs started in 1871. Elsewhere men could be engaged casually like the Rodney men at Brindley's Harecastle tunnel. The professionals were paid by the trip. Boats were sometimes linked together to be worked through in pairs or in a long train with two leggers on the leading boat only. Their occupational complaint was 'lighterman's bottom'.

Shafting was more popular because it was easier. The boatman had to push against the sides, roof or bottom, the sides being preferred in steamer days because the roof was so sooty. Some canals banned the use of shafts because of damage to brickwork or masonry, but the Grand Junction fitted special rails of wood 6" below water level on each side. Wooden chocks were secured to these at 9' intervals for the shafts to push against. Legging and shafting were not restricted to narrow boats. Both were the practice on the Leeds & Liverpool through Gannow and Foulridge and through Hincaster on the Lancaster, although here a rope was fixed to one side wall.

LOCOMOTIVE and TRACTOR HAULAGE: Steam locomotive haulage of canal boats was considered as early as 1830-31 by the Grand Junction, but no experiments were undertaken. In August 1839 half a mile of track was laid alongside the Forth & Clyde Canal near Camelon and an 0-4-0 mineral locomotive hauled canal boats with some success. However, due to the high cost, it was not pursued. In May 1888 the Shropshire Union laid a mile of 18" gauge track along a straight section of the Middlewich branch between Cholmondeston and Minshull locks, but later abandoned it.

Motor tractors offered canal haulage possibilities. There was one on the Forth & Clyde in early 1953, a three-wheeled machine towing oil barges for Shell-Mex. In the same year six tractors were put to work on the Regent's Canal by the British Transport Commission who undertook towage after about eighteen months of experiment. They could tow 80 ton capacity lighters and their use spread to the Lee and lower Grand Union. They were pneumatic tyred and petrol driven with a single cylinder four stroke air cooled motor of 5 or 8 h.p. A foot operated quick release for the towhook was fitted should the line catch. In 1963 the petrol tractors were replaced by Ransome machines with single cylinder 9 h.p. diesels.

MARINE ENGINES:

Steam: Powered propulsion in Great Britain was first tried in 1787 on the Hull River, followed by trials of William Symington's vessel on Dalswinton Loch in Dumfriesshire. He undertook further experiments on the Forth & Clyde in 1789, while in 1793 a steam cargo barge was put on the Sankey Brook Navigation and in 1797 on the Bridgewater. In 1802 came further trials on the Forth & Clyde. The Sankey pioneer was John Smith, and the 1802 Forth & Clyde boat was Symington's CHARLOTTE DUNDAS. Smith, because of the Watt patent had to have an atmospheric engine of Newcomen type, but this did not apply to Symington as the patent expired in 1800 and he used a single enclosed cylinder, the connecting rod driving the paddle shaft directly. On canals paddle steamers were disliked because of the damage to the banks, but on rivers they multiplied rapidly from about 1814. Machinery became more standardized in the 1820s, the problem being to fit the large cylinders then needed between the paddle shaft at deck level and the keelson. Commonest was the side lever engine introduced on the Clyde by Robert Napier in 1824. This was an inverted beam engine, but the beams had to be duplicated for each cylinder, the piston driving through a yoke. Less space consuming than the side lever was the oscillating cylinder engine, in which the piston rod worked directly on to the paddle shaft which carried the cranks. To achieve this the cylinders were made to rock on trunnions. Valve gear was perfected by Maudslay in 1827 and improved by John Penn in the late 1830s. Penn's modifications made the engine very popular and the type lasted into the twentieth century. An example built by Penn at Greenwich was the Thames steamer WATERMAN of the early 1840s with two cylinders of 24" diameter by 27" stroke. In William Fairbairn's twin hulled passenger canal packet LORD DUNDAS, built in 1831 for the Forth & Clyde, a reversion was made to the locomotive style layout of the CHARLOTTE DUNDAS. Later paddle engines were direct acting with cylinders inclined diagonally. Screw propulsion started to replace paddles in the 1840s, although paddles were kept for river work because they could work well in shallow water. The screw demanded a different layout and an easier space problem, since the shaft was low down. One solution was the neat vee adopted by the Leeds & Liverpool for their canal cargo steamers. But more general was the inverted engine with the cylinders directly above the propeller shaft. It was fitted to 'puffers' on the Forth & Clyde, packets on the Weaver, tugs on the Severn and steam keels on the Aire & Calder. On narrow canal steamers, space forced a tandem arrangement of cylinders, one above the other sharing a common piston rod and driving a single crank (86). To enable narrow cargo steamers to pay their way, the performance of the engine had to be improved. The answer was higher pressures which would permit smaller, neater, but still powerful engines using less fuel in smaller more efficient boilers. Early boilers had to be large to raise sufficient volumes of low pressure steam for the big cylinders. They had cavernous grates but a small heating surface. Use of tubes from the 1840s increased the heating surface and pressures could be safely increased when cylindrical boiler shells were made from the 1860s onwards. Higher pressures allowed compounding, introduced during the 1860s and applied to paddle and screw steamers until superseded by the triple expansion in larger vessels in the 1880s. Many small vessels continued to have the compound which gave sufficient power and economy for their needs. Compounding meant using steam twice over, in a high pressure cylinder followed by a low pressure and so using more of the energy in the steam and reducing the fuel needed.

157. Legging; the man lies on a legging board hooked to the foredeck.

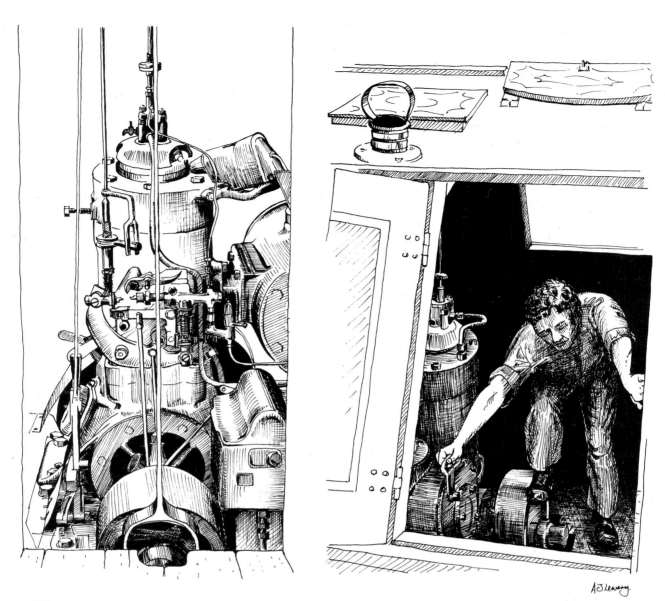

158. Left; single cylinder 15 h.p. Bolinder semi-diesel. View from aft which
shows the   eccentric driven fuel pump, throttle control, pre-heating blow
lamp, reverse lever and clutch. Right; kicking over the flywheel to start
the Bolinder. Note special hand grip on the silencer.

Before the adoption of oil and petrol engines just before the 1914-18 War, there had been
efforts to find other sources of propulsion. For passenger launches battery electric power
was tried. Disadvantages here were obvious; excessive weight and the need to recharge. The
Moritz-Immisch Electric Launch Co., of Hampton on the Thames had some built measuring
65' x 10' and drawing 22". The MALDEN displaced 12 tons while the VISCOUNTESS BURY of
1888, later on the Cam, had twin screws, each driven by an Immisch $7\frac{1}{2}$ h.p. motor. They
needed 200 accumulators for power. Immisch had their own generating plant aboard barges.
For a while, from the 1880s to about 1910, gas produced aboard by a coal or anthracite fed
apparatus was considered to have possibilities. Coal consumption was low and the boiler was
eliminated. In 1905-6 Thornycroft's fitted an anthracite burning producer into an old steam
narrow boat the DUCHESS, at their Chiswick works. The steam engine was replaced by a gas
engine and a full scale trial undertaken between London and Manchester. While the engine
worked well, producing the gas was a complex business attended by many problems. Another
ex-steam narrow boat, the VULCAN was given a Crossley gas engine between 1907 and 1909.
These units were economical but they took up as much room as a steamer's engine and boiler
and needed a skilled man to look after the producer.

Motor: More rewarding was the internal combustion engine. It could run without attention,
it took up little space and if a diesel or semi-diesel, was very economical on fuel. Steamers
were faster and more powerful but it was found that a motor narrow boat could also tow a
butty. By the 1900s light petrol spirit engines with electric ignition were available for marine
use, but more suitable for commercial craft was the so called 'semi-diesel' burning paraffin
or some other type of light oil. The first marine oil engine had been that of the Priestman
brothers of Hull in 1888. They fitted a four-stroke paraffin engine into a twenty foot launch
and followed it with others, one a double acting design. Dependent on electric spark ignition,
they were satisfactory for small craft, but commercial vessels demanded greater powers than
was practicable for such a design. The answer came with Akroyd **Stuart's** patents, the first of

which was taken out in 1886. He dispensed with ignition from an outside source, by using a combustion chamber or hot bulb on the cylinder head. This had to be preheated with a blow lamp, but was kept hot by the heat of compressed air and burning gas within the cylinder and this constant heat ensured ignition of the oil sprayed into the combustion chamber by the fuel pump. Stuart's patents formed the basis for the 'semi-diesel' engine which several makers made available in the 1900s. In this the air was compressed in the cylinder to some 200 p.s.i., considerably more than Stuart's original 30-35 p.s.i., but preheating with a blowlamp was still necessary, unlike Dr. Rudolf Diesel's engine where the air was compressed to 500 p.s.i. generating sufficient heat to ignite the oil unaided, so a start from cold was possible. Diesels stemming from Dr. Diesel's patent of 1892 were available in the 1900s for electric power generation, but marine applications were delayed, although one had been tried in a French canal boat as early as 1902-3. For inland waterway craft the vertical semi-diesel, using a more refined oil, seemed in the 1900s to offer more advantages. One of the makes most widely adopted was the two stroke Swedish Bolinder (158). This firm made their first marine oil engine in 1902, going on to produce a wide range of power units for ships, tugs, barges and fishing vessels. Other makes were Gardner of Manchester, Petter of Yeovil, Widdop of Keighley, and the Dutch Kromhout. The Petter burnt paraffin as did the Kelvin and Glenniffer, both Glasgow makes. Bolinders burning heavy oil or paraffin became most popular on the narrow canals. Fellows, Morton & Clayton fitted their first Bolinder to the LINDA in 1912 and remained faithful to the make until they gave up carrying in 1949. Most of these semi-diesels were single cylinder engines with cylinders of considerable bore. Starting was by preheating the combustion chamber and then in the case of the Bolinder by kicking over the flywheel, the foot pressing down on a spring loaded pin projecting from the rim (158). Gardners and Petters were started with a rope on the flywheel pin, the engine being bounced against the compression. The Bolinder was the only direct reversing among the smaller oil engines, the others had an epicyclic gear box. Bolinder reversal depended on pre-ignition of the mixture, achieved by bringing a second fuel pump temporarily into action, the drive to both pumps being by an eccentric on the crankshaft via a rocker arm. Bolinder running speed was about 450 r.p.m., the drive to the propeller being direct via a clutch. A disadvantage of these heavy single cylinder engines was vibration, particularly damaging to a wooden boat. For narrow boat operation 15 b.h.p. was most usual, sufficient to tow a butty.

Another problem was the need to alter hull design, particularly of narrow boats. The stern had to be reshaped to prevent propeller cavitation. To overcome this expense, some narrow boat carriers tried a petrol motor mounted on the cabin top. They were fitted at no sacrifice to cargo space and could be moved from boat to boat, but steering proved heavy work and the experiment was not continued. One make offered in the 1920s was the 'Peerless' a twin cylinder water cooled design of 16-20 h.p. On the Leeds & Liverpool the Widdop semi-diesel became the favourite engine, both twin and single cylinder examples, the twins causing less vibration. They ranged from 16 to 30 h.p. Some barges on the Calder & Hebble used 30 h.p. Bolinders, but Gardners have remained the most numerous on Yorkshire waterways, joined in recent years by Listers. From the 1930s the semi-diesel was replaced by the full diesel. Smaller multi-cylindered types, giving greater power in relation to their size, were becoming more generally available, working on the four-stroke cycle. Advantages were smoother running and compactness, but because they operated at higher revs, they needed a reduction gearbox. Russell Newbery, Gardner and National were favourite makes in narrow boats, while in the 1940s came the Lister JP. Widdop's turned over to full diesels at about this time and later in the 1950s came air cooled engines, again the Lister, the Petter and the Armstrong-Siddeley. Hitherto water cooling had been practically universal with attendant problems of blocked pipes and stuffed up filters.

Larger inland waterway craft followed deep sea practice with multi-cylinder full diesels, usually two-strokes. The motor vessels built in the late 1940s for the ICI Weaver fleet had four cylinder two-stroke Crossleys. Recent diesel developments have been marked by the use of inboard-outboard units, for example the Harbourmaster units of the Cawood Hargreaves pusher tugs on the Aire & Calder. Here the engine, a six cylinder Dorman diesel of 150 h.p., is mounted on deck, driving the propeller through two rightangles. The propeller part of the outfit can be swung clear of the water and does the steering via a hydraulic linkage. Manoeuvrability is remarkable, the tug going ahead or astern with equal facility. Having pushed the loaded compartment boats down to Ferrybridge, the tug returns at the head of a train of empties, in effect going astern all the way, since the hull is not turned round. For their pusher tugs, dealing with three 100 ton barges, the British Waterways Board have opted for twin inboard-outboard Schottel units. The engines are mounted on deck and drive through a double rightangle. Increased pleasure boating has meant increased interest in the smaller types of marine engine, particularly the outboard, of which there are many makes, mainly North American. Inboard-outboards are also growing in popularity. Used in pleasure craft, outboards have advantages in manoeuvrability and easy weed clearance from the propellor. Diesel power is almost universal for inboard pleasure craft engines, except the popular petrol Steuart Turner. Most outboards remain petrol driven.

159. An FMC steam narrow boat on the Braunston flight, Grand Junction Canal.

6.

Carrying, Carriers & Crews

CARRYING: Goods were carried by every navigation, none being purely passenger lines. On the rivers it was a loosely organised business, and it is doubtful if, in the seventeenth century, there were many large carrying fleets. Some boats were owned by merchants for carrying their own goods, thus coal factors had their own barges, while producers like millers had small fleets. Independent bargemasters would either hire their craft out or act as common carriers, picking up what cargoes they could. They would buy cargoes at one point to sell at another. Professor Willan explains this in his 'River Navigation in England 1600-1750' by describing the coal trade of the Great Ouse; the coal was bought at King's Lynn and sold at Bedford or St. Ives. In this case the boats were hired, the bargemen receiving freight charges. When carriage was the monopoly of the undertakers they would act as common carriers. Carriage by river navigation was universally cheaper than road in spite of monopolies on some rivers and the need to pay tolls, the monopolies working within an agreed rate structure. Tolls were the price of having an improved navigation, aggravated by extra dues demanded by millers for the passage of a boat through their locks and weirs. Roads had been free to all comers, although after the mid-eighteenth century most main highways were turnpiked. Canals were not usually hampered by a monopoly of carrying. The companies were seen as toll takers, like the turnpikes, providing and maintaining a road for all who would pay. Hence carrying was regarded as an independent venture by independent barge and boat owners, by merchants carrying their own goods and by producers. On the other hand there was the monopolistic Duke of Bridgewater who had built a canal at his own expense and who wanted it to pay. His solution was to have his own carrying fleet. Other canals followed suit and carrying departments were formed, or subsidiary companies, to make sure that traffic came to the new waterway. Canals' Acts did not disallow this. An alternative to direct carrying was adopted by the Calder & Hebble and the Don. They published freight charges as well as tolls and received cargo for dispatch which they put on the first suitable craft. Freight charges were paid to them and a proportion passed on to the carrier.

Apart from company backed fleets like Hugh Henshall & Co., there soon came to be large independent carriers. One of the biggest was Pickfords', road carriers who had started in the 1750s. Carrying companies proliferated in the earlier nineteenth century before railway competition, the newspapers were full of their advertisements and many famous names emerged such as Danks and Fellows. Organization of a large carrying fleet in the days of uncertain mails and no telephones was difficult. Poor accounting was another problem. However fleets large and small survived into the railway age. On the old rivers there was not much variation of the type of service provided, awkward millers and frequent shallows precluded speed, but the canals and improved navigations like the Aire & Calder gave more scope. Flyboats provided speedy delivery, sometimes associated with light road vehicles. Some boats had lock up facilities for valuable or tempting cargoes. A boat which, although independently owned, worked under regular contract, say to a canal company, was called a contract boat. The Rochdale used these craft from 1801 to 1804 for their Rochdale-Hull services. A bye trader was an independent carrier and in Yorkshire they talked of bye-keels meaning independently owned keels. Descriptive of a boat's employment were terms like bale boat for one carrying bales of cotton material or cloth, and the later gas and tar boats which were a distinctive type. In Ireland the bye traders were called hack boats and in South Wales hobblers. Whereas tolls were not allowed to go above the maxima laid down by a canal's or navigation's Act, there was no restriction on the freight charges. The charges would include the tolls the carrier had to pay plus payment for use of the boat. Carriers were allowed much more flexibility than the companies. Whereas a canal company could not offer a favoured customer special tolls, freight charges could be so adjusted, and a company with a carrying department could take advantage of this. Railway competition prompted the two Acts of 1845. One, the Canal Carriers Act specifically authorized canals and navigation companies to become carriers to give them the flexibility they needed. The other, the Canal Tolls Act, allowed them to vary tolls. The strict ton-mileage rate could be abandoned and different tolls charged on different parts of the line. This had been achieved to some extent by the granting of draw-backs, subsidizing certain goods for certain distances. Varied tolls would have the effect of encouraging traffic still more on a busy part of the canal, if a lower toll were offered, or a lower toll might encourage trade to develop on a quiet section of the waterway. Inland water-way traffic increased during the nineteenth century, but not as fast as railway tonnages. Long distance traffic on the main routes was maintained but railways killed the rural canals and navigations. Tolls were cut to retain traffic and carriers reduced their freight charges. Rate cutting (the combined toll and freight charge) happened on the major industrial waterways too. In other directions the railways were a stimulant, most notably to Birmingham and the Black Country system. Here with so many mines and factories served by water, the canals became railway feeders. Boatage services were started between factory and forge and railway goods station. The great companies were represented, the LNWR, the GWR, the Midland; the LNWR having 13 interchange basins. Elsewhere there were rail-canal interchange facilities on a smaller scale. Many canal companies who were carriers had rates agreements with the rail-ways, a conference system as in shipping, but bye traders could not achieve this.

Ever since the end of the 1914-18 War road motor competition had been a menace. More flexible than canal and rail, because of the large road mileage, lorries could provide a door to door service with which the others could not compete. Road competition had been a threat since the turnpikes of the eighteenth century, particularly when it was combined with steam packet services as on the Ouse and Humber. Carts and steam lorries were slow, although since the 1870s they benefited by freedom of toll and public highway maintenance. It was a different story with the motor lorry which has grown larger and faster. Roads have proved too much for most of the waterways, and for the bulk of the rail system. They killed the in-tensive short haul narrow boat traffics of the Black Country. Only the larger waterways could offer competitive services, the Severn, the Aire & Calder, the Trent and the Lee, for the size of vessel became a vital factor, added to its speed and the efficiency with which the cargo could be handled. Roads replaced canals in Ireland, first in Ulster, then in Eire. The South Wales system had already succumbed to nineteenth century rail domination of the valleys, while the Forth & Clyde suffered in the depression from ironworks closures. Since the 1939-45 War the carrying picture became bleaker although the nationalized fleets were re-equipped with new craft. Traffic could not be maintained and the 1960s was a decade of increasing carry-ing failure. The Willow Wren organization was a last stand to justify narrow boats, but their economic usefulness had gone years before, except in the artificial conditions of War. There were other carrying ventures and the wide waterways of Yorkshire carry impressive tonn-ages of coal and oil. The Gloucester & Berkeley Ship Canal takes larger coasters and petrol barges, and the Weaver can accommodate 600 ton ships up to Winnington. New craft have been built, tankers and pusher tugs with 100 ton lighters.

CARRYING COMPANIES; General. They were numerous, from large firms like Fellows, Morton & Clayton (Plate 2) down to Mrs. Agnes Beech of Saltersford on the Trent & Mersey with half a dozen boats. She came into the 'number one' category; the dividing line between a number one and a company was vague, since small companies were privately owned by one person, a family or a partnership. Larger firms depended on outside investment, in later days they were limited liability companies. There were companies closely linked to a navi-gation proprietor, such as Gilbert, Worthington & Co., backed by the Duke of Bridgewater, himself a carrier. Their rivals were Hugh Henshall & Co., founded by 1770, at first separate but soon a subsidiary of the Trent & Mersey. It probably lasted until the takeover of the canal by the North Staffordshire Railway in 1846, carrying for Wedgwood and the potters. Whereas Hugh Henshall & Co., was a subsidiary of a canal company, some companies had carrying de-partments, the Rochdale from 1807 to 1811, distinct from their venture into carrying at the end of the nineteenth century. The Aire & Calder Navigation started to carry in the 1770s, having acquired the fleet of the last lessee of the river, Peter Burt, in 1774. After the canal Carriers Act of 1845 had authorized navigation proprietors to carry, more started up. The Grand Junction in 1848, the Grand Canal in Ireland the following year, the Trent Navigation in 1882 and in the early 1900s, the manager of the Calder & Hebble started the subsidiary Calder Carrying Co. Sometimes the navigation was in a sense the subsidiary of the carrying company. Thus the Stevens family were carriers on the Wey long before they bought the navigation in about 1900. Railway owned waterways were sometimes carried upon by their owners. The North Staffordshire Railway bought the Trent & Mersey in 1846 replacing Hugh Henshall with their own North Staffordshire Railway & Canal Carrying Co. On the Ashton, Peak Forest and Macclesfield, acquired in 1846-8 by what became in 1847 the Manchester, Sheffield & Lincolnshire Railway, the railway company soon started a carrying fleet which was run in connection with goods trains from a rail-canal interchange basin at Guide Bridge, with similar facilities at Ashton and at the Manchester London Road. The fleet was given up in 1892. Rail-canal interchange traffic was most important on the BCN where boats were operated by the Shropshire Union on behalf of the LNWR and by the GWR. The Midland Rail-way ran boats on the Kennet & Avon from Bath between 1884 and 1899 so as to penetrate GWR territory, while on the Yorkshire Derwent the NER as lessees had a couple of craft on their shamefully neglected navigation as late as 1915. In Ireland the Midland & Great Western Railway, owners of the Royal Canal since 1845, tried a carrying fleet in the 1870s. The bulk of carrying throughout inland navigation history was done by independent bye traders, who survived to modern times. Many fleets were owned by manufacturers for transporting raw materials and products, but could act as common carriers if not needed by the firm. They became numerous towards the end of the nineteenth century. Flour millers were prominent, for example Henry Leetham & Co., of York established in 1850. On a smaller scale were Griffiths, the Chester corn millers, with flats, narrow boats and 3 steam barges. Chemical companies made use of the waterways, large and small. The United Alkali Co., founded in 1890, had sailing flats and steam packets which used the St. Helens Canal. On the narrow canals a well known chemicals carrier was W. H. Cowburn & Cowpar Ltd., of Manchester, who made sulphuric acid carried in carboys. They had a fleet of horse boats until, in the 1930s, motor boats were introduced carrying acid in two long demountable tanks. In 1956 the firm ceased canal transport, having built up a road haulage fleet. On the Calder & Hebble the Bradford Dyers' Association operated motor barges to Brighouse, their last being BRADSYLDA built in 1954. On the Black Country system the electric power companies had their own craft which were eventually nationalized. Coal producers ran carrying fleets, notably the Wigan Coal & Iron Co., on the Leeds & Liverpool, the Bridgewater and the Lancaster Canals. Back in 1886 they had 70 canal boats but after the 1914-18 War the fleet was given up, many of the boats being bought by Thomas & William Wells of Wigan, two boatman brothers who started in a modest way in the 1920s but ended with a big fleet. On the Glamorganshire and other South Wales canals, collieries owned boats and so did the patent fuel works which made briquettes. The Star Fuel Co., of Blackweir near Cardiff was one of the last, closing in 1927. It was founded in 1874, eventually with four works in the Cardiff area and latterly 40 boats, some passing to the Glamorganshire Canal Co. Iron works had their own boats, notably the ironmasters of South Wales, the Crawshays of Cyfarthfa, the Guests of Dowlais and the Hills of Plymouth on the Glamorganshire. On the BCN Stewart & Lloyd's tube works at Halesowen ran a large fleet until 1969 to the nearby railway interchange basin and continued to use their boats within the works. Guest, Keen & Nettlefold's also worked day boats in the Black Country and in the north the steel works at Ellesmere Port owned by the Wolverhampton Corrugated Iron Co., had not only flats but special decked floats for the carriage of steel fabrications. Quarry owners and sand and gravel pit operators ran boats, for example the Glynceiriog Granite Co., on the Ellesmere Canal and H. & W. Scott, sand merchants of Toomebridge on the Lower Bann. Cement manufacturers had them, for example Charles Nelson & Co. Ltd., of Stockton, Warwickshire, with their 3 steam narrow boats. In Ireland some of the great malting firms on the Barrow had their own boats, for example Minch, Norton & Co. Ltd., while the Boyne Navigation was bought in 1915 by the Navan corn millers John Spicer & Co. Ltd. A completely independent carrying company was rare in Ireland. Cargoes were more certain if the boat was owned by a manufactory, for so much offered was seasonal, for example barley for the maltings and sugar beet.

Independent carriers were legion in England and some large ones emerged. In the North-West there were John Kenworthy & Sons who had fly-boats on the Leeds & Liverpool which connected with Glasgow and Dublin packets at Liverpool, J. & J. Veevers and the Rochdale & Halifax Merchants Co., both of which worked on the Rochdale, as did Kenworthy's. Well known Midlands carriers were Shipton & Co., who had wharves at Wolverhampton and in the City Road Basin on the Regent's Canal. On the Bristol route from the Midlands were Brown & Son who put a steam tug on the Severn in 1830, Skey & Bird, Belsham & Reynolds, the Reynolds being Mrs. Elizabeth Reynolds in partnership with her brother George Belsham. The Black Country and Birmingham system was used by myriads of carriers, great and small, on short haul services. Apart from the railway company boats running to the canal-rail interchange basins, most of the boats were operated by businesses, manufacturers and merchants. The coal factors had the greatest quantity, working between the pits and their wharves for domestic retailing by cart or direct to canalside factories. W. H. Bowater were big fuel distributors, with tugs as well as horses, smaller companies were John Toole of Bradley near Bilston, H. S. Pitts of Stourbridge, Arthur Cooper of Smethwick and S. T. Brant of Birmingham. Elwell & Brown of Tipton dealt in scrap metal as well as coal. The Wulfruna Coal Co., established in 1850 in Wolverhampton had coal factoring premises near Horseley Fields junction. Distinctive decoration was a necessity for the Black Country fleets, so that the boatman could quickly find the craft he was to take over. Johnson's Iron & Steel Co., of West Bromwich had a pair of eyes at the fore end and stern, Walls of Sneyd had a length of red brick wall painted at the fore end, and Samuel Pearson's of West Bromwich, bottle manufacturers, had a bottle painted horizontally on the top bend each side of the fore stempost. Many firms on the BCN were in business as steerers, supplying boats, men and horses to manufacturers. If the latter had their own boats, then the steerers would provide men and horses. One of the biggest was T. & S. Element of Oldbury, with their stables at Oldbury, Gravelly Hill, Aston and Stewponey on the Staffs. & Worcs. Canal. They also ran their own boats and concentrated on coal and sand traffics. Some firms simply hired out boats, notably James Yates of Norton Canes with a dock on the Cannock Extension Canal. In more modern times, steerers have provided tugs as well as horses, as did Peter Keay & Son of Walsall, while a noted tug operator was Ernest Thomas. Based at Birchills near Walsall, he built up a fleet of day boats from small beginnings. His father worked as a carrier on the Shropshire Union, Ernest Thomas himself carrying coal to Cadbury's factory at Knighton. In 1926 the latter acquired some of Bowater's boats and one of their motor tugs. Later he built tugs at Birchills.

If the carriers of the Birmingham system were one close knit group, then another was to be found on the Bridgewater and associated waterways. Here there were barge owners as well as narrow boat carriers, the former being led by the Bridgewater themselves. Frederick J. Abbott of Salford were once a Runcorn firm handling raw cotton and cotton pieces, along with in the 1920s, the Mersey-Humber Carrying Co., who had a fleet of old Shropshire Union and Rochdale Canal Co., barges, and Faulkner's of Manchester, the latter with twelve. Three narrow boat carriers were well remembered, J. E. Southern, Simpson Davies and Jonathan Horsefield, all in the coal trade with big heavy craft. Southern's carried to Barton and Old

Trafford power stations, their deep six plank narrow boats being docked by Simpson Davies at Runcorn. John Simpson himself was a coal merchant with 20 pairs of narrow boats and 3 flats in the 1930s. He supplied slack coal to the Runcorn chemical works including Castner-Kellner's, also carrying moulding sand and clay, his narrow boats crossing the Mersey to Widnes with the sand. Jonathan Horsefield probably started with one narrow boat building up a fleet of these and so called bastard boats, built like narrow boats but wide like a barge. His main customers for coal were Runcorn gas works, Lymm gas works and the Co-operative Societies at Runcorn and Lymm, but he also carried road chippings for Cheshire County Council. On the Potteries trade there were small operators as well as the long established and large Anderton Co. and the later Mersey, Weaver & Ship Canal Carrying Company. Some potteries had their own boats, for example J. & G. Meakin of Tunstall, carrying raw materials and crated ware. Then there was John Walley of Stoke-on-Trent with a small fleet of richly decorated craft carrying flints from Weston Point to the Potteries. Another Runcorn firm was Joseph Rayner, in the coal, salt and pottery materials trades, the family having had salt works at Winsford and Wincham. Rayner worked in with both the Anderton and Mersey, Weaver companies. Rayner's were in business until after the 1939-45 War and bought three ex-Grand Union Canal Carrying Co., motor boats in 1947 from the Stanton ironworks.

Midlands carriers were equally diverse. John Griffiths of Bedworth in Warwickshire was an operator of coal boats, large capacity narrow boats which could carry 30 tons. In the 1920s he had a fleet of 64, 36 of them working between the Midlands and London, short haul day boats forming the remainder. Griffiths himself was an ex-boatman. Later his fleet passed to the Warwickshire Canal Carrying Co., who had Charity dock at Bedworth which Griffiths himself managed. Further south A. Harvey-Taylor of Aylesbury was a well known coal carrier. The business started in 1923 but merged in 1955 with the Samuel Barlow Coal Company. L. B. Faulkner of Leighton Buzzard were coal and sand carriers but were better known for their boatyard and high standard of decorative painting carried out by Frank Jones. Yorkshire navigations were always the home of small operators, many keels being individually owned. While millers and merchants ran their own craft, there were plenty of small carriers. One such was Thomas E. Claxton of Castleford who ran steam and later motor barges from Hull to Castleford and Wakefield, their main latter day contract being grain to Allinson's flour mill at Castleford. The business was a father and son partnership. Existing smaller firms operate from such centres as Hull and Goole. Yorkshire waterways were busy enough to sustain large carrying fleets such as John Harker, while Ernest V. Waddington Ltd. of Swinton run a large fleet on the Sheffield and South Yorkshire. Inland waterway carrying has remained open to big and small operator and so is highly competitive. The large numbers of independent carriers have perhaps been a source of weakness, since on the waterways, carrying could never be controlled as on the railways. There was wasteful use of craft, and too much empty running. The trouble from the carriers' point of view was that they depended on the navigation proprietors; not only were they subservient to the latters' constricting toll structures, but they also depended for wharf and warehouse space on leasing arrangements with the navigation companies. Not until the Regulation of Railways Act of 1873 were the companies given powers to quote through tolls, although tolls had been varied from a fixed ton-mileage rate since the Canal Tolls Act of 1845. The carriers therefore, existed by arrangement with the owners, who were not themselves necessarily interested in carrying, but only in taking the tolls, a rather discouraging divergence of views.

NUMBER ONES: Most river barges were probably owned by their captains and immediate families, and many barge masters would have no more than half a dozen craft. Capital to invest in large fleets was limited, and earnings small. The owner-captain of a Yorkshire keel remains with the present motor craft although he does not call himself a 'number one'. Weaver sailing flats went by this term in later days since they were mostly captain and family owned, and number ones were common on the canals of South Wales, there called hobblers, some owning more than one boat. There were number ones on the Leeds & Liverpool, men who hired out their craft to carriers, providing their own horses and paying their own mates. The practice was called 'boat hire'. Another Leeds & Liverpool term was 'Captain boat', meaning a boat which had the same man all the while, although he did not necessarily own it. Number ones' boats received personal attention. As the owner was dependent on his craft he made sure she was frequently docked and painting and decoration achieved a high standard, especially lavish among the Midlands number ones. They were latterly and probably always had been a small group who concentrated on the coal trade from the Warwickshire field down to the John Dickinson paper mills on the Grand Junction near Watford, and also took coal down the Oxford Canal. They carried under a regular contract to the mills until the 1920s when the Samuel Barlow Coal Co., took over as factors, the cargoes being arranged by them and the number ones running as sub-contractors. On the Grand Junction the boats worked in pairs pulled by a single horse, a Shire, pairs carrying a better payload and passing together through the wide locks. On the Oxford Canal where coal cargoes were arranged by Samuel Barlow, the narrow locks demanded single boat working. Earnings were reasonable, but number ones had to save for docking, holiday times at collieries and mills, while a prolonged freeze up hit them hard. During the early 1930s a number one would earn with his family £21 to £22 per trip and could do a trip a week. Their work was killed on the Grand Junction in the late 1930s by the new Grand Union Canal Carrying Co., desperate to find work for its huge fleet, which it achieved by undercutting. Owner boatmen still relied on Samuel Barlow's for what work was available but gradually sold their boats, Barlow's buying them and employing their crews. Oxford Canal number ones lasted longer because the trade was too small to justify Grand Union participation. Joe Skinner was the last, retiring in 1959 and employing his mule 'Dolly' to the end. Most number ones went over to motor boats in the 1930s. There were number

160. Two boat captains prepare to settle a dispute over precedence with their fists, common enough on crowded canals. Note shawls and frilled bonnets.

ones on the Trent & Mersey including Mrs. Agnes Beech at Saltersford who had a small fleet of six horse boats in the coal trade, one horse pulling a pair as on the Grand Junction. Potter & Sons (Runcorn) Ltd of Hanley were a small carrying firm whose boatmen were called number ones because they were semi-independent. They either hired boats from Potter's or used their own boats under contract to the firm, but charged customers direct.

BOAT CONTROL: Carriers had various methods of recording the whereabouts of their fleet. Albert Wood of Sowerby Bridge used boards, one for broad and one for narrow boats. Down the left hand side were the craft and across the top, days of the week. The information came in daily from his offices at Hull, Goole and Manchester stating craft movements. The 1929 Grand Union had a more advanced method. On their system and neighbouring waterways there were reporting stations marked on a large map in the boat control centre at Bull's Bridge. Each boat was represented by an ivorine disc with different colours for loaded craft, empty craft, broken-down craft and independent carriers. Reports came in each morning and the discs were checked. If a disc showed no signs of movement, enquiries were made. Breakdowns were dealt with rapidly by fitters sent out in vans. It was continued by the Docks & Inland Waterways Executive. Nowadays the British Waterways Board cargo craft are controlled by telephone between depots and locks and bridges, with daily or even twice daily reports. On the Aire & Calder and part of the Sheffield & South Yorkshire, the board have their own telephone system.

BOAT PEOPLE: Possibly in the early nineteenth century boat people would have numbered 100,000 including the large numbers on the river barges, a considerable class back in the seventeenth century. Samuel Pepys enjoyed the company of the western bargemen of the Thames. He has left a portrait of self reliant, good humoured men. Their fellows manned trows, flats, keels, and wherries. As rivers were improved so barges penetrated further inland and by the 1850s the rivermen must have become a large and well known class. Crews were big, because the gear was difficult to handle, and labour was cheap. Hours of work were long and unrestricted, the aim being to get there, unload and secure another cargo as quickly as possible. It is not known how the river men were paid, very likely as the later canal boatmen were, by tonnage and mileage, or they may have had a regular weekly wage with bonuses for fast trips. It was customary for the captain to be paid by the carrying company, he finding and paying his own crew, a tradition which must stem from the days when most barges were owned by the captain and his family. Evidence for late eighteenth century weekly wages comes from the flatmen's threatened strike on the Mersey & Irwell in 1797. Employed by the company's carrying department they were placated by weekly wages of captain 16s, mate 13s, and hand 6 to 9s. The Mersey & Irwell were generous because, apart from the fast trip bonuses, there were yearly bounties for good behaviour and a cost of living allowance for captains with families in Liverpool or Manchester. Families lived ashore, although some of their menfolk could hardly have got home very often, but many river trips were short so that a house ashore was worth while. Women were probably carried aboard if accommodation was sufficient, as in Yorkshire keels. With the arrival of canals one assumes that river men extended their employment further afield. They and their sons had the knowledge and although new types of boats were introduced, the work would be along familiar lines. Flatmen on the Douglas in Lancashire became familiar with the Leeds & Liverpool. Later the canal men became more specialized, although those working down to the Severn from the Midlands were expert on the river, and Irish Grand Canal boatmen were at home on the Shannon, while the difficult Barrow was navigated by specialist 'Barrow boys'. Keelmen on the Humber were regarded as men of the highest experience, and the keels a nursery of seamen for the mine-sweepers of the 1914-18 War. River men were indeed impressed for naval service from the seventeenth to the early nineteenth century, although the carriers were often given 'protections' or exemptions. There is no evidence to support a gypsy background except for the similar boat and waggon decoration. Far more tenable is the river man working further afield, aided by others, not so expert but ready or forced to learn. These could have been farm workers, redundant due to enclosures, soldiers discharged after the Seven Years War (1756-63), men who stayed on the canal having helped make it, in fact the wide background that any industry draws upon. Canal boats were crewed in the same way as river craft. Whereas it was three men and a boy on the Trent, the boy being in the role of unofficial or official apprentice, on the Birmingham Canal one man and a boy, often father and son was sufficient. Canal company bye laws were explicit over the age of these people and their duties, the man to steer, the boy to lead the horse. Many trips were short so the crews would get home, but family boating was a means of economising. When freight rates fell, due to the trade depression after 1815 and later railway competition, the captain's wages fell. He could not pay his mate so took his wife aboard as unpaid assistant with the children as useful helpers, particularly with the horse. However this was by no means widespread. It did not lend itself to short haul work, for example on the Black Country system where crews changed boats often. It was rare in South Wales, again the trips were short, and rare in Ireland also. Scotland does not seem to have had any family boats and it is doubtful if there were many in East Anglia and the short canals and navigations of southern England. This leaves the North-West, Yorkshire and the Midlands. There were many family boats on the Leeds & Liverpool, Yorkshire keels with families aboard and houses ashore, and family Mersey flats on the Rochdale. The centre of family boating lay in the Midlands, in the long distance narrow boats. Their cabins were not ideal for families, but they survived to build up a race of specialist boatmen. Narrow boat people became an independent community (160). They intermarried and sons succeeded fathers as captains after unofficial apprenticeships. On the Shropshire Union the practice was for a boy of 15 to leave the family boat and go as mate to another captain, who would feed and clothe him. After a few years the boy would have a boat of his own with a mate or a wife. Training started very young, at the age of 3 children were learning how to steer a narrow boat standing on a stool.

Because they were on the move, narrow boat children never received any education, not so remarkable in the nineteenth century, but a distressing social flaw in the twentieth. Some families lived in a house and a boat, a practice which persisted among the Potteries boatmen while fly-boats and steamers which worked fly kept an all male crew. This could be a father and sons, the Grand Junction fly-boat STOURPORT described in 'Household Words', vol. 18 of 1858, was captained by Thomas Randall assisted by one son, another man and a youth. Randall only got home three times a year. The women brought decorative paintwork, the polished brass, the scrubbed fancy ropework, the lace edged plates and the Measham teapots to the narrow boats (160). On the other hand large families in small boat cabins meant squalor, and disease. Moreover the children were exploited, undertaking tasks beyond their strength at the locks and walking the towpath behind the horse. George Smith was successful in securing the Canal Boats Acts of 1877 and 1884 which regulated the squalor but the lack of education was never overcome. Medical facilities for the family boat people were never easily secured, confinements being a particular problem and about the only event a boatman would tie up for. Boat people were wary of doctors and hospitals. Moreover they could have no regular doctor and payment was a problem. Some doctors would not come to the boats, but matters eased with the National Health Service. Their great confidante was Sister Mary Ward of Stoke Bruerne who stayed almost to the end of narrow boat carrying, while from 1903 the Shropshire Union maintained a nurse at Ellesmere Port. Locks were a hazard, particularly in the dark and in wet weather. Some companies picked out coping edges with whitewash and it is practically universal to have the end of balance beams painted white. Even so people slipped in, to be crushed between boat and chamber side. Propellers were an extra hazard and the incidence of drowning seems high, particularly of women and children. Kicks from horses were common and windlasses and rack and pinion gear of paddles could also injure. The work was uniquely demanding. Hours of work remained long, the eight hour day being impossible to apply to the long distance canal carrying where wages depended on mileage and tonnage. Food was consumed when the wife had time to cook it. There was no question of tying up for meals. In motor narrow boat days a wife on the butty would pass a plate to her husband at the lock. Many boat people preferred sandwiches or cold meat at mid-day after a cooked bacon breakfast and would wait until tying up for tea with a cold supper later.

161. A narrow boat woman organizes her water supply with can and dipper.

If they were working late they would forego the tea and have fish and chips. These meals were well spaced since it was usual to fetch the horse from the stable at 5.00 a.m. and to be away at 6.00 a.m. after breakfast. Tying up was not until 6.00 or 8.00 p.m. and after tea the family would go to the pub or the pictures. Sundays were marked by a cooked lunch. Beef steak and onions was a favourite dish and stew, which they called 'lobby' short for lobscouse, an old seafaring term for a stew or hash. During the 1939-45 War the boat families found it difficult to draw their rations, because, being customers of no particular shop they could not claim to be regulars and had to give way to the locals. In the all-male boats the cooking was reduced to a minimum; beef, potatoes, bread and tea were the staple victuals, the tea had no milk but was sweetened with sugar. Bowls and not plates were used, the crew drinking out of the bowls. A description of fly-boat conditions in the 1920s explains how 20 lbs. of beef was cooked at one go to last the whole trip. When women were aboard, the cooking was better, and they were welcomed on the Yorkshire keels for this reason. Mersey flatmen used to take their food aboard in a wicker basket, provisions to last just a few days, for their trips were usually short. Wages were dependent on the twin yardsticks of tonnage carried and mileage travelled. Some carrying companies, for example Albert Wood on the Rochdale, paid a regular weekly wage to the captain plus extra for tonnage and mileage. The captain was responsible for the boat and its cargo, and the safe passage of both. A basic wage would cover spells of idleness through lack of cargo or frost. It was called sometimes the 'fall back' although some companies left their men to draw the dole. Tonnage and mileage made the boatmen work long hours to cram in as many trips as possible. On the other hand the Rochdale Canal Co., set fixed hours for their 'boaties'. Wages were worked out at so much per ton, dependent on the length of trip. Lighter cargoes, like crated earthenware commanded more tonnage money than coal. Tolls and tunnel tug charges were paid by the company. In the 1920s a narrow pair were earning £8 per week average for the boatman and his family, so he was well off if he was not paying a mate. In the 1950s pairs carrying coal from South Lancashire to Runcorn gasworks were earning £15 per week, good money then. They were doing three trips per week at 50 tons per trip at 2s per ton. They received nothing for empty running. Yorkshire keel captains were paid by thirds, or fourths depending on freight rates. Brokerage, port dues and tolls were deducted before the freight was thirded, then one third went to the owner and two thirds to the captain, who paid hire of horses and tugs, and the mates wages. Lower freight rates were divided into fourths, a quarter for the owner and three quarters for the captain. If the keel was owned by the captain then he took the whole freight. Sometimes the keel captain on a regular trade was given a lump sum, a third of which went to the owner, the shipper finding all expenses.

W. H. Pyne's engravings of river barge crews at the turn of the nineteenth century show a costume of breeches and thick stockings with rough jackets and waistcoats, loose neck-cloths and wide brimmed, floppy hats. The STOURPORT's crew, narrow boatmen of the mid-nineteenth century, wore fustian trousers, thick blue worsted stockings, heavy Blucher boots with hobnails and iron reinforcing pieces. They had plush jackets and waistcoats, red or brown being favourite colours, the waistcoats with fustian sleeves and pearl buttons. They liked gay silk neckcloths and they wore either a sailor's leather hat, round with a low crown, or a cap with a shiny peak. Fustian is a cotton fabric of coarse twill, often a corduroy, a moleskin or velveteen, while plush is a woollen cloth woven to look like velvet. The Blucher boots were leather half boots named after the Prussian marshal at Waterloo. Something like this costume remained into the twentieth century. Photographs of the early twentieth century. show men with full sleeved pleated shirts (97), moleskin waistcoats and silk neckerchiefs elaborately crossed and counter crossed. Belts were leather or woven in wool in bright contrasting colours and braces were likewise woven. Many men stiffened their caps with cane to extend the brim and clogs were common footwear. Leeds & Liverpool wives knitted guernsey sweaters for their menfolk. Women dressed impressively, with their long skirts, starched white pinafores, pleated blouses and elaborate bonnets with rows of shirring or frills, ribbons and trimmings. Shawls were common as a workday head-dress. The bonnets were worn at work too, the older women preferring black, the younger white. Photographs suggest high standards of personal cleanliness and neatness of dress. The towing mast of a narrow boat made an excellent prop for a clothes line. Boatmen in the motor age have overalls and blue slop jackets while wet weather gear was a heavy overcoat which sopped up the rain and took hours to dry in the engine room.

Cleanliness was vital in the cabins. Many must have been unbelievably squalid and over-crowded. Bed bugs were the worst enemy, exterminated by fumigation or 'stoving'. This was done at depots when boats were handed over from one crew to another. Bugs appeared in the cleanest cabins, brought by people off affected boats. In the nineteenth century it was common to see boat families encamped on the towpath while they put sulphur powder in a tin over a red hot cabin fire or lit formalin candles in later times. All openings had to be closed including the chimney and cracks sealed. Turf and wet sacks were used. Boat people evolved a vocabulary with a dialect founded on the district from which they came. Keelmen were undeniably Yorkshire, and many Leeds & Liverpool men spoke with a Wigan accent. Much of the vocabulary, particularly of place names was the result of mispronunciation, for they were not checked by the written word. Marsworth became 'Maffas' and Atherstone was 'Ariston'. Locks and pounds were christened by the boatmen quite independently of their geographical titles, by the name of a former lock keeper or the nature of the waterway itself. Wigram's 3 are the three Calcutt locks on the Warwick & Napton, while boatmen called the Wyrley & Essington Canal the 'gansey cut' because its bleakness demanded 'ganseys' or guernseys (jerseys) to be worn. In the closed community of the narrow canals, intermarriage has resulted in the perpetuation of names which may go back to the early days of the canal age. There are tribes of Andersons, Hollingsheads, Beecheys and Houghs, while a river example would be Deakin and Mills on the Weaver. Nicknames were frequent, as much used as the real surnames, thus the Andersons were 'Ironheads' and the Hollingsheads 'Charcoal'. In 1953 the Beechey family were operating no less than 11 pairs of narrow boats, including three where the wives were Beecheys. Boatmen knew little of the world away from the canal banks. Conversely the world knew little of them. No particular interest in their welfare seems to have been taken until the 1820s. Sunday boating was not encouraged and even forbidden at the start of the canal age, until the increased traffic of the early nineteenth century made many of the regulations dead letters. However with the religious revival of the late 1830s, Sunday working became widely condemned. The boatmen themselves joined the protests with demands for time off. This was the period when religion started to be taken to the wharf side, by missions and friendly societies. Little was achieved to solve the illiteracy problem. The Incorporated Seamen's & Boatmen's Friend Society had a day school at Birmingham while the Church of England Elementary School at Braunston took a fair percentage of canal boat children. At West Drayton in the 1930s an old wide boat was fitted up as a class room for Grand Junction children, and there was a wide boat too at Bull's Bridge in the 1950s. A last attempt to solve the problem of spasmodic school attendance was made in 1952 when Wood End Hall, Erdington, Birmingham was opened as a hostel and boarding school. It took 16 children who could go back to the boats for holidays. Missionary work among the narrow boat population continued to the end of carrying. Boatmen had a bad record, notably the 'Rodney' men who would be casually employed as extra hands. The casual leggers at Brindley's Harecastle tunnel were also called 'Rodney' men. Cheshire boatmen were strongly influenced by Methodism, ostracized any man who got a girl into trouble, but theft was endemic on rivers and canals. The bargemen stole from the dockyards, but more common was broaching of cargo and pilferage. Boats carrying wines and spirits had lock up holds. Every account of the canal age describes the fighting, mainly at locks for precedence (160). Swearing has for long been associated with bargemen, doubtless with reason.

On the other hand boat people were and are great respecters of privacy, necessary in the conditions of a busy wharf like Tyseley. Permission must be asked to cross over a boat, nobody peers inside a cabin, but knocks for attention. Narrow boatmen, although apparently so gregarious, rarely visited each other's cabins unless they had relatives to see. Meetings were on the towpath or in the pub, and it seems that families knew little of each other's business. During the 1939-45 War the Grand Union Canal Carrying Co., manned some boats with girl volunteers, a successful experiment which was extended to Fellows, Morton & Clayton. Some of the boat people were resentful, fearing call-up, but generally the girls, from a very different background were accepted. They were trained by Miss Eily Gayford and others, themselves originally trained by boat people, and at one time 11 volunteer pairs were working on the Grand Union.

CARGOES; Distribution of coal for industrial and domestic use was a problem in Britain. Everyone everywhere wanted it, to burn limestone, evaporate brine, brew beer, fire pottery, cook and above all keep warm. When steam power replaced water power and coke smelting became universal, the demand for coal multiplied apace. London had depended on sea coal from Durham and Northumberland, but before the canal age inland districts had to rely on the nearest river navigation and then carts. A solution was to improve a river further upstream. and a canal could extend the effective distribution area of a river. Complementary to canals pushing distribution of coal outwards were those built inwards to the coalfields. The bulk of latter day coal cargoes were grades of slack for automatic stokers. Pits in the Wigan area had sent cannel which burnt with a fierce candle-like flame, hence the name, while the South Wales canals carried culm a small anthracite used for lime burning, the larger anthracite being called stone coal. Steam coal was brought down by the Aberdare and Glamorganshire Canals from the 1830s, later in the form of briquettes for export to the navies and railways of the world, manufactured by patent fuel companies out of coal dust bonded by pitch. In Devon the Stover Canal handled the inferior lignite or brown coal from pits near Bovey Tracey. Coal measurement in the eighteenth century was far from standard. They spoke of baskets in Lancashire on the Douglas Navigation, each carrying 72 lbs. and priced according to the score "20". The Yorkshire waterways calculated by the tramroad waggon load, but the Don found in 1776 that coal owners were increasing waggon capacity above the accepted weight. The ton varied, based on a volume of coal, the Sankey Brook Navigation called a ton of coal 63 cu. ft. of coal which would actually weigh about 27 cwt. The Yorkshire ton was no less than 81 cu. ft. of coal. The coal from the Tyne and Wearside was submitted to very complex measures. Best known was the chaldron, by 1695 standardized in Newcastle to 53 cwt. In the later eighteenth century the word described a tramroad waggon of that capacity, a 'chaldron waggon', shortened simply to 'chaldron'. Variety led to fraud and in the early nineteenth century efforts were made to reduce the confusion. The Calder & Hebble from about 1801 worked by tonnage, a ton generally measured as 21 or 22 cwt to allow for loss through handling and pilferage. Competition in the coal trade was intense, where rival waterways offered coal from rival fields in the same area. Thus Oxford and the Thames valley were open to coal from Somerset, the Forest of Dean and the Moira field in Leicestershire. The canal companies would award subsidies called drawbacks, intended to reduce prices to the customer. Coal cargoes were sought by factors who either owned or hired boats under contract. The Samuel Barlow Coal Co., was a latter day coal factor or merchant for whom many of the number ones on the Grand Junction carried under contract. Many colliery companies had their own boats to distribute to their customers, for example the Moira Colliery Co., Bridgewater Collieries near Manchester and the pits of South Wales. The coal would be sold by the collieries or the factors to retail merchants for distribution or direct to customers. Associated with coal was iron ore and limestone. When local iron ore deposits were exhausted, for example round Merthyr Tydfil, then foreign ore came in, carried up from the 1830s by the Glamorganshire Canal. Limestone was for canals like the Peak Forest, their staple traffic. It was a flux to help the reduction of ore to molten iron, as lime in mortar, fertilizer and as limestone cut into paving or broken into road metalling. The demand was enormous as Britain's industries expanded from the 1850s; with industry went urban development and on the land, a corresponding agrarian revolution. At the end of the nineteenth century lime was in demand by the chemical industry, notably by Brunner, Mond and Co., at Winnington near Northwich as an ingredient of the Solvay process of making soda. To make full use of boats, limekilns were set up by canal and river wharves, very often at the terminal basin. Boats would bring coal, slack or culm, for the kilns and take away lime. Like coal, limestone could be handled in boxes as on the Peak Forest. Lime must be kept dry so loading at Bugsworth was done under sheds, but the stone was handled in the open. Land fertilization promoted many of the country's obscurer canals and river improvement schemes, notably in South-West England. The Bude and the Torrington are classic examples of canals built inwards from the coast to carry the fine yellow shell sand which had improvement properties. In Kent and Sussex the rivers, like the Arun and the Adur, and the canals carried chalk for spreading on the land. Similarly dung was sent up the Grand Junction and in the twentieth century 'shoddy muck' or slaughterhouse offal was sent from Manchester abbatoirs to Preston Brook for the land.

Moulding sand was a principal traffic on the Forth & Clyde along whose banks many foundries were built. One of the last canal traffics was bentonite, a type of clay imported from Italy for mould making and as a pottery raw material. Building stone for Tewkesbury Abbey was one of the earlier waterborne cargoes, coming up the Severn from Caen. Bricks were an important Yorkshire keel traffic, and slates were distributed from the ports by waterway, again the demand was from the new towns. Gravel and sand for building and roadstone were handled in large tonnages. Josiah Wedgewood promoted the Trent & Mersey for his pottery and potters provided most of the cargoes. The raw materials were in bulk, china clay from Cornwall being a white powder and the ball clay from Devon and Dorset cut into 35 lb. lumps. China clay was in use from the 1770s in the manufacture of porcelain, ball clay being added to give strength to the pottery 'body' and make it more workable. Each lump had a wooden spike in it for ease of handling by the lumpers who loaded the coasters at Teignmouth from the Stover and Hackney barges. Narrow boats carried china stone, feldspar, flints, and bones, also materials for the glazes, salt and potash, and colouring such as cobalt. They could be in bulk or bagged so that the boats carried a good tonnage. The traffic in crated pottery was not so successful. The crates were light and large and so the narrow boats were at a disadvantage, loading only 7 or 8 tons, plates being heaviest and jugs and teapots the most unhandy. Timber is an unstable cargo prone to slip sideways unless well secured, but because of its lightness it was stacked on deck as well as in the hold. Mainly a barge cargo, large tonnages were imported through King's Lynn and Wisbech and handled by fen lighters. Modern steel barges on the Lydney Canal took West African logs from Avonmouth to the plywood factory by the canal. Imported sawn timber was the sole latter day traffic on the Chelmer & Blackwater. Unrefined salt went in bulk (150), refined was bagged, great care being taken to keep it dry. Henry Seddon & Sons, the Middlewich salt producers packed their export salt, mainly for West Africa, in 40 lb. calico bags. These were stacked in their narrow boats surrounded by an insulation of straw with straw laid on top, to keep out moisture. The mast and stands, and the horizontal beams were wrapped in brown paper as an additional precaution and the boats well sheeted down.

Boats in Yorkshire and Lancashire carried textiles, the raw cotton and wool bales as well as finished goods. Some were called bale boats and much of this light cargo was carried on deck. Flats on the Rochdale Canal were designed with side decks wide enough for a bale of cotton. Most liquids were taken in barrels or carboys. Distribution was in small lots compared with modern demands, so the small containers (barrels or carboys) had their value. Tar was the exception, the first of the bulk tar carrying narrow boats appearing in the 1870s. Gas water for the production of ammonia, and oil were later carried in bulk. Today oil and petroleum are the mainstays of much of Britain's inland water transport. Tankers are economic if they are big enough, but apart from the Manchester Ship Canal, the maximum is 1,000 tons to the Quedgeley depot on the Gloucester & Sharpness Canal. 'Dracone' flexible containers were tried on this canal in the early 1960s: 150' long and 7' in diameter, they could carry 30,000 gallons of petroleum and were towed like a barge. Much traffic came under the general heading of merchandise, such as castings, tools, cordage, furniture, carpets, household and farm equipment, and glassware. Boats carried awkward loads like the cast iron segments for lining the Mersey tunnel brought from Stanton ironworks near Nottingham in the 1930s. On the Birmingham system the day boats carried forge and foundry products to the railway interchange basins or in the case of ships' anchors and chain cable, long distance boats went direct to Merseyside or London. There were no refrigerated boats for perishables but most went by fly-boat. Those on the Shropshire Union carried salmon, bacon, figs, oranges, onions, pineapples and pears. Sheep on the hoof went to Paddington by double decked boat, probably of broad beam to maintain stability, and the Grand in Ireland had a steam cattle boat based at Ballinasloe. Traffic for Cadbury's milk and chocolate factories was important. It included milk collection from farms, the churns being set on stands in the boat. Chocolate crumb (the dry powdered mixture of cocoa, sugar and evaporated milk) and mass (pure ground up cocoa) were bagged. Parcels traffic was carried by scheduled fly-boats and passenger packets. They ran almost a postal service and some waterways did carry mails. Then there were boats carrying explosives, for example on the Lee Navigation from the Royal Powder Mills at Waltham Abbey. These were specialised craft with an iron canopy over the hold space, but explosives were also taken by ordinary craft. On the Rochdale they had to fly red flags fore and aft. In their day the waterways carried everything, wines and spirits, Cheshire potatoes, Norfolk reeds, Ulster flax, Dublin porter, West Country cider, Portsmouth dockyard stores and when the railways were being built, large tonnages of rails, sleepers, ballast and other materials. Without the canals the railways could not have been built so quickly. Latter day cargoes have either been bulk or specialized contracts to water-side premises, such as lime juice to Rose's at Boxmoor. The railways took away the high toll merchandise and groceries now captured by roads, although Fellows, Morton & Clayton specialized to the end on competitive non-bulk goods. For the future, bulk traffic of raw materials and part finished products like chemicals must be the answer, although containers and lighters aboard ship systems offer a range of possibilities.

CARGO HANDLING: Much cargo had to be barrowed; a crane could manage sacks, barrels and boxes, but before the grab, could not handle loose stuff. Barrowing was slow, it took a full day for three men to unload a Leeds & Liverpool long boat with 60 tons of coal aboard, two shovelling and one wheeling and tipping. A narrow boat with 25 tons of coal aboard took two men about half a day to empty, the work getting harder as they had to throw higher over the gunwale. Bricks were tipped in and thrown out if sufficiently hard, but facing bricks were handled more carefully. Keels used derrick poles to unload coal, sand or stones with baskets hoisted by the anchor windlass. The derrick heel was secured to the foot of the mast by a strop, a gin wheel rigged from the derrick head and the derrick held by a topping lift and slewed and steadied by two guys. Large stones were handled by big tongs called clams, like those used to grip round timber. Baskets held about 2 cwt. and there would be two, one being filled, the other hoisted and tipped into a barrow or cart on the quay. In this way a gang of four or five men, one on the windlass, one or two filling and two wheeling and working the guys could unload coal at a rate of 9 tons or so per hour. Some derricks were horse worked. Keels employed them, the horse walking backwards and forwards along the quay. From the gin wheel the hoisting rope, a single whip, led to another block on the lutchet and so to the horse's swingletree. The horse would be urged forward to lift and it would be 'back up' to lower, 'pulling out with a horse' the operation was called.

Weaver steam packets had derricks, Plate 3, to deal with bagged cargo. Of the two drums on the steam winch, the port side one worked the topping lift, which was double with a sheave at the derrick head, and the starboard side the whip. This was led through one of two sheaves mounted on a cross-tree about a third of the way up the mast. From the derrick head, guys to port and starboard slewed the derrick as required. For many cargoes loading by chute was possible. Most coal was put aboard in this way at staithes overhanging the water (162). Loading would begin at the fore end, then the boat would be moved so that the coal descended into the middle and finally aft, the boat being moved again to level off evenly. It was usual to load a little by the head so that the steering remained easy with the helm not too fully immersed. Another advantage was that any water would run away from the after cabin. Unloading followed the same process in reverse, working from aft forwards, with grab or shovels. South Wales coal cargoes were loaded in two great heaps, one forward and one aft of the fixed middle beam, and briquettes were stacked in two piles. At Bugsworth on the Peak Forest there were waggon tipplers, treadmill operated. They tipped the limestone waggons bodily, hoisting them up at one end. Between the quay and the boat deflection

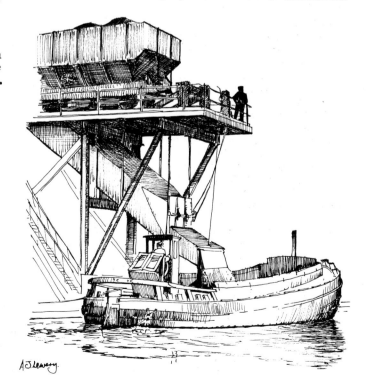

boards were laid to stop the stone rolling into the canal. As it was, the Peak Forest closed the basins for two weeks every summer to clean them out. Liquids went by barrel or carboy while tar was carried in bulk, pumped in and out. Waterways have benefited from advances in goods handling. On the wharf, fork lift trucks work in conjunction with pneumatic tyred cranes of up to 5 tons capacity. At depots like Brimsdown, Enfield on the Lee, overhead gantry cranes run out over the holds of lighters under the wharf canopies. At Leeds depot (Knostrop) a 32 ton derrick can handle containers between lorry and barge and at Weston Point and Sharpness derricks transfer containers to ships.

162.

British Oak coal staiths near Wakefield on the Calder & Hebble. Loading a 'West Country' motor barge of 80 tons capacity.

CRANES and HOISTS: From the fifteenth century treadmill cranes were in use on river quays and some survive including one on the wharf at Guildford. Renovated in 1972 and probably of eighteenth century origin, this has a jib which swings radially but will not luff, the former being more valuable for cargo work. Treadmills were safe and efficient because with men inside they could not lose control of the load, if they were strong enough to lift it they were strong enough to hold it. Warehouses made use of a fixed beam or cathead above the loading doors with a pulley block and single whip or rope. A double purchase could be contrived for heavier loads. These simple hoists could be operated by a hand windlass, by horse power via a sequence of sheaves so that the horse pulled horizontally, or by water power. Since it is difficult to stop a waterwheel precisely and impossible to reverse it, the drive was either by friction wheel or belt which could rapidly be put in and out of gear. Lowering of loads was controlled by a hand brake round a large diameter wooden wheel. Waterwheel powered hoists were employed at Rochdale Canal warehouses in Manchester. If the building was set back from the water, a gantry beam might be used projecting over the water with a carriage or crab running along it, with hoisting tackle. Weston Point had, until the reconstruction of the port after the 1939-45 War, a system of wooden gantries to unload and distribute the cargoes of flints, feldspar and china stone which came for transhipment to the Potteries. Coasting vessels unloaded by bucket into the trollies which ran on the gantries. Then they were pushed by hand and tipped as desired.

Transhipment became heavy at many wharves, between boat and cart or tramroad waggon, and between boats of different gauges. Cranes with double jibs were much used. In 1774 Josiah Wedgwood made a dinner service for the Empress Catherine II of Russia, and on one piece was a picture of Worsley basin. Two cranes are shown. One is a radial wharf crane bracketed to the side of a warehouse. This was a common arrangement, some large cranes of this type being built later on, for example the 10 ton lift one at Sowerby Bridge, with a lattice steel jib. The other Worsley crane has two horizontal jibs, or rather one horizontal jib with a pulley at each end, passing through an upright post free to rotate, being held by guys. One jib would be dropping its load, say a container box of coal on the quay, while the other would be lifting from a boat. A company would lease cranes to shippers and carriers, while at York in the Middle Ages there was a wharf crane owned by the corporation and usable by all on payment of a toll. Wooden freestanding wharf cranes were ponderous with the jib massively supported from a revolving post and heavily counterweighted. A few examples survive as at Bumblehole, Netherton, on the Dudley. In the nineteenth century came fixed jib cranes of the type associated with railway yards, with a geared hand windlass and swivelling about an iron post. Some, there was one at Newport on the Monmouthshire, had a double windlass arrangement. The operator wound a windlass at the foot of the crane which pulled round a large diameter wheel, on whose spindle was mounted the windlass for the crane rope, a type of reduction gearing. At canal maintenance yards where awkward loads like lock gates and bridge parts were handled, a derrick was needed with a luffing jib which could alter its radius.

Hydraulic cranes were introduced by William Armstrong in 1846. They had the advantage of compactness over the steam crane which was available at the same time. The hydraulic design embodied the jigger, an Armstrong idea which used a ram, but multiplied the effective length of the piston stroke by coupling the rod to a pulley block which was combined with a fixed pulley block on the cylinder head. The rope or chain passed round the sheaves in these blocks, usually three, multiplying the piston stroke six times, so a good lift could be obtained. For warehouse work the hydraulic crane was excellent and for fixed quayside installations. It was not mobile, although Armstrong had tried jointed hydraulic pipelines. Here the steam crane was at an advantage, self propelled on a railway chassis. Cranes were also mounted on boats for maintenance work and for cargo handling. Albert Wood, the Rochdale carrier had a steam crane boat, the BADEN POWELL for transhipping between keels and flats. The old Weaver sailing flat DARESBURY built in the late eighteenth century spent her last years as a crane boat for the Weaver Navigation maintenance fleet. Rail mounted steam cranes were put in at large centres like Ellesmere Port and Sharpness, and were common until replaced by pneumatic tyred diesel cranes, since the 1939-45 War. Many were fitted with grabs and large steam grab cranes were installed at power stations and gas works. Electric cranes were operating at Southampton in the 1890s, and electricity took over from hydraulic and steam power for large cranes. They were put on rail mountings for quayside work, for example at Weston Point in the 1920s, or fixed as at Westwood power station, Wigan. Goole is the home of the special hoists for the coal compartment boats (endpapers). Elsewhere coal was handled at drops above the quay where rail waggons would be tipped and the coal sent down chutes into the vessels (162). At Anderton there were salt chutes and hoists, later steam powered for pottery raw materials and crated ware. The so-called crate drops were counterbalanced hoists with chain tackle. More recently belt and bucket conveyors and pneumatic elevators came to handle many cargoes. Conveyors were introduced into the flour mills in the 1840s and pneumatic elevators to unload grain in the 1900s. On the waterways they have been used to discharge slack coal, while coal boats have been loaded by conveyor from lorry filled hoppers. The electric tippler at Ferrybridge C power station on the Aire & Calder receives a 170 ton compartment boat (39). Under the tippler the boat is hoisted on a counter-balanced cradle to a height of 40' and tipped, the unloading cycle taking 9 minutes. Up to 60 boats a day, 31,000 tons a week is the usual rate of unloading. At the other end of the scale Arddleen Wharf on the Montgomeryshire Canal had, until the end of its life in the 1930s, nothing more than a pulley block lashed to a tree.

AIRE & CALDER NAVIGATION, LEEDS. Until 1774 the Aire & Calder trustees leased their navigation. One of the lessees, Peter Birt, had a carrying fleet and remained the only lessee when the trustees bought him out in 1774. With the navigation in their own hands and much improved by the opening of the Selby canal in 1778 followed by other improvements, the trustees set up their own carrying business. They had taken over Peter Birt's boats, including his coal boats and in the 1780s they built sailing sloops for the Selby - Hull trade. Their carrying expanded, not only from Leeds and Wakefield to Hull, but on to the Calder & Hebble, and from 1794 on to the Leeds & Liverpool and Bradford Canals. Manchester was the principal market, either reached by road from Sowerby Bridge or via the very roundabout Trent and Trent & Mersey waterways, but later using the Rochdale Canal. Competition came from steam packets on the Ouse, Humber and Trent, served by road transport and fly-boats. The Aire & Calder started their own fly-boat services in 1821, all water carriers being much helped by the completion in 1826 of the Knottingley-Goole canal and the creation of the new port at Goole. The Aire & Calder put a steam tug into service on the navigation in 1831 to tow the fly-boats, two more soon joining it. Traffic benefited by the improvements made to the system by 1839, both up to Leeds and on the Calder line to Wakefield. On the other hand, carrying had become more competitive between water and road, the latter serving the Ouse steam packets. Because of this the Aire & Calder had followed a policy of reducing the number of their craft, particularly on the run between Goole & Hull, while on the navigation they concentrated on the more competitive fly-boats, some built of iron from the early 1840s. Railways at Goole, the first in 1848, hit the Aire & Calder hard. Agreements over rates were made but the Aire & Calder sought other ways of keeping traffic. For a while, from 1855 to 1857 they had a carrying fleet of narrow boats on the Huddersfield Canal, because Manchester traffic was hampered by the the Rochdale's lease to railway interests. However, the Huddersfield venture proved unsatisfactory because of Stanedge tunnel. Highly satisfactory on the other hand was the adoption of the compartment boat system, started in 1865 after a period of experiment. The Aire & Calder could now undercut rail carriage of coal and Goole grew as a coal exporting port; in 1899 the compartment boat fleet was handling nearly half a million tons of coal. These boats were operated by the navigation themselves, together with the tugs and hydraulic hoists at Goole. Some years before the compartment boat revolution the Aire & Calder had converted one of their fly-boats into a steamer to act as a cargo carrying tug and pull other flyboats. This was in 1852 and in 1857 they put on tugs to tow bye traders' boats. By the 1870s the Aire & Calder had a fleet of about a hundred carrying craft plus the compartment boats which numbered 401 at the end of the century. Merchandise traffic had increased and the Aire & Calder were now carrying now on the Barnsley Canal. As an extension, the Aire & Calder invested in seaborne commerce. After several false starts, the first in 1835, they eventually succeeded in establishing the Goole Steam Shipping Co., on a sound basis in 1865. It ran cargo liner services to Antwerp, Rotterdam, Dunkirk and Ghent, later extended to Hamburg, Copenhagen, Delfzyl, Amsterdam and Bruges. Supported by the L. & Y. the Goole S.S. was eventually bought by the Lancashire & Yorkshire Railway in 1904. The Aire & Calder inland fleet was able to survive the 1914-18 War. Compartment boat traffic continued to do well, as did merchandise handled by dumb barges towed by tugs, by tug towed fly-boats and by steam fly-boats working singly to Leeds and Barnsley. The old company's livery was dark green and white, their tugs and steamers having a white funnel with a black top. Few of their craft were named, just numbered.

ANDERTON Co., STOKE - on - TRENT. Alexander Reid & Co, a potteries carrying firm, had by the 1830s built up a traffic in pottery raw materials and crated ware between Weston Point and the Five Towns, everything being transhipped at Anderton. In 1836 they renamed themselves the Anderton Co., using narrow boats on the canal and flats on the river as Reid's must have done. In 1848 the Bridgewater trustees bought the Anderton Co., whose narrow boats then ran between Runcorn docks and the Potteries. It was a Bridgewater subsidiary until 1876 when the Bridgewater Navigation Co., sold it into private hands. In 1895 the Anderton Co., absorbed the canal carrying business of the North Staffordshire Railway, founded in 1847 as the North Staffordshire Railway & Canal Carrying Co. The partnership of W.H. Boddington and Edward Pamphilon, which had acquired the Anderton Co. in 1876, was replaced in 1898 by a limited company under the chairmanship of Harry Boddington, W.H.'s son. The Boddington family maintained control until 1954 when the Anderton was merged with the Mersey, Weaver & Ship Canal Carrying Co. Although parted from the Bridgewater, the Anderton Co. remained their agents in the potteries and their boats displayed the legend 'Bridgewater Navigation Route' on their cabin sides. The Anderton Co. specialised in pottery traffic, though flour, soda, coal and gravel were also carried. They had their own dock at Middleport, Burslem, where narrow boats were built and repaired. At one time their fleet numbered 175 narrow boats, all with black cabin sides, bordered by white and red, and white lettering. Decorative painting achieved a high standard, particularly after the 1914-18 War when William Hodgson produced the naturalistic roses associated with the 'knobstick' style, the name applied to the Anderton Co's boats and employees. Motor boats were introduced in the 1920s, the first being named WESTMINSTER, Anderton boats being called after countries, towns, rivers and girls' names. Horse boats remained until the 1950s, the last being on short haul work between the railway sidings at Cockshute Wharf, Stoke and Etruria. In 1958 the combined company was sold to the British Transport Commission who disposed of most of the boats.

Samuel BARLOW COAL Co., Ltd, BIRMINGHAM. Origins are obscure but this seems to have been started by a Coventry Canal owner-boatman 'Big Sam' Barlow towards the end of the nineteenth century. He built up a small fleet which by the 1900s was operating not only on local work, mainly coal but also some long distance services. Headquarters were on the Coventry Canal at Glascote near Tamworth, and Barlow did well enough by the end of the 1914-18 War to be taken over by W.H. Bowater, the Birmingham coal suppliers who had a large fleet of day boats and tugs. Under Bowater control, the Barlow fleet now called Samuel Barlow (Tamworth) Ltd, expanded further, the company acting as coal suppliers and arranging coal cargoes for several owner boatmen or number ones. Barlow's themselves carried coal to Banbury, Oxford, the power station at Uxbridge, Aylesbury dairy and the Ovaltine factory at King's Langley. At the same time they continued their day boat operations in the Birmingham - Coventry area, the day boats being built and repaired at their own dock at Amington Road, Glascote, established at about the time of the Bowater takeover. W.H. Bowater collapsed during the depression of the early 1930s but the Samuel Barlow fleet was saved by Raymond Stevens, formerly a clerk with Bowater's. He formed the Samuel Barlow Coal Co., Ltd, which continued as coal suppliers and canal carriers with the registered office in Birmingham. More long distance boats were built during the 1930's by Nurser's of Braunston. Motor boats were now introduced and the fleet by 1939 numbered up to 100 pairs, including day boats. In 1941 Samuel Barlow bought the Nurser Yard at Braunston, which continued to be managed by Frank Nurser. After the 1939-45 War trade declined because of road competition, although an effort was made to gain coal supply contracts by taking over carrying firms which had them, so during the 1950s they acquired among others, A. Harvey-Taylor of Aylesbury and their Glascote namesake S.E. Barlow. Meanwhile Samuel Barlow were expanding their fleet of motor vehicles, starting in the early 1950s. In the early 1960s the canal fleet was down to about 6 pairs of boats. The fleet and Braunston Dock were sold in 1962 to Blue Line Canal Cruisers who kept the boats in traffic until 1970 when the remaining contract was lost. In Barlow days they had dark green cabin sides with grained borders and the roses and castles for which Frank Nurser was renowned. Almost all the fleet were wooden craft and they bore a wide variety of names; islands, generals, admirals, and boys' and girls' names.

S.E. BARLOW, TAMWORTH. Confusingly also founded by a Coventry Canal boatman, 'Little Sam' Barlow, this firm was quite separate from the much bigger Samuel Barlow Coal Co., Ltd. The S.E. Barlow fleet started in the 1900s carrying coal from the Warwickshire field both to local and distant customers, including paper mills at the London end of the Grand Junction. S.E. Barlow had their own dock, Anchor Dock, on the Coventry Canal at Glascote near Tamworth. Here they built and repaired their own horse boats and in 1943 built the motor boat HOOD. Like Samuel Barlow, S.E. Barlow organised contracts for owner boatmen. During 1936 the Grand Union Canal Carrying Co., negotiated to buy the fleet, then about 15 pairs, but nothing came of this and the company continued independent until bought by the Samuel Barlow Coal Co., Ltd in the 1950s who retained the company name, but the boats were gradually withdrawn and by 1960 none remained. Like the Samuel Barlow boats, they had dark green cabin sides with grained borders.

James BARRACLOUGH & Co., Ltd, HULL. James Barraclough was a keel captain who in 1890 started to trade with his own keel TRIUMPH. More keels and sloops were acquired, the old family concern becoming a limited company in 1931. Sailing craft were kept in traffic until the 1940s and then unrigged, two of the last sloops both with steel hulls, the IVIE and THE SPRITE remaining as lighters in the 1970s. Meanwhile the Company had been acquiring motor craft, the first was the A VICTORY followed by the A TRIUMPH, both given an 'A' prefix because of other Victorys' and Triumphs' on the British register. Latterly the fleet totalled 11 motor craft and 5 dumb. Eight of the motor craft were of 250 ton capacity, three of 120 ton, Sheffield size, although they did not actually trade on the Sheffield & South Yorkshire Navigation. The dumb craft used for local work carried 140 tons. The large capacities of the motor craft had been achieved by lengthening. They could tow two dumb craft, although Barraclough's did have the motor tug FEAR NOT for this work. She also towed the sailing sloops up the Ancholme to Brigg. Coal and wheat were the principal cargoes, together with raw sugar to Brigg, but in the 1970s the bulk of their work was for Trent Wharfage at Gainsborough, carrying canned fruit and ferrous metals from Hull. Craft also went to York and Selby and up the Aire & Calder to Leeds and Wakefield. They had a grey top strake to the hull and a red rubbing bin. Coamings and wheelhouses were light brown and the hawse plates blue with black hawse pipes. They ceased trading in 1975.

Duke of BRIDGEWATER and his successors. The Duke's waterway was built to market his coal, so as soon as it was open in 1761 he started to carry, and when it was extended to Runcorn he handled general merchandise on the navigation and down the Mersey to Liverpool. His base was Castlefield, Manchester, with a terminal depot at Liverpool where in 1783 he completed the Duke's dock. Completion of the Trent & Mersey altered carrying on the Bridgewater. Hitherto the Duke had probably done all the carrying on his canal, both passenger and goods, his passenger boats having started as early as 1767. Now traders off the Trent & Mersey appeared at Castlefield, although the Duke retained most of the purely Bridgewater traffic. Most notable of the newcomers was the Trent & Mersey's own carrying subsidiary, Hugh Henshall & Co., later in competition with a firm the Duke supported, Gilbert, Worthington & Co., founded about 1790, trading between Manchester and Stockport. The Gilbert of the partnership was the son of the Duke's agent John Gilbert. It had been the intention that the Duke's barges should use the Trent & Mersey as far as Middlewich, but the tunnels were too narrow, so Preston Brook on his canal became the transhipment centre. He seems to have been exclusively a barge or flat owner, apart from his fleet of mine boats at Worsley. His boats were either bought or built at his dock at Worsley. At his death in 1803 he had a fleet of some 100 barges, plus the mine boats. The Duke's trustees continued his carrying policy and did well, in agreement with the Mersey & Irwell who had operated a fleet of flats from the 1730s. But the trustees failed to maintain a near monopoly of the Manchester, Runcorn, Liverpool traffic, for more bye traders appeared in the 1820s, among them the Rochdale & Halifax Merchant's Co., working from 1824 off the Rochdale Canal. The reason for the influx was clear, the Duke's canal had become part of the national network. Railway competition led to rate cutting and the small bye traders gave up. To keep traffic, the trustees found they had to fill the gap and their business extended, with barges and narrow boats on, for example, the Macclesfield Canal. A serious rate war started in 1848, when the Liverpool & Bury Railway was opened in competition with the Liverpool & Manchester. Freight charges went down to ridiculous levels, the great fear being that the railways would kill the bye traders. To protect them and therefore their own canal traffic, the trustees made these carriers their agents in 1849, being prepared to subsidize their losses and fixing their rates for them. Such a policy led the Bridgewater far afield. One agency agreement was made with a firm in Wolverhampton, Shipton & Co., and the Bridgewater had agencies at Stourport, Worcester, Gloucester and Bristol. Carriers were also acquired, the Rochdale & Halifax Merchants' Co., the Anderton Co., the Harrington Co., William Jackson & Sons and J. & J. Veevers & Co. This policy was continued when the Bridgewater was sold to railway interests in 1872. In 1875-6 new iron screw tugs appeared (45) able to tow three flats on the canal and work on the Mersey. The Bridgewater Navigation Co., formed in 1872, had a repair yard at the Sprinch in Runcorn, with 8 drydocks, Worsley having been left in the hands of the trustees for repair of the canal boats they still owned. In 1887 the Bridgewater Navigation Co., was bought by the Manchester Ship Canal Co. They worked the carrying fleet both on the canal and the part of the Mersey & Irwell that remained after construction of the ship canal. Bridgewater traffic was important to the new company, notably their cartage services based on Castlefield, and lighterage from the Manchester docks on to the canal system. Through traffic from the Mersey to Manchester suffered, but the ship canal had as many as 100 flats in the Bridgewater Department as late as the 1930s. The Bridgewater Department narrow boats gave overnight delivery service of parcels and perishables between Runcorn and Manchester. They worked fly with relays of horses and lasted until 1945. Passengers on any scale had ceased in the 1860s, but one craft continued to carry the odd passenger between Knott Mill at Castlefield and Stockton Heath near Warrington. This was the DUCHESS COUNTESS running as a parcels boat until about 1924. After 1948 the Bridgewater Department gave up most of its canal services, save for local work in Manchester and down the Irwell and ship canal to the depot at Howley Quay, Warrington. Barges also worked down to Runcorn and Liverpool via the ship canal. The old wooden craft were disposed of and new steel power and dumb barges were built at Northwich. However, more emphasis was put on the Bridgewater's road haulage fleet, based on Castlefield and all canal services ceased at the end of 1974.

'BRITISH WATERWAYS', LONDON. 'British Waterways' has been the short title under which the nationalised carrying fleet has operated since 1 January 1948, when the Docks & Inland Waterways Executive inherited the carrying fleets operated by the canal and river authorities and their subsidiaries. Independent carriers were not nationalised, although the British Transport Commission had powers to buy fleets by purchase and to licence new operators. The fleets which the D. & I. W. E. acquired included Canal Transport Ltd., on the Leeds & Liverpool, which became a wholly owned subsidiary of the Commission, the Aire & Calder carrying fleet, including tugs and compartment boats, the barges of the Trent Navigation Co., and the narrow boat fleet of the Grand Union Canal Carrying Co., while the day boats which were operated by the L.M.S.R. and G.W.R. in the Birmingham, Wolverhampton, Kidderminster and Stourport areas were run by British Railways. On the Severn the Commission bought the three river and channel general cargo barges which had been operated by the Severn & Canal Carrying Co., Ltd., as well as their tugs and narrow boats, and in 1949 they bought the fleet of Fellows, Morton & Clayton. Craft were built during the 1950s, high tensile steel short boats for the Leeds & Liverpool, steel narrow boats of larger capacity, diesel compartment boat tugs and motor barges for the Aire & Calder, 140 gross ton motor barges for the Trent, and a river and canal barge for the Severn, the SEVERN SIDE launched in 1952. The depot at Knostrop below Leeds was completed in 1958 with a 600ft quay, a depot at Rotherham on the Sheffield & South Yorkshire started in 1961 and later much enlarged by the British Waterways Board, an expansion at Brentford where between 1957 and 1960 the warehouse accommodation was more than doubled, and modernisation of warehousing at Meadow Lane and Trent Lane, Nottingham. In 1959 British Transport Waterways entered the container traffic with services from the West Riding via Knostrop and Hull to the Continent and from the Midlands via Nottingham or Regent's Canal Dock to the Continent. Both open and closed containers were offered. Services were not very successful as they created stowage and stability problems when loaded in barges. Knostrop can handle containers up to 40ft in length, and containers for road, rail and sea transport are loaded at many depots, for example in Birmingham. In 1963 the Board gave up most of their carrying on the Leeds & Liverpool and on the narrow Midlands canals, appreciating that there was no commercial future for the smaller waterways. On the wider waterways (commercial waterways under the 1968 Transport Act) the situation was different. Admittedly the Severn and Bristol Channel fleet were given up in 1969 but in Yorkshire the British Waterways Board were interested in the possibilities of push towing of large compartment boats. In 1970 an experimental train of three 100 ton boats was put into service on the Sheffield & South Yorkshire Navigation, followed in 1971 by another tug and two three-boat trains. Services were extended to the Trent and Aire & Calder. The older coal compartment boats inherited from the Aire & Calder Navigation maintain traffic down to Goole from Castleford and Doncaster although many have been withdrawn. Modern British Waterways Board Freight Services Division organization is arranged by groups under managers based at six centres. Each group operates several warehousing and distribution depots. Not all are water served, they were in the past, but now they depend on road vehicles, some of which are operated by the Board as at Nottingham. Customs facilities are offered as well as long and short term storage. Apart from the inland depots, the British Waterways Board have their docks, Weston Point, Sharpness and Gloucester. Much abuse was hurled at 'British Waterways' in their early days because of their choice of livery, predominantly yellow with blue lettering. However from 1949 the colours were reversed, a rich deep blue becoming predominant, plus a liberal use of transfers of the lifebuoy badge used by the Docks & Inland Waterways Executive, British Transport Waterways and British Waterways Board until the wave symbol was adopted in 1969. Funnels were black with a broad yellow band, changed to white in 1969, although this has never been standard. There is a 'British Waterways' house flag, blue with pairs of thin gold stripes parallel with the fly, top and bottom, and in the middle a ship's wheel in gold.

BRUNNER, MOND & Co., Ltd, NORTHWICH. Founded in 1873 (limited from 1881), by John Brunner of Liverpool and the German chemist Ludwig Mond, the company's aim was to develop the Solvay process of making caustic soda. The partners chose a site at Winnington Hall near Northwich for two reasons, local salt and the Weaver Navigation. In 1874 Brunner Mond became barge owners, with a fleet of locally built wooden flats, at first hired and bought second hand, but from 1880 new built. They also included four tank barges for gas water. They were all dumb craft, drawn by chartered tugs. In 1888 however they had a wooden steam packet built, the SHAMROCK, at Northwich, by Woodcock. She could tow up to three dumb barges and more steamers followed, some wood like the GWALIA, some iron framed like the SCOTIA and later ones wholly iron or steel. The packets and their attendant flats carried Winnington products down to Liverpool and Birkenhead for export. Return loads were coal for the works and raw materials such as limestone. Apart from the Weaver-Mersey traffic, Brunner Mond ran a fleet of horse drawn narrow boats between the limestone quarries and limekilns at Froghall on the Caldon Canal and their works, not only to Winnington, but also to the plant at Malkin's Bank near Sandbach. This works was closed in 1920 and the boats given up. Finally there was traffic between the Company's other soda ash plant at Lostock established in 1907, and Winnington, the boats going by the Anderton lift. This was handled by barges including the motor barges EVA and PADDY from the 1920s. Brunner Mond also had boats for dumping lime refuse, working between Winnington and the lime beds by the Weaver. They were dumb barges all with names beginning 'Wood' such as WOODLARK. The steam packets had a yellow funnel with a black top, continued for a time by I.C.I. The houseflag had the gold Brunner Mond crescent on a blue ground, with the initials B.M. & Co. also in gold under the crescent. As a distinguishing mark the boats had a white mast head.

CADBURY Bros., Ltd. In 1879 Richard and George Cadbury moved to factory premises at Bournville, south of Birmingham, adjacent to the Worcester & Birmingham Canal. The company established their own milk evaporating factories, at Knighton near Market Drayton in 1911 on the Shropshire Union and at Frampton-on-Severn in 1915 on the Gloucester & Berkeley, while in 1922 came a new process factory and store at Blackpole outside Worcester on the Worcester & Birmingham. To bring local milk to the Knighton factory. Cadbury's in 1912 commenced to operate a small fleet of horse boats each able to carry over 110 churns, collected from farms up and down the Shropshire Union. In the same year the firm started to carry chocolate crumb in bags, the dry mixture of cocoa, sugar and evaporated milk, from Knighton to Bournville in their own boats, with a return cargo of mass, also bagged, the pure ground cocoa needed at Knighton in the preparation of crumb. In 1916 they started to carry crumb and mass between Frampton and Bournville. Their boats were numbered, the motors being BOURNVILLE No. 1, No. 2 etc. The fleet never exceeded 9 long distance boats plus 3 or 4 milk boats at Knighton, although because of replacements the numbers reached 17. Their livery was the chocolate maroon of Cadbury's with the Company's name in their characteristic style. The long distance boats carried finished cocoa and chocolate to London and brought sugar from Liverpool and when the Blackpole factory started, took stored crumb from there to Bournville. In 1930 Cadbury's gave up their fleet, the work being taken over by the Severn & Canal Carrying Co., who handled the crumb traffic from Blackpole, Frampton and after 1945 some of that from Knighton, shared with Fellows, Morton & Clayton. Nationalization placed most of Cadbury's traffic in the hands of British Waterways, and crumb continued to be carried to Bournville until 1961 when the last cargoes arrived from Frampton, some of this being handled by the small private carrier Charles Ballinger of Gloucester. Between 1966 and 1968 Cadbury's revived their canal traffic when they sent large consignments of semi-extracted cocoa from Bournville to Regent's Canal Dock for shipment to Holland.

CANAL TRANSPORT Ltd, LIVERPOOL. In 1921 the Leeds & Liverpool gave up its fleet since it would no longer pay. Other carriers stepped in, notably Benjamin C. Walls of Skipton who built up quite a big fleet, converting a horse boat into a motor in 1924 and thereafter ordering many new motor boats. His craft were named after letters of the Greek alphabet. Also on the Yorkshire side was John Hunt & Sons (Leeds) Ltd. Later the Leeds & Liverpool Canal were keen to re-enter carrying and they were the force behind the 1930 amalgamation of Ben Walls, John Hunt, Lancashire Canal Transport Ltd of Eanam , Blackburn and the Liverpool Warehousing Co., Ltd, who acted as agents in Liverpool. The four firms, with half the capital subscribed by the Leeds & Liverpool, formed Canal Transport Ltd, and started a modernization programme. Steel and wooden motor boats were ordered, named after planets, birds and rivers. Canal Transport continued their constituents' leases of warehouse space from the canal company at Shipley, Leeds, Burnley, Church near Accrington, Blackburn and Wigan. Their headquarters were at Pall Mall basin, Liverpool and the canal company provided both the manager and secretary. Traffic, which included fly working, was in general cargoes, notably wool to Shipley from Liverpool, but up to the 1939-45 War the company was losing money. The War brought profits, but after 1945 losses were heavy. Canal Transport continued into nationalization as a wholly owned subsidiary of the Docks and Inland Waterways Executive. New craft continued to be built, wood and steel, the last of high tensile steel in 1952. After 1963 the boats ceased to be used for commercial carrying.

Thomas CLAYTON Ltd, OLDBURY. Carrying started in 1842 under, it is thought, William Clayton of Saltley, Birmingham, who handled general cargo, including liquids in barrels. Later in the nineteenth century the carriage of liquids became sufficiently important to be entrusted to a specialist subsidiary, Thomas Clayton, who ran bulk liquid narrow boats, starting their independent career in 1889 and remaining in canal carrying until 1966. The general carrying had gone to Fellows, Morton & Co., which became Fellows, Morton & Clayton in 1889. Another Clayton venture was a London subsidiary based on Paddington, which was latterly carrying refuse out of the capital and was bought by the Grand Union Carrying Co., in 1936. Brentford was the head office for both the Oldbury and Paddington firms which were known as Thomas Clayton (Oldbury) Ltd and Thomas Clayton (Paddington) Ltd. The former carried tar, oil and creosote throughout the Midlands canal system, between the Mersey and Manchester and the Black Country as well as from the London area. They operated between gas works and tar distilleries, oil storage installations and refineries. An important traffic was gas water, a gas works by-product from which ammonia is made. In the 1920s they had a fleet of 60 horse boats on both short haul traffic and long distance. Latterly the main runs were between Stanlow oil dock, near Ellesmere Port and Oldbury; Oldbury and Manchester where various grades of oil were loaded from deep sea tankers. They also took cargoes from the refineries at Stanlow and Trafford Park, Manchester. They discharged at the Shell-Mex depot at Langley, Oldbury. Their narrow boats were almost all wood, decked over to form a tank, and built by Nurser's of Braunston, Lees & Atkins of Polesworth and Rudkin Bros., of Leicester. One or two were iron, including the first motor in the fleet acquired in the mid- 1930s. At Oldbury the company had their own repair dock. The livery was red cabin side, bordered by yellow and green, the lettering being white. Naming was after rivers of the world in almost all cases, alphabetically so that DANE was an early boat and UMEA one of the last.

FELLOWS, MORTON & CLAYTON Ltd, Birmingham. Started in 1837 in Birmingham under James Fellows, the company sought merchandise and foodstuffs traffic rather than minerals. In about 1860 the famous Joshua Fellows succeeded his father later taking a partner, Frederick Morton. Expansion came in 1876 when the Grand Junction gave up carrying and they purchased many of the boats, followed by the London & Staffs. Carrying and the Midland & Counties Carrying fleets in the 1880s making a total of 379 narrow boats in 1885. In 1889 a third partner joined, Thomas Clayton. He was reorganising the family carrying business of William Clayton, which resulted in Fellows, Morton & Clayton taking over the general carrying side of Clayton's, while Thomas Clayton (Oldbury) Ltd remained separate, specialising in bulk liquids. The partners were keen to improve the canal route between London and the Trent. As the largest carriers on the Grand Junction, they persuaded the latter to buy the Grand Union and the Old Union, achieved in 1894. Because of their likely control over the whole water route between the Thames and the Derbyshire coalfield, the Grand Junction considered widening the locks at Watford and Foxton which Fellows, Morton advocated, so that they could use wide boats on their London to Leicester and Nottingham services. Fellows, Morton later turned to the Warwick Canals, the Warwick & Napton and Warwick & Birmingham, when in 1903 they offered to lease both and fit them for electric traction. London to Birmingham and Coventry and London to Leicester, Nottingham and Derby were their main routes, on which their steamers ran fly services, but 'Joshers' (as the boats were known after Joshua Fellows) also worked between Birmingham, Manchester and Liverpool, although much of the north western traffic was transhipped at Preston Brook. They had their own boat dock at Saltley, where they built and repaired boats and in 1896 they took over another at Uxbridge where wooden craft were built. Saltley built steam narrow boats for the fleet, some with engines of their own make, and after 1912, motor boats. After the 1914-18 War, the company started motor boat construction, some with low horse power engines for working singly. In 1920 the total fleet was 208 boats, 21 of these being steamers and 25 motor, but by the 1930s there were no steamers and few independent horse boats as many had been converted to motors. The post-war period was difficult for them and other carriers because of the 48 hour week. In 1923 the company were faced with a strike of boatmen over proposals to reduce rates. They were paid on piecework with a minimum figure if the man was idle. With the 48 hour week, fly services could no longer be properly worked, but the company retained the high class traffic in foodstuffs and non-ferrous metals which could be carried at lower rates than the railways offered. An important short haul was from Paddington to John Dickinson's paper mills at Croxley and Apsley, taking rags, waste and shavings and returning from the mills with paper for John Dickinson's Paddington depot. The boats were called 'paper dashers'; until 1927 this was a steamer and butty service, after that year it was worked by two motor and butty pairs. It finished in the 1950s. The firm stayed in business on a large scale because they could offer facilities like the railways. Between the Wars their main depots and offices were at London, Birmingham, Derby, Manchester, Liverpool, Leicester, Nottingham, Uxbridge, Dudley Port and Wolverhampton. Decline of canal carrying after the boom years of the Second World War forced them to sell their fleet to the Docks & Inland Waterways Executive and go into voluntary liquidation on 1 January 1949. The company colours were black and white with white lettering shaded blue. The steamers kept this livery but after the mid- 1920s, it was changed to red cabin side with a green and yellow border and white lettering. Steamers had titular names like SULTAN, but the others were called after birds, fish, animals, rivers, girls, and canal places.

FURLEY & Co., Ltd, GAINSBOROUGH. This is one of the oldest Trent and Humber carriers, founded in the 1770s as a wharfage business, a partnership of John Goodger and William Furley. Richard a son of William, built ships at Gainsborough and had shares in coasting vessels. The wharfage business did well with river and coastal services to Hull, Leeds, Wakefield, and London. During the ninteenth century, Furley's faced rail competition and were forced to diversify. Their salvation was the Russian hemp trade in which they set up as merchants with an office in Hull and also handled tar. Their interest in inland water transport revived in the 1870s when a partnership was formed between R.L.Furley and J.Fellows at Sheffield, with two keels on the Don. The fleet had grown to seven by 1888, including the steam keel BEE. In 1885 Furley's became agents for the Trent Navigation Co., and in 1914 a limited company. By this time the hemp trade was in decline, but the carrying business and wharfage as well as the warehousing were firmly entrenched. Sailing craft, some with iron hulls, were replaced between the wars by steel powered river craft, and after 1945 the company rebuilt their Gainsborough wharves and installed suction plant for unloading grain. Road vehicles were acquired and the Sheffield office closed, though one was opened in Lincoln for their grain trade up the Fossdyke. The traffic ended in 1972 because of the shallowness of this canal, 130 ton craft only being able to load 80 tons. However, in the 1970s the company were operating 1 power and 4 dumb craft between Gainsborough, Hull, Goole and York all capable of carrying up to 250 tons. The wharves and warehouses at Gainsborough handle grain, chemicals, hardboard, plywood, lead, zinc, animal foodstuffs, canned and dried fruit. Much of the carrying was of necessity subcontracted, but the black hulled Furley craft with their yellow coamings and wheelhouses were busy enough, although since 1975 they have been operated by Gilyott & Scott of Hull who have taken over all Furley's carrying business.

GAINSBOROUGH SHIPPING Co., Ltd. Gainsborough does a much increased river and coastal trade in the 1970s, one of the most energetic firms being Trent Wharfage who took over Watson's old shipyard at Beckingham in 1967. Barges were coming to the wharves that year, followed in 1968 by coasters, the main cargoes being grain, timber, metals, groundnuts and canned fruit for road distribution. Trent Wharfage have their own fleet of river craft running under the subsidiary Gainsborough Shipping Co, 9 motor craft and 4 dumb, plus others on charter. The motor craft carry up to 400 tons. Colours are blue and white and the craft work principally between Hull, Goole and Gainsborough.

GRAND CANAL Co., DUBLIN. From the early days Arthur Guinness had used the canal near his brewery, not with his own boats, but relying on the services of Thomas Berry & Co. A later arrival was the City of Dublin Steam Packet Co, founded in 1823. The Grand had run passenger packets on the canal since 1780, but did not start goods carrying until 1849, to keep traffic from the railways. They had been granted carrying powers since the Canal Carriers Act of 1845. The first services were from Dublin to Naas and up the Kilbeggan branch. By this time they had a steamer on the Shannon, a tug cum cargo vessel called the SHANNON which had started in 1846 and was later to carry passengers. Expansion of the Company's canal services came after 1851 when Thomas Berry and the City of Dublin S.P. gave up. The Grand bought their boats together with the former's depots at Tullamore and Shannon Harbour and the latter's premises at James Street Harbour, Dublin. In 1852 therefore, the Grand extended carrying throughout their system, to Shannon Harbour, on the river down to Limerick, or the Barrow line to Athy, and down the Barrow. Canal passenger services ceased in 1852, but cargoes rose to a peak in 1875. The company by then had more cargo steamers, one being a cattle boat operating from Ballinasloe. After 1875 the traffic fell, the Grand attempting to maintain tonnage by acquiring the carrying trade of the Barrow Navigation Co., north of Athy in 1878. By the 1880s competition became severe from the Great Southern & Western Railway who failed to keep rates agreements, while in the same decade Guinness' started to run their own barges on the Liffey, since they now had their own riverside quays. Previously they had sent export porter down the canal from the Guinness pond at James Street Harbour to Ringsend docks by Grand Canal Co., boats. Carrying revived under the chairmanship of James McCann, from 1891 to his death in 1904, and flourished until 1912. But the 1914-18 War and the upheaval at the birth of the Free State reduced trade, which revived during the 1939-45 War because of the fuel shortages affecting road transport. On the Shannon the company put a big motor barge into traffic, the ST.JAMES, built in 1938. She acted as a tug, towing Grand motor and dumb boats on the river and lakes. In 1945 she was joined by two ex-Severn motor barges renamed ST.BRIGID and ST.PATRICK. Over the years the Grand had built up a chain of 'stations' or wharves on the canal, on the Barrow and the Shannon. There were 50 of them, each with an agent to oversee traffic, attract business and report on the movement of craft. Regular services were run by the Company's boats, the principal ones being from Dublin to Limerick, Ballinasloe, Waterford, Carlow and Naas. In 1950 the Grand merged with Coras Iompair Eireann, Ireland's nationalised transport body, their lorries being absorbed in the CIE road fleet. CIE continued to carry, but their policy was retrenchment. The last CIE boat laden with Guinness left James Street Harbour in May 1960. Hulls of Grand boats were black with white washboards and grey cabin tops, the numbers being white on a red panel on the black at stem and stern on both sides, with the initials G.C.C. in red on the stern washboard. The Shannon power barges had a black funnel with a green band. CIE retained the colours.

GRAND UNION CANAL CARRYING Co., Ltd., LONDON. Formed in 1929, by the Grand Union to attract traffic. A small company, Associated Canal Carriers Ltd of Northampton, was bought in 1930 and modestly expanded, yet without profit. Another carrying subsidiary was formed in 1932, the Erewash Canal Carrying Co., to bring traffic to the Erewash, and Leicester and Loughborough Navigations, all bought by the Grand Union in 1932. In 1934 the Associated Canal Carriers changed its name to the Grand Union Canal Carrying Co., Ltd., and embarked on a large narrow-boat building programme. In 1936, Thomas Clayton (Paddington) Ltd and their rubbish boats were acquired and the purchase of S.E.Barlow proposed. In spite of new boats and traffic, notably iron and steel from the Continent to Birmingham and a good trade in acid, cheese and cement, carrying did not prosper, due to rail and road competition and the closure of small power stations on the Regent's Canal in favour of Battersea. Nearly half the boats were laid up, lack of crews being a problem, although traffic picked up by 1939 and was aided by the War, a new trade being Guinness from Park Royal Brewery, London to Birmingham. A small profit was made in 1946 by a fleet reduced to 79 pairs. Grand Union livery between 1934 and 1937 was two shades of blue and white, red being added in the latter year to mark the Coronation of George VI, while between 1943 and 1948 the colours were maroon, white and blue with white lettering. Little external decorative painting was favoured, although the old Associated Canal Carriers had lavish scroll work and elegant serif lettering.

HARGREAVES (WEST RIDING) Ltd., CASTLEFORD. At the beginning of the twentieth century James Hargreaves opened an office to trade in coal at the Midland Goods Yard, Hunslet, Leeds. The business prospered and in 1906 he bought Varley's Cosy Coal Co., at Crown Head Wharf, Leeds, adjacent to the River Aire. By 1910 he had had three wooden barges built by Riders at Victoria Bridge, to bring coal from various West Yorkshire collieries to his waterside depot. By 1922 the steam tug AIRE had been acquired to supplement the horses and coal was now being delivered by barge to waterside works in the Leeds area. In addition to the AIRE, the fleet was expanded by the purchase of new wooden and later steel barges to serve the area around Leeds. This included Kirkstall power station on the Leeds & Liverpool Canal for which trade the cargo carrying motor tug GEORGE and a number of other steel dumb craft were built in the late 1930s. In 1942 a further cargo carrying motor tug, the LAWSON, was added to the Leeds fleet and in 1947 the barging interests of Cawood Wharton were acquired. In the early 1950s a number of the Leeds dumb barges had engines installed and in 1953 the steam tug AIRE was scrapped. Leeds traffic was then carried in powered barges until 1965. Of particular importance was the traffic to Ferrybridge power stations. The Hargreaves interest in Ferrybridge commenced with the building of the first power station in 1927. The steam tug AUDREY (ex.SHH) was purchased in 1940 to tow the 4 larger 200 ton steel dumb barges which were built in 1939-40. From 1944 to 1954 a further 9 barges were built and from 1957 to 1962 15 more to meet the demand of the new Ferrybridge 'B' station. In 1958 a diesel tug, the ELSE MARGARETTA was built for the Ferrybridge traffic. In the 1950s Hargreaves acquired the Castleford dockyard from Richard Cliffe's, for the maintenance of their Ferrybridge and Leeds fleets and it was here that between 1960 and 1965 that 19 of the Ferrybridge dumb barges were converted to power by the installation of 45 and 60 h.p. Lister diesel engines. These eventually superseded the tugs which were withdrawn. A new company Cawoods Hargreaves Ltd. was formed in 1964 with Cawoods Wharton Ltd, to develop push towing for supplying coal to the new Ferrybridge 'C' power station. The fleet in 1973 consisted of 35 compartment barges and 9 tugs. The Calder & Hebble traffic of Hargreaves commenced in 1933 with the delivery of coal in hired barges, to Thornhill power station. Immediately after the war there was expansion, Hargreaves building new craft and buying up fleets. In 1948 the two largest fleets on that navigation were taken over, I. & J. Dutton and the Calder Carrying Co. Also acquired were the fleets of Thomas Clay & Sons, of Sowerby Bridge, W.D. Poppleton of Huddersfield and Ledgard Bridge dockyard, Mirfield, previously owned by the Calder & Hebble Navigation. On the Calder & Hebble, in addition to Thornhill power station, coal was delivered to Sowerby Bridge and Elland gas works, Huddersfield power station and Brighouse wharf. Seven new wooden barges were built at Mirfield, the last in 1955. These 'West Country' barges, now steel, measure 57'6" x 14'2". With the exception of deliveries to Thornhill power station, all Calder traffic has now ceased. Also there was the Hull fleet of Sheffield size barges 61'6" x 15'6" of 100 tons capacity operated on the Sheffield & South Yorkshire, Aire & Calder and latterly Calder & Hebble. The main traffic was then coal to Earle's cement works at Hull. The fleet was sold in 1970. Finally Hargreaves had an interest in canal transport in Lancashire when in 1951 they purchased Dean Waddington & Co., whose fleet delivered coal to the power stations at Blackburn and Wigan. These boats were disposed of in the 1960s when they sold the whole of their Lancashire coal interests to the British Fuel Co. In the 1970s, the barges, under Hargreaves (Industrial Services) Ltd of Castleford, are painted in the orange and black livery of the Group. The old livery was green and red.

John HARKER Ltd., KNOTTINGLEY specialised in bulk liquid transport on the Yorkshire navigations, the Trent, Manchester Ship Canal, Mersey, Severn, Gloucester & Sharpness Canal, Bristol Channel, Tyne and Tees. Their history goes back to the 1870s when in 1877 Messrs. Stainsby & Lyon founded the Aire tar distillery at Knottingley. Pitch was sent to Goole and Hull for export in barges owned by John Harker. Harker's craft also carried oil in casks. In 1913 the Harker business was reconstituted as J.W. Harker and J.W. Kipping, son and son in law of John Harker who died in 1911. In 1918 the fleet was bought by Stainsby & Lyon who named the company John Harker Ltd., and began experiments with bulk carriage of tar and oil in tank barges. During the 1920s they were operating dumb tank barges towed by tugs and one motor tank barge built in 1925 which also towed dumb craft. In 1926 they sold their Knottingley tar plant to Yorkshire Tar Distillers and concentrated on barge operation. In 1929 they took over two ship-yards in Knottingley where they continue to build barges and other craft for themselves and others, adding Gloucester Shipyard in 1939 and Sharpness in 1946. In 1936 Stainsby & Lyon went into liquidation to be replaced by the Lyon & Lyon organization, retaining the Harker name for barges and shipyards. The Severn & Canal Carrying Co., was bought in 1948, but the general cargo barges were sold to the British Transport Commission. By 1957 John Harker was carrying one and three-quarter million tons of liquids in 100 barges. In 1973 the fleet numbered some 60 barges, half of which were working up to Leeds, Wakefield, Newark and Nottingham from the Humber. The craft on the Leeds run, carrying oil under contract to Esso, had a maximum capacity of 520 tons. Liquid cargoes were not confined to petroleum, but included molasses, creosote and tar. The barges, painted grey, were named after dales with the suffix 'H', thus FARNDALE H. Their squat black funnels had a white square with a red 'H' surrounded by a circular red line. The houseflag had the addition of a red diagonal stripe from the top at the fly to the bottom at the hoist which was enclosed by the red circle, and similar to the white panel on the funnels. In 1976 the company gave up most of its inland waterway carrying, but retained the shipyards.

G.D. HOLMES Ltd., IMMINGHAM. Founded in the early 1890s this family firm started as a partner-ship of two brothers with two keels, SHAMROCK and GARLAND. Their home port was at Stainforth on the Don and later Goole. The family had about 15 keels and sloops in the 1930s, the later ones having steel hulls. Most of the traffic was bulk; sand, alum, potash, sulphur, raw wool from Hull to York, Leeds and Wakefield as well as up the Hull River and Trent. The family, a limited company from 1933, acted as sand merchants and took part in the construction of the training walls in the Lower Ouse, bringing stone from the chalk quarries at Cliff near Barton-on-Humber. Sail survived in the fleet until 1937, but by this time the firm had tugs and motor barges. In 1972 all were sold save for 3, suiting the load line regulations of the 1967 Merchant Shipping Act, which could trade as far down the Humber as Immingham where Holmes' moved in 1967. The largest MAUREEN ANNE W. had a capacity of 400 tons, the other two, GEORGE DYSON and JAMES JONES, 200 and 280 tons respectively. The colours were blue bulwarks and hawse plates, white topstrake and grained wheelhouse. The HIDDEKEL and the VISTA used to have red topstrakes with light oak coloured coamings and grained headledges. The last three barges were sold in 1975 but the company continue as shipbrokers and forwarding agents.

John HUNT & Sons (Leeds) Ltd, LEEDS. Founded in the 1860s by John Hunt of Leeds, the firm were carriers on the Aire & Calder between Hull and Leeds. John Hunt was joined by his two sons Joseph and Henry, and the company acted as merchants and carriers. They dealt in limestone and fodder for boat horses in Leeds and elsewhere, while their principal traffics were coal and vegetable oils to the soapworks of Watson's in Leeds. Among their customers for fodder were the horses on the Leeds & Liverpool Canal and they took the opportunity to enter the canal trade when the canal company closed its carrying department in 1921. They bought 5 horseboats from the Leeds & Liverpool and had 15 more built, named after animals such as FOX, BADGER, OTTER. The boats had a red livery, decorative paintwork being left to the crews. Leeds & Liverpool traffics were sugar from Liverpool, both raw and refined, much for Tetley's Leeds brewery, grain and glucose, with return loadings of cement from Earle's works at Hull for transhipping at Leeds and distribution along the line of the Leeds & Liverpool. As tenants of the Leeds & Liverpool Canal's warehouse space in Leeds, they were drawn into the Canal Transport organisation, founded in 1930 by the canal company. But Hunt continued on the Aire & Calder. From 1922 they replaced the wooden barges by steel. These were all dumb craft of 110 tons capacity towed by Aire & Calder Navigation tugs until in 1930 John Hunt built their first diesel craft. In the 1970s they operated five 250 ton steel diesel river craft averaging 110' x 17'6" x 7'6" loaded draught, named after members of the family. Traffics included copper ingots, pulp board and paper, the company leasing warehouse and wharf space from British Waterways at Dock Street, just below Leeds bridge. However in 1975 inland waterway carrying was given up. Associated with John Hunt from 1910 has been the Leeds, Goole & Hull Transport Co., Ltd., who have a considerable warehousing business in Leeds and nearby Ossett, and a fleet of road vehicles. This company offers storage and distribution and undertakes customs clearance at their shipping and forwarding agency at Hull.

William JACKSON & Sons, MANCHESTER, were important carriers on the Rochdale Canal during the 1840s, leasing warehouses and sheds at Sowerby Bridge, Rochdale and Manchester from the Canal Co. In 1845 Jackson's are known to have had 32 barges, 6 narrow boats and 120 horses, when they wanted to sell their business to the Rochdale, fearing that the canal would come under railway control. Later they accepted the protection of the Bridgewater trustees along with other carriers, becoming Bridgewater agents and later a subsidiary of the trustees and in 1872 of the Bridgewater Navigation Co. Between 1855 and 1876 the Rochdale Canal was leased to four railways who arranged a carrying department, but in 1875 the railway lessees gave up and the boats were bought by William Jackson. In 1891 Jackson's themselves were bought by the Rochdale Canal Co. Not long after, in 1894, two ex-Jackson boats were bought by Albert Wood a former clerk in Jackson's office at Sowerby Bridge. He kept his head office at Sowerby Bridge but established a Manchester branch. He had in the 1900s 35 Yorkshire keels able to work through from Liverpool and Manchester to Hull, 2 Mersey flats, and 13 narrow boats mainly trading on the Ashton and Peak Forest Canals. Wood kept the yellow livery of Jackson's boats and had his own repair dock for keels at Shepley Bridge, Mirfield. Although busy during the 1914-18 War, Wood gave up carrying in 1919 due to high costs and road transport competition.

LEEDS & LIVERPOOL CANAL Co. In 1845 the Canal Carriers Act legalised the establishment of carrying departments by canal companies. One was set up by the Leeds & Liverpool which was suffering from railway competition, to keep traffic on the canal and contribute to revenue although it was not expected to be profitable. Business was started in 1849 but was soon overtaken by the 1850 lease of tolls, warehouses and wharves to three railway companies. The carrying department was sold outright to the railways that same year, who continued it as the Leeds & Liverpool Carrying Co. It was railway policy to kill off the canal's bye traders and keep profitable traffic for themselves, but bye traders undercut them and were of value to the railways as providers of hired boats. These were more economical for one way traffics, since they could be hired for one journey, their owners finding the return cargo. When the railways' lease ended in 1874 the Leeds & Liverpool took up carrying with the prospects of increased business. Fly-boats were put on and steam tugs were in service from the early 1870s. Steam fly-boats appeared in the 1880s, able to tow horse drawn craft. Cargoes were mainly merchandise, including baled wool; coal and minerals being left to bye traders. The horse drawn fly-boats were always round stern craft with their all male crew working shifts and the boats were numbered, not named. The firm also had barges on the Mersey and a steam packet, the IRENE acquired in 1907. Services were maintained up to and during the 1914-18 War, for the latter part of which from 1917, the canal received a government subsidy. When this was withdrawn in 1920, the company found that carrying would no longer pay and gave up in 1921 leaving the field clear for bye traders. A return was made to carrying in 1930 when the company invested in Canal Transport Ltd.

MERSEY, WEAVER & SHIP CANAL CARRYING Co., Ltd, STOKE-ON-TRENT, was associated with the Mersey, Weaver & Northwich Carrying Co, both being subsidiaries of the Salt Union formed in 1888. Both operated flats on the Weaver and down to Liverpool, this company taking over the Salt Union fleet of narrow boats, together with their dock at Marston on the Trent & Mersey. The company concentrated on narrow boat work between Anderton and the Potteries, specializing in pottery raw materials and ware in crates. They had transhipment sheds and a warehouse at Anderton, the Salt Union carrying for them on the Weaver and towing their flats behind their own steam packets. A fly-boat service was operated between Liverpool, Anderton and the Potteries, 48 hours from the Mersey to Stoke, including transhipment at Anderton. It lasted until the 1930s when the Mersey, Weaver still had a few river flats based at Anderton. Mr. C.W. Shirley had for long been manager of the company and the Salt Union offered to sell it to him and in 1935 he bought it. In fly-boat days, the Mersey, Weaver used to take foodstuffs, fruit and Guinness up to the Potteries, but the staples were pottery materials upwards and some crated ware down to the Weaver and Runcorn. Flour was another traffic, also coal from Sideaway near Stoke down to Middlewich for Seddon's salt works and gravel from Trentham to Manchester. In the Potteries the company had a fleet of horse drays and like their rivals, the Anderton Co., a chain of depots in the Potteries. There were offices at Stoke, the head office, Northwich, Manchester and at Liverpool. The company had their own dock at Longport, Burslem where they built and repaired their own boats and those of other pottery carriers, including John Walley. Motor boats were introduced in the 1939-45 War, some of these being built at their dock. All were wood and followed the rounded cross section of the Anderton Co., craft. They had red cabin sides bordered with green and white lettering. Names were of rivers, countries, flowers, boys and girls; rivers perpetuating the Salt Union narrow boat names. In 1954 Mr. L.P. Shirley bought the Anderton Co., from the Boddington family and continued in the same pottery trade, until sold in 1958 to British Transport Waterways.

A. & A. PEATE Ltd, OSWESTRY. Although not boat owners until 1921, Peate's Maesbury Hall Mill had received grain by the Ellesmere Canal for many years, their business being founded in 1846. When the Shropshire Union gave up carrying in 1921, Peate's bought 11 of their horse drawn boats. One, the CRESSY became famous as L.T.C. Rolt's 'Narrow Boat'. Each brought 20 tons of grain per week to the mill from Ellesmere Port, returning with loads of roadstone from Vron quarries. The fleet was repaired by Jack Beech at his dock at Welsh Frankton and by J.H. Taylor & Sons of Chester who had taken over the Shropshire Union dock. Peate's kept the Shropshire Union livery of black cabin sides with white lettering. However, by 1932 the canal to Maesbury was silting up and it was no longer possible to use the boats and they were sold. Coal had also come to the mill by boat from Black Park Colliery, Chirk, Peate's using 20 tons per week. George Beck was the last carrier to Newtown and was caught on the wrong side when the canal burst near Frankton in February 1936. He carried on between Welshpool and Newtown for a further two years with his aptly named boat PERSEVERANCE.

PICKFORDS, MANCHESTER and LONDON. James Pickford had two sons, Matthew and Thomas. Matthew was a road carrier operating from Manchester who became interested in local canal transport during the 1780s. By 1794 he had opened a depot at Castlefield, Manchester. As the canal network spread his interests moved southward, to Birmingham and beyond. When the Grand Junction was fully open in 1805, Pickfords' ran canal services to London, with their depot at Paddington basin. Thomas Pickford had looked after the London end for the road haulage business while Matthew was in Manchester. Matthew died in 1799 and Thomas left in 1800, dying in 1811. Each had two sons; Matthew's sons, Thomas and Matthew remained in Manchester and those of Thomas, James and Matthew continued in London, all four taking over the partnership in 1801. They were interested in traffic to Leicester and made use of the Ashby Canal as far as Hinckley, carrying onwards to Leicester by road. As soon as the Grand Union was opened in 1814, they could reach Leicester by boat. However the road transport business was maintained and extensive services offered, including fly-vans between Manchester and London. On the canals most of the carrying was by narrow fly-boats, loaded with a variety of merchandise and granted licences by the canal companies to pass locks at night. On the Severn, Pickfords' operated trows down to Bristol, later via the Gloucester & Berkeley Canal when this opened in 1827. Their narrow fly-boats bore a large painted diamond on the side as a recognition mark. The completion of the Regent's in 1820 gave the firm new premises in the great City Road basin. At first they hired boat horses from contractors, but later had their own, a thousand by 1838, to work the complex fly-boat services. The four cousins continued as a family partnership until 1816 when, in the depression after the war, they got into difficulties. New capital was however raised and new partners assumed, control passing out of the hands of the four cousins. It was henceforward in the hands of the Baxendale family. In the 1820s and 30s they were the premier carriers on the London, Birmingham, Manchester canals. They also carried to Huddersfield in 1834-5 and to Liverpool when the locks on the Leeds & Liverpool's Leigh branch were lengthened to take narrow boats. By 1838 Pickfords had 116 boats and in 1842 they were considering steam craft after trials on the Grand Junction Canal. Completion of the Grand Junction Railway between the Liverpool & Manchester and Birmingham in 1838 and of the London & Birmingham early the following year encouraged them to enter rail transport to which some traffic was transferred. Also 1838 saw a failure of the water supply to Tring summit. The same year saw a new depot opened at Camden Town on an arm of the Regent's Canal which also served the line out of Euston. More and more of their traffic went over to rail in the 1840s, notably the lighter goods. In 1847 they became goods agents for the L. & N. W. Railway and gradually transferred all their business to rail and road. The canal fleet was gradually run down, the Grand Junction stepping into the vacuum created in 1848 opening their own carrying department. However their agency work for the railway lasted until 1901 and until that year they operated boatage services in South Staffordshire for the railway company.

ROCHDALE CANAL Co. In their early days, between 1807 and 1811 the Rochdale Co. tried carrying in a small way, but gave up as it failed to pay. When traffic was declining at the end of the nineteenth century they tried to revive canal transport by re-entering the carrying business. In 1888 they started with two steam barges or packets, adding more steamers, so that by 1892 they had 15 steam packets, 15 keels and flats and 38 narrow boats. Some of these craft were bought in 1891 by William Jackson & Sons who had long traded on the Rochdale. Many of the Rochdale's services were fly, including all the steam packets which operated on the tidal Mersey. The flats, steamers and narrow boats went no further east than Sowerby Bridge but the keels worked through from the Humber to Manchester, Runcorn and Liverpool. Flats were built by Rathbone's of Stretford and repaired both there and at the company's own dock at Castlefield, Manchester. Many were named after flowers and the steam packets after rivers. All bore a gay livery of white, red and light blue. High costs and the introduction of the 8 hour day forced them to give up carrying in 1921. Most of the boats were sold or leased to bye traders and former employees, who did well with them for a while.

SALT UNION Ltd., LONDON. Towards the end of the nineteenth century, British salt production had become so competitive that an effort was made to check the ruinous undercutting. Amalgamation was considered the answer and a London financial syndicate formed a combine of Cheshire, Worcestershire and Teeside firms into the Salt Union in 1888. Some of its constituents like Falk's founded in 1841, and Verdins founded in 1863 had already become carriers on the Weaver, while George Deakin was a river carrier who entered salt producing in 1846. Falk's introduced steam cargo vessels to the Weaver in 1864 and built some at their own shipyard. George Deakin had a shipyard which was kept on by the Salt Union for new construction and repairs, and by ICI for the latter until 1952. Other Winsford salters joined the Union later, for example George Hamlett & Sons after 1914, bringing more vessels to the combine. Some of the steam packets were iron, but most were wood and of considerable size, the largest being MONARCH of 1897, 121 ft. long. The powerful iron HERALD OF PEACE built in 1899 was used as a tug in addition to the official tugs FIREFLY of 1856 and WATER FLY of 1901. Livery of the packets was a black funnel and a red masthead with a white band as a recognition mark. Names were varied and the AUSTRIA was renamed ANTIGUA during the 1914-18 War, while DECEMPEDES referred to the 10 foot draught up to Winsford which Falk's wanted and got by 1890. The dumb barge fleet was more numerous, mostly craft 70 ft. long loading 80-90 tons. In 1937 the Salt Union fleet was absorbed by Imperial Chemical Industries. The Salt Union also had narrow boats on the Trent & Mersey and Bridgewater Canals, repaired at their own dock at Marston near Northwich. All were in the salt trade carrying to Manchester, up the Rochdale, and some being short narrow boats, down from Sowerby Bridge to Huddersfield via the Calder & Hebble and Sir John Ramsden's Canal. They also went up the Leeds & Liverpool to Church near Accrington. The boats had black cabin sides and yellow lettering with roses and castles confined to the interiors.

Henry SEDDON & Sons Ltd., MIDDLEWICH, was registered in 1907 though the company dates back to the 1890s when Henry Seddon bought a salt producing company at Middlewich. Because his salt works (there were later two), were both on the banks of the Trent & Mersey Canal, Seddon used water transport to Anderton where the salt was transhipped to Weaver vessels. Seddon operated his own narrow boats and from 1900 he had craft on the Weaver. The narrow boats also carried salt to Manchester and via the Manchester, Bolton & Bury Canal to Bolton and Radcliffe. They brought slack coal from the pits near Stoke-on-Trent to fire their open pans at Middlewich. Seddon acted as a general carrier when any boats were spare, taking china stone from Weston Point to the Potteries,   flour from Manchester to the

Potteries and grain up the Welsh canal to Grindley Brook and Whitchurch, all under contract to the Mersey, Weaver & Ship Canal Carrying Co. The narrow boat fleet was never more than 11, the craft being mostly built at Braunston by Nurser's or at Rickmansworth by Walker's, while repairs were done by a local man, Tommy Williams of King's lock Middlewich and later by the Anderton Co., Burslem. Two boats, the NEWS and the MAIL were large, carrying 30 tons of salt, the others carrying 20-21 tons. The first motor boat, SWEDEN, did not appear until 1948 and the company had horses until the 1950s with their stables at Middlewich. Between Middlewich and Anderton it was common for a motor boat to pull two butties. There were 4 motor boats. Most were named after animals and two after the daughters of Henry Seddon's son Roland, NORA and NELLIE. The livery was red cabin side with white lettering, a big white star device being a decorative feature. On the Weaver, Henry Seddon had two steam packets, WEAVER BELLE, Plate 3, and DANEHURST also built at Northwich, later in 1904. The WEAVER BELLE was paired with the large dumb barge GOWANBURN originally built for H. Ingram Thompson of Northwich in 1902 and later acquired by Seddon's. At Anderton they received the bagged salt from the narrow boats and took it down to Liverpool and Birkenhead for export. In October 1960 the narrow boat fleet was withdrawn. By that time WEAVER BELLE and GOWANBURN had been laid up and export cargoes were being handled by a small motor vessel, the ex-coaster PURBECK built in 1936. She was actually a Cerebos ship, this company having taken over Seddon's in 1952. In 1969 Cerebos became part of the Rank, Hovis, McDougall organisation, operating under the title RHM Foods, Middlewich.

SEVERN & CANAL CARRYING Co., Ltd, GLOUCESTER, can be traced back to at least 1798, to the firm of Yates and Dancks of Stourport who owned trows on the river. In 1804 this company was known as Samuel Danks & Co, and the Danks family remained proprietors of what came to be called the Severn & Canal Carrying Co. until the 1900s. In 1884 they commissioned the iron screw coaster ATALANTA to run up to Worcester. Between 1843 and 1876 they had assembled a fleet of 10 iron sailing trows, 'Danks trows' for river and coastal work. By 1890 Joshua Fellows of Fellows, Morton & Clayton, was a partner with Danks, and the company were running narrow boats to the Midlands which were towed on the Severn and on the Gloucester & Berkeley by their own tugs. However in 1890 they appealed to the Staffs & Worcs. Canal for financial assistance. The Canal company were willing to buy the fleet and hire it back, but the Severn & Canal carried on until 1906 when a new company was formed with strong Staffs.& Worcs. support. The tugs were transferred to the Sharpness, New Docks & Gloucester & Birmingham Navigation Co., which had been formed in 1874 and which in 1910 acquired a controlling interest in the Severn & Canal Carrying Co. In 1932 they commissioned a new cargo vessel for river and Bristol Channel work, the 119 gross ton SEVERN TRADER, followed by two others of similar size and five tankers of 92 tons gross, to capture a share in the growing Severn petroleum traffic. In 1942 the name of the company was changed to the Severn Carrying Co., and on nationalization in 1948 was bought by John Harker who was interested in the tankers. The British Transport Commission therefore bought back the three cargo vessels and in 1952 had a fourth built, the SEVERN SIDE, also acquiring the narrow boat fleet operating on the river, Staffs. & Worcs, and Worcester & Birmingham Canals. Motor boats were introduced after the 1914-18 War. Much of Cadbury's traffic was handled by the company whose chairman was at one time George Cadbury. Some narrow boats were just numbered, others named after places on the Severn like KEMPSEY and STOURPORT. Welded motor boats were named after trees. The narrow boats were blue and white, and the funnels of the river craft and ATALANTA were black with a large white S. Later tugs and motor barges were given a black funnel with a wide blue band edged with a narrow white band above and below. In the middle of the blue band was a white 'S'. Vessels of the Sharpness, New Docks Co. had a black funnel with a broad white band.

SHROPSHIRE UNION RAILWAYS & CANAL Co., CHESTER. Amalgamation of railway and canal interests in 1846 founded the Shropshire Union which enjoyed a few months independence before passing under L.N.W.R. control in 1847. The company immediately undertook carrying on their Autherley to Ellesmere Port line and on their Middlewich branch, but in 1849 this was extended to the whole system comprising the Ellesmere and Montgomeryshire Canals, and the Shrewsbury and later the Shropshire network. Thus extensive services were built up on their own canals with L.N.W.R. encouragement, since much of the system lay in rival territory. Both fly and ordinary boats were operated. from Birmingham and Wolverhampton to Ellesmere Port; a limestone traffic from Trevor and Llanymynech to iron works of the Wellington-Oakengates area, returning to Ruabon with iron ore from Golden Hill near Burslem, coal from the collieries of Denbighshire and a general merchandise trade. General trade from the Chester across to Liverpool was in Shropshire Union flats but towed by Bridgewater tugs. Towards the end of the 19th century, traffic on the Shropshire and Shrewsbury network declined and to save expense on the Trench plane, the Lilleshall Co's coal and iron trade was handled by the Shropshire Union at a rail connected wharf on the Humber Arm of the Newport branch. At about the same time the company expanded their traffic across the Mersey, buying two fleets of flats and establishing headquarters at Manchester Dock, Liverpool. After working trains of narrow boats for a while between Autherley and Ellesmere Port, tugs were confined to the lock free Chester- Ellesmere Port length. On the Mersey the company acquired tugs to handle the 101 flats which they had acquired by 1889. They also owned a few steam barges which worked between Nantwich, Chester, Ellesmere Port and Liverpool. In 1889, 395 narrow boats were owned by the company who were developing boatage services in the Black Country. Their day boat fleet carried between the canalside factories and the L.N.W.R. rail-canal interchange basins. They had road cartage services also in Chester, Birmingham and the Potteries. While traffic declined on the Welsh canals, between 1892 and 1912 much modernisation was undertaken at Ellesmere Port, because of the improvement in the Potteries trade with the opening of the Manchester Ship Canal and the increase in grain traffic. The 1900s were a busy time for the Shropshire Union since they had achieved a near monopoly over their system with 450 narrow boats in 1902. All was subsidized by the L.N.W.R. and during the 1914-18 War by the Government. In 1921 with higher costs and an attempt to apply the 8 hour day to boatmen, ended their carrying and all the craft were sold. Some were bought by local firms, while 100 went to the L.N.W.R., later the L.M.S.R., to continue boatage services in the Birmingham and the Wolverhampton areas. Although faithful to horses, the Shropshire Union did try motor narrow boats, the first being the HOOGHLI around 1910. Chester was the company headquarters both for the canals and the carrying fleets, served by a large dockyard there. Narrow boats were also built by outside firms like Nursers of Braunston and Lees & Atkins of Polesworth. The narrow boats had black cabin sides with a red bead and a white border and lettering. The flats had a white top strake at stem and stern, and a white gunwale. The windlass, tiller and rails were picked out in black and white.

TRENT NAVIGATION Co., NOTTINGHAM. To revive traffic on their shallow river, a carrying fleet was started in 1882. Craft were hired from Fellows, Morton & Clayton and Furley & Co., and steam tugs were bought. By the end of the year the Company were operating 16 keels and 9 dumb lighters. More craft were ordered, but the Trent went through a bad period and little was done for the carrying fleet until

Frank Rayner took over as engineer in 1896, later becoming general manager. New keels were built at the company's Newark dockyard and in the early 1900s the Navigation were carrying up to a fifth of all Trent cargoes. A daily service was provided from the Humber ports, to Newark and Nottingham,and from 1903, Loughborough, Leicester and Derby. Navigation Co., tugs were used down to Torksey, but were chartered from Hull for towage below. In Newark, Nottingham, Loughborough,Leicester and Hull they had horse drawn delivery lorries and warehousing. By 1915 the Company had a fleet of about 20 carrying craft including one motor craft, plus their tugs. In 1908 they had 12 built at Beckingham, opposite Gainsborough, and Goole, named TRENT No.1. etc. River reconstruction below Nottingham in the 1920s helped the carrying fleet. Lighters of 120 tons capacity were built and more powered river craft such as the 100 ton YARE and TYNE. The company opened a depot at Shardlow above Nottingham in 1932 and in 1948 the fleet was nationalized. Craft were named after rivers and had white bulwarks with a red bead, red coamings and green hatch covers. The funnels were black.

Ernest V. WADDINGTON Ltd, Swinton. Based on the Sheffield & South Yorkshire Navigation, Waddington's, always a family business, were established in the 1820s and have been barge builders also. Horse hauled and sailing keels and sloops were replaced by diesel craft between the wars, with steel hulls of 90-100 tons capacity, the maximum for the locks of the Sheffield & South Yorkshire. In the past a wide range of cargo was handled, coal, grain, timber and chemicals. In 1973, still with a large fleet of 60 craft, Waddingtons handled coal between Cadeby colliery and Doncaster power station. They also serve the steel industry from Humber ports and bring grain to the local flour mills. The firm has a wharf and warehouse at Eastwood, Rotherham, established during the 1950s and since much expanded. Here cargoes to and from Humber ports are handled. The Swinton boatyard has not built new craft since the 1950s, but is busy on repairs. The boats are brown, light grey and blue with a variety of names.

A. WANDER & Co.,Ltd., KING'S LANGLEY, better known as the Ovaltine Co, this firm built their factory and egg farm at King's Langley north of Watford in 1923, on the Grand Junction Canal. Coal for the steam plant came from Warwickshire, the firm hiring boats in addition to those under contract. In 1925 they started running their own boats, built by Walker's of Rickmansworth who undertook their repairs. Eight narrow boat pairs were commissioned and the company took some from the Grand Union Canal Carrying Co. They were a smart fleet with dark blue cabin sides edged by maroon and white. Both the cabin side and cratch advertised 'Drink Delicious Ovaltine'. In 1956 the factory changed to oil firing and the boats were given up.

John H. WHITAKER (Holdings) Ltd, HULL, began modestly in 1885, trading with two wooden craft and one sailing billyboy. These were traded locally by J.H. Whitaker who later went into partnership with James A. Whitaker and T.P. Bullard. Expansion came gradually with more wooden craft, which in 1907 included 3 double skinned wooden tankers for the lighterage of creosote in Hull. In 1910 the partnership became a limited company and soon after began to carry petroleum products in drums, mainly paraffin. A steam tug, CAWOOD was acquired in 1912 to handle their lighters, and is still in service in the 1970s though motorized. Horses were used for canal work until 1936. Early moves towards diversification came in 1917 when Whitaker's acquired two shipyards on the Hull and formed the subsidiary Yorkshire Dry Dock Co.,Ltd. After the 1914-18 War new steel lighters were ordered from Thorne and Beverley of up to 200 tons capacity, two of which were used for vegetable oil. Bulk liquid traffics developed in the 1920s, notably bunkering oil fired steamers from dumb craft, the company not having powered tankers until 1937, though the motor barge COALITE had been in service from 1933. The first self propelled tanker VINCIT was Gardner powered. By 1939 they had a fleet of 45 craft on the Humber and associated waterways. In 1950 a new building programme was started at their own and other yards and by 1973 the fleet comprised 32 tankers, three of them dumb for vegetable oils and 11 dry cargo craft, all motorized. Additionally there were three barges on the Clyde, one at Belfast and a coaster. The Humber fleet works locally and since 1976 has been augmented by the purchase of some Harker and Cory tank craft used both for bunkering ships in Hull and working up the Trent, Ouse and Aire & Calder but not on the Sheffield & South Yorkshire. HUMBER RENOWN and HUMBER ENTERPRISE are the maximum size for the Aire & Calder, 180' long carrying 480 tons on the river. Other tankers are smaller, 143' long carrying up to 320 tons. Principal dry cargoes are oil seeds, soya beans and cased goods. Whitaker's craft are red with mast colour wheelhouses. Management is now in the hands of the fourth generation and family names are often used for the craft. The houseflag is red and green divided vertically with red at the hoist and is pennant shaped. In the red there is a white bordered black roundel with a white 'W' on it. The company have interests in bulk liquid storage and road tankers.

WILLOW WREN CANAL CARRYING Co., Ltd., BRENTFORD. A final effort to revive narrow boat carrying was made in 1952 by Leslie Morton who had been manager of the Grand Union Carrying Co.He was generously backed by Captain Vivien Bulkeley-Johnson and started with two pairs, expanded to 8 by about 1955, engaged principally on the coal trade from Cannock to Hayes. The end of most narrow boat carrying by the nationalized fleet in 1963 gave the firm, now reconstituted as Willow Wren Canal Transport Services, the opportunity to hire 40 pairs from the British Waterways Board to keep the traffic which the latter had surrendered. Willow Wren succeeded in carrying increased tonnage. In 1968 Captain Bulkeley-Johnson died, but Leslie Morton carried on, now leasing the boats to the boatmen in return for a weekly rent. The boatmen earned the freights paying a percentage to the firm, but the company saved on maintenance and fuel costs which were paid by the boatmen. The system worked after Leslie Morton's death in 1968 until the company ceased to carry in 1970, finding it impossible to make narrow boat carrying pay on the basis of properly costed maintenance and depreciation, while offering competitive wages. Boats were named after birds and bore a large representation of a willow wren on the cabin side and sometimes on the cratch. The livery was red, green and yellow. From 1963 a separate fleet worked from Anderton on the Trent & Mersey with hired boats. In 1967 this fleet was reconstituted as the Anderton Canal Carrying Co.

Albert WOOD. See William Jackson & Sons.

Engineers and Personalities

Profile of Francis Egerton,
the 3rd Duke of Bridgewater

ADAMSON, Daniel, 1821-1890. From Shildon Co. Durham, Adamson was a pupil of Timothy Hackworth on the Stockton & Darlington Railway and became manager of the locomotive works. In 1850 he came to Cheshire to manage a foundry at Stockport but soon set up his own engineering works at Newton near Hyde, at the same time investing in iron and steel elsewhere. He took up the cause of the Manchester Ship Canal and called a meeting at his house, The Towers, Didsbury, on 27 June 1882. He became chairman of the company and led it through the long struggle to gain its Act. When the company failed to raise its capital, there was a crisis which ended in 1887 with the reconstruction of the board of directors and the resignation of Adamson as chairman in favour of Lord Egerton of Tatton. Adamson did not have the confidence of the commercial world and was a difficult colleague. However he continued to support the canal until his death.

ALLNUTT, Zachary. As superintendent or manager and receiver of tolls for the Thames Commissioners, he was a highly placed waterways offical. His father, Henry Allnutt had been clerk to the authority in the 1770s. Zachary was an enthusiast for inland navigation and in 1810 published at his own expense his "Useful and Correct Accounts of the Navigation of the Rivers and Canals West of London". This small volume describes the Thames and adjacent waterways, giving distances, opening hours and information on wharves, types of craft and commodities carried. There is a map and tables of tolls with specimen freight charges by water and road.

ASHLEY, Henry, Senior, c.1630-1700. A Huntingdon tanner who in 1674 secured the lease of the Great Ouse and carried on improvements Arnold Spencer had been forced to give up because of the Civil War. By 1687 he had restored the navigation to Great Barford and in 1689 extended it to Bedford. He and his son Henry did well from tolls for they were proprietors of the whole river above St. Neots, financing and supervising all improvements.

ASHLEY, Henry, Junior, 1654-1730. The younger Ashley probably worked with his father on the Great Ouse improvements, but in 1700 he was appointed undertaker of the Lark, improving the river for navigation between Mildenhall and Bury St. Edmunds. He assigned his rights to tolls to Bury St. Edmunds and remained as engineer. In 1720 he rebuilt the staunch on the Great Ouse below St. Ives.

ASHTON, John, 1711-1759. A Liverpool merchant and owner of the Dungeon salt works on the Mersey near Speke Hall, Ashton became the main subscriber to the Sankey Brook Navigation. As a salt refiner he was interested in cheaper waterborne coal from pits around St. Helens. With the Sankey open in 1757 Ashton was concerned with the markets for the coal, and he and John Blackburne, proprietor of the Liverpool salt works and the other main promoter of the Sankey, pressed for improvements to the Weaver which were commenced in 1758.

BAIRD, Hugh, 1770-1827, was a citizen of Glasgow and assistant engineer during the construction of the Crinan Canal, having worked as a contractor to finish the Ulverston Canal. From the Crinan he moved to the Forth & Clyde, as the canal's maintenance engineer, and it was in 1813, during his tenure of office, that he put forward plans supported by Telford, for a canal from the Forth & Clyde into Edinburgh. The Edinburgh & Glasgow Union went ahead with Baird as engineer, and opened in 1822.

BARNES, James, of Banbury appears first on the final phase of the Oxford Canal from Banbury to Oxford, begun in 1786. He moved from the Oxford to make the first survey in 1792 for what became the Grand Junction, followed by William Jessop. Barnes' line, although approved by Jessop was altered later by the committee. Barnes became resident engineer and stayed until 1805 when the canal was finished. Barnes had been involved with Blisworth tunnel and encouraged Jessop to build a new tunnel when the first attempts were given up in 1796. During 1793 the Grand Junction ordered Barnes to do a survey of the northern Oxford in an attempt to show that company how their canal could be shortened and widened to the same gauge as the Grand Junction, but this was never done and Barnes' survey during the same year, of what became the Newport Pagnell Canal off the Grand Junction, had to wait until 1813 before it was considered again. During his Grand Junction employment, Barnes did surveys for the continuance of the Leicestershire & Northamptonshire Union in 1799, stuck at Gumley Debdale, near Market Harborough. Outside the Midlands Barnes was engineer of the Llanelly Dock & Railway authorized in 1802, and in 1809 was a contractor for part of the Severn & Wye tramroad.

BARTHOLOMEW, William Hamond, 1831-1919. William succeeded his father Thomas Hamond Bartholomew appointed in 1825, as engineer on the Aire & Calder, on the latter's death in 1853. His uncle was Charles Bartholomew and engineer of the Don Navigation. In 1876 William also became general manager, formally retiring in 1895 although now a director, remaining on the board until just before his death. Though best remembered for his compartment boats, he did much for the Yorkshire Ouse, being called repeatedly to advise the trustees, in 1866 on Naburn lock, again in 1871 and in 1880 on the condition of the river. When in 1884 the lower Ouse to Trent Falls was placed under Aire & Calder control, Bartholomew directed the improvements including the training walls made by the new authority, while from 1891 he supervised building of the New Junction Canal between the Aire & Calder and the Sheffield & South Yorkshire Navigation. During his time, much was done for Goole, and as late as 1909 at the age of 78 he planned the dock extension which was completed in 1912. Between 1880 and 1904 he was chairman of the Goole S.S. Co., founded in 1864 and backed by the Aire & Calder and the L. & Y. Railway.

BENTLEY, Thomas, 1731-1780. A Liverpool warehouse owner and merchant, Bentley met Josiah Wedgwood in 1762 and in 1769 went into partnership, moving the following year to London to organise sales of china. His was the scientific mind in the business which guided Wedgewood craftsmanship. He supported Wedgwood in the promotion of the Trent & Mersey Canal, in 1765 writing "A View of the Advantages of Inland Navigation, with a plan of a Navigable Canal intended for a Communication between the ports of Liverpool and Hull".

BERRY, Henry, 1720-1812, came from a dissenting family in the St. Helens district, and was employed as a clerk and assistant to Thomas Steers, the builder of Liverpool's first wet dock. He probably helped Steers between 1736 and 1741 during the latter's work on the Newry Navigation, and on Steers' death in 1750 assumed his mantle as Liverpool's dock engineer. In 1755 he was given leave by Liverpool Corporation to survey the proposed Sankey Brook Navigation which he completed in 1757 with William Taylor. On the Sankey, Berry built the first English double locks, a staircase of two, at Blackbrook near Gerard's Bridge. Later Berry was involved in surveys to improve the Weaver which had deteriorated and new locks were built to his designs at Pickerings and probably at Saltersford. He later returned to dock construction in Liverpool and in 1769 did surveys for the Leeds & Liverpool Canal.

BEVAN, Benjamin, from Leighton Buzzard, appears to have been one of the Grand Junction engineers prior to the full opening in 1805. He is remembered for the Ouse aqueducts at Wolverton. He was involved with estimates for the three arched structure which looked like a series of big culverts through the high embankment, which collapsed in 1808. Although temporarily replaced by a wooden trunk, Bevan laid the foundation stone for a new aqueduct of stone with a cast iron trough in 1809 which was opened in 1811. He is also known for work on the Grand Union for which he did final surveys before the Act of 1809. Bevan became the engineer and also acted as engineer of the small Newport Pagnell Canal. Between 1812 and 1843 he was consulted on the Great Ouse between St. Ives and Bedford.

BRADSHAW, Robert Haldane, 1759-1835. A maligned figure, he has been condemned as an avaricious profiteer. He joined the public service after legal training and by 1800 had become the legal agent to the third Duke of Bridgewater, succeeding Thomas Gilbert. The Duke by his will, appointed Bradshaw superintendent of the trust created to control the canal, which he already supervised, plus the industrial properties and estates. Bradshaw took his duties seriously ; overwork was his problem and he would not delegate, although well assisted by Benjamin Sothern and later by his son Captain James Bradshaw, Royal Navy. Bradshaw was devoted to the canal but he was prevented from using much of the profits for capital improvement by the Duke's will, under which they were left to the second Marquess of Stafford who had his own and other canal schemes. The Duke's canal remained in trust for his second son, but declined. By 1828 however, he was able to complete new locks at Runcorn and other works, so that the canal was in a better position to face the railway challenge. This Bradshaw regarded with bitter hostility, to the extent of impeding the surveyors as they passed through the south Lancashire estates; meanwhile the Marquess of Stafford decided to support the railway. In 1831 Bradshaw had a stroke and by 1833 his son believed that he was no longer fit to continue. He retired in 1834 and died the following year.

BRIDGEWATER, Duke of. See EGERTON, Francis, 3rd Duke of Bridgewater.

BRINDLEY, James, 1716-1772, was born near Buxton, Derbyshire, the son of a farm labourer. He had a limited education and was a labourer until apprenticed at the age of 17 to Abraham Bennett, a Macclesfield wheel and millwright. He proved a better craftsman than his employer and worked on a variety of water powered silk and paper mills. He set up in 1742 as a millwright in Leek. His watermill jobs included the planning of weirs, leats, and reservoirs, features demanded by a canal. He drained Wet Earth colliery at Clifton, near Manchester and by 1753 had installed a waterwheel fed by a leat which became Fletcher's Canal. In the late 1750s Brindley met Lord Gower's estate agent Thomas Gilbert when called to repair a pump at Trentham and it was Gower and his associates who asked Brindley to survey a possible canal from Stoke-on-Trent to Wilden Ferry on the navigable Trent, done in 1758. The following year he was brought to the Bridgewater works by Thomas' brother John who introduced him to the Duke. The canal plans had already been made and cutting started, Brindley being paid as a part time assistant engineer from 1 July 1759. From 1761, Brindley was surveying onwards for the line to the Mersey which he never saw completed. Meanwhile he was exerting his ingenuity over the mines at Worsley and the basin at Castlefield opened in 1765. He built a water powered ventilating system for the mines and a waterwheel to hoist boxes of coal to street level at Castlefield from the canal basin tunnelled out below. By the mid-1760s he was becoming an inland navigation expert. Thus, although not enthusiastic about river navigations, Brindley was called in 1764 to advise on the improvement of Witton Brook, a tributary of the Weaver below Northwich. Because of his 1758 survey for a Stoke to Wilden Ferry canal, he was called in again when the project was revived by Wedgwood in 1765. With this canal, the Trent & Mersey, which he surveyed for the Bill, Brindley made his name. Authorized in 1766 it was then an undertaking of daunting novelty. On it Brindley laid down the features which were to characterize the whole Midlands network. The 7 ft. lock width led to the special 'narrow boat' which was further limited by the shallow channel and limited headroom in Harecastle tunnel, thus establishing the loading gauge for much of the English system. Another feature established was the single line tunnel without a towpath; because the tunnel was so long and expensive it had to be built as cheaply as possible. He standardized a canal overbridge design using a segmental arch and curving each face wall outwards to the abutments to resist earth pressure. He never tried a skew bridge, being careful to have roads cross the canal at a right angle. Cheapness and caution were his twin mottoes. To satisfy the first he laid his line to follow contours and avoid earthworks, to satisfy the second he built on a massive scale, notably aqueducts. He and his assistant Simcock followed the contours to an excessive degree on the Birmingham and the Oxford Canals, arguing that they would serve more people in that way, although others said that the canal company would exact more tolls for the increased mileage! The massive aqueducts were needed to carry the great weight of water in its bed of puddle and for safety and economy, Brindley crossed rivers at a low level with low arches. Parallel with the Trent & Mersey, he had to give time to the allied Staffs. & Worcs. but he left the work to his assistants, in this case Samuel Simcock and the elder Thomas Dadford. He rushed from scheme to scheme as more canals were projected while his assistants undertook each canal in his name. He became the arch consultant and every project tried to gain his blessing to help secure public support and parliamentary approval. Wedgwood in 1767 thought he was doing far too much and some canal committees complained of his inattention. The previous year he had surveyed for the Rochdale which was dropped until the 1790s, another lapsed project of 1766 being the Loughborough Navigation. In 1772 Brindley died from a chill caught while surveying the Caldon, but up to his death he was incredibly busy. He surveyed for the Birmingham, Droitwich, Coventry and Oxford in 1767 and all four were authorized in 1768-9 with him as engineer. The Birmingham was poorly laid out with a short high summit level of only a mile. Brindley was not good on water supplies, relying on drainage from the mines to feed the summits of the Trent & Mersey and the Coventry. On the latter he fell foul of the committee in 1769 and was dismissed as the works were not proceeding well. He also resigned from the Oxford, but withdrew his letter and stayed on. The Droitwich and the Staffs. & Worcs. were the only two of all his projects he saw completed and the Chesterfield he hardly started. He was consulted on the Leeds & Liverpool and made engineer on passage of the Act, but he declined the post in favour of Longbotham who originally suggested the route. In Yorkshire Brindley became, from 1765 until probably the following year, engineer to the Calder & Hebble in succession to Smeaton who later returned. Also in the 1760s Brindley advised the Yorkshire Don on their navigation and designed new bridges for the Dutch River section. In 1763 he advised on the cost of a Stainforth to Keadby canal. He was consulted in 1767-8 on a canal from the collieries of south west Durham to the Tees, for which Whitworth did a survey. In the south he was called by the City of London to consider Thames improvements in 1770. He proposed a bypass canal for the lower reaches, the Reading-Monkey Island-Isleworth scheme. He and R. Whitworth had been south before in 1768-9 and this encouraged people to plan canals, for example the Andover. In 1768 Brindley looked over a possible canal between Salisbury and Southampton water, but nothing was done since he had no further time, although another survey was made by an assistant in 1771. Brindley was also drawn to consider canals between the English and Bristol Channels for which Whitworth did surveys. Finally he went to Scotland to look out routes between Forth and Clyde. He was commissioned by the Carron ironworks to find a line which would be more useful to them than Smeaton's on which work had already started. Brindley with all his commitments became wealthy. As engineer of the Trent & Mersey he was paid £200 a year and also £200 from the Oxford, £200 from the Birmingham and £150 from the Coventry all at the same time. He had colliery interests at Golden Hill above Harecastle and lived in some style. He married late in life, in 1765, Anne Henshall and his brother-in-law took over on the Trent & Mersey, and the Chesterfield. He invested in his own canals, he and his brother John being major share-holders in the Trent & Mersey, while James invested in the Oxford and the Chesterfield. Smiles says he had no pleasures, but thought all the time of mechanics. He was deservedly called by John Phillips the 'ingenious Mr. Brindley.'

BRYDONE, John, 1841-1899. Appointed in 1884 as the first inspector under the Canal Boats Acts, he made the Acts work, but the tone of his first report was too dramatic for his superiors and his contacts with them became more and more perfunctory. He did well in the field with his team of 100 odd local inspectors who made regular inspections and frequent prosecutions; in 1893 seven to eight thousand boats of all types were given 31,280 inspections, about 4 per boat per year. He died from overwork at the age of 58.

BULL, Samuel, was assistant engineer to Edmund Lingard on the Coventry Canal in 1769, later moving to the Birmingham where he surveyed for the Warwick & Birmingham in 1792-3 in which the Birmingham were naturally interested. He was also concerned with the Warwick & Napton.

CARTWRIGHT, Thomas, died 1810. Appointed engineer of the Worcester & Birmingham in 1791, he stayed until 1807. Meanwhile he had been doing work for the Brecknock & Abergavenny since 1802. In his time with the Worcester & Birmingham he had done work for the Stratford Canal, superintending King's Norton tunnel.

CASTLE, Richard, died 1751. Believed to be a Huguenot refugee, Castle turned up in Ireland in the late 1720s. He was an architect and was probably invited to Ireland to work on a mansion in Co.Fermanagh. By 1728 he was in Dublin as an assistant to E.L. Pearce, one of the country's leading architects who was made Surveyor General for Ireland. In this capacity Pearce was involved with the newly (1729) appointed groups of commissioners in each province, who were expected to further a series of river improvements and canal schemes. Castle appealed to the commissioners for work in a long 'Essay on Artifical Navigation' written in 1730 which was a statement of his own knowledge of canal construction gleaned from observation on the continent. He succeeded for he was put in charge of the pioneer Newry Navigation authorized in 1731, under general direction from Pearce. When the latter died in 1733, Castle remained in sole charge of the Newry and is credited with the first stone chambered lock in Ireland, but in 1736 he was dismissed, to be replaced by Thomas Steers.

CHAPMAN, William, 1749-1832. A civil engineer from Newcastle-upon-Tyne although brought up at Whitby, he had a career involving canals, harbours and railways. From 1783 he was assistant to William Jessop on the Grand Canal in Ireland. He later became responsible for the branch down to the Liffey from James Street Harbour which he re-routed as a circular line round the south of the city. In 1787 he surveyed the Nore Navigation in Co. Kilkenny, and in 1791 did a survey of the Shannon from Killaloe to Lough Allen. His best work was on the Barrow Navigation. Between 1787 and 1789 Chapman had been resident engineer of the Kildare Canal Co., and built the Naas line off the Grand Canal. Chapman turned to writing and in 1797 published 'Observations on the Various Systems of Canal Navigation' as an answer to Robert Fulton's " Treatise on the improvement of Canal Navigation" of 1796. Chapman was unfavourably impressed with the ideas of Fulton for small canals and small boats with wheels. He says tub-boats would be difficult to manage in a wind and unable to carry their full tonnage of any light cargo because they would become un-stable. He favoured broad boats and suggested how they might carry tramroad wagons. On the completion of his Irish commitments in 1796 he returned to survey the Driffield Navigation in the East Riding of Yorkshire. This included improvements to the River Hull and drainage associated with the Hull; acting as engineer. In 1797 he surveyed the Keyingham navigable drains south-east of Hull where he proposed close coupled tub-boats as described in his 'Observations', carrying coal and lime in containers. In 1800 as a drainage expert he was called in over the extension of the Derwent Navigation, and advised the landowners bordering the Don, fearful of the effect navigation improvement might have on their land. Two years later Chapman built Grovehill lock at the junction of the Beverley Beck with the River Hull and reported on the Pocklington Canal. More important was his survey for the Sheffield Canal in 1814 where he was made to take a route of which he disapproved because of its difficulty and expense. As early as 1795 he had reported on a Newcastle-Carlisle-Maryport canal which he advocated for military and civil use. He was to realise part of this dream when he became consulting engineer to the Carlisle Canal. He was not a success with the Carlisle committee and in 1822 was dismissed because he was severely critical of the work of one of the subordinate engineers.

CLOWES, Josiah, c.1736-1795, was from Middlewich in Cheshire, starting his canal career as a contractor on the Trent & Mersey in 1775, later carrying on this canal. In 1778 he was made engineer to the Chester Canal but was dismissed for slackness. Clowes redeemed his reputation when in 1783 he became resident engineer on the Thames & Severn under Robert Whitworth. His main concern was Sapperton tunnel but it 1789 after endless difficulties tunnel and canal were ready. As resident engineer to the Thames & Severn, he designed new locks for the river above Oxford. Because of his tunnel success Clowes moved to the Dudley in 1789, his main responsibility being the unfinished tunnel, started in 1785 which he completed in 1792. He continued as engineer of their Selly Oak line, authorized in 1793, in which year he became engineer to the Stratford. Further afield Clowes had done survey work on the Gloucester & Berkeley Ship Canal before its Act of 1793 and it that year he was made engineer of the Shrewsbury. He had since 1790, been engineer to the Herefordshire & Gloucestershire on which he stayed until his death in 1795. On the Shrewsbury he designed Berwick tunnel and started to built a masonry aqueduct over the Tern at Longdon. His death came about the time when floods destroyed the works, his successor Telford building in iron.

CRAWSHAY, Richard, 1739-1810, and sons. Crawshay came from Normanton in Yorkshire, but moved to London; in about 1777 he became a partner with Anthony Bacon, an ironmaster from Whitehaven who had leased land and built furnaces at Cyfarthfa, near Merthyr Tydfil. When Bacon died in 1786 Crawshay took over and soon became the most powerful of the Merthyr ironmasters. When the Glamorganshire Canal was suggested Richard Crawshay led the promotion and was the most substantial shareholder with the canal almost a Crawshay subsidiary. In 1809 he gave financial aid to the Brecknock & Abergavenny Canal to enable it to be finished. This was probably because his nephew Joseph Bailey was to take over the Nant-y-glo ironworks, which needed the canal. Richard's son William (1764-1834) had been on the Glamorganshire committee since 1798 but quarrelled with their chairman and was off it between 1814 and 1818. He was chairman himself in 1822, the year he handed over the chair to his son William Crawshay II (1788-1867). In 1819 the Crawshays acquired the Hirwaun ironworks at the head of the Aberdare valley, which made them take a big shareholding in the Aberdare Canal. William Crawshay presided over the Glamorganshire when it was at its zenith in the mid 1830s, but made the mistake of standing by the canal when railway proposals were made. William II remained chairman of the Glamorganshire until his death in 1867. His son Robert (1817-1879) continued as chairman, but the canal was in a poor way. When it was sold to the Marquess of Bute, the Crawshays severed their canal interest both here and in the Aberdare.

CROSLEY, William, (senior) died 1796, came from Brighouse and was associated with Rennie. In 1791 he worked under Rennie on the latter's first survey of the Rochdale for the 1792 Bill having done some preliminary work, and the 1793 Bill. Jessop took over and Crosley worked as resident engineer under him until his death. He was also Rennie's assistant surveyor for the Lancaster Canal on its authorization in 1792.

CROSLEY, William (junior), had a more varied career, becoming resident engineer on the Rochdale in 1802 under Jessop, he remained with the company until 1809 when he moved to South Wales to complete the Brecknock & Abergavenny and to work on tramroads in the area. In 1811 he joined the Worcs. & Birmingham as engineer, finishing the summit level to Tardebigge and continuing down the locks to Worcester. In 1817 he became resident engineer of the North End of the Lancaster when work was starting on the long delayed extension to Kendal. He took charge of Hincaster tunnel and the works at Killington reservoir, the extension being opened in 1819. In 1820 he was made superintendent of the whole Lancaster and built the Glasson Dock branch. In 1826 he became engineer to the projected Macclesfield under Telford who took no part after the initial surveys, so the Macclesfield Canal is the work of William Crosley junior.

CUBITT, Sir William, 1785-1861, a Norfolk man from Bacton on the coast near North Walsham, his father ran a windmill. In 1807 William patented his windmill sails whose shutters could be controlled by a single striking rod. He set up in business as a millwright and in 1812 became a partner in Ransome's of Ipswich. In 1826 he moved to London. His first canal work was for the Oxford when he was consultant for the straightening programme between Braunston and Hawkesbury, completed in 1834. Connected with the Oxford was his 1832 survey for the proposed Central Union Canal from the Worcester & Birmingham via the Warwick and Birmingham to the Oxford. He was also connected with the grandiose London & Birmingham Canal scheme of 1836. In 1833 Cubitt succeeded the ageing Telford as engineer to the Birmingham & Liverpool Junction, finishing Shelmore embankment. He also took over the Ulster from Telford. Telford as engineer to the Ellesmere & Chester had recommended improvements at Ellesmere Port which were carried out by Cubitt as his successor with William Provis as contractor. He was consulted on improvements to the Weaver, which he much admired, in the 1830s, recommending deepening, straightening and duplicate locks. He worked on the Witham, the Welland, the Suffolk Stour, the Nene and was an advocate of the Norwich & Lowestoft Navigation and a new port at Lowestoft. In South Wales, he reported in 1836 on the Monmouthshire Canal above Pontymoile and in 1839 completed the West Bute dock in Cardiff. In 1840 he was appointed engineer to the Severn Improvement Association and when a Severn Commission was formed in 1842, Cubitt became chief engineer. In 1847 improvements were sufficiently complete for tolls to be charged and Cubitt now left his deputy Edward Leader Williams (senior) as sole engineer, remaining as consultant. He was also an important railway engineer.

DADFORD, Thomas (senior), died 1809. Father and son, also Thomas, were responsible for much canal construction, particularly in South Wales. The elder Dadford, possibly from Stewponey near Stourbridge, started his career as assistant to Brindley in the Midlands. With another of Brindley's team, Samuel Simcock, he did the engineering on the Staffs. & Worcs. He also worked with Simcock and with Robert Whitworth on the Birmingham. Later he became engineer and surveyor to the Dudley Canal staying until 1783 but was consulted when the Dudley planned to extend via a tunnel to join the Birmingham. Works progressed badly, under the contractor John Pinkerton and in 1787 both Dadford and Pinkerton were suspended. In 1784 he advised on the Coventry's aqueduct over the Tame. In 1782 Dadford and his son had recommended improvements to the Trent, previous to William Jessop's survey and in 1789 Thomas senior acted as a cutting contractor on the Cromford Canal together with the elder Thomas Sheasby under Jessop and Benjamin Outram. Later Dadford activities were confined to Wales and the Borders, now being regularly assisted by the sons, particularly Thomas. Both father and son Thomas carried on as contractors as well as engineers, and on the Glamorganshire they undertook the twin tasks, assisted by the elder Sheasby, which they finished in 1794, but later the elder Dadford and Sheasby were arrested on orders from the company after a dispute about a breach they refused to repair unless money was advanced. This was refused so they withdrew their men and left. Later Robert Whitworth arbitrated and found against the company. The elder Dadford's final canal was the Montgomeryshire, succeeding his son John as engineer, his problems being the aqueducts over the Vyrnwy and the Rhiw. Like other engineers, the Dadfords were shareholders in the canals they planned and built, investing in the Neath and the Aberdare.

DADFORD, Thomas (junior) died 1806. He was associated with his father's many schemes but also worked on his own account. While his father was engineer of the Dudley, he was busy on the Stourbridge from 1776 to his resignation in 1781. Earlier in 1774 he had surveyed for the Stroudwater with John Priddey, the ex-resident engineer of the Droitwich. The Dadfords worked together in South Wales as well as independently. The younger surveyed and was engineer to the Leominster Canal. He worked with his father on the Glamorganshire, but left to be made engineer of the Neath in 1791 having surveyed it the previous year with his father and brother John. Young Thomas remained until 1792 when he left to become engineer of the Monmouthshire. Bearing in mind that he was still engineer of the Leominster, the Monmouthshire made him give them three quarters of his time, in case he got caught up in any more projects. This was to happen after his survey, on Monmouthshire orders, of the Brecknock & Abergavenny, whose part-time engineer he became in 1795, remaining until 1800. During the 1793 mania period, he worked on two schemes which were eventually built as tramroads from the Brecknock & Abergavenny, to Hereford and to the Wye. In 1797 he surveyed the extension of the Neath Canal to Giant's Grave and in 1800 did a re-survey of the Aberdare Canal although cutting was delayed until 1810. In Mid-Wales, he helped his brother John who was engineer on the Montgomeryshire from 1794 to 1797 when he left for America. John Dadford had built a tramroad from the Brecknock & Abergavenny Canal up the Clydach valley, opened in 1794 and had in 1790, helped in survey work for the Neath and in 1792 the Aberdare canals. A James Dadford, probably a younger brother of Thomas, was for a while engineer of the Gloucester & Berkeley from 1797 to 1800.

DARWIN, Dr. Erasmus, 1731-1802. As a doctor he practised at Lichfield, later Derby, and was a founder member of the Lunar Society. His friendship with Wedgwood stimulated his interest in canals. In about 1765 it seems to have been Darwin who encouraged Wedgwood to proceed with planning the Trent & Mersey to the Potteries. He did some practical work in the 1760s devising a canal lock and had ideas for a lift in 1779.

DODD, Ralph 1756-1822. With more vision than practical ability, Dodd, a Londoner, had an unhappy career as an engineer. In 1795 his "Account of the principal Canals in the known World, with reflections on the great utility of Canals" was published, he had the year before invented a canal cutting machine and done a survey for a canal from the Tyne to the Solway. In 1796 he planned an extension of the Wear navigation to Durham and a canal between the Wear and the Tyne. He also surveyed a canal from Stockton to the colliery area west of Darlington. His most ambitious canal was the Thames & Medway. He had proposals for the Croydon Canal involving inclined planes but never became its engineer. He was engineer of the third of his proposals, the Grand Surrey, but was dismissed the following year. Robert Dodd was clerk of works. He was re-employed on the Grand Surrey later to do small jobs. It was possibly his son Barrodale Robert Dodd who came up with the final Tyne-Solway scheme in 1810.

DUCART, Davis, died c.1778. Of probable Franco-Italian descent, the name a corruption of Daviso de Arcort, he was an architect and engineer who worked for the King of Sardinia, later settling in Ireland as Davis Ducart, the name variously spelt. Practising as an architect, Ducart designed the Customs House in the town of Limerick and a number of mansions before he became engineer of the colliery extension of the Coalisland Canal in Co. Tyrone, where in 1777 he built the first inclined plane on a British waterway.

DUNDAS, Sir Lawrence c.1710-1781 and DUNDAS, Thomas, 1st Baron Dundas, 1741-1820. The Dundas family of Stirlingshire were supporters of the Stewarts but changed allegiance at the time of the '45 rising, to the extent of Lawrence becoming a supplier of Cumberland's army. He remained a contractor to the army retiring in 1762 with a large fortune. His seat was West Kerse by the Carron and on the route of the proposed Forth & Clyde Canal. He supported it, becoming a shareholder and committee chairman. He pressed for a modification of the canal's entry into the Forth via a cut parallel with the Carron. Like his father, Thomas Dundas also supported the canal, having a large shareholding, and the name Port Dundas given to the Glasgow terminus. He promoted William Symington's successful 1802 experiments with the steam paddle tug CHARLOTTE DUNDAS, named after his third daughter.

EGERTON, Francis, 3rd Duke of Bridgewater 1736-1803. Father of British inland navigation, he was the last of seven sons and four daughters by two wives of Scroop Egerton, the first Duke of Bridgewater who died in 1745. Scroop was succeeded by John, Francis' elder brother, but he died in 1748 leaving Francis as the 3rd Duke at the age of 11. He was placed under the guardianship of his uncle John, 4th Duke of Bedford, his brother-in-law Lord Gower (then Viscount Trentham) and his kinsman Samuel Egerton. In 1757 at the age of 21 he succeeded to estates in Hertfordshire, Northamptonshire, Shropshire and Lancashire. The Lancashire estates, centred on Worsley near Manchester, held a particular interest because of their coal. Various schemes had been attempted to make marketing of the coal easier and he revived these with the encouragement of the Worsley estate agent John Gilbert. He believed in canals for bulk haulage and was fortunately rich enough to be able to finance it. His 1759 Act for a canal from Worsley to Salford, with another line to the Mersey & Irwell at Hollins Ferry below Barton, passed unopposed. The former was constructed and expanded as the Bridgewater Canal, eventually controlling the north-western outlet for the whole of the Midlands system. With Lord Gower, Thomas Gilbert and Brindley he was a major investor in the Trent & Mersey, and his concern for this waterway and his own line to Runcorn had caused him to refuse the Chester Canal's proposed junction with the Trent & Mersey at Middlewich. In north-east Cheshire the Duke had countered in 1765 with a scheme for an independent canal from Macclesfield to the Weaver, for it would contribute nothing to his revenue, but he later became involved with the Leeds & Liverpool, Lancaster and Rochdale plans. He was not keen on the Rochdale at first and refused the junction at Castlefield until in 1792 he heard of a Trans-Pennine extension of the Manchester, Bolton & Bury which would bypass the Rochdale. The Duke was on good terms with the Lancaster Canal and welcomed their plans for extending to Worsley. The Duke's Leigh branch was open by about 1799 to which he welcomed the Leeds & Liverpool from Wigan, but his death in 1803 stopped negotiations. At Worsley he developed extensive underground canals to serve the mines and was associated with the East Shropshire enterprises of Earl Gower & Co. The Duke was impressed with steam navigation and met the enthusiastic Robert Fulton who in 1796-7 superintended the building of a canal steam boat at Worsley. The Duke was going to order 8 tugs from William Symington after the demonstration given by the CHARLOTTE DUNDAS in 1802, but in 1803 the Duke died and the order was cancelled. He left the canal and the colliery properties and the Lancashire and Northamptonshire estates under the care of three trustees, headed by the canal manager and legal agent R.H. Bradshaw, the income from these going to Gower's eldest son George. Lord Gower himself, since 1786 Marquess of Stafford, also died in 1803. The Bridgewater title became extinct, although under the Duke's will, Francis, the second son of George, on the latter's death in 1833, took the name and arms of Egerton when he succeeded to the inheritance.

EGERTON, Lord Francis, 1st Earl of Ellesmere, 1800-1857. Born the second son, as Lord Francis Leveson-Gower,, of the second Marquess of Stafford, Lord Francis was named by the will of the 3rd Duke of Bridgewater as life renter after his father, of the Duke's canal and collieries at Worsley and of the Lancashire and Northamptonshire estates, all in trust. Lord Francis had to take the name and arms of Egerton. Lord Francis entered on his inheritance in 1833. It proved a trying one, for Lord Francis had to suffer in succession two difficult superintendents of the trust, who as chief of the trustees had been given autocratic powers. As squire of Worsley he treated his employees well, building schools and churches. This policy cost money and he had no great capital of his own and so was dependent on the income from the trust which he used to the full and little was set aside for developing the canal or the mines. The trust too had little capital and Lord Francis had to pay for canal and dock works at Runcorn and Liverpool. His greatest achievement was the purchase of the Mersey & Irwell Navigation in 1844 to stop the rate war.

EGREMONT, Earl of, see Wyndham, George O'Brien.

ELLESMERE, Earl of, see Egerton, Lord Francis.

EVANS, Richard, died 1802, was entirely concerned with Irish works. He was responsible in the 1780s for Shannon improvements between Jamestown and Killaloe. He was also occupied with a canal parallel with the River Erne from the coast up to the Lower Lough Erne, but little was done on this. In about 1785 he succeeded General Tarrant as resident engineer of the Grand and was responsible for the Leinster aqueduct over the Liffey. He stayed with the Grand until about 1798, and was employed on the Royal until his death, though nearly dismissed for incompetence. He built the aqueducts over the Rye Water and the Boyne.

EYES, John, died 1773. A land surveyor, he is chiefly remembered for his map making and detailed survey of the Liverpool area. His first work for inland navigation was a survey in 1740-1 of the River Calder, with Thomas Steers. He did another survey in 1758 for a navigation further up to Sowerby Bridge. In the 1760s he surveyed for an extension of the Sankey Brook Navigation to Fidler's Ferry, where a second Mersey entrance was made. In 1769 he worked on the Leeds & Liverpool with R. Melling to lay out a line more pleasing to the canal's Liverpool supporters than Longbotham's.

FAIRBAIRN, Sir William, Bart, 1789-1874, came from Kelso in Roxburghshire where his father was a farm servant. He was apprenticed as a millwright and in 1811 was employed in Newcastle. About 1813 he moved to Manchester and in 1817 established a partnership with James Lillie as textile machinery manufacturers. He did well and devoted much time to improving waterwheels. In 1834 he provided waterwheel driven pumps for the Carlisle Canal. In the 1830s he turned to shipbuilding in iron and the possibilities of powered iron canal craft. He took a close interest in the Forth & Clyde Canal's passenger boat trials of July 1830 and obtained an order for a twin hulled iron passenger steamer. This was the LORD DUNDAS completed in 1831 the year that Fairbairn published his "Remarks on Canal Navigation", a detailed description of the Forth & Clyde trials and the earlier ones on the Paisley canal. Another steamer, the MANCHESTER, converted from an iron passage boat, with a stern paddle, was used on the Forth. He did not think steam justified on the narrow canals but advocated iron construction because of its lightness. In 1832 he built a swift iron boat to carry passengers, the LANCASHIRE WITCH, for the Manchester, Bolton & Bury Canal. Having built boats in sections at Manchester, he moved on to the Thames at Millwall in 1835, but returned to Manchester in 1849 where he built boilers and locomotives, becoming a baronet in 1869.

FITZWILLIAM, William (Wentworth), 4th Earl Fitzwilliam, 1748-1833. A Yorkshire colliery owner, he was by inheritance owner of the Yorkshire Derwent Navigation, bought in 1715 by his great uncle Thomas Wentworth. He had his own plans for improving the river and from 1808 took over management from the last lessees, his own boats carrying estate produce. He ran the Navigation efficiently and faced railways with a well maintained river. Before the railway age he had encouraged waterways to the coalfields. His uncle, the last Marquess of Rockingham had planned a canal in 1769 from the Don to his collieries near Rotherham, the Greasbrough Canal. Completed about 1780, the main traffic was coal from Park Gate colliery, one of those inherited by Earl Fitzwilliam. He supported the Dearne & Dove Canal which served his Elsecar colliery by a branch opened in 1799 and in 1815 subscribed £1000 for the long delayed Sheffield Canal.

FLETCHER, Matthew, 1731-1808. Second son of Jacob Fletcher, a mine owner on the outskirts of Bolton, Matthew took up mine engineering with John Heathcote of Salford, for whom he sunk Wet Earth colliery near Clifton in the 1740s. In the early 1760s Matthew became lessee of this and other Heathcote properties together with mineral rights in the Clifton area. He was concerned with getting the coal away and became a committee member of the Manchester, Bolton & Bury Canal, doing the first survey for this canal in 1790. He supervised construction with the engineer Charles Roberts who was dismissed in 1793 and replaced by Fletcher's nephew John Nightingale. He also subscribed to the 1792 scheme to extend the Manchester, Bolton & Bury from Bury to the Rochdale at Sladen, or beyond. He enlarged the mill leat at Wet Earth and Botany Bay collieries forming Fletcher's Canal. In 1799 as chairman of the Mersey & Irwell, he had to turn against the Manchester, Bolton & Bury to defeat their Bill for an aqueduct over the Irwell and a junction with the Bridgewater, a possible reason for his dismissal from the Bolton & Bury's committee in 1801, the year he received a silver cup in recognition of his services from the Mersey & Irwell. At this time he was being consulted as a mining expert by the Huddersfield Canal over Stanedge tunnel.

FLETCHER, Samuel, died 1804 and others. A family of Fletchers was employed on the Leeds & Liverpool. They came from Bradford and one, James Fletcher, assisted Whitworth on the Yorkshire side when the latter became engineer in 1790. This James could have been the brother of Samuel Fletcher who in 1795 became the canal's resident engineer under Whitworth. Samuel Fletcher helped his brother Joseph on the canal works between Burnley and Sheffield near Accrington, over which Samuel had full control after Whitworth's death in 1799. After Samuel's own death in 1804, Joseph and Samuel's son James carried on as joint surveyors of the canal. James Fletcher had a long career with the Leeds & Liverpool remaining as engineer until his death in 1844. He was succeeded by Walmsley Stanley whose assistant was another Fletcher, Thomas, possibly James' son.

FORTREY, Samuel 1622-1681. Son of a London merchant, he held a court appointment under Charles II. In 1663 he published "England's Interest and Improvement" and in 1672 made a contract with the Corporation of Lincoln to improve the Fossdyke, sharing costs and profits with them. In 1675, after the Fossdyke works had been completed, he was appointed to improve the Wiltshire Avon as a salaried official under Salisbury Corporation, but not much was done until later under a private group.

FULTON, Robert, 1765-1815 was born in Pennsylvania, with an Irish father. He became a successful artist, moving to London in 1786 to gain a wider reputation. Here he met men of eminence including the Duke of Bridgewater and the third Earl of Stanhope, sharing the latter's interest in steam navigation. Stanhope was also interested in the Bude canal about which Fulton wrote to him, amplifying the Earls' ideas on inclined planes. Fulton took his ideas to the Peak Forest Canal when in 1794 he accepted a contract for cutting part of it, and sufficiently impressed them with proposals for tub-boats, inclined planes and an iron aqueduct over the Goyt, that they sent their engineer Outram, probably with Fulton, to look at existing working planes in East Shropshire. The company asked Fulton to write down his ideas and the well known "Treatise on the Improvement of Canal Navigation" of 1796 resulted. This book advocated small boat canals throughout the country, overcoming changes of level by lifts and inclined planes. The novelty was his suggestion for wheeled boats, first described in his patent of 1794, both tub boats and his larger 30' long market and 'dispatch' or fly boats. His planes would save the cost of aqueducts, with inclines descending each side of the valley, crossing at low level by means of a single arched bridge or by a plane spanning the river at a steep angle to gain height on one side. A further idea was to use a 'horizontal' plane to cross a valley, thereby saving the cost and materials for an aqueduct. Fulton never built from his designs. Reverting to steam navigation he directed the construction of a paddle tug at Worsley which was successfully tried in about 1797 although abandoned a couple of years later. In 1797 he left for France and later America.

GILBERT, John, 1724-1795. A Staffordshire man, he was the son of a small landowner at Cotton near Alton in the Churnet valley. He was apprenticed to the Boulton hardware works at Snow Hill, Birmingham, where he became friendly with young Matthew Boulton. John's elder brother Thomas was land agent to Lord Gower and chief legal agent to the Duke of Bridgewater, and John himself entered the Duke's service as land agent for the Worsley estate. He had mining experience and proposed extending as an underground navigation, the drainage sough system of John Massey, agent at Worsley between about 1721 and 1745. The Duke agreed with Gilbert and the latter also surveyed for a proposed canal to Salford which received its Act in 1759. Brindley joined this project as assistant engineer.   Gilbert also handled the Duke's Worsley finances raising much of the canal capital himself, and by 1762 he and Brindley had prepared surveys for an extension towards Liverpool. As engineer of the new line Gilbert was helped by Brindley and Thomas Morris from Liverpool. Gilbert's son John took over much of the estate work, succeeding him as agent. In 1764 he had, with Gower and Thomas Gilbert, formed Earl Gower & Co., to develop the Earl's east Shropshire mineral resources, building the Donnington Wood Canal with navigational soughs into the coal mines, and branch canals to the limestone quarries. He was involved in the Shropshire Canal promotion and sat on the committee. He subscribed to the Shrewsbury and was a committee member in his last year. He followed his brother, the Duke and Gower by subscribing to the Trent & Mersey, though neither Gilbert joined the committee at first. His mining experience took him to the Speedwell lead mine near Castleton in Derbyshire, where he drove the navigation sough between 1774 and 1778. He had mining interests in the Alston area, in 1771 planning two underground canals at Middle Fell, although the rock was found too hard, but a second venture started in 1776 was later opened as the Nent Force Level. He was involved, with his son in the canal and river carrying firm John Gilbert & Co., also using coastal craft. In 1782 the younger John started canal carrying with Jonathan Worthington, a road carrier to Bristol. In his last years he worked on inclined planes, designing one for the underground levels at Worsley, completed in 1797 and possibly a similar one for Donnington Wood underground canals.

GILBERT, Thomas, 1720-1798 was the elder brother of John Gilbert. Trained in law, he was called to the bar in 1744. He entered the service of Lord Gower as his land agent at Trentham, becoming also principal legal agent for Gower's brother-in-law the Duke of Bridgewater. In 1759 he introduced Brindley to the Duke. He became the member of parliament for Newcastle-under-Lyme in 1763. He was also chairman of the committee considering the Bill for the Trent & Mersey, to which he subscribed, later joining the canal's committee. He developed many interests, a quarry at Caldon Low, farms and became a major subscriber to the Shropshire Canal with Earl Gower, and with his co-partners to the Shrewsbury Canal. He was a parliamentary reformer and in 1782 secured a Poor Law Act named after him.

GILES, Francis, 1787-1847. With his brother Netlam, Francis Giles was one of the John Rennie team involved with many of the master's projects. In 1811 they surveyed for a canal from the Croydon to the Arun Navigation at Newbridge, and in 1812 on a Bedford-Grand Junction canal link. The brothers had worked for Rennie on the Kent & Sussex Junction Canal project of 1809, followed in 1815 by surveys for the Portsmouth & Arundel. Francis Giles helped Rennie over the Aire & Calder in the latter's last years, and carried on after his death in 1821, planning improvements on the Leeds line. After John Rennie's death Francis Giles worked for the two sons when they judged the merits of the 1824-5 schemes for ship canals between the Thames and Portsmouth. In 1825 Francis Giles was made engineer of a projected canal from the Kennet & Avon to the Basingstoke, while in 1815 he had been involved with a revival of the 1802 Western Union Canal scheme between the Kennet & Avon and the Grand Junction. He was therefore party to many schemes, but little achievement. He was however engineer to the Ivel's extension to Shefford and to the Hertford Union, the short canal between the Regent's and the Lee Navigation. Following this, he was the engineer of the extension of the Sankey Brook Navigation from Fidler's Ferry to Widnes opened in 1833. He was involved with what became the Birmingham & Warwick Junction Canal, having been proposed as engineer to its predecessor the Union scheme of 1830. He succeeded Telford as engineer to the Exchequer Bill Loan Commissioners.

GOWER, Lord. See Leveson-Gower.

GRANTHAM, John, c. 1775-1833. Formerly a cavalry officer, he became one of John Rennie's team. As an engineer he worked for Rennie on the Shannon when Rennie was ordered to do a survey in 1821 for flood relief and drainage. He was impressed with the traffic possibilities, for in 1826 he formed the Shannon Steam Packet Co., which attracted the attention of Charles Wye Williams who bought Grantham's passenger steamer, forming the Inland Navigation Co. Latterly his son John assisted him.

GREEN, James, did most of his work in the West Country, but probably had Midlands origins because it may have been his father James Green who assisted the younger Thomas Dadford to build the Stourbridge. The son worked in the Midlands, surveying the Stourbridge Extension Canal in 1836, but Green's first completed canal was the Bude, with its 6 inclined planes, successful enough to encourage the Rolle family to build the Torrington with an inclined plane, James Green being the engineer. In 1823 he surveyed for a tub-boat canal from the coast at Looe up to Liskeard, but his ideas were not adopted, the canal being built for barges. Green was then busy on his greatest single work, the improvement of the Exeter Ship Canal. In 1821 he had surveyed a tub-boat canal from the Tone to Beer on the south Devon coast, and in 1827 a canal up to Newton Abbot. In 1828 he was working on a proposed ship canal in Cardiff for Lord Bute, later altered to become Bute docks. Most impressive was his London & Birmingham Canal project of 1836 from the Stratford to the Regent's. By application of tub-boat standards, he rescued two moribund canals in the 1830s,, the Grand Western isolated near Tiverton and the Chard Canal. The Chard committee however replaced Green as their engineer by Sydney Hall, recommended by William Cubitt. Green was called in 1833 to rescue the Kidwelly & Llanelly Canal which he extended to Burry Port as an ordinary boat canal, then cutting an extension up the Gwendraeth Fawr valley for tub-boats using inclined planes.

GREEN, James. There may have been four James Greens as canal engineers. Best known is the nineteenth century West Country engineer. The father, or yet another James Green was engineer to both the completed Dudley and the Stourbridge as a joint post from 1801. Outside this family was James Green of Wollaton near Nottingham. He was a land surveyor working for Lord Middleton. In 1791 he became resident engineer after he was called to survey the Nottingham Canal under Jessop who was ill. In 1793 he laid out a line for a proposed extension of the Ashby Canal to Swadlincote with tramroads on to the collieries. When the Grantham Canal was authorized in that year, Green became resident engineer from the Trent as far as the Leicestershire boundary.

GREGSON, Samuel c. 1763-1846 and GREGSON, Bryan Padgett, died 1872. The father, Samuel, helped to form the Lancaster Canal Company in 1791 when he was appointed clerk, a post which he retained until his death. As soon as parts of the canal were open he took the opportunity of using it as a trader. Although accused of receiving favourable treatment, his activities helped the canal to gain traffic. On his father's death, the son B. P. Gregson became clerk and dealt with the complex canal-railway politics of this period for which a grateful company fixed his salary at not less than £1000 a year. Because of his experience in railway affairs, Gregson accepted the managership of the Edinburgh & Glasgow Railway in 1846. He also acted for a few years from 1847 as carrying manager for the Grand Junction. He died in office after serving 60 years.

GRESLEY, Sir Nigel, Bart, died 1787. Owner of collieries at Apedale, 3miles from Newcastle-under-Lyme,

Sir Nigel and his son built a private canal from the mines into the town completed in about 1776. Sir Nigel's son, Sir Nigel Bowyer Gresley was promoter of the Newcastle-under-Lyme Junction Canal and inherited the private canal from his father. He had collieries too near Swadlincote so he was interested in the Ashby Canal and a promoter of the 1796 scheme for the Commercial Canal. The private canal passed on Sir Nigel Bowyer Gresley's death in 1808 to his son Sir Roger who died in 1837. About ten years before Sir Roger's death, ownership of the canal passed to a cousin, Richard Edensor Heathcote, husband of Sir Roger's half sister Emma and a partner in the Apedale mines.

GRUNDY, John, 1719-1783. He was born at Congerstone, near Market Bosworth in Leicestershire. He worked on the Witham in 1744, 1753 and 1761. He was consulted on the Blyth Navigation in Suffolk in 1759 and in 1765 became engineer of the Louth Navigation which he had surveyed as early as 1756. In Yorkshire, he undertook dock building at Hull and during the 1760s surveyed the Swale and Bedale Beck. He also surveyed for the Driffield Navigation enlarging on Smeaton's proposals. Finally Grundy, who also reported on the Chesterfield Canal, was called in to make the Market Weighton Canal. John Smith had done the survey and was appointed consulting engineer, but Grundy came to check and alter his work, becoming engineer in 1773 and Smith left. Grundy had been associated with Smeaton in the 1760s on drainage work on the Hull and was one of the early band of engineers who called themselves the Smeatonians, or Smeatonian Society.

HADLEY, John, flourished 1700, was from West Bromwich and an expert engineer on waterwheel driven pumps. He was associated with George Sorocold who in 1694-5 was building waterworks at Leeds, and probably Sorocold was asked by the Aire & Calder Navigation to recommend an engineer. He must have suggested Hadley, for he did the surveys before the act of 1699 and was appointed engineer at the high fee of £420 on its passage. Hadley's achievement was notable, for the first boat reached Leeds at the end of 1700, while the Calder line was finished in 1702. He was also asked in 1699 to look over the Ouse below York. Here he followed the recommendations of Thomas Surbey whom the City of York had called in earlier in 1699.

HARMSWORTH, Alexander John, 1868-1947, was the eldest son of a Basingstoke Canal carpenter. He followed his father's trade although also a carter and bargeman on the Basingstoke Canal and Thames. In the 1890s he developed a pleasure boat hire business on the Basingstoke at Ash Vale, becoming a carrier on the canal in 1902. During the 1914-18 War, the fleet was enlarged to handle extra traffic to Aldershot and timber to Woking. In 1923 he bought the canal from William Carter and carried on with the coal and timber traffic to Woking until 1949. He died in 1947 and in 1949 the canal was auctioned by the family, who continued to operate barges on the Thames and Wey until 1966.

HATHERTON, 1st Baron. See Littleton, Edward John.

HEATHCOTE, Sir John Edensor, 1757-1822. Son-in-law of Sir Nigel Gresley Bart, he was involved in mines near Newcastle-under-Lyme and in the Irwell Valley near Salford, inherited from his great uncle John Heathcote. Much of these had been leased to Matthew Fletcher, but he retained local interests and became involved with the promotion of the Manchester, Bolton & Bury Canal. He was a principal subscriber and sat on the canal's committee. He was one of the promotors of the Newcastle-under-Lyme Junction Canal. His eldest son Richard Edensor Heathcote, born about 1781, married his cousin Emma Gresley, to form a second marriage link between the Heathcotes and the Gresleys, gaining for Richard Heathcote, ownership of Gresley's canal in the 1820s, also called Heathcote's Canal.

HENSHALL, Hugh, c.1734-1816. His father, John Henshall, was a land surveyor and worked with Brindley on the Trent & Mersey surveys. Hugh had become Brindley's pupil and from 1765 his brother-in-law when the 49 year old bachelor married Hugh's 19 year old sister Anne. When Brindley died in 1772 Henshall took over his works, for he was a competent canal engineer. On the passage of the Trent & Mersey's Act he was appointed clerk of works under his brother-in-law as engineer. He became involved with other Brindley Canals, in 1765-66 he and Samuel Simcock, were surveying for the proposed Staffs. & Worcs., and he also probably worked on the Chesterfield. When Brindley died in 1772 Henshall took over the Trent & Mersey bringing it to a successful completion in 1777, and also acted as a consultant on the Chesterfield. Apart from canal engineering, Henshall lent his name to the carrying subsidiary of the Trent & Mersey. The Mersey & Irwell Navigation consulted him on flooding in 1787 and again in 1793 while in 1790 he did survey work for the proposed Manchester, Bolton & Bury. He was a considerable subscriber to this canal and was on its committee from 1791 to 1796. He also subscribed heavily to the Bury & Sladen project. In 1791 he was altering the line of the Herefordshire & Gloucestershire, making it go by way of Newent. Then in 1793 he was working for Jessop on surveys for the Grand Western, and the following year with the younger Thomas Dadford laid out a tramroad feeder for the Brecknock & Abergavenny, his only tramroad.

HODGKINSON, John, was a kinsman of Benjamin Outram whose mother was a Hodgkinson and likewise came from Derbyshire. His family, like the Outrams, were supporters of the Cromford Canal in which both men were involved with the first proposals of 1787. Hodgkinson trained as an engineer under Outram on the Ashby Canal tramroad and became a capable builder of them. His canal work was more limited. He did the Newport extension of the Monmouthshire, 1804-8 and worked on the Brecknock & Abergavenny. There was also a Samuel Hodgkinson, described as an 'eminent engineer'. In 1819 he advised the Stratford upon Avon Canal on water supply, in 1820 surveyed the Stourbridge Extension Canal and in 1822 reported on the Earlswood reservoir for the Stratford.

HOMFRAY, Francis, 1725-c.1789, and sons. Of Yorkshire and Welsh descent, Francis Homfray became established as an ironmaster in Worcestershire and at Broseley, near Coalbrookdale. In the early 1780s he was invited into South Wales by another Broseley ironmaster, John Guest. He came to Merthyr in 1782 with his three sons Jeremiah, Thomas and Samuel. An ironworks was started at Penydarren in 1784 and it is thought he was behind the promotion of the Glamorganshire Canal with other ironmasters, although much overtopped by Richard Crawshay. One son, Jeremiah was a shareholder in the Aberdare Canal and in the Brecknock & Abergavenny, although he sold his Aberdare shares before the canal was cut. Samuel was caught up in quarrels with Richard Crawshay over the conduct of the Glamorganshire Canal affairs, quarrels which led to the promotion by Samuel and others of the Penydarren tramroad opened in 1802, to bypass the upper length of the canal. Like Jeremiah he was an Aberdare shareholder but sold his stock. In 1800 he and others started the Tredegar ironworks which was to be joined to the coast at Newport by tramroad.

HORE, John, c.1690-1762, came from a family of maltsters of Newbury, Berkshire. With his father, he was one of the proprietors of the proposed Kennet Navigation, in 1718 being appointed surveyor and engineer for the improvements. Between 1718 and 1723 Hore supervised the building of locks and artifical cuts from Reading up to Newbury. By 1724 the Kennet was open, but the following year he had a dispute with the undertakers over payment and his rights as a wharf proprietor at Newbury. He left the river, going as engineer to the Bristol Avon, which he may have already surveyed. The Avon work was completed in 1727. Next he surveyed the Stroudwater suggesting an 8 mile lateral canal. No work was done and in 1733 he surveyed the Chelmer. This proved abortive and he found himself in reduced circumstances. However, in 1734, the Kennet took him back as maintenance engineer and he was restored to his Newbury wharf business. His son, born in 1730, became resident engineer under John Rennie of the Kennet & Avon Canal.

HUSTLER, John, died 1790. A Quaker wool merchant from Bradford, Hustler was persuaded by the Halifax engineer John Longbotham to consider a canal from Leeds to Liverpool. Hustler was appointed treasurer at Bradford, James Hollingshead being treasurer at Liverpool. In 1771 Hustler became sole treasurer. He was a promoter of the Bradford Canal and had colliery interests near Wigan, Hustler's tramroad being built from Billinge down to the Leeds & Liverpool at Gathurst in 1788.

HOUSTON, William, 1781-c.1850, of Johnstone Castle, Renfrew became a member of the committee of the Glasgow, Paisley & Johnstone Canal. He improved on the canal's passenger boats designing a craft based on a gig used in rowing matches. It was placed in service about 1830 and was followed by others, some of iron, which made sensational reductions in the timings between Glasgow and Paisley. Called swift or gig boats, they were widely adopted.

JAMES, William, 1771-1837. A far sighted man, he has been called the 'Father of Railways', a title which is generally awarded to George Stephenson. Long before his railway schemes he had been interested in canals. In 1797 he surveyed the line of the Stratford Canal and in 1800 was on the committee, later becoming chairman. His energy secured completion of the canal. In 1812 James took charge of operations also spending a good deal of his own money on the work, while the following year he personally bought the Upper Avon Navigation which in 1816 was linked with the completed canal in Stratford. By then James was in financial difficulty, owing money to the Stratford Canal on which he ran a carrying fleet. In 1820 he had to leave the canal committee and in 1823 was declared bankrupt, selling the Upper Avon the following year. He died a poor man at Bodmin in Cornwall.

JESSOP, Josias, died 1826. Son of William Jessop, he was associated with some of his father's works, for example he was resident engineer of the harbour improvements at Bristol. This was in 1803, but he did not undertake any canal works until 1810 when he probably became engineer of the Lydney Canal and the Severn & Wye tramroad over to Lydbrook on the Wye. He did not stay to complete the canal, leaving in 1811. His greatest success was the survey of the Cromford & High Peak Railway which he engineered like the canal which had been first intended, with gradients overcome by inclined planes. He did surveys for the Wey & Arun Junction Canal and became its engineer. He was also consulted in 1813 about the extension of the Montgomeryshire from Garthmyl to Newtown. He did the surveys for this Western Branch, authorized in 1815, with probably a local man, John Williams as his resident engineer.

JESSOP, William, 1745-1814. William Jessop became the greatest expert during his lifetime on British canal construction and river improvement. During his career he was consulted about practically every major scheme, but he was a modest man taking the blame for mistakes and even offering to pay for them. Technically he was competent, ensuring his canals had plenty of water. He saw the economic value of river navigations and broad canals, and most of his were successful. His father Josias worked as an engineer at Plymouth dockyard, and William was born at Plymouth. His father helped Smeaton build the third Eddystone lighthouse as resident engineer. His father died in 1761 but fortunately for William, now 16, he was taken under the care of Smeaton. Jessop was trained as an engineer, unique at that time and was soon given responsibility. Under Smeaton he surveyed the Ure and the Ripon Canal and was put in charge of the works. In 1769-70 he helped Smeaton with his second and successful improvement on the Calder & Hebble, and in 1773 he accompanied him to Ireland to rescue the Grand Canal. Jessop stayed as consulting engineer paying occasional visits from England. From 1772 he worked for Smeaton on improvements to the Aire & Calder Navigation, notably the Selby canal, bypassing the lower Aire which he surveyed before the act of 1774, acting as resident engineer under Smeaton's direction. In 1779 he reported on Smeaton's proposals for lock improvement on the Calder & Hebble, a case of the pupil teaching the master. He was put in charge of the works, all completed by 1785. Back on the Aire & Calder, Jessop had not been regularly employed since completion of the Selby canal, but was consulted on the other improvements which had been authorized along with the Selby line by the Act of 1774. These were completed on both the Leeds and Wakefield lines by 1785. In the 1790s he advised on improvements at Selby and designed a toll swing bridge over the Ouse in 1791. He became engineer of the Aire & Calder satellite, the Barnsley Canal which included his largest masonry aqueduct. He was too busy to do the Dearne & Dove survey in 1792, but in 1799 surveyed the little Leven Canal. In south Yorkshire Jessop built the short Greasbrough Canal, having altered Smeaton's line. In 1801 he did a survey for a proposed extension of the Don on to Sheffield, eventually built as the Sheffield Canal after his death, he also reported on large scale improvements for the Don. In 1795 he had worked with William Chapman on a Tyne-Solway canal. Apart from Yorkshire his main area of operations became the East Midlands. In 1777 he was called on to report on the state of the Loughborough Navigation, recommending improvements. From 1783 he was working on the Trent, remaining as engineer all his life. The navigation was declared finished in 1801, his greatest river undertaking. He had as contractors, the Pinkertons, who served under him on the Basingstoke and on the Sussex Ouse and whom he helped to secure the contract for Dudley tunnel. In 1784 he was consulted on the Severn, commissioned by the Staffs. & Worcs. Canal and in 1789 did a Thames survey. He worked on improvement of the Sussex Ouse in 1788 and 3 years later on the Western Rother for the third Earl of Egremont. From 1788 he was continuously engaged in the East Midlands, although parallel projects were afoot in Shropshire, Yorkshire, Lancashire and the South. There was the Cromford Canal serving the Butterley ironworks in which he was a partner with Outram and others from 1790. These works supplied parts for lock gates, paddle gear and tramroad rails and also plates for the first cast iron aqueduct, completed in 1796 on the Derby Canal. On the Cromford Jessop built two major aqueducts and both gave trouble. He surveyed for the Nottingham, but retired for a spell in 1791, ill with a poisoned face, but became engineer in 1792 and was by then engineer of the Leicester Navigation and also the Cromford. It was the time of the canal mania and in 1793 he took on two large projects, the Grand Junction and the Ellesmere, but all paid him well. He had received £250 a year for part-time work on the Selby canal, he got £350 from the Cromford, 3 guineas a day from the Nottingham, £350 a year from the Leicester and probably £500 a year from the Grand Junction. From 1793 he became involved with the Derby and the Grantham, while he surveyed what became the Nutbrook and the Oakham. He had already guided the younger Christopher Staveley's survey of the Melton Mowbray Navigation and as early as 1787 he planned for a canal and tramroad to serve the Ashby-de-la-Zouch area. In 1794, with Robert Whitworth he did the parliamentary survey for the Ashby. The Grand Junction was his longest single canal and his greatest challenge. He was forced to abandon Blisworth tunnel in 1796, but encouraged by Rennie, Whitworth and his resident engineer James Barnes he tried again on a different line, this time successfully. He was engaged at the same time on the Ellesmere. Third of his canal achievements was the Rochdale built at this time. He superintended construction throughout, unlike the Ellesmere which he left in 1801, while on the Grand Junction he was not in regular attendance after 1797. In the south he surveyed the line of the Basingstoke and was their consultant engineer, he reported on the Somersetshire Coal Canal and in 1793 on the Grand Western. In East Anglia he reported in 1791 on the Horncastle Canal and in 1792 surveyed the Caistor. He also reported about this time on the Ipswich & Stowmarket Navigation, the River Gipping. Jessop laid out the West India docks on the Thames and the Floating Harbour at Bristol. Moreover he was an ironmaster keen on tramroads. He was responsible for the ill-fated Forest Line of the Leicester Navigation, part canal and part tramroad and the Surrey Iron Railway. He died at 69 having had a stroke, at Butterley.

KILLALY, John, died 1832. He was one of the engineers along with John Brownrigg to the Directors - General of Inland Navigation in Ireland appointed in 1800. Before this post he worked as resident engineer on the Grand Canal. Under the Directors-General he worked on the Shannon, completing in 1822 the Lough Allen Canal, although better known for the Ulster Canal, which he surveyed in 1814-15, starting in 1825.

KINDERLEY, Nathaniel. His father Charles Kinderley proposed in 1720 that training walls should be built below Wisbech to improve the outfall of the Nene. He suggested a cut on the Ouse above King's Lynn, eventually opened in 1821 as Eau Brink Cut. His son also pressed for Nene and Ouse improvements, in 1751 producing "Ancient and Present State of the Navigation of the Towns of Lyn, Wisbech, Spalding and Boston" which advocated combining the Welland and Nene outfalls. The Nene works were carried out by 1773 and named Kinderley's Cut. On the Cheshire Dee, he was appointed undertaker for the new channel from Chester to the estuary and for reclamation of the marshes. The channel was completed in 1737, but because of estuary siltation failed to compete with Liverpool.

KIRKHOUSE, William. George Kirkhouse, William's grandfather came from Gateshead to South Wales as a mining engineer. William became a mining engineer, working in the Llanelly district and in Pembrokeshire. His first canal work was a survey for a possible extension of the Neath Canal to Port Talbot. He however had the more important task of engineer to Mr. George Tennant's canals.

LEADER WILLIAMS, Edward, (senior), died 1879. He came into prominence as the sub-engineer of the Severn Improvement Association formed in 1840 which was followed by the Commission of 1842. By 1847 Leader Williams was the engineer in charge with Cubitt in an advisory role. He was later involved with improvements at Gloucester finished by the end of 1871. His son Edward helped on the Severn in the early days from 1844 to 1846. Another son Alfred ran a tug business on the Severn which was taken over from about 1861 by the Staffs.& Worcs. Canal, Alfred becoming manager of the Canal's carrying fleet.

LEADER WILLIAMS, Sir Edward, 1828-1910. Distinguished son of a capable father, the younger Edward, was born at Worcester. In 1846, after his Severn apprenticeship he worked on the Great Northern Railway. In 1849 he became resident engineer for the harbour works at Shoreham in Sussex, moving in 1852 to take charge of the Dover pier. In 1856 he was made engineer of the Weaver Navigation and soon showed himself a forward thinking man who could fit a waterway into the railway age, planning improvements to encourage steam coasters to use the waterway. His river plans were completed in 1865 but work was delayed until Delamere dock, Weston Point, was ready. He also suggested the Anderton lift, although the design was prepared by Edwin Clark. Leader Williams did not stay to see it completed because in 1872 he moved to the Bridgewater, although continuing to advise the Weaver trustees. In 1872 the Bridgewater had been sold to railway interests and they called upon Leader Williams to become engineer and general manager; his first improvement was to introduce steam canal tugs. He undertook improvements at Runcorn, but left in 1879. He was invited in 1882 to advise the committee promoting the Manchester Ship Canal, and his plan for a canal with locks was accepted and he was made engineer. One of his last works was the completion in 1893 of the Barton swing aqueduct to carry the Bridgewater over the Ship Canal which was opened in 1894. He was knighted for this work, remaining engineer of the canal until 1905 when he retired, although still playing a consultative role in his final years.

LEATHER, George. He was a Bradford man whose work was mostly confined to Yorkshire, and his greatest success was his modernization of the Aire & Calder with his father, George. The son surveyed the Derwent in 1810 for Earl Fitzwilliam and the two of them superintended improvement works above Malton. He went on to survey the Pocklington Canal in 1813-14 and after the 1815 Act became engineer.   For most of the rest of his career he was involved with the Aire & Calder, at first under John Rennie. Rennie laid out the Knottingley - Goole canal but Leather built it. He was called in on associated projects, for example in 1817 he surveyed a possible canal from the Aire to the Don, nothing came of this but he made some improvements under the Act of 1821. In 1826 he completed the Knottingley-Goole Canal and to him should be given the credit for the port and town of Goole. In the 1830s he was busy on further Aire & Calder· improvements above the Knottingley Canal entrance at Ferrybridge. He had already done a certain amount of work on the Leeds line in the earlier 1820s. The Calder line to Wakefield was ready in 1839 and included the cast iron aqueduct at Stanley Ferry designed by Leather. Another Leather, John, was, associated in a move to improve the Aire in Leeds to extend the navigation to Armley.

LEVESON-GOWER, Granville. Earl Gower, 1st Marquess of Stafford, 1721-1803. A name as closely linked with canal development as the Duke of Bridgewater, whose favourite sister Louisa married Gower in 1748 as his second wife. Gower acted as the Duke's guardian together with Samuel Egerton and the 4th Duke of Bedford, so the Duke of Bridgewater was a frequent visitor to Gower's Staffordshire seat Trentham Park near Stoke. As proprietor of collieries, iron mines and limestone quarries in Staffordshire and Shropshire, Gower was very wealthy. He was a good business man and followed his brother-in-law's lead in the development of inland waterways, probably at the suggestion of their stewards the Gilbert brothers.   As early as 1758 Gower with others had asked Brindley to survey a canal from Stoke-on-Trent to the Mersey. To this Gower lent his patronage, of value because of his association with the Duke. Gower from 1759 also organised parliamentary support for the Bridgewater Canal acts, at the same time building a canal to serve his quarries at Lilleshall and Donnington Wood in Shropshire. In 1764 with John and Thomas Gilbert he formed Earl Gower & Co to undertake the canal and operate the mines and quarries. In 1802 after the death of the Gilberts, Earl Gower & Co., became the Lilleshall Partnership forerunner of the Lilleshall Co.

LEVESON-GOWER, George Granville, Earl Gower, 2nd Marquess of Stafford, 1st Duke of Sutherland 1758- 1833. Succeeding his father as Marquess of Stafford in 1803, he inherited his father's estate, and the life rent of his uncle the Duke of Bridgewater's estate, becoming a 'leviathan of wealth'; this included the mines and the canal, and the Lilleshall estate with the Donnington Wood Canal of his father. Two thirds of the county of Sutherland came to him by marriage in 1785. Though he favoured railways, he supported the Birmingham & Liverpool Junction Canal. Though the Liverpool & Manchester Railway would compete with his own Bridgewater Canal, his withdrawal of opposition secured the railway its Act in 1826.

LINGARD, Thomas, died 1836. An Edmund Lingard succeeded Joseph Parker as engineer of the Coventry Canal in 1770. He then worked on the Stroudwater, succeeding John Priddey in about 1776, although he was dismissed in 1777. He may have been an ancestor, even the father of Thomas Lingard, who became manager of the Mersey & Irwell Navigation in 1814. Under his regime the Mersey & Irwell was well run,

Lingard designing an iron lighter decked over for timber cargoes, in the 1830s. He was succeeded by a T. O. Lingard, probably his son, who wanted to improve the canal as a ship canal to Manchester and commissioned surveys, but no action followed. Instead he was involved in a rates crisis with the Bridgewater and the railways which led in 1844 to the transfer of the Mersey & Irwell to Bridgewater control.

LITTLETON, Edward John, 1st Baron Hatherton, 1791-1863. Originally called Walhouse, he assumed the name Littleton on the death of his great uncle Sir Edward Littleton in 1812, to whose Staffordshire estates he succeeded, centred on Teddesley Park near Cannock. Sir Edward had been an original subscriber to the Staffs. & Worcs, a promoter of the Thames & Severn and a shareholder in the Leominster. Edward John took over his great uncle's Thames & Severn interests and in 1812 was an original subscriber to the North Wilts Canal. Returning to local waterways he was, at least from 1826, on the committee of the Staffs. & Worcs., Canal. Later he became chairman, the Hatherton branch to the Cannock coalfield being named after him. In 1840 he was elected chairman of the committee formed to press for the establishment of the Severn Commission. He remained chairman of the Staffs. & Worcs., until his death. His grandson born in 1842, Edward George Percy, the 3rd baron, was on the canal's committee from 1868 and chairman from 1888 until his death in 1930. The committee boat of 1898, named LADY HATHERTON honoured his wife.

LOCH, James, 1780-1855. James Loch was the son of a poor Scots laird, but trained at Edinburgh University and practised as a barrister, becoming an expert on property conveyancing and estate management. The latter secured for him in 1813 the post of principal agent to the second Marquess of Stafford. Unlike Bradshaw, superintendent of the Duke of Bridgewater's trust, Loch was not antagonistic to railways. As agent he had to protect the canal interests of the Marquess, but may well have influenced the latter's decision in 1825 to invest heavily in the Liverpool & Manchester Railway and in the proposed Birmingham & Liverpool Junction Canal and Loch was given a seat on both boards as a result. In 1834 he was able to secure Bradshaw's retirement and in 1837 the dismissal of his successor Sothern. From 1837 to his death in 1855 Loch himself was superintendent, but he was too busy to exercise personal supervision. His greatest achievement for the Bridgewater was to secure its control by direct purchase in 1844, of the Mersey & Irwell Navigation. Loch now became principal agent of the Mersey & Irwell. He was also a member of the Ellesmere & Chester Canal's board, for this in 1845 absorbed the Birmingham & Liverpool Junction and he became involved with the formation of the Shropshire Union.

LONGBOTHAM, John, died 1801. From Halifax and a pupil of John Smeaton, in 1766 Longbotham suggested a Leeds-Liverpool canal. He did a survey for a route which was approved by the Yorkshire promoters and later by James Brindley. Brindley was made chief engineer and Longbotham clerk of works, but because Brindley did not take up the appointment, Longbotham became chief engineer in addition, but was soon to be involved with projects elsewhere. Already in 1768 he had tried to serve his native Halifax by planning a canal from the Calder & Hebble above Brighouse to a point just short of the town. This was followed by two other local canal surveys from the Calder & Hebble. In 1772 he worked on a proposed canal from Leeds to Selby on the Ouse to bypass the Aire. Other interests were coal mines at Upholland near Wigan while as soon as the canal was open from Liverpool to Newburgh in 1774, Longbotham started a passenger packet service. He was dismissed from the Leeds & Liverpool in 1775 mainly because his accounts were at fault. His canal career was not ended, in about 1787 he was doing surveys for the proposed Lancaster Canal, on a route which would cut round the shores of Morecambe Bay. Then in the early 1790s he surveyed for the extended Bury & Sladen scheme and then returned to the Leeds & Liverpool, in difficulties at its summit level. In 1792 he did preparatory surveys for the Grand Western to cross Devon and Somerset and worked on the Bristol & Western from the Avon to Taunton.

McCANN, James, 1840-1904. A man of many parts, he started his career in the Hibernian Bank, Dublin, but became a stockbroker, retiring to improve his estates around Navan, Co. Meath in the 1890's. He was concerned at the high inland charges for transport of agricultural produce imposed by the railways. It was probably this that led him to champion inland waterways, becoming chairman of the Grand Canal Co. in 1891 and doing much to restore traffic. He also helped to form the new Boyne Navigation Co. in 1894 which he hoped would benefit the town of Navan at the head of this waterway. He remained chairman of the Grand until his death and was succeeded by his son until the canal was taken over by the CIE in 1950.

MACKELL, Robert, died 1779. He appears to have been involved with three preliminary surveys for the Forth & Clyde Canal. His canal would have been shallow, but Smeaton's ship canal proposals were accepted. Mackell became resident engineer in 1768 and seems to have been very quarrelsome and in some respects slack and corrupt. He pushed ahead and gained a change of line near Glasgow which saved expense. Quarrelling to the last he died with the canal still incomplete. He was also involved with projected canals in Strathmore and Clackmannanshire before his post with the Forth & Clyde.

McNIVEN, Charles. A Manchester man, first described as an architect, he did the parliamentary survey for the Manchester, Bolton & Bury Canal and was on the committee from 1791 to 1814 although never engineer. He worked on the Haslingden Canal project about 1793, but in 1794 he is heard of as a contractor with Robert Fulton for part of the Peak Forest; at the same time he was contracting for the Rochdale between Castlefield and Piccadilly. McNiven soon dropped out of the Fulton partnership, for he was probably by now working for the Mersey & Irwell Navigation. Later he was probably the engineer of the Runcorn & Latchford.

MALLET, John, c.1638. A Somerset landowner, he was wealthy enough to finance improvements to the rivers Parrett and Tone acting as surveyor and supervisor of the works.

MORRIS, Thomas. A Liverpool man, he was one of the Duke's team on the Bridgewater and was responsible for the embankment across the Bollin valley near Altrincham. His son Thomas worked for the Mersey & Irwell Navigation on the surveys for the Runcorn & Latchford Canal. The younger Morris was called in by the Weaver trustees for the Weston canal and basin at Weston Point, but the work was started in 1807 by their own engineer.

MYLNE, Robert, 1734-1811. His father was city surveyor for Edinburgh and called himself an architect, which profession Robert followed with some success, adding a considerable engineering practice. In 1767 he was made engineer to the New River Co, an appointment he held until his death. As an expert on water by virtue of his New River work he was consulted during the canal age. Thus in 1786 he gave evidence before a Bill to improve the Severn, and did a survey in 1790 of the river followed by some improvement works. During the following year he was recommending improvements to the Thames, including replacement of flash locks by pound locks. In 1792 he made what must have been a lightning post-chaise trip to Yorkshire to look over the line of the Stainforth & Keadby and Dearne & Dove Canals. It occupied four days while he spent one on the Sheffield Canal, although this did not go forward for many years. In 1793 he surveyed a canal from Bristol to Cirencester for the Thames & Severn, which was never built, and became engineer of the Gloucester & Berkeley Ship Canal after an initial survey and what turned out to be a serious under estimate. Because of his misleading costing and his quarrels with the resident engineer who was James Dadford, Mylne was dismissed in 1797 by the Gloucester committee. He was probably responsible for the elegant porticoed bridgemen's cottages on this canal. He was involved in surveys for the Grand Western, revising earlier lines of Robert Whitworth and Longbotham. Mylne worked on the Ouse above King's Lynn and designed harbours at Yarmouth and Wells in Norfolk.

NEWDIGATE, Sir Roger, 1719-1806. A colliery owner near Nuneaton in Warwickshire, he extended a system of small canals to transport coal from his mines at Griff, and carry materials on his Arbury estate, possibly started by his father, Sir Richard, who had proposed a canal to link the Trent and Severn. He was also an original shareholder in the Coventry Canal and the family had colliery interests in the Kirk Hallam district of Derbyshire. This second marriage, in 1776, was to Hester Margaretta, sister of Edward Miller Mundy of Shipley Hall near Kirk Hallam, likewise a colliery owner. These connections involved Sir Roger with the promotion of the Nutbrook Canal from the Erewash up to Shipley.

NIGHTINGALE, John, died 1814, was a nephew of Matthew Fletcher, planner of the Manchester, Bolton & Bury Canal. Its engineer, Charles Roberts, was found unsatisfactory and was dismissed in 1793. Fletcher as superintendent, gained the job for Nightingale. Later Nightingale left for the Mersey & Irwell Navigation. In about 1805 he was made their first manager cum engineer at the full-time salary of £500 a year, a high figure for the period. He started the Mersey & Irwell's passenger services between Manchester and Runcorn with new packet boats in 1807.

OMER, Thomas, was an engineer appointed by the Commissioners of Inland Navigation, for Ireland. Omer surveyed for and started many river improvements and tried some canal works. In 1755 he was working on the Shannon and on the Nore in Co Kilkenny, the works including a four mile canal built by his assistant William Ockenden. In about 1760 he was working on the Barrow and in Ulster from 1756 he worked on the Lagan. His improvements on the Boyne started in 1759 were not very satisfactory. His Grand Canal work had to be redone by later engineers, but he did complete the Newry Ship Canal in 1769.

OUTRAM, Benjamin, 1764-1805, was an ironmaster from Alfreton, Derbyshire, which led him to specialise in iron tramroads and from 1790 he was a partner in the Butterley Co., with Jessop and others. Prior to this he had been Jessop's assistant on the Cromford Canal. Later he became engineer for the Nutbrook Canal which had been surveyed by Jessop. A year earlier in 1792, Outram's assistant Thomas Brown had presented estimates for the Ashton Canal and in 1798 Outram contracted to cut the Ashton's extension to join the Rochdale. He was also involved with the Peak Forest and the Huddersfield acting as engineer. On the Huddersfield he tackled Stanedge tunnel with skill and energy but it was incomplete when he left in 1801. On the Peak Forest he is remembered for the 100 ft. high aqueduct at Marple and built the first iron aqueduct in the country on the Derby Canal. His later career was taken up with tramroads. Because of shortage of funds he built a tramroad down what later became Marple locks on the Peak Forest. In 1801 he reported on what became the Severn & Wye Railway from Lydney to Lydbrook via the Forest of Dean, and in 1799 recommended a tramroad at Combe Hay to link the two levels of the Somersetshire Coal Canal. He was responsible for the development of the flanged rail or plateway, but did not invent it.

OVERTON, George, probably trained as a colliery engineer, later owning collieries. He was a partner in the the Hirwaun ironworks above Aberdare and did some canal and much tramroad engineering. He came from Llanelly near Crickhowell. His first notable work was the Penydarren tramroad from Merthyr ironworks down to the Glamorganshire Canal opened in 1802. Because of his interest in the Hirwaun ironworks, from c.1806 until liquidation in 1812, he was interested in the Aberdare Canal and took over as engineer in 1811. Later he worked on Glamorganshire projects, proposing improvements in 1821 so that the canal could accommodate more deep sea ships in Cardiff.

OWEN, Richard, 1744-1830, came from Flixton on the Lancashire-Cheshire border. He started his engineering career in 1768 under the Duke of Bridgewater, and joined the Leeds & Liverpool in 1774. As the engineer from 1777, the Rufford branch was built and the canal reached Wigan, but he was discharged in 1782 and went to the Lagan Navigation which was struggling to reach Lough Neagh, building the section from Sprucefield to Ellis' Gut on the lough.

PALMER, William. A citizen of York, he was responsible for much early improvement to Yorkshire rivers. In 1722 with Joseph Atkinson and Joshua Mitchell he surveyed the Don from Doncaster to Sheffield as well as the lower river below Doncaster, showing that navigation was possible to Sheffield. The Don Act passed in 1726 and he was probably in charge of works above Doncaster and possibly below. He did surveys from York to Trent Falls on the Yorkshire Ouse, before the Act of 1727 and became engineer of the works. He achieved increased depth by narrowing the channel so that tidal scour was increased. Palmer was also consulted on Beverley Beck and in 1736 asked to do a survey of the Aire & Calder.

PERROTT, George, died 1780 and George Perrott his nephew, died 1806. A London lawyer of Yorkshire birth, George Perrott bought the Avon below Evesham in 1763 and undertook extensive repairs. His sucessful management of the river is evident today for the fine house he built in Bridge Street, Pershore, stands. On his death the river passed to his nephew, an Indian nabob, who returned to England in 1781. The nephew supported the Stratford Canal, sitting on the committee and becoming treasurer. He hoped that it would join the Avon, but never lived to see this. His son G.W.Perrott suceeded as owner, dying in 1831 and was in turn succeeded by Edmund Thomas Perrott.

PHILLIPS, John, an Essex man, he was a surveyor and builder, but had canal cutting experience since he seems to have worked on Harecastle tunnel and the Leeds & Liverpool. He retained an admiration for Brindley which colours his canal writings. In 1785 he published his "Treatise on Inland Navigation" about his proposed canal from London to Norwich and King's Lynn. Of much wider appeal was his 1792 book "A General History of Inland Navigation, Foreign and Domestic". This could not have come out at a better time, as the canal mania was getting under way. The book describes in detail the expanding canal system of the British Isles and its value to commerce, the first to do so, and it went through five editions.

PINKERTON, John died 1813, and James. Among the better known canal contractors, they seem to have come from the East Riding of Yorkshire, for James Pinkerton is first heard of in 1768 as a joint contractor for the Driffield Navigation. Then the brothers moved to the Market Weighton Canal authorized in 1772. From the mid-1770s the Pinkertons were associated with William Jessop's many works. Between 1775 and 1778 they were engaged on the Selby canal from the Aire to the Ouse. Then they moved to the Erewash in Derbyshire and cut it quickly, for it was open in 1779. Jessop employed John Pinkerton on the Calder & Hebble in 1779 to make the Shepley Bridge-Mirfield cut, and in 1785 John extended the Battye Ford cut above Mirfield. Both Jessop and John Pinkerton had a personal interest in the Calder & Hebble because they were joint owners of the dry dock at Mirfield and a colliery nearby. From 1783 the Pinkertons were under Jessop on the Trent and it was Jessop who in 1785 secured them the Dudley tunnel contract, given to John. Here they do not seem to have been successful for in 1787 John was stopped and the Canal took over.

At the same time as the Dudley, John Pinkerton was working on the Birmingham & Fazeley from 1786 to 1789, the year it was opened, though he was dismissed before completion. He had also contracted for the Broadwaters extension of the Birmingham Canal. From 1790 they were working for Jessop on the Sussex Ouse, being already on the Basingstoke Canal. Their Ouse work was bad. But Jessop had John Pinkerton on the Barnsley Canal and from 1792 he was contractor for parts of the Lancaster Canal with John Murray of Colne and both worked on the Ulverston Canal from 1793, but they gave up both contracts in 1795. John Pinkerton worked on the Gloucester & Berkeley and another Pinkerton after 1819 worked on the tunnel at Strood for the Thames & Medway. Brother James became engineer of the Kidwelly & Llanelly.

POWNALL, Robert, c.1715-1780. He became clerk of the Weaver navigation at Winsford in 1735 but seems to have been promoted because in 1757 he was surveying for improvements. A year later he was appointed inspector and superintendent of the navigation and rebuilt the lock and weir at Pickerings which had failed though only just completed by Henry Berry. In 1761 he became toll-collector at Northwich and accountant as well as engineer. He planned the deepening of Witton Brook, carried out in 1765. He resigned as toll-collector in 1778 but retained the other posts until his death.

PRAED, William 1749-1823. A member of the banking firm of Praed & Co. of Truro, he was a member of Parliament. He married in 1778 one of the Tyringhams from Tyringham near Newport Pagnell and moved to London banking, retaining his Cornish interests. As a Buckinghamshire landowner and banker, he led the promotion of the Grand Junction Canal, on the passage of its Act becoming chairman. He was a considerable shareholder, remaining as chairman until his death. He joined the committee of the Coventry over which the Grand Junction appears to have had influence, while he chaired the first promotion meeting in 1808 of the Grand Union. His son William Tyringham Praed was likewise a banker, his firm Praed & Box being treasurers of the Grand Junction.W.T. Praed joined the Grand Junction committee in 1809 and the Grand Union as soon as it was authorized. He influenced the Grand Union until the 1860s, while William stayed on the committee of the Grand Junction until his death (1846),while the last Praed did not leave until 1906.

PRIDDEY, John, served under Brindley on the Droitwich as resident engineer. He then moved to the Oxford as assistant clerk of works. In 1774 he surveyed for the Stroudwater with the younger Thomas Dadford and in 1781 did an early survey for the Thames & Severn before Whitworth was called in.

PRIESTLEY, Joseph (senior), c.1741-1817. He became book keeper to the clerk of works and accountant of the Leeds & Liverpool in 1770. In 1772 he acted as general manager and secretary of the company and after Robert Whitworth's death, engineer. He lived to see completion of the canal for which he had worked so hard and died in office at the age of 74.

PRIESTLEY, Joseph (junior), c.1767-1852. Son of Joseph Priestley, he became manager of the Wiltshire & Berkshire Canal. He became a shareholder in this and the North Wilts., Canal. He was on the committee of the Severn & Wye Railway & Canal Co., also. In 1816 he became chief clerk and land agent to the Aire & Calder Navigation with his office at Wakefield, remaining until retiring in 1851, a period which saw many improvements. He is best remembered for his book, an "Historical Account of the Navigable Rivers, Canals and Railways of Great Britain", of 1831, describing each company in alphabetical order. The book survived as a 'vade mecum' for canal and railway officials, carriers and manufacturers. The descriptions cover the authorizing act, route, length, engineering details, scale of tolls and nature of traffic.

PROVIS, William Alexander, died 1848. Probably the son of Henry Provis, a district engineer on the Grand Junction from 1802 to 1816, William was one of Telford's team and appears in 1810 as a draughtsman, preparing plans for the proposed Stamford Junction Navigation. He was on the Wyrley & Essington in 1826, surveying for a link between this and the Staffs. & Worcs., and also worked on a new reservoir for the latter. He estimated in 1828 for a canal from Aylesbury to Abingdon to meet the Wilts. & Bucks.,an old idea, and in 1829 was involved with J.U.Rastrick and William Fowler in surveys for the Stourbridge Extension Canal. He is best known as a contractor from 1829 for the Birmingham & Liverpool Junction. He also contracted for the Newport branch and Knighton reservoir. In 1836 he became contractor for the new works at Ellesmere Port under Cubitt.

RASTRICK, John Urpeth, 1780-1856. Among the earlier railway engineers, he came from Morpeth in Northumberland. His father was a mechanical engineer and the son went about 1801 to work at Ketley iron foundry. Later he was a partner with John Hazeldine at an ironworks in Bridgnorth. At the same time he completed the Shutt End Railway opened in 1829 and was called on to survey a canal line to Shut End (the modern spelling) from the Stourbridge Canal, but this was dropped, later revived as the Stourbridge Extension Canal for which he surveyed and estimated but declined to be engineer. He was at this time engineer of the Staffs. & Worcs., and had been involved with the Leominster Canal's ideas to reach the Severn via a tramroad. In Leicestershire he was consulted in 1833 over reviving the Forest line of the Leicester Navigation by building a tramroad to Charnwood collieries.

RAYNER, Frank, died 1945. Born in Nottingham, his province was the Trent, which he joined in 1887 as a junior engineer, at a time when the river's fortunes were at a low ebb. In 1896 he became engineer to the Trent Navigation and later general manager. He undertook some much needed improvements, but real modernization did not come until after the Act of 1906. He returned in 1919 from war service to find the river in danger of complete closure, but saved by Nottingham Corporation. He resigned in 1928 because of ill health but remained consultant engineer and was given a seat on the board which he retained until death.

RENNIE John, 1761-1821, and sons George Rennie, 1791-1866, and Sir John Rennie 1794-1874. John Rennie came from a prosperous East Lothian farming family and was apprenticed to a local millwright, Andrew Meikle. He started himself in 1799 as a millwright, but took time off to attend Edinburgh University. In 1783 he did a tour of engineering works in England including a visit to Boulton & Watt, whose service he entered the following year, being put in charge of mill work at the new steam driven Albion flour mills at Blackfriars, London. Completion of the mills brought Rennie international fame and many other commissions. He built his first bridge in 1784 in Mid-Lothian and in 1788 was making his first canal surveys for three waterway schemes which proved abortive, from Bishop's Stortford to the Little Ouse, from Basingstoke to Salisbury and from Bury St. Edmunds to the Suffolk Stour. In 1790 he became involved with the major Kennet & Avon scheme for which he did surveys, becoming engineer in 1794. It was his biggest single work, but not well engineered, the summit level being too short. He used ornamental masonry work of Bath stone which gave trouble as it was unseasoned, but the aqueducts were successful. In 1791 he was introduced to the Lancaster and the Rochdale. The Rochdale took him on because William Jessop and Robert Whitworth were too busy, although Rennie had not yet built a canal. On the Rochdale he was assisted by William Crosley who probably did most of the work, as he had already done some surveys. Certainly for the 1794 Bill he did most of the work, Rennie having little connection with the canal by that time. On the Lancaster, Rennie did the surveys and became engineer when the Act passed. In 1792 he reported on the Ipswich & Stowmarket Navigation and directed surveys of the Chelmer. In 1799 he advised

on the Horncastle Canal and in 1801 reported on the Ancholme, with which his son Sir John was to be
associated in 1824, the new lock and sluice at South Ferriby being completed in 1844 to Sir John's design.
The elder Rennie was engineer of the Crinan and at the same time surveyed for the Caledonian. He worked on the Glasgow, Paisley & Johnstone in 1800, on a scheme for a canal parallel with Loch Ken in
Kirkcudbrightshire, schemes in the 1790s for canals in central Scotland, and acted as consultant to the
Aberdeenshire Canal. In the North of England, he surveyed the Ulverston Canal of which he became the
engineer in 1793. He was also later associated with the High Peak Junction Canal between the Peak Forest
and the Cromford. He did a survey in 1810 but the canal was not built. In 1795 he advised on the Foss
Navigation and found the work of their engineer, Moon, very poor, so the latter was dismissed. In the
South he had! grandiose ideas for inland water communication. Following the Kennet & Avon, he directed
William Smith's surveys for the Somersetshire Coal Canal and was himself responsible for laying out a
continuation of the Kennet & Avon from Bath to Bristol, but it was not built because of local opposition. He
was interested in a canal to join the English and Bristol Channels, surveying and becoming engineer of the
Grand Western. In 1809 he was recommending a small ship canal from Seaton, Devon across to Combwich
at the mouth of the Parrett and in 1810 varied his ideas when he surveyed a canal from Taunton to Bristol
as part of a London to Exeter inland navigation route. Another interest was water communication between
the Thames and the Channel. Having advised on the Croydon Canal, he proposed in 1803, to extend it to
Portsmouth. In 1809 he advised the Thames Commissioners on the river between Staines and Boulter's
Lock, locks being built as a result. Then there was the Grand Southern scheme of 1810 from the Medway
to Portsmouth and the Weald of Kent Canal scheme in 1812. When the Portsmouth & Arundel was authorized
in 1817 Rennie was the engineer. He was also consultant for the Royal Military Canal and reported on a
scheme to flood the Lee valley as an anti-invasion measure. The Aire & Calder called on him to improve
their line to the Humber and his report laid down plans for what became the Knottingley-Goole Canal. He
also worked on improvements to the Leeds line which were carried out after his death. At the same time,
1819, that he was on the Aire & Calder, Rennie produced a scheme for a bypass canal for the lower Don,
this never went ahead. In 1812 and 1816 he was called on to advise on a canal from the Tees to the
collieries of south-west Durham. In Ireland he advised on the expensive Royal Canal, in 1808 made a
survey for a canal from Larne to Lough Neagh, and in 1821, surveyed the Shannon. He was also a notable
harbour and dock engineer with London Docks and Plymouth breakwater to his credit. He also designed
London bridge which was completed by his son in 1830, the year the latter was knighted. He was consulted on Fens drainage and worked on the Witham from 1801 and the Fossdyke from 1804. More was done
by his son Sir John. The elder Rennie co-operated with Telford on the Eau Brink Cut to improve the Great
Ouse above King's Lynn and the Nene Outfall built after his death.

His sons George and Sir John did less canal engineering, but were eminent in other fields. In 1825 they
surveyed a canal from London to Portsmouth and were consulted over rival proposals of Elmes and Cundy.
In 1846 Sir John was involved with the abortive Langstone Docks and Ship Canal project at Portsmouth. They
also reported on the unsatisfactory state of the Portsmouth & Arundel Canal in 1827, recommending dredging
Portsea Creek. Sir John was called on by the Aire & Calder in 1824 to recommend improvements and in
1837 he surveyed a possible ship canal from Liverpool to Warrington which could be extended to Manchester.
He was consulted on improvements to the Newry Ship Canal and the minor Glastonbury ship canal for which
he revised the original plans in 1828. In 1834 Denver sluice was rebuilt to Sir John's designs, while in
1839 he put forward an ambitious and typically Rennie idea for a common Wash outfall for the Witham,
Welland, Nene and Ouse.

REYNOLDS, William, 1758-1803, was associated with the Darbys of Coalbrookdale and was the son of Richard
Reynolds, a Bristol iron merchant, who in 1757 married Hannah Darby grand-daughter of the first Abraham. On his
marriage he acquired a half share in the new Ketley works and in 1758 his son William was born. William
became manager at the age of about 28 and brought a scientific mind to ironfounding and better transport.
Tramroads were introduced to eastern Shropshire, the Coalbrookdale Co. casting rails as early as 1767,
but for bulk haulage, canals were more attractive. However canals were a problem in this hilly country
where water drained away through mine workings, and were only possible because Reynolds built to a
small gauge for tub-boats which could be carried down inclined planes. His first plane, the first in England,
was completed in 1788 on his private canal from Oakengates down to Ketley for which, as he said, he was
'head and subschemer, Engineer & Director'. At about this time he completed the Wombridge
Canal, but more ambitious was his promotion of the publicly subscribed Shropshire Canal for which he acted
as engineer. He also subscribed to the much larger Shrewsbury Canal. Here he provided the design and
ironwork for the aqueduct over the Tern at Longdon.

RHODES, Thomas, 1789-1868. One of the Telford team, Rhodes worked as resident engineer on the
Caledonian until 1822, when he moved to Wales to take charge of the chain link assembly for the Menai
suspension bridge. In 1831 he surveyed the Shannon from its source to Limerick on behalf of a
Government Commission. In 1841 he did some survey work on the Barrow. In 1836 he surveyed the Severn
for a proposed Severn Navigation Co, one of several concerns trying to improve this difficult river. In
the same year on behalf of the Staffs. & Worcs., he surveyed a canal from Hinksford to the Stourbridge
Extension. Two years earlier he had been on the Yorkshire Ouse, making a detailed survey from Linton
lock above York, to Selby. He surveyed the Yorkshire Derwent in 1837 and improvements were made.

ROBINSON, Thomas, c.1730, In 1730 he was appointed 'surveyor general' of the Weaver works to start the
improvements sanctioned in 1721. His appointment was ended in 1735, but he advised as late as 1753.

ROLLE, John, Lord Rolle, 1750-1842. With estates in north Devon the family were keen to improve them
by use of lime and sea sand as fertilisers. Denys Rolle projected a tub-boat canal up to Torrington for
this task in 1793, but died in 1797 and nothing was done until 1823 when the canal was cut by his son John.

ROOTH, John, c.1800. A Manchester canal carrier, he was keen to start in business on the Ashton and
Huddersfield Canals. In 1800 Stanedge tunnel was incomplete, but he started carrying on the Lancashire
side. The Huddersfield took him on as superintendent for this side from February 1801 and by April was
superintendent of the whole canal. By October he was in charge of Stanedge tunnel and using direct
labour on two headings he completed the tunnel in 1811. He remained superintendent or agent until 1817
when he was dismissed to make way for a younger man.

SANDYS, Sir William, c.1600-1669. Aptly nicknamed William 'Water-work' Sandys, he came from Fladbury
near Evesham on the Avon which he improved using his own time, money and engineering knowledge. Granted
Letters Patent by Charles I in 1636, Sandys, aided by the local influence of his cousin Lord Windsor, had
completed the work by 1639. He was by this time a Member of Parliament but in 1641 lost his seat and his
control of the Avon, accused of establishing a monopoly by virtue of his right to charge tolls on the river.
He had ideas of improving the Arrow down from Redditch and Alcester, possibly the Warwickshire Stour,
and certainly he had been granted powers to improve the Teme, but the Civil War prevented any work.

After the Restoration, he was appointed in 1664 to make the Wye and Lugg navigable. His work did not last and by the end of the century the rivers had reverted to their unimproved state.

SANER, John Arthur, 1864-1952. In 1885 L.B. Wells was succeeded on the Weaver by Saner as engineer and later also as manager until 1934. Under Wells and Saner the navigation improvements recommended by Leader Williams were carried out. Saner converted the Anderton lift to electric power and designed the two electric swing bridges at Northwich, and later the floating swing bridges at Sutton and Acton. He advocated a modern waterways system in Britain in his paper to the Institution of Civil Engineers in November 1905. It described how they should be modernized and extended, anticipating the 1906-9 Royal Commission.

SHEASBY, Thomas (senior), The Thomas Sheasbys, father and son formed a partnership quite often working together. The elder Sheasby was associated with the elder Dadford on the Coventry who also advised on the aqueduct over the Tame near Fazeley, but Sheasby built it. He worked for the Birmingham & Fazeley on their part of the Coventry, from Fazeley to Whittington Brook and was, along with John Pinkerton a contractor for the Birmingham & Fazeley itself. From 1789 to 1791 he worked with the elder Dadford as a contractor on the Cromford. He then moved to South Wales, working with the Dadfords on the Glamorganshire as engineer contractors. In 1792 Sheasby moved to the Neath Canal, succeeding the younger Thomas Dadford. Then in 1794 he was arrested with the elder Dadford by the Glamorganshire company. They had refused to repair a breach unless money was advanced and withdrew their men. This ended Sheasby's employment by the Neath. Although not at first the Swansea's engineer, he took over in 1796, having acted as assistant to Charles Roberts from 1795. He stayed until 1799 and was succeeded by his son who had been helping since 1796. The younger Thomas left in 1802.

SIMCOCK, Samuel, was one of Brindley's pupils and assistants. Simcock (or Simcox) like the others, did the real work, while Brindley rushed from scheme to scheme. Simcock with Hugh Henshall, surveyed the line of the Staffs. & Worcs., before its Act of 1766 and afterwards, although Brindley superintended, Simcock and Thomas Dadford senior were the men on the spot. Again when the Birmingham was authorized, Brindley was made engineer but Simcock, Dadford and Robert Whitworth acted for him and similarly Simcock laid out the line and superintended cutting of the Oxford. The winding course between Brinklow and Banbury was probably his work. He worked with Robert Whitworth to finish the Oxford, surveying from Banbury to Oxford in 1779. Later he was a member of a syndicate including Samuel Weston, formed to complete the Oxford out of their own resources, but only repair work was done.

SMEATON, John, 1724-1792. Britain's first professional civil engineer, in 1771 he and his associates formed the Smeatonian Society, predecessor of the Institution of Civil Engineers founded in 1818. His father was a lawyer in Leeds and Smeaton was intended to follow the same profession. He could not settle and his father released him with a generous allowance. Established in London, Smeaton entered the workshop of an instrument maker. In 1750 he set up his own instrument making business which was not successful. He researched into windmill sails and waterwheels, building 4 windmills and 43 watermills during his life, all overshadowed by his completion of the Eddystone Rock lighthouse off Plymouth. While engaged on the lighthouse he was invited to undertake his first navigation work on the Calder in the West Riding. He was too busy to go in 1756, but did a survey the following year based on earlier work of Thomas Steers and John Eyes. When the Calder & Hebble Act passed, Smeaton was made part-time engineer. The Eddystone was completed in August 1759 and Smeaton arrived on the Calder in May 1760. His assistant was Joseph Nickalls who had worked on the lighthouse and on the locks they used the same kind of quick drying cement. Smeaton was not appreciated on the Calder for, in 1765 he was replaced by Brindley. Although opened to Salterhebble in 1767 the navigation was closed the following year because of flood damage. Smeaton had already returned to do repairs before the floods and he was associated with moves to reopen the navigation. In 1779 he recommended lock alterations. During the 1760s he was surveying the Ouse above York, proposing the lock at Linton, and looked over the Ure, the improvement Acts passing in 1767. In 1765 he advised on the upper Hull and a navigation to Driffield, authorized in 1767. In 1766 he surveyed the Great Ouse to Denver and was associated with Yeoman in a report on the Lee Navigation. He had in 1762 surveyed the Chelmer with which Yeoman became involved. Also in about 1762 he had advised on the Fossdyke in Lincoln, while in 1760 he had reported on the Louth Navigation. As early as 1761 Smeaton was giving some thought to the Trent-Mersey canal, considering a canal to join the Weaver. More rewarding were his Scottish and Irish associations. In 1764 he was asked by the Government to survey a canal between the Forth and the Clyde, he proposed two routes for small craft and later ships. He was made engineer with the quarrelsome Mackell under him, and resigned in 1773, having built a splendid summit level. He was asked to help on the Grand in 1771 and went in 1773, taking his young assistant William Jessop. They revised the lock work and built across the Bog of Allen, but his shallow cut was to need considerable embanking to overcome subsidence. He examined Jessop's report on the inclined planes on the Coalisland Canal extension, then returning to England. In 1772 he had reported on improvements for the Aire & Calder proposing dredging, new cuts, locks and two canals to bypass much of the lower river, resulting in the Selby canal. In his last years he engineered canals in the Birmingham area. He built the Birmingham Co's Broadwaters line part way to Walsall and the Birmingham & Fazeley, opened in 1789. His last work was lowering of Brindley's summit at Smethwick to the Wolverhampton level, accomplished by 1790. In 1778 he put forward ideas for a navigation between Bude and the Tamar using rivers and a canal, and suggested a canal or tramroad to serve Cann quarries near Plymouth, while in 1775 he reported on what became the Nent Force level into Alston mines. He also built bridges and harbours, notably Ramsgate.

SMITH, George, of Coalville, 1831-1895. Born near Tunstall, the son of a Staffordshire brickmaker, he worked from the age of 7 in a brickyard, owning one near Longnor, before he moved into Leicestershire as a brickyard manager, from 1857 at Coalville near Ashby-de-la-Zouch, identifying himself with the place so that he always signed himself George Smith of Coalville. He was an ardent philanthropist and felt himself 'marked out by Divine Providence for special work', the salvation of child labour in the brickyards. In 1873 he plunged into a crusade for the salvation of the children of the canal boats. He started a press campaign culminating in the appearance in 1875 of his book 'Our Canal Population. A Cry from the Boat Cabins'. As a result of his work aided by that of the factory inspectors, a government Bill, the Canal Boats Act, was passed in 1877. Smith saw the Act as inadequate, in 1880 leaving Coalville for Welton near Daventry and continuing his work. He produced a second book, 'Canal Adventures by Moonlight'. An amending Bill was introduced in 1881, finally passing in 1884, ordering local authorities to carry out regular inspections.

SMITH, George Samuel Fereday, 1812-1878. James Loch became superintendent of the Duke of Bridgewater's trust in 1837 and for the canal and collieries needed a competent deputy. He approached William Smith, mine agent to the trustees of the first Earl of Dudley, but the trust would not release him and instead he got his son George, only 25 years old but of proven ability. Smith brought enthusiasm for improvement and modernisation but was frustrated by Loch. Smith was anxious to proceed with improvements at Runcorn but nothing was done until after Loch's death in 1855. The new superintendent was the Earl of Ellesmere's third son, the Hon. Algernon Fulke Egerton, who knew nothing of canals and relied heavily on Smith, who proceeded rapidly with the Runcorn & Weston Canal, a new tidal basin and the Alfred dock hydraulic cranes.

SMITH, William, 1769-1839. From Oxfordshire, he trained as a surveyor, working in 1793 under John Rennie. In 1795 he became surveyor under William Bennett of the Somersetshire Coal Canal,, having the previous year toured the country inspecting canal and tramroad works. Smith had a parallel interest, that of geology, which much aided his canal surveying. He discovered the basic principles of rock strata and in 1801 published a map showing the rock formations of England and Wales. By this time he had left the Canal, sacked because he mixed private and Canal business. He was recalled in 1811-12 to deal with leakage, at a time when he was engineer to the improvement works on the Sussex Ouse. Later he surveyed for the Aire & Dun scheme and the Went & Wakefield. His main concern was now geology, publishing a great strata map in 1815, and raising English geology to a serious science.

SOROCOLD, George, died 1717. Variously spelt Sorrowcold, Seracoll and Seracold, he probably came from Derby where he displayed various talents, rehanging church bells, in 1692-3 providing the town with a water supply and in 1702 preparing plans to make the Derwent navigable up to Derby. Earlier he had built a waterworks for Leeds (1694-5) and worked on surveys for the Yorkshire Derwent (1695-1700), and undertook improvements to London Bridge water pumps. His claim to national fame was England's first wet dock at Rotherhithe completed in 1700.

SOTHERN, James, His father Benjamin had served the third duke of Bridgewater as manager of works as early as 1782, and on the Duke's death in 1803 Benjamin became principal agent and inspector of the navigation, in effect general manager, until 1826. His superior was Robert Haldane Bradshaw who in 1813 took on the young James Sothern as personal assistant. In 1832 Bradshaw made him principal agent and in 1833 deputy superintendent in succession to his son. When in 1834 Bradshaw was persuaded to retire, Loch, agent to the trust's life renter, had to accept him as superintendent. He proved exceptionally unsatisfactory as he wanted to be independent of Loch and Lord Francis Egerton, the latter paying him to retire in 1837.

SPENCER, Arnold, 1587-1655. Born at Cople near Bedford, he inherited local estates and in 1618 was granted Letters Patent to improve his local river, the Great Ouse between St. Ives and St. Neots. He planned and undertook the task at his own expense and by about 1631 the works were ready. He then pressed on to Bedford but only reached Great Barford. The Civil War (1642-1645) ruined him and he had to mortgage the navigation. It also prevented any work on the Suffolk Stour for which he obtained Letters Patent in 1638.

STANHOPE, Charles, 3rd Earl Stanhope, 1753-1816. He was a man of science being elected a Fellow of the Royal Society at 19. His work was very diverse. His interest in canals was aroused as his land at Holsworthy would benefit from the proposed tub-boat canal from Bude Bay. He gave much thought to the planes needed and with his ideas in mind it was resurveyed in 1793. He was also a promotor of the Regent's Canal favouring locks with side ponds to Congreve's lift. Earlier he had backed the Nutbrook Canal which would serve his ironworks at Dale.

STAVELEY, Christopher (senior). The father worked under William Jessop on the Leicester Navigation reporting on the project in 1790. The younger Staveley became surveyor of the works under Jessop, while the father was made engineer on completion in 1795. Previously the elder Christopher had worked with John Varley on the parliamentary survey for the Leicestershire & Northamptonshire Union, authorized in 1793.

STAVELEY, Christopher (junior), died 1827. The Staveleys stuck to local Leicestershire projects, in 1790 the younger Christopher under Jessop's direction surveyed for the Wreak navigation to Melton Mowbray, following this up with surveys for the Oakham Canal again under Jessop. He became engineer of the Oakham but gave it up in 1797. He stayed with the Leicestershire until his death, as engineer and superintendent and was succeeded by his son Edward who had been appointed joint engineer with his father in 1825. The son bolted in 1833 with £1400 owing to the company. Neither it nor Edward Staveley could be traced.

STEERS, Thomas, c. 1672-1750. Originally an army officer, probably an engineer, Steers may have lived for a while in the Low Countries, although he came from Kent. He settled in Rotherhithe and worked under George Sorocold on England's first wet dock. It was completed in 1700 and Steers became involved with Sorocold in planning a wet dock for Liverpool, in 1709 being put in charge of construction. In 1712 he surveyed the rivers Mersey and Irwell, promoting it as a navigation and acting as engineer. He also surveyed the Douglas from the Ribble to Wigan and later became principal promoter of this navigation. He was also involved with the Weaver which received its Act in 1721. Apart from schemes in north-west England;   assisted: Henry Berry between 1736 and 1741, surveying and building a summit level canal in Ulster from the Bann above Portadown over to Newry, completed as the Newry Navigation, the first canal with a summit level in Britain. Steers however did not start the project. He surveyed Worsley Brook about 1736, for the Mersey & Irwell, who wanted to make the Brook navigable. Finally in 1740-1, with John Eyes he planned the proposed Calder & Hebble Navigation from Wakefield to Halifax.

STEVENS, Harry William, 1887-1970. For about 150 years the barge owning Stevens family of Guildford were connected with the Wey Navigation, from 1812 when William Stevens became lock keeper at Triggs, to 1963 when Harry Stevens decided to pass the river to the National Trust, his family having acquired it c. 1900.

TELFORD, Thomas, 1757-1834. Born in Eskdale near Langholm, he was a stonemason, helping to build local bridges and farmhouses before moving to Edinburgh and in 1782, London. He was lucky to be noticed by William Pulteney who gave Telford several commissions, as a kind of building surveyor or even as architect, planning and estimating for alterations. In 1784 he was working on buildings in Portsmouth dockyard and two years later restored Shrewsbury Castle owned by Pulteney. At Shrewsbury in 1788 Pulteney got him the job of Surveyor of Public Works for the County of Salop, so Telford had come a long way in 6 years. In 1793 he was made 'General Agent, Surveyor, Engineer, Architect and Overlooker of the Works' of the newly authorized Ellesmere Canal, part-time under Jessop, the principal engineer and retaining his County Surveyor's post. Two years later, in 1795, he was made engineer to the Shrewsbury Canal, on Josiah Clowes' death. He remained on the Ellesmere until 1805, when Pontcysyllte was completed. With experience embracing bridge, road and canal construction he was increasingly in demand. Since 1796 he had been associated with the British Fisheries Society, which was committed to rehabilitation of the Highlands. On their instructions he prepared plans in 1801-2 for what became the Caledonian Canal, for which he was appointed engineer. It was a hard struggle involving the greatest earthworks and structures he was ever called upon to undertake, and from 1816 he was also responsible for the Crinan Canal. He also carried out other road and bridge works in the Highlands completed in 1824. Telford   advised and helped with the Glasgow, Paisley & Johnstone and the Edinburgh & Glasgow Union, on the latter helping the engineer Hugh Baird to such an extent that the aqueducts were copies of Telford's   at Chirk.

Telford went over to Sweden to survey the Göta canal. This was built on the Caledonian model and opened in 1832. In 1809 he was called to advise on the Weaver's Weston Canal and basin. In 1810 he was consulted on the Holyhead road. The works were completed in 1826 with the opening of Menai and Conway suspension bridges. He was appointed consultant engineer to the Exchequer Bill Loan Commissioners in 1817. He had to vet schemes applying for help, bringing him into contact with many canals. He examined the Bude and took charge of the Gloucester & Berkeley, where work resumed in 1819. In Ireland he looked over the Ulster Canal. He was consulted about 1818 on a projected canal to Knaresborough and in 1825 surveyed for an extension of the Gloucester & Berkeley, the so-called Worcester & Gloucester Union. The previous year he had worked on the English & Bristol Channels Ship Canal survey and commenced a scheme to improve the Kentish Stour, as well as reporting on the Scarsdale & High Peak proposal. He was involved in the Wirral ship canal scheme from the Mersey to the Dee and was engineer of the proposed London & Birmingham Junction Canal. In 1824 he surveyed the Birmingham Canal Navigations' main line for much needed improvements. He suggested the twin towpaths, the cutting at Smethwick and the cast iron overbridges. As their consulting engineer, he recommended the improvements for the Ellesmere which were made at Ellesmere Port after his death. He laid out the line of the Middlewich branch and in 1827 rebuilt the two Beeston locks on the Chester Canal. His Birmingham work led him to consider a new canal to the Mersey which would join at Nantwich with the Ellesmere and Chester. This the Birmingham & Liverpool Junction, proved to be his last canal work. He was too old to take much part in the work giving place to William Cubitt in 1833. Contemporary with this canal work, he was completing a new Harecastle tunnel for the Trent & Mersey. Telford was connected with the Macclesfield Canal, carrying out a survey in 1825. He was asked in 1827 to report on the Aire & Calder's proposed improvements to their navigation above Ferrybridge both to Leeds and to Wakefield. His most notable recommendation was the aqueduct over the Calder at Stanley Ferry. He worked with the elder John Rennie to build Eau Brink Cut on the Great Ouse, which was completed in 1821, and undertook drainage work in the North Level. He partnered the younger John Rennie in another project of his father's, a new outfall for the Nene, started in 1827.

TENNANT, George, 1765-1832. His father was a solicitor in Wigan but George became interested in South Wales affairs when he bought the Rhyddings estate near Neath in 1816, followed by Cadoxton Lodge. He then made the largest private canal system in the country except for the Bridgewater. He opened the Red Jacket canal in 1818, followed by a connection built at great expense to himself, to join the Neath Canal, completed in 1824, the year he published "Neath and Swansea Red Jacket & Neath Canals. Narrative of some Particulars relating to their formation etc.", a book describing his works. He happily paid his workmen but was glad that nobody else's money was involved, since he was not too sanguine about prospects.

THOMAS, Hubert and Thomas, Gordon Cale. Hubert Thomas was appointed engineer of the Grand Junction Canal in 1864 and was responsible for the Slough branch. He remained as engineer until 1891 when he was succeeded by his son Gordon Cale Thomas. Hubert now became company secretary and took part in the purchase by the Grand Junction of the Leicestershire & Northamptonshire Union and Grand Union Canals. G. C. Thomas was involved with plans to widen the Leicester line and he planned the Foxton inclined plane, with his cousin B. J. Thomas of Thomas & Taylor, civil engineering consultants of Westminster. Construction began in 1898 with B. J. Thomas as resident engineer. Both father and son worked on the water supply to Tring summit. Owing to suspect accounts G. C. Thomas was dismissed in 1916; he then joined the army. Hubert Thomas had retired in 1905.

TOWNSEND, Chauncy, was a wealthy merchant and London alderman, as well as Member of Parliament for Westbury, Wilts. He became interested in mineral development in South Wales about 1749, leasing coal at Eaglesbush near Neath and later developed coal workings west of the Tawe valley. It was here in the Llanelly area that he had canals built feeding down to the Loughor River, the Dafen and the Yspitty in about 1770, both later owned by General Warde and named after the latter.

TRAIL, John, was apparently an engineer of some experience as he was engaged as a contractor in 1768 and later in 1772, engineer when the Grand Canal Co. was formed. He said he was an expert at building waterways through bog land, but ran into difficulties with lock work. His task was to replace the earlier efforts of Thomas Omer. After considerable dissension with the company over accounts, he resigned in 1777.

TURNER, Joseph, was employed by the Chester Canal as engineer from 1779 to at least 1794. He was a member of the committee from 1778 to 1805, suggesting he was an amateur engineer. In 1791 with John Duncombe, he surveyed for the projected Ellesmere Canal. He may have been related to another engineer, William Turner, who worked on the Ellesmere.

TURNER, William. A Warrington man described as an architect, he was involved in the Ellesmere Canal, producing a route in 1791, later helping Jessop with the parliamentary survey and becoming assistant engineer with John Duncombe. Probably an amateur, he was responsible for the design of the masonry aqueduct at Pontcysyllte and for that first suggested at Chirk. When proposals for cast iron aqueducts were accepted, Turner's work was scrapped.

VARLEY, John, was one of Brindley's team. In 1769 he did a survey for the Greasbrough Canal off the Don near Rotherham. Then he comes to notice as clerk of works on the Chesterfield, becoming resident engineer on Brindley's death, under Hugh Henshall's superintendence, who found his Norwood tunnel work far from satisfactory. As engineer of the Erewash he got his accounts muddled and his levels wrong and was dismissed in 1780. However in 1791 he did an early survey for what became the Nutbrook on behalf of the Erewash. Working under William Jessop on surveying the Leics. & Northants., Union, in 1792, he later became resident engineer and met trouble in Saddington tunnel. In 1800 he was considered as a contractor for Stanedge tunnel, since he was already on the canal doing flood control work. He did a little in the tunnel, but the company ordered him to cease because of his poor reputation.

VERMUYDEN, Sir Cornelius, c. 1590-1677. Vermuyden, by his drainage works, created a new pattern of waterways in the West Riding of Yorkshire and the Fens. He came from the island of Tholen in Zeeland, but in 1624 was naturalized in England. His first English work was to repair the breach at Dagenham on the Thames. King James I invited him to undertake drainage both in the Fens and on Hatfield Chase, east of Doncaster. He started the latter in 1626 with Dutch partners under an agreement with Charles I. Their work diverted the Don's Trent outlet into the Aire channel resulting in flooding on the lower Aire and they were compelled to cut a new channel for the Don parallel with the Aire. He was knighted for his success in 1629. His largest task was draining the Level between the Great Ouse and the Nene. The first stage was completed in 1637, the second, for Charles I, who in 1639 replaced the Earl of Bedford as Undertaker. He cut the two Bedford rivers as straight drainage channels from Earith to Denver. In 1655 he quarrelled with the 5th Earl of Bedford and left the works. He had other interests, a lead mine at Wirksworth, Derbyshire and estates on Sedgemoor and at Malvern.

WALKER, James, 1781-1862. Born at Falkirk, he started his engineering career in 1800 under his uncle

Ralph Walker who was then working on the East and West India docks on the Thames. James became an expert and was appointed engineer to the Commercial docks on the Thames in 1806. In Scotland he worked under Telford repairing the Crinan Canal between 1816 and 1818, and later on the Caledonian. He was consulted over improvement of the Severn, preparing a report for the Gloucester & Berkeley Canal in 1841 and in 1852 for the Admiralty. Another James Walker, a grandson of Ralph Walker, worked on the Birmingham canals, completing the Bentley Canal in 1843 and the Tame Valley in 1844. Between 1855 and 1858 he was in charge of the Netherton tunnel works. In 1836 he may have been the engineer of the abortive Tonbridge-Penshurst canal.

WATT, James, 1736-1819, is little rememembered as a competent canal surveyor. In 1767 he was joint surveyor of a canal between the Forth and Clyde and in 1769-70 surveyed the Monkland Canal, accepting the superintendence of its construction. In 1770 he was surveying a canal from Perth to Forfar, followed by surveys on the Clyde and at Port Glasgow. In 1771 he surveyed Ayr harbour and the proposed Crinan Canal as well as one from Arrochar on Loch Long to Tarbet on Loch Lomond. In 1773 he surveyed the rivers Forth, Gudie and Devon for navigation, also a canal from Paisley to Hurlet, a canal across Kintyre from Campbeltown to Macrihanish and finally a canal through the Great Glen, eventually built as the Caledonian. The turning point in his career occurred in 1773; a financial panic caused work on the Monkland to cease, his Scottish patron John Roebuck, for whom he had built his first steam engine, went bankrupt, while in the September his wife died. The following year he moved to Matthew Boulton's works in Birmingham, but he continued to be associated with canals; he was on the committee of the Birmingham Canal Navigations from 1804 until his death, while in 1788 he had judged, with John Wilkinson, designs of inclined planes for the Shropshire Canal.

WEDGWOOD, Josiah, 1730-1795. Born the thirteenth child of a family of Burslem potters, Josiah although crippled from smallpox, became a practical potter at an early age, apprenticed to his brother Thomas. In about 1759 he set up on his own at Ivy House, Burslem. He was successful, moving in 1762 to Bell Works, Burslem. He welcomed the idea of a canal and in 1765 with Dr. Erasmus Darwin and Thomas Bentley, he started promoting the Trent & Mersey Canal. After Brindley's survey, Wedgwood enlisted the patronage of Lord Gower. When the Act passed he became treasurer although not an original shareholder, possibly because he wished to appear disinterested. With the line of the canal fixed he was able to select a site on the waterway for his new factory, Etruria works, opened in 1769.

WELDON, Robert, died 1805. A native of Lichfield, with ideas on canal boat lifts, demonstrating a model of one in 1794 at Oakengates, Shropshire, as the result of an approach by Weldon to the Somersetshire Coal Canal. The latter were impressed enough to build a trial lift at Combe Hay. One of the trials was watched by the Prince of Wales, but it was not a success and he faded into obscurity. See under lifts.

WESTON, Sir Richard, 1591-1652. A landowner of Sutton in Surrey, he became one of the new baronets in 1622. To facilitate transport between Surrey and London, notably of flour and timber, he made plans to improve the Wey in 1635, up to Guildford. The Civil War (1642-45) prevented this and as he was a royalist Catholic he fled to Flanders in 1644, but returned in 1649 and started work in 1651 on the Wey. He died before completion and it was finished in 1653 by his son George.

WESTON, Samuel, started under Brindley as a survey staff holder and then did cutting contract work on the Leeds & Liverpool. He surveyed for the Chester Canal in 1770 and became its engineer, but was dismissed in 1774 after evidence of bad workmanship. In 1785 the Oxford company commissioned him to survey the Cherwell from Banbury to Oxford and the River Swift between Cosford near Rugby and Lutterworth with a view to a navigation. In 1786 he, Simcock and four others were preparing to form a syndicate to complete the Oxford from their own resources but it never got under way and only repairs were done. Later, with Simcock, he surveyed the Hampton Gay Canal (London & Western). He and his son John Weston were contractors on the Wirral line of the Ellesmere between 1793 and 1796.

WHITWORTH, Robert (senior), died 1799. Second only to William Jessop in the number of schemes he undertook, he was trained under Brindley, becoming an accomplished draughtsman, assisting Simcock and Dadford on the Birmingham. Also under Brindley's direction he was surveying for the Oxford in 1768. He was associated with the elder Dadford again on the Coventry Canal's extension from Atherstone to Fazeley. Brindley entrusted him with a great deal of work. Thus, in 1768 he was advising on the Lagan Navigation, surveying for a canal later built as the Stockton & Darlington Railway and the following year surveying a canal from the Exe to Uphill near Weston-super-Mare. In 1770 he surveyed one to Andover and worked on Brindley's Thames improvement schemes, surveying the canal from Reading down to Monkey Island and Isleworth. In 1788 he returned to do the parliamentary survey for the Andover and in 1793 worked on another English & Bristol Channels scheme. Finally under Brindley, he worked out a line for the Lancaster. In 1774 he reported on the scheme which became the Herefordshire & Gloucestershire, and in 1777 he looked over a possible Leominster Canal which had been preceded by work for the Stourbridge and Dudley Canals in 1775. First of his own waterways was the Thames & Severn for which he did preliminary surveys in 1781, proposing a canal from Tewkesbury to Lechlade, later resurveying along the line adopted. He became engineer but because of other work he left it to his resident Josiah Clowes. In the 1780s; Whitworth was involved with the Ashby Canal, the Oakham and above all the Forth & Clyde, also in 1784 doing surveys for the Gloucester & Berkeley, but too busy to follow this one up. On the Ashby he worked with his son, Robert, making a survey and estimate in 1781; nothing was done until 1792 when they became joint engineers. In 1797 their services were ended probably because they were not giving the Ashby sufficient time. In 1785 the elder Whitworth made a survey for the Oakham Canal, although the line adopted was different. In 1785 also he was made engineer of the Forth & Clyde and his greatest single work was his aqueduct over the Kelvin. He left his son Robert to complete this canal while he went to the Leeds & Liverpool with which he had been associated from about 1769 when he checked Longbotham's line for Brindley. In 1789 he was called upon to report on how the canal should be completed, advising the summit level tunnel at Foulridge. As engineer from 1790, he was assisted by his younger son William and between them they took the canal over the top and down the Lancashire side. He was also busy elsewhere, surveying the Wye for possible improvements and checking early Kennet & Avon surveys. He worked on surveys for the Grand Western and the Dorset & Somerset, on a canal from Leith to the Clyde, later to be truncated to the Edinburgh & Glasgow Union, and in 1795 on the Commercial Canal project from the Chester at Nantwich to the Ashby. But in 1791 he refused to become involved with the Rochdale preparations, and in 1795 had his Leeds & Liverpool salary halved to 300 guineas because of his work elsewhere, which in that year included the Herefordshire & Gloucestershire which he took over on Clowes' death. He had in 1792 been asked to survey for the proposed Dearne & Dove but was too busy to do more than watch over the work of John Thompson, but he became engineer on Thompson's death and stayed until his own death. In 1795 he inspected progress of another Don satellite, the Stainforth & Keadby, two years later surveying the Don itself for improvements. In 1797 he reported on Ralph Dodd's plans for a canal from Durham down to the navigable part of the Wear with a branch to the Tyne and possibly from Stella on the Tyne to Hexham. His son William pursued a modest course as engineer of the Wilts. & Berks., on its sanction in 1796, and was possibly helped by his father. William also engineered the North Wilts., Canal. The younger Robert apart from earlier work helping his father, was employed in about 1800 to survey for a small ship canal to Canterbury from St. Nicholas Bay, west of Margate, and one of the sons finished the Dearne & Dove, opened in 1804.

WILLIAMS, Charles Wye, 1779-1866. He was trained in law in Dublin. A capable business man he directed a bleaching works in his early twenties, later moving to shipping ventures. He was impressed by steam navigation and became associated with the engineer John Grantham who from 1822 was working on flood control on the Shannon. In 1826 Grantham introduced a river steam packet subsequently acquired by Williams who intended to extend the service to Carrick. He led pleas for better inland waterways, publishing in 1831 his "Observations on the Inland Navigation of Ireland". Meanwhile he set up a steamer depot at Killaloe and ordered some vessels from William Laird at Birkenhead, the first craft the yard built. After three iron barges ordered between 1829 and 1832, came the iron paddler LADY LANSDOWNE in 1833. His Shannon fleet eventually numbered 9 vessels and were operated as the Inland Steam Navigation Co. and after 1840 were associated with the City of Dublin S.P. Co., which had been founded in 1823 which he had started under his own name to run a service from Dublin to Liverpool.

WILLIAMS, Henry, from Ketley, Shropshire, he was probably associated with William Reynolds in building the Ketley inclined plane in 1788. Next he designed those for the Shropshire Canal, qualifying for a part of the award the company gave for the best models and drawings submitted. He became surveyor of the canal in 1794 and stayed until he retired in 1839, one of the longest managerial careers in the canal age. From 1797 he was also superintendent and engineer of the adjacent Shrewsbury Canal, with an inclined plane at Trench, over which he was doubtless consulted.

WOODHOUSE, John. From Ashby-de-la-Zouch, he was a contractor on the Grand Junction. He worked on Blisworth tunnel and may have been bankrupted by it. A relative, Jonathan, partnered him at Blisworth and erected the steam pumps for the Grand Junction at Tringford. Once he gave up contracting he joined Grand Junction as engineer of the Northern district from 1805 to 1809. He was also considered as engineer for the Grand Union, but Bevan was chosen. He designed a lift which he offered in 1808 to the Worcs. & Birmingham Canal and in 1809 he was appointed their engineer, being succeeded by the younger William Crosley. He stayed to undertake cutting contracts, until at least 1814. Later he appears as resident engineer on the Gloucester & Berkeley, appointed at a time when Telford took over, but Telford soon secured his dismissal as he was buying inferior stone from his son.

WYNDHAM, George O'Brien, 3rd Earl of Egremont, 1751-1837. Owner of Petworth House, large estates in Sussex and lead mines and coal mines in Cumberland from where he derived his title. He was never inclined to politics but was a patron of the arts and dedicated to agricultural improvement. The latter led him to support inland waterways and in 1791 promoted as sole proprietor the Western Rother Navigation with a branch canal to near Petworth, completed in 1794, in which year he became chairman of the Arun Navigation which was joined by the Rother at Stopham. From 1810 he began promoting the Wey & Arun Canal and was later principal shareholder in the Portsmouth & Arundel by which he lost heavily. He was chairman until his death of the Arun Navigation, Wey & Arun Canal and the Rother, the latter two bringing in rewarding dividends.

YARRANTON, Andrew, 1616-1684. Coming from Astley on the Severn, near Stourport, he seems to have been a man of wide interest and capabilities. He was keen on industrial development, perceiving how industry needed efficient transport to flourish. He owned ironworks on the Dick Brook near Astley, and made the brook navigable in the 1650s at his own expense. Later he was engineer on the Worcestershire Stour for Lord Windsor, but he was unable to continue after 1667 for lack of money, although his son Robert tried to extend the works below Kidderminster. During the Commonwealth he put forward a scheme to improve the Salwarpe to Droitwich, while in 1664 he was a member of a syndicate granted a section of the Upper Avon by Lord Windsor which they improved. A century before Brindley, he was planning a national waterway system; his Stour improvements were part of his scheme to link the Severn and Trent, while he had ideas of a Thames-Severn water route surveyed by his son. He also wanted to improve the Dee and surveyed the Chelmer. Towards the end of his life he published his plans for industry and for Navigation in "England's Improvement by Sea and Land", the first part appearing in 1677 and the second in 1686.

YEOMAN, Thomas, c.1700-1781. Among the earliest of professional civil engineers, he was the first to be president, from 1771 to 1780, of the Society of Civil Engineers, predecessor of the Institution. He followed John Hore in surveying the Chelmer, in 1765 publishing plans to make the river navigable. In 1764 he was elected an F.R.S. and from 1766 he was working with Smeaton on the Lee in Hertfordshire; their surveys were followed by improvements carried out by Yeoman, who also improved the Stort. He was consulted about fen drainage, publishing a report on the Ancholme in 1766, on the North Level in 1769 and the outfall of the Wisbech River or rather the Nene. In 1769 he did a survey for a canal from the Aire to Selby and his last task was a survey in 1775 of the Stroudwater, having reported on the Oxford Canal in 1774-5 and in 1775 also helped Robert Whitworth with the Stourbridge.

163. Pool Lock aqueduct takes the Trent & Mersey's Hall Green branch over their main line Red Bull flight to join the Macclesfield.

354

Appendix C;

LOCK Terms

164. Lock hut (above) at Beeston on the Chester Canal, with a cover for stop planks in the foreground. Feeders; the channel off the Peasey beck (left), which feeds the Lancaster Canal at Crooklands near Kendal.

GENERAL

COMMON LOCK; a pound lock (see below). DOUBLE LOCK; a two rise staircase a term found particullarly in Ireland where they count as one lock only. DRAW; to raise or open a lock paddle, or in the fens, a staunch. DROP; to lower, close or in the Fens set or 'shut in' a paddle or a staunch. FLUSHING; running water into a lock to stir a boat which is grounded or jammed. Rapid opening and shutting of the paddles causes a sudden and often effective surge of water. FOREBAY; the breast wall and upper sill, a term found on the Leeds & Liverpool and elsewhere. HALF LOCK; West Midlands and West Country term for a watergate or staunch, not a flash lock because it is used to dam a weir to make a level, not release a flash. It is called a half lock because it is half a pound lock. HEAD; the upper or top end of a pound lock by the upper water level. LEVEL; a level is made when two reaches of water either side of a lock or weir attain equal height. LIFT; boatman's term for a lock staircase, for example Etruria lift, a two rise staircase on the Caldon Canal. LOCK DISTANCE POST; To prevent dispute, posts were sometimes set up 15 or 20 yards from the head or tail of a lock. The first boat to pass either post took the lock. LOCK PEN or LOCK PIT: Yorkshire and East Midlands word for pound lock chamber. To pen means the operation of locking. NAVIGATION GATE; a watergate or staunch but not a flash lock (see flash locks.). NAVIGATION WEIR; the same, but can also be applied to a flash lock. PLANK STAUNCH; a very simple type of East Anglian staunch composed of planks laid one above the other. POUND; a stretch of water on a canal, called a pool on the Leeds & Liverpool. REACH; a stretch of water between locks on a river navigation. RISER; one of the locks in a staircase or the staircase itself. Two rise locks are generally called a staircase pair. SIDE LOCK; a junction lock linking a river and canal when the two run parallel. SOSS; another word for sluice, thus Misterton soss on the Idle. STAUNCH or STANCH; East Anglian word for watergate (see under Flash Locks). TAIL; the lower or bottom end of a pound lock by the lower water level. TIDE LOCK; sited to overcome the difference in level between fresh water and tidal water, also called a TIDE GATE. Their fall may be either way depending on the level of the fresh water and the state of the tide, so a double set of gates is fitted, mitred in each direction (see Locks, tide locks). This could be another name for a river lock where the river is tidal, or indeed a sea lock. Tide gates are simply a single set of gates. TURNPIKE: River Lee term for staunch see Locks, flash locks. WATERGATE: West Midlands word for a staunch or navigation gate (see Locks, flash locks). WEIR; artificial barrier across a river to impound water either for navigational or milling purposes. Also applied to canals as a barrier to control flow of water, see under Weirs.

LOCK PARTS.

APRON; the part of the lock bottom where the sills are fixed. BALANCE BEAM; projecting beams to balance the lock gates and provide leverage for moving them. Balance pole is equally common. BALANCE POLE was officially used by the Glamorganshire in 1810. BARS; horizontal members in the framework of a lock gate. BREAST; the end wall of a lock on top of which the upper sill is fixed. It is the riser if the lock is seen as a step. BREAST POST; the upright timber of a lock gate away from the heel post at the lock side, also called the breast beam. BUMPING PIECES; wooden or iron guards on lock gates and on the breast wall to protect the structure from damage by boats. In 1802 the Monmouthshire used the term bumping blocks. BYE-WASH; the weir stream bypassing a lock, a Rochdale Canal term of 1840, but also in general use in the north, notably in Yorkshire. CHAMBER; the body of a pound lock enclosed by gates at each end. CHECK PIN; a special curved horn shaped pin on the lock side, to hold the check straps of boats entering a lock, so called and so shaped on the Rochdale Canal, and on the Calder & Hebble Navigation. CLAPPING POST; vertical sill against which a single gate closes, old word used on the Staffs. & Worcs., Canal in 1835. CLAP QUOIN; modern term for Clapping Post. COIN POST; old Staffs. & Worcs., word of 1835 for the heel post of a lock gate. COLLAR; metal strap, anchored to the lock side, to hold the heel in position. COYN or COIN; the hollow quoin in which the heel post is recessed, late eighteenth and early nineteenth century spellings. CULVERT; the tunnel by which water is fed or drained from a lock chamber, the lock weir stream may also be culverted. DOOR; Fens word for a lock gate, a Fenman would speak of a sluice door and he would also talk of sea doors meaning tide gates, as opposed to navigation doors meaning ordinary lock gates. He called the vertically lifting door at a staunch a clough (pronounced clow). The Erewash Canal also used 'door' for gate in 1779. EYE; another Fens term, the opening closed by a sluice gate or a lock paddle or rather in the Fens a slat or slacker. To shoot the eye of a sluice actually meant taking a boat through the doors. GALLEY BEAM; found on East Anglian staunches as an extension of the gateposts where these were used to hang gates by means of pintle hinges. The beam uniting the extensions kept the gateposts upright, called a lintel on the Suffolk Stour. GUDGEON; an old word found in Rees' "Cyclopaedia"(1819) to describe the pin projecting from the foot of the heel post of a lock gate, which rotates in a pot in the lock bottom. GUILLOTINE; vertically closing lock gate, called a shutter in the Fens, see Locks, pound locks. HEAD GATES; the upper or top gates of a lock. HEAD POST; the same as breast post, the upright timber of a lock gate away from the heel post, applied to single gates. HEEL POST; the upright post of a lock gate which fits against the lock side. HOLLOW QUOIN; vertical recess of stone or

165. 'Strapping' a narrow boat round the turn from the Coventry to the Oxford at Hawkesbury or Sutton Stop. The boatman is using a bridle on the horse line to bring the point of tow forward, while he will ease the fore end round by a strap to the post on the bank.

iron or rarely specially moulded brick in which the lock gates heel post turns, held by water pressure. JACK HEAD; an old word, used on the Cromford Canal in 1804, to describe a lock gate's head post. LINTEL; see galley beam (above). LOCK TUNNELL; the Dudley Canal in 1777 described a hollow quoin as a lock tunnell. MITRE POST; on mitred pairs of gates the head posts are so called. POINTING DOORS; Fenland term for mitred gates as opposed to shutters or guillotine gates. POT; the socket in which the gudgeon or tan pin turns. SILL; against this ledge the bottom of the lock gate beds; the depth of water above the sills indicates the navigable depth of the lock, for these are the highest projections above the lock bottom. SNUBBING POST; an old Chester Canal word used in 1808 to describe a strapping post. STRAPPING POST; designed to hold the check strap of a boat entering the lock, mounted either on the lock side or on the top gate. There are strapping posts at the head and tail of the chamber and along the sides. The Forth & Clyde used a swivelling hook, the Rochdale a curved iron pin, a check pin (see above) STRIDE; the same as a galley beam, a Thames word. TAIL GATES; the lower or bottom gates of a lock. TAN PIN; the pin at the foot of a lock gate heel post, turning in the pot. WING WALLS; the flanking walls at the lock tail, often protected by guards to avoid damage from boats.

PADDLES and PADDLE GEAR.

BREAST RACKS; Irish words for gate paddles. CLOUGH; pronounced clow and so spelt at the end of the eighteenth century. This was a North Country word, although used in 1771 on the Staffs. & Worcs, for a paddle. Found on the Leeds & Liverpool, also on the Calder & Hebble, the Don, the Erewash (1785) and the Cromford Canal (1804), but not the Rochdale. It was also a Fens word for the sluice of a weir and indeed for the door or gate of a vertically rising staunch. COUGH; Derbyshire word for paddle, used on the Nutbrook Canal. DANDY PADDLE; top gate paddle, Trent & Mersey boatman's term. FLASHER; a gate paddle, a word certainly used on the Glamorganshire, also called a FLY PADDLE. JACK CLOUGH; Leeds & Liverpool top ground paddle, also called a side clough or box clough. JACK POST; Glamorganshire Canal term for ground paddle. LAND RACKS; Irish term for ground paddles. OVERFALLS; the fixed weir sills alongside an East Anglian staunch, or the second set of paddles above the first in a paddle and rimer flash lock. PADDLE BAR; the shaft or rod linking the paddle with the operating mechanism. RIMERS; the vertical and detachable guides for paddles in a paddle and rimer flash lock. SHUTTER; Fens word for a vertically rising staunch or sluice gate, synonymous with clough or door. It is thus used to describe a guillotine lock gate. SLACKER; Fens word for a paddle. SLAT; the same as Slacker. SLIDES; Dudley Canal word for paddles in 1789, meaning the actual paddles, not the operating gear. VALVE; the same as slides, also used at the same time on the Coventry Canal.

166. Locks with side ponds at Atherstone, Coventry Canal, on the flight of 11.

Appendix **D.**

167. Grafton steam dredger on the Shropshire Union. Note the large cylinder for working the grab which is secured to a horizontal beam raised and lowered by the crane.

C.V.Wain

ART & WATERWAYS

Waterways attracted landscape artists of the eighteenth century because they were something new, and engravings of the engineering achievements of the canal age sold well. They sometimes resorted to tricks to achieve necessary panoramic effects, the foreground being viewed at normal eye level, but the background as from a bird. This is well illustrated by a view of Stourport in the 1770s engraved by Peter Mazell, after a painting by James Sherriff where a tree in the foreground is seen from the ground, whereas the Severn and the locks, basins and warehouses of Stourport are observed from above. The aqueducts and tunnels of the canal age appealed to the artist and his public. Barton aqueduct was popular, the graving by Robert Pollard (1755-1838) being the best known, with a rigged vessel crossing, towed by two horses. This looks like artistic licence, because no sailing craft with her mast up could possibly travel the Bridgewater with its low bridges. The artist was trying to illustrate the scope of inland navigation afforded and to achieve full dramatic effect he felt obliged to give the craft sails. Portrayal varied from the delicate coloured aquatints of John Claude Nattes (c.1765-1822) who drew scenes at Worsley and whose Dundas aqueduct is well known, to a crude drawing of Sapperton tunnel by an unknown artist. This is a water colour of the pinnacled western portal sketched in August 1788 before the water was let in. Topographical canal prints continued into the nineteenth century until overlaid by their railway rivals and eventually extinguished by the camera. John Hassell's 'Tour of the Grand Junction' of 1819 is an example of a published sketch book; inaccurate drawings of locks and boats intermingled with a travelogue. More impressive are the series of engravings by Thomas Shepherd of scenes on the Regents Canal of 1827-8 which feature Pickfords' boats, locks, Islington tunnel and City Road Basin with accuracy. By this time other aspects besides topography were attracting artists. W.H.Pyne (1769-1843) was a competent figure painter whose "Microcosm or a Picturesque Delineation of the Arts, Agriculture, Manufactures, etc. of Great Britain", published in 1808, was intended as a drawing book for the instruction of amateurs. He features road and inland water transport, with sketches of the Thames western barges and coastal craft. E.W.Cooke (1811-1880) whose folio of etchings, "Shipping & Craft" completed publication in 1829, was an accurate ship portraitist. Fortunately he has included two of Pickfords' narrow boats in one of his Thames scenes. In the nineteenth century technical drawing was executed as a work of art. The plates illustrating the articles in Rees "Cyclopaedia" (1819) fall into this category. Very impressive are the meticulously shaded working drawings prepared by James Green of his lifts on the Grand Western Canal, illustrating his paper in Vol.2, 1838 of the "Transactions" of the Institution of Civil Engineers. Better known are the plates in the "Atlas" of Telford accompanying his "Life" published in 1838, recording his engineering achievements. Also portrayed were rivers; the Ouse and its shipping at York and an early eighteenth century panorama of the Aire below Leeds showing the cuts and locks. The new port of Goole appeared in an engraving of about 1830, while the paintings of James Stark were engraved to illustrate J.W.Robberd's "Scenery of the Rivers of Norfolk" published in 1834. Ireland had a competent topographical artist in William C.E. Stokes who in 1842 published "A Pictorial Survey and Tourist's Guide to Lough Derg", a folio volume of panoramic scenes which included Killaloe pier and two paddle steamers alongside. John Constable's (1776-1837) scenes on the Suffolk Stour were accurate. The painting 'Flatford Mill' illustrates the Stour lighter well, unchanged in design from Constable's time to the 1920s. The 'Leaping Horse' shows how Stour boat horses had to jump over the stiles which intersected the navigation's towpath, while 'The White Horse' illustrates a lighter ferrying her horse on her foredeck to the other bank. With the recent upsurge in waterway interest there has been a canal art revival, both Emett and Thelwell having used narrow boats in cartoons, and in L.T.C.Rolt's "Narrow Boat" much of the delight lies in the wood engravings of D.J.Watkins-Pitchford.

SOCIETIES & CLUBS

Nowadays with pleasure boating dominant on a large mileage, boat clubs flourish. These, apart from their social functions, have mooring facilities leased out to their members and some possess boat slipways for launching and repair. The earliest, founded in 1942, is the North Cheshire Cruising Club on the Macclesfield Canal at High Lane near Stockport. The idea of voluntary labour for canal repair really got going with the Stratford Canal restoration of the early 1960s and soon many preservation societies were formed. The 'new navvies', at first formed into the London Working Party Group, did great work on the Stourbridge and the Kennet & Avon. Other groups followed and in 1966 a magazine "Navvies Notebook" was started, later shortened to "Navvies". More unity came in 1970 with the formation of a parent body, the Waterway Recovery Group, who organize labour, arrange for hire of plant and advise on methods of attack.

The historian has been helped by the availability of documents, collected since inland transport has been nationalized, in the archives of British Transport Historical Records, now part of the Public Record Office. Since 1954 there has been the Railway & Canal Historical Society with its quarterly 'Journal' and monthly single sheet 'Bulletin', its regional meetings and its excursions. The founding of the Waterways Museum at Stoke Bruerne in 1962 is further evidence of the historical trend, and growth of waterways collections in other museums, for example Manchester and Cusworth Hall near Doncaster. Guildford Council have preserved the treadmill crane by the Wey, and Ironbridge Gorge Museum Trust are determined to save the Longdon cast iron aqueduct. Craft have been restored to their old colours, Fellows, Morton & Clayton, the Shropshire Union and the Grand Union Canal Carrying Co. Steam vessel preservation is encouraged by the Steam Boat Association of Great Britain, founded in 1971 and a canal boat museum was opened at Ellesmere Port in 1976.

GENERAL INCLUDING ART & SOME RECREATION.
British Waterways Board. CANAL ARCHITECTURE IN
BRITAIN (1976).
Calvert, R. INLAND WATERWAYS OF BRITAIN (1963).
De Maré, E. THE CANALS OF ENGLAND (1951). Excellent
photographs.
Eyre, F. & Hadfield C. ENGLISH RIVERS & CANALS (1945).
Gagg, J. CANALS IN CAMERA. 2 volumes. (1970-1971).
Hadfield, C. INTRODUCING CANALS (1955).
THE CANAL AGE (1968). General account of
the age throughout the world.
Harris, R. CANALS AND THEIR ARCHITECTURE (1969) A
good pictorial survey.
Jenkins, J. G. "Commercial Salmon Fishing in Welsh Rivers"
in FOLK LIFE 9.
Klingender, F. D. ART AND THE INDUSTRIAL REVOLUTION
(1947).
McKnight, H. CANALS, LOCKS AND CANAL BOATS (1974).
SHELL BOOK OF INLAND WATERWAYS an
encyclopaedia (1975).
Ransom, P. J. G. WATERWAYS RESTORED (1974).
Robertson, H. R. LIFE ON THE UPPER THAMES (1875).
Rolt, L. T. C. THE INLAND WATERWAYS OF ENGLAND
(1950). Long standing general account.
Russell, R. LOST CANALS OF ENGLAND AND WALES (1971).
WATERSIDE PUBS (1975).
Seaman, K. CANAL FISHING (1971).
Smith, P. WATERWAYS HERITAGE (1971). A collection of
facsimile material of the canal age and after.
Ware, M. CANALSIDE CAMERA 1845-1930 (1975).

HISTORY.

Anon. THE HISTORY OF INLAND NAVIGATION (1766).
Arnott, W. G. THE ORWELL ESTUARY (1954).
Astbury, A. K. THE BLACK FENS (1958) republished (1970).
Barker, T. C. "The Sankey Navigation" Trans. LANCASHIRE
and CHESHIRE ANTIQUARIAN SOCIETY in
Vol. 100 (1948).
Broadbridge, S. R. BIRMINGHAM CANAL NAVIGATIONS
1786-1846. (1974).
Burton, Antony. THE CANAL BUILDERS (1972).
Came, HISTORY OF THE CHELMER & BLACKWATER
NAVIGATION.
Chard History Group. THE CHARD CANAL. Publication No. 1
(1967)
Clew, K. R. THE DORSET & SOMERSET CANAL (1971).
THE KENNET & AVON CANAL (1968).
THE SOMERSETSHIRE COAL CANAL AND
RAILWAYS (1970)
Dalby, L. J. THE WILTS & BERKS CANAL (1971).
Delany, V. T. H. & D. R. THE CANALS OF THE SOUTH OF
IRELAND (1966).
Delany, R. THE GRAND CANAL (of Ireland) (1973).
Duckham, B. F. NAVIGABLE RIVERS OF YORKSHIRE (1964)
THE YORKSHIRE OUSE (1967).
Ewans, M. C. THE HAYTOR GRANITE TRAMWAY AND THE
STOVER CANAL (1966).
"A Brief History of the River Ivel Navigation
in THE LOCK GATE, Journal of the Great
Ouse Restoration Society, Vol. 1, No. 3. (1962),
Vol. 1, No. 4. (1962), Vol. 1. No. 5. (1962), Vol. 1.,
No. 6. (1963), Vol. 1. No. 7. (1963).
Falk, Bernard. THE BRIDGEWATER MILLIONS (1942).
Faulkner, A. H. THE GRAND JUNCTION CANAL (1973).
Flanagan, P. J. THE BALLINAMORE & BALLYCONNELL
CANAL (1972).
Hadfield, C. BRITISH CANALS, 4th Edition, (1969).
THE CANALS OF THE EAST MIDLANDS 2nd.
Edition (1970).
THE CANALS OF SOUTH AND SOUTH EAST
ENGLAND (1969).
THE CANALS OF SOUTH WALES AND THE
BORDERS. 2nd Edition (1967).
THE CANALS OF SOUTH WEST ENGLAND
(1967).
THE CANALS OF THE WEST MIDLANDS. 2nd
Edition (1967).
THE CANALS OF YORKSHIRE AND NORTH
EAST ENGLAND. 2 volumes. (1972-1973).
Hadfield, C. & Biddle, G. THE CANALS OF NORTH WEST
ENGLAND. 2 Volumes (1970).
Hadfield, C. & Norris, J. WATERWAYS TO STRATFORD
2nd edition (1968).
Handford, M. STROUDWATER CANAL Vol. 1. 1729-1763.
(1976).

Harris, H. THE GRAND WESTERN CANAL (1973).
Harris, H. & Ellis, Monica. THE BUDE CANAL (1972).
Hill, Sir Francis. GEORGIAN LINCOLN (1966). For the
Fossdyke and Witham, a magnificent
study of local history.

169. Two Humber keels with their sails set.

168. Weirs and sluices: lagoon below the headbank of Rudyard reservoir, Trent & Mersey
Canal, compensating slot weir to the right
and long weir sill for the feed to the left
and in the foreground.

Appendix E ; Bibliography

Household, H. THE THAMES & SEVERN CANAL (1969).
Jackman, W. T. THE DEVELOPMENT OF TRANSPORT IN
    MODERN ENGLAND (1914). Reprinted 1962
    with bibliography brought up to date.
Leech, Sir Bosdin. HISTORY OF THE MANCHESTER SHIP
    CANAL 2 Vols. (1907). A mammoth acc-
    ount of the building of the canal.
Lindsay, Jean. THE CANALS OF SCOTLAND (1968).
McCutcheon, A. W. THE CANALS OF THE NORTH OF
    IRELAND (1965).
    "Inland Navigations of Northern Ireland"
    TECHNOLOGY AND CULTURE Vol. 6.
    Vol. 6. No. 4.   (1965).
Malster, R. W. "The Norwich River" in THE NORFOLK
    SAILOR No. 6 (1963).
    "Norfolk Navigations" THE NORFOLK
    SAILOR No. 11 (1966).
Marriage, J. E. "The Chelmer & Blackwater Navigation"
    EAST ANGLIAN MAGAZINE. January 1958.
Mather, F. C. AFTER THE CANAL DUKE (1970).
Mutton, N. "Eardington Forges and Canal Tunnel" INDUSTRI-
    ARCHAEOLOGY Vol. 7. No. 1. (1970).
Paar, H. W. THE SEVERN & WYE RAILWAY (1963).
Phillips, J. A GENERAL HISTORY OF INLAND NAVIGATION
    FOREIGN AND DOMESTIC. (1792) Reprinted.
Priestley, J. HISTORICAL ACCOUNT OF THE NAVIGABLE
    RIVERS, CANALS AND RAILWAYS THROUGH-
    OUT GREAT BRITAIN. (1831). Reprinted.
Rolt, L. T. C. NAVIGABLE WATERWAYS (1969).
Spencer, H. LONDON'S CANAL (1962).
Stevens, P. A. THE LEICESTER LINE (1972).
Stevenson, P. THE NUTBROOK CANAL (1971).
Summers, Dorothy. THE GREAT OUSE (1973).
Tew, D. H. THE OAKHAM CANAL (1967).
Thacker, F. S. THE THAMES HIGHWAY: GENERAL HISTORY
    (1914) Reprinted.
    THE THAMES HIGHWAY: LOCKS AND WEIRS
    (1920) Reprinted.
Tomlinson, V. I. "The Manchester, Bolton & Bury Canal"
    Navigation and Railway Company, 1790-1845"
    Trans. LANCASHIRE & CHESHIRE
    ANTIQUARIAN SOCIETY. Vol. 75 & 76.
                                    (1965-66).
    "Salford Activities connected with the
    Bridgewater Navigation. Trans. LANCS. &
    CHESHIRE ANTIQUARIAN SOCIETY
                            Vol. 66. (1956-7).
Tye, W. "The Ipswich & Stowmarket Navigation". EAST
    ANGLIAN MAGAZINE. July 1954.
Vine, P. A. L. LONDON'S LOST ROUTE TO BASINGSTOKE
                                    (1968).
    THE ROYAL MILITARY CANAL (1972).
    LONDON'S LOST ROUTE TO THE SEA (1965).
Waller, A. J. R. THE SUFFOLK STOUR (1957).
Waters, B. SEVERN TIDE (1947).
Weaver, C. P. "The Arbury Canals" J. RAILWAY & CANAL
    HISTORICAL SOCIETY. Vol. 16. No's 1 and 2
                                    (1970).
Willan, T. S. THE EARLY HISTORY OF THE DON
    NAVIGATION (1965).
    "The Navigation of the Great Ouse between
    St. Ives and Bedford in the Seventeenth Century"
    PUBLICATIONS OF THE BEDFORDSHIRE HIST-
    ORICAL RECORD SOCIETY, Vol. 24. (1946).
    RIVER NAVIGATION IN ENGLAND, 1600-1750.
                                    (1936).
    THE NAVIGATION OF THE RIVER WEAVER IN
    THE EIGHTEENTH CENTURY (1951).
Williams, W. H. Articles on the Canals of East Shropshire
    in the SHROPSHIRE MAGAZINE, July 1951 and
    May, June, July, and August 1954.
Wilson, E. ELLESMERE AND LLANGOLLEN CANAL (1976).

THE CONTEMPORARY SCENE

Cadbury, G. & Dobbs, S. P. CANALS AND INLAND WATER-
                            WAYS. (1929).
Forbes, L. A. & Ashford, W. H. R. OUR WATERWAYS. A
    HISTORY OF INLAND NAVIGATION CONSIDER-
    ED AS A BRANCH OF WATER CONSERVANCY.
                            (1906).
Jeans, J. S. WATERWAYS AND WATER TRANSPORT IN
    DIFFERENT COUNTRIES (1890). An advocate
    for state control.
McLeod, R. M. "Social Policy and the Floating Population" in
    PAST AND PRESENT. Journal of Historical
    Studies. No's 33-35 (1966). The working of the
    Canal Boats Acts.
Palmer, J. E. BRITISH CANALS: PROBLEMS AND
    POSSIBILITIES (1910). A reply to Pratt, below,
    recommending state assistance.

Pratt, E. A. BRITISH CANALS: IS THEIR RESUSCITATION
    PRACTICABLE? (1906).
    CANALS AND TRADERS (1910) Both books are
    critical of canal modernisation, written by a
    railwayman.
    SCOTTISH CANALS AND WATERWAYS (1922).
Saner, J. A. "On Waterways in Great Britain". Proc. I. of
    Civil Engineers. Vol. 163, Part 1. (1905-6).
Smith, G. OUR CANAL POPULATION (1875) Reprint 1975.
    CANAL ADVENTURES BY MOONLIGHT (1881).
Thompson, H. G. THE CANAL SYSTEM OF ENGLAND (1902).
    Pleading for a modernized system.
Yarranton, A. ENGLAND'S IMPROVEMENT BY SEA AND
    LAND. Two parts 1677 and 1686.

BIOGRAPHIES

Addis, J. P. THE CRAWSHAY DYNASTY (1957).
Banks, A. G. & Schofield, R. B. BRINDLEY AT WET EARTH
    COLLIERY (1968). Of value for details of
    Matthew Fletcher.
Boucher, C. T. G. BRINDLEY (1970).
    JOHN RENNIE (1761-1821). (1963).
Broadbridge, S. R. "John Pinkerton and the Birmingham
    Canals". TRANSPORT HISTORY Vol. 6. No. 1.
                                    (1971).
Brown, R. S. "Maps and plans of Liverpool and District by
    the Eyes family of Surveyors". Trans. of the
    HISTORIC SOCIETY OF LANCASHIRE AND
    CHESHIRE Vol. 62. (1910).
Delany, D. R. "John Trail, Grand Canal Engineer". JOURNAL
    OF THE CO. KILDARE ARCHAEOLOGICAL
    SOCIETY Vol. 14. No. 5. (1970).
Gibb, Sir Alexander. THE STORY OF TELFORD: THE RISE
    OF CIVIL ENGINEERING (1935).
Harris, L. E. "Sir Cornelius Vermuyden, an evaluation and
    appreciation". Trans. of the NEWCOMEN
    SOCIETY. Vol. 27 (1949).
    VERMUYDEN AND THE FENS (1953).
Harris, S. A. "Henry Berry, (1720-1812, Liverpool's Second
    Dock Engineer". Trans. of the HISTORIC
    SOCIETY OF LANCASHIRE AND CHESHIRE.
    Vol. 89. (1937).
Hodder, Edwin. GEORGE SMITH OF COALVILLE (1896).
King-Hele, D. ERASMUS DARWIN (1963).
Lindsay, J. "Robert Mackell and the Forth & Clyde Canal"
    TRANSPORT HISTORY Vol. 1. No. 3. (1968).
Lunar Society Guide to Exhibition, Birmingham, City Museum
    (1966). Useful short biographies of members.
Malet, H. THE CANAL DUKE (1961).
Meteyard, E. THE LIFE OF JOSIAH WEDGWOOD (1865).
Peet, H. "Thomas Steers, the Engineer of Liverpool's First
    Dock'. Trans. of the HISTORIC SOCIETY OF
    LANCASHIRE AND CHESHIRE Vol. 82 (1930).
Petree, J. P. "Charles Wye Williams (1780-1866). A Pioneer
    in Steam Navigation and Fuel Efficiency". Trans.
    of the NEWCOMEN SOCIETY. Vol. 39 (1966-7).
Phillips, E. A HISTORY OF THE PIONEERS OF THE WELSH
    COALFIELD (1925). Biographies of Chauncy
    Townsend and William Kirkhouse.
Raistrick, A. A DYNASTY OF IRONFOUNDERS (1953). A
    history of the Darbys of Coalbrookdale and
    useful for details of William Reynolds.
Rolt, L. T. C. THOMAS TELFORD (1958).
    JAMES WATT (1962).
Scholfield, R. E. THE LUNAR SOCIETY OF BIRMINGHAM
                                    (1963).
Skempton, A. W. "The Engineers of the English River
    Navigations, 1620-1760". Trans. of the
    NEWCOMEN SOCIETY, Vol. 29 (1953). Brief bio-
    graphies of the principal waterways engineers.
    "William Chapman (1749-1832) Civil Engineer"
    Trans. of the NEWCOMEN SOCIETY Vol. 46,
                                    (1973-4).
Simmons, J. PARISH AND EMPIRE (1952). A chapter on
    William Jessop.
Smiles, S. LIVES OF THE ENGINEERS. (1861). 2 Volumes
    Brindley, John Rennie (the elder) and Telford
                                    Reprinted.
Williamson, F. "George Sorocold of Derby". J. of the
    DERBYSHIRE ARCHAEOLOGICAL AND
    NATURAL HISTORY SOCIETY Vol. 57 (new
    series vol. 10) (1936).
Wright, E. C. "The Early Smeatonians". Trans. of the
    NEWCOMEN SOCIETY. Vol. 18. (1937-1938).
    Biographies of John Grundy, John Golborne
    and Thomas Yeoman.

ALSO NOTE THE DICTIONARY OF NATIONAL BIOGRAPHY
for many eminent promoters of inland waterways and for
some of the engineers.

ENGINEERING & WATERWAY FEATURES

Anderson, J. VIEW OF THE AGRICULTURE OF THE
    COUNTY OF ABERDEEN (1794). A description
    of his boat lift.

Appendix E ; Bibliography

The house magazines of the nationalized waterways are very useful for engineering works. They are as follows:-

LOCK & QUAY   September 1949 to December 1954, Docks & Inland Waterways Executive, British Transport Commission Monthly.

WATERWAYS   September 1955 to September/Oct. 1969. British Transport Waterways and British Waterways Board. Monthly and bi-monthly.

WATERWAYS NEWS. April 1971 to date. British Waterways Board. Monthly.

Brewster, D. EDINBURGH ENCYCLOPAEDIA. (1830). Vol. 15. "Navigation Inland".

Castle, R. "Essay on Artificial Navigation, 1730.", edited by J. H. Farrington. TRANSPORT HISTORY Vol. 5. No's 1 and 2 (1972).

Chapman, W. OBSERVATIONS ON THE VARIOUS SYSTEMS OF CANAL NAVIGATION (1797). Answer to Fulton (see below).

Clark, R. H. "The Staunches and Navigation of the Little Ouse River". Trans. of the NEWCOMEN SOCIETY Vol. 30. (1957).

Clegg, H. "The Third Duke of Bridgewater's Canal Works in Manchester". Trans. of the LANCASHIRE AND CHESHIRE ANTIQUARIAN SOCIETY Vol. 65 (1955).

Darby, H. C. THE DRAINING OF THE FENS (1956) Reprinted 1968.

Dupin, Baron Charles. THE COMMERCIAL POWER OF GREAT BRITAIN; EXHIBITING A COMPLETE VIEW OF THE PUBLIC WORKS OF THIS COUNTRY. 2 volumes (1825) Translated from French.

Dutens, J. MEMOIRES SUR LES TRAVAUX PUBLIQUES D'ANGLETERRE (1819).

Encyclopaedia Britannica. Notable articles on waterways occur in the 3rd edition (1803), 7th edition (1842), 8th edition (1858), 11th edition (1911).

The Engineer. "The Anderton electric lift". 24th July 1908.

Engineering. "The Foxton inclined plane". 25th Jan. 1901.

Fulton, R. TREATISE ON THE IMPROVEMENT OF CANAL NAVIGATION (1796).

Green, J. "Description of the perpendicular lifts as erected on the Grand Western Canal". Trans. of the INSTITUTION OF CIVIL ENGINEERS. Vol. 2. (1838).

Leach, E. A TREATISE OF UNIVERSAL INLAND NAVIGATIONS, AND THE USE OF ALL SORTS OF MINES. (1790)...... Plainly demonstrating the Possibility of making any River and Stream of Running Water in the World Navigable, by Canals of New Construction, without Locks and Dams etc.

Lewis, M. J. T. "Flashlocks on English Waterways". INDUSTRIAL ARCHAEOLOGY Vol. 6. No. 3. (1969).

Jarvis, P. N. "Flashlocks: an addendum". INDUSTRIAL ARCHAEOLOGY Vol. 7. No. 2. (1970).

McEwan, J. F. "Locomotive Haulage on the Forth & Clyde Canal 1839". J. of the STEPHENSON LOCOMOTIVE SOCIETY Vol 48. No. 560. (1972).

Institution of Civil Engineers. "Anderton Hydraulic Lift". Minutes of Proceedings, Vol. 45.

Needham, J. "China and the invention of the pound lock". Trans. of the NEWCOMEN SOCIETY Vol. 36 (1963-4)

Von Oeynhausen, C. & von Dechen, H, "Report on Railways in England in 1826-7". Trans. of the NEWCOMEN SOCIETY. Vol. 29 (1953).

Oxford History of Technology. Vols 3 & 4, (1957). Harris, L. E. "Land Drainage and Reclamation", Skempton, A. W. "Canals and River Navigations before 1750", both in Vol. 3. Doorman, G., "Dredging", Hadfield, C. "Canals: Inland Waterways of the British Isles", Pilkington, R. "Canals: Inland Waterways outside Britain" all in Vol. 4. Also useful information on surveying in other chapters.

Plymley, J. GENERAL VIEW OF THE AGRICULTURE OF SHROPSHIRE (1803). "Canals" by Thomas Telford, 1797.

Rees, A. CYCLOPAEDIA. (1819). "Canals" written by John Farey in 1905.

Richardson, A. "Water Supplies to Tring Summit". J. of the RAILWAY & CANAL HISTORICAL SOCIETY, Vol. 15. No's 2 and 3. (1969).

Stevenson, D. CANAL AND RIVER ENGINEERING (1872).

Tew, D. H. "Canal Lifts and Inclined Planes". Trans. of the NEWCOMEN SOCIETY Vol. 28. (1951-2).

Thorn, R. B. THE DESIGN OF LAND DRAINAGE WORKS (1959).

Tomlinson, V. I. "Early Warehouses on Manchester Waterways". Trans. of the LANCASHIRE & CHESHIRE ANTIQUARIAN SOCIETY. Vol. 71. (1961).

Vernon-Harcourt, L. F. RIVERS & CANALS. 1st Edition, 1882, (2 vols), Second edition enlarged 1896. (2 vols).

Williams, W. H. "Canal Inclined Planes of East Shropshire" INDUSTRIAL ARCHAEOLOGY Vol. 2. No. 2. (1965).

BOATS.

Aire & Calder. Brochure c. 1930. Useful description of compartment boats.

Benham, H. ONCE UPON A TIDE (1955). Details of billyboys and other east coast craft.

Carr, F. G. G. SAILING BARGES (1951).

Chaplin, T. A SHORT HISTORY OF THE NARROW BOAT, (1967). Revised 1974.

Clark, R. BLACK SAILED TRADERS (1961). Reprinted. Norfolk keels and wherries.

Cooke, E. W. SHIPPING AND CRAFT (1829). Engravings of river, coastal and seagoing vessels.

D'Arcy, G. PORTRAIT OF THE GRAND CANAL (1969). Details of traffic and boats on this Irish Canal.

Fairbairn, W. REMARKS ON CANAL NAVIGATION, ILLUSTRATIVE OF THE ADVANTAGES OF THE USE OF STEAM AS A MOVING POWER ON CANALS (1831).

Farr, G. E. "Severn Navigation and the Trow". MARINER'S MIRROR. Vol. 32 (1966).

Frank, J. "Humber Keels". MARINER'S MIRROR. Part 1, Vol. 41 (1955) and Part 2, Vol. 44 (1958).

Green, G. C. THE NORFOLK WHERRY (1953) 2nd Edition.

Greenhill, B. "The Story of the Severn Trow" MARINER'S MIRROR Vol. 26 (1940).

Harmsworth. T. BOATS FROM THE BASINGSTOKE'S PAST (1969). Surrey & Hants Canal Society.

Hollingshead, J. His account of a fly-boat journey on the Grand Junction is in HOUSEHOLD WORDS Vol. 18 (1858). Reprinted as ON THE CANAL in (1974).

Hughes W. Article on wharf boats on the Black Country canals in CUTTINGS, the magazine of the Shropshire Union Canal Society, Spring 1968.

Jones, B. THE UNSOPHISTICATED ARTS (1951) Canal boat decoration.

Lewery, A. J. NARROW BOAT PAINTING (1974).

Liverpool Museums SHIPPING GALLERY HANDBOOK AND GUIDE Part II (1935). Mersey and Weaver flats.

McKnight, H. CANAL AND RIVER CRAFT IN PICTURES (1969).

McNeill, D. B. COASTAL PASSENGER STEAMERS AND INLAND NAVIGATIONS IN THE NORTH OF IRELAND. N0. 3. Transport Handbook Belfast (now Ulster) Museum, 1960.

Malster, R. W. WHERRIES AND WATERWAYS (1972).

Norton, P. THE END OF THE VOYAGE (1959). Description of Tamar sailing barges.

O'Connor, J. CANALS, BARGES AND PEOPLE (1950).

Paget-Tomlinson, E. W. MERSEY & WEAVER FLATS (1972).

Pengelley, A. HISTORY OF CALSTOCK (1955). Description of Tamar sailing barges.

Wheat, G. LEEDS & LIVERPOOL CANAL CRAFT (1973).

Wilson, J. K. & Faulkner, A. H. FENLAND BARGE TRAFFIC (1972).

Wilson, R. J. BOATYARDS & BOATBUILDING (1974). Details of narrow boat construction.

CARRIERS AND BOAT PEOPLE.

Bellamy, J. M. "The History of Furley & Co. Ltd". (1963). Thesis: Dept. of Economics, Hull University.

Broadbridge, S. R. "Living Conditions on Midland Canal Boats". TRANSPORT HISTORY Vol. 3. No. 1. (1970).

Faulkner, A. H. FMC, FELLOWS, MORTON & CLAYTON (1975). THE 'GEORGE' AND THE 'MARY' (1973). History of the Grand Union Canal Carrying Co

Fletcher, T. LIFE ON THE HUMBER (1975).

Gayford, E. AMATEUR BOATWOMAN (1973). Training boat crews. 1941-45.

Halfpenny, E. " 'Pickfords'. Expansion and Crisis in the Early Ninteenth Century". BUSINESS HISTORY Vol. 1. (1958-9).

Hanson, H. "The Economic and Social Conditions of Canal Boatmen" (1973). Thesis, University of Manchester. Published as: CANAL BOATMEN 1760-1914. (1975).

Smith, P. L. 'ETHEL' & 'ANGELA JANE' (1976). Commercial carrying on the Calder & Hebble.

Wilkinson, T. HOLD ON A MINUTE (1967). Working narrow boats in the late 1940's.

Wilson, E. A. "Maesbury Hall Mill". SHROPSHIRE MAGAZINE Vol. 6. No. 4. (1955). The fleet of A. & A. Peate Ld.

Wilson, R. J. KNOBSTICKS (1974). Commercial carrying on the Trent & Mersey. LIFE AFLOAT (1976).

Appendix E; Bibliography

Wilson, R.J. ROSES & CASTLES. (1976). Narrow boat painting.
THE NUMBER ONES (1971).

PLACES OF PARTICULAR WATERWAY INTEREST.

Beckwith, I. "Gainsborough the Industrial Archaeology of a Lincolnshire Town".
Chaplin, P. THE THAMES AT HAMPTON (1967).
Corbett, J. THE RIVER IRWELL (1907).
Dean, R.J. THE ELLESMERE CANAL PACKET. Notes for a tour of the Railway and Canal Historical Society, Details of Chester and Ellesmere Port. (1967).
Gardiner, F.J. HISTORY OF WISBECH (1898).
Lamb, B. THE PEAK FOREST CANAL AND TRAMWAY. A discourse in maps; features the canal, the Bugsworth Complex and the tramroad. Privately published no date.
Moss, I.P. FAREWELL TO WALTON SUMMIT. Notes for a tour of the Railway & Canal Historical Society (1968) Lancaster Canal (South End).
Mullineux, F. "The Duke of Bridgewater's Underground Canals at Worsley". Trans. of the LANCASHIRE & CHESHIRE ANTIQUARIAN SOCIETY Vol. 71. (1961).

TRAMROADS

Baxter, B. STONE BLOCKS AND IRON RAILS (1966).
Lewis, M.J.T. EARLY WOODEN RAILWAYS (1970).

TRAVELOGUES AND GUIDES, JOURNALS AND MAPS.

Aickman, R. KNOW YOUR WATERWAYS (No date).
Anon. THE WATERWAY TO LONDON, AS EXPLORED IN THE 'WANDERER' AND 'RANGER' ETC. (1869).
Aubertin, C.J. A CARAVAN AFLOAT. (Circa 1918).
Ball, E. & P.W. HOLIDAY CRUISING ON THE THAMES (1970).
Bliss, W. THE HEART OF ENGLAND BY WATERWAY (1933).
Canoeing expedition.
CANOEING (1934).
RAPID RIVERS (1935). Canoeing.
Bonthron, P. MY HOLIDAYS ON INLAND WATERWAYS (1916).
'Bumps' A TRIP THROUGH THE CALEDONIAN CANAL (1861). Privately printed.
Carr, Sir John. THE STRANGER IN IRELAND: OR A TOUR INTO SOUTHERN AND WESTERN PARTS OF THAT COUNTRY IN THE YEAR 1805 (1806).
Dashwood, J.B. THE THAMES TO THE SOLENT BY CANAL AND SEA, OR THE LOG OF THE UNA BOAT 'CAPRICE'. (1868).
Doughty, H.M. OUR WHERRY IN WENDISH LANDS (1892). A Norfolk pleasure wherry in North Germany.
Edwards, L.A. HOLIDAY CRUISING ON THE BROADS AND FENS (1972).
Geikie, Sir Archibald. SCOTTISH REMINISCENCES (1904) Passenger packet journey.
Hadfield, C. THE CANAL ENTHUSIAST'S HANDBOOK No. 1. (editor). (1970-1) and No. 2. (1972).
Hadfield, C. WATERWAY SIGHTS TO SEE (1976).
Hadfield, C. & Streat, M. HOLIDAY CRUISING ON INLAND WATERWAYS (1971).
Harvey, R. THE SHANNON AND ITS LAKES. (1896).
Hassall, J. A TOUR OF THE GRAND JUNCTION CANAL IN 1819. Reprinted.
Head, Sir George. A HOME TOUR THROUGH THE MANUFACTURING DISTRICTS OF ENGLAND IN THE SUMMER OF 1835. Reprinted.
Liley, J. JOURNEYS OF THE 'SWAN' (1971). Entertaining account of narrow boat cruising.
Lloyd, M. & A. THROUGH ENGLAND'S WATERWAYS (1948) Canal cruising immediately pre-nationalization.
Malet, H. VOYAGE IN A BOWLER HAT (1960). Irish waterways.
Owen, D.E. WATER HIGHWAYS (1967).
WATER RALLIES (1969).
WATER BYWAYS (1973).
Prothero, F.E. & Clark, W.A. OARSMAN'S GUIDE TO RIVERS AND CANALS (1896).
'Red Rover' CANAL AND RIVER: A CANOE CRUISE FROM LEICESTERSHIRE TO GREENHITHE (1873).
Ransom, P.J.G. HOLIDAY CRUISING IN IRELAND (1971).
Rolt, L.T.C. NARROW BOAT (1944). Reprinted. Famous work which has attracted so many to the canals.
GREEN AND SILVER (1949). Irish waterways.
Rowbotham, F.W. THE SEVERN AND ITS BORE (1967).
Scott James, R.A. AN ENGLISHMAN IN IRELAND (c. 1911).
Seymour, J. SAILING THROUGH ENGLAND (1956).
VOYAGE INTO ENGLAND (1966).
Southey, R. JOURNAL OF A TOUR IN SCOTLAND IN 1819 Not published until 1929.
Taylor, C. THE CAMBRIDGESHIRE LANDSCAPE (1973).
Thurston, E.T. THE FLOWER OF GLOUCESTER (1911). Reprinted.

Weeton, E. MISS WEETON'S JOURNAL OF A GOVERNESS Vol. 1.1807-1811, Vol. 2. 1811-1825, as reprinted.
Westall, G. INLAND CRUISING ON THE RIVERS AND CANALS OF ENGLAND AND WALES. (1908).
Young, A. A SIX MONTHS TOUR THROUGH THE NORTH OF ENGLAND. 2nd edition 1770.

Literary

Ash, Bernard FITCHETT'S INN (1955). The Trent & Mersey.
Cordell, A. SONG OF THE EARTH (1969). South Wales Canals.
Herbert, A.P. THE WATER GIPSIES (1930).
Jerome, J.K. THREE MEN IN A BOAT (1889).
Meade, L.T. WATER GYPSIES (c. 1895). Strongly moral tale.
Peacock, T.L. CROTCHET CASTLE (1831). Occasional whimsical canal references.
Pearse, Rev. G.M. ROB RAT: A STORY OF BARGE LIFE (1878). Linked with the writings of George Smith.
Reade, A. LIFE ON THE CUT (1889).
Smith, E. MAIDEN'S TRIP (1949). Experiences of a trainee boatwoman 1939-45.
Trollope, A. THE KELLYS AND THE O'KELLYS. (1848).
Woolfitt, S. IDLE WOMEN (1947). See above.

Legal

Boyle, W. & Waghorn, T. THE LAW RELATING TO TRAFFIC ON RAILWAYS AND CANALS (1901) 3 vols. Acts, reports of select committees and cases.

Guides, Journals and Maps.

Allnutt, Z. USEFUL AND CORRECT ACCOUNTS OF THE NAVIGATION OF THE RIVERS AND CANALS WEST OF LONDON (1810).
De Salis, H.R. CHRONOLOGY (1897). A chronology of inland waterway events.
BRADSHAW'S CANALS AND NAVIGABLE RIVERS. 1st. edition 1904, but reprinted.
Edwards, L.A. INLAND WATERWAYS OF GREAT BRITAIN AND IRELAND (1962 and 1972, except Ireland).
Guides: Very numerous locally published guides. Also from 1956, the 'British Waterways' Inland cruising booklets (16 titles), since 1972 superseded by 4 British Waterways Board and Nicholson's guides covering England and Wales. Also Ladyline guides 1972-3.
Inland Waterways Association. BULLETIN for information also their own guides.
Kennet & Avon Canal Trust: Series of booklets on various aspects of the canal.

Journals

Newspapers and Journals of historical value are: ARIS'S BIRMINGHAM GAZETTE, BERROW'S WORCESTER JOURNAL and LEEDS INTELLIGENCER. Also periodicals: THE GENTLEMAN'S MAGAZINE and technical press such as ENGINEERING etc. CANALS AND WATERWAYS was the monthly business journal from 1919-1924.

Modern journals of value for current events:- MOTOR BOAT AND YACHTING, fortnightly from 1904. WATERWAYS WORLD, monthly from 1972. YACHTING AND BOATING WEEKLY.

Maps

Imray's Chart of the Rivers Cam and Ouse.
Imray's Chart of the River Nene.
Stanford's Inland Cruising Map (England & Wales).
Stanford's Map of the Thames from Richmond to Lechlade.
Stanford's Canoeing Map of England and Wales.
Bord Failte Eireann (Irish Tourist Board) the Shannon.
Shell Mex & B.P. THE SHANNON GUIDE.
Wilson W.E. INLAND WATERWAYS OF GREAT BRITAIN (1939) Revised by L.A. Edwards, 1962. (see above)

Official Publications in order of Date.

Royal Society of Arts. REPORT on the Canal Conference (May 1888).
Royal Commission on Canals and Inland Navigations of the United Kingdom. REPORT, 12 volumes (1907-11) H.M.S.O.
Ministry of Health Departmental Committee, "living-in on canal boats". MINUTES OF EVIDENCE (1921) H.M.S.O.
Royal Commission 1930. The Co-ordination and Development of Transport, FINAL REPORT (1931) H.M.S.O.
CANALS AND INLAND WATERWAYS; Rusholme Board of Survey, British Transport Commission (1955).
REPORT of the Committee of inquiry into Inland Waterways, (the Bowes Report). 1958. H.M.S.O.
British Waterways Board. THE FUTURE OF THE WATERWAYS. An interim report, 1964.
British Waterways Board. FACTS ABOUT THE WATERWAYS (1965).
Ministry of Transport. TRANSPORT POLICY (1966) H.M.S.O.
Ministry of Transport. BRITISH WATERWAYS: RECREATION AND AMENITY (1967). H.M.S.O.
British Waterways Board. LEISURE AND THE WATERWAYS (1967).

Dept. of the Environment. REORGANIZATION OF WATER AND SEWAGE SERVICES: GOVERNMENT PROPOSALS AND ARRANGEMENTS FOR CONSULTATION (1971).

Appendix F ;

Canal and River Navigation Terms.

BALLASTING. Dredging by hand with a scoop or a bag at the end of a long pole, only soft stuff being handled. The term derives from the use of the dredgings for ships' ballast.

BARGE WALK. Thameside word for a towpath.

CATCHWATER DRAIN. An artifical drainage channel.

CLAMP UP. To freeze up.

COTTING and RODING. Cutting and taking out rushes or weeds in a river or dyke, a Fens term.

CRADGING. Strengthening a bank with turf or reeds, a Fens term.

DROWN. A flood in the Fens.

DYDLE. Norfolk word for dredging and reed cutting. A dydle was a scoop with a bag, the scoop being faced with a cutting edge like a hoe.

EAU. An artificial drainage and navigation waterway in the Fens. Eau is pronounced 'o'.

FLASH. An open stretch of water where a river broadens, such as Winsford flashes. It also means a lake formed by mining subsidence such as Leigh flash, or where a canal has widened out due to subsidence, such as the flash at Billinge Green on the Trent & Mersey near Northwich.

FLOODBANK. An earthwork set well back from the river's natural bank, and built to contain flood water, protecting surrounding land.

FRESH. On the Severn the 'fresh' (plural freshes) is the floodwater coming downstream. Before improvements of the 1840s the 'fresh' was vital to navigation.

GOIT or GOYT. A north of England term for a watercourse, particularly a mill leat, thus 'head goyt' is a headrace and 'tail goyt' a tailrace. The Lincolnshire term 'gowt' is similar.

HAIN. Higher; in Norfolk; the water is 'hain' today.

HALING SIDE. The towpath side of the river in the Fens.

HALING WAY. Fens and East Anglian word for a towpath, but also used in Yorkshire.

HARD. A shallow reach, Norfolk.

HEAD LEVEL. Summit level, a term found in Northern Ireland.

HYTHE. A quay or wharf, thus Clayhithe near Cambridge.

LASHER. A weir, South of England word.

LATERAL CANAL. One running alongside and supplied from a river, such as the Sankey Brook Navigation.

LEAM. A drainage and navigation waterway and the area it drains.

LOCK SPIT. The initial excavation of a canal, a shallow trench linking the slope holes which were dug every two or three chains on each side of the proposed cut.

MUDDING. Dredging by hand.

NIP. A narrow place on the Trent.

PILL. A tidal creek with a soft mud bottom. The word is the Welsh pwll (pool), anglicised.

POOL. North of England term for a canal pound, certainly used on the Leeds & Liverpool, eg. Marton pool.

QUARRAGE. The small rise and fall of the tide at the upper limit of tidal influence on the Severn, which may occasionally reach the foot of Diglis weir just below Worcester.

QUEACHES. Used to describe wet spots by a canal. Queachy; an old word for boggy.

REACH. The stretch of river between two locks or on the tidal Thames any open stretch.

REED ROND. A reed bank, Norfolk.

RHYNE. A drainage ditch, Somerset, sometimes navigable for small craft. Pronounced rheen.

ROCKING. Boatman's term for deep cutting, certainly used on the Shropshire Union.

ROND. A river bank in Norfolk.

SCEND. Space between a vessel's keel and river bottom. A certain depth must be allowed for efficient operation of the propeller and the plunging of a vessel in disturbed water.

SLOPE. The fall of a river's surface expressed in feet and inches per mile, thus the Calder in Yorkshire has a slope of 90 inches per mile, which is steep.

SLOPE HOLES. Following the surveyor's pegs, the canal cutters made nicks in the ground every two or three chains on each side of the canal's course. They were joined up by lock spits.

SLUB or SLUTCH. Dredged mud.

SOUGH. Pronounced 'suff', a tunnel driven in to drain a mine working or canal workings when tunneling.

SPARKUBELS. Used in the Worsley mines for the timber framings of the sough, spar meaning frame and kubel, cupola, or arched roof of the sough.

STAKE. To moor, a Fenland term.

TOE. The bottom of a bank or embankment.

TRACKWAY. The towing path, Irish term.

TYING POINT. The shallowest point on a navigation, say the bottom sill of a lock. If a boat could float over it she could go anywhere on the navigation.

VALLEY. Boatman's term for embankment, because it crosses a valley.

WASH LANDS. The ground between a river's natural bank and its flood bank, inundated at times of flood.

WATERS MEETING. A canal junction, that at Stretford being so called where the line to Runcorn leaves that to Manchester on the Bridgewater Canal.

WIDE or WIDE WATER. Widened out places on a line of a canal.

WINDING HOLE. Pronounced like a gale of wind, these wide places allowed a boat to wind or turn round. They were carefully sited where boats could see each other. They often had to be at wharves while there were some special winding holes for tunnel tugs. To-day they are often very shallow and only recommended winding points should be attempted.

WORKING TURNS or WAITING TURNS at locks when water was short. The canal company could enforce this method of working, whereby each boat requiring to proceed either up or down had to wait for another coming the opposite way should the lock be set against it. In this way the lock could be fully used and no water turned to waste.

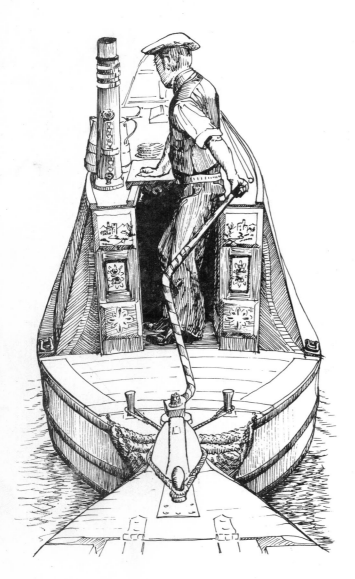

Above; the elegantly carved date stone of La Touche bridge, Portobello, Dublin, on the Grand's Circular line to Ringsend.

Left; a 'cross strapped' pair. The butty behaves like a trailer, without much need for steering.

Below; a Preston-Kendal swift boat at Hincaster wharf, Lancaster Canal.